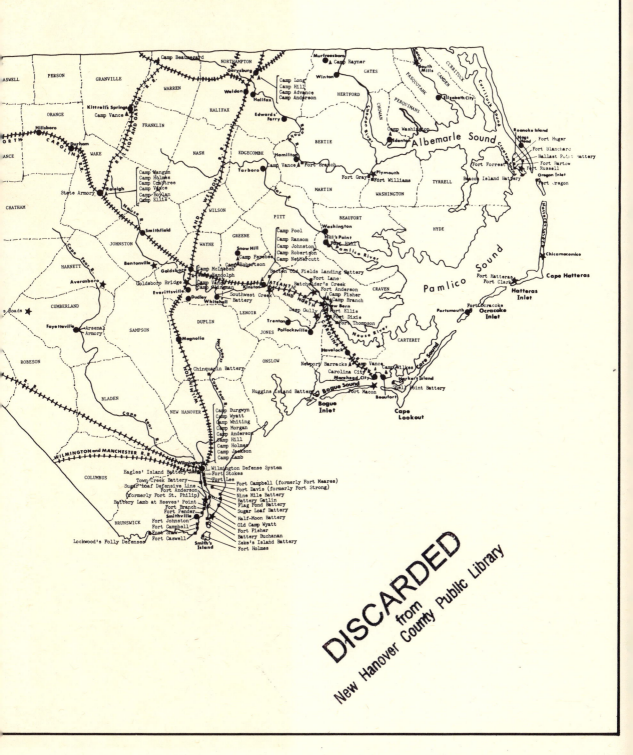

NORTH CAROLINA TROOPS
1861-1865
A ROSTER

Photograph of John Hoyle Howey and his father, William Howey, both of whom served in Company K, Thirtieth Regiment N.C. Troops. Photograph furnished by David L. King, Jr., Matthews, North Carolina.

North Carolina Troops
1861-1865
A Roster

Compiled By
Weymouth T. Jordan, Jr.

Unit Histories By
Louis H. Manarin

VOL. VIII
INFANTRY

27th-31st
REGIMENTS

RALEIGH, NORTH CAROLINA

DIVISION OF ARCHIVES AND HISTORY

1981

©1981 by North Carolina Division of Archives and History

Printed by

The B & J Typesetting Service, Charlotte

Bound by

The North Carolina State University Print Shop, Raleigh

ISBN 0-86526-013-3 (Volume VIII)
ISBN 0-86526-005-2 (Set)

PREFACE

This volume is the eighth in a projected series of fourteen volumes containing the names and service records of North Carolinians who served in the Confederate and Union armed forces during the Civil War.

Begun in February, 1961, the project to compile a North Carolina Civil War roster grew out of the work of the North Carolina Confederate Centennial Commission under the direction of its chairman, the late Colonel Hugh Dortch, and its executive secretary, Norman C. Larson. Dr. Louis H. Manarin, editor of the first three volumes, was initially a member of the Confederate Centennial Commission.

At the termination of the commission in June, 1965, the roster project was transferred to the State Department of Archives and History (which later became, under state government reorganization, the Division of Archives and History of the Department of Cultural Resources). Dr. Manarin remained head of the project until January, 1970, when he was succeeded in the post of editor by Weymouth T. Jordan, Jr. Dr. Manarin has continued his service to the North Carolina Civil War Roster Project as author of the unit histories that appear in this volume.

To Weymouth Jordan and Louis Manarin; to Secretary Sara W. Hodgkins of the Department of Cultural Resources; to William S. Price, Jr., acting director of the Division of Archives and History; to Memory F. Mitchell, chief of the Historical Publications Section; and to the staff of the roster project, I wish to express my appreciation for their efforts in making possible this memorial to the service, courage, and sacrifice of the brave soldiers from our state who fought and died for North Carolina.

October 30, 1980

JAMES B. HUNT, JR.
Governor of North Carolina

CONTENTS

INTRODUCTION

The principal source of information for the individual service records contained in this volume is the compiled military service records on file in Record Group 109 in the National Archives, Washington, D.C., and available on microfilm at the North Carolina Division of Archives and History in Raleigh. Record Group 109 is composed of individual service record envelopes for each North Carolina soldier in which are filed data cards containing information abstracted from primary Civil War records. Envelopes are filed numerically by regiment or battalion and then alphabetically by surname. Primary records from which service record information was abstracted include company muster rolls, payrolls, rosters, appointment books, hospital registers, prison registers and rolls, parole registers, and inspection reports. Some envelopes contain primary documents such as enlistment and discharge papers, pay vouchers, requisitions, court-martial proceedings, and personal correspondence. In addition to the foregoing source materials, the North Carolina Roll of Honor, compiled by the state adjutant general during the war and containing service record information on thousands of North Carolina soldiers, was loaned to federal authorities in Washington at the time Record Group 109 was compiled, and its contents were abstracted and incorporated into the record group.

A second National Archives source utilized in this volume was the Papers of and Relating to Military and Civilian Personnel, 1861-1865. This collection consists of cards and manuscripts collected and compiled for inclusion in Record Group 109 but not filed, for various reasons, in the envelopes for individual soldiers.

Material obtained from the National Archives was supplemented by records in the North Carolina state archives. These included muster rolls for periods not covered by muster rolls on file at the National Archives, bounty rolls, state pension applications filed by Confederate veterans and their widows, and records of the office of the state adjutant general. Information relative to Confederate service was abstracted from membership applications, Cross of Honor certificates, and Cross of Military Service certificates in the possession of the North Carolina Division of the United Daughters of the Confederacy and from Confederate gravestone records compiled by the same organization. Also utilized were published registers of Hollywood Cemetery, Richmond, Virginia; Stonewall Cemetery, Winchester, Virginia; the cemeteries at Sharpsburg, Maryland, and Gettysburg, Pennsylvania; and unpublished registers compiled for various Northern cemeteries by the Office of the Quartermaster General, United States Army, in 1912 and 1914.

Because of the shortcomings of the *Roster of North Carolina Troops in the War Between the States,* edited by John W. Moore (Raleigh: [State of North Carolina], 4 volumes, 1882), hereinafter cited as Moore's *Roster,* that source and local rosters compiled from it were not used except for auxiliary purposes such as those of cross-reference. However, service record information was abstracted from *Histories of the Several Regiments and Battalions from North Carolina in the Great War, 1861-'65* (Raleigh and Goldsboro: State of North Carolina, 5 volumes,

1901), by Walter Clark, hereinafter cited as Clark's *Regiments*; from *Reminiscences of the Guilford Grays, Co. B, 27th N.C. Regiment* (Washington, D.C.: R. O. Polkinhorn, 1883), by John A. Sloan; and from *Experience of a Confederate Chaplain, 1861-1864* (n.p., n.d.), by Alexander Davis Betts of the 30th Regiment N.C. Troops. Casualty reports were abstracted from 1861-1865 issues of various North Carolina newspapers, and service record information was received from descendants of Civil War veterans, from professional and lay historians, and from other private individuals. Two final sources that remained almost untouched because of lack of time and staff were the 1860 census of North Carolina and Civil War letters and diaries in the North Carolina state archives and in other manuscript repositories.

Information abstracted from the foregoing sources was arranged and consolidated for each member of each unit for which a roster appears in this volume. The method adopted for presenting regimental rosters and listing the names and service records of individual soldiers is as follows:

Regimental field officers (Colonels, Lieutenant Colonels, Majors), as well as regimental staff officers (Adjutants, Assistant Quartermasters, Assistant Commissaries of Subsistence, Surgeons, Chaplains, Ensigns) and regimental noncommissioned officers (Sergeants Major, Quartermaster Sergeants, Commissary Sergeants, Ordnance Sergeants, Hospital Stewards) are grouped together by rank under a major heading entitled Field and Staff. Within their respective rank-groups their names and service records are listed chronologically by date of rank. Members of the regimental band are listed alphabetically at the end of the Field and Staff section.

Rosters of the companies (usually ten in number) of which the regiment was composed follow the Field and Staff section and are divided into two *major* subsections consisting of (1) Officers and (2) Noncommissioned Officers and Privates. Within the Officers subsection are two *minor* subsections for (i) Captains and (ii) Lieutenants. Captains are listed chronologically by date of rank; Lieutenants are listed alphabetically. All soldiers whose names and service records appear in the subsection for Noncommissioned Officers and Privates are listed alphabetically regardless of their date of rank and whether they were Sergeants, Corporals, or Privates.

Following the last company roster is a Miscellaneous section containing the names and service records of soldiers who were members of the regiment but whose records do not indicate the company in which they served. (Personal names, including given names as well as surnames, are spelled throughout as they were spelled in primary records, the only exceptions being when a signature was available or when the soldier's descendants provided information concerning his name. A number of oddities and corruptions have inevitably occurred, and the index has been extensively cross-referenced to assist the researcher in locating names that may appear in corrupted form.)

In composing the service records contained in this volume, the editor has cited as the enlistment date for each soldier the date of enlistment that was recorded for him on the earliest surviving muster roll of the company in which he served. The place of enlistment was derived from the same source. Actually, there were at least five dates on which a soldier might be reported to have entered service: the date he enrolled for military service; the date he enlisted or was conscripted; the date he reported for duty; the date his unit was mustered into state service; and the date his unit was mustered into Confederate service. Similarly, the place of enlistment might be reported as the town or county where he enrolled for military service; the town or county where he enlisted or was conscripted; the town, county, or camp where he joined the unit to which he was assigned; or the camp of instruction to which he was assigned. No standard procedure was followed by company clerks in citing either date or place of enlistment, and individual clerks sometimes altered arbitrarily their previous procedure. It is a frequent occurrence, therefore, for several conflicting enlistment dates and places of enlistment to appear in the primary records of a single soldier, and, in such circumstances, the procedure outlined above for determining and standardizing enlistment dates and places of enlistment has been deemed the most advisable.

All references to counties are as of 1861-1865 boundaries. In instances where primary records indicate that an individual was born in a county that had not been formed at the time of the individual's birth, an asterisk appears after the county (*e.g.*, Born in Alamance County*), and the assumption can probably be made that the individual in question was born at a locality that later became a part of the county cited.

Records pertaining to the age at date of enlistment of individual soldiers have proved so contradictory and unreliable that, in the absence of a reason to favor one source over another, the editor has arbitrarily adopted the practice of selecting for inclusion in the service records in this volume the youngest age among the possibilities available. (However, in the case of soldiers under the age of 18, the oldest age has been selected.) Apparently, the widespread illiteracy extant among North Carolina soldiers often extended to ignorance of exact birthdates. The latter rarely appear in primary Civil War records, and it is suggestive that North Carolina state pension applications filed long after the cessation of hostilities often reflect age discrepancies similar to those that are evident in the primary records of the war. The age-at-date-of-enlistment problem is further complicated by the fact that each soldier, like all mortals, was two different ages during any given calendar year, which of the two depending on whether or not his birthday had already passed. Thus, a Confederate hospital record indicating that a soldier was 28 years old in May, 1864, does not reveal whether he was 24 or 25 when he enlisted in July, 1861. The editor's procedure in such cases is to quote the source in brackets at the end of the service record (*e.g.*, [Confederate hospital records dated May, 1864, give his age as 28]).

All references to cities and towns are as of their 1861-1865 designations; however, in instances where the place-name has been changed the 1861-1865 designation is followed by the current designation in parentheses—*e.g.*, Smithville (Southport). North Carolina counties, cities, towns, etc., are not followed by reference to the state except for clarity (*e.g.*, Greensboro; but Washington, North Carolina). Counties and localities in other states are followed by the state only on the first occasion that they are mentioned in a service record. West Virginia place names are cited as being in West Virginia only if the date of the reference is on or subsequent to June 20, 1863, the date West Virginia was admitted to the Union. If the reference is prior to that date, the locality is cited as being in Virginia; hence, some place names may be listed in West Virginia in one service record but in Virginia in a second service record. In a few cases it proved impossible to ascertain the state in which a hamlet or geographical feature was located, either because no such place could be located at all or because two or more places with the same name were located in two or more states and no evidence was available as to which of the places was the one intended. Such place names appear in quotation marks in this volume (*e.g.*, ''Table Knob,'' or ''Warrenton'').

Causes of death, reasons for discharge, and other information that sometimes is unsavory or unheroic, and thus unwelcome to later generations, is presented in quotation marks in order to emphasize its authenticity and, perhaps, channel any dismay of the soldier's descendants in the direction of the original document. Information that is ambiguous, contradictory, unverifiable, or of doubtful accuracy is presented in quotation marks and will normally be found in brackets at the end of a service record. Brackets are used also to enclose editorial corrections, interpolations, comments, and cross-references, and they are employed at the end of some service records to convey information that it would have been difficult, illogical, or awkward to present in the body of the service record.

The phrase ''on or about'' is used when the date of a historic event such as a battle has been supplied by the editor or is cited in primary records as having taken place on a date that only approximates the date on which the event actually occurred (*e.g.*, Wounded at Gettysburg, Pennsylvania, on or about July 5, 1863.) This phrase is used also when an event which is not a verified or verifiable historical fact is cited in primary records as having occurred on two or more dates which are more or less consecutive, the date cited being the one which seems most probably correct on the basis of available evidence (*e.g.*, Died at Raleigh on or about April 8, 1864.) In instances where there is no reason to favor one such date as being more probably correct than another, hyphenated dates are given if the dates are more or less consecutive (*e.g.*, Died at Raleigh, April 2-8, 1864.) When such dates are not more or less consecutive they are cited individually (*e.g.*, Died at Raleigh on April 2 or June 5, 1864.) Hyphenated dates preceded by ''in'' indicate a single event that occurred during the period in question (*e.g.*, Hospitalized at Goldsboro in July-August, 1863); but dates preceded by ''during'' indicate a condition that prevailed throughout the period in question (*e.g.*, Hospitalized at Goldsboro during July-August, 1863.) Again, this system was found necessary because in many instances the exact date of an event could not be determined.

The phrase ''present or accounted for'' is used to indicate that a soldier was either present for duty or absent for reasons other than desertion or extended absence without leave (*i.e.*, sixty days or more). Desertion and absence without leave were apparently considered synonymous terms by many company clerks; hence, a soldier who absented himself without authorization but returned of his own accord sixty days later might be listed as a deserter in the records of one company, while a soldier who absented himself from another company for the same period under identical circumstances might be listed as absent without leave. The editor has judged it best not to standardize these terms, however inequitable the prevailing Civil War system may now seem, and references to desertion or absence without leave that appear in this volume are, in the overwhelming majority of cases, quoted directly from primary sources. Because of space limitations, no reference whatever is made to unauthorized absences of less than sixty days except in the case of chronic deserters.

The phrase "no further records" is used at the end of a service record when there is doubt as to the manner in which a soldier's military career terminated (*e.g.*, Company muster rolls indicate he was discharged at Weldon on May 9, 1864; however, medical records indicate he died in hospital at Weldon on May 30, 1864. No further records.) Use of this phrase does not indicate that there are literally no further records extant but that there are no further records pertaining to the most important aspects of a soldier's military career. Additional records pertaining to hospitalizations for minor complaints, authorized leaves of absence, issuance of clothing, and other comparatively insignificant episodes exist, often in quantity, for almost every soldier whose service record appears in this volume.

During the twenty years since the inception of the roster project rules of capitalization, punctuation, and style have changed considerably; for example, it is no longer considered good form to capitalize an individual's title or rank unless it appears before his name. However, except in those few instances where a new system provided greater clarity or seemed distinctly advantageous, systems employed in earlier volumes have been retained. One particularly noticeable punctuation oddity that perhaps should be mentioned specifically involves the use in the possessive case of singular nouns ending in "s." Personal names are rendered "s's" (*e.g.*, Jones's men), but, on the theory that the historic spelling of a place-name cannot be altered by a change in modern rules of punctuation, place-names ending in the possessive are rendered without the final "s" (*e.g.*, Jones' Mill, Virginia).

The chronic editorial problem of cross-referencing the service records of soldiers who served in two or more units also would appear to merit discussion at this point. A specific case may serve best to illustrate the difficulties involved and the precautions that should be taken by users of ***North Carolina Troops.*** Private William T. Wood enlisted originally in Company B, 17th Regiment N.C. Troops (2nd Organization). In November, 1862, he was transferred to Company A, 8th Regiment N.C. State Troops. His service record in the roster for Company B, 17th Regiment should conclude, therefore, with a statement that he was transferred to Company A, 8th Regiment in November, 1862; and his service record in the roster for Company A, 8th Regiment should begin with a statement that he served previously in Company B, 17th Regiment and was transferred to the 8th Regiment in November, 1862. Unfortunately, as often happens in the case of transferees, there was no record in the files of the 8th Regiment of Private Wood's previous service in the 17th Regiment, and the roster of the 8th Regiment was already in print when his previous service in the 17th Regiment was discovered in the records of the latter unit; hence, the appropriate cross-reference was omitted in the roster of the 8th Regiment. In an attempt to circumvent cross-referencing problems of the foregoing type, an effort was made to locate records of dual service for soldiers whose careers either began abruptly in mid-war or terminated inexplicably a year or more before the fighting ceased; however, for a variety of technical reasons it was not always possible to locate or conclusively identify additional records for such individuals. Therefore, until a revised edition of **North Carolina Troops** is published, reference should be made to the index to each volume in this series (or to the master index that will be published at its conclusion) whenever the service record of a soldier begins or terminates in a manner that does not preclude previous or later service in another unit.

I would like to express my sincere appreciation to those persons who have contributed to the publication of this volume:

—Mrs. Memory F. Mitchell, chief of the Historical Publications Section of the Division of Archives and History, provided valuable support, guidance, and counsel.

—Miss Flora J. Hatley, editorial assistant (October, 1978-April, 1980) and later editorial secretary/typist (May-September, 1980) of the roster project, typed much of the manuscript for this volume, assisted in proofreading the manuscript and page proof, successfully undertook many research projects for the editor, and performed all of her editorial and clerical duties with unflagging dedication. Her predecessor, Mrs. Saralyn G. Page, served briefly (August-October, 1979). Miss Mary V. McMillan produced a large quantity of high-quality work while serving as a summer typist (May-June, 1980).

—Mrs. Patricia R. Johnson, editorial secretary/typist of the roster project from January, 1978, through July, 1979, typed most of the manuscript for this volume, performed most of the accuracy checks that were made on the manuscript, and, after her promotion to another position in the Historical Publications Section, made an additional and much-appreciated contribution by assisting with the proofreading.

—Mr. S. H. Harrington of Erwin, North Carolina, provided information concerning the local designations of several companies for which rosters are published in this volume.

Weymouth T. Jordan, Jr.
Editor

September 10, 1980

NORTH CAROLINA TROOPS
1861-1865
A ROSTER

27th REGIMENT N.C. TROOPS

Attempts to organize this unit as the 9th Regiment N.C. Volunteers began in June, 1861; however, before the organizational process was completed three of the regiment's ten companies were transferred, and three new companies were assigned to replace them. Shortly thereafter, four more companies were transferred. The six remaining companies were then organized into a battalion, and Captain George B. Singletary was elected Lieutenant Colonel. The battalion organization was temporary, but from June until September, 1861, when the regiment was organized, the battalion was referred to as Singletary's Battalion. In July a new company was attached to the battalion, and the three companies that had been transferred in June were reassigned to the unit in September. The regiment was finally organized on September 28, 1861, for twelve months' service and was designated the 27th Regiment N.C. Troops.

On the date the regiment was organized Companies A, B, and G were stationed at Fort Macon, in Carteret County, and Companies C, D, E, H, I, and K were on duty at Camp Gatlin, near New Bern. The tenth company, Company F, was stationed at Fort Ellis, below New Bern, where its members were being trained as artillerymen; a detachment from Company F was transferred to Fort Lane, on the Neuse River above New Bern, on or about October 1. The companies remained at their various posts until February 26, 1862, when Companies A, B, and G were ordered to Camp Gatlin; Company F joined the remainder of the regiment at Camp Gatlin prior to March 1, 1862.

After Roanoke Island fell to a Federal force under General Ambrose E. Burnside on February 8, 1862, Burnside moved up the Neuse, attacked the Confederate line below New Bern on March 14, and drove the defenders from the field. The 27th Regiment was on the left of the line between a defensive work called Fort Thompson and the Beaufort County road; but, except for some skirmishing and sharpshooting, it was not actively engaged. Major John A. Gilmer, Jr., reported the regiment's activities to Colonel Charles C. Lee, commander of the Confederate left wing, as follows (*Official Records*, Series I, Vol. IX, pp. 257-259):

On the morning of the 13th, pursuant to orders from your headquarters, I marched the Twenty-seventh Regiment to the river bank, about 100 yards above Fort Thompson, arriving about an hour before daybreak. Forming the regiment in line of battle at that point I awaited orders.

About 7 o'clock I received orders to retire a short distance toward the river, to avoid any shot and shell that might be thrown in the direction of Fort Thompson. The regiment was immediately moved a short distance to the left and rear.

While in this position I received orders to march the regiment to the breastworks and line the same on the left near Fort Thompson, which was immediately done. The regiment remained (covering the breastworks, principally in one rank, for the distance of 300 or 400 yards from Fort Thompson) all the day and night of the 13th; were aroused and placed in position at the works twice during the night. Numbers of shell and shot were thrown from the gunboats of the enemy during the evening of the 13th, most of which, however, passed beyond the works.

On the morning of the 14th the regiment was again placed in position to await the approach of the enemy, whom I supposed to be in force in the woods in front of the works. I was informed by Captain [Benjamin T.] Barden [Bardin], whose company [K] had been sent out the evening before as a portion of the picket guard, that the enemy was advancing on the county road to our right.

About 6.30 or 7 a.m. the fire of the enemy began beyond our right and continued vigorously during the entire engagement. The fire was immediately returned by the artillery stationed beyond the right of the Twenty-seventh and continued unabated. I commanded the regiment to retain their fire until ordered to fire by me.

A short time after the firing began on the right the bombardment again began from the gunboats of the enemy, directed principally toward Fort Thompson and the portion of the breastworks behind which the Twenty-seventh was stationed. Thus situated, the regiment manfully and cheerfully sustained the shower of shell and shot from the gunboats for two and a half hours, during which but 1 man was killed and 3 stunned.

Between 10 and 11 a.m. I discovered that the troops stationed immediately on the right of the Twenty-seventh were falling back, which movement I discovered was being followed by two or three companies of the Twenty-seventh, on the right. I immediately hastened to my right and ordered the two retreating companies back to the trenches. I then gave my entire command the order to fire by file, designating at the same time the direction in which I perceived the enemy advancing in great numbers.

I then hastened to meet you, whom I perceived advancing along the lines to the left. You informed me that our right had been turned and I must fall back. I then ordered the regiment to retire, which was done in tolerable order by most of the companies on the left. I ordered those companies which were together to march through Camp Gatlin to the railroad bridge, where the greater part of the right assembled and halted. I hastened then to the left, beyond Camp Fisher, to find out what were the plans of our troops, supposing that a stand was to be made at that point. Finding our forces retreating, I returned to the right and passed with them over the bridge to the railroad depot, where the companies were again formed, agreeably to orders I had received from the assistant adjutant-general.

At the depot we were ordered to fall back still farther, when I placed the regiment on the march toward Kinston, under command of my senior captain. I joined the regiment again where the railroad is crossed by the county road above New Berne, and again joined them at Tuscarora, whence I proceeded with them to Kinston, partly on foot and partly by means of the cars which were sent back to take us up.

. . . .

P. S.—It is, perhaps, proper for me to add that about 30 of the Twenty-seventh were detailed to operate Latham's battery in conjunction with Captain [Alexander C.] Latham's company. These 30 men were in the hottest of the engagement, and several of them seriously injured but none killed.

During the battle and the subsequent retreat the regiment lost 4 men killed, 8 wounded, and 42 missing.

With New Bern lost, the Confederate force fell back to Kinston, where the 27th Regiment was assigned to the First Brigade, commanded by General Samuel G. French. In addition to this regiment, the brigade was composed of the 7th Regiment N.C. State Troops, 26th Regiment N.C.

Troops, 35th Regiment N.C. Troops, Major L. H. Rogers's battalion, and seven companies of foot artillery. The regiment left Kinston for Camp Blackjack, eight miles west of Kinston, on March 22, 1862; a week later it moved to Camp South West, five miles east of Kinston. In April the regiment, which was mustered in originally for twelve months' service, was reorganized to serve for the duration of the war and was assigned to General Robert Ransom's brigade. In addition to this regiment, the brigade was composed of the 25th Regiment N.C. Troops, 26th Regiment N.C. Troops, 35th Regiment N.C. Troops, and several cavalry units which were soon transferred.

The regiment was stationed at Camp South West during April and May and assisted in the destruction of the Atlantic & North Carolina Railroad from Kinston to Core Creek. On May 31 the regiment departed by rail for Richmond, Virginia; it arrived on June 1 and was sent immediately to the battlefield at Seven Pines, which it reached too late to take part in the fighting. The regiment was ordered to Drewry's Bluff the next day to join General John G. Walker's brigade. In addition to the 27th Regiment, Walker's brigade was composed of the 2nd Battalion Georgia Infantry, 3rd Regiment Arkansas Infantry, 30th Regiment Virginia Infantry, 46th Regiment N.C. Troops, and the 57th Regiment Virginia Infantry.

The 27th Regiment remained at Drewry's Bluff constructing fortifications until June 26, when orders were received to reinforce General Benjamin Huger's division north of the James River near King's School House, where the opening engagement of the Seven Days' battles had occurred on the previous day. Colonel Van H. Manning, senior colonel in command of Walker's brigade after Walker was injured on July 1, reported the brigade's activities during the Seven Days' as follows (*Official Records*, Series I, Vol. XI, pt. 2, p. 915):

> Thursday night, June 26, orders were received from the Secretary of War for the Fourth Brigade, Brig. Gen. J. G. Walker commanding, to cross the James River and re-enforce Major-General [Benjamin] Huger's division. The brigade, composed of the Third Arkansas, Thirtieth Virginia, Fifty-seventh Virginia, Twenty-seventh North Carolina, and Forty-sixth North Carolina Regiments, Second Georgia Battalion, Capts. D. A. French's and J. R. Branch's light batteries, and Captain Goodwin's cavalry company—in all amounting to about 4,000 men and officers—crossed the pontoon bridge, and reached General Huger about 12 m. on Friday, June 27. While with General Huger's division the Fifty-seventh Regiment Virginia Volunteers was relieved from duty with this brigade, and in its place Col. R. C. Hill's Forty-eighth Regiment North Carolina Troops was substituted.
>
> Friday night the brigade was ordered to cross the Chickahominy on a bridge thrown across the stream by the enemy, which was accomplished in good order by noon Saturday, and the command moved down and bivouacked on the battle-field of the day before, where they remained until Sunday morning, when orders were received to recross the Chickahominy and report to Major-General Huger again. The troops were crossed by daylight Sunday morning and proceeded at once to General Huger's division.
>
> Orders came in the afternoon of Sunday to move down the river road. The column was immediately put in motion, and after an exceedingly fatiguing march reached General [Theophilus H.] Holmes' division in the evening, in the vicinity of the pontoon

bridge across [the] James River.

> Monday, June 30, the brigade moved forward about 5 or 6 miles and formed line of battle on a very commanding hill, in order to check the reported advance of the enemy.
>
> In the afternoon of Monday the brigade was advanced and came into action with the enemy about 5 p.m. A heavy fire of artillery was kept up between a section of Captain French's battery, under Lieutenant Cooper, a section of Captain Branch's battery, under Lieut. M. A. Martin, and the enemy's numerous batteries advantageously posted on Malvern Hill. Unfortunately, our troops were under the range of the enemy's gunboats, which kept up an incessant fire with guns of the heaviest caliber with extraordinary precision. The firing ceased before dark, except an occasional shot, and about 9 o'clock the command returned to its original position.
>
> Nothwithstanding the exceedingly heavy fire the brigade was exposed to during the evening of the 30th comparatively few casualties occurred, 20 men having been wounded, 1 of whom has since died.
>
> During the greater part of Tuesday, July 1, the brigade remained in line of battle on Warren's Hill. In the afternoon an advance was ordered. The command moved forward in line of battle for about half a mile, when they were halted and remained in line during the night.
>
> It is proper to state here that the brigadier-general commanding [John G. Walker] met with a painful accident on Tuesday evening, which incapacitated him to retain command of the brigade, and as senior colonel I was assigned command.
>
> On Wednesday evening at 5 o'clock orders were received for the brigade to move back to Drewry's Bluff. After a fatiguing march through a drenching rain and over muddy roads we reached the bluff safely by daylight Thursday morning.

During the Seven Days' battles the regiment lost six men wounded.

Walker's brigade returned to its former camp at Drewry's Bluff on July 3. On July 6 this regiment and the 2nd Battalion Georgia Infantry marched to Petersburg, where they remained until ordered to Fort Powhatan, on the James River below City Point, on July 8. After shelling a Federal transport on July 11, the two units returned to Petersburg. On July 31 and August 1 they took part in the bombardment of General George B. McClellan's base at Harrison's Landing. The entire brigade was ordered to Richmond on August 20 and went into camp at Camp Lee. On August 26 it was sent by rail with General Robert Ransom's brigade to Rapidan Station, near Orange Court House; at about the same time the two brigades were organized into a division under the command of General Walker. Command of Walker's former brigade devolved once more on the senior colonel, Van H. Manning. On September 1 Walker's division moved from Rapidan Station to join the Army of Northern Virginia near Leesburg, where General Lee was preparing to cross the Potomac River into Maryland. The army began fording the river on September 4; the 27th Regiment, in the rear guard, crossed on September 8.

Upon reaching Frederick, Maryland, two days later the army halted, and Lee dispatched General Thomas J. Jackson to capture Harpers Ferry while General James Longstreet's corps, of which Walker's division was a part, moved to Hagerstown. On September 9 Walker moved his division from Monocacy Junction, near Frederick, to the mouth of the Monocacy River under orders to destroy the aqueduct of the Chesapeake and Ohio Canal. The aqueduct was captured after a brief skirmish with its Federal defenders, but efforts to destroy the facility proved futile. Under orders from Lee to assist Jackson at Harpers Ferry, Walker then recrossed the Potomac and marched towards Loudoun Heights southeast of the town. On the evening of September 12 Walker positioned this regiment and the 30th Regiment Virginia Infantry atop Loudoun Heights and placed the remainder of his division on the right bank of the Potomac to prevent the enemy from escaping by that route. Across the river General Lafayette McLaws's division, reinforced by General Richard H. Anderson's division, occupied Maryland Heights while Jackson's troops occupied Bolivar Heights west of Harpers Ferry. Surrounded, the Federal garrison surrendered on September 15 after a brief resistance.

With the fall of Harpers Ferry, Lee ordered the army to concentrate at Sharpsburg, where the Federal army under General McClellan was ponderously massing for an attack. When Walker's division arrived on the field on September 16 it was positioned on the right flank of Lee's line. On the morning of September 17 the Confederate left under General Jackson was vigorously assaulted, and Walker's division was ordered to reinforce Jackson. General Walker reported the division's movements and activities as follows (*Official Records*, Series I, Vol. XIX, pt. 1, pp. 914-916):

Soon after 9 a.m., I received orders from General Lee, through Colonel [A.L.] Long, of his staff, to hasten to the extreme left, to the support of Major-General Jackson. Hastening forward, as rapidly as possible, along the rear of our entire line of battle, we arrived, soon after 10 o'clock, near the woods which the commands of Generals [John B.] Hood and [Jubal A.] Early were struggling heroically to hold but gradually and sullenly yielding to the irresistible weight of overwhelming numbers. Here we at once formed line of battle, under a sharp artillery fire, and, leaving the Twenty-seventh North Carolina and Third Arkansas Regiments to hold the open space between the woods and Longstreet's left, the division, with [Robert] Ransom's brigade on the left, advanced in splendid style, firing and cheering as they went, and in a few minutes cleared the woods, strewing it with the enemy's dead and wounded. Colonel Manning, with the Forty-sixth and Forty-eighth North Carolina and Thirtieth Virginia, not content with the possession of the woods, dashed forward in gallant style, crossed the open fields beyond, driving the enemy before him like sheep, until, arriving at a long line of strong post and rail fences, behind which heavy masses of the enemy's infantry were lying, their advance was checked; and it being impossible to climb over these fences under such a fire, these regiments, after suffering a heavy loss, were compelled to fall back to the woods, where the Forty-sixth and Forty-eighth North Carolina Regiments were quickly reformed, but the Thirtieth Virginia, owing to some unaccountable misunderstanding of orders, except Captain [John M.] Hudgin's company, went entirely off the field, and, as a regiment, was not again engaged during the day. Captain [W. A.] Smith, of my staff, and myself succeeded in gathering up portions of it, which, acting with the Forty-sixth North Carolina, afterward did good service.

Just before the falling back of these regiments, the gallant Colonel Manning was severely wounded and was compelled to leave the field, relinquishing the command of the brigade to the next in rank, Col. E. D. Hall, of the Forty-sixth North Carolina Regiment.

The Forty-eighth North Carolina Regiment, Col. R. C. Hill commanding, after reforming, was sent by me, with [D. A.] French's and [J. R.] Branch's light batteries, to re-enforce General [J.E.B.] Stuart, on the extreme left, who was specially charged by General Jackson with the task of turning the enemy's right.

The falling back of a portion of Manning's brigade enabled the enemy to temporarily reoccupy the point of woods near the position assigned to Colonel [John R.] Cooke, commanding the Twenty-seventh North Carolina and the Third Arkansas Regiments, upon whom the enemy opened a galling fire of musketry, which was replied to with spirit; but the enemy having the cover of the woods while Colonel Cooke's command was on the open ground, this officer very properly drew them back to a corn-field and behind a rail fence, which gave them partial protection. From this position they kept up an effective fire upon the enemy, driving his artillerists from a battery they were attempting to get into position to bear upon Colonel Cooke's command. They afterward succeeded in getting off with their guns, but abandoned two caissons filled with rifle ammunition, from which Captain French that night replenished his exhausted limber-chests.

Early in the afternoon, Major-General Longstreet directed Colonel Cooke, with his own regiment (Twenty-seventh North Carolina) and the Third Arkansas, to charge the enemy, who was threatening his front, as if to pass through the opening between the point of timber held by Ransom's brigade and Longstreet's left. This order was promptly obeyed in the face of such a fire as troops have seldom encountered without running away, and with a steadiness and unfaltering gallantry seldom equaled. Battery after battery, regiment after regiment opened their fire upon them, hurling a torrent of missiles through their ranks, but nothing could arrest their progress, and three times the enemy broke and fled before their impetuous charge. Finally they reached the fatal picket-fences before alluded to. To climb over them, in the face of such a force and under such a fire, would have been sheer madness to attempt, and their ammunition being now almost exhausted, Colonel Cooke, very properly, gave the order to fall back, which was done in the most perfect order, after which the regiments took up their former position, which they continued to hold until night.

After holding its position virtually without ammunition for more than two hours, during which time a Federal attack was expected momentarily, the regiment was relieved and marched to the rear. Resupplied with ammunition and fresh water, it returned to a reserve position on the left, where it was subjected to heavy shelling. Although severely crippled, the Confederate line held during the terrible day-long battle of September 17. The next day the two armies rested on the field, and during the night of September 18 the Army of Northern Virginia retired across the Potomac and went into camp. During the Maryland campaign the regiment lost 31 men killed and 168 wounded.

The Army of Northern Virginia remained in the Shenandoah Valley until the Army of the Potomac began crossing the Blue Ridge Mountains on October 26, 1862. On October 28 Lee ordered Longstreet's corps, of which

Walker's division was still a part, to move east of the mountains to Culpeper Court House and Jackson's corps to move closer to Winchester. When it became apparent that the Federal army, now commanded by General Ambrose E. Burnside, was concentrating on the Rappahannock River across from Fredericksburg, Lee ordered Longstreet's corps to take a position on the heights overlooking the town while Jackson's men went into line on Longstreet's right. During this movement General Walker was transferred and General Robert Ransom was placed in command of the division. Colonel John R. Cooke of the 27th Regiment was promoted to brigadier general and assigned to command Walker's old brigade. The 3rd Regiment Arkansas Infantry and the 30th Regiment Virginia Infantry were transferred, and the 15th Regiment N.C. Troops (5th Regiment N.C. Volunteers) was assigned to the brigade on November 26. Cooke's brigade was thus composed of the 15th Regiment N.C. Troops (5th Regiment N.C. Volunteers), 27th Regiment N.C. Troops, 46th Regiment N.C. Troops, and the 48th Regiment N.C. Troops.

When Ransom's division arrived at Fredericksburg on November 19 it was placed in a supporting position behind the artillery on Marye's Heights and Willis' Hill. During the fighting at Fredericksburg on December 13 General Cooke was wounded, and Colonel Edward D. Hall of the 46th Regiment N.C. Troops assumed command of the brigade. Colonel Hall reported the brigade's activities during the battle as follows (*Official Records*, Series I, Vol. XXI, pp. 629-630):

> Early on the morning of the 11th instant, the brigade, under the command of General Cooke, was ordered to the front, opposite Fredericksburg, where we remained in position until about 12 o'clock Saturday, the 13th, at which time the engagement was going on in our front. The brigade was formed in line of battle as follows: The Twenty-seventh on the right; Forty-eighth next; Forty-sixth next; Fifteenth on the left. We moved into action by regiments. After advancing about 200 yards under a heavy fire of shell and musketry, we arrived at the crest of Willis' Hill, which overlooks the battle-field, on which hill several batteries were placed. With the exception of the Twenty-seventh, the brigade was halted on the crest of the hill, and delivered its fire on the advancing column of the enemy, who was then engaged in making a furious assault on our front lines, which were covered by a long stone wall at the foot of the hill, which assault, on the arrival of the brigade, was repulsed, with great loss to the enemy. The enemy that time succeeded in getting up to within 40 yards of the wall. After the repulse of the enemy, the Forty-sixth was moved down the hill behind the [wall], supporting [T.R.R.] Cobb's brigade, the Twenty-seventh and Forty-sixth remaining behind the fence, and the Forty-eighth and Fifteenth on the top of the hill all day. Six different times during the day did the enemy advance his heavily re-enforced columns, and each time was driven back with immense loss. The action ceased at night, when the brigade was withdrawn, and resumed the position they occupied previous to the action.

During the battle the regiment lost three men killed and twelve wounded.

Cooke's brigade was ordered to South Carolina on January 3, 1863, and moved via Richmond, Goldsboro, and Burgaw to Wilmington. From Wilmington it was sent by rail to Charleston and then to Coosawhatchie. At Coosawhatchie the brigade was placed under the command of General P. G. T. Beauregard, commander of the Third Military District, Department of South Carolina, Georgia, and Florida.

In the late winter and early spring of 1863 the Federals were applying pressure at a number of points along the Atlantic coast and were preparing to launch an attack against Charleston. The latter, which took place on April 7, was exclusively naval and was beaten off by the Confederate defenders without undue difficulty. During the engagement Cooke's brigade was in a supporting position but did not see any action.

On April 23 the brigade left Coosawhatchie for Wilmington, where it arrived on April 26. Five days later the brigade moved to Kinston to reinforce General D. H. Hill's command, which had just failed in attempts to recapture New Bern and Washington, North Carolina. On May 22 Cooke's brigade was sent to the support of the 56th Regiment N.C. Troops, which was being severely handled by a superior force at Gum Swamp. After forcing the enemy to withdraw, Cooke's brigade returned to Kinston. Shortly thereafter it was ordered to Richmond, where it arrived on June 8.

During the Gettysburg campaign in late June and early July, 1863, Cooke's brigade remained in the defenses around Richmond under the command of General Arnold Elzey. One regiment, the 46th Regiment N.C. Troops, was sent to Hanover Junction while the remainder of the brigade was stationed on the Meadow Bridge Road, north of Richmond. Two regiments were later sent to New Bridge, on the South Anna River, and, when a Federal force advanced against that position, General Cooke was dispatched there with the remainder of his brigade on July 4. After halting the Federals, Cooke's men remained on the South Anna until ordered to Fredericksburg when the Army of Northern Virginia returned to Virginia in mid-July after the Gettysburg campaign. In early September the brigade was relieved and returned to Hanover Junction, where it remained until ordered to Gordonsville on or about September 27. At Gordonsville it rejoined the Army of Northern Virginia and was assigned to Henry Heth's division of A. P. Hill's corps.

At the time that Cooke's brigade joined Heth's division on or about October 3, 1863, the Army of Northern Virginia was defending the Rapidan River line while the Army of the Potomac was in position on the Rappahannock River line; and when Lee learned in early October that the Federal army had been weakened in order to send reinforcements to take part in the Chattanooga campaign, he moved to strike the enemy's right flank in the vicinity of the Rapidan River. That maneuver compelled the Federal commander, General George G. Meade, to retire toward Centreville. As the rear guard of Meade's army was passing through Bristoe Station on October 14, Heth's division of Hill's corps came onto the field. Without waiting for the rest of his division to come up or pausing to reconnoiter, Hill ordered an attack; and the brigades of Cooke and General William W. Kirkland, unaware that they were heavily outnumbered, advanced down an open hill toward Federal troops entrenched behind a railroad embankment. Cooke's and Kirkland's brigades, swept by the murderous fire of three Federal divisions, were repulsed with decimating casualties. During the fighting General Cooke was wounded, and Colonel Edward D. Hall of the 46th Regiment N.C. Troops assumed command of the brigade. Colonel Hall reported the battle as follows (*Official Records*, Series I, Vol. XXIX, pt. 1, pp. 434-436):

I have the honor to report that on the 14th instant, on arriving within 1 or 2 miles of Bristoe Station, the brigade formed a line of battle on the right of the road in the following order: First, Forty-sixth North Carolina; second, Fifteenth North Carolina; third, Twenty-seventh North Carolina; and the Forty-eighth North Carolina on the left. After forming we advanced through a very thick undergrowth. On clearing the woods and arriving in the first opening the brigade was halted a few moments to correct the alignment. The enemy was discovered massed upon our left beyond the railroad and to the left of the road leading to the station. Being then in command of the extreme right regiment, I immediately discovered that the enemy was in heavy force on my right and busily engaged in getting in position. In a few moments we were ordered to advance, and soon after the enemy's skirmishers commenced firing on my right flank. I discovered the line of battle behind the railroad, extending as far on my right as I could see; also a mass of troops lying perpendicular to the road and on the side next to us, from which body an advance was made on my right in considerable numbers. I then sent word to General Cooke that I was much annoyed by the fire and seriously threatened. I sent my right company to engage the skirmishers on my right, but they were soon driven in. I then changed the front of my regiment on the first company and checked their advance.

The brigade had again halted just before getting under fire, and I moved back just in time to join the line in its final advance. Soon after getting under fire I found that the left of the brigade had commenced firing as they advanced, which was taken up along the whole line.

Shortly afterward information was brought me that General Cooke was wounded and that I was in command. I ordered my regiment to cease firing and passed up to the center of the brigade, stopping the firing as I went. The brigade was then within 200 yards of the railroad. On getting on the top of the hill, I found the brigade suffering from a heavy flank fire of artillery from the right. The number of guns I cannot say; evidently more than one battery. Also the guns on the left and rear of the railroad had an enfilading fire on us. The musketry fire from the line of railroad was very heavy. I soon saw that a rapid advance must be made or a withdrawal. I chose the former. I passed the word to the right regiments to charge, which was done in what I conceive to be in good style. The fourth regiment was somewhat confused, but I sent the lieutenant-colonel commanding word to follow the line, which he did with about two-thirds of his regiment, the balance giving way.

The brigade charged up to within 40 yards of the railroad, and from the severity of the fire, and from their seeing the extreme left of the line falling back, they fell back—the two right regiments in good order, the third (Twenty-seventh North Carolina) in an honorable confusion, from the fact that between one-half and two-thirds of the regiment had been killed and wounded, they being in a far more exposed position than the other two regiments and having gone farther. The Forty-eighth, in advancing, encountered the whole line falling back. I halted the brigade in the first field we came to, about 400 yards from the enemy's line, from which position we fell back beyond the second field on seeing the enemy

come out on our right and left. After a short time the brigade of General [Joseph R.] Davis joined us on the right, when we again advanced to within 400 yards of the enemy, and on seeing the right brigade halt I halted, where we remained during the night.

As there was a battery of artillery lost during the engagement, and from its proximity to the brigade the loss may be laid to it, I will state that I knew nothing of the guns being there until we had fallen back to the second field. The guns may have been in our rear, but they must certainly have been placed there after we advanced; and in retreating, our losses both by casualties and straggling, shortened our line so much that with the addition of one of General Kirkland's regiments (Forty-fourth North Carolina), which joined our left, the left of the brigade was some distance to the right of the guns. On learning the guns were there and in danger, I dispatched a portion of one regiment to the relief, but the guns had been taken off before the relief arrived.

I would respectfully state that I have been with the brigade during some of the heaviest engagements of the war, and have never seen the men more cool and determined, and that their falling back resulted from no fault of theirs, but from the great superiority in number and position of the enemy, and entire want of support, both in rear and prolongation of our lines.

During the battle the 27th Regiment lost 30 men killed and 174 wounded.

No further attempts were made to attack the enemy at Bristoe Station, and during the night the Federal rear guard continued its retreat to Centreville. Lee retired to the Rappahannock but, after battles at Rappahannock Bridge and Kelly's Ford on November 7, returned to the Rapidan. On November 26 Meade began moving his army to cross the Rapidan below Lee's position, and Lee shifted his forces eastward to intercept the Federals. By November 29 Lee's men were strongly entrenched at Mine Run, and Meade, unable to locate a vulnerable point against which to launch an attack, also began entrenching. On the morning of December 2 Lee sent an attack force composed of Cadmus M. Wilcox's and Richard H. Anderson's divisions against what he believed to be an exposed Federal flank; however, when the Confederates moved out they found that the Federal army had retreated. A pursuit was undertaken, but Meade recrossed the Rapidan unmolested. Lee then ordered his troops into winter quarters, and the 27th Regiment spent the winter of 1863-1864 on picket along the Rapidan and in camp with Cooke's brigade near Orange Court House.

The brigade was still in camp near Orange Court House when the Federal army, now commanded by General U. S. Grant, began crossing the lower Rapidan on the morning of May 4, 1864, and entered an area of dense woods and tangled undergrowth known as the Wilderness. When news of Grant's crossing was received, Lee ordered Hill's corps to move toward the enemy by the Plank Road and Richard S. Ewell's corps to advance on Hill's left down the Orange Turnpike. Longstreet's corps, at Gordonsville, was instructed to move up on Hill's right. On the morning of May 5 Hill's column, with Kirkland's brigade in the lead, encountered Federal cavalry at Parker's Store and succeeded in forcing the enemy back. Hill's men then occupied the crossroads at Parker's Store. Immediately north of the Orange Turnpike, Ewell encountered the enemy in corps strength, and Hill ordered Heth's division to deploy across the Plank Road in anticipation of a Federal attack. Cooke's brigade was placed in the center of the Confederate line with Kirkland's brigade behind it in reserve. At 4:00 P.M. elements of the Federal II Corps attacked Heth's position and were repulsed with the aid of Kirkland's brigade after desperate fighting. After repelling repeated Federal assaults, the Confederates went over to the attack but were unable to dislodge the enemy. Severe fighting continued until Wilcox's division arrived on the scene and succeeded in stabilizing the Confederate line. During the night Cooke's battered brigade was withdrawn and placed in reserve to the left rear of Heth's position on the left of the road. Wilcox's division took up position on the right of the road.

At 5:00 A.M. the next morning, May 6, Federal columns struck the Confederate line in front and on the left flank. Thirteen Federal brigades fell upon Hill's eight brigades with such suddenness and violence that there was scarcely time for resistance, and the entire line fell back in disorder. Kirkland's men then rallied on Cooke's brigade, and other units joined in support of Cooke's position, but the Federals broke through again and a general rout followed. Only the timely arrival of Longstreet's corps, moving up to reinforce Hill, prevented the collapse of the right wing of Lee's army. The Federal assault was blunted and driven back, and Hill's men, after re-forming behind Longstreet, were dispatched to close a gap on the left of Longstreet's line. The battle continued on Longstreet's front until night brought an end to the fighting. During the Wilderness battle of May 5-6, 1864, the 27th Regiment sustained heavy but unreported losses in killed and wounded.

Late in the evening of May 7 it became apparent that Grant's army was on the march toward Spotsylvania Court House, and throughout the night of May 7-8 Lee's men pushed southeastward in a race with the Federals to that vital crossroad. The race was narrowly won by the Confederates on the morning of May 8, and a strong defensive line was quickly constructed. Hill's corps, under the temporary command of General Jubal A. Early, was positioned on the right of the line with Ewell's corps in the center and Longstreet's corps, under the temporary command of General Richard H. Anderson, on the left. Heth's division occupied the extreme right of the Confederate position until May 10, when it was moved to the extreme left of the line to attack an exposed Federal flank. After inconclusive fighting with Federal troops under the command of General Francis C. Barlow, Heth's men returned to their original position on the Confederate right on the morning of May 11.

Early on the morning of May 12 the Federals launched a sudden attack against a convex, U-shaped salient in the center of the Confederate line, overran the salient at its apex, and began driving the survivors back. After severe hand-to-hand fighting, Confederate reinforcements managed to check the Federal assault while a new line was constructed across the base of the salient. Cooke's brigade was not involved in the vicious fighting at the so-called "Mule Shoe" but extended its front in order to cover the area vacated by reinforcements sent to stem the Federal attack.

After several more unsuccessful attempts against the Confederate line during the next week, General Grant began moving eastward; Lee then moved his army to the North Anna River to a point just north of Hanover Junction, where he blocked the Federal route of advance. Several days of inconclusive fighting, in which Heth's division was not directly involved, convinced Grant of the tactical inferiority of his position on the North Anna, and on the night of May 26-27 he recrossed the river and moved eastward toward the Pamunkey.

Lee began shifting his army southward as soon as it was learned that Grant was again on the march, and on May 27 Ewell's corps, temporarily commanded by General Early (General Hill had returned to the command of his own corps on May 21), marched some twenty-four miles and entrenched between Beaver Dam Creek and Pole Green Church. Longstreet's corps, still under the command of Anderson, came up on Early's right, and Hill's corps extended the line on Early's left. On May 30, under orders from Lee, Early moved to attack the Federal left at Bethesda Church. The attack failed to turn the Federal flank but revealed that the enemy was moving again to the Confederate right.

The two armies began concentrating at Cold Harbor, where new fighting broke out on June 1. The next day two of Hill's divisions, commanded by Cadmus M. Wilcox and William Mahone, were ordered to leave their position on the left of the Confederate line and go to the support of Anderson, on the right. While Wilcox and Mahone moved to anchor the Confederate right, Heth's division, still in its original position on the left, joined Ewell's (Early's) corps in an attack which, after some initial success, was beaten off by Federal reinforcements.

At 4:30 A.M. on June 3 the Federals launched a three-pronged frontal attack against the six-mile-long Confederate line. Three separate assaults against Heth's well-entrenched division were bloodily repulsed, and at other points along the line the swarming Federal attackers were beaten off with equally devastating casualties. At about 11:00 A.M. the Federal assaults ceased, but infantry and artillery fire continued from defensive positions until 1:00 P.M. Heth's division was ordered to the right to rejoin Hill's corps at Turkey Hill in late afternoon, but the three-day battle of Cold Harbor was over, and more than 12,000 Federals were dead or wounded.

The two armies settled into defensive positions, where they remained until Grant began to move south toward the James River on June 12. Lee followed on June 13 and made contact with the enemy at Riddell's Shop the same day. A defensive line was established, but no general engagement followed. Grant then crossed the James and moved against Petersburg. Hill's corps arrived at Petersburg on June 18 and went into position on the extreme right of the line, which was thereby extended to the Petersburg & Weldon Railroad. Heth's division began entrenching and remained in the line until July 28, when it was ordered to the north side of the James to confront a Federal advance that was later revealed to be a feint. Heth's division returned to the Petersburg line on August 2 after the withdrawal of the Federal feint and the failure of Grant's Petersburg mine assault on July 30. Heth's men then enjoyed three weeks of relative quiet.

In mid-August, 1864, General Grant ordered an extension of his line to the west, and on August 18 a Federal force occupied Globe Tavern on the vital Petersburg & Weldon Railroad. Hill's corps was engaged at Globe Tavern on August 18-21 in an unsuccessful effort to dislodge the Federals. South of Globe Tavern a Federal force which had occupied Reams' Station and was destroying the railroad south of that point was attacked by Hill on August 25. An assault by two brigades was repulsed, but a stronger attack on the Federal right in which Cooke's brigade took part succeeded in breaking the Federal line. Some 2,000 men and nine pieces of artillery were captured, and the Federals were driven from the field in disorder. Hill's corps returned to the Petersburg trenches that night. According to an officer who served in the 27th Regiment, the strength of the regiment was now reduced to approximately seventy men.

Heth's division did not see action again until September 30 when the Confederates, in an unsuccessful attempt to prevent Grant from extending his line westward from Globe Tavern, were defeated at Jones' Farm. On October 27 a Federal force attempted to cut the Boydton Plank Road and the South Side Railroad by gaining possession of the high ground north of Hatcher's Run at Burgess' Mill. Hill concentrated Heth's and William Mahone's divisions and General Wade Hampton's cavalry force to oppose this advance and, while Heth's men held the Confederate center, sent Mahone to strike the Federal right while Hampton moved against the left. Mahone's attack failed, but the simultaneous attack on the left achieved a measure of success and was pressed vigorously until dark. The Federals withdrew the next day, and Cooke's brigade marched to a camp near Hatcher's Run and went into winter quarters.

On December 8 Cooke's brigade, with the remainder of Hill's corps, was ordered to Belfield to oppose a Federal advance on the Petersburg & Weldon Railroad. Marching through sleet and snow, the Confederates arrived at a point a few miles from Belfield where they learned that the Federals had retired. Hill then attempted to cut off the enemy's retreat and intercepted the Federal cavalry at Jarratt's Station. After a brief skirmish the Confederates pushed on, only to find that the Federal infantry was three hours ahead of them and could not be overtaken. Hill then called off the pursuit. After bivouacking for the night Hill started back to Hatcher's Run, which he reached on the afternoon of December 13. Except for picket duty, Cooke's brigade was involved in no further action or activities for the remainder of the year.

Early in February, 1865, General Grant ordered a move on the left of his line to secure a position on the Boydton Plank Road at Hatcher's Run. Cooke's brigade led an assault on this new Federal position on February 5 but, finding itself inadequately supported by a brigade on its left flank which failed to assume its assigned position, Cooke's men fell back in the face of mounting Federal pressure. After more skirmishing on February 6, the brigade returned to its former camp.

Following almost two months of relative quiet, during which they were subjected to privation, bitter cold, and the occasional attention of Federal artillerymen and sharpshooters, Cooke's men marched to Petersburg on the night of March 24-25 and were formed in line to take part in an attack on Fort Stedman, a key Federal fortification whose capture would endanger Grant's line of supply and help relieve the intensifying pressure on the Richmond-Petersburg defenses. Cooke's brigade was held in reserve during the Confederate assault which, after some initial success, was shattered by a massive Federal counterattack. The brigade then returned to its former camp.

On March 26 General Phil Sheridan's powerful cavalry command, under orders from Grant, crossed the James River and rode towards Petersburg. This movement, which threatened to unhinge the right flank of the Richmond-Petersburg defense system, was thwarted temporarily on March 31 when a Confederate force under George E. Pickett drove Sheridan's cavalry back from Dinwiddie Court House. Pickett then retired to Five Forks, where a defensive position was established to anchor the extreme right of Lee's line. On April 1 Federal infantry and cavalry surprised Pickett at Five Forks and drove a wedge between his force and the Confederate line at Hatcher's Run. Pickett's men were then overpowered and driven from the field with heavy casualties, and an avenue of advance was opened to the flank and rear of the Petersburg defenses.

On April 2 the Federals launched a general attack against the Confederate line, broke through to the left of Cooke's brigade, and swept down the trenches. Cooke's men fell back to the second line of defense, where they were subjected to infantry and artillery fire. General Lee, aware that Richmond could no longer be held, ordered a general evacuation that night.

The Army of Northern Virginia, now a shadow of its former self, began to retreat westward toward Amelia Court House on the evening of April 2. Almost immediately the 27th Regiment and three other North Carolina regiments (the 13th, 22nd, and 49th) were cut off from the main body of the army while defending a ford of the Appomattox River. After retreating upstream in the face of enemy pressure, crossings of the swollen Appomattox and its Deep Creek tributary were safely accomplished, and contact was reestablished with Lee's retreating columns on April 4. (At that time the officers of the 27th Regiment reorganized the depleted unit into a battalion of two companies commanded by Lieutenant Colonel Joseph C. Webb; the companies were commanded by Major Calvin Herring and Captain John A. Sloan.)

On April 5 the weary and half-starved Confederates, under hit-and-run attack by Federal cavalry, reached Amelia Court House, only to find that the vital supplies ordered sent there had not arrived. At Sayler's Creek the next day the rear guard of the army was cut off and destroyed, with the loss of approximately a third of Lee's remaining force. The 27th Regiment skirmished that day with Federal cavalry and on April 6 was involved in savage fighting in defense of a Confederate wagontrain. The army continued to reel westward until April 9, 1865, when its last route of retreat was blocked. General Lee surrendered at Appomattox Court House that day. One hundred seventeen members of the 27th Regiment N.C. Troops were present to receive their paroles.

FIELD AND STAFF

COLONELS

SINGLETARY, GEORGE BADGER

Previously served as Captain of Company H of this regiment and as Lieutenant Colonel of Singletary's Battalion. [See regimental history, page 1.] Elected Colonel on September 28, 1861, and transferred to the Field and Staff. Resigned on December 16, 1861, after he was court-martialed (and convicted) for "conduct prejudicial to good order and military discipline." Later served as Colonel of the 44th Regiment N.C. Troops.

SLOAN, JOHN

Previously served as Captain of Company B of this regiment. Elected Lieutenant Colonel on September 28, 1861, and transferred to the Field and Staff. Elected Colonel on December 23, 1861. Present or accounted for until he was defeated for reelection when the regiment was reorganized in April, 1862.

COOKE, JOHN ROGERS

Born at Jefferson Barracks, Missouri, and was by occupation a U.S. Army officer prior to enlisting at age 29. Elected Colonel on April 24, 1862. Wounded "no less than seven times" in unspecified battles prior to November 1, 1862, when he was promoted to Brigadier General and transferred.

SINGLETARY, RICHARD W.

Previously served as Captain of Company H of this

regiment. Elected Lieutenant Colonel on March 18, 1862, and transferred to the Field and Staff. Wounded at Sharpsburg, Maryland, September 17, 1862. Returned to duty on an unspecified date. Promoted to Colonel on November 1, 1862. Resigned on or about December 5, 1862, by reason of disability from wounds. Later served as Captain of Company H, 44th Regiment N.C. Troops.

GILMER, JOHN ALEXANDER, Jr.

Previously served as 2nd Lieutenant of Company B of this regiment. Elected Major on January 6, 1862, and transferred to the Field and Staff. Promoted to Lieutenant Colonel on November 1, 1862, and was promoted to Colonel on December 5, 1862. Wounded in the leg at Fredericksburg, Virginia, December 13, 1862. Returned to duty on an unspecified date. Wounded in the left leg at Bristoe Station, Virginia, October 14, 1863. Reported absent wounded until January 11, 1865, when he was retired to the Invalid Corps by reason of disability from wounds received at Bristoe Station.

WHITFIELD, GEORGE F.

Previously served as Captain of Company C of this regiment. Promoted to Major on November 1, 1862, and transferred to the Field and Staff. Promoted to Lieutenant Colonel on or about December 5, 1862. Wounded in the right leg at or near Bristoe Station, Virginia, October 14, 1863. Returned to duty on an unspecified date. Wounded in the head at or near Cold Harbor, Virginia, June 3, 1864. Promoted to Colonel on January 11, 1865, while absent wounded. Reported absent wounded through February, 1865.

LIEUTENANT COLONELS

SINGLETARY, THOMAS C.

Previously served as 3rd Lieutenant of Company E of this regiment. Elected Major on September 28, 1861, and transferred to the Field and Staff. Elected Lieutenant Colonel on January 6, 1862. Present or accounted for until he resigned on or about March 12, 1862. Reason he resigned not reported. Later served as Colonel of the 44th Regiment N.C. Troops.

WEBB, JOSEPH C.

Previously served as Captain of Company G of this regiment. Promoted to Major on or about December 5, 1862, and transferred to the Field and Staff. Wounded in the arm and/or left side at Wilderness, Virginia, May 6, 1864. Returned to duty prior to November 1, 1864. Promoted to Lieutenant Colonel on January 11, 1865. Present or accounted for until he surrendered at Appomattox Court House, Virginia, April 9, 1865.

MAJOR

HERRING, CALVIN

Previously served as Captain of Company D of this regiment. Promoted to Major and transferred to the Field and Staff on January 11, 1865. Present or accounted for until he surrendered at Appomattox Court House, Virginia, April 9, 1865.

ADJUTANTS

JOYNER, JASON P.

Born in Pitt County where he enlisted. Appointed Adjutant (3rd Lieutenant) on April 19, 1861. Present or accounted for until elected Captain on November 18, 1861, and transferred to Company E of this regiment.

WILSON, WILLIAM P.

Previously served as 3rd Lieutenant of Company B of this regiment. Appointed Adjutant on June 1, 1862. Died at Greensboro on or about March 3, 1863, of disease. "He was a most worthy young man, and an excellent officer."

KNIGHT, WALTER ASHLAND

Previously served as Private in Company A of this regiment. Appointed Adjutant on March 23, 1863, and transferred to the Field and Staff. Killed at Reams' Station, Virginia, August 25, 1864. [See also Sergeants Major's section below.]

PITTMAN, THADDEUS E.

Previously served as Sergeant Major of this regiment. [See Sergeants Major's section below.] Appointed Adjutant (1st Lieutenant) on August 25, 1864. Present or accounted for until he surrendered at Appomattox Court House, Virginia, April 9, 1865.

ASSISTANT QUARTERMASTER

WHITE, JOSHUA W.

Previously served as 2nd Lieutenant of Company F of this regiment. Appointed Assistant Quartermaster on or about September 5, 1861. Present or accounted for until he was appointed Assistant Quartermaster of Brigadier General John R. Cooke's brigade on or about September 15, 1864, and transferred.

ASSISTANT COMMISSARY OF SUBSISTENCE

MORRILL, WILLIAM H.

Previously served as Captain of Company E of this regiment. Appointed Assistant Commissary of Subsistence (Captain) on November 2, 1861, and transferred to the Field and Staff. Present or accounted for until promoted to Assistant Commissary of Subsistence of Brigadier General John R. Cooke's brigade on July 16, 1863, and transferred.

SURGEONS

BLOW, WILLIAM J.

Appointed Surgeon on or about October 8, 1861. "Dropped" on April 22, 1862, by reason of "having refused to appear for examination before the Army Medical Board at Goldsboro."

TURNER, HECTOR

Appointed Surgeon of this regiment in May, 1862. No further records.

HOLT, WILLIAM A.

Appointed Assistant Surgeon on or about October 2, 1861. Promoted to Surgeon on September 26, 1862. Transferred to the 4th Regiment Virginia Infantry prior to January 1, 1863.

HOWARD, E. LLOYD

Resided in Maryland. Appointed Surgeon on November 2, 1862. Present or accounted for until he surrendered at Appomattox Court House, Virginia, April 9, 1865.

ASSISTANT SURGEONS

HALSEY, ROBERT S.
Appointed Assistant Surgeon to rank from June 3, 1861. Reported present with the regiment in May-July, 1862. Transferred to an unspecified artillery battalion on an unspecified date.

HUNT, LEANDER GWYNN
Previously served as Hospital Steward of this regiment. [See Hospital Stewards' section below.] Appointed Assistant Surgeon on June 23, 1862. Captured at Hatcher's Run, Virginia, April 1-2, 1865. Confined at Old Capitol Prison, Washington, D.C., until transferred to Johnson's Island, Ohio, May 1, 1865. Released at Johnson's Island on June 18, 1865, after taking the Oath of Allegiance.

CHAPLAIN

FAIRLEY, DAVID S.
Resided in Cumberland County. Appointed Chaplain on February 10, 1863. Resigned on or about December 8, 1863. Reason he resigned not reported.

ENSIGN

STORY, WILLIAM C.
Previously served as Private in Company B of this regiment. Appointed Ensign (Lieutenant) on April 28, 1864, and transferred to the Field and Staff. Wounded in the arm at Spotsylvania Court House, Virginia, May 10, 1864. Returned to duty prior to November 1, 1864. Present or accounted for through February, 1865.

SERGEANTS MAJOR

WHITFIELD, JAMES G.
Previously served as Private in Company D of this regiment. Promoted to Sergeant Major on July 19, 1861, and transferred to the Field and Staff. Present or accounted for until he was reduced to ranks on February 15, 1862, and transferred back to Company D of this regiment.

SLOAN, JOHN A.
Served as Sergeant in Company B of this regiment. Reported on duty as acting Sergeant Major from May 1, 1861, until January 14, 1862, when he was elected 2nd Lieutenant and transferred back to Company B. Later served as Captain of Company B.

DUPREE, R. W.
Previously served as 1st Sergeant of Company H of this regiment. Promoted to Sergeant Major on February 19, 1862, and transferred to the Field and Staff. Present or accounted for until wounded in the breast and captured at Sharpsburg, Maryland, September 17, 1862. Confined at Fort McHenry, Maryland, and at Fort Monroe, Virginia. Paroled and transferred to Aiken's Landing, James River, Virginia, October 25, 1862, for exchange. Declared exchanged at Aiken's Landing on November 10, 1862. No further records.

KNIGHT, WALTER ASHLAND
Served as Private in Company A of this regiment. Detailed as acting Sergeant Major and transferred to the Field and Staff on September 20, 1862. Reported on duty as acting Sergeant Major through November, 1862. Transferred back to Company A on an unspecified date. [See also Adjutants' section above.]

WEATHERLY, ROBERT D.
Previously served as Corporal in Company B of this regiment. Promoted to Sergeant Major on March 27, 1863, and transferred to the Field and Staff. Wounded in the groin and hip at Bristoe Station, Virginia, October 14, 1863. Hospitalized at Richmond, Virginia, where he died on October 24, 1863 of wounds and "erysipelas." "Bob was a noble boy, and bravest of the brave. Fear was no word in his vocabulary. He was always at his post, and though slight in stature, his form was ever seen in the thickest of the fight."

PITTMAN, THADDEUS E.
Previously served as Sergeant in Company A of this regiment. Promoted to Sergeant Major in October, 1863, and transferred to the Field and Staff. Wounded at Wilderness, Virginia, May 5, 1864. Appointed Adjutant of the regiment on August 25, 1864. [See Adjutants' section above.]

WARD, WILLIAM E.
Previously served as Sergeant in Company I of this regiment. Promoted to Sergeant Major on August 25, 1864, and transferred to the Field and Staff. Present or accounted for until he surrendered at Appomattox Court House, Virginia, April 9, 1865.

QUARTERMASTER SERGEANTS

EDWARDS, DAVID H.
Previously served as Private in Company B of this regiment. Promoted to Quartermaster Sergeant on December 1, 1862, and transferred to the Field and Staff. Captured in Caroline County, Virginia, on or about May 20, 1864. Confined at Point Lookout, Maryland, until paroled and transferred to Aiken's Landing, James River, Virginia, where he was received on March 16, 1865, for exchange. Paroled at Greensboro subsequent to April 26, 1865.

STRAYHORN, SIDNEY G.
Served as Private in Company G of this regiment. Detailed as Quartermaster Sergeant on May 20, 1864, and transferred to the Field and Staff. Wounded in the shoulder "in Virginia" in June, 1864. Transferred back to Company G subsequent to February 28, 1865.

ORDNANCE SERGEANT

LINDSAY, ANDREW DAVID
Previously served as Private in Company B of this regiment. Promoted to Ordnance Sergeant on April 1, 1862, and transferred to the Field and Staff. Present or accounted for until he surrendered at Appomattox Court House, Virginia, April 9, 1865.

HOSPITAL STEWARDS

HUNT, LEANDER GWYNN
Previously served as Private in Company B of this regiment. Promoted to Hospital Steward on May 18, 1862, and transferred to the Field and Staff. Appointed Assistant Surgeon of the regiment on June 23, 1862. [See Assistant Surgeons' section above.]

MATTOCKS, C. J.

Previously served as Private in Company I of this regiment. Promoted to Hospital Steward on June 20, 1862, and transferred to the Field and Staff. Present or accounted for until discharged on August 1, 1862, by reason of disability.

PARKS, CHARLES M.

Previously served as Private in Company G of this regiment. Promoted to Hospital Steward on August 1, 1862, and transferred to the Field and Staff. Captured at Sharpsburg, Maryland, September 17, 1862, after he was left behind to attend the wounded. Paroled prior to November 1, 1862. Returned to duty on an unspecified date. Present or accounted for until he surrendered at Appomattox Court House, Virginia, April 9, 1865.

BAND

ALDRIDGE, BENNETT FRANKLIN, Musician

Previously served as Private in Company C of this regiment. Promoted to Musician in September-October, 1864, and transferred to the regimental band. Present or accounted for through February, 1865.

BRILEY, JAMES A., Musician

Previously served as Musician in Company H of this regiment. Transferred to the regimental band in November, 1862-October, 1864. Captured at Deep Creek, Virginia, April 3, 1865. Confined at Point Lookout, Maryland, until released on June 23, 1865, after taking the Oath of Allegiance.

BURROUGHS, WILLIAM H. H., Musician

Previously served as Corporal in Company G of this regiment. Promoted to Musician (Drummer) on November 1, 1863, and transferred to the regimental band. Present or accounted for until he surrendered at Appomattox Court House, Virginia, April 9, 1865.

DICKSON, SAMUEL A., Musician

Previously served as Private in Company G of this regiment. Promoted to Musician on August 1, 1862, and transferred to the regimental band. Present or accounted for until he surrendered at Appomattox Court House, Virginia, April 9, 1865.

FAIRCLOTH, MATTHEW, Musician

Previously served as Private in Company A of this regiment. Promoted to Musician in November, 1862-October, 1864, and transferred to the regimental band. Reduced to ranks subsequent to February 28, 1865, and transferred back to Company A.

HIGGINS, EDWARD B., Musician

Previously served as Private in Company B of this regiment. Promoted to Musician on or about August 1, 1862, and transferred to the regimental band. Present or accounted for until captured near Petersburg, Virginia, April 2, 1865. Confined at Point Lookout, Maryland, until released on June 13, 1865, after taking the Oath of Allegiance.

JONES, RICHARD E., Musician

Previously served as Private in Company A of this regiment. Promoted to Musician in September-October, 1862, and transferred to the regimental band. Captured at Petersburg, Virginia, April 3, 1865. Confined at Point Lookout, Maryland, until released on June 28, 1865, after taking the Oath of Allegiance.

KINSEY, JOHN L., Musician

Previously served as Private in Company I of this regiment. Promoted to Musician in November, 1862-October, 1864, and transferred to the regimental band. Present or accounted for through February, 1865.

LIPSCOMB, SAMUEL M., Musician

Previously served as Private in Company B of this regiment. Promoted to Musician on or about August 1, 1862, and transferred to the regimental band. Present or accounted for until he surrendered at Appomattox Court House, Virginia, April 9, 1865.

MANKER, GUILFORD, Musician

Previously served as Private in Company H of this regiment. Promoted to Musician in September-October, 1864, and transferred to the regimental band. Captured at Hatcher's Run, Virginia, April 2, 1865. Confined at Point Lookout, Maryland, until released on June 29, 1865, after taking the Oath of Allegiance.

SLOAN, THOMAS J., Musician

Previously served as Sergeant in Company B of this regiment. Promoted to Musician on August 1, 1862, and transferred to the regimental band. Present or accounted for until paroled at Greensboro in 1865.

SPENCE, JAMES A., Chief Musician

Previously served as Private in Company D of this regiment. Promoted to Musician (Fifer) in May-June, 1862, and transferred to the regimental band. Promoted to Musician (Drummer) in July-August, 1862. Promoted to Chief Musician in November, 1862-October, 1864. Captured at Petersburg, Virginia, April 3, 1865. Confined at Point Lookout, Maryland, until released on June 20, 1865, after taking the Oath of Allegiance.

SUGGS, JOHN H., Musician

Previously served as Private in Company C of this regiment. Promoted to Musician on September 1, 1862, and transferred to the regimental band. Wounded at Sharpsburg, Maryland, September 17, 1862. Returned to duty on an unspecified date. Surrendered at Appomattox Court House, Virginia, April 9, 1865.

TURNER, SAMUEL D., Musician

Previously served as Private in Company K of this regiment. Promoted to Musician in September-October, 1862, and transferred to the regimental band. Captured at Sutherland's Station, Virginia, on or about April 3, 1865. Confined at Point Lookout, Maryland, until released on June 20, 1865, after taking the Oath of Allegiance.

COMPANY A

This company, known as the "Goldsboro Rifles," was raised in Wayne County and enlisted at Fort Macon in Carteret County on April 15, 1861. It was mustered into service on June 13, 1861, and was later assigned to the 27th Regiment as Company A. After joining the regiment the company functioned as a part of the regiment, and its history for the war period is reported as a part of the regimental history.

The information contained in the following company roster was compiled principally from company muster rolls for June 13, 1861-October, 1862, and September, 1864-February, 1865. No company muster rolls were found for November, 1862-August, 1864, or for the period after February, 1865. Valuable information was obtained also from primary records such as the Roll of Honor, medical records, prisoner of war records, discharge certificates, and pension applications, and from secondary sources such as postwar rosters and histories, cemetery records, and records of the United Daughters of the Confederacy.

OFFICERS

CAPTAINS

CRATON, MARSHALL D.
Born in Rutherford County and resided in Wayne County prior to enlisting at age 31. Elected Captain on or about April 15, 1861. Present or accounted for until November 6, 1861, when he was elected Lieutenant Colonel of the 35th Regiment N.C. Troops and transferred to that unit.

PHILLIPS, STEPHEN D.
Resided in Wayne County and enlisted at age 40. Elected 3rd Lieutenant on or about April 15, 1861, and was elected 2nd Lieutenant on July 5, 1861. Elected Captain on November 21, 1861. Present or accounted for until he was defeated for reelection when the regiment was reorganized in April, 1862.

BRYAN, JAMES D.
Resided in Wayne County and enlisted at age 21, April 15, 1861. Mustered in as Corporal and was appointed acting Orderly Sergeant on May 5, 1861. Elected 3rd Lieutenant on July 5, 1861, and was elected 2nd Lieutenant on November 21, 1861. Elected Captain on April 22, 1862. Present or accounted for until wounded in the right thigh at or near Bristoe Station, Virginia, on or about October 14, 1863. Right leg amputated. Died in hospital at Richmond, Virginia, October 30, 1863, of wounds.

BRYAN, JOHN D.
Resided in Wayne County and enlisted at age 25, April 15, 1861. Mustered in as Private and was promoted to Sergeant in March-April, 1862. Promoted to 1st Sergeant on April 22, 1862, and was elected 3rd Lieutenant on October 1, 1862. Promoted to Captain on October 31, 1863. Present or accounted for until he resigned on October 6, 1864. Letter of resignation indicates he resigned because "I have unintentionally incurred the displeasure of my Brigade Commander [and] therefore ask that I may be permited [sic] to join some other command."

LIEUTENANTS

ANDREWS, WILLIAM S. G., 2nd Lieutenant
Born at Woodbury, Connecticut, and resided in Wayne County where he was by occupation a merchant prior to enlisting at age 39. Elected 2nd Lieutenant on April 15, 1861. Present or accounted for until June 24, 1861, when he was appointed Captain of Company F, 10th Regiment N.C. State Troops (1st Regiment N.C. Artillery), to rank from May 16, 1861, and transferred to that unit.

BORDEN, WILLIAM H., 2nd Lieutenant
Resided in Wayne County and enlisted at age 20, April 15, 1861. Mustered in as Private and was promoted to Sergeant on September 23, 1861. Promoted to 1st Sergeant on November 21, 1861, and was appointed 2nd Lieutenant on February 20, 1862. Present or accounted for until transferred to Company E, 50th Regiment N.C. Troops, on or about March 7, 1862.

DENMARK, JOEL J., 2nd Lieutenant
Resided in Wayne County and enlisted at age 19, June 12, 1861. Mustered in as Private and was promoted to Corporal on October 1, 1862. Elected 2nd Lieutenant on January 31, 1863. Present or accounted for until killed at Bristoe Station, Virginia, October 14, 1863.

HOOKS, BOAZ F., 3rd Lieutenant
Resided in Wayne County and enlisted at age 30, April 15, 1861. Mustered in as Corporal and was promoted to 1st Sergeant on July 5, 1861. Elected 3rd Lieutenant on November 21, 1861. Present or accounted for until he was defeated for reelection when the regiment was reorganized in April, 1862. Later served as Major of an unspecified North Carolina reserve battalion.

HUNT, STEPHEN MONROE, 1st Lieutenant
Born in Beaufort County and resided in Wayne County prior to enlisting at age 24. Elected 1st Lieutenant on or about April 15, 1861. Present or accounted for until he was defeated for reelection when the regiment was reorganized in April, 1862. "Died from war injury" on December 2, 1863. Place and date injured not reported. Place of death not reported.

NOBLES, RICHARD L., 3rd Lieutenant
Resided in Pitt County and enlisted at age 22, August 19, 1861. Mustered in as Private and was elected 3rd Lieutenant on April 22, 1862. Present or accounted for until wounded and reported captured at Sharpsburg, Maryland, September 17, 1862. Died on September 20, 1862, of wounds. Place of death not reported.

PARKER, JOHN G., 1st Lieutenant
Resided in Wayne County and enlisted at age 31, April 15, 1861. Mustered in as Private and was appointed 2nd Lieutenant on April 22, 1862. Present or accounted for until captured in Maryland on or about September 15, 1862. Confined at Fort Delaware, Delaware, until transferred to Aiken's Landing, James River, Virginia, October 2, 1862, for exchange. Declared exchanged at Aiken's Landing on November 10, 1862. Returned to duty on an unspecified date. Promoted to 1st Lieutenant on or about October 24, 1863. Present or accounted for until he surrendered at Appomattox Court House, Virginia, April 9, 1865.

SLOCUMB, THOMAS WRIGHT, 1st Lieutenant
Born in Wayne County and was by occupation a cadet at the military institute in Charlotte prior to enlisting at Fort Macon at age 19, June 1, 1861. Mustered in as Private and was promoted to Sergeant on November 21, 1861. Elected 1st Lieutenant on April 22, 1862. Present or accounted for until he resigned on September 25, 1862, by reason of ill health. Later served as Private in Company H, 9th Regiment N.C. State Troops (1st Regiment N.C. Cavalry).

WHITLEY, NEEDHAM LAFAYETTE, 2nd Lieutenant
Resided in Johnston County and enlisted at age 23, May 1, 1861. Mustered in as Private and was promoted to Corporal on or about March 1, 1862. Captured at New

Bern on March 14, 1862. Confined at Fort Columbus, New York Harbor. Exchanged prior to July 1, 1862. Promoted to Sergeant on October 1, 1862, and was appointed 2nd Lieutenant on October 31, 1864. Present or accounted for until he surrendered at Appomattox Court House, Virginia, April 9, 1865.

NONCOMMISSIONED OFFICERS AND PRIVATES

ANDRES, WILLIAM H., Private
Born in Edgecombe County and resided in Wayne County where he was by occupation a farmer prior to enlisting at Fort Macon at age 37, June 1, 1861. Present or accounted for until discharged on July 16, 1862, by reason of being overage.

AYCOCK, LARRY, Private
Resided in Wayne County and enlisted at Fort Macon at age 20, May 1, 1861. Present or accounted for until he surrendered at Appomattox Court House, Virginia, April 9, 1865.

BAKER, JOHN B., 1st Sergeant
Born in Wayne County where he resided prior to enlisting at Fort Macon at age 18, April 15, 1861. Mustered in as Private and was promoted to Corporal on September 1, 1861. Promoted to Sergeant on April 22, 1862. Present or accounted for until wounded in the leg and captured at Sharpsburg, Maryland, September 17, 1862. Confined at Fort McHenry, Maryland, until transferred to Fort Monroe, Virginia, October 20, 1862. Transferred to Aiken's Landing, James River, Virginia, October 25, 1862, for exchange. Declared exchanged at Aiken's Landing on November 10, 1862. Returned to duty on an unspecified date. Promoted to 1st Sergeant prior to November 1, 1864. Present or accounted for until captured on the South Side Railroad, near Petersburg, Virginia, April 2, 1865. Confined at Hart's Island, New York Harbor, April 7, 1865. Released on June 18, 1865, after taking the Oath of Allegiance.

BANES, ELI, Private
Resided in Wayne County and enlisted at Fort Macon at age 20, June 12, 1861. Present or accounted for through December, 1863. No further records.

BEST, REGDON, Private
Resided in Wayne County and enlisted at age 23, April 15, 1861. No further records.

BOYETT, STEPHEN, Private
Born in Duplin County and resided in Wilson County where he was by occupation a cooper prior to enlisting at Fort Macon at age 36, April 15, 1861. Present or accounted for until discharged on July 16, 1862, by reason of being overage. [May have served later in Company C, 43rd Regiment N.C. Troops.]

BROWN, LEONARD, Private
Enlisted in Wake County on June 20, 1864, for the war. Present or accounted for through February, 1865. [North Carolina pension records indicate he was wounded in July, 1864.]

BRYAN, JOSEPH H., Private
Enlisted in Wake County on July 15, 1862, for the war. Present or accounted for until transferred to Company C, 16th Battalion N.C. Cavalry, December 3, 1864, in exchange for Private William M. Westry. [Private Bryan's service record was omitted in Volume II of this series.]

BUMPASS, GEORGE W., Private
Previously served in Company C, 16th Battalion N.C. Cavalry. Transferred to this company on January 31, 1865. Wounded in the right foot and captured on an unspecified date. Hospitalized at Farmville, Virginia, April 7, 1865. Paroled at Farmville on April 11-21, 1865.

CARTER, GREEN, Private
Resided in Stanly County and enlisted at age 35, February 21, 1863, for the war. Died in hospital at Richmond, Virginia, October 16, 1863, of "febris typhoides." [North Carolina pension records indicate he was wounded in an unspecified engagement.]

CHESTNUT, WILLIAM, Private
Resided in Wayne County and enlisted at Fort Macon at age 21, June 1, 1861. Present or accounted for until captured at Sharpsburg, Maryland, on or about September 17, 1862. Confined at Fort McHenry, Maryland. Paroled and transferred to City Point, Virginia, where he was received November 21, 1862, for exchange. Returned to duty on an unspecified date. Captured at Bristoe Station, Virginia, October 14, 1863. Confined at Old Capitol Prison, Washington, D.C. Transferred to Point Lookout, Maryland, October 27, 1863. Died at Point Lookout on August 14, 1864. Cause of death not reported.

CLINGLE, ANDREW, Private
Born in Gaston County and enlisted at age 18. Place and date of enlistment not reported. Deserted to the enemy on or about September 12, 1864.

COBB, BRYANT, Private
Resided in Wayne County and enlisted at age 23, April 15, 1861. No further records.

COBB, JOHN D., Private
Resided in Wayne County and enlisted at age 25, April 15, 1861. No further records.

COBB, WILLIAM H., Private
Resided in Wayne County and enlisted at age 20, April 15, 1861. No further records.

COGDELL, DANIEL, Private
Resided in Wayne County and enlisted at Fort Macon at age 33, April 15, 1861. Present or accounted for until June 24, 1861, when he was appointed 1st Lieutenant of Company F, 10th Regiment N.C. State Troops (1st Regiment N.C. Artillery), and transferred to that unit.

COLE, MALCOM, Private
Previously served in Company D, 49th Regiment N.C. Troops. Enlisted in this company in Wayne County on April 1, 1864, for the war. Present or accounted for until wounded at or near Wilderness, Virginia, in May, 1864. Returned to duty prior to November 1, 1864. Transferred to Company D, 49th Regiment N.C. Troops, January 7, 1865.

COLLINS, GEORGE W., Private
Enlisted in Wake County on May 20, 1863, for the war. Present or accounted for through February, 1865.

COOR, HOPTON H., Private
Resided in Wayne County and enlisted at Fort Macon at age 19, April 15, 1861. Mustered in as Sergeant but was reduced to ranks on September 23, 1861. Present or accounted for until April 22, 1862, when he was elected 1st Lieutenant of Company K of this regiment. Later served as Captain of Company K.

CRAWFORD, HARRISON W., Private
Born in Wayne County where he resided as a carpenter prior to enlisting at Fort Macon at age 26, May 1, 1861. Present or accounted for until September 7, 1861, when he broke his right leg while on detail as a laborer. Discharged on May 12, 1862, by reason of "deformity of the right leg."

CROWELL, JOEL, Private
Resided in Stanly County and enlisted at age 35, February 21, 1863, for the war. Present or accounted for until July 2, 1864, when he died in hospital at Richmond, Virginia, of "pneumonia."

CURRIE, HENRY B., Private
Resided in Moore County and enlisted in Wake County on April 1, 1864, for the war. Present or accounted for until hospitalized at Richmond, Virginia, May 26, 1864, with a gunshot wound. Place and date wounded not reported. Returned to duty prior to November 1, 1864. Present or accounted for until captured at Hatcher's Run, Virginia, March 31, 1865. Confined at Point Lookout, Maryland, April 2, 1865. Released at Point Lookout on June 24, 1865, after taking the Oath of Allegiance.

DAVIS, DANIEL, Private
Born in Wayne County where he resided as a farmer prior to enlisting at Fort Macon at age 34, June 1, 1861. Present or accounted for until he "cut off his hand while at home on furlough" in March-April, 1862. Discharged on May 26, 1862, by reason of disability.

DAVIS, WILLIAM E., Private
Resided in Wayne County and enlisted at Fort Macon at age 22, May 1, 1861. Present or accounted for until wounded in the head at Cold Harbor, Virginia, June 3, 1864. Returned to duty in November-December, 1864, but was retired to the Invalid Corps on December 22, 1864, by reason of disability from wounds.

DAVIS, WILLIAM R., Private
Resided in Wayne County and enlisted at Fort Macon at age 20, June 1, 1861. Present or accounted for until October 14, 1863, when he was captured at Bristoe Station, Virginia. Confined at Old Capitol Prison, Washington, D.C., until transferred to Point Lookout, Maryland, October 27, 1863. Died at Point Lookout on February 27, 1865, of "chronic diarrhoea."

DEANS, WILLIAM, Sergeant
Resided in Wayne County and enlisted at Fort Macon at age 20, June 12, 1861. Mustered in as Private and was promoted to Sergeant on November 30, 1864. Present or accounted for until February 22, 1865, when he was reported absent without leave.

DEES, JOHN T., Corporal
Resided in Wayne County and enlisted at Fort Macon at age 19, June 12, 1861. Mustered in as Private and was promoted to Corporal in November, 1862-October,

1864. Present or accounted for until wounded in the leg on or about June 15, 1864. Battle in which wounded not reported. Reported absent wounded through February, 1865.

DENMARK, STEPHEN H., Corporal
Born in Wayne County where he resided prior to enlisting at Fort Macon at age 24, April 15, 1861. Mustered in as Private and was promoted to Corporal on an unspecified date. Present or accounted for until August 23, 1861, when he was discharged by reason of having been appointed clerk of the court of Wayne County. [May have served later in Captain Nelson's Independent N.C. Company (Local Defense).]

DIVINE, JOHN FRANCIS, Quartermaster Sergeant
Resided in Wayne County and enlisted at Fort Macon at age 33, April 15, 1861. Mustered in as Private and was promoted to Quartermaster Sergeant on June 24, 1861. Appointed Quartermaster (Captain) of Fort Macon on July 15, 1861, and was discharged from this regiment.

DRY, ADAM, Private
Resided in Stanly County and enlisted in Wake County at age 35, March 12, 1863, for the war. Present or accounted for until wounded at or near Wilderness, Virginia, in May, 1864. Returned to duty prior to November 1, 1864. Present or accounted for until he deserted to the enemy on or about March 18, 1865. Confined at Washington, D.C., March 24, 1865. Released on an unspecified date after taking the Oath of Allegiance.

DUKES, JAMES, Private
Resided in Wayne County and enlisted at age 36, April 15, 1861. No further records.

DUNAHUE, WILLIAM, Private
Resided in Lenoir County and enlisted at Fort Macon at age 24, August 12, 1861. Present or accounted for until June 20, 1862, when he was discharged. Reason discharged not reported.

DYER, ISHAM R., Private
Resided in Wayne County and enlisted at Fort Macon at age 46, April 15, 1861. Mustered in as Sergeant but was reduced to ranks in March-April, 1862. Present or accounted for until July 16, 1862, when he was discharged by reason of being overage.

EDGERTON, JAMES G., Private
Place and date of enlistment not reported. Captured at or near Pine Level on or about April 12, 1865. Paroled at Raleigh on April 22, 1865.

EVERITT, SAMUEL S., Private
Resided in Wayne County and enlisted at Fort Macon at age 18, June 1, 1861. Discharged on August 22, 1861, but reenlisted in the company on February 1, 1863, for the war. Present or accounted for until December 3, 1864, when he was transferred to Company C, 16th Battalion N.C. Cavalry, in exchange for Private William H. Oliver.

FAIRCLOTH, MATTHEW, Private
Resided in Wayne County and enlisted at Fort Macon at age 23, June 12, 1861. Mustered in as Private. Promoted to Musician in November, 1862-October, 1864, and transferred to the regimental band. Reduced to ranks

and transferred back to this company subsequent to February 28, 1865. Captured near Petersburg, Virginia, April 2, 1865. Confined at Point Lookout, Maryland, until June 27, 1865, when he was released after taking the Oath of Allegiance.

FAIRCLOTH, WILLIAM H., Private
Resided in Wayne County and enlisted at Fort Macon at age 21, April 15, 1861. Present or accounted for until he was killed in an unspecified engagement on June 10, 1864.

FAULK, HOSEA, Private
Resided in Union County and enlisted in Wake County at age 18, May 20, 1863, for the war. Present or accounted for until wounded in the left thigh at Reams' Station, Virginia, August 25, 1864. Reported absent on furlough through February, 1865. Paroled at Charlotte in May, 1865.

FLOWERS, WILLIAM, Private
Resided in Wayne County and enlisted at Fort Macon at age 22, June 1, 1861. Present or accounted for until killed at Wilderness, Virginia, May 5, 1864.

FOREMAN, STEPHEN D., Private
Previously served in Company I, 52nd Regiment N.C. Troops. Enlisted in this company in Wake County at age 37, March 12, 1863, for the war. Present or accounted for until captured at Hatcher's Run, Virginia, March 31, 1865. Confined at Point Lookout, Maryland, until released on June 26, 1865, after taking the Oath of Allegiance. [North Carolina pension records indicate he was wounded at Bristoe Station, Virginia, on an unspecified date.]

FURILL, J., Private
Resided in Wayne County and enlisted at age 24, April 15, 1861. No further records.

GARDNER, JAMES B., Private
Resided in Craven County and enlisted at Fort Macon at age 28, August 26, 1861. Present or accounted for until wounded in the knee at Bristoe Station, Virginia, October 14, 1863. Hospitalized at Richmond, Virginia, until December 1, 1863, when he was furloughed for sixty days. No further records.

GOODWIN, RICHARD, Private
Resided in Wayne County and enlisted at age 21, April 22, 1861. No further records.

GRICE, STEPHEN M., Private
Resided in Wayne County and enlisted at Fort Macon at age 18, May 1, 1861. Present or accounted for until he died in hospital at Richmond, Virginia, June 18, 1864, of a gunshot wound. Place and date wounded not reported.

GULLICK, JAMES WHARTON, Corporal
Resided in Wayne County and enlisted at age 24, April 15, 1861. Mustered in as Corporal. Present or accounted for until May 16, 1861, when he was appointed 3rd Lieutenant of Company H, 2nd Regiment N.C. State Troops, and transferred to that unit.

GUY, J. A., Private
Place and date of enlistment not reported. Paroled at Farmville, Virginia, April 11-21, 1865.

HAMMEL, LOUIS, Private
Enlisted at Fort Macon on April 15, 1861. Present or accounted for until discharged "by surgeon" on June 14, 1861. Reason discharged not reported.

HARDIN, WILLIAM H., Private
Previously served in Company C, 16th Battalion N.C. Cavalry. Transferred to this company on February 8, 1865. Captured at Hatcher's Run, Virginia, March 25, 1865. Confined at Point Lookout, Maryland, until released on June 27, 1865, after taking the Oath of Allegiance.

HARMON, RAIFORD, Private
Born in Johnston County and resided in Wayne County where he was by occupation a farmer prior to enlisting at Fort Macon at age 35, August 29, 1861. Present or accounted for until July 16, 1862, when he was discharged by reason of being overage.

HOFFMAN, LEWIS, Private
Resided in Wayne County and enlisted at Fort Macon at age 28, April 15, 1861. Present or accounted for until discharged on or about October 4, 1862, by reason of "having never acquired a domicile."

HOLLOMAN, EZEKIEL, Private
Born in Wayne County where he resided prior to enlisting at Fort Macon at age 19, June 12, 1861. Present or accounted for until wounded in the right thumb at Fredericksburg, Virginia, December 13, 1862. Returned to duty on January 13, 1863. Killed at Bristoe Station, Virginia, October 14, 1863.

HOLLOMAN, RICHARD, Private
Resided in Wayne County and enlisted at Fort Macon at age 21, June 12, 1861. Present or accounted for until captured at New Bern on March 14, 1862. Confined at Fort Columbus, New York Harbor. Exchanged on an unspecified date. Killed at Wilderness, Virginia, May 5, 1864.

HOLLOMAN, WILLIAM, Private
Resided in Wayne County and enlisted at age 19, April 15, 1861. No further records.

HOLLOWELL, WILLIAM G., Private
Resided in Wayne County and enlisted at Fort Macon at age 21, April 15, 1861. Present or accounted for until wounded in the left leg at Bristoe Station, Virginia, October 14, 1863. Left leg amputated. Reported absent wounded until August 9, 1864, when he was retired to the Invalid Corps.

HOLT, CALVIN A., Sr., Private
Enlisted in Wake County on April 20, 1864, for the war. Present or accounted for through February, 1865; however, he was reported absent sick during most of that period.

HOLT, SAMUEL, Private
Resided in Wayne County and enlisted at age 35, April 15, 1861. No further records.

HOWARD, JOSEPH D., Private
Born in Wayne County where he resided prior to enlisting at Fort Macon at age 31, May 15, 1861. Present or accounted for until killed at Bristoe Station, Virginia,

October 14, 1863.

HOWELL, JAMES, Private
Resided in Wayne County and enlisted at age 24, April 25, 1861. No further records.

HOWELL, ROBERT PHILLIPS, Private
Born in Wayne County where he resided prior to enlisting at Fort Macon at age 21, April 15, 1861. Present or accounted for until appointed Quartermaster on August 8, 1862, and transferred to an unspecified unit or post. Later served as Assistant Quartermaster (Captain) of the 62nd Regiment Georgia Cavalry.

HOWELL, WILLIAM, Private
Resided in Wayne County and enlisted at Fort Macon at age 46, April 15, 1861. Present or accounted for until July 16, 1862, when he was discharged by reason of being overage. [May have served later in Company D, 1st Battalion N.C. Local Defense Troops.]

HOWELL, WILLIAM M., Private
Born in Wayne County where he resided as a farmer prior to enlisting at Fort Macon at age 20, May 15, 1861. Present or accounted for until killed at Sharpsburg, Maryland, September 17, 1862.

HUGHES, WILLIAM, Private
Resided in Wayne County and enlisted at Fort Macon at age 23, May 15, 1861. Present or accounted for until captured at Bristoe Station, Virginia, October 14, 1863. Confined at Old Capitol Prison, Washington, D.C., until transferred to Point Lookout, Maryland, October 27, 1863. Confined at Point Lookout until February 24, 1865, when he was paroled and transferred to Aiken's Landing, James River, Virginia, for exchange.

JONES, RICHARD E., Private
Resided in Wayne County and enlisted at Fort Macon at age 18, April 15, 1861. Mustered in as Private and was promoted to Corporal on April 22, 1862. Reduced to ranks on August 25, 1862. Promoted to Musician in September-October, 1862, and transferred to the regimental band.

KELLEY, J., Private
Resided in Wayne County and enlisted at age 30, April 15, 1861. No further records.

KENNEDY, JOHN BRYAN, Private
Born in Wayne County where he resided as a farmer prior to enlisting at Fort Macon at age 17, April 15, 1861. Present or accounted for until transferred to Company I, 35th Regiment N.C. Troops, February 1, 1862.

KENNEDY, JOHN THOMAS, Private
Born in Wayne County where he resided as a farmer prior to enlisting at Fort Macon at age 36, April 15, 1861. Present or accounted for until he was elected 1st Lieutenant of Company I, 35th Regiment N.C. Troops, October 11, 1861.

KILPATRICK, SIMON B., Corporal
Resided in Pitt County and enlisted at Fort Macon at age 30, August 26, 1861. Mustered in as Private and was promoted to Corporal in November, 1862-May, 1864. Present or accounted for until wounded in the left hand at or near Wilderness, Virginia, on or about May 5,

1864. Returned to duty prior to November 1, 1864. Present or accounted for until he surrendered at Appomattox Court House, Virginia, April 9, 1865.

KING, ALLEN, Private
Born in Wayne County where he resided as a farmer prior to enlisting at Fort Macon at age 19, June 1, 1861. Present or accounted for until wounded in the right arm and captured at Sharpsburg, Maryland, September 17, 1862. Right arm amputated. Confined at Fort McHenry, Maryland. Transferred to Aiken's Landing, James River, Virginia, where he was received on October 19, 1862, for exchange. Discharged on November 6, 1862, by reason of disability.

KNIGHT, WALTER ASHLAND, Private
Resided in Wayne County and enlisted at Fort Macon at age 17, June 1, 1861. Reported on duty with the Field and Staff of this regiment as acting Sergeant Major from September 20, 1862, through November, 1862. Transferred back to this company on an unspecified date. Appointed Adjutant on March 23, 1863, and assigned to permanent duty with the Field and Staff.

KORNEGAY, J. F., Sergeant
Resided in Wayne County and enlisted at age 27, April 15, 1861. Promotion record not reported. No further records.

LANNON, JAMES, Private
Born at Ruth Common, Ireland, and resided in Wilson County where he was by occupation a miner prior to enlisting at Fort Macon at age 35, August 8, 1861. Present or accounted for until July 16, 1862, when he was discharged by reason of being overage.

McCOTTER, GEORGE BADGER, Private
Resided in Pitt County and enlisted at Fort Macon at age 20, August 26, 1861. Present or accounted for until appointed 2nd Lieutenant to rank from August 31, 1863, and transferred to Company G, 1st Battalion N.C. Local Defense Troops.

McINTYRE, ROBERT T., Sergeant
Resided in New Hanover County and enlisted at Fort Macon at age 24, May 1, 1861. Mustered in as Private. Present or accounted for until wounded at Sharpsburg, Maryland, September 17, 1862. Retired from service on an unspecified date. Reason he was retired not reported. Reenlisted in the company on or about February 1, 1865, and was promoted to Sergeant the same date. Present or accounted for through February, 1865.

McLEAN, NEIL, Private
Resided in Moore County and enlisted in Wake County on April 1, 1864, for the war. Present or accounted for until wounded at Wilderness, Virginia, May 5, 1864. Returned to duty in November-December, 1864. Present or accounted for until captured at or near Fort Stedman, Virginia, March 25, 1865. Confined at Point Lookout, Maryland, until released on June 29, 1865, after taking the Oath of Allegiance.

MANESS, JOHN L., Private
Enlisted in Wake County on April 1, 1864, for the war. Present or accounted for through February, 1865; however, he was reported absent sick during most of that period.

MASSEY, ASA B., Private

Resided in Wayne County and enlisted at Fort Macon at age 31, May 1, 1861. Mustered in as Private and was promoted to Corporal on July 5, 1861. Reported missing on September 12, 1862, and was captured by the enemy on an unspecified date. Paroled at Warrenton, Virginia, November 9, 1862. Received at City Point, Virginia, November 18, 1862, for exchange. Reduced to ranks in November, 1862-October, 1864. Deserted near Petersburg, Virginia, November 30, 1864.

MATTOX, WILLIAM R., Private

Resided in Wayne County and enlisted at Fort Macon at age 31, April 15, 1861. Present or accounted for until wounded at Sharpsburg, Maryland, September 17, 1862. Company records do not indicate whether he returned to duty. Died near Goldsboro on June 28, 1863. Cause of death not reported.

MEWBORN, WILLIAM P., Private

Born in Lenoir County where he resided as a farmer prior to enlisting at Fort Macon at age 18, August 26, 1861. Present or accounted for until discharged on May 26, 1862, by reason of "chronic hepatitis." Later served in Company E, 1st Battalion N.C. Local Defense Troops.

MILLS, SIMEON, Private

Resided in Union County and enlisted in Wake County at age 37, May 20, 1863, for the war. Reported absent without leave from October 1, 1863, until he returned to duty on August 15, 1864. Wounded at Reams' Station, Virginia, August 25, 1864. Reported absent wounded through February, 1865.

MOORE, GEORGE J., Private

Born in Wayne County where he resided as a druggist prior to enlisting at Fort Macon at age 30, April 15, 1861. Present or accounted for until discharged on May 25, 1862, by reason of being a druggist. Later served as 2nd Lieutenant of Company D, 63rd Regiment N.C. Troops (5th Regiment N.C. Cavalry).

MOORE, J. G., Private

Resided in Wayne County and enlisted at age 25, April 15, 1861. No further records.

MOORE, JOHN SAUNDERS, Private

Resided in Wayne County and enlisted at Fort Macon at age 27, April 15, 1861. Present or accounted for until discharged on July 15, 1861. Reason discharged not reported.

MOORE, STYRING SCARBORO, Private

Resided in Wayne County and enlisted at Fort Macon at age 22, July 21, 1861. Present or accounted for until appointed Chaplain on September 15, 1862, and transferred to the Field and Staff of the 26th Regiment N.C. Troops.

MOSELEY, W. CICERO, Private

Resided in Lenior County and enlisted at Fort Macon at age 18, August 26, 1861. Present or accounted for until he died in hospital at Richmond, Virginia, November 21, 1863, of a gunshot wound of the thigh. Place and date wounded not reported.

MUSGRAVE, NEEDHAM WHITLEY, Private

Born in Wayne County where he resided prior to enlisting at Fort Macon at age 21, June 1, 1861. Mustered in as Private. Present or accounted for until wounded in the right foot at Bristoe Station, Virginia, October 14, 1863. Returned to duty prior to November 1, 1864, and was promoted to Corporal on November 30, 1864. Reduced to ranks on an unspecified date. Transferred to Company C, 16th Battalion N.C. Cavalry, February 8, 1865. [Private Musgrave's service record was omitted in Volume II of this series.]

MUSGRAVE, WILLIAM T., Private

Resided in Wayne County and enlisted at Fort Macon at age 18, June 1, 1861. Present or accounted for until wounded in the jaw at Wilderness, Virginia, May 5, 1864. Returned to duty subsequent to February 1, 1865. Captured at or near Fort Stedman, Virginia, March 25, 1865. Confined at Point Lookout, Maryland, until released on June 29, 1865, after taking the Oath of Allegiance.

NASH, JOHN, Private

Resided in Union County and enlisted in Wake County at age 36, May 20, 1863, for the war. Present or accounted for through February, 1865.

NORMELL, L., Private

Resided in Wayne County and enlisted on April 15, 1861. Discharged on May 1, 1861. Reason discharged not reported.

OLIVER, WILLIAM H., Private

Previously served in Company C, 16th Battalion N.C. Cavalry. Transferred to this company on December 3, 1864, in exchange for Private Samuel S. Everitt. Present or accounted for until captured at Hatcher's Run, Virginia, March 31, 1865. Confined at Point Lookout, Maryland, until released on June 22, 1865, after taking the Oath of Allegiance.

O'NEAL, J. B., Private

Place and date of enlistment not reported. Paroled at Farmville, Virginia, April 11-21, 1865.

OVERMAN, EZEKIEL, Private

Previously served in Company D, 13th Battalion N.C. Infantry. Transferred to this company on or about May 22, 1863, in exchange for Private Wilie B. Wright. Captured at or near Fort Stedman, Virginia, March 25, 1865. Confined at Point Lookout, Maryland, until released on June 29, 1865, after taking the Oath of Allegiance.

OVERMAN, JOHN, Private

Resided in Wayne County and was by occupation a farmer prior to enlisting at Fort Macon at age 20, June 12, 1861. Present or accounted for until captured at New Bern on March 14, 1862. Confined at Fort Columbus, New York Harbor. Exchanged on an unspecified date. Returned to duty in November, 1862. Captured at Petersburg, Virginia, April 3, 1865. Confined at Hart's Island, New York Harbor, until released on June 19, 1865, after taking the Oath of Allegiance.

OVERMAN, THOMAS C., Corporal

Resided in Wayne County and enlisted at Fort Macon at age 21, May 1, 1861. Mustered in as Private. Reported absent without leave from August 17 through October, 1862. Returned to duty on an unspecified date. Wounded at Wilderness, Virginia on or about May 5,

1864. Returned to duty on an unspecified date and was promoted to Corporal on October 31, 1864. Deserted to the enemy on or about March 18, 1865. Confined at Washington, D.C., until released on or about March 24, 1865, after taking the Oath of Allegiance.

PARKER, JAMES H., Private
Born in Wayne County where he resided as a farmer prior to enlisting at Fort Macon at age 27, April 15, 1861. Mustered in as Corporal but was reduced to ranks in March-April, 1862. Present or accounted for until wounded at Sharpsburg, Maryland, September 17, 1862. Returned to duty subsequent to October 31, 1862. Killed at Bristoe Station, Virginia, October 14, 1863.

PARKER, NATHAN B., Private
Born in Wayne County where he resided as a farmer prior to enlisting at Fort Macon at age 25, April 15, 1861. Mustered in as Private and was promoted to Corporal on August 8, 1861. Reduced to ranks on August 22, 1862. Present or accounted for until wounded and captured at Sharpsburg, Maryland, September 17, 1862. Died at "Smith's Farm" on September 21, 1862, of wounds.

PARKER, RICHARD B., Sergeant
Resided in Wayne County and enlisted at Fort Macon at age 21, April 15, 1861. Mustered in as Private and was promoted to Sergeant on October 31, 1864. Surrendered at Appomattox Court House, Virginia, April 9, 1865.

PARKER, WILLIAM R., Private
Born in Sampson County and resided in Wayne County where he was by occupation a farmer prior to enlisting at Fort Macon at age 37, June 25, 1861. Present or accounted for until discharged on May 26, 1862, by reason of disability.

PARRISH, EZEKIEL, Private
Resided in Guilford County and enlisted in Wake County on August 15, 1864, for the war. Present or accounted for until captured at Hatcher's Run, Virginia, April 2, 1865. Confined at Point Lookout, Maryland, until released on June 17, 1865, after taking the Oath of Allegiance.

PARRISH, SIDNEY A., Private
Enlisted in Wake County on August 15, 1864, for the war. Present or accounted for until he died in hospital at Richmond, Virginia, December 16, 1864. Cause of death not reported.

PATRICK, FREDERICK COX, Private
Resided in Wayne County and enlisted at Fort Macon at age 31, June 12, 1861. Present or accounted for until discharged on August 20, 1862. Reason discharged not reported.

PEACOCK, JOSEPH, Private
Resided in Wayne County and enlisted at Fort Macon at age 19, May 12, 1861. Wounded in the hand at Wilderness, Virginia, on or about May 5, 1864. Returned to duty prior to November 1, 1864. Present or accounted for until he surrendered at Appomattox Court House, Virginia, April 9, 1865.

PERDUE, ADAM M., Private
Enlisted in Wake County on August 15, 1864, for the war. Present or accounted for until he died on February

18, 1865, of disease. Place of death not reported.

PHILLIPS, THOMAS B., Private
Resided in Wayne County and enlisted at Fort Macon at age 22, August 12, 1861. Present or accounted for until captured at or near Sharpsburg, Maryland, on or about September 17, 1862. Requested that he not be exchanged and was apparently released on his promise not to rejoin the Confederate Army. [North Carolina pension records indicate he was wounded at New Bern on March 17, 1862; was wounded in the left arm and shoulder at "Gettysburg, Pennsylvania, May 31, 1862"; and was discharged after the battle of Gettysburg, July 1-3, 1863.]

PHILMORE, E. K., Private
Resided in Union County and enlisted in Lenoir County at age 39, May 23, 1863, for the war. Wounded in the left leg at or near Bristoe Station, Virginia, October 14, 1863. Left leg amputated. Hospitalized at Richmond, Virginia, until January 26, 1864, when he was furloughed for sixty days. No further records.

PHILMORE, JACOB, Private
Resided in Union County and enlisted at age 36, May 23, 1863, for the war. Wounded at or near Wilderness, Virginia, on or about May 5, 1864. Returned to duty on an unspecified date. Killed at or near Reams' Station, Virginia, on or about August 23, 1864.

PIKE, JOHN W., Private
Resided in Wayne County and enlisted at Fort Macon at age 18, May 12, 1861. Present or accounted for until hospitalized at Richmond, Virginia, May 7, 1864, with a gunshot wound of the left hand. Place and date wounded not reported. Returned to duty prior to August 25, 1864, when he was wounded at Reams' Station, Virginia. Reported absent wounded through February, 1865.

PIKE, NATHAN U., Private
Resided in Wayne County and enlisted at Fort Macon at age 25, May 15, 1861. Captured at Hatcher's Run, Virginia, April 2, 1865. Confined at Point Lookout, Maryland, until released on June 17, 1865, after taking the Oath of Allegiance.

PINER, GEORGE P., Private
Resided in Carteret County and enlisted at Fort Macon at age 25, April 15, 1861. "Mortally wounded in the head" at Cold Harbor, Virginia, June 3, 1864. Place and date of death not reported.

PITTMAN, THADDEUS E., Sergeant
Born in Cabarrus County and resided in Wayne County where he was by occupation a student prior to enlisting at Fort Macon at age 17, April 15, 1861. Mustered in as Private and was promoted to Sergeant on April 22, 1862. Promoted to Sergeant Major in October, 1863, and transferred to the Field and Staff of this regiment.

POWELL, HENRY, Private
Born in Wayne County where he resided as a farmer prior to enlisting at Fort Macon at age 23, June 12, 1861. Present or accounted for until he died in hospital at Richmond, Virginia, on or about January 7, 1863, of "typhoid fever."

PRIDGEN, JAMES A., Private
Resided in Lenoir County and enlisted at Fort Macon at

age 21, May 15, 1861. Present or accounted for until discharged on August 2, 1862, after providing a substitute. [May have served later as Corporal in Company K, 1st Battalion N.C. Local Defense Troops.]

REGISTER, DANIEL, Private
Previously served in Company C, 7th Regiment N.C. State Troops. Enlisted in this company in Lenoir County on February 10, 1863, for the war as a substitute. Wounded at or near Wilderness, Virginia, on or about May 5, 1864. Returned to duty prior to November 1, 1864. Present or accounted for until captured at or near Petersburg, Virginia, April 2, 1865. Confined at Hart's Island, New York Harbor, until released on June 19, 1865, after taking the Oath of Allegiance.

RENTBRON, J. H., ———
Resided in Wayne County. Place and date of enlistment not reported. Paroled at Goldsboro on May 13, 1865.

RHODES, BRYANT J., Sergeant
Resided in Wayne County and enlisted at Fort Macon at age 21, May 1, 1861. Mustered in as Private and was promoted to Sergeant on July 16, 1862. Present or accounted for until wounded at Sharpsburg, Maryland, September 17, 1862. Reported absent wounded through November, 1862. Returned to duty on an unspecified date. Wounded mortally at or near Wilderness, Virginia, on or about May 7, 1864. Place and date of death not reported.

RIGGS, AZARIAH J., 1st Sergeant
Born in New York City and resided in Wayne County where he was by occupation a builder prior to enlisting at Fort Macon at age 39, June 12, 1861. Mustered in as 1st Sergeant. Present or accounted for until June 24, 1861, when he was appointed 1st Lieutenant of Company F, 10th Regiment N.C. State Troops (1st Regiment N.C. Artillery), and transferred to that unit.

RILEY, NATHANIEL, Private
Enlisted in Wake County on March 1, 1864, for the war. Present or accounted for until wounded at or near Wilderness, Virginia, on or about May 5, 1864. Returned to duty prior to November 1, 1864. Deserted to the enemy on or about March 18, 1865. Confined at Washington, D.C., until released on or about March 24, 1865, after taking the Oath of Allegiance. Records of the Federal Provost Marshal dated March-April, 1865, give his age as 28.

RIVES, BENJAMIN B., Sergeant
Born in Pitt County and resided in Wayne County where he was by occupation a farmer prior to enlisting at Fort Macon at age 49, April 15, 1861. Mustered in as Private and was promoted to Sergeant on July 5, 1861. Present or accounted for until discharged on June 16, 1862, by reason of being overage.

ROBBINS, SOLOMON, Private
Resided in New Hanover County and enlisted at Petersburg, Virginia, January 15, 1865, for the war. Present or accounted for until he deserted to the enemy on April 6, 1865. Confined at Washington, D.C. Released on or about April 21, 1865.

ROBERTS, JAMES B., Sergeant
Resided in Wayne or Lincoln County and enlisted at

Fort Macon at age 17, June 15, 1861. Mustered in as Private and was promoted to Corporal on August 25, 1862. Promoted to Sergeant in June-August, 1864. Wounded in the right forearm at Reams' Station, Virginia, August 25, 1864. Returned to duty in January-February, 1865. Captured at Hatcher's Run, Virginia, April 2, 1865. Confined at Point Lookout, Maryland, until released on June 17, 1865, after taking the Oath of Allegiance.

ROBERTS, JOHN T., Private
Resided in Wayne County and enlisted at Fort Macon at age 19, April 15, 1861. Hospitalized at Richmond, Virginia, August 29, 1864, with a gunshot wound of the right arm. Place and date wounded not reported. Returned to duty in November-December, 1864. Surrendered at Appomattox Court House, Virginia, April 9, 1865.

ROBERTS, NATHAN W., Private
Enlisted in Rowan County on January 2, 1864, for the war. Present or accounted for through February, 1865.

RODGERS, THOMAS D., Private
Resided in Union County and enlisted in Wake County at age 37, May 21, 1863, for the war. Captured at Hatcher's Run, Virginia, April 2, 1865. Confined at Point Lookout, Maryland, until released on June 17, 1865, after taking the Oath of Allegiance.

RODGERS, V. A., Private
Previously served in Company K of this regiment. Enlisted in this company in New Hanover County on May 1, 1863, for the war. Paroled at Lynchburg, Virginia, April 14, 1865. [Name appears on a medical certificate dated February 23, 1865, which states he was suffering from a gunshot wound of the left leg. Place and date wounded not reported.]

RODGERS, WILLIAM R., Private
Enlisted at Camp Stokes on December 8, 1864, for the war. Present or accounted for until he deserted on February 19, 1865.

ROUNTREE, WILLIAM F., Private
Resided in Lenoir County and enlisted at Fort Macon at age 18, August 26, 1861. Present or accounted for through February, 1865. Deserted prior to March 19, 1865.

ROYALL, WILLIAM S., Private
Born in Chesterfield County, Virginia, and resided in Wayne County where he was by occupation a merchant prior to enlisting at Fort Macon at age 38, May 1, 1861. Mustered in as Sergeant but was reduced to ranks in March-April, 1862. Present or accounted for until discharged on April 30, 1862, by reason of "disease of the lower part of the spine from an injury received by the explosion of the steamer *Johnson* near Fort Macon."

SASSER, EDWARD B., Private
Resided in Wayne County and enlisted at Fort Macon at age 24, June 1, 1861. Died in hospital at Richmond, Virginia, January 17, 1864, of a gunshot wound of the knee joint and gangrene. Place and date wounded not reported.

SAULS, JOSIAH, Corporal
Born in Wayne County where he resided as a coach

painter prior to enlisting at Fort Macon at age 26, April 15, 1861. Mustered in as Private and was promoted to Corporal on April 22, 1862. Hospitalized at Richmond, Virginia, December 15, 1862, with a gunshot wound of the head. Place and date wounded not reported. Returned to duty on January 8, 1863. Captured at Bristoe Station, Virginia, October 14, 1863. Confined at Old Capitol Prison, Washington, D.C., until transferred to Point Lookout, Maryland, October 27, 1863. Released at Point Lookout on February 22, 1864, after joining the U.S. Army. Assigned to Company F, 1st Regiment U.S. Volunteer Infantry. Later served in Company C, 1st Regiment U.S. Volunteer Infantry.

SMITH, CHARLES, Private
Resided in Wayne County and enlisted at Fort Macon at age 37, June 18, 1861. Present or accounted for until he was reportedly captured at Sharpsburg, Maryland, September 17, 1862; however, records of the Federal Provost Marshal do not substantiate that report. Hospitalized at Richmond, Virginia, December 6, 1862, with "stricture." Company muster rolls dated September-December, 1864, indicate he was absent sick. Detailed for light duty at Salisbury in January-February, 1865.

SMITH, CHARLES F., Private
Born in Prussia and was by occupation a physician prior to enlisting at Fort Macon at age 33, May 1, 1861. Present or accounted for until discharged on May 14, 1862, by reason of "chronic orchitis."

SMITH, STEPHEN J., Private
Born in Wayne County where he resided as a farmer prior to enlisting at Fort Macon at age 19, June 12, 1861. Present or accounted for until killed at Sharpsburg, Maryland, September 17, 1862.

SMITH, WILLIAM E., Private
Enlisted in Wake County on August 15, 1864, for the war. Present or accounted for until he deserted to the enemy on or about February 21, 1865.

SMITH, WILLIS H., Private
Previously served in Company D, 49th Regiment N.C. Troops. Transferred to this company on January 7, 1865. Failed to report for duty and was listed as a deserter prior to March 1, 1865.

SNIPES, TOBIAS, Private
Born in Wayne County where he resided prior to enlisting at Fort Macon at age 24, May 1, 1861. Present or accounted for until wounded at Sharpsburg, Maryland, September 17, 1862. Died in hospital at Goldsboro on February 18, 1863. Cause of death not reported.

STEGALL, GEORGE W., Private
Resided in Union County and enlisted in Wake County at age 19, May 20, 1863, for the war. Wounded in the right leg at Bristoe Station, Virginia, October 14, 1863. Surrendered at Appomattox Court House, Virginia, April 9, 1865.

TADLOCK, WILLIAM, Private
Resided in Wake County where he enlisted at age 34, August 15, 1864, for the war. Present or accounted for until captured at Hatcher's Run, Virginia, April 2, 1865. Confined at Point Lookout, Maryland, until released on

June 21, 1865, after taking the Oath of Allegiance.

TAYLOR, WILLIAM, Private
Resided in Wayne County and enlisted at Fort Macon on June 1, 1861. Present or accounted for until discharged on September 24, 1862, by reason of being a "mail agent."

THOMPSON, THOMAS, Private
Resided in Wayne County and enlisted at Fort Macon at age 26, May 1, 1861. Present or accounted for until wounded at Sharpsburg, Maryland, September 17, 1862. Returned to duty on an unspecified date. Deserted to the enemy on or about March 18, 1865. Confined at Washington, D.C., until released on or about March 24, 1865, after taking the Oath of Allegiance.

THOMPSON, WILLIAM A., Private
Resided in Wayne County and enlisted at Fort Macon on April 15, 1861. Present or accounted for until February, 1862, when he was appointed Captain of Company E, 62nd Regiment Georgia Cavalry, and transferred to that unit.

WALTERS, W. RILEY, Private
Resided in Wayne County and enlisted at Fort Macon at age 27, June 12, 1861. Present or accounted for until discharged on July 16, 1862. Reason discharged not reported.

WARD, HENRY, Private
Resided in Wayne County and enlisted at Fort Macon at age 20, April 15, 1861. Present or accounted for until he deserted on May 26, 1861. Later served in Company D, 2nd Regiment N.C. State Troops.

WARD, RICHARD, Private
Resided in Wayne County and was by occupation a cooper prior to enlisting at Fort Macon at age 28, May 15, 1861. Wounded in the right arm at or near Bristoe Station, Virginia, on or about October 14, 1863. Wounded in the wrist at Wilderness, Virginia, on or about May 5, 1864. Wounded in the right hand near Petersburg, Virginia, on an unspecified date in 1864. Present or accounted for from September-October, 1864, through February, 1865. Surrendered at Appomattox Court House, Virginia, April 9, 1865.

WARRICK, EZEKIEL, Private
Resided in Wayne County and enlisted at Fort Macon at age 21, June 12, 1861. Wounded in the leg at Bristoe Station, Virginia, October 14, 1863. Reported absent wounded through October, 1864. Detailed for light duty in November-December, 1864. Reported on detail through February, 1865.

WARRICK, HEZEKIAH, Private
Resided in Wayne County and enlisted at Fort Macon at age 23, June 12, 1861. Reported absent wounded through October, 1864. Detailed for light duty in November-December, 1864. Reported absent on detail through February, 1865.

WASHINGTON, J. A., Sergeant
Resided in Wayne County and enlisted at age 25, April 15, 1861. No further records.

WATSON, LEONIDAS E., Private
Enlisted in Orange County on March 15, 1864, for the

war. Present or accounted for until wounded in the right shoulder at Wilderness, Virginia, on or about May 5, 1864. Returned to duty prior to August 21, 1864, when he was wounded in the left hand at the Weldon Railroad, near Petersburg, Virginia. Returned to duty in November-December, 1864. Present or accounted for until he deserted on January 3, 1865.

WESTBROOK, JOSEPH T., Private
Resided in Sampson County and enlisted in Wake County at age 33, February 29, 1863, for the war. Captured at Bristoe Station, Virginia, October 14, 1863. Confined at Old Capitol Prison, Washington, D.C., until transferred to Point Lookout, Maryland, October 27, 1863. Paroled at Point Lookout and transferred to Aiken's Landing, James River, Virginia, February 24, 1865, for exchange.

WESTRY, WILLIAM M., Private
Previously served in Company C, 16th Battalion N.C. Cavalry. Transferred to this company on December 3, 1864, in exchange for Private Joseph H. Bryan. Captured at or near Fort Stedman, Virginia, March 25, 1865. Confined at Point Lookout, Maryland, until released on June 21, 1865, after taking the Oath of Allegiance.

WITKINS, W., Private
Resided in Wayne County. Place and date of enlistment not reported. Paroled at Goldsboro on May 2, 1865.

WOODS, MICHAEL, 1st Sergeant
Born in Wayne County where he resided as a clerk prior to enlisting at Fort Macon at age 24, April 15, 1861. Mustered in as Private and was promoted to Sergeant on April 22, 1862. Promoted to 1st Sergeant on October 1, 1862. Wounded in the "left hypochondriac region" at Bristoe Station, Virginia, October 14, 1863. Retired to the Invalid Corps on July 10, 1864.

WORREL, ERVIN, Private
Resided in Wayne County and enlisted at Fort Macon at age 26, June 18, 1861. Present or accounted for until discharged on July 16, 1862. Reason discharged not reported.

WRIGHT, ESICK ARNOLD, Private
Previously served in Company I, 35th Regiment N.C. Troops. Transferred to this company on February 1, 1862. Discharged on August 3, 1862, by reason of "disability caused by a fracture of the right arm." Place and date injured not reported. Later reenlisted in Company I, 35th Regiment N.C. Troops.

WRIGHT, WILIE B., Private
Resided in Wayne County and enlisted at Fort Macon at age 17, April 15, 1861. Mustered in as Private and was promoted to Corporal on an unspecified date. Reduced to ranks "by request" on August 8, 1861. Present or accounted for until transferred to Company D, 13th Battalion N.C. Infantry, on or about May 22, 1863, in exchange for Private Ezekiel Overman.

COMPANY B

This company, known as the "Guilford Grays," was organized at Greensboro on January 9, 1860. It was mustered into service on June 20, 1861, and was later assigned to the 27th Regiment as Company B. After joining the regiment the company functioned as a part of the regiment, and its history for the war period is reported as a part of the regimental history.

The information contained in the following company roster was compiled principally from company muster rolls for June 20, 1861-October, 1862, and September, 1864-February, 1865. No company muster rolls were found for November, 1862-August, 1864, or for the period after February, 1865. Valuable information was obtained also from primary records such as the Roll of Honor, medical records, prisoner of war records, discharge certificates, and pension applications, and from secondary sources such as postwar rosters and histories, cemetery records, and records of the United Daughters of the Confederacy.

OFFICERS

CAPTAINS

SLOAN, JOHN
Resided in Guilford County. Elected Captain on or about April 20, 1861. Present or accounted for until he was elected Lieutenant Colonel on September 28, 1861, and transferred to the Field and Staff of this regiment. Later served as Colonel of this regiment.

ADAMS, WILLIAM
Born in Guilford County where he resided as an attorney prior to enlisting at Fort Macon at age 25. Elected 1st Lieutenant on or about April 20, 1861, and was elected Captain on or about October 4, 1861. Present or accounted for until shot through the abdomen and killed on September 17, 1862, while "fighting nobly on the bloody field of Sharpsburg," Maryland.

SLOAN, JOHN A.
Resided in Guilford County and enlisted at Fort Macon at age 22, April 20, 1861. Mustered in as Sergeant. Detailed as acting Sergeant Major of this regiment and transferred to the Field and Staff on May 1, 1861. Elected 2nd Lieutenant on January 14, 1862, and transferred back to this company. Elected 1st Lieutenant on April 22, 1862, and was promoted to Captain on September 17, 1862. Wounded at Wilderness, Virginia, on or about May 5, 1864. Returned to duty prior to November 1, 1864. Present or accounted for until he surrendered at Appomattox Court House, Virginia, April 9, 1865.

LIEUTENANTS

CAMPBELL, CHARLES A., 2nd Lieutenant
Resided in Guilford County where he enlisted at age 22, April 20, 1861. Mustered in as Private and was promoted to Corporal on April 22, 1862. Promoted to Sergeant on August 1, 1862. Wounded in the arm at Sharpsburg, Maryland, September 17, 1862. Returned to duty on October 11, 1862. Elected 2nd Lieutenant on December 11, 1863. Present or accounted for until killed "on skirmish line" at Pole Green Church, Virginia, June 2, 1864.

GIBSON, RUFUS B., 1st Lieutenant
Resided in Guilford County and enlisted at Fort Macon at age 20, April 20, 1861. Mustered in as Private. Captured at Sharpsburg, Maryland, September 17, 1862. Confined at Fort Delaware, Delaware, until transferred to Aiken's Landing, James River, Virginia, October 2, 1862, for exchange. Declared exchanged at

Aiken's Landing on November 10, 1862. Promoted to Corporal on December 18, 1863. Wounded at Bristoe Station, Virginia, October 14, 1863. Elected 1st Lieutenant on December 7, 1864. Paroled at Greensboro in 1865.

GILMER, JOHN ALEXANDER, Jr., 2nd Lieutenant
Resided in Guilford County and enlisted at Fort Macon at age 23. Elected 3rd Lieutenant on or about April 20, 1861, and was elected 2nd Lieutenant on October 5, 1861. Present or accounted for until he was elected Major on January 6, 1862, and transferred to the Field and Staff of this regiment. Later served as Colonel of this regiment.

GRAHAM, BENJAMIN G., 2nd Lieutenant
Resided in Guilford County and enlisted at Fort Macon at age 23, April 20, 1861. Mustered in as Corporal and was promoted to Sergeant on October 31, 1861. Promoted to 1st Sergeant on April 22, 1862, and was elected 3rd Lieutenant on September 22, 1862. Promoted to 2nd Lieutenant on October 14, 1863. Resigned on October 25, 1864. Reason he resigned not reported.

HANNER, FRANK A., 1st Lieutenant
Resided in Guilford County and enlisted at Fort Macon at age 26, April 20, 1861. Mustered in as Private and was elected 3rd Lieutenant on April 22, 1862. Promoted to 2nd Lieutenant on September 17, 1862, and was promoted to 1st Lieutenant on October 14, 1863. Hospitalized at Richmond, Virginia, May 30, 1864, with a gunshot wound. Place and date wounded not reported. Died in hospital at Richmond on June 4, 1864, of wounds and "dysenteria chron[ic]."

McKNIGHT, JOHN H., 1st Lieutenant
Resided in Guilford County where he enlisted at age 18, April 20, 1861. Mustered in as Private and was promoted to Sergeant on October 5, 1861. Elected 2nd Lieutenant on April 22, 1862, and was promoted to 1st Lieutenant on September 17, 1862. Present or accounted for until killed at Bristoe Station, Virginia, October 14, 1863. "He fell . . . foremost in the charge; was left on the field, and captured by the enemy. On the morning of the 15th, we found his body in the thicket beyond the railroad, where the enemy had left him to die. Here we buried him. His remains were afterwards removed, and interred in the cemetery at Greensboro."

MOREHEAD, JAMES T., Jr., 1st Lieutenant
Resided in Guilford County and was by occupation a farmer prior to enlisting at Fort Macon at age 21. Elected 2nd Lieutenant on or about April 20, 1861, and was elected 1st Lieutenant on October 15, 1861. Present or accounted for until he was defeated for reelection when the regiment was reorganized in April, 1862. Later served as Captain of Company C, 45th Regiment N.C. Troops.

WILSON, WILLIAM P., 3rd Lieutenant
Resided in Guilford County and enlisted at Fort Macon at age 24, April 20, 1861. Mustered in as 1st Sergeant and was elected 3rd Lieutenant on October 5, 1861. Present or accounted for until he was defeated for reelection when the regiment was reorganized in April, 1862. Later served as Adjutant of this regiment.

NONCOMMISSIONED OFFICERS AND PRIVATES

ARCHER, WASHINGTON D., Private
Born in Guilford County where he resided as a trader prior to enlisting at Fort Macon at age 30, June 9, 1861. Present or accounted for until wounded at Sharpsburg, Maryland, September 17, 1862. Returned to duty prior to December 13, 1862, when he was killed at Fredericksburg, Virginia. "A splendid specimen of a soldier."

AYER, HENRY W., Private
Resided in Iredell County and enlisted at age 28, May 15, 1863, for the war. Transferred to Company C, 48th Regiment N.C. Troops, March 1, 1864.

AYERS, HARDY L., Private
Resided in Guilford County and enlisted at Fort Macon at age 18, April 20, 1861. Present or accounted for until wounded at Sharpsburg, Maryland, September 17, 1862. Returned to duty on an unspecified date. Wounded in the left leg at Reams' Station, Virginia, August 25, 1864. Left leg amputated. Retired to the Invalid Corps on November 12, 1864.

AYERS, JAMES, Private
Resided in Guilford County and enlisted at Fort Macon at age 20, April 20, 1861. Present or accounted for until discharged on or about May 12, 1862, by reason of disability.

BOLING, RICHARD G., Private
Resided in Guilford County and enlisted at Fort Macon at age 19, April 20, 1861. Present or accounted for until he died in hospital at Richmond, Virginia, January 10, 1863, of "pneumonia" and/or "phthisis."

BOONE, HENRY M., Private
Resided in Guilford County and enlisted at Fort Macon at age 20, May 1, 1861. Wounded and captured at Bristoe Station, Virginia, October 14, 1863. Confined at Old Capitol Prison, Washington, D.C., until transferred to Point Lookout, Maryland, October 27, 1863. Paroled at Point Lookout and transferred to Aiken's Landing, James River, Virginia, February 24, 1865, for exchange. Paroled again at Greensboro on May 24, 1865.

BROOKS, THOMAS D., Private
Place and date of enlistment not reported. Discharged prior to July 1, 1861. Reason discharged not reported.

BROWN, JOSEPH E., Private
Place and date of enlistment not reported. Discharged prior to July 1, 1861. Reason discharged not reported.

BROWN, PETER M., Private
Resided in Guilford County and enlisted at Fort Macon at age 24, April 20, 1861. Present or accounted for until wounded in the right hip and captured at Sharpsburg, Maryland, September 17, 1862. Confined at Fort McHenry, Maryland, and at Fort Monroe, Virginia. Received at Aiken's Landing, James River, Virginia, October 25, 1862, for exchange. Declared exchanged at Aiken's Landing on November 10, 1862. Returned to duty on an unspecified date. Surrendered at Appomattox Court House, Virginia, April 9, 1865.

BROWN, R. D., Private
Resided in Guilford County and enlisted at Fort Macon

at age 22, August 1, 1861. Present or accounted for until he died in hospital at Richmond, Virginia, September 21, 1862, of ''febris typhoides.''

BRYAN, WILLIAM L., Corporal
Resided in Guilford County and enlisted at age 19, April 20, 1861. Mustered in as Private and was promoted to Corporal on September 21, 1862. Present or accounted for until he died in camp near Fredericksburg, Virginia, December 17, 1862, of ''typhoid pneumonia.''

BURNSIDE, BENJAMIN F., Private
Resided in Guilford County where he enlisted at age 17, February 25, 1862. Present or accounted for until wounded in the left leg and captured at Sharpsburg, Maryland, September 17, 1862. Confined at Fort McHenry, Maryland. Received at Aiken's Landing, James River, Virginia, October 22, 1862, for exchange. Declared exchanged at Aiken's Landing on November 10, 1862. Wounded in the head at Cold Harbor, Virginia, June 3, 1864. Returned to duty on or about October 1, 1864, and was detailed as a teamster. Reported absent on detail through February, 1865. Paroled at Greensboro on May 13, 1865.

BURNSIDES, WILSON W., Private
Resided in Guilford County and enlisted at Camp Holmes at age 38, July 15, 1862, for the war. Wounded in the thigh at Bristoe Station, Virginia, October 14, 1863. Died on or about December 28, 1864, of wounds. Place of death not reported.

CANNADY, JOHN, Private
Resided in Guilford County and enlisted at Fort Lane or at Greensboro at age 27, February 27, 1862. Killed at Bristoe Station, Virginia, October 14, 1863.

CAUSEY, JOSEPH H., Private
Resided in Guilford County and enlisted at Camp Stokes on October 24, 1864, for the war. Present or accounted for until captured at Hatcher's Run, Virginia, March 31, 1865. Confined at Point Lookout, Maryland, until released on June 24, 1865, after taking the Oath of Allegiance.

CHEELY, ALLISON C., Sergeant
Resided in Guilford County and enlisted at Fort Macon at age 24, April 20, 1861. Mustered in as Private and was promoted to Corporal on August 1, 1862. Promoted to Sergeant on November 1, 1862. Wounded in the right arm at Reams' Station, Virginia, August 25, 1864. Right arm amputated. Retired to the Invalid Corps on November 7, 1864. Paroled at Greensboro on May 1, 1865.

CHILCUTT, FRANK G., Private
Resided in Guilford County and enlisted at Fort Macon at age 24, August 1, 1861. Wounded in the right arm at Wilderness, Virginia, May 5, 1864. Right arm amputated. Retired to the Invalid Corps on December 15, 1864.

CLAPP, ISRAEL W., Private
Resided in Guilford County and enlisted at Fort Macon at age 23, June 11, 1861. Present or accounted for until discharged on May 12, 1862, by reason of disability.

CLAPP, WILLIAM C., Private
Resided in Guilford County and enlisted at Fort Macon

at age 19, June 11, 1861. Present or accounted for until he died ''at home'' on August 3, 1862, of disease.

CLARK, D. LOGAN, Private
Resided in Guilford County and enlisted at Fort Lane or at Greensboro at age 26, February 28, 1862. Present or accounted for until captured at New Bern on March 14, 1862. Confined at Fort Columbus, New York Harbor. Exchanged on an unspecified date. Discharged in June, 1862, by reason of disability.

COBLE, ALFRED F., Private
Born in Guilford County where he resided prior to enlisting at Fort Macon at age 19, May 4, 1861. Present or accounted for until killed at Sharpsburg, Maryland, September 17, 1862.

COBLE, JOHN HENRY, Private
Resided in Guilford County and enlisted at Fort Lane or at Greensboro at age 19, February 25, 1862. Wounded at Bristoe Station, Virginia, October 14, 1863. Returned to duty on an unspecified date. Wounded at or near Petersburg, Virginia, June 15, 1864. Reported absent wounded or absent on furlough through January, 1865. Paroled at Greensboro on May 4, 1865.

COBLE, ROBERT S., Private
Born in Guilford County where he resided prior to enlisting at Fort Macon at age 22, May 4, 1861. Present or accounted for until he died at Frederick, Maryland, September 12, 1862, of fever.

COLE, JAMES R., Private
Resided in Guilford County. Place and date of enlistment not reported. Transferred to Company F, 19th Regiment N.C. Troops (2nd Regiment N.C. Cavalry), on or about June 10, 1861.

COLLINS, JOHN D., Corporal
Resided in Guilford County and enlisted at Fort Macon at age 20, April 20, 1861. Mustered in as Private and was promoted to Corporal in November-December, 1861. Present or accounted for until he died at Camp Jackson, near Drewry's Bluff, Virginia, July 17, 1862, of ''typhoid fever.''

COLTRAIN, DANIEL B., Private
Enlisted in Guilford County on October 20, 1863, for the war. Wounded at Wilderness, Virginia, on or about May 5, 1864. Wounded in the heel at Cold Harbor, Virginia, June 3, 1864. Returned to duty prior to November 1, 1864. Deserted to the enemy on or about March 23, 1865. Confined at Washington, D.C., until released on or about March 29, 1865, after taking the Oath of Allegiance.

COLTRAIN, JOHN, Private
Born in Guilford County where he resided prior to enlisting at Fort Lane or at Greensboro at age 25, February 27, 1862. Present or accounted for until captured at New Bern on March 14, 1862. Confined at Fort Columbus, New York Harbor. Exchanged prior to September 1, 1862. Returned to duty on an unspecified date. Captured at Bristoe Station, Virginia, October 14, 1863. Confined at Old Capitol Prison, Washington, D.C., until transferred to Point Lookout, Maryland, October 27, 1863. Paroled at Point Lookout on May 3, 1864, and transferred to Aiken's Landing, James River,

Virginia, where he was received May 8, 1864, for exchange. Returned to duty on an unspecified date. Killed at Reams' Station, Virginia, August 25, 1864.

COLTRAIN, ROBERT L., Private
Resided in Guilford County and enlisted at Fort Lane or at Greensboro at age 25, February 28, 1862. Present or accounted for until discharged on or about July 23, 1862, by reason of disability.

COOK, WILLIAM D., Private
Resided in Guilford County and enlisted at age 27, April 20, 1861. Died at Greensboro on June 5, 1861, of "typhoid fever."

CRIDER, HENRY, Private
Resided in Guilford County and enlisted in Lenoir County at age 27, April 12, 1862. Wounded at Sharpsburg, Maryland, on or about September 17, 1862. Returned to duty prior to November 1, 1862. Killed at Bristoe Station, Virginia, October 14, 1863.

CROWSON, CYRUS M., Private
Resided in Guilford County where he enlisted at age 18, August 4, 1863, for the war. "Shot through both legs" at Bristoe Station, Virginia, October 14, 1863. Returned to duty on an unspecified date. Deserted to the enemy on or about March 17, 1865. Confined at Washington, D.C., until released on or about March 24, 1865, after taking the Oath of Allegiance.

CROWSON, E. M., Sergeant
Born in Guilford County where he resided prior to enlisting at Fort Macon or at Greensboro at age 21, April 20, 1861. Mustered in as Private and was promoted to Sergeant on August 1, 1862. Captured at Bristoe Station, Virginia, October 14, 1863. Confined at Old Capitol Prison, Washington, D.C., October 15, 1863. Transferred to Point Lookout, Maryland, October 27, 1863. Died at Point Lookout on or about January 23, 1864, of "chronic diarrhoea."

CRUTCHFIELD, PAUL W., Private
Resided in Guilford County where he enlisted at age 17, June 1, 1862, for the war as a substitute for Private B. N. Smith. Present or accounted for until captured at Sharpsburg, Maryland, September 17, 1862. Confined at Fort Delaware, Delaware. Paroled and transferred to Aiken's Landing, James River, Virginia, October 2, 1862, for exchange. Declared exchanged at Aiken's Landing on November 10, 1862. Returned to duty on an unspecified date. Company records indicate he was captured at Bristoe Station, Virginia, October 14, 1863; however, records of the Federal Provost Marshal do not substantiate that report. Company records indicate he was in confinement at Point Lookout, Maryland, through December, 1864. Paroled at Greensboro on May 1, 1865.

DAVIS, JAMES C., Private
Born in Guilford County where he resided prior to enlisting at Fort Macon at age 17, June 11, 1861. Died at Fort Macon on August 29, 1861, of "typhoid fever."

DENNIS, JAMES, Private
Resided in Guilford County and enlisted at age 24, July 20, 1862, for the war. Wounded at Sharpsburg, Maryland, September 17, 1862. Discharged on May 15, 1863, by reason of disability.

DENNIS, WILLIAM, Private
Resided in Guilford County and enlisted at Camp Holmes at age 28, July 20, 1862, for the war. Captured at or near Fort Stedman, Virginia, March 25, 1865. Confined at Point Lookout, Maryland, until released on June 12, 1865, after taking the Oath of Allegiance.

DENNIS, WILLIAM D., Private
Resided in Guilford County and enlisted at Fort Macon at age 26, June 15, 1861. Wounded in the face at Bristoe Station, Virginia, October 14, 1863. Returned to duty on an unspecified date. Captured at Hatcher's Run, Virginia, March 31, 1865. Confined at Point Lookout, Maryland, until released on June 1, 1865, after taking the Oath of Allegiance.

DICK, PRESTON P., Private
Enlisted in Guilford County on March 1, 1864, for the war. Deserted to the enemy subsequent to February 28, 1865. Reported in confinement in a Federal prison at Richmond, Virginia, April 10, 1865.

DODSON, SILAS C., Private
Resided in Guilford County where he enlisted at age 27, June 1, 1861. Surrendered at Appomattox Court House, Virginia, April 9, 1865.

DONNELL, ROBERT L., Private
Born in Guilford County where he resided prior to enlisting at Fort Macon at age 24, May 4, 1861. Present or accounted for until wounded in the leg and captured at Sharpsburg, Maryland, September 17, 1862. Leg amputated. Died in hospital at Chester, Pennsylvania, November 6, 1862, of "exhaustion."

DONNELL, WILLIAM H., Private
Resided in Guilford County where he enlisted on February 18, 1864, for the war. Wounded at Wilderness, Virginia, on or about May 5, 1864. Returned to duty on or about August 9, 1864. Present or accounted for until captured at Hatcher's Run, Virginia, March 31, 1865. Confined at Point Lookout, Maryland, until released on June 12, 1865, after taking the Oath of Allegiance.

DUVALL, W. G., Private
Place and date of enlistment not reported. "Served with the company until June, 1861." No further records.

EDWARDS, DAVID H., Private
Resided in Guilford County and enlisted at Fort Macon at age 25, June 1, 1861. Present or accounted for until promoted to Quartermaster Sergeant on December 1, 1862, and transferred to the Field and Staff of this regiment.

EDWARDS, JAMES M., Private
Born in Guilford County where he resided prior to enlisting at Fort Lane at age 19, March 4, 1862. Present or accounted for until killed at Sharpsburg, Maryland, September 17, 1862.

EDWARDS, JAMES T., Private
Resided in Guilford County and enlisted at Fort Macon at age 23, May 1, 1861. Present or accounted for until killed at Sharpsburg, Maryland, September 17, 1862.

ERWIN, FRANK, Private
Place and date of enlistment not reported. "Served with

the company until June, 1861." No further records.

FORBIS, H. SMILEY, Private
Resided in Guilford County and enlisted at Fort Macon at age 29, June 15, 1861. Present or accounted for until wounded at Sharpsburg, Maryland, September 17, 1862. Returned to duty on an unspecified date. Died in hospital at Lynchburg, Virginia, March 13, 1864, of "diarrhoea chronica."

FORBIS, HUGH RUFUS, Corporal
Previously served in Company G of this regiment. Transferred to this company with the rank of Private prior to September 1, 1861. Captured at Sharpsburg, Maryland, September 17, 1862. Confined at Fort Delaware, Delaware. Paroled and transferred to Aiken's Landing, James River, Virginia, October 2, 1862, for exchange. Declared exchanged at Aiken's Landing on November 10, 1862. Returned to duty on November 25, 1862, and was promoted to Corporal on December 20, 1862. Wounded in the hip at Bristoe Station, Virginia, October 14, 1863. Hospitalized at Richmond, Virginia, where he died on October 27, 1863, of wounds.

FOUST, DANIEL Q., Private
Resided in Guilford County and enlisted at Camp Stokes on October 24, 1864, for the war. Present or accounted for until captured at Hatcher's Run, Virginia, March 31, 1865. Confined at Point Lookout, Maryland, until released on June 26, 1865, after taking the Oath of Allegiance.

FOUST, JACOB, Private
Enlisted at Camp Stokes on February 5, 1865, for the war. Present or accounted for until captured near Petersburg, Virginia, April 2, 1865. Confined at Hart's Island, New York Harbor, where he died on April 26, 1865, of "typhoid fever."

GANT, JAMES H., Private
Born in Guilford County where he resided prior to enlisting at Fort Macon at age 27, August 1, 1861. Died in hospital at Richmond, Virginia, on or about February 26, 1863, of disease.

GILMER, JOHN, ———
Negro. North Carolina pension records indicate that he served in this company.

GORRELL, HENRY CLAY, Private
Born in Guilford County where he resided as a druggist prior to enlisting at age 22, April 20, 1861. Elected 1st Lieutenant of 2nd Company E, 2nd Regiment N.C. State Troops, to rank from May 16, 1861, and transferred to that unit.

GRAY, SAMUEL E. B., Private
Born in Guilford County where he resided prior to enlisting in Guilford County at age 20, February 28, 1862. Present or accounted for until wounded at Sharpsburg, Maryland, September 17, 1862. Returned to duty prior to November 1, 1862. Wounded at Bristoe Station, Virginia, October 14, 1863. Returned to duty on an unspecified date. Wounded at Wilderness, Virginia, on or about May 5, 1864. Returned to duty prior to September 13, 1864, when he was killed "in trenches" near Petersburg, Virginia.

GREENE, WALTER, Private
Resided in Guilford County and enlisted at Fort Macon

at age 19, April 20, 1861. Wounded at Bristoe Station, Virginia, October 14, 1863. Returned to duty on an unspecified date. Surrendered at Appomattox Court House, Virginia, April 9, 1865.

GREESON, THOMAS R., Private
Resided in Guilford County where he enlisted at age 19, February 28, 1862. Present or accounted for until captured at Frederick, Maryland, September 9, 1862. Confined at Fort Delaware, Delaware. Paroled and transferred to Aiken's Landing, James River, Virginia, October 2, 1862, for exchange. Declared exchanged at Aiken's Landing on November 10, 1862. Returned to duty on February 10, 1863. Wounded at Wilderness, Virginia, May 5, 1864. Returned to duty prior to November 1, 1864. Present or accounted for until he deserted to the enemy on or about February 6, 1865. Confined at Washington, D.C., until released on or about February 13, 1865, after taking the Oath of Allegiance.

GRETTER, MICHAEL, Private
Resided in Guilford County and enlisted at Fort Macon at age 27, May 4, 1861. Present or accounted for until he was detailed as brigade Commissary Sergeant on March 18, 1862, and transferred. Reported absent on detail through February, 1865.

HACKETT, JAMES, Private
Resided in Guilford County and enlisted at Camp Holmes at age 40, August 16, 1864, for the war. Present or accounted for until captured near Petersburg, Virginia, April 2, 1865. Confined at Point Lookout, Maryland, until released on June 27, 1865, after taking the Oath of Allegiance.

HALL, HUGH A., Private
Born in Guilford County where he resided as a farmer prior to enlisting in Guilford County at age 20, February 28, 1862. Present or accounted for until he died in hospital at Richmond, Virginia, September 19, 1862, of "febris typhoides."

HALL, JAMES S., Private
Resided in Guilford County where he enlisted at age 29, February 28, 1862. Present or accounted for until wounded at Sharpsburg, Maryland, September 17, 1862. Returned to duty prior to November 1, 1862. Died at Hardeeville, South Carolina, on or about April 15, 1863, of disease. "A good soldier."

HAMPTON, ROBERT F., Private
Resided in Guilford County and enlisted at Fort Macon at age 18, May 4, 1861. Wounded in the thigh and arm after volunteering to bring up ammunition at Cold Harbor, Virginia, June 3, 1864. Died on or about July 28, 1864, of wounds. Place of death not reported.

HANNER, WILLIAM D., Private
Resided in Guilford County and enlisted at age 36, February 28, 1862. Discharged on May 22, 1862, by reason of being overage. Later served in Company I, 63rd Regiment N.C. Troops (5th Regiment N.C. Cavalry).

HARDIN, JAMES M., Private
Resided in Guilford County and enlisted at Fort Macon at age 23, June 10, 1861. Present or accounted for until

captured at or near Sharpsburg, Maryland, on or about September 19, 1862, after having been left behind to attend the wounded. Confined at Fort McHenry, Maryland, and at Fort Monroe, Virginia. Paroled and transferred to Aiken's Landing, James River, Virginia, where he was received November 2, 1862, for exchange. Declared exchanged at Aiken's Landing, November 10, 1862. Returned to duty prior to December 13, 1862, when he was wounded in the thigh at Fredericksburg, Virginia. Detailed as a teamster on July 7, 1863. Rejoined the company on April 22, 1864. Wounded at Wilderness, Virginia, May 5, 1864. Returned to duty prior to November 1, 1864. Present or accounted for until he surrendered at Appomattox Court House, Virginia, April 9, 1865.

HEATH, ROBERT F., Private
Enlisted at Camp Holmes on August 16, 1864, for the war. Deserted on September 27, 1864, but returned to duty on December 14, 1864. Deserted to the enemy on or about March 23, 1865. Confined at Washington, D.C., until released on or about March 29, 1865, after taking the Oath of Allegiance.

HIATT, SAMUEL S., Corporal
Resided in Guilford County and enlisted at Fort Macon at age 17, June 15, 1861. Mustered in as Private. Wounded at Wilderness, Virginia, May 5, 1864. Returned to duty prior to November 1, 1864. Promoted to Corporal on February 1, 1865. Present or accounted for through February, 1865. Paroled at Greensboro on an unspecified date in 1865.

HIGGINS, EDWARD B., Private
Resided in Guilford County where he enlisted at age 24, May 1, 1861. Present or accounted for until promoted to Musician on or about August 1, 1862, and transferred to the regimental band.

HINES, GIDSON D., Private
Born in Guilford County where he resided as a teacher prior to enlisting at Fort Macon at age 27, May 4, 1861. Present or accounted for until he deserted on June 4, 1862. Company records do not indicate whether he returned to duty; however, he was discharged on August 7, 1862, by reason of "amputation of left forearm, in consequence of gunshot injury." Place and date injured not reported.

HOAD, ABRAHAM, Private
Resided in Guilford County and enlisted at age 30, February 28, 1862. Present or accounted for until discharged on May 21, 1862, under the provisions of the Conscription Act.

HOPKINS, WALTER, Private
Place and date of enlistment not reported. Paroled at Greensboro on May 12, 1865.

HORNEY, WILLIAM A., Private
Resided in Guilford County where he enlisted at age 20, May 14, 1862, for the war. Present or accounted for until wounded at Sharpsburg, Maryland, September 17, 1862. Returned to duty subsequent to November 30, 1862. Wounded in the left leg at Wilderness, Virginia, May 5, 1864. Leg amputated. Retired to the Invalid Corps on November 5, 1864. Paroled at Greensboro on May 4, 1865.

HOWLETT, GEORGE W., Sergeant
Born in Guilford County where he resided as a trader prior to enlisting in Guilford County at age 25, April 20, 1861. Mustered in as Sergeant. Present or accounted for until discharged on July 23, 1862, by reason of "neuralgia of the face and head [which has] much impaired his sight."

HUNT, LEANDER GWYNN, Private
Resided in Guilford County and enlisted at Fort Macon at age 25, May 1, 1861. Present or accounted for until captured at New Bern on March 14, 1862. Confined at Fort Columbus, New York Harbor. Exchanged prior to May 18, 1862, when he was promoted to Hospital Steward and transferred to the Field and Staff of this regiment.

HUNT, WILLIAM J. H., Private
Resided in Yadkin County and enlisted at Martinsburg, Virginia, at age 18, September 22, 1862, for the war. Wounded at Wilderness, Virginia, on or about May 5, 1864. Returned to duty prior to June 3, 1864, when he was killed by a sharpshooter at Cold Harbor, Virginia.

HUNTER, SAMUEL A., Private
Resided in Guilford County and enlisted at Fort Macon at age 24, June 11, 1861. Present or accounted for until killed "by a fragment of shell" at New Bern on March 14, 1862. "A noble and most worthy young gentleman."

HUNTER, WILLIAM F., Private
Resided in Guilford County and enlisted at Fort Macon at age 22, June 11, 1861. Present or accounted for until wounded at Sharpsburg, Maryland, September 17, 1862. Returned to duty prior to November 1, 1862. Wounded in the thigh and right arm at Bristoe Station, Virginia, October 14, 1863. Right arm amputated. Died in hospital at Richmond, Virginia, on or about November 9, 1863, of wounds.

ISLEY, LEWIS N., Private
Resided in Guilford County where he enlisted at age 28, February 28, 1862. Wounded in both thighs at Bristoe Station, Virginia, October 14, 1863. Returned to duty subsequent to January 1, 1864. Surrendered at Appomattox Court House, Virginia, April 9, 1865.

JONES, RICHARD B., Private
Resided in Guilford County and enlisted at age 38, February 28, 1862. Present or accounted for until discharged on May 22, 1862, by reason of being overage.

JORDAN, SAMUEL B., 1st Sergeant
Born in Harford County, Maryland, and resided in Maryland where he was by occupation a tobacconist prior to enlisting at Fort Macon at age 34, April 20, 1861. Mustered in as Sergeant and was promoted to 1st Sergeant on October 5, 1861. Present or accounted for until captured at New Bern on March 14, 1862. Confined at Fort Columbus, New York Harbor. Paroled and transferred to Aiken's Landing, James River, Virginia, where he was exchanged on August 5, 1862. Discharged on August 21, 1862, by reason of being "from the state of Maryland."

KELLOGG, HENRY G., Private
Resided in Guilford County and enlisted at Fort Macon at age 21, August 1, 1861. Present or accounted for until January, 1863, when he was detailed for duty with the

brigade commissary department. Reported on detail with the commissary department at Salisbury from January, 1864, through February, 1865.

KIRKMAN, FRANKLIN N., Private
Resided in Guilford County and enlisted at age 25, February 28, 1862. Present or accounted for until discharged on May 22, 1862, under the provisions of the Conscription Act. Paroled at Greensboro on May 10, 1865.

KIRKMAN, WILLIAM N., Private
Born in Guilford County where he resided prior to enlisting in Guilford County at age 17, March 1, 1862. Killed "in trenches" near Petersburg, Virginia, September 27, 1864.

KLUTTS, ALFRED W., Corporal
Resided in Guilford County and enlisted at Fort Macon at age 24, April 20, 1861. Mustered in as Private. Wounded at Sharpsburg, Maryland, September 17, 1862. Returned to duty prior to November 1, 1862. Promoted to Corporal on December 18, 1863. Wounded at Wilderness, Virginia, on or about May 5, 1864. Returned to duty on an unspecified date. Promoted to 1st Sergeant on September 19, 1864, but was reduced to the rank of Corporal on December 4, 1864. Deserted to the enemy on or about January 18, 1865. Confined at Washington, D.C., until released on or about January 24, 1865, after taking the Oath of Allegiance.

LANE, ISAAC F., Private
Born in Guilford County where he resided as a farmer prior to enlisting at Fort Macon at age 25, May 4, 1861. Present or accounted for until he died at Leesburg on February 18, 1863, of disease.

LEMMONS, GEORGE W., Private
Resided in Guilford County and enlisted at Fort Macon at age 24, August 1, 1861. Captured at Bristoe Station, Virginia, October 14, 1863. Confined at Old Capitol Prison, Washington, D.C., until transferred to Point Lookout, Maryland, October 27, 1863. Paroled at Point Lookout on or about February 10, 1865, and transferred to Cox's Wharf, James River, Virginia, where he was received February 14-15, 1865, for exchange. Surrendered at Appomattox Court House, Virginia, April 9, 1865.

LEMONS, JAMES M., Private
Born in Guilford County where he resided prior to enlisting in Guilford County at age 18, May 1, 1862, for the war. Present or accounted for until wounded at Sharpsburg, Maryland, September 17, 1862. Company records do not indicate whether he returned to duty; however, he died "at his home" on March 1, 1863, of disease.

LINDSAY, ANDREW DAVID, Private
Resided in Guilford County and enlisted at Fort Macon at age 22, April 20, 1861. Present or accounted for until promoted to Ordnance Sergeant on April 1, 1862, and transferred to the Field and Staff of this regiment.

LINDSAY, ED. B., Private
Resided in Guilford County and enlisted at Fort Macon at age 17, June 10, 1861. Present or accounted for until discharged on May 22, 1862, by reason of being underage. Later served as 1st Lieutenant of Company

K, 63rd Regiment N.C. Troops (5th Regiment N.C. Cavalry).

LINDSAY, JED HARPER, Jr., 1st Sergeant
Resided in Guilford County and enlisted at Fort Macon at age 21, April 20, 1861. Mustered in as Private and was promoted to Corporal prior to September 1, 1861. Promoted to Sergeant on April 22, 1862, and was promoted to 1st Sergeant on September 21, 1862. Appointed Adjutant of the 45th Regiment N.C. Troops on November 3, 1862, and transferred.

LINDSAY, ROBERT HENRY, Private
Resided in Guilford County and enlisted at age 24, April 20, 1861. Died in camp "shortly afterwards." Cause of death not reported.

LINEBERRY, LOUIS S., Private
Born in Randolph County and resided in Yadkin County prior to enlisting in Guilford County at age 17, August 17, 1862, for the war as a substitute for Private Henry S. Puryear. Wounded at Bristoe Station, Virginia, October 14, 1863. Returned to duty on an unspecified date and was killed at Wilderness, Virginia, May 5, 1864. "A most excellent soldier."

LIPSCOMB, SAMUEL M., Private
Resided in Guilford County and enlisted at Fort Macon at age 22, April 20, 1861. Promoted to Musician on or about August 1, 1862, and transferred to the regimental band.

LLOYD, THOMAS E., Private
Resided in Guilford County where he enlisted at age 17, January 26, 1863, for the war as a substitute for Private Samuel William Henry Smith. Reported absent without leave in July, 1863. Company muster roll dated November-December, 1864, states he was "killed at home being a deserter" on an unspecified date; however, North Carolina pension records indicate that he survived the war. No further records.

McADOO, WALTER D., Private
Resided in Guilford County and enlisted at Fort Macon at age 21, May 4, 1861. Present or accounted for until wounded at Sharpsburg, Maryland, September 17, 1862. Transferred to Company A, 53rd Regiment N.C. Troops, February 16, 1863.

McBRIDE, WILLIAM A., Private
Enlisted at Camp Holmes on May 31, 1864, for the war. Present or accounted for until he surrendered at Appomattox Court House, Virginia, April 9, 1865.

McCONNELL, DANIEL W., 1st Sergeant
Resided in Guilford County where he enlisted at age 18, July 4, 1863, for the war. Mustered in as Private and was promoted to 1st Sergeant on July 15, 1864. Wounded by a shell "while lying sick in a field hospital" in September, 1864. Died on or about September 18, 1864. Place of death not reported.

McCUISTON, JOHN FRANKLIN, Corporal
Resided in Guilford County where he enlisted at age 18, June 22, 1863, for the war. Mustered in as Private and was promoted to Corporal on February 1, 1865. Captured at Hatcher's Run, Virginia, April 2, 1865. Confined at Point Lookout, Maryland, until released on June 29, 1865, after taking the Oath of Allegiance.

McDOWELL, JOHN W., Private

Resided in Guilford County and enlisted at Fort Macon at age 30, April 20, 1861. Present or accounted for until wounded at Sharpsburg, Maryland, September 17, 1862. Returned to duty on an unspecified date. Wounded at Bristoe Station, Virginia, October 14, 1863. Returned to duty on an unspecified date. Captured at Hatcher's Run, Virginia, April 2, 1865. Confined at Point Lookout, Maryland, until released on June 29, 1865, after taking the Oath of Allegiance.

McFARLAND, WILLIAM, Private

Born in Guilford County where he resided prior to enlisting in Guilford County at age 19, February 28, 1862. Present or accounted for until killed at Sharpsburg, Maryland, September 17, 1862.

McLAIN, WILLIAM H., Private

Born in Guilford County where he resided as a farmer prior to enlisting in Guilford County at age 22, February 28, 1862. Present or accounted for until he died in a hospital at Winchester, Virginia, October 24, 1862, of disease.

McLEAN, JOSEPH E., Private

Resided in Guilford County where he enlisted at age 27, May 6, 1862, for the war. Present or accounted for until wounded at Sharpsburg, Maryland, September 17, 1862. Returned to duty on an unspecified date. Captured at or near Fort Stedman, Virginia, March 25, 1865. Confined at Point Lookout, Maryland, where he died on May 31, 1865, of "diarrhoea."

McLEAN, ROBERT B., Private

Resided in Guilford County and enlisted at Fort Macon at age 19, June 11, 1861. Wounded at Bristoe Station, Virginia, October 14, 1863. Returned to duty on an unspecified date. Wounded at Wilderness, Virginia, May 5, 1864. Returned to duty prior to November 1, 1864. Captured at or near Fort Stedman, Virginia, March 25, 1865. Confined at Point Lookout, Maryland, until released on June 3, 1865, after taking the Oath of Allegiance.

McLEAN, SAMUEL F., Private

Born in Guilford County where he resided prior to enlisting in Guilford County at age 29, May 26, 1862, for the war. Killed at Wilderness, Virginia, May 5, 1864.

McNAIRY, JOHN W., Private

Resided in Guilford County and enlisted at Fort Macon at age 19, June 15, 1861. Present or accounted for until wounded at Sharpsburg, Maryland, September 17, 1862. Returned to duty on an unspecified date. Wounded in the left leg at Bristoe Station, Virginia, October 14, 1863. Left leg amputated. Retired to the Invalid Corps on November 19, 1864.

MARSH, JAMES M., Private

Resided in Guilford County and enlisted at Fort Macon at age 20, June 13, 1861. Captured at Bristoe Station, Virginia, October 14, 1863. Confined at Old Capitol Prison, Washington, D.C., until transferred to Point Lookout, Maryland, October 27, 1863. Arrived at Point Lookout on October 28, 1863. Paroled at Point Lookout on May 3, 1864, and transferred to Aiken's Landing, James River, Virginia, where he was received May 8, 1864, for exchange. Returned to duty on June 18, 1864.

Present or accounted for until he deserted to the enemy on or about March 23, 1865. Confined at Washington, D.C., until released on or about March 29, 1865, after taking the Oath of Allegiance.

MAY, LEMUEL, Private

Resided in Guilford County where he enlisted at age 26, February 28, 1862. Wounded at Wilderness, Virginia, on or about May 5, 1864. Returned to duty on an unspecified date. Captured at Farmville, Virginia, October 6, 1865. Confined at Newport News, Virginia, until released on June 27, 1865, after taking the Oath of Allegiance.

MAY, WILLIAM H., Private

Resided in Guilford County where he enlisted at age 21, May 6, 1862, for the war. Wounded in the right side at Bristoe Station, Virginia, October 14, 1863. Returned to duty on an unspecified date. Wounded at Wilderness, Virginia, on or about May 5, 1864. Returned to duty prior to November 1, 1864. Captured at Hatcher's Run, Virginia, April 2, 1865. Confined at Hart's Island, New York Harbor, until released on June 18, 1865.

NELSON, JOHN W., Private

Born in Guilford County where he resided prior to enlisting at Fort Macon at age 26, May 1, 1861. Present or accounted for until he died in a hospital at Charleston, South Carolina, March 17, 1863, of "fever."

ORRELL, ADOLPHUS LAFAYETTE, Sr., Private

Resided in Guilford County and enlisted at Fort Macon at age 22, April 20, 1861. Wounded at Bristoe Station, Virginia, October 14, 1863. Transferred to the C.S. Navy on April 1, 1864.

ORRELL, JAMES A., Private

Resided in Guilford County and enlisted at Fort Macon at age 20, May 1, 1861. Captured at Frederick, Maryland, September 9, 1862. Exchanged on an unspecified date. Returned to duty on an unspecified date. Captured at Bristoe Station, Virginia, October 14, 1863. Confined at Old Capitol Prison, Washington, D.C., until transferred to Point Lookout, Maryland, October 27, 1863. Paroled at Point Lookout on or about November 1, 1864, and transferred to Venus Point, Savannah River, Georgia, where he was received November 15, 1864, for exchange. Returned to duty in January-February, 1865. Captured at or near Fort Stedman, Virginia, March 25, 1865. Confined at Point Lookout until released on June 3, 1865, after taking the Oath of Allegiance.

OWEN, WILBUR F., Private

Resided in Guilford County and enlisted at Fort Macon at age 22, June 11, 1861. Captured at Bristoe Station, Virginia, October 14, 1863. Confined at Old Capitol Prison, Washington, D.C., until transferred to Point Lookout, Maryland, October 27, 1863. Paroled at Point Lookout and transferred to Aiken's Landing, James River, Virginia, for exchange. Returned to duty in November-December, 1864. Present or accounted for until captured at Amelia Court House, Virginia, April 5, 1865. Confined at Point Lookout until released on June 29, 1865, after taking the Oath of Allegiance.

PAISLEY, WILLIAM M., Sergeant
Born in Guilford County where he resided prior to enlisting at Fort Macon at age 19, April 20, 1861. Mustered in as Private and was promoted to Corporal on August 1, 1862. Promoted to Sergeant on September 21, 1862. Wounded in the breast at "Gary's Farm," Virginia, June 15, 1864. "Sergeant Paisley, at the head and slightly in advance of his company, was shot by a sharpshooter, and fell mortally wounded. He was carried from the field and sent to the hospital in Richmond, [Virginia]. There he suffered and lingered until the 13th of July, when he died in the arms of his broken hearted father. . . ."

PEARCE, JAMES R., Corporal
Resided in Guilford County and enlisted at Fort Macon at age 21, April 20, 1861. Mustered in as Private. Captured at Bristoe Station, Virginia, October 14, 1863. Confined at Old Capitol Prison, Washington, D.C., until transferred to Point Lookout, Maryland, October 27, 1863. Paroled at Point Lookout and transferred to City Point, Virginia, April 17, 1864, for exchange. Returned to duty on an unspecified date. Promoted to Corporal on December 14, 1864. Present or accounted for until captured at or near Sutherland's Station, Virginia, April 2, 1865. Confined at Hart's Island, New York Harbor, until released on June 18, 1865, after taking the Oath of Allegiance.

POE, WILLIAM E., Private
Resided in Guilford County where he enlisted at age 19, February 28, 1862. Present or accounted for until paroled at Greensboro on May 16, 1865.

PORTER, CHARLES E., Private
Resided in Guilford County and enlisted at Fort Macon at age 23, April 20, 1861. Reported absent sick from September-October, 1861, through February, 1862. Discharged on May 12, 1862, by reason of disability. Died at Greensboro on an unspecified date of disease.

PRATHER, LOVETT L., Private
Resided in Guilford County and was by occupation a teacher prior to enlisting at Fort Macon at age 29, August 1, 1861. Present or accounted for until wounded in the arm at Sharpsburg, Maryland, September 17, 1862. Discharged on March 26, 1863, by reason of disability.

PURYEAR, HENRY S., Private
Resided in Yadkin County and enlisted at Fort Macon at age 20, May 1, 1861. Present or accounted for until discharged on or about August 17, 1862, after providing Private Louis S. Lineberry as a substitute.

RANKIN, JOSEPH W., Private
Resided in Guilford County and was by occupation a farmer prior to enlisting at Fort Macon at age 19, May 1, 1861. Wounded at Sharpsburg, Maryland, September 17, 1862. Returned to duty on an unspecified date. Wounded in the lungs at Bristoe Station, Virginia, October 14, 1863. Died in hospital at Richmond, Virginia, October 24, 1863, of wounds.

REED, JOHN W., Private
Resided in Guilford County and enlisted at Fort Macon at age 20, June 15, 1861. Present or accounted for until transferred to Company K, 48th Regiment N.C. Troops, December 4, 1862.

REITZEL, HENRY C., Private
Resided in Guilford County and enlisted at Camp Stokes on October 26, 1864, for the war. Present or accounted for until captured at Hatcher's Run, Virginia, March 31, 1865. Confined at Point Lookout, Maryland, until released on June 17, 1865, after taking the Oath of Allegiance.

RHODES, THOMAS J., 1st Sergeant
Resided in Guilford County and enlisted at Fort Macon at age 19, June 23, 1861. Mustered in as Private and was promoted to Corporal on December 17, 1862. Promoted to Sergeant on February 20, 1864, and was promoted to 1st Sergeant on or about February 1, 1865. Present or accounted for until he surrendered at Appomattox Court House, Virginia, April 9, 1865.

RICKS, PLEASANT A., Private
Resided in Guilford County where he enlisted at age 17, May 1, 1862, for the war as a substitute for Private John E. Wharton. Died in hospital at Lynchburg, Virginia, March 12, 1864, of "typhoid fever."

ROBINSON, SAMUEL, Private
Place and date of enlistment not reported. "Served with the company until June, 1861." No further records.

SCOTT, JAMES S., Private
Resided in Guilford County and enlisted at Fort Macon at age 22, May 1, 1861. Wounded at Reams' Station, Virginia, August 25, 1864. Returned to duty subsequent to February 28, 1865. Wounded near Burgess' Mill, Virginia, on an unspecified date. Died on May 6, 1865, of wounds. Place of death not reported.

SEATS, WILLIAM, Private
Resided in Guilford County where he enlisted at age 27, February 28, 1862. Died at Winchester, Virginia, on or about September 24, 1862, of disease.

SHARPE, EDWIN TONKIE, Private
Resided in Guilford County where he enlisted at age 19, May 7, 1863, for the war. Surrendered at Appomattox Court House, Virginia, April 9, 1865.

SHEPHERD, J. PAISLEY, Private
Resided in Guilford County where he enlisted at age 25, February 28, 1862. Present or accounted for until wounded at Sharpsburg, Maryland, September 17, 1862. Returned to duty on an unspecified date. Captured at Bristoe Station, Virginia, October 14, 1863. Confined at Old Capitol Prison, Washington, D.C., until transferred to Point Lookout, Maryland, October 27, 1863. Paroled at Point Lookout and transferred to Aiken's Landing, James River, Virginia, September 22, 1864, for exchange. Died at or near Richmond, Virginia, on or about September 23, 1864. Cause of death not reported.

SHULER, EMSLEY F., Private
Resided in Guilford County where he enlisted at age 31, May 6, 1862, for the war. Wounded in the left hip at Bristoe Station, Virginia, October 14, 1863. Reported absent wounded and "disabled" through February, 1865.

SILER, JOHN RANDOLPH, Private
Resided in Chatham County and enlisted at Camp

Holmes at age 18, July 18, 1862, for the war. Wounded in the neck at Wilderness, Virginia, May 5, 1864. Returned to duty in November-December, 1864. Present or accounted for until captured at Hatcher's Run, Virginia, March 31, 1865. Confined at Point Lookout, Maryland, until released on June 19, 1865, after taking the Oath of Allegiance.

SLOAN, GEORGE J., Private
Resided in Guilford County and enlisted at Fort Macon at age 25, April 20, 1861. Died at Fort Macon on July 31, 1861, of disease.

SLOAN, THOMAS J., Sergeant
Resided in Guilford County and enlisted at Fort Macon at age 23, April 20, 1861. Mustered in as Corporal and was promoted to Sergeant on January 14, 1862. Promoted to Musician and transferred to the regimental band on August 1, 1862.

SMITH, B. N., Private
Resided in Guilford County where he enlisted at age 28, February 28, 1862. Present or accounted for until discharged on or about June 1, 1862, after providing Private Paul W. Crutchfield as a substitute.

SMITH, JOHN H., Private
Resided in Guilford County where he enlisted at age 19, February 28, 1862. Present or accounted for until he died in camp near Petersburg, Virginia, August 8, 1862, of disease.

SMITH, R. LEYTON, Private
Born in Guilford County where he resided as a farmer prior to enlisting in Guilford County at age 22, February 28, 1862. Present or accounted for until killed at Sharpsburg, Maryland, September 17, 1862.

SMITH, RICHARD S., Sergeant
Resided in Guilford County where he enlisted at age 21, August 8, 1861. Mustered in as Private. Wounded at Bristoe Station, Virginia, October 14, 1863. Returned to duty on an unspecified date. Promoted to Corporal on February 20, 1864, and was promoted to Sergeant on February 1, 1865. Present or accounted for until captured at Sutherland's Station, Virginia, April 2, 1865. Confined at Hart's Island, New York Harbor, until released on June 18, 1865, after taking the Oath of Allegiance.

SMITH, SAMUEL WILLIAM HENRY, Private
Resided in Guilford County and enlisted at Fort Macon at age 19, August 8, 1861. Discharged on or about January 26, 1863, after providing Private Thomas E. Lloyd as a substitute.

SOCKWELL, JOHN T., Private
Resided in Guilford County and enlisted at Fort Macon at age 18, August 1, 1861. Killed at Bristoe Station, Virginia, October 14, 1863.

STANLEY, ANDREW L., Private
Resided in Guilford County and enlisted at Fort Macon at age 21, June 11, 1861. Present or accounted for until wounded at Sharpsburg, Maryland, September 17, 1862. Returned to duty on an unspecified date. Captured at Bristoe Station, Virginia, October 14, 1863. Confined at Old Capitol Prison, Washington, D.C.,

until released on December 17, 1863, after taking the Oath of Allegiance. He was the "champion forager" of General John R. Cooke's brigade.

STEINER, WILLIAM U., Sergeant
Resided in Guilford County where he enlisted at age 31, April 20, 1861. Mustered in as Private and was promoted to Corporal on or about January 14, 1862. Promoted to Sergeant on April 22, 1862. Wounded at Bristoe Station, Virginia, October 14, 1863. Returned to duty on an unspecified date. Wounded at Wilderness, Virginia, on or about May 5, 1864. Returned to duty prior to August 25, 1864, when he was wounded at Reams' Station, Virginia. Reported absent wounded through February, 1865. Paroled at Greensboro on May 9, 1865.

STERLING, EDWARD G., Private
Resided in Guilford County and enlisted at Fort Macon at age 21, April 20, 1861. Present or accounted for until he died at Greensboro on September 6, 1861, of "typh[oi]d fever."

STORY, WILLIAM C., Private
Resided in Guilford County and enlisted at Fort Macon at age 19, June 11, 1861. Present or accounted for until appointed Ensign (Lieutenant) on April 28, 1864, and transferred to the Field and Staff of this regiment. ["Complimented in special orders for gallantry at Bristoe" Station, Virginia, October 14, 1863.]

STRATFORD, CHRISTOPHER WALLACE, Sergeant
Resided in Guilford County where he enlisted at age 26, May 1, 1861. Mustered in as Private and was promoted to Corporal on August 1, 1862. Wounded at Bristoe Station, Virginia, October 14, 1863. Returned to duty on an unspecified date. Promoted to Sergeant on December 18, 1863. Wounded at Wilderness, Virginia, May 5, 1864. Reported absent wounded through February, 1865. Paroled at Greensboro on May 1, 1865.

STRATFORD, EMSLEY W., Private
Resided in Guilford County and enlisted at Fort Macon at age 22, May 1, 1861. Wounded at Reams' Station, Virginia, August 25, 1864. Returned to duty in November-December, 1864. Present or accounted for through February, 1865.

SUMMERS, WILLIAM M., Private
Resided in Guilford County and enlisted at Fort Macon at age 26, May 1, 1861. Wounded in the forehead and/or right elbow at Bristoe Station, Virginia, October 14, 1863. Returned to duty on an unspecified date. Present or accounted for through February, 1865. Paroled at Burkeville Junction, Virginia, April 14-17, 1865. [North Carolina pension records indicate he was wounded in August, 1864.]

SWEITZ, EDWARD, Private
Enlisted on April 20, 1861, as a substitute for Private J. H. Tarpley. No further records.

SWIFT, T., Private
Place and date of enlistment not reported. Discharged on May 22, 1862. Reason discharged not reported.

TARPLEY, J. H., Private
Place and date of enlistment not reported. Discharged on or about April 20, 1861, after providing Private

Edward Sweitz as a substitute.

TATE, ROBERT B., Private
Resided in Guilford County and enlisted at Fort Macon at age 25, June 11, 1861. Present or accounted for until wounded at Sharpsburg, Maryland, September 17, 1862. Returned to duty on an unspecified date. Wounded in the head at Wilderness, Virginia, May 5, 1864. Died in hospital near Parker's Store, Spotsylvania County, Virginia, June 19, 1864, of wounds.

THOM, JOEL J., Sergeant
Resided in Guilford County and enlisted at Greensboro at age 18, May 10, 1862, for the war. Mustered in as Private and was promoted to Corporal on June 1, 1864. Promoted to Sergeant on or about February 1, 1865. Present or accounted for until he surrendered at Appomattox Court House, Virginia, April 9, 1865.

THOMAS, JAMES C., ———
Enlisted on April 20, 1861. Discharged on June 10, 1861, "on account of injuries received while in service." Place and date injured not reported.

UNDERWOOD, WILLIAM W., Private
Born in Rockingham County and resided in Guilford County where he was by occupation a farmer prior to enlisting in Guilford County at age 28, February 28, 1862. Present or accounted for until wounded and captured at Sharpsburg, Maryland, September 17, 1862. Died on September 29, 1862, of wounds. Place of death not reported.

WEATHERLY, ROBERT D., Corporal
Born in Guilford County where he resided prior to enlisting at Fort Macon at age 21, April 20, 1861. Mustered in as Private and was promoted to Corporal on November 1, 1862. Promoted to Sergeant Major on March 27, 1863, and transferred to the Field and Staff of this regiment.

WEIR, SAMUEL PARK, Private
Born in Guilford County and was by occupation a divinity student prior to enlisting at Fort Macon at age 22, April 20, 1861. Present or accounted for until appointed 2nd Lieutenant and transferred to Company F, 46th Regiment N.C. Troops, April 24, 1862.

WESTBROOK, CHARLES WALL, Corporal
Resided in Guilford County and enlisted at Fort Macon at age 23, May 1, 1861. Mustered in as Private and was promoted to Corporal on August 1, 1862. Performed the duties of Chaplain until December 20, 1862. Present or accounted for until January 8, 1864, when he was promoted to Chaplain and transferred to another unit. [Corporal Westbrook was known as the "fighting parson" and "preached as he shot, without fear and to the mark."]

WHARTON, JOHN E., Private
Resided in Guilford County where he enlisted at age 27, April 20, 1861. Present or accounted for until discharged on or about May 1, 1862, after providing Private Pleasant A. Ricks as a substitute. Later served as Captain of Company K, 63rd Regiment N.C. Troops (5th Regiment N.C. Cavalry).

WILEY, JAMES R., Private
Born in Guilford County where he resided as a student prior to enlisting in Guilford County at age 20, February 28, 1862. Present or accounted for until discharged on February 1, 1863, by reason of "chronic rheumatism."

WILLIAMS, JOHN WASHINGTON, Private
Resided in Guilford County where he enlisted at age 25, February 28, 1862. Wounded at Wilderness, Virginia, May 5, 1864. Returned to duty prior to August 25, 1864, when he was wounded at Reams' Station, Virginia. Returned to duty prior to November 1, 1864. Present or accounted for until he deserted to the enemy on or about March 23, 1865. Confined at Washington, D.C., until released on or about March 29, 1865, after taking the Oath of Allegiance.

WILSON, JAMES L., Private
Resided in Guilford County and enlisted at Fort Macon at age 22, July 19, 1861. Wounded and captured at Sharpsburg, Maryland, September 17, 1862. Confined at Fort Delaware, Delaware, until transferred to Aiken's Landing, James River, Virginia, October 2, 1862, for exchange. Declared exchanged at Aiken's Landing on November 10, 1862. Returned to duty on an unspecified date. Wounded in the side at Wilderness, Virginia, May 5, 1864. Returned to duty prior to November 1, 1864. Present or accounted for until he deserted to the enemy on or about January 18, 1865. Confined at Washington, D.C., until released on or about January 24, 1865, after taking the Oath of Allegiance.

WINBOURNE, STEPHEN D., Corporal
Resided in Guilford County where he enlisted at age 27, April 28, 1862, for the war. Mustered in as Private. Wounded at Sharpsburg, Maryland, September 17, 1862. Returned to duty prior to November 1, 1862. Promoted to Corporal on February 1, 1865. Captured at Sutherland's Station, Virginia, April 2, 1865. Confined at Hart's Island, New York Harbor, until released on June 19, 1865, after taking the Oath of Allegiance.

WINFREE, J. R., Private
Resided in Guilford County and enlisted at age 36, February 28, 1862. No further records.

WINFREE, W. C., Private
Enlisted at age 35, in February, 1862. Discharged on May 22, 1862, under the provisions of the Conscription Act.

WOODBURN, THOMAS MONROE, Private
Born in Guilford County and resided in Guilford or Bladen County prior to enlisting at Fort Macon at age 20, June 10, 1861. Present or accounted for until wounded at Sharpsburg, Maryland, September 17, 1862. Returned to duty prior to November 1, 1862. Captured at Bristoe Station, Virginia, October 14, 1863. Confined at Old Capitol Prison, Washington, D.C., until transferred to Point Lookout, Maryland, October 27, 1863. Paroled at Point Lookout on or about October 30, 1864, and transferred to Venus Point, Savannah River, Georgia, where he was received November 15, 1864, for exchange. No further records.

WOODS, J. K., Private
Enlisted at Fort Macon on May 4, 1861. Present or accounted for through February, 1862. No further records.

WOOLEN, GEORGE H., Private

Born in Guilford County where he resided prior to enlisting in Guilford County at age 23, April 28, 1862, for the war. Present or accounted for until wounded at Sharpsburg, Maryland, September 17, 1862. Returned to duty on an unspecified date. Captured at Bristoe Station, Virginia, October 14, 1863. Confined at Old Capitol Prison, Washington, D.C., until transferred to Point Lookout, Maryland, February 3, 1864. Died at Point Lookout on or about September 18, 1864. Cause of death not reported.

WORRELL, RICHARD B., 1st Sergeant

Resided in Guilford County and enlisted at Fort Macon at age 19, April 20, 1861. Mustered in as Private. Captured at Bristoe Station, Virginia, October 14, 1863. Confined at Old Capitol Prison, Washington, D.C., until transferred to Point Lookout, Maryland, October 27, 1863. Paroled at Point Lookout and transferred to Aiken's Landing, James River, Virginia, May 3, 1864, for exchange. Returned to duty prior to September 14, 1864, when he was promoted to Corporal. Promoted to 1st Sergeant on December 4, 1864. Deserted to the enemy on or about January 18, 1865. Confined at Washington, D.C., until released on or about January 24, 1865, after taking the Oath of Allegiance.

YOUNG, SAMUEL S., Private

Born in Guilford County where he resided as a farmer prior to enlisting in Guilford County at age 19, February 28, 1862. Present or accounted for until killed at Sharpsburg, Maryland, September 17, 1862.

COMPANY C

This company, known as the "North Carolina Guards," was raised in Lenoir County and enlisted in April, 1861. On April 28, 1861, the company was ordered to Fort Macon, but it was not received into service and returned home. It was then ordered to New Bern, where it was mustered into service on June 6, 1861; it was later assigned to the 27th Regiment as Company C. After joining the regiment the company functioned as a part of the regiment, and its history for the war period is reported as a part of the regimental history.

The information contained in the following company roster was compiled principally from company muster rolls for June 6, 1861-June, 1862; September-October, 1862; and September, 1864-February, 1865. No company muster rolls were found for July-August, 1862; November, 1862-August, 1864; or for the period after February, 1865. Valuable information was obtained also from primary records such as the Roll of Honor, medical records, prisoner of war records, discharge certificates, and pension applications, and from secondary sources such as postwar rosters and histories, cemetery records, and records of the United Daughters of the Confederacy.

OFFICERS

CAPTAINS

WHITFIELD, GEORGE F.

Resided in Lenoir County where he enlisted at age 31. Elected Captain on April 17, 1861. Present or accounted for until appointed Major on November 1, 1862, and transferred to the Field and Staff of this regiment. Later served as Colonel of this regiment.

WOOTEN, EDWARD G.

Resided in Lenoir County where he enlisted at age 24, May 6, 1862, for the war. Mustered in as Private and was elected 2nd Lieutenant on September 22, 1862. Promoted to Captain on December 1, 1862. Wounded in the shoulder at Fredericksburg, Virginia, December 13, 1862. Returned to duty on an unspecified date. Present or accounted for until paroled at Farmville, Virginia, April 11-21, 1865.

LIEUTENANTS

BIZZELL, WOOTEN, 1st Lieutenant

Resided in Wayne County and enlisted in Lenoir County at age 32, April 17, 1861. Mustered in with an unspecified rank and was promoted to Sergeant on May 1, 1861. Elected 3rd Lieutenant in August, 1862, and was promoted to 2nd Lieutenant on September 18, 1862. Promoted to 1st Lieutenant on October 14, 1863. Captured in hospital at Richmond, Virginia, April 3, 1865.

FOSS, LOUIS, 2nd Lieutenant

Resided in Lenoir County where he enlisted at age 26, April 17, 1861. Mustered in as Private and was promoted to Sergeant on February 18, 1862. Reduced to ranks in May-June, 1862, but was elected 2nd Lieutenant on or about October 14, 1862. Paroled at Burkeville Junction, Virginia, April 14-17, 1865.

ROUSE, THOMAS W., 2nd Lieutenant

Resided in Lenoir County where he enlisted at age 30. Elected 3rd Lieutenant on April 17, 1861, and was elected 2nd Lieutenant on or about August 22, 1861. Present or accounted for until he died in a hospital at Petersburg, Virginia, August 6, 1862, of "bilious fever."

WATERS, BENJAMIN, 1st Lieutenant

Resided in Lenoir County where he enlisted at age 32. Elected 2nd Lieutenant on April 17, 1861. Promoted to 1st Lieutenant on September 18, 1862. Present or accounted for until captured in an unspecified engagement in [September], 1862. Confined at Fort Delaware, Delaware, until transferred to Aiken's Landing, James River, Virginia, October 2, 1862, for exchange. Declared exchanged at Aiken's Landing on November 10, 1862. Died on October 16, 1863. Place and cause of death not reported.

WOOTEN, JOHN PUGH, 1st Lieutenant

Resided in Lenoir County where he enlisted at age 35. Elected 1st Lieutenant on April 17, 1861. Present or accounted for until wounded at Sharpsburg, Maryland, September 17, 1862. Died at Sharpsburg on September 18, 1862, of wounds.

NONCOMMISSIONED OFFICERS AND PRIVATES

ALDRIDGE, BARRINGTON HOWELL, Private

Born in Greene County and resided in Lenoir County where he was by occupation a shoemaker prior to enlisting in Lenoir County at age 25, May 6, 1862. Detailed as a shoemaker during much of the war. Reported on duty with Company B, 2nd Battalion Virginia Infantry (Local Defense) in June, 1863, and July, 1864. Deserted to the enemy on or about December 27, 1864. Confined at Washington, D.C., until released on or about January 3, 1865, after taking the Oath of

Allegiance.

ALDRIDGE, BENNETT FRANKLIN, Private
Resided in Lenoir County where he enlisted at age 18, April 17, 1861. Wounded at Bristoe Station, Virginia, October 14, 1863. Returned to duty on an unspecified date. Present or accounted for until promoted to Musician in September-October, 1864, and transferred to the regimental band.

ALDRIDGE, JESSE B., Private
Resided in Lenoir County where he enlisted on April 17, 1861. Reported on detail as a shoemaker from April, 1864, through February, 1865. Took the Oath of Allegiance at Richmond, Virginia, April 11, 1865.

ALDRIDGE, JOSEPH, Private
Resided in Lenoir County where he enlisted at age 19, May 6, 1862, for the war. Present or accounted for through February, 1865. Captured by the enemy on an unspecified date. Confined at Point Lookout, Maryland, until released on June 23, 1865, after taking the Oath of Allegiance. [North Carolina pension records indicate he was wounded at Orange Court House, Virginia, in 1863.]

ALDRIDGE, RICHARD H., Private
Resided in Lenoir County where he enlisted at age 21, April 17, 1861. Hospitalized at Charlottesville, Virginia, October 18, 1863, with a gunshot wound. Place and date wounded not reported. Furloughed on November 3, 1863. No further records.

BARROW, JAMES F., Private
Resided in Lenoir County where he enlisted at age 18, April 17, 1861. Present or accounted for until he died at "Camp Jackson" on July 10, 1862. Cause of death not reported.

BARROW, JESSE H., Private
Resided in Lenoir County where he enlisted at age 29, April 25, 1861. Wounded in the right elbow at Bristoe Station, Virginia, October 14, 1863. Reported absent wounded through December, 1864. Returned to duty in January-February, 1865, but was retired to the Invalid Corps on March 6, 1865, by reason of disability.

BARROW, SIMON P., Private
Resided in Lenoir County and enlisted at New Bern at age 22, June 20, 1861. Killed at Wilderness, Virginia, on or about May 5, 1864.

BELL, GEORGE, Private
Enlisted at Fort Lane on August 31, 1861. Discharged on April 3, 1863. Reason discharged not reported. Later served as Corporal in Company D, 1st Battalion N.C. Local Defense Troops.

BELL, JAMES H., Private
Resided in Lenoir County and enlisted at Coosawhatchie, South Carolina, at age 17, March 3, 1863, for the war. Wounded in the left arm at or near Spotsylvania Court House, Virginia, on or about May 8, 1864. Returned to duty prior to January 1, 1865. Present or accounted for until captured at Hatcher's Run, Virginia, March 31, 1865. Confined at Point Lookout, Maryland, until released on June 23, 1865, after taking the Oath of Allegiance.

BELL, JOSHUA H., Sergeant
Resided in Lenoir County where he enlisted at age 25, April 17, 1861. Mustered in as Private and was promoted to Corporal on May 1, 1861. Promoted to Sergeant in March-April, 1862, but was reduced to ranks in May-June, 1862. Reappointed Sergeant on September 1, 1862. Present or accounted for until killed "in Virginia" in June, 1864.

BENTON, JAMES, Sergeant
Born in Lenoir County where he resided as a farmer prior to enlisting in Lenoir County at age 40, April 17, 1861. Mustered in with an unspecified rank and was promoted to Sergeant on May 1, 1861. Present or accounted for until he died "at home" on February 18, 1862, of "typhoid fever."

BIZZELL, WILLIAM B., Private
Resided in Duplin County and enlisted in Lenoir County at age 18, June 3, 1863, for the war. Captured at Farmville, Virginia, April 6, 1865. Confined at Newport News, Virginia, until released on June 27, 1865, after taking the Oath of Allegiance.

BLIZZARD, JOHN M., Private
Born in Lenoir County and was by occupation a farmer prior to enlisting in Wake County on August 3, 1861. Present or accounted for until he died "at home" on or about June 26, 1862. Cause of death not reported. Death records dated July 23, 1862, give his age as 30.

BOLDING, SPENCER, Private
Resided in Lenoir County where he enlisted at age 34, April 17, 1861. Killed at Wilderness, Virginia, on or about May 5, 1864.

BOON, CALEB, Private
Resided in Lenoir County where he enlisted at age 23, April 17, 1861. Present or accounted for until captured at New Bern on March 14, 1862. Confined at Fort Columbus, New York Harbor. Paroled and transferred to Aiken's Landing, James River, Virginia, where he was received July 12, 1862, for exchange. Declared exchanged at Aiken's Landing on August 5, 1862. Present or accounted for through October, 1862. No further records.

BRAXTON, ISAAC B., Private
Resided in Lenoir County where he enlisted at age 20, May 6, 1862, for the war. Wounded at Wilderness, Virginia, on or about May 5, 1864. Returned to duty prior to June 3, 1864, when he was wounded in the left shoulder at Cold Harbor, Virginia. Returned to duty in January-February, 1865. Present or accounted for through February, 1865.

BROCK, JOSEPH, Private
Resided in Duplin County and enlisted in Lenoir County at age 34, May 6, 1862, for the war. Present or accounted for through June, 1863. Deserted on an unspecified date. Apprehended on an unspecified date and was court-martialed "for deserting [his] comrades, and taking up arms on the enemy's side." Hanged at Kinston on February 15, 1864.

BROWN, POWELL, Private
Resided in Lenoir County where he enlisted at age 34, April 17, 1861. Present or accounted for until wounded at Sharpsburg, Maryland, September 17, 1862.

Returned to duty on an unspecified date. Deserted on December 8, 1864, but returned to duty on January 27, 1865. Deserted again on February 7, 1865.

BURKETT, JOHN W., Private
Resided in Lenoir County where he enlisted at age 33, April 17, 1861. Deserted on August 6, 1861. Returned to duty prior to November 1, 1861. Deserted on May 30, 1862. Returned to duty on an unspecified date. Deserted on December 8, 1864.

CASEY, WILLIAM B., Sergeant
Resided in Lenoir County where he enlisted at age 23, April 25, 1861. Mustered in as Private and was promoted to Corporal on May 1, 1862. Hospitalized at Charlottesville, Virginia, October 18, 1863, with a gunshot wound. Place and date wounded not reported. Returned to duty on October 28, 1863. Promoted to Sergeant on October 1, 1864. Captured at or near Sutherland's Station, Virginia, April 2, 1865. Confined at Point Lookout, Maryland, until released on June 26, 1865, after taking the Oath of Allegiance.

COLLIES, ETHELDRED, Private
Resided in Lenoir County where he enlisted at age 25, April 17, 1861. Present or accounted for until wounded in the leg at Fredericksburg, Virginia, December 13, 1862. Company records do not indicate whether he returned to duty; however, he was retired to the Invalid Corps on September 29, 1864.

DAVIS, JAMES F., Private
Born in Wayne County and resided in Lenoir County where he was by occupation a farmer prior to enlisting in Craven County at age 17, July 2, 1861. Discharged on July 17, 1862, by reason of being underage.

DAWSON, BENJAMIN, Private
Resided in Lenoir County where he enlisted at age 24, April 20, 1861. Mustered in as Private and was promoted to Corporal on July 10, 1861. Promoted to Sergeant on May 1, 1862. Present or accounted for until wounded in the right arm and captured at Sharpsburg, Maryland, September 17, 1862. Hospitalized at Frederick, Maryland, until transferred to Fort McHenry, Maryland. Paroled at Fort McHenry and transferred to Aiken's Landing, James River, Virginia, where he was received October 30, 1862, for exchange. Declared exchanged at Aiken's Landing on November 10, 1862. Reduced to ranks on an unspecified date. Reported absent wounded until July 6, 1864, when he was retired to the Invalid Corps by reason of disability.

DAWSON, SIMON, Private
Resided in Lenoir County where he enlisted at age 26, April 17, 1861. Present or accounted for until wounded at Sharpsburg, Maryland, September 17, 1862. Returned to duty on an unspecified date. Wounded at Bristoe Station, Virginia, October 14, 1863. Returned to duty on an unspecified date. Wounded at Reams' Station, Virginia, August 25, 1864. Reported absent wounded through February, 1865.

DAWSON, THOMAS, Private
Resided in Lenoir County where he enlisted at age 21, May 6, 1862, for the war. Present or accounted for until wounded in the right hand at Sharpsburg, Maryland, September 17, 1862. Returned to duty on an unspecified date. Deserted on December 8, 1864.

EDGLEY, JOHN, Private
Resided in Lenoir County where he enlisted at age 27, April 17, 1861. Wounded at Wilderness, Virginia, on or about May 5, 1864. Returned to duty on an unspecified date. Deserted to the enemy on or about March 16, 1865. Confined at Washington, D.C., until released on or about March 24, 1865, after taking the Oath of Allegiance.

ELMORE, WILLIAM, Private
Resided in [Nash County] and enlisted at Camp Holmes at age 18, July 27, 1864. Present or accounted for until captured at Hatcher's Run, Virginia, March 31, 1865. Confined at Point Lookout, Maryland, until released on June 12, 1865, after taking the Oath of Allegiance.

FARMER, WILLIAM, Private
Born in Greene County and was by occupation a farmer prior to enlisting in Lenoir County on May 6, 1862, for the war. Present or accounted for until wounded at Sharpsburg, Maryland, September 17, 1862. Discharged on January 22, 1863, by reason of "anchylosis knee joint." Discharge certificate gives his age as 27.

FIELDS, BARTHOLOMEW, Private
Resided in Lenoir County where he enlisted at age 19, April 17, 1861. Present or accounted for until wounded in the right leg and captured at Sharpsburg, Maryland, September 17, 1862. Right leg amputated. Hospitalized at Frederick, Maryland. Exchanged on or about March 4, 1863. Reported absent wounded until July 5, 1864, when he was retired to the Invalid Corps.

FIELDS, BENNETT C., Private
Resided in Lenoir County where he enlisted at age 31, April 17, 1861. Present or accounted for until wounded at Sharpsburg, Maryland, September 17, 1862. Returned to duty on an unspecified date. Wounded in the left arm at Wilderness, Virginia, May 6, 1864. Returned to duty prior to November 1, 1864. Present or accounted for until captured at Hatcher's Run, Virginia, March 31, 1865. Confined at Point Lookout, Maryland, until released on June 3, 1865, after taking the Oath of Allegiance.

FIELDS, JESSE, Private
Born in Lenoir County where he resided as a farmer prior to enlisting in Craven County at age 17, July 15, 1861. Present or accounted for until discharged on July 17, 1862, by reason of being underage. Later served in Company D, 1st Battalion N.C. Local Defense Troops.

FIELDS, L. H., Private
Resided in Lenoir County where he enlisted at age 17, May 6, 1862, for the war. Wounded in the left shoulder at Wilderness, Virginia, on or about May 5, 1864. Returned to duty on or about July 20, 1864. Wounded in the right shoulder at Reams' Station, Virginia, on or about August 25, 1864. Reported absent on detached service from September-October, 1864, through February, 1865. Surrendered at Appomattox Court House, Virginia, April 9, 1865.

FIELDS, ROBERT C., Private
Enlisted in Lenoir County on April 17, 1861. Mustered in as Private and was promoted to Sergeant on May 1,

1861. Reduced to ranks in March-April, 1862. Wounded in the breast at Fredericksburg, Virginia, December 13, 1862. Returned to duty on an unspecified date. Wounded at Bristoe Station, Virginia, October 14, 1863. Reported absent wounded until August 4, 1864, when he was retired to the Invalid Corps. Paroled at Greensboro on May 9, 1865.

FULLER, SAMUEL D., Private
Resided in Lenoir County where he enlisted at age 27, May 6, 1862, for the war. Died in hospital at Richmond, Virginia, September 20, 1864, of wounds. Place and date wounded not reported.

FULLER, WILLIAM W., Private
Born in Lenoir County where he resided as a mechanic prior to enlisting in Lenoir County at age 34, April 17, 1861. Present or accounted for until discharged on July 17, 1862, by reason of being overage. Later served as Sergeant in Company D, 1st Battalion N.C. Local Defense Troops.

GRADY, CHAUNCY GRAHAM, Private
Resided in Lenoir County where he enlisted at age 17, April 17, 1861. Mustered in as Private and was promoted to Corporal on May 1, 1862. Reduced to ranks subsequent to February 28, 1865. Captured at Sutherland's Station, Virginia, April 2, 1865. Confined at Hart's Island, New York Harbor, until released on June 19, 1865, after taking the Oath of Allegiance.

GRANT, HENRY, Private
Enlisted at Camp Holmes on October 20, 1864, for the war. Present or accounted for until he surrendered at Appomattox Court House, Virginia, April 9, 1865.

GRANT, JESSE, Private
Enlisted at Camp Holmes on October 25, 1864, for the war. Present or accounted for until he surrendered at Appomattox Court House, Virginia, April 9, 1865.

HAM, EZEKIEL, Private
Born in Wayne County and was by occupation a farmer prior to enlisting in Lenoir County on April 17, 1861. Present or accounted for until discharged on July 17, 1862, by reason of being overage. Discharge certificate gives his age as 46. [May have served later in Company K, 66th Regiment N.C. Troops.]

HERRING, BENJAMIN FRANKLIN, Private
Born in Lenoir County where he resided as a farmer prior to enlisting in Lenoir County at age 34, April 17, 1861. Present or accounted for until discharged on July 17, 1862, by reason of being overage. Later served as Sergeant in Company D, 1st Battalion N.C. Local Defense Troops.

HERRING, EDWARD M., Private
Resided in Lenoir County where he enlisted at age 21, April 25, 1861. Present or accounted for until killed at Sharpsburg, Maryland, September 17, 1862.

HERRING, JOHN W., Private
Place and date of enlistment not reported. Died at Petersburg, Virginia, July 19, 1862. Cause of death not reported.

HERRING, LEONIDAS, Private
Resided in Lenoir County where he enlisted at age 32,

May 6, 1862, for the war. Present or accounted for until he died in hospital at Petersburg, Virginia, July 26, 1862, of ''meningitis.''

HERRING, THOMAS, Private
Resided in Lenoir County where he enlisted at age 22, May 6, 1862, for the war. Wounded in the right eye at or near Petersburg, Virginia, on or about September 15, 1864. Reported absent wounded through December, 1864. Returned to duty in January-February, 1865. Hospitalized at Richmond, Virginia, March 3, 1865, with a gunshot wound of the right side. Place and date wounded not reported. Captured in hospital at Richmond, Virginia, April 3, 1865, and was paroled on or about April 22, 1865.

HILL, ALEXANDER, Private
Resided in Lenoir County and enlisted at Camp Holmes on August 31, 1864, for the war. Present or accounted for until captured near Petersburg, Virginia, April 2, 1865. Confined at Point Lookout, Maryland, until released on June 27, 1865, after taking the Oath of Allegiance.

HILL, HARDY, Private
Enlisted in Lenoir County on May 6, 1862, for the war. Discharged on an unspecified date. Reason discharged not reported. [May have served later in Company G, 1st Battalion N.C. Local Defense Troops.]

HILL, JAMES L., Private
Resided in Lenoir County where he enlisted at age 20, February 1, 1863, for the war. Hospitalized at Richmond, Virginia, June 4, 1864, with a gunshot wound. Place and date wounded not reported. Returned to duty prior to November 1, 1864. Present or accounted for until paroled at Greensboro on May 1, 1865.

HILL, NATHAN B., Jr., Sergeant
Born in Lenoir County where he resided as a farmer prior to enlisting in Lenoir County on April 25, 1861. Mustered in as Private and was promoted to Sergeant on September 1, 1862. Died on October 22, 1862. Place and cause of death not reported. [Death records give his age as 21.]

HILL, NATHAN B., Sr., Private
Resided in Lenoir County where he enlisted at age 30, April 17, 1861. Present or accounted for through November, 1862.

HINES, CHARLES C., Private
Resided in Lenoir County where he enlisted at age 30, April 25, 1861. Present or accounted for through December, 1861. [North Carolina pension records indicate he was wounded in an unspecified battle.] No further records.

HINES, JAMES A., Private
Born in Duplin County and resided in Wayne County where he was by occupation a farmer prior to enlisting in Lenoir County at age 22, April 25, 1861. Present or accounted for until wounded in the right ankle and captured at Sharpsburg, Maryland, September 17, 1862. Paroled on September 27, 1862. Discharged on April 12, 1863, by reason of disability from wounds.

HINES, JAMES A., Private
Enlisted at Orange Court House, Virginia, November

26, 1863, for the war. Hospitalized at Charlottesville, Virginia, December 1, 1863, with a gunshot wound. Place and date wounded not reported. Returned to duty on December 12, 1863. Reported on detached service at Richmond, Virginia, from December 29, 1863, through February, 1865. Captured in hospital at Richmond on April 3, 1865, and was paroled on April 20, 1865.

HINES, JAMES M., Private
Born in Wayne County and resided in Lenoir County where he was by occupation a farmer prior to enlisting in Wake County at age 17, August 6, 1861. Present or accounted for until discharged on July 17, 1862, by reason of being underage.

HINES, JOHN, Private
Resided in Wayne County and enlisted in Lenoir County at age 20, April 25, 1861. Killed at Fredericksburg, Virginia, December 13, 1862.

HINES, SAMUEL, Corporal
Resided in Wayne County and enlisted in Lenoir County at age 24, April 25, 1861. Mustered in as Private and was promoted to Corporal in November, 1862-October, 1864. Wounded on an unspecified date and was hospitalized at Richmond, Virginia, on or about April 2, 1865. Captured in hospital at Richmond on April 3, 1865. Transferred to Newport News, Virginia, April 23, 1865. Released at Newport News on June 30, 1865, after taking the Oath of Allegiance.

HINSON, GEORGE A., Private
Born in Wayne County where he resided as a farmer prior to enlisting in Craven County at age 30, October 3, 1861, as a substitute for Corporal Benjamin F. Sutton. Present or accounted for until he died in hospital at New Bern on December 12, 1861, of "typhoid fever."

HINSON, JOE HENRY, ———
North Carolina pension records indicate that he served in this company.

HOLMES, HENRY, Private
Resided in Greene County and enlisted in Lenoir County at age 23, April 17, 1861. Wounded in the head in Virginia in June, 1864. Died of wounds. Place and date of death not reported.

JUMP, JOHN W., Private
Resided in Lenoir County where he enlisted at age 28, April 17, 1861. Present or accounted for until he died in hospital at Petersburg, Virginia, July 20, 1862, of "diarrhoea chronica."

KENNEDY, JOHN T., Private
Born in Lenoir County and was by occupation a farmer prior to enlisting in Lenoir County on April 17, 1861. Present or accounted for until he died at Camp Mangum on August 29, 1861, of "typhoid fever." Death records give his age as 21.

KENNEDY, ROBERT H., Private
Resided in Lenoir County where he enlisted at age 21, April 17, 1861. Wounded in the left thigh at Bristoe Station, Virginia, October 14, 1863. Left leg amputated at the thigh. Reported absent wounded until August 17, 1864, when he was retired to the Invalid Corps.

KOONCE, JOHN E., Private
Enlisted at Orange Court House, Virginia, at age 17,

April 17, 1864, for the war. Wounded at Wilderness, Virginia, on or about May 5, 1864. Hospitalized at Richmond, Virginia. Furloughed on September 2, 1864. Company muster roll dated January-February, 1865, indicates that he had not been heard from since the date of his furlough. [North Carolina pension records indicate that he survived the war.]

LASSITER, STEPHEN, Private
Resided in Lenoir County where he enlisted at age 28, April 17, 1861. Mustered in with an unspecified rank and was promoted to 1st Sergeant on May 1, 1861. Reduced to ranks prior to July 20, 1861. Discharged on July 27, 1861. Reason discharged not reported. Later served as 2nd Lieutenant of 1st Company I, 36th Regiment N.C. Troops (2nd Regiment N.C. Artillery).

LOVITT, HILARY, Private
Resided in Lenoir County where he enlisted at age 28, April 17, 1861. Last reported in the records of this company on March 23, 1864.

MOORE, J. C., Private
Place and date of enlistment not reported. Company records dated July, 1862, indicate he was sick at home. No further records.

NELSON, WILLIAM B., Private
Was by occupation a farmer prior to enlisting in Lenoir County on April 25, 1861. Present or accounted for until discharged on July 17, 1862, by reason of being overage. Discharge certificate gives his age as 42.

OUTLAW, JAMES B., Corporal
Resided in Duplin County and was by occupation a farmer prior to enlisting in Wake County at age 21, August 3, 1861. Mustered in as Private and was promoted to Corporal in November, 1862-June, 1864. Wounded in the left arm at Cold Harbor, Virginia, June 3, 1864. Reported absent wounded until February 11, 1865, when he returned to duty. Captured at Farmville, Virginia, April 6, 1865. Confined at Newport News, Virginia, until released on June 27, 1865, after taking the Oath of Allegiance.

PEAL, GEORGE W., Private
Enlisted at Camp Holmes on October 20, 1864, for the war. Present or accounted for until he deserted on February 7, 1865.

PEAL, MORDECAI, 1st Sergeant
Born in Wayne County where he resided as a farmer prior to enlisting in Lenoir County at age 24, April 17, 1861. Mustered in as Private and was promoted to Corporal on May 1, 1861. Promoted to 1st Sergeant on July 20, 1861. Hospitalized at Charlottesville, Virginia, October 18, 1863, with a gunshot wound. Place and date wounded not reported. Returned to duty on an unspecified date. Captured at or near Sutherland's Station, Virginia, April 2, 1865. Confined at Point Lookout, Maryland, until released on June 16, 1865, after taking the Oath of Allegiance.

PERDEW, JOSHUA, Private
Resided in Lenoir County and enlisted in Wake County at age 21, August 3, 1861. Present or accounted for until wounded at Sharpsburg, Maryland, September 17, 1862. Returned to duty on an unspecified date.

Captured at Bristoe Station, Virginia, October 14, 1863. Confined at Old Capitol Prison, Washington, D.C., until transferred to Point Lookout, Maryland, October 27, 1863. Paroled at Point Lookout and transferred to Aiken's Landing, James River, Virginia, September 18, 1864, for exchange.

PERDEW, WILLIAM, Private
Born in Lenoir County where he resided as a farmer prior to enlisting in Lenoir County at age 45, April 17, 1861. Present or accounted for until discharged on July 17, 1862, by reason of being overage.

PERDUE, THOMAS, Private
Resided in Lenoir County and enlisted in Craven County at age 17, July 15, 1861. Present or accounted for until wounded in the head and/or right shoulder at Sharpsburg, Maryland, September 17, 1862. Returned to duty on an unspecified date. Paroled at Appomattox Court House, Virginia, April 9, 1865. [North Carolina pension records indicate he was wounded in the left knee at Fredericksburg, Virginia, on an unspecified date.]

POTTER, ALEXANDER, Private
Enlisted in Lenoir County on April 25, 1861. Present or accounted for through November, 1862. No further records.

POTTER, JAMES, Private
Resided in Lenoir County where he enlisted at age 28, April 17, 1861. Wounded in the left shoulder at Fredericksburg, Virginia, December 13, 1862. Returned to duty on January 12, 1863. Wounded in the left leg at Reams' Station, Virginia, August 25, 1864. Retired from service on November 8, 1864.

POTTER, JOHN, Private
Resided in Lenoir County where he enlisted at age 30, April 17, 1861. Wounded at Sharpsburg, Maryland, September 17, 1862. Returned to duty on an unspecified date. Wounded at Wilderness, Virginia, on or about May 5, 1864. Deserted on August 25, 1864.

POTTER, JORDAN, Private
Resided in Lenoir County and enlisted in Craven County at age 21, July 15, 1861. Wounded at Wilderness, Virginia, on or about May 5, 1864. Returned to duty prior to June 15, 1864, when he was wounded in the arm at or near Petersburg, Virginia. Hospitalized at Richmond, Virginia, August 27, 1864, with a gunshot wound of the left leg. Place and date wounded not reported. Reported absent wounded or absent sick through February, 1865. [North Carolina pension records indicate he was wounded at Bristoe Station, Virginia, on an unspecified date.]

PRICE, N. G., Private
Resided in Wayne County. Place and date of enlistment not reported. Paroled at Goldsboro on May 2, 1865.

RADFORD, PATRICK, Private
Resided in Greene County and enlisted in Lenoir County at age 28, April 17, 1861. Mustered in as Private and was promoted to Musician on May 1, 1862. Reduced to ranks on November 1, 1862. Wounded in the arm in Virginia in June, 1864. Returned to duty prior to November 1, 1864. Captured near Petersburg, Virginia, April 2, 1865. Confined at Point Lookout,

Maryland, until released on June 17, 1865, after taking the Oath of Allegiance.

ROUSE, JOHN G., Private
Resided in Lenoir County where he enlisted at age 22, April 17, 1861. Died in hospital at Hanover Junction, Virginia, August 31, 1863. Cause of death not reported.

ROUSE, JOSHUA L., Private
Born in Lenoir County where he resided as a farmer prior to enlisting in Lenoir County at age 18, April 17, 1861. Present or accounted for until discharged on June 18, 1862, by reason of disability. Later served as Corporal in Company D, 1st Battalion N.C. Local Defense Troops. [North Carolina pension records indicate he was wounded at New Bern in 1861.]

ROUSE, SIMON B., Private
Resided in Lenoir County where he enlisted at age 40, April 16, 1861. Present or accounted for until he died on January 15, 1862. Place and cause of death not reported.

ROUSE, WILLIAM H., Corporal
Resided in Lenoir County where he enlisted at age 23, April 17, 1861. Mustered in as Private and was promoted to Corporal on May 1, 1862. Wounded in the left wrist at Wilderness, Virginia, on or about May 5, 1864. Returned to duty prior to November 1, 1864. Deserted on February 7, 1865.

RUSSELL, J. B., ———
Place and date of enlistment not reported. Discharged on or about April 16, 1861, after providing Private Levi Russell (his brother) as a substitute.

RUSSELL, LEVI, Private
Enlisted in Lenoir County on April 16, 1861, as a substitute for J. B. Russell (his brother). Present or accounted for through July, 1862. No further records.

SASSER, JAMES A., Private
Resided in Lenoir County where he enlisted at age 20, April 17, 1861. Deserted on December 8, 1864. Went over to the enemy on or about March 16, 1865. Confined at Washington, D.C., until released on or about March 24, 1865, after taking the Oath of Allegiance.

SASSER, RIGDON, Private
Resided in Lenoir County where he enlisted at age 23, May 6, 1862, for the war. Present or accounted for through February, 1865.

SAVAGE, DAVID, Private
Resided in Lenoir County where he enlisted at age 20, April 25, 1861. Wounded at Wilderness, Virginia, on or about May 5, 1864. Returned to duty prior to October 2, 1864, when he was killed in a "skirmish." Place of death not reported.

SEYMORE, JAMES, Private
Resided in Lenoir County where he enlisted at age 34, April 25, 1861. Deserted to the enemy on or about March 18, 1865. Confined at Washington, D.C., until released on or about March 24, 1865, after taking the Oath of Allegiance.

SEYMORE, JOHN, Private
Resided in Lenoir County where he enlisted at age 30,

April 17, 1861. Present or accounted for until killed at Sharpsburg, Maryland, September 17, 1862.

SKINNER, NATHANIEL, Private

Resided in Lenoir County where he enlisted at age 22, April 17, 1861. Mustered in as Private and was promoted to Musician on May 1, 1862. Reduced to ranks in July-October, 1862. Wounded in the left arm at Wilderness, Virginia, on or about May 5, 1864. Deserted to the enemy on or about October 25, 1864. Released on November 11, 1864, after taking the Oath of Allegiance at City Point, Virginia, October 31, 1864.

SPENCE, OLIVER, Private

Born in Lenoir County and was by occupation a farmer prior to enlisting in Craven County at age 47, October 3, 1861, as a substitute. Present or accounted for until discharged on July 17, 1862, by reason of being overage.

STANTON, APPOLAS, Private

Born in Wilson County* and was by occupation a farmer prior to enlisting in Lenoir County on April 25, 1861. Present or accounted for until captured at South Mountain, Maryland, September 14, 1862. Confined at Fort Delaware, Delaware, where he died on October 19, 1862. Cause of death not reported.

SUGGS, JOHN H., Private

Resided in Lenoir County where he enlisted at age 24, April 17, 1861. Present or accounted for until promoted to Musician on September 1, 1862, and transferred to the regimental band.

SUGGS, JOSHUA F., Private

Resided in Lenoir County and was by occupation a farmer prior to enlisting in Lenoir County at age 26, May 6, 1862, for the war. Present or accounted for until wounded in the shoulder at Sharpsburg, Maryland, September 17, 1862. Returned to duty on an unspecified date. Captured at Bristoe Station, Virginia, October 14, 1863. Confined at Old Capitol Prison, Washington, D.C., until transferred to Point Lookout, Maryland, October 27, 1863. Paroled at Point Lookout and transferred to City Point, Virginia, where he was received March 20, 1864, for exchange. Returned to duty on an unspecified date. Present or accounted for through February, 1865.

SUTTON, ALEXANDER, Private

Resided in Lenoir County where he enlisted at age 20, April 25, 1861. Captured at Bristoe Station, Virginia, October 14, 1863. Confined at Old Capitol Prison, Washington, D.C., until transferred to Point Lookout, Maryland, October 27, 1863. Paroled at Point Lookout and transferred to Cox's Wharf, James River, Virginia, where he was received February 14-15, 1865, for exchange.

SUTTON, BENJAMIN F., Corporal

Resided in Lenoir County where he enlisted at age 22, April 17, 1861. Mustered in as Private and was promoted to Corporal on May 1, 1861. Present or accounted for until discharged on or about October 3, 1861, after providing Private George A. Hinson as a substitute.

SUTTON, FRANCIS MARION, Sergeant

Resided in Lenoir County where he enlisted at age 24, April 17, 1861. Mustered in as Private and was promoted to Sergeant on May 1, 1862. Reduced to ranks in July-September, 1862, but was reappointed Sergeant on September 17, 1862. Deserted on February 7, 1865.

SUTTON, HENRY, Private

Resided in Lenoir County and enlisted at Fort Lane at age 23, September 3, 1861. Present or accounted for until killed at Sharpsburg, Maryland, September 17, 1862.

SUTTON, JESSE, Private

Resided in Lenoir County and was by occupation a farmer prior to enlisting in Lenoir County at age 22, April 17, 1861. Wounded in the chest and neck at Bristoe Station, Virginia, October 14, 1863. Reported absent wounded until September 29, 1864, when he was retired to the Invalid Corps. [North Carolina pension records indicate he was wounded in the left leg at Gaines' Farm, Virginia, on an unspecified date and was wounded in the left side at Fredericksburg, Virginia, on an unspecified date.]

SUTTON, JOHN W., Private

Resided in Lenoir County and enlisted in Craven County at age 18, July 15, 1861. Present or accounted for until he died in a hospital at Petersburg, Virginia, July 19, 1862, of "bilious fever."

SUTTON, JOSIAH, Sergeant

Born in Lenoir County where he resided as a farmer prior to enlisting at age 26, April 17, 1861. Mustered in as Private and was promoted to Sergeant on January 23, 1865. Present or accounted for through February, 1865.

SUTTON, LEMUEL H., Private

Resided in Lenoir County where he enlisted at age 28, April 17, 1861. Present or accounted for until wounded in the arm at Sharpsburg, Maryland, September 17, 1862. Reported absent wounded until July 26, 1864, when he was retired to the Invalid Corps.

SUTTON, RICHARD, Private

Resided in Lenoir County where he enlisted at age 18, April 17, 1861. Present or accounted for until he surrendered at Appomattox Court House, Virginia, April 9, 1865.

SUTTON, WILLIAM I., Sergeant

Resided in Lenoir County where he enlisted at age 19, April 17, 1861. Mustered in with an unspecified rank and was promoted to Sergeant on May 1, 1861. Captured at or near Sutherland's Station, Virginia, April 2, 1865. Confined at Point Lookout, Maryland, until released on June 3, 1865, after taking the Oath of Allegiance.

TILGHMAN, JAMES, Private

Resided in Lenoir County where he enlisted at age 17, May 6, 1862, for the war. Present or accounted for through October, 1862. No further records.

TRIPP, JOHN, Private

Resided in Lenoir County and enlisted in Craven

County at age 19, July 15, 1861. Present or accounted for through November, 1862. No further records.

WADE, JAMES HAMPTON, Private
Resided in Greene County and enlisted in Lenoir County at age 28, April 25, 1861. Present or accounted for until wounded in the left thigh at Wilderness, Virginia, on or about May 5, 1864. Returned to duty prior to November 1, 1864. Present or accounted for until captured at Sutherland's Station, Virginia, April 2, 1865. Confined at Hart's Island, New York Harbor, until released on or about June 20, 1865, after taking the Oath of Allegiance.

WARTERS, ASA T., Private
Born in Lenoir County where he resided as a farmer prior to enlisting in Lenoir County at age 34, April 17, 1861. Present or accounted for until discharged on July 16, 1862, by reason of being overage. Later served as 1st Sergeant of Company D, 1st Battalion N.C. Local Defense Troops.

WATERS, BRYANT, Private
Born in Lenoir County where he resided as a farmer prior to enlisting in Lenoir County at age 17, April 17, 1861. Present or accounted for through February, 1865.

WATERS, JOHN B., Private
Resided in Lenoir County where he enlisted at age 18, April 17, 1861. Present or accounted for until November, 1862, when he was reported absent without leave.

WATERS, RODERICK, Private
Resided in Lenoir County where he enlisted at age 23, April 17, 1861. Mustered in as Private and was promoted to Corporal on July 20, 1861. Reduced to ranks in May-June, 1862. Present or accounted for until he was transferred to the C.S. Navy on or about April 6, 1864.

WATERS, THOMAS, Private
Born in Lenoir County where he resided prior to enlisting in Lenoir County at age 18, April 17, 1861. Present or accounted for until he died in hospital at Staunton, Virginia, December 20, 1862, of "diarrhoea chronica."

WATERS, WILLIAM H., Private
Resided in Lenoir County where he enlisted at age 32, May 6, 1862, for the war. Present or accounted for until he died at Petersburg, Virginia, July 23, 1862. Cause of death not reported.

WATERS, WILLIS, Private
Resided in Lenoir County where he enlisted at age 18, April 17, 1861. Mustered in as Corporal but was reduced to ranks prior to September 1, 1861. Deserted to the enemy on or about March 16, 1865. Confined at Washington, D.C., until released on or about March 24, 1865, after taking the Oath of Allegiance.

WHITFIELD, JOHN W., Private
Resided in Lenoir County where he enlisted at age 29, May 6, 1862, for the war. Wounded at or near Spotsylvania Court House, Virginia, May 10, 1864. Reported absent wounded until August 25, 1864, when he was retired to the Invalid Corps.

WHITFIELD, JOSEPH P., Private
Resided in Duplin County and enlisted at Orange Court House, Virginia, at age 25, April 7, 1863, for the war. Retired to the Invalid Corps on December 22, 1864.

WIGGINS, BRYAN, Private
Enlisted in Lenoir County on April 17, 1861. Present or accounted for until discharged on July 17, 1862, by reason of being overage. Later served in Company D, 1st Battalion N.C. Local Defense Troops.

WILLIAMS, THOMAS, Private
Resided in Lenoir County and enlisted at Camp Holmes on August 31, 1864, for the war. Present or accounted for until captured at Hatcher's Run, Virginia, March 31, 1865. Confined at Point Lookout, Maryland, until released on June 21, 1865, after taking the Oath of Allegiance.

WILLIS, WILLIAM R., Private
Enlisted in Wayne County on May 25, 1861. Present or accounted for until killed at Sharpsburg, Maryland, September 17, 1862.

WINES, JAMES, Private
Resided in Lenoir County and enlisted in Craven County at age 29, June 25, 1861. Wounded in the arm at Fredericksburg, Virginia, December 13, 1862. Returned to duty on an unspecified date. Wounded at Wilderness, Virginia, on or about May 5, 1864. Returned to duty prior to November 1, 1864. Deserted on December 8, 1864.

WOOLERSON, RICHARD, Private
Born in Lenoir County where he resided prior to enlisting in Lenoir County at age 30, April 17, 1861. Present or accounted for until he died in hospital at Richmond, Virginia, December 18, 1862, of "diarrhoea chron[ic]."

WOOTEN, BENJAMIN, Corporal
Resided in Lenoir County where he enlisted at age 18, April 17, 1861. Mustered in as Private and was promoted to Corporal on May 1, 1862. Present or accounted for through January 8, 1863. No further records.

WOOTEN, SHADE, Sergeant
Born in Lenoir County and resided in Greene County where he was by occupation a farmer prior to enlisting in Lenoir County at age 21, May 6, 1862, for the war. Mustered in as Private and was promoted to Sergeant in November, 1862-October, 1864. Wounded in the finger in Virginia in June, 1864. Returned to duty prior to August 15, 1864, when he was wounded in the head in battle near Petersburg, Virginia. Reported absent wounded until January 20, 1865, when he was discharged by reason of "a gunshot wound . . . fracturing the left parietal bone, severing the longitudinal sinus, occasioning partial paralysis of the left side. He is troubled with the severest cerebral pain and is unable to undergo any exertion without producing mental disturbance."

COMPANY D

This company, known as the "Tuckahoe Braves," was raised in Lenoir County where it enlisted on April 27, 1861. It was mustered into service on June 20, 1861, and was later assigned to the 27th Regiment as Company D. After joining the regiment the company functioned as a part of the regiment, and its history for the war period is reported as a part of the regimental history.

The information contained in the following company roster was compiled principally from company muster rolls for June 20, 1861-October, 1862, and September, 1864-February, 1865. No company muster rolls were found for November, 1862-August, 1864, or for the period after February, 1865. Valuable information was obtained also from primary records such as the Roll of Honor, medical records, prisoner of war records, discharge certificates, and pension applications, and from secondary sources such as postwar rosters and histories, cemetery records, and records of the United Daughters of the Confederacy.

OFFICERS

CAPTAINS

WOOTEN, WILLIAM T.
Enlisted in Lenoir County. Elected Captain on April 27, 1861. Present or accounted for until he died on or about February 19, 1862. Place and cause of death not reported.

HERRING, CALVIN
Resided in Lenoir County where he enlisted. Elected 2nd Lieutenant on April 27, 1861, and was elected Captain on or about February 21, 1862. Wounded in the chest and right side at Bristoe Station, Virginia, October 14, 1863. Returned to duty on an unspecified date. Wounded at Wilderness, Virginia, on or about May 5, 1864. Returned to duty prior to August 25, 1864, when he was wounded at Reams' Station, Virginia. Returned to duty in November-December, 1864. Promoted to Major on January 11, 1865, and transferred to the Field and Staff of this regiment.

LIEUTENANTS

DAVIS, JAMES G., 1st Lieutenant
Enlisted in Lenoir County. Elected 1st Lieutenant on April 27, 1861. Present or accounted for until he was defeated for reelection on or about April 22, 1862. Later served as Private in Company B, 8th Battalion N.C. Partisan Rangers.

HARPER, CORNELIUS, 2nd Lieutenant
Resided in Lenoir County. Elected 3rd Lieutenant on April 27, 1861, and was promoted to 2nd Lieutenant on February 21, 1862. Present or accounted for until he surrendered at Appomattox Court House, Virginia, April 9, 1865.

JONES, GEORGE W., 1st Lieutenant
Resided in Lenoir County where he enlisted on April 27, 1861. Mustered in as Private and was promoted to Sergeant on May 5, 1861. Promoted to 1st Sergeant on July 19, 1861. Elected 2nd Lieutenant on April 22, 1862, and was promoted to 1st Lieutenant on December 4, 1862. Present or accounted for until he surrendered at Appomattox Court House, Virginia, April 9, 1865.

NUNN, BENJAMIN F., 1st Lieutenant
Enlisted in Craven County on June 27, 1861. Mustered in as Private and was elected 2nd Lieutenant on February 21, 1862. Elected 1st Lieutenant on April 22, 1862. Present or accounted for until wounded at Sharpsburg, Maryland, September 17, 1862. Died on an unspecified date prior to January 1, 1863, of wounds. Place of death not reported.

WORLEY, THOMAS F., 3rd Lieutenant
Enlisted in Lenoir County on April 27, 1861. Mustered in as Private and was elected 3rd Lieutenant on December 24, 1862. Wounded in the right foot at Bristoe Station, Virginia, October 14, 1863. Reported absent wounded until December 23, 1864, when he was retired to the Invalid Corps.

NONCOMMISSIONED OFFICERS AND PRIVATES

BASDEN, DAVID C., Private
Enlisted in Lenoir County on May 18, 1861. Present or accounted for until he deserted on or about February 24, 1865. [Medical records dated 1862 give his age as 27.]

BASDEN, E. H., Private
Previously served in Company A, 40th Regiment N.C. Troops (3rd Regiment N.C. Artillery). Transferred to this company on October 1, 1861. Present or accounted for until he died near Culpeper Court House, Virginia, November 1, 1862, of "ch[ronic] diarrhoea."

BELK, PETER R., Private
Previously served in Company F, 2nd Regiment N.C. Junior Reserves. Transferred to this company on July 28, 1864. Present or accounted for until captured at or near Sutherland's Station, Virginia, on or about April 2, 1865. Confined at Point Lookout, Maryland, until released on or about June 23, 1865, after taking the Oath of Allegiance.

BLIZZARD, ALFRED B., Private
Enlisted in Lenoir County on May 18, 1861. Present or accounted for until he surrendered at Appomattox Court House, Virginia, April 9, 1865.

BLIZZARD, HOSEA P., Private
Enlisted in Lenoir County on May 18, 1861. Present or accounted for until he died at or near Richmond, Virginia, on or about December 1, 1862, of "catarrhus."

BROWN, WILLIAM L., Private
Enlisted in Lenoir County on May 18, 1861. Present or accounted for until he deserted on May 30, 1862. Returned to duty on or about August 20, 1863. Captured at Bristoe Station, Virginia, October 14, 1863. Confined at Old Capitol Prison, Washington, D.C., until transferred to Point Lookout, Maryland, October 27, 1863. Paroled at Point Lookout and transferred to Aiken's Landing, James River, Virginia, February 24, 1865, for exchange. Reported in hospital at Richmond, Virginia, March 3, 1865.

BUTLER, W. R., Private
Place and date of enlistment not reported. Captured in hospital at Richmond, Virginia, April 3, 1865. No further records.

CARTER, B. A., Private
Enlisted in Lenoir County on April 27, 1861. Present or accounted for until wounded at Wilderness, Virginia, on or about May 5, 1864. No further records.

CARTER, ILA J., Private
Born in Duplin County where he resided as a farmer prior to enlisting in Lenoir County on April 27, 1861. Present or accounted for until discharged on July 16, 1862, by reason of being overage. Discharge certificate gives his age as 36. Later served in Company A, 40th Regiment N.C. Troops (3rd Regiment N.C. Artillery).

CARTER, JOHN H., Private
Enlisted in Lenoir County on April 27, 1861. Present or accounted for until wounded at New Bern on March 14, 1862. Returned to duty prior to September 17, 1862, when he was wounded at Sharpsburg, Maryland. Reported absent wounded through November, 1862. [May have served later in Company C, 1st Battalion N.C. Local Defense Troops.]

CARTER, WILLIAM B., Private
Resided in Lenoir County where he enlisted on April 27, 1861. Present or accounted for until wounded at Sharpsburg, Maryland, September 17, 1862. Returned to duty on an unspecified date. Wounded at Wilderness, Virginia, on or about May 5, 1864. Returned to duty prior to November 1, 1864. Present or accounted for until captured at Hatcher's Run, Virginia, March 31, 1865. Confined at Point Lookout, Maryland, until released on June 24, 1865, after taking the Oath of Allegiance.

CHEEK, JOHN F., Private
Enlisted at Camp Holmes on July 31, 1864, for the war. Present or accounted for until he deserted to the enemy on or about March 18, 1865. Confined at Washington, D.C., until released on or about March 24, 1865, after taking the Oath of Allegiance.

COBLE, SIMON P., Private
Enlisted at Camp Holmes on June 23, 1864, for the war. Present or accounted for until he deserted on September 29, 1864.

CUNNINGHAM, HENRY, Private
Enlisted in Lenoir County on April 27, 1861. Mustered in as Private and was promoted to Corporal on September 8, 1861. Reduced to ranks on April 22, 1862. Wounded at Wilderness, Virginia, on or about May 5, 1864. Detailed for light duty at Richmond, Virginia, September 17, 1864. Reported absent on detail through February, 1865.

CUNNINGHAM, IVY, Private
Enlisted in Lenoir County on April 27, 1861. Present or accounted for until he died in hospital at Gordonsville, Virginia, December 2, 1862, of "febris typhoides."

CUNNINGHAM, JESSE, Private
Enlisted at Orange Court House, Virginia, March 1, 1864, for the war. Hospitalized at Richmond, Virginia, June 2, 1864, with a gunshot wound. Place and date wounded not reported. Returned to duty prior to November 1, 1864. Present or accounted for until he died in hospital at Raleigh on January 20, 1865, of "diarrhoea ch[ronic]."

DAVENPORT, JOHN, Private
Born in Lenoir County and was by occupation a farmer prior to enlisting in Lenoir County on April 27, 1861. Present or accounted for until discharged on July 16, 1862, by reason of being overage. Discharge certificate gives his age as 45.

DAVENPORT, LOUIS, Private
Enlisted in Lenoir County on April 27, 1861. Present or accounted for until he died in hospital at Richmond, Virginia, February 24, 1865, of "typh[oid] feb[ris]."

DAVENPORT, WILLIAM, Private
Enlisted in Lenoir County on April 27, 1861. Wounded at Wilderness, Virginia, May 5, 1864. Returned to duty on or about February 25, 1865. Captured at Kinston on March 19, 1865. No further records.

DAVIS, JARMAN, Private
Enlisted at Camp Holmes on November 23, 1863, for the war. Present or accounted for until he surrendered at Appomattox Court House, Virginia, April 9, 1865.

DAVIS, JOHN Z., Corporal
Enlisted in Lenoir County on May 18, 1861. Mustered in as Corporal. Deserted on August 4, 1861. [May have served later as 1st Lieutenant of Company A, 40th Regiment N.C. Troops (3rd Regiment N.C. Artillery).]

DAVIS, MALACIAH, Private
Born in Lenoir County and enlisted in Craven County on August 1, 1861. Present or accounted for until killed at Sharpsburg, Maryland, September 17, 1862.

DAVIS, ROBERT W., Private
Born in Lenoir County where he enlisted on April 27, 1861. Present or accounted for until wounded at Sharpsburg, Maryland, September 17, 1862. Died "at home" on February 11, 1863, of "pneumonia."

DAVIS, SETH, Private
Born in Duplin County and was by occupation a farmer prior to enlisting at Fort Lane on October 2, 1861. Present or accounted for until discharged on July 16, 1862, by reason of being overage. Discharge certificate gives his age as 40.

DAVIS, WILLIAM T., Private
Enlisted in Lenoir County on April 27, 1861. Mustered in as Private and was promoted to Commissary Sergeant on August 27, 1861. Reduced to ranks in January-February, 1862. Present or accounted for until he died at Dearsville, Virginia, September 17, 1862. Cause of death not reported.

DEAVER, RICHARD, Private
Enlisted in Lenoir County on May 18, 1861. Mustered in as Private and was promoted to Corporal on April 22, 1862. Wounded at Sharpsburg, Maryland, September 17, 1862. Returned to duty on an unspecified date. Reduced to ranks in November, 1862-October, 1863. Captured at Bristoe Station, Virginia, October 14, 1863. Confined at Old Capitol Prison, Washington, D.C., until transferred to Point Lookout, Maryland, October 27, 1863. Died at Point Lookout on or about December 15, 1864, of "gangrene."

FREEMAN, WILLIAM J., Private
Born in Lenoir County where he resided as a farmer prior to enlisting in Lenoir County at age 31, April 27, 1861. Wounded in the neck and right shoulder at Bristoe Station, Virginia, October 14, 1863. Returned to duty on an unspecified date. Captured at Farmville, Virginia, April 6, 1865. Confined at Newport News, Virginia, until released on June 27, 1865, after taking

the Oath of Allegiance.

GOODMAN, EZEKIEL, Private
Enlisted in Craven County on June 2, 1861. Died in hospital at Richmond, Virginia, January 29, 1864, of "anaemia" following the amputation of his right leg at the thigh. Place and date injured not reported.

GRADY, GEORGE W., Private
Enlisted in Lenoir County on April 27, 1861. Present or accounted for until he deserted to the enemy on or about March 18, 1865. Confined at Washington, D.C., until released on or about March 24, 1865, after taking the Oath of Allegiance. [North Carolina pension records indicate he was wounded at New Bern on March 14, 1862.]

GRADY, JAMES B., Private
Born in Lenoir County where he enlisted on April 27, 1861. Present or accounted for until he died on March 14, 1863, of disease. Place of death not reported.

GRADY, LEWIS, Private
Enlisted in Lenoir County on April 27, 1861. Present or accounted for until discharged on November 2, 1861, by reason of "sickness."

GRAY, BENAJA, Private
Enlisted at Orange Court House, Virginia, April 27, 1864, for the war. Present or accounted for until hospitalized at Richmond, Virginia, May 18, 1864, with a shell wound of the right thigh. Place and date wounded not reported. Returned to duty prior to November 1, 1864. Present or accounted for through February, 1865. Died in hospital at Richmond on or about June 2, 1865. Cause of death not reported.

GRAY, JOHN ROBERT, Corporal
Enlisted in Lenoir County at age 26, April 27, 1861. Mustered in as Private and was promoted to Corporal on May 5, 1861. Reduced to ranks on April 22, 1862. Present or accounted for until wounded at Sharpsburg, Maryland, September 17, 1862. Returned to duty on an unspecified date. Promoted to Corporal in November, 1862. Surrendered at Appomattox Court House, Virginia, April 9, 1865.

HARDY, GEORGE E., Corporal
Born in Lenoir County where he enlisted on May 18, 1861. Mustered in as Private and was promoted to Corporal on April 22, 1862. Present or accounted for until killed at Sharpsburg, Maryland, September 17, 1862.

HARDY, JAMES, Private
Enlisted in Lenoir County on May 3, 1862, for the war. Wounded in the left thigh at Bristoe Station, Virginia, October 14, 1863. Returned to duty on an unspecified date. Surrendered at Appomattox Court House, Virginia, April 9, 1865.

HARDY, JOHN W., Private
Enlisted in Lenoir County on April 27, 1861. Died in hospital at Richmond, Virginia, on or about September 11, 1864, of "diarrhoea chron[ic]."

HARPER, WINDAL T., Private
Born in Lenoir County where he resided as a farmer prior to enlisting in Lenoir County on April 27, 1861.

Discharged on or about April 26, 1862, by reason of "chronic ulceration of the bowels." Discharge certificate gives his age as 21. Later served as Corporal in Company K, 61st Regiment N.C. Troops.

HARPER, ZACHARIAH, Sergeant
Enlisted at Fort Lane on September 13, 1861. Mustered in as Private and was promoted to Corporal in November, 1862-November, 1863. Hospitalized at Charlottesville, Virginia, October 18, 1863, with a gunshot wound. Place and date wounded not reported. Returned to duty on an unspecified date. Promoted to Sergeant in November, 1863-October, 1864. Hospitalized at Farmville, Virginia, April 7, 1865, with a gunshot wound of the right forearm. "Home paroled" on June 12, 1865.

HATLEY, JAMES W., Private
Born in Stanly County* and was by occupation a miner prior to enlisting at age 38, February 28, 1863, for the war. Hospitalized at Richmond, Virginia, December 19, 1863, with a gunshot wound of the head. Place and date wounded not reported. Died in hospital at Richmond on December 22, 1863, of wounds.

HAZARD, SAMUEL, Private
Enlisted in Lenoir County at age 37, April 27, 1861. Transferred to the C.S. Navy on April 1, 1864.

HEATH, WILLIAM, Private
Born in Lenoir County and was by occupation a farmer prior to enlisting in Lenoir County on April 27, 1861. Present or accounted for until discharged on April 22, 1863, by reason of "pulmonary disease which has shortened his constitution & rendered him unfit for any kind of duty."

HERRING, JAMES W., Private
Born in Wayne County and was by occupation a farmer prior to enlisting at Fort Lane on September 12, 1861. Present or accounted for until discharged on July 16, 1862, by reason of being overage. Reenlisted in the company on August 15, 1863. Hospitalized at Richmond, Virginia, April 3, 1865, with a gunshot wound. Place and date wounded not reported. Captured in hospital at Richmond on April 3, 1865. No further records.

HINES, JOSEPH, Sergeant
Born in Lenoir County and was by occupation a farmer prior to enlisting in Lenoir County at age 20, April 27, 1861. Mustered in as Private and was promoted to Sergeant on February 21, 1862. Discharged on April 16, 1863, by reason of "chronic diarrhoea and tuberculosis." Discharge certificate gives his age as 20. Died in hospital at Danville, Virginia, April 20, 1863.

HINES, THOMAS, Private
Enlisted in Lenoir County on April 27, 1861. Deserted on July 14, 1861. Reported under arrest in November-December, 1861. Court-martialed on or about December 24, 1861. Returned to duty in January-February, 1862. Present or accounted for until he deserted on or about May 5, 1862.

HOPEWELL, JAMES H., Private
Enlisted in Lenoir County on April 27, 1861. Died in hospital at Charlottesville, Virginia, August 30, 1863, of "diarr[hoea] chronica."

HOUSTON, WILLIAM, Private
Born in Duplin County and was by occupation a farmer prior to enlisting at Fort Lane on September 12, 1861. Present or accounted for until discharged on July 16, 1862, by reason of being overage. Discharge certificate gives his age as 40. Later served in Company H, 1st Battalion N.C. Local Defense Troops.

HOWARD, ISAAC J., Private
Born in Lenoir County where he enlisted on April 27, 1861. Present or accounted for until he died at Camp Gatlin on November 5, 1861, of "congestive chill."

HOWARD, JOHN, Private
Enlisted in Lenoir County on April 27, 1861. Present or accounted for until he deserted on or about May 30, 1861.

HOWARD, JOHN ROBERT, Corporal
Enlisted in Lenoir County at age 17, April 27, 1861. Mustered in as Private. Present or accounted for until wounded in the thigh at Sharpsburg, Maryland, September 17, 1862. Returned to duty on an unspecified date. Promoted to Corporal in November, 1862-August, 1864. Hospitalized at Charlottesville, Virginia, October 18, 1863, with a gunshot wound. Place and date wounded not reported. Returned to duty in November-December, 1864. Present or accounted for until he surrendered at Appomattox Court House, Virginia, April 9, 1865.

JONES, WILLIAM S., Corporal
Born in Lenoir County where he enlisted on April 27, 1861. Mustered in as Private and was promoted to Corporal on April 22, 1862. Present or accounted for until he died in hospital at Petersburg, Virginia, September 15, 1862, of "typhoid fever."

KORNEGAY, STEPHEN H., Corporal
Enlisted in Lenoir County on May 18, 1861. Mustered in as Private and was promoted to Corporal in November, 1862-October, 1864. Present or accounted for until he surrendered at Appomattox Court House, Virginia, April 9, 1865.

LAMBERT, JOHN H., Private
Born in Lenoir County where he enlisted on April 27, 1861. Present or accounted for until he died at Camp Gatlin on January 28, 1862. Cause of death not reported.

LAWSON, JOHN A., Private
Resided in Stokes County and enlisted at Camp Holmes on September 2, 1864, for the war. Present or accounted for until captured at Hatcher's Run, Virginia, March 31, 1865. Confined at Point Lookout, Maryland, until released on June 28, 1865, after taking the Oath of Allegiance.

LAWSON, M. J., Commissary Sergeant
Enlisted in Lenoir County on April 27, 1861. Mustered in as Private and was promoted to Commissary Sergeant in September-October, 1862. Present or accounted for until he died in hospital at Farmville, Virginia, on or about November 12, 1862, of "camp fever."

LAWSON, TUCKER, Private
Enlisted at Camp Holmes on September 2, 1864, for the

war. Present or accounted for until he deserted on October 5, 1864.

LEE, DAVID C., Private
Resided in Lenoir County where he enlisted on April 27, 1861. Present or accounted for until wounded in the left thigh at Hatcher's Run, Virginia, March 31, 1865. Hospitalized at Richmond, Virginia, where he was captured on April 3, 1865. Transferred to Point Lookout, Maryland, where he was hospitalized on May 6, 1865. Released on or about June 26, 1865, after taking the Oath of Allegiance.

LEE, ISAAC E., Sergeant
Enlisted in Lenoir County on May 18, 1861. Mustered in as Private and was promoted to Sergeant on July 19, 1861. Killed at Bristoe Station, Virginia, October 14, 1863.

LEE, JACOB W., Sergeant
Born in Lenoir County where he enlisted on April 27, 1861. Mustered in as Private and was promoted to Sergeant on May 5, 1861. Died at Camp Gatlin on or about February 18, 1862. Cause of death not reported.

MILLER, ELIAS, Private
Resided in Davidson County and enlisted at Camp Holmes on March 1, 1864, for the war. Captured at or near Fort Stedman, Virginia, March 25, 1865. Confined at Point Lookout, Maryland, until released on June 29, 1865, after taking the Oath of Allegiance.

MIZELL, AUGUSTUS, Private
Enlisted on September 26, 1864, for the war. Deserted on October 25, 1864.

MOODY, JAMES M., Private
Born in Duplin County and was by occupation a farmer prior to enlisting in Lenoir County on May 18, 1861. Present or accounted for until discharged on July 16, 1862, by reason of being overage. Discharge certificate gives his age as 45.

MOODY, JOHN, Private
Resided in Duplin County and enlisted in Lenoir County on May 18, 1861. Mustered in as Musician (Drummer) but was reduced to ranks on April 22, 1862. Wounded in the hip at Wilderness, Virginia, on or about May 5, 1864. Returned to duty prior to November 1, 1864. Present or accounted for until captured at or near Sutherland's Station, Virginia, April 2, 1865. Confined at Point Lookout, Maryland, until released on June 29, 1865, after taking the Oath of Allegiance. [Medical records dated 1863 give his age as 23.]

MOORE, SIDNEY D., Private
Resided in Union County and enlisted at Camp Holmes on September 3, 1864, for the war. Present or accounted for until captured at or near Fort Stedman, Virginia, March 25, 1865. Confined at Point Lookout, Maryland, until released on June 15, 1865, after taking the Oath of Allegiance.

MOSLEY, WILLIAM, Private
Enlisted in Lenoir County on May 5, 1862, for the war. Present or accounted for until wounded at Sharpsburg, Maryland, September 17, 1862. Died at Staunton, Virginia, September 20, 1862, of wounds.

NEWMAN,WILLIAM, Private
Born in Lenoir County. Place and date of enlistment not reported. Died "at home" on July 19, 1861, of "measles."

NOAH, GEORGE M., Private
Resided in Alamance County and enlisted at Camp Holmes on July 31, 1864, for the war. Present or accounted for until captured at or near Fort Stedman, Virginia, March 25, 1865. Confined at Point Lookout, Maryland, until released on June 15, 1865, after taking the Oath of Allegiance.

NUNN, HENRY S., 1st Sergeant
Resided in Lenoir County where he enlisted at age 17, April 27, 1861. Mustered in as Private and was promoted to Sergeant on April 22, 1862. Promoted to 1st Sergeant in November-December, 1864. Surrendered at Appomattox Court House, Virginia, April 9, 1865.

NUNN, JESSE I., 1st Sergeant
Born in Lenoir County where he enlisted on April 27, 1861. Mustered in as Private and was promoted to Sergeant on May 5, 1861. Promoted to 1st Sergeant on April 22, 1862. Died in hospital at Staunton, Virginia, October 31, 1862, of "phthisis pulmonalis."

OUTLAW, WILLIAM, Private
Enlisted in Lenoir County on May 12, 1862, for the war. Present or accounted for until wounded at Sharpsburg, Maryland, September 17, 1862. Apparently captured at or near Sharpsburg the same date. Paroled at Keedysville, Maryland, September 20, 1862. Returned to duty prior to November 1, 1862. Captured at Bristoe Station, Virginia, October 14, 1863. Confined at Old Capitol Prison, Washington, D.C., until transferred to Point Lookout, Maryland, October 27, 1863. Paroled at Point Lookout on May 3, 1864, and transferred to Aiken's Landing, James River, Virginia, where he was received May 8, 1864, for exchange. Returned to duty prior to November 1, 1864. Present or accounted for through December, 1864.

PARKER, WILSON B., Private
Enlisted in Lenoir County on April 27, 1861. Died at Richmond, Virginia, on or about June 29, 1863, of "diarrhoea chron[ic]."

PHILLIPS, DAVID, Private
Born in Lenoir County and was by occupation a farmer prior to enlisting in Lenoir County on May 18, 1861. Died on January 18, 1863. Place and cause of death not reported. [Death records dated 1863 give his age as 24.]

PHILLIPS, JESSE, Private
Born in Lenoir County where he enlisted on May 18, 1861. Present or accounted for until he died in hospital at New Bern on January 1, 1862, of "pneumonia."

POTTER, ABNER J., Private
Previously enlisted in Company E, 61st Regiment N.C. Troops, but never reported for duty with that unit. Enlisted in this company in Lenoir County on April 28, 1862, for the war. Captured and paroled at Warrenton, Virginia, September 29, 1862. Died at Fredericksburg, Virginia, December 3, 1862, of "pneumonia."

POTTER, DANIEL, Private
Born in Duplin County and enlisted in Lenoir County on April 27, 1861. Present or accounted for until he died in hospital at Richmond, Virginia, on or about September 18, 1862, of "febris typhoides."

POTTER, DRURY, Private
Born in Lenoir County where he enlisted on April 27, 1861. Killed at Reams' Station, Virginia, August 25, 1864.

POTTER, JESSE, Private
Previously enlisted in Company E, 61st Regiment N.C. Troops, but never reported for duty with that unit. Enlisted in this company in Lenoir County on April 28, 1862, for the war. Present or accounted for until wounded at Sharpsburg, Maryland, September 17, 1862. Returned to duty on an unspecified date. Wounded at Wilderness, Virginia, on or about May 5, 1864. Returned to duty prior to November 1, 1864. Present or accounted for until captured at Fort Stedman, Virginia, March 25, 1865. Confined at Point Lookout, Maryland, until released on June 17, 1865, after taking the Oath of Allegiance.

PRICE, STEPHEN H., Private
Enlisted at Camp Holmes on September 1, 1864, for the war. Present or accounted for until he died at or near Richmond, Virginia, on or about January 11, 1865. Cause of death not reported.

QUINN, DAVID, Private
Enlisted in Lenoir County on April 27, 1861. Wounded in the leg at Gray's Farm, Virginia, May 10, 1864. Leg amputated. Reported absent wounded until November 28, 1864, when he was retired to the Invalid Corps.

QUINN, GEORGE, Private
Born in Duplin County and was by occupation a blacksmith prior to enlisting in Lenoir County on May 18, 1861. Mustered in as Musician (Drummer) but was reduced to ranks on April 22, 1862. Discharged on July 16, 1862, by reason of being overage. Discharge certificate gives his age as 36. Reenlisted in the company on December 29, 1864. Present or accounted for through February, 1865.

QUINN, JAMES, Private
Enlisted in Lenoir County on April 27, 1861. Present or accounted for until wounded at Sharpsburg, Maryland, September 17, 1862. Returned to duty on an unspecified date. Surrendered at Appomattox Court House, Virginia, April 9, 1865.

QUINN, JOHN A., Private
Was by occupation a laborer prior to enlisting in Lenoir County on April 27, 1861. Wounded in the thigh at Bristoe Station, Virginia, October 14, 1863. Hospitalized at Richmond, Virginia, where he died on November 8, 1863, of wounds.

ROGERS, REUBEN C., Private
Enlisted in Stanly County on February 2, 1863, for the war. Wounded in the right leg at or near Petersburg, Virginia, on or about October 1, 1864. Died in hospital at Richmond, Virginia, November 1, 1864, of wounds.

ROUSE, THOMAS A., Sergeant
Enlisted in Lenoir County on May 18, 1861. Mustered in as Corporal and was promoted to Sergeant on April 22, 1862. Present or accounted for until wounded and

captured at or near Sharpsburg, Maryland, on or about September 17, 1862. Confined at Fort McHenry, Maryland. Paroled and transferred to Aiken's Landing, James River, Virginia, where he was received November 2, 1862, for exchange. Declared exchanged at Aiken's Landing on November 10, 1862. Returned to duty on an unspecified date. Present or accounted for until transferred to Company I, 9th Regiment N.C. State Troops (1st Regiment N.C. Cavalry), February 25, 1865. [Service record does not appear in Volume II of this series.]

SMITH, ARROW, Private
Resided in Warren County and enlisted at Camp Holmes on January 3, 1865, for the war. Present or accounted for until captured at or near Sutherland's Station, Virginia, on or about April 2, 1865. Confined at Point Lookout, Maryland, until released on June 20, 1865, after taking the Oath of Allegiance.

SMITH, HENRY E., Private
Resided in Lenoir County where he enlisted on April 27, 1861. Wounded in the side at Wilderness, Virginia, on or about May 5, 1864. Returned to duty prior to November 1, 1864. Present or accounted for until captured at or near Sutherland's Station, Virginia, on or about April 2, 1865. Confined at Point Lookout, Maryland, until released on June 20, 1865, after taking the Oath of Allegiance.

SMITH, IRA, Private
Resided in Lenoir County where he enlisted on May 18, 1861. Present or accounted for until wounded in the left elbow at Sharpsburg, Maryland, September 17, 1862. Reported absent wounded through November, 1862. Transferred to Company K, 61st Regiment N.C. Troops, on or about June 9, 1863.

SMITH, JONAS W., Private
Born in Duplin County and enlisted in Lenoir County on April 27, 1861. Present or accounted for until he died in hospital at or near Staunton, Virginia, on or about October 31, 1862, of "febris typhoides."

SPENCE, JAMES A., Private
Resided in Lenoir County where he enlisted on April 27, 1861. Promoted to Musician (Fifer) in May-June, 1862, and transferred to the regimental band. [North Carolina pension records indicate he was wounded at New Bern on an unspecified date.]

STANLEY, JESSE, Private
Previously served in Company A, 40th Regiment N.C. Troops (3rd Regiment N.C. Artillery). Transferred to this company on June 21, 1861. Present or accounted for until discharged on or about October 8, 1861, by reason of disability. Later reenlisted in Company A, 40th Regiment N.C. Troops (3rd Regiment N.C. Artillery).

STANLY, JOHN, Private
Previously served in an unspecified company of the 17th Regiment N.C. Troops (1st Organization). Transferred to this company on September 8, 1861. No further records. [Service record does not appear in Volume VI of this series.]

STARBER, J. F., Private
Place and date of enlistment not reported. Captured at New Bern on March 14, 1862. Reported in confinement at Fort Columbus, New York Harbor, June 2, 1862. Paroled and exchanged on an unspecified date. Hospitalized at Richmond, Virginia, July 31, 1863. No further records.

STRAY, R., Private
Place and date of enlistment not reported. Captured in hospital at Richmond, Virginia, April 3, 1865. Reported in hospital at Richmond on May 28, 1865. No further records.

STROUD, CURTIS, Private
Enlisted in Lenoir County on April 27, 1861. Present or accounted for until captured in hospital at Richmond, Virginia, April 3, 1865. Paroled on April 22, 1865.

STROUD, DANIEL, Private
Born in Lenoir County and was by occupation a farmer prior to enlisting in Lenoir County on April 27, 1861. Present or accounted for until wounded in the left shoulder at Sharpsburg, Maryland, September 17, 1862. Returned to duty on an unspecified date. Hospitalized at Danville, Virginia, on or about August 8, 1864, with a gunshot wound of the leg. Place and date wounded not reported. Returned to duty on December 2, 1864. Present or accounted for through March 15, 1865. [North Carolina pension records indicate he was wounded in the groin at Bristoe Station, Virginia, October 14, 1863, and was wounded at Manassas Gap, Virginia, on an unspecified date. Company records dated 1865 give his age as 21.]

STROUD, EVERETT, Private
Born in Lenoir County where he enlisted on April 27, 1861. Present or accounted for until he died at Richmond, Virginia, December 24, 1862, of "pneumonia."

STROUD, LUTSON, Private
Enlisted in Lenoir County on April 27, 1861. Wounded in the right buttock in an unspecified engagement on November 27, 1863. Returned to duty prior to May 5-7, 1864, when he was wounded in the groin and captured at Wilderness, Virginia. Exchanged prior to June 29, 1864. Returned to duty prior to November 1, 1864. Present or accounted for through February, 1865.

STROUD, SAMUEL S., Private
Enlisted in Lenoir County on April 27, 1861. Wounded in the right leg at Wilderness, Virginia, on or about May 5, 1864. Returned to duty prior to November 1, 1864. Present or accounted for until he surrendered at Appomattox Court House, Virginia, April 9, 1865.

SWINSON, GEORGE L., Private
Born in Duplin County and was by occupation a farmer prior to enlisting at Fort Lane on September 12, 1861. Present or accounted for until discharged on July 16, 1862, by reason of being overage. Discharge certificate gives his age as 36. Later served in Company H, 1st Battalion N.C. Local Defense Troops.

TAYLOR, AMOS, Private
Previously served in the "Wilson Light Infantry." Transferred to this company on June 27, 1861. Died on December 12, 1862. Place and cause of death not reported.

TAYLOR, DANIEL G., Sergeant
Enlisted in Lenoir County on May 5, 1862, for the war.

Mustered in as Private and was promoted to Sergeant in November, 1862-October, 1863. Wounded in the left leg at Bristoe Station, Virginia, October 14, 1863. Reported absent wounded through October, 1864. Retired from service in November-December, 1864.

TAYLOR, ISAAC, Private
Previously served in the ''Wilson Light Infantry.'' Transferred to this company on June 27, 1861. Died at Petersburg, Virginia, on or about January 30, 1863, of ''colitis.''

TAYLOR, ISAAC E., Corporal
Resided in Lenoir County and was by occupation a laborer prior to enlisting in Lenoir County on May 18, 1861. Mustered in as Private and was promoted to Corporal on April 22, 1862. Present or accounted for until wounded in the left leg at Sharpsburg, Maryland, September 17, 1862. Returned to duty on an unspecified date. Wounded in the left foot at Bristoe Station, Virginia, October 14, 1863. Returned to duty on an unspecified date. Wounded in the left foot at Wilderness, Virginia, on or about May 5, 1864. Returned to duty prior to November 1, 1864. Present or accounted for until captured at or near Fort Stedman, Virginia, on or about March 25, 1865. Confined at Point Lookout, Maryland, until released on June 21, 1865, after taking the Oath of Allegiance. [Medical records dated 1862 give his age as 30.]

TAYLOR, JAMES, Private
Born in Lenoir County and was by occupation a farmer prior to enlisting in Lenoir County on April 27, 1861. Present or accounted for until discharged on July 16, 1862, by reason of being overage. Discharge certificate gives his age as 37. [May have served later in Company D, 1st Battalion N.C. Local Defense Troops.]

TAYLOR, JOHN L., Private
Born in Lenoir County where he resided as a farmer prior to enlisting in Lenoir County on April 27, 1861. Present or accounted for until he died at Camp Gatlin on March 11, 1862. Cause of death not reported. [Death records give his age as 42.]

TAYLOR, JOHN N., Private
Resided in Duplin County and enlisted in Lenoir County on May 18, 1861. Wounded in the right arm at Wilderness, Virginia, on or about May 5, 1864. Returned to duty on July 8, 1864. Captured at or near Hatcher's Run, Virginia, April 1, 1865. Confined at Point Lookout, Maryland, until released on June 21, 1865, after taking the Oath of Allegiance.

THOMAS, JAMES HAMILTON, Private
Enlisted at Camp Holmes at age 18, July 31, 1864, for the war. Wounded in the left shoulder at Reams' Station, Virginia, August 25, 1864. Returned to duty in November-December, 1864. Present or accounted for until he surrendered at Appomattox Court House, Virginia, April 9, 1865. [May have served previously in Company D, 4th Battalion N.C. Junior Reserves.]

TILGHMAN, JOSEPH, Private
Enlisted in Lenoir County on April 27, 1861. Mustered in as Private and was promoted to Corporal on May 5, 1861. Reduced to ranks on April 22, 1862. Deserted at Kinston on or about May 30, 1862.

TINDALL, ALLEN, Private
Born in Lenoir County where he enlisted on April 27, 1861. Present or accounted for until he died ''at home'' on November 25, 1861. Cause of death not reported.

TURNER, ARETAS, Private
Previously served in Company A, 40th Regiment N.C. Troops (3rd Regiment N.C. Artillery). Transferred to this company on July 21, 1861. Wounded in the back and captured at or near Bristoe Station, Virginia, on or about October 14, 1863. Confined at Old Capitol Prison, Washington, D.C., until transferred to Point Lookout, Maryland, October 27, 1863. Paroled at Point Lookout on May 3, 1864, and transferred to Aiken's Landing, James River, Virginia, where he was received May 8, 1864, for exchange. Retired from service on March 14, 1865, by reason of ''partial paralysis of the lower extremities'' resulting from wounds received at Bristoe Station.

TURNER, DAVID J., Private
Born in Duplin County and was by occupation a farmer prior to enlisting in Lenoir County on May 18, 1861. Present or accounted for until wounded at Sharpsburg, Maryland, September 17, 1862. Hospitalized at Richmond, Virginia, where he died on December 12, 1862, of ''variola confluent.'' Death records give his age as 28.

TURNER, GEORGE, Private
Resided in Duplin County and enlisted in Lenoir County on May 15, 1862, for the war. Wounded in the right hand at Wilderness, Virginia, on or about May 5, 1864. Returned to duty prior to November 1, 1864. Present or accounted for until captured near Petersburg, Virginia, April 2, 1865. Confined at Point Lookout, Maryland, until released on June 21, 1865, after taking the Oath of Allegiance.

WHITFIELD, JAMES G., Private
Enlisted in Lenoir County on May 5, 1861. Mustered in as Private. Promoted to Sergeant Major on July 19, 1861, and transferred to the Field and Staff of this regiment. Reduced to ranks on February 15, 1862, and transferred back to this company. Present or accounted for through April, 1862. No further records.

WOODY, JOHN M., Private
Previously served in Company G, 1st Regiment N.C. Junior Reserves. Enlisted in this company at Camp Holmes on September 3, 1864, for the war. Present or accounted for until he died in hospital at Richmond, Virginia, January 16, 1865, of ''dysentery jaundice.''

WOOTEN, JAMES B., Private
Enlisted in Lenoir County on April 27, 1861. Mustered in as Private and was promoted to Sergeant on May 5, 1861. Reduced to ranks on April 22, 1862. Present or accounted for until wounded at Sharpsburg, Maryland, September 17, 1862. Returned to duty on an unspecified date. Wounded in the left thigh at Wilderness, Virginia, on or about May 5, 1864. Left leg amputated at the thigh. No further records.

WORLEY, BRYANT, Private
Enlisted at Camp Jackson on June 14, 1862, for the war. Died ''at home'' on June 18, 1863, of ''dropsy.''

WORLEY, CURTIS, Private
Enlisted in Lenoir County on April 27, 1861. Mustered

in as Private and was promoted to Musician (Drummer) on April 22, 1862. Reduced to ranks in November, 1862-October, 1864. Surrendered at Appomattox Court House, Virginia, April 9, 1865.

WORLEY, WILLIAM S., Private
Born in Lenoir County where he enlisted on May 18, 1861. Died in hospital at Lynchburg, Virginia, April 25, 1864, of "pneumonia."

YARBROUGH, W. G., Private
Born in Stanly County and enlisted at Camp Holmes on March 1, 1864, for the war. Died "at home" on or about August 20, 1864, of disease.

COMPANY E

This company, known as the "Marlboro Guards," was raised in Pitt County and enlisted at Marlboro. The company was ordered to New Bern on May 18, 1861, and encamped at the fairgrounds; there, on June 19, twenty-seven members of the "Pitt Volunteers" (later Company H of this regiment) were transferred to the "Marlboro Guards" in order to bring it up to its authorized strength. The company was mustered in on June 21, 1861, and was later assigned to the 27th Regiment as Company E. After joining the regiment the company functioned as a part of the regiment, and its history for the war period is reported as a part of the regimental history.

The information contained in the following company roster was compiled principally from company muster rolls for June 21, 1861-April, 1862; July-October, 1862; and September, 1864-February, 1865. No company muster rolls were found for May-June, 1862; November, 1862-August, 1864; or for the period after February, 1865. Valuable information was obtained also from primary records such as the Roll of Honor, medical records, prisoner of war records, discharge certificates, and pension applications, and from secondary sources such as postwar rosters and histories, cemetery records, and records of the United Daughters of the Confederacy.

OFFICERS

CAPTAINS

MORRILL, WILLIAM H.
Enlisted in Pitt County. Elected Captain on April 20, 1861. Present or accounted for until appointed Assistant Commissary of Subsistence (Captain) on November 2, 1861, and transferred to the Field and Staff of this regiment.

JOYNER, JASON P.
Previously served as Adjutant (3rd Lieutenant) of this regiment. Elected Captain of this company on November 18, 1861. Present or accounted for until wounded at Sharpsburg, Maryland, September 17, 1862. Died on September 19, 1862, of wounds. Place of death not reported.

JOYNER, ROBERT W.
Born in Pitt County where he resided prior to enlisting at Kinston on or about April 1, 1862. Mustered in as Private and was elected 3rd Lieutenant on April 22, 1862. Promoted to Captain on September 19, 1862. Wounded in both legs and captured at or near Farmville, Virginia, on or about April 6, 1865. Paroled at Farmville on April 27, 1865.

LIEUTENANTS

BARRETT, JOSEPH B., 1st Lieutenant
Born in Pitt County and was by occupation a merchant. Elected 1st Lieutenant on or about April 29, 1861. Present or accounted for until killed at Sharpsburg, Maryland, September 17, 1862.

BARRETT, LYCURGUS J., 3rd Lieutenant
Enlisted in Pitt County on April 20, 1861. Mustered in as Corporal and was elected 3rd Lieutenant on October 7, 1861. Present or accounted for until he was defeated for reelection when the regiment was reorganized in April, 1862. Later served as Captain of Company H, 7th Regiment Confederate Cavalry.

ERNUL, McGREIGER, 1st Lieutenant
Previously served as an enlisted man in Company H of this regiment. Transferred to this company on an unspecified date with an unspecified rank. Promoted to Sergeant on June 19, 1861, and was elected 1st Lieutenant on September 28, 1862. Hospitalized at Richmond, Virginia, August 25, 1864, with a gunshot wound of the right arm. Place and date wounded not reported. Returned to duty prior to November 1, 1864. Present or accounted for until he surrendered at Appomattox Court House, Virginia, April 9, 1865.

HINES, AMOS J., 2nd Lieutenant
Born in Edgecombe County and resided in Pitt County prior to enlisting at age 25. Elected 2nd Lieutenant on April 29, 1861. Resigned prior to May 16, 1861, when he was appointed 1st Lieutenant of Company G, 8th Regiment N.C. State Troops. Later served as Captain of that unit.

MOORE, EDWARD, 2nd Lieutenant
Elected 2nd Lieutenant on April 29, 1861. Resigned on an unspecified date prior to January 1, 1862. Reason he resigned not reported.

SINGLETARY, THOMAS C., 3rd Lieutenant
Previously served as 3rd Lieutenant of Company H of this regiment. Transferred to this company on or about June 19, 1861. Present or accounted for until elected Major on September 28, 1861, and transferred to the Field and Staff of this regiment. Later served as Lieutenant Colonel of this regiment.

TYER, JAMES R., 2nd Lieutenant
Enlisted in Pitt County on April 20, 1861. Mustered in with an unspecified rank and was promoted to Sergeant on April 27, 1861. Promoted to 1st Sergeant on December 21, 1861. Present or accounted for until wounded at Sharpsburg, Maryland, September 17, 1862. Returned to duty on an unspecified date. Elected 2nd Lieutenant on September 29, 1862. Killed at Bristoe Station, Virginia, October 14, 1863.

WARREN, SILAS W., 2nd Lieutenant
Enlisted in Pitt County on April 20, 1861. Mustered in with an unspecified rank and was promoted to 1st Sergeant on April 27, 1861. Elected 3rd Lieutenant on November 18, 1861, and was promoted to 2nd Lieutenant on April 16, 1862. Present or accounted for until killed at Sharpsburg, Maryland, September 17, 1862.

WILLIAMS, JAMES T., 2nd Lieutenant
Resided in Pitt County where he enlisted on April 20, 1861. Mustered in as Private and was promoted to Musician in September-October, 1862. Elected 2nd Lieutenant on or about November 28, 1862. Promoted to 1st Lieutenant and transferred to Company I, 44th Regiment N.C. Troops, June 14, 1864.

NONCOMMISSIONED OFFICERS AND PRIVATES

ALLEN, JOHN M., Private
Born in Pitt County and was by occupation a miller prior to enlisting in Pitt County on April 20, 1861. Present or accounted for until he died "at home" on or about October 22, 1861. Cause of death not reported. Death records dated 1862 give his age at time of death as 19.

ALLEN, RICHARD B., Private
Born in Pitt County and was by occupation a farmer prior to enlisting in Pitt County on April 30, 1861. Present or accounted for through February, 1865. Furlough records dated 1865 give his age as 21.

ASKEW, NEEDHAM W., Private
Enlisted in Pitt County on April 20, 1861. Wounded at Wilderness, Virginia, on or about May 5, 1864. Retired to the Invalid Corps on December 22, 1864.

ASKEW, WILLIAM C., Private
Enlisted at Camp Gatlin on September 9, 1861. Wounded in the hand at Fredericksburg, Virginia, December 13, 1862. Returned to duty on an unspecified date. Wounded in the arm and chest at Wilderness, Virginia, May 5, 1864. Reported absent wounded until December 22, 1864, when he was retired to the Invalid Corps.

AVERY, RICHARD, Private
Enlisted in Pitt County at age 21, April 30, 1861. Present or accounted for until he deserted on February 19, 1865.

BAKER, ALLEN JOHNSON, Private
Resided in Pitt or Wilson County and enlisted in Lenoir County on May 15, 1862, for the war. Present or accounted for until wounded at Sharpsburg, Maryland, September 17, 1862. Returned to duty on an unspecified date. Wounded in the right thigh at Bristoe Station, Virginia, October 14, 1863. Returned to duty on an unspecified date. Captured at Farmville, Virginia, April 6, 1865. Confined at Newport News, Virginia, until released on June 27, 1865, after taking the Oath of Allegiance.

BAKER, J. B., Private
Born in Pitt County and enlisted in Lenoir County on May 15, 1862, for the war. Present or accounted for until killed at Sharpsburg, Maryland, September 17, 1862.

BAKER, JESSE J., Private
Resided in Pitt County and enlisted in Craven County on May 24, 1861. Wounded in the breast and arm at Wilderness, Virginia, on or about May 5, 1864. Returned to duty in November-December, 1864. Present or accounted for until captured near Petersburg, Virginia, February 6, 1865. Confined at Point Lookout, Maryland, until released on June 23, 1865, after taking the Oath of Allegiance.

BARRETT, EDWIN A., Corporal
Enlisted at Camp Gatlin on September 11, 1861. Mustered in as Private and was promoted to Corporal in September, 1862. Present or accounted for until wounded at Sharpsburg, Maryland, September 17, 1862. Returned to duty on an unspecified date. Wounded in the right thigh at Bristoe Station, Virginia, October 14, 1863. Company records do not indicate whether he returned to duty; however, he was transferred to Company H, 7th Regiment Confederate Cavalry, March 30, 1864.

BEALE, CADWALADER H., Private
Enlisted at Camp Gatlin on January 25, 1862. Discharged in March-April, 1862. Reason discharged not reported.

BLIZZARD, SAMUEL, Private
Place and date of enlistment not reported. Name appears as signature to a parole datelined Kinston, December 14, 1862. No further records.

BOON, JACOB, Private
Enlisted in Wake County on August 16, 1864, for the war. Present or accounted for until paroled at Greensboro on May 16, 1865.

BOWLES, BENJAMIN, Private
Enlisted in Wake County on May 25, 1864, for the war. Present or accounted for until transferred to Company G, 24th Regiment N.C. Troops (14th Regiment N.C. Volunteers), January 31, 1865.

BRANTLEY, HENRY, Sergeant
Enlisted in Pitt County on April 20, 1861. Mustered in as Corporal and was promoted to Sergeant on September 29, 1862. Present or accounted for until hospitalized at Richmond, Virginia, on or about April 2, 1865, with a wound. Place and date wounded not reported. Captured in hospital at Richmond on April 3, 1865. Died at Richmond on May 2, 1865. Cause of death not reported.

BREWER, JAMES, Private
Previously enlisted in Company H of this regiment. Transferred to this company on April 20, 1861. Promoted to Musician (Drummer) on June 20, 1861, but was reduced to ranks in November, 1862-October, 1863. Wounded in the head in Virginia in June, 1864. Returned to duty prior to August 25, 1864, when he was wounded at Reams' Station, Virginia. Returned to duty in November-December, 1864. Present or accounted for until wounded in the breast at or near Fort Stedman, Virginia, March 25, 1865. Captured in hospital at Richmond, Virginia, April 3, 1865. Transferred to Point Lookout, Maryland, where he arrived on May 6, 1865. Released on June 26, 1865, after taking the Oath of Allegiance.

BRYANT, WILLIAM, Private
Enlisted in Wake County on March 1, 1864, for the war. Present or accounted for through December, 1864.

BUCK, BENJAMIN A., Private
Previously served in Company H of this regiment. Transferred to this company on June 19, 1861. Killed in battle "in Virginia" in June, 1864.

CANNON, CALEB, Private
Enlisted in Wake County on March 31, 1864, for the war. Present or accounted for until hospitalized at Danville, Virginia, on or about March 30, 1865, with a gunshot wound of the left arm. Place and date wounded not reported. Returned to duty in November-December, 1864. Present or accounted for through December 31, 1864.

CANNON, JOHN C., Private
Previously served in Company H of this regiment. Transferred to this company on June 19, 1861. Present or accounted for through April 29, 1864.

CARR, ALBERT L., Sergeant
Enlisted at Camp Gatlin on September 12, 1861. Mustered in as Private and was promoted to Sergeant on September 29, 1862. Surrendered at Appomattox Court House, Virginia, April 9, 1865.

CASON, SAMUEL R., Corporal
Enlisted in Pitt County on April 20, 1861. Mustered in as Private and was promoted to Corporal in November, 1862-October, 1864. Wounded in the arm at Fredericksburg, Virginia, December 13, 1862. Returned to duty on an unspecified date. Surrendered at Appomattox Court House, Virginia, April 9, 1865.

CORBETT, DEMPSEY R., Private
Enlisted in Pitt County on April 20, 1861. Wounded in the face at Fredericksburg, Virginia, December 13, 1862. Returned to duty on an unspecified date. Wounded in the right ankle at Bristoe Station, Virginia, October 14, 1863. Retired to the Invalid Corps on August 2, 1864, by reason of disability from wounds received at Bristoe Station.

CORBETT, HOWELL, Private
Enlisted in Pitt County on April 20, 1861. Died in hospital at Richmond, Virginia, May 5, 1864, of a compound fracture of the thigh. Place and date injured not reported.

CORBETT, WILLIAM, Private
Enlisted in Pitt County on April 20, 1861. Wounded at Wilderness, Virginia, on or about May 5, 1864. Returned to duty prior to November 1, 1864. Present or accounted for until he surrendered at Appomattox Court House, Virginia, April 9, 1865.

COX, BRYANT, Private
Enlisted in Lenoir County on May 1, 1862, for the war. Deserted on February 19, 1865.

CRAWFORD, DAVID L., Private
Enlisted in Pitt County at age 21, April 30, 1861. Wounded in the hand at Fredericksburg, Virginia, December 13, 1862. Returned to duty on an unspecified date. Wounded at Wilderness, Virginia, on or about May 5, 1864. Returned to duty prior to November 1, 1864. Present or accounted for through February, 1865.

CRAWFORD, JAMES A., Private
Previously served in Company D, 4th Regiment N.C. State Troops. [Service record does not appear in Volume IV of this series.] Transferred to this company on June 6, 1861. Present or accounted for until wounded and captured at Sharpsburg, Maryland, September 17, 1862. No further records.

DAVIS, RICHARD B., Private
Born in Pitt County and enlisted at Camp Gatlin on September 9, 1861. Died at Camp Gatlin on October 27, 1861. Cause of death not reported.

DIXON, JOHN R., 1st Sergeant
Enlisted in Pitt County on May 22, 1861. Mustered in as Private and was promoted to Corporal on January 1, 1862. Promoted to Sergeant in September, 1862. Present or accounted for until wounded in the right arm and right thigh and captured at Sharpsburg, Maryland, September 17, 1862. Hospitalized at Philadelphia, Pennsylvania. Promoted to 1st Sergeant on September 28, 1862, while a prisoner of war. Transferred from Philadelphia to Fort Delaware, Delaware, on or about December 12, 1862. Paroled and transferred to City Point, Virginia, where he was received December 18, 1862, for exchange. Returned to duty on an unspecified date. Surrendered at Appomattox Court House, Virginia, April 9, 1865.

EDWARDS, WILLIAM BRYANT, Private
Enlisted in Wake County on August 12, 1864, for the war. Present or accounted for until he surrendered at Appomattox Court House, Virginia, April 9, 1865.

ELKS, CHARLES F., Private
Born in Pitt County and was by occupation a farmer prior to enlisting in Pitt County on May 6, 1861. Present or accounted for until killed at Sharpsburg, Maryland, September 17, 1862. Death records give his age as 21.

ELKS, JOHN, Private
Enlisted in Pitt County on May 6, 1861. Wounded in an unspecified engagement on June 10, 1864. Reported absent wounded through February, 1865.

GAY, WILLIAM R., Private
Enlisted at Camp Gatlin on September 9, 1861. Died in hospital at Richmond, Virginia, September 9, 1864, of a gunshot wound. Place and date wounded not reported.

GEARNER, WILLIAM, Private
Enlisted in Wake County on August 21, 1864, for the war. Present or accounted for until he surrendered at Appomattox Court House, Virginia, April 9, 1865.

GRIMMER, RUFUS R., Private
Previously served in Company H of this regiment. Transferred to this company on June 19, 1861. Present or accounted for until he surrendered at Appomattox Court House, Virginia, April 9, 1865.

GRIMSLEY, FRANK, Private
Previously served in Company H of this regiment. Transferred to this company on June 19, 1861. Present or accounted for until he died in hospital at Gordonsville, Virginia, November 27, 1862, of "pneumonia."

GRIMSLEY, WYATT, Private
Previously served in Company H of this regiment. Transferred to this company on June 19, 1861. Died in hospital at Richmond, Virginia, September 19, 1864, of "diarrhoea chron[ic]."

HADDOCK, HENRY C., Private
Previously served in Company H of this regiment.

Transferred to this company on June 19, 1861. Wounded at Reams' Station, Virginia, August 25, 1864. Reported absent wounded through December, 1864, Reported absent without leave during January-February, 1865.

HADDOCK, JOHN, Private
Previously served in Company H of this regiment. Transferred to this company on June 19, 1861. Present or accounted for until discharged on August 2, 1861. Reason discharged not reported.

HARRIS, ASA, Private
Previously served in Company H of this regiment. Transferred to this company on June 19, 1861. Present or accounted for until discharged on August 7, 1861, by reason of disability. [May have served later in Company C, 61st Regiment N.C. Troops.]

HARRIS, BAKER P., Private
Born in Warren County and enlisted in Pitt County on April 26, 1861. Present or accounted for until killed at Sharpsburg, Maryland, September 17, 1862.

HARRIS, JOHN, Private
Born in Pitt County and enlisted at Camp Gatlin on September 11, 1861. Present or accounted for until he died in hospital at Kinston on May 12, 1862. Cause of death not reported.

HARRIS, RICHARD, Private
Enlisted at Camp Gatlin at age 22, September 11, 1861. Reported absent wounded in September-October, 1864. Place and date wounded not reported. Returned to duty in January-February, 1865. Present or accounted for until he surrendered at Appomattox Court House, Virginia, April 9, 1865. [North Carolina pension records indicate he was wounded at Petersburg, Virginia, in March, 1864.]

HEMBY, JOHN J., Private
Enlisted in Pitt County on April 26, 1861. Present or accounted for until he was reported missing at New Bern on March 14, 1862.

HINSON, GRAY R., Private
Resided in Wilson County and enlisted in Pitt County on April 20, 1861. Present or accounted for through February, 1865; however, he was reported on duty as a teamster during most of that period. Captured at or near Fort Stedman, Virginia, March 25, 1865. Confined at Point Lookout, Maryland, until released on June 14, 1865, after taking the Oath of Allegiance.

HINSON, JESSE R., Private
Resided in Greene County and enlisted in Lenoir County at age 21, May 15, 1862, for the war. Wounded in the face at Wilderness, Virginia, on or about May 5, 1864. Returned to duty prior to November 1, 1864. Present or accounted for until captured at or near Sutherland's Station, Virginia, April 2, 1865. Confined at Point Lookout, Maryland, until released on June 28, 1865, after taking the Oath of Allegiance.

ISLEY, EMANUEL, Private
Enlisted in Wake County on August 16, 1864, for the war. Present or accounted for until February 9, 1865, when he was listed as a deserter. Returned to duty on an unspecified date. Surrendered at Appomattox Court

House, Virginia, April 9, 1865.

JAMES, CALVIN, Private
Previously served in Company H of this regiment. Transferred to this company on June 19, 1861. Present or accounted for until discharged on or about September 17, 1861, by reason of disability.

JAMES, JOHN W., Private
Enlisted in Pitt County on April 30, 1861. Captured at Bristoe Station, Virginia, October 14, 1863. Confined at Old Capitol Prison, Washington, D.C., until transferred to Point Lookout, Maryland, October 27, 1863. Paroled at Point Lookout and transferred to Cox's Wharf, James River, Virginia, where he was received February 13, 1865, for exchange.

JOLLY, BENJAMIN FRANKLIN, Private
Enlisted at Camp Holmes on May 5, 1864, for the war. Hospitalized at Richmond, Virginia, May 25, 1864, with a gunshot wound. Place and date wounded not reported. Returned to duty on July 7, 1864. Present or accounted for until he deserted on February 19, 1865.

JOLLY, JOSEPH H., Private
Enlisted in Pitt County on April 20, 1861. Present or accounted for until discharged in January-February, 1862, by reason of disability.

JONES, BRYANT, Private
Previously served in Company H of this regiment. Transferred to this company on June 19, 1861. Present or accounted for until killed at Sharpsburg, Maryland, September 17, 1862.

JONES, JAMES, Private
Enlisted at Camp Gatlin on September 12, 1861. Present or accounted for until he surrendered at Appomattox Court House, Virginia, April 9, 1865.

JONES, MATTHEW R., Private
Enlisted in Pitt County on April 20, 1861. Present or accounted for until he surrendered at Appomattox Court House, Virginia, April 9, 1865.

JONES, WILEY, Private
Enlisted at Camp Gatlin on September 9, 1861. Deserted on October 11, 1861.

JONES, WILLOUGHBY, Private
Resided in Pitt County where he enlisted on October 1, 1863, for the war. Captured at Hatcher's Run, Virginia, March 31, 1865. Confined at Point Lookout, Maryland, until released on June 28, 1865, after taking the Oath of Allegiance.

JOYNER, AMON, Corporal
Born in Pitt County where he enlisted on April 20, 1861. Mustered in as Private and was promoted to Corporal on September 19, 1862. Died at Hardeeville, South Carolina, March 27, 1863, of "ty[phoid] fever."

JOYNER, JOHN T., Sergeant
Born in Pitt County and was by occupation a farmer prior to enlisting in Pitt County on April 20, 1861. Mustered in with an unspecified rank and was promoted to Sergeant on May 20, 1861. Present or accounted for until discharged on July 16, 1862, by reason of being overage. Discharge certificate gives his age as 36. Later

served as Private in Company I, 41st Regiment N.C. Troops (3rd Regiment N.C. Cavalry).

KILPATRICK, FRANK M., Corporal
Previously served in Company H of this regiment. Transferred to this company on June 19, 1861, with the rank of Corporal. Present or accounted for until wounded in the left leg and captured at Sharpsburg, Maryland, September 17, 1862. Paroled on or about January 25, 1863. Returned to duty on an unspecified date. Surrendered at Appomattox Court House, Virginia, April 9, 1865.

KILPATRICK, JOHN B., Sergeant
Previously served in Company H of this regiment. Transferred to this company on June 19, 1861, with the rank of Corporal. Promoted to Sergeant on December 21, 1861. Captured at Frederick, Maryland, September 12, 1862. Confined at Fort Delaware, Delaware. Paroled and transferred to Aiken's Landing, James River, Virginia, October 2, 1862, for exchange. Declared exchanged at Aiken's Landing on November 10, 1862. Returned to duty on an unspecified date. Wounded at Reams' Station, Virginia, August 25, 1864. Returned to duty subsequent to December 31, 1864. Paroled at Lynchburg, Virginia, April 15, 1865.

KILPATRICK, WILLIAM JAMES, Private
Previously served in Company H of this regiment. Transferred to this company on June 19, 1861. Present or accounted for until wounded at Sharpsburg, Maryland, September 17, 1862. Returned to duty on an unspecified date. Captured at Bristoe Station, Virginia, October 14, 1863. Confined at Old Capitol Prison, Washington, D.C., until transferred to Point Lookout, Maryland, October 27, 1863. Paroled at Point Lookout on January 17, 1865, and transferred to Boulware's Wharf, James River, Virginia, where he was received January 21, 1865, for exchange. Returned to duty prior to March 31, 1865, when he was captured at Hatcher's Run, Virginia. Confined at Point Lookout until released on June 14, 1865, after taking the Oath of Allegiance.

KILPATRICK, WILLIAM P., Private
Previously served in Company H of this regiment. Transferred to this company on June 19, 1861. Present or accounted for until wounded at Sharpsburg, Maryland, September 17, 1862. No further records.

LANG, JOHN A., Private
Enlisted at Camp Gatlin at age 17, September 9, 1861. Wounded at Wilderness, Virginia, May 5, 1864. Returned to duty prior to November 1, 1864. Present or accounted for through February, 1865.

LANG, ROBERT J., Corporal
Resided in Pitt County where he enlisted on April 26, 1861. Mustered in as Private and was promoted to Corporal on September 1, 1862. Wounded in the groin at Bristoe Station, Virginia, October 14, 1863. Returned to duty on an unspecified date. Wounded at Wilderness, Virginia, on or about May 5, 1864. Returned to duty prior to November 1, 1864. Present or accounted for until he surrendered at Appomattox Court House, Virginia, April 9, 1865.

LAUGHINGHOUSE, CASWELL, Private
Previously served in Company H of this regiment. Transferred to this company on June 19, 1861.

Wounded at Wilderness, Virginia, on or about May 5, 1864. Returned to duty prior to June 1, 1864. Killed "in Virginia" in June, 1864.

LEGGETT, JOHN, Private
Enlisted in Pitt County on April 20, 1861. Reported absent without leave on June 15, 1861, but returned to duty on or about July 10, 1861. Present or accounted for until he deserted in March-April, 1862.

LOCK, HENRY CLAY, Private
Enlisted at Camp Holmes on August 18, 1864, for the war. Present or accounted for through February, 1865.

McGOWAN, J. J., Private
Previously served in Company H of this regiment. Transferred to this company on June 19, 1861. Captured at Hatcher's Run, Virginia, March 31, 1865. Confined at Point Lookout, Maryland, until released on June 29, 1865, after taking the Oath of Allegiance.

McKEEL, EDWARD, Private
Previously served in Company H of this regiment. Transferred to this company on or about June 19, 1861. Discharged on September 5, 1861, by reason of disability.

MIXON, JOHN, Private
Enlisted in Pitt County on April 30, 1861. Present or accounted for until wounded in the shoulder and breast at New Bern on March 14, 1862. "The ball pass[ed] entirely through his body. He has the ball and says he intends to kill a Yankee with it if he ever gets well." Returned to duty on an unspecified date. Hospitalized at Richmond, Virginia, May 18, 1864, with a gunshot wound of the left leg. Place and date wounded not reported. Left leg amputated. Died in hospital at Richmond on June 5, 1864, of wounds.

MOBLEY, JAMES T., Private
Previously served in Company H of this regiment. Transferred to this company on June 19, 1861. Present or accounted for until March 14, 1862, when he was reported absent sick. Reported absent sick through October, 1862. No further records.

MOBLEY, ROBERT T., Private
Born in Edgecombe County and enlisted in Pitt County on April 20, 1861. Present or accounted for until he died at Camp Gatlin on January 9, 1862. Cause of death not reported.

MOBLEY, W. G., Private
Previously served in Company H of this regiment. Transferred to this company on June 19, 1861. Present or accounted for until he deserted on August 1, 1861.

MOORE, JOHN, Private
Enlisted in Pitt County on April 20, 1861. Present or accounted for until wounded in both thighs and captured at Sharpsburg, Maryland, September 17, 1862. Exchanged at City Point, Virginia, January 26, 1863. Company records do not indicate whether he returned to duty; however, he was retired to the Invalid Corps on August 9, 1864.

MOORE, TURNER, Private
Enlisted at Camp Gatlin on September 9, 1861. Present or accounted for until wounded at Sharpsburg,

Maryland, September 17, 1862. Returned to duty on an unspecified date. Wounded in the head at Wilderness, Virginia, on or about May 5, 1864. Returned to duty prior to September 3, 1864, when he was killed in an unspecified engagement.

MORGANSTEEN, CHARLES, Private
Enlisted in Pitt County on May 6, 1861. "Drowned at New Bern" on June 26, 1861.

MURPHREY, RICHARD K., Private
Born in Pitt County where he enlisted on April 20, 1861. Killed at Bristoe Station, Virginia, October 14, 1863.

MURPHY, JESSE J., Private
Resided in Greene County and enlisted in Wayne County on May 5, 1863, for the war. Captured at or near Fort Stedman, Virginia, March 25, 1865. Confined at Point Lookout, Maryland, until released on June 29, 1865, after taking the Oath of Allegiance.

MUSE, WILLIS, Private
Resided in Beaufort County. Place and date of enlistment not reported. Captured in hospital at Richmond, Virginia, April 3, 1865. Transferred to Newport News, Virginia, April 23, 1865. Released on June 14, 1865, after taking the Oath of Allegiance.

NICHOLS, JAMES, Private
Enlisted at Camp Gatlin on August 2, 1864, for the war. Present or accounted for until he deserted on February 9, 1865.

NICHOLS, MOSES, Private
Previously served in Company D, 4th Regiment N.C. State Troops. [Service record omitted in Volume IV of this series.] Transferred to this company on June 6, 1861. Wounded in the right leg at Bristoe Station, Virginia, October 14, 1863. Right leg amputated. Retired to the Invalid Corps on August 13, 1864.

NICHOLS, SILAS, Private
Enlisted in Pitt County at age 20, April 30, 1861. Wounded in the left shoulder at Wilderness, Virginia, on or about May 5, 1864. Reported absent without leave in September-October, 1864, and was listed as a deserter in January-February, 1865.

NOBLES, BENJAMIN, Private
Previously served in Company H of this regiment. Transferred to this company on June 19, 1861. Present or accounted for until he died in hospital at Kinston on May 1, 1862. Cause of death not reported.

NOBLES, WILEY F., Private
Born in Pitt County where he enlisted at age 18, May 6, 1861. Wounded in the right leg at Bristoe Station, Virginia, October 14, 1863. Returned to duty on an unspecified date. Wounded in the jaw and right shoulder at Wilderness, Virginia, on or about May 5, 1864. Returned to duty on an unspecified date but was retired to the Invalid Corps on November 10, 1864.

NORRIS, JOHN, Private
Born in Pitt County where he enlisted on May 6, 1861. Reported absent without leave from June 16, 1861, until September 15, 1861. Killed at Bristoe Station, Virginia, on or about October 14, 1863.

PARKER, CHARLES W., Private
Born in Pitt County where he enlisted on April 30, 1861. Present or accounted for until killed at Sharpsburg, Maryland, September 17, 1862.

PARKER, EDWARD S., Private
Resided in Wayne or Pitt County and enlisted in Pitt County at age 21, April 20, 1861. Wounded in the left thigh at Bristoe Station, Virginia, October 14, 1863. Reported absent wounded or absent sick through February, 1865. Deserted on an unspecified date. Reported in confinement at Libby Prison, Richmond, Virginia, April 10, 1865.

PARKER, JAMES P., Private
Enlisted in Pitt County on April 20, 1861. Killed at Bristoe Station, Virginia, October 14, 1863.

PARKER, ROBERT H., Private
Enlisted in Pitt County on May 26, 1861. Present or accounted for until wounded at Sharpsburg, Maryland, September 17, 1862. Company records do not indicate that he returned to duty prior to September-October, 1864, when he was reported absent on furlough of disability. Returned to duty in January-February, 1865, but was retired to the Invalid Corps on February 3, 1865.

PATRICK, ALBERT H., Private
Enlisted at Camp Holmes on August 2, 1864, for the war. Present or accounted for until he died in hospital at Richmond, Virginia, on or about December 28, 1864, of "feb[ris] typh[oides]."

PHILLIPS, JOHN M., Corporal
Born in Pitt County where he enlisted on April 20, 1861. Mustered in as Private and was promoted to Corporal on October 31, 1861. Present or accounted for until he died in hospital at Petersburg, Virginia, on or about July 14, 1862, of "meningitis."

PHILLIPS, SETH, Private
Enlisted in Pitt County on May 24, 1861. Present or accounted for until wounded at Sharpsburg, Maryland, September 17, 1862. Returned to duty on an unspecified date. Present or accounted for through February, 1865.

PIERCE, WILEY B., Private
Enlisted at Camp Gatlin at age 17, September 11, 1861. Present or accounted for until wounded in the left foot at Sharpsburg, Maryland, September 17, 1862. Returned to duty on an unspecified date. Captured at Bristoe Station, Virginia, October 14, 1863. Confined at Old Capitol Prison, Washington, D.C., until transferred to Point Lookout, Maryland, October 27, 1863. Paroled at Point Lookout on February 18, 1865, and transferred to Boulware's Wharf, James River, Virginia, where he was received February 20-21, 1865, for exchange. [North Carolina pension records indicate he was wounded in the back at "Horse Shoe" on an unspecified date and was wounded in the thigh at Fredericksburg, Virginia, in 1865.]

PUGH, JAMES A., Private
Previously served in Company C, 1st Regiment N.C. Junior Reserves. Enlisted in this company at Camp Holmes on July 27, 1864, for the war. Present or accounted for until wounded in the right knee at Reams'

Station, Virginia, August 25, 1864. Reported absent wounded until March 11, 1865, when he deserted from hospital at Richmond, Virginia.

REITZEL, MICHAEL M., Private
Resided in Guilford County and enlisted at Camp Holmes on August 16, 1864, for the war. Present or accounted for until captured at or near Fort Stedman, Virginia, March 25, 1865. Confined at Point Lookout, Maryland, until released on June 17, 1865, after taking the Oath of Allegiance.

RINGOLD, JAMES, Private
Previously served in Company H of this regiment. Transferred to this company on June 19, 1861. Present or accounted for until discharged on April 30, 1862, by reason of being underage. Discharge certificate gives his age as 17. [North Carolina pension records indicate he was wounded at Chancellorsville, Virginia, on an unspecified date.]

SHIVERS, ALGERNON, Private
Previously served in Company H of this regiment. Transferred to this company on June 19, 1861. Wounded in the left leg and/or left shoulder at Wilderness, Virginia, on or about May 5, 1864. Hospitalized at Richmond, Virginia, until furloughed for sixty days on May 22, 1864. No further records.

SMITH, BURTON A., Private
Born in Pitt County and was by occupation a farmer prior to enlisting in Pitt County on April 20, 1861. Wounded in the head at Fredericksburg, Virginia, December 13, 1862. Died at or near Richmond, Virginia, on or about December 17, 1862, of wounds and/or "typhoid fever." Death records give his age as 28.

SMITH, HENRY CLAY, Private
Resided in Greene County and enlisted at Camp Gatlin on February 11, 1862. Captured at or near Fort Stedman, Virginia, March 25, 1865. Confined at Point Lookout, Maryland, until released on June 20, 1865, after taking the Oath of Allegiance.

SMITH, JOHN I., Private
Enlisted in Pitt County on April 20, 1861. Wounded at Wilderness, Virginia, on or about May 5, 1864. Died in hospital at Richmond, Virginia, May 17, 1864, of wounds.

SUMMERS, ELIAS, Private
Enlisted at Camp Holmes on August 16, 1864, for the war. Present or accounted for until he died at "Heth's division hospital" on December 22, 1864, of disease.

SUMMERS, PETER H., Private
Enlisted at Camp Holmes on August 29, 1864, for the war. Present or accounted for until he surrendered at Appomattox Court House, Virginia, April 9, 1865.

TAYLOR, WILLIAM L., Private
Previously served in Company H of this regiment. Transferred to this company on June 19, 1861. Present or accounted for until wounded and captured at Sharpsburg, Maryland, September 17, 1862. Paroled on September 27, 1862. Returned to duty on an unspecified date. Died in hospital at Richmond, Virginia, November 21, 1863, of pneumonia following the amputation of his leg. Place and date injured not reported.

THOMAS, ROBERT H., Private
Enlisted in Wake County on October 12, 1864, for the war. Present or accounted for through February, 1865.

TUGWELL, LEVI, Private
Enlisted at Camp Gatlin on September 9, 1861. Deserted on September 15, 1861.

TYER, JOHN E., Sergeant
Enlisted in Pitt County on April 26, 1861. Mustered in as Private and was promoted to Corporal on December 21, 1861. Promoted to Sergeant on January 1, 1862. Wounded at Sharpsburg, Maryland, September 17, 1862. Returned to duty on an unspecified date. Surrendered at Appomattox Court House, Virginia, April 9, 1865.

WALL, JOHN, Private
Enlisted in Craven County on June 10, 1861. Present or accounted for until he deserted on June 30, 1862.

WALSTON, JOHN D., Corporal
Enlisted in Pitt County on April 20, 1861. Mustered in as Private. Wounded at Sharpsburg, Maryland, September 17, 1862. Returned to duty on an unspecified date. Promoted to Corporal in November, 1862-July, 1863. Surrendered at Appomattox Court House, Virginia, April 9, 1865.

WARD, JOSEPH T., Private
Enlisted in Pitt County on April 30, 1861. Wounded in the left thigh at or near Reams' Station, Virginia, on or about August 23, 1864. Reported absent wounded until furloughed for sixty days on February 11, 1865.

WILLIAMS, SAMUEL, Private
Previously served in Company H of this regiment. Transferred to this company on June 19, 1861. Died at Camp Gatlin on or about November 26, 1861. Cause of death not reported.

WILLIAMS, SHADE, Private
Previously served in Company H of this regiment. Transferred to this company on June 19, 1861. Wounded and captured at Sharpsburg, Maryland, September 17, 1862. Confined at Fort McHenry, Maryland. Paroled and transferred to Aiken's Landing, James River, Virginia, where he was received October 25, 1862, for exchange. Declared exchanged at Aiken's Landing on November 10, 1862. Returned to duty on an unspecified date. Wounded at Wilderness, Virginia, on or about May 5, 1864. Died in hospital at Staunton, Virginia, May 28, 1864, of wounds.

WILLOUGHBY, WILLIAM JOSEPH, Private
Born in Pitt County and was by occupation a farmer prior to enlisting in Pitt County on April 30, 1861. Mustered in as Private and was promoted to Musician (Drummer) on June 20, 1861. Reduced to ranks in November-December, 1861. Present or accounted for until discharged on July 16, 1862, by reason of being underage. Discharge certificate gives his age as 16.

WORTHINGTON, AMBROSE J., Private
Enlisted in Pitt County on May 25, 1861. Present or accounted for until wounded at Sharpsburg, Maryland, September 17, 1862. Died in hospital at Richmond,

Virginia, October 30, 1862, of "febris."

WRIGHT, JOHN, Private
Enlisted at Camp Holmes on May 23, 1864, for the war. Present or accounted for until he died in hospital at or near Richmond, Virginia, on or about January 30, 1865, of "diarrhoea ch[ronic]."

COMPANY F

This company, known as the "Perquimans Beauregards," was raised in Perquimans County and enlisted at Hertford. The company was composed initially of both infantry and cavalry contingents but was soon converted to a standard infantry organization. The company was mustered in on May 16, 1861; it remained in camp in Perquimans County until ordered to New Bern on July 3. On July 19 the company departed on board the steamer *Curlew* and traveled to New Bern via the Perquimans River, Albemarle and Pamlico sounds, and the Neuse River. Upon its arrival the company was assigned to a battalion which later became the 27th Regiment N.C. Troops, and the Perquimans Beauregards became Company F of that unit. After joining the regiment the company functioned as a part of the regiment, and its history for the war period is reported as a part of the regimental history.

The information contained in the following company roster was compiled principally from company muster rolls for May 16, 1861-October, 1862; March-April, 1863; September, 1863-February, 1864; and September-December, 1864. No company muster rolls were found for November, 1862-February, 1863; May-August, 1863; March-August, 1864; or for the period after December, 1864. Valuable information was obtained also from primary records such as the Roll of Honor, medical records, prisoner of war records, discharge certificates, and pension applications, and from secondary sources such as postwar rosters and histories, cemetery records, and records of the United Daughters of the Confederacy.

OFFICERS

CAPTAINS

NIXON, WILLIAM
Enlisted in Perquimans County. Elected Captain on or about May 16, 1861. Present or accounted for until he was defeated for reelection when the regiment was reorganized in April, 1862.

JONES, THOMAS D.
Was by occupation a clerk prior to enlisting in Perquimans County. Elected 3rd Lieutenant on May 16, 1861, and was elected 2nd Lieutenant on August 20, 1861. Elected Captain on April 22, 1862. Wounded in the abdomen and kidney at Bristoe Station, Virginia, October 14, 1863. Hospitalized at Richmond, Virginia, where he died on November 7, 1863, of wounds.

SKINNER, BENJAMIN S.
Resided in Perquimans County where he enlisted on May 16, 1861. Mustered in as Sergeant and was elected 2nd Lieutenant on April 22, 1862. Wounded at Sharpsburg, Maryland, September 17, 1862. Returned to duty on an unspecified date. Promoted to 1st Lieutenant on November 15, 1862, and was promoted to Captain on November 8, 1863. Killed at Reams' Station, Virginia, August 25, 1864.

LIEUTENANTS

MARTIN, THOMAS DUNCAN, 1st Lieutenant
Born in Pasquotank County where he resided as a doctor prior to enlisting in Perquimans County at age 46. Elected 1st Lieutenant on or about May 16, 1861. Detailed in hospital in New Bern on or about July 1, 1861. Reported absent on detail at New Bern until transferred to a hospital at Goldsboro on or about February 15, 1862. Defeated for reelection on or about April 22, 1862.

MEBANE, WILLIAM A., 2nd Lieutenant
Resided in Perquimans County where he enlisted on May 16, 1861. Mustered in as Private and was elected 3rd Lieutenant on April 22, 1862. Wounded at Sharpsburg, Maryland, September 17, 1862. Returned to duty on an unspecified date. Captured at Bristoe Station, Virginia, October 14, 1863. Confined at Old Capitol Prison, Washington, D.C. Promoted to 2nd Lieutenant on October 16, 1863, while a prisoner of war. Transferred from Old Capitol Prison to Johnson's Island, Ohio, November 11, 1863. Released on June 12, 1865, after taking the Oath of Allegiance. Records of the Federal Provost Marshal dated 1865 give his age as 32.

NIXON, FRANCIS, 3rd Lieutenant
Resided in Perquimans County where he enlisted on May 16, 1861. Mustered in as Sergeant. Captured at New Bern on March 14, 1862. Confined at Fort Columbus, New York Harbor. Exchanged on an unspecified date. Promoted to Quartermaster Sergeant on May 1, 1862, and was elected 3rd Lieutenant on November 28, 1862. Wounded in the right leg at Bristoe Station, Virginia, October 14, 1863. Reported absent wounded until October 5, 1864, when he was retired to the Invalid Corps.

RIDDICK, ELBERT T., 1st Lieutenant
Enlisted in Perquimans County on May 16, 1861. Mustered in as 1st Sergeant and was elected 3rd Lieutenant on November 15, 1861. Elected 1st Lieutenant on April 22, 1862. Present or accounted for until wounded at Sharpsburg, Maryland, September 17, 1862. Died on November 15, 1862, of wounds. Place of death not reported.

WHITE, JOSHUA W., 2nd Lieutenant
Enlisted in Perquimans County. Appointed 2nd Lieutenant to rank from May 16, 1861. Appointed Assistant Quartermaster on or about September 5, 1861, and transferred to the Field and Staff of this regiment.

WILSON, WILLIAM A., 3rd Lieutenant
Enlisted in Perquimans County on May 16, 1861. Mustered in as Corporal and was promoted to Sergeant on November 15, 1861. Elected 3rd Lieutenant on September 1, 1864. Present or accounted for through December, 1864.

NONCOMMISSIONED OFFICERS AND PRIVATES

ALBERTSON, JOSEPH, Private
Enlisted in Perquimans County on May 16, 1861. Present or accounted for through July 26, 1864; however, he was reported on duty as a teamster during most of that period.

ALBERTSON, THOMAS, Private
Born in Perquimans County where he enlisted on May 16, 1861. Present or accounted for until he died "at home" on June 1, 1862. Cause of death not reported.

ALDRIDGE, WILLIAM, Private
Resided in Union County and enlisted in Wake County or at Petersburg, Virginia, November 1, 1864, for the war. Present or accounted for through January 5, 1865. Captured by the enemy on an unspecified date. Confined at Point Lookout, Maryland, until released on or about June 22, 1865, after taking the Oath of Allegiance.

ARRINGTON, HENDERSON, Private
Enlisted in Perquimans County on September 1, 1861. Present or accounted for through December, 1864.

BANKS, WILLIAM H., Private
Enlisted in Perquimans County on May 16, 1861. Present or accounted for until July-August, 1862, when he deserted.

BARCLIFT, JAMES M., Private
Enlisted in Perquimans County on May 16, 1861. Present or accounted for through October, 1862. No further records.

BARCLIFT, JOSEPH G., Sergeant
Enlisted in Perquimans County on May 16, 1861. Mustered in as Private. Present or accounted for until captured at Frederick, Maryland, September 12, 1862. Confined at Fort Delaware, Delaware. Transferred to Aiken's Landing, James River, Virginia, October 2, 1862, for exchange. Declared exchanged at Aiken's Landing on November 10, 1862. Returned to duty on an unspecified date. Wounded in the right wrist at Bristoe Station, Virginia, October 14, 1863. Returned to duty prior to January 1, 1864. Promoted to Sergeant on September 1, 1864. Present or accounted for through December, 1864.

BARKER, DANIEL L., Private
Born in Randolph County and was by occupation a farmer prior to enlisting in Wake County on December 7, 1863, for the war. Present or accounted for until discharged on March 12, 1864, by reason of "general debility, dropsy, & deafness." Discharge certificate gives his age as 46.

BELL, H. F., Private
Enlisted in Randolph County on December 3, 1863, for the war. Present or accounted for until he died in hospital at Richmond, Virginia, October 14, 1864, of "colitas [*sic*] acuta."

BENTON, THOMAS J., Private
Born in Perquimans County where he enlisted on May 16, 1861. Present or accounted for until wounded at Sharpsburg, Maryland, September 17, 1862. Died on September 18, 1862, of wounds. Place of death not reported.

BERRY, JOHN A., 1st Sergeant
Enlisted in Perquimans County on September 1, 1861. Mustered in as Private and was promoted to 1st Sergeant on May 1, 1862. Present or accounted for until wounded at Wilderness, Virginia, on or about May 5, 1864.

BILLUPS, JOSEPH R., Private
Enlisted in Perquimans County at age 16, May 1, 1862, for the war. Present or accounted for until wounded in the left ankle and captured at Sharpsburg, Maryland, September 17, 1862. Hospitalized at Frederick, Maryland. Paroled and transferred to Aiken's Landing, James River, Virginia, where he was received October 22, 1862, for exchange. Declared exchanged at Aiken's Landing on November 10, 1862. Reported absent wounded or absent on detail through February, 1865.

BILLUPS, ROBERT L., Private
Resided in Perquimans County where he enlisted on May 16, 1861. Present or accounted for until wounded in the side and captured at Sharpsburg, Maryland, September 17, 1862. Hospitalized at Frederick, Maryland. Paroled and transferred to Aiken's Landing, James River, Virginia, where he was received October 22, 1862, for exchange. Declared exchanged at Aiken's Landing on November 10, 1862. Present or accounted for until captured at Bristoe Station, Virginia, October 14, 1863. Confined at Old Capitol Prison, Washington, D.C., until transferred to Point Lookout, Maryland, October 27, 1863. Paroled at Point Lookout and transferred to Cox's Wharf, James River, Virginia, where he was received October 15, 1864, for exchange. Company records do not indicate whether he returned to duty; however, he was paroled in "eastern Virginia" on April 30, 1865.

BOYCE, JOHN A., Private
Enlisted in Perquimans County on July 1, 1861. Present or accounted for until captured at New Bern on March 14, 1862. Confined at Fort Columbus, New York Harbor. Paroled and transferred to Aiken's Landing, James River, Virginia, where he was received on July 12, 1862, for exchange. Declared exchanged at Aiken's Landing on August 5, 1862. Returned to duty prior to September 1, 1862. Present or accounted for until captured at Bristoe Station, Virginia, October 14, 1863. Confined at Old Capitol Prison, Washington, D.C., until transferred to Point Lookout, Maryland, October 27, 1863. Arrived at Point Lookout on October 28, 1863. Paroled at Point Lookout and transferred to Aiken's Landing on February 24, 1865, for exchange. No further records.

BOYCE, WILLIAM, Private
Born in Perquimans County and was by occupation a farmer prior to enlisting in Perquimans County on May 16, 1861. Present or accounted for until discharged on July 16, 1862, by reason of being overage. Discharge certificate gives his age as 35.

BRASWELL, CHURCHWELL, Private
Enlisted in Wake County on May 30, 1864, for the war. Present or accounted for through December, 1864.

BUNDY, JESSE, Private
Enlisted in Perquimans County on May 16, 1861. Present or accounted for until wounded at Sharpsburg, Maryland, September 17, 1862. Returned to duty on an unspecified date. Wounded at Wilderness, Virginia, on or about May 5, 1864. Company records do not indicate whether he returned to duty; however, he was reported "sick at hospital" from October 25, 1864, through December, 1864. No further records.

BUNDY, MORDECAI, Private
Enlisted in Perquimans County on September 1, 1861. Present or accounted for until wounded in the "bowels" at Bristoe Station, Virginia, October 14, 1863. Hospitalized at Richmond, Virginia, where he died on November 4, 1863, of wounds.

BURGESS, JOSEPH J., Private
Born in Currituck County and was by occupation an artist prior to enlisting in Perquimans County on May 16, 1861. Present or accounted for until discharged on April 28, 1862, by reason of "left inguinal hernia." Discharge certificate gives his age as 30. Rejoined the company on an unspecified date (apparently subsequent to December 31, 1864) as a sutler. Surrendered at Appomattox Court House, Virginia, April 9, 1865.

BURNHAM, RICHARD A., Private
Enlisted in Perquimans County on May 16, 1861. Present or accounted for until he died at Goldsboro on April 1, 1862. Cause of death not reported.

BURROW, J., Private
Enlisted in Randolph County on December 3, 1863, for the war. Listed as a deserter and dropped from the rolls of the company prior to January 1, 1864.

BURROW, W., Private
Enlisted in Randolph County on December 3, 1863, for the war. Listed as a deserter and dropped from the rolls of the company prior to January 1, 1864.

BURTON, BARCELL, Private
Enlisted in Randolph County on December 3, 1863, for the war. Present or accounted for until he died while "on sick furlough" on December 3, 1864. Place and cause of death not reported.

CALVERT, WILLIAM, Private
Resided in Polk County and enlisted in Wake County on November 23, 1864, for the war. Present or accounted for until he deserted to the enemy on or about January 7, 1865. Confined at Washington, D.C., until released on or about January 11, 1865, after taking the Oath of Allegiance.

CARDEN, LEVI W., Private
Enlisted in Wake County on May 1, 1864, for the war. Captured near Hanover, Virginia, May 24, 1864. Confined at Point Lookout, Maryland, where he died on August 10, 1864. Cause of death not reported.

CHESHIRE, JAMES, Private
Enlisted in Wake County on November 23, 1864, for the war. Present or accounted for through December, 1864.

CRAVEN, B. YANCEY, Private
Enlisted in Randolph County on December 3, 1863, for the war. Present or accounted for until wounded at Wilderness, Virginia, on or about May 5, 1864. Returned to duty prior to November 1, 1864. Present or accounted for through December, 1864. Paroled at Greensboro on May 18, 1865.

CROSS, WILLIAM M., Private
Enlisted in Randolph County on December 3, 1863, for the war. Present or accounted for until wounded at Wilderness, Virginia, on or about May 5, 1864. Returned to duty prior to November 1, 1864. Deserted

on December 9, 1864.

CULP, WILLIAM E., Private
Resided in Cabarrus County and enlisted in Stanly County on March 1, 1863, for the war. Present or accounted for until transferred to Company A, 8th Regiment N.C. State Troops, May 1, 1863.

DAVIS, JAMES A., Private
Resided in Union County and enlisted in Wake County on May 30, 1864, for the war. Present or accounted for until he deserted to the enemy on or about January 7, 1865. Confined at Washington, D.C., until released on or about January 11, 1865, after taking the Oath of Allegiance.

DESHIELDS, LUTHER, Private
Enlisted at Coosawhatchie, South Carolina, February 28, 1863, for the war. Present or accounted for until he died at Hardeeville, South Carolina, April 16, 1863. Cause of death not reported.

DINKENS, BRYAN, Private
Enlisted in Wake County on May 20, 1863, for the war. Present or accounted for until wounded in the right knee at Bristoe Station, Virginia, October 14, 1863. Reported absent wounded through December, 1863. Detailed for hospital duty in January-February, 1864, and was reported absent on detail through December, 1864. Captured at Raleigh on April 13, 1865, and was paroled at Raleigh on April 22, 1865. [Medical records dated 1864 give his age as 43.]

DIXON, JAMES, Private
Enlisted in Wake County on November 23, 1864, for the war. Died at the "div[ision] hos[pital]" on December 2, 1864. Cause of death not reported.

ELLIOTT, AUGUSTUS, Private
Enlisted in Perquimans County on May 16, 1861. Present or accounted for through March 12, 1864. No further records.

ETHERIDGE, HENRY C., Private
Enlisted in Perquimans County on May 16, 1861. Present or accounted for until discharged on or about September 15, 1861, by reason of "sickness." Enlisted in Company K of this regiment on May 15, 1862.

FLEETWOOD, ELISHA, Private
Born in Perquimans County and was by occupation a farmer prior to enlisting in Perquimans County on September 1, 1861. Present or accounted for until discharged on July 16, 1862, by reason of being underage. Discharge certificate gives his age as 17.

FLEETWOOD, THOMAS J., Corporal
Enlisted in Perquimans County on September 1, 1861. Mustered in as Private. Present or accounted for until wounded in the breast and left arm at Wilderness, Virginia, on or about May 5, 1864. Promoted to Corporal subsequent to November 30, 1864. Reported absent wounded through December, 1864. Paroled at Greensboro subsequent to April 29, 1865.

FOSTER, FRANCIS A., Private
Enlisted in Perquimans County on May 16, 1861. Present or accounted for until wounded at Wilderness, Virginia, on or about May 5, 1864. Hospitalized at

Lynchburg, Virginia, where he died on May 24, 1864, of a gunshot wound.

GODFREY, HENRY C., Private
Born in Perquimans County and was by occupation a student prior to enlisting in Perquimans County on May 16, 1861. Present or accounted for until discharged on July 16, 1862, by reason of the expiration of his term of service. Discharge certificate gives his age as 17.

GOODMAN, THOMAS E., Sergeant
Enlisted in Perquimans County on May 16, 1861. Mustered in as Private and was promoted to Corporal on November 1, 1863. Present or accounted for until wounded in the left elbow at Wilderness, Virginia, on or about May 4, 1864. Returned to duty on an unspecified date. Promoted to Sergeant on September 1, 1864. Captured near Petersburg, Virginia, October 1, 1864. Confined at Point Lookout, Maryland, until paroled and transferred to Boulware's Wharf, James River, Virginia, where he was received January 21, 1865, for exchange.

GOODWIN, THOMAS J., Sergeant
Born in Perquimans County where he enlisted on May 16, 1861. Mustered in as Private and was promoted to Sergeant on February 12, 1862. Present or accounted for until he died in camp near Petersburg, Virginia, August 4, 1862. Cause of death not reported.

GRIFFIN, WILLIAM F., Private
Born in Perquimans County where he enlisted on May 16, 1861. Present or accounted for until wounded at Sharpsburg, Maryland, September 17, 1862. Hospitalized at Mount Jackson, Virginia, where he died on November 2, 1862, of wounds and "pneumonia."

HAITHCOCK, JESSE, Private
Enlisted in Stanly County on March 1, 1863, for the war. Present or accounted for until he deserted on December 9, 1864. Paroled at Albemarle on May 19, 1865.

HALL, JOHN A., Private
Enlisted in Randolph County on December 3, 1863, for the war. Present or accounted for until wounded at Wilderness, Virginia, on or about May 5, 1864. Returned to duty prior to November 1, 1864. Present or accounted for through December, 1864. Paroled at Greensboro on May 15, 1865.

HATLEY, NOAH, Private
Enlisted in Wake County on February 3, 1864, for the war. Present or accounted for until wounded in the left arm on or about July 8, 1864. Reported absent wounded through December, 1864.

HENDRICKS, CALVIN, Private
Born in Perquimans County and was by occupation a farmer prior to enlisting in Perquimans County on May 16, 1861. Present or accounted for until discharged on July 16, 1862, by reason of being overage. Discharge certificate gives his age as 35. Reenlisted in the company on August 18, 1862. Wounded at Sharpsburg, Maryland, September 17, 1862. Returned to duty prior to May 1, 1863. Present or accounted for until captured at Bristoe Station, Virginia, October 14, 1863. Confined at Old Capitol Prison, Washington, D.C., until transferred to Point Lookout, Maryland, October 27,

1863. Paroled at Point Lookout and transferred to Aiken's Landing, James River, Virginia, February 24, 1865, for exchange.

HOBBS, ALEXANDER B., Private
Born in Perquimans County and was by occupation a farmer prior to enlisting in Perquimans County on May 16, 1861. Mustered in as Private. Promoted to 1st Sergeant on September 12, 1861, but was reduced to ranks on or about November 1, 1861. Present or accounted for until discharged on July 20, 1862, by reason of "pulmonary consumption." Discharge certificate gives his age as 23.

HOBBS, DAVID R., Sergeant
Enlisted in Perquimans County on May 16, 1861. Mustered in as Private and was promoted to Corporal on September 1, 1861. Present or accounted for until wounded in the head at or near Bristoe Station, Virginia, on or about October 14, 1863. Returned to duty and was promoted to Sergeant on or about November 1, 1863. Present or accounted for until wounded in both thighs at Wilderness, Virginia, May 5, 1864. Reported absent wounded through December, 1864.

HOLLOWELL, JOHN B., Private
Enlisted in Perquimans County on May 1, 1862, for the war. Present or accounted for until captured at Bristoe Station, Virginia, October 14, 1863. Confined at Old Capitol Prison, Washington, D.C., until transferred to Point Lookout, Maryland, October 27, 1863. Paroled at Point Lookout and transferred to Aiken's Landing, James River, Virginia, February 24, 1865, for exchange.

HUMPHRIES, ALFRED, Private
Enlisted in Perquimans County on September 1, 1861. Present or accounted for until wounded at Sharpsburg, Maryland, September 17, 1862. Reported absent without leave during March-April, 1863. Returned to duty prior to November 1, 1863. Present or accounted for until wounded on or about August 20, 1864. Reported absent wounded through December, 1864.

HUMPHRIES, THOMAS, Private
Enlisted in Perquimans County on September 1, 1861. Present or accounted for through February, 1862. No further records.

IVEY, NATHAN, Private
Enlisted in Perquimans County on May 16, 1861. Present or accounted for until discharged on December 23, 1861, by reason of disability.

JACKSON, WILLIAM L., Private
Born in Perquimans County and was by occupation a farmer prior to enlisting in Perquimans County on May 16, 1861. Present or accounted for until wounded at Fredericksburg, Virginia, December 13, 1862. Company records do not indicate whether he returned to duty; however, he deserted to the enemy prior to October 20, 1863, when he was received at Fort Monroe, Virginia. Released on October 27, 1863, apparently after taking the Oath of Allegiance. Records of the Federal Provost Marshal dated 1863 give his age as 28.

JONES, WILLIAM F., 1st Sergeant
Born in Perquimans County and was by occupation a

draftsman prior to enlisting in Perquimans County on May 16, 1861. Mustered in as 1st Sergeant. Present or accounted for until discharged on February 11, 1862, by reason of "promotion in the navy." Discharge certificate gives his age as 21.

JORDAN, EDWARD M., Corporal
Enlisted in Perquimans County on May 16, 1861. Mustered in as Private and was promoted to Corporal on July 1, 1861. Present or accounted for until transferred to Company C, 19th Regiment N.C. Troops (2nd Regiment N.C. Cavalry), August 12, 1861. Later served as 2nd Lieutenant of that unit.

JORDAN, JOHN P., Private
Enlisted in Perquimans County on May 16, 1861. Present or accounted for until transferred to Company C, 19th Regiment N.C. Troops (2nd Regiment N.C. Cavalry), August 12, 1861.

KEATON, JOSEPH, Private
Enlisted in Perquimans County on May 16, 1861. Present or accounted for until wounded at Sharpsburg, Maryland, September 17, 1862. Returned to duty prior to November 1, 1862. Present or accounted for through December, 1864.

KNIGHTS, JAMES, Private
Enlisted in Perquimans County on May 16, 1861. Present or accounted for until wounded and captured at Sharpsburg, Maryland, September 17, 1862. Confined at Fort Delaware, Delaware, where he died on November 20, 1862, of disease.

KNIGHTS, JOSHUA, Private
Enlisted in Perquimans County on May 16, 1861. Present or accounted for until killed at Bristoe Station, Virginia, October 14, 1863.

KNIGHTS, WILLIAM, Private
Born in Perquimans County where he enlisted on May 16, 1861. Present or accounted for until wounded in the leg and captured at Sharpsburg, Maryland, September 17, 1862. Confined at Fort McHenry, Maryland. Paroled and transferred to Aiken's Landing, James River, Virginia, October 22, 1862, for exchange. Declared exchanged at Aiken's Landing on November 10, 1862. Died in Perquimans County on January 1, 1863. Cause of death not reported.

LACY, GEORGE H., Private
Enlisted in Perquimans County on May 16, 1861. Present or accounted for until wounded at Spotsylvania Court House, Virginia, May 10, 1864. Returned to duty prior to November 1, 1864. Present or accounted for until paroled at Greensboro on May 1, 1865.

LANE, CHARLES A., Private
Enlisted in Perquimans County on May 16, 1861. Present or accounted for until September 17, 1863, when he was reported absent without leave. Listed as a deserter in November-December, 1863. Returned to duty prior to May 6, 1864, and was wounded at Wilderness, Virginia. No further records. [North Carolina pension records indicate he survived the war and was wounded at Sharpsburg, Maryland, on or about September 17, 1862.]

LANE, EDMUND, Private
Born in Perquimans County where he enlisted on May

16, 1861. Present or accounted for until wounded at Sharpsburg, Maryland, September 17, 1862. Died on or about September 19, 1862, of wounds. Place of death not reported.

LANE, ELIAS, Private
Enlisted in Perquimans County on May 16, 1861. Present or accounted for until killed at Bristoe Station, Virginia, October 14, 1863.

LANE, HENRY H., Private
Enlisted in Perquimans County on May 16, 1861. Present or accounted for until January-February, 1864, when he was reported absent without leave. [North Carolina pension records indicate he was wounded at Reams' Station, Virginia, in August, 1864.]

LANE, JOSHUA, Private
Enlisted in Perquimans County on May 16, 1861. Present or accounted for until wounded and captured at Sharpsburg, Maryland, September 17, 1862. Hospitalized at Frederick, Maryland, where he died on November 27, 1862, of wounds. Federal hospital records give his age as 22.

LANE, NEHEMIAH, Private
Enlisted in Perquimans County on May 16, 1861. Present or accounted for until wounded at Sharpsburg, Maryland, September 17, 1862. Died of wounds. Place and date of death not reported.

LANNING, ROBERT, Private
Enlisted in Wake County on May 1, 1864, for the war. Present or accounted for until he surrendered at Appomattox Court House, Virginia, April 9, 1865.

LAUGHLIN, SETH W. N., Private
Enlisted in Wake County on September 1, 1864, for the war. Company muster roll dated September-October, 1864, indicates he was a "Quaker and will not sign the pay rolls." Died in hospital at Richmond, Virginia, December 8, 1864. Cause of death not reported.

LEIGH, LEE W., Private
Enlisted in Wake County on May 10, 1864, for the war. Present or accounted for until paroled at Greensboro on May 1, 1865.

LEMMOND, W. T., Private
Previously served in Company F, 2nd Regiment N.C. Junior Reserves. Transferred to this company on September 2, 1864. Present or accounted for until paroled at Greensboro on May 1, 1865.

LONG, W. A., Private
Previously served in Company F, 2nd Regiment N.C. Junior Reserves. Transferred to this company on September 2, 1864. Present or accounted for until he died in hospital at Richmond, Virginia, October 31, 1864, of "diarrhoea chron[ic]."

MALLORY, WILLIAM S., 1st Sergeant
Born at Norfolk, Virginia, and resided in Perquimans County where he enlisted at age 15, May 16, 1861. Mustered in as Private. Present or accounted for until discharged on July 16, 1862, by reason of being underage. Reenlisted in the company on an unspecified date. Present or accounted for until wounded and

captured at Bristoe Station, Virginia, October 14, 1863. Confined at Old Capitol Prison, Washington, D.C., until transferred to Point Lookout, Maryland, October 27, 1863. Paroled at Point Lookout on May 3, 1864, and transferred to Aiken's Landing, James River, Virginia, where he was received May 8, 1864, for exchange. Returned to duty on an unspecified date and was promoted to 1st Sergeant on September 1, 1864. Present or accounted for until paroled at Greensboro on May 1, 1865.

MAY, JONATHAN, Private
Enlisted in Wake County on May 1, 1864, for the war. Captured at Spotsylvania Court House, Virginia, May 12, 1864. Confined at Point Lookout, Maryland, where he died on August 18, 1864. Cause of death not reported.

MILLER, JOHN, Private
Enlisted in Perquimans County on May 16, 1861. Present or accounted for until wounded at Wilderness, Virginia, on or about May 5, 1864. Company records do not indicate whether he returned to duty; however, he was issued clothing on July 25, 1864. No further records.

MISENHEIMER, WILLIAM A., Private
Born in Cabarrus County and was by occupation a farmer prior to enlisting in Stanly County on March 1, 1863, for the war. Present or accounted for until wounded in the right knee at Bristoe Station, Virginia, October 14, 1863. Reported absent wounded or absent on light duty until November-December, 1864, when he rejoined the company. Retired from service on March 21, 1865, by reason of disability from wounds received at Bristoe Station. Retirement papers give his age as 20. Paroled at Albemarle on May 19, 1865.

MOFFAT, DENNIS, Private
Resided in Randolph County where he enlisted on December 3, 1863, for the war. Deserted on December 12, 1863. Returned from desertion on September 20, 1864. Deserted to the enemy on or about October 1, 1864. Confined at Washington, D.C., until released on or about October 10, 1864, after taking the Oath of Allegiance.

MOORE, ANDREW, Private
Enlisted in Wake County on an unspecified date. First listed in the records of this company on December 7, 1864, when he was reported sick in hospital. No further records.

MULLEN, JAMES W., Sergeant
Born in Perquimans County and was by occupation a farmer prior to enlisting in Perquimans County on May 16, 1861. Mustered in as Sergeant and was promoted to 1st Sergeant on February 12, 1862. Reduced to the rank of Sergeant in May-June, 1862. Present or accounted for until discharged on July 16, 1862, by reason of being overage. Discharge certificate gives his age as 36.

MULLEN, JOSEPH, Corporal
Enlisted in Perquimans County on July 18, 1861. Mustered in as Private and was promoted to Corporal on September 18, 1862. Present or accounted for until paroled at Greensboro on April 29, 1865.

MUNDEN, THOMAS, Private
Enlisted in Perquimans County on September 1, 1861.

Present or accounted for until wounded at Bristoe Station, Virginia, October 14, 1863. Returned to duty in January-February, 1864. Present or accounted for through January 11, 1865.

MYERS, WILLIAM S., Corporal
Born in Perquimans County where he enlisted on May 16, 1861. Mustered in as Private and was promoted to Corporal on July 15, 1861. Present or accounted for until killed at Sharpsburg, Maryland, September 17, 1862.

NEWBY, GEORGE D., Corporal
Enlisted in Perquimans County on May 16, 1861. Mustered in as Private and was promoted to Corporal on November 16, 1861. Present or accounted for until discharged on or about August 18, 1862, after providing a substitute.

NICHOLSON, THOMAS, Private
Enlisted in Perquimans County on May 16, 1861. Present or accounted for until captured at Bristoe Station, Virginia, October 14, 1863. Confined at Old Capitol Prison, Washington, D.C., until transferred to Point Lookout, Maryland, October 27, 1863. Paroled at Point Lookout on May 3, 1864, and transferred to Aiken's Landing, James River, Virginia, where he was received May 8, 1864, for exchange. Reported absent on sick furlough through December, 1864.

NIXON, HENRY H., Private
Born in Perquimans County where he enlisted on July 1, 1861. Present or accounted for until he died in camp near Petersburg, Virginia, July 31, 1862. Cause of death not reported.

NIXON, JAMES R., Private
Born in Perquimans County and was by occupation a farmer prior to enlisting in Perquimans County on May 16, 1861. Present or accounted for until captured by the enemy in September-October, 1862. Confined at Baltimore, Maryland, and at Fort Monroe, Virginia. Paroled and transferred to Aiken's Landing, James River, Virginia, where he was received October 12, 1862, for exchange. Discharged on April 22, 1863, by reason of "chronic diarrhoea." Discharge certificate gives his age as 29.

NIXON, NATHAN W., Private
Enlisted in Perquimans County at age 20, July 1, 1861. Present or accounted for until discharged on October 5-6, 1861. Reason discharged not reported.

NIXON, THOMAS R., Private
Enlisted in Perquimans County on July 1, 1861. Present or accounted for until he was captured in September, 1862, after he was "found sick" near Buckeytown [Buckletown?], [West] Virginia. Paroled on or about September 26, 1862. Returned to duty prior to May 1, 1863. Present or accounted for until he died in hospital at Lynchburg, Virginia, January 3, 1864, of "diarrhoea chron[ic]."

OBERMAN, ISAIAH, Private
Enlisted in Perquimans County on May 16, 1861. Present or accounted for until wounded at Bristoe Station, Virginia, October 14, 1863. Returned to duty in January-February, 1864. Present or accounted for through December, 1864.

OWNLEY, WILLIAM F., Private
Enlisted in Perquimans County on May 16, 1861. Present or accounted for until he died in hospital at Petersburg, Virginia, February 23, 1863, of "effects of vaccination."

PARKER, JACOB HENRY, Corporal
Born in Perquimans County where he enlisted at age 19, August 20, 1862, for the war. Mustered in as Private and was promoted to Corporal subsequent to December 31, 1864. Present or accounted for until paroled at Greensboro on May 1, 1865.

PARKER, JAMES E., Private
Enlisted in Perquimans County on May 16, 1861. Present or accounted for through February, 1864. No further records.

PERRY, THOMAS J., Private
Enlisted in Perquimans County on May 16, 1861. Present or accounted for until wounded at Sharpsburg, Maryland, September 17, 1862. Company records indicate he was captured at Sharpsburg; however, records of the Federal Provost Marshal do not substantiate that report. No further records.

PHILLIPS, JOEL, Private
Enlisted in Wake County on September 15, 1864, for the war. Deserted on October 1, 1864. No further records.

PLYLER, DANIEL, Private
Enlisted in Stanly County on March 1, 1863, for the war. Present or accounted for until wounded in the left leg at Bristoe Station, Virginia, October 14, 1863. Reported absent wounded until August 19, 1864, when he was retired to the Invalid Corps.

POE, F. H., Private
Enlisted in Wake County on February 2, 1864, for the war. Present or accounted for until he died in hospital at Lynchburg, Virginia, June 18, 1864, of "febris typhoides."

PRICE, JOSEPH H., Private
Previously served in Company A, 8th Regiment N.C. State Troops. Transferred to this company on May 1, 1863. Killed at Wilderness, Virginia, on or about May 5, 1864.

REGAN, HENRY C., Private
Enlisted in Wake County on May 30, 1864, for the war. Present or accounted for until paroled at Greensboro on May 1, 1865.

RIDDICK, JOSEPH H., Private
Enlisted in Perquimans County on July 1, 1861. Present or accounted for until discharged on or about August 1, 1862, after providing a substitute.

RIDDICK, THOMAS, Private
Enlisted in Perquimans County on September 1, 1861. Present or accounted for until killed at Bristoe Station, Virginia, October 14, 1863.

RIDDICK, THOMAS T., Corporal
Enlisted in Perquimans County on May 16, 1861. Mustered in as Private and was promoted to Corporal on August 20, 1862. Present or accounted for until wounded in the left thigh and captured at Sharpsburg, Maryland, September 17, 1862. Confined at various Federal hospitals until confined at Fort McHenry, Maryland. Paroled at Fort McHenry and transferred to City Point, Virginia, where he was received May 2, 1863, for exchange. Reported absent wounded until January 28, 1864, when he was discharged by reason of disability.

RUSH, A. G., Private
Enlisted in Randolph County on December 3, 1863, for the war. Discharged on December 26, 1863, by reason of being a member of the Society of Friends.

SCAFF, WILLIAM E., Private
Enlisted in Perquimans County on July 1, 1861. Present or accounted for until captured at Petersburg, Virginia, October 1, 1864. Confined at Point Lookout, Maryland, until released on June 3, 1865, after taking the Oath of Allegiance.

SEXTON, SIMON, Private
Enlisted in Perquimans County on September 1, 1861. Present or accounted for until he died on June 21, 1864. Place and cause of death not reported.

SHARPE, D. P., Private
Enlisted in Wake County on April 13, 1864, for the war. Wounded at or near Wilderness, Virginia, on or about May 5, 1864. Reported absent wounded through December, 1864.

SKINNER, BENJAMIN F., Private
Enlisted in Perquimans County on May 16, 1861. Mustered in as Corporal and was promoted to Sergeant in November-December, 1861. Reduced to the rank of Corporal in January-February, 1862, and was reduced to ranks in March-April, 1862. Present or accounted for until paroled at Greensboro on May 1, 1865.

SKINNER, WILLIAM J., Private
Enlisted in Perquimans County on May 16, 1861. Never mustered into the company and was dropped from the rolls on or about January 1, 1862.

SMALL, CHARLES C., Private
Previously served in Company I, 17th Regiment N.C. Troops (1st Organization). Enlisted in this company on August 20, 1862, for the war. Present or accounted for until wounded in the "body" at Fredericksburg, Virginia, December 13, 1862. Returned to duty prior to May 1, 1863. Present or accounted for until captured at Bristoe Station, Virginia, October 14, 1863. Confined at Old Capitol Prison, Washington, D.C., until transferred to Point Lookout, Maryland, October 27, 1863. Paroled at Point Lookout and transferred to Aiken's Landing, James River, Virginia, February 24, 1865, for exchange. Paroled in "eastern Virginia" on April 25, 1865.

SMALL, GEORGE W., Private
Enlisted in Perquimans County on May 16, 1861. Mustered in as Musician (Drummer) but was reduced to ranks in March-April, 1862. Present or accounted for until killed in Virginia in June, 1864.

SMALL, ROBERT P., Private
Enlisted in Perquimans County at age 33, May 16, 1861. Present or accounted for until wounded in the chest and left arm at Sharpsburg, Maryland, September

17, 1862. Discharged on March 30, 1863. Reason discharged not reported.

STACY, JOSEPH, Private
Resided in Hertford County and enlisted on May 1, 1862, for the war. Present or accounted for until wounded in the left leg and captured at Sharpsburg, Maryland, September 17, 1862. Hospitalized at Frederick, Maryland, where he died on November 12, 1862, of "pneumonia." Death records give his age as 16.

STEPHENS, JOHN W., Private
Resided in Stokes County and enlisted in Wake County on November 23, 1864, for the war. Present or accounted for until he deserted to the enemy on or about January 7, 1865. Confined at Washington, D.C., until released on or about January 11, 1865, after taking the Oath of Allegiance.

STEVENSON, JOSEPH R., Private
Enlisted in Perquimans County on May 16, 1861. Present or accounted for through December, 1861. No further records.

STEVENSON, NATHAN, Private
Born in Perquimans County and was by occupation a farmer prior to enlisting in Perquimans County on May 16, 1861. Present or accounted for until discharged on April 28, 1862, by reason of "rheumatism." Discharge certificate give his age as 36.

SUMNER, WILLIAM T., Corporal
Born in Perquimans County where he enlisted on May 16, 1861. Mustered in as Private and was promoted to Corporal on August 5, 1862. Present or accounted for until killed at Bristoe Station, Virginia, October 14, 1863.

SUTTON, WILLIAM, Private
Enlisted in Wake County on November 1, 1863, for the war. Present or accounted for until wounded at or near Spotsylvania Court House, Virginia, May 10, 1864. Reported absent wounded through December, 1864.

SYLVESTER, JOSEPH, Private
Born in Perquimans County where he enlisted on May 16, 1861. Present or accounted for until he died at Winchester, Virginia, November 8, 1862. Cause of death not reported.

TRUEBLOOD, JOSHUA L., Private
Born in Pasquotank County and was by occupation a farmer prior to enlisting in Perquimans County on September 1, 1861. Present or accounted for until discharged on July 16, 1862, by reason of being underage. Discharge certificate gives his age as 17.

TURNER, JACOB, Private
Born in Perquimans County and was by occupation a farmer prior to enlisting in Perquimans County on May 16, 1861. Present or accounted for until discharged on July 16, 1862, by reason of being overage. Discharge certificate gives his age as 35.

TURNER, RICHARD HENRY, Private
Enlisted in Perquimans County on May 16, 1861. Present or accounted for until wounded and captured at Sharpsburg, Maryland, September 17, 1862. Paroled at Keedysville, Maryland, September 20, 1862. Reported

absent without leave through April, 1863. No further records.

WARD, LEMUEL, Private
Enlisted in Wake County on September 1, 1864, for the war. Present or accounted for until paroled at Greensboro on May 16, 1865.

WEEKS, THOMAS B., Sergeant
Enlisted in Perquimans County on May 16, 1861. Mustered in as Private and was promoted to Sergeant in November, 1862-April, 1863. Present or accounted for until wounded in the face at Fredericksburg, Virginia, December 13, 1862. Returned to duty prior to May 1, 1863. Present or accounted for until wounded at Wilderness, Virginia, on or about May 5, 1864. Hospitalized at Richmond, Virginia, where he died on May 12, 1864, of wounds.

WESTMORELAND, JOHN B., Private
Enlisted in Wake County on May 30, 1864, for the war. Present or accounted for until he died in hospital at Richmond, Virginia, October 7, 1864. Cause of death not reported.

WHITE, ANDERSON M., Private
Enlisted in Perquimans County on May 16, 1861. Present or accounted for until discharged on August 18, 1862. Reason discharged not reported.

WHITE, ANDERSON M., Private
Enlisted in Perquimans County at age 27, September 1, 1861. Present or accounted for until captured at Bristoe Station, Virginia, October 14, 1863. Confined at Old Capitol Prison, Washington, D.C., until transferred to Point Lookout, Maryland, October 27, 1863. Paroled at Point Lookout and transferred to Aiken's Landing, James River, Virginia, February 24, 1865, for exchange. [North Carolina pension records indicate he was wounded in both ankles at Petersburg, Virginia, in November, 1863.]

WHITE, CALEB, Sergeant
Born in Perquimans County where he enlisted on May 16, 1861. Mustered in as Private and was promoted to 1st Sergeant on November 1, 1861. Reduced to ranks prior to January 1, 1862, but was promoted to Corporal in March-April, 1862. Promoted to Sergeant on August 5, 1862. Present or accounted for until captured at Winton on May 31, 1863. Confined at Fort Monroe, Virginia. Paroled and transferred to City Point, Virginia, July 16, 1863, for exchange. Was reportedly transferred to Company D, 66th Regiment N.C. Troops, in November-December, 1863; however, records of that unit do not indicate that he served therein. No further records.

WHITE, ERIE, Private
Enlisted in Perquimans County on May 16, 1861. Present or accounted for until he died in hospital at Richmond, Virginia, January 19, 1864, of "pneumonia."

WHITE, HENRY E., Private
Enlisted in Perquimans County on August 1, 1862, for the war. Present or accounted for until wounded and captured at Sharpsburg, Maryland, September 17, 1862. Paroled at Keedysville, Maryland, September 20, 1862. Reported absent wounded or absent without leave

through April, 1863. No further records.

WHITE, ISAIAH, Private
Born in Chowan County and was by occupation a sailer prior to enlisting in Hertford County on May 16, 1861. Present or accounted for until discharged on July 16, 1862, by reason of being overage. Discharge certificate gives his age as 36.

WHITE, JOHN A., Private
Born in Perquimans County and was by occupation a farmer prior to enlisting in Perquimans County on September 1, 1861. Present or accounted for until captured at or near Sharpsburg, Maryland, on or about September 17, 1862. Confined at various Federal prisons until paroled and transferred to Aiken's Landing, James River, Virginia, October 27, 1862, for exchange. Declared exchanged at Aiken's Landing on November 10, 1862. Returned to duty prior to May 1, 1863. Present or accounted for until killed at Wilderness, Virginia, on or about May 5, 1864.

WHITE, JOHN W., Private
Enlisted in Perquimans County on May 1, 1864, for the war. Present or accounted for through December, 1864.

WHITE, JOSEPH H., Corporal
Enlisted in Perquimans County on May 16, 1861. Present or accounted for until captured at or near Sharpsburg, Maryland, on or about September 17, 1862. Confined at Fort McHenry, Maryland, and at Fort Monroe, Virginia. Paroled and transferred for exchange on October 27, 1862. Returned to duty prior to November 1, 1862. Present or accounted for until he died on September 17, 1864. Place and cause of death not reported.

WHITE, THEOPHILUS, Sergeant
Enlisted in Perquimans County on May 16, 1861. Mustered in as Private and was promoted to Sergeant on May 1, 1862. Present or accounted for until captured at Bristoe Station, Virginia, October 14, 1863. Confined at Old Capitol Prison, Washington, D.C., until transferred to Point Lookout, Maryland, October 27, 1863. Paroled at Point Lookout and transferred to Aiken's Landing, James River, Virginia, February 24, 1865, for exchange. Paroled at Greensboro on May 1, 1865.

WHITE, TIMOTHY, Private
Enlisted in Perquimans County at age 20, May 16, 1861. Present or accounted for until wounded in the left side at Sharpsburg, Maryland, September 17, 1862. Returned to duty prior to November 1, 1862. Present or accounted for until captured at Bristoe Station, Virginia, October 14, 1863. Confined at Old Capitol Prison, Washington, D.C., until transferred to Point Lookout, Maryland, October 27, 1863. Paroled at Point Lookout and transferred for exchange on or about October 30, 1864. Company records do not indicate whether he returned to duty; however, North Carolina pension records indicate that he survived the war.

WHITE, WILLIAM FRANK, Private
Enlisted in Perquimans County at age 21, May 16, 1861. Never mustered into service and was dropped from the rolls of the company on or about January 1, 1862. [North Carolina pension records indicate he was wounded in the arm at Camden Court House, North Carolina, in 1863.]

WILLIAMS, WILLIAM T., Private
Born in Perquimans County and was by occupation a farmer prior to enlisting in Perquimans County on May 16, 1861. Present or accounted for until discharged on July 16, 1862, by reason of being overage. Discharge certificate gives his age as 35.

WINSLOW, WILLIAM A., Private
Born in Perquimans County where he enlisted on June 1, 1861. Present or accounted for until he died in hospital at Kinston on May 28, 1862. Cause of death not reported.

WOOD, GEORGE H., Private
Born in Perquimans County and was by occupation a farmer prior to enlisting in Perquimans County on September 1, 1861. Present or accounted for until discharged on July 16, 1862, by reason of the expiration of his term of service. Discharge certificate gives his age as 17.

WOOD, JOSEPH R., Private
Born in Perquimans County and was by occupation a merchant prior to enlisting in Perquimans County on May 16, 1861. Present or accounted for until discharged on July 16, 1862. Reason discharged not reported. Discharge certificate gives his age as 28.

WOOLEY, JOEL, Private
Enlisted in Wake County on May 30, 1864, for the war. Present or accounted for until wounded at Reams' Station, Virginia, August 25, 1864. Returned to duty in November-December, 1864. Present or accounted for through December, 1864.

COMPANY G

This company, known as the "Orange Guards," was organized as a militia unit at Hillsborough, Orange County, on October 1, 1855. It was mustered into state service on June 22, 1861, and was later assigned to the 27th Regiment as Company G. After joining the regiment the company functioned as a part of the regiment, and its history for the war period is reported as a part of the regimental history.

The information contained in the following company roster was compiled principally from company muster rolls for June 22, 1861-October, 1862, and September, 1864-February, 1865. No company muster rolls were found for November, 1862-August, 1864, or for the period after February, 1865. Valuable information was obtained also from primary records such as the Roll of Honor, medical records, prisoner of war records, discharge certificates, and pension applications, and from secondary sources such as postwar rosters and histories, cemetery records, and records of the United Daughters of the Confederacy.

OFFICERS

CAPTAINS

JONES, PRIDE
Enlisted in Orange County. Elected Captain on or about April 20, 1861. Present or accounted for until he resigned on or about August 15, 1861.

WEBB, JOSEPH C.
Born in Greene County, Alabama, and resided in Orange County where he was by occupation a druggist prior to enlisting in Orange County at age 25. Appointed 1st Lieutenant on April 20, 1861, and was

elected Captain on August 17, 1861. Present or accounted for until promoted to Major on or about December 5, 1862, and transferred to the Field and Staff of this regiment. Later served as Lieutenant Colonel of this regiment.

WHITTED, JAMES Y.

Born in Orange County and was by occupation a tobacco manufacturer prior to enlisting at age 25. Appointed 3rd Lieutenant on or about April 20, 1861, and was elected 1st Lieutenant on August 17, 1861. Wounded in the right knee and captured at Sharpsburg, Maryland, September 17, 1862. Paroled and transferred to Aiken's Landing, James River, Virginia, where he was received November 5, 1862, for exchange. Declared exchanged at Aiken's Landing on November 10, 1862. Elected Captain on December 5, 1862. Resigned on April 7, 1863, by reason of disability from wounds received at Sharpsburg.

DICKSON, STEPHEN

Born in Orange County where he resided as a clerk prior to enlisting in Orange County at age 23, April 20, 1861. Mustered in as Private and was elected 2nd Lieutenant on or about July 5, 1861. Elected 1st Lieutenant on December 5, 1862, and was promoted to Captain on April 25, 1863. Wounded in the right lung at Bristoe Station, Virginia, October 14, 1863. Returned to duty on or about January 4, 1864. Reported absent sick during September-October, 1864. Retired to the Invalid Corps on November 2, 1864, by reason of disability from wounds received at Bristoe Station. Paroled at Greensboro on May 3, 1865.

GRAHAM, JAMES AUGUSTUS

Was by occupation a student prior to enlisting in Orange County at age 20, April 20, 1861. Mustered in as Corporal and was promoted to Sergeant on May 8, 1861. Promoted to Orderly Sergeant on July 19, 1861, and was elected 3rd Lieutenant on August 17, 1861. Elected 2nd Lieutenant on December 5, 1862, and was promoted to 1st Lieutenant on April 25, 1863. Wounded in the knee at Bristoe Station, Virginia, October 14, 1863. Returned to duty on an unspecified date. Wounded in the right thigh and/or left knee at Wilderness, Virginia, May 5, 1864. Returned to duty prior to November 1, 1864. Promoted to Captain on November 2, 1864. Present or accounted for until he surrendered at Appomattox Court House, Virginia, April 9, 1865.

LIEUTENANTS

GRAHAM, JOHN WASHINGTON, 2nd Lieutenant

Born in Orange County where he resided as a lawyer and college professor prior to enlisting at age 22. Appointed 2nd Lieutenant on April 20, 1861. Present or accounted for until he was appointed Aide-de-Camp to Brigadier General R. C. Gatlin on June 21, 1861, and transferred. Later served as Captain of Company D, 56th Regiment N.C. Troops.

PATTERSON, ROBERT D., 2nd Lieutenant

Born in Orange County where he resided as a farmer prior to enlisting at Fort Macon at age 29, June 18, 1861. Mustered in as Private. Wounded in the head at Fredericksburg, Virginia, December 13, 1862. Returned to duty on an unspecified date. Elected 3rd Lieutenant on April 30, 1863. Wounded in the abdomen at Bristoe

Station, Virginia, October 14, 1863. Returned to duty on March 17, 1864. Furloughed again on account of wounds on March 28, 1864. Reported absent wounded or absent sick through February, 1865; however, he was promoted to 2nd Lieutenant on September 8, 1864.

STRAYHORN, THOMAS J., 2nd Lieutenant

Born in Orange County where he resided as a merchant prior to enlisting in Orange County at age 30, April 20, 1861. Mustered in as Private and was promoted to 2nd Lieutenant on April 25, 1863. Wounded in the right shoulder at Reams' Station, Virginia, August 25, 1864. Hospitalized at Richmond, Virginia, where he died on September 7, 1864, of wounds.

NONCOMMISSIONED OFFICERS AND PRIVATES

ADAMS, MEREDITH, Corporal

Born in Orange County and was by occupation a shoemaker prior to enlisting in Orange County at age 29, December 11, 1862, for the war. Mustered in as Private. Wounded in the foot at or near Yellow Tavern, Virginia, on or about August 21, 1864. Returned to duty prior to November 1, 1864. Promoted to Corporal on January 1, 1865. Present or accounted for until he surrendered at Appomattox Court House, Virginia, April 9, 1865.

ANDERSON, JAMES B., Private

Previously served in Company G, 1st Regiment N.C. Junior Reserves. Transferred to this company on September 3, 1864. Died in hospital at Richmond, Virginia, September 27, 1864, of "pneumonia typh[oid]."

ANDERSON, WILLIAM W., Private

Born in Orange County and was by occupation a carpenter or farmer prior to enlisting in Orange County on April 20, 1861. Mustered in as Sergeant but was reduced to ranks "at his own request" on July 24, 1861. Present or accounted for until discharged on May 14, 1862, by reason of "an injury of the right knee." Place and date injured not reported. Discharge certificate gives his age as 22.

BENNETT, LORENZO L., Private

Born in Orange County and was by occupation a farmer prior to enlisting in Orange County at age 28, May 12, 1862, for the war. Present or accounted for until he died at Winchester, Virginia, October 21, 1862, of "typhoid pneumonia."

BLALOCK, CHESLEY H., Private

Born in Orange County and was by occupation a farmer prior to enlisting at Camp Holmes at age 30, July 17, 1862, for the war. Captured at Bristoe Station, Virginia, October 14, 1863. Confined at Old Capitol Prison, Washington, D.C., until transferred to Point Lookout, Maryland, October 27, 1863. Died at Point Lookout on or about August 1, 1864. Cause of death not reported.

BOGGS, JEHU F., Private

Born in Orange County and was by occupation a farmer prior to enlisting in Orange County at age 17, April 20, 1861. Hospitalized at Richmond, Virginia, May 13, 1864, with a gunshot wound. Place and date wounded not reported. Returned to duty on an unspecified date. Surrendered at Appomattox Court House, Virginia,

April 9, 1865.

BORLAND, WILLIAM G., Private
Born in Orange County and was by occupation a farmer prior to enlisting in Orange County at age 27, April 20, 1861. Present or accounted for until discharged on July 15, 1862, after providing Private John Mowatt as a substitute. Later served in Company K, 2nd Regiment N.C. Home Guards.

BROWN, ASA, Private
Born in Orange County and was by occupation a brickmason prior to enlisting in Orange County at age 23, March 3, 1862. Present or accounted for until he died in hospital at Richmond, Virginia, November 28, 1862, of "pneumonia."

BROWN, EVANS, Private
Born in Duplin or Orange County and was by occupation a farmer prior to enlisting in Orange County at age 42, August 19, 1863, for the war. Wounded in the right arm at Bristoe Station, Virginia, October 14, 1863. Right arm amputated. Reported absent wounded until March 22, 1865, when he was retired by reason of disability.

BROWN, WILSON, Private
Previously served in Company E, 31st Regiment N.C. Troops. Enlisted in this company in Orange County at age 49, May 26, 1863, for the war as a substitute for Private William Lipscomb. Present or accounted for until he surrendered at Appomattox Court House, Virginia, April 9, 1865.

BROWNING, JAMES M., Private
Born in Caswell County and was by occupation a farmer prior to enlisting at Fort Macon on June 18, 1861. Captured at Bristoe Station, Virginia, October 14, 1863. Confined at Old Capitol Prison, Washington, D.C., until transferred to Point Lookout, Maryland, October 27, 1863. Died at Point Lookout on January 11, 1864, of "chronic diarrhoea" and/or "pneumonia."

BURROUGHS, WILLIAM H. H., Corporal
Born in Orange County and was by occupation a farmer prior to enlisting at Fort Macon at age 19, June 18, 1861. Mustered in as Private and was promoted to Corporal on September 17, 1862. Promoted to Musician (Drummer) on November 1, 1863, and transferred to the regimental band.

CAIN, THOMAS R., Private
Resided in Orange County and enlisted at age 27, April 20, 1861. Appointed Assistant Commissary of Subsistence (Captain) of the 13th Regiment N.C. Troops (3rd Regiment N.C. Volunteers) and transferred to that unit on or about May 16, 1861.

CAMPBELL, WILLIAM H., Private
Born in Orange County where he enlisted at age 17, April 20, 1861. Mustered in as Private and was promoted to Color Bearer on July 1, 1862. Reduced to ranks on April 17, 1863. Killed at Bristoe Station, Virginia, October 14, 1863.

CAPE, WILLIAM T., Private
Born in Orange County and was by occupation a carpenter prior to enlisting at Fort Macon at age 21, May 7, 1861. Present or accounted for through February

27, 1865; however, he was reported absent on detail or absent sick during most of that period. Deserted to the enemy on February 28-March 1, 1865. Confined at Washington, D.C., until released on or about March 6, 1865, after taking the Oath of Allegiance. "He never smelt gunpowder."

CARMICHAEL, THOMAS C., Sergeant
Born in Orange County and was by occupation a clerk prior to enlisting in Orange County at age 20, April 20, 1861. Mustered in as Sergeant but was reduced to ranks on May 8, 1861. Promoted to Sergeant on February 1, 1862. Present or accounted for until wounded in the leg at Sharpsburg, Maryland, September 17, 1862. Died near Sharpsburg on September 19, 1862, of wounds.

CHEEK, ADOLPH W., Private
Enlisted on April 20, 1861. Discharged prior to September 1, 1861. Reason discharged not reported.

CHEEK, ROBERT H., Private
Born in Orange County and was by occupation a carpenter prior to enlisting at Fort Macon at age 21, May 7, 1861. Present or accounted for until August 1, 1862, when he was reported absent without leave. Returned to duty on or about January 1, 1863. Present or accounted for through February, 1865; however, he was reported absent sick during much of that period.

CLARK, FRED P., Private
Born in Orange County and was by occupation a farmer prior to enlisting at Fort Macon at age 18, June 18, 1861. Present or accounted for until wounded in the thigh at Sharpsburg, Maryland, September 17, 1862. Returned to duty on or about January 29, 1863. Wounded in the foot at Bristoe Station, Virginia, October 14, 1863. Returned to duty on December 9, 1863. Wounded in the arm near Petersburg, Virginia, June 15, 1864. Returned to duty on an unspecified date. Reported on detached duty at Graham from September 28, 1864, until March 4, 1865, when he rejoined the company. Paroled at Greensboro on May 27, 1865.

CLARK, JOHN K., Private
Born in Orange County and was by occupation a farmer prior to enlisting at Fort Macon at age 24, May 7, 1861. Wounded in the thigh at Bristoe Station, Virginia, October 14, 1863. Hospitalized at Richmond, Virginia, where he died on November 2, 1863, of wounds and "erysipelas."

COLLINS, SAMUEL, Musician
Born in Rockbridge County, Virginia, and resided in Orange County where he enlisted on April 20, 1861. Transferred to Company B, 1st Regiment N.C. State Troops, June 8, 1861.

COOLEY, CHARLES S., Private
Born in Orange County where he resided as a cabinetmaker prior to enlisting in Orange County at age 22, April 20, 1861. Present or accounted for until wounded in the arm at Sharpsburg, Maryland, September 17, 1862. Returned to duty on an unspecified date. Wounded in the hand at Bristoe Station, Virginia, October 14, 1863. Returned to duty on an unspecified date. Wounded at Wilderness, Virginia, on or about May 5, 1864. Returned to duty in July, 1864. Reported absent on detached duty from October 20, 1864, through February, 1865. Rejoined the company prior to

April 2, 1865, when he was captured near Petersburg, Virginia. Confined at Point Lookout, Maryland, until released on June 10, 1865, after taking the Oath of Allegiance.

COOLEY, JAMES LEONIDAS, Corporal
Born in Orange County where he resided as a harness maker prior to enlisting in Orange County at age 18, April 20, 1861. Mustered in as Private. Present or accounted for until captured at Sharpsburg, Maryland, September 17, 1862. Confined at Fort Delaware, Delaware. Paroled and transferred to Aiken's Landing, James River, Virginia, October 2, 1862, for exchange. Declared exchanged at Aiken's Landing on November 10, 1862. Returned to duty on January 3, 1863. Promoted to Corporal on September 1, 1864. Captured near Petersburg, Virginia, April 2, 1865. Confined at Point Lookout, Maryland, until released on June 24, 1865, after taking the Oath of Allegiance.

COOLEY, JOSEPH G. B., Private
Previously served in Company H, 24th Regiment N.C. Troops (14th Regiment N.C. Volunteers). Transferred to this company on January 5, 1865, in exchange for Private Lemuel K. Woodward. Present or accounted for until captured at or near Petersburg, Virginia, on or about April 3, 1865. Confined at Hart's Island, New York Harbor, until released on June 16, 1865, after taking the Oath of Allegiance.

COOLEY, THOMAS L., ———
Resided in Orange County and enlisted on April 20, 1861. Discharged or transferred prior to June 24, 1861, when he enlisted in Company B, 6th Regiment N.C. State Troops, with the rank of Sergeant. Later served as 1st Lieutenant of that unit.

COPLEY, GEORGE W., Private
Born in Orange County and was by occupation a grocer prior to enlisting at Fort Macon at age 16, June 1, 1861. Captured at Bristoe Station, Virginia, October 14, 1863. Confined at Old Capitol Prison, Washington, D.C., until transferred to Point Lookout, Maryland, October 27, 1863. Paroled at Point Lookout on February 18, 1865, and transferred to Boulware's Wharf, James River, Virginia, where he was received February 20-21, 1865, for exchange.

CRABTREE, PORTER, Private
Enlisted on April 20, 1861. Discharged prior to September 1, 1861. Reason discharged not reported. [May have served later in Company I, 57th Regiment N.C. Troops.]

CRABTREE, SAMUEL H., Private
Born in Orange County and was by occupation an overseer prior to enlisting at Camp Holmes at age 31, January 24, 1864, for the war. Wounded in the leg at Reams' Station, Virginia, August 25, 1864. Hospitalized at Richmond, Virginia, where he died on October 25, 1864, of wounds and "fever."

CRABTREE, WILLIAM A., Private
Born in Orange County and was by occupation a coach maker prior to enlisting in Orange County at age 25, April 20, 1861. Deserted to the enemy on or about March 1, 1865. Confined at Washington, D.C., until released on or about March 6, 1865, after taking the Oath of Allegiance.

CRABTREE, WILLIAM H., Private
Born in Orange County and was by occupation a farmer prior to enlisting in Orange County at age 18, March 25, 1864, for the war. Wounded in the hip at Wilderness, Virginia, May 5, 1864. Returned to duty on or about September 6, 1864. Present or accounted for until he deserted to the enemy on or about March 1, 1865. Confined at Washington, D.C., until released on or about March 6, 1865, after taking the Oath of Allegiance.

DAVIS, RODERICK C., Private
Born in Chatham County and was by occupation a clerk prior to enlisting at Fort Macon at age 22, June 18, 1861. Present or accounted for until discharged on July 13, 1862. Reason discharged not reported. Conscripted and was reassigned to this company on July 14, 1863. Killed at Wilderness, Virginia, May 5, 1864.

DELANEY, MARTIN, Private
Was by occupation a hostler prior to enlisting at Fort Macon at age 22, May 7, 1861. Wounded in the right arm at Wilderness, Virginia, May 5, 1864. Right arm amputated on May 15, 1864. Died in hospital at Lynchburg, Virginia, on or about May 29, 1864, of "pyaemia."

DICKSON, SAMUEL A., Private
Born in Orange County and was by occupation a clerk prior to enlisting in Orange County at age 22, April 20, 1861. Promoted to Musician on August 1, 1862, and transferred to the regimental band.

DICKSON, WILLIAM J., Private
Previously served in Company D, 2nd Regiment N.C. Junior Reserves. Enlisted in this company on May 26, 1864, for the war. Present or accounted for until wounded in the right arm at Hatcher's Run, Virginia, February 5, 1865. Hospitalized at Richmond, Virginia, until furloughed for thirty days on March 28, 1865.

DOROTHY, GEORGE M., Private
Born in Orange County and was by occupation a farmer prior to enlisting at Fort Macon at age 24, August 31, 1861. Wounded in the knee at Bristoe Station, Virginia, October 14, 1863. Returned to duty on an unspecified date. Wounded in the face at Wilderness, Virginia, May 5, 1864. Returned to duty on December 7, 1864. Present or accounted for until hospitalized at Charlotte on April 7, 1865, with a gunshot wound of the head. Returned to duty the next day. No further records.

DUNNEGAN, CHARLES LEWIS, Private
Born in Orange County where he resided as a farmer prior to enlisting in Orange County at age 18, September 24, 1863, for the war. Wounded in the shoulder at Wilderness, Virginia, May 5, 1864. Returned to duty on an unspecified date. Wounded in the left leg at Reams' Station, Virginia, August 25, 1864. Returned to duty on November 16, 1864. Present or accounted for until captured at or near Fort Stedman, Virginia, March 25, 1865. Confined at Point Lookout, Maryland, until released on June 26, 1865, after taking the Oath of Allegiance.

DUNNEGAN, LORENZO, Private
Enlisted in Orange County on May 16, 1862, for the war. Captured at Bristoe Station, Virginia, October 14,

1863. Confined at Old Capitol Prison, Washington, D.C., until transferred to Point Lookout, Maryland, October 27, 1863. Died at Point Lookout on November 5, 1863. Cause of death not reported.

DUNNEGAN, TIMOTHY C., Private
Born in Orange County and was by occupation a farmer prior to enlisting at Fort Macon at age 21, July 12, 1861. Present or accounted for until he died in hospital at Winchester, Virginia, October 27, 1862, of "typhoid fever."

DURHAM, ELISHA, Private
Born in Orange County and was by occupation a blacksmith prior to enlisting at Camp Holmes at age 38, October 19, 1864, for the war. Present or accounted for until captured near Petersburg, Virginia, on or about April 7, 1865. Confined at Point Lookout, Maryland, where he died on June 5, 1865. Cause of death not reported.

DUSKIN, G. M., Private
Enlisted on April 20, 1861. Discharged prior to September 1, 1861. Reason discharged not reported.

FAUCETT, ALBERT G., Private
Born in Orange County and was by occupation a carpenter prior to enlisting in Orange County on July 4, 1861. Present or accounted for until discharged on September 24, 1861. Reason discharged not reported. Later served as Captain of Company A, 66th Regiment N.C. Troops.

FAUCETT, ED STRUDWICK, Private
Born in Orange County and was by occupation a farmer prior to enlisting at Fort Macon at age 18, July 31, 1861. Wounded in the thigh at Bristoe Station, Virginia, October 14, 1863. Captured by the enemy at Bristoe Station the same date but was "left by them in their flight." Hospitalized at Richmond, Virginia. Returned to duty on January 24, 1864. Killed at or near Yellow Tavern, Virginia, on or about August 21, 1864.

FAUCETT, JAMES N., Private
Born at Memphis, Tennessee, and was by occupation a clerk prior to enlisting at Fort Macon at age 19, August 4, 1861. Present or accounted for until wounded in the leg at Sharpsburg, Maryland, September 17, 1862. Returned to duty on January 1, 1863. Captured at Bristoe Station, Virginia, October 14, 1863. Confined at Old Capitol Prison, Washington, D.C., until transferred to Point Lookout, Maryland, October 27, 1863. Paroled at Point Lookout on or about February 10, 1865, and transferred to Cox's Wharf, James River, Virginia, where he was received February 14-15, 1865, for exchange. Returned to duty on an unspecified date. Surrendered at Appomattox Court House, Virginia, April 9, 1865.

FAUCETT, THOMAS, Private
Born in Orange County and was by occupation a shoemaker prior to enlisting in Orange County at age 17, April 20, 1861. Transferred to "Captain J. W. Latt's Company, Wright's Battalion," May 29, 1863, in exchange for Private Albert J. Forrest.

FAUCETT, WILLIAM A., Private
Born in Orange County and was by occupation a farmer prior to enlisting at Fort Macon at age 22, June 18, 1861.

Present or accounted for until he surrendered at Appomattox Court House, Virginia, April 9, 1865.

FORBIS, HUGH RUFUS, Private
Resided in Guilford County and enlisted at Fort Macon at age 27, April 20, 1861. Present or accounted for until transferred to Company B of this regiment prior to September 1, 1861.

FORREST, ALBERT J., Private
Previously served in "Captain Latt's Company, Wright's Battalion." Transferred to this company on May 29, 1863, in exchange for Private Thomas Faucett. Wounded in the hand at Wilderness, Virginia, May 5, 1864. Returned to duty on or about July 1, 1864. Present or accounted for until captured near Petersburg, Virginia, April 2, 1865. Confined at Point Lookout, Maryland, until released on June 26, 1865, after taking the Oath of Allegiance.

FORREST, JAMES A., Private
Previously served in Mallett's North Carolina Battalion (Camp Guard). Transferred to this company on April 7, 1863. Captured at Bristoe Station, Virginia, October 14, 1863. Confined at Old Capitol Prison, Washington, D.C., until transferred to Point Lookout, Maryland, February 3, 1864. Paroled at Point Lookout and transferred to City Point, Virginia, April 27, 1864, for exchange. Hospitalized at Richmond, Virginia, where he died on May 1, 1864, of "ch[ronic] diarrhoea."

GATTIS, JAMES A., Private
Previously served in Mallett's North Carolina Battalion (Camp Guard). Transferred to this company on April 7, 1863. Killed at Bristoe Station, Virginia, October 14, 1863.

GATTIS, WILLIAM A., Private
Previously served as Corporal in Company D, 1st Regiment N.C. Infantry (6 months, 1861). Enlisted in this company in Orange County on February 8, 1863, for the war. Wounded in the thigh at Bristoe Station, Virginia, October 14, 1863. Returned to duty on an unspecified date. Wounded in the hip at Wilderness, Virginia, May 5, 1864. Returned to duty on an unspecified date. Wounded in the left hip at Reams' Station, Virginia, August 25, 1864. Reported absent wounded through February, 1865.

GORDON, DAVID THOMAS, Corporal
Born in Caswell or Orange County and was by occupation a brickmason prior to enlisting at Fort Macon at age 35, June 18, 1861. Mustered in as Private and was promoted to Corporal on February 10, 1862. Present or accounted for until discharged on July 16, 1862, by reason of being overage.

HALEY, JASPER I., Private
Born in Orange County and was by occupation a carpenter prior to enlisting at Fort Macon at age 18, June 18, 1861. Wounded in the hand at Bristoe Station, Virginia, October 14, 1863. Returned to duty on January 3, 1864. Present or accounted for through February, 1865; however, he was reported absent on detail during most of that period. Paroled at Greensboro on May 18, 1865.

HALL, THOMAS J., Sergeant
Born in Orange County where he resided as a farmer prior to enlisting at Fort Macon at age 17, May 14, 1861.

Mustered in as Private. Present or accounted for until wounded in the shoulder at Sharpsburg, Maryland, September 17, 1862. Promoted to Corporal on September 17, 1862, "for bravery and good conduct in battle of Sharpsburg." Returned to duty on an unspecified date. Captured at Bristoe Station, Virginia, October 14, 1863. Confined at Old Capitol Prison, Washington, D.C., until transferred to Point Lookout, Maryland, October 27, 1863. Promoted to Sergeant on August 6, 1864, while a prisoner of war. Paroled at Point Lookout on or about September 18, 1864, and transferred to Aiken's Landing, James River, Virginia, for exchange. Returned to duty on December 20, 1864. Captured at or near High Bridge, Virginia, on or about April 6, 1865. Confined at Newport News, Virginia, until released on or about June 26, 1865, after taking the Oath of Allegiance.

HALL, WILLIAM H., Private

Born in Orange County where he resided as a farmer prior to enlisting at Fort Macon at age 21, September 1, 1861. Died "at home" or at Petersburg, Virginia, July 28, 1864, of "consumption."

HAMLET, JOHN, Private

Enlisted on April 20, 1861. Discharged prior to September 1, 1861. Reason discharged not reported.

HANNER, JOHN ERWIN, Private

Born in Orange County and was by occupation a farmer prior to enlisting at Fort Macon at age 21, May 14, 1861. Wounded in the little finger of the left hand and captured at Bristoe Station, Virginia, October 14, 1863. Confined at Old Capitol Prison, Washington, D.C., until transferred to Point Lookout, Maryland, October 27, 1863. Paroled at Point Lookout on April 27, 1864, and transferred to City Point, Virginia, where he was received April 30, 1864, for exchange. Returned to duty on July 3, 1864. Wounded in the shoulder at Yellow Tavern, Virginia, August 21, 1864. Returned to duty prior to November 1, 1864. Present or accounted for until captured near Petersburg, Virginia, April 2, 1865. Confined at Point Lookout until released on June 3, 1865, after taking the Oath of Allegiance.

HANNER, SAMUEL F., Private

Born in Orange County and was by occupation a farmer prior to enlisting in Orange County at age 16, February 12, 1865, for the war. Killed "in skirmish line" near Hatcher's Run, Virginia, March 30, 1865.

HANNER, WILLIAM P., Private

Born in Orange County and was by occupation a farmer prior to enlisting in Orange County at age 18, November 24, 1862, for the war. Died in hospital at Danville, Virginia, February 19, 1863, of "variola."

HATCH, OLIN F., Sergeant

Born in Orange County and resided in Wake County where he was by occupation a carpenter prior to enlisting in Orange County at age 22, April 20, 1861. Mustered in as Private and was promoted to Corporal on July 19, 1861. Promoted to Sergeant on February 10, 1862. Wounded in the left leg at Wilderness, Virginia, May 5, 1864. Returned to duty in August, 1864. Present or accounted for until captured near Petersburg, Virginia, April 2, 1865. Confined at Point Lookout, Maryland, until released on June 27, 1865, after taking the Oath of Allegiance.

HAUGHTON, JOHN LAWRENCE, Private

Born in Chatham County where he resided as a planter prior to enlisting at Fort Macon at age 21, May 15, 1861. Left the company under unknown circumstances prior to October 7, 1861, when he was appointed 2nd Lieutenant of Company E, 41st Regiment N.C. Troops (3rd Regiment N.C. Cavalry).

HAYES, JAMES ALEXANDER, Private

Born in Orange County and was by occupation a shoemaker prior to enlisting in Orange County at age 19, April 20, 1861. Present or accounted for until wounded in the face and eye at Sharpsburg, Maryland, September 17, 1862. Reported absent wounded or absent on detail through February, 1863. Died in hospital at Goldsboro on or about March 5, 1863, of "pneumonia" and/or "erysipelas."

HAYES, JOHN SIDNEY, Corporal

Born at Knoxville, Tennessee, and resided in Orange County where he was by occupation a printer prior to enlisting in Orange County at age 20, April 20, 1861. Mustered in as Private and was promoted to Corporal on July 24, 1861. Present or accounted for until August 8, 1862, when he was reportedly transferred to Company E, 3rd Regiment Tennessee Volunteers. Records of the latter unit do not indicate that he served therein. No further records.

HAYES, WILLIAM A., Musician

Born in Orange County and was by occupation a clerk prior to enlisting in Orange County at age 18, December 11, 1862, for the war. Mustered in as Private. Reported absent on detail as an orderly from June 1, 1863, through October, 1864. Promoted to Musician on November 1, 1864. Present or accounted for until he surrendered at Appomattox Court House, Virginia, April 9, 1865. "Crossed Hatcher's Run below Burgess Mill, April 1, 1865, under heavy fire, and brought us the news of the break of the Confederate lines and the orders for retreat."

HEDGEPETH, ABRAHAM W., Private

Born in Orange County and was by occupation a harness maker prior to enlisting in Orange County at age 18, December 11, 1862, for the war. Wounded in the arm and abdomen at Gary's Farm, Virginia, June 15, 1864. Returned to duty on or about September 22, 1864. Present or accounted for until he surrendered at Appomattox Court House, Virginia, April 9, 1865.

HILL, JOHN T., Private

Born in Orange County and was by occupation a coach maker prior to enlisting in Orange County at age 23, April 20, 1861. Mustered in as Private and was promoted to Corporal on July 19, 1861. Promoted to Sergeant on August 17, 1861, but was reduced to ranks "at his own request" on February 10, 1862. Present or accounted for until wounded in the thigh near Hatcher's Run, Virginia, April 1, 1865. Captured near Hatcher's Run on April 2, 1865. Confined at Point Lookout, Maryland, until released on June 27, 1865, after taking the Oath of Allegiance.

HOLLOWAY, BENJAMIN F., Private

Born in Henrico County, Virginia, and was by occupation a blacksmith prior to enlisting in Orange County at age 30, April 20, 1861. Mustered in as Corporal but was reduced to ranks "at his own request" on July 24, 1861. Present or accounted for until discharged on June 30, 1862. Reason discharged not reported. Reenlisted in the company on October 20, 1864. Present or accounted for until killed at Hatcher's Run, Virginia, February 5, 1865.

HOLLOWAY, JOHN, Private
Born in Henrico County, Virginia, and resided in Orange County where he was by occupation a blacksmith prior to enlisting at Camp Holmes at age 38, October 19, 1864, for the war. Present or accounted for until wounded in the breast and captured at Sayler's Creek, Virginia, April 6, 1865. Confined at various Federal hospitals. Hospitalized at Washington, D.C., May 2, 1865. Released on June 14, 1865, after taking the Oath of Allegiance.

HOLLOWAY, SAMUEL T., Private
Born in Henrico County, Virginia, and was by occupation a blacksmith prior to enlisting in Orange County at age 26, April 20, 1861. Present or accounted for until discharged on June 30, 1862. Reason discharged not reported.

HOPKINS, WILLIAM J., Private
Born in Orange County and was by occupation a farmer prior to enlisting in Orange County at age 19, April 20, 1861. Present or accounted for until killed at Sharpsburg, Maryland, September 17, 1862.

HUGHES, JAMES H., Private
Previously served in Mallett's North Carolina Battalion (Camp Guard). Transferred to this company on April 7, 1863. Wounded near Petersburg, Virginia, June 15, 1864. Hospitalized at Richmond, Virginia, where he died on June 16, 1864, of wounds.

ISARD, JOHN, Private
Born in Orange County and was by occupation a shoemaker prior to enlisting in Orange County at age 36, March 3, 1862. Detailed as a shoemaker at Danville, Virginia, November 18, 1862. Rejoined the company on March 5, 1864. Discharged on March 12, 1864, by reason of disability. Paroled at Greensboro on May 15, 1865.

IVY, SIDNEY M., Private
Resided in Anderson District, South Carolina, and was by occupation a harness maker prior to enlisting in Orange County at age 21, April 20, 1861. Mustered in as Private and was promoted to Corporal on July 19, 1861. Promoted to Sergeant on July 24, 1861. Captured at Bristoe Station, Virginia, October 14, 1863. Confined at Old Capitol Prison, Washington, D.C., until transferred to Point Lookout, Maryland, October 27, 1863. Promoted to 1st Sergeant on August 6, 1864, while a prisoner of war. Paroled at Point Lookout on October 11, 1864, and transferred to Cox's Wharf, James River, Virginia, where he was received October 15, 1864, for exchange. Returned to duty on December 25, 1864. Captured near Town Creek, Virginia, February 20, 1865. Confined at Point Lookout on February 28, 1865. Reduced to ranks while a prisoner of war. Released at Point Lookout on June 28, 1865, after taking the Oath of Allegiance.

JACKSON, JACOB, Private
Born in Orange County and was by occupation a "daguerrean artist" prior to enlisting at Fort Macon at age 22, June 26, 1861. Present or accounted for until killed at Sharpsburg, Maryland, September 17, 1862.

JOHNSON, BENJAMIN J., Private
Born in Chatham County where he resided as a farmer prior to enlisting at Fort Macon at age 23, June 18, 1861. Captured near Petersburg, Virginia, April 2, 1865. Confined at Point Lookout, Maryland, until released on June 28, 1865, after taking the Oath of Allegiance.

JONES, JAMES E., Private
Enlisted on April 20, 1861. Discharged prior to September 1, 1861. Reason discharged not reported.

JOY, SIDNEY M., Private
Enlisted on April 20, 1861. Discharged prior to September 1, 1861. Reason discharged not reported.

KIRKLAND, ALEXANDER M., ———
Resided in Orange County and was by occupation a "gentleman" prior to enlisting on April 20, 1861. Left the company under unknown circumstances prior to May 20, 1861, when he was appointed 2nd Lieutenant of Company A, 6th Regiment N.C. State Troops.

KIRKLAND, JOHN Q., Jr., ———
Enlisted at age 24, April 15, 1861. Left the company under unknown circumstances prior to July 19, 1861, when he was appointed Assistant Quartermaster (Captain) of the 5th Regiment N.C. State Troops.

LACK, JOHN PIERRE, Private
Resided in Orange County where he enlisted at age 25, April 20, 1861. Present or accounted for until promoted to 1st Sergeant and transferred to Company D, 1st Regiment N.C. State Troops, on or about July 15, 1861. Later served as 3rd Lieutenant of that unit.

LATTA, WILLIAM G., Private
Born in Orange County and was by occupation a farmer prior to enlisting in Orange County at age 26, December 8, 1863, for the war. Died in hospital at Richmond, Virginia, May 15, 1864. Cause of death not reported.

LIPSCOMB, WILLIAM, Private
Born in Orange County and was by occupation a farmer prior to enlisting at Fort Macon at age 19, August 4, 1861. Present or accounted for until discharged on May 26, 1863, after providing Private Wilson Brown as a substitute.

LOCKHART, SAMUEL P., Private
Born in Orange County and was by occupation a farmer prior to enlisting in Orange County at age 18, May 4, 1862, for the war. Wounded at Bristoe Station, Virginia, October 14, 1863. Returned to duty on January 31, 1864. Killed at or near Yellow Tavern, Virginia, August 21, 1864.

LYNCH, L. GEORGE, ———
Enlisted on April 20, 1861. Left the company under unknown circumstances prior to September 1, 1861. Later served as Captain of an unspecified militia unit.

McCAULEY, HENRY C., Private
Born in Orange County and was by occupation a farmer prior to enlisting in Orange County at age 35, April 20, 1861. Present or accounted for until discharged on July 16, 1862, by reason of being overage.

McCAULEY, WILLIAM H., Private

Born in Orange County and was by occupation a farmer prior to enlisting in Orange County at age 17, April 20, 1861. Captured at Bristoe Station, Virginia, October 14, 1863. Confined at Old Capitol Prison, Washington, D.C., until transferred to Point Lookout, Maryland, October 27, 1863. Released at Point Lookout on February 15, 1864, after taking the Oath of Allegiance and joining the U.S. Army. Assigned to Company G, 1st Regiment U.S. Volunteer Infantry.

MARKHAM, SANDERS L., Private

Born in Orange County and was by occupation a farmer prior to enlisting in Orange County at age 19, April 28, 1862, for the war. Present or accounted for until he died in Orange County on or about December 15, 1862, of "typhoid fever."

MEBANE, CORNELIUS, Private

Born in Orange County and enlisted at age 21, April 21, 1861. Left the company under unknown circumstances prior to June 10, 1861, when he enlisted in Company F, 6th Regiment N.C. State Troops.

MEBANE, DAVID A., Private

Born in Orange County and was by occupation a farmer prior to enlisting at age 31, April 21, 1861. Left the company under unknown circumstances prior to June 10, 1861, when he enlisted in Company F, 6th Regiment N.C. State Troops.

MEBANE, THOMAS H., Private

Born in Orange County where he resided prior to enlisting at Camp Holmes at age 23, June 30, 1864, for the war. Wounded in the hand at or near Yellow Tavern, Virginia, August 21, 1864. Reported absent wounded until November 14, 1864, when he was detailed at the arsenal at Salisbury. Captured at Salisbury on April 12, 1865. Confined at Camp Chase, Ohio, May 2, 1865. Released on June 13, 1865, after taking the Oath of Allegiance.

MEBANE, WILLIAM A., Private

Enlisted at age 24, April 21, 1861. Discharged prior to June 2, 1861, when he enlisted in Company F, 6th Regiment N.C. State Troops. Later served as 2nd Lieutenant of that unit.

MERRITT, GEORGE W., Private

Previously served in Mallett's North Carolina Battalion (Camp Guard). Transferred to this company on April 7, 1863. Killed at Bristoe Station, Virginia, October 14, 1863.

MERRITT, JOSEPH, Jr., Private

Enlisted in Orange County on March 3, 1862. Present or accounted for through June, 1862. No further records.

MERRITT, JOSEPH J., Private

Born in Orange County and was by occupation a miller prior to enlisting at Camp Holmes at age 32, October 19, 1864, for the war. Present or accounted for until wounded in the hand near Hatcher's Run, Virginia, "in the night of March 31, 1865." Paroled at Greensboro on May 16, 1865.

MERRITT, LAFAYETTE, Private

Born in Chatham County and resided in Orange

County where he was by occupation a farmer prior to enlisting at Fort Macon at age 20, June 18, 1861. Present or accounted for until wounded in the stomach and captured at Sharpsburg, Maryland, September 17, 1862. Paroled on September 27, 1862. Reported absent wounded until April 18, 1863, when he returned to duty. Furloughed on May 12, 1863, by reason of disability from wounds. Returned to duty on February 2, 1864. Detailed for light duty at Hillsborough on April 4, 1864. Reported absent on detail through February, 1865.

MILES, GEORGE F., Private

Born in Orange County and was by occupation a blacksmith prior to enlisting at Fort Macon at age 19, May 15, 1861. Died in hospital at Richmond, Virginia, June 30, 1863, of "fever."

MILES, JAMES, Corporal

Born in Orange County and was by occupation a farmer prior to enlisting at Fort Macon at age 22, May 15, 1861. Mustered in as Private. Present or accounted for until wounded in the hip at Sharpsburg, Maryland, September 17, 1862. Returned to duty on an unspecified date. Promoted to Corporal on November 1, 1863. Wounded in the shoulder at Wilderness, Virginia, May 5, 1864. Hospitalized at Gordonsville, Virginia. Transferred to Charlottesville, Virginia, or Lynchburg, Virginia, May 9, 1864. Presumed dead and dropped from the rolls of the company on January 31, 1865, having not been heard from since May 9, 1864. No further records.

MILLER, SANDERS H., Private

Born in Orange County and was by occupation a farmer or carpenter prior to enlisting at Fort Macon at age 35, September 17, 1861. Present or accounted for until discharged on July 15, 1862, by reason of being overage.

MINOR, W. H., Private

Place and date of enlistment not reported. Listed in regimental records dated September, 1862. No further records.

MITCHELL, JAMES, Private

Previously served in Mallett's North Carolina Battalion (Camp Guard). Transferred to this company on April 7, 1863. Wounded in the breast near Spotsylvania Court House, Virginia, May 10, 1864. Returned to duty on October 12, 1864. Present or accounted for until he deserted to the enemy on or about March 18, 1865. Confined at Washington, D.C., until released on or about March 24, 1865, after taking the Oath of Allegiance.

MOWATT, JOHN, Private

Born in Kenderdenshire[?], Scotland, and was by occupation a shoemaker prior to enlisting in Orange County on July 15, 1862, for the war as a substitute for Private William G. Borland. Wounded at Bristoe Station, Virginia, October 14, 1863. Returned to duty on December 8, 1863. Detailed as regimental shoemaker on September 25, 1864. Reported absent on detail through February, 1865. Captured near Petersburg, Virginia, April 2, 1865. Confined at Point Lookout, Maryland, until released on June 3, 1865, after taking the Oath of Allegiance.

NASH, FREDERICK, Jr., Private

Born in Orange County and was by occupation a lawyer

prior to enlisting in Orange County at age 23, February 8, 1863, for the war. Appointed acting Inspector General of Kirkland's brigade on October 11, 1863, and transferred. Rejoined the company on February 3, 1864. Appointed Inspector General of Kirkland's brigade to rank from February 24, 1864, and transferred.

NASH, SAMUEL S., Private

Born in Orange County where he resided as a student prior to enlisting in Orange County at age 20, February 28, 1865, for the war. Captured at Hatcher's Run, Virginia, March 31, 1865. Confined at Point Lookout, Maryland, until released on June 15, 1865, after taking the Oath of Allegiance.

NELSON, SAMUEL L., Private

Born in Orange County and was by occupation a farmer prior to enlisting at Fort Macon at age 18, May 15, 1861. Present or accounted for until discharged on May 27, 1862, by reason of "chronic diarrhoea." Reenlisted in the company on February 8, 1863. Wounded in the right leg at Bristoe Station, Virginia, October 14, 1863. Returned to duty on December 20, 1864. Present or accounted for until he surrendered at Appomattox Court House, Virginia, April 9, 1865.

NEWMAN, WILLIAM HENRY, Corporal

Born in Orange County and was by occupation a brickmason prior to enlisting at Fort Macon at age 16, July 31, 1861. Mustered in as Private. Wounded in the face and leg at Bristoe Station, Virginia, October 14, 1863. Promoted to Corporal on November 1, 1863. Reported absent wounded until December 10, 1864, when he returned to duty. Retired to the Invalid Corps on December 15, 1864, by reason of disability from wounds.

NEWTON, WESLEY J., Private

Born in Virginia and was by occupation a shoemaker prior to enlisting at Camp Holmes at age 29, October 19, 1864, for the war. Present or accounted for until captured near Petersburg, Virginia, April 2, 1865. Confined at Point Lookout, Maryland, until released on June 6, 1865, after taking the Oath of Allegiance.

NICHOLS, STEVEN, Private

Enlisted on April 20, 1861. Discharged prior to September 1, 1861. Reason discharged not reported.

NORWOOD, ALVIS, Private

Born in Orange County where he enlisted on May 10, 1862, for the war. Killed in battle near Richmond, Virginia, June 15, 1864.

NUNN, WILLIAM H., Private

Born in Orange County and was by occupation a farmer prior to enlisting in Orange County at age 22, September 5, 1862, for the war. Wounded in the neck near Petersburg, Virginia, June 15, 1864. Returned to duty on November 8, 1864. Present or accounted for until he surrendered at Appomattox Court House, Virginia, April 9, 1865. [May have served previously in Company D, 1st Regiment N.C. Infantry (6 months, 1861).]

PARKS, CHARLES M., Private

Born in Orange County and was by occupation a clerk prior to enlisting in Orange County at age 19, April 20, 1861. Promoted to Hospital Steward on August 1, 1861,

and transferred to the Field and Staff of this regiment.

PARKS, DAVID C., Private

Born in Orange County and was by occupation a merchant prior to enlisting in Orange County at age 28, December 11, 1862, for the war. Present or accounted for until he surrendered at Appomattox Court House, Virginia, April 9, 1865.

PATTERSON, WILLIE T., Private

Born in Orange County and was by occupation a farmer prior to enlisting at Fort Macon at age 20, June 18, 1861. Present or accounted for until wounded in the leg and captured at Sharpsburg, Maryland, September 17, 1862. Leg amputated. Hospitalized at Frederick, Maryland. Paroled and transferred to City Point, Virginia, where he was received May 2, 1863, for exchange. Reported absent wounded until August, 1864, when he was retired from service.

PAUL, ALFRED N., Private

Born in Orange County and was by occupation a farmer prior to enlisting at Fort Macon at age 20, June 1, 1861. Present or accounted for until he died in hospital at Richmond, Virginia, January 12, 1863, of "pneumonia."

PAUL, DAVID C., Private

Previously served in Company D, 1st Regiment N.C. State Troops. Enlisted in this company in Orange County on April 2, 1863, for the war. Wounded in the right hip at Wilderness, Virginia, May 5, 1864. Returned to duty on July 28, 1864. Wounded in the hip at Reams' Station, Virginia, August 25, 1864. Returned to duty on January 10, 1865. Deserted to the enemy on or about March 1, 1865. Confined at Washington, D.C., until released on or about March 6, 1865, after taking the Oath of Allegiance.

PEARSON, WILLIAM FRANK, Private

Previously served in Mallett's North Carolina Battalion (Camp Guard). Transferred to this company on April 7, 1863. Killed at Bristoe Station, Virginia, October 14, 1863.

PICKETT, HENRY, Private

Previously served in Mallett's North Carolina Battalion (Camp Guard). Transferred to this company on April 7, 1863. Wounded in the arm and right leg at Bristoe Station, Virginia, October 14, 1863. Right leg amputated. Reported absent wounded until August 24, 1864, when he was retired from the service by reason of disability.

PILAND, PHILLIP A., Private

Born in Northampton County and was by occupation a shoemaker prior to enlisting in Orange County at age 27, May 16, 1862, for the war. Present or accounted for until he died in hospital at Petersburg, Virginia, on or about July 14, 1862, of "cerebro meningitis." [May have served previously in Company D, 1st Regiment N.C. Infantry (6 months, 1861).]

RAINEY, JOSIAH, Private

North Carolina pension records indicate that he served in this company.

RAY, T. MURPHY, Private

Born in Chatham County and was by occupation a

farmer prior to enlisting in Orange County at age 26, February 8, 1863, for the war. Wounded in the hand at Wilderness, Virginia, May 5, 1864. Returned to duty prior to November 1, 1864. Present or accounted for until he died "at home" on March 5, 1865, of "fever."

RAY, WILLIAM R., Private
Born in Orange County and was by occupation a farmer prior to enlisting in Orange County at age 44, August 19, 1863, for the war. Wounded in the arm and captured at Bristoe Station, Virginia, October 14, 1863. Confined at Old Capitol Prison, Washington, D.C., until transferred to Point Lookout, Maryland, October 27, 1863. Paroled at Point Lookout and transferred to Aiken's Landing, James River, Virginia, September 18, 1864. Hospitalized at Richmond, Virginia, where he died on September 24, 1864, of "dysenteria acute."

REESE, JOSEPH, Private
Enlisted on April 20, 1861. Discharged prior to September 1, 1861. Reason discharged not reported.

RICHARDS, HIRAM, Private
Born in Orange County where he enlisted on April 20, 1861. Discharged on December 2, 1861. Reason discharged not reported. Discharge certificate gives his age as 17.

RICHARDS, ROSCOE, Sergeant
Born in Orange County and was by occupation a brickmason prior to enlisting in Orange County at age 18, April 20, 1861. Mustered in as Private and was promoted to Corporal on July 15, 1862. Present or accounted for until wounded in the hand at Sharpsburg, Maryland, September 17, 1862. Returned to duty on an unspecified date. Wounded in the hand at Wilderness, Virginia, May 5, 1864. Returned to duty prior to May 10, 1864, when he was wounded in the arm near Spotsylvania Court House, Virginia. Promoted to Sergeant on August 6, 1864, and returned to duty on August 7, 1864. Present or accounted for until he surrendered at Appomattox Court House, Virginia, April 9, 1865.

ROBERTS, JOHN S., Corporal
Born in Orange County and was by occupation a farmer prior to enlisting in Orange County at age 19, April 20, 1861. Mustered in as Private. Wounded in the shoulder at Wilderness, Virginia, May 5, 1864. Returned to duty on an unspecified date. Promoted to Corporal on August 6, 1864. Killed at Reams' Station, Virginia, August 25, 1864.

ROBSON, MILTON B., Private
Born in Orange County and was by occupation a farmer prior to enlisting at Fort Macon at age 29, June 18, 1861. Killed at Fredericksburg, Virginia, December 13, 1862.

ROGERS, WILLIAM H., Private
Born in Orange County where he resided as a farmer prior to enlisting in Orange County at age 18, April 28, 1862, for the war. Captured at Hatcher's Run, Virginia, March 31, 1865. Confined at Point Lookout, Maryland, until released on June 17, 1865, after taking the Oath of Allegiance.

RUFFIN, THOMAS, Jr., ———
Resided in Alamance County and enlisted at age 36, April 20, 1861. Left the company under unknown

circumstances prior to May 8, 1861, when he was elected Captain of Company E, 13th Regiment N.C. Troops (3rd Regiment N.C. Volunteers).

SCARLETT, JOHN B., Private
Born in Orange County and was by occupation a brickmason prior to enlisting at Fort Macon at age 24, May 1, 1861. Mustered in as Private. Captured at Bristoe Station, Virginia, October 14, 1863. Confined at Old Capitol Prison, Washington, D.C., until transferred to Point Lookout, Maryland, October 27, 1863. Paroled and transferred for exchange on or about March 10, 1864. Returned to duty on May 10, 1864. Promoted to Corporal on August 6, 1864, and was promoted to Sergeant on November 15, 1864. Reduced to ranks subsequent to February 28, 1865.

SCARLETT, SAMUEL J., Private
Born in Orange County and was by occupation a carpenter prior to enlisting in Orange County at age 22, April 20, 1861. Present or accounted for until discharged on April 30, 1862, by reason of "the loss of his right eye." Place and date injured not reported. Reenlisted in the company on July 13, 1863. Wounded near Hatcher's Run, Virginia, March 31, 1865, and was captured near Petersburg, Virginia, April 2, 1865. Confined at Point Lookout, Maryland, until released on June 3, 1865, after taking the Oath of Allegiance.

SCARLETT, THOMAS J., Corporal
Enlisted on April 20, 1861. Promotion record not reported. Discharged prior to September 1, 1861. Reason discharged not reported.

SCOTT, JAMES, Private
Enlisted on April 20, 1861. Discharged prior to September 1, 1861. Reason discharged not reported.

SHARP, ELI, Private
Born in Orange County and was by occupation a farmer prior to enlisting at Camp Holmes at age 40, October 19, 1864, for the war. Present or accounted for until he surrendered at Appomattox Court House, Virginia, April 9, 1865.

SHIELDS, CHARLES J., Private
Born in Orange County and was by occupation a machinist prior to enlisting at Fort Macon at age 27, May 7, 1861. Captured at Bristoe Station, Virginia, October 14, 1863. Confined at Old Capitol Prison, Washington, D.C., until transferred to Point Lookout, Maryland, October 27, 1863. Paroled at Point Lookout and transferred to Aiken's Landing, James River, Virginia, September 18, 1864, for exchange. Hospitalized at Richmond, Virginia, where he died on September 24, 1864, of "diarrhoea chronica."

SHIELDS, JAMES S., Private
Born in Orange County and was by occupation a miller prior to enlisting at Fort Macon at age 30, May 7, 1861. Killed at Bristoe Station, Virginia, October 14, 1863.

SHIELDS, WILLIAM THOMAS, Private
Born in Orange County and was by occupation a manufacturer or farmer prior to enlisting in Orange County at age 22, May 12, 1862, for the war. Present or accounted for until wounded in the left hip and captured at Sharpsburg, Maryland, September 17, 1862. Paroled on September 30, 1862. Returned to duty on April 5,

1863. Present or accounted for through March 10, 1865; however, he was reported absent on light duty during much of that period. Retired to the Invalid Corps on March 11, 1865, by reason of disability from wounds received at Sharpsburg.

SIMMS, HUBBARD H., Private
Enlisted on April 21, 1861. Left the company under unknown circumstances prior to September 1, 1861.

SIMS, THOMAS E., Private
Born in Orange County and was by occupation a farmer prior to enlisting in Orange County at age 16, March 26, 1862. Wounded in the side near Petersburg, Virginia, June 15, 1864. Hospitalized at Richmond, Virginia, where he died on or about June 16, 1864, of wounds.

SKIPPER, SAMUEL, Private
Place and date of enlistment not reported. Deserted to the enemy on or about August 31, 1864. Confined at Washington, D.C., until released on or about September 1, 1864, after taking the Oath of Allegiance.

SMITH, ALEXANDER A., Private
Born in Orange County and was by occupation a farmer prior to enlisting at Camp Holmes at age 31, October 19, 1864, for the war. Present or accounted for until paroled at Greensboro on May 16, 1865.

SMITH, JOSEPH A., Private
Born in Orange County and was by occupation a farmer prior to enlisting in Orange County at age 42, February 24, 1864, for the war. Wounded in the shoulder at Wilderness, Virginia, May 5, 1864. Reported absent wounded or absent on detail until February 4, 1865, when he rejoined the company. Present or accounted for until he surrendered at Appomattox Court House, Virginia, April 9, 1865.

SNEED, JAMES M., Private
Born in Person County and was by occupation a farmer prior to enlisting in Orange County at age 22, March 7, 1862. Present or accounted for until wounded in the ankle at Sharpsburg, Maryland, September 17, 1862. Returned to duty on May 21, 1863, but was discharged on June 16, 1863, by reason of disability from wounds.

STRAIN, WILLIAM H. H., Private
Born in Orange County and was by occupation a farmer prior to enlisting at Fort Macon at age 19, June 18, 1861. Wounded in the face at Bristoe Station, Virginia, October 14, 1863. Reported absent wounded until January 20, 1864, when he was detailed for light duty at Hillsborough. Rejoined the company on March 30, 1864. Hospitalized at Richmond, Virginia, October 27, 1864, with an unspecified complaint. Captured in hospital at Richmond on April 3, 1865. Confined at Newport News, Virginia, April 23, 1865. Released at Newport News on June 30, 1865, after taking the Oath of Allegiance.

STRAYHORN, EGBERT H., Private
Born in Orange County and was by occupation a farmer prior to enlisting in Orange County at age 29, July 5, 1862, for the war. Wounded in the neck at Wilderness, Virginia, May 5, 1864. Hospitalized at Danville, Virginia, June 29, 1864, with chronic diarrhoea. Died in hospital at Danville on July 1, 1864, of ''convulsions.''

STRAYHORN, Q. GREEN, Private
Born in Orange County and was by occupation a farmer prior to enlisting in Orange County at age 26, February 8, 1863, for the war. Wounded in the shoulder near Petersburg, Virginia, June 15, 1864. Hospitalized at Richmond, Virginia, where he died on July 20, 1864, of wounds.

STRAYHORN, SIDNEY G., Private
Born in Orange County and was by occupation a farmer prior to enlisting at Fort Macon at age 27, June 18, 1861. Wounded in the ankle at Bristoe Station, Virginia, October 14, 1863. Returned to duty on January 18, 1864. Detailed as regimental Quartermaster Sergeant on May 20, 1864, and transferred to the Field and Staff. Reported absent on detail through February, 1865. Rejoined the company on an unspecified date. Surrendered at Appomattox Court House, Virginia, April 9, 1865.

STRUDWICK, WILLIAM, ———
Enlisted on April 20, 1861. Left the company under unknown circumstances prior to September 1, 1861.

SYKES, WILLIAM J., Private
Born in Alamance County* and was by occupation a farmer prior to enlisting in Orange County at age 17, August 15, 1863, for the war. Hospitalized at Petersburg, Virginia, June 20, 1864, with ''con[tinued] fever'' and ''pneumonia'' and died on July 7, 1864.

TERRY, WILLIAM L., Private
Born in Orange County and was by occupation a farmer prior to enlisting at Fort Macon at age 24, July 12, 1861. Present or accounted for until wounded at Sharpsburg, Maryland, September 17, 1862. Returned to duty on November 25, 1862. Died in hospital at Richmond, Virginia, January 3, 1863, of ''febris typhoides.''

THOMAS, JOHN, Private
Previously served in Mallett's North Carolina Battalion (Camp Guard). Transferred to this company on April 7, 1863. Died in hospital at Richmond, Virginia, April 26, 1864. Cause of death not reported.

THOMPSON, DAVID, Corporal
Born in Orange County and was by occupation a farmer prior to enlisting at Fort Macon at age 19, June 18, 1861. Mustered in as Private. Present or accounted for until wounded in the neck at Sharpsburg, Maryland, September 17, 1862. Returned to duty prior to November 1, 1862. Wounded at Bristoe Station, Virginia, October 14, 1863. Returned to duty on December 9, 1863. Promoted to Corporal on November 15, 1864. Present or accounted for until paroled at Greensboro on May 16, 1865.

THOMPSON, JOHN F., Private
Born in Orange County and was by occupation a farmer prior to enlisting in Orange County at age 21, April 20, 1861. Mustered in as Private and was promoted to Corporal on July 24, 1861. Promoted to Sergeant on September 17, 1862. Wounded in the arm at Fredericksburg, Virginia, December 13, 1862. Returned to duty on April 30, 1863. Reduced to ranks on August 1, 1864. Wounded in the head at Sutherland's Station, Virginia, April 2, 1865. Surrendered at Appomattox Court House, Virginia, April 9, 1865.

THOMPSON, WALTER A., Private

Born in Orange County and was by occupation a merchant prior to enlisting at Fort Macon at age 48, April 27, 1861. Present or accounted for until discharged on July 21, 1862, by reason of being overage.

THOMPSON, WILLIAM, Private

Born in Alamance County* and was by occupation a farmer prior to enlisting in Orange County at age 41, August 15, 1863, for the war. Wounded in the shoulder, leg, jaw, both arms, and left side at Bristoe Station, Virginia, October 14, 1863. Returned to duty on an unspecified date. Wounded in the head at Wilderness, Virginia, May 5, 1864. Returned to duty on September 24, 1864. Present or accounted for until he surrendered at Appomattox Court House, Virginia, April 9, 1865.

TURNER, JULIAN S., Private

Enlisted on April 20, 1861. Discharged prior to September 1, 1861. Reason discharged not reported.

WADDELL, GUION W., Private

Born in Orange County and was by occupation a farmer prior to enlisting at Camp Holmes at age 24, October 18, 1864, for the war. Present or accounted for until he surrendered at Appomattox Court House, Virginia, April 9, 1865.

WALKER, GEORGE A., Private

Born in Orange County where he resided as a farmer prior to enlisting in Orange County at age 20, March 3, 1862. Present or accounted for until wounded in the arm at Sharpsburg, Maryland, September 17, 1862. Returned to duty on March 4, 1863. Captured at Sutherland's Station, Virginia, on or about April 4, 1865. Confined at Point Lookout, Maryland, until released on June 21, 1865, after taking the Oath of Allegiance.

WARD, THOMAS F., Private

Previously served in Company G, 1st Regiment N.C. Junior Reserves. Transferred to this company on September 3, 1864. Present or accounted for until he surrendered at Appomattox Court House, Virginia, April 9, 1865.

WARREN, BEDFORD B., Private

Born in Orange County and was by occupation a farmer prior to enlisting at Fort Macon at age 20, June 1, 1861. Captured at Bristoe Station, Virginia, October 14, 1863. Confined at Old Capitol Prison, Washington, D.C., until transferred to Point Lookout, Maryland, October 27, 1863. Paroled at Point Lookout and transferred to Cox's Wharf, James River, Virginia, where he was received February 14-15, 1865, for exchange. Returned to duty on April 2, 1865, and was captured near Petersburg, Virginia, the same date. Confined at Point Lookout until released on June 3, 1865, after taking the Oath of Allegiance.

WATSON, CHARLES J., Private

Born in Orange County where he resided as a farmer prior to enlisting at Fort Macon at age 17, May 7, 1861. Captured at Bristoe Station, Virginia, October 14, 1863. Confined at Old Capitol Prison, Washington, D.C., until transferred to Point Lookout, Maryland, October 27, 1863. Paroled at Point Lookout on October 11, 1864, and transferred to Cox's Wharf, James River,

Virginia, where he was received October 15, 1864, for exchange. Returned to duty on January 7, 1865. Present or accounted for until captured near Petersburg, Virginia, April 2, 1865. Confined at Point Lookout until released on June 21, 1865, after taking the Oath of Allegiance.

WATSON, ORRIN A., Private

Born in Orange County and was by occupation a clerk prior to enlisting in Orange County at age 19, April 20, 1861. Present or accounted for until killed at Sharpsburg, Maryland, September 17, 1862.

WATSON, RICHARD B., Private

Born in Orange County and was by occupation a farmer prior to enlisting at Fort Macon at age 27, June 1, 1861. Present or accounted for until he died in hospital at Charlottesville, Virginia, November 17, 1862, of "typhoid pneumonia."

WATSON, WESLEY F., ———

Born in Orange County and was by occupation a carpenter. Place and date of enlistment not reported. Discharged on May 19, 1861. Reason discharged not reported. Later served in Company D, 1st Regiment N.C. State Troops.

WEAVER, WILEY, Private

Born in Granville County and was by occupation a farmer prior to enlisting in Orange County at age 42, September 4, 1863, for the war. Died in hospital at Gordonsville, Virginia, March 3, 1864, of "typhoid fever" and/or "pneumonia."

WEBB, JAMES, Private

Enlisted in Orange County on May 14, 1862, for the war. Transferred to Company K, 59th Regiment N.C. Troops (4th Regiment N.C. Cavalry), October 25, 1864, in exchange for Private Lemuel K. Woodward.

WEINAND, JOSEPH, Private

Born in Germany and enlisted in Orange County on April 20, 1861. Present or accounted for until captured at New Bern on March 14, 1862. Confined at Fort Columbus, New York Harbor. Paroled and transferred to Aiken's Landing, James River, Virginia, where he was received July 26, 1862. Declared exchanged at Aiken's Landing on August 5, 1862. Discharged on November 7, 1862, by reason of having "never acquired a domicile." Paroled at Danville, Virginia, June 28, 1865.

WHITTED, JEHU R., Private

Born in Orange County and was by occupation a farmer prior to enlisting in Orange County at age 20, May 4, 1862, for the war. Present or accounted for until wounded in the spine and left shoulder at Sharpsburg, Maryland, September 17, 1862. Returned to duty on May 29, 1863. Present or accounted for through November 30, 1864; however, he was reported absent on light duty during most of that period. Retired to the Invalid Corps on December 1, 1864, by reason of disability from wounds received at Sharpsburg. Paroled at Greensboro on May 2, 1865.

WHITTED, THOMAS BYRD, Private

Born in Orange County and was by occupation a clerk prior to enlisting in Orange County at age 23, April 20, 1861. Mustered in as Corporal and was promoted to

Sergeant on July 19, 1861. Present or accounted for until wounded at Sharpsburg, Maryland, September 17, 1862. Returned to duty prior to November 1, 1862. Wounded in the left eye at Wilderness, Virginia, May 5, 1864. Reported absent wounded until September 17, 1864, when he was detailed for light duty at Hillsborough. Reduced to ranks on November 15, 1864. Reported absent on detail through February, 1865. Paroled at Greensboro on May 15, 1865.

WILKERSON, URIAH M., Private
Born in Orange County and was by occupation a farmer prior to enlisting in Orange County at age 38, February 8, 1863, for the war. Captured at Bristoe Station, Virginia, October 14, 1863. Confined at Point Lookout, Maryland, where he died on or about January 17, 1864, of "chronic diarrhoea."

WILLIAMS, JAMES E., Private
Born in Orange County and was by occupation a grocer prior to enlisting in Orange County at age 22, April 20, 1861. Mustered in as Private and was promoted to Sergeant on July 19, 1861. Promoted to 1st Sergeant on August 17, 1861, but was reduced to ranks on August 2, 1864. Wounded in the head at Reams' Station, Virginia, August 25, 1864. Hospitalized at Petersburg, Virginia, where he died on September 3, 1864, of wounds.

WOLF, JOHN M., Musician
Was by occupation a carpenter prior to enlisting in Orange County at age 32, April 20, 1861. Promotion record not reported. Discharged on June 12, 1861, by reason of "ill health."

WOOD, JOHN F., Private
Born in Caswell County and was by occupation a farmer prior to enlisting at Fort Macon at age 21, June 10, 1861. Killed at Spotsylvania Court House, Virginia, May 10, 1864.

WOODS, GEORGE W., Private
Born in Orange County and was by occupation a farmer prior to enlisting in Orange County at age 20, February 24, 1862. Present or accounted for until wounded and captured at Sharpsburg, Maryland, September 17, 1862. Died at Sharpsburg on September 27, 1862, of wounds.

WOODS, HUGH P., Corporal
Born in Orange County and was by occupation a farmer prior to enlisting at Fort Macon at age 21, May 14, 1861. Mustered in as Private and was promoted to Corporal on August 17, 1861. Killed at Bristoe Station, Virginia, October 14, 1863.

WOODS, JOSEPH E., Private
Born in Orange County and was by occupation a farmer prior to enlisting at Fort Macon at age 18, July 12, 1861. Killed at Bristoe Station, Virginia, October 14, 1863.

WOODS, JOSEPH H., Private
Born in Orange County where he resided as a harness maker prior to enlisting at Fort Macon at age 27, July 4, 1861. Wounded in the left thigh at Bristoe Station, Virginia, October 14, 1863. Reported absent wounded until November 24, 1864, when he was detailed for light duty at Hillsborough. Reported absent on detail through February, 1865.

WOODS, SAMUEL KNOX, Private
Born in Orange County and was by occupation a farmer prior to enlisting in Orange County at age 17, November 24, 1862, for the war. Captured at Bristoe Station, Virginia, October 14, 1863. Confined at Old Capitol Prison, Washington, D.C., until transferred to Point Lookout, Maryland, October 27, 1863. Paroled at Point Lookout on November 1, 1864, and transferred to Venus Point, Savannah River, Georgia, where he was received November 15, 1864, for exchange. Returned to duty on February 12, 1865. Present or accounted for until he surrendered at Appomattox Court House, Virginia, April 9, 1865.

WOODS, WILLIAM DOKE, Private
Born in Orange County where he resided as a farmer prior to enlisting at Fort Macon at age 25, June 1, 1861. Wounded in the left hip and knee at Bristoe Station, Virginia, October 14, 1863. Returned to duty on February 27, 1864. Detailed as an ambulance driver on April 15, 1864, by reason of being unfit for field service. Returned to duty on October 20, 1864. Present or accounted for until he surrendered at Appomattox Court House, Virginia, April 9, 1865.

WOODWARD, LEMUEL K., Private
Previously served in Company K, 59th Regiment N.C. Troops (4th Regiment N.C. Cavalry). Transferred to this company on October 25, 1864, in exchange for Private James Webb. Present or accounted for until transferred to Company H, 24th Regiment N.C. Troops (14th Regiment N.C. Volunteers), January 5, 1865, in exchange for Private Joseph G. B. Cooley.

COMPANY H

This company, known as the "Pitt Volunteers," was raised in Pitt County. It was mustered in on June 1, 1861, and was later assigned to the 27th Regiment as Company H. After joining the regiment the company functioned as a part of the regiment, and its history for the war period is reported as a part of the regimental history.

The information contained in the following company roster was compiled principally from company muster rolls for June 1, 1861-October, 1862, and September, 1864-February, 1865. No company muster rolls were found for November, 1862-August, 1864, or for the period after February, 1865. Valuable information was obtained also from primary records such as the Roll of Honor, medical records, prisoner of war records, discharge certificates, and pension application, and from secondary sources such as postwar rosters and histories, cemetery records, and records of the United Daughters of the Confederacy.

OFFICERS

CAPTAINS

SINGLETARY, GEORGE BADGER
Resided in Pitt County. Elected Captain on August 20, 1861. Served as Lieutenant Colonel of Singletary's Battalion during June-September, 1861. [See the history of the 27th Regiment, page 1 above.] Elected Colonel of this regiment on September 28, 1861.

SINGLETARY, RICHARD W.
Resided in Pitt County where he enlisted. Elected 1st Lieutenant on April 26, 1861, and was elected Captain on or about September 28, 1861. Present or accounted

for until elected Lieutenant Colonel on March 18, 1862, and transferred to the Field and Staff of this regiment. Later served as Colonel of this regiment.

WILLIAMS, JOSEPH A.

Was by occupation a farmer prior to enlisting in Pitt County on April 20, 1861. Mustered in with an unspecified rank and was promoted to Sergeant on April 26, 1861. Promoted to 1st Sergeant on May 26, 1861, and was elected 1st Lieutenant on June 25, 1861. Elected Captain on March 18, 1862. Present or accounted for until wounded in the hip at Fredericksburg, Virginia, December 13, 1862. Returned to duty on an unspecified date. Hospitalized at Richmond, Virginia, October 19, 1863, with a gunshot wound of the abdomen. Place and date wounded not reported. Died on November 24, 1863. Place and cause of death not reported. Death records dated 1863 give his age as 24.

MANKER, JAMES F.

Resided in Pitt County where he enlisted on April 20, 1861. Mustered in as Private and was promoted to 1st Sergeant on September 26, 1861. Elected 3rd Lieutenant on February 3, 1862, and was elected 1st Lieutenant on or about April 22, 1862. Promoted to Captain on November 25, 1863. Killed at or near Globe Tavern, Virginia, on or about August 21, 1864.

PRICE, HENRY F.

Resided in Pitt County where he enlisted on April 20, 1861. Mustered in as Private and was elected 3rd Lieutenant on April 22, 1862. Present or accounted for until wounded at Sharpsburg, Maryland, September 17, 1862. Returned to duty on an unspecified date and was promoted to 2nd Lieutenant on November 18, 1862. Promoted to 1st Lieutenant on November 25, 1863, and was promoted to Captain on August 21, 1864. Wounded in the back at Reams' Station, Virginia, August 25, 1864. Returned to duty prior to November 1, 1864. Present or accounted for until he surrendered at Appomattox Court House, Virginia, April 9, 1865.

LIEUTENANTS

BERNARD, WILLIAM, 2nd Lieutenant

Elected 2nd Lieutenant on or about August 20, 1861. Resigned prior to January 1, 1862. Reason he resigned not reported.

COX, GUILFORD W., 3rd Lieutenant

Enlisted in Pitt County on April 20, 1861. Mustered in with an unspecified rank and was promoted to 1st Sergeant on April 26, 1861. Elected 3rd Lieutenant on May 26, 1861. Present or accounted for until appointed Captain of Company C, 13th Battalion N.C. Infantry, on or about January 28, 1862, and transferred to that unit.

GASKINS, CHARLES PERRY, 2nd Lieutenant

Enlisted in Pitt County at age 22, April 20, 1861. Mustered in with an unspecified rank and was promoted to Sergeant on May 4, 1861. Promoted to 1st Sergeant on June 25, 1861, and was elected 2nd Lieutenant on September 5, 1861. Resigned on April 4, 1863, by reason of "having been cited to appear before an examining board to stand an examination for the position I now hold." [North Carolina pension records indicate he was wounded at Fredericksburg, Virginia, in 1862. May

have served later as 1st Sergeant of Company F, 1st Battalion N.C. Local Defense Troops.]

JOHNSTON, JOHN H., 2nd Lieutenant

Resided in Pitt County where he enlisted on April 20, 1861. Mustered in as Private and was promoted to Corporal on April 26, 1861. Promoted to Sergeant on May 3, 1861, and was promoted to 1st Sergeant on February 19, 1862. Elected 2nd Lieutenant on March 18, 1862. Defeated for reelection when the regiment was reorganized in April, 1862. Later served as Sergeant Major of the 44th Regiment N.C. Troops.

O'HAGAN, CHARLES JAMES, 1st Lieutenant

Born in County Londonderry, Ireland, and resided in Pitt County where he was by occupation a physician prior to enlisting at age 40. Elected 1st Lieutenant on August 20, 1861. Appointed Assistant Surgeon of the 9th Regiment N.C. State Troops (1st Regiment N.C. Cavalry) on October 23, 1861, and transferred to that unit.

SINGLETARY, THOMAS C., 3rd Lieutenant

Resided in Pitt County where he enlisted. Elected 3rd Lieutenant on or about April 20, 1861. Present or accounted for until transferred to Company E of this regiment on or about June 19, 1861.

SMITH, RICHARD O., 1st Lieutenant

Resided in Pitt or Lenoir County and enlisted in Pitt County on April 20, 1861. Mustered in as Private and was promoted to Sergeant on February 19, 1862. Promoted to 1st Sergeant on March 18, 1862, and was appointed 3rd Lieutenant on November 25, 1863. Promoted to 2nd Lieutenant on April 30, 1864, and was promoted to 1st Lieutenant on August 21, 1864. Died on September 25, 1864. Place and cause of death not reported.

WHITLEY, SAMUEL A., 2nd Lieutenant

Resided in Pitt or Edgecombe County and enlisted in Pitt County on April 20, 1861. Mustered in as Private and was promoted to Corporal on May 26, 1861. Promoted to Sergeant on September 6, 1861, and was promoted to 1st Sergeant in November, 1862-October, 1863. Wounded in the right thigh at Bristoe Station, Virginia, October 14, 1863. Returned to duty on an unspecified date. Wounded at Wilderness, Virginia, on or about May 5, 1864. Returned to duty on an unspecified date. Elected 2nd Lieutenant on December 7, 1864. Present or accounted for until captured at Sayler's Creek, Virginia, April 6, 1865. Confined at Old Capitol Prison, Washington, D.C., until transferred to Johnson's Island, Ohio, April 21, 1865. Released on June 20, 1865, after taking the Oath of Allegiance.

NONCOMMISSIONED OFFICERS AND PRIVATES

ABRAMS, JOSEPH, Private

Enlisted in Pitt County on April 20, 1861. Present or accounted for until wounded at Sharpsburg, Maryland, September 17, 1862. Reported absent wounded through November, 1862. No further records.

ADAMS, DAVID C., Private

Enlisted in Pitt County on April 20, 1861. Present or accounted for until wounded at Sharpsburg, Maryland, September 17, 1862. Returned to duty on an unspecified date. Deserted on December 10, 1864.

ADAMS, EDWARD, Private

Enlisted in Pitt County on April 20, 1861. Present or accounted for until wounded at Sharpsburg, Maryland, September 17, 1862. Returned to duty on an unspecified date. Wounded in the left arm at Wilderness, Virginia, on or about May 5, 1864. Returned to duty prior to November 1, 1864. Deserted on December 10, 1864.

ADAMS, FOREMAN, Private

Enlisted in Pitt County on April 20, 1861. Present or accounted for until wounded at Sharpsburg, Maryland, September 17, 1862. Returned to duty on October 29, 1862. Deserted to the enemy on or about February 19, 1865. Confined at Washington, D.C., until released on or about February 21, 1865, after taking the Oath of Allegiance.

BARNHILL, A. J., Private

Resided in Pitt County and enlisted at Camp Holmes on November 8, 1864, for the war. Present or accounted for until captured at Farmville, Virginia, April 6, 1865. Confined at Newport News, Virginia, until released on June 27, 1865, after taking the Oath of Allegiance. [May have served previously in Company I, 40th Regiment N.C. Troops (3rd Regiment N.C. Artillery).]

BEVILL, ARCHIE, Private

Enlisted at Camp Holmes on November 8, 1864, for the war. Present or accounted for until he surrendered at Appomattox Court House, Virginia, April 9, 1865.

BRANCH, ALFRED, Private

Enlisted in Granville County on April 20, 1861. Captured at Bristoe Station, Virginia, October 14, 1863. Confined at Old Capitol Prison, Washington, D.C., until transferred to Point Lookout, Maryland, October 27, 1863. Paroled at Point Lookout and transferred to Cox's Wharf, James River, Virginia, where he was received February 14-15, 1865, for exchange.

BREWER, JAMES, Private

Resided in Pitt County and enlisted on April 20, 1861. Transferred to Company E of this regiment the same date.

BRILEY, IRVIN, Private

Enlisted in Craven County on July 1, 1861. Present or accounted for through February, 1865.

BRILEY, JAMES A., Musician

Resided in Pitt County where he enlisted on April 20, 1861. Mustered in as Musician. Transferred to the regimental band in November, 1862-October, 1864.

BRITTON, W. H., Private

Born in Pitt County and enlisted in Craven County on July 15, 1861. Present or accounted for until he died "at home" on December 29, 1862. Cause of death not reported.

BROOKS, JAMES F., Private

Enlisted in Pitt County on April 20, 1861. Wounded at Bristoe Station, Virginia, October 14, 1863. Reported absent wounded until December 15, 1864, when he was retired to the Invalid Corps by reason of disability.

BROOMS, MASON, Private

Born in Greene County and was by occupation a farmer prior to enlisting in Pitt County on April 20, 1861. Present or accounted for until discharged on July 16, 1862. Reason discharged not reported. Discharge certificate gives his age as 36.

BUCK, BENJAMIN A., Private

Enlisted in Pitt County on April 20, 1861. Present or accounted for until transferred to Company E of this regiment on June 19, 1861.

BUCK, JAMES H., Private

Born in Pitt County where he enlisted on April 20, 1861. Present or accounted for until he died at Camp Gatlin on December 27, 1861, of "pneumonia."

BULLOCK, WILEY, Private

Born in Pitt County and was by occupation a farmer prior to enlisting in Pitt County on April 20, 1861. Present or accounted for until discharged on July 16, 1862, by reason of being overage. Discharge certificate gives his age as 37.

BULLOCK, WILLIAM, Private

Enlisted in Pitt County on April 20, 1861. Captured at Hanover Junction, Virginia, May 24, 1864. Confined at Point Lookout, Maryland, where he died on August 7, 1864. Cause of death not reported.

BURNEY, JOHN H., Private

Born in Pitt County and was by occupation a farmer prior to enlisting in Wake County on August 15, 1861. Present or accounted for until discharged on August 4, 1862, by reason of "disability to perform the duties of a soldier." Discharge certificate gives his age as 26. Later served as Corporal in Company E, 1st Battalion N.C. Local Defense Troops.

BURNEY, WILLIAM C., Corporal

Enlisted in Pitt County on April 20, 1861. Mustered in as Private and was promoted to Corporal on May 26, 1861. Present or accounted for until he surrendered at Appomattox Court House, Virginia, April 9, 1865.

CANNON, JOHN C., Private

Enlisted on April 20, 1861. Present or accounted for until transferred to Company E of this regiment on June 19, 1861.

CHERRY, JOHN H., Sergeant

Enlisted in Pitt County at age 21, April 20, 1861. Mustered in as Private and was promoted to Sergeant in November, 1862-October, 1864. Present or accounted for through February, 1865.

CHERRY, W. L., Private

Enlisted in Pitt County on April 20, 1861. Present or accounted for until wounded at Sharpsburg, Maryland, September 17, 1862. Returned to duty on an unspecified date. Hospitalized at Richmond, Virginia, June 2, 1864, with a gunshot wound of the leg or left lung. Place and date wounded not reported. Died in hospital at Richmond on June 7, 1864, of wounds.

CLARK, JOHN, Private

Enlisted in Craven County on July 15, 1861. Present or accounted for until discharged on September 15, 1861. Reason discharged not reported.

CLARK, JOSEPH H., Private
Enlisted in Craven County on July 15, 1861. Wounded at Wilderness, Virginia, on or about May 5, 1864. Returned to duty prior to November 1, 1864. Present or accounted for through February, 1865.

COGGINS, MECAM M., Private
Enlisted in Craven County on July 15, 1861. Present or accounted for until wounded and captured at or near Sharpsburg, Maryland, on or about September 17, 1862. Confined at Fort Delaware, Delaware, and at Fort Monroe, Virginia. Exchanged on or about April 1, 1863. Returned to duty on an unspecified date. Killed at or near Petersburg, Virginia, October 1, 1864.

CONGLETON, HENRY R., Private
Previously served in Company C, 17th Regiment N.C. Troops (1st Organization). Transferred to this company on July 25, 1861. Present or accounted for until wounded and captured at or near Frederick, Maryland, on or about September 12, 1862. Hospitalized at Frederick until transferred to Fort Delaware, Delaware, on or about September 22, 1862. Paroled at Fort Delaware and transferred to Aiken's Landing, James River, Virginia, October 2, 1862, for exchange. Declared exchanged at Aiken's Landing on November 10, 1862. Returned to duty prior to December 13, 1862, when he was wounded in the arm at Fredericksburg, Virginia. Company records do not indicate whether he rejoined the company; however, he was reported on detail for hospital duty in September-October, 1864. Retired to the Invalid Corps on December 15, 1864.

CORBIT, REDDING, Private
Born in Pitt County where he enlisted on April 20, 1861. Present or accounted for until he died at Camp Gatlin on November 9 or November 29, 1861, of "pneumonia."

CORBITT, IVEY, Private
Enlisted in Pitt County on April 20, 1861. Wounded at Reams' Station, Virginia, August 25, 1864. Retired to the Invalid Corps on December 6, 1864. Paroled at Greensboro on May 1, 1865.

COX, HYRAM, Private
Enlisted in Pitt County on April 20, 1861. Present or accounted for until he died at Petersburg, Virginia, August 17, 1862. Cause of death not reported.

COX, JESSE A., Private
Born in Pitt County and was by occupation a farmer prior to enlisting in Pitt County on April 20, 1861. Present or accounted for until discharged on July 16, 1862, by reason of being overage. Discharge certificate gives his age as 37. Later served in Company E, 1st Battalion N.C. Local Defense Troops.

DAVENPORT, McG., Private
Enlisted in Pitt County on April 20, 1861. Captured at Bristoe Station, Virginia, October 14, 1863. Confined at Old Capitol Prison, Washington, D.C., until transferred to Point Lookout, Maryland, October 27, 1863. Paroled at Point Lookout and transferred to Aiken's Landing, James River, Virginia, February 24, 1865, for exchange.

DAVIS, JAMES H., Private
Resided in Guilford County and enlisted at Camp Holmes on November 8, 1864, for the war. Captured at Hatcher's Run, Virginia, April 2, 1865. Confined at

Hart's Island, New York Harbor, until released on June 18, 1865, after taking the Oath of Allegiance.

DEAL, HENRY, Private
Enlisted in Craven County on August 1, 1861. Present or accounted for until he deserted in June, 1862.

De LOACH, BENJAMIN, Private
Born in Pitt County and was by occupation a farmer prior to enlisting in Pitt County on April 20, 1861. Present or accounted for until he died in hospital at Richmond, Virginia, November 30, 1862, of "typhoid fever."

DELOACH, JESSE R., Private
Born in Pitt County where he enlisted on April 20, 1861. Died on October 14, 1863. Place and cause of death not reported. Death records give his age as 26.

De LOACH, PEYTON, Private
Enlisted in Pitt County on April 20, 1861. Present or accounted for until he died in hospital at Huguenot Springs, Virginia, December 13, 1862. Cause of death not reported.

DUPREE, R. W., 1st Sergeant
Enlisted in Pitt County on April 20, 1861. Mustered in as Private and was promoted to Sergeant on September 6, 1861. Promoted to 1st Sergeant on February 3, 1862. Present or accounted for until promoted to Sergeant Major on February 19, 1862, and transferred to the Field and Staff of this regiment.

EDWARDS, W. N., Private
Enlisted in Pitt County on April 20, 1861. Wounded at Wilderness, Virginia, on or about May 5, 1864. Hospitalized at Gordonsville, Virginia, where he died on May 22, 1864, of wounds.

ERNUL, McGREIGER, ———
Enlisted on April 20, 1861. Transferred to Company E of this regiment prior to June 19, 1861. Later served as 1st Lieutenant of Company E.

EVANS, GUSTAVIUS, Private
Enlisted in Pitt County on April 20, 1861. Mustered in as Private and was promoted to Corporal on July 15, 1861. Reduced to ranks in January-February, 1862. Present or accounted for until wounded at Sharpsburg, Maryland, September 17, 1862. Returned to duty on an unspecified date. Wounded at Wilderness, Virginia, on or about May 5, 1864. Returned to duty prior to November 1, 1864. Present or accounted for until he surrendered at Appomattox Court House, Virginia, April 9, 1865.

EWELL, JAMES J., Private
Born in Pitt County and was by occupation a farmer prior to enlisting in Pitt County on April 20, 1861. Present or accounted for until discharged on July 16, 1862, by reason of being overage. Discharge certificate gives his age as 36. Later served in Company E, 1st Battalion N.C. Local Defense troops.

FLEMING, LEONIDAS, Private
Resided in Pitt County and enlisted at Camp Holmes at age 19, January 23, 1865, for the war. Present or accounted for until captured at Farmville, Virginia, April 6, 1865. Confined at Newport News, Virginia,

until released on June 27, 1865, after taking the Oath of Allegiance.

FLEMING, PETER, Corporal

Enlisted in Pitt County on April 20, 1861. Mustered in as Private and was promoted to Corporal in January-February, 1862. Present or accounted for until wounded at Sharpsburg, Maryland, September 17, 1862. Returned to duty on an unspecified date. Wounded in the thigh in Virginia in June, 1864. Hospitalized at Richmond, Virginia, where he died on July 12, 1864. Cause of death not reported.

FLEMING, ROBERT R., Corporal

Enlisted in Pitt County on April 20, 1861. Mustered in as Private. Present or accounted for until wounded in the left forearm at Sharpsburg, Maryland, September 17, 1862. Returned to duty on an unspecified date. Promoted to Corporal in November-December, 1864. Surrendered at Appomattox Court House, Virginia, April 9, 1865.

FOUST, EMANUEL C., Private

Resided in Guilford County and enlisted at Camp Holmes on April 8, 1864, for the war. Present or accounted for until he deserted to the enemy on or about February 6, 1865. Confined at Washington, D.C., until released on or about February 13, 1865, after taking the Oath of Allegiance.

GARRIS, WILLIAM BRYANT, Private

Enlisted in Pitt County on April 20, 1861. Wounded at Wilderness, Virginia, May 5, 1864. Reported absent wounded through February, 1865.

GRIFFIN, JOHN A., Private

Enlisted in Pitt County at age 20, April 27, 1861. Present or accounted for until captured at New Bern on March 14, 1862. Confined at Fort Columbus, New York Harbor. Exchanged on an unspecified date. Returned to duty in July-August, 1862. Captured at Bristoe Station, Virginia, October 14, 1863. Confined at Old Capitol Prison, Washington, D.C., until transferred to Point Lookout, Maryland, October 27, 1863. Paroled at Point Lookout and transferred to Aiken's Landing, James River, Virginia, February 24, 1865, for exchange. Reported in hospital at Richmond, Virginia, March 3, 1865. [North Carolina pension records indicate that he survived the war.]

GRIMMER, RUFUS R., Private

Enlisted in Pitt County on April 20, 1861. Present or accounted for until transferred to Company E of this regiment on June 19, 1861.

GRIMSLEY, FRANK, Private

Born in Greene County and enlisted in Pitt County on April 20, 1861. Present or accounted for until transferred to Company E of this regiment on June 19, 1861.

GRIMSLEY, WYATT, Private

Enlisted in Pitt County on April 20, 1861. Present or accounted for until transferred to Company E of this regiment on June 19, 1861.

HADDOCK, BURTON A., Private

Enlisted in Pitt County on April 20, 1861. Deserted on or about April 1, 1864.

HADDOCK, HENRY C., Private

Enlisted in Pitt County on April 20, 1861. Present or accounted for until transferred to Company E of this regiment on June 19, 1861.

HADDOCK, JOHN, Private

Enlisted in Pitt County on April 20, 1861. Present or accounted for until transferred to Company E of this regiment on June 19, 1861.

HARDEE, JOHN B., Private

Enlisted in Pitt County on April 20, 1861. Present or accounted for until discharged on October 1, 1861. Reason discharged not reported.

HARDEE, JOSEPH J., Private

Born in Pitt County where he enlisted on April 20, 1861. Present or accounted for until wounded at or near Sharpsburg, Maryland, on or about September 17, 1862. Confined at Fort McHenry, Maryland, and at Fort Monroe, Virginia. Paroled and transferred to Aiken's Landing, James River, Virginia, where he was received October 25, 1862, for exchange. Declared exchanged at Aiken's Landing on November 10, 1862. Died "at home" on December 18, 1862. Cause of death not reported.

HARRINGTON, JOAB, Private

Born in Pitt County and was by occupation a farmer prior to enlisting in Pitt County on April 20, 1861. Present or accounted for until discharged on July 16, 1862, by reason of being overage. Discharge certificate gives his age as 35. Later served in Company E, 1st Battalion N.C. Local Defense Troops.

HARRIS, ASA, Private

Enlisted in Pitt County on April 20, 1861. Present or accounted for until transferred to Company E of this regiment on June 19, 1861.

HATHAWAY, NATHANIEL H., Private

Born in Pitt County and was by occupation a farmer prior to enlisting in Pitt County on April 20, 1861. Present or accounted for until discharged on July 16, 1862, by reason of being overage. Discharge certificate gives his age as 35. Later served as Sergeant in Company E, 1st Battalion N.C. Local Defense Troops.

HERRINGTON, FRANK, Private

Resided in Wayne County and enlisted in Pitt County at age 25, April 20, 1861. Present or accounted for until he deserted on May 31, 1862. Returned to duty prior to September 1, 1862. Wounded at Sharpsburg, Maryland, September 17, 1862. Returned to duty on an unspecified date. Wounded at Bristoe Station, Virginia, October 14, 1863. Died of wounds. Place and date of death not reported.

HERRINGTON, JAMES, Private

Resided in Pitt County and enlisted in Craven County on July 15, 1861. Present or accounted for until wounded at Sharpsburg, Maryland, September 17, 1862. Returned to duty on an unspecified date. Captured at or near Fort Stedman, Virginia, March 25, 1865. Confined at Point Lookout, Maryland, until released on June 27, 1865, after taking the Oath of Allegiance.

HERRINGTON, L. W., Private

Enlisted in Lenoir County on May 9, 1862, for the war.

Wounded at Bristoe Station, Virginia, October 14, 1863. Died of wounds the same date. Place of death not reported.

HIGHSMITH, THOMAS, Private
Born in Pitt County and was by occupation a farmer prior to enlisting in Pitt County on April 20, 1861. Present or accounted for until he died in hospital at Petersburg, Virginia, August 30, 1862, of "remittent fever." Death records give his age as 21.

HOBBS, J. H., Private
Born in Greene County and was by occupation a farmer prior to enlisting in Pitt County on April 20, 1861. Present or accounted for until discharged on July 17, 1862, by reason of "disability to perform the duties of a soldier." Discharge certificate gives his age as 28.

HOFF, W. A., Private
Enlisted in Craven County on May 1, 1861. Present or accounted for until he died on September 8, 1861. Place and cause of death not reported.

HOUSE, JOHN F., Sergeant
Born in Pitt County and was by occupation a farmer prior to enlisting in Pitt County on April 20, 1861. Mustered in as Private and was promoted to Sergeant on September 6, 1861. Present or accounted for until discharged on November 17, 1862, by reason of "disease of the aortic valves & consequent dropsy." Discharge certificate gives his age as 22.

HOUSE, M. J., Private
Born in Pitt County and was by occupation a farmer prior to enlisting in Pitt County on April 20, 1861. Present or accounted for until discharged on July 16, 1862, by reason of being underage. Discharge certificate gives his age as 17. [May have served later in Company E, 17th Regiment N.C. Troops (2nd Organization).]

HUMBER, WILLIAM H., Private
Enlisted at Petersburg, Virginia, July 5, 1864, for the war. Present or accounted for until he surrendered at Appomattox Court House, Virginia, April 9, 1865.

JAMES, CALVIN, Private
Enlisted in Pitt County on April 20, 1861. Present or accounted for until transferred to Company E of this regiment on June 19, 1861.

JAMES, JOSEPH W. G., Private
Enlisted in Pitt County on April 20, 1861. Present or accounted for until he died in Maryland on September 15, 1862. Cause of death not reported.

JAMES, MATTHEW A., Private
Enlisted in Lenoir County on May 3, 1862, for the war. Present or accounted for until wounded at Sharpsburg, Maryland, September 17, 1862. Returned to duty on an unspecified date. Surrendered at Appomattox Court House, Virginia, April 9, 1865.

JAMES, REUBEN S., Private
Enlisted at Petersburg, Virginia, October 1, 1864, for the war. Present or accounted for until he surrendered at Appomattox Court House, Virginia, April 9, 1865.

JOHNSTON, G. S., Private
Enlisted in Pitt County on August 20, 1861. Present or accounted for until wounded at Sharpsburg, Maryland, September 17, 1862. Returned to duty on an unspecified date. Wounded in the leg at Gum Swamp on May 22, 1863. Leg amputated. Reported absent wounded through October, 1864. Reported absent on detail at Tarboro from December 1, 1864, through February, 1865. Paroled at Greensboro on May 3, 1865.

JONES, BRYANT, Private
Born in Pitt County where he enlisted on April 20, 1861. Present or accounted for until transferred to Company E of this regiment on June 19, 1861.

JOYNER, BENJAMIN, Private
Born in Pitt County and was by occupation a farmer prior to enlisting in Pitt County on April 20, 1861. Present or accounted for until discharged on December 1, 1862, by reason of "hydrocele." Discharge certificate gives his age as 23.

KILPATRICK, FRANK M., Corporal
Enlisted in Pitt County on April 20, 1861. Mustered in as Private and was promoted to Corporal on June 19, 1861. Transferred to Company E of this regiment the same date.

KILPATRICK, JOHN B., Corporal
Enlisted in Pitt County on April 20, 1861. Mustered in as Private and was promoted to Corporal on June 19, 1861. Transferred to Company E of this regiment on or about the same date.

KILPATRICK, WILLIAM JAMES, Private
Resided in Pitt County where he enlisted on April 20, 1861. Present or accounted for until transferred to Company E of this regiment on June 19, 1861.

KILPATRICK, WILLIAM P., Private
Enlisted in Pitt County on April 20, 1861. Present or accounted for until transferred to Company E of this regiment on June 19, 1861.

LAUGHINGHOUSE, CASWELL, Private
Enlisted in Pitt County on April 20, 1861. Present or accounted for until transferred to Company E of this regiment on June 19, 1861.

LAWRENCE, PETER P., Private
Enlisted in Pitt County on April 20, 1861. Wounded at Wilderness, Virginia, on or about May 5, 1864. Rejoined the company in November-December, 1864. Present or accounted for until he surrendered at Appomattox Court House, Virginia, April 9, 1865.

LITTLE, ICHABOD H., Sergeant
Enlisted in Craven County on July 15, 1861. Mustered in as Private. Present or accounted for until wounded at Sharpsburg, Maryland, September 17, 1862. Returned to duty on an unspecified date. Promoted to Sergeant in November, 1862-October, 1864. Surrendered at Appomattox Court House, Virginia, April 9, 1865.

McCOY, ROBERT A., Private
Enlisted at Camp Holmes on October 23, 1864, for the war. Present or accounted for until transferred to Company I, 59th Regiment N.C. Troops (4th Regiment

N.C. Cavalry), December 5, 1864. [Service record omitted in Volume II of this series.]

McGOWAN, J. J., Private
Resided in Pitt County where he enlisted on April 20, 1861. Present or accounted for until transferred to Company E of this regiment on June 19, 1861.

McGOWNS, BENTON P., Private
Born in Pitt County and was by occupation a workman prior to enlisting in Pitt County on April 20, 1861. Present or accounted for until he died in hospital at Kinston on April 8, 1862. Cause of death not reported.

McKEEL, EDWARD, Private
Enlisted in Pitt County on April 20, 1861. Present or accounted for until transferred to Company E of this regiment on or about June 19, 1861.

MANKER, GUILFORD, Private
Resided in Pitt County where he enlisted on April 20, 1861. Promoted to Musician in September-October, 1864, and transferred to the regimental band.

MANNING, J. S. L., Private
Enlisted in Pitt County on April 20, 1861. Present or accounted for until wounded at Sharpsburg, Maryland, September 17, 1862. Died at Winchester, Virginia, November 5, 1862. Cause of death not reported.

MATTHEWS, JOSIAH, Private
Enlisted in Lenoir County on May 3, 1862, for the war. Killed at or near Petersburg, Virginia, June 15, 1864.

MAYO, FREDERICK, Corporal
Enlisted in Pitt County on April 20, 1861. Mustered in as Private and was promoted to Corporal on September 18, 1862. Present or accounted for through October, 1862. No further records.

MAYO, JAMES E., Private
Born in Pitt County where he resided as a farmer prior to enlisting in Pitt County on April 20, 1861. Present or accounted for until wounded in the left arm at Sharpsburg, Maryland, September 17, 1862. Company records do not indicate whether he returned to duty; however, he was discharged on April 3, 1863, by reason of disability from wounds. Later served in Company B, 16th Regiment N.C. Troops (6th Regiment N.C. Volunteers).

MOBLEY, JAMES T., Private
Enlisted in Pitt County on April 20, 1861. Present or accounted for until transferred to Company E of this regiment on June 19, 1861.

MOBLEY, W. G., Private
Enlisted in Pitt County on April 20, 1861. Present or accounted for until transferred to Company E of this regiment on June 19, 1861.

MOORE, ASA, Private
Resided in Pitt County where he enlisted on April 20, 1861. Captured at or near Fort Stedman, Virginia, March 25, 1865. Confined at Point Lookout, Maryland, until released on June 15, 1865, after taking the Oath of Allegiance.

MOORE, SAMUEL, Sergeant
Resided in Pitt County and enlisted in Craven County

on June 16, 1861. Mustered in as Private and was promoted to Corporal on May 18, 1862. Promoted to Sergeant on September 18, 1862. Wounded at Wilderness, Virginia, on or about May 5, 1864. Returned to duty prior to November 1, 1864. Present or accounted for until captured at or near Fort Stedman, Virginia, March 25, 1865. Confined at Point Lookout, Maryland, until released on June 29, 1865, after taking the Oath of Allegiance.

NELSON, HENRY E., Sergeant
Enlisted in Pitt County on April 20, 1861. Mustered in as Private. Present or accounted for until wounded in the left arm at Sharpsburg, Maryland, September 17, 1862. Returned to duty on an unspecified date. Promoted to Sergeant in November, 1862-October, 1863. Wounded in the left thigh at Bristoe Station, Virginia, October 14, 1863. Reported absent wounded through October, 1864. Elected 2nd Lieutenant of Company F, 2nd Regiment N.C. Junior Reserves, November 22, 1864, and transferred to that unit.

NELSON, JAMES H., Private
Enlisted in Pitt County on April 20, 1861. Present or accounted for until killed at Sharpsburg, Maryland, September 17, 1862.

NELSON, JOHN G., Private
Born in Craven County and was by occupation a farmer prior to enlisting in Pitt County on April 20, 1861. Present or accounted for until discharged on July 16, 1862, by reason of being overage. Discharge certificate gives his age as 44.

NOBLES, BENJAMIN, Private
Born in Pitt County where he enlisted on April 20, 1861. Present or accounted for until transferred to Company E of this regiment on June 19, 1861.

OVERTON, W. R., Private
Enlisted in Pitt County on April 20, 1861. Present or accounted for until he was wounded "slightly" at Wilderness, Virginia, in May, 1864. No further records.

OXLEY, ELBERT H., Corporal
Enlisted in Pitt County on April 20, 1861. Mustered in as Private and was promoted to Corporal in November, 1862-March, 1864. Wounded at Reams' Station, Virginia, August 25, 1864. Reported absent wounded through February, 1865.

OXLEY, WILKES, Private
Enlisted in Pitt County on April 20, 1861. Present or accounted for until wounded at Sharpsburg, Maryland, September 17, 1862. Returned to duty on an unspecified date. Wounded at Wilderness, Virginia, May 5, 1864. Reported absent wounded until he deserted on or about August 1, 1864.

PAGE, JOHN, Private
Enlisted in Lenoir County at age 22, May 9, 1862, for the war. Present or accounted for until killed at Sharpsburg, Maryland, September 17, 1862.

PAGE, JOHN J., Private
Resided in Pitt County where he enlisted at age 18, April 20, 1861. Captured at or near Fort Stedman, Virginia, March 25, 1865. Confined at Point Lookout, Maryland,

until released on June 16, 1865, after taking the Oath of Allegiance.

PAGE, VINCENT, Private
Enlisted in Pitt County on April 20, 1861. Died in hospital at Richmond, Virginia, June 28, 1863, of "pneumonia."

PAGE, WILLIAM H., Private
Place and date of enlistment not reported. Captured at New Bern on March 14, 1862. Confined at Fort Columbus, New York Harbor. Exchanged on an unspecified date. Died in hospital at Richmond, Virginia, on or about July 1, 1863, of "pneumonia" and/or "febris typhoides."

PARKER, PLEASANT, Private
Enlisted in Craven County on July 15, 1861. Present or accounted for until discharged in July-August, 1862, by reason of disability.

PARKER, W. H., Private
Born in Pitt County and was by occupation a mechanic prior to enlisting in Pitt County on April 20, 1861. Present or accounted for until discharged on September 25, 1861, by reason of "chronic rheumatism." Discharge certificate gives his age as 31.

PEARCE, WILLIAM S., Private
Resided in Wilson County and enlisted at Petersburg, Virginia, at age 28, July 5, 1864, for the war. Present or accounted for until captured at or near Fort Stedman, Virginia, March 25, 1865. Confined at Point Lookout, Maryland, until released on June 17, 1865, after taking the Oath of Allegiance.

PEEL, WILLIAM J., Private
Resided in Martin County and enlisted in Lenoir County on May 13, 1862, for the war. Wounded in both legs at Bristoe Station, Virginia, October 14, 1863. Returned to duty prior to November 1, 1864. Present or accounted for through February, 1865.

POLLARD, JAMES A., Private
Previously served in Company E, 55th Regiment N.C. Troops. Enlisted in this company at Camp Holmes on October 22, 1864, for the war. Present or accounted for until captured at Hatcher's Run, Virginia, March 31, 1865. Confined at Point Lookout, Maryland, until released on June 17, 1865, after taking the Oath of Allegiance.

QUARTERMUS, JAMES BENJAMIN, Sr., Private
Enlisted in Pitt County on April 20, 1861. Wounded in the left leg and right hand at Wilderness, Virginia, May 5, 1864. Reported absent on light duty from September-October, 1864, through February, 1865. Records of the Federal Provost Marshal indicate he was a deserter who took the Oath of Allegiance at or near Washington, D.C., on or about April 12, 1865.

RANDOLPH, JOHN E., Private
Enlisted in Pitt County at age 29, April 20, 1861. Mustered in as Private and was promoted to Sergeant on July 15, 1861. Promoted to Quartermaster Sergeant on August 27, 1861, but was reduced to ranks on May 2, 1862. Present or accounted for until wounded in the ankle at Sharpsburg, Maryland, September 17, 1862. Returned to duty on an unspecified date. Wounded in the wrist and hand at Reams' Station, Virginia, August 25, 1864. Reported absent wounded through February, 1865. Returned to duty prior to April 9, 1865, when he surrendered at Appomattox Court House, Virginia.

RANDOLPH, RICHARD, Private
Enlisted in Pitt County on April 20, 1861. Wounded at Wilderness, Virginia, on or about May 5, 1864. Last reported in the records of this company on August 23, 1864.

RINGOLD, JAMES, Private
Born in Pitt County and was by occupation a farmer prior to enlisting in Pitt County on April 20, 1861. Present or accounted for until transferred to Company E of this regiment on June 19, 1861.

ROBINSON, BRACY, Private
Enlisted in Pitt County on April 20, 1861. Died in hospital at Richmond, Virginia, May 1, 1864, of "diarrhoea chro[nic]."

ROLLINS, JOHN R., 1st Sergeant
Enlisted in Pitt County on April 20, 1861. Mustered in as Private. Present or accounted for until wounded at Sharpsburg, Maryland, September 17, 1862. Returned to duty on an unspecified date. Promoted to Corporal in November, 1862-March, 1864. Promoted to 1st Sergeant in November-December, 1864. Present or accounted for until he surrendered at Appomattox Court House, Virginia, April 9, 1865.

ROUNTREE, ERASTUS, Private
Place and date of enlistment not reported. Surrendered at Appomattox Court House, Virginia, April 9, 1865.

SHIVERS, ALGERNON, Private
Enlisted in Pitt County on April 20, 1861. Transferred to Company E of this regiment on June 19, 1861.

SMITH, D. C., Private
Enlisted in Pitt County on April 20, 1861. Killed at Bristoe Station, Virginia, October 14, 1863.

SMITH, JOSHUA W., Sergeant
Enlisted in Pitt County on April 20, 1861. Mustered in as Private and was promoted to Sergeant in November-December, 1864. Paroled at Burkeville Junction, Virginia, April 14-17, 1865.

SMITH, STEPHEN, Private
Enlisted in Pitt County on April 20, 1861. Present or accounted for until captured at New Bern on or about March 14, 1862. No further records.

SMITH, ZENO, Private
Enlisted in Craven County on August 1, 1861. Present or accounted for until he died on February 27, 1862. Place and cause of death not reported.

SPRINGER, WILEY, Private
Resided in Stanly County and enlisted at Camp Holmes on August 31, 1864, for the war. Present or accounted for until he deserted to the enemy on or about October 24, 1864. Confined at Washington, D.C., until released on or about November 12, 1864, after taking the Oath of Allegiance.

STANCIL, WILLIAM H., Private
Born in Pitt County and was by occupation a farmer

prior to enlisting in Craven County on July 15, 1861. Present or accounted for until wounded in the leg and captured at Sharpsburg, Maryland, on or about September 17, 1862. Paroled on or about October 27, 1862. Returned to duty on an unspecified date. Wounded at Wilderness, Virginia, May 5, 1864. Confederate medical records indicate he was retired to the Invalid Corps on February 1, 1865; however, records of the Federal Provost Marshal indicate he surrendered at Appomattox Court House, Virginia, April 9, 1865. Company records dated 1865 give his age as 20. No further records.

STOCKS, WILLIAM A., Private
Born in Pitt County and was by occupation a farmer prior to enlisting in Pitt County on April 20, 1861. Present or accounted for until discharged on July 16, 1862, by reason of being overage. Discharge certificate gives his age as 46. Later served in Company E, 1st Battalion N.C. Local Defense Troops.

STOKES, DAVID W., Private
Enlisted in Pitt County on April 20, 1861. Died in hospital at Richmond, Virginia, on or about January 1, 1864, of a gunshot wound of the thigh. Place and date wounded not reported.

STOKES, JAMES, Private
Resided in Pitt County where he enlisted on April 20, 1861. Captured near Petersburg, Virginia, April 2, 1865. Confined at Point Lookout, Maryland, until released on June 20, 1865, after taking the Oath of Allegiance.

STOKES, JOHN A., Private
Enlisted in Pitt County on April 20, 1861. Wounded at Wilderness, Virginia, on or about May 5, 1864. Returned to duty on an unspecified date. Wounded at Reams' Station, Virginia, August 25, 1864. Hospitalized at Richmond, Virginia, where he died on October 11, 1864, of wounds.

STOKES, S. A., Private
Enlisted in Pitt County on April 20, 1861. Killed at Wilderness, Virginia, on or about May 5, 1864.

SUMRELL, W. J., Private
Enlisted in Pitt County at age 17, April 20, 1861. Present or accounted for until wounded in the left arm at Sharpsburg, Maryland, September 17, 1862. Returned to duty on an unspecified date. Wounded in the left thigh at Wilderness, Virginia, on or about May 5, 1864. Returned to duty prior to November 1, 1864. Present or accounted for until paroled at Burkeville Junction, Virginia, April 14-17, 1865.

TAYLOR, WILLIAM L., Private
Born in Pitt County where he enlisted on April 20, 1861. Present or accounted for until transferred to Company E of this regiment on June 19, 1861.

TEEL, G. D., Corporal
Enlisted in Pitt County on April 20, 1861. Mustered in as Private and was promoted to Corporal on April 26, 1861. Present or accounted for until reported missing at Sharpsburg, Maryland, September 17, 1862. No further records.

TEEL, McG., Private
Enlisted in Pitt County on April 20, 1861. Present or

accounted for through February, 1865.

THIGPEN, JESSE L., Private
Enlisted in Pitt County on April 20, 1861. Wounded at Wilderness, Virginia, on or about May 5, 1864. Returned to duty prior to August 25, 1864, when he was wounded in the right shoulder at Reams' Station, Virginia. Reported absent wounded or absent on detail through February, 1865.

TUCKER, M. W., Private
Enlisted in Pitt County on April 20, 1861. Died in hospital at Lynchburg, Virginia, January 19, 1863, of "hepatitis."

TYSON, BENJAMIN FRANKLIN, Private
Born in Pitt County and was by occupation a mechanic prior to enlisting in Pitt County on April 20, 1861. Present or accounted for until discharged on July 16, 1862, by reason of being underage. Discharge certificate gives his age as 17.

VENDRICK, JOHN A., Corporal
Resided in Pitt County where he enlisted on April 20, 1861. Mustered in as Private. Present or accounted for until wounded at Sharpsburg, Maryland, September 17, 1862. Returned to duty on an unspecified date. Promoted to Corporal in November, 1862-October, 1864. Wounded at Wilderness, Virginia, May 5, 1864. Returned to duty prior to November 1, 1864. Present or accounted for until captured at Sutherland's Station, Virginia, on or about April 2, 1865. Confined at Hart's Island, New York Harbor, where he died on April 28, 1865, of "typhoid fever."

VENDRICK, W. F., Sergeant
Enlisted in Pitt County on April 20, 1861. Mustered in as Private and was promoted to Sergeant on February 3, 1862. Present or accounted for through August, 1862. Company records indicate he was wounded and captured at Sharpsburg, Maryland, on or about September 17, 1862; however, records of the Federal Provost Marshal do not substantiate that report. No further records.

VENTERS, GEORGE W., Private
Born in Pitt County and was by occupation a farmer prior to enlisting in Pitt County on April 20, 1861. Present or accounted for until wounded and captured at Sharpsburg, Maryland, September 17, 1862. Paroled and transferred to Aiken's Landing, James River, Virginia, where he was received November 2, 1862, for exchange. Declared exchanged at Aiken's Landing on November 10, 1862. Company records dated November, 1862, give his age as 24. No further records. Later served in Company K, 1st Battalion N.C. Local Defense Troops.

WARREN, DRED A., Private
Resided in Pitt County where he enlisted on April 20, 1861. Mustered in as Musician but was reduced to ranks in January-February, 1862. Present or accounted for until discharged on February 28, 1862. Reason discharged not reported. Later served in Company C, 44th Regiment N.C. Troops.

WHITLEY, DANIEL, Private
Enlisted in Pitt County on April 20, 1861. Wounded in the right thigh at Reams' Station, Virginia, August 25,

1864. Right leg amputated. Reported absent wounded through February, 1865.

WHITLY, McG. D., Private
Enlisted in Pitt County on April 20, 1861. Present or accounted for until killed at Sharpsburg, Maryland, September 17, 1862.

WILLIAMS, JOHN A., Private
Born in Pitt County and was by occupation a farmer prior to enlisting in Pitt County on April 20, 1861. Present or accounted for until wounded in the face at Sharpsburg, Maryland, September 17, 1862. Returned to duty on an unspecified date. Wounded in the neck at Wilderness, Virginia, May 5, 1864. Returned to duty prior to November 1, 1864. Present or accounted for until discharged on February 4, 1865, by reason of being overage. Discharge certificate gives his age as 49. [North Carolina pension records indicate he was wounded in the left shoulder at Petersburg, Virginia, September 16, 1863.]

WILLIAMS, SAMUEL, Private
Born in Pitt County where he enlisted on April 20, 1861. Present or accounted for until transferred to Company E of this regiment on June 19, 1861.

WILLIAMS, SAMUEL W., Sergeant
Born in Pitt County and was by occupation a farmer prior to enlisting in Pitt County on April 20, 1861. Mustered in as Private and was promoted to Corporal on September 15, 1861. Promoted to Sergeant in March-April, 1862. Present or accounted for until killed at Sharpsburg, Maryland, September 17, 1862. Death records give his age as 23.

WILLIAMS, SHADE, Private
Enlisted in Pitt County on April 20, 1861. Present or accounted for until transferred to Company E of this regiment on June 19, 1861.

WILSON, EDWARD, Private
Born in Pitt County and was by occupation a laborer prior to enlisting at Orange Court House, Virginia, March 9, 1864, for the war. Wounded in the left ankle at Wilderness, Virginia, on or about May 5, 1864. Returned to duty prior to November 1, 1864. Present or accounted for until he deserted to the enemy on or about February 19, 1865. Confined at Washington, D.C., until released on or about February 21, 1865, after taking the Oath of Allegiance. Assigned to Company B, 4th Regiment U.S. Volunteer Infantry.

WILSON, STEPHEN A., Private
Enlisted in Pitt County on April 20, 1861. Present or accounted for until wounded at Sharpsburg, Maryland, September 17, 1862. Returned to duty prior to November 1, 1862. Deserted on December 10, 1864.

WITHERINGTON, TURNER, Private
Enlisted in Pitt County on April 20, 1861. Present or accounted for until wounded at Sharpsburg, Maryland, September 17, 1862. Returned to duty prior to December 13, 1862, when he was wounded in the face at Fredericksburg, Virginia. Returned to duty on an unspecified date. Wounded at Reams' Station, Virginia, August 25, 1864. Hospitalized at Richmond, Virginia, where he died on October 7, 1864, of wounds. Medical records dated 1862 give his age as 29.

WOLLARD, W. J., Private
Enlisted in Pitt County on April 20, 1861. Present or accounted for until he was reported missing at New Bern on or about March 14, 1862.

COMPANY I

This company, known as the "Southern Rights Infantry," was raised in Jones County. It was mustered in on June 17, 1861, and was later assigned to the 27th Regiment as Company I. After joining the regiment the company functioned as a part of the regiment, and its history for the war period is reported as a part of the regimental history.

The information contained in the following company roster was compiled principally from company muster rolls for June 17, 1861-October, 1862, and September, 1864-February, 1865. No company muster rolls were found for November, 1862-August, 1864, or for the period after February, 1865. Valuable information was obtained also from primary records such as the Roll of Honor, medical records, prisoner of war records, discharge certificates, and pension applications, and from secondary sources such as postwar rosters and histories, cemetery records, and records of the United Daughters of the Confederacy.

OFFICERS

CAPTAINS

WARD, WILLIAM P.
Enlisted in Jones County. Appointed Captain on June 17, 1861. Present or accounted for until he was defeated for reelection when the regiment was reorganized in April, 1862.

LARKINS, WILLIAM R.
Resided in New Hanover County and enlisted in Jones County on June 17, 1861. Mustered in with an unspecified rank and was appointed Sergeant on August 24, 1861. Elected Captain on April 22, 1862. Wounded in the right leg at Wilderness, Virginia, on or about May 5, 1864. Returned to duty on May 12, 1864. Died in hospital at Richmond, Virginia, August 1, 1864, of "dysentery."

JONES, KENNETH RAYNOR
Born in Jones County where he resided prior to enlisting in Jones County at age 19, June 17, 1861. Mustered in as Private and was elected 3rd Lieutenant on September 5, 1861. Elected 1st Lieutenant on April 22, 1862. Present or accounted for until wounded in the left arm at Sharpsburg, Maryland, September 17, 1862. Returned to duty on an unspecified date. Wounded in the right arm at or near Cold Harbor, Virginia, on or about June 3, 1864. Returned to duty prior to June 15, 1864, when he was wounded in the left leg at or near Petersburg, Virginia. Promoted to Captain on August 1, 1864. Reported absent wounded until he was captured at Raleigh on or about April 13, 1865. Paroled at Raleigh on May 16, 1865.

LIEUTENANTS

FOY, FRANKLIN, 2nd Lieutenant
Appointed 2nd Lieutenant on June 17, 1861. Present or accounted for until he was defeated for reelection when the regiment was reorganized in April, 1862. Later

served as 2nd Lieutenant of Company A, 8th Battalion N.C. Partisan Rangers.

MATTOCKS, GEORGE D., 2nd Lieutenant
Resided in Onslow County and enlisted at Camp Green on July 29, 1861. Mustered in as Private and was promoted to Corporal on July 1, 1862. Promoted to Sergeant in November, 1862-May, 1864. Wounded at Wilderness, Virginia, on or about May 5, 1864. Returned to duty prior to November 1, 1864. Appointed 2nd Lieutenant subsequent to February 28, 1865. Captured at the Appomattox River, Virginia, April 3, 1865. Confined at Old Capitol Prison, Washington, D.C., until transferred to Johnson's Island, Ohio, April 17, 1865. Released at Johnson's Island on June 19, 1865, after taking the Oath of Allegiance. Oath of Allegiance gives his age as 21.

NETHERCUTT, JOHN H., 1st Lieutenant
Enlisted in Jones County. Elected 1st Lieutenant on June 17, 1861. Present or accounted for until he was defeated for reelection when the regiment was reorganized in April, 1862. Later served as Captain of Company A, 8th Battalion N.C. Partisan Rangers.

RUSSELL, MAJOR, 1st Lieutenant
Resided in Onslow County and enlisted at Camp Green on July 23, 1861. Mustered in with an unspecified rank and was promoted to 1st Lieutenant on August 24, 1861. Reduced to the rank of Sergeant on April 23, 1862, but was promoted to 1st Sergeant on October 1, 1862. Elected 2nd Lieutenant on August 6, 1863. Promoted to 1st Lieutenant on July 30, 1864. Captured at the Appomattox River, Virginia, April 3, 1865. Confined at Old Capitol Prison, Washington, D.C., until transferred to Johnson's Island, Ohio, April 17, 1865. Released at Johnson's Island on June 19, 1865, after taking the Oath of Allegiance.

SMITH, JOSEPH A., 3rd Lieutenant
Enlisted in Jones County on June 17, 1861. Mustered in as Private and was promoted to Corporal on August 24, 1861. Promoted to Sergeant on November 23, 1861, and was elected 3rd Lieutenant on April 22, 1862. Present or accounted for until wounded in the left shoulder at Fredericksburg, Virginia, December 13, 1862. Reported absent wounded until he resigned on August 4, 1863, by reason of disability from wounds.

WARD, GEORGE W., 2nd Lieutenant
Resided in Onslow County and enlisted at Camp Green at age 26, July 23, 1861. Mustered in as Private and was promoted to Corporal on November 23, 1861. Elected 2nd Lieutenant on April 22, 1862. Wounded in the left arm at Cold Harbor, Virginia, June 3, 1864. Reported absent wounded through October, 1864. Company records indicate he was dropped from the rolls of the company in November-December, 1864. Records of the North Carolina Adjutant General indicate he was "cashiered" in 1864. No further records.

NONCOMMISSIONED OFFICERS AND PRIVATES

AMAN, STARKEY B., Private
Enlisted in Onslow County on May 1, 1862, for the war. Present or accounted for until captured at Humphrey's Station, Virginia, March 31, 1865. Confined at Point Lookout, Maryland, where he died on or about May 20,

1865, of ''chro[nic] diarrhoea.''

ANDREWS, JOHN B., Private
Born in Jones County and was by occupation a farmer prior to enlisting in Jones County on May 1, 1862, for the war. Present or accounted for until discharged on July 21, 1862, by reason of disability. Discharge certificate gives his age as 32. Later served in Company F, 1st Battalion N.C. Local Defense Troops.

ANDREWS, WILLIAM H., Corporal
Resided in Jones County where he enlisted at age 30, May 1, 1862, for the war. Mustered in as Private and was promoted to Corporal on November 1, 1864. Captured by the enemy on an unspecified date subsequent to February 28, 1865. Confined at Point Lookout, Maryland. Released at Point Lookout on June 23, 1865, after taking the Oath of Allegiance. [North Carolina pension records indicate he was wounded on March 30, 1865.]

BALLARD, J. L., Private
Born in Jones County and was by occupation a farmer prior to enlisting in Jones County on June 17, 1861. Present or accounted for until discharged on July 16, 1862, by reason of being underage.

BARBER, GEORGE M., Private
Enlisted at Camp Green on July 29, 1861. Present or accounted for until September 12, 1862, when he was reported absent without leave. Wounded and captured at or near Harpers Ferry, Virginia, on or about November 9, 1862. Confined at Fort McHenry, Maryland, until paroled and transferred to City Point, Virginia, where he was received November 21, 1862, for exchange. Returned to duty on an unspecified date. Wounded at Wilderness, Virginia, on or about May 5, 1864. Returned to duty prior to November 1, 1864. Deserted to the enemy on or about February 22, 1865. Confined at Washington, D.C., until released on or about February 24, 1865, after taking the Oath of Allegiance.

BARBER, J. F., Private
Born in Craven County and was by occupation a farmer prior to enlisting at Fort Lane on October 3, 1861. Present or accounted for until discharged on July 16, 1862, by reason of being overage. Discharge certificate gives his age as 38.

BARFIELD, ALEXANDER J., Private
Resided in Nash County and enlisted at Camp Green at age 21, June 17, 1861. Captured at or near Fort Stedman, Virginia, March 25, 1865. Confined at Point Lookout, Maryland, until released on June 24, 1865, after taking the Oath of Allegiance. [North Carolina pension records indicate he was wounded in the left arm at Wilderness, Virginia, on an unspecified date.]

BELL, J. A., Private
Born in Onslow County and was by occupation a farmer prior to enlisting at Camp Green on August 19, 1861. Mustered in as Musician but was reduced to ranks in May-June, 1862. Present or accounted for until discharged on May 26, 1862, by reason of disability. Discharge certificate gives his age as 45.

BRINKLE, P., Private
Enlisted at Petersburg, Virginia, July 22, 1862, for the

war as a substitute for Private William W. Franks. Deserted on or about August 21, 1862.

BRITTAIN, A. J., Private
Enlisted in Jones County on June 17, 1861. Present or accounted for through December, 1861. No further records. [May have served later in Company A, 8th Battalion N.C. Partisan Rangers.]

BROWN, JOHN, Private
Enlisted at Camp Vance on October 6, 1863, for the war. "Sent to hospital" on April 16, 1864. Reported absent sick through February, 1865. No further records.

BURKHART, JOHN W., Private
Enlisted in Wake County on February 22, 1864, for the war. Wounded at Wilderness, Virginia, on or about May 5, 1864. Company records do not indicate whether he returned to duty; however, he died in hospital at Richmond, Virginia, on or about September 24, 1864, of "pneumonia typh[oid]."

CIVILS, VINCENT, Private
Enlisted in Wayne County at age 35, June 17, 1861. Present or accounted for until March-April, 1862, when company records indicate he was captured by the enemy. Records of the Federal Provost Marshal do not substantiate that report. Returned to duty on an unspecified date. Surrendered at Appomattox Court House, Virginia, April 9, 1865.

COGGINS, EMANUEL J., Private
Resided in Davidson County and enlisted in Wake County on November 20, 1863, for the war. Hospitalized at Richmond, Virginia, June 2, 1864, with a gunshot wound. Place and date wounded not reported. Returned to duty on an unspecified date. Deserted to the enemy on or about October 9, 1864. Confined at Washington, D.C., until released on or about October 12, 1864, after taking the Oath of Allegiance.

COLEY, ISHAM, Private
Enlisted in Wake County on March 1, 1863, for the war. Present or accounted for through February, 1865.

CONAWAY, GEORGE W., Private
Enlisted in Wayne County at age 30, June 17, 1861. Present or accounted for until March-April, 1862, when company muster rolls indicate he was captured by the enemy. Records of the Federal Provost Marshal do not substantiate that report. Company records do not indicate whether he returned to duty; however, company muster rolls dated September, 1864-February, 1865, indicate he was captured by the enemy on January 31, 1864. Records of the Federal Provost Marshal do not substantiate that report. No further records.

CONAWAY, JOHN, Private
Born in Jones County and was by occupation a farmer prior to enlisting in Wayne County on June 17, 1861. Present or accounted for until discharged on April 25, 1862, by reason of "a chronic disease of his bowels, which was produced by an attack of typhoid fever." Discharge certificate gives his age as 36.

COOKE, ANDREW W., Private
Resided in Iredell County and enlisted at Camp Stokes at age 41, October 28, 1864, for the war. Present or accounted for until captured at Farmville, Virginia, April 6, 1865. Confined at Newport News, Virginia,

until released on June 30, 1865, after taking the Oath of Allegiance.

COX, GABRIEL P., Private
Born in Jones County where he resided as a farmer prior to enlisting at Fort Lane at age 41, September 3, 1861. Present or accounted for until discharged on July 16, 1862, by reason of being overage. Later served in Company F, 1st Battalion N.C. Local Defense Troops.

COX, HUGH B., Private
Previously served as Sergeant in Company H, 26th Regiment N.C. Troops. Enlisted in this company in Wake County on April 1, 1864, for the war. Wounded at Wilderness, Virginia, on or about May 5, 1864. Returned to duty on an unspecified date. Transferred to Company D, 48th Regiment N.C. Troops, on or about November 1, 1864.

CRISP, J. W., Private
Enlisted in Pitt County on June 17, 1861. Deserted prior to September 1, 1861.

CROSS, HENRY J., Private
Enlisted in Wake County on November 20, 1863, for the war. Deserted from hospital at Richmond, Virginia, on or about May 8, 1864. Hospitalized at Petersburg, Virginia, June 7, 1864, with typhoid pneumonia. Returned to duty prior to November 1, 1864. Present or accounted for until he deserted to the enemy on or about March 18, 1865. Confined at Washington, D.C., on or about March 21, 1865. [North Carolina pension records indicate he was wounded in 1864.] No further records.

DAVIS, J. S., Private
Enlisted at Fort Lane on September 1, 1861. Present or accounted for until he died on November 3, 1861. Place and cause of death not reported.

DEES, JOHN W., Private
Enlisted in Wake County at age 18, April 1, 1864, for the war. Present or accounted for until he surrendered at Appomattox Court House, Virginia, April 9, 1865.

EASTER, FELIX, Private
Enlisted in Wake County on April 1, 1864, for the war. Present or accounted for until he deserted to the enemy on or about March 17, 1865. Confined at Washington, D.C., until released on or about March 24, 1865, after taking the Oath of Allegiance.

EASTER, MICHAEL, Private
Enlisted in Wake County on April 1, 1864, for the war. "Sent to hospital" on July 28, 1864. Reported absent sick in hospital through February, 1865. No further records.

FONVILLE, C. D., Private
Enlisted at Camp Green on June 17, 1861. Present or accounted for until March-April, 1862, when company muster rolls indicate he was captured by the enemy. Records of the Federal Provost Marshal do not substantiate that report. Company records do not indicate that he returned to duty prior to March 1, 1865. Surrendered at Appomattox Court House, Virginia, April 9, 1865.

FORDHAM, DAVID G., Sergeant
Born in Jones County and enlisted at Camp Green on

August 19, 1861. Mustered in as Private and was promoted to Sergeant on April 23, 1862. Present or accounted for until he died in Jones County on April 24, 1862. Cause of death not reported.

FOSCUE, EDGAR MACON, Private
Enlisted in Jones County on June 17, 1861. Wounded at Bristoe Station, Virginia, October, 14, 1863. Discharged on March 17, 1864, by reason of disability from wounds.

FOSCUE, H. C., Private
Enlisted in Jones County on June 17, 1861. Present or accounted for until November, 1862, when he was "left at hospital in Richmond," Virginia. No further records.

FOY, T. D., Sergeant
Enlisted in Jones County on June 17, 1861. Mustered in with an unspecified rank and was promoted to Sergeant on August 24, 1861. No further records. [May have served later as 1st Sergeant of Captain John H. Daniel's Company, 8th Regiment N.C. Senior Reserves.]

FRANKS, WILLIAM W., Private
Born in Jones County and was by occupation a student prior to enlisting in Jones County on June 17, 1861. Mustered in as Private and was promoted to Corporal on August 24, 1861. Reduced to ranks on November 3, 1861. Present or accounted for until discharged on July 19, 1862, after providing Private P. Brinkle as a substitute. Discharge certificate gives his age as 21.

GALLIHER, JULIUS A., Private
Resided in Iredell County and enlisted at Camp Stokes at age 19, October 28, 1864, for the war. Present or accounted for until captured at Farmville, Virginia, April 6, 1865. Confined at Newport News, Virginia, until released on June 27, 1865, after taking the Oath of Allegiance.

GILBERT, JOHN H., Private
Resided in Jones County and was by occupation a farmer prior to enlisting at Camp Green on August 14, 1861. Present or accounted for until March-April, 1862, when company muster rolls indicate he was captured by the enemy. Records of the Federal Provost Marshal do not substantiate that report. Returned to duty on an unspecified date. "Wounded twice" at Bristoe Station, Virginia, October 14, 1863. Returned to duty on an unspecified date. Captured at Farmville, Virginia, April 6, 1865. Confined at Newport News, Virginia, until released on June 27, 1865, after taking the Oath of Allegiance. Medical records dated July, 1863, give his age as 16.

GILBURT, D. S., Private
Enlisted at Camp Green on August 20, 1861. Present or accounted for until March-April, 1862, when company muster rolls indicate he was captured by the enemy. Records of the Federal Provost Marshal do not substantiate that report. No further records.

GILLET, O. M., Private
Born in Massachusetts and was by occupation a painter prior to enlisting at Camp Green on June 17, 1861. Present or accounted for until discharged on July 16, 1862, by reason of being overage. Discharge certificate gives his age as 45.

GILLEY, ISAAC P., Private
Enlisted at Camp Green on June 17, 1861. Present or

accounted for until he "fell out on the march in Maryland" in September, 1862. Captured by the enemy on an unspecified date and was paroled on October 22, 1862; however, he apparently remained in Maryland. Records of the Federal Provost Marshal indicate he was arrested on or about June 1, 1863, at or near Catonsville, Maryland, where he was "using treasonable language & encouraging sympathy with the rebellion in every way." Paroled at Fort McHenry, Maryland, and transferred to Fort Monroe, Virginia, on or about June 26, 1863, for exchange. No further records.

GOFORTH, SAMUEL S., Private
Resided in Wilkes County where he enlisted on or about September 2, 1864, for the war. Present or accounted for until captured at Hatcher's Run, Virginia, March 31, 1865. Confined at Point Lookout, Maryland, until released on June 27, 1865, after taking the Oath of Allegiance.

GORDON, AMOS, Private
Enlistment date reported as June 17, 1861; however, he was not listed in the records of this company until February 24, 1864. Wounded at Wilderness, Virginia, on or about May 5, 1864. Returned to duty prior to August 25, 1864, when he was wounded at Reams' Station, Virginia. Died in hospital at Richmond, Virginia, September 5, 1864, of wounds.

HADNOT, J., Private
Enlisted at Camp Green on July 6, 1861. Present or accounted for until he deserted on March 14, 1862. Returned to duty on an unspecified date prior to May 4, 1863. Wounded at Wilderness, Virginia, on or about May 5, 1864. Returned to duty on June 2, 1864. No further records.

HALL, E. S., Private
Born in Jones County and was by occupation a farmer prior to enlisting in Jones County on June 17, 1861. Present or accounted for until discharged on July 21, 1862, by reason of disability. Discharge certificate gives his age as 23.

HALL, J. H., Private
Born in Duplin County and enlisted in Jones County on June 17, 1861. Present or accounted for until killed at Sharpsburg, Maryland, September 17, 1862.

HAMADY, WILLIAM, Private
Enlisted in Wake County on April 1, 1864, for the war. Died at Lynchburg, Virginia, May 8, 1864. Cause of death not reported.

HAY, CURTIS, Sergeant
Enlisted at Camp Green on June 17, 1861. Mustered in as Private and was promoted to Sergeant on April 23, 1862. Present or accounted for until wounded at Sharpsburg, Maryland, September 17, 1862. Returned to duty on an unspecified date. Captured at Bristoe Station, Virginia, October 14, 1863. Confined at Old Capitol Prison, Washington, D.C., until transferred to Point Lookout, Maryland, October 27, 1863. Paroled at Point Lookout on February 24, 1865, and transferred to Aiken's Landing, James River, Virginia, for exchange.

HAYWOOD, E. W., Private
Born in Jones County and was by occupation a teacher

prior to enlisting in Jones County on June 17, 1861. Mustered in with an unspecified rank and was promoted to Sergeant on August 24, 1861. Reduced to ranks on February 14, 1862, by court-martial. Reason he was court-martialed not reported. Present or accounted for until discharged on July 16, 1862, by reason of being overage. Discharge certificate gives his age as 36.

HESTER, ABRAHAM, Private
Enlisted at Camp Stokes on November 15, 1864, for the war. Present or accounted for through February, 1865.

HOWARD, W., Private
Born in Onslow County and enlisted at Camp Green on July 30, 1861. Killed at Bristoe Station, Virginia, October 14, 1863.

HUGGINS, COOPER, Private
Enlisted at Camp Green on August 7, 1861. Mustered in as Private and was promoted to 1st Sergeant on April 23, 1862. Reduced to ranks on September 24, 1862. Wounded at Wilderness, Virginia, on or about May 5, 1864. Returned to duty prior to January 1, 1865. Present or accounted for through February, 1865.

HYMAN, T., Private
Born in Craven County and was by occupation a farmer prior to enlisting at Camp Green on August 12, 1861. Present or accounted for until discharged on July 16, 1862, by reason of being overage. Discharge certificate gives his age as 37.

JENKINS, W. T., Private
Enlisted at Camp Gatlin on November 1, 1861. Died in hospital at Charlottesville, Virginia, March 30, 1863, of "phthisis pulmonalis."

JOHNSTON, JOHN FRANCIS, Private
Resided in Iredell County and enlisted at Camp Vance on October 28, 1864, for the war. Present or accounted for until captured at Hatcher's Run, Virginia, March 31, 1865. Confined at Point Lookout, Maryland, until released on June 28, 1865, after taking the Oath of Allegiance.

JONES, LEVI J., Private
Enlisted at Camp Green on June 17, 1861. Present or accounted for until he deserted on June 1, 1862. "Sent to hospital" on October 4, 1863, and was reported absent in hospital through February, 1865.

JONES, LEWIS, Private
Born in Jones County and was by occupation a farmer prior to enlisting in Jones County on May 1, 1862, for the war. Died in hospital at Lynchburg, Virginia, March 6, 1863, of "phthisis pulm[onalis]."

KILLINGSWORTH, WILLIAM F., Private
Enlisted at Camp Green on July 30, 1861. Captured at Bristoe Station, Virginia, October 14, 1863. Confined at Old Capitol Prison, Washington, D.C., until transferred to Point Lookout, Maryland, October 27, 1863. Paroled at Point Lookout and transferred to Boulware's Wharf, James River, Virginia, where he was received March 16, 1865, for exchange.

KING, CALVIN, Private
Enlisted in Wake County on April 1, 1864, for the war. Wounded in both legs at Wilderness, Virginia, on or

about May 5, 1864. Reported absent in hospital through February, 1865.

KING, FELIX, Private
Enlisted in Jones County on June 17, 1861. Wounded at or near Bristoe Station, Virginia, on or about October 14, 1863. Company records do not indicate whether he rejoined the company; however, he was detailed for light duty on July 25, 1864. Retired to the Invalid Corps on October 14, 1864, by reason of disability. Captured in hospital at Richmond, Virginia, April 3, 1865, and was paroled on April 23, 1865.

KINSEY, J. A., Private
Enlisted in Jones County on June 17, 1861. Present or accounted for until he deserted on or about September 1, 1861.

KINSEY, JOHN J., Private
Resided in Jones County where he enlisted on June 17, 1861. Captured at Kinston on March 10, 1865. Confined at Point Lookout, Maryland, until released on June 28, 1865, after taking the Oath of Allegiance.

KINSEY, JOHN L., Private
Enlisted in Jones County on June 17, 1861. Promoted to Musician in November, 1862-October, 1864, and transferred to the regimental band.

KINSEY, W. C., Private
Enlisted in Jones County on June 17, 1861. Mustered in as Private and was promoted to Corporal on November 2, 1861. Reduced to ranks on April 23, 1862. Present or accounted for through April, 1862. No further records.

KOONCE, LEWIS, Sergeant
Born in Jones County and enlisted at Camp Green on June 17, 1861. Mustered in as Private and was promoted to Corporal on May 1, 1862. Promoted to Sergeant on October 1, 1862. Died in hospital at Petersburg, Virginia, February 24, 1863, of "chr[onic] diarrhoea."

KOONCE, RICHARD H., Private
Resided in Jones County and enlisted at Fort Lane on October 18, 1861. Present or accounted for until wounded in the head at Sharpsburg, Maryland, September 17, 1862. Transferred to Company G, 2nd Regiment N.C. State Troops, on or about October 1, 1862. Reenlisted in this company in April-November, 1863. Transferred back to Company G, 2nd Regiment N.C. State Troops, November 5, 1863, in exchange for Private Edward M. Owens. [Service record in Volume III of this series is partially in error.]

KOONCE, SIMON EVERETTE, Private
Enlisted in Jones County on June 17, 1861. Present or accounted for through January 20, 1863. No further records.

LINDLEY, W. W., Private
Place and date of enlistment not reported. Discharged on July 2, 1864, by reason of being a member of the "Society of Friends."

LOVITT, JAMES M., Private
Enlisted at Camp Green on June 17, 1861. Wounded at Wilderness, Virginia, on or about May 5, 1864. Returned to duty prior to August 25, 1864, when he was wounded at or near Reams' Station, Virginia. Assigned

to light duty on November 25, 1864. Retired from service on January 13, 1865, by reason of disability.

LOVITT, WILLIAM, Private
Was by occupation a farmer prior to enlisting at Camp Green on August 19, 1861. Mustered in as Private. Present or accounted for until wounded at Sharpsburg, Maryland, September 17, 1862. Returned to duty on an unspecified date. Promoted to Corporal on October 1, 1862. Wounded in the right hand at Wilderness, Virginia, on or about May 5, 1864. Returned to duty prior to November 1, 1864. Promoted to Sergeant on January 1, 1865, but was reduced to ranks subsequent to February 28, 1865. Present or accounted for until he surrendered at Appomattox Court House, Virginia, April 9, 1865. [Medical records dated June, 1864, give his age as 33.]

LYON, WILLIAM A., Private
Enlisted in Wake County on April 1, 1864, for the war. Died in hospital at Richmond, Virginia, September 15, 1864, of "febris typhoides."

McDANIEL, WILLIAM L., Private
Born in Jones County and was by occupation a teacher prior to enlisting at Camp Green on June 17, 1861. Mustered in with an unspecified rank and was promoted to Sergeant on August 24, 1861. Reduced to ranks on November 2, 1861. Present or accounted for until discharged on July 16, 1862, by reason of being overage. Discharge certificate gives his age as 37.

McRAINEY, JOHN, Private
Born in Stanly County* and was by occupation a farmer prior to enlisting in Wake County at age 37, February 11, 1863, for the war. Present or accounted for through February, 1865.

MAIDES, JOSEPH F., Sergeant
Resided in Jones County and enlisted at Camp Green on June 17, 1861. Mustered in as Private and was promoted to Sergeant on April 23, 1862. Captured in hospital at Richmond, Virginia, April 3, 1865. Confined at Newport News, Virginia, until released on June 30, 1865, after taking the Oath of Allegiance.

MARSHALL, HENRY, Private
Enlisted in Onslow County on May 1, 1862. Hospitalized at Richmond, Virginia, October 21, 1863, with a gunshot wound. Returned to duty prior to November 1, 1864. Present or accounted for until he deserted on February 22, 1865.

MARSHALL, JAMES M., Corporal
Born in Craven County and was by occupation a farmer prior to enlisting in Jones County on June 17, 1861. Mustered in as Private and was promoted to Corporal on April 23, 1861. Present or accounted for until discharged on August 16, 1862, by reason of "hemorrhage of the lungs." Discharge certificate gives his age as 32.

MASON, GEORGE W., Corporal
Enlisted at Camp Green on June 17, 1861. Mustered in as Private. Present or accounted for until wounded at Sharpsburg, Maryland, September 17, 1862. Returned to duty on an unspecified date. Promoted to Corporal in November, 1862-February, 1864. Deserted to the enemy on or about February 22, 1865. Confined at

Washington, D.C., until released on or about February 24, 1865, after taking the Oath of Allegiance.

MATTOCKS, C. J., Private
Born in Onslow County and was by occupation a doctor prior to enlisting at Camp Green on July 23, 1861. Present or accounted for until promoted to Hospital Steward on June 20, 1862, and transferred to the Field and Staff of this regiment.

MEADOWS, H. C., ——
Place and date of enlistment not reported. First listed in the records of this company on September 30, 1862. Present or accounted for through November, 1862. No further records.

MEADOWS, ISAAC L., Private
Enlisted at Camp Green on August 19, 1861. Present or accounted for until he "fell out on the march in Maryland" and was captured on or about September 12, 1862. Confined at Old Capitol Prison, Washington, D.C. Paroled and transferred to Aiken's Landing, James River, Virginia, where he was received on or about September 27, 1862, for exchange. Declared exchanged at Aiken's Landing on November 10, 1862. Returned to duty on an unspecified date. Deserted on February 14, 1865.

MEADOWS, WILLIAM, Sergeant
Enlisted at Camp Green on August 19, 1861. Mustered in as Private and was promoted to Corporal on April 23, 1862. Reduced to ranks prior to July 1, 1862, but was promoted to Corporal in November, 1862-October, 1864. Wounded at or near Reams' Station, Virginia, August 25, 1864. Returned to duty in November-December, 1864. Promoted to Sergeant on January 1, 1865. Present or accounted for through February, 1865.

MESSER, EDWARD, Private
Enlisted at Camp Green at age 20, July 8, 1861. Captured near New Bern on February 24, 1864. Confined at Point Lookout, Maryland, until paroled and transferred to Venus Point, Savannah River, Georgia, where he was received November 15, 1864, for exchange. [North Carolina pension records indicate he was wounded in the right shoulder at Hanover, Virginia, in 1863.]

MILLER, JAMES P., Private
Enlisted at Camp Stokes on October 23, 1864, for the war. Present or accounted for until he surrendered at Appomattox Court House, Virginia, April 9, 1865.

MILLS, JULIUS C., Private
Enlisted in Wake County on April 1, 1864, for the war. Surrendered at Appomattox Court House, Virginia, April 9, 1865.

MILLS, NEWTON F., Private
Enlisted in Wake County on April 1, 1864, for the war. Present or accounted for through February, 1865.

MURPHEY, WILLIE, ——
Negro. Born in 1831. "Served during the Civil War as a servant under the command of Captain W. P. Ward." Resided in Jones County after the war.

NEAL, NATHANIEL S., Private
Enlisted at Camp Green on June 17, 1861. Mustered in

as Private and was promoted to Corporal on August 24, 1861. Promoted to Sergeant on November 2, 1861, but was reduced to ranks on April 22, 1862. Died in a field hospital on January 17, 1865. Place and cause of death not reported.

ODHAM, R., Private

Born in Onslow County and was by occupation a farmer prior to enlisting at Fort Lane on February 1, 1862. Present or accounted for until discharged on July 17, 1862, by reason of being underage. Discharge certificate gives his age as 14.

ODUM, ELISHA, Private

Enlisted in Onslow County on May 1, 1862, for the war. Deserted on February 20, 1865.

ODUM, JAMES P., Private

Born in Onslow County and was by occupation a farmer prior to enlisting at Camp Green on August 8, 1861. Present or accounted for until March 14, 1862, when he was listed as a deserter. Discharged on July 16, 1862, by reason of being overage. Discharge certificate gives his age as 43. [North Carolina pension records indicate he was wounded at Kinston on May 25, 1862.]

OLIVER, ABRAM R., Private

Enlisted at Camp Vance on August 13, 1864, for the war. Present or accounted for through February, 1865.

OWENS, D., Private

Enlisted at Camp Green on June 17, 1861. Present or accounted for until he was drowned at New Bern on December 15, 1861.

OWENS, EDWARD M., Private

Previously served in Company G, 2nd Regiment N.C. State Troops. Transferred to this company on November 5, 1863, in exchange for Private Richard H. Koonce. Deserted on February 14, 1865.

OWENS, H. J., Private

Enlisted at Camp Green on July 16, 1861. Present or accounted for until wounded in the breast at Fredericksburg, Virginia, December 13, 1862. Returned to duty on an unspecified date. Wounded at Bristoe Station, Virginia, October 14, 1863. Died October 30, 1863, of wounds. Place of death not reported.

PEARCE, THOMAS, Private

Resided in Union County and enlisted at Camp Stokes on October 25, 1864, for the war. Present or accounted for until captured at or near Fort Stedman, Virginia, March 25, 1865. Confined at Point Lookout, Maryland, until released on June 16, 1865, after taking the Oath of Allegiance.

PEED, JESSE J., Private

Previously served in Company E, 15th Regiment N.C. Troops (5th Regiment N.C. Volunteers). Transferred to this company on April 1, 1864. Wounded at Wilderness, Virginia, on or about May 5, 1864. Returned to duty prior to November 1, 1864. Present or accounted for until February 4, 1865, when he died in hospital at Richmond, Virginia, of "diarrhoea ch[ronic]."

PEGRAM, RICHARD G., Private

Place and date of enlistment not reported. First listed in the records of this company on April 3, 1864. Last listed in the records of this company on August 23, 1864.

PERRY, WILLIAM T., Private

Resided in Mecklenburg County and enlisted at Camp Green on June 17, 1861. Wounded in both legs at Bristoe Station, Virginia, October 14, 1863. Reported absent wounded until December 15, 1864, when he was retired to the Invalid Corps.

POLK, THOMAS J., Private

Enlisted in Wake County on November 20, 1863, for the war. Wounded in the left elbow at Wilderness, Virginia, on or about May 5, 1864. Returned to duty on May 11, 1864. Deserted on December 1, 1864.

POWELL, CHARLES, Private

Enlisted at Camp Lee on July 21, 1862, for the war. Deserted on July 24, 1862.

PROVOW, W. J., Private

Born in Onslow County and enlisted at Camp Green on August 4, 1861. Present or accounted for until he "fell out on the march in Maryland" and was captured on or about September 12, 1862. Confined at Old Capitol Prison, Washington, D.C. Paroled and transferred to Aiken's Landing, James River, Virginia, where he was received on or about September 27, 1862, for exchange. Declared exchanged at Aiken's Landing on November 10, 1862. Returned to duty on an unspecified date. Wounded at Bristoe Station, Virginia, October 14, 1863. Died on October 15, 1863, of wounds. Place of death not reported.

RHODES, A. E., Private

Enlisted at Fort Lane on September 26, 1861. Present or accounted for through October, 1862; however, he was reported absent sick or absent on detail as a Hospital Steward during much of that period. No further records.

RIGGS, I., Private

Born in Onslow County and was by occupation a farmer prior to enlisting at Camp Green on August 8, 1861. Mustered in as Musician but was reduced to ranks in January-February, 1862. Present or accounted for until he deserted on March 8, 1862. Discharged on July 16, 1862, by reason of being overage. Discharge certificate gives his age as 38.

ROBINSON, GEORGE D., Private

Enlisted at Camp Green at age 20, August 7, 1861. Present or accounted for until he surrendered at Appomattox Court House, Virginia, April 9, 1865.

ROBISON, S. W., Private

Enlisted in Pitt County on June 17, 1861. Deserted prior to September 1, 1861.

ROSS, H., Private

Enlisted in Pitt County on June 17, 1861. Deserted prior to September 1, 1861.

ROWE, LEVI F., Sergeant

Enlisted at Camp Green on August 15, 1861. Mustered in as Private and was promoted to Corporal on October 1, 1862. Promoted to Sergeant in November, 1862-February, 1864. Wounded at or near Reams' Station, Virginia, August 25, 1864. Died on August 30, 1864, of wounds. Place of death not reported.

RUSSELL, D. S., Corporal
Enlisted at Camp Green on August 17, 1861. Mustered in as Private and was promoted to Corporal in December, 1862-October, 1863. Captured at Bristoe Station, Virginia, October 14, 1863. Confined at Old Capitol Prison, Washington, D.C., until transferred to Point Lookout, Maryland, October 27, 1863. Paroled at Point Lookout and transferred to City Point, Virginia, April 27, 1864, for exchange. Returned to duty on an unspecified date. Hospitalized at Petersburg, Virginia, August 27, 1864, with a gunshot wound of the head. Place and date wounded not reported. Died in hospital at Petersburg on August 30, 1864, of wounds.

SCHILLING, CHARLES, Private
Enlisted at Camp Lee on July 21, 1862, for the war. Deserted on July 24, 1862.

SCOTT, HARDY O., Corporal
Born in Jones County and was by occupation a student prior to enlisting in Jones County on June 17, 1861. Mustered in as Private and was promoted to Corporal on April 23, 1862. Present or accounted for until discharged on July 16, 1862, by reason of being underage. Discharge certificate gives his age as 17.

SHUTE, H. S., Private
Born in Craven County and was by occupation a farmer prior to enlisting at Camp Green on August 20, 1861. Present or accounted for until discharged on May 26, 1862, by reason of disability. Discharge certificate gives his age as 46.

SIMPSON, J. D., Private
Born in Jones County and enlisted at Camp Green on July 15, 1861. Present or accounted for until he died at Raleigh on or about November 2, 1862. Cause of death not reported.

SMITH, HENRY, Private
Enlisted in Wake County on February 22, 1864, for the war. Died in hospital at Richmond, Virginia, April 23, 1864, of "pneumonia."

SMITH, JACOB, Private
Enlisted in Wake County on November 20, 1863, for the war. "Sent to hospital" on March 26, 1864. Reported absent sick through February, 1865.

SMITH, R., Private
Enlisted at Camp Green on August 1, 1861. Present or accounted for until discharged in January-February, 1862. Reason discharged not reported.

SPEAS, ISRAEL, Private
Enlisted in Wake County on April 1, 1864, for the war. Wounded at or near Wilderness, Virginia, on or about May 5, 1864. Reported absent wounded or absent sick through February, 1865.

SPRINGER, AARON, Private
Enlisted in Wake County on April 20, 1863, for the war. "Sent to hospital" on April 27, 1864. Reported absent in hospital through February, 1865.

SUMMERS, S. AUGUSTUS, Private
Enlisted in Rowan County on December 5, 1863, for the war. Deserted to the enemy on or about February 22, 1865. Confined at Washington, D.C., until released on

or about February 24, 1865, after taking the Oath of Allegiance.

SWARINGEN, GEORGE I., Private
Enlisted in Wake County on March 20, 1863, for the war. Deserted on September 30, 1864.

TAYLOR, J. R., Private
Enlisted in Jones County on June 17, 1861. Present or accounted for until discharged in January-February, 1862. Reason discharged not reported.

TAYLOR, W. B., Private
Enlisted at Camp Green on July 1, 1861. Present or accounted for through October, 1861. No further records.

TITUS, J. H., Private
Enlisted in Jones County on June 17, 1861. Killed at Bristoe Station, Virginia, October 14, 1863.

WARD, WILLIAM E., Sergeant
Enlisted in Jones County on June 17, 1861. Mustered in as Private and was promoted to Corporal on August 24, 1861. Promoted to Sergeant on August 1, 1862. Wounded in the head at Fredericksburg, Virginia, December 13, 1862. Returned to duty on an unspecified date. Promoted to Sergeant Major on August 25, 1864, and transferred to the Field and Staff of this regiment.

WATERS, D. T., Private
Enlisted in Jones County on May 1, 1862, for the war. Present or accounted for until he "fell out on the march in Maryland" in September, 1862. Captured by the enemy on an unspecified date and was paroled on December 23, 1862. No further records.

WEATHERINGTON, AMOS, Private
Enlisted at Camp Green on July 16, 1861. Present or accounted for until he deserted on March 14, 1862. Returned to duty on an unspecified date subsequent to October 31, 1862. Hospitalized on May 5, 1864, with an unspecified complaint. Returned to duty in November-December, 1864. Deserted on February 14, 1865.

WHITTY, G. W., Private
Born in Jones County where he enlisted on June 17, 1861. Present or accounted for until he died "at camp" on May 6, 1862. Cause of death not reported.

WILKERSON, E., Private
Born in Jones County and was by occupation a farmer prior to enlisting at Camp Green on June 17, 1861. Present or accounted for until discharged on July 16, 1862, by reason of being overage. Discharge certificate gives his age as 38. [May have served later in Company H, 1st Battalion N.C. Local Defense Troops.]

WILLIAMS, A., Private
Born in Jones County and enlisted at Fort Lane on September 11, 1861. Present or accounted for until he died at New Bern on or about April 26, 1862. Cause of death not reported.

WILLIAMS, STEPHEN, Private
Enlisted at Fort Lane on September 11, 1861. Captured at Bristoe Station, Virginia, October 14, 1863. Confined at Old Capitol Prison, Washington, D.C., until transferred to Point Lookout, Maryland, October 27,

1863. Paroled at Point Lookout and transferred to Aiken's Landing, James River, Virginia, February 24, 1865, for exchange.

WILLIAMSON, E., Private
Born in Jones County and was by occupation a sailor prior to enlisting in Onslow County on May 1, 1862, for the war. Present or accounted for until discharged on July 21, 1862. Reason discharged not reported. Discharge certificate gives his age as 35. [May have served later in Company H, 1st Battalion N.C. Local Defense Troops.]

WREN, JAMES R., Private
Enlisted at Fort Lane at age 30, September 3, 1861. Present or accounted for until he "fell out on the march in Maryland" in September, 1862. Returned to duty subsequent to November 30, 1862. Captured at Bristoe Station, Virginia, October 14, 1863. Confined at Old Capitol Prison, Washington, D.C., until transferred to Point Lookout, Maryland, February 3, 1864. Paroled at Point Lookout and transferred to Boulware's Wharf, James River, Virginia, where he was received February 20-21, 1865, for exchange.

COMPANY K

This company, known as the "Saulston Volunteers," was raised in Wayne County. It was mustered in on June 10, 1861, and was later assigned to the 27th Regiment N.C. Troops as Company K. After joining the regiment the company functioned as a part of the regiment, and its history for the war period is reported as a part of the regimental history.

The information contained in the following company roster was compiled principally from company muster rolls for June 10, 1861-October, 1862, and September, 1864-February, 1865. No company muster rolls were found for November, 1862-August, 1864, or for the period after February, 1865. Valuable information was obtained also from primary records such as the Roll of Honor, medical records, prisoner of war records, discharge certificates, and pension applications, and from secondary sources such as postwar rosters and histories, cemetery records, and records of the United Daughters of the Confederacy.

OFFICERS

CAPTAINS

BARDIN, BENJAMIN T.
Enlisted in Wayne County. Elected Captain on June 10, 1861. Present or accounted for until he was defeated for reelection when the regiment was reorganized in April, 1862.

GARDNER, JAMES M.
Born in Wayne County and was by occupation a farmer prior to enlisting in Wayne County on June 10, 1861. Mustered in as 1st Sergeant and was elected Captain on April 22, 1862. Present or accounted for until he resigned on July 17, 1862. Reason he resigned not reported. Later served as Captain of James M. Gardner's Company, 8th Regiment N.C. Senior Reserves.

COOR, HOPTON H.
Previously served as Private in Company A of this regiment. Elected 1st Lieutenant on April 22, 1862, and transferred to this company. Promoted to Captain on

July 18, 1862. Wounded at Wilderness, Virginia, on or about May 5, 1864. Resigned on August 11, 1864, because, after more than two years as Captain of the company, "I am now ordered before a military board for examination, doing me a great injustice." Later served as Private in Company D, 41st Regiment N.C. Troops (3rd Regiment N.C. Cavalry). [North Carolina pension records indicate he was wounded on July 24, 1864.]

PARKS, BERRY
Resided in Wayne County where he enlisted on June 10, 1861. Mustered in as Private and was elected 2nd Lieutenant on April 22, 1862. Promoted to 1st Lieutenant on July 18, 1862. Wounded in the left leg at Bristoe Station, Virginia, October 14, 1863. Returned to duty on an unspecified date. Promoted to Captain on August 30, 1864. Present or accounted for until he surrendered at Appomattox Court House, Virginia, April 9, 1865.

LIEUTENANTS

BARDIN, REDDIN C., 3rd Lieutenant
Enlisted in Wayne County. Elected 3rd Lieutenant on June 10, 1861. Present or accounted for until he was defeated for reelection when the regiment was reorganized in April, 1862. Later served as 1st Lieutenant of Company D, 8th Battalion N.C. Partisan Rangers. [Name rendered as Redding C. Barden in Volume II of this series.]

BARNES, BENNETT G., 1st Lieutenant
Resided in Wayne County where he enlisted on June 10, 1861. Mustered in as Private and was elected 3rd Lieutenant on April 22, 1862. Promoted to 2nd Lieutenant on or about July 18, 1862. Present or accounted for until wounded at Sharpsburg, Maryland, September 17, 1862. Company records indicate he was also captured at Sharpsburg; however, records of the Federal Provost Marshal do not substantiate that report. Reported absent wounded through November, 1862. Returned to duty on an unspecified date and was promoted to 1st Lieutenant on August 30, 1864. Present or accounted for through February, 1865.

HOWELL, DANIEL T., 1st Lieutenant
Enlisted in Wayne County. Elected 1st Lieutenant on June 10, 1861. Present or accounted for until he was defeated for reelection when the regiment was reorganized in April, 1862.

JOHNSON, GABRIEL S., 3rd Lieutenant
Enlisted in Wayne County on June 10, 1861. Mustered in as Private and was promoted to 1st Sergeant on August 5, 1862. Present or accounted for until wounded in the left forearm at Sharpsburg, Maryland, September 17, 1862. Captured at or near Sharpsburg on or about September 19, 1862. Confined at Fort McHenry, Maryland, and at Fort Monroe, Virginia. Paroled and transferred to Aiken's Landing, James River, Virginia, where he was received November 2, 1862, for exchange. Declared exchanged at Aiken's Landing on November 10, 1862. Returned to duty on an unspecified date. Appointed 3rd Lieutenant on February 10, 1863. Killed at Bristoe Station, Virginia, October 14, 1863. [Confederate hospital records give his age as 22.]

LANCASTER, ROBERT B., 3rd Lieutenant
Born in Wayne County where he enlisted on June 10,

1861. Mustered in as Private and was promoted to 1st Sergeant on April 22, 1862. Elected 3rd Lieutenant on August 5, 1862. Present or accounted for until he died at Petersburg, Virginia, September 24, 1862, of disease.

LEWIS, JOSEPH E., 2nd Lieutenant
Enlisted in Wayne County. Elected 2nd Lieutenant on June 10, 1861. Present or accounted for until he was defeated for reelection when the regiment was reorganized in April, 1862.

McINTYRE, A. J., 1st Lieutenant
Appointed 1st Lieutenant on June 16, 1861. Resigned on or about September 20, 1861. Reason he resigned not reported. [May have served later as Captain of Company K, 33rd Regiment N.C. Troops.]

NONCOMMISSIONED OFFICERS AND PRIVATES

ADAMS, ALSEY, Private
Born in Johnston County and was by occupation a laborer prior to enlisting in Wayne County on June 10, 1861. Present or accounted for until discharged on July 16, 1862, by reason of being overage. Discharge certificate gives his age as 36. [May have served later in Company D, 50th Regiment N.C. Troops.]

ALLEN, JAMES F., Private
Born in Union County. Place and date of enlistment not reported. Killed at Reams' Station, Virginia, August 25, 1864.

ALLEN, JOHN, Private
Resided in Union County and enlisted at Camp Holmes on May 27, 1863, for the war. Present or accounted for through February, 1865. Captured by the enemy on an unspecified date. Confined at Point Lookout, Maryland, until released on or about June 26, 1865, after taking the Oath of Allegiance.

BARDEN, ISAAC V., Private
Enlisted in Wayne County on June 10, 1861. Mustered in as Sergeant but was reduced to ranks on April 22, 1862. Present or accounted for until transferred to Company D, 8th Battalion N.C. Partisan Rangers, April 18, 1863.

BARDIN, WILLIAM, Private
Enlisted in Wayne County on June 10, 1861. Present or accounted for until he surrendered at Appomattox Court House, Virginia, April 9, 1865.

BAREFOOT, J. W., Sergeant
Resided in Wayne County. Place and date of enlistment not reported. Promotion record not reported. Paroled at Goldsboro in 1865.

BARNES, JOHN A., Private
Enlisted at Camp Smith at age 19, February 18, 1863, for the war. Wounded at Wilderness, Virginia, on or about May 5, 1864. Detailed as a nurse in hospital at Richmond, Virginia, September 24, 1864. Reported absent on detail through February, 1865. Captured in hospital at Richmond on April 3, 1865, and was paroled at or near Richmond on April 22, 1865.

BASS, BRYANT, Private
Enlisted in Wayne County on June 10, 1861. Present or

accounted for until discharged on or about May 25, 1862, by reason of being overage. [May have served later in Company A, 55th Regiment N.C. Troops.]

BASS, JOHN, Private
Born in Wayne County and was by occupation a farmer prior to enlisting in Wayne County on June 10, 1861. Present or accounted for until discharged on July 16, 1862, by reason of being overage. Discharge certificate gives his age as 35. Reenlisted in the company on March 1, 1864. Deserted on November 25, 1864. Hospitalized at Goldsboro on January 12, 1865, with a gunshot wound. Place and date wounded not reported. Died at Goldsboro on February 3, 1865, of wounds.

BEAMAN, EDWARD G., Sergeant
Enlisted in Wayne County on June 10, 1861. Mustered in as Private and was promoted to Sergeant on April 22, 1862. Wounded at Wilderness, Virginia, on or about May 5, 1864. Returned to duty prior to November 1, 1864. Present or accounted for through February, 1865.

BEAMAN, JAMES, Sergeant
Enlisted in Wayne County on June 10, 1861. Mustered in as Private and was promoted to Sergeant on April 22, 1862. Present or accounted for until wounded at Sharpsburg, Maryland, September 17, 1862. Died at or near Sharpsburg on September 21, 1862, of wounds.

BEDFORD, COUNCIL, Private
Born in Pitt County and was by occupation a farmer prior to enlisting in Wayne County on June 10, 1861. Present or accounted for until discharged on July 16, 1862, by reason of being overage. Discharge certificate gives his age as 44.

BEST, BENJAMIN S., Corporal
Enlisted in Wayne County on June 10, 1861. Mustered in as Private and was promoted to Corporal on January 1, 1865. Present or accounted for until he surrendered at Appomattox Court House, Virginia, April 9, 1865. [North Carolina pension records indicate he was wounded in the right arm on June 6, 1863.]

BEST, ROBERT H., Sergeant
Enlisted in Wayne County on June 10, 1861. Mustered in as Private. Present or accounted for until wounded at Sharpsburg, Maryland, September 17, 1862. Returned to duty on an unspecified date. Promoted to Sergeant in November, 1862-March, 1864. Killed at Wilderness, Virginia, May 5, 1864.

BEST, WILLIAM C., Private
Enlisted at Camp Holmes on August 3, 1864, for the war. Present or accounted for until transferred to Company A, 55th Regiment N.C. Troops, January 31, 1865, in exchange for Private Haywood Word. [May have served previously in Company A, 2nd Regiment N.C. Junior Reserves.]

BLOW, STEPHEN FARMER, Corporal
Enlisted in Wayne County on June 10, 1861. Mustered in as Private and was promoted to Corporal on April 22, 1862. Present or accounted for until wounded in the elbow at Sharpsburg, Maryland, September 17, 1862. Reported absent wounded through November, 1862.

BRACKIN, JULIUS A., ——
North Carolina pension records indicate that he served

in this company.

BRADBERRY, JOHN J., Private
Enlisted at Orange Court House, Virginia, December 20, 1863, for the war. Hospitalized at Richmond, Virginia, June 27, 1864, with a gunshot wound. Place and date wounded not reported. Returned to duty on October 1, 1864. Hospitalized at Richmond in April, 1865, with a gunshot wound of the back. Place and date wounded not reported. Captured in hospital at Richmond on April 3, 1865. Died in hospital at Richmond on April 27, 1865, of "inflammation of the lungs." [May have served previously as Captain of Company D, 13th Battalion N.C. Infantry.]

BUNN, DUNCAN, Private
Resided in Wayne County and enlisted at Orange Court House, Virginia, March 1, 1864, for the war. Captured at Goldsboro on March 18, 1865. Confined at Hart's Island, New York Harbor, until released on June 18, 1865, after taking the Oath of Allegiance.

CARLISLE, JOHN, Private
Enlisted in Wayne County on June 10, 1861. Present or accounted for until hospitalized at Charlottesville, Virginia, September 6, 1862, with a gunshot wound of the finger. Place and date wounded not reported. Finger amputated. Reported absent wounded through November, 1862. Returned to duty on an unspecified date. Reported absent sick in September-October, 1864, but returned to duty in November-December, 1864. Hospitalized at Richmond, Virginia, in February, 1865, and was apparently captured in hospital at Richmond on April 3, 1865. Transferred to the Federal Provost Marshal on April 14, 1865.

CHASE, ALLEN, Private
Enlisted in Wayne County on September 1, 1861. Present or accounted for until discharged on or about May 26, 1862. Reason discharged not reported.

CHASE, HENRY, Private
Enlisted in Wake County on December 1, 1863, for the war. Wounded at Wilderness, Virginia, on or about May 5, 1864. Reported absent wounded or absent sick through February, 1865. Deserted to the enemy on March 25, 1865. Confined at Washington, D.C., until released on or about April 5, 1865, after taking the Oath of Allegiance.

CHASE, STARLIN, Private
Born in Wayne County and was by occupation a farmer prior to enlisting in Wayne County on September 1, 1861. Present or accounted for until discharged on July 16, 1862, by reason of being underage. Discharge certificate gives his age as 16. Later served in Company D, 1st Battalion N.C. Local Defense Troops.

COBB, JAMES MONROE, Corporal
Born in Edgecombe County and enlisted in Wayne County on June 10, 1861. Mustered in as Corporal. Present or accounted for until he died at Goldsboro on April 1, 1862. Cause of death not reported.

COLEY, GABRIEL H., Private
Enlisted in Wayne County at age 24, May 15, 1862, for the war. Wounded in the thigh at Fredericksburg, Virginia, December 13, 1862. Returned to duty on an unspecified date. Wounded in the left hand at Wilderness, Virginia, on or about May 5, 1864. Reported absent wounded through February, 1865. [May have served previously in Company H, 9th Regiment N.C. State Troops (1st Regiment N.C. Cavalry).]

COLEY, JOHN C., Private
Enlisted in Wayne County at age 27, May 15, 1862, for the war. Deserted to the enemy on or about March 17, 1865. Confined at Washington, D.C., until released on or about March 24, 1865, after taking the Oath of Allegiance.

COLEY, PATRICK C., Private
Born in Wayne County and was by occupation a carpenter prior to enlisting in Wayne County on June 10, 1861. Present or accounted for until discharged on May 6, 1862, by reason of "right inguinal hernia." Discharge certificate gives his age as 22.

COMBS, ISAAC, Private
Born in Wayne County where he resided prior to enlisting on June 10, 1861. Present or accounted for until he died at or near Camp Gatlin on February 18, 1862. Cause of death not reported.

COMBS, JAMES, Private
Resided in Wayne County where he enlisted on June 10, 1861. Wounded in the arm in Virginia in June, 1864. Returned to duty prior to November 1, 1864. Deserted on December 8, 1864. Captured by the enemy at Goldsboro on March 24-25, 1865. Confined at Hart's Island, New York Harbor, until released on June 18, 1865, after taking the Oath of Allegiance.

COX, WILLIAM S., Private
Enlisted in Wake County on December 20, 1863, for the war. Wounded in the side and neck at or near Wilderness, Virginia, on or about May 5, 1864. Company records do not indicate whether he returned to duty; however, he died in hospital at Richmond, Virginia, November 15, 1864. Cause of death not reported.

CROCKER, ELI H., Private
Enlisted in Wayne County on June 10, 1861. Present or accounted for through May 15, 1864. Died in hospital at Lynchburg, Virginia, prior to November 1, 1864. Date and cause of death not reported.

DARDIN, CALVIN, Musician
Enlisted in Wayne County on June 10, 1861. Mustered in as Private and was promoted to Musician (Drummer) on April 22, 1862. Present or accounted for through October, 1862. [May have served later as Private in Company D, 8th Battalion N.C. Partisan Rangers.]

DARDIN, WILLIAM R., Private
Enlisted in Wayne County on June 10, 1861. Mustered in as Sergeant but was reduced to ranks on April 22, 1862. Present or accounted for until he died at Nahunta on September 18, 1862, of disease.

EDMUNDSON, JAMES CARRAWAY, Private
Enlisted in Wayne County at age 18, June 10, 1861. Mustered in as Private and was promoted to Corporal in November, 1862-October, 1864. Wounded in the foot in Virginia in June, 1864. Returned to duty prior to

November 1, 1864. Promoted to Sergeant on November 6, 1864, but was reduced to ranks subsequent to February 28, 1865. Deserted to the enemy on or about April 2, 1865. Confined at Washington, D.C., until released on or about April 5, 1865, after taking the Oath of Allegiance.

ELMORE, THOMAS, Private
Enlisted in Wayne County on June 10, 1861. Died in hospital at Gordonsville, Virginia, August 23, 1863, of "diarrhoea chr[onic]."

ETHERIDGE, DANIEL, 1st Sergeant
Born in Wayne County where he enlisted on June 10, 1861. Mustered in as Private and was promoted to Sergeant on April 22, 1862. Promoted to 1st Sergeant in November, 1862-October, 1864. Died in hospital at Richmond, Virginia, October 18, 1864, of "diarrhoea chron[ic]."

ETHERIDGE, HENRY C., Private
Previously served in Company F of this regiment. Enlisted in this company in Wayne County on May 15, 1862, for the war. Present or accounted for through November, 1862. Died in Wayne County on an unspecified date prior to December 5, 1864. Cause of death not reported.

ETHERIDGE, WILLIAM, Private
Enlisted in Wayne County on June 10, 1861. Wounded at Wilderness, Virginia, on or about May 5, 1864. Returned to duty prior to November 1, 1864. Present or accounted for through February, 1865.

ETHERIDGE, WILLIS, Private
Enlisted in Wayne County on June 10, 1861. Deserted on February 23, 1865. Went over to the enemy on March 24, 1865. Confined at Washington, D.C., until released on or about April 5, 1865, after taking the Oath of Allegiance.

EVANS, WILLIS, Private
Place and date of enlistment not reported. Deserted to the enemy on or about March 24, 1865.

GARDNER, JOSIAH, Sergeant
Enlisted in Wayne County on June 10, 1861. Mustered in as Private and was promoted to Sergeant in September-October, 1864. Deserted to the enemy on or about April 2, 1865. Confined at Washington, D.C., until released on or about April 5, 1865, after taking the Oath of Allegiance. [North Carolina pension records indicate he was wounded at Bristoe Station, Virginia, on or about October 14, 1863.]

GARDNER, WILLIAM, Private
Enlisted in Wayne County on June 10, 1861. Deserted on or about August 20, 1861.

GINN, JAMES HYRAM, Private
Enlisted in Wayne County on June 10, 1861. Wounded in the left hand at Wilderness, Virginia, on or about May 5, 1864. Reported absent wounded through February, 1865. Deserted to the enemy on or about March 24, 1865. Confined at Washington, D.C., until released on or about April 5, 1865, after taking the Oath of Allegiance.

GURLEY, WILLIAM H., Private
Born in Wayne County where he resided as a farmer

prior to enlisting in Wayne County on June 10, 1861. Present or accounted for until discharged on December 6, 1862, by reason of "pulmonary tuberculosis." Discharge certificate gives his age as 18. Reenlisted in the company on December 1, 1863. Wounded at Wilderness, Virginia, on or about May 5, 1864. Wounded in the breast at or near Petersburg, Virginia, June 15, 1864. Reported absent wounded through February, 1865. Captured by the enemy near Goldsboro on March 24, 1865. Confined at Point Lookout, Maryland, until released on June 27, 1865, after taking the Oath of Allegiance.

HAM, COUNCIL, Private
Born in Wayne County and was by occupation a farmer prior to enlisting in Wayne County on June 10, 1861. Died in hospital at Lynchburg, Virginia, January 2, 1863, of "diarrhoea chron[ic]." Death records give his age as 25.

HAM, JORDAN B., Private
Enlisted in Wayne County on June 10, 1861. Transferred to Company E, 62nd Regiment Georgia Cavalry, February 29, 1864.

HEAD, ASA, Private
Enlisted in Wayne County on August 5, 1861. Present or accounted for until discharged on May 25, 1862. Reason discharged not reported.

HEATH, S. A., Sergeant
Born in Wayne County and was by occupation a farmer prior to enlisting in Wayne County on May 15, 1862, for the war. Mustered in as Private and was promoted to Corporal in September, 1862. Promoted to Sergeant on October 1, 1862. Died in hospital at Petersburg, Virginia, January 15, 1863, of "typhoid fever." Death records give his age as 22.

HEFNER, DANIEL, ———
North Carolina pension records indicate that he served in this company.

HILL, JAMES P., Private
Born in Wayne County where he enlisted on June 10, 1861. Died "at his father's residence in Wayne County" on March 25, 1862. Cause of death not reported.

HINSON, RICHARD H., Private
Enlisted at Camp Holmes on October 18, 1864, for the war. Present or accounted for until he deserted on February 7, 1865. Went over to the enemy on or about March 24, 1865. Confined at Washington, D.C., until released on or about April 5, 1865, after taking the Oath of Allegiance.

HOLLAND, JOSEPH W., Private
Enlisted in Wayne County on June 10, 1861. Present or accounted for until wounded and captured at or near South Mountain, Maryland, on or about September 15, 1862. Confined at Fort Delaware, Delaware, until transferred to Aiken's Landing, James River, Virginia, October 2, 1862, for exchange. Declared exchanged at Aiken's Landing on November 10, 1862. Returned to duty on an unspecified date. Wounded at Wilderness, Virginia, on or about May 5, 1864. Returned to duty prior to November 1, 1864. Captured at or near Goldsboro on or about March 28-29, 1865. Confined at

Hart's Island, New York Harbor, until released on June 18, 1865, after taking the Oath of Allegiance.

HOLLAND, RUFUS H., Private
Resided in Wayne County where he enlisted at age 27, June 10, 1861. Mustered in as Corporal but was reduced to ranks on April 22, 1862. Present or accounted for through April 1, 1865; however, he was reported on detail as a shoemaker during much of that period. Captured near Petersburg, Virginia, April 2, 1865. Confined at Point Lookout, Maryland, until released on June 27, 1865, after taking the Oath of Allegiance. [North Carolina pension records indicate he was wounded at Knoxville, Tennessee, in 1863 and was wounded at Petersburg in 1864.]

HOLLAND, SIMON J., Private
Enlisted in Wayne County on June 10, 1861. Deserted to the enemy on or about March 18, 1865. Confined at Washington, D.C., until released on or about March 24, 1865, after taking the Oath of Allegiance.

HOOKS, HARDY, Private
Born in Wayne County and was by occupation a farmer prior to enlisting in Wayne County on June 10, 1861. Present or accounted for until discharged on July 16, 1862, by reason of being overage. Discharge certificate gives his age as 35. [May have served later in Company D, 8th Battalion N.C. Partisan Rangers.]

HORNE, THOMAS G., Private
Born in Edgecombe County and enlisted in Wayne County on September 1, 1861. Present or accounted for until killed at Sharpsburg, Maryland, September 17, 1862.

HOWELL, DANIEL T., Private
Enlisted in Wayne County on June 10, 1861. Present or accounted for through December, 1861. No further records.

HOWELL, STEPHEN, Private
Enlisted in Wayne County on June 10, 1861. Died in hospital at Richmond, Virginia, January 1, 1863, of ''variola.''

HUGHES, AUGUSTUS, Private
Born in Wayne County and was by occupation a farmer prior to enlisting in Wayne County on June 10, 1861. Present or accounted for until captured at New Bern on March 14, 1862. Confined at Fort Columbus, New York Harbor. Exchanged on or about [June 10], 1862. Returned to duty prior to September 17, 1862, when he was wounded in the left thigh and captured at Sharpsburg, Maryland. Confined at Fort McHenry, Maryland. Paroled and transferred to Aiken's Landing, James River, Virginia, where he was received October 23, 1862, for exchange. Declared exchanged at Aiken's Landing on November 10, 1862. Discharged on April 16, 1863, by reason of wounds received at Sharpsburg ''resulting in contraction of the muscles & inability on the part of the man to extend his leg.'' Discharge certificate gives his age as 30.

LAMBETH, DAVID H., Private
Enlisted at Camp Holmes on April 23, 1863, for the war. Wounded in the left arm and captured at or near Bristoe Station, Virginia, on or about October 14, 1863. Left arm amputated. Confined at various Federal hospitals

until confined at Old Capitol Prison, Washington, D.C., December 18, 1863. Transferred to Point Lookout, Maryland, February 3, 1864. Paroled at Point Lookout and transferred to City Point, Virginia, where he was received April 30, 1864, for exchange. Reported absent wounded until December 29, 1864, when he was retired to the Invalid Corps. [Medical records dated October-November, 1863, give his age as 19.]

LANCASTER, MONROE, Private
Born in Wayne County and was by occupation a farmer prior to enlisting in Wayne County on June 10, 1861. Present or accounted for until discharged on July 16, 1862, by reason of being underage. Discharge certificate gives his age as 16. [May have served later in Company C, 68th Regiment N.C. Troops.]

LANCASTER, WILLIAM T., Corporal
Resided in Wayne County where he enlisted on June 10, 1861. Mustered in as Private. Wounded in the hip at Wilderness, Virginia, on or about May 5, 1864. Returned to duty in November-December, 1864. Promoted to Corporal in January-February, 1865. Deserted to the enemy on February 7, 1865. Confined at Fort Monroe, Virginia. Transferred to Washington, D.C., April 2, 1865. Released at Washington on or about April 5, 1865, after taking the Oath of Allegiance.

LANGSTON, ALFRED L., Private
Enlisted in Wayne County on June 10, 1861. Wounded in the left thigh at Wilderness, Virginia, May 5, 1864. Returned to duty subsequent to February 28, 1865. Deserted to the enemy on or about March 25, 1865. Confined at Washington, D.C., until released on or about April 5, 1865, after taking the Oath of Allegiance.

LANGSTON, DANIEL T., Private
Born in Wayne County and was by occupation a farmer prior to enlisting in Wayne County on June 10, 1861. Present or accounted for until discharged on July 16, 1862, by reason of being underage. Discharge certificate gives his age as 17. [May have served later in Company D, 8th Battalion N.C. Partisan Rangers.]

LEWIS, JAMES, Private
Enlisted in Wake County on June 10, 1861. Mustered in as Sergeant but was reduced to ranks on April 22, 1862. Present or accounted for until September-October, 1862, when he was reported absent sick at Winchester, Virginia. Reported absent sick at Winchester through November, 1862.

LONG, JOHN C., Private
Previously served in Company B, 15th Regiment N.C. Troops (5th Regiment N.C. Volunteers). Transferred to this company on March 5, 1864. Wounded at Wilderness, Virginia, on or about May 5, 1864. Reported on detail as a guard from October 25, 1864, through February 7, 1865. Paroled at Charlotte on May 3, 1865.

LOVETT, LEWIS, Private
Resided in Wayne County where he enlisted on June 10, 1861. Deserted on December 8, 1864. Captured by the enemy at Goldsboro on March 24, 1865. Confined at Hart's Island, New York Harbor, until released on June 19, 1865, after taking the Oath of Allegiance.

McCARTER, OMA, Private
Enlisted in Wayne County on June 10, 1861. Present or

accounted for until discharged on July 16, 1862, by reason of being overage.

MARLOW, WILLIAM H., Private
Born in Edgecombe County and was by occupation a farmer prior to enlisting in Wayne County on June 10, 1861. Present or accounted for until discharged on April 28, 1862, by reason of "a fractured forearm." Place and date injured not reported. Discharge certificate gives his age as 58.

MATHEWS, DUNKIN L., Private
Enlisted in Nash County on February 28, 1863, for the war. Died in hospital at Richmond, Virginia, on or about September 16, 1864, of "diarrhoea chron[ic]."

MATTOX, JOHN J., Sergeant
Enlisted in Wayne County on June 10, 1861. Mustered in as Sergeant. Killed at Bristoe Station, Virginia, on or about October 14, 1863.

MOORE, NATHANIEL, Private
Enlisted in Wayne County on September 1, 1861. Court-martialed on or about December 24, 1861. Reason he was court-martialed not reported. Company muster roll dated January-February, 1862, states that he was present but indicates that his pay was stopped for desertion. Present or accounted for until May 27, 1862, when he deserted.

MULLIS, ANDREW J., Private
Enlisted at Camp Holmes on May 21, 1863, for the war. Detailed for guard duty at Charlotte on April 21, 1864. Reported absent on detail at Charlotte through February 7, 1865. Paroled at Charlotte on May 3, 1865.

MULLIS, CHARLES P., Private
Enlisted in Stokes County at age 31, November 3, 1864, for the war. Present or accounted for until he deserted on February 22, 1865.

MULLIS, TYSON, Private
Enlisted at Camp Holmes on May 20, 1863, for the war. Present or accounted for through February, 1865.

MUSGRAVE, WILLIAM H., Private
Enlisted in Wayne County on June 10, 1861. Present or accounted for until wounded at Sharpsburg, Maryland, September 17, 1862. Returned to duty on an unspecified date. Present or accounted for through April 20, 1864. No further records.

NEWSOM, BENNETT, Private
Enlisted in Wayne County on June 10, 1861. Present or accounted for until he died in hospital at Richmond, Virginia, October 21, 1862, of "diphtheria."

NEWSOM, JOAB, Corporal
Enlisted in Wayne County on May 15, 1862, for the war. Mustered in as Private. Present or accounted for until wounded at Sharpsburg, Maryland, September 17, 1862. Promoted to Corporal in September-October, 1862. Returned to duty subsequent to November 30, 1862. Wounded in the head in Virginia in June, 1864. Returned to duty prior to November 1, 1864. Present or accounted for until he deserted on February 22, 1865.

NEWSOM, JORDAN, Private
Enlisted in Wayne County on June 10, 1861. Present or

accounted for through February, 1865.

PARKS, AMAZIAH, Private
Previously served in Company I, 15th Regiment N.C. Troops (5th Regiment N.C. Volunteers). Transferred to this company on February 10, 1863, in exchange for Private David Peacock. Discharged on December 7, 1864, by reason of disability.

PARKS, JOSEPH E., Private
Born in Wayne County and was by occupation a farmer prior to enlisting in Wayne County on June 10, 1861. Present or accounted for until wounded and possibly captured at Sharpsburg, Maryland, September 17, 1862. Died at or near Sharpsburg on September 20, 1862, of wounds. Death records give his age as 27.

PATE, DAVID, Private
Enlisted at Camp Holmes on August 28, 1864, for the war. Present or accounted for until captured at Goldsboro on March 28, 1865. Took the Oath of Allegiance the same date.

PATE, STEPHEN W., Private
Enlisted at Camp Holmes on November 22, 1864, for the war. Present or accounted for until he deserted on February 22, 1865. Returned to duty on an unspecified date. Surrendered at Appomattox Court House, Virginia, April 9, 1865.

PATE, WILLIAM C., Private
Enlisted at Camp Holmes at age 16, November 22, 1864, for the war. Present or accounted for until discharged on February 4, 1865, by reason of being underage.

PEACOCK, BRYANT, Private
Enlisted in Wayne County on July 20, 1861. Present or accounted for through October, 1861. Deserted in November-December, 1861. Apprehended and was court-martialed on or about December 24, 1861. Returned to duty in January-February, 1862. Present or accounted for until discharged on or about May 25, 1862. Reason discharged not reported.

PEACOCK, DAVID, Private
Resided in Wayne County where he enlisted on June 10, 1861. Present or accounted for until transferred to Company I, 15th Regiment N.C. Troops (5th Regiment N.C. Volunteers), on or about February 10, 1863, in exchange for Private Amaziah Parks.

PEEL, SAMUEL A., Private
Enlisted in Wayne County at age 20, June 10, 1861. Deserted on February 7, 1865.

PERKINS, EZEKIEL, Private
Enlisted in Wayne County on June 10, 1861. Present or accounted for until he deserted on or about August 20, 1861.

PERKINS, FENEL, Private
Resided in Wayne County and enlisted at Petersburg, Virginia, at age 19, November 1, 1864, for the war. Present or accounted for until wounded in the left leg and captured at Hatcher's Run, Virginia, March 31, 1865. Confined at Point Lookout, Maryland, until released on June 16, 1865, after taking the Oath of

Allegiance.

PHILLIPS, RUFUS, Private
Born in Wayne County and was by occupation a farmer prior to enlisting in Wayne County on June 10, 1861. Died at Goldsboro on January 15, 1863. Cause of death not reported. Death records give his age as 26.

PLUNK, JACOB F., Private
Born in Gaston County and was by occupation a shoemaker prior to enlisting in Gaston County on March 5, 1863, for the war. Discharged on April 10, 1863, by reason of an injury to the hip joint suffered before he entered the service.

POLK, ANDREW J., Private
Enlisted at Camp Holmes on May 20, 1863, for the war. Deserted on December 8, 1864.

POTTER, THOMAS, Private
Born in Lenoir County and was by occupation a farmer prior to enlisting in Wayne County on June 10, 1861. Present or accounted for until discharged on November 3, 1862, by reason of "hypertrophy of heart." Discharge certificate gives his age as 23.

RADFORD, JOSHUA L., Private
Enlisted in Wayne County on June 10, 1861. Present or accounted for through November, 1862. No further records.

RODGERS, V. A., Private
Born in Greene County and resided in Wayne County where he was by occupation a carpenter prior to enlisting in Wayne County on June 10, 1861. Present or accounted for until discharged on July 16, 1862, by reason of being overage. Discharge certificate gives his age as 35. Later served in Company A of this regiment.

SASSER, STEPHEN L., Private
Enlisted in Wayne County on June 10, 1861. Reported absent without leave on April 30, 1864. Returned to duty in November-December, 1864. Deserted on February 20, 1865. Went over to the enemy on March 24, 1865. Confined at Washington, D.C., until released on or about April 6, 1865, after taking the Oath of Allegiance.

SASSER, TIPPO H., Private
Previously served in Company I, 35th Regiment N.C. Troops. Enlisted in this company at Camp Holmes on October 18, 1864, for the war. Present or accounted for until captured on the South Side Railroad, Virginia, April 2, 1865. Confined at Hart's Island, New York Harbor, until released on June 19, 1865, after taking the Oath of Allegiance.

SAULS, EDWIN M., Private
Enlisted in Wayne County on June 10, 1861. Present or accounted for until he surrendered at Appomattox Court House, Virginia, April 9, 1865.

SAULS, WILLIAM, Private
Enlisted in Wayne County on April 30, 1862, for the war. Deserted on February 7, 1865. Went over to the enemy at Goldsboro on March 23, 1865. Confined at Washington, D.C., until released on or about April 6, 1865, after taking the Oath of Allegiance. [May have served also in Company E, 62nd Regiment Georgia Cavalry.]

SAULS, WILLIAM R., Private
Enlisted in Wayne County on June 10, 1861. Mustered in as Private and was promoted to Corporal on April 22, 1862. Reduced to ranks in September-October, 1862. Wounded in the head at Fredericksburg, Virginia, December 13, 1862. Returned to duty on an unspecified date. Present or accounted for through June 6, 1864. No further records.

SAULS, WILLIAM RILEY, Private
Enlisted in Wayne County on June 10, 1861. Present or accounted for until captured at or near Sharpsburg, Maryland, on or about September 17, 1862. Confined at Fort Delaware, Delaware, until transferred to Aiken's Landing, James River, Virginia, October 2, 1862, for exchange. Declared exchanged at Aiken's Landing on November 10, 1862. Returned to duty on an unspecified date. Killed at Bristoe Station, Virginia, October 14, 1863.

SAVAGE, HAYWOOD, Private
Born in Wayne County and was by occupation a farmer prior to enlisting in Wayne County on June 10, 1861. Died near Pikeville on February 24, 1863. Cause of death not reported. Death records give his age as 20.

SHADDING, BURWELL, Private
Was by occupation a farmer prior to enlisting in Wayne County on June 10, 1861. Present or accounted for until discharged on July 16, 1862, by reason of being overage. Discharge certificate gives his age as 36.

SMITH, ANDREW J., Private
Enlisted at Camp Holmes on May 23, 1863, for the war. Deserted on February 2, 1865.

SMITH, ERASTUS, Private
Born in Wayne County and was by occupation a farmer prior to enlisting in Wayne County on June 10, 1861. Present or accounted for until discharged on May 8, 1862, by reason of "repeated attacks of rheumatism, rendering him completely helpless at times." Discharge certificate gives his age as 21.

SMITH, GEORGE, Private
Resided in Wayne County where he enlisted on June 10, 1861. Captured at Hatcher's Run, Virginia, March 31, 1865. Confined at Point Lookout, Maryland, until released on June 20, 1865, after taking the Oath of Allegiance.

SMITH, J. C., Private
Resided in Wayne County. Place and date of enlistment not reported. Paroled at Goldsboro on May 16, 1865.

SMITH, JAMES G., Sergeant
Resided in Wayne County where he enlisted on June 10, 1861. Mustered in as Private and was promoted to Sergeant subsequent to February 28, 1865. Captured on the South Side Railroad, near Petersburg, Virginia, April 2, 1865. Confined at Hart's Island, New York Harbor, until released on June 18, 1865, after taking the Oath of Allegiance.

SMITH, JAMES R., Private
Born in Wayne County and was by occupation a farmer prior to enlisting in Wayne County on June 10, 1861. Present or accounted for until he died in hospital at

Petersburg, Virginia, or at Williamsburg, Virginia, August 9, 1862, of "rem[ittent] febris."

SMITH, JOHN, Private
Enlisted in Wayne County on June 10, 1861. Wounded in the right arm at Cold Harbor, Virginia, June 3, 1864. Returned to duty in November-December, 1864. Deserted on February 7, 1865. Deserted to the enemy at Goldsboro on March 25, 1865. Confined at Washington, D.C., until released on or about April 5, 1865, after taking the Oath of Allegiance.

SMITH, JOHN F., Private
Enlisted in Wayne County on May 15, 1862, for the war. Wounded in the hip in Virginia in June, 1864. Returned to duty prior to November 1, 1864. Deserted on November 25, 1864.

SMITH, JOSIAH J., Private
Resided in Wayne County where he enlisted at age 30, June 10, 1861. Mustered in as Private and was promoted to Corporal on April 22, 1862. Reduced to ranks in November, 1862-March, 1864. Reported missing on October 27, 1864, and was reported under arrest in November-December, 1864. Court-martialed in January-February, 1865. Captured by the enemy at Hatcher's Run, Virginia, March 31, 1865. Confined at Point Lookout, Maryland, until released on June 20, 1865, after taking the Oath of Allegiance.

SMITH, JOSIAH P., Corporal
Enlisted in Wayne County on June 10, 1861. Mustered in as Private. Present or accounted for until wounded at Sharpsburg, Maryland, September 17, 1862. Returned to duty on an unspecified date. Promoted to Corporal in November, 1862-October, 1863. Retired to the Invalid Corps on April 15, 1864, by reason of disability.

SMITH, NEEDHAM J., 1st Sergeant
Born in Wayne County and was by occupation a farmer prior to enlisting in Wayne County on June 10, 1861. Mustered in as Corporal and was promoted to Sergeant in November, 1862-March, 1864. Wounded at Wilderness, Virginia, on or about May 5, 1864. Returned to duty prior to November 1, 1864. Promoted to 1st Sergeant on February 7, 1865. Present or accounted for through February, 1865.

SMITH, OLIVER, Private
Born in Wayne County and was by occupation a farmer prior to enlisting in Wayne County on June 10, 1861. Mustered in as Corporal but was reduced to ranks on April 22, 1862. Present or accounted for until discharged on July 16, 1862, by reason of being overage. Discharge certificate gives his age as 35.

SMITH, THADDEUS, Private
Enlisted in Wayne County on June 10, 1861. Captured at Hatcher's Run, Virginia, March 31, 1865. Confined at Point Lookout, Maryland, where he died on May 21, 1865, of "pneumonia."

SNIDER, PETER, Private
Enlisted at Camp Holmes on May 23, 1863, for the war. Wounded at Wilderness, Virginia, on or about May 5, 1864. Died in hospital at Richmond, Virginia, August 8, 1864. Cause of death not reported.

TAYLOR, JESSE, Private
Enlisted in Wayne County on September 1, 1861.

Wounded in the leg near Petersburg, Virginia, June 15, 1864. Leg amputated. Reported absent wounded through February, 1865.

TAYLOR, JOHN A., Private
Born in Wayne County where he resided as a mechanic prior to enlisting in Wayne County on June 10, 1861. Mustered in as Musician (Drummer) but was reduced to ranks on April 22, 1862. Present or accounted for until discharged on July 16, 1862, by reason of being overage. Discharge certificate gives his age as 42.

TAYLOR, T. A., Private
Resided in Wayne County. Place and date of enlistment not reported. Paroled at Goldsboro in 1865.

THOMAS, JOHN J., Private
Enlisted in Wayne County on June 10, 1861. Deserted on December 8, 1864. Went over to the enemy at Goldsboro on March 23, 1865. Confined at Washington, D.C. No further records.

THOMPSON, WILLIE, Private
Enlistment date reported as August 18, 1861; however, he was not listed in the records of this company until October, 1863. Rank reported as Sergeant on that date. Hospitalized at Richmond, Virginia, May 7, 1864, with a gunshot wound of the left hand. Place and date wounded not reported. Returned to duty prior to November 1, 1864, and was promoted to 1st Sergeant on that date. Reduced to ranks in January-February, 1865. Deserted on February 7, 1865. Returned to duty prior to April 9, 1865, when he surrendered at Appomattox Court House, Virginia.

TURNER, SAMUEL D., Private
Resided in Granville County and enlisted in Wayne County on September 1, 1861. Promoted to Musician in September-October, 1862, and transferred to the regimental band.

VICK, P. ELIJAH, Private
Born in Nash County and was by occupation a farmer prior to enlisting in Wayne County on June 10, 1861. Present or accounted for until discharged on July 16, 1862, by reason of being underage. Discharge certificate gives his age as 17. Enlisted in Company D, 8th Battalion N.C. Partisan Rangers, February 2, 1863. Transferred back to this company on April 19, 1863. Died in an unspecified North Carolina hospital on May 24, 1863, of "pneumonia."

WORD, HAYWOOD, Private
Previously served in Company A, 55th Regiment N.C. Troops. Transferred to this company on January 31, 1865, in exchange for Private William C. Best. Present or accounted for until paroled at Burkeville Junction, Virginia, April 14-17, 1865.

MISCELLANEOUS

Civil War records indicate that the following soldiers served in the 27th Regiment N.C. Troops; however, the companies in which they served are not reported.

BINKLEY, J. G., ———
Born in Forsyth County. Place and date of enlistment not reported. Killed at Reams' Station, Virginia, August

25, 1864. [May have served previously in Company B, 4th Battalion N.C. Junior Reserves.]

HILL, JOSHUA A., Private
Resided in Randolph County. Place and date of enlistment not reported. Deserted to the enemy on or about September 29, 1864. Confined at Washington, D.C., until released on or about October 1, 1864, after taking the Oath of Allegiance.

LINDLEY, FRANKLIN D., ———
North Carolina pension records indicate that he served in this regiment.

MEASLER, W. G., Private
Resided in Bertie County. Place and date of enlistment not reported. Deserted to the enemy on or about October 27, 1864. Confined at Fort Monroe, Virginia. Released on or about November 1, 1864, after taking the Oath of Allegiance.

THOMAS, J. W., Private
Place and date of enlistment not reported. Deserted to the enemy on or about [March 31,] 1865. Confined at Washington, D.C., until released on or about April 5, 1865, after taking the Oath of Allegiance.

THOMAS, ROBERT N., Private
Previously served in Company G, 24th Regiment N.C. Troops (14th Regiment N.C. Volunteers). Transferred to this regiment in January-February, 1865. No further records.

WEST, JAMES, Private
Place and date of enlistment not reported. Deserted to the enemy on or about [March 31,] 1865. Confined at Washington, D.C., until released on or about April 5, 1865, after taking the Oath of Allegiance.

28th REGIMENT N.C. TROOPS

This regiment was organized at Camp Fisher, near High Point, on September 21, 1861, for twelve months' service. On September 30 the regiment left for Wilmington, where it arrived on October 1 and was assigned to General Joseph R. Anderson's command. The regiment went into camp near the city on the Atlantic & North Carolina Railroad, constructed barracks, and was drilled in regimental formations and other military arts. Detachments from the regiment were sent to guard railroad bridges from Wilmington to Goldsboro and north to the Virginia line. On February 13, 1862, the regiment's strength was reported as 933 men. Six of the regiment's twelve-months companies were reorganized about that time to serve for the duration of the war.

On March 13, 1862, the 28th Regiment entrained for New Bern, which was under attack by a Federal force commanded by General Ambrose E. Burnside. The regiment arrived on the field too late to take part in the battle of March 14 but was placed in a rear-guard position to help cover the Confederate retreat. It then retired to Kinston. Six members of the regiment were reported missing during the New Bern campaign.

At Kinston, on March 17, the 28th Regiment was assigned to General Lawrence O'B. Branch's brigade along with the 18th Regiment N.C. Troops (8th Regiment N.C. Volunteers), 25th Regiment N.C. Troops, 33rd Regiment N.C. Troops, 37th Regiment N.C. Troops, John N. Whitford's foot artillery battalion, Alexander C. Latham's and Samuel R. Bunting's batteries, and Peter G. Evans's cavalry unit. The 25th Regiment N.C. Troops was transferred and the 7th Regiment N.C. State Troops was assigned to the brigade in its place shortly thereafter. Branch's brigade remained in the Kinston area for six weeks, during which time the foot artillery and cavalry units were reassigned. On April 12 the four remaining twelve-months' companies of the 28th Regiment were reorganized to serve for the duration of the war.

In early May, 1862, the situation in Virginia, where Federal armies were advancing in the Shenandoah Valley and on the peninsula between the James and York rivers, became so ominous that troops were transferred from North Carolina, and Branch's brigade was ordered to the vicinity of Gordonsville. The 28th Regiment entrained at Kinston on May 2 and on May 6 arrived at Rapidan Station, Virginia, where it went on picket duty. The regiment moved to Gordonsville on May 15 and rejoined the brigade. On May 16 the brigade was ordered toward the Shenandoah Valley; however, when it reached the foothills of the Blue Ridge Mountains it was ordered back to Gordonsville and then to Hanover Court House northeast of Richmond. There the brigade performed picket duty and attempted to watch the right flank of General George B. McClellan's Federal army near Richmond and another Federal force at Fredericksburg.

On May 26 General Branch moved his brigade from Hanover Court House to Slash Church, a position which was still between the two Federal forces but which afforded a direct route to Ashland should Branch be forced to retire. On the morning of May 27 Branch sent the 28th Regiment forward to Taliaferro's Mill, where it soon found itself cut off from the remainder of the brigade by a superior Federal force. Colonel James H. Lane of the 28th Regiment reported the ensuing action as follows (*Official Records*, Series I, Vol. XI, pt. 1, pp. 743-745):

In obedience to your [General Branch's] orders I proceeded to Taliaferro's Mill on the morning of the 27th of May with 890 of my regiment and a section of [Alexander C.] Latham's battery, commanded by

Lieut. J. R. Potts. While I was there, examining the ground for a suitable position for my forces information was received that the enemy was approaching in the direction of Hanover Court-House. I immediately retraced my steps, marching left in front, and throwing out a platoon of Company G as flankers, under Capt. George B. Johnston, to my right, the supposed direction of the enemy, while the other was thrown to my left and front, under Lieut. E. G. Morrow. It was not until we had nearly emerged from the pine thicket in front of Dr. Kinney's that we discovered some of the enemy ambushed in the same to our left, and where we were not expecting them. The regiment was immediately halted, faced by the rear rank, and wheeled to the right through the woods, pouring a deadly fire into a portion of the Twenty-fifth New York Regiment as they executed the movement. As soon as we cleared the thicket and appeared in the road running by Dr. Kinney's to Richmond another portion of the enemy, previously concealed in the wheat and behind the house immediately in front of us, opened a sharp fire, which was promptly returned by the Twenty-eighth.

The regiment was then ordered to charge, and did it most gallantly, many of them, shouting, leaped the ditch and high fence inclosing the field of wheat, while the rest rushed into the yard and around the house. The enemy, armed with Springfield rifles, were "flushed" like so much game, and dropped back into the wheat before our unerring marksmen. Here and in the woods we killed and wounded not less than 200 and took a large number of prisoners, only about 75 of whom we were able to send to the rear, and put in charge of a small detachment of cavalry from the Fourth Virginia Regiment, which was retiring from the mill. It was not until we had swept the Twenty-fifth New York Regiment before us and passed nearly across the wheat field that we found ourselves in the presence of a whole brigade, commanded by General [John H.] Martindale, about 400 yards distant from our extreme right—left as faced. The enemy opened a heavy fire on us from two batteries planted upon an eminence between the balance of your brigade and ourselves, but fortunately fired too high, and gave us time to reform in an open field on the opposite side of Dr. Kinney's dwelling and in a direction perpendicular to our previous position. Our flag-bearer was shot down while we were reforming, but one of his comrades seized the flag and bore it onward. It was here that I sent to you for re-enforcements, stating that we had been cut off by an overwhelming force. I also sent a courier to Hanover Court-House for assistance, with instructions to proceed to Hanover Junction, if none could be had there.

After we had reformed, the men, heated and excited, threw off their knapsacks, made heavier than usual by the drenching rain of the previous night, were advanced a short distance and made to lie down, while the section of artillery, previously planted in the road, was ordered to take a more commanding position in rear of the dwelling, between 600 and 700 yards from the enemy's guns; after which we opened a brisk and well-directed fire, forcing the enemy to withdraw one of his pieces, which was thrown forward a little on the same side of the road with ourselves. Lieutenant [John R.] Potts and the men under him behaved with great gallantry and must have done considerable execution. This unequal contest was

99

maintained for three long hours, in expectation of assistance either from you or Hanover Junction. During the artillery firing Capt. W. J. Montgomery, with his company, was ordered to the right to observe the enemy and check his advance up a hollow not far from the artillery, while Captain [George B.] Johnston, with a part of his company [G], was sent to the left to reconnoiter. Company B, under Capt. S. N. Stowe, and the remainder of Company G, under Lieutenant [Daniel F.] Morrow, was held as a support to our two pieces. Captain Montgomery soon informed me that the enemy were throwing a large force through a wooded ravine on our right to surround us. He was immediately recalled and ordered to follow the head of their line along a fence running parallel to the road, and the other companies of the regiment, except those named above, were directed to follow. After prolonging our line in this new direction, and finding the enemy still going on and throwing at the same time sharpshooters between our infantry and artillery up the hollow that Captain Montgomery was first ordered to defend, while their artillery was pouring a hot fire upon us (they having got our range), and as we could see a strong infantry reserve in rear of their batteries, it was deemed advisable to retire. I was not able to recall Captain Johnston from the left, and was forced to leave the dead and badly wounded on the field, together with an old ambulance, a two-horse wagon, and our knapsacks. The 12-pound brass howitzer also had to be left, as 1 of the horses was killed and 3 others badly wounded. We know the names of 7 killed and 15 wounded as we retreated across the field to the road under the enemy's fire, and a few in the woods where the engagement first commenced. Exposed all the previous night to a drenching rain, without tents, deprived of food, having marched over a horribly muddy road with unusually heavy knapsacks, and having fought bravely and willingly for three hours in anticipation of being re-enforced, we were not in a condition to retreat. Many of my brave men fell from exhaustion on the road-side, and I am sorry to inform you that many of them are still missing, but trust that in a few days the number will be greatly reduced, as some are finding their way back to camp daily.

We were pursued by infantry, artillery, and a regiment of cavalry beyond Hanover Court-House, where I received a dispatch from you stating that you had yourself engaged another portion of the enemy.

Guns were placed on the railroad hill formerly occupied by the Twenty-eighth Regiment as a camping ground, which prevented our retreating by the Ashland road, as we had anticipated, and forced us to take the right-hand road to Taylorsville, along which we were shelled a short distance. The cavalry pursued us beyond Colonel Wickham's farm, and were only prevented from making a charge by our throwing the regiment into a field and making it march along the fences, while Lieutenant Potts protected our rear with his Parrott gun.

We succeeded in reaching Taylorsville about sunset, and for three days we were endeavoring to join the rest of the command, and had scarcely anything to eat.

The exact number of casualties suffered by the 28th Regiment at Hanover Court House (the battle was known also as Taliaferro's Mill, Kinney's Farm, and Slash Church) was not reported, but the regiment mustered only 480 men on June 26. Over 400 men were captured; however, many of these were paroled and exchanged before the end of the year.

Early in June, 1862, Branch's brigade moved to a point about three miles north of Richmond and encamped on the Brook Turnpike. The brigade remained there until June 25, when it was ordered to the vicinity of Half Sink in preparation for an attack planned by General Robert E. Lee on the Federal right at Mechanicsville. Generals D. H. Hill's and James Longstreet's divisions were placed on the Mechanicsville Turnpike, and General A. P. Hill's division, of which Branch's brigade was a part, was positioned to the northwest on the Meadow Bridge road. Branch's men were on the left of A. P. Hill's line, and General T. J. Jackson's troops were moving up on Branch's left. Lee's plan called for A. P. Hill to advance on Mechanicsville on the morning of June 26 while Jackson moved forward on Hill's left. Once A. P. Hill's troops had cleared Meadow Bridge and the Mechanicsville Turnpike, D. H. Hill and Longstreet would cross the bridge to support Jackson and A. P. Hill respectively.

Lee's somewhat-too-complex plan to destroy the right wing of the Federal army misfired badly on June 26 when Jackson failed to reach his assigned position on time and A. P. Hill launched his scheduled attack without authorization from Lee. The activities of the 28th Regiment during the Battle of Mechanicsville were reported by Colonel Lane as follows (*Official Records*, Series I, Vol. XI, pt. 2, p. 892):

> I have the honor to report that on Wednesday, June 25, I left camp with my regiment, numbering 480, and, with the balance of your [Branch's] brigade, proceeded up the Telegraph road, crossed the Chickahominy on the morning of the 26th, and advanced toward Meadow Bridge. Two of my companies were ordered to Mrs. Crenshaw's bridge to apprise Lieutenant-Colonel [Robert F.] Hoke, with a portion of his regiment which was doing picket duty on the south side of the Chickahominy, that the way was clear. We then continued our march toward Mechanicsville. The fight had commenced on our reaching this place, and we were ordered to support a battery which was firing from the works to the left of the road. I had 1 man wounded that evening. We slept upon the field, and were held as a support again next morning, when the artillery opened upon us, and another one of my men was wounded.

During the night the Federals fell back to a defensive position at Gaines' Mill and then retired to Cold Harbor.

Early on the morning of June 27 the divisions of A. P. Hill and Longstreet moved against the center of the new enemy position while Jackson and D. H. Hill advanced against the Federal right. A. P. Hill's division was in the advance and made first contact. Longstreet's men then moved up on A. P. Hill's right while Jackson and D. H. Hill came in on A. P. Hill's left. Colonel Lane reported the 28th Regiment's movements during the Battle of Gaines' Mill as follows (*Official Records*, Series I, Vol. XI, pt. 2, pp. 892-893):

> As soon as it was ascertained that the enemy had abandoned his position and was in full retreat we were ordered to follow, and on reaching Cold Harbor the Seventh North Carolina Troops and my regiment were ordered into the woods to the left of the road leading to the battle-field. The Seventh preceded us, and when I was about to form my regiment on its left

a sharp fire, both of shell and infantry, was opened upon us, causing one of the wings of the Seventh to give way. On asking the cause of this, I was informed by some of the company officers of the Seventh, whose names I do not know, that Colonel [Reuben P.] Campbell [the commanding officer of the Seventh Regiment] had ordered them to fall back, and as there was a large pond of water in my rear, I led my regiment out of the woods by the left flank, when I met you [General Branch] and was ordered back. I then marched up the road and wheeled my entire regiment into the same piece of woods. Colonel [Charles C.] Lee followed with his regiment [the Thirty-seventh], which he intended posting to my right, but the enemy opened upon him just as he was about to turn the angle of the road and his right was thrown into confusion. This caused Companies D, A, and I, of the right wing, and Company H, to the left of the colors in my regiment, to give way. Company D promptly reformed and came into line; the other three companies, I am told, reformed and attached themselves for the remainder of the day to other regiments. They were not with me. Colonel Campbell's regiment, seven of my companies, Lieutenant [Lorenzo D.] Webb, of Company H, and a few rank and file from the three missing companies, engaged the enemy in the woods and were exposed to a hot fire, when fresh troops came up and relieved us temporarily. Maj. James Barbour, General [Arnold] Elzey's assistant adjutant-general, approached me soon afterward and requested me to take my command to the support of a portion of his forces, which had advanced into the open field in front of the woods. My command advanced most gallantly through the woods and into the open field, although exposed to a front and right enfilade infantry fire, and bravely remained there until General George B. Anderson's brigade debouched from the woods to our left and charged across the field. I ordered my men to cease firing when the brigade was nearly in front of us, and, forming on the right, assisted them in clearing the field of the enemy. At the advice of General Anderson, my men now being very much fatigued, I remained with a portion of his brigade in a somewhat sheltered position until night-fall, when I rejoined you.

Our loss in this engagement was 13 killed and 78 wounded.

Although the Confederates succeeded in driving the Federals from their positions, darkness and fatigue prevented a pursuit. The next day, June 28, was spent in bivouac on the battlefield.

On June 30 Lee launched another ill-coordinated attack against the retreating Federals, who were now protected in part by the "desolate mire" of White Oak Swamp. The Confederate assault, launched late in the afternoon, achieved a measure of success after hard fighting, but Lee was once again unable to exploit his advantage. Colonel Lane reported the 28th Regiment's part in the Battle of Frayser's Farm as follows (*Official Records*, Series I, Vol. XI, pt. 2, p. 893):

Sunday evening we recrossed the Chickahominy, and on Monday evening (the 30th) were among the first to engage the enemy; the whole brigade advanced, driving the foe before us, notwithstanding the character of the ground. My regiment, in its advance, had to pass through two skirts of woods

containing swampy ground, and an intermediate open field, in which there was a dwelling surrounded by a yard and garden; all of which, I am told, had been converted into a temporary breastwork by the enemy. All of my men behaved well in this action, notwithstanding they were exposed to a murderous fire of shell, grape, and small-arms. I did not remain with my regiment until the close of the fight, as a flesh-wound in the right cheek forced me to leave the field.

Our loss was 6 killed and 50 wounded.

The next day, July 1, Lee attacked the Federals again at Malvern Hill, a formidable defensive position to which they had withdrawn the previous night. Severe casualties were suffered by units of D. H. Hill's division in frontal assaults against entrenched Federal artillery, but Branch's brigade was not directly involved in the fighting and its losses were minor. Darkness brought an end to the fighting and to the last battle of the Seven Days', during which the Confederate capital was saved and the Federal army of General George B. McClellan was driven back to its base at Harrison's Landing on the James River. On July 8 Lee withdrew the Army of Northern Virginia to the vicinity of Richmond. The 28th Regiment, which went into action on June 26 with 480 men, lost nineteen men killed and 130 wounded during the Seven Days .

While at Richmond, Lee reorganized his army into two "commands" under Longstreet and Jackson, and A. P. Hill's division was assigned to Jackson's command. On July 13 Jackson was ordered to move with two of his divisions, under Charles S. Winder and Richard S. Ewell, to Gordonsville to intercept an advancing Federal army commanded by General John Pope. A. P. Hill's division, of which Branch's brigade was still a part, was ordered to join Jackson on July 27. While the remainder of the Army of Northern Virginia continued to keep watch on McClellan at Harrison's Landing, Jackson took the offensive against Pope. At Cedar Mountain, on August 9, Jackson attempted to destroy an isolated corps of Pope's army and was on the verge of a stinging defeat when Hill's division arrived to deliver a devastating counterattack. The activities of Branch's brigade at Cedar Mountain were reported by Colonel Lane, who assumed temporary command of the brigade after Branch was wounded, as follows (*Official Records*, Series I, Vol. XII, pt. 2, p. 220):

After a long, rapid, and weary march we reached the battle-field at Cedar Run on the afternoon of August 9, and took the position assigned us in line of battle by General Branch in the woods to the left of the road leading to the Run, the right of the Thirty-seventh resting on the road, the Twenty-eighth, Thirty-third, Eighteenth, and Seventh being on its left. The Twenty-eighth, Thirty-third, Eighteenth, and Thirty-seventh moved cheerfully and irresistibly forward and in perfect order through the woods upon the enemy, who had succeeded in flanking the First (Stonewall) Brigade, of General Jackson's division, which was rapidly giving way. The enemy's infantry were soon driven from the woods into the field beyond, and both infantry and cavalry were finally driven in great disorder from the scene of action. Many prisoners were taken, and many others deserted their colors and voluntarily surrendered themselves. After advancing in line beyond Cedar Run we were half-wheeled to the right and marched across the road through a field of corn and over an open field until we reached the left of the forces under Brig. Gen. W. B. Taliaferro, where we were halted. It was then dark, and the infantry firing had ceased in all directions.

During the entire engagement the officers and men behaved as well as could be desired, notwithstanding the disorderly manner in which some of the troops we were ordered to support fell back.

During the Battle of Cedar Mountain the 28th Regiment lost three men killed and twenty-six wounded.

Jackson's men remained on the battlefield until the night of August 11, when they were withdrawn to the vicinity of Gordonsville. The Federals then began to reinforce Pope, and Lee countered by sending troops from Richmond to the support of Jackson. On August 25 Jackson began a movement to flank Pope's army, which was now in position on the north side of the Rappahannock, and get astride its line of communications—the Orange & Alexandria Railroad. On August 26 Jackson succeeded in reaching Manassas Junction, a major Federal supply depot. After destroying the supplies and facilities at Manassas Junction, Jackson withdrew his force five miles northwest to Groveton and assumed a defensive position. Branch's brigade was placed on the left of the Confederate line along an unfinished branch of the Manassas Gap Railroad. Pope, the recipient of a continual stream of reinforcements as a result of McClellan's withdrawal from Harrison's Landing in mid-August, now rounded on Jackson, who was outnumbered by a margin of better than three to one. While Pope blundered about in search of Jackson, Lee hurried Longstreet's command to Jackson's support.

Fierce fighting, during which Jackson's men managed to hold their own, broke out at Groveton in the late afternoon of August 28. The next morning Pope launched a series of uncoordinated and ill-conceived frontal attacks which failed to dislodge Jackson from his strong position, and Branch's brigade was involved in severe fighting along the railroad cut. At about 11:00 A.M. Longstreet's corps arrived on the field and went into position on Jackson's right. The Confederate line, although sometimes hard-pressed, held in the face of piecemeal Federal assaults until sunset, when the fighting ceased. The next day, August 30, a new attack on Jackson was contained with the help of Longstreet's massed artillery; Longstreet then went over to the offensive and succeeded in enveloping the left flank of Pope's army. Fierce fighting continued until nightfall in the vicinity of Henry House Hill, the retention of which kept open the Federals' line of retreat and prevented a severe tactical defeat from becoming a disaster. Although not actively engaged on August 30, Branch's brigade was exposed to heavy artillery fire and suffered some casualties. Colonel Lane reported the activities of the brigade at the Battle of Second Manassas as follows (*Official Records*, Series I, Vol. XII, pt. 2, pp. 675-677):

Next day [August 28], after marching through Centreville and across Bull Run on the stone bridge road, we were ordered from the road to the right into a piece of woods fronting a large open field, in which one of our batteries was planted. As soon as the engagement was opened on our right General [James J.] Archer's brigade, which was in front of us, moved from the woods into the field up to and to the right of the battery, where it was halted. Our brigade also moved a short distance into the field in the same direction, when the enemy opened a left enfilade artillery fire upon us. General Branch then ordered the Twenty-eighth Regiment to continue its march

and directed me to halt it in rear of General Archer, while he moved the rest of his command some distance to the left. The whole brigade, with no protection whatever, stood this artillery fire for several hours in the open field. The Eighteenth at one time was ordered to the support of General Ewell, and was marched down, but as the enemy had been driven from the field it was not put in. None of us were actively engaged that day, and about night-fall the whole command was moved into the woods into the railroad cut, where we slept upon our arms.

Next day we were marched a circuitous route and brought back into an open field near the spot where we had spent the night. Captain [W. G.] Crenshaw, who was in command of his battery in front of us, notified General Branch of the presence of the enemy in our front. Captain [John McL.] Turner, of the Seventh, was immediately sent to the left of the battery with his company to act as skirmishers. Soon after General Branch ordered me to take command of the Twenty-eighth and Thirty-third Regiments and dislodge the enemy, who were in the woods beyond the field of corn. On passing beyond the small cluster of woods to the right of the Crenshaw Battery we saw the enemy retreating in confusion before Captain Turner's skirmishers. We continued to advance until we saw General [Maxcy] Gregg's brigade in the woods to our right. It was here that I learned the enemy was in force in the woods and that General Gregg had been ordered not to press them. I deemed it advisable to inform General Branch of these facts, and was ordered by him to remain where I was. I had three companies at the time deployed as skirmishers along the fence in front of us and connecting with those first sent out under Captain Turner. The enemy advanced upon General Gregg in strong force soon after we halted, and General Branch, with the rest of his command, advanced to his support. The Thirty-seventh first became actively engaged. The enemy opened a deadly fire upon this regiment. The Eighteenth, under Lieutenant-Colonel [T. J.] Purdie, and Seventh, under Captain [R. B.] MacRae, went to its assistance, and the enemy were driven in disorder beyond the railroad cut. The enemy were repulsed in two subsequent attempts to drive these regiments from their positions. The Thirty-third, under Colonel [Robert F.] Hoke, also fought well in the woods to the left of these regiments, and once gallantly advanced into the open field in front and drove the enemy back in disorder. Up to this time the Twenty-eighth had not been engaged, and as the other regiments were nearly out of ammunition, General Branch ordered it to join him, intending to make it cover his front. The order was not delivered properly, and the regiment went into action to the left of General [Charles W.] Field's brigade. It advanced boldly into the woods, driving the enemy before it, although exposed to a left enfilade and direct fire, but fell back when it found itself alone in the woods and unsupported. The men, however, rallied and reformed in the center of the open field and advanced a second time, when the enemy was not only driven beyond the cut, but entirely out of the woods. Never have I witnessed greater bravery and desperation than was that day displayed by this brigade. We were not actively engaged the next day, but held our position under a heavy artillery fire and very heavy skirmishing until late in the afternoon. We then followed up the enemy until about 10 p. m., advancing in line through a body of woods nearly to a large hospital, in which the enemy had left many of his wounded.

During the Battle of Second Manassas the 28th Regiment lost five men killed and forty-five wounded.

As the Federal army retired toward Washington, Lee ordered Jackson to attempt to turn the Federal right flank. Advance elements of Jackson's column encountered the enemy at Ox Hill late on the afternoon of September 1, 1862, and Branch's brigade was ordered forward to attack. In a blinding rainstorm the brigade advanced. A general battle then developed between Jackson's column and the Federal rear guard, but the latter held its position until nightfall and then retired under cover of darkness. Colonel Lane reported the Battle of Ox Hill as follows (*Official Records*, Series I, Vol. XII, pt. 2, p. 677):

> The pursuit was continued the whole of Sunday, and on Monday afternoon about 4 o'clock we came up with the enemy again at Ox Hill, near Fairfax Court-House, on the Alexandria and Winchester turnpike, when the engagement was immediately opened. This brigade pressed eagerly forward through an open field and a piece of woods to the edge of another field, where we were for a short time exposed to the enemy's infantry fire without being able to return it. An attempt was made to flank us on the right, and the Eighteenth Regiment was immediately detached from the center of the brigade and ordered to the right to prevent the movement, which it did, sustaining a deadly fire unsupported. The enemy's direct advance was through a field of corn, in which he sustained great loss, notwithstanding most of our guns fired badly on account of the heavy rain which fell during the engagement. On learning that our ammunition was nearly out General Branch made known the fact, and was ordered to hold his position at the point of the bayonet. We remained where we were until dark, when the whole command fell back to the field in rear of the woods. The Twenty-eighth, cold, wet, and hungry, was then ordered back to the field of battle to do picket duty for the night without fires. This engagement is regarded by this brigade as one of our severest. The enemy's infantry used a great many explosive balls.
>
> Our loss was 14 killed, 92 wounded, and 2 missing.

Lee abandoned any further attempts to cut off the Federal retreat and turned his army north to cross into Maryland. After moving through Leesburg, Branch's brigade crossed the Potomac River on September 4. On September 9 Lee issued orders for the movements of the army during the campaign and for the capture of Harpers Ferry by a strike force under Jackson. Jackson's command, of which Branch's brigade of A. P. Hill's division was still a part, was ordered to invest Harpers Ferry from the west; General Lafayette McLaws's division, reinforced by General Richard H. Anderson's division, was instructed to occupy Maryland Heights across the Potomac from Harpers Ferry; and General John G. Walker's division was ordered to occupy Loudoun Heights southeast of the town. The Harpers Ferry strike force was to rejoin Lee as soon as the town and its garrison had been secured; in the meantime, Longstreet's command was to advance in the direction of Hagerstown.

Jackson moved on September 10, crossed the Potomac near Williamsport the next day, and sent A. P. Hill's division against a Federal force at Martinsburg. The enemy retired as Hill entered Martinsburg on September

12. On September 13 Hill's men came in sight of Bolivar Heights, west of Harpers Ferry, where the badly outnumbered Federal defenders were strongly entrenched. By September 14 McLaws's and Walker's commands were in position, and the investment of Harpers Ferry was completed. On September 15, following a Confederate bombardment, the Federal garrison surrendered.

While Jackson was occupied at Harpers Ferry, Longstreet had been forced to withdraw from Hagerstown to defend the South Mountain gaps, where some of his units had taken a severe pounding on September 14. Lee then issued orders for his divided and outnumbered army to concentrate at Sharpsburg, and Jackson, after leaving A. P. Hill's division to receive the surrender of the Harpers Ferry garrison, rejoined Lee and Longstreet about noon on September 16. In the meantime the Federal commander, General George B. McClellan, was ponderously maneuvering his army into position to attack Lee at Sharpsburg. Fighting broke out there about sunrise on September 17, a day which was to prove the bloodiest of the war.

Hill's division left Harpers Ferry at 7:30 A.M. on September 17 and was on the march to Sharpsburg while the battle there was raging. A powerful attack on the right of Lee's line that afternoon was blunted by the timely arrival of Hill's men; and the Confederate line, although severely crippled, held during the terrible day-long fight. Colonel Lane reported the activities of Branch's brigade during the Battle of Sharpsburg as follows (*Official Records*, Series I, Vol. XIX, pt. 1, pp. 985-986):

> We left Harper's Ferry on September 17, and, after a very rapid and fatiguing march, recrossed the Potomac and reached Sharpsburg in time to participate in the fight. The entire brigade was ordered to the right, and, on reaching the field, the Twenty-eighth was detached by General A. P. Hill, in person, and sent on the road to the left leading to Sharpsburg to repel the enemy's skirmishers, who were advancing through a field of corn. The rest of the brigade moved nearly at right angles to our line, and on the enemy's flank. The Thirty-third, Seventh, and Thirty-seventh were the regiments principally engaged. They fought well, and assisted in driving back three separate and distinct columns of the enemy. The Eighteenth was not actively engaged. I was ordered, about sunset, to rejoin the brigade, and on doing so ascertained that General Branch had been killed. It was after sunset when I assumed command of the brigade. I found the Seventh, Thirty-seventh, and Thirty-third posted behind a stone fence, and the Eighteenth sheltered in a hollow in rear. I ordered the Twenty-eighth to the left of the line, but the order was delivered to the Eighteenth, which was posted to the left behind a rail fence, a portion of it being broken back to guard against a flank movement. The Twenty-eighth was posted to the left of the Seventh, in the opening caused by the withdrawal of a few Georgia troops. Although annoyed by the enemy's sharpshooters, we held our position until ordered to fall back, on the night of the 18th.

The following day the Army of Northern Virginia rested on the field until nightfall, when it retired across the Potomac. Branch's brigade, still under Colonel Lane of the 28th Regiment, was one of three brigades which formed the rear guard while the army crossed.

On the morning of September 20 the brigade marched

with Hill's division to the ford near Shepherdstown and assisted in driving the Federals back across the Potomac. During that action the division was subjected to heavy artillery fire. After taking part in the destruction of a portion of the Baltimore & Ohio Railroad, the division encamped near Bunker Hill with the rest of the army.

The Army of Northern Virginia remained in the Shenandoah Valley until the Army of the Potomac began crossing the Blue Ridge on October 26, 1862. On October 28 Lee ordered Longstreet's corps to move east of the mountains and Jackson's corps, of which Hill's division was still a part, to move closer to Winchester. (On November 1 Colonel Lane was promoted to brigadier general and assigned to command the brigade formerly commanded by Branch.) When it became apparent that the Federal army, under General Ambrose E. Burnside, was concentrating on the Rappahannock River opposite Fredericksburg, Lee ordered Longstreet's corps to take a position on the heights overlooking the town while Jackson's men went into line on Longstreet's right.

About 2:00 A.M. on December 11 the Federals began constructing bridges across the river at Fredericksburg, and on the night of December 12 they began crossing. Lane's brigade was in the left center of Jackson's position and posted in a woods which projected into the open ground in front of the main Confederate line. It was against that point that the Federals advanced on December 13. General Lane reported the activities of his brigade during the Battle of Fredericksburg as follows (*Official Records*, Series I, Vol. XXI, pp. 653-655):

At 6.30 o'clock on the morning of the 12th, we left our bivouac and took the position assigned us on the railroad, my right being about 250 yards to the left of the small piece of woods beyond the track, and my left resting on a dirt road which crosses the railroad near the point where it makes a bend. Several batteries were to my left and rear, and General [William D.] Pender some distance farther back, my left nearly covering his right. When I had made this disposition of my command, I rode to the right of General Archer's brigade, which was posted in the woods some 400 yards from the railroad, and informed Colonel [Peter] Turney, who was at that time commanding, that there was an open space between us of about 600 yards. I also informed General Gregg of this opening, his command, which was to have been my support, being on the military road opposite this opening and some 500 or 600 yards from the railroad. I subsequently met General A. P. Hill and spoke to him of our relative positions.

Nothing of interest occurred on Friday [December 12] and Friday night.

Saturday morning I ordered the Seventh and Eighteenth Regiments beyond the railroad, to support three batteries which had been placed on a hill immediately in their front. Lieutenant-Colonel [Junius L.] Hill at once approached the captain of one of these batteries, told him he would insure its safety against any attempt on the part of the enemy to capture it, and that he must let him know when he wished him to move to the front. As soon as the fog lifted, heavy skirmishing commenced along my whole line, and the enemy were seen advancing. Our skirmishers, with the exception of Captain [J. McLeod] Turner's company, on the left, fell back. The batteries just alluded to then opened with telling effect and checked their advance. During this firing Captain Turner withdrew his company, as his men

were suffering, and rejoined his regiment. Several pieces of artillery, after firing a few rounds, hurried from the field, saying they were choked. On intimation from one of the captains of the batteries, Lieutenant-Colonel Hill promptly moved his regiment to the crest of the hill in front of the artillery, and delivered a volley at the sharpshooters, who were in range, the artillery all limbering up and driving to the rear. The Seventh and Eighteenth both suffered from the enemy's artillery fire, and at times from their sharpshooters.

About two hours later the enemy advanced in strong force across the open field to the right of my front. Colonel [W. M.] Barbour, his regiment [the Thirty-seventh North Carolina] being on the right, informed me, through Adjutant [David W.] Oates, of the advance, and wished to know what he must do should he be flanked. On being ordered to hold his position as long as possible, he deflected his three right companies, and formed them to the rear, at right angles to the track. I at once sent my courier, Mr. [James W.] Shepperd, to inform General A. P. Hill that the enemy were advancing in force upon the opening, Captain [F. T.] Hawks having been previously sent to apprise him that their skirmishers were in front of the same. Eight regiments were seen to pass to my right, and another to move by the right flank by file left, between the small body of woods and the fence beyond the track. This last regiment then faced by the rear rank, and opened fire upon my right. The three right companies of the Thirty-seventh became hotly engaged, and General Gregg's command was soon after encountered on the military road. Although our right was turned by such a large force, our position was deemed too important to be given up without a blow, and nobly did both officers and men await the approach of another large force along our entire front. As this force was concealed from the Thirty-third, Eighteenth, and Seventh Regiments by the hill about 40 yards beyond the track, they were cautioned to reserve their fire. The Twenty-eighth and Thirty-third, however, had open, level ground in their front, and when the enemy had gotten within 150 yards of our line they opened a terrific and deadly fire upon them, repulsing their first and second lines and checking the third. These two regiments were subjected not only to a direct, but to right and left oblique fires, that portion of the enemy's force behind the hill nearest the Twenty-eighth firing upon them. As soon as the right of my command became engaged with such an overwhelming force, I dispatched Captain Hawks to General Gregg for reinforcements, with instructions, if he was unable to send them, to apply to General [Edward L.] Thomas, or anybody else whom he might see in command of troops, for assistance.

My whole command held their ground until the Twenty-eighth and Thirty-seventh had fired away not only their own ammunition, but that of their own dead and wounded, which in some cases was handed to them by their officers. When these regiments had ceased firing, the enemy, in column doubled on the center, bore down in mass from behind the hill upon the left of the Twenty-eighth and right of the Thirty-third, and the power of numbers forced them entirely across the railroad. The Twenty-eighth and Thirty-seventh, being flanked right and left, fell back in an orderly manner, and were resupplied with ammunition. A well-directed volley from the Thirty-third checked the enemy for a time, and Colonel [Clark M.] Avery [of that regiment] ordered a charge, but, being unsupported on his right, he countermanded the order and withdrew his regiment into the woods, about 75 yards from the railroad. The Eighteenth Regiment then fell back about 100 yards, the right companies firing into the foe until he reached the woods in the pursuit. The Seventh, being on the left, fell back about 50 yards in perfect order. During the greater part of the engagement the enemy's artillery played upon the woods in our rear. While awaiting re-enforcements, I sent my aide, Lieutenant [Oscar] Lane, to the left to tell Lieutenant Colonel Hill, if he could possibly be spared, to come to the assistance of my right, as it was heavily pressed. The right, however, was forced to fall back before the order could be delivered. General Thomas came to my assistance, but too late to save my line. He encountered the enemy in the edge of the woods, drove them back, and, with the Eighteenth and Seventh Regiments of my brigade on his left, chased them to their first position. The Thirty-third, in accordance with orders, held the position in the woods to which it had fallen back until I could move up the Twenty-eighth and Thirty-seventh, when all again resumed their positions on the railroad.

That night the whole brigade was aligned on the track, and skirmishers thrown forward preparatory to a general advance. After this order was countermanded, my command rested on their arms until morning, when, having already been on duty upward of forty-eight hours, there was heavy skirmishing along my whole front, a number of men being killed and wounded.

We formed a portion of the second line on Monday, and, as we occupied an exposed position, the men soon constructed a very good temporary breastwork of logs, bush, and dirt, behind which they rested until Tuesday morning, when it was ascertained that the enemy had all recrossed the Rappahannock.

At the Battle of Fredericksburg, on December 13, 1862, the 28th Regiment lost sixteen men killed and forty-nine wounded. Following the battle Lane's brigade went into winter quarters near Moss Neck, below Fredericksburg, where it remained on picket duty until April 30, 1863.

Early on the morning of April 28, 1863, the Army of the Potomac, now commanded by General Joseph Hooker, began crossing the Rappahannock River in the Wilderness area upstream from Fredericksburg; at the same time, a large Federal force at Fredericksburg under General John Sedgwick began to make apparent preparations for a crossing. Lee, concluding that the Federal activity at Fredericksburg was a feint, began moving the bulk of his army to oppose Hooker. A small force under General Jubal Early was left behind to prevent a crossing by Sedgwick. Jackson's corps, with A. P. Hill's division in the rear, moved down the Orange Plank Road in the direction of Chancellorsville on May 1 and, at a point about three miles from that place, found the enemy retiring. Advancing in two columns, the Confederates drove the Federals back to their defensive positions around Chancellorsville. Lane's brigade was not engaged in the fighting on May 1 but was formed in line of battle near Chancellorsville late that evening.

Early on the morning of May 2 Jackson's corps was dispatched by Lee to turn the exposed right flank of the Federal army; and, after hard marching, Jackson succeeded in reaching a point about four miles west of Chancellorsville on Hooker's flank. As his troops came up, Jackson deployed them in three lines for the attack. Hill's division was placed in the third line; Lane's brigade was in column on the Orange Turnpike and was ordered to move forward by the flank, eastward on the turnpike, as the lines advanced.

The attack began about 5:15 P.M., and the Federal troops, caught by surprise, fell back in disorder toward Chancellorsville. The first two Confederate lines merged and drove the enemy until strong resistance forced a halt for the night. The third line was exposed to artillery fire as it advanced and, after the attack stalled, it moved to the front and became the first line. Colonel Samuel D. Lowe reported the activities of the 28th Regiment during the night of May 2 and on the next day, when the Confederate attack resumed, as follows (*Official Records*, Series I, Vol. XXV, pt. 1, pp. 920-921):

By command of General Lane, I formed on the right of the brigade about 11 p.m., May 2, to the right of the Plank road, a little less than a mile in rear of Chancellorsville. The men rested on their arms in line of battle.

About 1 a.m., May 3, we found that the enemy were advancing upon our line with loud and continuous cheers. My men quietly awaited the charge till within good range, as I supposed, when they opened a tremendous fire upon the advancing column, which seemed to have the effect of halting them immediately. The charge was accompanied by a severe enfilading fire from a great many pieces of cannon, planted on a commanding position in the direction of Chancellorsville. Though the enemy extended his left flank far beyond our right, and my regiment was on the extreme right of our line, his left did not advance much more than his right, yet enough to show his intention of turning our right. This plan was probably defeated by two of my right companies, which were formed at right angles with the line on a large road. The officers of my regiment had been instructed to obey and repeat any orders coming from the left, and, when the fight had almost ceased, the command to fall back was started by some mistake near the left and repeated to the right. The regiment at once fell back a short distance without the least confusion, but without difficulty was reformed in its proper place. We took several prisoners, such was the confusion of the enemy and the close proximity of the contending forces; also a flag belonging to the Third Maine Volunteers, which was captured by Captain [Niven] Clark's company (E).

At 2 a.m. all was quiet, and we were permitted to rest till after daybreak. Near the time of sunrise their batteries again opened upon us, killing some of my men. In a very short time General Lane ordered me to advance my right by a change of direction to the left, which being done without halting, we charged forward in brigade line of battle, moving in a line nearly parallel to the Plank road toward Chancellorsville. When we approached the enemy's breastworks, which defended his batteries, we were met by such a storm of solid shot, grape, and canister as I never before witnessed. Here a brigade of Confederates, a little in advance and on my right, masked the front of my regiment, excepting two companies on my left. General Lane, being always present, perceived this, and ordered me to support the line in my front with whatever companies lapped it.

Companies B and G passed on with the brigade, when the line before me halted. After standing a murderous fire for some time, my men fell back with the line to a breastwork which we had just passed over, and formed promptly. They did not seem discouraged, though our loss had been very heavy. General Lane then ordered me to assist in holding this line if the enemy charged upon it. General [J. E. B.] Stuart now came dashing along the line, ordering us forward to a second charge. The whole line again advanced and fought with the most determined courage, the artillery and musketry mowing our men down, till suddenly the Yankees were discovered flanking my regiment on the right. As I then had no support, I withdrew, and formed the second time behind breastworks. Hearing that General Lane was forming the brigade on the Plank road, I reported to him to know if I should not join him. While absent, General Stuart again commanded the line forward, and my regiment charged through the same terrible artillery firing the third time, led by Captain [Edward F.] Lovill, Company A, to the support of our batteries, which had just got into position on the hill from which those of the enemy had been driven.

On May 3 the entire Confederate line converged on Chancellorsville and forced the Federals to retire. Once Chancellorsville was occupied, Hill's division was ordered to entrench. It occupied its new position until Hooker's army recrossed the Rappahannock. Lee then moved his army back to Fredericksburg. During the Battle of Chancellorsville the 28th Regiment lost twelve men killed and seventy-seven wounded.

Following the Chancellorsville campaign and the death of Jackson, the Army of Northern Virginia was reorganized into three corps under Generals James Longstreet, Richard S. Ewell, and A. P. Hill. William D. Pender was promoted to the command of Hill's former division, and Lane's brigade was placed under Pender. Thus the 28th Regiment was now a part of Lane's brigade of Pender's division of Hill's 3rd Corps.

On June 3, 1863, General Lee put his army in motion toward the Shenandoah Valley to begin the campaign that would end at Gettysburg. General Ewell's corps moved first and was followed by Longstreet's corps. Hill's corps remained temporarily at Fredericksburg to watch the Federal forces opposite the town. On June 13 Ewell's corps defeated an enemy force at Winchester, and Longstreet's corps occupied Culpeper Court House. The Federals evacuated their Fredericksburg position the same day, and Hill's corps was ordered to move north. Ewell's corps crossed the Potomac into Maryland on June 16 and was followed by Hill's corps, which began fording the river at Shepherdstown on June 24. On the afternoon of June 27 Hill's corps arrived at Fayetteville, Pennsylvania. Longstreet's corps was at Chambersburg, just west of Fayetteville, that day, and Ewell's corps was advancing on Carlisle about thirty miles to the northeast. Hill's corps was ordered to move to Cashtown, about twelve miles southeast of Fayetteville, on June 29, and Longstreet was directed to follow on June 30. Ewell's corps was directed to rejoin the army at Cashtown or Gettysburg, as circumstances required. During the evening of June 30 General Hill arrived at Cashtown with Pender's division and decided to advance on Gettysburg, about seven miles to the southeast, with Pender's and General Henry Heth's divisions the next morning. At daylight on July 1 the two divisions, with Heth's men in the lead, moved toward Gettysburg. Federal

cavalry under the command of General John Buford delayed the Confederate advance, and when Federal infantry in strength were encountered near Gettysburg a general battle developed. After a hard fight the Confederates, reinforced by Ewell's timely arrival from Carlisle, drove the Federals through the streets of Gettysburg to Cemetery Hill south of the town. General Lane reported the activities of his brigade on July 1 as follows (*Official Records*, Series I, Vol. XXVII, pt. 2, pp. 664-665):

I have the honor to report that, on the morning of July 1, we moved from South Mountain, Pa., through Cashtown, in the direction of Gettysburg, and formed line of battle in rear of the left of Heth's division, about 3 miles from the latter place, to the left of the turnpike, in the following order: Seventh, Thirty-seventh, Twenty-eighth, Eighteenth, and Thirty-third North Carolina Regiments, the right of the Seventh resting on the road. After marching nearly a mile in line of battle, we were ordered to the right of the road, and formed on the extreme right of the light division [Pender's].

Here I ordered the Seventh Regiment to deploy as a strong line of skirmishers some distance to my right and at right angles to our line of battle, to protect our flank, which was exposed to the enemy's cavalry. [James J.] Pettigrew's and [James J.] Archer's brigades were in the first line, immediately in our front. We were soon ordered forward again after taking this position, the Seventh Regiment being instructed to move as skirmishers by the left flank. In advancing, we gained ground to the right, and, on emerging from the woods in which Pettigrew's brigade had been formed, I found that my line had passed Archer's, and that my entire front was unmasked.

We then moved forward about a mile, and as the Seventh Regiment had been detained a short time, Colonel Barbour threw out 40 men, under Captain [D. L.] Hudson, to keep back some of the enemy's cavalry, which had dismounted and were annoying us with an enfilade fire. We moved across this open field at quick time until a body of the enemy's cavalry and a few infantry opened upon us from the woods subsequently occupied by [W. J.] Pegram's battalion of artillery, when the men gave a yell, and rushed forward at a double-quick, the whole of the enemy's force beating a hasty retreat to Cemetery Hill.

My right now extended into the woods above referred to, and my left was a short distance from the Fairfield road. On passing beyond the stone fence and into the peach orchard near McMillan's house, I was ordered by General Pender not to advance farther unless there was another general forward movement. As I could see nothing at that time to indicate such a movement, and as one of the enemy's batteries on Cemetery Hill was doing us some damage, I ordered the brigade back a few yards, that the left might take shelter behind the stone fence.

We remained in this position that night. . . .

As Longstreet came up with his corps, Lee ordered him into position on Hill's right. With Ewell's corps on his left, Hill thus held the center of the Confederate line. On July 2 Longstreet and Ewell assaulted, with inconclusive results, the left and right wings respectively of the Federal army, which was now under the command of General George G. Meade. Conditions were relatively quiet on General Lane's part of the line, and he reported his brigade's activities for that day as follows (*Official Records*, Series I, Vol. XXVII, pt. 2, p. 665):

[The] next day, before the heavy artillery firing commenced, I ordered the Thirty-third and Eighteenth Regiments to the left of Lieutenant-Colonel [John J.] Garnett's battalion of artillery, that they might be better sheltered and at the same time be out of the enemy's line of fire.

In the afternoon, I was ordered by General Pender to take possession of the road in my front with my skirmishers, if possible. Fresh men were thrown forward, and the whole, under Maj. O. N. Brown, of the Thirty-seventh, executed the order very handsomely, driving the enemy's skirmishers, and occupying the road along our entire front. With the exception of the gallantry displayed by our skirmishers, nothing of interest occurred in my command on the 2d.

General Pender was wounded during the action of July 2 and was succeeded as division commander by General Lane, who was in turn succeeded by General Isaac Trimble on July 3. (Lane then returned to the command of his brigade.) On that day Pender's (Trimble's) division was ordered to support Heth's division, commanded by General James J. Pettigrew after Heth was wounded on July 1, in an attack on the Federal center on Cemetery Ridge. The assault force consisted of Heth's (Pettigrew's) division on the left supported by Pender's (Trimble's) division, and George E. Pickett's division on the right supported by Cadmus M. Wilcox's brigade on his right rear. Lane's brigade was on the left of Trimble's line, which was shorter than Pettigrew's line. General Lane reported the assault as follows (*Official Records*, Series I, Vol. XXVII, pt. 2, pp. 666-667):

Now in command of my own brigade, I moved forward to the support of Pettigrew's right, through the woods in which our batteries were planted, and through an open field about a mile, in full view of the enemy's fortified position, and under a murderous artillery and infantry fire.

As soon as Pettigrew's command gave back, [W. L. J.] Lowrance's brigade and my own, without ever having halted, took position on the left of the troops which were still contesting the ground with the enemy. My command never moved forward more handsomely. The men reserved their fire, in accordance with orders, until within good range of the enemy, and then opened with telling effect, repeatedly driving the cannoneers from their pieces, completely silencing the guns in our immediate front, and breaking the line of infantry which was formed on the crest of the hill. We advanced to within a few yards of the stone wall, exposed all the while to a heavy raking artillery fire from the right. My left was here very much exposed, and a column of the enemy's infantry was thrown forward in that direction, which enfiladed my whole line. This forced me to withdraw my brigade, the troops on my right having already done so. We fell back as well as could be expected, reformed immediately in rear of the artillery, as directed by General Trimble, and remained there until the following morning.

Following the failure of the Pickett-Pettigrew Charge on July 3, Lee held his army in position to receive an expected attack. On the night of July 4 the army began its retreat,

and Pender's division, once more under the command of Lane after Trimble was wounded and captured on July 3, fell back toward Hagerstown by way of Fairfield. At Hagerstown on July 11 the brigade formed a line of battle as Lee's army assumed a defensive position. The next day the division was consolidated with the division of General Heth, who had returned to duty, and General Lane returned to the command of his brigade. When the army began crossing the Potomac on the night of July 13, Heth's men were ordered to act as rear guard. General Lane reported the ensuing action as follows (*Official Records*, Series I, Vol. XXVII, pt. 2, p. 667):

The retreat from Hagerstown the night of the 13th was even worse than that from Gettysburg. My whole command was so exhausted that they all fell asleep as soon as they were halted—about a mile from the pontoon bridge at Falling Waters. Just as we were ordered to resume our march, the troops of Heth's division that occupied the breastworks in our rear as a rear guard were attacked by the enemy's cavalry. I at once ordered my command to fix bayonets, as our guns were generally unloaded, and moved down the road after General [Edward L.] Thomas, but was soon halted by General Heth's order, and subsequently made to take a position in line of battle, to allow those brigades that were engaged to withdraw. I threw out a very strong line of skirmishers along our whole front, under Lieutenant [James M.] Crowell, of the Twenty-eighth, with instructions not to fire until the enemy got close upon him, and to fall back gradually when he saw the main line retiring toward the river. The Eighteenth Regiment, under Colonel [John D.] Barry, was deployed to the right as skirmishers, and Colonel [Clark M.] Avery had supervision of the right wing, so as to enable me to be apprised of the movements of the enemy more readily. As soon as the other brigades withdrew, a large force moved to our right, and as our left was also threatened, I lost no time in falling back, which was done in excellent order.

Our thanks are due to Lieutenant Crowell and the officers and men under him for the stubbornness with which they contested every inch of ground against the enemy's mounted and dismounted cavalry, thereby enabling us to effect a crossing without the brigade being engaged. Lieutenant Crowell's command was the last organized body to cross the bridge.

The army retreated to the vicinity of Bunker Hill and Darkesville, where it halted. During the Gettysburg campaign the 28th Regiment lost twelve men killed and ninety-two wounded.

When the Federal army crossed into Virginia in mid-July, Lee moved his army east of the Blue Ridge Mountains to interpose it between the enemy and Richmond. By August 4, the Army of Northern Virginia occupied the Rapidan River line, and the Army of the Potomac had taken position on the Rappahannock. At about that time General Cadmus M. Wilcox was promoted and placed in command of the division of General Pender, who died on July 18 of wounds received at Gettysburg. Thus the 28th Regiment was now a part of Lane's brigade of Wilcox's division of Hill's corps.

In October, 1863, Lee learned that the Army of the Potomac had been weakened in order to send additional forces to take part in the Chattanooga campaign, and he therefore moved to strike the Federals in the vicinity of the Rapidan River. That advance compelled the Federal commander, General Meade, to retire toward Centreville. As the rear guard of Meade's army was passing through Bristoe Station on October 14, Heth's division of Hill's corps came onto the field. Without waiting to reconnoiter or for the rest of his corps to come up, Hill ordered an attack against what quickly proved to be a greatly superior enemy force. Heavy casualties were sustained by two brigades of Heth's division, after which the Federals continued their withdrawal unmolested. Wilcox's division was formed in line of battle during the fighting at Bristoe Station but did not advance.

Lee now retired to the Rappahannock and, after battles at Rappahannock Bridge and Kelly's Ford on November 7, fell back to the Rapidan. On November 26 Meade began moving his army to cross the Rapidan below Lee's position, and Lee shifted his forces eastward to intercept the Federals. By November 29 Lee's men were strongly entrenched at Mine Run, and Meade, unable to locate a vulnerable point against which to launch an attack, also began entrenching. On the morning of December 2 Lee sent an attack force composed of Wilcox's and Richard H. Anderson's divisions against what he believed to be an exposed Federal flank; however, when the Confederates moved out they discovered that the Federal army had retreated. A pursuit was undertaken, but Meade recrossed the Rapidan unmolested. Both armies went into winter quarters. Lane's brigade returned to a camp it established earlier at Liberty Mills, on the Rapidan above Fredericksburg; there it spent the winter of 1863-1864.

The brigade was still in camp at Liberty Mills on the morning of May 4, 1864, when the Army of the Potomac, now under the strategic direction of General U. S. Grant, began crossing the lower Rapidan and entered a thicket- and vine-choked woods of dense scrub oak and pine known as the Wilderness. When news of Grant's crossing was received, Lee ordered Hill's corps to move eastward from Orange Court House by the Orange Plank Road while Ewell's corps, south of Morton's Ford, moved in a parallel direction on Hill's left on the Orange Turnpike. Longstreet's corps, near Gordonsville, was instructed to move up on Hill's right on the Catharpin road.

On the morning of May 5 Hill's column, with Heth's division in the lead, encountered Federal cavalry near Parker's Store and succeeded in forcing the enemy back. Immediately north of Hill, on the Orange Turnpike, Ewell encountered the enemy in corps strength. Hill ordered Heth's division to deploy in line of battle across the Orange Plank Road and directed Wilcox to lead his division off to the left and make contact with Ewell's right. Wilcox posted Alfred M. Scales's and Samuel McGowan's brigades on a low eminence known as Chewning Plateau and moved his other two brigades, under Lane and Edward L. Thomas, further to the left to link up with Ewell.

At 4:00 P.M. on May 5 elements of the Federal II Corps assaulted Heth's line in such strength that Heth was forced to commit his reserve brigade and then call for reinforcements. Scales's and McGowan's brigades were ordered to Heth's assistance and were followed shortly by the brigades of Lane and Thomas. After severe fighting, during which Lane's and Scales's brigades thwarted a Federal effort to turn the Confederate flank, the outnumbered defenders were able to stabilize their precarious position. Darkness brought an end to the battle, and during the night the line was re-formed. Lane's brigade was placed in a reserve position behind Scales's brigade to the right of the Orange Plank Road.

At 5:00 A.M. the next morning, May 6, Federal columns struck Hill's line in front and on the left flank. Thirteen Federal brigades fell upon Hill's eight brigades with such suddenness and violence that there was scarcely time for resistance, and the entire Confederate line fell back in disorder. The second line was unable to hold also, and a general rout followed. Only the timely arrival of Longstreet's corps, moving up to reinforce Hill, prevented the collapse of the right wing of Lee's army. The Federal assault was blunted and driven back, and Hill's men, after re-forming behind Longstreet, were dispatched to the vicinity of Chewning Plateau to close the gap between Longstreet and Ewell. During the Wilderness battles of May 5-6 the 28th Regiment lost eighty-eight men killed and wounded.

Late on the evening of May 7 it became apparent that Grant's army was on the march southeastward toward Spotsylvania Court House, and throughout the night Lee's men pushed in the same direction in a race with the Federals to that vital crossroad. The race was narrowly won by the Confederates on the morning of May 8, and a strong defensive line was quickly constructed. Hill's corps, under temporary command of General Jubal Early, was positioned on the right of the line with Ewell's corps in the center and Longstreet's corps, under temporary command of General Richard H. Anderson, on the left. Lane's brigade was on the left of Hill's (Early's) line and was connected with Ewell's line at a convex, U-shaped salient known as the "Mule Shoe." This position came under sudden, violent attack early on the morning of May 12; and, while the Confederate defenders, aided by reinforcements, held back the Federals in desperate, hand-to-hand fighting, a new line was quickly constructed across the base of the salient. The original line was then abandoned, and the Federal attacks ceased. Lane's brigade was actively engaged throughout the bloody battle; the 28th Regiment lost its colors and 126 men killed and wounded.

After several more unsuccessful attempts against the Confederate line at Spotsylvania Court House, General Grant began moving eastward; Lee then shifted his army to the North Anna River at a point just north of Hanover Junction, where he blocked the Federal route of advance. At Jericho Mills on May 23 Wilcox's division was engaged with the Federal V Corps, under General G. K. Warren, as it crossed the North Anna. During this action the 28th Regiment lost thirty men killed and wounded.

The center of Lee's line was now anchored on the North Anna with the flanks drawn back so that the line formed an inverted V. Grant crossed a force on May 24 and moved against both wings of the Confederate army; however, he was unable to push back the Confederate center. With his army dangerously divided into three parts and separated by the river, Grant found it expedient to withdraw, and during the night of May 26-27 the Federals recrossed the North Anna and moved eastward to the Pamunkey.

Lee began shifting his army eastward as soon as it was learned that Grant was again on the march, and on May 27 Ewell's corps, temporarily commanded by General Jubal Early, marched some twenty-four miles and entrenched between Beaver Dam Creek and Pole Green Church. Longstreet's (Anderson's) corps came up on Early's right, and Hill's corps extended the left of Early's line. On May 30, under orders from Lee, Early moved to attack the Federal left at Bethesda Church. The attack failed to turn the Federal left but revealed that the enemy was moving once again to the Confederate right.

The two armies began concentrating at Cold Harbor, where new fighting broke out on June 1. The next day two of Hill's divisions, commanded by Wilcox and William

Mahone, were ordered to leave their positions on the left of the Confederate line and go to the support of Anderson, on the right. After taking part in the occupation of Turkey Hill, Wilcox was ordered to extend the Confederate line to the Chickahominy. On June 3 Grant launched a massive and murderously unsuccessful general assault against the six-mile-long Confederate position. Only Wilcox's division, on the right extremity of the line, was not engaged in the devastating rebuff meted out to the attacking Federals.

The two armies settled into defensive positions, where they remained until Grant began moving south toward the James River on June 12. Lee followed on June 13 and made contact with the enemy at Riddell's Shop the same day. A defensive line was established, but no general engagement followed. Grant then crossed the James and moved against Petersburg. Hill's corps remained north of the James until ordered to move to Petersburg, where it arrived on June 18 and was sent into position on the extreme right of the Confederate defensive system. On June 22 Lane's brigade took part in an engagement on the Jerusalem Plank Road that prevented the Federals from gaining a lodgment on the vital Petersburg & Weldon Railroad.

On June 25 Lane's and McGowan's brigades of Wilcox's division were sent back north of the James to relieve two brigades of Heth's division, and the 28th Regiment was engaged at Gravel Hill on July 28. On August 16 the entire brigade was involved in a battle at Fussell's Mill, where the Federals made an abortive attempt to break through the Confederate defenses. Soon afterwards Wilcox's men were transferred south of the James to their original position on the Confederate right and took part, with the rest of Hill's corps, in a minor victory over the Federals at Reams' Station on August 25. The 28th Regiment did not see action again until September 30 at Jones Farm where Grant, now firmly established on the Petersburg & Weldon Railroad at Globe Tavern, made a successful attempt to extend his constricting lines still farther to the west. After dark the regiment retired to entrenchments near the Jones House, where it went into winter quarters in mid-November.

On December 8 Lane's brigade, with the remainder of Hill's corps, was ordered to Belfield to oppose a Federal effort to cut the Petersburg & Weldon Railroad well to the south of Richmond. Marching through sleet and snow, the Confederates arrived at a point a few miles from Belfield where they learned that the Federals had retired. Hill then attempted to cut off the enemy's retreat and intercepted the Federal cavalry at Jarratt's Station. After a brief skirmish the Confederates pushed on, only to find that the Federal infantry was three hours ahead of them and could not be overtaken. Hill then called off the pursuit. After bivouacking for the night Hill started back to his camp at Hatcher's Run, which he reached on the afternoon of December 13. The 28th Regiment saw no further action for the remainder of the year.

Early in February, 1865, Grant ordered a move on the left of his line to secure a position on the Boydton Plank Road at Hatcher's Run. Hill's troops were engaged on February 5 but were unsuccessful in preventing the Federal advance. Wilcox's division was then moved further to the right as the already overextended Confederates lengthened their line to cover the latest Federal extension.

On March 26 General Phil Sheridan's powerful cavalry command, under orders from Grant, crossed the James River and rode towards Petersburg. This movement, which threatened to unhinge the right flank of the Richmond-Petersburg defense system, was thwarted temporarily on

March 31 when a Confederate force under George E. Pickett drove Sheridan's cavalry back from Dinwiddie Court House. Pickett then retired to Five Forks, where a defensive position was established to anchor the extreme right of Lee's line. On April 1 Federal infantry and cavalry surprised Pickett at Five Forks and drove a wedge between his force and the Confederate line at Hatcher's Run. Pickett's men were then overpowered and driven from the field with heavy casualties, and an avenue of advance was opened to the flank and rear of the Petersburg defenses. On April 2 the Federals launched a general attack against the Confederate line, broke through, and swept down the trenches. General Lane reported the activities of his brigade from April 1 until the surrender at Appomattox Court House on April 9 as follows (*Official Records*, Series I, Vol. XLVI, pt. 1, pp. 1285-1286):

I have the honor to report that on the night of the 1st of April four regiments of my brigade, with intervals between the men varying from six to ten paces, were stretched along the works between Battery Gregg and Hatcher's Run in the following order from right to left: Twenty-eighth, Thirty-seventh, Eighteenth, Thirty-third [North Carolina Infantry], the right of the Twenty-eighth resting near the brown house in front of General [William] MacRae's [sic] winter quarters, and the left of the Thirty-third on the branch near Mrs. Banks'.

The enemy commenced shelling my line from several batteries about 9 o'clock that night; the picket-lines in my front opened fire at a quarter to 2 the following morning. The skirmishers from McGowan's brigade, who covered the works held by my command, were driven in at a quarter to 5 o'clock. My line was pierced by the enemy in strong force at the ravine in front of the right of the Thirty-seventh, near General McGowan's headquarters. The Twenty-eighth, enfiladed on the left by this force and on the right by the force that had previously broken the troops to our right, was forced to fall back to the plank road. The enemy on its left took possession of this road, and forced it to fall still farther back to the Cox road, where it skirmished with the enemy and supported a battery of artillery, by order of Brigadier-General [William N.] Pendleton. The other regiments fought the enemy between McGowan's winter quarters and those occupied by my brigade, and were driven back. They then made a stand in the winter quarters of the right regiment of my command, but were again broken, a part retreating along the works to the left and the remainder going to the rear. These last, under Colonel [Robert H.] Cowan [Eighteenth Regiment N.C. Troops], made a stand on the hill to the right of Mrs. Banks', but were forced back to the plank road, along which they skirmished for some time, and then fell back to the Cox road, where they supported a battery of artillery, by order of Lieutenant-General Longstreet. That portion of my command which retreated along the works to the left made two more unsuccessful attempts to resist the enemy, the last stand being made in the Church road leading to the Jones house. It then fell back to Battery Gregg and the battery to its left, but under Major [Thomas J.] Wooten and assisted by a part of Thomas' brigade it soon after charged the enemy, by order of Major-General Wilcox, and cleared the works as far as the branch on which the left of the Thirty-third rested the night previous. Here we were rejoined by Colonel Cowan, and we deployed as skirmishers to the left of the Church road and perpendicular to the works, but did not hold this position long, as we were attacked by a strong line of skirmishers, supported by two strong lines of battle. A part of us retreated to Battery Gregg, and the rest to the new line of works near the dam. Battery Gregg was subsequently attacked by an immense force, and fell after the most gallant and desperate defense. Our men bayoneted many of the enemy as they mounted the parapet. After the fall of this battery the rest of my command along the new line was attacked in front and flank, and driven back to the old line of works running northwest from Battery 45, where it remained until the evacuation of Petersburg. We were here rejoined by the Twenty-eighth, under Captain [T. James] Linebarger.

On the afternoon of the 3d we crossed the Appomattox at Goode's Bridge, bivouacked at Amelia Court-House on the 4th, and on the 5th formed line of battle between Amelia Court-House and Jetersville, where our sharpshooters, under Major Wooten, became engaged. Next day, while resting in Farmville, we were ordered back to a fortified hill to support our cavalry, which was hard pressed, but before reaching the hill the order was countermanded. We moved rapidly through Farmville, and sustained some loss from the artillery fire while crossing the river near that place. That afternoon we formed line of battle, facing to the rear, between one and two miles from Farmville, and my sharpshooters were attacked by the enemy. During the night we resumed our march, and on the 9th, while forming line of battle, we were ordered back and directed to stack our arms, as the Army of Northern Virginia had been surrendered.

When the army was paroled on April 12, 230 members of the 28th Regiment were present.

FIELD AND STAFF

COLONELS

LANE, JAMES HENRY
Previously served as Lieutenant Colonel of the 1st Regiment N.C. Infantry (6 months, 1861). Transferred to this regiment upon appointment as Colonel on September 21, 1861. Wounded at Frayser's Farm, Virginia, June 30, 1862, and at Malvern Hill, Virginia, July 1, 1862. Promoted to Brigadier General on November 1, 1862, and transferred.

LOWE, SAMUEL D.
Previously served as Captain of Company C of this regiment. Appointed Major on April 12, 1862, and transferred to the Field and Staff. Captured at Hanover Court House, Virginia, May 27, 1862. Confined at Fort Columbus, New York Harbor. Promoted to Lieutenant Colonel on June 11, 1862, while a prisoner of war. Transferred from Fort Columbus to Johnson's Island, Ohio, where he arrived on June 21, 1862. Transferred to Vicksburg, Mississippi, where he was received on September 20, 1862, for exchange. Promoted to Colonel on November 1, 1862. Returned to duty prior to January 1, 1863. Wounded in the left thigh at Gettysburg, Pennsylvania, July 1-3, 1863. Regimental records do not indicate whether he returned to duty. Retired to the Invalid Corps on July 8, 1864, by reason of "general debility accompanied with a predisposition to phthisis

pulmonalis. He is suffering with [a] cough & can not undergo but little physical exertion."

SPEER, WILLIAM H. ASBURY
Previously served as Captain of Company I of this regiment. Appointed Major on November 1, 1862, and transferred to the Field and Staff. Promoted to Lieutenant Colonel on March 12, 1863. Wounded at Chancellorsville, Virginia, May 2-3, 1863. Returned to duty prior to July 1-3, 1863, when he was wounded at Gettysburg, Pennsylvania. Returned to duty on an unspecified date. Promoted to Colonel on July 9, 1864. Wounded in the head at Reams' Station, Virginia, August 25, 1864. Hospitalized at Petersburg, Virginia, where he died on August 29, 1864, of wounds.

LIEUTENANT COLONELS

LOWE, THOMAS L.
Previously served as Captain of Company C of this regiment. Elected Lieutenant Colonel on September 21, 1861, and transferred to the Field and Staff. Died on or about June 10, 1862, of "fever." Place of death not reported.

BARRINGER, WILLIAM DAVIDSON
Previously served as Captain of Company E of this regiment. Appointed Major on October 18, 1862, and transferred to the Field and Staff. Promoted to Lieutenant Colonel on November 1, 1862. Captured at Fredericksburg, Virginia, December 13, 1862. Exchanged on or about December 17, 1862. Resigned on March 2, 1863, by reason of "a predisposition to inflammation of the mucous membrane." "A gallant officer."

MAJORS

REEVES, RICHARD E.
Previously served as Captain of Company A of this regiment. Elected Major on September 21, 1861, and transferred to the Field and Staff. Defeated for reelection when the regiment was reorganized on April 12, 1862.

MONTGOMERY, WILLIAM JAMES
Previously served as Captain of Company D of this regiment. Appointed Major on June 12, 1862. Resigned on September 29, 1862, by reason of "a severe and long continued attack of spermatorrhoea."

STOWE, SAMUEL N.
Previously served as Captain of Company B of this regiment. Appointed Major on April 16, 1863, and transferred to the Field and Staff. Wounded at Gettysburg, Pennsylvania, July 1-3, 1863. Returned to duty on an unspecified date. Retired to the Invalid Corps on December 13, 1864, by reason of disability.

ADJUTANTS

McRAE, DUNCAN A.
Previously served as 3rd Lieutenant of Company E of this regiment. Appointed Adjutant (1st Lieutenant) on October 18, 1861, and transferred to the Field and Staff. Resigned on January 6, 1863. Reason he resigned not reported.

FOLGER, ROMULUS S.
Previously served as 2nd Lieutenant of Company I of

this regiment. Appointed Adjutant (2nd Lieutenant) on January 7, 1863, and transferred to the Field and Staff. Promoted to Adjutant (1st Lieutenant) on an unspecified date. Surrendered at Appomattox Court House, Virginia, April 9, 1865.

ASSISTANT QUARTERMASTERS

THOMPSON, GEORGE S.
Previously served as Private in Company G of this regiment. Appointed Assistant Quartermaster (Captain) on October 18, 1861, and transferred to the Field and Staff. Promoted to Brigade Quartermaster (Major) on January 23, 1863, and transferred.

PARKER, DURANT A.
Previously served as Captain of Company D of this regiment. Appointed Assistant Quartermaster (Captain) on May 2, 1863, and transferred to the Field and Staff. Transferred to the 1st Regiment Confederate Engineering Troops with the rank of Assistant Quartermaster (Captain) on August 19, 1864.

ASSISTANT COMMISSARY OF SUBSISTENCE

GIBBON, NICHOLAS
Resided in Mecklenburg County. Appointed Assistant Commissary of Subsistence (Captain) on October 18, 1861. Present or accounted for until he was "reassign[ed]" on or about September 17, 1863.

SURGEONS

GIBBON, ROBERT
Resided in Mecklenburg County and enlisted in New Hanover County. Appointed Surgeon of this regiment on or about September 25, 1861. Present or accounted for until he was appointed Senior Surgeon of General James H. Lane's brigade on or about January 29, 1864.

McREE, JAMES FERGUS
Previously served as Surgeon of the 3rd Regiment N.C. State Troops. Appointed Surgeon of this regiment on an unspecified date in 1864. "Relieved" prior to October 1, 1864.

GAITHER, WILLIAM WILEY
Previously served as Assistant Surgeon of the 26th Regiment N.C. Troops. Appointed Surgeon on November 4, 1864, to rank from September 2, 1864, and transferred to this regiment. Present or accounted for through February, 1865.

ASSISTANT SURGEONS

COX, F.
Appointed Assistant Surgeon on September 21, 1861. Served with the regiment "but a short time." No further records.

LUCKEY, FRANCIS N.
Resided in Rowan County. Appointed Assistant Surgeon on September 25, 1861. Appointed Surgeon of the 25th Regiment N.C. Troops on or about March 31, 1862, and transferred.

BARHAM, W. R.
Appointed Assistant Surgeon in April, 1862. Served with the regiment "but a short time." [North Carolina Civil War newspapers indicate he was captured at or near Hanover Court House, Virginia, on or about May 27, 1862, "while in attendance on some of our wounded men, who had been necessarily left behind." Records of the Federal Provost Marshal do not substantiate the report of his capture.] No further records.

LANE, THOMAS B.
Resided in Virginia. Appointed Assistant Surgeon on June 25, 1862. Promoted to Surgeon and transferred to the 18th Regiment N.C. Troops (8th Regiment N.C. Volunteers), March 19, 1863.

MAYO, M. LEWIS
Resided in Virginia. Appointed Assistant Surgeon of this regiment on or about May 2, 1863. Transferred to hospital at Charlotte in January, 1865, and was paroled at Charlotte in May, 1865.

CHAPLAINS

BRENT, OSCAR J.
Resided in Guilford County. Appointed Chaplain of this regiment on October 18, 1861. Resigned on July 21, 1862, by reason of "ill health."

KENNEDY, F. MILTON
Born in South Carolina and resided in Mecklenburg County prior to enlisting at age 28. Appointed Chaplain of this regiment on December 6, 1862. Transferred to Charlotte for duty as Hospital Chaplain on April 6, 1864.

HENKLE, D. L.
Enlisted at age 18. Appointed Chaplain of this regiment on December 30, 1864. Surrendered at Appomattox Court House, Virginia, April 9, 1865.

ENSIGN

LITTLE, JUNIUS PINKNEY
Previously served as Private in Company C of this regiment. Appointed Ensign (1st Lieutenant) on May 2, 1864, and transferred to the Field and Staff. Captured at Spotsylvania Court House, Virginia, May 12, 1864. Confined at Point Lookout, Maryland. Transferred to Elmira, New York, August 10, 1864. Released on June 16, 1865, after taking the Oath of Allegiance.

SERGEANTS MAJOR

LOWE, MILTON A.
Previously served as Sergeant of Company C of this regiment. Promoted to Sergeant Major on October 17, 1861, and transferred to the Field and Staff. Elected 3rd Lieutenant on August 4, 1862, and transferred back to Company C.

LOWE, JOHN F.
Resided in Mecklenburg County where he enlisted at age 25, December 1, 1862, for the war. Mustered in as Sergeant Major. Killed at Fredericksburg, Virginia, December 13, 1862. "He was a brave and good man."

SMITH, DAVID B.
Previously served as Private in Company B of this regiment. Promoted to Sergeant Major in January, 1863, and transferred to the Field and Staff. Elected 2nd

Lieutenant of Company H of this regiment on April 6, 1863, and transferred to that unit.

RANKIN, WILLIAM RUFUS

Previously served as Private in Company B of this regiment. Promoted to Sergeant Major on April 29, 1863, and transferred to the Field and Staff. Wounded at Gettysburg, Pennsylvania, July 1-3, 1863. Returned to duty on an unspecified date. Surrendered at Appomattox Court House, Virginia, April 9, 1865.

QUARTERMASTER SERGEANTS

KELLY, JOHN C.

Previously served as Ordnance Sergeant of Company F of this regiment. Promoted to Quartermaster Sergeant on October 9, 1861, and transferred to the Field and Staff. Discharged on June 10, 1862, by reason of "predisposition to disease of the lungs, accompanied with debility."

MOOSE, EDMUND

Previously served as Sergeant in Company D of this regiment. Promoted to Quartermaster Sergeant in May-December, 1862, and transferred to the Field and Staff. Appointed 2nd Lieutenant on March 28, 1863, and transferred back to Company D.

LOWE, TULLIUS C.

Previously served as Private in Company H of this regiment. Promoted to Quartermaster Sergeant in May, 1863-October, 1864, and transferred to the Field and Staff. Surrendered at Appomattox Court House, Virginia, April 9, 1865.

COMMISSARY SERGEANT

MAUNEY, WILLIAM ANDREW

Previously served as Private in Company B of this regiment. Promoted to Commissary Sergeant in October, 1861, and transferred to the Field and Staff. Captured at Hanover Court House, Virginia, May 27, 1862. Confined at Fort Monroe, Virginia, and at Fort Columbus, New York Harbor. Paroled and transferred to Aiken's Landing, James River, Virginia, where he was received on July 12, 1862, for exchange. Declared exchanged at Aiken's Landing on August 5, 1862. Returned to duty prior to January 1, 1863. Paroled at Charlotte on May 3, 1865.

ORDNANCE SERGEANT

JOHNSTON, GABRIEL P.

Previously served as Private in Company G of this regiment. Promoted to Ordnance Sergeant on December 9, 1861, and transferred to the Field and Staff. Present or accounted for until June, 1864, when he was reported absent sick. Reported absent sick through February, 1865.

HOSPITAL STEWARDS

ABERNATHY, JOHN A.

Previously served as Private in Company H of this regiment. Promoted to Hospital Steward on or about December 28, 1861, and transferred to the Field and Staff. Captured at Hanover Court House, Virginia, on or about May 27, 1862. Confined at Fort Monroe,

Virginia. Transferred to Fort Delaware, Delaware, June 9, 1862. Paroled and transferred for exchange on an unspecified date. Transferred back to Company H upon election as 1st Lieutenant on or about August 2, 1862.

BARKER, LARKIN JONES

Previously served as Sergeant in Company I of this regiment. Promoted to Hospital Steward on an unspecified date subsequent to February 28, 1863, and transferred to the Field and Staff. Reported on duty as Hospital Steward during September, 1864-February, 1865. Surrendered at Appomattox Court House, Virginia, April 9, 1865.

COMPANY A

This company, known as the "Surry Regulators," was raised in Surry County and enlisted at Dobson on May 4, 1861. It was then mustered into service and assigned to the 28th Regiment as Company A. After joining the regiment the company functioned as a part of the regiment, and its history for the war period is reported as a part of the regimental history.

The information contained in the following roster of the company was compiled principally from company muster rolls for August 1, 1861-October 31, 1862; January-February, 1863; and September, 1864-February, 1865. No company muster rolls were found for May 4-July 31, 1861; November-December, 1862; March, 1863-August, 1864; or for the period after February, 1865. Valuable information was obtained also from primary records such as the Roll of Honor, medical records, prisoner of war records, discharge certificates, and pension applications, and from secondary sources such as postwar rosters and histories, cemetery records, and records of the United Daughters of the Confederacy.

OFFICERS

CAPTAINS

REEVES, RICHARD E.

Resided in Surry County and enlisted at age 40. Appointed Captain on May 4, 1861. Present or accounted for until he was elected Major on September 21, 1861, and transferred to the Field and Staff of this regiment.

NORMAN, WILLIAM M.

Resided in Surry County where he enlisted on May 4, 1861. Mustered in as 1st Sergeant and was appointed 1st Lieutenant on July 8, 1861. Promoted to Captain on or about September 21, 1861. Present or accounted for until he was defeated for reelection in April, 1862. Later served as Captain of 2nd Company A, 2nd Regiment N.C. State Troops.

LOVELL, EDWARD F.

Resided in Surry County where he enlisted at age 19, May 4, 1861. Mustered in as Private and was elected 2nd Lieutenant on October 4, 1861. Promoted to Captain on April 9, 1862. Wounded in the right arm at Gettysburg, Pennsylvania, July 1-3, 1863. Returned to duty on an unspecified date. Wounded in both thighs at Jones' Farm, Virginia, September 30, 1864. Reported absent wounded until December 17, 1864, when he was reported absent without leave. Returned to duty subsequent to February 28, 1865. Present or accounted for until he surrendered at Appomattox Court House,

Virginia, April 9, 1865.

LIEUTENANTS

DOBSON, LEANDER H., 3rd Lieutenant
Resided in Surry County where he enlisted at age 44. Appointed 3rd Lieutenant on May 4, 1861. Present or accounted for until he was defeated for reelection when the regiment was reorganized in April, 1862.

DUNNIGAN, A. C., 1st Lieutenant
Enlisted in Surry County. Appointed 1st Lieutenant on May 4, 1861. Present or accounted for until he resigned on or about July 6, 1861. Reason he resigned not reported.

FOLGER, ROMULUS S., 1st Lieutenant
Resided in Surry County where he enlisted at age 20, May 4, 1861. Mustered in as Private and was promoted to 1st Sergeant prior to September 3, 1861. Elected 1st Lieutenant on September 3, 1861. Present or accounted for until he resigned on April 9, 1862. Reason he resigned not reported. Later served as 2nd Lieutenant of Company I of this regiment.

LAFFOON, NATHAN D., 2nd Lieutenant
Resided in Surry County where he enlisted. Appointed 2nd Lieutenant on May 4, 1861. Present or accounted for until he resigned on September 6, 1861. Reason he resigned not reported. Later served as 2nd Lieutenant of Company B, 2nd Battalion N.C. Infantry.

NIXON, F. M., 3rd Lieutenant
Resided in Surry County where he enlisted at age 25, May 4, 1861. Mustered in as Private and was promoted to Sergeant prior to November 1, 1861. Reduced to ranks in April, 1862. Wounded at Gaines' Mill, Virginia, June 27, 1862. Returned to duty on an unspecified date. Promoted to 1st Sergeant on July 1, 1862, and was appointed 3rd Lieutenant on September 21, 1862. Present or accounted for through February, 1865.

NORMAN, MATTHEW H., 2nd Lieutenant
Resided in Surry County where he enlisted at age 18, May 4, 1861. Mustered in as Sergeant and was appointed 2nd Lieutenant on April 9, 1862. Captured at or near Liberty Mills, Virginia, on or about September 22, 1863. Confined at Old Capitol Prison, Washington, D.C., until transferred to Johnson's Island, Ohio, November 11, 1863. Released at Johnson's Island on June 12, 1865, after taking the Oath of Allegiance.

SNOW, JAMES S., 3rd Lieutenant
Resided in Surry County where he enlisted at age 34, May 4, 1861. Mustered in as Corporal and was appointed 3rd Lieutenant on April 9, 1862. Present or accounted for until he resigned on June 15, 1862, by reason of "the affliction of my family and [because] I am over thirty-five years of age." Resignation accepted on August 20, 1862.

THOMPSON, ELIJAH T., 1st Lieutenant
Resided in Surry County where he enlisted at age 26, May 4, 1861. Mustered in as Sergeant and was promoted to 1st Sergeant on January 12, 1862. Appointed 1st Lieutenant on April 9, 1862. Present or accounted for until wounded in the foot at the Battle of Second Manassas, Virginia, August 28-30, 1862.

Returned to duty prior to November 1, 1862. Wounded in the left thigh and captured at Gettysburg, Pennsylvania, July 3-5, 1863. Confined at Baltimore, Maryland, and at Chester, Pennsylvania, until transferred to Johnson's Island, Ohio, August 31, 1863. Transferred to Point Lookout, Maryland, April 22, 1864. Transferred to Fort Delaware, Delaware, June 23, 1864. Paroled at Fort Delaware on September 14, 1864, and transferred to Aiken's Landing, James River, Virginia, September 18, 1864, for exchange. Returned to duty in November-December, 1864, but was retired to the Invalid Corps on January 31, 1865, by reason of disability.

NONCOMMISSIONED OFFICERS AND PRIVATES

ADKINS, ROBERT, Private
Resided in Surry County and enlisted in Forsyth County at age 26, March 22, 1862. Roll of Honor indicates he was captured at Hanover Court House, Virginia, on or about May 27, 1862; however, records of the Federal Provost Marshal do not substantiate that report. Hospitalized at Richmond, Virginia, July 2, 1862, with a gunshot wound of the back. Place and date wounded not reported. Returned to duty on July 3, 1862. Wounded at the Battle of Second Manassas, Virginia, on or about August 28-30, 1862. Died at Middleburg, Virginia, September 2-3, 1862. Cause of death not reported.

ALBERTY, LEMUEL B., Private
Resided in Surry County where he enlisted at age 19, March 18, 1862. Captured in hospital at Richmond, Virginia, April 3, 1865. Confined at Newport News, Virginia, on or about April 23, 1865. Released on June 30, 1865, after taking the Oath of Allegiance.

ANTHONY, HENRY G., Sergeant
Resided in Surry County where he enlisted at age 19, May 4, 1861. Mustered in as Private. Wounded in the left hip in Virginia in May, 1864. Battle in which wounded not reported. Returned to duty prior to November 1, 1864. Promoted to Sergeant subsequent to February 28, 1865. Surrendered at Appomattox Court House, Virginia, April 9, 1865.

ANTHONY, M. C., ———
North Carolina pension records indicate that he served in this company.

ASHBURN, J. L., ———
North Carolina pension records indicate that he served in this company.

ASHBURN, JAMES W., Private
Resided in Surry County where he enlisted at age 18, March 18, 1862. Present or accounted for until captured at Hanover Court House, Virginia, May 27, 1862. Confined at Fort Columbus, New York Harbor. Exchanged at Aiken's Landing, James River, Virginia, August 5, 1862. Returned to duty prior to November 1, 1862. Wounded in the left leg near Petersburg, Virginia, September 20, 1864. Returned to duty prior to November 1, 1864. Present or accounted for until captured near Petersburg on April 2, 1865. Confined at Fort Delaware, Delaware, until released on June 19, 1865, after taking the Oath of Allegiance.

ASHBURN, JOHN, Private

Born in Surry County where he resided as a farmer prior to enlisting in Surry County at age 18, March 18, 1862. Present or accounted for until discharged on October 2, 1862, by reason of "phthisis pulmonalis . . . in both lungs with frequent hemorrhages. . . ."

ATKINSON, CHARLES H., Sergeant

Resided in Surry County where he enlisted at age 19, May 4, 1861. Mustered in as Private and was promoted to Sergeant on October 5, 1861. Reduced to ranks on April 9, 1862. Captured at Hanover Court House, Virginia, May 27, 1862. Confined at Fort Columbus, New York Harbor. Exchanged at Aiken's Landing, James River, Virginia, August 5, 1862. Returned to duty in January-February, 1863. Promoted to Sergeant in March, 1863-October, 1864. Wounded at Chancellorsville, Virginia, May 2-3, 1863. Returned to duty on September 18, 1863. Deserted to the enemy on or about February 23, 1865. No further records.

AXUM, SAMUEL I., Private

Born in Yadkin County* and resided in Surry County where he was by occupation a farmer prior to enlisting in Surry County at age 26, March 18, 1862. Present or accounted for until captured at Hanover Court House, Virginia, May 27, 1862. Confined at Fort Columbus, New York Harbor. Exchanged at Aiken's Landing, James River, Virginia, August 5, 1862. Died "at home" in Surry County on December 12, 1862. Cause of death not reported.

BELTON, JAMES R., Private

Resided in Surry County where he enlisted at age 34, May 4, 1861. Captured at Spotsylvania Court House, Virginia, May 12, 1864. Confined at Point Lookout, Maryland, until transferred to Elmira, New York, August 12, 1864. Died at Elmira on March 11, 1865, of "pleurisy."

BENNETT, WILLIAM T., Corporal

Resided in Surry County and enlisted on May 4, 1861. Mustered in as Corporal. Died at Garysburg on June 16, 1861. Cause of death not reported.

BENSON, JOHN W., Private

Resided in Surry County where he enlisted at age 28, March 18, 1862. Hospitalized at Richmond, Virginia, January 19, 1863, with a gunshot wound of the loins. Place and date wounded not reported. Returned to duty prior to July 1-3, 1863, when he was wounded in the left leg and right side at Gettysburg, Pennsylvania. Captured at Gettysburg on July 5, 1863. Hospitalized at Chester, Pennsylvania, until transferred to Point Lookout, Maryland, where he arrived on October 4, 1863. Paroled at Point Lookout and transferred to City Point, Virginia, where he was received March 6, 1864, for exchange. Reported absent on detached service in September-October, 1864. Rejoined the company in November-December, 1864. Present or accounted for until captured near Petersburg, Virginia, April 2, 1865. Confined at Fort Delaware, Delaware, until released on June 19, 1865, after taking the Oath of Allegiance.

BLACKWOOD, JULIUS T., Private

Resided in Surry County where he enlisted at age 16, March 18, 1862. Present or accounted for until captured at Hanover Court House, Virginia, on or about May 27, 1862. Confined at Fort Columbus, New York Harbor.

Exchanged at Aiken's Landing, James River, Virginia, August 5, 1862. Hospitalized at Charlottesville, Virginia, September 18, 1862, with a gunshot wound. Place and date wounded not reported. Returned to duty on an unspecified date. Captured at Gettysburg, Pennsylvania, July 3, 1863. Confined at Fort Delaware, Delaware, until transferred to Point Lookout, Maryland, October 15-18, 1863. Paroled at Point Lookout on February 18, 1865, and transferred to Boulware's Wharf, James River, Virginia, where he was received February 20-21, 1865, for exchange. [North Carolina pension records indicate he was wounded in the mouth on an unspecified date.]

BLACKWOOD, WILLIAM S., Corporal

Resided in Surry County where he enlisted at age 17, March 18, 1862. Mustered in as Private and was promoted to Corporal on April 9, 1862. Captured at or near Frayser's Farm, Virginia, on or about June 30, 1862. Confined at Fort Columbus, New York Harbor. Transferred to Fort Delaware, Delaware, July 9, 1862. Exchanged at Aiken's Landing, James River, Virginia, August 5, 1862. Hospitalized at Charlottesville, Virginia, September 18, 1862, with a gunshot wound. Place and date wounded not reported. Returned to duty on or about November 1, 1862. Wounded in the back and/or left thigh and captured at Gettysburg, Pennsylvania, July 1-3, 1863. Hospitalized at Gettysburg and at Chester, Pennsylvania. Paroled at Chester and transferred to City Point, Virginia, where he was received September 23, 1863, for exchange. Returned to duty on an unspecified date. Captured at Gravel Hill, Virginia, July 28, 1864. Confined at Point Lookout, Maryland, until transferred to Elmira, New York, August 8, 1864. Released at Elmira on June 16, 1865, after taking the Oath of Allegiance. [North Carolina pension records indicate he was wounded in the head on an unspecified date.]

BLEDSOE, TERRELL B., Musician

Born in Surry County where he resided as a farmer prior to enlisting in Surry County at age 38, May 4, 1861. Mustered in as Musician (Fifer). Present or accounted for until discharged on May 1, 1862, by reason of being overage.

BOBBITT, ANDREW J., Private

Resided in Grayson County, Virginia, and enlisted in Surry County at age 27, May 8, 1861. Wounded at Gettysburg, Pennsylvania, July 1-3, 1863. Returned to duty on an unspecified date. Wounded in the left arm near Petersburg, Virginia, April 2, 1865. Hospitalized at Richmond, Virginia, where he was captured on April 3, 1865. Transferred to Point Lookout, Maryland, May 2, 1865. Released at Point Lookout on June 26, 1865, after taking the Oath of Allegiance.

BRANNOCK, JAMES, Private

Resided in Surry County where he enlisted at age 23, May 4, 1861. Mustered in as Musician (Drummer) but was reduced to ranks in May-October, 1862. Surrendered at Appomattox Court House, Virginia, April 9, 1865.

BRAY, ARTHUR, Private

Resided in Surry County and enlisted in Guilford County at age 25, May 4, 1861. Wounded and captured at Gettysburg, Pennsylvania, July 3, 1863. Confined at Fort Delaware, Delaware, until transferred to Point

Lookout, Maryland, October 15-18, 1863. Paroled at Point Lookout on or about November 1, 1864. Received at Venus Point, Savannah River, Georgia, November 15, 1864, for exchange.

BRAY, CALVIN T., Private
Resided in Surry County where he enlisted at age 21, May 4, 1861. Mustered in as Musician but was reduced to ranks prior to November 1, 1861. Listed as a deserter on May 12, 1862. Hospitalized at Richmond, Virginia, July 2, 1862, with a wound of the hand. Place and date wounded not reported. Returned to duty prior to March 1, 1863. Deserted on April 4, 1863.

BRAY, EDWARD W., Private
Resided in Surry County where he enlisted at age 24, May 4, 1861. Captured at Hanover Court House, Virginia, May 27, 1862. Confined at Fort Monroe, Virginia, and at Fort Columbus, New York Harbor. Exchanged at Aiken's Landing, James River, Virginia, August 5, 1862. Returned to duty on an unspecified date. Wounded at Chancellorsville, Virginia, May 2-3, 1863. Deserted on July 25, 1863.

BRAY, L. W., Private
Place and date of enlistment not reported. Discharged on July 17, 1861, by reason of disability. [May have served later in Company C, 5th Regiment N.C. Senior Reserves.]

BRINKLEY, JOHN H., Corporal
Resided in Surry County where he enlisted at age 23, May 10, 1861. Mustered in as Private and was promoted to Corporal in May-July, 1862. Hospitalized at Richmond, Virginia, July 2, 1862, with a gunshot wound of the left knee. Place and date wounded not reported. Left leg amputated on July 12, 1862. Died in hospital at Richmond on August 4, 1862, of wounds.

BROWN, BARNABAS, Private
Resided in Surry County where he enlisted at age 23, March 18, 1862. Present or accounted for until captured at Hanover Court House, Virginia, on or about May 27, 1862. Confined at Fort Delaware, Delaware. Exchanged at Aiken's Landing, James River, Virginia, August 5, 1862. Died in hospital at Mount Jackson, Virginia, November 7, 1862, of "diarrhoea chronica."

BROWN, JAMES, Private
Resided in Surry County where he enlisted at age 18, May 4, 1861. Present or accounted for until hospitalized at Richmond, Virginia, July 2, 1862, with a gunshot wound of the left shoulder. Place and date wounded not reported. Returned to duty on July 3, 1862. Wounded in the shoulder at the Battle of Second Manassas, Virginia, on or about August 28, 1862. Deserted from hospital at Danville, Virginia, September 21, 1862. Returned to duty prior to March 1, 1863. Surrendered at Appomattox Court House, Virginia, April 9, 1865.

BULLIN, EDMUND, Private
Resided in Surry County where he enlisted at age 26, May 4, 1861. Present or accounted for until January-February, 1863, when he was reported sick in hospital. No further records.

BULLIN, GEORGE, Private
Resided in Surry County where he enlisted on January 18, 1864, for the war. Captured near Petersburg,

Virginia, April 2, 1865. Confined at Fort Delaware, Delaware, until released on June 19, 1865, after taking the Oath of Allegiance.

BULLIN, JOEL, Private
Resided in Surry County where he enlisted at age 20, May 10, 1861. Present or accounted for until he died at Wilmington on March 11, 1862. Cause of death not reported.

BURRIS, LEE H., Private
Born in Surry County where he resided as a farmer prior to enlisting in Surry County at age 21, May 4, 1861. Present or accounted for until captured at Hanover Court House, Virginia, May 27, 1862. Confined at Fort Monroe, Virginia, and at Fort Columbus, New York Harbor. Paroled and transferred to Aiken's Landing, James River, Virginia, where he was received July 12, 1862, for exchange. Declared exchanged at Aiken's Landing on August 5, 1862. Deserted in August, 1862. Returned to duty subsequent to February 28, 1863. Captured at Wilderness, Virginia, May 6, 1864. Confined at Point Lookout, Maryland, until released on May 28, 1864, after joining the U.S. Army. Assigned to Company I, 1st Regiment U.S. Volunteer Infantry.

CAIN, CORNELIUS, 1st Sergeant
Resided in Virginia and enlisted in Surry County at age 19, May 4, 1861. Mustered in as Corporal but was reduced to ranks on October 3, 1861. Promoted to 1st Sergeant on or about April 9, 1862. Present or accounted for until killed at Frayser's Farm, Virginia, June 30, 1862.

CAVE, JOHN, Private
Born in Surry County where he resided as a farmer prior to enlisting in Surry County at age 31, May 18, 1861. Present or accounted for until discharged on December 16, 1861, by reason of "general debility caused from anemia. . . ." [North Carolina pension records indicate he was wounded in an unspecified battle in 1864.]

CENTER, WILSON, Private
Resided in Surry County where he enlisted at age 25, March 18, 1862. Killed at Gettysburg, Pennsylvania, July 1-3, 1863.

CHANDLER, ANDREW J., Private
Resided in Surry County where he enlisted at age 27, March 18, 1862. Killed at Gettysburg, Pennsylvania, July 3, 1863.

CHANDLER, JOHN, Private
Born in Patrick County, Virginia, and resided in Surry County where he was by occupation a farmer prior to enlisting in Surry County at age 31, March 18, 1862. Discharged on April 15, 1863, by reason of "chronic rheumatism & contraction of left leg [and] imbecility of mind."

CHILDRESS, HIRAM, Private
Born in Surry County where he resided as a farmer prior to enlisting in Surry County at age 20, March 18, 1862. Present or accounted for until discharged on July 7, 1862, by reason of "anemia & dropsy of the lower extremities. . . ."

CHILDRESS, JOHN H., Private
Born in Surry County where he resided prior to enlisting

in Surry County at age 19, May 10, 1861. Present or accounted for until captured at Hanover Court House, Virginia, May 27, 1862. Confined at Fort Monroe, Virginia, and at Fort Columbus, New York Harbor. Paroled and transferred to Aiken's Landing, James River, Virginia, where he was received July 12, 1862, for exchange. Declared exchanged at Aiken's Landing on August 5, 1862. Wounded at Gettysburg, Pennsylvania, July 1-3, 1863. Returned to duty on August 27, 1863. Killed at Wilderness, Virginia, May 5, 1864.

CHILDRESS, STEPHEN, Private
Resided in Surry County where he enlisted at age 49, March 18, 1862. Present or accounted for until he "went home on furlough" on or about October 11, 1862, "and stayed there."

COCKERHAM, COLUMBUS C., Private
Resided in Surry County where he enlisted at age 25, May 4, 1861. Present or accounted for until discharged on May 12, 1862, after providing Private Jonathan Gentry as a substitute.

COCKERHAM, JESSE W., Sergeant
Resided in Surry County where he enlisted at age 28, May 4, 1861. Mustered in as Private and was promoted to Corporal on November 4, 1861. Reduced to ranks on or about April 8, 1862. Present or accounted for until captured at Hanover Court House, Virginia, May 27, 1862. Confined at Fort Monroe, Virginia, and at Fort Columbus, New York Harbor. Paroled and transferred to Aiken's Landing, James River, Virginia, where he was received July 12, 1862, for exchange. Declared exchanged at Aiken's Landing on August 5, 1862. Returned to duty on an unspecified date and was promoted to Sergeant in November, 1862-February, 1863. Killed at Gettysburg, Pennsylvania, July 3, 1863.

COCKERHAM, JOHN, Private
Born in Surry County where he enlisted on March 18, 1864, for the war. Captured at Spotsylvania Court House, Virginia, May 12, 1864. Confined at Point Lookout, Maryland, until transferred to Elmira, New York, August 8, 1864. Died at Elmira on September 22, 1864, of "chronic diarrhoea."

COCKERHAM, WILLIAM, Private
Resided in Surry County where he enlisted at age 25, May 4, 1861. Wounded at or near Chancellorsville, Virginia, May 3, 1863. Returned to duty on an unspecified date. Captured at or near Wilderness, Virginia, on or about May 12, 1864. Confined at Point Lookout, Maryland. Transferred to Elmira, New York, August 8, 1864. Arrived at Elmira on August 12, 1864. Paroled at Elmira on March 14, 1865, and transferred to Boulware's Wharf, James River, Virginia, where he was received March 18-21, 1865, for exchange.

COCKERHAM, WILLIAM H., Private
Resided in Surry County where he enlisted at age 18, May 4, 1861. Present or accounted for until killed at or near Frayser's Farm, Virginia, June 30, 1862.

COCKLEREESE, JULIUS, Private
Born in Orange County and resided in Surry County where he was by occupation a farmer prior to enlisting in Surry County at age 20, May 4, 1861. Present or accounted for until discharged on November 20, 1861,

by reason of "bronchitis."

COE, ARNOLD, Private
Born in Surry County where he resided as a farmer prior to enlisting in Surry County at age 22, March 18, 1862. Reported absent without leave in January-February, 1863. Surrendered at Appomattox Court House, Virginia, April 9, 1865. [North Carolina pension records indicate he was wounded on May 14, 1864.]

COLLINS, HEZEKIAH W., Private
Resided in Surry County where he enlisted at age 27, May 4, 1861. Present or accounted for until he surrendered at Appomattox Court House, Virginia, April 9, 1865.

COLLINS, JAMES M., Private
Resided in Surry County where he enlisted at age 22, May 4, 1861. Reported absent wounded in September-October, 1864. Place and date wounded not reported. Retired to the Invalid Corps on January 11, 1865, by reason of disability.

COPELAND, DRURY H., Private
Resided in Surry County where he enlisted at age 35, May 4, 1861. Present or accounted for until he died at Wilmington on or about January 5, 1862. Cause of death not reported.

COPELAND, JAMES M., Private
Resided in Surry County where he enlisted at age 23, May 4, 1861. Present or accounted for until he died at Kinston on May 19, 1862, of disease.

CUNNINGHAM, NICHOLAS F., Private
Resided in Surry County where he enlisted at age 33, May 4, 1861. Present or accounted for through February, 1863. No further records.

CUNNINGHAM, SHADRACH M., Private
Resided in Surry County where he enlisted at age 18, May 4, 1861. Captured at or near Wilderness, Virginia, on or about May 12, 1864. Confined at Point Lookout, Maryland, until transferred to Elmira, New York, August 8, 1864. Paroled at Elmira on March 2, 1865, and transferred for exchange. Hospitalized at Richmond, Virginia, March 6, 1865, and was furloughed for thirty days on March 8, 1865.

CUNNINGHAM, WILLIAM F., Private
Resided in Surry County where he enlisted at age 21, May 4, 1861. Wounded in the right shoulder at Chancellorsville, Virginia, May 1-3, 1863. Returned to duty on an unspecified date. Reported absent without leave on May 1, 1864. Returned to duty on October 11, 1864. Present or accounted for until captured near Petersburg, Virginia, April 2, 1865. Confined at Fort Delaware, Delaware, until released on June 19, 1865, after taking the Oath of Allegiance.

DAVIS, DRURY K., Private
Resided in Surry County where he enlisted at age 31, May 4, 1861. Present or accounted for until he died at Wilmington on December 29, 1861, of disease.

DAVIS, WILLIAM J., Private
Born in Rockingham County and resided in Surry County where he enlisted at age 20, May 4, 1861. "Killed in skirmish" at Deep Bottom, Virginia, July 27,

1864.

DRAUGHN, C., Private
Place and date of enlistment not reported. Surrendered at Appomattox Court House, Virginia, April 9, 1865.

DRAUGHN, ISAAC, Private
Born in Surry County where he resided as a farmer prior to enlisting in Surry County at age 20, May 4, 1861. Present or accounted for through February, 1865.

DRAUGHN, JOHN, Private
Born in Surry County. Place and date of enlistment not reported. Killed at Wilderness, Virginia, May 5, 1864.

DRAUGHN, WILLIAM, Private
Resided in Surry County where he enlisted at age 24, March 18, 1862. Present or accounted for until he was "arrested" on February 26, 1865. No further records.

EDWARDS, DANIEL, Private
Resided in Surry County where he enlisted at age 36, March 18, 1862. Present or accounted for until captured at Hanover Court House, Virginia, May 27, 1862. Confined at Fort Monroe, Virginia, and at Fort Columbus, New York Harbor. Paroled and transferred to Aiken's Landing, James River, Virginia, where he was received July 12, 1862, for exchange. Declared exchanged at Aiken's Landing on August 5, 1862. Reported absent sick through February, 1863. Died on an unspecified date. Place and cause of death not reported.

ELLIS, HENDERSON, Private
Resided in Surry County where he enlisted on November 1, 1864, for the war. Present or accounted for until captured near Petersburg, Virginia, April 2, 1865. Confined at Fort Delaware, Delaware, until released on June 19, 1865, after taking the Oath of Allegiance.

FOWLER, JOHN, Private
Resided in Surry County where he enlisted at age 18, March 18, 1862. Present or accounted for until he died in hospital at Kinston on May 6, 1862, of disease.

FREEMAN, MARK H., Private
Resided in Surry County where he enlisted at age 29, May 4, 1861. Wounded in the right side "in Virginia" on June 28, 1864. Returned to duty in November-December, 1864. Present or accounted for until he surrendered at Appomattox Court House, Virginia, April 9, 1865.

GATES, ALBERT L., Private
Resided in Surry County where he enlisted at age 27, May 4, 1861. Present or accounted for until he surrendered at Appomattox Court House, Virginia, April 9, 1865.

GATES, MARTIN C., Private
Resided in Surry County and enlisted at age 18, February 28, 1863, for the war. Wounded at Chancellorsville, Virginia, May 2-3, 1863. No further records.

GATES, SOLOMON G., Private
Born in Surry County where he resided as a farmer prior to enlisting in Surry County at age 18, May 4, 1861. Wounded and captured at Gettysburg, Pennsylvania,

July 3-4, 1863. Confined at Fort McHenry, Maryland, and at Fort Delaware, Delaware, until transferred to Point Lookout, Maryland, on or about October 18, 1863. Died at Point Lookout on January 16, 1864. Cause of death not reported.

GENTRY, JONATHAN, Private
Resided in Surry County where he enlisted on May 12, 1862, for the war as a substitute for Private Columbus C. Cockerham. Deserted prior to November 1, 1862. Returned to duty in March, 1863-October, 1864. Captured near Petersburg, Virginia, April 2, 1865. Confined at Hart's Island, New York Harbor, until released on June 19-20, 1865, after taking the Oath of Allegiance.

GENTRY, WILEY B., Private
Born in Surry County where he resided as a farmer prior to enlisting in Surry County at age 23, May 4, 1861. Present or accounted for until discharged on April 23, 1862, by reason of "intermittent and chronic rheumatism" resulting in the contraction of one of his legs.

GLOSSCOE, COLVIN W., Private
Resided in Surry County where he enlisted at age 19, March 18, 1862. Captured at Hanover Court House, Virginia, on or about May 28, 1862. Paroled and transferred to Aiken's Landing, James River, Virginia, where he was received June 26, 1862, for exchange. Declared exchanged at Aiken's Landing on August 5, 1862. Died in hospital at Richmond, Virginia, on or about October 1, 1862, of "phthisis pulmon[alis]."

GOLDEN, THOMAS, Private
Resided in Surry County where he enlisted at age 33, May 4, 1861. Present or accounted for until he died in hospital at Richmond, Virginia, August 9, 1862, of "chronic diarrhoea."

GRIFFITH, JAMES H., Private
Born in Franklin County, Virginia, and resided in Surry County where he was by occupation a farmer prior to enlisting in Surry County at age 31, May 13, 1861. Present or accounted for until discharged on January 7, 1862, by reason of "chronic rheumatism."

GRIGG, WILLIAM A., Private
Resided in Surry County where he enlisted at age 23, May 13, 1861. Present or accounted for until captured at Hanover Court House, Virginia, May 27, 1862. Confined at Fort Monroe, Virginia, and at Fort Columbus, New York Harbor. Paroled and transferred to Aiken's Landing, James River, Virginia, where he was received July 12, 1862, for exchange. Declared exchanged at Aiken's Landing on August 5, 1862. Died in hospital at Petersburg, Virginia, August 13, 1862, of "ty[phoid] febris."

HARDY, CHARLES, Private
Resided in Surry County where he enlisted on January 18, 1864, for the war. Captured near Petersburg, Virginia, April 2, 1865. Confined at Fort Delaware, Delaware, until released on June 19, 1865, after taking the Oath of Allegiance.

HARDY, JOHN H., Jr., Private
Born in Surry County where he resided as a farmer prior to enlisting in Surry County at age 18, May 4, 1861.

Wounded at Chancellorsville, Virginia, May 2-3, 1863. Returned to duty prior to July 1-5, 1863, when he was wounded in the left leg and captured at Gettysburg, Pennsylvania. Hospitalized at Davids Island, New York Harbor. Transferred to Fort Wood, Bedloe's Island, New York Harbor, prior to November 1, 1863. Transferred to Point Lookout, Maryland, on or about January 10, 1864. Paroled at Point Lookout on or about March 3, 1864, and transferred to City Point, Virginia, where he was received March 6, 1864, for exchange. Reported absent sick in September-October, 1864, and was reported absent without leave in November-December, 1864. Retired from service on February 4, 1865, by reason of wounds received at Gettysburg resulting in "extensive loss of bone & atrophy of the muscles."

HARE, JAMES E., Private
Resided in Surry County and was by occupation a farmer prior to enlisting in Surry County at age 19, March 18, 1862. Wounded on or about August 21, 1862. Returned to duty subsequent to February 28, 1863. Reportedly transferred to Company A, 2nd Regiment South Carolina Artillery, January 25, 1864. [Roll of Honor indicates he was wounded on the Rappahannock River, Virginia, October 24, 1862.]

HARRIS, ALFRED L., Private
Born in Surry County where he resided as a farmer prior to enlisting in Surry County at age 32, May 4, 1861. Present or accounted for until discharged on July 7, 1862, by reason of disability following "pneumonia."

HARRIS, JOHN, Private
Born in Pitt County and resided in Surry County where he was by occupation a farmer prior to enlisting in Surry County at age 39, March 18, 1862. Captured at Hanover Court House, Virginia, May 27, 1862. Confined at Fort Monroe, Virginia, and at Fort Columbus, New York Harbor. Exchanged on an unspecified date. Died in hospital at Richmond, Virginia, January 27, 1863. Cause of death not reported.

HARRIS, LEMUEL B., Private
Resided in Surry County where he enlisted at age 21, May 4, 1861. Present or accounted for until he deserted on August 1, 1862.

HAWKS, DICKERSON, Private
Resided in Surry County where he enlisted at age 23, March 18, 1862. Present or accounted for until paroled at Lynchburg, Virginia, April 13, 1865.

HAWKS, WILLIAM, Private
Resided in Surry County and enlisted in Carroll County, Virginia, at age 21, March 18, 1862. Present or accounted for until he died in hospital at Richmond, Virginia, September 1, 1862, of "febris typhoides."

HIATT, GEORGE W., Private
Resided in Surry County where he enlisted at age 21, March 18, 1862. Present or accounted for until captured at or near Hanover Court House, Virginia, on or about May 27, 1862. Confined at Fort Monroe, Virginia, and at Fort Delaware, Delaware. Paroled and transferred to Aiken's Landing, James River, Virginia, June 9, 1862, for exchange. Declared exchanged at Aiken's Landing on August 5, 1862. Returned to duty prior to November 1, 1862. Company records indicate he was captured at

Deep Bottom, Virginia, July 10, 1864; however, records of the Federal Provost Marshal do not substantiate that report. No further records.

HILL, LORENZO H., Private
Born in Surry County where he resided prior to enlisting in Surry County at age 20, March 18, 1862. Reported absent without leave from October 1, 1862, until January, 1863. Hospitalized at Richmond, Virginia, May 25, 1864, with a gunshot wound of the right hand. Place and date wounded not reported. Returned to duty on June 27, 1864. Died in hospital at Richmond on August 25, 1864. Cause of death not reported.

HODGES, HENRY, Private
Born in Surry County where he resided prior to enlisting in Surry County at age 17, March 18, 1862. Hospitalized at Richmond, Virginia, May 24, 1864, with a gunshot wound of the left shoulder. Place and date wounded not reported. Died in hospital at Richmond on May 30, 1864, of wounds.

HODGES, JAMES R., Private
Resided in Surry County where he enlisted at age 31, May 4, 1861. Present or accounted for until wounded in the head at Cedar Mountain, Virginia, August 9, 1862. Returned to duty in January-February, 1863. Furloughed for sixty days on April 30, 1863. Reported absent without leave through February, 1865.

HODGES, JOEL W., Private
Resided in Surry County where he enlisted at age 21, March 18, 1862. Present or accounted for through June 17, 1864. No further records.

HODGES, PLEASANT H., Private
Resided in Surry County where he enlisted at age 21, May 4, 1861. Present or accounted for until wounded at Cedar Mountain, Virginia, August 9, 1862. Deserted from hospital prior to November 1, 1862. Returned to duty on an unspecified date. Captured near Petersburg, Virginia, April 2, 1865. Confined at Fort Delaware, Delaware, until released on June 19, 1865, after taking the Oath of Allegiance.

HODGES, TYRE, Private
Resided in Surry County where he enlisted at age 36, May 5, 1861. Captured near Petersburg, Virginia, April 2, 1865. Confined at Fort Delaware, Delaware, until released on June 19, 1865, after taking the Oath of Allegiance.

HOLDER, JAMES H., Private
Resided in Surry County where he enlisted at age 18, March 18, 1862. Present or accounted for through April, 1862. Deserted from hospital on an unspecified date. Died "at home." Date and cause of death not reported.

HOLDER, JAMES M., Private
Resided in Surry County where he enlisted at age 18, March 18, 1862. Present or accounted for until wounded at Cedar Mountain, Virginia, on or about August 9, 1862. Hospitalized at Danville, Virginia. Deserted from hospital at Danville on September 22, 1862.

HOLDER, JESSE A., Sergeant
Resided in Surry County where he enlisted at age 18, March 18, 1862. Mustered in as Private and was

promoted to Corporal on September 1, 1864. Promoted to Sergeant subsequent to February 28, 1865. Surrendered at Appomattox Court House, Virginia, April 9, 1865. [North Carolina pension records indicate he was wounded at Fredericksburg, Virginia, October 3, 1863.]

HOLYFIELD, BIRD, 1st Sergeant
Resided in Surry County where he enlisted at age 23, May 4, 1861. Mustered in as Private and was promoted to 1st Sergeant on September 23, 1861. Died at Wilmington on January 11, 1862. Cause of death not reported.

HOLYFIELD, COLUMBUS C., Private
Resided in Surry County where he enlisted at age 24, May 4, 1861. Mustered in as Private and was promoted to Sergeant on April 10, 1862. Reported absent without leave on or about May 26, 1864. Reduced to ranks on September 1, 1864. Reported absent without leave through February, 1865.

HOLYFIELD, H., ———
North Carolina pension records indicate that he served in this company.

HOLYFIELD, WATSON B., 1st Sergeant
Born in Surry County where he resided as a farmer prior to enlisting in Surry County at age 20, May 4, 1861. Mustered in as Private. Present or accounted for until wounded in the right elbow at Gaines' Mill, Virginia, June 27, 1862. Returned to duty on an unspecified date and was promoted to 1st Sergeant on September 21, 1862. Wounded in the back and right hand at Wilderness, Virginia, May 5, 1864. Returned to duty prior to August 25, 1864, when he was wounded in the right shoulder at Reams' Station, Virginia. Reported absent wounded until he was retired from service on or about February 22, 1865, by reason of "gunshot wound of the right shoulder rendering the arm useless."

HOOTS, J., ———
Place and date of enlistment not reported. Died in hospital at Richmond, Virginia, August 7, 1864, of disease.

HUDSON, MARTIN C., Private
Enlisted in Surry County on March 18, 1862. Present or accounted for through February, 1865; however, he was reported absent sick during much of that period.

ISAACS, GODFREY, Private
Enlisted in Surry County on November 1, 1864, for the war. Wounded at Petersburg, Virginia, on an unspecified date. Present or accounted for until he surrendered at Appomattox Court House, Virginia, April 9, 1865.

ISAACS, N. J., ———
North Carolina pension records indicate that he served in this company.

JERRELL, RUFUS A., Private
Resided in Surry County and was by occupation a farmer prior to enlisting in Surry County at age 22, March 18, 1862. Wounded in the left leg at Ox Hill, Virginia, September 1, 1862. Reported absent wounded through October, 1862. Listed as a deserter in January-February, 1863. Returned to duty on an unspecified

date. Wounded in the left eye and/or both arms at or near Jericho Mills, Virginia, on or about May 23, 1864. Returned to duty in November-December, 1864. Deserted to the enemy on or about February 24, 1865. Confined at Washington, D.C., until released on or about February 27, 1865, after taking the Oath of Allegiance.

JOHNSON, THOMAS, Private
Born in Surry County where he resided as a shoemaker prior to enlisting in Surry County at age 35, March 18, 1862. Discharged on April 4, 1863, by reason of "phthisis pulmonalis." Hospitalized at Richmond, Virginia, where he died on April 25, 1863, of "phthisis pulmonalis" and/or "smallpox."

KEY, ANDREW JACKSON, Private
Enlisted in Surry County at age 17, October 12, 1864, for the war. Present or accounted for until he surrendered at Appomattox Court House, Virginia, April 9, 1865.

KEY, JAMES R., Private
Resided in Surry County where he enlisted at age 26, March 18, 1862. Present or accounted for until killed at Hanover Court House, Virginia, May 27, 1862.

KEY, JOHN A., Private
Resided in Surry County where he enlisted at age 38, May 4, 1861. Captured near Petersburg, Virginia, April 2, 1865. Confined at Fort Delaware, Delaware, until released on June 19, 1865, after taking the Oath of Allegiance.

KEY, MARTIN V., Corporal
Resided in Surry County where he enlisted at age 18, May 4, 1861. Mustered in as Private and was promoted to Corporal in May, 1862. Present or accounted for until killed at Hanover Court House, Virginia, May 27, 1862.

KEY, R. J., Private
Enlisted in Surry County on March 18, 1862. Present or accounted for until killed at Hanover Court House, Virginia, May 27, 1862.

KEY, SAMUEL C., Private
Resided in Surry County where he enlisted at age 24, May 4, 1861. Present or accounted for until reported absent without leave on or about February 7, 1865.

LANDID, J. F., Private
Place and date of enlistment not reported. Paroled at Farmville, Virginia, April 11-21, 1865.

LINVILLE, BERRY, Private
Resided in Surry County where he enlisted at age 24, May 4, 1861. Present or accounted for until transferred to Company B, 2nd Battalion N.C. Infantry, October 23, 1862.

LONGBOTTOM, MANOR, Private
Resided in Surry County where he enlisted at age 22, May 4, 1861. Captured near Petersburg, Virginia, April 2, 1865. Confined at Fort Delaware, Delaware, until released on June 19, 1865, after taking the Oath of Allegiance.

LOVILL, HENRY P., Private
Born in Surry County where he resided as a farmer prior

to enlisting in Surry County at age 22, May 4, 1861. Mustered in as Sergeant but was reduced to ranks prior to November 1, 1861. Present or accounted for until appointed 2nd Lieutenant of Company A, 54th Regiment N.C. Troops, March 20, 1862.

McGEE, JAMES L., Private
Enlisted in Surry County on January 18, 1864, for the war. Surrendered at Appomattox Court House, Virginia, April 9, 1865.

McGUFFIN, WILLIAM A., Private
Resided in Surry County where he enlisted at age 18, May 16, 1861. Present or accounted for until killed at or near Frayser's Farm, Virginia, on or about June 30, 1862.

McKINNIE, JESSE, Corporal
Resided in Surry County and enlisted at age 21, March 18, 1862. Mustered in as Private and was promoted to Corporal on September 10, 1862. Killed at Chancellorsville, Virginia, May 3, 1863.

McROBERTS, BENJAMIN, Private
Resided in Surry County where he enlisted at age 30, May 16, 1861. Present or accounted for until he deserted in May-October, 1862.

MARION, AZARIAH, Private
Resided in Surry County where he enlisted at age 18, March 18, 1862. Present or accounted for until hospitalized at Richmond, Virginia, July 2, 1862, with a gunshot wound of the right side. Place and date wounded not reported. Returned to duty prior to March 1, 1863. Discharged in March, 1863. Reason discharged not reported. [North Carolina pension records indicate he was wounded in the right hip at Richmond in July, 1863.]

MARION, JEREMIAH, Private
Resided in Surry County where he enlisted at age 25, May 13, 1861. Present or accounted for until he died at High Point on August 24-25, 1861, of disease.

MARION, NATHAN J., Private
Resided in Surry County and enlisted at age 19, May 4, 1861. Present or accounted for until he died at Garysburg on August 19, 1861. Cause of death not reported.

MARION, SIDNEY, Private
Born in Surry County where he resided as a trader prior to enlisting in Surry County at age 22, May 13, 1861. Present or accounted for until discharged on September 24, 1861, by reason of disability.

MARSH, JOHN, Private
Resided in Surry County and enlisted at "Wough Hill" or at Dobson at age 24, March 18, 1862. Present or accounted for until hospitalized at Richmond, Virginia, July 2, 1862, with a "contused wound." Place and date wounded not reported. Returned to duty on an unspecified date. Captured at Fredericksburg, Virginia, December 13, 1862. Exchanged on December 17, 1862. Returned to duty prior to March 1, 1863. Died in hospital at Staunton, Virginia, July 11, 1863, of "febris typhoides."

MARSH, WILLIAM, Private
Resided in Surry County where he enlisted at age 20, March 18, 1862. Present or accounted for until captured at Hanover Court House, Virginia, May 27, 1862. Confined at Fort Monroe, Virginia, and at Fort

Columbus, New York Harbor. Received at Aiken's Landing, James River, Virginia, July 12, 1862, for exchange. Declared exchanged at Aiken's Landing on August 5, 1862. Returned to duty prior to November 1, 1862. Wounded in the left shoulder at Gettysburg, Pennsylvania, July 1-3, 1863. Returned to duty on an unspecified date. Captured at or near Jericho Ford, Virginia, on or about May 23, 1864. Confined at Elmira, New York. Released on an unspecified date.

MARSH, WILLIAM H., Private
Resided in Surry County where he enlisted at age 17, March 18, 1862. Wounded in the hand at Gettysburg, Pennsylvania, July 3, 1863. Returned to duty on August 4, 1863. Present or accounted for through February, 1865.

MOODY, WOODSON R., Corporal
Resided in Surry County where he enlisted at age 21, May 4, 1861. Mustered in as Private and was promoted to Corporal in November, 1862-February, 1863. Present or accounted for through February, 1865.

MOORE, ELIJAH, Private
Resided in Surry County where he enlisted at age 30, May 13, 1861. Present or accounted for until he surrendered at Appomattox Court House, Virginia, April 9, 1865.

MOORE, THOMAS H., Private
Resided in Surry County where he enlisted at age 21, May 13, 1861. Captured near Petersburg, Virginia, April 2, 1865. Confined at Fort Delaware, Delaware, until released on June 19, 1865, after taking the Oath of Allegiance. [North Carolina pension records indicate he was wounded in the head and left side at Petersburg in 1864.]

MOSELEY, HENRY D., Private
Born in Surry County where he resided as a farmer prior to enlisting in Surry County at age 40, May 4, 1861. Mustered in as Sergeant but was reduced to ranks on October 4, 1861. Present or accounted for until discharged on or about May 2, 1862, by reason of being overage.

NANCE, RICHARD S., Private
Born in Yadkin County* and resided in Surry County where he was by occupation a farmer prior to enlisting in Surry County at age 22, May 4, 1861. Present or accounted for until wounded in the left arm at Malvern Hill, Virginia, July 1, 1862. Left arm amputated. Discharged on January 26, 1863, by reason of disability.

NIXON, NATHANIEL G., Private
Born in Surry County where he enlisted on March 24, 1864, for the war. Killed at Jericho Ford, Virginia, May 23, 1864.

NIXON, WILLIAM P., Private
Resided in Surry County where he enlisted at age 21, May 4, 1861. Wounded in the left shoulder at Fredericksburg, Virginia, December 13, 1862. Returned to duty subsequent to March 26, 1863. Surrendered at Appomattox Court House, Virginia, April 9, 1865.

NORMAN, ANSEL P., Private
Resided in Surry County where he enlisted at age 30, March 18, 1862. Present or accounted for until he deserted on August 1, 1862.

NORMAN, THOMAS P., Private
Born in Surry County where he resided prior to enlisting

in Surry County at age 20, March 18, 1862. Present or accounted for until he deserted on August 1, 1862. Listed as a deserter through February, 1863. Company records do not indicate whether he returned to duty. Died in hospital at Gordonsville, Virginia, on or about August 31, 1864, of a gunshot wound and/or "asthma."

NORTON, JAMES S., Private
Resided in Surry County where he enlisted at age 33, March 18, 1862. Present or accounted for until he died in hospital at Richmond, Virginia, August 26, 1862, of disease.

PARKS, WILLIAM CALVIN, Private
Resided in Surry County where he enlisted at age 32, March 18, 1862. Present or accounted for until captured at Hanover Court House, Virginia, May 27, 1862. Confined at Fort Monroe, Virginia, and at Fort Columbus, New York Harbor. Transferred to Aiken's Landing, James River, Virginia, where he was received July 12, 1862, for exchange. Declared exchanged at Aiken's Landing on August 5, 1862. Returned to duty prior to August 27-30, 1862, when he was wounded in the thigh at or near Manassas, Virginia. Reported absent without leave in January-February, 1863. Company records do not indicate whether he returned to duty; however, he was transferred to the C.S. Navy on or about April 3, 1864.

PARSONS, ALBERT, Private
Resided in Surry County where he enlisted at age 22, March 18, 1862. Present or accounted for until captured at Hanover Court House, Virginia, May 27, 1862. Confined at Fort Columbus, New York Harbor. Paroled and transferred to Aiken's Landing, James River, Virginia, where he was received July 12, 1862, for exchange. Died on or about August 3, 1862, of disease. Place of death not reported.

PARSONS, DANIEL C., Private
Resided in Surry County where he enlisted at age 25, March 18, 1862. Present or accounted for until he died "at home" on or about November 19, 1862. Cause of death not reported.

PATTERSON, HARRISON, Sergeant
Resided in Surry County where he enlisted at age 20, March 18, 1862. Mustered in as Private. Present or accounted for until captured at Hanover Court House, Virginia, May 27, 1862. Confined at Fort Monroe, Virginia, and at Fort Columbus, New York Harbor. Paroled and transferred to Aiken's Landing, James River, Virginia, where he received July 12, 1862, for exchange. Declared exchanged at Aiken's Landing on August 5, 1862. Returned to duty prior to November 1, 1862. Promoted to Corporal on June 1, 1863. Wounded in the right leg at Wilderness, Virginia, on or about May 5, 1864. Wounded in the left arm at Spotsylvania Court House, Virginia, in May, 1864. Promoted to Sergeant on September 1, 1864. Present or accounted for through February, 1865. [North Carolina pension records indicate he was wounded in the left leg at Petersburg, Virginia, on an unspecified date.]

PEDIGO, JAMES S., Private
Born in Patrick County, Virginia, and resided in Surry County where he was by occupation a mechanic prior to enlisting in Surry County at age 37, May 4, 1861.

Present or accounted for until discharged on or about May 1, 1862, by reason of being overage.

PEEL, THOMAS, Private
Resided in Surry County where he enlisted at age 22, May 4, 1861. Present or accounted for until wounded in the arm at the Battle of Second Manassas, Virginia, August 27-30, 1862. Hospitalized at Middleburg, Virginia, or at Upperville, Virginia, where he died on September 6 or September 29, 1862, of wounds.

PENDRY, J. F., ⸻
North Carolina pension records indicate that he served in this company.

PHILLIPS, JOHN W., Private
Resided in Surry County where he enlisted at age 17, March 18, 1862. Wounded in both knees and captured at Spotsylvania Court House, Virginia, May 12, 1864. Confined at Point Lookout, Maryland, until transferred to Elmira, New York, August 10, 1864. Released at Elmira on June 19, 1865, after taking the Oath of Allegiance.

POINDEXTER, A. L., ⸻
North Carolina pension records indicate that he served in this company.

POOL, HENRY G., Private
Born in Scotland and resided in Surry County where he enlisted at age 27, May 4, 1861. Present or accounted for until captured at Hanover Court House, Virginia, on or about May 27, 1862. Confined at Fort Monroe, Virginia, and at Fort Columbus, New York Harbor. Paroled and transferred to Aiken's Landing, James River, Virginia, where he was received July 12, 1862, for exchange. Declared exchanged at Aiken's Landing on August 5, 1862. Died in hospital at Petersburg, Virginia, prior to November 1, 1862. Cause of death not reported.

PORTIS, JOHN, Private
Resided in Surry County where he enlisted at age 22, May 4, 1861. Present or accounted for until captured by the enemy in September, 1862. Confined at Washington, D.C. Paroled and transferred to Aiken's Landing, James River, Virginia, where he was received on or about September 27, 1862, for exchange. Declared exchanged at Aiken's Landing on November 10, 1862. Deserted prior to March 1, 1863.

PUCKET, JAMES M., Private
Resided in Surry County where he enlisted at age 28, March 18, 1862. Present or accounted for until captured at Hanover Court House, Virginia, May 27, 1862. Confined at Fort Monroe, Virginia. Paroled and transferred to Aiken's Landing, James River, Virginia, where he was received September 1, 1862, for exchange. Declared exchanged at Aiken's Landing on November 10, 1862. Reported absent sick in January-February, 1863. Died in hospital at Danville, Virginia, on or about March 15, 1863, of "dyspepsia."

PUCKETT, HUGH, Private
Resided in Surry County where he enlisted at age 20, March 18, 1862. Present or accounted for until wounded in the right leg and captured at Hanover Court House, Virginia, May 27, 1862. Right leg amputated. Confined at various Federal hospitals. Paroled and transferred to Aiken's Landing, James River, Virginia,

where he was received September 1, 1862, for exchange. Discharged on September 6, 1862, by reason of disability.

QUINN, ISAAC, Private
Resided in Surry County where he enlisted at age 18, May 4, 1861. Present or accounted for until he died at Wilmington on or about January 21, 1862, of disease.

REID, IRVIN, Sergeant
Resided in Surry County where he enlisted at age 23, May 4, 1861. Mustered in as Private and was promoted to Sergeant on April 10, 1862. Present or accounted for until wounded at Cedar Mountain, Virginia, on or about August 9, 1862. Reported absent without leave on October 31, 1862. Returned to duty subsequent to February 28, 1863. Wounded at Chancellorsville, Virginia, May 2-3, 1863. Reported absent wounded in September-October, 1864, and was reported absent without leave in November-December, 1864. Returned to duty in January-February, 1865. Captured near Petersburg, Virginia, April 2, 1865. Confined at Point Lookout, Maryland, until released on June 17, 1865, after taking the Oath of Allegiance.

REID, ISAAC, Private
Resided in Surry County where he enlisted at age 22, March 18, 1862. Deserted on August 1, 1862. Returned to duty on or about October 31, 1862. Died in hospital at Richmond, Virginia, May 30, 1863, of ''feb[ris] typhoid.''

REID, JACOB F., Private
Resided in Surry County where he enlisted at age 28, May 4, 1861. Reported absent sick from April 30, 1863, through February, 1865.

REID, JOHN, Private
Resided in Surry County where he enlisted at age 24, March 18, 1862. Captured at Hanover Court House, Virginia, on or about May 27, 1862. Received at Aiken's Landing, James River, Virginia, June 26, 1862, for exchange. Declared exchanged at Aiken's Landing on August 5, 1862. Captured at Spotsylvania Court House, Virginia, May 12, 1864. Confined at Point Lookout, Maryland, until transferred to Elmira, New York, August 10, 1864. Released at Elmira on May 29, 1865, after taking the Oath of Allegiance.

RIGGAN, JOSEPH M., Private
Resided in Surry County and enlisted at age 28, May 4, 1861. Died at Garysburg on August 8, 1861, of disease.

RIGGS, CHRISTOPHER C., Sergeant
Born in Surry County where he resided as a farmer prior to enlisting in Surry County at age 22, May 4, 1861. Mustered in as Private. Hospitalized at Richmond, Virginia, May 24, 1864, with a gunshot wound. Place and date wounded not reported. Returned to duty on an unspecified date. Promoted to Sergeant on September 1, 1864. Wounded in the left arm near Jones' Farm, Virginia, September 30, 1864. Left arm amputated. Retired from service on February 4, 1865, by reason of disability.

RIGGS, GEORGE W., Private
Enlisted in Surry County on May 4, 1861. Present or accounted for until killed at the Battle of Second Manassas, Virginia, August 29, 1862.

RIGGS, THOMAS J., Private
Resided in Surry County where he enlisted on February 18, 1864, for the war. Hospitalized at Richmond, Virginia, June 6, 1864, with a gunshot wound. Place and date wounded not reported. Returned to duty prior to November 1, 1864. Present or accounted for until captured near Petersburg, Virginia, April 2, 1865. Confined at Point Lookout, Maryland, until released on June 17, 1865, after taking the Oath of Allegiance.

RING, ADAM, Private
Resided in Surry County where he enlisted at age 20, March 18, 1862. Present or accounted for until hospitalized at Charlottesville, Virginia, September 12, 1862, with a gunshot wound. Place and date wounded not reported. Returned to duty in January-February, 1863. Captured near Petersburg, Virginia, April 2, 1865. Confined at Fort Delaware, Delaware, until released on June 19, 1865, after taking the Oath of Allegiance. [North Carolina pension records indicate he was wounded by a ''falling limb at Manassas,'' Virginia, on an unspecified date.]

RING, STEPHEN, Private
Born in Surry County where he enlisted on December 20, 1863, for the war. Killed at Jericho Ford, Virginia, May 23, 1864.

RING, WILLIAM, Private
Resided in Surry County and enlisted at age 37, May 4, 1861. Died on August 6, 1861, of disease. Place of death not reported.

ROBERTS, PLEASANT H., Private
Resided in Surry County where he enlisted at age 19, May 4, 1861. Wounded in the thigh and captured at Hanover Court House, Virginia, May 27, 1862. Died at Gaines' Mill, Virginia, June 2, 1862, of wounds.

SHARPLIN, J., Private
Place and date of enlistment not reported. Hospitalized at Richmond, Virginia, March 28, 1865, with a gunshot wound of the right leg. Place and date wounded not reported. Captured in hospital at Richmond on April 3, 1865. No further records.

SHOUSE, FREDERICK, Private
Resided in Forsyth County and enlisted in Davidson County at age 33, September 17, 1861. Present or accounted for until killed at Frayser's Farm, Virginia, June 30, 1862.

SHREVE, ROBERT J., Private
Resided in Surry County where he enlisted at age 24, May 13, 1861. Present or accounted for until he died in hospital at Richmond, Virginia, in June-October, 1862. Cause of death not reported.

SHROPSHIRE, JEREMIAH, Private
Resided in Surry County where he enlisted at age 22, May 20, 1861. Wounded in the right leg near Petersburg, Virginia, March 27, 1865. Hospitalized at Richmond, Virginia, where he was captured by the enemy on April 3, 1865. Transferred to Point Lookout, Maryland, where he was received on May 12, 1865. Released on or about June 28, 1865, after taking the Oath of Allegiance.

SMITH, DAVID P., Private

Resided in Surry County where he enlisted at age 19, May 13, 1861. Present or accounted for until wounded in the arm at the Battle of Second Manassas, Virginia, August 27-30, 1862. Returned to duty on December 29, 1862. Killed at Gettysburg, Pennsylvania, July 3, 1863.

SMITH, FREEMAN, Private

Resided in Surry County where he enlisted at age 47, March 18, 1862. Company muster roll dated May 1-October 31, 1862, states he was captured and paroled; however, records of the Federal Provost Marshal do not substantiate that report. Listed as a deserter in January-February, 1863. Returned to duty on an unspecified date. Captured at Spotsylvania Court House, Virginia, May 12, 1864. Confined at Point Lookout, Maryland, until transferred to Elmira, New York, August 10, 1864. Died at Elmira on February 22, 1865, of "chro[nic] diarrhoea."

SNOW, FROST, Jr., Corporal

Resided in Surry County where he enlisted at age 18, May 4, 1861. Mustered in as Private and was promoted to Corporal on October 4, 1861. Reduced to ranks on April 9, 1862, but was promoted to Corporal on August 10, 1862. Wounded in the arm and captured at Spotsylvania Court House, Virginia, May 12, 1864. Confined at Old Capitol Prison, Washington, D.C., until transferred to Fort Delaware, Delaware, June 15, 1864. Released at Fort Delaware on June 19, 1865, after taking the Oath of Allegiance.

SNOW, SHADRICK, Private

Resided in Surry County where he enlisted at age 18, March 18, 1862. Present or accounted for until he died in hospital at Lynchburg, Virginia, July 8, 1862, of "febris."

SOUTHARD, LEVI, Private

Resided in Surry County where he enlisted at age 35, March 18, 1862. Captured at Gravel Hill, Virginia, July 28, 1864. Confined at Point Lookout, Maryland, until transferred to Elmira, New York, August 8, 1864. Died at Elmira on April 6, 1865, of "pneumonia."

SPRINKLE, THOMAS A., Private

Resided in Surry County where he enlisted at age 26, March 18, 1862. Captured at Gettysburg, Pennsylvania, July 3, 1863. Confined at Fort Delaware, Delaware, until transferred to Point Lookout, Maryland, October 15-18, 1863. Paroled at Point Lookout and transferred to City Point, Virginia, where he was received April 30, 1864, for exchange. Reported absent sick from September-October, 1864, until January 18, 1865, when he returned to duty. Reported absent sick during February, 1865.

STANLEY, HENDERSON D., Private

Place and date of enlistment not reported. Wounded in the left arm at Petersburg, Virginia, April 2, 1865. Left arm amputated. Hospitalized at or near Petersburg and was captured by the enemy on April 3, 1865. Hospitalized at Fort Monroe, Virginia, May 17, 1865, and was transferred on June 21, 1865.

STANLY, JAMES, Private

Born in Surry County where he resided as a farmer prior to enlisting in Surry County at age 26, May 4, 1861. Present or accounted for until discharged on January 18, 1862, by reason of "chronic rheumatism."

STANLY, JOHN H., Private

Resided in Surry County where he enlisted at age 22, May 4, 1861. Killed at Chancellorsville, Virginia, May 3, 1863.

STANLY, JOSEPH N., Private

Resided in Surry County and enlisted at age 21, May 4, 1861. Present or accounted for until he died at High Point on August 15, 1861. Cause of death not reported.

STANLY, OLIVER, Private

Resided in Surry County where he enlisted at age 22, March 18, 1862. Wounded in the right hip near Petersburg, Virginia, April 1, 1865. Hospitalized at Farmville, Virginia, where he was captured by the enemy on an unspecified date. Paroled at Farmville on April 11-21, 1865.

STANLY, SOLOMON, Sergeant

Resided in Surry County where he enlisted at age 21, May 13, 1861. Mustered in as Private and was promoted to Sergeant on April 10, 1862. Present or accounted for until he died in hospital at Richmond, Virginia, September 9, 1862, of "icterus."

STANTLIFF, OLIVER, Private

Resided in Surry County where he enlisted at age 35, March 18, 1862. Present or accounted for until captured at Hanover Court House, Virginia, May 27, 1862. Confined at Fort Monroe, Virginia, and at Fort Columbus, New York Harbor. Paroled and transferred to Aiken's Landing, James River, Virginia, where he was received July 12, 1862, for exchange. Declared exchanged at Aiken's Landing on August 5, 1862. Reported absent sick on October 31, 1862. Reported absent without leave in January-February, 1863. Returned to duty on an unspecified date. Reported absent without leave from July 1, 1864, through February, 1865.

STOKER, THOMAS A., Private

Resided in Surry County and enlisted at "Judesville" at age 20, March 18, 1862. Present or accounted for until he died "at home" on November 19, 1862, of disease.

STRANGE, JOHN R., —————

North Carolina pension records indicate that he served in this company.

TATE, JAMES, Private

Resided in Surry County where he enlisted at age 39, May 4, 1861. Captured at or near Liberty Mills, Virginia, September 22, 1863. Confined at Old Capitol Prison, Washington, D.C., until transferred to Point Lookout, Maryland, September 26, 1863. Transferred to Elmira, New York, August 16, 1864. Paroled at Elmira and transferred to Boulware's Wharf, James River, Virginia, where he was received March 18-21, 1865, for exchange.

THOMPSON, CHARLES T., Sergeant

Resided in Surry County where he enlisted at age 25, May 4, 1861. Mustered in as Private and was promoted to Sergeant on January 12, 1862. Died in hospital at Richmond, Virginia, June 3, 1864, of "febris typh[oid]."

THOMPSON, GEORGE W., Private

Resided in Surry County where he enlisted at age

18, May 4, 1861. Present or accounted for until he deserted on August 1, 1862.

TILLEY, JAMES L., Private
Resided in Surry County where he enlisted at age 16, March 18, 1862. Present or accounted for until wounded in the right leg at or near Gaines' Mill, Virginia, on or about June 27, 1862. Reported absent wounded through February, 1863. Reported absent without leave from July 1, 1863, through February, 1865.

TURNER, SAMUEL H., Private
Resided in Surry County and enlisted at age 27, May 4, 1861. Died at Garysburg on July 12, 1861, of disease.

VENABLE, JOSEPH, Private
Born in Surry County where he resided as a farmer prior to enlisting in Surry County at age 39, May 4, 1861. Present or accounted for until discharged on or about May 1, 1862, by reason of being overage.

VENABLE, JOSHUA, Private
Enlisted in Surry County on November 1, 1864, for the war. Present or accounted for through February, 1865.

WALKER, ELISHA, Private
Resided in Surry County where he enlisted at age 21, March 18, 1862. Present or accounted for until he died in camp at Richmond, Virginia, July 3, 1862, of disease.

WALKER, JOSEPH HARRISON, Private
Resided in Surry County where he enlisted at age 22, March 18, 1862. Present or accounted for until he deserted on August 1, 1862. Returned to duty subsequent to October 31, 1862. Reported present for duty in January-February, 1863. Wounded "in Virginia" on August 16, 1864. Returned to duty prior to November 1, 1864. Present or accounted for through February, 1865.

WHITAKER, ANDREW J., Private
Resided in Surry County where he enlisted at age 34, March 18, 1862. Present or accounted for until wounded at Ox Hill, Virginia, September 1, 1862. Returned to duty on an unspecified date. Present or accounted for through February, 1865.

WHITAKER, DAVID, Private
Born in Surry County where he resided as a farmer prior to enlisting in Surry County at age 30, March 18, 1862. Present or accounted for until discharged on July 21, 1862, by reason of "weak lungs and chronic cough."

WHITAKER, LEWIS, Private
Born in Surry County where he resided as a farmer prior to enlisting in Surry County at age 21, March 18, 1862. Present or accounted for until discharged on July 7, 1862, by reason of "chronic affection of the lungs."

WHITAKER, THOMAS J., Private
Resided in Surry County where he enlisted at age 17, March 18, 1862. Present or accounted for until he died in hospital at Danville, Virginia, August 14, 1862, of "febris typhoides."

WHITE, HEWEL L., Private
Resided in Surry County where he enlisted at age 22, May 4, 1861. Died in hospital at Lynchburg, Virginia, November 25, 1863, of "diarrhoea chron[ic]."

WHITE, JAMES P., Private
Resided in Surry County where he enlisted at age 27, May 4, 1861. Present or accounted for until he died in hospital at Lynchburg, Virginia, August 12, 1862, of "febris typhoides."

WHITE, RICHARD C., Private
Born in Surry County where he resided as a farmer prior to enlisting in Surry County at age 24, March 18, 1862. Present or accounted for until discharged on June 3, 1862, by reason of "abcess of the chest."

WHITE, ROBERT, Jr., Private
Resided in Surry County where he enlisted at age 30, May 4, 1861. Mustered in as Private and was promoted to Corporal on November 1, 1861. Promoted to Sergeant in November-December, 1861. Reduced to the rank of Corporal on January 25, 1862, and was reduced to ranks in May-October, 1862. Captured near Petersburg, Virginia, April 2, 1865. Confined at Fort Delaware, Delaware, until released on June 19, 1865, after taking the Oath of Allegiance. [North Carolina pension records indicate he was wounded in the right leg at Williamsport, Maryland, in July, 1863.]

WHITE, SWAN, Private
Born in Surry County where he resided prior to enlisting in Surry County on January 15, 1864, for the war. Captured at or near Spotsylvania Court House, Virginia, on or about May 12, 1864. Confined at Point Lookout, Maryland, where he died on June 19, 1864, of "dysentery acute."

WHITE, WILLIAM J., Private
Resided in Surry County where he enlisted at age 26, May 4, 1861. Mustered in as Corporal but was reduced to ranks on November 2, 1861. Wounded in the abdomen and captured at Gettysburg, Pennsylvania, July 1-3, 1863. Exchanged on an unspecified date. Hospitalized at Richmond, Virginia, October 2, 1864, with a gunshot wound of the back and left side. Place and date wounded not reported. Returned to duty in January-February, 1865. Present or accounted for until he surrendered at Appomattox Court House, Virginia, April 9, 1865. [North Carolina pension records indicate he was wounded in the right leg at Petersburg, Virginia, in 1864.]

WILLIAMS, JOHN W., Private
Resided in Surry County where he enlisted at age 18, February 18, 1863, for the war. Captured near Spotsylvania Court House, Virginia, May 12, 1864. Confined at Point Lookout, Maryland, until transferred to Elmira, New York, August 10, 1864. Released at Elmira on November 5, 1864, on instructions from the "C.C.G.P."

WILMOTH, AMBROSE, Private
Resided in Surry County where he enlisted at age 35, March 18, 1862. Present or accounted for through February, 1865.

WOOD, DEMPSON, Private
Resided in Surry County where he enlisted at age 19, May 4, 1861. Captured near Petersburg, Virginia, April 2, 1865. Confined at Fort Delaware, Delaware, until released on June 19, 1865, after taking the Oath of

Allegiance.

WOOD, RANSOM, Private

Resided in Surry County where he enlisted at age 29, March 18, 1862. Wounded in the right hand and right shoulder and captured at Gettysburg, Pennsylvania, July 1-5, 1863. Hospitalized at Davids Island, New York Harbor, until transferred to Fort Delaware, Delaware, April 19, 1864. Paroled at Fort Delaware on September 14, 1864, and transferred to Varina, Virginia, where he was received September 22, 1864, for exchange. Retired to the Invalid Corps on December 21, 1864, by reason of disability.

WOOD, SILAS W., Private

Resided in Surry County where he enlisted at age 22, May 4, 1861. Present or accounted for until captured at or near Harrison's Landing, Virginia, on or about June 28-30, 1862. Confined at Fort Columbus, New York Harbor, and at Fort Delaware, Delaware. Paroled and transferred to Aiken's Landing, James River, Virginia, July 12, 1862, for exchange. Declared exchanged at Aiken's Landing on August 5, 1862. Returned to duty prior to November 1, 1862. Present or accounted for through February, 1865.

YORK, LITTLE C., Private

Resided in Surry County and was by occupation a farmer prior to enlisting in Surry County at age 14, March 18, 1862. Wounded in the forehead and thigh and captured at Gettysburg, Pennsylvania, July 3-5, 1863. Confined at Fort McHenry, Maryland, and at Fort Delaware, Delaware. Paroled and transferred to City Point, Virginia, where he was received August 1, 1863, for exchange. Returned to duty on an unspecified date. Reported present for duty from September-October, 1864, through February, 1865. Surrendered at Appomattox Court House, Virginia, April 9, 1865.

COMPANY B

This company, known as the "Gaston Invincibles," was raised in Gaston County and enlisted at Dallas on July 30, 1861. It was then mustered into service and assigned to the 28th Regiment as Company B. After joining the regiment the company functioned as a part of the regiment, and its history for the war period is reported as a part of the regimental history.

The information contained in the following roster of the company was compiled principally from company muster rolls for August 1-December, 1861; February 29-October 31, 1862; January-February, 1863; and September, 1864-February, 1865. No company muster rolls were found for January-February 28, 1862; November-December, 1862; March, 1863-August, 1864; or for the period after February, 1865. Valuable information was obtained also from primary records such as the Roll of Honor, medical records, prisoner of war records, discharge certificates, and pension applications, and from secondary sources such as postwar rosters and histories, cemetery records, and records of the United Daughters of the Confederacy.

OFFICERS

CAPTAINS

EDWARDS, THOMAS H.

Resided in Orange or Gaston County and enlisted in Gaston County. Appointed Captain to rank from July 30, 1861. Present or accounted for until he was defeated for reelection when the regiment was reorganized on February 27, 1862.

STOWE, SAMUEL N.

Resided in Gaston County where he enlisted at age 38. Appointed 1st Lieutenant on July 30, 1861, and was elected Captain on February 27, 1862. Present or accounted for until captured at Hanover Court House, Virginia, May 27, 1862. Confined at Fort Monroe, Virginia, and at Fort Columbus, New York Harbor. Transferred to Johnson's Island, Ohio, where he arrived on June 21, 1862. Paroled and transferred to Vicksburg, Mississippi, September 1, 1862. Arrived at Vicksburg on September 20, 1862. Declared exchanged at Aiken's Landing, James River, Virginia, November 10, 1862. Returned to duty prior to December 13, 1862. Present or accounted for until April 16, 1863, when he was promoted to Major "for gallant conduct at Fredericksburg," Virginia, and transferred to the Field and Staff of this regiment.

SMITH, THOMAS T.

Resided in Gaston County where he enlisted at age 29, July 30, 1861. Mustered in as Sergeant and was appointed 2nd Lieutenant on February 27, 1862. Promoted to 1st Lieutenant on December 14, 1862, and was promoted to Captain on April 16, 1863. Wounded in the left thigh at Gettysburg, Pennsylvania, July 3, 1863. Returned to duty on an unspecified date. Killed at Reams' Station, Virginia, August 25, 1864.

RHYNE, ROBERT D.

Resided in Gaston County where he enlisted at age 20, July 30, 1861. Mustered in as Private and was elected 3rd Lieutenant on February 27, 1862. Promoted to 2nd Lieutenant on December 14, 1862, and was promoted to 1st Lieutenant on April 16, 1863. Wounded at Chancellorsville, Virginia, May 2-3, 1863. Returned to duty on an unspecified date. Wounded at Reams' Station, Virginia, August 25, 1864. Promoted to Captain the same date. Reported absent wounded through February, 1865.

LIEUTENANTS

CLONINGER, WILEY W., 1st Lieutenant

Resided in Gaston County where he enlisted on July 30, 1861. Mustered in as 1st Sergeant and was elected 1st Lieutenant on February 27, 1862. Present or accounted for until wounded at Fredericksburg, Virginia, December 13, 1862. Died in a field hospital on December 14, 1862, of wounds. "A brave officer."

COSTNER, HIRAM J., 3rd Lieutenant

Resided in Gaston County where he enlisted at age 22, July 30, 1861. Mustered in as Private. Captured at Hanover Court House, Virginia, May 27, 1862. Confined at Fort Monroe, Virginia, and at Fort Columbus, New York Harbor. Paroled and transferred to Aiken's Landing, James River, Virginia, where he was received July 12, 1862, for exchange. Declared exchanged at Aiken's Landing on August 5, 1862. Promoted to 1st Sergeant on November 13, 1862, and was elected 3rd Lieutenant on December 18, 1862. Wounded at Jericho Mills, Virginia, May 23, 1864. Died on May 25, 1864, of wounds. Place of death not reported.

ORMAND, ROBERT DIXON, 2nd Lieutenant

Resided in Gaston County and enlisted at Camp Fisher at age 27, August 20, 1861. Mustered in as Private. Wounded in the shoulder and/or arm at the Battle of Second Manassas, Virginia, August 28-30, 1862. Returned to duty prior to November 1, 1862. At Chancellorsville, Virginia, May 1-3, 1863, the enemy "shot a bomb under me . . . & blew me up"; however, he was apparently not seriously injured. Appointed 2nd Lieutenant on May 11, 1863. Wounded at Falling Waters, Maryland, July 14, 1863. Returned to duty on an unspecified date. Wounded in the side and/or right shoulder at Spotsylvania Court House, Virginia, May 12, 1864. Returned to duty prior to November 1, 1864. Present or accounted for until he surrendered at Appomattox Court House, Virginia, April 9, 1865.

PEGRAM, EDWARD LARKIN, 2nd Lieutenant

Resided in Gaston County where he enlisted. Appointed 2nd Lieutenant on July 30, 1861, but was defeated for reelection on February 27, 1862. Reenlisted in the company with the rank of Private on April 30, 1863. [See Noncommissioned Officers and Privates' section below.]

SMITH, DAVID B., 3rd Lieutenant

Resided in Gaston or Cleveland County and was by occupation a mechanic prior to enlisting in Gaston County at age 25. Appointed 3rd Lieutenant on July 30, 1861. Present or accounted for until he was defeated for reelection when the regiment was reorganized on February 27, 1862. Reenlisted in the company with the rank of Private on December 13, 1862. [See Noncommissioned Officers and Privates' section below.]

WHITE, ROBERT ADAM, 1st Lieutenant

Born in Gaston County* where he resided prior to enlisting in Gaston County at age 20, July 30, 1861. Mustered in as Sergeant and was promoted to 1st Sergeant on February 27, 1862. Reduced to ranks on November 12, 1862. Promoted to Sergeant in March, 1863-October, 1864. Wounded in the leg at Jericho Mills, Virginia, May 23, 1864. Returned to duty prior to November 1, 1864. Elected 2nd Lieutenant on January 12, 1865, and was promoted to 1st Lieutenant on January 23, 1865. Present or accounted for until he surrendered at Appomattox Court House, Virginia, April 9, 1865.

NONCOMMISSIONED OFFICERS AND PRIVATES

ABERNATHY, ALONZO, Private

Resided in Gaston County and enlisted in Wake County at age 18, September 3, 1863, for the war. Captured near Petersburg, Virginia, April 2, 1865. Confined at Hart's Island, New York Harbor, until released on June 17, 1865, after taking the Oath of Allegiance.

ABERNATHY, J. R., Private

Resided in Gaston County and enlisted at age 39, September 3, 1863, for the war. Transferred to the C.S. Navy on April 3, 1864.

ABERNATHY, MILES L., Private

Resided in Gaston County and enlisted in Wake County at age 36, April 30, 1863, for the war. Captured near Petersburg, Virginia, April 2, 1865. Confined at Hart's Island, New York Harbor, until released on or about June 18, 1865, after taking the Oath of Allegiance.

ABERNATHY, S. M., Private

Born in Gaston County* where he resided prior to enlisting in Gaston County at age 19, March 29, 1862. Wounded in the right thigh at Wilderness, Virginia, May 5, 1864. Right leg amputated. Hospitalized at Charlottesville, Virginia, where he died on May 27, 1864, of wounds.

ALLISON, JASPER L., Private

Resided in Gaston County where he enlisted at age 23, July 30, 1861. Captured at Fredericksburg, Virginia, December 13, 1862. Exchanged on or about December 17, 1862. Returned to duty prior to March 1, 1863. Present or accounted for through February, 1865.

ALLISON, WILLIAM T., Private

Born in Gaston County* where he resided as a farmer prior to enlisting in Gaston County at age 21, July 30, 1861. Present or accounted for until captured at Hanover Court House, Virginia, May 27, 1862. Confined at Fort Monroe, Virginia, and at Fort Columbus, New York Harbor. Paroled and transferred to Aiken's Landing, James River, Virginia, where he was received July 12, 1862, for exchange. Declared exchanged at Aiken's Landing on August 5, 1862. Returned to duty prior to November 1, 1862. Present or accounted for until he surrendered at Appomattox Court House, Virginia, April 9, 1865.

ARMSTRONG, DANIEL M., Private

Enlisted at Liberty Mills, Virginia, April 9, 1864, for the war. Present or accounted for through February, 1865.

ARMSTRONG, J. L., Private

Born in Gaston County* where he resided as a farmer prior to enlisting in Gaston County at age 18, March 29, 1862. Present or accounted for until he died at Sulpher Springs, Virginia, July 27, 1862, of disease.

ARMSTRONG, JAMES, Private

Resided in Gaston County where he enlisted at age 24, March 29, 1862. Died at Rapidan, Virginia, May 4, 1862. Cause of death not reported.

BALDEN, ANDREW J., Private

Born in Gaston County and enlisted at Liberty Mills, Virginia, March 5, 1864, for the war. Wounded in the left shoulder at Reams' Station, Virginia, August 25, 1864. Returned to duty prior to November 1, 1864. Present or accounted for until he surrendered at Appomattox Court House, Virginia, April 9, 1865.

BEARD, W. S., Private

Resided in Gaston County where he enlisted at age 20, March 29, 1862. Captured at Fredericksburg, Virginia, December 13, 1862. Confined at Old Capitol Prison, Washington, D.C., where he died on or about April 10, 1863, of "typhoid fever."

BEATY, ANDREW, Corporal

Born in Gaston County* where he resided prior to enlisting in Gaston County at age 27, July 30, 1861. Mustered in as Private and was promoted to Corporal on February 27, 1862. Present or accounted for until wounded in the left arm at Gaines Mill, Virginia, June 27, 1862. Left arm amputated. Discharged on July 22,

1862.

BEATY, JAMES F., Private
Born in Gaston County* where he resided as a farmer prior to enlisting in Gaston County at age 18, July 30, 1861. Captured at Fredericksburg, Virginia, December 13, 1862. Paroled on or about December 17, 1862. Returned to duty prior to March 1, 1863. Surrendered at Appomattox Court House, Virginia, April 9, 1865.

BEATY, JONATHAN P., Private
Resided in Gaston County and enlisted in Wake County at age 44, September 4, 1863, for the war. Captured at or near Spotsylvania Court House, Virginia, May 12, 1864. Confined at Point Lookout, Maryland, until transferred to Elmira, New York, August 8, 1864. Died at Elmira on November 26, 1864, of "scorbutus."

BEATY, R. M., Private
Born in Gaston County* where he resided prior to enlisting in Gaston County at age 18, July 30, 1861. Present or accounted for until captured at Hanover Court House, Virginia, May 27, 1862. Confined at Fort Monroe, Virginia, and at Fort Columbus, New York Harbor. Exchanged on an unspecified date. Returned to duty prior to November 1, 1862. Killed at Fredericksburg, Virginia, December 13, 1862.

BELL, JOSEPH C., Private
Enlisted at Liberty Mills, Virginia, February 16, 1864, for the war. Present or accounted for until he surrendered at Appomattox Court House, Virginia, April 9, 1865.

BELL, LORENSE M., Private
Born in Gaston County* where he resided as a farmer prior to enlisting in Gaston County at age 18, July 30, 1861. Present or accounted for until wounded in the left hand at Frayser's Farm, Virginia, June 30, 1862. Left arm amputated below the elbow. Reported absent wounded until November 25, 1863, when he was discharged.

BEST, A. J., Private
Born in Gaston County* where he resided as a farmer prior to enlisting in Gaston County at age 28, March 29, 1862. Present or accounted for through February, 1863. Discharged from service on March 28, 1864, by reason of "a gunshot causing the loss of left hand." Place and date injured not reported.

BLALOCK, J. B., Private
Born in York District, South Carolina, and resided in Cleveland County where he was by occupation a farmer prior to enlisting at Camp Fisher at age 26, September 18, 1861. Present or accounted for until wounded in the right arm at Cedar Mountain, Virginia, August 9, 1862. Right arm amputated. Discharged on October 5, 1862.

BOYD, WILLIAM, Private
Resided in Gaston County where he enlisted at age 25, July 30, 1861. Present or accounted for until he died at Wilmington on April 2, 1862, of "typhoid fever."

CANLEY, J. W., Private
Resided in Gaston County where he enlisted at age 22, July 30, 1861. Present or accounted for until he died in hospital at Danville, Virginia, August 21-22, 1862, of

"chronic diarrhoea."

CARPENTER, CALEB, Private
Resided in Gaston County and enlisted in Lenoir County at age 20, March 19, 1862. Present or accounted for until captured at Fredericksburg, Virginia, December 13, 1862. Paroled on or about December 17, 1862. Returned to duty prior to March 1, 1863. Wounded at Chancellorsville, Virginia, May 2-3, 1863. Returned to duty on an unspecified date. Surrendered at Appomattox Court House, Virginia, April 9, 1865.

CARPENTER, F. T., Private
Resided in Gaston County where he enlisted at age 20, July 30, 1861. Present or accounted for until wounded in the shoulder at Cedar Mountain, Virginia, August 9, 1862. Returned to duty in November-December, 1862. Captured at Fredericksburg, Virginia, December 13, 1862. Paroled on or about December 17, 1862. Returned to duty subsequent to February 28, 1863. Wounded and captured at Gettysburg, Pennsylvania, July 1-5, 1863. Died at Gettysburg on July 18, 1863, of wounds.

CARPENTER, JOHN C., Private
Resided in Gaston County where he enlisted at age 18, July 30, 1861. Present or accounted for until captured at Hanover Court House, Virginia, May 27, 1862. Confined at Fort Monroe, Virginia, and at Fort Columbus, New York Harbor. Paroled and transferred to Aiken's Landing, James River, Virginia, where he was received July 12, 1862, for exchange. Declared exchanged at Aiken's Landing on August 5, 1862. Returned to duty prior to November 1, 1862. Wounded and captured at Fredericksburg, Virginia, December 13, 1862. Paroled on or about December 17, 1862. Returned to duty prior to March 1, 1862. Captured near Petersburg, Virginia, April 2, 1865. Confined at Hart's Island, New York Harbor, until released on June 17, 1865, after taking the Oath of Allegiance.

CARPENTER, JOHN T., Sergeant
Born in Gaston County* where he resided prior to enlisting in Gaston County at age 21, July 30, 1861. Mustered in as Private. Present or accounted for until captured at Hanover Court House, Virginia, May 27, 1862. Confined at Fort Monroe, Virginia, and at Fort Columbus, New York Harbor. Paroled and transferred to Aiken's Landing, James River, Virginia, where he was received July 12, 1862, for exchange. Declared exchanged at Aiken's Landing on August 5, 1862. Returned to duty prior to November 1, 1862. Promoted to Corporal in February, 1863, and was promoted to Sergeant in March, 1863-October, 1864. Wounded in the left leg near Petersburg, Virginia, April 2, 1865. Captured by the enemy on an unspecified date and was paroled at Farmville, Virginia, April 11-21, 1865. [North Carolina pension records indicate he was wounded in the leg in 1864.]

CARPENTER, MARCUS, Private
Resided in Gaston County and enlisted at Liberty Mills, Virginia, February 5, 1864, for the war. Captured at Dinwiddie Court House, Virginia, April 5, 1865. Confined at Point Lookout, Maryland, until released on June 24, 1865, after taking the Oath of Allegiance.

CARPENTER, MICHAEL, Private
Enlisted at Liberty Mills, Virginia, at age 18, May 1,

1864, for the war. Present or accounted for until he surrendered at Appomattox Court House, Virginia, April 9, 1865. [North Carolina pension records indicate he was wounded on April 2, 1865.]

CARPENTER, WILLIAM H., Private

Born in Gaston County* where he resided prior to enlisting in Gaston County at age 18, July 30, 1861. Present or accounted for until captured at Hanover Court House, Virginia, May 27, 1862. Confined at Fort Monroe, Virginia, and at Fort Columbus, New York Harbor. Paroled and transferred to Aiken's Landing, James River, Virginia, where he was received July 12, 1862, for exchange. Declared exchanged at Aiken's Landing on August 5, 1862. Returned to duty prior to November 1, 1862. Wounded at Gettysburg, Pennsylvania, July 1-3, 1863. Returned to duty on July 31, 1863. Wounded in the chest ''in Virginia'' in May, 1864. Hospitalized at Gordonsville, Virginia, where he died on May 23, 1864, of wounds.

CARROLL, T. L., Private

Born in Gaston County* where he resided as a farmer prior to enlisting in Gaston County at age 21, August 5, 1861. Present or accounted for until he died in hospital at Lynchburg, Virginia, July 24, 1862, of ''chron[ic] diarrhoea'' and/or wounds. Place and date wounded not reported.

CARSON, JOHN B., 1st Sergeant

Born in Gaston County* where he resided as a farmer prior to enlisting in Gaston County at age 26, July 30, 1861. Mustered in as Corporal but was reduced to ranks on February 28, 1862. Present or accounted for until captured at Hanover Court House, Virginia, May 27, 1862. Confined at Fort Monroe, Virginia, and at Fort Columbus, New York Harbor. Paroled and transferred to Aiken's Landing, James River, Virginia, where he was received July 12, 1862, for exchange. Declared exchanged at Aiken's Landing on August 5, 1862. Returned to duty prior to November 1, 1862. Promoted to 1st Sergeant on December 18, 1862. Wounded in the left arm at Chancellorsville, Virginia, May 3, 1863. Left arm amputated. Discharged on January 2, 1864.

CARSON, RUFUS WATSON, Corporal

Born in Lincoln County and resided in Gaston County prior to enlisting at Bunker Hill, Virginia, at age 19, October 5, 1862, for the war. Mustered in as Private. Present or accounted for until wounded in the head, shoulder, and right arm at Fredericksburg, Virginia, December 13, 1862. Returned to duty prior to March 1, 1863. Promoted to Corporal on October 1, 1864. Surrendered at Appomattox Court House, Virginia, April 9, 1865.

CLARKE, MILAN A., Private

Enlisted at Liberty Mills, Virginia, March 15, 1864, for the war. Present or accounted for until he surrendered at Appomattox Court House, Virginia, April 9, 1865.

CLEMMER, E. J., Private

Resided in Gaston County where he enlisted at age 24, July 30, 1861. Present or accounted for until wounded in the thigh at Chancellorsville, Virginia, May 1-3, 1863. Hospitalized at Richmond, Virginia, where he died on or about September 25, 1863, of ''erysipelas succe[e]ding to comp[oun]d fracture of thigh.''

CLEMMER, G. A., Private

Resided in Gaston County where he enlisted at age 21, July 30, 1861. Present or accounted for until killed at Fredericksburg, Virginia, December 13, 1862.

CLEMMER, JOHN L., 1st Sergeant

Resided in Gaston County where he enlisted at age 18, July 30, 1861. Mustered in as Private and was promoted to 1st Sergeant on October 1, 1864. Captured near Petersburg, Virginia, April 2, 1865. Confined at Point Lookout, Maryland, until released on June 24, 1865, after taking the Oath of Allegiance.

CLEMMER, LEANDER R., Private

Resided in Gaston County where he enlisted at age 18, July 30, 1861. Present or accounted for until he surrendered at Appomattox Court House, Virginia, April 9, 1865.

CLONINGER, D. R., Private

Born in Gaston County* where he resided as a farmer prior to enlisting in Gaston County at age 48, March 29, 1862. Present or accounted for until captured at Fredericksburg, Virginia, December 13, 1862. Paroled on or about December 17, 1862. Returned to duty prior to March 1, 1863. Discharged on December 31, 1863, by reason of ''chronic rheumatism and infirmness of advanced age.''

CLONINGER, JAMES S., Private

Resided in Gaston County and enlisted in New Hanover County at age 21, March 14, 1862. Present or accounted for until captured at Hanover Court House, Virginia, May 27, 1862. Confined at Fort Monroe, Virginia, and at Fort Columbus, New York Harbor. Paroled and transferred to Aiken's Landing, James River, Virginia, where he was received July 12, 1862, for exchange. Declared exchanged at Aiken's Landing on August 5, 1862. Returned to duty prior to November 1, 1862. Captured at Fredericksburg, Virginia, December 13, 1862. Paroled on or about December 17, 1862. Returned to duty prior to March 1, 1863. Promoted to Corporal in March-July, 1863. Wounded in the right elbow and captured at Gettysburg, Pennsylvania, July 1-5, 1863. Hospitalized at Gettysburg until transferred to Davids Island, New York Harbor, July 17-24, 1863. Paroled at Davids Island and transferred to City Point, Virginia, where he was received September 16, 1863, for exchange. Reduced to ranks on an unspecified date. Retired to the Invalid Corps on May 2, 1864, by reason of disability.

CLONINGER, L. A., Private

Born in Gaston County* where he resided prior to enlisting in Gaston County at age 18, March 29, 1862. Killed at Reams' Station, Virginia, August 25, 1864.

CLONINGER, SIDNEY, Sergeant

Born in Gaston County* where he resided as a farmer prior to enlisting in Gaston County at age 34, March 29, 1862. Mustered in as Private. Present or accounted for until captured at Hanover Court House, Virginia, May 27, 1862. Confined at Fort Monroe, Virginia, and at Fort Columbus, New York Harbor. Paroled and transferred to Aiken's Landing, James River, Virginia, where he was received July 12, 1862, for exchange. Declared exchanged at Aiken's Landing on August 5, 1862. Returned to duty prior to November 1, 1862, and was promoted to Sergeant on November 5, 1862. Wounded at Fredericksburg, Virginia, December 13, 1862. Hospitalized at Richmond, Virginia, where he died on January 9, 1863, of wounds.

CLONINGER, VALENTINE, Private
Enlisted at Liberty Mills, Virginia, February 25, 1864, for the war. Present or accounted for until hospitalized at Richmond, Virginia, May 25, 1864, with rubeola. Reported absent sick through February, 1865.

CONNER, Y. L., Private
Place and date of enlistment not reported. Hospitalized at Richmond, Virginia, April 2, 1865. Captured in hospital at Richmond on April 3, 1865. Transferred to the Federal Provost Marshal on April 14, 1865.

COSTNER, JOHN H., Private
Resided in Gaston County where he enlisted at age 21, July 30, 1861. Wounded in the left leg and captured at Spotsylvania Court House, Virginia, May 12, 1864. Hospitalized at Washington, D.C. Transferred to Elmira, New York, August 28, 1864. Paroled at Elmira on October 11, 1864, and transferred to Venus Point, Savannah River, Georgia, where he was received November 15, 1864, for exchange. No further records.

COSTNER, JONAS L., Private
Resided in Gaston County where he enlisted at age 18, July 30, 1861. Present or accounted for until captured at Hanover Court House, Virginia, May 27, 1862. Confined at Fort Monroe, Virginia, and at Fort Columbus, New York Harbor. Paroled and transferred to Aiken's Landing, James River, Virginia, where he was received July 12, 1862, for exchange. Declared exchanged at Aiken's Landing on August 5, 1862. Returned to duty prior to November 1, 1862. Captured in hospital at Richmond, Virginia, April 3, 1865. Confined at Newport News, Virginia, April 24, 1865. Released on June 27, 1865, after taking the Oath of Allegiance. [North Carolina pension records indicate he was wounded in April, 1862.]

CRENSHAW, J. B., Private
Resided in Gaston County where he enlisted at age 18, July 30, 1861. Wounded in the right thigh and captured at Gettysburg, Pennsylvania, July 1-2, 1863. Right leg amputated. Died in hospital at Gettysburg on July 4, 1863, of wounds.

CROUSOR, V. O., ———
Place and date of enlistment not reported. Died in hospital at Richmond, Virginia, June 1, 1864. Cause of death not reported.

DAVIS, ALBERT CARTWRIGHT, Private
Resided in Gaston County where he enlisted at age 29, March 29, 1862. Present or accounted for until captured at Hanover Court House, Virginia, May 27, 1862. Confined at Fort Monroe, Virginia, and at Fort Columbus, New York Harbor. Paroled and transferred to Aiken's Landing, James River, Virginia, where he was received July 12, 1862, for exchange. Declared exchanged at Aiken's Landing on August 5, 1862. Returned to duty in November, 1862-February, 1863. Wounded at or near Fussell's Mill, Virginia, on or about August 18, 1864. Reported absent sick through February, 1865.

DAVIS, JAMES, Private
Born in Rutherford County and resided in Gaston County where he was by occupation a farmer prior to enlisting in Gaston County at age 45, March 29, 1862. Present or accounted for until wounded at Gaines' Mill, Virginia, June 27, 1862. Discharged on September 29, 1862, by reason of "cicatrices of the left arm, thigh, and fleshy part of the leg, effects of scrofula causing lameness. . . ." Later served in Company E, 5th Regiment N.C. Senior Reserves.

DAVIS, O. W., Private
Born in Gaston County* where he resided as a carpenter prior to enlisting at Camp Fisher at age 30, September 18, 1861. Discharged on July 20, 1863, by reason of "consolidation of whole of right lung and perfect aphonia, with general debility. . . ."

DICKSON, J. R., Private
Resided in Gaston County where he enlisted at age 18, July 30, 1861. Present or accounted for until captured at Fredericksburg, Virginia, December 13, 1862. Paroled on or about December 17, 1862. Returned to duty prior to March 1, 1863. Deserted in August, 1863.

FALLS, JOHN JAMES, Corporal
Resided in Cleveland County and enlisted at Camp Fisher at age 22, September 18, 1861. Mustered in as Private. Present or accounted for until captured at Hanover Court House, Virginia, May 27, 1862. Confined at Fort Monroe, Virginia, and at Fort Columbus, New York Harbor. Paroled and transferred to Aiken's Landing, James River, Virginia, where he was received July 12, 1862, for exchange. Declared exchanged at Aiken's Landing on August 5, 1862. Returned to duty prior to November 1, 1862. Promoted to Corporal in November-December, 1862. Captured at Fredericksburg, Virginia, December 13, 1862. Paroled on December 17, 1862. Returned to duty prior to March 1, 1863. Wounded at Chancellorsville, Virginia, on or about May 3, 1863. Died of wounds. Place and date of death not reported.

FARRAR, NATHANIEL P., Private
Resided in Gaston County where he enlisted at age 34, July 30, 1861. Captured near Petersburg, Virginia, April 2, 1865. Confined at Point Lookout, Maryland, until released on June 26, 1865, after taking the Oath of Allegiance.

FITE, J. C., Private
Resided in Gaston County and enlisted at age 18, February 18, 1863, for the war. Died in hospital at Richmond, Virginia, June 22, 1863, of "febris typh[oid]."

FLEMING, JAMES HENDERSON, ———
North Carolina pension records indicate that he served in this company.

FLOYD, JOHN A., Private
Resided in Gaston County where he enlisted at age 20, July 30, 1861. Present or accounted for until captured at Hanover Court House, Virginia, May 27, 1862. Confined at Fort Monroe, Virginia, and at Fort Columbus, New York Harbor. Paroled and transferred to Aiken's Landing, James River, Virginia, where he was received July 12, 1862, for exchange. Declared exchanged at Aiken's Landing on August 5, 1862.

Returned to duty in November, 1862-February, 1863. Wounded in the right foot and captured at Gettysburg, Pennsylvania, July 3-5, 1863. Hospitalized at Gettysburg and at Baltimore, Maryland. Confined at Point Lookout, Maryland, April 25, 1864. Paroled at Point Lookout on or about November 1, 1864, and transferred to Venus Point, Savannah River, Georgia, where he was received November 15, 1864, for exchange. No further records.

FORD, JOHN N., Private
Resided in Gaston County where he enlisted at age 40, July 30, 1861. Captured near Petersburg, Virginia, April 2, 1865. Confined at Point Lookout, Maryland, until released on June 26, 1865, after taking the Oath of Allegiance.

FORD, LAUSON H., Private
Resided in Gaston County and enlisted at Camp Fisher at age 23, September 18, 1861. Present or accounted for until captured at Hanover Court House, Virginia, on or about May 27, 1862. Confined at Fort Monroe, Virginia. Paroled and transferred to Aiken's Landing, James River, Virginia, where he was received July 12, 1862, for exchange. Declared exchanged at Aiken's Landing on August 5, 1862. Returned to duty in November, 1862-February, 1863. Surrendered at Appomattox Court House, Virginia, April 9, 1865.

FOSTER, TILMON M., Sergeant
Resided in Gaston County where he enlisted at age 20, July 30, 1861. Mustered in as Private and was promoted to Corporal on February 27, 1862. Present or accounted for until wounded in the arm at Cedar Mountain, Virginia, August 9, 1862. Returned to duty in November, 1862-February, 1863. Wounded at Chancellorsville, Virginia, May 1-3, 1863. Returned to duty prior to July 1-5, 1863, when he was wounded and captured at Gettysburg, Pennsylvania. Confined at Davids Island, New York Harbor, July 17-24, 1863. Paroled and transferred to City Point, Virginia, where he was received September 16, 1863, for exchange. Returned to duty on an unspecified date. Promoted to Sergeant in September, 1863-October, 1864. Surrendered at Appomattox Court House, Virginia, April 9, 1865.

FOY, JESSE S., Private
Born in Gaston County* where he resided as a farmer prior to enlisting in Gaston County at age 32, July 30, 1861. Present or accounted for until captured at Hanover Court House, Virginia, May 27, 1862. Confined at Fort Monroe, Virginia, and at Fort Columbus, New York Harbor. Paroled and transferred to Aiken's Landing, James River, Virginia, where he was received July 12, 1862, for exchange. Declared exchanged at Aiken's Landing on August 5, 1862. Returned to duty prior to November 1, 1862. Captured near Petersburg, Virginia, April 2, 1865. Confined at Point Lookout, Maryland, until released on June 26, 1865, after taking the Oath of Allegiance.

FRIDAY, ANDREW S., Private
Resided in Gaston County where he enlisted at age 20, July 30, 1861. Present or accounted for until captured at Hanover Court House, Virginia, May 27, 1862. Confined at Fort Monroe, Virginia, and at Fort Columbus, New York Harbor. Exchanged on or about [August 1,] 1862. Returned to duty prior to November 1,

1862. Captured at Fredericksburg, Virginia, December 13, 1862. Paroled on or about December 17, 1862. Returned to duty prior to March 1, 1863. Wounded in the thigh at or near Petersburg, Virginia, on or about June 21, 1864. Returned to duty in November-December, 1864. Deserted to the enemy on or about January 20, 1865. Confined at City Point, Virginia, until released on or about January 23, 1865, after taking the Oath of Allegiance.

FRIDAY, J. H., Private
Resided in Gaston County where he enlisted at age 19, March 29, 1862. Present or accounted for until he died at Richmond, Virginia, July 17, 1862, of disease.

FRONEBARGER, D. A., Private
Born in Gaston County* where he resided prior to enlisting in Gaston County at age 18, July 30, 1861. Present or accounted for until captured at Hanover Court House, Virginia, May 27, 1862. Confined at Fort Monroe, Virginia, and at Fort Columbus, New York Harbor. Paroled and transferred to Aiken's Landing, James River, Virginia, where he was received July 12, 1862, for exchange. Declared exchanged at Aiken's Landing on August 5, 1862. Returned to duty prior to November 1, 1862. Killed at Fredericksburg, Virginia, December 13, 1862, "by a gunshot through the head."

GAMBLE, FRANKLIN W., Private
Resided in Gaston County where he enlisted at age 18, March 29, 1862. Present or accounted for until captured at Hanover Court House, Virginia, May 27, 1862. Confined at Fort Monroe, Virginia, and at Fort Columbus, New York Harbor. Paroled and transferred to Aiken's Landing, James River, Virginia, where he was received July 12, 1862, for exchange. Declared exchanged at Aiken's Landing on August 5, 1862. Died in hospital at Richmond, Virginia, September 2, 1862, of "pneumonia typh[oid]."

GAMBLE, W. A., Private
Resided in Gaston County where he enlisted at age 22, March 29, 1862. Present or accounted for until killed at Hanover Court House, Virginia, May 27, 1862.

GASTON, ROSS MARCIUS, Private
Resided in Gaston County where he enlisted at age 15, July 30, 1861. Mustered in as Musician but was reduced to ranks subsequent to December 31, 1864. Surrendered at Appomattox Court House, Virginia, April 9, 1865.

GRICE, JOHN LITTLEBERRY, Private
Resided in Gaston County where he enlisted at age 25, July 30, 1861. Present or accounted for until captured near Hanover Court House, Virginia, May 27, 1862. Confined at Fort Monroe, Virginia, and at Fort Columbus, New York Harbor. Exchanged on an unspecified date. Returned to duty in November, 1862-February, 1863. Wounded at Chancellorsville, Virginia, May 2-3, 1863. Returned to duty on an unspecified date. Wounded in the left hip at Spotsylvania Court House, Virginia, May 12, 1864. Returned to duty prior to November 1, 1864. Present or accounted for until captured near Petersburg, Virginia, April 2, 1865. Confined at Point Lookout, Maryland, until released on June 27, 1865, after taking the Oath of Allegiance.

GROVES, CALEB C., Private
Resided in Gaston County and enlisted at Liberty Mills,

Virginia, March 5, 1864, for the war. Captured near Petersburg, Virginia, April 2, 1865. Confined at Point Lookout, Maryland, until released on June 27, 1865, after taking the Oath of Allegiance.

GROVES, JAMES L., Private

Born in Gaston County* where he resided prior to enlisting in Gaston County at age 21, July 30, 1861. Present or accounted for until captured at Hanover Court House, Virginia, May 27, 1862. Confined at Fort Monroe, Virginia, and at Fort Columbus, New York Harbor. Paroled and transferred to Aiken's Landing, James River, Virginia, July 12, 1862, for exchange. Declared exchanged at Aiken's Landing on August 5, 1862. Returned to duty prior to November 1, 1862. Deserted on May 28, 1864, but returned to duty on August 28, 1864. Present or accounted for until captured near Petersburg, Virginia, April 2, 1865. Confined at Point Lookout, Maryland, until released on June 27, 1865, after taking the Oath of Allegiance.

HAMILTON, J. T., Private

Resided in Gaston County and enlisted at Camp Fisher at age 21, August 12, 1861. Present or accounted for until he died at Wilmington on March 14, 1862, of "typhoid fever."

HAND, SAMUEL JASPER, Private

Resided in Gaston County and enlisted at Camp Fisher at age 20, September 18, 1861. Hospitalized at Charlottesville, Virginia, September 23, 1862, with a gunshot wound of the right arm. Place and date wounded not reported. Right arm amputated. Reported absent wounded until July 5, 1864, when he was retired to the Invalid Corps.

HARRIS, WILEY O., Private

Resided in Gaston County where he enlisted at age 30, August 6, 1861. Present or accounted for until captured at or near Hanover Court House, Virginia, on or about May 28-31, 1862. Confined at Fort Delaware, Delaware. Exchanged at Aiken's Landing, James River, Virginia, August 5, 1862. Returned to duty on an unspecified date. Hospitalized at Richmond, Virginia, May 25, 1864, with a gunshot wound of the right leg. Place and date wounded not reported. Returned to duty on June 18, 1864. Captured in hospital at Richmond on April 3, 1865. Confined at Newport News, Virginia, April 23, 1865. Released on June 30, 1865, after taking the Oath of Allegiance.

HAWKINS, WILLIS R., Private

Resided in Gaston County where he enlisted at age 27, July 30, 1861. Present or accounted for until captured at Fredericksburg, Virginia, December 13, 1862. Paroled on or about December 17, 1862. Returned to duty prior to March 1, 1863. Captured at Gettysburg, Pennsylvania, July 1-3, 1863. Confined at Davids Island, New York Harbor, until paroled and transferred to City Point, Virginia, where he was received September 16, 1863, for exchange. Returned to duty on an unspecified date. Reported absent on detached service on April 4, 1864. Furloughed on April 28, 1864. Reported absent on furlough through February, 1865.

HINES, GEORGE, Corporal

Born in Gaston County* where he resided prior to enlisting at Camp Fisher at age 24, September 18, 1861. Mustered in as Private. Wounded in the head and

captured at Gettysburg, Pennsylvania, July 3-5, 1863. Blinded in the right eye as a result of his wounds. Hospitalized at Davids Island, New York Harbor, until paroled and transferred to City Point, Virginia, where he was received August 28, 1863, for exchange. Returned to duty on an unspecified date. Wounded in the arm at Spotsylvania Court House, Virginia, May 12, 1864. Returned to duty prior to November 1, 1864. Promoted to Corporal on February 1, 1865. Present or accounted for until he surrendered at Appomattox Court House, Virginia, April 9, 1865.

HINES, JOHN B., Private

Enlisted at Liberty Mills, Virginia, January 19, 1864, for the war. Surrendered at Appomattox Court House, Virginia, April 9, 1865.

HOFFMAN, JOHN CEPHAS, Sergeant

Born in Gaston County* where he resided prior to enlisting in Gaston County at age 20, August 6, 1861. Mustered in as Private. Present or accounted for until captured at Hanover Court House, Virginia, May 27, 1862. Confined at Fort Monroe, Virginia, and at Fort Columbus, New York Harbor. Paroled and transferred to Aiken's Landing, James River, Virginia, where he was received July 12, 1862, for exchange. Declared exchanged at Aiken's Landing on August 5, 1862. Returned to duty prior to November 1, 1862. Captured at Fredericksburg, Virginia, December 13, 1862. Paroled on December 17, 1862. Returned to duty prior to March 1, 1863. Promoted to Corporal in March, 1863-October, 1864. Wounded in the right leg at Wilderness, Virginia, on or about May 5, 1864. Returned to duty prior to November 1, 1864. Promoted to Sergeant on February 1, 1865. Present or accounted for through February, 1865. [North Carolina pension records indicate he was wounded at Chancellorsville, Virginia, in 1863.]

HOFFMAN, JOHN H., Private

Resided in Gaston County where he enlisted at age 21, July 30, 1861. Present or accounted for until wounded at the Battle of Second Manassas, Virginia, August 28-30, 1862. Reported absent wounded through October, 1862. Reported on detail as a guard at Hanover Junction, Virginia, in January-February, 1863. Returned to duty on an unspecified date. Present or accounted for from September-October, 1864, through February, 1865.

HOFFMAN, THOMAS F., Private

Born in Gaston County* where he resided prior to enlisting in Gaston County at age 19, July 30, 1861. Present or accounted for until captured at Fredericksburg, Virginia, December 13, 1862. Paroled on or about December 17, 1862. Returned to duty prior to March 1, 1863. Killed at Wilderness, Virginia, May 5, 1864.

HOVIS, G. F., Private

Resided in Gaston County where he enlisted at age 28, July 30, 1861. Present or accounted for until he died at Wilmington on January 14, 1862. Cause of death not reported.

HOVIS, JAMES P., Private

Resided in Gaston County and enlisted in Wake County at age 18, September 3, 1863, for the war. Surrendered at Appomattox Court House, Virginia, April 9, 1865.

HOVIS, MARTIN VAN BUREN, Private

Resided in Gaston County where he enlisted at age 21, August 6, 1861. Present or accounted for until captured at Fredericksburg, Virginia, December 13, 1862. Paroled on or about December 17, 1862. Returned to duty on or about March 1, 1863. Captured near Petersburg, Virginia, April 2, 1865. Confined at Point Lookout, Maryland, until released on June 27, 1865, after taking the Oath of Allegiance.

HUFFSTETLER, EPHRIAM M., Private

Resided in Gaston County where he enlisted at age 25, August 6, 1861. Present or accounted for until he surrendered at Appomattox Court House, Virginia, April 9, 1865.

HUFFSTETLER, JOSHUA, Private

Born in Gaston County* where he resided prior to enlisting in Gaston County at age 31, March 29, 1862. Present or accounted for until captured at Hanover Court House, Virginia, May 27, 1862. Confined at Fort Monroe, Virginia, and at Fort Columbus, New York Harbor. Paroled and transferred to Aiken's Landing, James River, Virginia, where he was received July 12, 1862, for exchange. Declared exchanged at Aiken's Landing on August 5, 1862. Returned to duty prior to November 1, 1862. Wounded and captured at Gettysburg, Pennsylvania, July 1-4, 1863. Hospitalized at Davids Island, New York Harbor, July 17-24, 1863. Paroled and transferred to City Point, Virginia, where he was received September 27, 1863, for exchange. Returned to duty on an unspecified date. Killed near Petersburg, Virginia, June 23, 1864.

HUFFSTETLER, WILLIAM A., Private

Resided in Gaston County where he enlisted at age 22, March 29, 1862. Present or accounted for until captured at Hanover Court House, Virginia, May 27, 1862. Confined at Fort Monroe, Virginia, and at Fort Columbus, New York Harbor. Paroled and transferred to Aiken's Landing, James River, Virginia, where he was received July 12, 1862, for exchange. Declared exchanged at Aiken's Landing on August 5, 1862. Returned to duty prior to November 1, 1862. Killed at Fredericksburg, Virginia, December 13, 1862.

HUTCHINGS, C. B., Private

Resided in Yadkin County. Place and date of enlistment not reported. Deserted to the enemy on an unspecified date and was confined at Louisville, Kentucky, August 9, 1864. Took the Oath of Allegiance at Louisville on August 16, 1864.

JENKINS, ANDREW JACKSON, Private

Resided in Gaston County where he enlisted at age 26, July 30, 1861. Mustered in as Corporal but was reduced to ranks on February 28, 1862. Present or accounted for until captured at Hanover Court House, Virginia, May 27, 1862. Confined at Fort Monroe, Virginia, and at Fort Columbus, New York Harbor. Paroled and transferred to Aiken's Landing, James River, Virginia, where he was received July 12, 1862, for exchange. Declared exchanged at Aiken's Landing on August 5, 1862. Returned to duty on or about October 10, 1862, when he was detailed as brigade blacksmith. Reported absent on detail through February, 1865. Surrendered at Appomattox Court House, Virginia, April 9, 1865.

JENKINS, CALEB A., Private

Resided in Gaston County and enlisted at Camp Fisher

at age 18, September 17, 1861. Present or accounted for until he died on or about December 31, 1861. Place and cause of death not reported.

JENKINS, E. W., Private

Resided in Gaston County where he enlisted at age 24, July 30, 1861. Present or accounted for until he died at Wilmington on January 4, 1862. Cause of death not reported.

JENKINS, GEORGE W., Private

Resided in Gaston County where he enlisted at age 22, July 30, 1861. Present or accounted for until he died at Richmond, Virginia, on or about August 8, 1862. Cause of death not reported.

JENKINS, RUFUS M., Private

Born in Gaston County* where he resided prior to enlisting in Gaston County at age 24, July 30, 1861. Present or accounted for until captured at Fredericksburg, Virginia, December 13, 1862. Paroled on or about December 17, 1862. Returned to duty prior to March 1, 1863. Captured at Gettysburg, Pennsylvania, July 3, 1863. Confined at Fort Delaware, Delaware, until transferred to Point Lookout, Maryland, October 15-18, 1863. Paroled at Point Lookout on or about February 13, 1865, and transferred to Cox's Wharf, James River, Virginia, where he was received February 14-15, 1865, for exchange.

KISER, CALEB, Private

Resided in Gaston County where he enlisted at age 18, July 30, 1861. Present or accounted for until wounded in the leg at Gaines' Mill, Virginia, June 27, 1862. Died "at home" on July 28, 1862, of wounds and/or disease.

KISER, HENRY, Private

Resided in Gaston County and enlisted at Liberty Mills, Virginia, March 15, 1864, for the war. Captured near Petersburg, Virginia, April 2, 1865. Confined at Point Lookout, Maryland, until released on June 28, 1865, after taking the Oath of Allegiance.

KISER, MICHAEL, Private

Resided in Gaston County where he enlisted at age 18, July 30, 1861. Bayoneted in the right shoulder and captured at Fredericksburg, Virginia, December 13, 1862. Paroled on December 14, 1862. Returned to duty prior to March 1, 1863. Surrendered at Appomattox Court House, Virginia, April 9, 1865.

LANIER, ALEXANDER, Private

Resided in Gaston County where he enlisted at age 23, July 30, 1861. Present or accounted for until discharged on or about October 26, 1861, "for cutting off three of his fingers."

LAWING, WILLIAM A., Private

Born in Gaston County* where he resided as a farmer prior to enlisting in Gaston County at age 31, July 30, 1861. Present or accounted for until captured at Fredericksburg, Virginia, December 13, 1862. Paroled on or about December 17, 1862. Returned to duty prior to March 1, 1863. Wounded in the jaw and captured at Gettysburg, Pennsylvania, July 1-4, 1863. Hospitalized at Gettysburg until transferred to a hospital at Baltimore, Maryland, on or about September 14, 1863. Paroled at Baltimore and transferred to City Point, Virginia, where he was received September 27, 1863, for exchange. Reported absent wounded until he was detailed for hospital duty on or about February 25, 1864. Discharged on March 28, 1864, by reason of ''a gunshot wound of the face causing the loss of right side of the lower jaw.''

LEEPER, FRANKLIN W., Corporal

Resided in Gaston County and enlisted at age 31, March 14, 1862. Mustered in as Private. Present or accounted for until captured at Fredericksburg, Virginia, December 13, 1862. Paroled on or about December 17, 1862. Returned to duty prior to March 1, 1863. Wounded in the forearm and captured at Gettysburg, Pennsylvania, July 1-4, 1863. Hospitalized at Gettysburg until transferred to Davids Island, New York Harbor, July 17-24, 1863. Paroled at Davids Island and transferred for exchange on an unspecified date. Received for exchange on or about August 31, 1863. Promoted to Corporal in September, 1863-October, 1864. Surrendered at Appomattox Court House, Virginia, April 9, 1865.

LEWIS, JOHN J., Private

Resided in Gaston County where he enlisted at age 18, March 29, 1862. Surrendered at Appomattox Court House, Virginia, April 9, 1865.

LEWIS, W. F., Private

Resided in Gaston County where he enlisted at age 19, July 30, 1861. Wounded in the leg and captured at Gettysburg, Pennsylvania, July 1-5, 1863. Hospitalized at Gettysburg where he died on July 17, 1863, of wounds.

LINEBARGER, A. C., Corporal

Resided in Gaston County where he enlisted at age 22, July 30, 1861. Mustered in as Corporal. Present or accounted for until he died at Wilmington on or about January 20, 1862, of disease.

LINEBARGER, DAVIS A., Private

Born in Gaston County* where he resided prior to enlisting in Gaston County at age 30, July 30, 1861. Mustered in as Corporal but was reduced to ranks in January-April, 1862. Present or accounted for until captured at Fredericksburg, Virginia, December 13, 1862. Paroled on or about December 17, 1862. Returned to duty prior to March 1, 1863. Wounded in the right hand at Gettysburg, Pennsylvania, July 1-3, 1863. Right hand amputated. Company records do not indicate that he was discharged; however, North Carolina pension records indicate that he survived the war.

LINGERFELT, JACOB, Private

Born in Gaston County* where he resided as a farmer prior to enlisting in Gaston County at age 21, July 30, 1861. Present or accounted for until captured at Hanover Court House, Virginia, on or about May 28-31, 1862. Confined at Fort Delaware, Delaware. Exchanged at Aiken's Landing, James River, Virginia, August 5, 1862. Returned to duty prior to November 1, 1862. Wounded in the abdomen, right hip, and/or right foot at Fredericksburg, Virginia, December 13, 1862. Discharged on February 13, 1864, by reason of disability from wounds.

LOGAN, G. M., Private

Resided in Gaston County where he enlisted at age 18,

July 30, 1861. Wounded and captured at Gettysburg, Pennsylvania, July 1-4, 1863. Hospitalized at Davids Island, New York Harbor, July 17-24, 1863. Died at Davids Island on August 15, 1863, of ''pyaemia.''

LOVE, SAMUEL WILSON, Sergeant

Born in Lincoln County and resided in Gaston County where he was by occupation a farmer prior to enlisting in Gaston County at age 27, July 30, 1861. Mustered in as Sergeant. Present or accounted for until wounded in the left leg at Gaines' Mill, Virginia, June 27, 1862. Hospitalized at Richmond, Virginia, where he died on July 25, 1862, of wounds.

McARVER, FRANKLIN HARPER, Private

Resided in Gaston County and enlisted at Camp Fisher at age 20, August 21, 1861. Present or accounted for until captured at Hanover Court House, Virginia, May 27, 1862. Confined at Fort Monroe, Virginia, and at Fort Columbus, New York Harbor. Paroled and transferred to Aiken's Landing, James River, Virginia, where he was received July 12, 1862, for exchange. Declared exchanged at Aiken's Landing on August 5, 1862. Returned to duty in November, 1862-February, 1863. Surrendered at Appomattox Court House, Virginia, April 9, 1865.

McCAY, ALEXANDER R., Private

Resided in Gaston County and was by occupation a farmer prior to enlisting in Gaston County at age 40, July 30, 1861. Reported on detail as a teamster from June 9, 1863, through February, 1865. Captured at Amelia Court House, Virginia, April 5, 1865. Confined at Point Lookout, Maryland, until released on June 5, 1865, after taking the Oath of Allegiance.

McINTOSH, ISAAC L., Private

Resided in Gaston County where he enlisted at age 31, July 30, 1861. Present or accounted for until captured at Fredericksburg, Virginia, December 13, 1862. Paroled on or about December 17, 1862. Returned to duty prior to March 1, 1863. Wounded in the foot and captured at Gettysburg, Pennsylvania, July 1-5, 1863. Hospitalized at Davids Island, New York Harbor, July 17-24, 1863. Paroled and transferred to City Point, Virginia, where he was received September 16, 1863, for exchange. Reported absent wounded through February, 1865. Paroled at Charlotte on May 15, 1865.

McKEE, J. W., Private

Born in Gaston County* where he resided prior to enlisting in Gaston County at age 38, July 30, 1861. Present or accounted for until wounded at Fredericksburg, Virginia, December 13, 1862. Died at Fredericksburg on December 14, 1862, of wounds.

McLURE, JOHN J., Private

Resided in Gaston County where he enlisted at age 18, March 29, 1862. Present or accounted for until captured at Hanover Court House, Virginia, May 27, 1862. Confined at Fort Monroe, Virginia, and at Fort Columbus, New York Harbor. Paroled and transferred to Aiken's Landing, James River, Virginia, where he was received July 12, 1862, for exchange. Declared exchanged at Aiken's Landing on August 5, 1862. Returned to duty prior to November 1, 1862. Died in a hospital at Richmond, Virginia, on or about January 18, 1863, of ''pneumonia.''

MAUNEY, JAMES E., Private

Enlisted at Liberty Mills, Virginia, May 1, 1864, for the

war. Hospitalized at Richmond, Virginia, June 16, 1864, with a gunshot wound. Place and date wounded not reported. Furloughed for thirty days on July 30, 1864. Returned to duty prior to November 1, 1864. Captured in hospital at Richmond on April 3, 1865. No further records.

MAUNEY, PETER, Private
Born in Cleveland County and resided in Gaston County where he enlisted at age 18, March 29, 1862. Present or accounted for until killed at Shepherdstown, Virginia, September 20, 1862.

MAUNEY, WILLIAM ANDREW, Private
Born in Cleveland County and resided in Gaston County where he enlisted at age 19, August 6, 1861. Present or accounted for until promoted to Commissary Sergeant in October, 1861, and transferred to the Field and Staff of this regiment.

MENDENHALL, E. B., Private
Resided in Gaston County where he enlisted at age 24, July 30, 1861. Present or accounted for until he died "on the march" near Smithfield, Virginia, October 28, 1862, of "apoplexy."

MILLER, DENNIS, Private
Resided in Gaston County where he enlisted at age 25, July 30, 1861. Present or accounted for until he died in hospital at Richmond, Virginia, November 19, 1862, of "typhoid fever."

MILLER, WILLIAM A., Private
Born in York District, South Carolina, and resided in Gaston County where he enlisted at age 20, July 30, 1861. Present or accounted for until wounded at Gaines' Mill, Virginia, June 27, 1862. Returned to duty in November, 1862-February, 1863. Died in hospital at Liberty, Virginia, June 24, 1864, of "pneumonia."

MORROW, JOHN A., Private
Resided in Gaston County where he enlisted at age 20, July 30, 1861. Present or accounted for until captured at Fredericksburg, Virginia, December 13, 1862. Paroled on or about December 17, 1862. Returned to duty prior to March 1, 1863. Wounded at Chancellorsville, Virginia, May 2-3, 1863. Returned to duty prior to July 1-5, 1863, when he was wounded and captured at Gettysburg, Pennsylvania. Hospitalized at Chester, Pennsylvania, July 19, 1863. Paroled and transferred to City Point, Virginia, where he was received September 23, 1863, for exchange. Returned to duty on an unspecified date. Captured near Petersburg, Virginia, July 29-30, 1864. Confined at Point Lookout, Maryland, until transferred to Elmira, New York, August 8, 1864. Paroled at Elmira and transferred back to Point Lookout on October 11, 1864. Transferred to Venus Point, Savannah River, Georgia, where he was received November 15, 1864, for exchange. Returned to duty prior to January 1, 1865. Retired to the Invalid Corps on January 18, 1865, by reason of disability.

MORROW, WILLIAM J., Private
Born in Gaston County and enlisted at Liberty Mills, Virginia, March 15, 1864, for the war. Died at Spotsylvania Court House, Virginia, May 22, 1864. Cause of death not reported.

MURPHY, JOHN F., Private
Born in Gaston County* where he resided as a farmer prior to enlisting in Gaston County at age 21, July 30, 1861. Present or accounted for until hospitalized at Richmond, Virginia, July 2, 1862, with a gunshot wound of the hand. Place and date wounded not reported. Returned to duty on August 17, 1862. Wounded in the finger and/or arm at the Battle of Second Manassas, Virginia, August 27-30, 1862. Returned to duty prior to November 1, 1862. Wounded at Chancellorsville, Virginia, May 2-3, 1863. Returned to duty prior to July 1-5, 1863, when he was wounded and captured at Gettysburg, Pennsylvania. Hospitalized at Davids Island, New York Harbor, on an unspecified date. Paroled and transferred to City Point, Virginia, where he was received September 8, 1863, for exchange. Returned to duty on an unspecified date. Wounded in the left leg near Petersburg, Virginia, September 16, 1864. Left leg amputated. Reported absent wounded until February 15, 1865, when he was retired by reason of disability.

MURRAY, JOHN O., Private
Resided in Lincoln County where he enlisted at age 18, March 9, 1863, for the war. Wounded at Chancellorsville, Virginia, May 1-3, 1863. Returned to duty prior to July 1-3, 1863, when he was wounded at Gettysburg, Pennsylvania. Returned to duty on an unspecified date. Wounded "in Virginia" May 5-14, 1864. Returned to duty on an unspecified date. Captured at Amelia Court House, Virginia, April 3, 1865. Confined at Point Lookout, Maryland, until released on June 29, 1865, after taking the Oath of Allegiance.

NEAGLE, J. L. K., Corporal
Born in Mecklenburg County and resided in Gaston County where he was by occupation a farmer prior to enlisting in Gaston County at age 22, July 30, 1861. Mustered in as Private and was promoted to Corporal in January-April, 1862. Present or accounted for until killed at Fredericksburg, Virginia, December 13, 1862, "by a gunshot . . . near the heart."

NEIL, CHRISTOPHER, Corporal
Born in Gaston County* where he resided prior to enlisting in Gaston County at age 20, July 30, 1861. Mustered in as Private. Present or accounted for until captured at Hanover Court House, Virginia, May 27, 1862. Confined at Fort Monroe, Virginia, and at Fort Columbus, New York Harbor. Paroled and transferred to Aiken's Landing, James River, Virginia, where he was received July 12, 1862, for exchange. Declared exchanged at Aiken's Landing on August 5, 1862. Returned to duty prior to November 1, 1862. Captured at Fredericksburg, Virginia, December 13, 1862. Paroled on or about December 17, 1862. Returned to duty prior to March 1, 1863. Promoted to Corporal in March-December, 1863. Wounded at Chancellorsville, Virginia, May 2-3, 1863. Returned to duty prior to July 3, 1863, when he was captured at Gettysburg, Pennsylvania. Hospitalized at Chester, Pennsylvania, with an unspecified complaint. Paroled and transferred to City Point, Virginia, where he was received September 22, 1863, for exchange. Returned to duty on an unspecified date. Wounded in the left leg at or near Stoke's Farm, Virginia, on or about May 28, 1864. Hospitalized at Richmond, Virginia, where he died on or about September 26, 1864, of wounds.

NEILL, PETER, Private
Resided in Gaston County where he enlisted at age 22, August 6, 1861. Wounded in the thigh and captured at Gettysburg, Pennsylvania, July 3, 1863. Hospitalized at Chester, Pennsylvania. Paroled and transferred to City Point, Virginia, where he was received August 20, 1863, for exchange. Returned to duty on an unspecified date. Wounded in the right thigh and captured near Petersburg, Virginia, April 2, 1865. Hospitalized at Fort Monroe, Virginia, April 4, 1865. Transferred on June 11, 1865. [North Carolina pension records indicate that he survived the war.]

NICHOLS, ABRAHAM S., Private
Resided in Gaston County where he enlisted at age 18, July 30, 1861. Present or accounted for until captured at Hanover Court House, Virginia, May 27, 1862. Confined at Fort Monroe, Virginia, and at Fort Columbus, New York Harbor. Paroled and transferred to Aiken's Landing, James River, Virginia, where he was received July 12, 1862, for exchange. Declared exchanged at Aiken's Landing on August 5, 1862. Returned to duty prior to November 1, 1862. Captured at Fredericksburg, Virginia, December 13, 1862. Paroled on or about December 17, 1862. Returned to duty prior to March 1, 1863. Wounded and captured at Gettysburg, Pennsylvania, July 1-5, 1863. Hospitalized at Davids Island, New York Harbor, July 17-24, 1863. Paroled at Davids Island and transferred to City Point, Virginia, where he was received August 28, 1863, for exchange. Returned to duty on an unspecified date. Reported present for duty during September-December, 1864. Died at the "brigade hospital" on January 29, 1865, of disease.

NICHOLS, WILLIAM A., Private
Born in Gaston County and was by occupation a farmer prior to enlisting at Liberty Mills, Virginia, February 16, 1864, for the war. Wounded in the leg and captured at Wilderness, Virginia, on or about May 6, 1864. Exchanged on an unspecified date. Returned to duty in November-December, 1864. Present or accounted for through February, 1865. [Company records dated 1865 give his age as 18.]

PAYSOUR, DAVID RUFUS, Private
Born in Gaston County* where he resided as a blacksmith prior to enlisting in Gaston County at age 23, July 30, 1861. Present or accounted for until wounded in the right arm at Cedar Mountain, Virginia, August 9, 1862. Right arm amputated. Discharged on February 12, 1863, by reason of disability.

PEGRAM, EDWARD LARKIN, Private
Previously served as 2nd Lieutenant of this company. [See Lieutenants' section above.] Defeated for reelection on February 27, 1862. Reenlisted in the company with the rank of Private on April 30, 1863. Wounded in the face at Gettysburg, Pennsylvania, July 1-3, 1863. Returned to duty on an unspecified date. Reported on detail as a wagonmaster from February 25, 1864, through February, 1865.

PERKINS, JOHN, Private
Resided in Gaston County where he enlisted at age 22, July 30, 1861. Present or accounted for until he deserted on April 27, 1863. Returned to duty on an unspecified date. Transferred to the C.S. Navy on April 3, 1864.

PERKINS, MICHAEL C., Private
Resided in Gaston County where he enlisted at age 26, July 30, 1861. Present or accounted for until captured at Hanover Court House, Virginia, May 27, 1862. Received at Aiken's Landing, James River, Virginia, July 12, 1862, for exchange. Declared exchanged at Aiken's Landing on August 5, 1862. Returned to duty in November, 1862-February, 1863. Wounded in the right leg at Reams' Station, Virginia, August 25, 1864. Reported absent wounded through February, 1865.

RANKIN, WILLIAM RUFUS, Private
Previously served as Major of the 37th Regiment N.C. Troops. Enlisted in this company in Wake County on April 7, 1863, for the war. Promoted to Sergeant Major on April 29, 1863, and transferred to the Field and Staff of this regiment.

RANKIN, WILLIAM WASHINGTON, Private
Enlisted at Liberty Mills, Virginia, at age 19, February 15, 1864, for the war. Present or accounted for until he surrendered at Appomattox Court House, Virginia, April 9, 1865.

RATCHFORD, J. H., Private
Born in Gaston County* where he resided prior to enlisting in Gaston County at age 26, July 30, 1861. Present or accounted for until wounded at Gaines' Mill, Virginia, June 27, 1862. Died at Richmond, Virginia, July 20, 1862, of wounds.

RATCHFORD, JOHN G., Private
Born in Gaston County* where he resided prior to enlisting in Gaston County at age 24, March 17, 1862. Present or accounted for until wounded in the left hip and captured at Fredericksburg, Virginia, December 13, 1862. Hospitalized at Washington, D.C. Paroled and transferred to City Point, Virginia, where he was received March 29, 1863, for exchange. Returned to duty on an unspecified date. Wounded in the face at Reams' Station, Virginia, August 25, 1864. Hospitalized at Petersburg, Virginia, where he died on August 30, 1864, of wounds.

RHYNE, ALEXANDER A., Private
Resided in Gaston County where he enlisted at age 27, July 30, 1861. Present or accounted for until captured at Hanover Court House, Virginia, May 27, 1862. Confined at Fort Monroe, Virginia, and at Fort Columbus, New York Harbor. Paroled and transferred to Aiken's Landing, James River, Virginia, where he was received July 12, 1862, for exchange. Declared exchanged at Aiken's Landing on August 5, 1862. Returned to duty on an unspecified date. Wounded and captured at Gettysburg, Pennsylvania, July 1-5, 1863. Hospitalized at Chester, Pennsylvania. Paroled and transferred to City Point, Virginia, September 17, 1863, for exchange. Returned to duty on an unspecified date. Reported present for duty during September, 1864-February, 1865. Captured in hospital at Richmond, Virginia, April 3, 1865. Confined at Newport News, Virginia, April 24, 1865. Released on June 30, 1865, after taking the Oath of Allegiance.

RHYNE, ALFRED M., Corporal
Resided in Gaston County where he enlisted at age 18, July 30, 1861. Mustered in as Private. Present or

accounted for until captured at or near Sharpsburg, Maryland, on or about September 17, 1862. Confined at Fort McHenry, Maryland, and at Fort Monroe, Virginia. Paroled and transferred to Aiken's Landing, James River, Virginia, where he was received October 22, 1862, for exchange. Declared exchanged at Aiken's Landing on November 10, 1862. Returned to duty prior to March 1, 1863. Reported present for duty during September, 1864-February, 1865. Promoted to Corporal on October 1, 1864. Surrendered at Appomattox Court House, Virginia, April 9, 1865.

RHYNE, AMBROSE, Private

Born in Gaston County* where he resided prior to enlisting in Gaston County at age 24, August 5, 1861. Present or accounted for until wounded in the forehead near Richmond, Virginia, in June, 1862. Returned to duty prior to November 1, 1862. Captured at Fredericksburg, Virginia, December 13, 1862. Paroled on or about December 17, 1862. Returned to duty on or about March 1, 1863. Reported present for duty during September, 1864-February, 1865. Surrendered at Appomattox Court House, Virginia, April 9, 1865.

RHYNE, GEORGE C., Private

Resided in Gaston County where he enlisted at age 31, August 6, 1861. Present or accounted for until captured at Hanover Court House, Virginia, on or about May 27, 1862. Confined at Fort Monroe, Virginia, and at Fort Columbus, New York Harbor. Paroled and transferred to Aiken's Landing, James River, Virginia, where he was received July 12, 1862, for exchange. Declared exchanged at Aiken's Landing on August 5, 1862. Returned to duty prior to November 1, 1862. Wounded in the elbow and captured at Spotsylvania Court House, Virginia, May 12, 1864. Confined at various Federal hospitals until confined at Old Capitol Prison, Washington, D.C., September 24, 1864. Transferred to Elmira, New York, October 24, 1864. Arrived at Elmira on October 27, 1864. Paroled at Elmira on February 9, 1865, and transferred to Boulware's Wharf, James River, Virginia, where he was received February 20-21, 1865, for exchange.

RUTLEDGE, RUBURTUS GAMWELL, Private

Previously served in Company H, 37th Regiment N.C. Troops. Enlisted in this company at Liberty Mills, Virginia, March 15, 1864, for the war. Present or accounted for until hospitalized at Petersburg, Virginia, August 26, 1864, with a gunshot wound of the right thigh. Place and date wounded not reported. Returned to duty in January-February, 1865. Present or accounted for through February, 1865.

SANDERS, THOMAS L., Private

Resided in Gaston County where he enlisted at age 18, July 30, 1861. Present or accounted for until captured at Hanover Court House, Virginia, May 27, 1862. Confined at Fort Monroe, Virginia, and at Fort Columbus, New York Harbor. Paroled and transferred to Aiken's Landing, James River, Virginia, where he was received July 12, 1862, for exchange. Declared exchanged at Aiken's Landing on August 5, 1862. Returned to duty prior to November 1, 1862. Surrendered at Appomattox Court House, Virginia, April 9, 1865.

SARVICE, ALEXANDER, Private

Enlisted at Liberty Mills, Virginia, April 1, 1864, for the war. Wounded "in Virginia" in May, 1864. Reported absent wounded through February, 1865.

SARVICE, F. A., Private

Enlisted at age 19, in February, 1864, for the war. Wounded in the leg at Wilderness, Virginia, on or about May 5, 1864. [North Carolina pension records indicate that he survived the war.] No further records.

SARVIS, JOHN R., Private

Born in Gaston County* where he resided prior to enlisting in Gaston County at age 18, March 29, 1862. Present or accounted for until captured at Hanover Court House, Virginia, May 27, 1862. Confined at Fort Monroe, Virginia, and at Fort Columbus, New York Harbor. Paroled and transferred to Aiken's Landing, James River, Virginia, where he was received July 12, 1862, for exchange. Declared exchanged at Aiken's Landing on August 5, 1862. Returned to duty prior to November 1, 1862. Wounded in the right eye at Gettysburg, Pennsylvania, July 1-3, 1863. Returned to duty on an unspecified date. Wounded in the left thigh at Reams' Station, Virginia, August 25, 1864. Returned to duty in January-February, 1865. Captured in hospital at Richmond, Virginia, April 3, 1865. Confined at Newport News, Virginia, April 24, 1865. Released on June 30, 1865, after taking the Oath of Allegiance.

SHIELDS, ISAAC WILSON, Private

Resided in Gaston County where he enlisted at age 22, July 30, 1861. Present or accounted for until captured at Hanover Court House, Virginia, May 27, 1862. Confined at Fort Monroe, Virginia, and at Fort Columbus, New York Harbor. Paroled and transferred to Aiken's Landing, James River, Virginia, where he was received July 12, 1862, for exchange. Declared exchanged at Aiken's Landing on August 5, 1862. Returned to duty prior to November 1, 1862. Wounded in the right leg and captured at Gettysburg, Pennsylvania, July 3-5, 1863. Hospitalized at Davids Island, New York Harbor, July 17-24, 1863. Paroled and transferred to City Point, Virginia, where he was received September 16, 1863, for exchange. Returned to duty on an unspecified date. Surrendered at Appomattox Court House, Virginia, April 9, 1865.

SHIELDS, JAMES D. C., Private

Resided in Gaston County and enlisted in Iredell County at age 18, February 25, 1863, for the war. Mustered in as Private. Promoted to Musician in November-December, 1864, but was reduced to ranks subsequent to February 28, 1865. Surrendered at Appomattox Court House, Virginia, April 9, 1865.

SHRUM, JOHN A., Private

Resided in Gaston County where he enlisted at age 20, July 30, 1861. Present or accounted for until he surrendered at Appomattox Court House, Virginia, April 9, 1865.

SIFFORD, DANIEL M., Private

Resided in Gaston County and enlisted in Lenoir County at age 32, April 8, 1862. Present or accounted for until captured at Hanover Court House, Virginia, May 27, 1862. Confined at Fort Monroe, Virginia, and at Fort Columbus, New York Harbor. Exchanged on an unspecified date subsequent to July 31, 1862. Returned to duty prior to November 1, 1862. Captured at Fredericksburg, Virginia, December 13, 1862. Paroled on or about December 17, 1862. Returned to duty prior to March 1, 1863. Detailed as brigade blacksmith on February 1, 1863. Reported absent on detail through February, 1865. Surrendered at Appomattox Court House, Virginia, April 9, 1865.

SMITH, DAVID B., Private

Previously served as 3rd Lieutenant of this company. [See Lieutenants' section above.] Defeated for reelection as 3rd Lieutenant on February 27, 1862. Reenlisted in the company with the rank of Private on December 13, 1862. Promoted to Sergeant Major in January, 1863, and transferred to the Field and Staff of this regiment.

SMITH, LAWSON M., Private

Resided in Gaston County where he enlisted at age 21, July 30, 1861. Captured at or near Spotsylvania Court House, Virginia, on or about May 12, 1864. Confined at Point Lookout, Maryland, until transferred to Elmira, New York, August 10, 1864. Released at Elmira on June 19, 1865, after taking the Oath of Allegiance.

SMITH, NOAH, Private

Resided in Gaston County where he enlisted at age 18, July 30, 1861. Present or accounted for until captured at Hanover Court House, Virginia, May 27, 1862. Confined at Fort Monroe, Virginia, and at Fort Columbus, New York Harbor. Paroled and transferred to Aiken's Landing, James River, Virginia, July 12, 1862, for exchange. Declared exchanged at Aiken's Landing on August 5, 1862. Returned to duty prior to November 1, 1862. Present or accounted for through February, 1863. Deserted on an unspecified date but returned from desertion on September 27, 1864. Rejoined the company in November-December, 1864. Present or accounted for through February, 1865.

SMITH, P. H., Private

Resided in Gaston County and was by occupation a mechanic prior to enlisting in Gaston County at age 32, July 30, 1861. Present or accounted for until captured at Hanover Court House, Virginia, May 27, 1862. Confined at Fort Monroe, Virginia, and at Fort Columbus, New York Harbor. Paroled and transferred to Aiken's Landing, James River, Virginia, where he was received July 12, 1862, for exchange. Declared exchanged at Aiken's Landing on August 5, 1862. Returned to duty prior to November 1, 1862. "Instantly killed" at Fredericksburg, Virginia, December 13, 1862.

SMITH, WILLIAM A., Private

Resided in Gaston County where he enlisted at age 18, July 30, 1861. Present or accounted for until he surrendered at Appomattox Court House, Virginia, April 9, 1865.

STEELMAN, WILLIAM, ———

North Carolina pension records indicate that he served in this company.

STONE, ROBERT B., Private

Resided in Gaston County where he enlisted at age 23, July 30, 1861. Captured at Falling Waters, Maryland, on or about July 14, 1863. Confined at Old Capitol Prison, Washington, D.C., until transferred to Point Lookout, Maryland, August 8, 1863. Paroled at Point Lookout on March 16, 1864, and transferred to City Point, Virginia, where he was received March 20, 1864, for exchange. Returned to duty prior to November 1,

1864. Present or accounted for until he surrendered at Appomattox Court House, Virginia, April 9, 1865.

STOWE, BEVERLY F., Private

Resided in Gaston County where he enlisted at age 37, July 30, 1861. Present or accounted for until captured at Hanover Court House, Virginia, May 27, 1862. Confined at Fort Monroe, Virginia, and at Fort Columbus, New York Harbor. Paroled and transferred to Aiken's Landing, James River, Virginia, where he was received July 12, 1862, for exchange. Declared exchanged at Aiken's Landing on August 5, 1862. Died at Petersburg, Virginia, August 5, 1862, of disease.

STOWE, T. B., Private

Born in Gaston County* where he resided prior to enlisting in Gaston County at age 31, July 30, 1861. Present or accounted for until captured at Hanover Court House, Virginia, on or about May 27, 1862. Confined at Fort Monroe, Virginia, and at Fort Columbus, New York Harbor. Paroled and transferred to Aiken's Landing, James River, Virginia, where he was received July 12, 1862, for exchange. Declared exchanged at Aiken's Landing on August 5, 1862. Returned to duty prior to November 1, 1862. Killed at Spotsylvania Court House, Virginia, May 12, 1864.

STROUP, JOSEPH H., Private

Resided in Gaston County where he enlisted at age 30, July 30, 1861. Captured at Spotsylvania Court House, Virginia, May 12, 1864. Confined at Point Lookout, Maryland, until transferred to Elmira, New York, August 8, 1864. Paroled at Elmira on October 11, 1864, and transferred to Venus Point, Savannah River, Georgia, where he was received November 15, 1864, for exchange. Captured in hospital at Richmond, Virginia, April 3, 1865. Confined at Newport News, Virginia, April 23, 1865. Released on June 30, 1865, after taking the Oath of Allegiance.

STROUP, MOSES, Private

Resided in Gaston County where he enlisted at age 22, July 30, 1861. Present or accounted for until captured at Hanover Court House, Virginia, on or about May 27, 1862. Confined at Fort Monroe, Virginia, and at Fort Columbus, New York Harbor. Paroled and transferred to Aiken's Landing, James River, Virginia, where he was received July 12, 1862, for exchange. Declared exchanged at Aiken's Landing on August 5, 1862. Returned to duty prior to November 1, 1862. Captured at Fredericksburg, Virginia, December 13, 1862. Paroled on or about December 17, 1862. Returned to duty prior to March 1, 1863. Wounded in the right foot and captured at Gettysburg, Pennsylvania, July 1-5, 1863. Hospitalized at Chester, Pennsylvania. Paroled and transferred to City Point, Virginia, where he was received September 23, 1863, for exchange. Returned to duty prior to May 12, 1864, when he was captured at Spotsylvania Court House, Virginia. Confined at Point Lookout, Maryland, until transferred to Elmira, New York, August 8, 1864. Released at Elmira on or about June 19, 1865, after taking the Oath of Allegiance.

SUGGS, L. L., Corporal

Born in Gaston County* where he resided as a farmer prior to enlisting in Gaston County at age 19, July 30, 1861. Mustered in as Private and was promoted to Corporal in November, 1862-February, 1863. Wounded in the right arm at Chancellorsville, Virginia, May 3,

1863. Discharged on January 16, 1864, by reason of disability from wounds.

THOMAS, JOHN F., Private
Resided in Gaston County and enlisted in Mecklenburg County at age 18, August 18, 1863, for the war. Present or accounted for until he surrendered at Appomattox Court House, Virginia, April 9, 1865.

THOMAS, WILLIAM R., Private
Resided in Gaston County where he enlisted at age 19, March 29, 1862. Present or accounted for until captured at Hanover Court House, Virginia, May 27, 1862. Confined at Fort Monroe, Virginia, and at Fort Columbus, New York Harbor. Paroled and transferred to Aiken's Landing, James River, Virginia, where he was received July 12, 1862, for exchange. Declared exchanged at Aiken's Landing on August 5, 1862. Returned to duty prior to December 13, 1862, when he was captured at Fredericksburg, Virginia. Paroled on or about December 17, 1862. Returned to duty prior to March 1, 1863. Surrendered at Appomattox Court House, Virginia, April 9, 1865.

THOMPSON, FRANCIS WILBURN, Private
Born in Lincoln County and resided in Gaston County prior to enlisting in New Hanover County at age 29, March 14, 1862. Present or accounted for until captured at Hanover Court House, Virginia, May 27, 1862. Confined at Fort Monroe, Virginia, and at Fort Columbus, New York Harbor. Paroled and transferred to Aiken's Landing, James River, Virginia, where he was received July 12, 1862, for exchange. Declared exchanged at Aiken's Landing on August 5, 1862. Returned to duty prior to November 1, 1862. Wounded and captured at Gettysburg, Pennsylvania, July 3-4, 1863. Confined at Fort Delaware, Delaware. Transferred to Point Lookout, Maryland, October 15-18, 1863. Paroled at Point Lookout and transferred to Aiken's Landing where he was received on May 8, 1864, for exchange. Returned to duty prior to November 1, 1864. Reported absent on detail as a clerk to the brigade Quartermaster from November 10, 1864, through February, 1865.

THORNBURG, JACOB L., Private
Resided in Gaston County where he enlisted at age 20, March 29, 1862. Present or accounted for until he surrendered at Appomattox Court House, Virginia, April 9, 1865.

TORRENCE, HUGH A., Sergeant
Resided in Gaston County where he enlisted at age 21, July 30, 1861. Mustered in as Sergeant. Present or accounted for until wounded at Frayser's Farm, Virginia, June 30, 1862. Returned to duty in November, 1862-February, 1863. Wounded in the left eye and captured at Gettysburg, Pennsylvania, July 1-5, 1863. Hospitalized at Gettysburg until transferred to Davids Island, New York Harbor, July 17-24, 1863. Paroled at Davids Island and transferred to City Point, Virginia, where he was received August 28, 1863, for exchange. Reported absent wounded until he was detailed for light duty as a hospital guard on or about April 6, 1864. Rejoined the company on August 9, 1864. Present or accounted for through February, 1865. Wounded in the head and captured on an unspecified date. Hospitalized at Fort Monroe, Virginia. Released on or about June 18, 1865.

TUCKER, G. B., ———
North Carolina pension records indicate that he served in this company.

WARREN, J. T., Private
Born in Gaston County* where he resided as a farmer prior to enlisting in Gaston County at age 21, March 29, 1862. Present or accounted for until wounded in the left leg at Cedar Mountain, Virginia, August 9, 1862. Discharged on September 25, 1862, by reason of "contraction & atrophy of the left leg."

WEBB, GEORGE, Private
Resided in Gaston County where he enlisted at age 21, March 29, 1862. Present or accounted for until wounded at the Battle of Second Manassas, Virginia, August 29, 1862. Died the same day at Richmond, Virginia, of wounds.

WELLS, GEORGE, Private
Enlisted in Gaston County on March 29, 186[2]. Present or accounted for until killed at the Battle of Second Manassas, Virginia, August 29, 1862.

WHITE, E. M., Private
Born in Gaston County* where he resided prior to enlisting in Gaston County at age 22, July 30, 1861. Present or accounted for until captured at Hanover Court House, Virginia, on or about May 27, 1862. Confined at Fort Monroe, Virginia, and at Fort Columbus, New York Harbor. Paroled and transferred to Aiken's Landing, James River, Virginia, where he was received July 12, 1862, for exchange. Declared exchanged at Aiken's Landing on August 5, 1862. Returned to duty prior to November 1, 1862. Captured at Fredericksburg, Virginia, December 13, 1862. Paroled on or about December 17, 1862. Died in hospital at Richmond, Virginia, January 16, 1863, of "erysipelas."

WHITE, JOHN E., Sergeant
Resided in Gaston County and was by occupation a farmer prior to enlisting in Gaston County at age 29, July 30, 1861. Mustered in as Private and was promoted to Sergeant on February 27, 1862. Present or accounted for until wounded in the head at Gaines' Mill, Virginia, June 27, 1862. Returned to duty prior to November 1, 1862. Captured at Gettysburg, Pennsylvania, July 4, 1863. Confined at Fort Delaware, Delaware. Transferred to Point Lookout, Maryland, October 15-18, 1863. Died in hospital at Point Lookout on or about November 3, 1863, of "chronic diarrhoea."

WHITESIDE, M. C., Private
Resided in Gaston County where he enlisted on July 30, 1861. Present or accounted for until discharged on February 15, 1862, by reason of disability.

WHITESIDES, E. L., Sergeant
Born in Gaston County* where he resided prior to enlisting in Gaston County at age 27, July 30, 1861. Mustered in as Private and was promoted to Corporal on February 27, 1862. Promoted to Sergeant in January, 1863. Killed at Spotsylvania Court House, Virginia, May 12, 1864.

WHITESIDES, WILLIAM E., Private
Resided in Gaston County where he enlisted at age 23,

July 30, 1861. Present or accounted for until he surrendered at Appomattox Court House, Virginia, April 9, 1865.

WILLIS, MARTIN V. S., Private
Resided in Gaston County where he enlisted at age 21, July 30, 1861. Present or accounted for until he deserted on April 29, 1863. Returned from desertion on September 27, 1864. Reported in confinement through December, 1864. Returned to duty on an unspecified date. Surrendered at Appomattox Court House, Virginia, April 9, 1865. [North Carolina pension records indicate he was wounded in the right shoulder at "Malvern Hill, Virginia, April 1, 1862."]

WILSON, LEROY L., Private
Resided in Gaston County where he enlisted at age 20, March 29, 1862. Present or accounted for until captured at Fredericksburg, Virginia, December 13, 1862. Paroled on or about December 17, 1862. Reported absent in hospital through February, 1863. Returned to duty prior to July 14, 1863, when he was wounded and captured at Falling Waters, Maryland. Paroled at Baltimore, Maryland, August 23, 1863, and transferred to City Point, Virginia, where he was received August 24, 1863, for exchange. Reported on detached service at Charlotte from December 20, 1863, through December, 1864. Rejoined the company in January-February, 1865. Surrendered at Appomattox Court House, Virginia, April 9, 1865.

WYATT, WYLEY A., Private
Resided in Gaston County where he enlisted at age 21, July 30, 1861. Present or accounted for until captured at Hanover Court House, Virginia, May 27, 1862. Confined at Fort Monroe, Virginia, and at Fort Columbus, New York Harbor. Paroled and transferred to Aiken's Landing, James River, Virginia, where he was received July 12, 1862, for exchange. Declared exchanged at Aiken's Landing on August 5, 1862. Returned to duty prior to November 1, 1862. Captured at Fredericksburg, Virginia, December 13, 1862. Exchanged on or about December 17, 1862. Returned to duty prior to March 1, 1863. Transferred to the C.S. Navy on April 3, 1864.

COMPANY C

This company, known as the "South Fork Farmers," was raised in Catawba County and enlisted at Newton. It was mustered into service on August 13, 1861, and assigned to the 28th Regiment as Company C. After joining the regiment the company functioned as a part of the regiment, and its history for the war period is reported as a part of the regimental history.

The information contained in the following roster of the company was compiled principally from company muster rolls for August 13-December, 1861; March, 1862-April, 1863; and September, 1864-February, 1865. No company muster rolls were found for January-February, 1862; May, 1863-August, 1864; or for the period after February, 1865. Valuable information was obtained also from primary records such as the Roll of Honor, medical records, prisoner of war records, discharge certificates, and pension applications, and from secondary sources such as postwar rosters and histories, cemetery records, and records of the United Daughters of the Confederacy.

OFFICERS
CAPTAINS

LOWE, THOMAS L.
Resided in Catawba County and enlisted at age 31. Appointed Captain on August 13, 1861. Elected Lieutenant Colonel on September 21, 1861, and transferred to the Field and Staff of this regiment.

LOWE, SAMUEL D.
Resided in Lincoln County and was by occupation a merchant prior to enlisting in Catawba County at age 29. Appointed 1st Lieutenant on or about August 13, 1861, and was promoted to Captain on September 26, 1861. Present or accounted for until April 12, 1862, when he was appointed Major and transferred to the Field and Staff of this regiment. Later served as Colonel of this regiment.

LINEBARGER, T. JAMES
Resided in Catawba County where he enlisted at age 23, August 13, 1861. Mustered in as Private and was appointed 2nd Lieutenant on September 26, 1861. Elected 1st Lieutenant on February 27, 1862, and was promoted to Captain on April 14, 1862. Present or accounted for until wounded at Fredericksburg, Virginia, December 13, 1862. Returned to duty prior to March 1, 1863. Wounded at Chancellorsville, Virginia, May 2-3, 1863. Returned to duty prior to July 1-3, 1863, when he was wounded in the groin at Gettysburg, Pennsylvania. Returned to duty on October 1, 1864. Present or accounted for until he surrendered at Appomattox Court House, Virginia, April 9. 1865.

LIEUTENANTS

AUSTIN, E. COLEMAN, 2nd Lieutenant
Resided in Catawba County where he enlisted on August 13, 1861. Mustered in as Sergeant but was reduced to ranks in January-February, 1862. Promoted to Corporal on February 27, 1862. Captured at Hanover Court House, Virginia, May 27, 1862. Confined at Fort Monroe, Virginia. Exchanged at Aiken's Landing, James River, Virginia, August 5, 1862. Returned to duty prior to November 1, 1862. Appointed 2nd Lieutenant on November 17, 1862. Killed at Gettysburg, Pennsylvania, July 3, 1863. "A good officer."

CLINE, EPHRAIM ELCANAH, 3rd Lieutenant
Resided in Catawba County where he enlisted. Appointed 3rd Lieutenant on August 13, 1861. Present or accounted for until he was defeated for reelection on February 27, 1862. Later served as Sergeant of Company E, 57th Regiment N.C. Troops.

GILBERT, JACOB H., 1st Lieutenant
Resided in Catawba County where he enlisted. Appointed 2nd Lieutenant on August 13, 1861, and was promoted to 1st Lieutenant on September 27, 1861. Present or accounted for until he was defeated for reelection on February 27, 1862. Later served as 2nd Lieutenant of Company E, 57th Regiment N.C. Troops.

KENT, JOHN, 1st Lieutenant
Resided in Catawba County and enlisted at Camp Fisher on September 9, 1861. Mustered in as Private and was promoted to Sergeant on October 17, 1861. Elected 2nd Lieutenant on February 27, 1862, and was promoted to 1st Lieutenant on April 14, 1862. Died at

Brook Church, near Richmond, Virginia, July 14, 1862, of ''fever.''

KINCAID, JAMES, 2nd Lieutenant

Resided in Lincoln County and enlisted at Camp Fisher on August 26, 1861. Mustered in as Sergeant and was promoted to 1st Sergeant on February 27, 1862. Appointed 3rd Lieutenant on April 14, 1862, and was promoted to 2nd Lieutenant on or about July 14, 1862. Present or accounted for until he died ''at home'' on December 7, 1862, of disease. ''A gallant officer.''

LOWE, MILTON A., 3rd Lieutenant

Born in Lincoln County where he resided as a merchant prior to enlisting in Catawba County at age 19, August 13, 1861. Mustered in as Sergeant. Appointed Sergeant Major on October 17, 1861, and transferred to the Field and Staff of this regiment. Elected 3rd Lieutenant on August 4, 1862, and transferred back to this company. Promoted to 1st Lieutenant on or about November 14, 1862, and transferred to Company H of this regiment.

THRONEBURG, MARCUS AUGUSTUS, 1st Lieutenant

Resided in Catawba County where he enlisted on August 13, 1861. Mustered in as 1st Sergeant and was appointed 2nd Lieutenant on February 27, 1862. Captured at Hanover Court House, Virginia, May 27, 1862. Confined at Fort Monroe, Virginia, and at Fort Columbus, New York Harbor. Transferred to Fort Delaware, Delaware, June 21, 1862. Exchanged on July 10, 1862. Promoted to 1st Lieutenant on or about July 15, 1862. Wounded in the head and/or left hip at Reams' Station, Virginia, August 25, 1864. Reported absent wounded through December, 1864. Reported present but sick in January-February, 1865.

THRONEBURG, MATHIAS MILLER, 2nd Lieutenant

Resided in Catawba County where he enlisted at age 23, August 13, 1861. Mustered in as Private and was promoted to Sergeant on February 27, 1862. Wounded in the neck at Gaines' Mill, Virginia, June 27, 1862. Returned to duty prior to November 1, 1862. Promoted to 2nd Lieutenant on July 3, 1863. Surrendered at Appomattox Court House, Virginia, April 9, 1865.

WILLIAMS, JOHN WESLEY, 2nd Lieutenant

Resided in Catawba County where he enlisted on August 13, 1861. Mustered in as Private and was promoted to Corporal on November 25, 1862. Promoted to Sergeant on April 1, 1863, and was appointed 2nd Lieutenant on September 14, 1863. Surrendered at Appomattox Court House, Virginia, April 9, 1865.

NONCOMMISSIONED OFFICERS AND PRIVATES

ABERNATHY, J. HENRY, Private

Resided in Lincoln or Gaston County and enlisted at Camp Fisher on September 5, 1861. Present or accounted for until captured at Hanover Court House, Virginia, May 27, 1862. Confined at Fort Monroe, Virginia, and at Fort Columbus, New York Harbor. Exchanged at Aiken's Landing, James River, Virginia, August 5, 1862. Returned to duty prior to November 1, 1862. Captured near Petersburg, Virginia, April 2, 1865. Confined at Hart's Island, New York Harbor, until released on June 18, 1865, after taking the Oath of Allegiance.

ABERNATHY, J. SMITH, Private

Born in Catawba County where he enlisted on March 14, 1864, for the war. Died at Richmond, Virginia, July 21, 1864, of disease.

ABERNATHY, SIDNEY M., Private

Enlisted in Catawba County on August 12, 1863, for the war. Reported missing in action on May 1, 1864. No further records.

ABERNATHY, WILLIAM H., Private

Enlisted in Mecklenburg County on March 5, 1864, for the war. Reported missing in action on May 12, 1864. No further records.

ABERNETHY, GIDEON A., Sergeant

Resided in Burke County and enlisted in Catawba County on August 13, 1861. Mustered in as Private and was promoted to Corporal on September 1, 1862. Reduced to ranks on February 20, 1863. Promoted to Sergeant in May, 1863-October, 1864. Present or accounted for through February, 1865.

ASBURY, SIDNEY M., Private

Resided in Lincoln County and enlisted in Catawba County at age 18, August 12, 1863, for the war. Wounded and captured at or near Spotsylvania Court House, Virginia, on or about May 12, 1864. Confined at Point Lookout, Maryland, until transferred to Elmira, New York, August 8, 1864. Released at Elmira on June 19, 1865, after taking the Oath of Allegiance.

ASBURY, WILLIAM H., Private

Resided in Catawba County and enlisted in Mecklenburg County on March 5, 1864, for the war. Captured at or near Spotsylvania Court House, Virginia, May 12, 1864. Confined at Point Lookout, Maryland, until transferred to Elmira, New York, August 8, 1864. Released at Elmira on June 27, 1865, after taking the Oath of Allegiance.

BARGER, ALLEN, Private

Resided in Catawba County where he enlisted at age 22, March 15, 1862. Captured at Hanover Court House, Virginia, May 27, 1862. Confined at Fort Monroe, Virginia, and at Fort Columbus, New York Harbor. Exchanged at Aiken's Landing, James River, Virginia, August 5, 1862. Present or accounted for until transferred to the C.S. Navy on April 3, 1864.

BARGER, DAVID, Private

Previously served in Company H of this regiment. Transferred to this company in February, 1865. Wounded in the left thigh at Petersburg, Virginia, on an unspecified date. Captured by the enemy on an unspecified date prior to April 4, 1865, when he was reported in hospital at Fort Monroe, Virginia. Released on July 20, 1865, after taking the Oath of Allegiance. [Records of the Federal Provost Marshal dated 1865 give his age as 22.]

BARGER, GILBERT A., Private

Resided in Catawba County where he enlisted on May 6, 1864, for the war. Present or accounted for until captured near Petersburg, Virginia, April 2, 1865. Confined at Fort Delaware, Delaware, until released on June 19, 1865, after taking the Oath of Allegiance.

BARGER, JOSIAH W., Private

Resided in Catawba County where he enlisted on March 15, 1862. Captured at Hanover Court House, Virginia, May 27, 1862. Confined at Fort Monroe, Virginia, and at Fort Columbus, New York Harbor. Exchanged at Aiken's Landing, James River, Virginia, August 5, 1862. Returned to duty prior to January 1, 1863. Died at Guinea Station, Virginia, May 29, 1863, of disease.

BARGER, MARCUS, Private

Resided in Catawba County where he enlisted at age 25, March 15, 1862. Captured at Hanover Court House, Virginia, May 27, 1862. Confined at Fort Monroe, Virginia, and at Fort Columbus, New York Harbor. Exchanged at Aiken's Landing, James River, Virginia, August 5, 1862. Returned to duty prior to November 1, 1862. Captured at Petersburg, Virginia, April 2, 1865. Confined at Fort Delaware, Delaware, until released on June 19, 1865, after taking the Oath of Allegiance.

BARGER, MOSES, Private

Resided in Catawba County and enlisted at Camp Fisher on September 9, 1861. Present or accounted for until he died in hospital at Charlottesville, Virginia, on or about May 21, 1862, of "typhoid fever."

BARGER, NOAH, Private

Resided in Catawba County where he enlisted at age 22, March 15, 1862. Paroled at Farmville, Virginia, April 11-21, 1865.

BOLCH, AARON, Corporal

Resided in Catawba County where he enlisted on August 13, 1861. Mustered in as Private. Present or accounted for until captured at Hanover Court House, Virginia, May 27, 1862. Confined at Fort Monroe, Virginia, and at Fort Columbus, New York Harbor. Exchanged at Aiken's Landing, James River, Virginia, August 5, 1862. Returned to duty prior to November 1, 1862. Wounded and captured at Gettysburg, Pennsylvania, July 3-5, 1863. Hospitalized at Davids Island, New York Harbor. Paroled and transferred to City Point, Virginia, where he was received September 27, 1863, for exchange. Returned to duty on an unspecified date. Promoted to Corporal on December 1, 1864. Present or accounted for until he surrendered at Appomattox Court House, Virginia, April 9, 1865.

BOLCH, ABEL, Private

Resided in Catawba County where he enlisted on March 15, 1862. Wounded at Gaines' Mill, Virginia, June 27, 1862. Returned to duty prior to November 1, 1862. Captured near Petersburg, Virginia, April 2, 1865. Confined at Hart's Island, New York Harbor, until released on June 18, 1865, after taking the Oath of Allegiance.

BOLCH, EMANUEL, Private

Resided in Catawba County where he enlisted on March 15, 1862. Present or accounted for until he died in hospital at Lovingston, Virginia, August 15-17, 1862, of "febris typhoides."

BOLCH, HENRY C., Private

Enlisted in Catawba County on January 21, 1865, for the war. Wounded in the left leg and captured at or near Petersburg, Virginia, on or about April 2, 1865. Hospitalized at Fort Monroe, Virginia, until released on

or about July 13, 1865, after taking the Oath of Allegiance. [Federal hospital records dated 1865 give his age as 17.]

BOLCH, JORDAN, Private

Enlisted in Catawba County on April 14, 1864, for the war. Present or accounted for until he surrendered at Appomattox Court House, Virginia, April 9, 1865.

BOLCH, LOGAN, Private

Resided in Catawba County where he enlisted on March 14, 1863, for the war. Wounded and captured at Gettysburg, Pennsylvania, July 2-3, 1863. Hospitalized at Chester, Pennsylvania, where he died on September 30, 1863, of "exhaustion." [A pension application filed by his widow states that Private Bolch enlisted as a nurse "but could not endure that and he then was put into regular service."]

BOLCH, MARCUS, Private

Resided in Catawba County where he enlisted on August 13, 1861. Wounded at the Battle of Second Manassas, Virginia, August 28-30, 1862. Returned to duty prior to March 1, 1863. Wounded at Chancellorsville, Virginia, May 2-3, 1863. Returned to duty prior to July 18, 1863. Surrendered at Appomattox Court House, Virginia, April 9, 1865.

BOLCH, PHILIP H., Private

Enlisted in Catawba County on January 21, 1865, for the war. Surrendered at Appomattox Court House, Virginia, April 9, 1865.

BOLCH, WILLIAM, Private

Resided in Catawba County where he enlisted on March 15, 1862. Died in hospital at Farmville, Virginia, July 15, 1862, of "diarrhoea."

BOWMAN, CALVIN M., Private

Born in Catawba County where he resided prior to enlisting in Catawba County at age 18, March 15, 1862. Captured at Spotsylvania Court House, Virginia, May 12, 1864. Confined at Point Lookout, Maryland, until transferred to Elmira, New York, August 8, 1864. Paroled at Elmira on October 11, 1864, and transferred to Venus Point, Savannah River, Georgia, where he was received November 15, 1864, for exchange. Died "at home" on November 22, 1864, of disease.

BUMGARNER, ALLEN L., Private

Resided in Catawba County where he enlisted on August 13, 1861. Captured at Hanover Court House, Virginia, May 27, 1862. Confined at Fort Monroe, Virginia, and at Fort Columbus, New York Harbor. Exchanged at Aiken's Landing, James River, Virginia, August 5, 1862. Returned to duty prior to November 1, 1862. Surrendered at Appomattox Court House, Virginia, April 9, 1865.

BUMGARNER, DAVID A., Private

Resided in Catawba County where he enlisted on March 15, 1862. Captured at Hanover Court House, Virginia, May 27, 1862. Confined at Fort Monroe, Virginia, and at Fort Columbus, New York Harbor. Exchanged at Aiken's Landing, James River, Virginia, August 5, 1862. Returned to duty prior to November 1, 1862. Wounded at Chancellorsville, Virginia, May 1-3, 1863. Returned to duty on an unspecified date. Wounded in the back and captured at Gravel Hill,

Virginia, July 28, 1864. Confined at Point Lookout, Maryland. Paroled and transferred to Boulware's Wharf, James River, Virginia, March 18, 1865, for exchange.

BUMGARNER, SIDNEY A., Private
Resided in Catawba County where he enlisted on August 13, 1861. Present or accounted for until he died at Richmond, Virginia, August 1, 1862. Cause of death not reported.

CAMPBELL, ADOLPHUS L., Private
Resided in Catawba County where he enlisted on August 13, 1861. Present or accounted for until wounded at Chancellorsville, Virginia, May 2-3, 1863. Returned to duty prior to July 1-3, 1863, when he was wounded in the left shoulder and captured at Gettysburg, Pennsylvania. Hospitalized at Gettysburg where he died on July 15-18, 1863, of wounds.

CAMPBELL, WILLIAM A., Private
Born in Catawba County* where he resided as a farmer prior to enlisting in Catawba County on August 13, 1861. Present or accounted for until discharged on December 23, 1861, by reason of "scrotal hernia of the right side." Discharge certificate gives his age as 21.

CARTER, JAMES W., Private
Resided in Catawba County where he enlisted on March 14, 1864, for the war. Wounded in the back "in Virginia" in May, 1864. Returned to duty prior to November 1, 1864. Present or accounted for until captured near Petersburg, Virginia, April 2, 1865. Confined at Fort Delaware, Delaware, until released on June 19, 1865, after taking the Oath of Allegiance.

CARTER, JOSHUA C., Private
Resided in Catawba County where he enlisted at age 26, August 13, 1861. Wounded at Chancellorsville, Virginia, May 2-3, 1863. Returned to duty on or about June 28, 1863. Present or accounted for through November 27, 1864; however, he was reported on detail as a teamster during most of that period. Rejoined the company on November 28, 1864. Present or accounted for until he surrendered at Appomattox Court House, Virginia, April 9, 1865.

CHILDERS, FRANKLIN A., Private
Resided in Lincoln County and enlisted at Camp Fisher on August 26, 1861. Present or accounted for until he died at Wilmington on March 4, 1862, of disease.

CLINE, ADOLPHUS, Private
Resided in Catawba County where he enlisted on April 6, 1864, for the war. Present or accounted for until captured in hospital at Richmond, Virginia, April 3, 1865. Transferred to Newport News, Virginia, April 23, 1865. Released on June 30, 1865, after taking the Oath of Allegiance.

CLINE, ALFRED J., Private
Resided in Catawba County where he enlisted at age 18, August 13, 1861. Captured at Richmond, Virginia, April 3, 1865. Transferred to Newport News, Virginia, where he arrived on April 24, 1865. Released on an unspecified date. Paroled at Greensboro on May 2, 1865.

CLINE, AMBROSE, Private
Born in Catawba County* where he resided prior to

enlisting in Catawba County at age 24, March 14, 1863, for the war. Died near Richmond, Virginia, June 6, 1864, of wounds. Place and date wounded not reported.

CLINE, J. TIMOTHY, Private
Resided in Catawba County where he enlisted on February 12, 1864, for the war. Present or accounted for until captured near Petersburg, Virginia, April 2, 1865. Confined at Fort Delaware, Delaware, until released on June 19, 1865, after taking the Oath of Allegiance.

CLINE, JOHN L. H., Private
Resided in Catawba County where he enlisted at age 18, February 18, 1863, for the war. Deserted on June 5, 1863. Returned to duty on an unspecified date. Captured at Spotsylvania Court House, Virginia, May 12, 1864. Confined at Point Lookout, Maryland, where he died on June 19, 1864. Cause of death not reported.

CLINE, MAXWELL A., Private
Resided in Catawba County where he enlisted at age 19, August 13, 1861. Deserted on June 5, 1863. Returned to duty on an unspecified date. Captured at Spotsylvania Court House, Virginia, May 12, 1864. Confined at Point Lookout, Maryland, until transferred to Elmira, New York, August 8, 1864. Released on May 19, 1865, after taking the Oath of Allegiance.

CLINE, MONROE J., Private
Resided in Catawba County where he enlisted on August 13, 1861. Captured at Hanover Court House, Virginia, May 27, 1862. Confined at Fort Monroe, Virginia, and at Fort Columbus, New York Harbor. Paroled and transferred to Aiken's Landing, James River, Virginia, where he was received July 12, 1862, for exchange. Declared exchanged at Aiken's Landing on August 5, 1862. Returned to duty prior to November 1, 1862. Captured at Winchester, Virginia, on or about December 2, 1862. Paroled on December 4, 1862. Died in hospital at Petersburg, Virginia, December 27, 1862, of "feb[ris] typh[oid]."

CLIPPARD, JOHN, Private
Born in Catawba County* where he resided as a farmer prior to enlisting in Catawba County at age 27, March 15, 1862. Wounded in the jaw at Wilderness, Virginia, May 5, 1864. Returned to duty on December 1, 1864. Retired to the Invalid Corps on December 28, 1864, by reason of disability.

CONNELL, SIDNEY J., Private
Born in Lincoln County where he resided as a farmer prior to enlisting at Camp Fisher at age 21, August 26, 1861. Wounded at the Battle of Second Manassas, Virginia, August 28-30, 1862. Returned to duty prior to November 1, 1862. Wounded at Gettysburg, Pennsylvania, July 1-3, 1863. Returned to duty on an unspecified date. Surrendered at Appomattox Court House, Virginia, April 9, 1865.

CONRAD, HENRY A., Private
Born in Catawba County where he resided prior to enlisting in Catawba County at age 16, August 13, 1861. Killed at Gravel Hill, Virginia, July 28, 1864.

COOK, ABEL, Musician
Resided in Catawba County and enlisted at Camp Fisher on September 9, 1861. Mustered in as Private

and was promoted to Musician in January-April, 1862. Wounded in the left hip at Wilderness, Virginia, May 5, 1864. Reported absent wounded through February, 1865. [Confederate hospital records dated November, 1862, give his age as 39.]

COOK, LAWSON OBEDIAH, Private
Born in Lincoln County and resided in Catawba County where he enlisted at age 32, March 15, 1862. Wounded at Gettysburg, Pennsylvania, July 1-3, 1863. Returned to duty on an unspecified date. Surrendered at Appomattox Court House, Virginia, April 9, 1865.

DEAL, JUNIUS, Private
Resided in Catawba County where he enlisted at age 17, August 13, 1861. Present or accounted for until wounded at the Battle of Second Manassas, Virginia, August 28-30, 1862. Died at Middlebury, Virginia, August 31, 1862, of wounds.

DEAL, LEVI, Private
Resided in Catawba County where he enlisted on March 9, 1863, for the war. Wounded at Chancellorsville, Virginia, May 3, 1863. Died in hospital at Richmond, Virginia, June 10, 1863, of ''feb[ris] typhoides'' and/or ''super double pneumonia.''

DRUM, DAVID J., Private
Born in Catawba County where he resided as a farmer prior to enlisting in Catawba County on August 13, 1861. Wounded in the finger at the Battle of Second Manassas, Virginia, on or about August 27, 1862. Returned to duty prior to November 1, 1862. Wounded at Gettysburg, Pennsylvania, July 1-3, 1863. Returned to duty on an unspecified date. Wounded in the right leg at Reams' Station, Virginia, August 25, 1864. Right leg amputated. Retired from service on February 3, 1865, by reason of disability. Retirement papers give his age as 21.

DRUM, JOSEPH M., Private
Resided in Catawba County where he enlisted on March 15, 1862. Wounded at Gaines' Mill, Virginia, June 27, 1862. Returned to duty prior to August 29, 1862, when he was killed at the Battle of Second Manassas, Virginia. ''A most gallant soldier.''

ECKARD, CYRUS, Private
Resided in Catawba County where he enlisted on August 13, 1861. Captured at Hanover Court House, Virginia, on or about May 27, 1862. Confined at Fort Monroe, Virginia, and at Fort Columbus, New York Harbor. Died at Fort Columbus on June 22, 1862, of ''febris typhoides.'' Records of the Federal Provost Marshal dated 1862 give his age as 24.

ECKARD, RUFUS, Sergeant
Resided in Catawba County where he enlisted on August 13, 1861. Mustered in as Corporal and was promoted to Sergeant on February 27, 1862. Captured at Hanover Court House, Virginia, May 27, 1862. Confined at Fort Monroe, Virginia, and at Fort Columbus, New York Harbor. Exchanged on an unspecified date. Returned to duty prior to November 1, 1862. Killed at Fredericksburg, Virginia, December 13, 1862. [Records of the Federal Provost Marshal dated 1862 give his age as 27.]

EDWARDS, ADOLPHUS D., Private
Resided in Lincoln County and enlisted at Camp Fisher

at age 18, August 26, 1861. Captured at Hanover Court House, Virginia, May 27, 1862. Confined at Fort Monroe, Virginia, and at Fort Columbus, New York Harbor. Paroled and transferred to Aiken's Landing, James River, Virginia, where he was received July 12, 1862, for exchange. Declared exchanged at Aiken's Landing on August 5, 1862. Returned to duty prior to November 1, 1862. Wounded in the left leg at Jericho Mills, Virginia, May 23, 1864. Left leg amputated. Reported absent wounded through February, 1865.

FISHER, GEORGE, Private
Resided in Catawba County where he enlisted on March 15, 1862. Present or accounted for through April, 1862. No further records.

FLOWERS, NOAH T., Sergeant
Resided in Catawba County where he enlisted on August 13, 1861. Mustered in as Corporal and was promoted to Sergeant on February 27, 1862. Hospitalized at Richmond, Virginia, June 11, 1862, with ''paralysis [and] typhoid fever.'' Died in hospital at Richmond on or about June 25, 1862.

FRADY, ANDREW J., Private
Resided in Catawba County where he enlisted on August 13, 1861. Surrendered at Appomattox Court House, Virginia, April 9, 1865.

FRY, EPHRAIM N., Private
Born in Catawba County* where he resided as a farmer prior to enlisting in Catawba County at age 37, August 13, 1861. Wounded in the forehead at Gettysburg, Pennsylvania, July 1-3, 1863. Returned to duty on an unspecified date. Retired from service on February 8, 1865, by reason of ''ulceration of the tibia causing extension & incurable ulcers of the legs.''

FRY, JACOB A., Private
Resided in Catawba County and enlisted at Camp Fisher on September 2, 1861. Captured at Gettysburg, Pennsylvania, July 1-3, 1863. Confined at Fort Delaware, Delaware, until transferred to Point Lookout, Maryland, October 15-18, 1863. Paroled at Point Lookout on February 18, 1865, and transferred to Boulware's Wharf, James River, Virginia, where he was received February 20-21, 1865, for exchange. [North Carolina pension records indicate he was wounded in September, 1862.]

FULBRIGHT, JOHN, Private
Resided in Catawba County where he enlisted on March 14, 1863, for the war. Died in hospital at Richmond, Virginia, January 3, 1864, of ''febris typhoides'' or ''orchitis.''

GABRIEL, A. ALONZO, Sergeant
Born in Catawba County where he resided as a farmer prior to enlisting in Catawba County at age 18, March 15, 1862. Mustered in as Private. Captured at Hanover Court House, Virginia, May 27, 1862. Confined at Fort Monroe, Virginia, and at Fort Columbus, New York Harbor. Paroled and transferred to Aiken's Landing, James River, Virginia, where he was received July 12, 1862, for exchange. Declared exchanged at Aiken's Landing on August 5, 1862. Returned to duty prior to November 1, 1862. Promoted to Sergeant on January 1, 1863. Transferred to Company K, 23rd Regiment N.C. Troops (13th Regiment N.C. Volunteers), March 21,

1863.

GOINS, PHILIP P., Private

Resided in Catawba County where he enlisted at age 17, August 13, 1861. Captured at Hanover Court House, Virginia, May 27, 1862. Confined at Fort Monroe, Virginia, and at Fort Columbus, New York Harbor. Paroled and transferred to Aiken's Landing, James River, Virginia, where he was received July 12, 1862, for exchange. Declared exchanged at Aiken's Landing on August 5, 1862. Returned to duty prior to November 1, 1862. Wounded at Chancellorsville, Virginia, May 1-3, 1863. Returned to duty on an unspecified date. Wounded in the right hand at Jones' Farm, Virginia, September 30, 1864. Returned to duty on December 2, 1864. Captured near Petersburg, Virginia, April 2, 1865. Confined at Fort Delaware, Delaware, until released on June 19, 1865, after taking the Oath of Allegiance. [North Carolina pension records indicate he was wounded at Fredericksburg, Virginia, and at Wilderness, Virginia, on unspecified dates.]

GOODSON, JAMES, Private

Born in Catawba County where he resided prior to enlisting in Catawba County at age 17, August 13, 1861. Wounded in the shoulder at Frayser's Farm, Virginia, June 30, 1862. Returned to duty on July 5, 1862. Died at Richmond, Virginia, June 1, 1864, of wounds. Place and date wounded not reported.

GRICE, HENRY LEE, Private

Born in Catawba County where he resided as a farmer prior to enlisting in Catawba County at age 18, August 12, 1863, for the war. Killed at Reams' Station, Virginia, August 25, 1864.

GRICE, JAMES M., Sergeant

Resided in Catawba County and enlisted at Camp Fisher on September 2, 1861. Mustered in as Private. Captured at Hanover Court House, Virginia, May 27, 1862. Confined at Fort Monroe, Virginia, and at Fort Columbus, New York Harbor. Paroled and transferred to Aiken's Landing, James River, Virginia, where he was received July 12, 1862, for exchange. Declared exchanged at Aiken's Landing on August 5, 1862. Wounded at Fredericksburg, Virginia, on or about December 13, 1862. Returned to duty prior to March 1, 1863. Wounded at Chancellorsville, Virginia, May 1-3, 1863. Returned to duty on an unspecified date. Promoted to Sergeant in May, 1863-October, 1864. Wounded at Gettysburg, Pennsylvania, July 1-3, 1863. Returned to duty on an unspecified date. Present or accounted for through February, 1865.

HAGER, SIMON, Private

Resided in Lincoln County and enlisted at Camp Fisher on September 5, 1861. Died at Brook Church, Virginia, July 8, 1862, of "typhoid fever."

HARWELL, WATSON A., Private

Resided in Catawba County where he enlisted on March 14, 1863, for the war. Mortally wounded and "left on the field" at Gettysburg, Pennsylvania, July 3, 1863.

HASS, JOHN A., Private

Resided in Catawba County where he enlisted at age 21, August 13, 1861. Wounded in the right shoulder at Chancellorsville, Virginia, May 1-3, 1863. Returned to

duty on February 12, 1864; however, he was retired to the Invalid Corps on April 8, 1864, by reason of disability.

HASS, SIDNEY, Private

Born in Catawba County and was by occupation a farmer prior to enlisting at Richmond, Virginia, at age 18, February 6, 1864, for the war. Wounded in the arm on an unspecified date. Arm amputated. Reported absent wounded or absent sick through February, 1865.

HAUN, NEWTON D., Private

Resided in Catawba County where he enlisted on March 15, 1862. Present or accounted for until he was reported missing and "supposed to have been killed" at Gettysburg, Pennsylvania, July 3, 1863. [Records of the Federal Provost Marshal indicate that he may have been paroled at Morganton on May 16, 1865.]

HEFNER, DAVID, Private

Born in Catawba County* where he resided prior to enlisting in Catawba County at age 33, August 13, 1861. Shot four times (including once in the left side) and captured at Gettysburg, Pennsylvania, July 1-5, 1863. Hospitalized at Davids Island, New York Harbor, until paroled and transferred to City Point, Virginia, where he was received September 27, 1863, for exchange. Returned to duty on an unspecified date. Surrendered at Appomattox Court House, Virginia, April 9, 1865.

HEFNER, GEORGE, Private

Resided in Catawba County where he enlisted at age 29, March 15, 1862. Present or accounted for until he surrendered at Appomattox Court House, Virginia, April 9, 1865.

HEFNER, LEVI, Private

Resided in Catawba County where he enlisted at age 21, August 13, 1861. Present or accounted for until wounded at Ox Hill, Virginia, September 1, 1862. Returned to duty prior to November 1, 1862. Wounded at Fredericksburg, Virginia, December 13, 1862. Returned to duty prior to March 1, 1863. Captured at Spotsylvania Court House, Virginia, May 12, 1864. Confined at Point Lookout, Maryland, until transferred to Elmira, New York, August 10, 1864. Released on July 7, 1865, after taking the Oath of Allegiance.

HEFNER, MARCUS, Private

Resided in Catawba County where he enlisted at age 18, August 13, 1861. Captured at Hanover Court House, Virginia, May 27, 1862. Confined at Fort Monroe, Virginia, and at Fort Columbus, New York Harbor. Paroled and transferred to Aiken's Landing, James River, Virginia, where he was received July 12, 1862, for exchange. Declared exchanged at Aiken's Landing on August 5, 1862. Returned to duty prior to November 1, 1862. Killed at Chancellorsville, Virginia, May 3, 1863.

HEFNER, SERENUS, Private

Resided in Catawba County where he enlisted at age 20, August 13, 1861. Captured at Hanover Court House, Virginia, May 27, 1862. Confined at Fort Monroe, Virginia, and at Fort Columbus, New York Harbor. Paroled and transferred to Aiken's Landing, James River, Virginia, where he was received July 12, 1862, for exchange. Declared exchanged at Aiken's Landing on August 5, 1862. Returned to duty prior to November 1, 1862. Wounded in the left foot at Jones' Farm, Virginia,

September 30, 1864. Returned to duty on January 24, 1865. Surrendered at Appomattox Court House, Virginia, April 9, 1865.

HEFNER, WILSON W., Private

Resided in Catawba County where he enlisted at age 17, March 15, 1862. Captured at Hanover Court House, Virginia, May 27, 1862. Received at Aiken's Landing, James River, Virginia, July 12, 1862, for exchange. Declared exchanged at Aiken's Landing on August 5, 1862. Returned to duty prior to November 1, 1862. Wounded at Chancellorsville, Virginia, May 1-3, 1863. Returned to duty on an unspecified date. Present or accounted for through February, 1865.

HERMAN, ABEL, Private

Born in Catawba County where he resided prior to enlisting in Catawba County on August 13, 1861. Wounded at Chancellorsville, Virginia, May 2-3, 1863. Returned to duty prior to July 14, 1863, when he was captured at Falling Waters, Maryland. Confined at Old Capitol Prison, Washington, D.C., until transferred to Point Lookout, Maryland, August 8, 1863. Transferred to Elmira, New York, August 16, 1864. Died at Elmira on September 12, 1864, of "chronic diarrhoea."

HERMAN, D. ALEXANDER, Private

Resided in Catawba County where he enlisted on March 15, 1862. Died in hospital at Gordonsville, Virginia, May 27, 1862, of "typhoid fever."

HERMAN, DANIEL J., Private

Resided in Catawba County where he enlisted on May 6, 1864, for the war. Captured at Petersburg, Virginia, April 3, 1865. Confined at Hart's Island, New York Harbor, where he died on June 15, 1865, of "typhoid fever."

HERMAN, DANIEL M., Corporal

Resided in Catawba County where he enlisted at age 24, August 13, 1861. Mustered in as Private. Captured at Hanover Court House, Virginia, May 27, 1862. Confined at Fort Monroe, Virginia, and at Fort Columbus, New York Harbor. Paroled and transferred to Aiken's Landing, James River, Virginia, where he was received July 12, 1862, for exchange. Declared exchanged at Aiken's Landing on August 5, 1862. Returned to duty prior to November 1, 1862. Wounded at Chancellorsville, Virginia, May 1-3, 1863. Returned to duty on an unspecified date. Promoted to Corporal on December 1, 1864. Surrendered at Appomattox Court House, Virginia, April 9, 1865.

HERMAN, GEORGE DANIEL, Corporal

Born in Catawba County* where he resided prior to enlisting in Catawba County at age 22, August 13, 1861. Mustered in as Private. Wounded at the Battle of Second Manassas, Virginia, August 28-30, 1862. Returned to duty prior to November 1, 1862. Promoted to Corporal on September 1, 1863. Killed at Wilderness, Virginia, May 5, 1864.

HERMAN, JAMES NOAH, Private

Enlisted in Catawba County on August 6, 1864, for the war. Present or accounted for through February, 1865.

HERMAN, JOSEPH, Private

Born in Catawba County where he enlisted on March 24, 1864, for the war. Died "at home" on August 27, 1864, of disease.

HERMAN, PHANUEL J., Sergeant

Born in Catawba County* where he resided as a farmer prior to enlisting in Catawba County at age 23, August 13, 1861. Mustered in as Private. Captured at Hanover Court House, Virginia, May 27, 1862. Confined at Fort Monroe, Virginia, and at Fort Columbus, New York Harbor. Paroled and transferred to Aiken's Landing, James River, Virginia, where he was received July 12, 1862, for exchange. Declared exchanged at Aiken's Landing on August 5, 1862. Returned to duty prior to November 1, 1862. Promoted to Corporal on March 25, 1863. Wounded and captured at Gettysburg, Pennsylvania, July 1-4, 1863. Hospitalized at Davids Island, New York Harbor, July 17-24, 1863. Paroled at Davids Island and transferred to City Point, Virginia, where he was received September 8, 1863, for exchange. Promoted to Sergeant on or about September 9, 1863. Surrendered at Appomattox Court House, Virginia, April 9, 1865.

HERMAN, RUFUS D., Private

Resided in Catawba County where he enlisted at age 17, August 13, 1861. Captured at Gravel Hill, Virginia, July 28, 1864. Confined at Point Lookout, Maryland, until transferred to Elmira, New York, August 8, 1864. Released at Elmira on July 3, 1865, after taking the Oath of Allegiance. [Roll of Honor indicates he was wounded and captured in an unspecified battle.]

HERMAN, WILLIAM HENRY, Private

Resided in Catawba County where he enlisted on March 15, 1862. Died in hospital at Richmond, Virginia, July 8, 1862, of "diarrhoea ch[ronic]."

HERMON, J. S., Private

Place and date of enlistment not reported. Surrendered at Appomattox Court House, Virginia, April 9, 1865.

HOLLER, ADLEY D., Private

Previously served in 1st Company G, 6th Regiment South Carolina Infantry. Transferred to this company on March 30, 1864. Wounded at Gravel Hill, Virginia, July 28, 1864. Returned to duty on November 19, 1864. Present or accounted for until he surrendered at Appomattox Court House, Virginia, April 9, 1865.

HOLLER, LEMUEL, Private

Resided in Catawba County where he enlisted on March 15, 1862. Captured at Hanover Court House, Virginia, May 27, 1862. Confined at Fort Monroe, Virginia, and at Fort Columbus, New York Harbor. Paroled and transferred to Aiken's Landing, James River, Virginia, where he was received July 12, 1862, for exchange. Declared exchanged at Aiken's Landing on August 5, 1862. Returned to duty prior to November 1, 1862. Wounded and captured at Gettysburg, Pennsylvania, July 1-5, 1863. Hospitalized at Davids Island, New York Harbor, until paroled and transferred to City Point, Virginia, where he was received September 16, 1863, for exchange. Returned to duty on an unspecified date. Present or accounted for through February, 1865.

HOUSTON, JACOB F., Corporal

Resided in Catawba County where he enlisted at age 25, March 15, 1862. Mustered in as Private. Present or accounted for until wounded at Shepherdstown,

Virginia, September 20, 1862. Returned to duty prior to November 1, 1862. Wounded at Gettysburg, Pennsylvania, July 1-3, 1863. Returned to duty on an unspecified date. Promoted to Corporal on December 1, 1864. Surrendered at Appomattox Court House, Virginia, April 9, 1865.

HOUSTON, JOHN M., Private
Born in Catawba County where he resided as a farmer prior to enlisting in Catawba County at age 18, August 13, 1861. Captured at Hanover Court House, Virginia, May 27, 1862. Paroled and transferred to Aiken's Landing, James River, Virginia, where he was received July 12, 1862, for exchange. Declared exchanged at Aiken's Landing on August 5, 1862. Returned to duty prior to November 1, 1862. Surrendered at Appomattox Court House, Virginia, April 9, 1865.

HOUSTON, MARTIN L., Private
Resided in Catawba County where he enlisted at age 22, August 13, 1861. Present or accounted for until wounded in the leg at Gaines' Mill, Virginia, June 27, 1862. Hospitalized at Richmond, Virginia, where he died on July 17, 1862, of wounds.

HOWARD, FRANKLIN W., Private
Was by occupation a farmer prior to enlisting in Catawba County on January 1, 1864, for the war. Surrendered at Appomattox Court House, Virginia, April 9, 1865. [Confederate medical records dated June, 1864, give his age as 25.]

HUFFMAN, DANIEL W., Private
Resided in Catawba County where he enlisted at age 18, August 13, 1861. Present or accounted for until wounded in the chest at the Battle of Second Manassas, Virginia, August 27-30, 1862. Returned to duty prior to November 1, 1862. Captured at Spotsylvania Court House, Virginia, May 12, 1864. Confined at Point Lookout, Maryland, until transferred to Elmira, New York, August 10, 1864. Released at Elmira on June 19, 1865, after taking the Oath of Allegiance.

HUFFMAN, ELIJAH, Private
Resided in Catawba County where he enlisted at age 28, March 15, 1862. Captured at Hanover Court House, Virginia, May 27, 1862. Confined at Fort Monroe, Virginia, and at Fort Columbus, New York Harbor. Paroled and transferred to Aiken's Landing, James River, Virginia, where he was received July 12, 1862, for exchange. Declared exchanged at Aiken's Landing on August 5, 1862. Died "at home" on December 10, 1862, of disease.

HUFFMAN, ELIJAH J., Private
Resided in Catawba County where he enlisted on March 15, 1862. Captured at Hanover Court House, Virginia, May 27, 1862. Confined at Fort Monroe, Virginia, and at Fort Columbus, New York Harbor. Paroled and transferred to Aiken's Landing, James River, Virginia, where he was received July 12, 1862, for exchange. Declared exchanged at Aiken's Landing on August 5, 1862. Returned to duty on an unspecified date. Died at Camp Gregg, Virginia, June 6, 1863, of "typhoid pneumonia."

HUFFMAN, GEORGE F., Private
Enlisted in Catawba County on August 24, 1864, for the war. Hospitalized at Farmville, Virginia, April 9, 1865,

with a gunshot wound. Place and date wounded not reported. Died in hospital at Farmville on April 25, 1865, of wounds.

HUFFMAN, JEREMIAH, Private
Resided in Catawba County where he enlisted at age 26, August 13, 1861. Wounded in the hip at Gaines' Mill, Virginia, June 27, 1862. Returned to duty prior to November 1, 1862. "Left at Gettysburg, Pennsylvania, sick" on July 3, 1863, and was captured by the enemy. Died in hospital at Gettysburg on October 20, 1863, of "febris typhoides."

HUFFMAN, JOHN F., Private
Resided in Catawba County where he enlisted at age 20, August 13, 1861. Present or accounted for until wounded severely at Gaines' Mill, Virginia, June 27, 1862. Failed to rejoin the company and was "supposed to be dead."

HUFFMAN, LEVI L., Private
Resided in Catawba County and was by occupation a farmer prior to enlisting in Catawba County at age 22, August 13, 1861. Captured at Winchester, Virginia, on or about December 2, 1862. Confined at Camp Chase, Ohio, March 4, 1863. Paroled and transferred to City Point, Virginia, where he was received April 1, 1863, for exchange. Wounded in the shoulder "in Virginia" in May, 1864. Returned to duty prior to November 1, 1864. Captured in hospital at Richmond, Virginia, April 3, 1865. Transferred to Newport News, Virginia, April 23, 1865. Released at Newport News on June 30, 1865, after taking the Oath of Allegiance.

HUFFMAN, MARCUS J., Private
Resided in Catawba County where he enlisted at age 18, March 15, 1862. Captured at Hanover Court House, Virginia, May 27, 1862. Confined at Fort Monroe, Virginia, and at Fort Columbus, New York Harbor. Died in hospital at Fort Columbus on July 1-2, 1862, of "febris typhoides."

HUNEYCUTT, SOLOMON, Private
Resided in Catawba County where he enlisted at age 36, March 15, 1862. Captured at Hanover Court House, Virginia, May 27, 1862. Confined at Fort Monroe, Virginia, and at Fort Columbus, New York Harbor. Paroled and transferred to Aiken's Landing, James River, Virginia, where he was received July 12, 1862, for exchange. Declared exchanged at Aiken's Landing on August 5, 1862. Returned to duty prior to November 1, 1862. Wounded at Chancellorsville, Virginia, on or about May 2, 1863. Returned to duty on an unspecified date. Reported on detail at Richmond, Virginia, during September, 1864-February, 1865, by reason of disability. Surrendered at Appomattox Court House, Virginia, April 9, 1865.

KAYLER, ALFRED A., Private
Enlisted in Catawba County on February 12, 1864, for the war. Wounded in the chin at Jericho Mills, Virginia, May 23, 1864. Returned to duty on December 3, 1864, but was retired to the Invalid Corps on December 28, 1864, by reason of disability. Detailed for hospital duty at Danville, Virginia, January 2, 1865. [Confederate medical records dated January, 1865, give his age as 19.]

KAYLER, GEORGE E., Sergeant
Resided in Catawba County where he enlisted on

August 13, 1861. Mustered in as Corporal and was promoted to Sergeant on September 1, 1862. Died in hospital at Jordan's Springs, near Winchester, Virginia, on or about July 19, 1863. Cause of death not reported. "A gallant soldier."

KILLIAN, CALVIN M., Private
Resided in Catawba County where he enlisted on August 13, 1861. Present or accounted for until wounded at Frayser's Farm, Virginia, June 30, 1862. Died on July 1, 1862, of wounds. Place of death not reported.

KILLIAN, CASPER E., Private
Enlisted in Catawba County on February 9, 1864, for the war. Surrendered at Appomattox Court House, Virginia, April 9, 1865.

KILLIAN, ELIJAH, Private
Resided in Catawba County and was by occupation a blacksmith prior to enlisting in Catawba County on August 13, 1861. Captured at Gettysburg, Pennsylvania, July 1-4, 1863. Confined at Davids Island, New York Harbor. Paroled and transferred to City Point, Virginia, where he was received September 8, 1863, for exchange. Returned to duty on an unspecified date. Paroled at Lynchburg, Virginia, April 13, 1865.

KILLIAN, JOSEPH E., Private
Born in Catawba County where he resided prior to enlisting in Catawba County at age 18, March 15, 1862. Captured at Hanover Court House, Virginia, May 27, 1862. Confined at Fort Monroe, Virginia, and at Fort Columbus, New York Harbor. Paroled and transferred to Aiken's Landing, James River, Virginia, where he was received July 12, 1862, for exchange. Declared exchanged at Aiken's Landing on August 5, 1862. Returned to duty prior to November 1, 1862. Wounded at Gettysburg, Pennsylvania, July 1-3, 1863. Returned to duty on an unspecified date. Killed at Reams' Station, Virginia, August 25, 1864.

KINCAID, DAVID, 1st Sergeant
Resided in Lincoln County and enlisted at Camp Fisher on August 26, 1861. Mustered in as Private and was promoted to Corporal on February 27, 1862. Promoted to 1st Sergeant on April 14, 1862. Wounded at Ox Hill, Virginia, September 1, 1862. Returned to duty on or about March 20, 1863. Wounded at Chancellorsville, Virginia, May 1-3, 1863. Returned to duty on an unspecified date. Wounded and captured at Gettysburg, Pennsylvania, July 1-2, 1863. Hospitalized at Gettysburg until transferred to Chester, Pennsylvania, where he arrived on July 17, 1863. Paroled at Chester and transferred to City Point, Virginia, where he was received September 23, 1863, for exchange. No further records.

LAEL, ABEL, Private
Born in Catawba County where he resided as a farmer prior to enlisting in Catawba County at age 18, August 12, 1863, for the war. Surrendered at Appomattox Court House, Virginia, April 9, 1865.

LAEL, CICERO, Private
Resided in Catawba County where he enlisted at age 19, March 15, 1862. Wounded at Ox Hill, Virginia, September 1, 1862. Returned to duty prior to November 1, 1862. Wounded and captured at Gravel Hill,

Virginia, on or about July 28, 1864. Confined at Point Lookout, Maryland, until transferred to Elmira, New York, August 8, 1864. Died at Elmira on January 4, 1865, of "pneumonia."

LAEL, POLYCARP, Private
Resided in Catawba County where he enlisted at age 18, March 9, 1863, for the war. Wounded in the thigh at Spotsylvania Court House, Virginia, May 12, 1864. Returned to duty on November 6, 1864. Transferred to Company H of this regiment on February 1, 1865.

LEWIS, JAMES, Private
Place and date of enlistment not reported. Paroled at Salisbury on May 12, 1865.

LINEBARGER, AVERY P., Private
Resided in Catawba County where he enlisted at age 18, March 15, 1862. Wounded at Shepherdstown, Virginia, September 20, 1862. Returned to duty prior to January 1, 1863. Captured at or near Deep Bottom, Virginia, on or about July 27, 1864. Confined at Point Lookout, Maryland, until transferred to Elmira, New York, August 16, 1864. Died at Elmira on September 21, 1864, of "typhoid fever."

LINEBARGER, FREDERICK MIDDLETON, Private
Resided in Catawba County where he enlisted on October 25, 1864, for the war. Captured in hospital at Richmond, Virginia, April 3, 1865. Transferred to Newport News, Virginia, April 23, 1865. Released at Newport News on June 30, 1865, after taking the Oath of Allegiance. [North Carolina pension records indicate he was "slightly wounded once or twice."]

LINEBARGER, JACOB A., Private
Previously served in Company K, 23rd Regiment N.C. Troops (13th Regiment N.C. Volunteers). Transferred to this company on March 21, 1863. Wounded at Chancellorsville, Virginia, May 2-3, 1863. Returned to duty prior to July 1-3, 1863, when he was wounded at Gettysburg, Pennsylvania. Died on July 5, 1863, of wounds. Place of death not reported.

LINEBARGER, LEVI M., 1st Sergeant
Resided in Catawba County where he enlisted at age 18, March 15, 1862. Mustered in as Private and was promoted to Sergeant on January 22, 1863. Promoted to 1st Sergeant in May, 1863-October, 1864. Present or accounted for through February, 1865.

LINEBARGER, M. MONROE, Private
Enlisted in Catawba County on November 16, 1863, for the war. Surrendered at Appomattox Court House, Virginia, April 9, 1865.

LINK, EPHRAIM M., Private
Resided in Catawba County where he enlisted on March 15, 1862. Captured at Hanover Court House, Virginia, May 27, 1862. Confined at Fort Monroe, Virginia, and at Fort Columbus, New York Harbor. Paroled and transferred to Aiken's Landing, James River, Virginia, where he was received July 12, 1862, for exchange. Declared exchanged at Aiken's Landing on August 5, 1862. Returned to duty prior to November 1, 1862. Wounded on July 1-3, 1863, at Gettysburg, Pennsylvania, and "left there." Company records indicate he was presumed to have died of wounds received at Gettysburg.

LITTLE, JOSHUA A., Sergeant
Born in Catawba County* where he resided prior to enlisting in Catawba County at age 20, August 13, 1861. Mustered in as Corporal and was promoted to Sergeant on February 17, 1862. Wounded at Ox Hill, Virginia, September 1, 1862. Returned to duty prior to March 1, 1863. Wounded in the right thigh and captured at or near Gravel Hill, Virginia, July 28, 1864. Right leg amputated. Died in hospital at City Point, Virginia, October 9, 1864, of wounds.

LITTLE, JUNIUS PINKNEY, Private
Resided in Catawba County where he enlisted at age 16, August 13, 1861. Wounded at Frayser's Farm, Virginia, June 30, 1862. Returned to duty prior to November 1, 1862. Wounded at Chancellorsville, Virginia, May 3, 1863, "while gallantly bearing the colors in the charge on the [enemy's] works." Returned to duty on an unspecified date. Appointed Ensign (1st Lieutenant) on May 2, 1864, and transferred to the Field and Staff of this regiment. [Complimented for gallantry while carrying the regimental colors at Hanover Court House, Mechanicsville, Cold Harbor, Frayser's Farm, and Fredericksburg.]

MARTIN, JAMES W., Private
Resided in Lincoln County and enlisted at Camp Fisher on September 5, 1861. Wounded in the thigh at the Battle of Second Manassas, Virginia, August 27-30, 1862. Leg amputated. Hospitalized at Lynchburg, Virginia, where he died on September 27, 1862, of wounds and/or "typhoid fever." Roll of Honor indicates that he was a "most gallant soldier."

MARTIN, ROBERT N. M., Private
Resided in Lincoln County and enlisted at Camp Fisher on September 5, 1861. Captured at Hanover Court House, Virginia, May 27, 1862. Confined at Fort Monroe, Virginia, and at Fort Columbus, New York Harbor. Died in hospital at Fort Columbus on July 16, 1862, of "febris typhoides."

MARTIN, WILLIAM A., Private
Resided in Catawba County where he enlisted at age 25, August 13, 1861. Wounded "by an exploding shell from a gunboat" near Frayser's Farm, Virginia, June 30, 1862. Returned to duty prior to November 1, 1862. Wounded in the left arm and shoulder at Gettysburg, Pennsylvania, July 3, 1863. Returned to duty on an unspecified date. Wounded in the head, pelvis, and right leg near Petersburg, Virginia, on or about August 18, 1864. Returned to duty on September 27, 1864. Present or accounted for until he surrendered at Appomattox Court House, Virginia, April 9, 1865. [At Fredericksburg, Virginia, December 13, 1862, Private Martin "cooly sat on the (railroad) track and called to his comrades to watch the Yankee colors, then fired and down they went. This was done repeatedly."]

MILLER, CALEB, Corporal
Resided in Catawba County where he enlisted on March 15, 1862. Mustered in as Private and was promoted to Corporal on April 15, 1862. Died at Richmond, Virginia, December 1, 1862, of "smallpox."

MILLER, DAVID E., Private
Resided in Catawba County where he enlisted on March 14, 1863, for the war. Wounded at Wilderness,

Virginia, May 5, 1864. Retired to the Invalid Corps on December 28, 1864, by reason of disability.

MILLER, HIRAM A., Private
Resided in Catawba County where he enlisted on March 15, 1862. Wounded in the hand at Frayser's Farm, Virginia, June 30, 1862. Returned to duty prior to January 1, 1863. Wounded at Chancellorsville, Virginia, May 2-3, 1863. Returned to duty prior to July 1-5, 1863, when he was wounded and captured at Gettysburg, Pennsylvania. Hospitalized at Davids Island, New York Harbor, July 17-24, 1863. Paroled at Davids Island and transferred to City Point, Virginia, where he was received September 16, 1863, for exchange. Returned to duty on an unspecified date. Transferred to the C.S. Navy on April 3, 1864.

MILLER, MARCUS, Private
Born in Catawba County where he resided prior to enlisting in Catawba County on August 13, 1861. Killed at Spotsylvania Court House, Virginia, May 12, 1864.

MILLER, SAMUEL E., Private
Born in Catawba County where he resided as a farmer prior to enlisting at Camp Fisher on September 9, 1861. Died at Lynchburg, Virginia, January 6, 1863, of "diarrhoea chron[ic]" and/or "phthisis pulmonalis."

MILLER, WILLIAM J., Private
Resided in Catawba County where he enlisted on August 13, 1861. Killed at Gettysburg, Pennsylvania, July 3, 1863. "A most gallant soldier."

MOORE, JOHN A., Private
Resided in Catawba County where he enlisted on August 13, 1861. Wounded at Hanover Court House, Virginia, May 27, 1862. Died at Richmond, Virginia, on or about June 10-11, 1862, of wounds.

PITTS, CONRAD, Private
Born in Catawba County where he resided prior to enlisting in Catawba County on August 13, 1861. Wounded "in Virginia" May 5-14, 1864. Hospitalized at Staunton, Virginia, where he died on June 17, 1864, of wounds.

PITTS, W. HENRY, Private
Resided in Catawba County where he enlisted on August 13, 1861. Died in hospital at Farmville, Virginia, August 31, 1862, of "typhoid fever."

POLK, JOHN, ———
Negro. Served as "body guard to Colonel Samuel Lowe" of this regiment.

POLLARD, HIRAM, Private
Resided in Catawba County and enlisted at Camp Fisher at age 34, September 9, 1861. Wounded in both arms at the Battle of Second Manassas, Virginia, August 27-30, 1862. Returned to duty prior to January 1, 1863. Wounded in the arm "in Virginia" in May, 1864. Returned to duty prior to November 1, 1864. Captured near Petersburg, Virginia, April 2, 1865. Confined at Fort Delaware, Delaware, until released on June 19, 1865, after taking the Oath of Allegiance.

POOVEY, A. LEVI, Private
Resided in Catawba County where he enlisted at age 18, January 27, 1863, for the war. Wounded in the face and

right arm and captured at Gettysburg, Pennsylvania, July 1-5, 1863. Hospitalized at Gettysburg until transferred to Davids Island, New York Harbor, July 17-24, 1863. Paroled at Davids Island and transferred to City Point, Virginia, where he was received September 8, 1863, for exchange. Returned to duty on an unspecified date. Paroled at Farmville, Virginia, April 11-21, 1865.

POOVEY, DAVID A., Private
Resided in Catawba County where he enlisted at age 22, March 15, 1862. Captured at Hanover Court House, Virginia, May 27, 1862. Confined at Fort Columbus, New York Harbor. Paroled and exchanged on an unspecified date. Returned to duty prior to November 1, 1862. Wounded at Chancellorsville, Virginia, May 1-3, 1863. Returned to duty prior to July 3, 1863, when he was reported missing and was "supposed to have been killed" at Gettysburg, Pennsylvania. No further records.

POOVEY, HENRY F., Private
Resided in Catawba County where he enlisted on March 14, 1863, for the war. Killed at Gettysburg, Pennsylvania, July 3, 1863.

POOVEY, JOSIAH A., Sr., Private
Resided in Catawba County where he enlisted at age 19, March 15, 1862. Wounded at Gettysburg, Pennsylvania, July 3, 1863. Returned to duty on an unspecified date. Surrendered at Appomattox Court House, Virginia, April 9, 1865.

POOVEY, JULIUS A., Private
Resided in Catawba County where he enlisted at age 18, January 27, 1863, for the war. Wounded in the left leg at Chancellorsville, Virginia, May 1, 1863. Returned to duty on July 1, 1863. Wounded in the head at Wilderness, Virginia, on or about May 3, 1864. Returned to duty on an unspecified date. Surrendered at Appomattox Court House, Virginia, April 9, 1865.

POOVEY, LAWSON A., Private
Enlisted in Catawba County on May 6, 1864, for the war. Surrendered at Appomattox Court House, Virginia, April 9, 1865.

POOVEY, TAYLOR, Private
Enlisted in Catawba County on September 1, 1864, for the war. Surrendered at Appomattox Court House, Virginia, April 9, 1865.

POOVEY, WILLIAM F., Private
Resided in Catawba County where he enlisted at age 35, September 1, 1862, for the war. Died in hospital at Lynchburg, Virginia, on or about December 6, 1862, of "febris typhoides."

POOVY, HIRAM H., Private
Resided in Catawba County where he enlisted at age 24, March 15, 1862. Wounded in the right arm at Jones' Farm, Virginia, September 30, 1864. Returned to duty on November 18, 1864. Surrendered at Appomattox Court House, Virginia, April 9, 1865.

POOVY, WILLIAM H. H., Private
Resided in Catawba County where he enlisted at age 20, August 13, 1861. Wounded at Shepherdstown, Virginia, September 20, 1862. Returned to duty prior to March 1, 1863. Surrendered at Appomattox Court House,

Virginia, April 9, 1865.

PROPST, ALFRED, Private
Resided in Catawba County where he enlisted on August 13, 1861. Died in hospital at Lynchburg, Virginia, January 29, 1863, of "typ[hoi]d pneumonia." "He was a brave boy."

PRYOR, DAVID, Private
Resided in Lincoln County and enlisted at Camp Fisher on August 26, 1861. Captured at Hanover Court House, Virginia, May 27, 1862. Confined at Fort Monroe, Virginia, and at Fort Columbus, New York Harbor. Paroled and transferred to Aiken's Landing, James River, Virginia, where he was received July 12, 1862, for exchange. Declared exchanged at Aiken's Landing on August 5, 1862. Returned to duty prior to November 1, 1862. Reported missing and was "supposed to have been killed" at Gettysburg, Pennsylvania, July 3, 1863.

PRYOR, SAMUEL, Private
Resided in Lincoln County and enlisted at Camp Fisher on August 26, 1861. Captured at Hanover Court House, Virginia, May 27, 1862. Confined at Fort Monroe, Virginia, and at Fort Columbus, New York Harbor. Paroled and transferred to Aiken's Landing, James River, Virginia, where he was received July 12, 1862, for exchange. Declared exchanged at Aiken's Landing on August 5, 1862. Returned to duty prior to November 1, 1862. Wounded and captured at Gettysburg, Pennsylvania, July 1-4, 1863. Hospitalized at Davids Island, New York Harbor. Paroled at Davids Island and transferred to City Point, Virginia, where he was received September 16, 1863, for exchange. Returned to duty on an unspecified date. Captured at the Appomattox River, Virginia, April 3, 1865. Confined at Hart's Island, New York Harbor, April 11, 1865. Transferred to Davids Island on July 1, 1865. Released on July 11, 1865, after taking the Oath of Allegiance.

PRYOR, SIDNEY, Private
Born in Lincoln County where he resided as a farmer prior to enlisting in Catawba County at age 18, March 15, 1862. Discharged on June 15, 1862, by reason of "anemia accompanied with general debility."

PUNCH, JOSEPH L., Private
Born in Catawba County where he resided as a farmer prior to enlisting in Catawba County on August 13, 1861. Discharged on June 15, 1862, by reason of "general muscular debility." Discharge certificate gives his age as 19. [May have served later in Company A, 23rd Regiment N.C. Troops (13th Regiment N.C. Volunteers).]

PUNCH, ROBERT W., Private
Resided in Catawba County and enlisted at Camp Fisher on September 9, 1861. Wounded at Hanover Court House, Virginia, May 27, 1862. Returned to duty prior to November 1, 1862. Wounded in the abdomen at Fredericksburg, Virginia, December 13, 1862. Hospitalized at Richmond, Virginia, where he died on December 16, 1862, of wounds. "A good soldier."

PUNCH, WILLIAM S., Private
Resided in Catawba County and enlisted at Camp Fisher on September 9, 1861. Captured at Hanover Court House, Virginia, May 27, 1862. Confined at Fort Monroe, Virginia, and at Fort Columbus, New York

Harbor. Paroled and transferred to Aiken's Landing, James River, Virginia, where he was received July 12, 1862, for exchange. Declared exchanged at Aiken's Landing on August 5, 1862. Returned to duty prior to November 1, 1862. Died "at home" on July 15, 1863, of disease.

RADER, WILLIAM PINKNEY, Private
Resided in Catawba County where he enlisted on August 13, 1861. Captured at Hanover Court House, Virginia, May 27, 1862. Confined at Fort Monroe, Virginia, and at Fort Columbus, New York Harbor. Paroled and transferred to Aiken's Landing, James River, Virginia, where he was received July 12, 1862, for exchange. Declared exchanged at Aiken's Landing on August 5, 1862. Returned to duty prior to January 1, 1863. Surrendered at Appomattox Court House, Virginia, April 9, 1865.

REYNOLDS, F. HARVEY, Private
Resided in Catawba County where he enlisted on March 15, 1862. Died in hospital at Liberty, Virginia, November 19, 1862, of disease.

REYNOLDS, JAMES A., Private
Resided in Catawba County and enlisted at Camp Fisher on September 2, 1861. Captured at Hanover Court House, Virginia, May 27, 1862. Confined at Fort Monroe, Virginia, and at Fort Columbus, New York Harbor. Paroled and transferred to Aiken's Landing, James River, Virginia, where he was received July 12, 1862, for exchange. Declared exchanged at Aiken's Landing on August 5, 1862. Returned to duty prior to November 1, 1862. Reported missing and was "supposed to have been killed" at Gettysburg, Pennsylvania, July 3, 1863.

RICK, JOHN, Private
Enlisted in Catawba County on October 17, 1864, for the war. Present or accounted for through February, 1865.

RINK, HENRY, Private
Resided in Catawba County where he enlisted on March 15, 1862. Wounded in the forearm and captured at Hanover Court House, Virginia, May 27, 1862. Hospitalized at Fort Monroe, Virginia, where he died on July 6, 1862, of wounds. [Records of the Federal Provost Marshal dated May-July, 1862, give his age as 32.]

SEABOCH, GEORGE W., Private
Resided in Catawba County and enlisted at Camp Fisher at age 33, September 9, 1861. Captured at Hanover Court House, Virginia, May 27, 1862. Confined at Fort Monroe, Virginia, and at Fort Columbus, New York Harbor. Paroled and transferred to Aiken's Landing, James River, Virginia, where he was received July 12, 1862, for exchange. Declared exchanged at Aiken's Landing on August 5, 1862. Returned to duty prior to March 1, 1863. Present or accounted for through February, 1865.

SEABOCH, JOHN PINKNEY, Private
Resided in Catawba County and enlisted at Camp Fisher at age 20, September 9, 1861. Present or accounted for until killed at Gaines' Mill, Virginia, June 27, 1862.

SEABOCH, WILLIAM H., Private
Born in Catawba County where he resided prior to enlisting in Catawba County at age 18, March 15, 1862. Captured at Hanover Court House, Virginia, May 27, 1862. Confined at Fort Monroe, Virginia, and at Fort Columbus, New York Harbor. Paroled and transferred to Aiken's Landing, James River, Virginia, where he was received July 12, 1862, for exchange. Declared exchanged at Aiken's Landing on August 5, 1862. Returned to duty prior to November 1, 1862. Killed at Jones' Farm, Virginia, September 30, 1864.

SEITZ, LABAN M., Private
Born in Catawba County where he resided as a farmer prior to enlisting in Catawba County on March 15, 1862. Wounded in the right hand at Sharpsburg, Maryland, September 17, 1862. Two fingers amputated. Discharged on January 26, 1863, by reason of disability.

SEITZ, MARCUS, Private
Resided in Catawba County where he enlisted on March 15, 1862. Hospitalized at Richmond, Virginia, September 27, 1862, with a gunshot wound. Place and date wounded not reported. Returned to duty in January-February, 1863. Mortally wounded at Chancellorsville, Virginia, May 3, 1863, and died the same date.

SETZER, FRANKLIN A., Private
Resided in Catawba County where he enlisted on August 13, 1861. Mustered in as Sergeant but was reduced to ranks on or about February 28, 1862. Captured at Hanover Court House, Virginia, May 27, 1862. Confined at Fort Monroe, Virginia, and at Fort Columbus, New York Harbor. Paroled and transferred to Aiken's Landing, James River, Virginia, where he was received July 12, 1862, for exchange. Declared exchanged at Aiken's Landing on August 5, 1862. Returned to duty prior to March 1, 1863. Present or accounted for through February, 1865.

SHORT, JOHN, Private
Resided in Catawba County and enlisted at Camp Fisher at age 18, September 2, 1861. Captured at Hanover Court House, Virginia, May 27-28, 1862. Confined at Fort Monroe, Virginia, and at Fort Columbus, New York Harbor. Died at Fort Columbus on July 30, 1862. Cause of death not reported.

SIGMAN, ALFRED P., Private
Resided at "Hickory Station" and enlisted in Catawba County on April 14, 1864, for the war. Captured at Spotsylvania Court House, Virginia, May 12, 1864. Confined at Point Lookout, Maryland, until transferred to Elmira, New York, August 10, 1864. Released at Elmira on June 27, 1865, after taking the Oath of Allegiance.

SIGMAN, ISAIAH, Private
Resided in Catawba County where he enlisted on March 15, 1862. Died at Charlottesville, Virginia, May 29, 1862, of "typhoid pneumonia."

SIGMAN, MARTIN M., Private
Resided in Catawba County where he enlisted on March 15, 1862. Wounded at Cedar Mountain, Virginia, August 9, 1862. Returned to duty prior to January 1, 1863. Captured at Spotsylvania Court House, Virginia, May 12, 1864. Confined at Point Lookout,

Maryland, until transferred to Elmira, New York, August 10, 1864. Died at Elmira on November 14, 1864, of "chronic diarrhoea."

SIGMAN, MAXWELL A., Corporal
Resided in Catawba County where he enlisted on August 13, 1861. Mustered in as Private. Captured at Hanover Court House, Virginia, May 27, 1862. Confined at Fort Monroe, Virginia, and at Fort Columbus, New York Harbor. Paroled and transferred to Aiken's Landing, James River, Virginia, where he was received July 12, 1862, for exchange. Declared exchanged at Aiken's Landing on August 5, 1862. Returned to duty prior to November 1, 1862. Promoted to Corporal on March 25, 1863. Wounded in the left leg and captured at Gettysburg, Pennsylvania, July 3-5, 1863. Hospitalized at Davids Island, New York Harbor, July 17-24, 1863. Paroled at Davids Island and transferred to City Point, Virginia, where he was received October 28, 1863, for exchange. Company records do not indicate whether he returned to duty; however, he was retired to the Invalid Corps on April 15, 1864, by reason of disability.

SIMMONS, NOAH, Private
Resided in Catawba County where he enlisted on March 14, 1863, for the war. Captured at Wilderness, Virginia, May 12, 1864. Confined at Point Lookout, Maryland, until transferred to Elmira, New York, August 10, 1864. Died at Elmira on April 10, 1865, of "chro[nic] diarr[hoea]."

SIPE, DAVID, Private
Resided in Catawba County where he enlisted on August 13, 1861. Killed at Gettysburg, Pennsylvania, July 3, 1863.

SIZEMORE, JOHN E., Private
Resided in Catawba County where he enlisted on August 13, 1861. Wounded and captured at Hanover Court House, Virginia, May 27, 1862. Confined at Fort Monroe, Virginia, where he died on or about June 30, 1862, of wounds. [Records of the Federal Provost Marshal dated May-June, 1862, give his age as 32.]

SMYER, JONES S., Musician
Resided in Catawba County and enlisted at Camp Fisher at age 25, September 2, 1861. Mustered in as Private and was promoted to Musician in January-April, 1862. Wounded and captured at Chancellorsville, Virginia, May 1-4, 1863. Died at Governor's Island, New York Harbor, of wounds. Date of death not reported.

SPENCER, ELI, Private
Resided in Catawba County where he enlisted on August 13, 1861. Wounded at Cedar Mountain, Virginia, August 9, 1862. Returned to duty prior to January 1, 1863. Present or accounted for through November 20, 1863.

SPENCER, J. PINKNEY, Private
Resided in Catawba County where he enlisted on August 13, 1861. Wounded in the hand at Gaines' Mill, Virginia, June 27, 1862. Returned to duty prior to November 1, 1862. Present or accounted for until he surrendered at Appomattox Court House, Virginia, April 9, 1865. [North Carolina pension records indicate he was wounded at Turkey Ridge, near Richmond,

Virginia, on an unspecified date.]

SPENCER, SIDNEY E., Private
Enlisted in Catawba County on February 17, 1864, for the war. Present or accounted for until he surrendered at Appomattox Court House, Virginia, April 9, 1865.

STARR, EDMOND JONES, Private
Born in Catawba County and enlisted in Rowan County on February 2, 1864, for the war. Hospitalized at Richmond, Virginia, June 16, 1864, with a gunshot wound. Place and date wounded not reported. Died in hospital at Richmond on July 5, 1864, of wounds and/or disease.

STARR, ELON M., Private
Resided in Catawba County where he enlisted on March 14, 1863, for the war. Captured in hospital at Richmond, Virginia, April 3, 1865. Paroled at Richmond on or about April 25, 1865.

STARR, J. ABEL, Private
Resided in Catawba County where he enlisted on March 14, 1863, for the war. Surrendered at Appomattox Court House, Virginia, April 9, 1865.

STARR, JACOB S. D., Private
Resided in Catawba County and enlisted in Rowan County on February 2, 1864, for the war. Captured on the South Side Railroad, near Petersburg, Virginia, April 2, 1865. Confined at Hart's Island, New York Harbor, until released on June 17, 1865, after taking the Oath of Allegiance.

SUMMIT, HEGLAR P., Private
Resided in Catawba County and enlisted at Camp Fisher at age 21, September 2, 1861. Captured by the enemy in an unspecified engagement and was confined at an unspecified Federal prison on September 14, 1862. Paroled and transferred to Aiken's Landing, James River, Virginia, where he was received September 27, 1862, for exchange. Declared exchanged at Aiken's Landing on November 10, 1862. Returned to duty prior to March 1, 1863. Captured at Spotsylvania Court House, Virginia, May 12, 1864. Confined at Point Lookout, Maryland, until transferred to Elmira, New York, August 10, 1864. Died at Elmira on November 16, 1864, of "chronic diarrhoea."

THRONEBURG, JONATHAN S., Private
Resided in Catawba County and enlisted at Camp Stokes on October 24, 1864, for the war. Present or accounted for until captured in hospital at Richmond, Virginia, April 3, 1865. Transferred to Newport News, Virginia, April 23, 1865. Released on June 30, 1865, after taking the Oath of Allegiance.

TOWNSON, AARON ELIJAH, Private
Born in Catawba County where he resided prior to enlisting in Catawba County at age 17, March 15, 1862. Captured at Hanover Court House, Virginia, May 27, 1862. Confined at Fort Monroe, Virginia, and at Fort Columbus, New York Harbor. Paroled and transferred to Aiken's Landing, James River, Virginia, where he was received July 12, 1862, for exchange. Declared exchanged at Aiken's Landing on August 5, 1862. Returned to duty prior to November 1, 1862. Surrendered at Appomattox Court House, Virginia, April 9, 1865.

TOWNSON, SOLOMON, Private
Resided in Catawba County where he enlisted at age 25, March 15, 1862. Captured at Hanover Court House, Virginia, May 27, 1862. Confined at Fort Monroe, Virginia, and at Fort Columbus, New York Harbor. Paroled and transferred to Aiken's Landing, James River, Virginia, where he was received July 12, 1862, for exchange. Declared exchanged at Aiken's Landing on August 5, 1862. Died in hospital "in Virginia" on August 10, 1862, of "febris typhoides."

TURBYFILL, ELAM A., Private
Resided in Catawba County where he enlisted at age 19, March 15, 1862. Died in hospital at Richmond, Virginia, June 5-12, 1862. Cause of death not reported.

TURBYFILL, ELKANA, Corporal
Born in Catawba County* where he resided prior to enlisting in Catawba County at age 32, August 13, 1861. Mustered in as Private and was promoted to Corporal on September 1, 1862. Wounded at Chancellorsville, Virginia, May 2-3, 1863. Company records do not indicate whether he returned to duty. Died "at home" on June 28, 1864. Cause of death not reported.

TURBYFILL, JOHN L., Musician
Resided in Catawba County and enlisted at Camp Fisher at age 21, September 10, 1861. Mustered in as Private. Wounded at Mechanicsville, Virginia, June 26, 1862. Returned to duty prior to November 1, 1862. Promoted to Musician in May, 1863-October, 1864. Surrendered at Appomattox Court House, Virginia, April 9, 1865.

TURBYFILL, JONAS A., Private
Resided in Catawba County where he enlisted at age 25, August 13, 1861. Present or accounted for through April, 1862. No further records.

TURNER, DAVID H., Private
Enlisted at Camp Stokes on October 31, 1864, for the war. Present or accounted for through February, 1865. [North Carolina pension records indicate he was "presumed dead on retreat from Petersburg, Virginia," April 4, 1865.]

TURNER, GEORGE L., Private
Born in Catawba County* where he resided prior to enlisting in Catawba County at age 21, August 13, 1861. Died in hospital at Lynchburg, Virginia, June 14, 1863, of "pneumonia."

TURNER, JOHN, Private
Born in Catawba County where he enlisted on August 6, 1864, for the war. Died in hospital at Richmond, Virginia, October 27, 1864, of "febris typhoides."

TURNER, LABAN CICERO, Private
Resided in Catawba County and was by occupation a civil engineer prior to enlisting in Catawba County at age 18, March 15, 1862. Present or accounted for through February, 1865.

WAGNER, BENJAMIN, Private
Resided in Catawba County where he enlisted on March 14, 1863, for the war. Killed at Chancellorsville, Virginia, May 3, 1863.

WAGNER, NOAH P., Private
Born in Catawba County where he resided prior to enlisting in Catawba County at age 20 on March 15, 1862. Captured at Hanover Court House, Virginia, May 27, 1862. Confined at Fort Monroe, Virginia, and at Fort Columbus, New York Harbor. Paroled and transferred to Aiken's Landing, James River, Virginia, where he was received July 12, 1862, for exchange. Declared exchanged at Aiken's Landing on August 5, 1862. Returned to duty prior to November 1, 1862. Died at Richmond, Virginia, July 24, 1864, of disease.

WAGNER, THOMAS J., Private
Resided in Catawba County where he enlisted at age 22, August 13, 1861. Captured at Hanover Court House, Virginia, May 27, 1862. Confined at Fort Monroe, Virginia, and at Fort Columbus, New York Harbor. Paroled and transferred to Aiken's Landing, James River, Virginia, where he was received July 12, 1862, for exchange. Declared exchanged at Aiken's Landing on August 5, 1862. Returned to duty prior to November 1, 1862. Wounded at Gravel Hill, Virginia, July 28, 1864. Reported absent wounded through February, 1865. Captured in hospital at Richmond, Virginia, April 3, 1865. Transferred to Newport News, Virginia, April 23, 1865. Released on June 14, 1865, after taking the Oath of Allegiance.

WATTS, RUFUS, Private
Born in Catawba County* where he resided as a farmer prior to enlisting at Camp Fisher on September 2, 1861. Present or accounted for until discharged on April 25, 1862, by reason of "dyspepsia." Discharge certificate gives his age as 33.

WILSON, BENJAMIN F., Private
Resided in Catawba County and enlisted at Camp Fisher on September 10, 1861. Died in hospital at Lynchburg, Virginia, May 30, 1862, of "chr[onic] diarrhoea."

WILSON, H., Private
Place and date of enlistment not reported. Captured near Petersburg, Virginia, April 2, 1865. Confined at Fort Delaware, Delaware, April 4, 1865. No further records.

WRIGHT, SAMUEL, Private
Resided in Catawba County where he enlisted at age 28, March 15, 1862. Wounded at Chancellorsville, Virginia, May 2-3, 1863. Listed as a deserter on an unspecified date. Returned to duty on September 23, 1863. Wounded at Spotsylvania Court House, Virginia, May 21, 1864. Returned to duty on September 5, 1864. Captured near Petersburg, Virginia, April 2, 1865. Confined at Fort Delaware, Delaware, until released on June 19, 1865, after taking the Oath of Allegiance.

YOUNT, ABEL M., Private
Resided in Catawba County where he enlisted on August 13, 1861. Present or accounted for until he surrendered at Appomattox Court House, Virginia, April 9, 1865.

YOUNT, DANIEL P., Private
Born in Catawba County where he resided as a farmer prior to enlisting in Catawba County on March 15, 1862. Discharged on June 15, 1862, by reason of "general debility and a want of physical ability for active

service." Discharge certificate gives his age as 19. Later served in Company E, 12th Regiment N.C. Troops (2nd Regiment N.C. Volunteers).

YOUNT, DAVID, Private
Born in Catawba County* where he resided as a farmer prior to enlisting in Catawba County at age 41, August 13, 1861. Discharged on May 1, 1862, under the provisions of the Conscription Act. Later served in Company E, 12th Regiment N.C. Troops (2nd Regiment N.C. Volunteers).

YOUNT, LABAN A., Private
Resided in Catawba County and enlisted at Camp Fisher on September 9, 1861. Killed at Chancellorsville, Virginia, May 3, 1863. "A most gallant soldier."

YOUNT, LAWSON M., Private
Born in Catawba County* where he resided as a farmer prior to enlisting in Catawba County at age 30, August 13, 1861. Wounded in the head at Gaines' Mill, Virginia, June 27, 1862. Discharged on December 5, 1862, by reason of "general debility and rheumatism."

YOUNT, NOAH, Private
Resided in Catawba County where he enlisted on March 14, 1863, for the war. Wounded at Chancellorsville, Virginia, May 2-3, 1863. Returned to duty on an unspecified date. Reported on detail as "Wagon Sergeant" from July 1, 1864, through February, 1865. Surrendered at Appomattox Court House, Virginia, April 9, 1865.

COMPANY D

This company, known as the "Stanly Yankee Hunters," was raised in Stanly County and enlisted at Albemarle. It was mustered into service on July 29, 1861, and assigned to the 28th Regiment as Company D. After joining the regiment the company functioned as a part of the regiment, and its history for the war period is reported as a part of the regimental history.

The information contained in the following roster of the company was compiled principally from company muster rolls for July 29, 1861-April, 1862; June 30-December, 1862; and September, 1864-February, 1865. No company muster rolls were found for May-June 29, 1862; January, 1863-August, 1864; or for the period after February, 1865. Valuable information was obtained also from primary records such as the Roll of Honor, medical records, prisoner of war records, discharge certificates, and pension applications, and from secondary sources such as postwar rosters and histories, cemetery records, and records of the United Daughters of the Confederacy.

OFFICERS

CAPTAINS

MONTGOMERY, WILLIAM JAMES
Resided in Stanly County where he enlisted at age 26. Appointed Captain on July 29, 1861. Present or accounted for until appointed Major on June 12, 1862, and transferred to the Field and Staff of this regiment.

PARKER, DURANT A.
Resided in Stanly County where he enlisted at age 33. Appointed 1st Lieutenant on July 29, 1861, and was promoted to Captain on June 12, 1862. Appointed

Assistant Quartermaster (Captain) on May 2, 1863, and transferred to the Field and Staff of this regiment.

RANDLE, JOHN W.
Resided in Stanly County where he enlisted at age 23. Appointed 2nd Lieutenant on July 29, 1861, and was promoted to 1st Lieutenant on June 12, 1862. Promoted to Captain on May 2, 1863. Wounded at Gettysburg, Pennsylvania, July 1-3, 1863. Died on July 10, 1863, of wounds. Place of death not reported.

EUDY, MOSES J.
Resided in Stanly County and enlisted at age 25, July 29, 1861. Mustered in as Corporal and was promoted to Sergeant in February, 1863. Appointed 2nd Lieutenant on August 1, 1863, and was promoted to Captain on September 27, 1863. Hospitalized at Charlottesville, Virginia, May 12, 1864, with a gunshot wound in the left foot. Place and date wounded not reported. Returned to duty prior to November 1, 1864. Present or accounted for until captured near Petersburg, Virginia, April 2, 1865. Confined at Old Capitol Prison, Washington, D.C., until transferred to Johnson's Island, Ohio, April 9, 1865. Released at Johnson's Island on June 18, 1865, after taking the Oath of Allegiance.

LIEUTENANTS

LOWDER, LINDSEY, 3rd Lieutenant
Resided in Stanly County where he enlisted at age 26, July 29, 1861. Mustered in as Sergeant and was elected 3rd Lieutenant on July 27, 1862. Wounded in the left leg at Chancellorsville, Virginia, May 3, 1863. Company records do not indicate whether he returned to duty. Resigned on April 11, 1864, by reason of disability from wounds received at Chancellorsville. "He was a good soldier."

MOOSE, EDMUND, 1st Lieutenant
Resided in Stanly County where he enlisted at age 28, July 29, 1861. Mustered in as Sergeant. Promoted to Quartermaster Sergeant in May-December, 1862, and transferred to the Field and Staff of this regiment. Appointed 2nd Lieutenant on March 28, 1863, and transferred back to this company. Promoted to 1st Lieutenant on May 2, 1863. Wounded and captured at Gettysburg, Pennsylvania, July 1-5, 1863. Hospitalized at Baltimore, Maryland. Transferred to hospital at Chester, Pennsylvania, July 20, 1863. Died in hospital at Chester on September 27, 1863, of "exhaustion."

PARKER, HOWELL A., 1st Lieutenant
Resided in Stanly County where he enlisted at age 18, July 29, 1861. Mustered in as Private and was promoted to Corporal on November 16, 1862. Promoted to Sergeant in February, 1863, and was promoted to 1st Sergeant on August 1, 1863. Elected 2nd Lieutenant on June 1, 1864, and was promoted to 1st Lieutenant in January-February, 1865. Wounded in action on an unspecified date subsequent to February 28, 1865. Reported in hospital at Richmond, Virginia, April 2, 1865. Captured in hospital at Richmond on April 3, 1865, and was paroled on May 11, 1865.

RAMSEY, GILLIAM O., 2nd Lieutenant
Resided in Stanly County where he enlisted at age 22. Appointed 3rd Lieutenant on July 29, 1861, and was promoted to 2nd Lieutenant on July 12, 1862. Present or accounted for until he resigned on December 28, 1862,

by reason of "chronic rheumatism."

NONCOMMISSIONED OFFICERS
AND PRIVATES

AKARD, MORGAN E., Private
Resided in Alexander County and enlisted at Camp Holmes on December 3, 1864, for the war. Captured near Petersburg, Virginia, April 2, 1865. Confined at Point Lookout, Maryland, until released on June 22, 1865, after taking the Oath of Allegiance.

ALMOND, ERVIN, Private
Resided in Stanly County and enlisted in Guilford County at age 30, September 18, 1861. Captured at Hanover Court House, Virginia, May 27, 1862. Confined at Fort Columbus, New York Harbor. Exchanged on an unspecified date. Returned to duty prior to November 1, 1862. Captured at Gettysburg, Pennsylvania, on or about July 3, 1863. Confined at Fort Delaware, Delaware, until transferred to Point Lookout, Maryland, October 15-18, 1863. Paroled at Point Lookout on February 18, 1865, and transferred to Boulware's Wharf, James River, Virginia, where he was received February 20-21, 1865, for exchange. Company records do not indicate whether he returned to duty. Paroled at Charlotte on May 11, 1865.

ARY, GEORGE W., Private
Resided in Rowan County and enlisted in Stanly County at age 32, March 15, 1862. Hospitalized at Richmond, Virginia, April 27, 1863, with a gunshot wound. Place and date wounded not reported. Company records do not indicate whether he returned to duty and served in the field; however, he was reported absent on detached service at Richmond from April, 1863, through February, 1865. [North Carolina pension records indicate he was wounded in the left hand and left leg "in Virginia" on an unspecified date.]

ARY, HENRY, Private
Resided in Stanly County where he enlisted at age 20, March 15, 1862. Reported absent wounded during September-October, 1864. Place and date wounded not reported. Retired to the Invalid Corps on December 28, 1864, by reason of disability. Paroled at Salisbury on May 24, 1865.

AUSTEN, W. C., Private
Resided in Halifax County. Place and date of enlistment not reported. Paroled at Grenada, Mississippi, on or about May 22, 1865.

BARBEE, AARON, Private
Born in Stanly County where he resided as a farmer prior to enlisting in Stanly County at age 20, July 29, 1861. Wounded in the wrist at Gaines' Mill, Virginia, June 27, 1862. Returned to duty on an unspecified date. Present or accounted for from September-October, 1864, through February, 1865. Surrendered at Appomattox Court House, Virginia, April 9, 1865.

BARBEE, HIRAM, Private
Resided in Stanly County where he enlisted at age 19, March 15, 1862. Present or accounted for until he surrendered at Appomattox Court House, Virginia, April 9, 1865.

BARBEE, JAMES C., Private
Resided in Stanly County where he enlisted at age 19,

July 29, 1861. Captured at Hanover Court House, Virginia, May 27, 1862. Confined at Fort Monroe, Virginia, and at Fort Columbus, New York Harbor. Died at Fort Columbus on June 7, 1862, of "febris typhoides."

BLACKWELDER, ALEXANDER, Private
Resided in Stanly County where he enlisted at age 24, July 29, 1861. Killed at Frayser's Farm, Virginia, June 30, 1862.

BLALOCK, HENRY, Private
Resided in Stanly County and enlisted at Camp Stokes on October 31, 1864, for the war. Captured near Petersburg, Virginia, April 2, 1865. Confined at Point Lookout, Maryland, until released on June 23, 1865, after taking the Oath of Allegiance.

BOLICK, DAVID, Private
Resided in Catawba County and enlisted at Camp Stokes on October 28, 1864, for the war. Hospitalized at Richmond, Virginia, April 2, 1865, with an unspecified wound. Place and date wounded not reported. Captured in hospital at Richmond on April 3, 1865. Transferred to Newport News, Virginia, April 23, 1865. Released at Newport News on June 30, 1865, after taking the Oath of Allegiance.

BOLTON, ATLAS, Private
Resided in Stanly County where he enlisted at age 22, July 29, 1861. Died at Richmond, Virginia, on or about August 1, 1862, of disease.

BOLTON, CALVIN C., Private
Resided in Stanly County where he enlisted at age 28, March 15, 1862. Listed as a deserter on September 14, 1863. Returned to duty on an unspecified date. Captured at Spotsylvania Court House, Virginia, May 12, 1864. Confined at Point Lookout, Maryland, until transferred to Elmira, New York, August 8, 1864. Died at Elmira on September 30, 1864, of "pneumonia."

BOLTON, TERRELL, Private
Resided in Stanly County where he enlisted at age 25, July 29, 1861. Wounded in the left leg and captured at or near Wilderness, Virginia, on or about May 6, 1864. Confined at Old Capitol Prison, Washington, D.C., until transferred to Elmira, New York, October 25, 1864. Paroled at Elmira on February 9, 1865, and transferred to Boulware's Wharf, James River, Virginia, where he was received February 20-21, 1865, for exchange.

BULLIN, JOHN A., Private
Resided in Stanly County where he enlisted at age 29, July 29, 1861. Killed at Hanover Court House, Virginia, May 27, 1862.

BURLEYSON, ADAM, Private
Enlisted at Camp Holmes on October 15, 1864, for the war. Surrendered at Appomattox Court House, Virginia, April 9, 1865.

BURLEYSON, JOHN W., Private
Resided in Stanly County where he enlisted at age 22, July 29, 1861. Captured at Waterloo, Virginia, September 8, 1863. Confined at Old Capitol Prison, Washington, D.C., until released on or about September

26, 1863, after taking the Oath of Allegiance.

BUTNER, C. T., Private
Place and date of enlistment not reported. Hospitalized at Richmond, Virginia, March 31, 1865, with a gunshot wound of the left side. Captured in hospital at Richmond on April 3, 1865. Paroled on May 19, 1865.

CALLAWAY, ALFRED S., Private
Resided in Stanly County where he enlisted at age 34, July 29, 1861. Died in hospital at Lynchburg, Virginia, February 15 or April 7, 1863, of disease.

CANUP, DANIEL, Private
Resided in Stanly County where he enlisted at age 19, March 15, 1862. Died at Richmond, Virginia, July 15, 1862, of disease.

CANUP, DAVID, Private
Resided in Stanly County and enlisted at age 36, July 29, 1861. Died on September 20, 1861, of disease. Place of death not reported.

CARPENTER, ALLEN, Private
Resided in Stanly County where he enlisted at age 19, July 29, 1861. Present or accounted for until he surrendered at Appomattox Court House, Virginia, April 9, 1865.

CARPENTER, CHURCHWELL, Private
Resided in Stanly County where he enlisted at age 17, July 29, 1861. Killed at Gettysburg, Pennsylvania, July 3, 1863.

CARPENTER, ROBERT W., Private
Born in Stanly County and enlisted at Liberty Mills, Virginia, March 1, 1864, for the war. Died in hospital at Lynchburg, Virginia, May 18, 1864, of "diarrhoea chronica."

CARTER, JOSIAH L., Sergeant
Resided in Stanly County where he enlisted at age 36, July 29, 1861. Mustered in as Sergeant. "Murdered at Wilmington" on or about December 21, 1861.

CLAYTON, JAMES F., Private
Resided in Stanly County where he enlisted at age 21, July 29, 1861. Killed at Frayser's Farm, Virginia, June 30, 1862. "Was one of the best soldiers."

COLEY, LEVI, Private
Born in Stanly County* where he resided prior to enlisting in Stanly County at age 35, July 29, 1861. Hospitalized at Richmond, Virginia, May 25, 1864, with a gunshot wound of the right leg. Place and date wounded not reported. Died in hospital at Richmond on June 2-3, 1864, of wounds and "disease of kidney."

CRAYTON, JOHN A., Private
Resided in Stanly County where he enlisted at age 28, July 29, 1861. Mustered in as Corporal but was reduced to ranks in January-April, 1862. Killed at Chancellorsville, Virginia, May 3, 1863. "A medal was presented to his friends for his bravery."

CRAYTON, URIAH, Corporal
Resided in Stanly County where he enlisted at age 22, July 29, 1861. Mustered in as Private and was promoted to Corporal on August 15, 1863. Surrendered at

Appomattox Court House, Virginia, April 9, 1865. [North Carolina pension records indicate he was wounded in an unspecified battle.]

CRAYTON, WILLIAM, Private
Resided in Stanly County where he enlisted at age 33, July 29, 1861. Died in hospital at Richmond, Virginia, June 24, 1862, of disease.

CROWELL, DAVID D., Private
Resided in Stanly County where he enlisted at age 24, July 29, 1861. Killed at Gaines' Mill, Virginia, June 27, 1862. "A good soldier."

CROWELL, DOCTOR F., Private
Resided in Stanly County where he enlisted at age 21, July 29, 1861. Died in hospital at Brook Church, Virginia, July 26, 1862, of disease.

CROWELL, JAMES, Private
Born in Stanly County* where he resided as a farmer prior to enlisting at age 34, July 29, 1861. Discharged on May 1, 1862, because his company had "more than the maximum number [of men] allowed by law."

CROWELL, JOHN M., Private
Resided in Stanly County where he enlisted at age 19, March 15, 1862. Captured at Hanover Court House, Virginia, May 27, 1862. Confined at Fort Monroe, Virginia, and at Fort Columbus, New York Harbor. Paroled and transferred to Aiken's Landing, James River, Virginia, where he was received July 12, 1862, for exchange. Declared exchanged at Aiken's Landing on August 5, 1862. Returned to duty prior to November 1, 1862. Captured near Petersburg, Virginia, April 2, 1865. Confined at Point Lookout, Maryland, until released on June 24, 1865, after taking the Oath of Allegiance.

CROWELL, JOHN T., Private
Resided in Stanly County where he enlisted at age 25, March 15, 1862. Captured at Hanover Court House, Virginia, May 27, 1862. Confined at Fort Monroe, Virginia, and at Fort Columbus, New York Harbor. Paroled and transferred to Aiken's Landing, James River, Virginia, where he was received July 12, 1862, for exchange. Declared exchanged at Aiken's Landing on August 5, 1862. Company records do not indicate whether he returned to duty. Died in hospital near Richmond, Virginia, May 28 or June 2, 1863, of disease.

CROWELL, WILLIAM H., Private
Resided in Stanly County where he enlisted at age 22, July 29, 1861. Hospitalized at Richmond, Virginia, April 2, 1865, with an unspecified wound. Captured in hospital at Richmond on April 3, 1865. Transferred to Newport News, Virginia, April 23, 1865. Released on June 30, 1865, after taking the Oath of Allegiance.

CRUSE, WILLIAM G. A., Private
Resided in Cabarrus County and enlisted at Liberty Mills, Virginia, at age 18, March 1, 1864, for the war. Captured near Petersburg, Virginia, April 2, 1865. Confined at Point Lookout, Maryland, until released on June 24, 1865, after taking the Oath of Allegiance.

DAVIS, DAVID D., Private
Resided in Stanly or Cabarrus County and was by occupation a farmer prior to enlisting in Stanly County at age 18, July 29, 1861. Present or accounted for until

transferred to Company K of this regiment in February, 1862.

DAVIS, GEORGE W., Private
Resided in Stanly or Cabarrus County and enlisted in Stanly County at age 20, July 29, 1861. Present or accounted for until transferred to Company K of this regiment in February, 1862.

DAVIS, HENRY, Private
Resided in Stanly County where he enlisted at age 18, March 15, 1862. Died in hospital at Lynchburg, Virginia, on or about June 9, 1862, of "febris typhoides."

DAVIS, JAMES W., Private
Resided in Stanly County where he enlisted at age 19, March 15, 1862. Hospitalized at Richmond, Virginia, July 2, 1862, with a gunshot wound of the left thigh. Place and date wounded not reported. Returned to duty prior to November 1, 1862. Wounded in the right leg and captured at Gettysburg, Pennsylvania, July 1-4, 1863. Hospitalized at Gettysburg until transferred to Davids Island, New York Harbor, July 17-24, 1863. Paroled at Davids Island and transferred to City Point, Virginia, where he was received September 8, 1863, for exchange. Returned to duty on an unspecified date. Captured at Petersburg, Virginia, April 3, 1865. Confined at Hart's Island, New York Harbor, until released on June 19, 1865, after taking the Oath of Allegiance.

De BERRY, JOHN M., Corporal
Resided in Stanly County where he enlisted at age 17, July 29, 1861. Mustered in as Private and was promoted to Musician subsequent to October 31, 1861. Promoted to Corporal on December 5, 1861. Died in hospital at Huguenot Springs, Virginia, or at Lynchburg, Virginia, September 1-3, 1862, of "febris typhoides."

EASLEY, JAMES M., Sergeant
Resided in Stanly County where he enlisted at age 19, July 29, 1861. Mustered in as Private and was promoted to Sergeant on August 1, 1862. Killed at Gettysburg, Pennsylvania, July 3, 1863.

EPPS, CASWELL G., Private
Resided in Stanly County where he enlisted at age 33, March 15, 1862. Captured near Petersburg, Virginia, July 29, 1864. Confined at Point Lookout, Maryland, until transferred to Elmira, New York, August 8, 1864. Released at Elmira on July 3, 1865, after taking the Oath of Allegiance.

EUDY, HENRY H., Private
Previously served in Company G, 1st Regiment N.C. Junior Reserves. Transferred to this company on October 15, 1864. Captured near Petersburg, Virginia, April 2, 1865. Confined at Point Lookout, Maryland, until released on June 12, 1865, after taking the Oath of Allegiance.

FARR, EPHRIAM, Private
Resided in Stanly County where he enlisted at age 21, July 29, 1861. Discharged on September 21, 1861. Reason discharged not reported.

FINK, MOSES, Private
Resided in Stanly County where he enlisted at age 30,

July 29, 1861. Wounded at Malvern Hill, Virginia, July 1, 1862. Died at Richmond, Virginia, the same day of wounds.

FISHER, CHARLES T., Private
Resided in Stanly County where he enlisted at age 17, March 15, 1862. Hospitalized at Richmond, Virginia, March 28, 1865, with a gunshot wound of the leg. Place and date wounded not reported. Captured in hospital at Richmond on April 3, 1865. Released on or about June 21, 1865, after taking the Oath of Allegiance.

FOULKS, JOHN M., Private
Resided in Stanly County where he enlisted at age 18, July 29, 1861. Killed at Cedar Mountain, Virginia, August 9, 1862. "A good soldier."

FRALEY, ALEX A., Private
Enlisted in Stanly County on February 1, 1865, for the war. Present or accounted for through February, 1865.

FRICK, C. J., Private
Resided in Stanly County where he enlisted at age 18, March 15, 1862. Killed at Frayser's Farm, Virginia, June 30, 1862.

FULKS, JAMES, Private
Enlisted at Camp Stokes on October 31, 1864, for the war. Captured near Petersburg, Virginia, April 2, 1865. Confined at Point Lookout, Maryland, until released on June 26, 1865, after taking the Oath of Allegiance.

FURR, ALLEN M., Private
Resided in Stanly County where he enlisted at age 16, July 29, 1861. Killed at Fredericksburg, Virginia, December 13, 1862.

FURR, WILSON M., Private
Resided in Stanly County where he enlisted at age 28, March 15, 1862. Wounded in the head and captured at Wilderness, Virginia, May 6, 1864. Hospitalized at Washington, D.C. Confined at Old Capitol Prison, Washington, September 7, 1864. Transferred to Fort Delaware, Delaware, September 19, 1864. Released on June 19, 1865, after taking the Oath of Allegiance.

GREENE, WILLIAM E., Private
Resided in Stanly County and enlisted at Camp Gregg, Virginia, at age 36, April 7, 1863, for the war. Captured in hospital at Richmond, Virginia, April 3, 1865. Confined at Point Lookout, Maryland, until released on or about June 26, 1865, after taking the Oath of, Allegiance.

HARRIS, THOMAS A., 1st Sergeant
Resided in Stanly County where he enlisted at age 29, July 29, 1861. Mustered in as Corporal and was promoted to Sergeant in January-April, 1862. Promoted to 1st Sergeant in January, 1863-October, 1864. Present or accounted for through March 27, 1865.

HARVIL, JOHN W., Private
Born in Moore County and resided in Stanly County where he was by occupation a farmer prior to enlisting in Stanly County at age 40, July 29, 1861. Discharged on March 5, 1862, by reason of "loss of hearing to such a degree that it is impossible for him to hear the commands."

HATLEY, JOHN, Private

Resided in Stanly County and enlisted at Camp Stokes on October 31, 1864, for the war. Captured near Petersburg, Virginia, April 2, 1865. Confined at Point Lookout, Maryland, until released on June 27, 1865, after taking the Oath of Allegiance.

HATLEY, JOHN M., Private

Resided in Stanly County and enlisted in Guilford County at age 29, September 18, 1861. Killed at Gettysburg, Pennsylvania, July 3, 1863.

HERREN, DARLIN, Private

Born in Catawba County* and resided in Stanly County where he enlisted at age 27, July 29, 1861. Hospitalized at Richmond, Virginia, July 2, 1862, with a gunshot wound of the right forefinger. Place and date wounded not reported. Company records do not indicate whether he returned to duty. Died "at home" on August 15, 1864. Cause of death not reported.

HILLIARD, SILAS, Private

Resided in Stanly County where he enlisted at age 24, March 15, 1862. Captured at Hanover Court House, Virginia, May 27, 1862. Confined at Fort Monroe, Virginia, and at Fort Columbus, New York Harbor. Paroled and transferred to Aiken's Landing, James River, Virginia, where he was received July 12, 1862, for exchange. Declared exchanged at Aiken's Landing on August 5, 1862. Returned to duty prior to November 1, 1862. Died in hospital at Staunton, Virginia, or Winchester, Virginia, November 30, 1862, of "pneumonia."

HINSHAW, WILLIAM A., Private

Enlisted at Camp Holmes on October 16, 1864, for the war. Paroled at Burkeville Junction, Virginia, April 14-17, 1865.

HINSON, GEORGE, Private

Resided in Stanly County where he enlisted at age 25, July 29, 1861. Died at Middleburg, Virginia, September 12, 1862, of wounds. Place and date wounded not reported.

HINSON, NOAH L., Private

Resided in Stanly County where he enlisted at age 24, July 29, 1861. Present or accounted for through February, 1865; however, he was reported absent on detail as a shoemaker or nurse during much of that period.

HOPKINS, JAMES F., Private

Born in Stanly County* where he resided prior to enlisting in Stanly County at age 28, July 29, 1861. Died at Staunton, Virginia, July 3, 1862, of "gastro enteritis."

HOPKINS, JAMES F., Jr., Private

Resided in Stanly County where he enlisted at age 24, July 29, 1861. Died in hospital at Winchester, Virginia, on or about November 22, 1862, of "smallpox."

HOPKINS, JOHN F., Private

Resided in Stanly County where he enlisted at age 36, July 29, 1861. Captured at Hanover Court House, Virginia, May 27, 1862. Confined at Fort Monroe, Virginia, and at Fort Columbus, New York Harbor. Paroled and transferred to Aiken's Landing, James River, Virginia, where he was received July 12, 1862, for exchange. Declared exchanged at Aiken's Landing on August 5, 1862. Returned to duty prior to November 1, 1862. Wounded at Reams' Station, Virginia, August 25, 1864. Hospitalized at Petersburg, Virginia, where he died on October 2, 1864, of wounds.

HOPKINS, THOMAS, Private

Born in Stanly County* where he resided as a miner prior to enlisting in Stanly County at age 49, September 10, 1861. Discharged on April 30, 1862, by reason of being overage.

HOWELL, JAMES M., Private

Resided in Stanly County where he enlisted at age 20, March 1, 1862. Hospitalized at Richmond, Virginia, June 30, 1862, with two fingers amputated. Place and date injured not reported. Company records do not indicate whether he returned to duty. Company muster roll dated January-February, 1865, indicates he was captured on July 3, 1863; however, records of the Federal Provost Marshal do not substantiate that report. No further records.

HUFFMAN, NELSON C., Private

Resided in Catawba County and enlisted at Camp Stokes on October 28, 1864, for the war. Captured near Petersburg, Virginia, April 2, 1865. Confined at Point Lookout, Maryland, until released on June 27, 1865, after taking the Oath of Allegiance.

HULIN, NEWTON A., Private

Resided in Stanly County where he enlisted at age 20, July 29, 1861. Captured at Hanover Court House, Virginia, May 27, 1862. Confined at Fort Monroe, Virginia, and at Fort Columbus, New York Harbor. Paroled and transferred to Aiken's Landing, James River, Virginia, where he was received July 12, 1862, for exchange. Declared exchanged at Aiken's Landing on August 5, 1862. Returned to duty prior to November 1, 1862. Wounded at Chancellorsville, Virginia, May 1-4, 1863. Hospitalized at Richmond, Virginia, where he died on June 5, 1863, of a gunshot wound. "He was a dutiful soldier."

HULIN, THOMAS B., Sergeant

Resided in Stanly County where he enlisted at age 22, July 29, 1861. Mustered in as Private and was promoted to Corporal in March-April, 1862. Promoted to Sergeant on July 27, 1862. Wounded in the abdomen at Fredericksburg, Virginia, December 13, 1862. Died in hospital at Richmond, Virginia, December 18, 1862, of wounds.

HUNEYCUTT, HENRY, Private

Resided in Stanly County where he enlisted at age 24, July 29, 1861. Captured at Hanover Court House, Virginia, May 27, 1862. Confined at Fort Monroe, Virginia, and at Fort Columbus, New York Harbor. Paroled and transferred to Aiken's Landing, James River, Virginia, where he was received July 12, 1862, for exchange. Declared exchanged at Aiken's Landing on August 5, 1862. Returned to duty prior to November 1, 1862. Wounded in the head and captured at Gettysburg, Pennsylvania, July 3, 1863. Confined at Fort Delaware, Delaware. Transferred to Point Lookout, Maryland, October 15-18, 1863. Paroled at Point Lookout and transferred to Cox's Wharf, James River, Virginia, where he was received February 14-15, 1865, for exchange.

HUNEYCUTT, JOHN W., Private
Resided in Stanly County where he enlisted at age 26, July 29, 1861. Killed at Chancellorsville, Virginia, May 3, 1863.

HUNEYCUTT, JOSEPH, ———
North Carolina pension records indicate that he served in this company.

HUNEYCUTT, LINDSEY L., Private
Born in Union County* where he resided as a farmer prior to enlisting in Union County at age 21, July 29, 1861. Captured at Hanover Court House, Virginia, May 27, 1862. Confined at Fort Monroe, Virginia, and at Fort Columbus, New York Harbor. Paroled and transferred to Aiken's Landing, James River, Virginia, where he was received July 12, 1862, for exchange. Declared exchanged at Aiken's Landing on August 5, 1862. Returned to duty on an unspecified date. Deserted on July 1, 1863. Returned to duty prior to May 6, 1864, when he was captured at Wilderness, Virginia. Confined at Point Lookout, Maryland, until released on June 25, 1864, after joining the U.S. Army. Assigned to Company C, 1st Regiment U.S. Volunteer Infantry.

JAMES, WILLIAM C., Private
Enlisted at Camp Stokes on October 31, 1864, for the war. Present or accounted for until he surrendered at Appomattox Court House, Virginia, April 9, 1865.

KENNEDY, WILLIAM G., Private
Enlisted at Camp Stokes on October 31, 1864, for the war. Present or accounted for through February, 1865.

KIMBALL, WILLIAM W., Private
Enlisted at Camp Stokes on October 31, 1864, for the war. Hospitalized at Richmond, Virginia, on or about April 2, 1865, with an unspecified wound. Place and date wounded not reported. Captured in hospital at Richmond on April 3, 1865. Paroled on April 26, 1865.

KIRK, JOHN S., 1st Sergeant
Born in Stanly County* where he resided as a carpenter prior to enlisting in Stanly County at age 38, July 29, 1861. Mustered in as 1st Sergeant. Wounded in the elbow at or near Frayser's Farm, Virginia, on or about June 30, 1862. Returned to duty prior to January 1, 1863, but was discharged on February 23, 1863, by reason of disability from wounds.

KIRK, THOMAS F., Private
Resided in Stanly County where he enlisted at age 18, July 29, 1861. Captured at Hanover Court House, Virginia, May 27, 1862. Confined at Fort Monroe, Virginia, and at Fort Columbus, New York Harbor. Paroled and transferred to Aiken's Landing, James River, Virginia, where he was received July 12, 1862, for exchange. Declared exchanged at Aiken's Landing on August 5, 1862. Returned to duty prior to November 1, 1862. Wounded at Chancellorsville, Virginia, May 2-3, 1863. Returned to duty on an unspecified date. Reported absent without leave in September-October, 1864. Returned to duty in November-December, 1864. Captured near Petersburg, Virginia, April 2, 1865. Confined at Point Lookout, Maryland, until released on or about June 28, 1865, after taking the Oath of Allegiance.

LEFLER, CHARLES, Corporal
Born in Stanly County where he resided prior to enlisting in Stanly County at age 20, July 29, 1861. Mustered in as Private and was promoted to Corporal on December 1, 1862. Died "at home" on September 4, 1864. Cause of death not reported.

LEFLER, COLEMAN, Sergeant
Resided in Stanly County where he enlisted at age 23, July 29, 1861. Mustered in as Private. Captured at Hanover Court House, Virginia, May 27, 1862. Confined at Fort Monroe, Virginia, and at Fort Columbus, New York Harbor. Paroled and transferred to Aiken's Landing, James River, Virginia, where he was received July 12, 1862, for exchange. Declared exchanged at Aiken's Landing on August 5, 1862. Returned to duty prior to November 1, 1862. Promoted to Corporal on December 1, 1862. Promoted to Sergeant in July, 1863-February, 1864. Wounded in the right leg and captured near Petersburg, Virginia, March 27, 1865. Right leg amputated. Hospitalized at Point Lookout, Maryland. Released at Point Lookout on or about June 28, 1865, after taking the Oath of Allegiance.

LEFLER, DANIEL A., Private
Resided in Stanly County where he enlisted on February 1, 1865, for the war. Captured near Petersburg, Virginia, April 2, 1865. Confined at Hart's Island, New York Harbor, until released on or about June 17, 1865, after taking the Oath of Allegiance. Hospitalized at New York City on June 19, 1865, but was "sent south" on June 22, 1865.

LEFLER, MARTIN ALEXANDER, Private
Resided in Stanly County where he enlisted at age 25, July 29, 1861. Died in hospital at Richmond, Virginia, July 26-27, 1862, of "typhoid fever."

LEFLER, MONROE, Private
Born in Stanly County where he resided prior to enlisting at Camp Gregg, Virginia, March 26, 1863, for the war. Killed at Wilderness, Virginia, May 5, 1864.

LILLY, ARMSTEAD, Private
Born in Stanly County where he resided as a farmer prior to enlisting in Stanly County at age 19, July 29, 1861. Discharged on December 14, 1861, by reason of "chronic disease of the lungs."

LINEBARGER, WILLIAM ALEXANDER, Private
Previously served in Company G, 12th Regiment N.C. Troops (2nd Regiment N.C. Volunteers). Transferred to this company on February 8, 1865. Reported absent wounded in February, 1865. Paroled at Statesville on May 26, 1865.

LIPE, LEVI, Private
Resided in Stanly County and enlisted at Camp Stokes on October 31, 1864, for the war. Captured near Petersburg, Virginia, April 2, 1865. Confined at Point Lookout, Maryland, until released on June 28, 1865, after taking the Oath of Allegiance.

LITTLE, OLMSTEAD, Private
Resided in Stanly County and was by occupation a farmer prior to enlisting in Stanly County at age 32, March 15, 1862. Wounded in the right hand at Chancellorsville, Virginia, May 2-3, 1863. Returned to duty on an unspecified date. Reported present for duty in

September-October, 1864. Captured at or near Petersburg, Virginia, on or about April 4, 1865. Confined at Point Lookout, Maryland, until released on June 28, 1865, after taking the Oath of Allegiance.

LOVE, JOHN, Private
Resided in Stanly County where he enlisted at age 22, March 15, 1862. Died at Richmond, Virginia, or at Charlottesville, Virginia, August 23, 1862, of disease.

LOVE, MARTIN, Private
Resided in Stanly County where he enlisted at age 22, March 15, 1862. Died at Danville, Virginia, November 27, 1862, of ''erysipelas.''

LOWDER, MALACHAI, Sergeant
Resided in Stanly County where he enlisted at age 21, July 29, 1861. Mustered in as Private and was promoted to Corporal on November 16, 1862. Promoted to Sergeant on December 18, 1862. Company records indicate he was captured on July 3, 1863; however, records of the Federal Provost Marshal do not substantiate that report. No further records.

LYERLY, JACOB C., Private
Resided in Stanly County where he enlisted at age 21, July 29, 1861. Died in hospital at Lovingston, Virginia, on or about August 21, 1862, of ''febris typhoides.''

LYERLY, JACOB H., Corporal
Resided in Stanly County where he enlisted at age 22, July 29, 1861. Mustered in as Private and was promoted to Corporal on December 1, 1862. Died at Lynchburg, Virginia, August 10 or August 31, 1863, of ''ty[phoid] fever.''

LYERLY, JACOB H., Corporal
Resided in Stanly County where he enlisted at age 18, March 15, 1862. Mustered in as Private and was promoted to Corporal on December 1, 1864. Present or accounted for until he surrendered at Appomattox Court House, Virginia, April 9, 1865.

McDANIEL, DAVID, Private
Resided in Stanly County where he enlisted at age 38, March 15, 1862. Captured near Petersburg, Virginia, April 2, 1865. Confined at Hart's Island, New York Harbor, until released on June 17, 1865, after taking the Oath of Allegiance.

McLESTER, ALEXANDER G., Private
Resided in Stanly County where he enlisted at age 21, July 29, 1861. Discharged ''in the fall of 1863'' by reason of ''fistula.'' [North Carolina pension records indicate he was wounded at Guinea Station, Virginia, in November, 1862.]

MARKE, A. P., Private
Place and date of enlistment not reported. Captured in hospital at Richmond, Virginia, April 3, 1865, and was paroled on April 20, 1865.

MAULDIN, BENJAMIN R., Private
Resided in Stanly County where he enlisted at age 22, July 29, 1861. Wounded in the head and captured at Gettysburg, Pennsylvania, July 1-4, 1863. Hospitalized at Davids Island, New York Harbor, July 17-24, 1863. Paroled at Davids Island and transferred to City Point, Virginia, where he was received September 8, 1863, for

exchange. Returned to duty on an unspecified date. Reported present for duty in September-October, 1864. Paroled at Farmville, Virginia, April 11-21, 1865.

MAULT, ISAAC C., Private
Born in Stanly County and enlisted at Camp Gregg, Virginia, at age 18, April 27, 1863, for the war. Died on December 13, 1864. Place and cause of death not reported.

MAULT, JAMES P., Private
Resided in Stanly or Rowan County and enlisted in Stanly County at age 21, March 15, 1862. Wounded in the left lung and captured at Gettysburg, Pennsylvania, July 1-4, 1863. Hospitalized at Davids Island, New York Harbor. Paroled and transferred to City Point, Virginia, where he was received September 8, 1863, for exchange. Detailed for light duty on June 23, 1864. Reported absent on detail through February, 1865. Paroled at Salisbury on June 14, 1865.

MILLER, A. S., Private
Resided in Stanly County and enlisted at age 23, July 29, 1861. ''Rejected when mustered in service.''

MILLER, ADAM D., Private
Resided in Stanly County where he enlisted at age 19, March 15, 1862. Present or accounted for through December, 1862. Died ''in the United States'' in July, 1863. Cause of death not reported.

MILLER, ARTHUR K., Private
Born . in Stanly County* where he resided as a blacksmith prior to enlisting in Stanly County at age 22, July 29, 1861. Captured at Hanover Court House, Virginia, May 27, 1862. Confined at Fort Monroe, Virginia, and at Fort Columbus, New York Harbor. Paroled and transferred to Aiken's Landing, James River, Virginia, where he was received July 12, 1862, for exchange. Declared exchanged at Aiken's Landing on August 5, 1862. Returned to duty prior to November 1, 1862. Captured at Chancellorsville, Virginia, May 3, 1863. Confined at Washington, D.C. Paroled and transferred to City Point, Virginia, where he was received May 13, 1863, for exchange. Captured at Gettysburg, Pennsylvania, July 3, 1863. Confined at Fort Delaware, Delaware, until transferred to Point Lookout, Maryland, October 15-18, 1863. Released on January 25, 1864, after taking the Oath of Allegiance and joining the U.S. Army. Assigned to Company D, 1st Regiment U.S. Volunteer Infantry.

MILLER, ROLAND C., Private
Resided in Stanly County and was by occupation a farmer prior to enlisting in Stanly County at age 25, March 15, 1862. Mustered in as Private and was promoted to Corporal in January, 1863-June, 1864. Wounded in the left hand at ''South Anna bridge,'' Virginia, in 1863. Reported absent without leave in September-October, 1864. Returned to duty on or about November 30, 1864, and was reduced to ranks the same date. Retired from service on January 4, 1865, by reason of disability of the left hand.

MILLER, THOMAS A. G., Private
Enlisted at Camp Stokes on December 13, 1864, for the war. Present or accounted for through February, 1865.

MOOSE, ALEXANDER F., Corporal
Resided in Stanly County where he enlisted at age 22,

July 29, 1861. Mustered in as Corporal. Died "at home" on November 5, 1862, of disease. "A noble soldier."

MOOSE, HENRY D., Private
Resided in Stanly County where he enlisted at age 19, July 29, 1861. Died at Wilmington on January 27, 1862. Cause of death not reported.

MORRIS, DAVID A., Private
Born in Stanly County where he resided as a farmer prior to enlisting in Stanly County on March 15, 1862. Wounded in the hip at Gaines' Mill, Virginia, June 27, 1862. Discharged on February 23, 1863, by reason of disability. Reenlisted in the company on March 1, 1864. Captured near Petersburg, Virginia, April 2, 1865. Confined at Point Lookout, Maryland, until released on June 29, 1865, after taking the Oath of Allegiance.

MORRIS, DOCTOR M., Private
Born in Stanly County where he resided as a farmer prior to enlisting in Stanly County at age 20, July 29, 1861. Discharged on December 14, 1861, by reason of "rheumatism."

MORRIS, J. F., Private
Enlisted in Stanly County on March 15, 1862. Died in hospital at Lynchburg, Virginia, July 25, 1862, of "phthisis pulmonalis."

MORRIS, WILSON C., Private
Born in Stanly County* where he resided as a farmer prior to enlisting in Stanly County at age 24, March 15, 1862. Wounded in the right foot and captured at Gettysburg, Pennsylvania, July 1-5, 1863. Hospitalized at Davids Island, New York Harbor. Paroled and transferred to City Point, Virginia, where he was received August 28, 1863, for exchange. Returned to duty on an unspecified date. Hospitalized at Richmond, Virginia, February 23, 1864, with a gunshot wound of the left hand. Place and date wounded not reported. Returned to duty on April 7, 1864. Discharged on April 18, 1864, by reason of "disease of the heart."

MORTON, EDMUND D., Private
Resided in Stanly County where he enlisted at age 23, July 29, 1861. Died at Guinea Station, Virginia, February 4, 1863, of disease.

MORTON, W. B., Private
Born in Stanly County* where he resided as a "daguerrean artist" prior to enlisting in Stanly County at age 27, July 29, 1861. Discharged on January 27, 1862, by reason of "a protracted attack of pneumonia followed by a chronic cough and diarrhoea." Died on January 30, 1862, of disease. Place of death not reported.

MOSS, JAMES R., ———
North Carolina pension records indicate that he served in this company.

MURPHY, JAMES, Private
Resided in Catawba County and enlisted at Camp Stokes on October 28, 1864, for the war. Present or accounted for until transferred to Company G, 12th Regiment N.C. Troops (2nd Regiment N.C. Volunteers), February 8, 1865.

NEWBY, WILLIAM, Private
Resided in Stanly County where he enlisted at age 32.

March 15, 1862. Deserted on September 14, 1863. Returned to duty on an unspecified date. Captured at Wilderness, Virginia, May 12, 1864. Confined at Point Lookout, Maryland, until released on May 30, 1864, after taking the Oath of Allegiance and joining the U.S. Army. Unit to which assigned not reported.

NOBLES, THOMAS, Private
Born in Stanly County* where he resided as a farmer prior to enlisting in Stanly County at age 26, July 29, 1861. Wounded in the side and/or right hand at Frayser's Farm, Virginia, June 30, 1862. Discharged on February 23, 1863, by reason of disability from wounds.

PALMER, WILLIAM A., Private
Born in Stanly County* where he resided as a farmer prior to enlisting in Stanly County at age 38, July 29, 1861. Discharged on April 30, 1862, by reason of being overage.

PARKER, GEORGE A., Private
Resided in Stanly County where he enlisted at age 24, March 15, 1862. Died "at home" on or about December 30, 1862, of disease.

PARKER, JAMES A., Corporal
Resided in Stanly County where he enlisted at age 21, July 29, 1861. Mustered in as Private and was promoted to Corporal in November-December, 1861. Killed near Richmond, Virginia, July 25, 1862.

PENNINGTON, NELSON C., Private
Resided in Stanly County where he enlisted at age 20, July 29, 1861. Captured at Hanover Court House, Virginia, May 27, 1862. Confined at Fort Monroe, Virginia, and at Fort Columbus, New York Harbor. Paroled and transferred to Aiken's Landing, James River, Virginia, where he was received July 12, 1862, for exchange. Declared exchanged at Aiken's Landing on August 5, 1862. Returned to duty prior to November 1, 1862. Wounded in the left shoulder and captured at Gettysburg, Pennsylvania, July 1-5, 1863. Hospitalized at Davids Island, New York Harbor, July 17-24, 1863. Paroled at Davids Island and transferred to City Point, Virginia, where he was received September 16, 1863, for exchange. Returned to duty on an unspecified date. Reported on detached service as a hospital guard at Richmond, Virginia, from June 29, 1864, through February, 1865. Captured in hospital at Richmond on April 3, 1865, and was paroled at Richmond on April 24, 1865.

PERRY, BENJAMIN, Private
Resided in Stanly County where he enlisted at age 18, July 29, 1861. Wounded in the hand at the Battle of Second Manassas, Virginia, on or about August 27-30, 1862. Returned to duty prior to November 1, 1862. Wounded and captured at Gettysburg, Pennsylvania, July 3-5, 1863. Confined at Fort Delaware, Delaware. Paroled and transferred to City Point, Virginia, where he was received August 1, 1863, for exchange. Died in hospital at Petersburg, Virginia, on or about August 30, 1863, of wounds and/or "dysenteria chr[onic]."

PETERSON, CHARLES J., Private
Resided in Gaston County and enlisted at Camp Stokes on October 27, 1864, for the war. Captured near Petersburg, Virginia, April 2, 1865. Confined at Point

Lookout, Maryland, until released on June 16, 1865, after taking the Oath of Allegiance.

PETERSON, JOHN, Private
Resided in Catawba County and enlisted at Camp Stokes on October 28, 1864, for the war. Captured near Petersburg, Virginia, April 2, 1865. Confined at Point Lookout, Maryland, until released on June 16, 1865, after taking the Oath of Allegiance.

PLYLER, DANIEL W., Corporal
Resided in Stanly County where he enlisted at age 20, July 29, 1861. Mustered in as Private. Wounded at Ox Hill, Virginia, September 1, 1862. Returned to duty prior to November 1, 1862. Promoted to Corporal in January, 1863-October, 1864. Surrendered at Appomattox Court House, Virginia, April 9, 1865.

PLYLER, EDMOND A., Private
Enlisted at Liberty Mills, Virginia, March 1, 1864, for the war. Surrendered at Appomattox Court House, Virginia, April 9, 1865.

PLYLER, HENRY D., Private
Resided in Stanly County where he enlisted at age 18, March 15, 1862. Captured at Hanover Court House, Virginia, on or about May 28, 1862. Confined at Fort Monroe, Virginia. Received at Aiken's Landing, James River, Virginia, July 12, 1862, for exchange. Declared exchanged at Aiken's Landing on August 5, 1862. Returned to duty prior to November 1, 1862. Hospitalized at Petersburg, Virginia, June 23, 1864, with a gunshot wound. Place and date wounded not reported. Returned to duty on August 17, 1864. Surrendered at Appomattox Court House, Virginia, April 9, 1865.

PRITCHARD, STARLING, Private
Resided in Stanly County where he enlisted at age 35, July 29, 1861. Died in hospital at Richmond, Virginia, May 19, 1863, of "typh[oid] pneumonia." "A good soldier."

PRUITT, JACOB, Private
Enlisted at Liberty Mills, Virginia, March 1, 1864, for the war. Wounded in the left knee at Wilderness, Virginia, on or about May 5-6, 1864. Returned to duty prior to November 1, 1864. Surrendered at Appomattox Court House, Virginia, April 9, 1865.

RICHIE, JOHN, Private
Resided in Stanly County where he enlisted at age 21, March 15, 1862. Captured near Petersburg, Virginia, April 2, 1865. Confined at Point Lookout, Maryland, until released on June 17, 1865, after taking the Oath of Allegiance.

RIDENHOUR, FRANKLIN A., Private
Resided in Stanly County where he enlisted at age 34, July 29, 1861. Hospitalized at Petersburg, Virginia, June 23, 1864, with a gunshot wound. Place and date wounded not reported. Returned to duty prior to November 1, 1864. Captured near Petersburg on April 2, 1865. Confined at Point Lookout, Maryland, until released on June 17, 1865, after taking the Oath of Allegiance. [North Carolina pension records indicate he was wounded in the right leg at Petersburg on an unspecified date.]

RIDENHOUR, WILLIAM, Private
Resided in Stanly County where he enlisted at age 20, July 29, 1861. Wounded at or near Sharpsburg, Maryland, on or about September 16, 1862. Died at Shepherdstown, Virginia, September 30, 1862, of wounds. "A good soldier."

RITCHIE, MARVEL, Sergeant
Resided in Stanly County where he enlisted at age 16, July 29, 1861. Mustered in as Private. Wounded in the right heel and left thigh near Richmond, Virginia, in June, 1862. Returned to duty prior to November 1, 1862. Promoted to Corporal on November 16, 1862. Promoted to Sergeant in January, 1863-October, 1864. Wounded in the left side at Gettysburg, Pennsylvania, July 1-3, 1863. Returned to duty on an unspecified date. Wounded in the foot near Petersburg, Virginia, on an unspecified date. Returned to duty on an unspecified date. Reported present for duty from September-October, 1864, through February 17, 1865. Surrendered at Appomattox Court House, Virginia, April 9, 1865.

ROGERS, MADISON M., Private
Resided in Stanly County where he enlisted on February 1, 1865, for the war. Captured near Petersburg, Virginia, April 2, 1865. Confined at Point Lookout, Maryland, until released on June 19, 1865, after taking the Oath of Allegiance.

ROWLAND, COLUMBUS W., Private
Resided in Stanly County where he enlisted at age 23, March 15, 1862. Wounded near Richmond, Virginia, on an unspecified date. Returned to duty on an unspecified date. Reported absent on detached service at Charlotte from September-October, 1864, through February, 1865. No further records.

ROWLAND, MATHIAS, Private
Born in Stanly County* where he resided as a farmer prior to enlisting in Stanly County at age 52, July 29, 1861. Discharged on June 19, 1862, by reason of "general debility and advanced age."

RUDASILL, JOHN, Private
Enlisted at Camp Stokes on October 28, 1864, for the war. Surrendered at Appomattox Court House, Virginia, April 9, 1865.

SAFLEY, WILLIAM W., Private
Born in Stanly County where he resided as a farmer prior to enlisting in Stanly County at age 20, July 29, 1861. Wounded in the left leg and right hip at Gaines' Mill, Virginia, June 27, 1862. Left leg amputated. Discharged on February 23, 1863, by reason of disability.

SELL, J. P., Private
Born in Stanly County* where he resided as a farmer prior to enlisting in Stanly County at age 32, March 15, 1862. Discharged on February 23, 1863, by reason of "prolapsis ani of seven months standing."

SELL, JOHN E., Private
Resided in Stanly County where he enlisted at age 26, May 6, 1862, for the war. Present or accounted for until reported missing at Gettysburg, Pennsylvania, July 3, 1863. No further records.

SELL, RICHMOND, Private
Born in Rowan County and resided in Stanly County

where he was by occupation a farmer prior to enlisting in Stanly County at age 42, July 29, 1861. Present or accounted for until discharged on or about July 16, 1862, by reason of "disability."

SELL, SAMUEL, Private
Resided in Stanly County and was by occupation a "minor" prior to enlisting in Stanly County at age 21, March 15, 1862. Paroled at Salisbury on May 20, 1865.

SIDES, ALEXANDER, Jr., Private
Born in Stanly County where he resided as a farmer prior to enlisting in Stanly County at age 20, July 29, 1861. Present or accounted for through February, 1865.

SIDES, ALEXANDER, Sr., Private
Resided in Stanly County where he enlisted at age 42, July 29, 1861. Captured and paroled at Warrenton, Virginia, September 29, 1862. Returned to duty on an unspecified date. Captured at Gettysburg, Pennsylvania, on or about July 3, 1863. Confined at Fort Delaware, Delaware, until transferred to Point Lookout, Maryland, October 15-18, 1863. Paroled at Point Lookout on February 18, 1865. Transferred to Boulware's Wharf, James River, Virginia, where he was received on or about February 20, 1865, for exchange. Returned to duty on an unspecified date. Captured near Petersburg, Virginia, April 2, 1865. Confined at Point Lookout until released on June 20, 1865, after taking the Oath of Allegiance.

SIDES, CHARLES W., Private
Resided in Stanly County where he enlisted at age 19, March 15, 1862. Captured at Fredericksburg, Virginia, December 13, 1862. Exchanged on or about December 17, 1862. Returned to duty on an unspecified date. Wounded in the thigh and captured at Gettysburg, Pennsylvania, July 1-4, 1863. Hospitalized at Davids Island, New York Harbor. Paroled and transferred to City Point, Virginia, where he was received September 27, 1863, for exchange. Returned to duty on an unspecified date. Reported absent sick in September-October, 1864, and was reported present for duty during November, 1864-February, 1865. Captured near Petersburg, Virginia, April 2, 1865. Confined at Point Lookout, Maryland, until released on June 30, 1865, after taking the Oath of Allegiance.

SIDES, GREEN H., Private
Resided in Stanly County and enlisted at Liberty Mills, Virginia, February 1, 1864, for the war. Wounded at Wilderness, Virginia, May 5, 1864. Returned to duty prior to November 1, 1864. Present or accounted for through February, 1865. Captured in hospital at Richmond, Virginia, April 3, 1865. Transferred to Newport News, Virginia, April 23, 1865. Released on June 14, 1865, after taking the Oath of Allegiance.

SIDES, HENRY C., Private
Resided in Stanly County where he enlisted at age 29, July 29, 1861. Roll of Honor indicates he was killed at the Battle of Second Manassas, Virginia, August 29, 1862; however, the *Raleigh Register* of September 24, 1862, indicates he was wounded in the finger at Ox Hill, Virginia, September 1, 1862. Company muster roll dated June 30-October 31, 1862, indicates he died on September 17, 1862, of wounds received in an unspecified engagement. No further records.

SIDES, HENRY W., Private
Enlisted at Camp Holmes on October 22, 1864, for the war. Present or accounted for through February, 1865. [May have served previously in Company A, 4th Regiment N.C. State Troops.]

SIDES, JACOB, Private
Resided in Stanly County where he enlisted at age 32, March 15, 1862. Killed at or near Gaines' Mill, Virginia, on or about June 28, 1862.

SIDES, JAMES A., Private
Resided in Stanly County where he enlisted at age 20, July 29, 1861. Present or accounted for through February, 1865.

SIDES, JOSEPH, Private
Resided in Stanly County where he enlisted at age 29, July 29, 1861. Wounded in the left side near Richmond, Virginia, on an unspecified date. Captured at or near Gettysburg, Pennsylvania, on or about July 3, 1863. Confined at Fort Delaware, Delaware, until transferred to Point Lookout, Maryland, October 15-18, 1863. Paroled at Point Lookout on February 18, 1865, and transferred to Boulware's Wharf, James River, Virginia, where he was received on or about February 20, 1865, for exchange.

SIDES, WILLIAM W., Private
Resided in Stanly County where he enlisted at age 18, September 18, 1861. Captured at Fredericksburg, Virginia, December 13, 1862. Exchanged on or about December 17, 1862. Returned to duty on an unspecified date. Deserted on September 14, 1863. Returned to duty prior to May 12, 1864, when he was captured at or near Spotsylvania Court House, Virginia. Confined at Point Lookout, Maryland, until released on May 30, 1864, after joining the U.S. Army. Unit to which assigned not reported.

SMITH, DOCTOR E., Private
Resided in Stanly County where he enlisted at age 18, July 29, 1861. Wounded and captured at Gettysburg, Pennsylvania, July 3, 1863. Hospitalized at Chester, Pennsylvania, where he died on August 21, 1863, of "pyaemia."

SMITH, JOSIAH, Private
Resided in Stanly County where he enlisted at age 24, July 29, 1861. Present or accounted for through April, 1862. Enlisted in Company H, 42nd Regiment N.C. Troops, on or about May 12, 1862. Transferred back to this company on May 1, 1863. Captured at Spotsylvania Court House, Virginia, May 12, 1864. Reported in confinement at Elmira, New York, September 30, 1864. [Roll of Honor indicates that he "deserted twice."] No further records.

STOKER, ROBERT, Private
Born in Stanly County* where he resided prior to enlisting in Stanly County at age 39, July 29, 1861. Wounded at Fredericksburg, Virginia, December 13, 1862. Returned to duty on an unspecified date. Captured at or near Gettysburg, Pennsylvania, on or about July 4, 1863. Confined at Fort Delaware, Delaware, until transferred to Point Lookout, Maryland, October 15-18, 1863. Died at Point Lookout on December 23, 1863. Cause of death not reported.

TALLY, FRANCIS W., Sergeant
Resided in Stanly County where he enlisted at age 21, July 29, 1861. Mustered in as Private and was promoted to Corporal on August 15, 1863. Promoted to Sergeant in September, 1863-October, 1864. Surrendered at Appomattox Court House, Virginia, April 9, 1865.

TALLY, MARTIN V. B., Private
Resided in Stanly County where he enlisted at age 20, July 29, 1861. Captured at Hanover Court House, Virginia, May 27, 1862. Confined at Fort Monroe, Virginia, and at Fort Columbus, New York Harbor. Paroled and transferred to Aiken's Landing, James River, Virginia, where he was received July 12, 1862, for exchange. Declared exchanged at Aiken's Landing on August 5, 1862. Died in hospital at Richmond, Virginia, on or about October 19, 1862, of "fevris typh[oid]."

TOLBERT, HARRISON F., Private
Born in Stanly County where he resided as a farmer prior to enlisting in Stanly County at age 20, July 29, 1861. Captured on or about September 1, 1862. Confined at Fort Monroe, Virginia. Paroled and transferred to Aiken's Landing, James River, Virginia, where he was received September 7, 1862, for exchange. Declared exchanged at Aiken's Landing on September 21, 1862. Returned to duty prior to November 1, 1862. Captured at Spotsylvania Court House, Virginia, May 12, 1864. Confined at Point Lookout, Maryland, until released on May 30, 1864, after taking the Oath of Allegiance and joining the U.S. Army. Assigned to Company I, 1st Regiment U.S. Volunteer Infantry.

TREECE, PETER, Private
Born in Stanly County* where he resided as a farmer prior to enlisting in Stanly County at age 32, March 15, 1862. Wounded in the middle finger of the right hand at Sharpsburg, Maryland, September 17, 1862. Deserted from hospital at Danville, Virginia, January 23, 1863. Reported absent sick in September-October, 1864. Returned to duty in November-December, 1864. Retired from service on March 1, 1865, by reason of "ch[ronic] bronchitis & organic disease of the heart."

TURNER, FERDINAND G., Private
Resided in Stanly County where he enlisted at age 20, July 29, 1861. Captured at Hanover Court House, Virginia, May 27, 1862. Confined at Fort Monroe, Virginia, and at Fort Columbus, New York Harbor. Paroled and transferred to Aiken's Landing, James River, Virginia, where he was received July 12, 1862, for exchange. Declared exchanged at Aiken's Landing on August 5, 1862. Returned to duty prior to November 1, 1862. Retired to the Invalid Corps on April 15, 1864. Rejoined the company on September 15, 1864. Captured near Petersburg, Virginia, April 2, 1865. Confined at Point Lookout, Maryland, until released on June 20, 1865, after taking the Oath of Allegiance.

TURNER, JAMES E., Private
Resided in Stanly County where he enlisted at age 22, March 15, 1862. Deserted to the enemy on or about April 1, 1865. Took the Oath of Allegiance at Washington, D.C., on or about April 6, 1865.

UNDERWOOD, JOHN HUBBERT, Private
Enlisted at Camp Stokes at age 18, October 28, 1864, for the war. Surrendered at Appomattox Court House,

Virginia, April 9, 1865.

VANHOY, JOHN A., ———
North Carolina pension records indicate that he served in this company.

WAISNER, WILSON D., Private
Resided in Stanly County where he enlisted at age 28, July 29, 1861. Killed at Fredericksburg, Virginia, December 13, 1862.

WALLACE, GEORGE, Private
Resided in Stanly County where he enlisted at age 18, July 29, 1861. Killed at the Battle of Second Manassas, Virginia, August 27-30, 1862.

WALLACE, JOHN, Private
Resided in Stanly County where he enlisted at age 18, September 10, 1861. Killed at Gaines' Mill, Virginia, June 27, 1862.

WHITAKER, JAMES A., Private
Born in Stanly County* where he resided as a farmer prior to enlisting in Stanly County at age 23, July 29, 1861. Wounded at Cedar Mountain, Virginia, August 9, 1862. Returned to duty on an unspecified date. Wounded in the right thigh and captured at Gettysburg, Pennsylvania, on or about July 3, 1863. Hospitalized at Chester, Pennsylvania. Paroled and transferred to City Point, Virginia, where he was received September 23, 1863, for exchange. Discharged on March 21, 1864, by reason of wounds received at Gettysburg.

WILES, MARGAMIN, Private
Resided in Stanly County where he enlisted at age 43, March 15, 1862. Died on October 9-10, 1862, of disease. Place of death not reported.

WILES, WILLIAM, Private
Resided in Stanly County where he enlisted at age 23, March 15, 1862. Wounded in the finger at the Battle of Second Manassas, Virginia, August 27-30, 1862. Returned to duty prior to November 1, 1862. Hospitalized at Richmond, Virginia, June 5, 1864, with a gunshot wound. Place and date wounded not reported. Returned to duty on October 1, 1864. Paroled at Salisbury on or about July 10, 1865.

YOW, TIMOTHY, Private
Resided in Stanly County where he enlisted at age 25, March 15, 1862. Wounded near Richmond, Virginia, on an unspecified date. Returned to duty on an unspecified date. Retired from service on October 20, 1864. Reason he was retired not reported. [North Carolina pension records indicate he was wounded at Ox Hill, Virginia, June 26, 1863.]

YOW, WILLIAM C., Private
Resided in Stanly County where he enlisted at age 21, July 29, 1861. Wounded in the right thigh and/or right side at Spotsylvania Court House, Virginia, on or about May 12, 1864. Returned to duty prior to November 1, 1864. Captured near Petersburg, Virginia, April 2, 1865. Confined at Point Lookout, Maryland, until released on June 22, 1865, after taking the Oath of Allegiance. [North Carolina pension records indicate he suffered a bayonet wound in the right side at Seven Pines, Virginia, on an unspecified date.]

COMPANY E

This company, known as the "Montgomery Grays," was raised in Montgomery County and enlisted at Troy on August 1, 1861. It was then mustered into service and assigned to the 28th Regiment as Company E. After joining the regiment the company functioned as a part of the regiment, and its history for the war period is reported as a part of the regimental history.

The information contained in the following roster of the company was compiled principally from company muster rolls for August 1, 1861-October 31, 1862, and September, 1864-February, 1865. No company muster rolls were found for November, 1862-August, 1864, or for the period after February, 1865. Valuable information was obtained also from primary records such as the Roll of Honor, medical records, prisoner of war records, discharge certificates, and pension applications, and from secondary sources such as postwar rosters and histories, cemetery records, and records of the United Daughters of the Confederacy.

OFFICERS

CAPTAINS

BARRINGER, WILLIAM DAVIDSON
Resided in Montgomery County where he enlisted at age 26. Appointed Captain on August 1, 1861. Promoted to Major on October 18, 1862, and transferred to the Field and Staff of this regiment. Later served as Lieutenant Colonel of this regiment.

CLARK, NIVEN
Resided in Montgomery County where he enlisted at age 26, August 1, 1861. Mustered in as 1st Sergeant and was appointed 3rd Lieutenant on November 9, 1861. Promoted to 1st Lieutenant on February 28 or April 9, 1862. Wounded near Richmond, Virginia, on or about [June] 29, 1862. Returned to duty on an unspecified date. Promoted to Captain on October 18, 1862. Killed at Spotsylvania Court House, Virginia, May 12, 1864.

GREEN, THOMAS S.
Resided in Montgomery County where he enlisted at age 20, August 1, 1861. Mustered in as Private and was promoted to Sergeant on November 9, 1861. Appointed 3rd Lieutenant on October 7, 1862, and was promoted to 2nd Lieutenant on October 18, 1862. Wounded at Chancellorsville, Virginia, May 2-3, 1863. Returned to duty on an unspecified date. Promoted to Captain on May 12, 1864. Wounded in the left thigh at Reams Station, Virginia, August 25, 1864. Reported absent wounded until January 9, 1865, when he resigned by reason of disability from wounds.

LIEUTENANTS

EWING, JAMES WILLIAM, 1st Lieutenant
Resided in Montgomery County where he enlisted at age 27. Appointed 1st Lieutenant on August 1, 1861. Defeated for reelection on February 28, 1862. Elected 2nd Lieutenant on September 5, 1862, and was promoted to 1st Lieutenant on October 18, 1862. Wounded in the left leg at Fredericksburg, Virginia, December 13, 1862. Resigned on August 27, 1863, by reason of "atrophy of the left leg." "A gallant officer."

HURLEY, ELIAS, 2nd Lieutenant
Resided in Montgomery County where he enlisted at age 27, August 1, 1861. Mustered in as Sergeant and was promoted to 1st Sergeant on November 9, 1861. Reduced to ranks in March-April, 1862, but was elected 2nd Lieutenant on November 1, 1862. Wounded at Gettysburg, Pennsylvania, July 1-3, 1863. Returned to duty on an unspecified date. Captured at Wilderness, Virginia on or about May 6, 1864. Confined at Fort Delaware, Delaware. Transferred to Point Lookout, Maryland, October 6, 1864. Transferred to Washington, D.C., November 2, 1864. Transferred back to Fort Delaware on December 16, 1864. Paroled at Fort Delaware and transferred to City Point, Virginia, where he was received February 27, 1865, for exchange.

McRAE, DUNCAN A., 3rd Lieutenant
Resided in Montgomery County and enlisted at age 24. Appointed 3rd Lieutenant on August 1, 1861. Promoted to Adjutant (1st Lieutenant) on October 18, 1861, and transferred to the Field and Staff of this regiment.

McRAE, JAMES LAWRENCE, 3rd Lieutenant
Resided in Montgomery County where he enlisted at age 30, August 1, 1861. Mustered in as Sergeant and was elected 3rd Lieutenant on February 28, 1862. Resigned on July 23, 1862, but continued to serve in the company with the rank of Private. [See Noncommissioned Officers and Privates' section below.]

TOWNSEND, SOLOMON RICHARDSON, 1st Lieutenant
Resided in Richmond County and enlisted in Montgomery County at age 26. Appointed 2nd Lieutenant on August 1, 1861, and was promoted to 1st Lieutenant on April 9, 1862. Resigned on August 17, 1862, by reason of "rheumatism" and "an attack of a low form of fever."

WILLIAMS, ISAAC, 2nd Lieutenant
Resided in Montgomery or Chatham County and enlisted in Montgomery County at age 24, August 1, 1861. Mustered in as Ensign (Private) and was promoted to Corporal in January-February, 1862. Promoted to 1st Sergeant in March-April, 1862. Captured at Hanover Court House, Virginia, on or about May 27, 1862. Confined at Fort Monroe, Virginia, and at Fort Columbus, New York Harbor. Paroled and transferred to Aiken's Landing, James River, Virginia, where he was received July 12, 1862, for exchange. Declared exchanged at Aiken's Landing on August 5, 1862. Returned to duty prior to November 1, 1862. Elected 2nd Lieutenant on December 20, 1863. Captured at Gravel Hill, Virginia, July 28, 1864. Confined at Old Capitol Prison, Washington, D.C. Transferred to Fort Delaware, Delaware, where he arrived August 12, 1864. No further records.

NONCOMMISSIONED OFFICERS AND PRIVATES

ALLEN, DAWSON B., Private
Resided in Montgomery County where he enlisted at age 28, March 10, 1862. Mustered in as Private. Wounded and captured at Gettysburg, Pennsylvania, July 1-4, 1863. Hospitalized at Davids Island, New York Harbor. Paroled and transferred to City Point, Virginia, where he was received September 8, 1863, for exchange. Returned to duty on an unspecified date. Promoted to Sergeant in September, 1863-October, 1864. Reduced to ranks subsequent to February 28, 1865. Captured in hospital at Richmond, Virginia, April 3, 1865.

Transferred to Newport News, Virginia, April 23, 1865. Released on June 16, 1865, after taking the Oath of Allegiance.

ANDREWS, CYRUS P., Private
Resided in Montgomery County where he enlisted at age 18, August 1, 1861. Killed at Gaines' Mill, Virginia, June 27, 1862, "while gallantly charging the enemy."

ANDREWS, N. K., Private
Resided in Montgomery County where he enlisted at age 25, March 1, 1862. Died in hospital at or near Mount Jackson, Virginia, December 8, 1862, of "diarrhoea chronica."

ANDREWS, SETH, Private
Resided in Montgomery County and enlisted in Wake County on February 10, 1864, for the war. Captured near Petersburg, Virginia, April 2, 1865. Confined at Point Lookout, Maryland, until released on June 22, 1865, after taking the Oath of Allegiance.

ANDREWS, THOMAS S., Private
Resided in Montgomery County where he enlisted at age 21, March 1, 1862. Died at Gordonsville, Virginia, September 30, 1862. Cause of death not reported.

BALLARD, GEORGE M., Private
Born in Montgomery County where he resided as a farmer prior to enlisting in Montgomery County at age 33, August 1, 1861. Mustered in as Corporal but was reduced to ranks in January-February, 1862. Discharged on April 14, 1862, by reason of "piles & general debi[li]ty."

BALLARD, JAMES H., Private
Resided in Montgomery County where he enlisted at age 26, August 1, 1861. Captured at Hanover Court House, Virginia, May 27, 1862. Confined at Fort Monroe, Virginia, and at Fort Columbus, New York Harbor. Paroled and transferred to Aiken's Landing, James River, Virginia, where he was exchanged on August 5, 1862. Returned to duty prior to November 1, 1862. Wounded in the ankle and captured at Gettysburg, Pennsylvania, July 1-3, 1863. Hospitalized at Gettysburg until transferred to Chester, Pennsylvania, on or about July 6, 1863. Died in hospital at Chester on September 20, 1863, of "pyaemia."

BALLARD, MILES M., Private
Resided in Montgomery County where he enlisted at age 21, August 1, 1861. Captured at Hanover Court House, Virginia, May 27, 1862. Confined at Fort Monroe, Virginia, and at Fort Columbus, New York Harbor. Exchanged at Aiken's Landing, James River, Virginia, August 5, 1862. Returned to duty on an unspecified date subsequent to October 31, 1862. Captured near Petersburg, Virginia, April 2, 1865. Confined at Point Lookout, Maryland. Transferred to Washington, D.C., July 24, 1865. Died in hospital at Washington on July 28, 1865, of "ch[ronic] diarrhoea & scurvy."

BALLARD, WILLIAM M., Sergeant
Resided in Montgomery County where he enlisted at age 38, March 1, 1862. Mustered in as Private and was promoted to Sergeant in November, 1862-May, 1864. Surrendered at Appomattox Court House, Virginia, April 9, 1865. [North Carolina pension applications

indicate he was wounded in the neck near Richmond, Virginia, May 1, 1864.]

BARRINGER, GEORGE E., Private
Resided in Cabarrus County and enlisted in Montgomery County at age 27, August 1, 1861. Present or accounted for through February, 1865. Apparently served as a courier for General James H. Lane during much of the war.

BASS, ALEXANDER W., Private
Resided in Union County and enlisted in Wake County at age 40, March 4, 1863, for the war. Captured at Gettysburg, Pennsylvania, July 3, 1863. Confined at Fort Delaware, Delaware. Transferred to Point Lookout, Maryland, October 15-18, 1863. Paroled at Point Lookout and transferred to Aiken's Landing, James River, Virginia, September 18, 1864, for exchange. Hospitalized at Richmond, Virginia, September 22, 1864, with chronic diarrhoea and was furloughed for sixty days on or about October 4, 1864.

BEAN, WILLIAM, Private
Resided in Randolph County. Place and date of enlistment not reported. Captured at Petersburg, Virginia, April 3, 1865. Confined at Hart's Island, New York Harbor, until released on or about June 19, 1865, after taking the Oath of Allegiance.

BENNETT, ALEXANDER, Private
Resided in Union County and enlisted in Wake County at age 25, October 2, 1862, for the war. Wounded at Chancellorsville, Virginia, May 2-3, 1863. Returned to duty on an unspecified date. Captured at Spotsylvania Court House, Virginia, May 12, 1864. Confined at Point Lookout, Maryland, where he died on June 6, 1864. Cause of death not reported.

BIRD, COLIN, Private
Born in Montgomery County where he resided as a blacksmith prior to enlisting in Montgomery County at age 35, August 1, 1861. Discharged on December 9, 1861, by reason of "phthisis."

BIRD, ROBERT H., Private
Resided in Montgomery County where he enlisted at age 19, August 1, 1861. Wounded at Gaines' Mill, Virginia, on or about June 27, 1862. Returned to duty prior to November 1, 1862. Wounded in the arm and captured at Spotsylvania Court House, Virginia, May 12, 1864. Hospitalized at Washington, D.C., where he died on May 30, 1864, of wounds.

BREWER, ELI H., Private
Born in Montgomery County where he resided prior to enlisting in Montgomery County at age 30, August 1, 1861. Killed at Chancellorsville, Virginia, May 3, 1863.

BREWER, OLIVER C., Private
Resided in Montgomery County where he enlisted at age 19, March 4, 1863, for the war. Wounded and captured at Gettysburg, Pennsylvania, July 3-5, 1863. Hospitalized at Chester, Pennsylvania. Paroled and transferred to City Point, Virginia, where he was received September 23, 1863, for exchange. Returned to duty on an unspecified date. Captured at or near Pickett's Farm, Virginia, July 21, 1864. Confined at Point Lookout, Maryland, July 28, 1864. Released on

June 24, 1865, after taking the Oath of Allegiance.

BROWN, ROBERT B., Private
Resided in Montgomery County where he enlisted at age 40, March 10, 1862, as a substitute. Reported absent without leave from August 26, 1862, until December 1, 1862. Captured near Petersburg, Virginia, April 2, 1865. Confined at Point Lookout, Maryland, until released on June 23, 1865, after taking the Oath of Allegiance.

CALLAIS, JAMES M., Private
Resided in Montgomery County where he enlisted at age 23, August 1, 1861. Died at Gordonsville, Virginia, October 1, 1862. Cause of death not reported.

CALLAIS, JOSIAH, Private
Resided in Montgomery County where he enlisted at age 22, August 1, 1861. Wounded and captured at Gettysburg, Pennsylvania, July 1-2, 1863. Died at Gettysburg on July 25, 1863, of wounds.

CALLAIS, WILLIAM, Private
Resided in Montgomery County where he enlisted at age 21, August 1, 1861. Hospitalized at Wilmington on August 16, 1862, with a "puncture" wound. Place and date injured not reported. Returned to duty on August 18, 1862. Died at Hanover Junction, Virginia, on or about May 4, 1863, of "pneumonia."

CHANCEY, J. H., Private
Resided in Montgomery County where he enlisted at age 21, March 6, 1862. Died at Richmond, Virginia, July 13, 1862, of disease.

CHANCEY, L. N., Private
Resided in Montgomery County where he enlisted at age 23, March 6, 1862. Killed at Gaines' Mill, Virginia, June 27, 1862.

CHANCEY, W. H., Private
Resided in Montgomery County where he enlisted at age 20, March 6, 1862. Died in hospital at Richmond, Virginia, August 26-27, 1862, of "contin[ued] fever."

CHAUNCY, DAVID E. D., Private
Resided in Montgomery County where he enlisted at age 32, August 1, 1861. Present or accounted for through August 11, 1863. No further records.

CHAUNCY, MARTIN A., Private
Resided in Montgomery County where he enlisted at age 22, August 1, 1861. Wounded in the hand at Frayser's Farm, Virginia, June 30, 1862. Reported absent wounded through October, 1862. Hospitalized at Richmond, Virginia, June 21, 1863, with chronic diarrhoea and was transferred to another hospital in Richmond on or about August 15, 1863. No further records.

CHISHOLM, MOSES, Private
Enlisted in Wake County on March 28, 1864, for the war. Surrendered at Appomattox Court House, Virginia, April 9, 1865.

CHISHOLM, WILLIAM J., Corporal
Previously served in Company F, 44th Regiment N.C. Troops. Joined this company in March-August, 1862, "without a transfer." Mustered in as Private. Promoted to Corporal in November, 1862-July, 1864. Present or

accounted for until paroled at Farmville, Virginia, April 11-21, 1865.

CLARK, B. Y., Private
Place and date of enlistment not reported. Paroled at Greensboro on or about May 5, 1865.

COGGIN, DANIEL H., Corporal
Born in Montgomery County where he resided as a farmer prior to enlisting in Montgomery County at age 20, August 1, 1861. Mustered in as Corporal. Discharged on October 15, 1862, by reason of "organic disease of heart."

COOK, J. R., Private
Resided in Montgomery County where he enlisted at age 21, March 1, 1862. Died at Lynchburg, Virginia, on or about August 12, 1862, of disease.

COOK, LEWIS, Private
Resided in Montgomery County where he enlisted at age 27, August 1, 1861. Wounded at Chancellorsville, Virginia, May 2-3, 1863. Returned to duty on an unspecified date. Wounded at Wilderness, Virginia, May 5, 1864. Returned to duty on December 14, 1864. Paroled at Troy on May 22, 1865.

COOK, NATHANIEL L., Private
Resided in Montgomery County where he enlisted at age 23, August 1, 1861. Hospitalized at Richmond, Virginia, June 29, 1862, with a gunshot wound of the head. Place and date wounded not reported. Returned to duty prior to November 1, 1862. Wounded in the left arm and captured at Gettysburg, Pennsylvania, July 1-3, 1863. Died in hospital at Gettysburg on September 1, 1863, of wounds.

COOK, WILLIAM, Private
Resided in Montgomery County where he enlisted at age 19, August 1, 1861. Died at Wilmington on February 22, 1862. Cause of death not reported.

CRANFORD, JOSHUA A., 1st Sergeant
Resided in Montgomery County where he enlisted at age 27, August 1, 1861. Mustered in as Private and was promoted to 1st Sergeant in November, 1862-July, 1864. Captured at or near Pickett's Farm, Virginia, on or about July 21, 1864. Confined at Point Lookout, Maryland, July 28, 1864. Paroled and transferred to Venus Point, Savannah River, Georgia, where he was received November 15, 1864, for exchange. Returned to duty in January-February, 1865. Surrendered at Appomattox Court House, Virginia, April 9, 1865.

DAVIS, ROBERT, Private
Born in Montgomery County where he resided as a farmer prior to enlisting in Montgomery County at age 40, August 1, 1861. Discharged on December 23, 1861, by reason of "inguinal hernia."

De BERRY, BENJAMIN, Private
Resided in Montgomery County where he enlisted at age 19, August 1, 1861. Died at Wilmington in January, 1862. Cause of death not reported.

De BERRY, DAVID D., Private
Enlisted at Liberty Mills, Virginia, at age 20, February 22, 1864, for the war. Captured at or near Spotsylvania Court House, Virginia, on or about May 10, 1864.

Confined at Point Lookout, Maryland, until transferred to Elmira, New York, July 8, 1864. Paroled at Elmira on October 11, 1864, and transferred to Venus Point, Savannah River, Georgia, where he was received November 15, 1864, for exchange.

De BERRY, JOHN, Private
Resided in Montgomery County where he enlisted at age 20, August 1, 1861. Died in hospital at Richmond, Virginia, July 30, 1862, of disease.

DICKSON, W. H., Private
Place and date of enlistment not reported. Surrendered at Appomattox Court House, Virginia, April 9, 1865.

DUNN, JAMES T., Private
Previously served in Company E, 1st Regiment N.C. Junior Reserves. Transferred to this company on January 20, 1865. Deserted on February 22, 1865.

DUNN, WILLIAM A., Private
Resided in Montgomery County where he enlisted at age 20, March 10, 1862. Died in hospital at Gordonsville, Virginia, May 9, 1862, of "pneumonia."

DUNN, WILLIAM J., Sergeant
Resided in Montgomery County where he enlisted at age 24, August 1, 1861. Mustered in as Private and was promoted to Sergeant on September 20, 1862. Died "in the Valley of Virginia" on November 1, 1862. Cause of death not reported.

DUNN, WILLIAM J., Jr., Private
Enlisted in Montgomery County on March 1, 1862. No further records.

FRASER, JOHN H., Sergeant
Resided in Montgomery County where he enlisted at age 19, August 1, 1861. Mustered in as Private and was promoted to Sergeant in November, 1862-May, 1864. Reported missing in action at Spotsylvania Court House, Virginia, May 12, 1864. No further records.

FRASER, WILLIAM T., Private
Enlisted in Wake County on February 10, 1864, for the war. Wounded at Gravel Hill, Virginia, July 28, 1864. Returned to duty on November 28, 1864. Present or accounted for through February, 1865.

GADD, JESSE, Private
Resided in Montgomery County where he enlisted at age 56, August 1, 1861. Died at Wilmington on January 10 or January 21, 1862. Cause of death not reported.

GADD, WILLIAM, Private
Resided in Montgomery County where he enlisted at age 35, August 1, 1861. Wounded at Gettysburg, Pennsylvania, July 1-3, 1863. Returned to duty on an unspecified date. Hospitalized at Petersburg, Virginia, June 25, 1864, with a gunshot wound. Place and date wounded not reported. Returned to duty on September 20, 1864. Deserted to the enemy on or about February 10, 1865. Confined at Washington, D.C. Released on or about February 16, 1865, after taking the Oath of Allegiance.

GARDNER, WILLIAM G., Private
Resided in Montgomery County where he enlisted at age 19, August 1, 1861. Died in hospital at Richmond, Virginia, July 11, 1862, of "typhoid fever."

GIBSON, JAMES T., Private
Born in Richmond County where he resided as a farmer prior to enlisting in New Hanover County at age 27, January 28, 1862. Present or accounted for through February, 1865.

GREEN, JOEL, Private
Enlisted in Wake County on November 5, 1864, for the war. Captured near Petersburg, Virginia, April 2, 1865. Confined at Point Lookout, Maryland, where he died on May 31, 1865, of "consumption."

GREEN, ROBERT E., Private
Resided in Montgomery County where he enlisted at age 17, March 10, 1862. Died in hospital at Charlottesville, Virginia, on or about May 31, 1862, of "typhoid pneumonia."

GREEN, WILLIAM T., Private
Resided in Montgomery County where he enlisted at age 20, August 1, 1861. Captured at the Battle of Second Manassas, Virginia, August 28-30, 1862. Paroled and transferred to Aiken's Landing, James River, Virginia, where he was received September 7, 1862, for exchange. Declared exchanged at Aiken's Landing on September 21, 1862. Returned to duty on an unspecified date. Deserted in February, 1865. Returned to duty on an unspecified date. Surrendered at Appomattox Court House, Virginia, April 9, 1865. [North Carolina pension records indicate he was wounded on September 10, 1863.]

HAITHCOCK, E. W., ———
North Carolina pension records indicate that he served in this company.

HALL, B. L., Private
Born in Montgomery County where he resided prior to enlisting at Camp Gregg, Virginia, February 1, 1863, for the war. Killed at Wilderness, Virginia, May 6, 1864.

HALL, ELISHA, Private
Resided in Montgomery County where he enlisted at age 26, August 1, 1861. Mustered in as Corporal. Captured at Hanover Court House, Virginia, May 27, 1862. Confined at Fort Monroe, Virginia, and at Fort Columbus, New York Harbor. Paroled and transferred to Aiken's Landing, James River, Virginia, where he was received July 12, 1862, for exchange. Declared exchanged at Aiken's Landing on August 5, 1862. Returned to duty prior to November 1, 1862. Reduced to ranks in November, 1862-October, 1864. Wounded at Chancellorsville, Virginia, May 2-3, 1863. Returned to duty on an unspecified date. Deserted on August 15, 1863. Returned to duty prior to May 6, 1864, when he was wounded at Wilderness, Virginia. Reported absent without leave from November 11, 1864, through February, 1865.

HALL, JOHN W., Private
Resided in Montgomery County where he enlisted at age 23, August 1, 1861. Captured at Hanover Court House, Virginia, May 27, 1862. Confined at Fort Monroe, Virginia, and at Fort Columbus, New York Harbor. Paroled and transferred to Aiken's Landing, James River, Virginia, where he was received July 12, 1862, for exchange. Declared exchanged at Aiken's Landing on August 5, 1862. Company records do not

indicate whether he returned to duty. Reported absent without leave from October 18, 1864, through February, 1865.

HALTON, REUBIN J., Private
Previously served in Company E, 1st Regiment N.C. Junior Reserves. Transferred to this company on January 20, 1865. Surrendered at Appomattox Court House, Virginia, April 9, 1865.

HANEY, JOHN ALLEN, Private
Resided in Union County and enlisted in Wake County at age 25, October 2, 1862, for the war. Present or accounted for until August 5, 1864, when he was reported absent without leave. [North Carolina pension records indicate he was wounded at Petersburg, Virginia, July 7, 1864.]

HARPER, JAMES N., Private
Resided in Montgomery County where he enlisted at age 26, August 1, 1861. Captured at Spotsylvania Court House, Virginia, May 12, 1864. Confined at Point Lookout, Maryland, until transferred to Elmira, New York, August 10, 1864. Released at Elmira on June 19, 1865, after taking the Oath of Allegiance.

HARRIS, ELI, Private
Born in Montgomery County where he resided as a farmer prior to enlisting at age 22, August 1, 1861. Wounded in the left thigh at Gaines' Mill, Virginia, June 27, 1862. Discharged on February 12, 1863, by reason of disability from wounds. Paroled at Troy on May 23, 1865.

HARRIS, ELI T., Private
Resided in Montgomery County where he enlisted at age 18, March 10, 1862. Died in hospital at Charlottesville, Virginia, June 9, 1862, of "pneumonia."

HASTEN, JOHN C., Private
Enlisted in Wake County on October 2, 1862, for the war. Wounded in the thigh and captured at Gettysburg, Pennsylvania, July 3, 1863. Hospitalized at Gettysburg where he died on July 7, 1863, of wounds.

HASTY, W. F., Private
Resided in Union County and enlisted at age 30, October 2, 1862, for the war. Deserted on June 5, 1863. Captured by the enemy at Culpeper, Virginia, August 3, 1863. Confined at Old Capitol Prison, Washington, D.C., until released on September 24, 1863, after taking the Oath of Allegiance.

HAYWOOD, WILSON, Private
Resided in Montgomery County where he enlisted at age 31, August 1, 1861. Died at Wilmington on January 5 or January 14, 1862. Cause of death not reported.

HENDERSON, JEHU S., Private
Resided in Montgomery County and enlisted at age 18, March 4, 1862. Died at Guinea Station, Virginia, June 8, 1863. Cause of death not reported.

HENDERSON, JOEL G., Private
Resided in Montgomery County where he enlisted at age 18, August 1, 1861. Present or accounted for until transferred to Company K, 34th Regiment N.C. Troops, March 12, 1864, in exchange for Private Calvin Macon.

HESTER, JEREMIAH M., Private
Resided in Montgomery or Forsyth County and enlisted in Montgomery County at age 19, August 1, 1861. Wounded at Chancellorsville, Virginia, May 2-3, 1863. Returned to duty on an unspecified date. Detailed for light duty at Staunton, Virginia, March 18, 1864. Reported absent on detail through February, 1865. Captured by the enemy on an unspecified date. Confined at Wheeling, West Virginia, on or about March 12, 1865. Released on or about March 13, 1865, after taking the Oath of Allegiance.

HESTER, STEPHEN, Private
Resided in Union County and enlisted in Wake County at age 21, October 2, 1862, for the war. Captured at Spotsylvania Court House, Virginia, May 12, 1864. Confined at Point Lookout, Maryland, until transferred to Elmira, New York, August 10, 1864. Died at Elmira on September 20, 1864, of "pneumonia."

HIGHT, CHARNAL, Private
Resided in Montgomery County and enlisted in Wake County on November 19, 1864, for the war. Captured at the Appomattox River, Virginia, April 3, 1865. Confined at Hart's Island, New York Harbor, until released on or about June 20, 1865, after taking the Oath of Allegiance.

HIGHT, SAMUEL, Private
Resided in Montgomery County where he enlisted at age 22, August 1, 1861. Hospitalized at Richmond, Virginia, July 1, 1862, after being "bruised by bomb." Place and date injured not reported. Returned to duty prior to November 1, 1862. Retired to the Invalid Corps on November 23, 1864, by reason of disability.

HILL, JESSE LEE, Private
Resided in Montgomery County where he enlisted at age 22, August 1, 1861. Present or accounted for until he surrendered at Appomattox Court House, Virginia, April 9, 1865.

HOWELL, JAMES, Private
Born in Montgomery County where he resided as a farmer prior to enlisting in Montgomery County at age 67, August 1, 1861. Discharged on December 8, 1862, by reason of "bronchitis and chronic diarrh[o]ea."

HUDSON, HENRY H., Private
Resided in Montgomery County where he enlisted at age 20, August 1, 1861. Died in hospital at Richmond, Virginia, October 25, 1862, of disease.

HUDSON, JOHN D., Private
Resided in Montgomery County where he enlisted at age 19, March 1, 1862. Captured at Burkeville, Virginia, April 3, 1865. Confined at Point Lookout, Maryland, until released on June 27, 1865, after taking the Oath of Allegiance. [North Carolina pension records indicate he was wounded on July 20, 1862.]

HUNSUCKER, GEORGE HENDERSON, Private
Resided in Montgomery County where he enlisted at age 28, March 4, 1862/1863, for the war. Wounded at Gettysburg, Pennsylvania, July 1-3, 1863. Captured at Williamsport, Maryland, July 4, 1863. Hospitalized at Chester, Pennsylvania. Paroled and transferred to City Point, Virginia, where he was received August 17, 1863, for exchange. Reported on light duty as a hospital nurse

from July 1 through September 30, 1864. Rejoined the company on October 9, 1864. Present or accounted for through February, 1865.

HUNSUCKER, JOHN A., Private
Resided in Montgomery County where he enlisted at age 23, August 1, 1861. Killed at Chancellorsville, Virginia, May 3, 1863.

HURT, MASON A., Private
Born in Montgomery County where he resided as a farmer prior to enlisting in Montgomery County at age 25, August 1, 1861. Wounded at Chancellorsville, Virginia, May 2-3, 1863. Returned to duty on an unspecified date. Reported present for duty from September-October, 1864, through February 20, 1865, when he was furloughed for eighteen days. Paroled at Troy on May 23, 1865.

INGRAM, WILLIAM B., Private
Enlisted at Camp Stokes on November 5, 1864, for the war. Surrendered at Appomattox Court House, Virginia, April 9, 1865.

JOHNSON, THOMAS, Private
Resided in Montgomery County where he enlisted at age 37, August 1, 1861. Captured in hospital at Richmond, Virginia, April 3, 1865. Confined at Newport News, Virginia, until released on June 15, 1865, after taking the Oath of Allegiance.

KESTER, MOSES M., Private
Enlisted in Wake County on October 16, 1863, for the war. Died in hospital at Richmond, Virginia, February 19, 1864, of "febris typhoides."

KING, HIRAM D., Private
Resided in Henderson County. Place and date of enlistment not reported. Deserted to the enemy on or about March 20, 1864. Confined at Knoxville, Tennessee. Released on or about October 7, 1864, after taking the Oath of Allegiance.

LASSITER, JAMES A., Private
Resided in Montgomery County where he enlisted at age 25, August 1, 1861. Present or accounted for through February, 1865.

LEACH, ALEXANDER M., Private
Born in Montgomery County where he resided prior to enlisting in Montgomery County at age 21, August 1, 1861. Died in hospital at Richmond, Virginia, December 18, 1862, of "pneumonia."

LEDBETTER, JOHN A., Private
Resided in Montgomery County where he enlisted at age 43, March 1, 1862. Present or accounted for until he surrendered at Appomattox Court House, Virginia, April 9, 1865.

LEMONS, ARCHIBALD, Private
Enlisted in Wake County on November 17, 1864, for the war. Deserted in February, 1865. Returned to duty on an unspecified date. Surrendered at Appomattox Court House, Virginia, April 9, 1865.

LEMONS, MALCOLM, Private
Resided in Montgomery County where he enlisted at age 33, August 1, 1861. Deserted in February, 1865.

Returned to duty on an unspecified date. Surrendered at Appomattox Court House, Virginia, April 9, 1865.

LISK, JOSIAH T., Private
Resided in Montgomery County and enlisted in Lenoir County at age 19, March 20, 1862. Present or accounted for until he surrendered at Appomattox Court House, Virginia, April 9, 1865.

LISK, WASHINGTON, Private
Resided in Montgomery County where he enlisted at age 45, August 1, 1861. Died in hospital at Richmond, Virginia, August 3-6, 1862, of "feb[ris] typhoides."

LISK, WILLIAM T., Musician
Resided in Montgomery County where he enlisted at age 29, August 1, 1861. Mustered in as Musician. Present or accounted for until he surrendered at Appomattox Court House, Virginia, April 9, 1865.

LOTHROP, WILLIAM H., Private
Resided in Union County and enlisted in Wake County at age 25, October 2, 1862, for the war. Captured at or near Gravel Hill, Virginia, July 28, 1864. Confined at Point Lookout, Maryland, until transferred to Elmira, New York, August 8, 1864. Transferred to a hospital at Baltimore, Maryland, on or about October 13, 1864. Died in hospital at Baltimore on December 19, 1864, of "chronic diarrhoea."

LUTHER, GODFREY W., Private
Resided in Montgomery or Randolph County and enlisted in Montgomery County at age 21, August 1, 1861. Wounded in both thighs at Fredericksburg, Virginia, December 13, 1862. Hospitalized at Richmond, Virginia. Furloughed for ninety days on March 26, 1863. Returned to duty on an unspecified date. Reported on light duty at Staunton, Virginia, from March 10, 1864, through February, 1865. "Arrested" by the enemy on March 10, 1865. Confined at Wheeling, West Virginia, on or about March 12, 1865. Released on or about March 12, 1865, after taking the Oath of Allegiance.

LUTHER, JESSE M., Private
Resided in Montgomery County where he enlisted at age 23, August 1, 1861. Captured at or near Gravel Hill, Virginia, July 28, 1864. Confined at Point Lookout, Maryland, until transferred to Elmira, New York, August 8, 1864. Arrived at Elmira on August 12, 1864. Paroled at Elmira on March 14, 1865, and transferred to Boulware's Wharf, James River, Virginia, where he was received March 18-21, 1865, for exchange.

McAULAY, ANGUS M., Private
Resided in Montgomery County where he enlisted at age 27, August 1, 1861. Mustered in as Corporal but was reduced to ranks in March-April, 1862. Captured at Hanover Court House, Virginia, May 27, 1862. Confined at Fort Monroe, Virginia, and at Fort Columbus, New York Harbor. Paroled and transferred to Aiken's Landing, James River, Virginia, July 12, 1862, for exchange. Declared exchanged at Aiken's Landing on August 5, 1862. Returned to duty prior to November 1, 1862. Hospitalized at Richmond, Virginia, May 16, 1864, with a gunshot wound of the left thigh. Place and date wounded not reported. Returned to duty on September 3, 1864. Captured near Petersburg, Virginia, April 2, 1865. Confined at Point Lookout, Maryland, until released on June 29, 1865, after taking the Oath of Allegiance.

McAULAY, H. W., Private
Resided in Montgomery County where he enlisted at age 25, August 1, 1861. Died at Wilmington on December 31, 1861. Cause of death not reported.

McAULAY, JOHN T., Private
Previously served as 2nd Lieutenant and Sergeant in Company E, 1st Regiment N.C. Junior Reserves. Transferred to this company with the rank of Private on January 20, 1865. Surrendered at Appomattox Court House, Virginia, April 9, 1865.

McAULAY, MARTIN A., Private
Enlisted in Wake County on November 5, 1864, for the war. Captured in hospital at Richmond, Virginia, April 3, 1865. Transferred to Newport News, Virginia, April 23, 1865. Died at Newport News on June 1, 1865, of "chronic diarrhoea" and/or "rubeola."

McCASKILL, JAMES, Private
Born in Montgomery County where he resided as a farmer prior to enlisting in Montgomery County at age 53, March 6, 1862, as a substitute. Captured at Hanover Court House, Virginia, May 27, 1862. Confined at Fort Monroe, Virginia, and at Fort Columbus, New York Harbor. Paroled and transferred to Aiken's Landing, James River, Virginia, where he was received July 12, 1862, for exchange. Declared exchanged at Aiken's Landing on August 5, 1862. Company records do not indicate whether he returned to duty. Discharged on November 21, 1863, by reason of "varicose veins of leg & infirmities of old age."

McDANIEL, JOHN, Private
Previously served in an unspecified junior reserves regiment. Transferred to this company on January 20, 1865. Captured in hospital at Petersburg, Virginia, April 3, 1865. Died in hospital at Petersburg on April 7, 1865. Cause of death not reported.

McDONALD, HOWELL G., Private
Resided in Montgomery County where he enlisted at age 21, August 1, 1861. Captured near Petersburg, Virginia, June 22, 1864. Confined at Point Lookout, Maryland, where he died on April 20, 1865, of "chronic diarrhoea."

McINNIS, EVANDER J., Private
Born in Montgomery County where he resided prior to enlisting in Montgomery County at age 19, August 1, 1861. Wounded and captured at Gettysburg, Pennsylvania, July 3, 1863. Hospitalized at Chester, Pennsylvania, where he died on July 12, 1863. Cause of death not reported.

McKAY, ROBERT B., Sergeant
Resided in Montgomery County and enlisted in Guilford County at age 18, September 25, 1861. Mustered in as Private and was promoted to Sergeant in November, 1862-October, 1864. Captured near Petersburg, Virginia, April 2, 1865. Confined at Point Lookout, Maryland, until released on June 29, 1865, after taking the Oath of Allegiance.

McKENZIE, JAMES A., Private
Resided in Montgomery County where he enlisted at age 24, August 1, 1861. Present or accounted for until he surrendered at Appomattox Court House, Virginia,

April 9, 1865.

McLEAN, JOHN, Private
Resided in Montgomery County where he enlisted at age 26, August 1, 1861. Captured at the Battle of Second Manassas, Virginia, August 28-30, 1862. Confined at Fort Monroe, Virginia. Paroled and transferred to Aiken's Landing, James River, Virginia, where he was received September 7, 1862, for exchange. Declared exchanged at Aiken's Landing on September 21, 1862. Company records do not indicate whether he returned to duty. Died in hospital at Richmond, Virginia, February 18, 1863, of "pneumonia."

MACON, CALVIN, Private
Previously served in Company K, 34th Regiment N.C. Troops. Transferred to this company on March 12, 1864, in exchange for Private Joel G. Henderson. Deserted in February, 1865. Returned to duty on an unspecified date. Surrendered at Appomattox Court House, Virginia, April 9, 1865.

McRAE, GEORGE W., Private
Resided in Montgomery County where he enlisted at age 19, August 1, 1861. Wounded in the right arm at Reams' Station, Virginia, August 25, 1864. Retired to the Invalid Corps on December 21, 1864, by reason of disability.

McRAE, JAMES LAWRENCE, Private
Previously served as 3rd Lieutenant of this company. Resigned as 3rd Lieutenant on July 23, 1862, and was reduced to the rank of Private. Wounded at Gettysburg, Pennsylvania, July 1-3, 1863. Returned to duty on an unspecified date. Reported present for duty from September-October, 1864, through February, 1865. Captured near Petersburg, Virginia, April 2, 1865. Confined at Point Lookout, Maryland, until released on June 29, 1865, after taking the Oath of Allegiance. [See also the Lieutenants' section above.]

MASK, J. F., Private
Resided in Montgomery County where he enlisted at age 18, March 20, 1862. Died in hospital at Lynchburg, Virginia, June 6, 1862, of "typhoid fever."

MASON, JOHN T., Sergeant
Resided in Montgomery County where he enlisted at age 27, August 1, 1861. Mustered in as Sergeant. Killed at Gaines' Mill, Virginia, or at Frayser's Farm, Virginia, June 27-30, 1862. "A cheerful soldier."

MATHERSON, MALCOLM D., Private
Born in Moore County and resided in Montgomery County prior to enlisting in Wake County on November 5, 1864, for the war. Captured near Petersburg, Virginia, April 2, 1865. Confined at Fort Delaware, Delaware, until released on June 19, 1865, after taking the Oath of Allegiance.

MATHESON, JOHN L., Corporal
Resided in Montgomery County and was by occupation a blacksmith prior to enlisting in Montgomery County at age 17, August 1, 1861. Mustered in as Private. Wounded in the thigh at Gaines' Mill, Virginia, June 27, 1862. Returned to duty prior to November 1, 1862. Promoted to Corporal in July, 1863-October, 1864. Captured near Petersburg, Virginia, April 2, 1865. Confined at Point Lookout, Maryland, until released on June 29, 1865, after taking the Oath of Allegiance.

MILLS, HIRAM M., Private
Resided in Montgomery County where he enlisted at age 30, August 1, 1861. Died in hospital at Richmond, Virginia, June 15, 1862, of "remit[tent] fever."

MORGAN, GEORGE H., Private
Resided in Montgomery County where he enlisted at age 18, March 4, 1863, for the war. Captured at Spotsylvania Court House, Virginia, May 12, 1864. Confined at Point Lookout, Maryland, until transferred to Elmira, New York, August 10, 1864. Released at Elmira on June 27, 1865, after taking the Oath of Allegiance.

MORRIS, GREEN RICHARDSON, Private
Resided in Montgomery County where he enlisted at age 27, August 1, 1861. Company records indicate he was captured at the Battle of Second Manassas, Virginia, August 28-30, 1862; however, records of the Federal Provost Marshal do not substantiate that report. Company records do not indicate whether he served with the company after October 31, 1862. Transferred to Company B, 14th Regiment N.C. Troops (4th Regiment N.C. Volunteers), April 14, 1864.

MORRIS, JAMES C., Private
Born in Montgomery County where he resided as a farmer prior to enlisting in Montgomery County at age 30, August 1, 1861. Discharged on December 30, 1861, by reason of "chronic rheumatism."

MORRIS, SAMPSON, Private
Resided in Montgomery County where he enlisted at age 32, August 1, 1861. Wounded at Gettysburg, Pennsylvania, July 1-3, 1863. Returned to duty on an unspecified date. Wounded in the left knee at Jones' Farm, Virginia, September 30, 1864. Reported absent without leave from December 25, 1864, through February, 1865. Paroled at Troy on May 22, 1865.

MUNN, MARTIN A., Sergeant
Resided in Montgomery County where he enlisted at age 28, August 1, 1861. Mustered in as Private and was promoted to Sergeant on September 8, 1862. Wounded at Shepherdstown, Virginia, September 20, 1862. Died at Winchester, Virginia, September 25, 1862, of wounds.

NICHOLS, NOAH W., Private
Resided in Montgomery County where he enlisted at age 18, August 1, 1861. Captured near Petersburg, Virginia, April 2, 1865. Confined at Point Lookout, Maryland, until released on June 29, 1865, after taking the Oath of Allegiance.

PARKER, JOHN C., Private
Resided in Montgomery County where he enlisted at age 23, August 1, 1861. Reported missing and "supposed to be dead" at Gettysburg, Pennsylvania, July 3, 1863.

PARNELL, H. H., Private
Born in Montgomery County where he resided as a farmer prior to enlisting in Montgomery County at age 19, March 10, 1862. Discharged on December 25, 1863, by reason of "disease of the heart."

PARNELL, LARKIN N., Private
Resided in Montgomery County where he enlisted at

age 25, August 1, 1861. Died at Wilmington on November 19, 1861. Cause of death not reported.

PARSONS, THOMAS A., Private
Resided in Montgomery County where he enlisted at age 21, August 1, 1861. Deserted in February, 1865. Returned to duty on an unspecified date. Surrendered at Appomattox Court House, Virginia, April 9, 1865.

PHILLIPS, WILLIAM, Private
Resided in Montgomery County where he enlisted at age 19, August 1, 1861. Reported missing and "supposed to be dead" at Gettysburg, Pennsylvania, July 3, 1863.

PITMAN, JOHN A., Private
Resided in Montgomery County where he enlisted at age 22, August 1, 1861. Died in hospital at Richmond, Virginia, on or about June 3, 1863, of "feb[ris] typhoid."

REDEN, JAMES A., Private
Previously served in Company F, 44th Regiment N.C. Troops. Enlisted in this company "without a transfer" in March-May, 1862. Captured at Hanover Court House, Virginia, May 27, 1862. Confined at Fort Monroe, Virginia, and at Fort Columbus, New York Harbor. Paroled and transferred to Aiken's Landing, James River, Virginia, where he was received July 12, 1862, for exchange. Declared exchanged at Aiken's Landing on August 5, 1862. Returned to duty prior to November 1, 1862. Captured at Gettysburg, Pennsylvania, July 3, 1863. Confined at Fort Delaware, Delaware. Released on May 3, 1865, after taking the Oath of Allegiance.

RICHARDSON, JOHN T., Private
Resided in Montgomery County where he enlisted at age 26, August 1, 1861. Died at Wilmington on December 30, 1861, of disease.

ROBERSON, THOMAS C., Private
Previously served in Company E, 1st Regiment N.C. Junior Reserves. Transferred to this company on January 20, 1865. Surrendered at Appomattox Court House, Virginia, April 9, 1865.

ROBINSON, JOHN L., Private
Born in Montgomery County where he resided as a farmer prior to enlisting in Montgomery County at age 19, August 1, 1861. Discharged on February 25, 1862, by reason of "inguinal hernia of the right side." [North Carolina pension records indicate he was wounded in the face near Petersburg, Virginia, June 30, 1862.]

ROBINSON, LIVINGSTON, Private
Resided in Montgomery County where he enlisted at age 33, August 1, 1861. Killed at Fredericksburg, Virginia, December 13, 1862.

ROPER, JOHN W., Private
Resided in Montgomery County where he enlisted at age 21, August 1, 1861. Hospitalized at Richmond, Virginia, December 16, 1862, with a gunshot wound. Place and date wounded not reported. Died in hospital at Richmond on March 18, 1863, of "varioloid & gangre[ne]."

RUSSELL, JASON, Private
Resided in Montgomery County and enlisted at age 40,

March 4, 1863, for the war. Died at Salisbury on July 18, 1863. Cause of death not reported.

RUSSELL, JOSEPH C., Private
Resided in Montgomery County where he enlisted at age 30, March 10, 1862. Captured at Hanover Court House, Virginia, May 27, 1862. Confined at Fort Monroe, Virginia, and at Fort Columbus, New York Harbor. Paroled and transferred to Aiken's Landing, James River, Virginia, where he was received July 12, 1862, for exchange. Declared exchanged at Aiken's Landing on August 5, 1862. Company records do not indicate whether he returned to duty. Died in hospital in Lynchburg, Virginia, April 9, 1863, of "diarrhoea ch[ronic]."

SCARBOROUGH, BENJAMIN F., Private
Enlisted at Liberty Mills, Virginia, February 15, 1864, for the war. Wounded in the hip at Jones' Farm, Virginia, September 30, 1864. Returned to duty in January-February, 1865. Present or accounted for through February, 1865.

SEDBERRY, JOHN A., Private
Resided in Montgomery County where he enlisted at age 31, August 1, 1861. Wounded at or near Frayser's Farm, Virginia, on or about June 30, 1862. Returned to duty prior to November 1, 1862. Captured at Gettysburg, Pennsylvania, July 3, 1863. Confined at Fort Delaware, Delaware. Transferred to Point Lookout, Maryland, October 15-18, 1863. Died at Point Lookout on December 27, 1863. Cause of death not reported.

SIDES, CALVIN T., Private
Previously served in Company B, 14th Regiment N.C. Troops (4th Regiment N.C. Volunteers). Transferred to this company on April 14, 1864. Captured at Fussell's Mill, Virginia, August 16, 1864. Confined at Point Lookout, Maryland, until paroled and transferred to Boulware's Wharf, James River, Virginia, where he was received March 16, 1865, for exchange.

SMART, E. M., Private
Resided in Montgomery County where he enlisted at age 25, March 10, 1862. Died in hospital at Richmond, Virginia, June 22, 1862, of disease.

SMART, G. H., Private
Resided in Montgomery County where he enlisted at age 23, March 10, 1862. Died at Winchester, Virginia, November 30, 1862. Cause of death not reported.

SMART, JOSEPH A., Corporal
Resided in Montgomery County where he enlisted at age 24, August 1, 1861. Mustered in as Private and was promoted to Corporal in March-April, 1862. Died in hospital at Richmond, Virginia, December 1, 1862, of "pneumonia."

SMITH, CALVIN, Corporal
Resided in Montgomery County where he enlisted at age 30, August 1, 1861. Mustered in as Private. Captured at Hanover Court House, Virginia, May 27, 1862. Confined at Fort Monroe, Virginia, and at Fort Columbus, New York Harbor. Paroled and transferred to Aiken's Landing, James River, Virginia, where he was received July 12, 1862, for exchange. Declared exchanged at Aiken's Landing on August 5, 1862. Returned to duty prior to November 1, 1862. Promoted to Corporal in July, 1863-May, 1864. Captured at

Spotsylvania Court House, Virginia, May 12, 1864. Confined at Point Lookout, Maryland. Paroled and transferred to Cox's Wharf, James River, Virginia, where he was received on or about February 14, 1865, for exchange. Company records do not indicate whether he returned to duty. Paroled at Troy on May 22, 1865.

SMITH, GREEN, Private
Born in Montgomery County where he resided as a farmer prior to enlisting in Montgomery County at age 22, August 1, 1861. Wounded in the right arm at Fredericksburg, Virginia, December 13, 1862. Company records do not indicate whether he returned to duty. Discharged on December 25, 1863, by reason of disability from wounds.

SMITH, JOHN R., Private
Resided in Montgomery County where he enlisted at age 23, August 1, 1861. Hospitalized at Richmond, Virginia, July 1, 1862, with a gunshot wound of the hand. Place and date wounded not reported. Returned to duty prior to November 1, 1862. Died at Guinea Station, Virginia, January 17-19, 1863. Cause of death not reported.

SMITH, REUBEN, Private
Resided in Montgomery County where he enlisted at age 29, March 10, 1862. Died in hospital at Lynchburg, Virginia, September 2, 1862, of "typhoid fever."

SMITH, THOMAS R., Private
Born in Montgomery County where he resided prior to enlisting in Montgomery County at age 33, August 1, 1861. Killed at Spotsylvania Court House, Virginia, May 12, 1864.

SMITH, W. A., Private
Resided in Montgomery County and enlisted in New Hanover County at age 32, March 12, 1862. Wounded and captured at Gettysburg, Pennsylvania, July 1-3, 1863. Died at Gettysburg on July 11, 1863, of wounds.

SMITH, WILLIAM D., Private
Resided in Montgomery County where he enlisted at age 19, March 10, 1862. Wounded in the chest at Fredericksburg, Virginia, December 13, 1862. Returned to duty prior to May 2-3, 1863, when he was wounded at Chancellorsville, Virginia. Returned to duty on an unspecified date. Reported present for duty from September-October, 1864, through January, 1865. Deserted in February, 1865. Returned to duty on an unspecified date. Surrendered at Appomattox Court House, Virginia, April 9, 1865.

STAFFORD, J. A., Private
Born in Montgomery County where he resided prior to enlisting in Montgomery County at age 25, March 10, 1862. Died at Richmond, Virginia, December 11, 1862, of "pneumonia."

STAFFORD, JOHN M., Private
Resided in Montgomery or Randolph County and enlisted in Lenoir County at age 21, March 20, 1862. Captured at Gettysburg, Pennsylvania, July 1-3, 1863. Confined at Fort Delaware, Delaware. Transferred to Point Lookout, Maryland, October 15-18, 1863. Released at Point Lookout on June 20, 1865, after taking the Oath of Allegiance.

STUTTS, MATHEW H., Corporal
Resided in Montgomery County where he enlisted at age 20, August 1, 1861. Mustered in as Private and was promoted to Corporal in November, 1862-October, 1864. Deserted on February 2, 1865. Returned to duty on an unspecified date. Surrendered at Appomattox Court House, Virginia, April 9, 1865.

TEAL, THOMAS FRANK, Private
Resided in Montgomery County where he enlisted at age 26, August 1, 1861. Wounded at or near Gaines' Mill, Virginia, on or about June 27, 1862. Died at Richmond, Virginia, July 1-2, 1862, of wounds.

THOMPSON, JAMES, Private
Born in Montgomery County and enlisted in Wake County on November 26, 1863, for the war. Died in hospital at Gordonsville, Virginia, March 27, 1864, of "pneumonia."

TIPPET, WILLIAM, Corporal
Born in England and resided in Montgomery County where he enlisted at age 30, August 1, 1861. Mustered in as Private and was promoted to Corporal in March-April, 1862. Captured at Hanover Court House, Virginia, May 27, 1862. Confined at Fort Monroe, Virginia, and at Fort Columbus, New York Harbor. Paroled and transferred to Aiken's Landing, James River, Virginia, where he was received July 12, 1862, for exchange. Declared exchanged at Aiken's Landing on August 5, 1862. Returned to duty prior to November 1, 1862. Hospitalized at Richmond, Virginia, December 19, 1862, with an unspecified complaint. No further records.

TOLBERT, PINKNEY T., Private
Resided in Montgomery County where he enlisted at age 35, August 1, 1861. Deserted on August 15, 1863. Returned to duty on an unspecified date. Reported present for duty from September-October, 1864, through February, 1865. Captured near Petersburg, Virginia, April 2, 1865. Confined at Point Lookout, Maryland, until released on June 20, 1865, after taking the Oath of Allegiance.

TOWNSEND, BENJAMIN J., Sergeant
Resided in Richmond County and enlisted in Montgomery County at age 21, August 1, 1861. Mustered in as Sergeant. Killed at Cedar Mountain, Virginia, August 9, 1862.

USERY, JAMES, Private
Resided in Montgomery County where he enlisted at age 19, August 1, 1861. Wounded at Gaines' Mill, Virginia, June 27, 1862. Returned to duty on an unspecified date. Deserted in February, 1865. Returned to duty on an unspecified date. Surrendered at Appomattox Court House, Virginia, April 9, 1865.

USHER, JOHN B., Private
Born in Montgomery County where he resided as a farmer prior to enlisting in Lenoir County at age 23, April 10, 1862. Discharged on March 13, 1863, by reason of "physical disability."

WADE, EDWIN P., Private
Resided in Montgomery County where he enlisted at age 21, August 1, 1861. Wounded in the lungs at Cedar Mountain, Virginia, August 9, 1862. Died in hospital at

Charlottesville, Virginia, on or about September 1, 1862, of wounds.

WADE, JAMES W., Private
Resided in Montgomery County and enlisted in Lenoir County at age 19, March 20, 1862. Wounded in the arm and captured at Gettysburg, Pennsylvania, July 1-4, 1863. Hospitalized at Gettysburg until transferred to Davids Island, New York Harbor, July 17-24, 1863. Paroled at Davids Island and transferred to City Point, Virginia, where he was received October 28, 1863, for exchange. Reported absent wounded until he was retired to the Invalid Corps on October 13 or December 21, 1864, by reason of disability.

WAESNER, G. W., Private
Resided in Montgomery County where he enlisted at age 27, March 10, 1862. Died in hospital at Lynchburg, Virginia, June 22, 1863, of "pneumonia."

WAESNER, SOLOMON E., Private
Resided in Montgomery County where he enlisted at age 25, May 23, 1862, for the war. Wounded in the right hip and captured at Gettysburg, Pennsylvania, July 1-3, 1863. Died in hospital at Gettysburg on August 18, 1863. Cause of death not reported.

WAISNER, DAVID W., Private
Resided in Montgomery County and enlisted in Lenoir County at age 22, March 20, 1862. Captured at Hanover Court House, Virginia, May 27, 1862. Confined at Fort Monroe, Virginia, and at Fort Columbus, New York Harbor. Paroled and transferred to Aiken's Landing, James River, Virginia, where he was received July 12, 1862, for exchange. Declared exchanged at Aiken's Landing on August 5, 1862. Returned to duty prior to November 1, 1862. Captured at Gettysburg, Pennsylvania, July 3, 1863. Hospitalized at Chester, Pennsylvania, July 17, 1863. Paroled and transferred to City Point, Virginia, where he was received August 20, 1863, for exchange. Returned to duty on an unspecified date. Wounded and captured at Gravel Hill, Virginia, July 28, 1864. Confined at Point Lookout, Maryland, on or about December 3, 1864. Paroled and transferred to Boulware's Wharf, James River, Virginia, where he was received March 18, 1865, for exchange.

WARNER, JAMES A., Private
Born in Montgomery County where he resided as a farmer prior to enlisting in Montgomery County at age 23, August 1, 1861. Discharged on November 13, 1861, or February 27, 1862, by reason of "varicocele of both sides."

WARNER, WILLIAM G., Musician
Resided in Montgomery County where he enlisted at age 27, August 1, 1861. Mustered in as Musician. Died in hospital at Montgomery White Sulphur Springs, Virginia, February 6, 1863, of "diarrhoea chronica."

WEBB, BENJAMIN R., Private
Resided in Richmond County and enlisted in Montgomery County at age 23, August 1, 1861. Died at Berryville, Virginia, November 6, 1862, of disease.

WELCH, JOHN J., Private
Resided in Guilford County and enlisted in Wake County on October 16, 1863, for the war. Captured near

Petersburg, Virginia, April 2, 1865. Confined at Point Lookout, Maryland, until released on June 21, 1865, after taking the Oath of Allegiance.

WILLIAMS, RANDOLPH S., Private
Enlisted at Camp Stokes on November 17, 1864, for the war. Surrendered at Appomattox Court House, Virginia, April 9, 1865.

WILSON, JOHN, Private
Enlisted in Wake County on October 3, 1863, for the war. Present or accounted for through February, 1865.

YARBOROUGH, THOMAS, Private
Resided in Montgomery County where he enlisted at age 30, March 18, 1862. Hospitalized at Richmond, Virginia, February 22, 1864, with "variola" and died on March 7, 1864.

COMPANY F

This company, known as the "Yadkin Boys," was raised in Yadkin County and enlisted at East Bend. It was mustered into service on June 18, 1861, and assigned to the 28th Regiment as Company F. After joining the regiment the company functioned as a part of the regiment, and its history for the war period is reported as a part of the regimental history.

The information contained in the following roster of the company was compiled principally from company muster rolls for June 18-December, 1861; May-December, 1862; and September, 1864-February, 1865. No company muster rolls were found for January-April, 1862; January, 1863-August, 1864; or for the period after February, 1865. Valuable information was obtained also from primary records such as the Roll of Honor, medical records, prisoner of war records, discharge certificates, and pension applications, and from secondary sources such as postwar rosters and histories, cemetery records, and records of the United Daughters of the Confederacy.

OFFICERS

CAPTAINS

KENYON, JOHN HENDRICKS
Resided in Yadkin County and was by occupation a physician prior to enlisting in Yadkin County at age 33. Appointed Captain on June 18, 1861. Resigned on March 28, 1862, in order to apply for a medical position. Appointed Assistant Surgeon of the 66th Regiment N.C. Troops on August 16, 1862.

APPERSON, THOMAS V.
Resided in Yadkin County where he enlisted at age 23. Appointed 1st Lieutenant on June 18, 1861, and was elected Captain on April 12, 1862. Wounded in the left leg and captured at Hanover Court House, Virginia, May 27, 1862. Hospitalized at Portsmouth Grove, Rhode Island, July 7, 1862. Transferred to Fort Monroe, Virginia, September 17, 1862. Paroled and transferred to Aiken's Landing, James River, Virginia, where he was received on or about September 23, 1862, for exchange. Declared exchanged at Aiken's Landing on November 10, 1862. Returned to duty prior to January 1, 1863. Resigned on January 26, 1865, by reason of ill health and in order to serve in the cavalry.

LIEUTENANTS

CONRAD, JOHN T., 1st Lieutenant
Resided in Yadkin County and enlisted at Camp Enon at age 23, August 10, 1861. Mustered in as Private and was promoted to 2nd Lieutenant on September 5, 1861. Elected 1st Lieutenant on April 12, 1862. Present or accounted for through December, 1862. Furloughed home on an unspecified date and "remained overtime." Dropped from the rolls of the company on or about April 27, 1863.

CORNELIUS, JOHN H., 3rd Lieutenant
Resided in Yadkin County and enlisted at Camp Enon at age 23, August 10, 1861. Mustered in as Private and was promoted to Corporal on October 10, 1861. Appointed 3rd Lieutenant on April 12, 1862. Wounded in the right thigh and captured at Hanover Court House, Virginia, May 27, 1862. Hospitalized at New York City. Transferred to Fort Delaware, Delaware, August 23, 1862. Paroled and transferred to Aiken's Landing, James River, Virginia, October 2, 1862, for exchange. Declared exchanged at Aiken's Landing on November 10, 1862. Resigned on March 29, 1863, by reason of wounds received at Hanover Court House.

MARLER, WILLIAM A., 2nd Lieutenant
Resided in Yadkin County where he enlisted at age 22. Appointed 3rd Lieutenant on June 18, 1861. Defeated for reelection on April 12, 1862. Enlisted in Company H, 63rd Regiment N.C. Troops (5th Regiment N.C. Cavalry), July 18, 1862, with the rank of Private. Transferred back to this company in June, 1863, upon appointment as 2nd Lieutenant to rank from April 9, 1863. Captured at Gettysburg, Pennsylvania, July 3, 1863. Confined at Fort Delaware, Delaware. Transferred to Johnson's Island, Ohio, July 18, 1863. Paroled at Johnson's Island and transferred to Cox's Wharf, James River, Virginia, where he was received March 22, 1865, for exchange.

POINDEXTER, JOHN H., 2nd Lieutenant
Resided in Yadkin County where he enlisted at age 32. Appointed 2nd Lieutenant on June 18, 1861. Resigned on or about September 5, 1861; however, he continued to serve in the company as a Private and was later promoted to Sergeant. [For additional information see page 182 of this volume.]

STARLING, JAMES M., 3rd Lieutenant
Resided in Yadkin County where he enlisted at age 22, June 18, 1861. Mustered in as Private and was promoted to Sergeant in January-June, 1862. Reduced to the rank of Corporal on an unspecified date but was promoted to Sergeant on September 26, 1862. Reported absent wounded in November-December, 1862. Place and date wounded not reported. Returned to duty on an unspecified date. Appointed 3rd Lieutenant on May 11, 1863. Present or accounted for through February, 1865.

TRUELOVE, JOHN GEORGE, 1st Lieutenant
Resided in Yadkin County where he enlisted at age 29, June 18, 1861. Mustered in as Private and was appointed 2nd Lieutenant on April 12, 1862. Promoted to 1st Lieutenant on April 27, 1863. Wounded in the neck at Gettysburg, Pennsylvania, July 1-3, 1863. Returned to duty on an unspecified date. Wounded in the abdomen near Petersburg, Virginia, June 22, 1864. Hospitalized at Richmond, Virginia. Furloughed on August 11, 1864. Returned to duty on an unspecified

date. Wounded at Jones' Farm, Virginia, September 30, 1864. Died on October 11, 1864, of wounds. Place of death not reported.

NONCOMMISSIONED OFFICERS AND PRIVATES

ADAMS, BENJAMIN F., Private
Born in Yadkin County* where he resided as a farmer prior to enlisting in Yadkin County at age 20, June 18, 1861. Captured at or near Gettysburg, Pennsylvania, July 1-5, 1863. Confined at Davids Island, New York Harbor. Paroled and transferred to City Point, Virginia, where he was received September 16, 1863, for exchange. Returned to duty on an unspecified date. Captured at or near Pickett's Farm, Virginia, on or about July 21-22, 1864. Confined at Point Lookout, Maryland. Released on October 18, 1864, after joining the U.S. Army. Assigned to Company D, 4th Regiment U.S. Volunteer Infantry.

ADAMS, ELAM J., Private
Resided in Yadkin County where he enlisted at age 20, March 4, 1862. Reported absent without leave during July-December, 1862. Returned to duty on an unspecified date. Reported present for duty from September-October, 1864, through February, 1865. Captured near Petersburg, Virginia, April 2, 1865. Confined at Point Lookout, Maryland, until released on June 22, 1865, after taking the Oath of Allegiance.

ALDERMAN, IRA H., Private
Resided in Alamance County and enlisted in Forsyth County at age 26, October 1, 1862, for the war. Transferred to the C.S. Navy on April 3, 1864. [North Carolina pension records indicate he was wounded at Fredericksburg, Chancellorsville, and Gettysburg.]

APPERSON, JOHN ALVIS, Musician
Resided in Yadkin County where he enlisted at age 18, February 1, 1863, for the war. Mustered in as Private and was promoted to Musician prior to January 1, 1865. Present or accounted for through February, 1865.

APPERSON, PETER A., 1st Sergeant
Resided in Yadkin County where he enlisted at age 20, June 18, 1861. Mustered in as Private and was promoted to Sergeant in January-June, 1862. Wounded near Richmond, Virginia, June 25-July 1, 1862. Returned to duty prior to September 1, 1862, when he was wounded in the finger and/or back at Ox Hill, Virginia. Returned to duty on an unspecified date. Promoted to 1st Sergeant on December 1, 1862. Wounded in the right shoulder and captured at Gettysburg, Pennsylvania, July 1-4, 1863. Hospitalized at Davids Island, New York Harbor. Paroled and transferred to City Point, Virginia, where he was received September 16, 1863, for exchange. Returned to duty on an unspecified date. Reported absent sick in September-December, 1864. Returned to duty in January-February, 1865. Captured near Petersburg, Virginia, April 2, 1865. Confined at Point Lookout, Maryland, until released on June 22, 1865, after taking the Oath of Allegiance.

APPERSON, WILLIAM H., Ordnance Sergeant
Resided in Yadkin County where he enlisted at age 35, June 18, 1861. Mustered in as Corporal and was promoted to Ordnance Sergeant on October 9, 1861. Hospitalized at Wilmington on or about February 15,

1862, with typhoid fever and died on February 19-20, 1862.

BAKER, H. C., Private
Born in Yadkin County* where he resided as a student prior to enlisting in Yadkin County at age 17, April 12, 1862, as a substitute. Wounded in the right leg at Gaines' Mill, Virginia, June 27, 1862. Right leg amputated. Discharged on February 19, 1863.

BEAN, ALFORD MONROE, Private
Resided in Yadkin County and enlisted at Camp Gregg, Virginia, at age 30, February 18, 1863, for the war. Deserted on June 5, 1863. [North Carolina pension records indicate he was wounded in May, 1863.]

BEAN, H. T., ——
North Carolina pension records indicate that he served in this company.

BEAN, WILEY J., Private
Resided in Yadkin County and enlisted at Camp Gregg, Virginia, at age 23, February 18, 1863, for the war. Deserted on June 5, 1863. Returned to duty on September 15, 1864. Captured in hospital at Richmond, Virginia, April 3, 1865. Transferred to Newport News, Virginia, April 23, 1865. Died at Newport News on May 8 or June 24, 1865, of "chronic diarrhoea."

BINKLEY, JOHN W., Private
Resided in Yadkin County where he enlisted at age 25, June 18, 1861. Captured near Petersburg, Virginia, April 2, 1865. Confined at Point Lookout, Maryland, until released on June 23, 1865, after taking the Oath of Allegiance.

BLAKELY, ELI Y., Private
Resided in Yadkin County where he enlisted on November 1, 1863, for the war. Reported absent without leave in September-October, 1864. Returned to duty in November-December, 1864. Captured near Petersburg, Virginia, April 2, 1865. Confined at Hart's Island, New York Harbor, until released on June 17, 1865, after taking the Oath of Allegiance.

BLAKELY, GEORGE W., Private
Resided in Yadkin County where he enlisted at age 22, June 18, 1861. Retired on February 18, 1865. Reason was retired not reported. [North Carolina pension records indicate he was "wounded at Reams' Station in 1862."]

BOVENDER, G. G., Private
Resided in Yadkin County where he enlisted at age 30, March 31, 1862. Wounded at Chancellorsville, Virginia, May 2-3, 1863. Died at Richmond, Virginia, May 5, 1863, of wounds.

BOVENDER, GEORGE W., Private
Resided in Yadkin County where he enlisted at age 37, June 18, 1861. Died "at home" on or about June 27, 1862. Cause of death not reported.

BOVENDER, JOHN R., Private
Resided in Yadkin County where he enlisted at age 16, June 18, 1861. Deserted on September 13, 1862. Returned to duty subsequent to December 31, 1862. Reported present with the company during September, 1864-February, 1865. Wounded in the right thigh at or

near Amelia Court House, Virginia, April 5, 1865. Reported in hospital at Danville, Virginia, April 6, 1865. [North Carolina pension records indicate that he survived the war.]

BRAN, HENRY T., Corporal
Resided in Yadkin County where he enlisted at age 18, June 18, 1861. Mustered in as Private and was promoted to Corporal on November 1, 1864. Captured near Petersburg, Virginia, April 2, 1865. Confined at Point Lookout, Maryland, until released on June 23, 1865, after taking the Oath of Allegiance.

BRAN, JOHN M., Private
Resided in Yadkin County where he enlisted at age 22, June 18, 1861. Died in hospital at Wilmington on December 29, 1861. Cause of death not reported.

BROWN, AZARIAH, Private
Resided in Rockingham County and enlisted in Yadkin County at age 21, March 25, 1862. Captured at or near Gettysburg, Pennsylvania, July 3-5, 1863. Confined at Fort Delaware, Delaware. Released on an unspecified date after taking the Oath of Allegiance and joining the U.S. Army. Assigned to Company G, 1st Regiment Connecticut Cavalry.

BROWN, JAMES K. P., Sergeant
Born in Yadkin County* where he resided as a farmer prior to enlisting in Yadkin County at age 16, June 18, 1861. Mustered in as Private and was promoted to Corporal on May 11, 1863. Promoted to Sergeant prior to November 1, 1864. Captured near Petersburg, Virginia, April 2, 1865. Confined at Point Lookout, Maryland, until released on June 23, 1865, after taking the Oath of Allegiance.

BROWN, JESSE F., Private
Resided in Yadkin County where he enlisted at age 18, June 18, 1861. Died in hospital at Richmond, Virginia, August 8, 1862, of "fev[er] typhoid & parotitis."

BROWN, JOHN C., Sergeant
Born in Yadkin County* where he resided prior to enlisting in Yadkin County at age 29, April 4, 1862. Mustered in as Private and was promoted to Sergeant prior to May 1, 1862. Captured in an unspecified battle in August-September, 1862. Received at Aiken's Landing, James River, Virginia, September 27, 1862, for exchange. Declared exchanged at Aiken's Landing on November 10, 1862. Returned to duty prior to January 1, 1863. Captured at Gettysburg, Pennsylvania, July 3, 1863. Confined at Fort Delaware, Delaware. Transferred to Point Lookout, Maryland, October 15-18, 1863. Hospitalized at Point Lookout on November 17, 1863, with smallpox and died on November 25, 1863.

BROWN, SQUIRE, Private
Born in Yadkin County* where he resided as a farmer prior to enlisting in Yadkin County at age 25, April 27, 1862, for the war. Reported absent without leave in November-December, 1862. Died at or near Camp Gregg, Virginia, February 15, 1863. Cause of death not reported.

CALVARD, BENJAMIN, Private
Born in Yadkin County* where he resided as a farmer prior to enlisting in Yadkin County at age 19, April 1,

1862. Wounded in the forearm and captured at Hanover Court House, Virginia, May 27, 1862. Confined at Fort Monroe, Virginia, and at Fort Columbus, New York Harbor. Transferred to Fort Delaware, Delaware, August 23, 1862. Paroled and transferred to Aiken's Landing, James River, Virginia, October 2, 1862, for exchange. Declared exchanged at Aiken's Landing on November 10, 1862. Reported absent wounded through December, 1862. Company records do not indicate whether he returned to duty; however, he was discharged on January 3, 1864, by reason of wounds received at Hanover Court House.

CARTER, EUGENE, Private
Resided in Yadkin County where he enlisted at age 17, June 18, 1861. Discharged on September 21, 1861, by reason of disability.

CARTER, JOHN A., Private
Born in Yadkin County* where he resided as a farmer prior to enlisting in Yadkin County at age 21, June 18, 1861. Discharged on January 12, 1862. Later served in Company A, 54th Regiment N.C. Troops.

CHOPLIN, JOSEPH, Sergeant
Resided in Yadkin County where he enlisted at age 23, June 18, 1861. Mustered in as Corporal and was promoted to Sergeant on April 12, 1861. Reported missing in action at Gaines' Mill, Virginia, June 27, 1862. No further records.

CHOPLIN, ROBERT, Private
Resided in Yadkin County where he enlisted at age 18, June 18, 1861. Wounded at Gaines' Mill, Virginia, June 27, 1862. Died at Richmond, Virginia, on or about August 3, 1862, of wounds and/or disease.

CHOPLIN, SIDNEY, Private
Born in Franklin County and resided in Yadkin County where he enlisted at age 24, June 18, 1861. Killed at Gettysburg, Pennsylvania, July 1-3, 1863.

CHOPLIN, WESLEY, Private
Resided in Yadkin County where he enlisted at age 21, June 18, 1861. Wounded in the left elbow at Ox Hill, Virginia, September 1, 1862. Reported absent wounded or absent with leave through December, 1862. Company records do not indicate whether he rejoined the company. Detailed as a hospital guard on October 17, 1863. Reported absent on detail through February, 1865. Paroled at Greensboro on May 3, 1865.

CLONINGER, M. H., Private
Place and date of enlistment not reported. Captured near Petersburg, Virginia, April 2, 1865. Confined at Point Lookout, Maryland, April 6, 1865. Released on June 3, 1865, after taking the Oath of Allegiance.

COLVARD, JOHN S., Private
Resided in Yadkin County where he enlisted at age 22, June 18, 1861. Deserted on June 3, 1863. Went over to the enemy on or about July 31, 1864. Took the Oath of Allegiance at Louisville, Kentucky, August 10, 1864.

COLVARD, THOMAS E., Private
Resided in Yadkin County and was by occupation a farmer prior to enlisting in Yadkin County at age 26, June 18, 1861. Hospitalized at Richmond, Virginia, December 15, 1862, with a gunshot wound of the

forefinger. Place and date wounded not reported. Transferred to hospital at Danville, Virginia, January 8, 1863. Deserted from hospital at Danville on March 24, 1863. Went over to the enemy on an unspecified date and was confined at Knoxville, Tennessee, July 31, 1864. Took the Oath of Allegiance at Louisville, Kentucky, August 10, 1864.

COLVARD, WILLIAM M., Private
Resided in Yadkin County where he enlisted at age 24, June 18, 1861. Present or accounted for through December, 1862. Deserted on June 5, 1863. Went over to the enemy on an unspecified date. Confined at Knoxville, Tennessee, July 31, 1864. Took the Oath of Allegiance at Louisville, Kentucky, August 10, 1864.

CONRAD, JAMES D., Private
Resided in Yadkin County and enlisted at age 18, July 1, 1863, for the war. Wounded and captured at Gettysburg, Pennsylvania, July 1-3, 1863. Died at Gettysburg on September 16, 1863, of wounds.

CORNELIUS, ALVIUS E., Private
Born in Forsyth County* and resided in Yadkin County where he was by occupation a farmer prior to enlisting in Yadkin County at age 20, June 18, 1861. Wounded in the ankle and/or right knee at Cedar Mountain, Virginia, August 9, 1862. Reported absent wounded through December, 1862. Company records do not indicate whether he returned to duty. Discharged on August 22, 1863, by reason of disability from wounds received at Cedar Mountain.

CORNELIUS, L. M., 1st Sergeant
Resided in Yadkin County and enlisted in New Hanover County at age 23, March 13, 1862. Mustered in as Private and was promoted to 1st Sergeant on April 12, 1862. Died in hospital at Staunton, Virginia, November 25, 1862, of ''febris typhoides.''

CRESON, SAMUEL D., Corporal
Resided in Yadkin County and enlisted at Camp Fisher at age 23, September 18, 1861. Mustered in as Private and was promoted to Corporal in January-June, 1862. Wounded at Gettysburg, Pennsylvania, July 1-3, 1863. Deserted to the enemy on September 10, 1863. Took the Oath of Allegiance at Knoxville, Tennessee, October 5, 1864.

CUZZENS, BLOOM S., Private
Resided in Yadkin County where he enlisted at age 25, June 22, 1861. Deserted on or about June 30, 1862.

CUZZENS, LEMUEL, Private
Resided in Yadkin County where he enlisted at age 22, June 18, 1861. Died in hospital at Richmond, Virginia, on or about July 18, 1862, of ''typhoid fever.''

DANNER, G. M., Private
Enlisted in Yadkin County on April 24, 1862, for the war. Killed at Gaines' Mill, Virginia, June 27, 1862.

DAVIS, DANIEL, Private
Resided in Yadkin County where he enlisted at age 26, June 18, 1861. Killed at Hanover Court House, Virginia, May 27, 1862.

DAVIS, JESSE, Private
Resided in Yadkin County where he enlisted on

November 5, 1863, for the war. Captured in hospital at Richmond, Virginia, April 3, 1865. Transferred to Newport News, Virginia, April 23, 1865. Released on June 30, 1865, after taking the Oath of Allegiance.

DAVIS, THOMAS W., Private
Born in Yadkin County* where he resided as a farmer prior to enlisting in Yadkin County at age 45, June 18, 1861. Discharged on November 7, 1861, by reason of ''ulcer upon the sole of the foot which has been in a state of ulceration for the last five months and interferes with the use of his foot.''

DIXON, WILLIAM S., Private
Resided in Yadkin County and enlisted in Alamance County at age 18, October 1, 1862, for the war. Wounded at Gettysburg, Pennsylvania, July 1-3, 1863. Returned to duty on an unspecified date. Present or accounted for through February, 1865.

DONATHAN, JOHN, Private
Resided in Yadkin or Surry County and enlisted in Yadkin County at age 17, April 1, 1862. Wounded in the left hand at Wilderness, Virginia, May 5, 1864. Returned to duty on an unspecified date. Hospitalized at Richmond, Virginia, October 2, 1864, with a gunshot wound of the left side. Place and date wounded not reported. Captured in hospital at Richmond on April 3, 1865. Confined at Newport News, Virginia, April 24, 1865. Released on June 16, 1865, after taking the Oath of Allegiance.

DONATHAN, LEWIS, Private
Born in Yadkin County* where he resided prior to enlisting in Yadkin County at age 18, June 18, 1861. Wounded at Cedar Mountain, Virginia, August 9, 1862. Died in hospital at Staunton, Virginia, September 3, 1862, of wounds.

DONATHAN, WILLIAM, Private
Resided in Yadkin County where he enlisted at age 50, June 18, 1861. Wounded in the knee and feet at Ox Hill, Virginia, September 1, 1862. Hospitalized at Charlottesville, Virginia, where he died on September 26, 1862, of ''erysipelas.''

DOUGLAS, ANDERSON, Private
Enlisted in Yadkin County on October 27, 1863, for the war. Wounded in the right arm at Reams' Station, Virginia, August 25, 1864. Right arm amputated. Reported absent wounded through February, 1865.

EDRDGTER, C. A., Private
Place and date of enlistment not reported. Captured in hospital at Richmond, Virginia, April 3, 1865. Reported still in hospital at Richmond on May 28, 1865. No further records.

FLEMING, JOHN W., ———
North Carolina pension records indicate that he served in this company.

FLETCHER, JOHN F., Corporal
Born in Yadkin County* where he resided as a shoemaker prior to enlisting in Yadkin County at age 18, June 18, 1861. Mustered in as Corporal. Discharged on March 12, 1862, by reason of ''inguinal hernia of the left side.''

FLINN, JESSE F., Private
Resided in Yadkin County and enlisted at Camp Enon at age 21, June 18, 1861. Deserted on April 4, 1863.

FLINN, WILLIAM C., Private
Born in Yadkin County* where he resided as a farmer prior to enlisting in Yadkin County at age 22, April 27, 1862, for the war. Discharged on July 21, 1862, by reason of "chronic cough accompanied with great debility."

FORTNER, ALEXANDER, Private
Resided in Yadkin County where he enlisted at age 21, June 18, 1861. Hospitalized at Charlottesville, Virginia, September 12, 1862, with a gunshot wound. Place and date wounded not reported. Returned to duty on or about November 1, 1862. Killed at Gettysburg, Pennsylvania, July 3, 1863.

FREEMAN, JOHN W., Private
Resided in Yadkin County where he enlisted at age 17, June 18, 1861. Died in hospital at Richmond, Virginia, September 5, 1862, of "febris typhoides."

GOUGH, MARTIN FRANKLIN, Private
Resided in Yadkin County where he enlisted at age 17, June 18, 1861. Wounded at Gettysburg, Pennsylvania, July 1-3, 1863. Returned to duty on an unspecified date. Present or accounted for through February, 1865.

GRABBS, LEWIS E., Private
Enlisted in Stokes County on December 19, 1864, for the war. Surrendered at Appomattox Court House, Virginia, April 9, 1865.

GREEN, MILES, Private
Place and date of enlistment not reported. Captured at Hanover Court House, Virginia, on or about May 27, 1862. Confined at Fort Monroe, Virginia, and at Fort Columbus, New York Harbor. Paroled and transferred to Aiken's Landing, James River, Virginia, where he was received July 12, 1862, for exchange. Declared exchanged at Aiken's Landing on August 5, 1862. Deserted on an unspecified date but was apprehended on or about August 29, 1862. No further records.

HALE, WILLIAM D., Private
Resided in Yadkin County where he enlisted at age 21, June 18, 1861. Reported absent wounded in November-December, 1862. Place and date wounded not reported. Returned to duty on an unspecified date. Wounded in the chest at Chancellorsville, Virginia, May 2-3, 1863. Returned to duty on an unspecified date subsequent to August 15, 1863. Captured at or near Pickett's Farm, Virginia, on or about July 21, 1864. Confined at Point Lookout, Maryland. Paroled and transferred to Venus Point, Savannah River, Georgia, where he was received November 15, 1864, for exchange. Captured at Savannah on December 21, 1864. Died in a Federal hospital at Savannah on January 25, 1865, of "debility."

HALL, JAMES SANFORD, Private
Enlisted in Yadkin County at age 24, April 27, 1864, for the war. Captured at or near Deep Bottom, Virginia, in August, 1864. Confined at Point Lookout, Maryland, until paroled and transferred to Venus Point, Savannah River, Georgia, where he was received November 15, 1864, for exchange. Reported absent sick through February, 1865.

HALL, LEWIS W., Private
Resided in Yadkin County where he enlisted at age 21, June 18, 1861. Deserted on or about January 2, 1862.

HALL, THOMAS, Private
Enlisted in Yadkin County on September 28, 1863, for the war. Deserted on May 4, 1864.

HALL, THOMAS G., Private
Enlisted in Yadkin County on April 27, 1864, for the war. Captured at or near Fussell's Mill, Virginia, on or about August 16, 1864. Confined at Point Lookout, Maryland. Paroled and transferred to Boulware's Wharf, James River, Virginia, where he was received March 18, 1865, for exchange.

HAUSER, ANDREW J., Private
Resided in Forsyth County and enlisted at Camp Enon at age 22, August 20, 1861. Died "at home" on or about February 12, 1862, of disease.

HAUSER, N. V., Private
Born in Forsyth County and enlisted in Wake County on April 27, 1864, for the war. Died in hospital at Richmond, Virginia, on or about August 7, 1864. Cause of death not reported.

HAYNES, WILLIAM M., Private
Enlisted in [Stokes County] on October 19, 1864, for the war. Present or accounted for through February, 1865.

HEAD, A. E., Private
Resided in Yadkin County where he enlisted at age 25, March 25, 1862. Wounded in the shoulder at Ox Hill, Virginia, September 1, 1862. Hospitalized at Danville, Virginia. Deserted from hospital at Danville on October 16, 1862. Returned to duty in January-July, 1863, but deserted again on July 19, 1863. No further records.

HEAD, BENJAMIN C., Private
Born in Yadkin County* where he resided as a farmer prior to enlisting in Yadkin County at age 26, June 18, 1861. Died "at home" on December 7, 1862, of disease.

HEAD, WILEY L., Private
Resided in Yadkin County where he enlisted at age 20, June 18, 1861. Died at Hanover Junction, Virginia, May 5, 1863, of "fever."

HICKS, DANIEL, Private
Resided in Forsyth County where he enlisted at age 26, March 17, 1862. Captured at or near Pickett's Farm, Virginia, on or about July 21, 1864. Confined at Point Lookout, Maryland. Exchanged on or about September 30, 1864. Reported absent sick through February, 1865.

HICKS, JOHN H., Private
Resided in Forsyth County where he enlisted at age 25, March 17, 1862. Wounded at Gettysburg, Pennsylvania, July 1-3, 1863. Returned to duty on an unspecified date. Wounded in the right leg at Wilderness, Virginia, in May, 1864. Returned to duty prior to November 1, 1864. Surrendered at Appomattox Court House, Virginia, April 9, 1865.

HICKS, JONATHAN, Private
Resided in Forsyth County where he enlisted at age 36, March 17, 1862. Captured at Hanover Court House,

Virginia, on or about May 27, 1862. Confined at Fort Monroe, Virginia, and at Fort Columbus, New York Harbor. Paroled and transferred to Aiken's Landing, James River, Virginia, where he was received on July 12, 1862, for exchange. Declared exchanged at Aiken's Landing on August 5, 1862. Reported absent without leave through December, 1862. Returned to duty on an unspecified date. Reported absent wounded in September-December, 1864. Place and date wounded not reported. Reported absent without leave from December 14, 1864, through February, 1865. Returned to duty on an unspecified date. Captured near Petersburg, Virginia, April 2, 1865. Confined at Point Lookout, Maryland, until released on June 27, 1865, after taking the Oath of Allegiance.

HICKS, THOMAS R., Private
Resided in Yadkin County where he enlisted at age 19, June 18, 1861. Killed at Gaines' Mill, Virginia, June 27, 1862.

HOOVER, W. V., Private
Place and date of enlistment not reported. Died in hospital at Farmville, Virginia, August 7, 1864, of "febris typhoides."

HUNT, RICHARD, Private
Resided in Yadkin or Guilford County and enlisted in Yadkin County at age 28, June 18, 1861. Deserted on June 5, 1863. Returned to duty on an unspecified date. Captured at Wilderness, Virginia, May 6, 1864. Confined at Point Lookout, Maryland. Transferred to Elmira, New York, August 10, 1864. Released at Elmira on May 19, 1865, after taking the Oath of Allegiance.

HUTCHENS, RICHARD H., Private
Resided in Yadkin County where he enlisted at age 20, June 18, 1861. Reported absent wounded in November-December, 1862. Place and date wounded not reported. Returned to duty on an unspecified date. Captured at or near Gettysburg, Pennsylvania, on or about July 1-5, 1863. Confined at Davids Island, New York Harbor. Paroled and transferred to City Point, Virginia, where he was received August 28, 1863, for exchange. Returned to duty on an unspecified date. Reported absent on detail from September-October, 1864, through February, 1865. Surrendered at Appomattox Court House, Virginia, April 9, 1865.

HUTCHENS, SAMUEL G., Private
Resided in Yadkin County where he enlisted at age 18, June 18, 1861. Furloughed for twenty days on December 7, 1862. Failed to return to duty.

HUTCHENS, WILLIAM D., Private
Born in Yadkin County* where he enlisted on November 5, 1863, for the war. Wounded in the breast near Petersburg, Virginia, June 22, 1864. Died at Petersburg on June 23, 1864, of wounds.

JOBE, JOHN T., Private
Resided in Alamance County and enlisted at Camp Gregg, Virginia, at age 27, February 18, 1863, for the war. Deserted prior to November 1, 1864.

JOYNER, DAVID W., Corporal
Resided in Yadkin County where he enlisted at age 23, June 18, 1861. Mustered in as Private. Captured at Hanover Court House, Virginia, May 27, 1862.

Confined at Fort Monroe, Virginia, and at Fort Columbus, New York Harbor. Paroled and transferred to Aiken's Landing, James River, Virginia, where he was received on July 12, 1862, for exchange. Declared exchanged at Aiken's Landing on August 5, 1862. Returned to duty prior to November 1, 1862. Promoted to Corporal in January, 1863-October, 1864. Captured near Petersburg, Virginia, April 2, 1865. Confined at Point Lookout, Maryland, until released on June 28, 1865, after taking the Oath of Allegiance.

JOYNER, JOHN S., Private
Resided in Yadkin County where he enlisted at age 18, June 18, 1861. Died in hospital at Richmond, Virginia, August 6, 1862, of "feb[ris] typhoides."

JOYNER, JOHN T., Private
Born in Yadkin County* where he resided as a farmer prior to enlisting in Yadkin County at age 17, April 23, 1862, for the war as a substitute. Discharged on July 24, 1862, by reason of disease of the left lung.

JOYNER, TIMOTHY, Private
Resided in Yadkin County where he enlisted at age 18, June 18, 1861. Wounded at Ox Hill, Virginia, September 1, 1862. Died "at home" on or about June 13, 1863, of wounds.

KELLY, JOHN C., Ordnance Sergeant
Born in Yadkin County* where he resided as a schoolteacher prior to enlisting in Yadkin County at age 44 in May, 1861. Mustered in as Ordnance Sergeant. Promoted to Quartermaster Sergeant on or about October 9, 1861, and transferred to the Field and Staff of this regiment.

KELLY, WILLIAM D., Private
Born in Yadkin County* where he resided prior to enlisting in Yadkin County at age 20, June 18, 1861. Mustered in as Corporal but was reduced to ranks in January-June, 1862. Wounded and captured at Gettysburg, Pennsylvania, July 3, 1863. Confined at Fort Delaware, Delaware. Transferred to Point Lookout, Maryland, October 15-18, 1863. Died at Point Lookout on March 10, 1864. Cause of death not reported.

KIRK, JAMES M., Private
Resided in Yadkin County where he enlisted at age 19, June 18, 1861. Captured near Petersburg, Virginia, April 2, 1865. Confined at Point Lookout, Maryland, until released on June 28, 1865, after taking the Oath of Allegiance.

KIRK, JOHN P., Private
Born in Yadkin County* where he enlisted on November 5, 1863, for the war. Killed at Wilderness, Virginia, May 5, 1864.

KITTLE, COSTIN, Private
Resided in Yadkin County where he enlisted at age 24, June 18, 1861. Mustered in as Musician (Fifer) but was reduced to ranks in July-October, 1862. Reported missing at Frayser's Farm, Virginia, June 30, 1862. No further records.

KITTLE, EUGENE, Private
Born in Yadkin County* where he resided as a farmer prior to enlisting in Yadkin County at age 26, June 18, 1861. Mustered in as Musician (Drummer) but was

reduced to ranks in January-June, 1862. Discharged on June 10, 1862, by reason of "chronic diarrhoea & debility."

KITTLE, JOSEPH, Private
Born in Yadkin County* where he resided as a carpenter prior to enlisting in Yadkin County at age 21, April 5, 1862. Discharged on July 7, 1862, by reason of "chronic disease of the lungs or phthisis pulmonalis."

LAY, PETER, Private
Resided in Alamance County where he enlisted at age 35, October 1, 1862, for the war. Wounded at Chancellorsville, Virginia, May 1-4, 1863. Returned to duty on an unspecified date. Reported absent sick in September-October, 1864. Returned to duty on an unspecified date. Reported absent sick from December 14, 1864, through February, 1865. Paroled at Greensboro on May 11, 1865.

LOGAN, H. A., Private
Resided in Yadkin County where he enlisted at age 21, April 27, 1862, for the war. Died "at home" on April 18, 1863. Cause of death not reported.

LOGAN, RICHARD M., Private
Resided in Yadkin County where he enlisted at age 26, June 18, 1861. Mustered in as Sergeant but was reduced to ranks in January-June, 1862. Promoted to Corporal in November-December, 1862. Reported absent without leave from September 1, 1863, through February, 1865. Reduced to ranks prior to November 1, 1864.

LYNCH, PLEASANT H., Private
Resided in Yadkin County where he enlisted at age 25, February 18, 1863, for the war. Deserted to the enemy on or about April 1, 1863. Confined at Fort Monroe, Virginia. Released on an unspecified date after taking the Oath of Allegiance.

McCOLLUM, JOHN, Private
Enlisted in Yadkin County on October 27, 1863, for the war. Reported absent without leave on August 1, 1864.

MARLER, JAMES N., Corporal
Resided in Yadkin County where he enlisted at age 16, August 5, 1861. Mustered in as Private and was promoted to Corporal on May 11, 1863. Captured near Petersburg, Virginia, April 2, 1865. Confined at Point Lookout, Maryland, until released on June 15, 1865, after taking the Oath of Allegiance.

MARLER, JOSEPH F., Private
Resided in Yadkin County where he enlisted at age 34, June 18, 1861. Captured at Wilderness, Virginia, or at Spotsylvania Court House, Virginia, May 6-12, 1864. Confined at Point Lookout, Maryland. Transferred to Elmira, New York, July 25, 1864. Died at Elmira on February 25, 1865, of "pneumonia."

MARTIN, BENNETT, Private
Born in Yadkin County* where he resided prior to enlisting in Yadkin County at age 29, February 1, 1863, for the war. Killed at Jericho Mills, Virginia, May 23, 1864.

MARTIN, GILBERT, Private
Born in Yadkin County* where he resided as a farmer prior to enlisting in Yadkin County at age 33, June 18,

1861. Discharged on November 7, 1861, by reason of "an affection of the spine of some eight years standing & which interferes with the use of his lower limbs. . . ."

MARTIN, JOHN H., Private
Enlisted in Yadkin County on April 27, 1864, for the war. Reported absent without leave on October 26, 1864.

MARTIN, REPS, Private
Born in Yadkin County* where he resided as a farmer prior to enlisting in Yadkin County at age 35, June 18, 1861. Mustered in as Sergeant but was reduced to ranks in January-June, 1862. Discharged on June 10, 1862, by reason of "predisposition to disease of the lungs, accompanied with a severe cough of long standing."

MATTHEWS, HENRY D., Private
Born in Yadkin County* where he enlisted on September 28, 1863, for the war. Killed at Wilderness, Virginia, May 5, 1864.

MATTHEWS, J. T. S., ———
North Carolina pension records indicate that he served in this company.

MATTHEWS, JOHN V., Private
Resided in Yadkin County where he enlisted on September 28, 1863, for the war. Captured near Petersburg, Virginia, April 2, 1865. Confined at Point Lookout, Maryland, until released on June 29, 1865, after taking the Oath of Allegiance.

MATTHEWS, T. C., ———
North Carolina pension records indicate that he served in this company.

MICHAELS, NICHOLAS, Private
Resided in Yadkin County where he enlisted at age 24, June 18, 1861. Wounded in the left hand and captured at or near Hanover Court House, Virginia, on or about May 27, 1862. Confined at Fort Monroe, Virginia, and at Fort Columbus, New York Harbor. Paroled and transferred to Aiken's Landing, James River, Virginia, where he was received July 12, 1862, for exchange. Declared exchanged at Aiken's Landing on August 5, 1862. Returned to duty in November-December, 1862. Deserted on May 27, 1864.

MILLER, WILLIAM HENRY, Private
Resided in Yadkin County where he enlisted at age 43, November 5, 1863, for the war. Captured in hospital at Richmond, Virginia, April 3, 1865. Confined at Point Lookout, Maryland. Released on or about June 26, 1865, after taking the Oath of Allegiance.

MITCHELL, HIRAM, Private
Resided in Yadkin County where he enlisted at age 22, June 18, 1861. Died in Yadkin County on or about February 25, 1862. Cause of death not reported.

MURPHY, ABRAHAM, Private
Born in Yadkin County* where he resided prior to enlisting in Yadkin County at age 28, June 18, 1861. Died at Camp Gregg, Virginia, March 6, 1863, of "pneumonia."

MURPHY, BENJAMIN, Private
Resided in Yadkin County where he enlisted at age 30,

November 5, 1863, for the war. Reported absent without leave from March 2, 1864, until September 10, 1864. Present or accounted for through February, 1865. Captured near Petersburg, Virginia, April 2, 1865. Confined at Point Lookout, Maryland, until released on June 29, 1865, after taking the Oath of Allegiance.

MURRAH, MILTON, Private
Resided in Yadkin County where he enlisted at age 22, June 18, 1861. Killed at Chancellorsville, Virginia, May 3, 1863.

MYERS, FREDERICK A., Sergeant
Resided in Yadkin County where he enlisted at age 21, June 18, 1861. Mustered in as Private and was promoted to Corporal in January-June, 1862. Promoted to Sergeant on May 11, 1863. Captured near Petersburg, Virginia, April 2, 1865. Confined at Point Lookout, Maryland, until released on June 29, 1865, after taking the Oath of Allegiance.

MYERS, GEORGE D., Private
Resided in Yadkin County where he enlisted at age 19, June 18, 1861. Wounded in the left shoulder at Ox Hill, Virginia, September 1, 1862. "Went home on furlough October 1, 1862, & never returned."

MYERS, WILLIAM H., Private
Resided in Yadkin County where he enlisted at age 17, November 5, 1863, for the war. Captured near Petersburg, Virginia, April 2, 1865. Confined at Point Lookout, Maryland. Released on June 29, 1865, after taking the Oath of Allegiance.

NANCE, JOSEPH W., Corporal
Resided in Yadkin County where he enlisted at age 31, June 18, 1861. Mustered in as Private and was promoted to Corporal in January, 1863-October, 1864. Captured near Petersburg, Virginia, July 29, 1864. Confined at Point Lookout, Maryland. Transferred to Elmira, New York, August 8, 1864. Died at Elmira on October 25, 1864, of "pneumonia."

NEAL, GEORGE W., Private
Resided in Forsyth County and enlisted in Alamance County at age 21, October 1, 1862, for the war. "Went home on furlough on April 28, 1864, & never returned."

NICHOLSON, JAMES G., Private
Resided in Yadkin County where he enlisted at age 27, June 18, 1861. Captured at Hanover Court House, Virginia, May 27, 1862. Confined at Fort Columbus, New York Harbor. Exchanged on an unspecified date. Returned to duty prior to November 1, 1862. Captured near Petersburg, Virginia, April 2, 1865. Confined at Point Lookout, Maryland. Released on June 29, 1865, after taking the Oath of Allegiance.

NORMAN, HENRY I., Private
Resided in Yadkin County where he enlisted at age 19, February 18, 1863, for the war. Deserted on September 12, 1863. Returned to duty on or about September 15, 1864. Captured near Petersburg, Virginia, April 2, 1865. Confined at Point Lookout, Maryland. Released on June 29, 1865, after taking the Oath of Allegiance.

NORMAN, WILLIAM, Private
Born in Yadkin County* where he resided as a farmer prior to enlisting at Yadkin County at age 36, June 18, 1861. Died at Camp Gregg, Virginia, March 25-26, 1863, of "pneumonia."

PACK, REASON A., Private
Resided in Forsyth County and enlisted at Camp Fisher at age 28, September 20, 1861. Wounded in the left thigh and left hand and captured at Gettysburg, Pennsylvania, July 1-5, 1863. Hospitalized at Davids Island, New York Harbor. Paroled and transferred to City Point, Virginia, where he was received August 28, 1863, for exchange. Returned to duty on an unspecified date. Reported absent without leave during September-December, 1864. Returned to duty in January-February, 1865. Captured in hospital at Richmond, Virginia, April 3, 1865. [North Carolina pension records indicate he was wounded at Petersburg, Virginia, and that he survived the war.]

PARKE, EBENEZER, Private
Previously served in Company H, 54th Regiment N.C. Troops. Transferred to this company on February 17, 1865. Captured near Petersburg, Virginia, April 2, 1865. Confined at Point Lookout, Maryland. Released on June 17, 1865, after taking the Oath of Allegiance.

PATTERSON, J. C., Private
Resided in Yadkin County. Place and date of enlistment not reported. Deserted to the enemy on an unspecified date. Took the Oath of Allegiance at Louisville, Kentucky, August 16, 1864.

PEAL, D., Private
Place and date of enlistment not reported. Hospitalized at Richmond, Virginia, March 28, 1865, with a gunshot wound of the right leg. Place and date wounded not reported. Captured in hospital at Richmond on April 3, 1865. No further records.

PETTITT, WILLIAM, Private
Born in Yadkin County* where he resided prior to enlisting in Yadkin County at age 36, August 15, 1861. Killed at Ox Hill, Virginia, September 1, 1862.

PHILLIPS, ABRAHAM, Private
Born in Yadkin County* and enlisted in Wake County on November 15, 1863, for the war. Killed at Wilderness, Virginia, May 5, 1864.

PHILLIPS, BENJAMIN A., Private
Born in Yadkin County* where he resided as a farmer prior to enlisting in Yadkin County on April 27, 1862, for the war. Wounded in the right arm at or near Wilderness, Virginia, on or about May 5, 1864. Right arm amputated. Retired from service on January 11, 1865, by reason of disability from wounds.

PHILLIPS, W. A., Private
Born in Yadkin County* where he resided as a farmer prior to enlisting in Yadkin County at age 23, April 24, 1862, for the war as a substitute. Discharged on June 23, 1862, by reason of "general debility."

POINDEXTER, ALEXANDER ROBY, ———
North Carolina pension records indicate that he served in this company.

POINDEXTER, CHARLES A., Private
Resided in Yadkin County where he enlisted on March 12, 1864, for the war. Captured in hospital at Richmond, Virginia, April 3, 1865. Transferred to Newport News, Virginia, April 23, 1865. Released on June 30, 1865, after taking the Oath of Allegiance.

POINDEXTER, ISAAC C., Sergeant
Resided in Yadkin County where he enlisted at age 23, June 18, 1861. Mustered in as Private and was promoted to Sergeant in January-April, 1862. Reduced to ranks on April 23, 1862. Promoted to Corporal on February 1, 1863, and was promoted to Sergeant in March-May, 1864. Captured at Wilderness, Virginia, or at Spotsylvania Court House, Virginia, in May, 1864. Confined at Point Lookout, Maryland, until transferred to Elmira, New York, August 15, 1864. Paroled at Elmira on March 14, 1865, and transferred to Boulware's Wharf, James River, Virginia, where he was received March 18-21, 1865, for exchange. Captured in hospital at Richmond, Virginia, April 3, 1865. Confined at Point Lookout until released on July 25, 1865, after taking the Oath of Allegiance.

POINDEXTER, JOHN H., Sergeant
Previously served as 2nd Lieutenant of this company. [See page 174 of this volume.] Resigned as 2nd Lieutenant on September 5, 1861, but continued to serve in the company with the rank of Private. Promoted to Corporal in January-June, 1862. Hospitalized at Richmond, Virginia, July 3, 1862, with a flesh wound of the hand. Place and date wounded not reported. Returned to duty on July 4, 1862. Promoted to Sergeant on July 16, 1862. Captured at Burkeville, Virginia, April 6, 1865. Confined at Point Lookout, Maryland. Released on June 17, 1865, after taking the Oath of Allegiance.

POINDEXTER, ROBY H., Private
Previously served in Company G of this regiment. Transferred to this company on or about September 28, 1863. Deserted on September 13, 1864.

POINDEXTER, THOMAS C. M., Private
Resided in Yadkin County where he enlisted at age 30, June 18, 1861. Mustered in as Sergeant but was reduced to ranks in January-June, 1862. Died in hospital at Richmond, Virginia, July 10, 1862, of "ty[phoid] fever."

POTTS, NICHOLAS H., Private
Resided in Yadkin County where he enlisted at age 19, June 20, 1863, for the war. Hospitalized at Richmond, Virginia, June 3, 1864, with a gunshot wound. Place and date wounded not reported. Furloughed on June 30, 1864. Reported absent without leave on August 28, 1864.

RANDLEMAN, AUGUSTUS T., Sergeant
Born in Forsyth County* where he resided prior to enlisting in Forsyth County at age 20, June 18, 1861. Mustered in as Private and was promoted to Corporal in November-December, 1862. Promoted to Sergeant on May 11, 1863. Wounded and captured at Gettysburg, Pennsylvania, July 1-4, 1863. Hospitalized at Davids Island, New York Harbor, where he died on July 23, 1863, of "hemorr[h]age lungs."

RASH, RICHARD M., Private
Born in [Yadkin County*] where he resided as a farmer prior to enlisting in Yadkin County at age 21, June 18, 1861. Captured at or near Fussell's Mill, Virginia, on or about August 16, 1864. Confined at Point Lookout, Maryland, until released on October 14-17, 1864, after taking the Oath of Allegiance and joining the U.S. Army. Assigned to Company B, 4th Regiment U.S. Volunteer Infantry.

RASH, ROBERT, Private
Resided in Yadkin County where he enlisted at age 19, June 18, 1861. Died in hospital at Wilmington on March 6, 1862, of "ty[phoid] fever" and/or "dysenteria chron[ic]."

ROBERTS, A. W., Private
Resided in Yadkin County and enlisted in Alamance County at age 25, October 1, 1862, for the war. Deserted in March, 1863.

SAWYER, EDWIN, ———
Negro. North Carolina pension applications indicate that he served in this company.

SHEPARD, GEORGE W., Private
Born in Franklin County and resided in Yadkin County where he enlisted at age 22, June 18, 1861. Captured at Fredericksburg, Virginia, December 13, 1862. Exchanged on December 17, 1862. Reported absent without leave prior to January 1, 1863. Returned to duty on an unspecified date but deserted again on June 23, 1863. Hospitalized at Richmond, Virginia, June 30, 1864. Company records do not indicate whether he returned to duty. Died "at home" on September 7 or October 1, 1864, of disease.

SHIPWASH, GEORGE W., Private
Resided in Yadkin County where he enlisted at age 24, June 18, 1861. Deserted on June 30, 1862. Returned to duty subsequent to December 31, 1862. Deserted again on July 19, 1863. Captured by the enemy at Culpeper, Virginia, December 4, 1863. Confined at Old Capitol Prison, Washington, D.C. Released on March 19, 1864, after taking the Oath of Allegiance. [Roll of Honor indicates he deserted three times.]

SHORES, JOHN, Private
Born in Yadkin County* and was by occupation a farmer prior to enlisting on November 11, 1863, for the war. Discharged on December 21, 1863, by reason of "double inguinal hernia." Discharge certificate gives his age as 43.

SIMPSON, ANDREW, Private
Born in Union County* and resided in Forsyth County where he was by occupation a farmer prior to enlisting in Union County at age 21, October 1, 1862, for the war. Discharged on January 17, 1863, by reason of "imbecility of mind."

SMITH, CHARLES, Private
Born in Forsyth County* where he resided prior to enlisting in Forsyth County at age 58, August 20, 1862, for the war as a substitute. Died at Camp Gregg, Virginia, April 5, 1863. Cause of death not reported.

SMITH, JOHN, Private
Enlisted in Yadkin County on May 8, 1862, for the war. Died in hospital at Richmond, Virginia, August 9, 1862, of "typhoid fever."

SPAINHOWER, JOHN W., Private
Resided in Stokes County and enlisted in Forsyth County on October 19, 1864, for the war. Captured near Petersburg, Virginia, April 2, 1865. Confined at Point Lookout, Maryland, until released on June 20, 1865, after taking the Oath of Allegiance.

SPEAS, WILLIAM H., Corporal
Resided in Yadkin County where he enlisted at age 22, June 18, 1861. Mustered in as Private and was promoted to Corporal on July 10, 1862. Died in hospital at or near Richmond, Virginia, on or about January 7, 1863. Cause of death not reported.

SPEER, ALEX, Private
Resided in Yadkin County where he enlisted at age 19, April 5, 1862. Captured near Petersburg, Virginia, April 2, 1865. Confined at Point Lookout, Maryland. Died at Point Lookout on May 8, 1865, of "diphtheria."

SPEER, JAMES D., Private
Resided in Yadkin County where he enlisted on November 5, 1863, for the war. Captured near Petersburg, Virginia, April 2, 1865. Confined at Point Lookout, Maryland, until released on June 20, 1865, after taking the Oath of Allegiance.

SPEER, LEWIS H., Private
Born in Yadkin County* and was by occupation a farmer prior to enlisting in Yadkin County on June 18, 1861. Hospitalized at Richmond, Virginia, July 2, 1862, with a gunshot wound of the right shoulder. Place and date wounded not reported. Returned to duty on July 3, 1862. Captured at or near Fussell's Mill, Virginia, on or about August 16, 1864. Confined at Point Lookout, Maryland, until released on October 16, 1864, after joining the U.S. Army. Assigned to Company C, 4th Regiment U.S. Volunteer Infantry.

SPEER, WILLIAM A., Private
Born in [Yadkin County*] where he resided as a farmer prior to enlisting in Yadkin County at age 17, April 10, 1862. Deserted on August 7, 1862. Returned to duty subsequent to December 31, 1862. Captured at or near Fussell's Mill, Virginia, on or about August 16, 1862. Confined at Point Lookout, Maryland, until released on October 16, 1864, after joining the U.S. Army. Assigned to Company E, 4th Regiment U.S. Volunteer Infantry

SPILLMAN, MATTHEW D., Private
Resided in Yadkin County where he enlisted at age 18, February 11, 1863, for the war. Wounded and captured at Spotsylvania Court House, Virginia, May 12, 1864. Confined at Old Capitol Prison, Washington, D.C., May 19, 1864. Transferred to Fort Delaware, Delaware, June 15, 1864. Released on June 19, 1865, after taking the Oath of Allegiance.

SPILLMAN, WILLIAM, Corporal
Resided in Yadkin County where he enlisted at age 20, June 18, 1861. Mustered in as Private. Reported absent wounded in July-October, 1862. Place and date wounded not reported. Returned to duty subsequent to December 31, 1862. Promoted to Corporal on May 11, 1863. Reported present for duty in September-October, 1864. Retired to the Invalid Corps on November 9, 1864, by reason of an unspecified disability.

SPILLMAN, WILLIAM H., Private
Resided in Yadkin County where he enlisted at age 21, April 28, 1862, for the war. Captured at Wilderness, Virginia, May 12, 1864. Confined at Point Lookout, Maryland. Transferred to Elmira, New York, August 10, 1864. Released at Elmira on June 21, 1865, after taking the Oath of Allegiance.

SPRINKLE, CLEM C., Private
Resided in Yadkin County where he enlisted at age 22, April 30, 1862, for the war. Captured in hospital at Richmond, Virginia, April 3, 1865. Confined at Point Lookout, Maryland, until released on or about June 28, 1865, after taking the Oath of Allegiance.

SPRINKLE, JOHN T., Private
Enlisted in Yadkin County on April 28, 1862, for the war. Died at Richmond, Virginia, on or about July 11, 1862, of wounds and/or disease. Place and date wounded not reported.

STRICKLAND, CARSON C., Private
Resided in Yadkin or Nash County and enlisted in Nash County at age 22, October 1, 1862, for the war. Reported absent wounded in November-December, 1862. Place and date wounded not reported. Returned to duty on an unspecified date. Wounded in the thigh near Petersburg, Virginia, June 22, 1864. Returned to duty prior to January 1, 1865. Captured at Hatcher's Run, Virginia, April 2, 1865. Confined at Point Lookout, Maryland. Released on June 19, 1865, after taking the Oath of Allegiance.

STRICKLAND, STEPHEN B., Private
Born in Yadkin County* where he resided prior to enlisting in Alamance County at age 20, October 1, 1862, for the war. Killed at Gettysburg, Pennsylvania, July 3, 1863.

TACKETT, B. FRANK, Private
Born in Yadkin County* where he resided prior to enlisting in Yadkin County at age 17, April 5, 1862. Reported absent without leave in November-December, 1862. Returned to duty on an unspecified date. Died at Camp Gregg, Virginia, April 19, 1863, of "pneumonia."

TACKETT, JAMES W., Private
Resided in Yadkin County where he enlisted at age 21, April 26, 1862, for the war. Wounded and captured at Gettysburg, Pennsylvania, July 1-5, 1863. Hospitalized at Davids Island, New York Harbor. Paroled and transferred to City Point, Virginia, where he was received on August 28, 1863, for exchange. Returned to duty on an unspecified date. Reported absent without leave on June 1, 1864. Returned to duty on or about August 13, 1864. Captured near Petersburg, Virginia, April 2, 1865. Confined at Point Lookout, Maryland, until released on June 21, 1865, after taking the Oath of Allegiance.

TACKETT, JOHN W., Private
Resided in Yadkin County where he enlisted at age 20, June 18, 1861. Captured at Gettysburg, Pennsylvania, July 3-4, 1863. Confined at Fort Delaware, Delaware. Transferred to Point Lookout, Maryland, October 15-18, 1863. Paroled at Point Lookout and transferred to City Point, Virginia, where he was received on March 20, 1864, for exchange. Reported absent without leave on April 20, 1864. Returned to duty on August 28, 1864. Captured near Petersburg, Virginia, April 2, 1865. Confined at Point Lookout until released on June 20, 1865, after taking the Oath of Allegiance.

TACKETT, THOMAS E., Private
Resided in Yadkin County where he enlisted at age 18, April 29, 1862, for the war. Wounded in the left thigh at Bethesda Church, Virginia, May 31, 1864. Returned to

duty in August-October, 1864. Captured near Petersburg, Virginia, April 2, 1865. Confined at Point Lookout, Maryland, until released on June 21, 1865, after taking the Oath of Allegiance.

TALLY, C. A., Private
Resided in Cabarrus County and enlisted in Mecklenburg County at age 31, October 1, 1862, for the war. Reported missing at Gettysburg, Pennsylvania, July 1-3, 1863. No further records.

TAYLOR, FRANCIS W., Private
Born in Yadkin County* where he resided prior to enlisting in Yadkin County at age 21, June 18, 1861. Died in hospital at Richmond, Virginia, on or about July 25, 1864, of disease.

TAYLOR, WILLIAM COLUMBUS, Private
Resided in Yadkin County where he enlisted at age 16, April 21, 1862, for the war as a substitute. Hospitalized at Danville, Virginia, on or about August 13, 1862, with pneumonia. Deserted from hospital on October 6, 1862. [North Carolina pension records indicate he was wounded at Richmond, Virginia, in June, 1862.]

THOMPSON, REECE, Private
Was by occupation a farmer prior to enlisting in Forsyth County on March 17, 186[2]. Died at Churchville, Virginia, December 4, 1862, of disease. Death records give his age as 35.

VESTAL, LARKIN HENRY, Private
Enlisted at Liberty Mills, Virginia, March 30, 1864, for the war. Transferred to Company H, 54th Regiment N.C. Troops, February 17, 1865.

WARD, S. BROWN, Private
Resided in Alamance County where he enlisted at age 30, October 1, 1862, for the war. Hospitalized at Richmond, Virginia, May 30, 1863, with typhoid fever. Died in hospital at Richmond on July 2, 1863.

WEBB, THOMAS P., Private
Resided in Yadkin County where he enlisted at age 19, June 18, 1861. Present or accounted for until February 10, 1865, when he was reported absent without leave.

WELCH, W. W., Private
Resided in Forsyth County where he enlisted at age 34, October 1, 186[2], for the war. Wounded at Chancellorsville, Virginia, May 2-3, 1863. Deserted from hospital in June, 1863.

WILLIAMS, GEORGE D., Private
Resided in Yadkin County where he enlisted at age 34, June 18, 1861. Mustered in as Sergeant but was reduced to ranks on April 15, 1862. Captured at Hanover Court House, Virginia, May 27, 1862. Confined at Fort Monroe, Virginia, and at Fort Columbus, New York Harbor. Paroled and transferred to Aiken's Landing, James River, Virginia, where he was received on July 12, 1862, for exchange. Declared exchanged at Aiken's Landing on August 5, 1862. Discharged on September 18, 1862. Reason discharged not reported.

WILLIAMS, JOHN L., Private
Resided in Yadkin County where he enlisted on October 27, 1863, for the war. Furloughed on February 21, 1864. Failed to return to duty and was listed as a deserter.

Went over to the enemy on an unspecified date. Took the Oath of Allegiance at Louisville, Kentucky, August 16, 1864.

WOMACK, ALLEN M., Private
Resided in Yadkin County and enlisted at Camp Enon at age 22, August 20, 1861. Wounded at Gaines' Mill, Virginia, June 27, 1862. Hospitalized at Richmond, Virginia, where he died on July 3-6, 1862, of wounds.

WOOTEN, THOMAS H., Private
Resided in Yadkin County where he enlisted at age 19, June 18, 1861. Wounded in the left thigh and captured at Gettysburg, Pennsylvania, July 3, 1863. Hospitalized at Chester, Pennsylvania. Paroled and transferred to City Point, Virginia, where he was received on September 23, 1863, for exchange. Returned to duty on an unspecified date. Reported absent without leave from September 22, 1864, through February, 1865.

YARBROUGH, ANDREW J., Private
Resided in Yadkin County where he enlisted at age 19, June 18, 1861. Captured near Petersburg, Virginia, April 2, 1865. Confined at Point Lookout, Maryland. Released on June 6, 1865.

COMPANY G

This company, known as the "Guards of Independence," was raised in Orange County where it enlisted on September 2, 1861. It was then mustered into service and assigned to the 28th Regiment as Company G. After joining the regiment the company functioned as a part of the regiment, and its history for the war period is reported as a part of the regimental history.

The information contained in the following roster of the company was compiled principally from company muster rolls for November, 1861-October 31, 1862, and September, 1864-February, 1865. No company muster rolls were found for September 2-October, 1861; November, 1862-August, 1864; or for the period after February, 1865. Valuable information was obtained also from primary records such as the Roll of Honor, medical records, prisoner of war records, discharge certificates, and pension applications, and from secondary sources such as postwar rosters and histories, cemetery records, and records of the United Daughters of the Confederacy.

OFFICERS

CAPTAINS

MARTIN, WILLIAM JOSEPH
Born at Richmond, Virginia, and resided in Orange County where he was by occupation a college professor prior to enlisting at age 30. Appointed Captain on September 2, 1861. Appointed Major to rank from April 28, 1862, and transferred to the 11th Regiment N.C. Troops (1st Regiment N.C. Volunteers). Later served as Colonel of the 11th Regiment N.C. Troops.

JOHNSTON, GEORGE BURGWYN
Previously served as Private in Company D, 1st Regiment N.C. Infantry (6 months, 1861). [Muster-out date cited in Volume III of this series is in error.] Appointed 1st Lieutenant of this company on September 2, 1861. Promoted to Captain on May 1, 1862. Captured at Hanover Court House, Virginia, on or about May 27, 1862. Confined at Fort Monroe, Virginia, and Fort

Columbus, New York Harbor. Transferred to Johnson's Island, Ohio, where he arrived June 21, 1862. Transferred to Vicksburg, Mississippi, September 1, 1862. Received at Vicksburg on September 20, 1862, for exchange. Declared exchanged at Aiken's Landing, James River, Virginia, November 10, 1862. Appointed Assistant Adjutant General of General James H. Lane's brigade on January 19, 1863, and transferred.

MORROW, ELIJAH GRAHAM

Resided in Orange County and enlisted at age 28. Appointed 2nd Lieutenant on September 2, 1861, and was promoted to 1st Lieutenant on May 1, 1862. Captured at Fredericksburg, Virginia, December 13, 1862. Exchanged on or about December 17, 1862. Promoted to Captain on January 19, 1863. Wounded at Chancellorsville, Virginia, May 2-3, 1863. Returned to duty prior to July 1-3, 1863, when he was wounded in the thigh and captured at Gettysburg, Pennsylvania. Leg amputated. Died in hospital at Gettysburg on July 19, 1863, of wounds.

McCAULEY, GEORGE W.

Resided in Orange County where he enlisted at age 29, September 2, 1861. Mustered in as Sergeant and was promoted to 1st Sergeant in March-April, 1862. Appointed 2nd Lieutenant on May 1, 1862, and was promoted to 1st Lieutenant on January 19, 1863. Promoted to Captain on July 19, 1863. Wounded in the right hip and captured near Petersburg, Virginia, April 2, 1865. Hospitalized at Washington, D.C. Released on or about June 9, 1865, after taking the Oath of Allegiance.

LIEUTENANTS

ANDREWS, HENRY CALVIN, 2nd Lieutenant

Resided in Orange County where he enlisted at age 36, September 2, 1861. Mustered in as Sergeant and was promoted to 1st Sergeant in May, 1862. Captured at Hanover Court House, Virginia, on or about May 27, 1862. Confined at Fort Monroe, Virginia, and at Fort Columbus, New York Harbor. Exchanged at Aiken's Landing, James River, Virginia, August 5, 1862. Returned to duty on an unspecified date. Appointed 2nd Lieutenant on April 18, 1863. Captured at or near Spotsylvania Court House, Virginia, on or about May 12, 1864. Confined at Fort Delaware, Delaware. Transferred to Hilton Head, South Carolina, August 20, 1864. Confined at Fort Pulaski, Georgia, October 20, 1864. Transferred to Charleston, South Carolina, where he was paroled on December 15, 1864. Reported absent sick in January, 1865. Retired to the Invalid Corps on February 24, 1865.

ANGERMAN, WILLIAM H., 2nd Lieutenant

Previously served as Private in Company F, 12th Regiment N.C. Troops (2nd Regiment N.C. Volunteers). Transferred to this company on March 4, 1863, with the rank of Private. Appointed Sergeant Major of the 33rd Regiment N.C. Troops on November 1, 1864, and transferred to that unit. Transferred back to this company upon appointment as 2nd Lieutenant on January 28, 1865. Surrendered at Appomattox Court House, Virginia, April 9, 1865.

EDWARDS, EDWIN S., 1st Lieutenant

Resided in Orange County where he enlisted at age 23, September 2, 1861. Mustered in as Sergeant. Captured

at or near Hanover Court House, Virginia, on or about May 27, 1862. Confined at Fort Monroe, Virginia, and Fort Columbus, New York Harbor. Paroled and transferred to Aiken's Landing, James River, Virginia, where he was received on July 12, 1862, for exchange. Declared exchanged at Aiken's Landing on August 5, 1862. Returned to duty prior to November 1, 1862. Appointed 2nd Lieutenant on January 13, 1863, and was promoted to 1st Lieutenant on July 19, 1863. Killed at Spotsylvania Court House, Virginia, May 21, 1864.

MORROW, DANIEL F., 1st Lieutenant

Born in Alamance County* where he resided as a student prior to enlisting in Orange County at age 19, September 2, 1861. Mustered in as Private and was promoted to Sergeant on March 1, 1862. Captured at Hanover Court House, Virginia, May 27, 1862. Confined at Fort Monroe, Virginia, and at Fort Columbus, New York Harbor. Paroled and transferred to Aiken's Landing, James River, Virginia, where he was received on July 12, 1862, for exchange. Declared exchanged at Aiken's Landing on August 5, 1862. Returned to duty on an unspecified date. Wounded at Chancellorsville, Virginia, May 2-3, 1863. Returned to duty on an unspecified date. Appointed 2nd Lieutenant on or about August 18, 1863. Promoted to 1st Lieutenant on January 28, 1865. Reported present for duty during September, 1864-February, 1865. Surrendered at Appomattox Court House, Virginia, April 9, 1865.

OLDHAM, WILLIAM P., 3rd Lieutenant

Resided in Orange County and enlisted at age 24. Appointed 3rd Lieutenant on September 2, 1861. Defeated for reelection on or about March 1, 1862. Later served as Captain of Company K, 44th Regiment N.C. Troops.

SCOTT, CALVIN, 3rd Lieutenant

Resided in Orange County where he enlisted at age 29, September 2, 1861. Mustered in as 1st Sergeant and was appointed 3rd Lieutenant on March 1, 1862. Wounded and captured at Hanover Court House, Virginia, on or about May 27, 1862. Confined at Fort Monroe, Virginia, and at Fort Columbus, New York Harbor. Transferred to Johnson's Island, Ohio, where he arrived June 21, 1862. Transferred to Vicksburg, Mississippi, September 1, 1862. Arrived at Vicksburg on September 20, 1862. Declared exchanged at Aiken's Landing, James River, Virginia, November 10, 1862. Resigned on January 5, 1863, by reason of "a bronchial affection."

NONCOMMISSIONED OFFICERS AND PRIVATES

ADAMS, JAMES B., Private

Resided in Orange County where he enlisted at age 19, September 2, 1861. Died at or near Chapel Hill on January 16, 1862, of disease.

ADAMS, WALTER, Private

Resided in Orange County where he enlisted at age 22, September 2, 1861. Died at Wilmington on January 1, 1862, of disease.

ANDREWS, JOHN C., Private

Born in Orange County where he resided as a bricklayer prior to enlisting in Orange County at age 18, December 20, 1861. Wounded at Chancellorsville, Virginia, May

2-3, 1863. Returned to duty on an unspecified date. Deserted on December 3, 1863. Returned to duty prior to May 12, 1864, when he was captured at or near Spotsylvania Court House, Virginia. Confined at Point Lookout, Maryland, until released on May 30, 1864, after joining the U.S. Army. Assigned to Company I, 1st Regiment U.S. Volunteer Infantry. Deserted from Federal service on August 1, 1864, and returned to duty with this company. Reported present for duty during September, 1864-February, 1865.

ANDREWS, RUFUS A., Private
Resided in Orange County where he enlisted at age 21, March 5, 1862. Died in hospital at Lynchburg, Virginia, on or about July 1, 1862, of "measles."

ATWATER, MATTHEW, Private
Enlisted in Orange County on October 19, 1864, for the war. Surrendered at Appomattox Court House, Virginia, April 9, 1865.

ATWATER, WESLEY, Private
Resided in Orange County where he enlisted on October 19, 1864, for the war. Captured near Petersburg, Virginia, April 2, 1865. Hospitalized at Baltimore, Maryland, April 22, 1865, "convalescent from febris remittens." Transferred to Fort McHenry, Maryland, May 9, 1865. Released at Fort McHenry on June 9, 1865, after taking the Oath of Allegiance. [Federal hospital records dated April-May, 1865, give his age as 44.]

BISHOP, JOHN, Private
Resided in Orange County where he enlisted at age 41, September 2, 1861. Captured at Hanover Court House, Virginia, May 27, 1862. Confined at Fort Monroe, Virginia, and at Fort Columbus, New York Harbor. Paroled and transferred to Aiken's Landing, James River, Virginia, where he was exchanged on August 5, 1862. Returned to duty prior to November 1, 1862. Captured at Fredericksburg, Virginia, December 13, 1862. Exchanged on or about December 17, 1862. Returned to duty on an unspecified date. Captured near Petersburg, Virginia, April 2, 1865. Confined at Point Lookout, Maryland, until released on June 23, 1865, after taking the Oath of Allegiance.

BROCKWELL, BENJAMIN, Private
Resided in Orange County where he enlisted at age 36, March 5, 1862. Captured at Fredericksburg, Virginia, December 13, 1862. Exchanged on or about December 17, 1862. Returned to duty on an unspecified date. Captured at Spotsylvania Court House, Virginia, May 12, 1864. Confined at Point Lookout, Maryland. Transferred to Elmira, New York, August 8, 1864. Released at Elmira on June 19, 1865, after taking the Oath of Allegiance.

BROCKWELL, JAMES I., Private
Resided in Orange County and was by occupation a farmer prior to enlisting in Orange County at age 21, December 20, 1861. Present or accounted for through February, 1865.

BROCKWELL, JOHN B., Private
Previously served in Company D, 1st Regiment N.C. Infantry (6 months, 1861). Enlisted in this company in Orange County at age 22, December 20, 1861. Deserted to the enemy on or about March 8, 1865. Confined at

Washington, D.C., until released on or about March 10, 1865, after taking the Oath of Allegiance.

BROCKWELL, JOSEPH JOSHUA, Private
Resided in Orange County where he enlisted at age 26, December 20, 1861. Present or accounted for through February, 1865.

BROCKWELL, WILLIAM B., Private
Resided in Orange County where he enlisted at age 38, March 5, 1862. Captured at Hanover Court House, Virginia, May 27, 1862. Confined at Fort Monroe, Virginia, and at Fort Columbus, New York Harbor. Paroled and transferred to Aiken's Landing, James River, Virginia, where he was exchanged on August 5, 1862. Returned to duty prior to November 1, 1862. Killed at Wilderness, Virginia, May 6, 1864.

CARDEN, JOHN W., Private
Enlisted in Orange County on March 1, 1864, for the war. Captured at Gravel Hill, Virginia, July 28, 1864. Confined at Point Lookout, Maryland. Transferred to Elmira, New York, August 8, 1864. Died at Elmira on October 1, 1864, of "chronic dysentery."

CARMODY, J., Private
Place and date of enlistment not reported. Surrendered at Appomattox Court House, Virginia, April 9, 1865.

CATES, DENNIS M., Private
Resided in Orange County where he enlisted at age 22, December 20, 1861. Captured at Hanover Court House, Virginia, May 27, 1862. Confined at Fort Columbus, New York Harbor. Paroled and transferred to Aiken's Landing, James River, Virginia, where he was received July 12, 1862, for exchange. Declared exchanged at Aiken's Landing on August 5, 1862. Returned to duty prior to November 1, 1862. Captured at Fredericksburg, Virginia, December 13, 1862. Exchanged on or about December 17, 1862. Returned to duty on an unspecified date. Captured at Spotsylvania Court House, Virginia, May 12, 1864. Confined at Point Lookout, Maryland. Transferred to Elmira, New York, August 10, 1864. Released at Elmira on June 19, 1865, after taking the Oath of Allegiance.

CATES, ENOCH C., Private
Resided in Orange County where he enlisted at age 19, September 2, 1861. Killed at Wilderness, Virginia, May 5, 1864.

CATES, JOHN M., Private
Resided in Orange County where he enlisted at age 18, September 2, 1861. Died at Wilmington on January 29, 1862, of disease.

CATES, RICHARD L., Private
Resided in Orange County where he enlisted at age 19, September 2, 1861. Wounded at Gaines' Mill, Virginia, June 27, 1862. Returned to duty subsequent to October 31, 1862. Captured at Falling Waters, Maryland, July 14, 1863. Confined at Point Lookout, Maryland. Paroled and transferred to Cox's Wharf, James River, Virginia, where he was received February 20-21, 1865, for exchange.

CHAVERS, SAMUEL, Private
Resided in Orange County where he enlisted at age 21, September 2, 1861. Captured at Fredericksburg,

Virginia, December 13, 1862. Exchanged on or about December 17, 1862. Discharged in January, 1863, by reason of being "of mixed blood." He was "a faithful soldier" and "fought in almost every battle from Hanover Court House to Fredericksburg."

CHEEK, JESSE H., Private
Resided in Orange County and enlisted at age 18, December 18, 1862, for the war. Wounded at Gettysburg, Pennsylvania, July 1-3, 1863. Died on July 16, 1863, of wounds. Place of death not reported.

CHEEK, JOHN W., Private
Enlisted in Orange County at age 18, February 1, 1865, for the war. Surrendered at Appomattox Court House, Virginia, April 9, 1865.

CHEEK, JULIUS M., Corporal
Resided in Orange County where he enlisted at age 23, September 2, 1861. Mustered in as Private and was promoted to Corporal in March-April, 1862. Captured at Hanover Court House, Virginia, May 27, 1862. Confined at Fort Monroe, Virginia, and at Fort Columbus, New York Harbor. Paroled and transferred to Aiken's Landing, James River, Virginia, where he was received on July 12, 1862, for exchange. Declared exchanged at Aiken's Landing on August 5, 1862. Returned to duty prior to November 1, 1862. Wounded in the shoulder and captured at Fredericksburg, Virginia, December 13, 1862. Exchanged on or about December 17, 1862. Transferred to Company I, 6th Regiment N.C. State Troops, March 18, 1863.

CHEEK, RUFFIN, Private
Resided in Orange County where he enlisted at age 45, September 2, 1861. Captured at Fredericksburg, Virginia, December 13, 1862. Exchanged on or about December 17, 1862. Discharged on September 6, 1864, by reason of being overage.

CHEEK, WILLIAM J. A., Private
Resided in Orange County where he enlisted at age 18, September 2, 1861. Captured at Hanover Court House, Virginia, on or about May 27, 1862. Confined at Fort Monroe, Virginia, and at Fort Columbus, New York Harbor. Paroled and transferred to Aiken's Landing, James River, Virginia, where he was received on July 12, 1862, for exchange. Declared exchanged at Aiken's Landing on August 5, 1862. Returned to duty on an unspecified date. Captured at Spotsylvania Court House, Virginia, May 12, 1864. Confined at Point Lookout, Maryland. Transferred to Elmira, New York, August 8, 1864. Released at Elmira on June 19, 1865, after taking the Oath of Allegiance.

CLARK, WILLIAM, Private
Born in Orange County where he resided as a shoemaker prior to enlisting in Orange County at age 22, September 2, 1861. Discharged on November 14, 1862, by reason of "chronic rheumatism."

CLARKE, JAMES R., Private
Born in Chatham County and resided in Orange County where he was by occupation a blacksmith prior to enlisting in Orange County at age 31, September 2, 1861. Discharged on October 9, 1861, by reason of "scrotal hernia of the right side. . . ."

COLE, JESSE W., Private
Resided in Orange County where he enlisted at age 20,

September 2, 1861. Wounded in the left leg at Gaines' Mill, Virginia, June 27, 1862. Left leg amputated. Retired to the Invalid Corps on May 19, 1864.

COLE, WILLIAM COMPTON, Private
Born in Chatham County and resided in Orange County where he was by occupation a farmer prior to enlisting in Orange County at age 18, December 20, 1861. Discharged on March 21, 1864, by reason of "chronic diarrhoea and general debility."

CRABTREE, DALLAS, Private
Resided in Orange County where he enlisted at age 16, in February, 1863, for the war. Captured at Spotsylvania Court House, Virginia, May 12, 1864. Confined at Point Lookout, Maryland. Paroled and transferred to Boulware's Wharf, James River, Virginia, where he was received on March 19, 1865, for exchange.

CRABTREE, JOHN, Private
Resided in Orange County where he enlisted at age 18, March 5, 1862. Deserted in August-September, 1862.

CRABTREE, NORWOOD, Private
Born in Orange County where he resided as a farmer prior to enlisting in Orange County at age 40, September 2, 1861. Discharged on February 7, 1863, by reason of "dropsy." [May have served later in Captain Mark Durham's Company, 3rd Battalion N.C. Senior Reserves.]

CRABTREE, SIMPSON, Private
Resided in Orange County where he enlisted at age 36, September 2, 1861. Captured at Hanover Court House, Virginia, on or about May 27, 1862. Confined at Fort Monroe, Virginia, and at Fort Columbus, New York Harbor. Paroled and transferred to Aiken's Landing, James River, Virginia, where he was received on July 12, 1862, for exchange. Declared exchanged at Aiken's Landing on August 5, 1862. Discharged in February, 1863, after providing a substitute.

CRABTREE, WILLIAM E., Private
Born in Granville County and resided in Orange County where he enlisted at age 23, September 2, 1861. Captured at Hanover Court House, Virginia, on or about May 27, 1862. Confined at Fort Monroe, Virginia, and at Fort Columbus, New York Harbor. Paroled and transferred to Aiken's Landing, James River, Virginia, where he was received on July 12, 1862, for exchange. Declared exchanged at Aiken's Landing on August 5, 1862. Returned to duty on an unspecified date. Killed at Gettysburg, Pennsylvania, July 3, 1863.

CRAIGE, JAMES F., Private
Resided in Orange County where he enlisted at age 25, September 2, 1861. Captured at Hanover Court House, Virginia, May 27, 1862. Confined at Fort Monroe, Virginia, and at Fort Columbus, New York Harbor. Paroled and transferred to Aiken's Landing, James River, Virginia, where he was received on July 12, 1862, for exchange. Declared exchanged at Aiken's Landing on August 5, 1862. Returned to duty prior to November 1, 1862. Captured at Spotsylvania Court House, Virginia, May 12, 1864. Confined at Point Lookout, Maryland. Transferred to Elmira, New York, August 8, 1864. Released at Elmira on July 3, 1865, after taking the Oath of Allegiance.

CRAWFORD, ADDISON, Private
Resided in Orange County where he enlisted at age 18, September 2, 1861. Captured at Fredericksburg, Virginia, December 13, 1862. Exchanged on or about December 17, 1862. Returned to duty on an unspecified date. Killed at Wilderness, Virginia, May 5, 1864.

CRAWFORD, HENRY C., Corporal
Resided in Orange County where he enlisted at age 18, December 20, 1861. Mustered in as Private. Captured at Hanover Court House, Virginia, on or about May 28, 1862. Confined at Fort Monroe, Virginia, and at Fort Columbus, New York Harbor. Exchanged on an unspecified date. Returned to duty on or about November 1, 1862. Captured at Fredericksburg, Virginia, December 13, 1862. Exchanged on or about December 17, 1862. Returned to duty on an unspecified date. Wounded in the left side at Chancellorsville, Virginia, May 2-3, 1863. Returned to duty on June 8, 1863. Promoted to Corporal on September 1, 1863. Captured at Wilderness, Virginia, May 12, 1864. Confined at Point Lookout, Maryland. Transferred to Elmira, New York, August 8, 1864. Released at Elmira on June 30, 1865, after taking the Oath of Allegiance.

CRAWFORD, ROBERT ALVIS, Private
Born in Orange County and was by occupation a farmer prior to enlisting in Orange County on February 13, 1864, for the war. Wounded in the left shoulder at Jones' Farm, Virginia, September 30, 1864. Retired from service on February 22, 1865, by reason of disability from wounds.

CRAWFORD, SAMUEL N., Private
Resided in Orange County where he enlisted at age 28, September 2, 1861. Wounded at Gettysburg, Pennsylvania, July 1-3, 1863. Returned to duty on an unspecified date. Reported present for duty during September, 1864-February, 1865. Surrendered at Appomattox Court House, Virginia, April 9, 1865.

DANIEL, LUCIEN, Private
Born in Orange County where he resided prior to enlisting in Orange County at age 20, September 2, 1861. Killed at Wilderness, Virginia, May 6, 1864.

DAVIS, SAMUEL B., Private
Resided in Orange County where he enlisted at age 35, January 1, 1863, for the war. Reported absent without leave during August-October, 1864. Returned to duty in November-December, 1864. Captured near Petersburg, Virginia, April 2, 1865. Confined at Point Lookout, Maryland. Released on June 12, 1865, after taking the Oath of Allegiance.

DOLEHITE, JOHN C., Private
Resided in Orange County where he enlisted at age 21, September 2, 1861. Captured at Fredericksburg, Virginia, December 13, 1862. Exchanged on or about December 17, 1862. Returned to duty on an unspecified date. Killed at Chancellorsville, Virginia, May 3, 1863.

DURHAM, ASHER S., Private
Resided in Orange County and enlisted at age 22, May 14, 1862, for the war. Wounded at Chancellorsville, Virginia, May 1-3, 1863. No further records.

DURHAM, BRYANT, Private
Resided in Orange County where he enlisted at age 22, March 5, 1862, for the war as a substitute. Captured at Fredericksburg, Virginia, December 13, 1862. Exchanged on or about December 17, 1862. Returned to duty on an unspecified date. Wounded at Chancellorsville, Virginia, May 2, 1863. Returned to duty on an unspecified date. Reported present for duty during November, 1864-February, 1865.

DURHAM, FRANKLIN R., Corporal
Enlisted in Orange County on October 31, 1864, for the war. Mustered in as Private and was promoted to Corporal on January 1, 1865. Surrendered at Appomattox Court House, Virginia, April 9, 1865.

DURHAM, JAMES G., Private
Resided in Orange County where he enlisted at age 19, September 2, 1861. Captured at Spotsylvania Court House, Virginia, May 12, 1864. Confined at Point Lookout, Maryland. Paroled and transferred to Cox's Wharf, James River, Virginia, where he was received February 14-15, 1865, for exchange.

DURHAM, JAMES S., 1st Sergeant
Resided in Orange County where he enlisted at age 19, September 2, 1861. Mustered in as Private. Captured at Fredericksburg, Virginia, December 13, 1862. Exchanged on or about December 17, 1862. Promoted to Corporal in March, 1863, and was promoted to 1st Sergeant on September 1, 1863. Hospitalized at Richmond, Virginia, May 8, 1864, with a gunshot wound of the right knee. Place and date wounded not reported. Returned to duty prior to November 1, 1864. Surrendered at Appomattox Court House, Virginia, April 9, 1865.

DURHAM, JOHN S., Private
Resided in Orange County where he enlisted on March 14, 1862. Wounded at Chancellorsville, Virginia, May 2-3, 1863. Returned to duty on an unspecified date. Captured at Spotsylvania Court House, Virginia, May 12, 1864. Confined at Elmira New York, until released on June 23, 1865, after taking the Oath of Allegiance.

DURHAM, JOSEPH H., Private
Resided in Orange County where he enlisted at age 28, September 2, 1861. Mustered in as Corporal but was reduced to ranks on or about April 9, 1862. Captured at Hanover Court House, Virginia, on or about May 27, 1862. Sent to Fort Monroe, Virginia. Received at Aiken's Landing, James River, Virginia, July 12, 1862, for exchange. Declared exchanged at Aiken's Landing on August 5, 1862. Returned to duty prior to November 1, 1862. Wounded in the left thigh and right arm and captured at Gettysburg, Pennsylvania, July 1-4, 1863. Hospitalized at Davids Island, New York Harbor. Transferred to Fort Monroe on January 5, 1864. Hospitalized at Point Lookout, Maryland, January 10, 1864. Paroled and transferred to City Point, Virginia, where he was received on August 30, 1864, for exchange. Retired to the Invalid Corps on November 7, 1864, by reason of disability.

DURHAM, ROBERT A., Corporal
Resided in Orange County where he enlisted at age 19, December 20, 1861. Mustered in as Private. Captured at Hanover Court House, Virginia, on or about May 27, 1862. Confined at Fort Monroe, Virginia, and at Fort Columbus, New York Harbor. Paroled and transferred to Aiken's Landing, James River, Virginia, where he

was received on July 12, 1862, for exchange. Declared exchanged at Aiken's Landing on August 5, 1862. Returned to duty prior to November 1, 1862. Promoted to Corporal on August 6, 1863. Captured at Spotsylvania Court House, Virginia, May 12, 1864. Confined at Point Lookout, Maryland. Transferred to Elmira, New York, August 8, 1864. Released at Elmira on June 19, 1865, after taking the Oath of Allegiance.

DURHAM, SIDNEY C., Private
Resided in Orange County where he enlisted on March 24, 1864, for the war. Captured at Hatcher's Run, Virginia, April 2, 1865. Confined at Point Lookout, Maryland, until released on June 26, 1865, after taking the Oath of Allegiance.

DURHAM, THOMAS MALEUS, Private
Resided in Orange County where he enlisted at age 22, September 2, 1861. Captured at Hanover Court House, Virginia, on or about May 27, 1862. Confined at Fort Monroe, Virginia, and at Fort Columbus, New York Harbor. Paroled and transferred to Aiken's Landing, James River, Virginia, where he was received on July 12, 1862, for exchange. Declared exchanged at Aiken's Landing on August 5, 1862. Returned to duty prior to November 1, 1862. Captured at Spotsylvania Court House, Virginia, May 12, 1864. Confined at Point Lookout, Maryland. Transferred to Elmira, New York, August 8, 1864. Released at Elmira on June 27, 1865, after taking the Oath of Allegiance.

DURHAM, WILLIAM J., Private
Born in Orange County where he resided prior to enlisting in Orange County at age 23, March 5, 1862. Wounded at Fussell's Mill, Virginia, August 16, 1864. Hospitalized at Richmond, Virginia, where he died on or about September 6, 1864, of wounds.

DURHAM, WILLIAM P., Private
Resided in Orange County where he enlisted at age 22, September 2, 1861. Captured at Spotsylvania Court House, Virginia, May 12, 1864. Confined at Point Lookout, Maryland. Paroled and transferred to Varina, Virginia, where he was received on September 22, 1864, for exchange. Returned to duty in November-December, 1864. Surrendered at Appomattox Court House, Virginia, April 9, 1865.

EDWARDS, HENRY A., Sergeant
Resided in Orange County where he enlisted at age 18, June 1, 1862, for the war. Mustered in as Private. Wounded in the left shoulder at Malvern Hill, Virginia, July 1, 1862. Returned to duty on or about March 30, 1863. Promoted to Sergeant in November, 1862-June, 1864. Surrendered at Appomattox Court House, Virginia, April 9, 1865.

EDWARDS, SAMUEL A., Private
Born in Orange County where he resided prior to enlisting in Orange County at age 22, March 5, 1862, as a substitute. Captured at Spotsylvania Court House, Virginia, May 12, 1864. Confined at Point Lookout, Maryland. Transferred to Elmira, New York, August 10, 1864. Died at Elmira on September 25, 1864, of "chronic diarrhoea."

EDWARDS, WILLIAM D. F., Sergeant
Resided in Orange County where he enlisted at age 20, September 2, 1861. Mustered in as Private and was promoted to Corporal on March 1, 1862. Captured at Hanover Court House, Virginia, on or about May 27, 1862. Confined at Fort Monroe, Virginia, and at Fort Columbus, New York Harbor. Paroled and transferred to Aiken's Landing, James River, Virginia, where he was received on July 12, 1862, for exchange. Declared exchanged at Aiken's Landing on August 5, 1862. Returned to duty prior to November 1, 1862. Captured at Fredericksburg, Virginia, December 13, 1862. Exchanged on or about December 17, 1862. Returned to duty on an unspecified date. Promoted to Sergeant in March, 1863. Wounded at Chancellorsville, Virginia, May 2-3, 1863. Returned to duty prior to July 1-5, 1863, when he was wounded and captured at Gettysburg, Pennsylvania. Hospitalized at Gettysburg and at Chester, Pennsylvania. Paroled and transferred to City Point, Virginia, where he was received on August 20, 1863, for exchange. Returned to duty on an unspecified date. Killed near Petersburg, Virginia, on or about June 23, 1864.

FAUCETTE, R. C. P., Private
Resided in Orange County where he enlisted at age 21, March 5, 1862. Died at or near Lynchburg, Virginia, on or about January 18-22, 1863, of disease.

FREEMAN, RICHARD C., Private
Resided in Franklin County and enlisted in Orange County at age 22, September 12, 1861. Discharged on September 3, 1862, by reason of "injury of the back and . . . stricture of the urethra."

GEAN, WILLIAM P., Private
Resided in Orange County where he enlisted at age 25, September 2, 1861. Present or accounted for through February, 1865.

HAYES, RICHARD T., Private
Born in Orange County where he resided as a farmer prior to enlisting in Orange County at age 20, September 2, 1861. Captured at or near Hanover Court House, Virginia, May 27, 1862. Confined at Fort Monroe, Virginia, and at Fort Columbus, New York Harbor. Paroled and transferred to Aiken's Landing, James River, Virginia, where he was received on July 12, 1862, for exchange. Declared exchanged at Aiken's Landing on August 5, 1862. Discharged on April 16, 1863, by reason of "loss of hearing following an attack of sickness."

HOLTON, WILLIAM B., Corporal
Resided in Orange County where he enlisted at age 18, September 2, 1861. Mustered in as Corporal. Killed at Fredericksburg, Virginia, December 13, 1862.

HOWARD, GEORGE W., Private
Resided in Orange County where he enlisted at age 20, March 5, 1862, as a substitute. Captured at Fredericksburg, Virginia, December 13, 1862. Exchanged on or about December 17, 1862. Returned to duty on an unspecified date. Reported present for duty during September, 1864-February, 1865. Surrendered at Appomattox Court House, Virginia, April 9, 1865. [North Carolina pension records indicate he was wounded at the Battle of Second Manassas, Virginia, in August, 1862.]

HOWARD, JAMES H., Private
Resided in Orange County where he enlisted at age 18,

September 2, 1861. Died at Camp Gregg, Virginia, March 22, 1863. Cause of death not reported.

HOWARD, SAMUEL, Private

Resided in Orange County where he enlisted at age 18, December 20, 1861. Died at Richmond, Virginia, June 22, 1862, of "typhoid fever."

HOWARD, THOMAS W., Private

Resided in Orange County where he enlisted at age 35, September 2, 1861. Wounded in the thigh and captured at Gettysburg, Pennsylvania, July 1-3, 1863. Leg amputated. Died in hospital at Gettysburg on July 19, 1863, of wounds.

HUNTER, ANDERSON, Private

Born in Orange County where he resided as a farmer prior to enlisting in Orange County at age 22, September 2, 1861. Discharged on December 14, 1861, by reason of "general debility resulting from anemia." [May have served later in Company G, 11th Regiment N.C. Troops (1st Regiment N.C. Volunteers).]

HUNTER, RICHARD, Private

Resided in Orange County where he enlisted at age 35, March 5, 1862. Wounded at Hanover Court House, Virginia, May 27, 1862, and "left on the field." Died of wounds. Place and date of death not reported.

JOHNSON, JAMES P., Private

Resided in Orange County where he enlisted at age 21, January 1, 1862. Present or accounted for until he surrendered at Appomattox Court House, Virginia, April 9, 1865.

JOHNSTON, GABRIEL P., Private

Resided in Orange County where he enlisted at age 19, September 2, 1861. Promoted to Ordnance Sergeant on December 9, 1861, and transferred to the Field and Staff of this regiment.

KENNEDY, JOHN, Private

Resided in Orange County where he enlisted at age 21, September 2, 1861. Present or accounted for through February, 1865.

KING, WILLIAM DUNCAN, Private

Resided in Orange County where he enlisted at age 20, September 2, 1861. Captured at Hanover Court House, Virginia, on or about May 27, 1862. Confined at Fort Monroe, Virginia, and at Fort Columbus, New York Harbor. Paroled and transferred to Aiken's Landing, James River, Virginia, where he was received on July 12, 1862, for exchange. Declared exchanged at Aiken's Landing on August 5, 1862. Discharged on September 21, 1862, by reason of "rigidity of muscles of arm."

KIRKLAND, SAMUEL D., Private

Resided in Orange County where he enlisted at age 19, September 17, 1861. Captured at or near Hanover Court House, Virginia, on or about May 28, 1862. Confined at Fort Monroe, Virginia, and at Fort Columbus, New York Harbor. Paroled and transferred to Aiken's Landing, James River, Virginia, where he was received on July 12, 1862, for exchange. Declared exchanged at Aiken's Landing on August 5, 1862. Returned to duty on an unspecified date. Reported absent on light duty in hospital at Richmond, Virginia, during September, 1864-February, 1865.

LLOYD, BUNK, Private

Resided in Orange County where he enlisted at age 16, in January, 1863, for the war as a substitute. Captured near Spotsylvania Court House, Virginia, May 10, 1864. Confined at Point Lookout, Maryland. Transferred to Elmira, New York, August 10, 1864. Died at Elmira on October 20, 1864, of "typhoid fever."

LLOYD, GREEN H., Private

Resided in Orange County where he enlisted at age 48, September 2, 1861. Captured at Frederick, Maryland, September 12, 1862. Confined at Fort Delaware, Delaware. Paroled and transferred to Aiken's Landing, James River, Virginia, where he was received on October 2, 1862, for exchange. Declared exchanged at Aiken's Landing on November 10, 1862. Discharged in January, 1863, after providing a substitute.

LLOYD, HENRY, Private

Resided in Orange County where he enlisted at age 18, March 5, 1862. Captured at Fredericksburg, Virginia, December 13, 1862. Exchanged on or about December 17, 1862. Returned to duty on an unspecified date. Captured at or near Spotsylvania Court House, Virginia, May 10-12, 1864. Confined at Point Lookout, Maryland. Transferred to Elmira, New York, August 10, 1864. Paroled at Elmira and transferred to the James River, Virginia, where he was received on March 2, 1865, for exchange. Hospitalized at Richmond, Virginia, with debilitas. Furloughed for thirty days on March 9, 1865.

LLOYD, HENRY W., Private

Resided in Orange County where he enlisted on March 24, 1864, for the war. Captured at or near Spotsylvania Court House, Virginia, on or about May 12, 1864. Confined at Point Lookout, Maryland. Transferred to Elmira, New York, August 10, 1864. Paroled at Elmira and transferred to Venus Point, Savannah River, Georgia, where he was received on November 15, 1864, for exchange. Returned to duty on or about January 1, 1865. Present or accounted for through February, 1865.

LLOYD, LUCIAN, Private

Resided in Orange County where he enlisted at age 21, September 2, 1861. Captured at Fredericksburg, Virginia, December 13, 1862. Exchanged on or about December 17, 1862. Returned to duty on an unspecified date. Wounded and captured at Gettysburg, Pennsylvania, July 3, 1863. Died at Gettysburg on or about July 10, 1863, of wounds.

LLOYD, LUCIUS J., Sergeant

Resided in Orange County where he enlisted at age 18, December 20, 1861. Mustered in as Private. Captured at Fredericksburg, Virginia, December 13, 1862. Exchanged on or about December 17, 1862. Returned to duty on an unspecified date. Promoted to Corporal on August 21, 1863. Captured at Wilderness, Virginia, May 12, 1864. Confined at Point Lookout, Maryland. Transferred to Elmira, New York, August 8, 1864. Paroled at Elmira and transferred to Venus Point, Savannah River, Georgia, where he was received on November 15, 1864, for exchange. Returned to duty on an unspecified date. Promoted to Sergeant on January 1, 1865. Surrendered at Appomattox Court House, Virginia, April 9, 1865.

McCAULEY, BENJAMIN, Private
Resided in Orange County where he enlisted at age 21, September 2, 1861. Killed at Frayser's Farm, Virginia, or at Malvern Hill, Virginia, June 30-July 1, 1862.

McCAULEY, MATHEW J. W., Private
Enlisted in Orange County on October 19, 1864, for the war. Discharged on November 27, 1864. Reason discharged not reported.

McCOLLUM, CHARLES, Private
Resided in Orange County where he enlisted on October 19, 1864, for the war. Captured in hospital at Richmond, Virginia, April 3, 1865. Transferred to Newport News, Virginia, April 23, 1865. Released on July 3, 1865, after taking the Oath of Allegiance.

MARCOM, WILLIAM W., Sergeant
Resided in Orange County where he enlisted on September 2, 1861. Mustered in as Private. Captured at Fredericksburg, Virginia, December 13, 1862. Exchanged on or about December 17, 1862. Returned to duty on an unspecified date. Promoted to Corporal on April 1, 1863. Wounded at Chancellorsville, Virginia, May 2-3, 1863. Returned to duty on an unspecified date. Promoted to Sergeant prior to January 24, 1864. Captured at or near Wilderness, Virginia, on or about May 6, 1864. Confined at Point Lookout, Maryland. Transferred to Elmira, New York, August 10, 1864. Released on June 27, 1865, after taking the Oath of Allegiance.

MARTIN, EDWARD A., Sergeant
Resided in Orange County where he enlisted at age 20, March 5, 1862. Mustered in as Private and was promoted to Sergeant on May 1, 1862. Captured at Hanover Court House, Virginia, May 27, 1862. Confined at Fort Monroe, Virginia, and at Fort Columbus, New York Harbor. Paroled and transferred to Aiken's Landing, James River, Virginia, where he was received on or about July 12, 1862, for exchange. Declared exchanged at Aiken's Landing on August 5, 1862. Returned to duty prior to November 1, 1862. Transferred to Company K, 11th Regiment N.C. Troops (1st Regiment N.C. Volunteers), August 1, 1863.

MERRITT, MORRIS G., Private
Resided in Orange County where he enlisted at age 18, September 17, 1861. Died in hospital at Richmond, Virginia, June 29, 1862, "of exhaustion in the battle of Cold Harbor [Gaines' Mill, Virginia]."

MOORE, JAMES J., Private
Resided in Orange County where he enlisted at age 19, March 5, 1862. Died in Orange County on or about November 23, 1862, of disease.

MORRIS, BAXTER B., Private
Resided in Orange County where he enlisted at age 21, March 5, 1862. Wounded in the knee and/or left thigh and captured at Hanover Court House, Virginia, May 27, 1862. Died in hospital at or near Fort Monroe, Virginia, on or about June 30, 1862, of wounds.

MORRIS, ISAAC J., Private
Resided in Orange County where he enlisted at age 24, March 5, 1862, as a substitute. Captured at or near Hanover Court House, Virginia, on or about May 27,

1862. Confined at Fort Monroe, Virginia, and at Fort Columbus, New York Harbor. Paroled and transferred to Aiken's Landing, James River, Virginia, where he was received on July 12, 1862, for exchange. Declared exchanged at Aiken's Landing on August 5, 1862. Returned to duty prior to November 1, 1862. Wounded in the left leg at or near Kelly's Ford, Virginia, on or about November 7, 1863. Hospitalized at Richmond, Virginia. Furloughed on February 10, 1864. Retired to the Invalid Corps on November 15, 1864, by reason of disability from wounds. [North Carolina pension records indicate he was wounded in the right knee at Gaines' Mill, Virginia, June 26, 1862, and was wounded in the left shoulder at Petersburg, Virginia, "April 26, 1865."]

MORRIS, JOHN A., Private
Born in Orange County where he resided prior to enlisting in Orange County at age 19, March 5, 1862. Captured at Hanover Court House, Virginia, on or about May 27, 1862. Confined at Fort Monroe, Virginia, and at Fort Columbus, New York Harbor. Paroled and transferred to Aiken's Landing, James River, Virginia, where he was received on July 12, 1862, for exchange. Declared exchanged at Aiken's Landing on August 5, 1862. Returned to duty prior to November 1, 1862. Captured at Fredericksburg, Virginia, December 13, 1862. Exchanged on or about December 17, 1862. Returned to duty on an unspecified date. Wounded at Chancellorsville, Virginia, May 2-3, 1863. Returned to duty prior to July 3, 1863, when he was killed at Gettysburg, Pennsylvania.

MORRIS, JOHN R., Private
Resided in Orange County where he enlisted at age 18, March 5, 1862. Captured at Fredericksburg, Virginia, December 13, 1862. Exchanged on or about December 17, 1862. Wounded in the right leg at Chancellorsville, Virginia, May 2, 1863. Company records do not indicate whether he returned to duty. Retired to the Invalid Corps on September 28, 1864.

MORROW, ALEXANDER, Private
Enlisted in Lenoir County on April 10, 1862. Captured at Hanover Court House, Virginia, May 27, 1862. Exchanged on or about August 12, 1862. No further records.

MORROW, RICHARD A., Private
Resided in Orange County where he enlisted at age 20, March 5, 1862. Captured at Hanover Court House, Virginia, on or about May 27, 1862. Confined at Fort Monroe, Virginia, and at Fort Columbus, New York Harbor. Paroled and transferred to Aiken's Landing, James River, Virginia, where he was received on July 12, 1862, for exchange. Declared exchanged at Aiken's Landing on August 5, 1862. Returned to duty prior to November 1, 1862. Wounded at Fredericksburg, Virginia, December 13, 1862. Died at Fredericksburg on December 14, 1862, of wounds. [May have served previously in Company D, 1st Regiment N.C. Infantry (6 months, 1861).]

NEVILL, JESSE, Sergeant
Resided in Orange County where he enlisted at age 19, September 2, 1861. Mustered in as Private. Captured at Hanover Court House, Virginia, May 27, 1862. Confined at Fort Monroe, Virginia, and at Fort Columbus, New York Harbor. Paroled and transferred

to Aiken's Landing, James River, Virginia, where he was received on July 12, 1862, for exchange. Declared exchanged at Aiken's Landing on August 5, 1862. Returned to duty prior to November 1, 1862. Captured at Fredericksburg, Virginia, December 13, 1862. Exchanged on or about December 17, 1862. Promoted to Corporal in January, 1863, and was promoted to Sergeant in April, 1863. Killed at Wilderness, Virginia, May 6, 1864.

PENDERGRASS, JOHN S., Private
Born in Orange County where he resided as a farmer prior to enlisting in Orange County at age 21, September 2, 1861. Captured at Hanover Court House, Virginia, May 27, 1862. Confined at Fort Monroe, Virginia, and at Fort Columbus, New York Harbor. Paroled and transferred to Aiken's Landing, James River, Virginia, where he was received on July 12, 1862, for exchange. Declared exchanged at Aiken's Landing on August 5, 1862. Returned to duty prior to November 1, 1862. Discharged on January 18, 1864, by reason of "organic disease of the heart."

PENDERGRASS, NATHANIEL, Private
Resided in Orange County where he enlisted at age 21, September 2, 1861. Wounded in the left hand at Chancellorsville, Virginia, May 2-3, 1863. Returned to duty on an unspecified date. Captured at Spotsylvania Court House, Virginia, May 12, 1864. Confined at Point Lookout, Maryland. Transferred to Elmira, New York, August 10, 1864. Paroled at Elmira and transferred for exchange on February 20, 1865. [North Carolina pension records indicate he was wounded in the knee at "Bull Run" on an unspecified date and was wounded in the right knee at Brandy Station, Virginia, on an unspecified date.]

PEOPLES, ALBERT, Private
Previously served in Company I of this regiment. Transferred to this company subsequent to October 31, 1864. No further records.

PHILLIPS, JAMES, Private
Enlisted in Orange County on March 15, 1864, for the war. Surrendered at Appomattox Court House, Virginia, April 9, 1865.

PICKARD, WILLIAM W., Private
Resided in Orange County where he enlisted at age 20, September 2, 1861. Wounded and captured at Fredericksburg, Virginia, December 13, 1862. Exchanged on or about December 17, 1862. Transferred to Company I, 6th Regiment N.C. State Troops, March 18, 1863.

POE, NAUFLET F., Private
Enlisted in Orange County on April 1, 1864, for the war. Captured at Spotsylvania Court House, Virginia, May 12, 1864. Confined at Elmira, New York. Transferred to Point Lookout, Maryland, where he arrived on October 14, 1864. Died at Point Lookout on October 30, 1864, of "chronic diarrhoea." [May have served previously in Company D, 1st Regiment N.C. Infantry (6 months, 1861).]

POE, NORFLEET H., Private
Resided in Orange County where he enlisted at age 23, December 20, 1861. Wounded at Gaines' Mill, Virginia, June 27, 1862. Hospitalized at Richmond,

Virginia, where he died on or about July 24, 1862, of wounds.

POE, REUBEN P., Private
Resided in Orange County where he enlisted at age 25, December 20, 1861. Captured at Spotsylvania Court House, Virginia, May 12, 1864. Confined at Point Lookout, Maryland. Transferred to Elmira, New York, August 10, 1864. Paroled at Elmira and transferred for exchange on October 11, 1864. Received at Venus Point, Savannah River, Georgia, November 15, 1864, for exchange. Returned to duty prior to January 1, 1865. Surrendered at Appomattox Court House, Virginia, April 9, 1865.

POE, STEPHEN A., Private
Resided in Orange County where he enlisted at age 19, December 20, 1861. Captured at Fredericksburg, Virginia, December 13, 1862. Exchanged on or about December 17, 1862. Returned to duty on an unspecified date. Reported present for duty during September, 1864-February, 1865. Surrendered at Appomattox Court House, Virginia, April 9, 1865.

POINDEXTER, PLEASANT HENDERSON, Private
Previously served in Company I, 6th Regiment N.C. State Troops. Transferred to this company in March-April, 1863. Wounded in the back at Gettysburg, Pennsylvania, July 1-3, 1863. Returned to duty on August 17, 1863. Reported present for duty during September, 1864-February, 1865. Surrendered at Appomattox Court House, Virginia, April 9, 1865.

POINDEXTER, ROBY H., Private
Resided in Yadkin County where he enlisted at age 27, September 15, 1862, for the war. Transferred to Company F of this regiment on or about September 28, 1863.

POINDEXTER, WILLIAM G. W., Private
Previously served in Company I, 6th Regiment N.C. State Troops. Transferred to this company on March 18, 1863. Wounded and captured at Gettysburg, Pennsylvania, July 3, 1863. Hospitalized at Gettysburg where he died on July 5, 1863, of wounds.

POWEL, MANLEY B., Private
Born in Orange County where he resided as a farmer prior to enlisting in Orange County at age 22, March 5, 1862. Died in hospital at Richmond, Virginia, on or about June 29, 1862, of "phthisis pulmonalis."

POWELL, WILLIAM H., Private
Born in Orange County where he resided as a farmer prior to enlisting in Orange County at age 18, September 17, 1861. Hospitalized at Richmond, Virginia, February 26, 1863, with a gunshot wound of the head. Place and date wounded not reported. Returned to duty on March 19, 1863. Deserted in May, 1863, but returned to duty on an unspecified date. Captured at or near Spotsylvania Court House, Virginia, on or about May 12, 1864. Confined at Point Lookout, Maryland. Released on May 30, 1864, after joining the U.S. Army. Assigned to Company I, 1st Regiment U.S. Volunteer Infantry.

QUAKENBUSH, FREDERICK S., Sergeant
Resided in Orange County where he enlisted at age 23, March 5, 1862. Mustered in as Private. Captured at

Fredericksburg, Virginia, December 13, 1862. Exchanged on or about December 17, 1862. Returned to duty prior to May 2-3, 1863, when he was wounded at Chancellorsville, Virginia. Returned to duty on an unspecified date. Captured at Spotsylvania Court House, Virginia, May 12, 1864. Confined at Point Lookout, Maryland. Transferred to Elmira, New York, August 14, 1864. Promoted to Sergeant subsequent to February 28, 1865, while a prisoner of war. Released at Elmira on June 27, 1865, after taking the Oath of Allegiance.

REEVES, JOHN W., Private
Born in Orange County where he resided as a tailor prior to enlisting in Orange County at age 18, September 17, 1861. Discharged on December 26, 1861, by reason of "general debility following an attack of measles."

RILEY, JOHN W., Private
Born in South Carolina and resided in Orange County where he enlisted at age 20, September 2, 1861. Captured at Fredericksburg, Virginia, December 13, 1862. Exchanged on or about December 17, 1862. Hospitalized at Richmond, Virginia, December 21, 1862, with a gunshot wound of the head. Place and date wounded not reported. Returned to duty on an unspecified date. Reported present for duty during September, 1864-February, 1865.

RIVERVILLE, J. J., Private
Place and date of enlistment not reported. Name appears on a list of prisoners paroled at Farmville, Virginia, April 11-21, 1865.

ROBERSON, HASTON M., Private
Resided in Orange County where he enlisted at age 24, September 2, 1861. Mustered in as Corporal but was reduced to ranks in March-April, 1862. Killed at Hanover Court House, Virginia, May 27, 1862.

ROBERSON, JOHN A., Private
Resided in Orange County where he enlisted at age 19, December 20, 1861. Captured at Hanover Court House, Virginia, May 27, 1862. Confined at Fort Monroe, Virginia, and at Fort Columbus, New York Harbor. Paroled and transferred to Aiken's Landing, James River, Virginia, where he was received on July 12, 1862, for exchange. Declared exchanged at Aiken's Landing on August 5, 1862. Returned to duty prior to November 1, 1862. Killed at Spotsylvania Court House, Virginia, May 18, 1864.

ROBERSON, THOMAS H., Private
Enlisted in Orange County on September 2, 1861. Killed at Shepherdstown, Virginia, September 20, 1862.

ROBERSON, THOMAS J., Private
Resided in Orange County where he enlisted at age 22, September 2, 1861. Reported on light duty as a guard at Charlotte from December, 1862, through February, 1865.

ROBERTSON, ALFRED G., Private
Resided in Orange County where he enlisted at age 21, September 2, 1861. Mustered in as Sergeant but was reduced to ranks in March-April, 1862. Reported on detail as an enrolling and enlisting officer from February 10, 1864, through February, 1865.

ROBERTSON, HENRY F., Private
Resided in Orange County where he enlisted at age 29, September 2, 1861. Killed at Shepherdstown, Virginia, September 20, 1862.

ROBERTSON, HENRY H., Private
Resided in Orange County where he enlisted at age 18, September 1, 1863, for the war. Surrendered at Appomattox Court House, Virginia, April 9, 1865.

RYAN, SAMUEL G., Sergeant
Resided in Orange County where he enlisted at age 19, March 5, 1862. Mustered in as Private. Captured at Hanover Court House, Virginia, May 27, 1862. Confined at Fort Monroe, Virginia. Received at Aiken's Landing, James River, Virginia, July 12, 1862, for exchange. Declared exchanged at Aiken's Landing on August 5, 1862. Returned to duty prior to November 1, 1862. Wounded at Gettysburg, Pennsylvania, July 1-3, 1863. Promoted to Sergeant on September 1, 1863. Detailed as a provost guard at Raleigh from December 19, 1863, through February, 1865.

SMITH, GEORGE, Private
Resided in Orange County where he enlisted at age 21, September 2, 1861. Captured at Hanover Court House, Virginia, on or about May 27, 1862. Confined at Fort Monroe, and at Fort Columbus, New York Harbor. Paroled and transferred to Aiken's Landing, James River, Virginia, where he was received on July 12, 1862, for exchange. Declared exchanged at Aiken's Landing on August 5, 1862. Returned to duty on an unspecified date. Captured at or near Wilderness, Virginia, on or about May 6, 1864. Confined at Point Lookout, Maryland. Transferred to Elmira, New York, August 10, 1864. Died at Elmira on October 25, 1864, of "chronic diarrhoea."

SMITH, JAMES L., Private
Resided in Orange County where he enlisted at age 19, September 2, 1861. Reported absent without leave from August, 1864, through February, 1865.

SMITH, MITCHELL, Private
Resided in Orange County where he enlisted at age 30, September 2, 1861. Captured at Hanover Court House, Virginia, on or about May 28, 1862. Confined at Fort Monroe, Virginia, and at Fort Columbus, New York Harbor. Paroled and transferred to Aiken's Landing, James River, Virginia, where he was received on July 26, 1862, for exchange. Declared exchanged at Aiken's Landing on August 5, 1862. Returned to duty on an unspecified date. Wounded in the foot and captured at Gettysburg, Pennsylvania, July 1-4, 1863. Confined at Fort Delaware, Delaware. Transferred to Point Lookout, Maryland, October 15-18, 1863. Paroled and transferred to Boulware's Wharf, James River, Virginia, where he was received on February 20-21, 1865, for exchange. Company records do not indicate whether he returned to duty. Paroled at Greensboro on May 10, 1865.

SNIPES, CALVIN P., Private
Resided in Orange County where he enlisted at age 20, September 2, 1861. Captured at Hatcher's Run, Virginia, April 2, 1865. Confined at Point Lookout, Maryland, until released on June 19, 1865, after taking the Oath of Allegiance.

SNIPES, JESSE B., Private
Resided in Orange County where he enlisted at age 24, September 2, 1861. Captured at Hanover Court House, Virginia, on or about May 27, 1862. Confined at Fort Monroe, Virginia, and at Fort Columbus, New York Harbor. Paroled and transferred to Aiken's Landing, James River, Virginia, where he was received on July 12, 1862, for exchange. Declared exchanged at Aiken's Landing on August 5, 1862. Returned to duty on an unspecified date. Died in hospital at Richmond, Virginia, on or about June 6, 1863, of "febris typhoides."

SNIPES, JOHN B., Corporal
Resided in Orange County where he enlisted at age 25, September 2, 1861. Mustered in as Corporal. Died at Goldsboro on or about March 21, 1862, of disease.

SNIPES, JOHN W., Private
Born in Orange County where he resided prior to enlisting in Orange County at age 18, September 2, 1863, for the war. Captured by the enemy on an unspecified date. Confined at Point Lookout, Maryland, where he died on June 27, 1864, of disease.

SNIPES, THOMAS E., Corporal
Resided in Orange County where he enlisted at age 22, March 5, 1862. Mustered in as Private and was promoted to Corporal on March 14, 1862. Wounded at Gaines' Mill, Virginia, June 27, 1862. Company records do not indicate whether he returned to duty. Transferred to Company G, 63rd Regiment N.C. Troops (5th Regiment N.C. Cavalry), August 18, 1863.

SPARROW, JAMES T., Private
Resided in Orange County where he enlisted at age 19, December 20, 1861. Captured near Petersburg, Virginia, June 22-30, 1864. Confined at Point Lookout, Maryland. Paroled and transferred to Varina, Virginia, where he was received on September 22, 1864, for exchange. Reported absent sick through February, 1865.

SPARROW, SIDNEY B., Private
Born in Orange County and was by occupation a farmer prior to enlisting in Orange County on April 15, 1864, for the war. Retired from service on March 8, 1865, by reason of "ascites & organic disease of the heart." Retirement papers give his age as 19.

STANFORD, WILLIAM G., Private
Resided in Orange County where he enlisted at age 19, September 2, 1861. Wounded and captured at Hanover Court House, Virginia, on or about May 27, 1862. Confined at Fort Monroe, Virginia, and at Fort Columbus, New York Harbor. Paroled and transferred to Aiken's Landing, James River, Virginia, where he was received on July 12, 1862, for exchange. Declared exchanged at Aiken's Landing on August 5, 1862. Returned to duty subsequent to October 31, 1862. Reported absent on light duty in hospital at Richmond, Virginia, from April, 1864, through February, 1865. Captured in hospital at Richmond on April 3, 1865. Paroled at Richmond on April 18, 1865.

STEPHENS, JOHN, Private
Enlisted in Orange County on April 15, 1864, for the war. Captured at Spotsylvania Court House, Virginia, May 12, 1864. Confined at Point Lookout, Maryland.

Transferred to Elmira, New York, August 10, 1864. Paroled and transferred to Boulware's Wharf, James River, Virginia, where he was received on March 15, 1865, for exchange.

STEPHENS, ROBERT H., Private
Resided in Orange County where he enlisted at age 22, September 2, 1861. Present or accounted for through February, 1865.

STRAUGHAN, GEORGE W., Private
Resided in Orange County where he enlisted at age 30, September 2, 1861. Captured at Fredericksburg, Virginia, December 13, 1862. Exchanged on or about December 17, 1862. Wounded at Wilderness, Virginia, May, 1864. Returned to duty prior to November 1, 1864. Captured near Petersburg, Virginia, April 2, 1865. Confined at Point Lookout, Maryland, until released on June 19, 1865, after taking the Oath of Allegiance.

STRAUGHAN, JULIAN R., Corporal
Resided in Orange County where he enlisted at age 31, September 2, 1861. Mustered in as Private and was promoted to Corporal in March-April, 1862. Killed at Gaines' Mill, Virginia, June 27, 1862.

STRAUGHAN, NATHAN R., Private
Resided in Orange County where he enlisted at age 19, September 2, 1861. Captured at Fredericksburg, Virginia, December 13, 1862. Exchanged on or about December 17, 1862. Captured at Chancellorsville, Virginia, May 3, 1863. Exchanged at City Point, Virginia, on or about May 13, 1863. Wounded at Gettysburg, Pennsylvania, July 1-3, 1863. Returned to duty on an unspecified date. Captured near Petersburg, Virginia, April 2, 1865. Confined at Point Lookout, Maryland. Released on June 19, 1865, after taking the Oath of Allegiance.

STRAUGHAN, WILEY H., Private
Resided in Orange County where he enlisted on October 19, 1864, for the war. Captured near Petersburg, Virginia, April 2, 1865. Confined at Point Lookout, Maryland, until released on June 19, 1865, after taking the Oath of Allegiance.

STROUD, JOHN B., Private
Born in Orange County where he resided as a farmer prior to enlisting in Orange County at age 25, September 2, 1861. Captured at Fredericksburg, Virginia, December 13, 1862. Exchanged on or about December 17, 1862. Discharged on March 28, 1864, by reason of "general debility and disease of the heart." Paroled at Raleigh on May 12, 1865.

STUBBINS, JOHN, Private
Resided in Orange County where he enlisted at age 19, September 2, 1861. Died at Wilmington on December 26, 1861, of "typhoid pneumonia."

SYKES, HENRY C., Private
Resided in Orange County where he enlisted at age 20, September 2, 1861. Captured at Fredericksburg, Virginia, December 13, 1862. Exchanged on or about December 17, 1862. Captured at Falling Waters, Maryland, July 14, 1863. Confined at Point Lookout, Maryland. Transferred to Elmira, New York, August 16, 1864. Paroled at Elmira and transferred to Boulware's Wharf, James River, Virginia, where he was received on

March 15, 1865, for exchange.

SYKES, JASPER J., Private
Enlisted in Orange County at age 20, October 19, 1864, for the war. Surrendered at Appomattox Court House, Virginia, April 9, 1865.

SYKES, JOHN A., Private
Resided in Orange County where he enlisted at age 19, September 2, 1861. Captured at Winchester, Virginia, on or about December 3, 1862. Paroled at Winchester on December 4, 1862. Died in hospital at Winchester on December 7, 1862, of "pneumonia typ[hoi]d."

SYKES, JOHNSON C., Private
Resided in Orange County where he enlisted at age 19, September 2, 1861. Captured at Hanover Court House, Virginia, on or about May 27, 1862. Confined at Fort Monroe, Virginia, and at Fort Columbus, New York Harbor. Paroled and transferred to Aiken's Landing, James River, Virginia, where he was received on July 12, 1862, for exchange. Declared exchanged at Aiken's Landing on August 5, 1862. Returned to duty prior to November 1, 1862. Hospitalized at Petersburg, Virginia, August 26, 1864, with a gunshot wound of the left foot. Place and date wounded not reported. Returned to duty in November-December, 1864. Present or accounted for through February, 1865.

TENNEY, OREGON BURNS, Private
Resided in Orange County where he enlisted at age 18, December 20, 1861. Wounded in both hands at Cedar Mountain, Virginia, August 9, 1862. Returned to duty subsequent to October 31, 1862. Surrendered at Appomattox Court House, Virginia, April 9, 1865.

THOMPSON, GEORGE S., Private
Resided in Orange County and enlisted at Orange Court House, Virginia, at age 22, September 2, 1861. Appointed Assistant Quartermaster (Captain) on October 18, 1861, and transferred to the Field and Staff of this regiment.

THOMPSON, JAMES O., Sergeant
Born in Alamance County* where he resided as a farmer prior to enlisting in Orange County at age 26, September 17, 1861. Mustered in as Private and was promoted to Sergeant on March 1, 1862. Discharged on December 25, 1863, by reason of "general debility of long standing."

THOMPSON, JAMES SIDNEY, Private
Resided in Alamance County and enlisted in Orange County at age 21, September 2, 1861. Wounded in the arm and thigh at Wilderness, Virginia, May 5-7, 1864. Died at Lynchburg, Virginia, May 31, 1864, of wounds.

THOMPSON, THOMAS H., Private
Enlisted in Orange County at age 19, October 19, 1864, for the war. Surrendered at Appomattox Court House, Virginia, April 9, 1865.

VANCE, JOHN, Private
Resided in Orange County and enlisted at age 20, December 20, 1861. Reported in hospital at Richmond, Virginia, in June-July, 1863, and in November, 1863. No further records.

VICKERS, JOSEPH G., Corporal
Resided in Orange County where he enlisted at age 19,

September 2, 1861. Mustered in as Private. Captured at Hanover Court House, Virginia, May 27, 1862. Confined at Fort Monroe, Virginia. Paroled and transferred to Aiken's Landing, James River, Virginia, where he was received on July 12, 1862, for exchange. Declared exchanged at Aiken's Landing on August 5, 1862. Returned to duty on an unspecified date. Promoted to Corporal in November, 1862-May, 1864. Captured at Spotsylvania Court House, Virginia, May 12, 1864. Confined at Point Lookout, Maryland. Transferred to Elmira, New York, August 10, 1864. Released on June 14, 1865, after taking the Oath of Allegiance.

WAITT, GEORGE N., Private
Resided in Orange County where he enlisted at age 18, September 2, 1861. Present or accounted for until he surrendered at Appomattox Court House, Virginia, April 9, 1865.

WARD, JOHN R., Private
Enlisted in Orange County on October 19, 1864, for the war. Transferred to Company G, 63rd Regiment N.C. Troops (5th Regiment N.C. Cavalry), March 8, 1865.

WARD, WILLIAM J., Private
Born in Orange County where he resided prior to enlisting in Orange County at age 26, December 20, 1861. Captured at Hanover Court House, Virginia, on or about May 27, 1862. Confined at Fort Monroe, Virginia, and at Fort Columbus, New York Harbor. Paroled and transferred to Aiken's Landing, James River, Virginia, where he was received on July 12, 1862, for exchange. Declared exchanged at Aiken's Landing on August 5, 1862. Returned to duty prior to November 1, 1862. Captured at or near Spotsylvania Court House, Virginia, May 12, 1864. Confined at Point Lookout, Maryland. Transferred to Elmira, New York, August 10, 1864. Died at Elmira on October 6, 1864, of "chronic diarrhoea."

WEAVER, JOHN THOMAS, Private
Resided in Orange County where he enlisted at age 21, September 2, 1861. Captured at Gravel Hill, Virginia, July 28, 1864. Confined at Point Lookout, Maryland. Transferred to Elmira, New York, August 8, 1864. Released at Elmira on June 19, 1865, after taking the Oath of Allegiance.

WORKMAN, GASTON B., Private
Enlisted in Orange County on December 16, 1863, for the war. Surrendered at Appomattox Court House, Virginia, April 9, 1865.

WORKMAN, HENRY N., Private
Born in Orange County where he resided prior to enlisting in Orange County at age 45, March 5, 1862. Died at Chapel Hill on August 12, 1864, of disease.

WORKMAN, SIDNEY M., Private
Resided in Orange County where he enlisted at age 18, September 17, 1861. Captured at Frederick, Maryland, September 12, 1862. Confined at Fort Delaware, Delaware. Paroled and transferred to Aiken's Landing, James River, Virginia, October 2, 1862, for exchange. Declared exchanged at Aiken's Landing on November 10, 1862. Returned to duty on an unspecified date. Captured at Spotsylvania Court House, Virginia, on or

about May 12, 1864. Confined at Point Lookout, Maryland. Transferred to Elmira, New York, August 10, 1864. Died at Elmira on February 1, 1865, of "variola."

COMPANY H

This company, known as the "Cleveland Regulators," was raised in Cleveland County where it was mustered into service on August 22, 1861. It was then assigned to the 28th Regiment as Company H. After joining the regiment the company functioned as a part of the regiment, and its history for the war period is reported as a part of the regimental history.

The information contained in the following roster of the company was compiled principally from company muster rolls for August 22-December, 1861; March-October 31, 1862; and September, 1864-February, 1865. No company muster rolls were found for January-February, 1862; November, 1862-August, 1864; or for the period after February, 1865. Valuable information was obtained also from primary records such as the Roll of Honor, medical records, prisoner of war records, discharge certificates, and pension applications, and from secondary sources such as postwar rosters and histories, cemetery records, and records of the United Daughters of the Confederacy.

OFFICERS

CAPTAINS

WRIGHT, WILLIAM W.

Previously served as 1st Sergeant of Company E, 12th Regiment N.C. Troops (2nd Regiment N.C. Volunteers). Appointed Captain of this company on August 22, 1861. Defeated for reelection on April 7, 1862.

BRIDGES, ISAAC O.

Resided in Cleveland County where he enlisted at age 30. Appointed 3rd Lieutenant on August 22, 1861. Promoted to Captain on April 7, 1862. Resigned on July 23, 1862, by reason of "chronic ulceration of the throat & mouth. . . ."

HOLLAND, GOLD GRIFFIN

Resided in Cleveland County where he enlisted at age 42, March 17, 1862. Mustered in as Private and was appointed 1st Lieutenant on April 7, 1862. Promoted to Captain on August 2, 1862. Surrendered at Appomattox Court House, Virginia, April 9, 1865. [The following story about Captain Holland is told in Clark's *Regiments*, Volume II, page 475: "After the battle (of Fredericksburg, Virginia, December 13, 1862) when Captain Holland . . . congratulated General (James H.) Lane on his escape, he added: 'And I am indebted to a biscuit for my own life.' Running his hand into his haversack, he drew forth a camp biscuit about the size of a saucer, cooked without salt or 'shortening' of any kind, and looking like horn when sliced—something that an ostrich could not digest—and there was a Yankee bullet only *half* imbedded in that wonderful biscuit."]

LIEUTENANTS

ABERNATHY, JOHN A., 1st Lieutenant

Resided in Gaston County and enlisted in New Hanover County at age 18 in August-December, 1861. Mustered in as Private. Promoted to Hospital Steward on or about December 28, 1861, and transferred to the Field and Staff of this regiment. Elected 1st Lieutenant and transferred back to this company on or about August 2, 1862. Died on or about October 8, 1862. Place and

cause of death not reported.

BRIDGES, BURREL H., 3rd Lieutenant

Resided in Cleveland County where he enlisted at age 18, August 22, 1861. Mustered in as Private and was promoted to Sergeant in January-April, 1862. Appointed 3rd Lieutenant on April 7, 1862. Resigned on October 3, 1862, by reason of "disability." [May have served later as 1st Sergeant of Company D, 55th Regiment N.C. Troops.]

GILBERT, WILLIAM W., 1st Lieutenant

Resided in Cleveland County where he enlisted at age 23. Appointed 1st Lieutenant on August 22, 1861. Dismissed from the service by a general court-martial in April, 1862. Reason he was court-martialed not reported.

GREEN, THOMAS FRANK, 3rd Lieutenant

Previously served as Private in Company E, 12th Regiment N.C. Troops (2nd Regiment N.C. Volunteers). Transferred to this company with the rank of Private on April 2, 1863. Elected 3rd Lieutenant on December 20, 1863. Surrendered at Appomattox Court House, Virginia, April 9, 1865.

LOWE, MILTON A., 1st Lieutenant

Previously served as 3rd Lieutenant of Company C of this regiment. Promoted to 1st Lieutenant on or about November 14, 1862, and transferred to this company. Captured at or near Gravel Hill, Virginia, on or about July 28, 1864. Confined at Old Capitol Prison, Washington, D.C. Transferred to Fort Delaware, Delaware, August 11, 1864. Paroled at Fort Delaware on October 6, 1864. Received at Cox's Wharf, James River, Virginia, October 15, 1864, for exchange. Returned to duty in November-December, 1864. Resigned on February 23, 1865. Reason he resigned not reported.

ROLLINS, DRURY D., 2nd Lieutenant

Resided in Cleveland County and enlisted at age 38. Appointed 2nd Lieutenant on August 22, 1861. Defeated for reelection when the regiment was reorganized on April 7, 1862. [May have served later in Company I, 34th Regiment N.C. Troops.]

SIMMONS, STEPHEN A., 3rd Lieutenant

Resided in Cleveland County where he enlisted at age 18, August 22, 1861. Mustered in as Private and was promoted to 1st Sergeant on April 7, 1862. Appointed 3rd Lieutenant on November 14, 1862. Killed at Gettysburg, Pennsylvania, July 3, 1863.

SMITH, DAVID B., 2nd Lieutenant

Previously served as Sergeant Major of this regiment. Elected 2nd Lieutenant and transferred to this company on April 6, 1863. Resigned on September 28, 1864, because "my company is small having only about fifteen (15) enlisted men for duty and having a full number of officers and being a professional mechanic I feel that I can be of far greater service to my country in such a capacity than as a commissioned officer over a handful of men. . . ."

WEBB, LORENZO DOW, 2nd Lieutenant

Resided in Cleveland County where he enlisted at age 20, March 17, 1862. Mustered in as Private and was appointed 2nd Lieutenant on April 7, 1862. Wounded in the right ankle at Gaines' Mill, Virginia, June 27,

1862. Company records do not indicate whether he returned to duty. Resigned on January 8, 1863, by reason of disability from wounds.

NONCOMMISSIONED OFFICERS AND PRIVATES

ABERNATHY, IRA, Private
Resided in Lincoln County and enlisted at age 36, October 2, 1862, for the war. Died in hospital at Charlottesville, Virginia, January 16, 1863, of "typhoid fever."

ALLISON, JAMES M., Private
Resided in Cleveland County where he enlisted at age 17, August 22, 1861. Wounded in the arm at Gaines' Mill, Virginia, or at Frayser's Farm, Virginia, June 27-30, 1862. Arm amputated. Discharged from service on February 2, 1864.

ARMSTRONG, JOSEPH, Private
Resided in Lincoln County and enlisted at Camp Holmes at age 35, October 28, 1862, for the war. Deserted from hospital at Richmond, Virginia, in June, 1863.

BARGER, DAVID, Private
Enlisted at Camp Hill on August 14, 1862, for the war. Mustered in as Corporal but was reduced to ranks in January-February, 1865. Transferred to Company C of this regiment in February, 1865.

BARNETT, CRAWFORD M., Private
Resided in Cleveland County where he enlisted at age 20, August 22, 1861. Present or accounted for until he surrendered at Appomattox Court House, Virginia, April 9, 1865.

BARNETT, WILLIAM T., Private
Resided in Cleveland County where he enlisted at age 31, August 22, 1861. Wounded in the shoulder at Gettysburg, Pennsylvania, July 1-3, 1863. Reported absent wounded or absent sick through February, 1865.

BELL, WILLIAM B., Private
Enlisted in Edgecombe County on September 1, 1863, for the war. Died in hospital at Charlottesville, Virginia, January 14, 1864, of "chro[nic] diarrh[oea]."

BLANTON, EDWARD M., Private
Born in Rutherford County and resided in Cleveland County where he was by occupation a farmer prior to enlisting in Cleveland County at age 47, August 22, 1861. Discharged on June 19, 1862, by reason of "advanced age & debility."

BLANTON, FRANCIS A., Private
Resided in Cleveland County where he enlisted at age 32, March 17, 1862. Captured at Hanover Court House, Virginia, May 27, 1862. Confined at Fort Monroe, Virginia, and at Fort Columbus, New York Harbor. Paroled and transferred to Aiken's Landing, James River, Virginia, where he was exchanged on August 5, 1862. Died in hospital at Petersburg, Virginia, on or about August 6, 1862, Cause of death not reported.

BLANTON, FRANK B., ———
North Carolina pension records indicate that he served in this company.

BLANTON, GEORGE W., Private
Resided in Cleveland County where he enlisted at age 18, August 22, 1861. Died near Richmond, Virginia, August 2, 1862, of disease.

BLANTON, JOHN, Private
Resided in Cleveland County where he enlisted at age 35, March 17, 1862. Died "at the field hosp[ita]l" near Richmond, Virginia, August 1, 1862, of wounds. Place and date wounded not reported.

BLANTON, JOSIAH S., Private
Previously served in Company C, 15th Regiment N.C. Troops (5th Regiment N.C. Volunteers). Transferred to this company on March 28, 1864. Captured at or near Wilderness, Virginia, on or about May 6, 1864. Confined at Point Lookout, Maryland. Transferred to Elmira, New York, August 15, 1864. Paroled and transferred to Venus Point, Savannah River, Georgia, where he was received on November 15, 1864, for exchange. Reported absent sick through February, 1865.

BLANTON, THOMAS J., Private
Born in Cleveland County* where he resided prior to enlisting in Cleveland County at age 49, August 22, 1861. Mustered in as Sergeant but was reduced to ranks in January-April, 1862. Captured at Hanover Court House, Virginia, May 27, 1862. Confined at Fort Monroe, Virginia, and at Fort Columbus, New York Harbor. Paroled and transferred to Aiken's Landing, James River, Virginia, where he was exchanged on August 5, 1862. Returned to duty on an unspecified date. Killed at Wilderness, Virginia, May 6, 1864.

BLANTON, WILLIAM, Private
Born in Rutherford County and resided in Cleveland County where he was by occupation a farmer prior to enlisting in Cleveland County at age 58, March 17, 1862. Discharged on June 19, 1862, by reason of "advanced age and want of physical ability to do duty."

BLANTON, WILLIAM T., Private
Resided in South Carolina and enlisted in Cleveland County at age 22, August 22, 1861. Hospitalized at Richmond, Virginia, June 23, 1862, with diarrhoea and typhoid fever and died on June 30, 1862, after he "drank cold water to great excess."

BOLCH, FRANKLIN, Private
Enlisted at Camp Vance on February 24, 1864, for the war. Surrendered at Appomattox Court House, Virginia, April 9, 1865.

BOLCH, NATHAN A., Private
Enlisted in Catawba County at age 18, February 1, 1865, for the war. Present or accounted for through February, 1865.

BOLCH, PHILIP, Private
Born in Catawba County and enlisted at Camp Vance on September 22, 1863, for the war. Died in hospital at Richmond, Virginia, on or about October 26, 1864, of a gunshot wound. Place and date wounded not reported.

BOLCH, WILLIAM H., Private
Previously served in Company E, McRae's Battalion N.C. Cavalry. Transferred to this company in June, 1864. Present or accounted for through February, 1865.

BOLLINGER, LEVI A., Private

Enlisted at Camp Vance on March 1, 1864, for the war. Captured at or near Pickett's Farm, Virginia, on or about July 21, 1864. Confined at Point Lookout, Maryland. Paroled and transferred to Boulware's Wharf, James River, Virginia, where he was received on March 16, 1865, for exchange.

BOWEN, JAMES D., Private

Born in Cleveland County where he resided as a farmer prior to enlisting in Cleveland County at age 20, March 17, 1862. Discharged on July 21, 1862, by reason of "a want of physical ability to do the duties of a soldier...."

BOWENS, ELIAS P., Private

Enlisted in Cleveland County on March 17, 1862. Present or accounted for through April, 1862.

BRADDY, JAMES, Private

Born in Rutherford County and resided in Cleveland County where he enlisted at age 35, August 22, 1861. Died in hospital near Richmond, Virginia, July 23, 1862, of disease.

BRIDGES, JAMES W., Private

Resided in Cleveland County where he enlisted at age 22, March 17, 1862. Died at the brigade hospital of General Lawrence O'B. Branch on July 11, 1862. Cause of death not reported.

BRIDGES, JOHN, Private

Born in Cleveland County* where he resided as a farmer prior to enlisting in Cleveland County at age 48, August 22, 1861. Discharged on June 19, 1862, by reason of "debility and advanced age."

BRIDGES, PRESTON, Private

Resided in Cleveland County where he enlisted at age 17, August 22, 1861. Captured at Hanover Court House, Virginia, May 27, 1862. Confined at Fort Monroe, Virginia, and at Fort Columbus, New York Harbor. Paroled and transferred to Aiken's Landing, James River, Virginia, where he was exchanged on August 5, 1862. Wounded in the buttock at Chancellorsville, Virginia, May 2-3, 1863. Returned to duty on an unspecified date. Captured at Petersburg, Virginia, April 3, 1865. Confined at Hart's Island, New York Harbor. Released on June 18, 1865, after taking the Oath of Allegiance.

BRIDGES, SAMUEL G. H., Private

Resided in Cleveland County where he enlisted at age 18, February 20, 1863, for the war. Wounded and captured at Gettysburg, Pennsylvania, July 1-5, 1863. Hospitalized at Chester, Pennsylvania, July 19, 1863. Paroled and transferred to City Point, Virginia, where he was received on August 20, 1863, for exchange. Returned to duty on an unspecified date. Surrendered at Appomattox Court House, Virginia, April 9, 1865.

BRIDGES, THOMAS S., Private

Born in Cleveland County and was by occupation a farmer prior to enlisting in Cleveland County on August 22, 1861. Discharged on June 23, 1862, by reason of "chronic rheumatism." Discharge certificate gives his age as 21. Reenlisted in the company on October 5, 1864. Surrendered at Appomattox Court House, Virginia, April 9, 1865.

BRIDGES, THOMAS WALLACE, Sergeant

Born in Cleveland County where he resided as a farmer prior to enlisting in Cleveland County at age 18, August 22, 1861. Mustered in as Private and was promoted to Sergeant in May-October, 1862. Wounded in the left arm at Chancellorsville, Virginia, May 3, 1863. Left arm amputated. Discharged from service on February 22, 1864, by reason of disability.

BURGESS, AMBROSE C., Private

Resided in Cleveland County where he enlisted at age 21, March 17, 1862. Captured at Hanover Court House, Virginia, May 27, 1862. Confined at Fort Monroe, Virginia, and at Fort Columbus, New York Harbor. Paroled and transferred to Aiken's Landing, James River, Virginia, where he was exchanged on August 5, 1862. Returned to duty on an unspecified date. Killed at Chancellorsville, Virginia, May 3, 1863.

BYARS, ELIAS, Private

Born in Cleveland County* where he resided prior to enlisting in Cleveland County at age 30, March 17, 1862. Killed at Spotsylvania Court House, Virginia, May 12, 1864.

CHAMPION, DAVID O. P., Private

Resided in Cleveland County where he enlisted at age 24, August 22, 1861. Present or accounted for until he surrendered at Appomattox Court House, Virginia, April 9, 1865.

CHAMPION, JAMES, Private

Resided in Cleveland County where he enlisted at age 17, March 17, 1862. Wounded at Fredericksburg, Virginia, December 13, 1862. Returned to duty on an unspecified date. Wounded in the right leg and captured at Gravel Hill, Virginia, July 28, 1864. Confined at various Federal hospitals until confined at Old Capitol Prison, Washington, D.C., September 7, 1864. Transferred to Fort Delaware, Delaware, September 19, 1864. Paroled and transferred to City Point, Virginia, where he was received on February 27, 1865, for exchange. Furloughed for sixty days on March 9, 1865.

CHAMPION, JAMES M., Private

Resided in Cleveland County where he enlisted at age 21, August 22, 1861. Wounded at Gaines' Mill, Virginia, June 27, 1862. Hospitalized at Richmond, Virginia, where he died on July 18, 1862, of wounds.

CHAMPION, JOHN G., Private

Resided in Cleveland County where he enlisted at age 18, August 22, 1861. Died near Gordonsville, Virginia, on or about December 10, 1862. Cause of death not reported.

CLINE, FRANKLIN, Private

Resided at "Hickory Station" and enlisted at Camp Holmes on October 9, 1863, for the war. Captured at Gravel Hill, Virginia, July 28, 1864. Confined at Point Lookout, Maryland. Transferred to Elmira, New York, August 8, 1864. Released at Elmira on May 29, 1865, after taking the Oath of Allegiance. [Prisoner of war records dated September, 1864, give his age as 46.]

CLINE, NOAH, Private

Born in Catawba County and enlisted at Camp Vance on February 24, 1864, for the war. Wounded in the left knee at Fussell's Mill, Virginia, August 16, 1864. Left leg amputated. Hospitalized at Richmond, Virginia, where he died on October 11-12, 1864, of wounds.

COBB, JESSE, Private
Resided in Cleveland County where he enlisted at age 17, March 17, 1862. Died in hospital at Lynchburg, Virginia, May 20, 1862, of "pneumonia."

COBB, THOMPSON, Private
Resided in Cleveland County where he enlisted at age 18, August 22, 1861. Captured at Hanover Court House, Virginia, May 27, 1862. Confined at Fort Monroe, Virginia, and at Fort Columbus, New York Harbor. Paroled and transferred to Aiken's Landing, James River, Virginia, where he was received on July 12, 1862, for exchange. Declared exchanged at Aiken's Landing on August 5, 1862. Returned to duty on an unspecified date. Captured by the enemy at an unspecified locality but was paroled on May 24, 1863. Hospitalized at Richmond, Virginia, on or about June 12, 1863, with a gunshot wound. Place and date wounded not reported. Company records do not indicate whether he returned to duty; however, he was reported absent sick from April, 1864, through February, 1865.

CONNOR, WILLIAM C., Private
Resided in Cleveland County where he enlisted at age 25, March 17, 1862. Died "at home" on April 16, 1863. Cause of death not reported.

COX, JOHN M., Private
Enlisted at Camp Vance on October 16, 1863, for the war. Captured at or near Gravel Hill, Virginia, on or about July 28, 1864. Confined at Point Lookout, Maryland. Transferred to Elmira, New York, where he arrived on August 12, 1864. Died at Elmira on or about September 5, 1864, of "chronic diarrhoea."

DAILY, JOHN J., Private
Resided in Cleveland County where he enlisted at age 30, August 22, 1861. Mustered in as Sergeant but was reduced to ranks in May-October, 1862. Captured at Spotsylvania Court House, Virginia, May 12, 1864. Confined at Point Lookout, Maryland. Transferred to Elmira, New York, August 8, 1864. Paroled at Elmira on February 9, 1865, and transferred to Boulware's Wharf, James River, Virginia, where he was received on February 20-21, 1865, for exchange.

DOBBINS, DANIEL, Private
Resided in Cleveland County where he enlisted at age 39, August 22, 1861. Discharged on November 2 or November 21, 1862. Reason discharged not reported.

DOBBINS, DILLIARD P., Private
Resided in Cleveland County where he enlisted at age 21, August 22, 1861. Wounded near Shepherdstown, Virginia, September 20, 1862. Returned to duty on an unspecified date. Captured in hospital at Richmond, Virginia, April 3, 1865. Transferred to Newport News, Virginia, April 23, 1865. Released at Newport News on June 30, 1865, after taking the Oath of Allegiance.

ELLISON, JAMES M., Private
Born in Cleveland County and was by occupation a farmer prior to enlisting in Cleveland County on August 22, 1861. Wounded in the right arm at or near Frayser's Farm, Virginia, June 30, 1862. Company records do not

indicate whether he returned to duty. Discharged on February 2, 1864, by reason of disability from wounds.

GILLASPIE, JONATHAN R., Private
Resided in Rutherford County where he enlisted at age 28, March 17, 1862. Died at Charlottesville, Virginia, May 14, 1862, of "pneumonia."

GILLESPIE, JAMES B., Corporal
Born in Cleveland County* and resided in Rutherford County where he was by occupation a farmer prior to enlisting in Cleveland County at age 22, March 17, 1862. Mustered in as Private and was promoted to Corporal on November 5, 1863. Hospitalized at Richmond, Virginia, May 28, 1864, with a gunshot wound of the left thigh. Place and date wounded not reported. Returned to duty prior to November 1, 1864. Present or accounted for until furloughed on February 20, 1865.

GILLESPIE, JOHN M., Private
Resided in Cleveland County where he enlisted at age 21, March 17, 1862. Wounded at or near Ox Hill, Virginia, on or about September 1, 1862. Returned to duty on an unspecified date. Wounded in the left wrist "in Virginia" on or about December 12, 1864. Reported absent wounded through February, 1865.

GILLESPIE, WILLIAM D., Private
Born in Cleveland County* where he resided prior to enlisting in Cleveland County at age 25, August 22, 1861. Died at Richmond, Virginia, July 17, 1862, of "typhoid fever."

GOLD, PERRY G., Corporal
Resided in Cleveland County where he enlisted at age 20, August 22, 1861. Mustered in as Private and was promoted to Sergeant in May-June, 1862. Reduced to ranks on July 7, 1862. Promoted to Corporal in November, 1862-October, 1864. Surrendered at Appomattox Court House, Virginia, April 9, 1865.

GREEN, DAVID O., Private
Resided in Cleveland County and enlisted in New Hanover County at age 24, October 6, 1861. Captured at Hanover Court House, Virginia, May 27, 1862. Confined at Fort Monroe, Virginia, and at Fort Columbus, New York Harbor. Paroled and transferred to Aiken's Landing, James River, Virginia, where he was received on July 12, 1862, for exchange. Declared exchanged at Aiken's Landing on August 5, 1862. Returned to duty on an unspecified date. Wounded at Chancellorsville, Virginia, May 2-3, 1863. Returned to duty on an unspecified date. Reported present for duty during September, 1864-February, 1865. Surrendered at Appomattox Court House, Virginia, April 9, 1865.

GREEN, EDMOND, Private
Resided in Cleveland County where he enlisted at age 20, August 22, 1861. Captured at Hanover Court House, Virginia, May 27, 1862. Confined at Fort Monroe, Virginia, and at Fort Columbus, New York Harbor. Paroled and transferred to Aiken's Landing, James River, Virginia, where he was exchanged on August 5, 1862. Returned to duty on an unspecified date. Died at Camp Gregg, Virginia, February 1, 1863. Cause of death not reported.

GREEN, EWELL, Private
Born in Cleveland County* where he resided as a

farmer prior to enlisting in Cleveland County at age 26, August 22, 1861. Discharged on December 26, 1861, by reason of "typhoid fever and acute rheumatism."

GREEN, GEORGE M., Private
Born in Cleveland County where he resided prior to enlisting in Cleveland County at age 18, August 22, 1861. Killed at Gettysburg, Pennsylvania, July 3, 1863.

GREEN, JAMES M., Sergeant
Resided in Cleveland County where he enlisted at age 34, August 22, 1861. Mustered in as Corporal and was promoted to Sergeant prior to November 1, 1861. Reduced to ranks in January-April, 1862. Promoted to Corporal in May-October, 1862, and was promoted to Sergeant in November, 1862-June, 1863. Surrendered at Appomattox Court House, Virginia, April 9, 1865.

GREEN, JAMES M., Sr., Private
Resided in Cleveland County where he enlisted at age 21, August 22, 1861. Present or accounted for until he surrendered at Appomattox Court House, Virginia, April 9, 1865.

GREEN, JAMES MOORE, Jr., Private
Resided in Cleveland County where he enlisted at age 18, August 22, 1861. Mustered in as Private. Captured at Hanover Court House, Virginia, May 27, 1862. Confined at Fort Monroe, Virginia, and at Fort Columbus, New York Harbor. Paroled and transferred to Aiken's Landing, James River, Virginia, where he was received on July 12, 1862, for exchange. Declared exchanged at Aiken's Landing on August 5, 1862. Returned to duty on an unspecified date. Promoted to Sergeant in November, 1862-June, 1863. Reduced to ranks in June-October, 1864. Surrendered at Appomattox Court House, Virginia, April 9, 1865.

GREEN, JOHN L., Private
Resided in Cleveland County where he enlisted at age 17, August 22, 1861. Wounded in the leg at Gettysburg, Pennsylvania, July 1-3, 1863. Reported absent wounded through October, 1864. Rejoined the company in November-December, 1864, but was detailed for light duty at Richmond, Virginia, in February, 1865. Surrendered at Appomattox Court House, Virginia, April 9, 1865.

GREEN, REUBEN H., Private
Enlisted at Camp Holmes on September 25, 1864, for the war. Surrendered at Appomattox Court House, Virginia, April 9, 1865.

GREEN, WILLIAM, Jr., Private
Born in Cleveland County where he resided as a farmer prior to enlisting in Cleveland County at age 20, March 17, 1862. Discharged on September 28, 1862, by reason of "tubercular phthisis."

GREEN, WILLIAM H., Private
Resided in Cleveland County where he enlisted at age 32, August 22, 1861. Died at Wilmington on or about February 2, 1862. Cause of death not reported.

HAMRICK, A. V., Private
Resided in Cleveland County and enlisted at age 23, August 22, 1861. Died at Wilmington on November 8, 1861. Cause of death not reported.

HAMRICK, ALFRED W., Private
Resided in Cleveland County where he enlisted at age 18, August 22, 1861. Wounded at the Battle of Second Manassas, Virginia, August 28, 1862. Returned to duty on an unspecified date. Reported present for duty during September, 1864-February, 1865. Captured near Petersburg, Virginia, April 2, 1865. Confined at Fort Delaware, Delaware. Released on June 19, 1865, after taking the Oath of Allegiance.

HAMRICK, ANDREW J., Private
Resided in Cleveland County where he enlisted at age 21, March 17, 1862. Died in hospital at Liberty, Virginia, on or about March 17, 1863, of "typhoid fever."

HAMRICK, ASA, Corporal
Resided in Cleveland County where he enlisted at age 21, August 22, 1861. Mustered in as Private and was promoted to Corporal on April 7, 1862. Captured at Hanover Court House, Virginia, May 27, 1862. Confined at Fort Monroe, Virginia, and at Fort Columbus, New York Harbor. Paroled and transferred to Aiken's Landing, James River, Virginia, where he was received on July 12, 1862, for exchange. Declared exchanged at Aiken's Landing on August 5, 1862. Returned to duty on an unspecified date. Wounded in the left thigh and captured at Spotsylvania Court House, Virginia, May 12, 1864. Left leg amputated. Hospitalized at Washington, D.C., where he died on June 13, 1864, of "exhaustion."

HAMRICK, JAMES BRYSON, Private
Enlisted in Cleveland County on March 1, 1864, for the war. Wounded and captured at Fussell's Mill, Virginia, on or about August 16, 1864. Confined at Point Lookout, Maryland. Paroled and transferred to City Point, Virginia, where he was received on November 15, 1864, for exchange. Reported absent sick through February, 1865.

HAMRICK, JAMES M., Private
Resided in Cleveland County where he enlisted at age 28, August 22, 1861. Transferred to Company E, 12th Regiment N.C. Troops (2nd Regiment N.C. Volunteers), April 24, 1863.

HAMRICK, JONATHAN, Private
Born in Cleveland County* where he resided as a farmer prior to enlisting in Cleveland County at age 40, March 17, 1862. Present or accounted for through February, 1865.

HAMRICK, M. N., Private
North Carolina pension records indicate that he served in this company.

HAMRICK, OLIVER A., Private
Resided in Cleveland County where he enlisted at age 19, August 22, 1861. Present or accounted for through October, 1862. Left the company without authorization on an unspecified date and enlisted in Company D, 55th Regiment N.C. Troops, prior to July 1, 1863.

HAMRICK, PRICE, Private
Resided in Cleveland County where he enlisted at age 23, March 17, 1862. Wounded at Spotsylvania Court House, Virginia, May 12, 1864. Reported absent

wounded through February, 1865. Paroled at Charlotte on May 1, 1865.

HARDIN, ALMON S., Private
Born in Cleveland County where he resided as a farmer prior to enlisting in Cleveland County at age 16, August 22, 1861. Discharged on June 19, 1862, by reason of "debility & anemia following a protracted attack of typhoid fever."

HARDIN, CRAYTON, Private
Records of Company E, 12th Regiment N.C. Troops (2nd Regiment N.C. Volunteers), indicate he was transferred to this company on April 24, 1863; however, records of this company do not indicate that he served herein.

HARDIN, ELIJAH, Private
Resided in Cleveland County where he enlisted at age 18, August 22, 1861. Died in hospital at Lynchburg, Virginia, on or about August 22, 1862, of "febris typhoides" and/or "phthisis pulmonalis."

HARDIN, JESSE, Private
Resided in Cleveland County where he enlisted at age 43, August 22, 1861. Discharged on September 5, 1863. Reason discharged not reported. [May have served later in Company H, 4th Regiment N.C. Senior Reserves.]

HARDIN, ORVILLE S., Private
Born in Cleveland County where he resided prior to enlisting in Cleveland County at age 19, August 22, 1861. Mustered in as Private and was promoted to Corporal on April 7, 1862. Reduced to ranks on an unspecified date. Killed at Spotsylvania Court House, Virginia, May 12, 1864.

HARRELL, JOHN H., Private
Born in Rutherford County and resided in Cleveland County where he was by occupation a farmer prior to enlisting in Cleveland County at age 44, March 17, 1862. Transferred to Company B, 34th Regiment N.C. Troops, November 18, 1864.

HAWKINS, CHARLES H., Musician
Resided in Cleveland County where he enlisted at age 21, August 22, 1861. Mustered in as Musician (Drummer). Died at Wilmington on or about January 19, 1862. Cause of death not reported.

HAWKINS, GEORGE M., Private
Born in Cleveland County* where he resided as a farmer prior to enlisting in Cleveland County at age 35, August 22, 1861. Discharged on July 25, 1862, by reason of "advanced age & physical inability to do duty."

HAWKINS, JOHN E., Private
Born in Cleveland County where he resided as a farmer prior to enlisting in Cleveland County at age 19, August 22, 1861. Discharged on July 25, 1862. Reason discharged not reported. Died in camp near Richmond, Virginia, July 29, 1862. Cause of death not reported.

HAWKINS, JOHN R., Private
Enlisted in Cleveland County at age 19, February 15, 1864, for the war. Surrendered at Appomattox Court House, Virginia, April 9, 1865.

HAWKINS, LEWIS J., Private
Resided in Cleveland County where he enlisted at age

23, August 22, 1861. Died at Wilmington on December 29, 1861, of disease.

HAWKINS, ORVEY C., Private
Resided in Cleveland County where he enlisted at age 25, March 17, 1862. Died on August 10, 1862. Place and cause of death not reported.

HAWKINS, RANSOM N., Sergeant
Resided in Cleveland County where he enlisted at age 23, August 22, 1861. Mustered in as Private and was promoted to Corporal on November 15, 1862. Promoted to Sergeant on December 20, 1862. Hospitalized at Danville, Virginia, on or about April 4, 1865, with a gunshot wound of the left hand. Place and date wounded not reported. Paroled at Charlotte on May 3, 1865.

HAWKINS, SAMUEL C., Private
Resided in Cleveland County where he enlisted at age 21, August 22, 1861. Mustered in as Musician (Fifer) but was reduced to ranks in January-April, 1862. Wounded at Cedar Mountain, Virginia, August 9, 1862. Hospitalized at Staunton, Virginia, where he died on August 20, 1862, of wounds.

HAWKINS, WILLIAM D., Private
Resided in Cleveland County where he enlisted at age 24, August 22, 1861. Killed at Chancellorsville, Virginia, May 3, 1863.

HAWKINS, WILLIAM J., Private
Born in Cleveland County* where he resided as a farmer prior to enlisting in Cleveland County at age 27, August 22, 1861. Wounded in the neck and right shoulder at Gravel Hill, Virginia, July 28, 1864. Retired from service on January 18, 1865, by reason of disability from wounds.

HELTON, DRAYTON, Private
Born in Rutherford County and resided in Cleveland County where he was by occupation a shoemaker prior to enlisting in Cleveland County at age 22, March 17, 1862. Discharged on October 25, 1862, by reason of "hypertrophy of heart."

HERMAN, DARIOUS L., Private
Records of Company E, McRae's Battalion N.C. Cavalry, indicate he was transferred to this company in June, 1864; however, records of this company do not indicate that he served herein.

HICKS, BENJAMIN P. G., Private
Resided in Cleveland County where he enlisted at age 34, March 17, 1862. Reported absent sick from February, 1864, through February, 1865. Captured in hospital at Richmond, Virginia, April 3, 1865. Transferred to Newport News, Virginia, April 23, 1865. Released on June 16, 1865, after taking the Oath of Allegiance.

HICKS, DAVID, Private
Resided in Cleveland County and enlisted at age 30, October 2, 1862, for the war. Died in hospital at Richmond, Virginia, June 4-5, 1863, of "feb[ris] typhoides."

HICKS, LEVI, Private
Resided in Cleveland County and enlisted at age 28,

October 2, 1862, for the war. Died in hospital at Richmond, Virginia, on or about June 5, 1863, of "feb[ris] typhoides."

HILL, JONATHAN F., Private
Resided in Cleveland County where he enlisted at age 19, August 22, 1861. Mustered in as Corporal but was reduced to ranks in May-July, 1862. Died in hospital at Richmond, Virginia, July 8, 1862, of "feb[ris] typh[oides]."

HOLLAND, JAMES C., Sergeant
Born in Cleveland County where he resided prior to enlisting in Cleveland County at age 19, August 22, 1861. Mustered in as Private and was promoted to Corporal in January-July, 1863. Wounded at Gettysburg, Pennsylvania, July 1-3, 1863. Returned to duty on or about August 4, 1863. Promoted to Sergeant on an unspecified date. Hospitalized at Richmond, Virginia, May 24, 1864, with a gunshot wound of the left thigh. Place and date wounded not reported. Died in hospital at Richmond on June 18, 1864, of wounds.

HOLLAND, JEROME W., Private
Resided in Cleveland County and enlisted at age 29, October 2, 1862, for the war. Hospitalized at Richmond, Virginia, December 15, 1862, with a gunshot wound of the middle finger of the right hand. Place and date wounded not reported. Died "at home" on January 11, 1863. Cause of death not reported.

HOLLAND, PHINEAS A., Private
Resided in Cleveland County where he enlisted at age 18, August 22, 1861. "Fell out" near Orange Court House, Virginia, August 13, 1862. Returned to duty subsequent to October 31, 1862. Captured at or near Jericho Mills, Virginia, on or about May 24, 1864. Confined at Point Lookout, Maryland. Transferred to Elmira, New York, July 8, 1864. Transferred back to Point Lookout on an unspecified date. Paroled at Point Lookout and transferred to Varina, Virginia, where he was received on September 22, 1864, for exchange. Reported absent sick through February, 1865.

HOLLAND, THOMAS J., 1st Sergeant
Resided in Cleveland County where he enlisted at age 18, August 22, 1861. Mustered in as Private and was promoted to Sergeant on February 8, 1862. Reduced to ranks prior to May 1, 1862. Wounded at or near Mechanicsville, Virginia, on or about June 27, 1862. Returned to duty subsequent to October 31, 1862. Promoted to 1st Sergeant in May, 1863. Reported present for duty during September, 1864-February, 1865. Surrendered at Appomattox Court House, Virginia, April 9, 1865.

HOLLER, J. C., Private
Previously served in Company E, McRae's Battalion N.C. Cavalry. Transferred to this company in June, 1864. Killed at Fussell's Mill, Virginia, August 16, 1864.

HOPPER, H., Private
Place and date of enlistment not reported. Surrendered at Appomattox Court House, Virginia, April 9, 1865.

HOPPER, JOHN A., Private
Enlisted at Camp Stokes on October 4, 1864, for the

war. Deserted on February 22, 1865.

HOPPER, LANSFORD M., Private
Resided in Cleveland County where he enlisted on September 22, 1863, for the war. Transferred to Company I, 34th Regiment N.C. Troops, November 18, 1864.

HORTON, WILLIAM P., Private
Resided in South Carolina and enlisted in Cleveland County at age 21, August 22, 1861. Died at Wilmington on February 4, 1862. Cause of death not reported.

HUGHES, A. J., Private
Resided in Cleveland County and enlisted at age 21, March 17, 1862. No further records.

HUGHES, BERRY E., Corporal
Resided in Cleveland County where he enlisted at age 20, August 22, 1861. Mustered in as Private and was promoted to Corporal in November, 1862-July, 1863. Captured at Gettysburg, Pennsylvania, July 3-4, 1863. Confined at Fort Delaware, Delaware, where he died on September 25, 1863. Cause of death not reported.

HUGHES, JAMES E., Private
Resided in Cleveland County where he enlisted at age 18, December 20, 1862, for the war. Wounded in the right hand at Chancellorsville, Virginia, May 1-3, 1863. Returned to duty on an unspecified date. Captured at Spotsylvania Court House, Virginia, May 12, 1864. Confined at Point Lookout, Maryland. Transferred to Elmira, New York, July 25, 1864. Released at Elmira on June 27, 1865, after taking the Oath of Allegiance.

HUMPHRIES, PERRY G., Private
Resided in Cleveland County where he enlisted at age 29, August 22, 1861. Wounded at Chancellorsville, Virginia, May 2-3, 1863. Company records do not indicate whether he returned to duty. Last reported in the records of this company on November 29, 1863, when he was hospitalized at Richmond, Virginia, with an unspecified complaint. [May have served later in Company C, 15th Regiment N.C. Troops (5th Regiment N.C. Volunteers).]

INGLE, LEVI, Private
Resided in Lincoln County and enlisted at Camp Holmes at age 30, October 2, 1862, for the war. Died in hospital at Richmond, Virginia, June 10, 1863, of "pneumonia."

JENKINS, LINZAY G., Private
Born in Chester District, South Carolina, and resided in Cleveland County where he enlisted at age 54, March 17, 1862. Discharged on June 19, 1862, by reason of "advanced age & a want of physical ability to do duty."

JOLLEY, BENJAMIN A., Private
Resided in Cleveland County where he enlisted at age 30, August 22, 1861. Died in hospital at Lynchburg, Virginia, May 26, 1862, of "camp fever."

JOLLEY, CLINGMAN C., Private
Resided in Rutherford County and enlisted in Cleveland County at age 19, August 22, 1861. Captured at Hanover Court House, Virginia, May 27, 1862. Confined at Fort Monroe, Virginia, and at Fort Columbus, New York Harbor. Paroled and transferred

for exchange. Died on August 4, 1862, "on a steamboat coming up James River to Richmond."

JOLLEY, JAMES P., Private
Resided in Cleveland County where he enlisted at age 34, March 17, 1862. Wounded near Shepherdstown, Virginia, on or about September 20, 1862. Died at Winchester, Virginia, September 30, 1862, of wounds and/or disease.

JOLLEY, JESSE L., 1st Sergeant
Resided in Cleveland County where he enlisted at age 28, August 22, 1861. Mustered in as Private and was promoted to 1st Sergeant on November 14, 1862. Killed at Chancellorsville, Virginia, May 3, 1863.

JOLLEY, LEANDER O., Private
Born in Cleveland County* and resided in Rutherford County where he was by occupation a farmer prior to enlisting in Cleveland County at age 34, August 22, 1861. Discharged on December 7, 1861, by reason of "a deformity in one of his feet."

JOLLEY, MEREDITH M., Sergeant
Resided in Rutherford County and enlisted in Cleveland County at age 18, March 10, 1862. Mustered in as Private and was promoted to Corporal in May, 1862. Wounded at Gettysburg, Pennsylvania, July 1-3, 1863. Returned to duty on an unspecified date. Promoted to Sergeant in August, 1863-October, 1864. Wounded at Fussell's Mill, Virginia, August 16, 1864. Returned to duty prior to November 1, 1864. Surrendered at Appomattox Court House, Virginia, April 9, 1865.

JOLLEY, WILLIAM A., Private
Resided in Cleveland County where he enlisted at age 34, August 22, 1861. Killed at Ox Hill, Virginia, September 1, 1862.

JONES, ROBERT, Private
Resided in Cleveland County where he enlisted at age 17, August 22, 1861. Died in hospital at Raleigh on September 1, 1862, of "febris typhoides."

JONES, WILLIAM J., Private
Resided in Cleveland County where he enlisted at age 20, March 17, 1862. Present or accounted for through February, 1865.

KILLIAN, ANTHONY, Private
Born in Columbus County and was by occupation a farmer prior to enlisting at Camp Vance on September 23, 1863, for the war. Present or accounted for through February, 1865. [Furlough records dated February, 1865, give his age as 37.]

LAEL, POLYCARP, Private
Previously served in Company C of this regiment. Transferred to this company on February 1, 1865. Surrendered at Appomattox Court House, Virginia, April 9, 1865.

LAIL, SIDNEY, Private
Resided in Burke County and enlisted at Camp Holmes on September 20, 1863, for the war. Hospitalized at Richmond, Virginia, May 16, 1864, with a gunshot wound. Place and date wounded not reported. Returned to duty prior to November 1, 1864. Captured near Petersburg, Virginia, April 2, 1865. Confined at Fort

Delaware, Delaware, until released on June 19, 1865, after taking the Oath of Allegiance.

LEDBETTER, ANONOMOUS, Private
Resided in Cleveland County where he enlisted at age 32, March 17, 1862. Died at Lynchburg, Virginia, on or about January 24, 1863. Cause of death not reported.

LEE, DRURY B., Private
Born in Cleveland County where he resided as a farmer prior to enlisting in Cleveland County at age 19, March 17, 1862. Discharged on April 23, 1863, by reason of "anchylosis of knee joint."

LEE, JOHN W., Private
Born in Cleveland County where he resided prior to enlisting in Cleveland County at age 20, March 17, 1862. Killed at Gettysburg, Pennsylvania, July 3, 1863.

LEE, WALTER E., Private
Resided in Cleveland County where he enlisted at age 40, March 17, 1862. Died in hospital at Richmond, Virginia, June 3, 1863, of "pleuritis."

LEE, WATSON E., Private
Born in Cleveland County* where he resided prior to enlisting in Cleveland County at age 23, March 17, 1862. Killed at Gettysburg, Pennsylvania, July 3, 1863.

LEE, WILLIAM W., Private
Resided in Cleveland County and was by occupation a farmer prior to enlisting in Cleveland County at age 21, March 17, 1862. Wounded in the abdomen and side at Reams' Station, Virginia, August 25, 1864. Returned to duty in November-December, 1864. Captured at Petersburg, Virginia, April 3, 1865. Confined at Hart's Island, New York Harbor. Released on or about June 20, 1865, after taking the Oath of Allegiance.

LOVELACE, JAMES L., Private
Resided in Cleveland County where he enlisted at age 18, March 17, 1862. Captured at Hanover Court House, Virginia, May 27, 1862. Confined at Fort Monroe, Virginia, and at Fort Columbus, New York Harbor. Paroled and transferred to Aiken's Landing, James River, Virginia, where he was received on July 12, 1862, for exchange. Declared exchanged at Aiken's Landing on August 5, 1862. Returned to duty on an unspecified date. Captured at Warrenton, Virginia, or at Middleburg, Virginia, August 25-26, 1863. Confined at Old Capitol Prison, Washington, D.C., September 3, 1863. Transferred to Point Lookout, Maryland, September 26, 1863. Exchanged on or about March 14, 1864. Returned to duty prior to November 1, 1864. Surrendered at Appomattox Court House, Virginia, April 9, 1865.

LOWE, SIDNEY H., Private
Resided in Lincoln County where he enlisted at age 18, August 11, 1863, for the war. Present or accounted for through February, 1865.

LOWE, TULLIUS C., Private
Resided in Lincoln County where he enlisted at age 19, May 9, 1863, for the war. Promoted to Quartermaster Sergeant prior to November 1, 1864, and transferred to the Field and Staff of this regiment.

McBRAYER, SAMUEL C., 1st Sergeant
Born in Rutherford County and resided in Cleveland

County where he enlisted at age 20, August 22, 1861. Mustered in as 1st Sergeant. Discharged on January 30, 1862, by reason of "an attack of typhoid pneumonia producing disease threatening the development of tubercular phthisis."

McCRAW, ALMEREIN, Private
Born in Cleveland County where he resided prior to enlisting in Cleveland County at age 20, August 22, 1861. Killed at Spotsylvania Court House, Virginia, May 12, 1864.

McGINNIS, JAMES L. B., Private
Resided in Rutherford County and enlisted in Cleveland County at age 16, August 22, 1861. Wounded and captured at Gettysburg, Pennsylvania, July 3, 1863. Hospitalized at Gettysburg. Transferred to hospital at Chester, Pennsylvania, July 14, 1863. Died in hospital at Chester on September 5, 1863, of "hemorrhage."

McKINNEY, JOSEPH D., Private
Resided in Cleveland County where he enlisted at age 17, August 22, 1861. Died at Wilmington on or about February 15, 1862. Cause of death not reported.

McSWAIN, BENJAMIN F., Private
Resided in Cleveland County where he enlisted at age 43, August 22, 1861. Discharged on September 23, 1864. Reason discharged not reported.

McSWAIN, BURRELL B., Private
Resided in Cleveland County where he enlisted at age 33, March 17, 1862. Wounded at Cedar Mountain, Virginia, August 9, 1862. Returned to duty subsequent to October 31, 1862. Wounded at Chancellorsville, Virginia, May 1-3, 1863. Returned to duty prior to July 1-3, 1863, when he was wounded at Gettysburg, Pennsylvania. Company records do not indicate whether he rejoined the company. Reported on duty as a hospital guard at Charlotte from August 19, 1864, through February, 1865.

McSWAIN, DAVID L., Private
Resided in Cleveland County where he enlisted at age 22, March 17, 1862. Captured at Hanover Court House, Virginia, May 27, 1862. Confined at Fort Monroe, Virginia, and at Fort Columbus, New York Harbor. Paroled and transferred to Aiken's Landing, James River, Virginia, where he was received on July 12, 1862, for exchange. Declared exchanged at Aiken's Landing on August 5, 1862. Died at Richmond, Virginia, August 29, 1862. Cause of death not reported.

McSWAIN, GEORGE W., Private
Resided in Cleveland County where he enlisted at age 32, March 17, 1862. Died "at home" on or about February 11, 1863, of "chronic rheumatism and diarrhoea."

McSWAIN, JAMES, Private
Enlisted in Cleveland County on August 22, 1861. Hospitalized at Wilmington on or about February 25, 1862, with "febris typhoides" and died on March 3, 1862.

McSWAIN, ROBERT E., Private
Resided in Cleveland County where he enlisted at age 23, March 17, 1862. Wounded at Gaines' Mill,

Virginia, on or about June 27, 1862. Hospitalized at Raleigh where he died on September 5, 1862, of wounds and/or "febris typhoides."

McSWAIN, WILLIAM D., Private
Resided in Cleveland County where he enlisted at age 40, March 17, 1862. Wounded at Ox Hill, Virginia, September 1, 1862. Returned to duty on an unspecified date. Died in hospital at Richmond, Virginia, October 30, 1864, of a gunshot wound of the hand followed by the amputation of his arm. Place and date wounded not reported.

McWEBB, JOHN, Private
Born in Cleveland County where he resided as a farmer prior to enlisting in Cleveland County at age 21, March 17, 1862. Discharged on September 14, 1863, by reason of "hypertrophy with dilation of left ventricle of heart, attended with great debility [and] chronic diarrhoea."

MARTIN, ABRAM M., Private
Born in Cleveland County where he resided as a farmer prior to enlisting in Cleveland County at age 21, March 17, 1862. Discharged on September 27, 1862, by reason of "pulmonary consumption destroying a good part of the right lung."

MARTIN, WELDON H., Private
Resided in Cleveland County where he enlisted at age 23, March 17, 1862. Present or accounted for through February, 1865.

MATHENEY, JOHN, Corporal
Resided in Lincoln County and enlisted in Cleveland County at age 19, August 22, 1861. Mustered in as Private and was promoted to Corporal in May-August, 1862. Died in a field hospital near Richmond, Virginia, August 9, 1862. Cause of death not reported.

MATHENEY, LEWIS H., Sergeant
Born in Cleveland County* and resided in Lincoln County where he enlisted at age 29, August 22, 1861. Mustered in as Private and was promoted to Corporal prior to November 1, 1861. Promoted to Sergeant prior to May 1, 1862. Killed at Wilderness, Virginia, May 6, 1864.

MATHENY, DAVID, ———
North Carolina pension records indicate that he served in this company.

MILLER, ABEL A., Private
Born in Catawba County and enlisted at Camp Vance on February 24, 1864, for the war. Died at Richmond, Virginia, or at Lynchburg, Virginia, May 2-6, 1864, of "c[hronic] bronchitis."

MILLER, DAVID, Private
Enlisted at Camp Vance on August 22, 1863, for the war. Present or accounted for through February, 1865.

MILLER, JONES M., Private
Previously served in Company E, 12th Regiment N.C. Troops (2nd Regiment N.C. Volunteers). Transferred to this company in March-April, 1864. Surrendered at Appomattox Court House, Virginia, April 9, 1865.

MOORE, DAVID O. H. P., Private
Enlisted at Camp Vance on October 5, 1864, for the

war. Surrendered at Appomattox Court House, Virginia, April 9, 1865.

MOORE, GEORGE M., Jr., Private
Enlisted in Cleveland County at age 17, January 10, 1864, for the war. Wounded in the left foot at Reams' Station, Virginia, August 25, 1864. Left foot amputated. Reported absent wounded through February, 1865.

MOORE, GEORGE M., Sr., Private
Enlisted at Camp Holmes on October 9, 1864, for the war. Surrendered at Appomattox Court House, Virginia, April 9, 1865.

NEAL, JAMES, Private
Born in Cleveland County* where he resided as a miller prior to enlisting in Cleveland County at age 28, March 17, 1862. Died in hospital at Lynchburg, Virginia, on or about May 23, 1862, of "rubeola."

OWEN, ELIAS P., Private
Resided in Cleveland County where he enlisted at age 40, March 17, 1862. Died in hospital at Lynchburg, Virginia, July 29, 1862, of "typhoid fever."

PADGETT, JAMES C., Private
Resided in Rutherford County and enlisted in Cleveland County on March 10, 1862. Captured near Petersburg, Virginia, April 2, 1865. Confined at Fort Delaware, Delaware, until released on June 19, 1865, after taking the Oath of Allegiance.

PADGETT, JOHN H., Private
Resided in Cleveland County where he enlisted at age 24, March 17, 1862. Wounded at Gaines' Mill, Virginia, on or about June 27, 1862. Died in hospital at Richmond, Virginia, July 20, 1862, of wounds.

PADGETT, LORENZO G., Private
Resided in Rutherford County and enlisted in Cleveland County at age 30, March 17, 1862. Died in hospital at Charlotte on or about April 13, 1863, of "diarrhoea ch[ronic]."

PALMER, CHARLES W., Private
Resided in Cleveland County where he enlisted at age 19, March 17, 1862. Killed at Chancellorsville, Virginia, May 3, 1863.

PETERSON, PETER J., Private
Born in Catawba County and enlisted on March 1, 1864, for the war. Died in hospital at Staunton, Virginia, May 20, 1864, of a gunshot wound. Place and date wounded not reported.

PINSON, DAVID G., Private
Enlisted in Cleveland County on August 22, 1861. Died at Wilmington on February 8, 1862. Cause of death not reported.

POWELL, MARCUS D., Private
Resided in Cleveland County where he enlisted at age 30, August 22, 1861. Mustered in as Corporal but was reduced to ranks subsequent to April 30, 1862. Killed at the Battle of Second Manassas, Virginia, August 28-29, 1862.

PRUETT, JAMES C., Sr., Private
Resided in Cleveland County where he enlisted at age 23, March 17, 1862. Present or accounted for until he surrendered at Appomattox Court House, Virginia, April 9, 1865.

PRUETT, JOHN, Private
Enlisted at Camp Holmes on September 25, 1864, for the war. Surrendered at Appomattox Court House, Virginia, April 9, 1865.

PRUETT, THOMAS J., Private
Resided in Cleveland County where he enlisted at age 24, March 17, 1862. Died at Camp Gregg, Virginia, or at Guinea Station, Virginia, January 5, 1863. Cause of death not reported.

PRUETT, WILLIAM T., Private
Resided in Cleveland County where he enlisted at age 17, March 17, 1862. Wounded in the right leg at Gettysburg, Pennsylvania, July 1-3, 1863. Reported absent wounded through January 28, 1864. Reported on duty as a hospital guard at Charlotte during September, 1864-February, 1865. Paroled at Charlotte in May, 1865.

RADER, JONAS MONROE, Private
Enlisted at Camp Vance at age 16, March 1, 1864, for the war. Wounded in the left leg at Spotsylvania Court House, Virginia, on or about May 12, 1864. Retired to the Invalid Corps on January 14, 1865.

ROBESON, WILLIAM R., Private
Resided in Cleveland County where he enlisted at age 29, March 17, 1862. Died in hospital at Richmond, Virginia, September 4, 1862, of "dyspepsia."

ROLLINS, DOCTOR O., Private
Born in Cleveland County* where he resided as a farmer prior to enlisting in Cleveland County at age 27, August 22, 1861. Transferred to Company I, 34th Regiment N.C. Troops, in September-October, 1864.

ROLLINS, JAMES J., Sergeant
Resided in Cleveland County where he enlisted at age 27, August 22, 1861. Mustered in as Corporal and was promoted to Sergeant in May-October, 1862. Wounded in the left leg and right shoulder and captured at Gettysburg, Pennsylvania, July 1-3, 1863. Died in a Federal field hospital near Gettysburg on July 22, 1863, of wounds.

ROLLINS, NOAH J., Private
Resided in Cleveland County where he enlisted at age 25, August 22, 1861. Wounded in the left hip at Ox Hill, Virginia, September 1, 1862. Company records do not indicate whether he rejoined the company. Reported on detail as a guard in November-December, 1864. Retired to the Invalid Corps on December 28, 1864.

SCRUGGS, LORENZO B., Private
Resided in Cleveland County and was by occupation a farmer prior to enlisting in Cleveland County at age 28, August 22, 1861. Wounded in the left hand at the Battle of Second Manassas, Virginia, August 28-30, 1862. Returned to duty on an unspecified date. Deserted near Chancellorsville, Virginia, on an unspecified date. Returned to duty on an unspecified date. Captured at Spotsylvania Court House, Virginia, May 12, 1864. Confined at Point Lookout, Maryland. Transferred to Elmira, New York, August 10, 1864. Paroled at Elmira

and transferred to Venus Point, Savannah River, Georgia, where he was received on November 15, 1864, for exchange.

SIGMON, JESSE A., Private
Enlisted in Catawba County on February 1, 1865, for the war. Present or accounted for through February, 1865.

SIMPSON, ALLISON, Private
Resided in Wilkes County and enlisted at age 25, October 2, 1862, for the war. Died in hospital at Guinea Station, Virginia, January 30 or July 30, 1863. Cause of death not reported.

TATE, KINCHEN T., Private
Resided in Cleveland County where he enlisted at age 18, March 17, 1862. Discharged in November, 1862. Reason discharged not reported. Later served in Company C, 15th Regiment N.C. Troops (5th Regiment N.C. Volunteers).

WEBB, CHARLES E., Private
Resided in Cleveland County where he enlisted at age 28, August 22, 1861. Hospitalized at Richmond, Virginia, May 25, 1864, with a gunshot wound of the left hand. Place and date wounded not reported. Returned to duty prior to November 1, 1864. Reported absent wounded in January-February, 1865. Place and date wounded not reported. [North Carolina pension records indicate that he survived the war.]

WEBB, JOHN Mc., ———
North Carolina pension records indicate that he served in this company.

WEBB, WILLIS J., Private
Resided in Cleveland County where he enlisted at age 20, March 17, 1862. Wounded in the left hand at Wilderness, Virginia, May 6, 1864. Returned to duty in November-December, 1864. Present or accounted for through February, 1865. Captured in hospital at Richmond, Virginia, April 3, 1865. Transferred to Newport News, Virginia, April 23, 1865. Released on June 30, 1865, after taking the Oath of Allegiance.

WEIR, M. S., Private
Place and date of enlistment not reported. Paroled at Charlotte in May, 1865.

WILLIAMS, JAMES W., Private
Born in Rutherford County and resided in Cleveland County where he was by occupation a farmer prior to enlisting in Cleveland County at age 29, August 22, 1861. Discharged on November 8, 1861, by reason of "a scrotal hernia of the right side."

WILSON, ALBERT C., Private
Resided in Cleveland County where he enlisted at age 18, May 10, 1862, for the war. Died in hospital at Charlottesville, Virginia, May 31, 1862, of "pneumonia."

WILSON, DAVID P., Private
Enlisted at Camp Vance on March 1, 1864, for the war. Present or accounted for through February, 1865.

WILSON, GEORGE W., Private
Resided in South Carolina and enlisted in Cleveland County at age 22, March 17, 1862. Captured at Hanover Court House, Virginia, May 27, 1862. Confined at Fort Monroe, Virginia, and at Fort Columbus, New York Harbor. Paroled and transferred to Aiken's Landing, James River, Virginia, where he was received on July 12, 1862, for exchange. Declared exchanged at Aiken's Landing on August 5, 1862. Returned to duty on an unspecified date. Killed at Fredericksburg, Virginia, December 13, 1862.

WILSON, JAMES T., Private
Resided in Cleveland County where he enlisted at age 21, August 22, 1861. Wounded in the face and neck and captured at Gettysburg, Pennsylvania, July 1-4, 1863. Hospitalized at Gettysburg. Transferred to hospital at Davids Island, New York Harbor, July 17-24, 1863. Paroled at Davids Island and transferred to City Point, Virginia, where he was received on September 8, 1863, for exchange. Returned to duty on May 8, 1864. Wounded at Fussell's Mill, Virginia, August 16, 1864. Returned to duty in November-December, 1864. Paroled at Farmville, Virginia, April 11-21, 1865.

WRIGHT, ABNER B., Private
Resided in Cleveland County where he enlisted at age 26, August 22, 1861. Mustered in as Sergeant. Reduced to ranks on an unspecified date. Transferred to Company E, 12th Regiment N.C. Troops (2nd Regiment N.C. Volunteers), April 24, 1863.

YARBORO, LEWIS H., Private
Resided in Cleveland County where he enlisted at age 23, March 17, 1862. Wounded in the left hand at or near Wilderness, Virginia, on or about May 3, 1864. Returned to duty in November-December, 1864. Wounded in the left wrist at Petersburg, Virginia, April 2, 1865. Captured in hospital at Richmond, Virginia, April 3, 1865. Paroled on April 23, 1865.

COMPANY I

This company, known as the "Yadkin Stars," was raised in Yadkin County where it was mustered into service on August 13, 1861. It was then assigned to the 28th Regiment as Company I. After joining the regiment the company functioned as a part of the regiment, and its history for the war period is reported as a part of the regimental history.

The information contained in the following roster of the company was compiled principally from company muster rolls for August 13-December, 1861; May-October, 1862; January-February, 1863; and September, 1864-February, 1865. No company muster rolls were found for January-April, 1862; November-December, 1862; March, 1863-August, 1864; or for the period after February, 1865. Valuable information was obtained also from primary records such as the Roll of Honor, medical records, prisoner of war records, discharge certificates, and pension applications, and from secondary sources such as postwar rosters and histories, cemetery records, and records of the United Daughters of the Confederacy.

OFFICERS

CAPTAINS

SPEER, WILLIAM H. ASBURY
Resided in Yadkin County where he enlisted at age 30. Appointed Captain on August 13, 1861. Captured at

Hanover Court House, Virginia, May 27, 1862. Confined at Fort Monroe, Virginia, and at Fort Columbus, New York Harbor. Transferred to Johnson's Island, Ohio, where he arrived on an unspecified date. Paroled and transferred to Vicksburg, Mississippi, where he was received on September 20, 1862, for exchange. Appointed Major on November 1, 1862, and transferred to the Field and Staff of this regiment.

BOHANNON, NEAL
Resided in Yadkin County where he enlisted at age 31, August 13, 1861. Mustered in as Sergeant and was promoted to 1st Sergeant on October 8, 1861. Appointed 1st Lieutenant on April 12, 1862. Captured at Hanover Court House, Virginia, May 27, 1862. Confined at Fort Monroe, Virginia, and at Fort Columbus, New York Harbor. Exchanged on an unspecified date. Promoted to Captain on November 1, 1862. Died "in Virginia" on or about June 20, 1863, of "typhoid fever." He was "a brave and good officer."

BOHANNON, SIMON S.
Resided in Yadkin County where he enlisted at age 26, August 13, 1861. Mustered in as Sergeant and was appointed 2nd Lieutenant on April 12, 1862. Promoted to 1st Lieutenant on November 1, 1862, and was promoted to Captain on June 20, 1863. Wounded at Gettysburg, Pennsylvania, July 1-3, 1863. Returned to duty on an unspecified date. Captured at Spotsylvania Court House, Virginia, on or about May 12, 1864. Confined at Fort Delaware, Delaware. Transferred to Hilton Head, South Carolina, on an unspecified date. Transferred back to Fort Delaware where he arrived on March 12, 1865. Released on June 16, 1865, after taking the Oath of Allegiance.

LIEUTENANTS

FOLGER, ROMULUS S., 2nd Lieutenant
Previously served as 1st Lieutenant of Company A of this regiment. Appointed 2nd Lieutenant of this company on or about January 7, 1863, but was appointed Adjutant (2nd Lieutenant) to rank from the same date and transferred to the Field and Staff of this regiment.

HOLCOMB, DANIEL F., 1st Lieutenant
Resided in Yadkin County where he enlisted at age 25. Appointed 1st Lieutenant on August 13, 1861. Defeated for reelection when the regiment was reorganized on April 12, 1862. Continued to serve in this company with the rank of Private. [For additional information see page 213 of this volume.]

HOLCOMB, JOHN T., 3rd Lieutenant
Born in Yadkin County* where he resided prior to enlisting in Yadkin County at age 22. Elected 3rd Lieutenant on August 13, 1861. Defeated for reelection when the regiment was reorganized on April 12, 1862. Continued to serve in this company with the rank of Private. [For additional information see page 213 of this volume.]

LONG, FREDERICK, 2nd Lieutenant
Resided in Yadkin County where he enlisted at age 21. Appointed 2nd Lieutenant on August 13, 1861. Wounded in the back at Shepherdstown, Virginia, September 20, 1862. Died at Winchester, Virginia,

October 23, 1862, of wounds. "He was a brave and gallant officer."

SNOW, JORDAN H., Jr., 1st Lieutenant
Resided in Yadkin County where he enlisted at age 29, August 13, 1861. Mustered in as Private and was elected 3rd Lieutenant on January 3, 1863. Promoted to 1st Lieutenant on June 20, 1863. Wounded in the right thigh at Gettysburg, Pennsylvania, July 3, 1863. Returned to duty on an unspecified date. Captured at or near Pickett's Farm, Virginia, on or about July 21, 1864. Confined at Point Lookout, Maryland, July 28, 1864. Transferred to Old Capitol Prison, Washington, D.C., August 4, 1864. Transferred to Fort Delaware, Delaware, August 11, 1864. Released on June 17, 1865, after taking the Oath of Allegiance.

THOMPSON, SAMUEL TUNSTALL, 2nd Lieutenant
Previously served as 1st Sergeant of Company K, 23rd Regiment N.C. Troops (13th Regiment N.C. Volunteers). Transferred to this company in September-October, 1863, upon appointment as 2nd Lieutenant to rank from April 11, 1863. Surrendered at Appomattox Court House, Virginia, April 9, 1865.

TODD, LEANDER A., 3rd Lieutenant
Resided in Yadkin County where he enlisted at age 24, March 8, 1862. Mustered in as Private and was elected 3rd Lieutenant on October 20, 1863. Surrendered at Appomattox Court House, Virginia, April 9, 1865.

NONCOMMISSIONED OFFICERS AND PRIVATES

ARMSTRONG, MERIDETH T., Private
Resided in Yadkin County where he enlisted at age 40, August 13, 1861. Captured at Hanover Court House, Virginia, May 27, 1862. Confined at Fort Columbus, New York Harbor. Exchanged at Aiken's Landing, James River, Virginia, August 5, 1862. Wounded in the thigh at the Battle of Second Manassas, Virginia, August 27-30, 1862. Discharged on or about November 21, 1862, under the provisions of the Conscription Act.

ASHLY, BURGESS H., Private
Resided in Yadkin County where he enlisted at age 40, August 13, 1861. Deserted on June 18, 1863. Returned to duty on December 13, 1864. Deserted on January 11, 1865.

ATWOOD, GEORGE W., Corporal
Resided in Yadkin County where he enlisted at age 18, August 13, 1861. Mustered in as Private and was promoted to Corporal on April 12, 1862. Killed at Gaines' Mill, Virginia, June 27, 1862.

ATWOOD, JESSE C., Private
Resided in Yadkin County where he enlisted at age 19, March 8, 1862. Died in hospital at Richmond, Virginia, March 6, 1864, of "febr[is] typhoides."

BAITY, PLEASANT H., Private
Resided in Yadkin County where he enlisted at age 18, March 8, 1862. Wounded at Gettysburg, Pennsylvania, July 1-3, 1863. Returned to duty on an unspecified date. Reported present for duty during September, 1864-February, 1865.

BAITY, WILLIAM W., Private
Resided in Yadkin County where he enlisted at age 20,

August 13, 1861. Died at Winchester, Virginia, on or about December 8, 1862, of "fever."

BARKER, LARKIN JONES, Sergeant
Resided in Yadkin County where he enlisted at age 18, August 13, 1861. Mustered in as Sergeant. Promoted to Hospital Steward in March, 1863-October, 1864, and transferred to the Field and Staff of this regiment.

BEGGARLY, JERRY, Private
Born in Surry County and resided in Yadkin County where he was by occupation a saddler prior to enlisting in Yadkin County at age 27, August 13, 1861. Discharged on October 17, 1861, by reason of "scrotal hernia in both sides."

BENGE, JOHN, Private
Born in Surry County and resided in Yadkin County where he was by occupation a farmer prior to enlisting in Yadkin County at age 20, August 13, 1861. Discharged on May 1, 1862, by reason of "epilepsy."

BENGE, NATHAN, Private
Resided in Yadkin County where he enlisted at age 18, August 13, 1861. Captured at Spotsylvania Court House, Virginia, May 12, 1864. Confined at Point Lookout, Maryland. Transferred to Elmira, New York, August 8, 1864. Paroled at Elmira and transferred to Venus Point, Savannah River, Georgia, where he was received on November 15, 1864, for exchange. Died "at home" on January 5, 1865. Cause of death not reported.

BRACHLEY, WILLIAM, ———
Place and date of enlistment not reported. Deserted to the enemy on January 15, 1865. Took the Oath of Allegiance at Beverly, West Virginia, April 19, 1865. Records of the Federal Provost Marshal give his age as 21.

BREWBAKER, ALEXANDER, Private
Resided in Yadkin County where he enlisted at age 21, March 8, 1862. Deserted on April 5, 1863.

BREWBAKER, WASHINGTON, Private
Resided in Yadkin County where he enlisted at age 34, March 8, 1862. Deserted on August 5, 1862.

BRINDLE, JAMES FREE, Sergeant
Resided in Yadkin County where he enlisted at age 23, August 13, 1861. Mustered in as Private and was promoted to Corporal on June 11, 1862. Promoted to Sergeant in March, 1863-October, 1864. Captured near Petersburg, Virginia, April 2, 1865. Confined at Fort Delaware, Delaware. Released on June 19, 1865, after taking the Oath of Allegiance.

BRINDLE, MARK, Private
Resided in Yadkin County and was by occupation a farmer prior to enlisting in Yadkin County at age 18, August 13, 1861. Wounded in the arm, thigh, and finger at the Battle of Second Manassas, Virginia, August 27-30, 1862. Returned to duty on March 6, 1863. Captured near Petersburg, Virginia, April 2, 1865. Confined at Hart's Island, New York Harbor, until released on June 18, 1865, after taking the Oath of Allegiance.

BROWN, ROBERT W., Private
Resided in Yadkin County where he enlisted at age 19,

August 13, 1861. Wounded in the right shoulder at Frayser's Farm, Virginia, June 30, 1862. Died in hospital at Richmond, Virginia, August 13, 1862, of wounds.

BRYANT, STEPHEN H., Private
Resided in Yadkin County where he enlisted at age 23, March 8, 1862. Wounded at the Battle of Second Manassas, Virginia, August 27-30, 1862. Transferred to Company A, 44th Regiment N.C. Troops, in March-December, 1863.

BUCHANNON, WILLIAM, Private
Resided in Yadkin County where he enlisted at age 22, August 13, 1861. Captured at Hanover Court House, Virginia, May 27, 1862. Confined at Fort Monroe, Virginia, and at Fort Columbus, New York Harbor. Paroled and transferred to Aiken's Landing, James River, Virginia, where he was exchanged on August 5, 1862. Failed to return to duty and was reported absent without leave on or about October 31, 1862. Returned to duty in January-February, 1863. Reported missing at Gettysburg, Pennsylvania, July 1-3, 1863. No further records.

BUNDY, HENRY, Private
Resided in Yadkin County where he enlisted at age 23, August 13, 1861. Captured at Hanover Court House, Virginia, May 27, 1862. Confined at Fort Monroe, Virginia, and at Fort Columbus, New York Harbor. Paroled and transferred to Aiken's Landing, James River, Virginia, where he was exchanged on August 5, 1862. Returned to duty prior to November 1, 1862. Captured at Gettysburg, Pennsylvania, July 3, 1863. Confined at Fort Delaware, Delaware. Transferred to Point Lookout, Maryland, October 15-18, 1863. Released at Point Lookout on January 25, 1864, after joining the U.S. service. Unit to which assigned not reported.

BUNDY, NATHAN, Private
Resided in Yadkin County where he enlisted at age 21, March 8, 1862. Captured at Hanover Court House, Virginia, May 27, 1862. Confined at Fort Monroe, Virginia, and at Fort Columbus, New York Harbor. Paroled and transferred to Aiken's Landing, James River, Virginia, where he was exchanged on August 5, 1862. Reported absent without leave prior to November 1, 1862. Listed as a deserter on October 1, 1863.

BURGESS, EDWARD T., ———
North Carolina pension records indicate that he served in this company.

BURNS, JOHN, Private
Enlisted in Yadkin County on August 13, 1861. Present or accounted for through December, 1861. No further records.

CALAWAY, CHARLES M., Private
Resided in [Yadkin County] and enlisted at Liberty Mills, Virginia, December 20, 1863, for the war. Captured near Petersburg, Virginia, April 2, 1865. Confined at Fort Delaware, Delaware. Released on June 7, 1865, after taking the Oath of Allegiance.

CARLTON, SANDFORD B., Private
Resided in Yadkin County where he enlisted at age 19,

August 13, 1861. Captured at Hanover Court House, Virginia, May 27, 1862. Confined at Fort Monroe, Virginia, and at Fort Columbus, New York Harbor. Paroled and transferred to Aiken's Landing, James River, Virginia, where he was received on July 12, 1862, for exchange. Declared exchanged at Aiken's Landing on August 5, 1862. Wounded at Chancellorsville, Virginia, May 1-3, 1863. Company records do not indicate whether he returned to duty. Reported absent sick in September-October, 1864, and was reported absent without leave from November 15, 1864, through February, 1865.

CARTER, MILES, Private

Resided in Yadkin County and enlisted at Liberty Mills, Virginia, February 29, 1864, for the war. Captured near Petersburg, Virginia, April 2, 1865. Confined at Fort Delaware, Delaware, until released on June 19, 1865, after taking the Oath of Allegiance.

CARTER, WILLIAM M., Private

Previously served in Company B, 38th Regiment N.C. Troops. Transferred to this company on March 29, 1863. Wounded and captured at Gettysburg, Pennsylvania, July 3, 1863. Confined at Fort Delaware, Delaware. Transferred to Point Lookout, Maryland, October 15-18, 1863. Died at Point Lookout on August 24, 1864. Cause of death not reported.

CARTRIGHT, THOMAS D., Private

Enlisted at Camp Vance on November 4, 1863, for the war. Reported on detail as a shoemaker at Richmond, Virginia, from January 8, 1864, through February, 1865. Captured in hospital at Richmond on April 3, 1865. Paroled on May 3, 1865.

CASEY, DANIEL C., Sergeant

Resided in Yadkin County where he enlisted at age 20, August 13, 1861. Mustered in as Private and was promoted to Sergeant on April 12, 1862. Wounded in the shoulder at the Battle of Second Manassas, Virginia, August 27-30, 1862. Returned to duty prior to March 1, 1863. Captured at Chancellorsville, Virginia, May 3, 1863. Paroled and transferred to City Point, Virginia, where he was received on May 13, 1863, for exchange. Returned to duty prior to July 3, 1863, when he was captured at Gettysburg, Pennsylvania. Confined at Fort Delaware, Delaware. Transferred to Point Lookout, Maryland, October 15-18, 1863. Released at Point Lookout on January 25, 1864, after taking the Oath of Allegiance and joining the U.S. service. Unit to which assigned not reported.

CHAPPEL, CALVIN J., Private

Enlisted at Camp Gregg, Virginia, at age 26, February 28, 1863, for the war. Reported absent without leave from October, 1864, through February, 1865. [North Carolina pension records indicate he was wounded at or near Chancellorsville, Virginia, May 4, 1863. May have served previously in Company G, 44th Regiment N.C. Troops.]

CHAPPEL, LEWIS J., Private

Born in Yadkin County where he resided as a farmer prior to enlisting in Yadkin County at age 24, August 13, 1861. Transferred to Company B, 38th Regiment N.C. Troops, January 10, 1862.

CHAPPEL, WILLIAM, Private

Resided in Yadkin County and was by occupation a farmer prior to enlisting at Camp Holmes on November 14, 1862, for the war. Captured at or near Pickett's Farm, Virginia, on or about July 21, 1864. Confined at Point Lookout, Maryland, July 28, 1864. Released on May 13, 1865, after taking the Oath of Allegiance.

CHAPPELL, J. C., Private

Resided in Yadkin County and enlisted at age 18, February 28, 1863, for the war. Deserted on June 18, 1863.

CHAPPELL, JAMES R., Private

Resided in Yadkin County where he enlisted at age 30, August 13, 1861. Wounded in both thighs and both hips and captured at Wilderness, Virginia, on or about May 6, 1864. No further records.

CHILDERS, JAMES F., Private

Born in Surry County and resided in Yadkin County where he was by occupation a farmer prior to enlisting in Yadkin County at age 23, August 13, 1861. Discharged on December 14, 1861, by reason of "varicocele."

CHILDRESS, WILLIAM H., Private

Resided in Yadkin County where he enlisted at age 19, August 13, 1861. Captured at Hanover Court House, Virginia, May 27, 1862. Confined at Fort Monroe, Virginia, and at Fort Columbus, New York Harbor. Paroled and transferred to Aiken's Landing, James River, Virginia, where he was received on July 12, 1862, for exchange. Declared exchanged at Aiken's Landing on August 5, 1862. Returned to duty prior to November 1, 1862. Wounded at Gettysburg, Pennsylvania, July 1-3, 1863. Returned to duty on an unspecified date. Captured near Petersburg, Virginia, April 2, 1865. Confined at Fort Delaware, Delaware, until released on June 19, 1865, after taking the Oath of Allegiance.

COCKERHAM, DAVID, Corporal

Resided in Yadkin County where he enlisted at age 30, August 13, 1861. Mustered in as Private and was promoted to Corporal in March, 1863-October, 1864. Captured at New Bern on March 14, 1862. Confined at Fort Columbus, New York Harbor. Paroled and transferred to Aiken's Landing, James River, Virginia, where he was received on July 12, 1862, for exchange. Declared exchanged at Aiken's Landing on August 5, 1862. Returned to duty subsequent to February 28, 1863. Captured near Petersburg, Virginia, April 2, 1865. Confined at Point Lookout, Maryland. Released on June 24, 1865, after taking the Oath of Allegiance.

COMER, JAMES Q., Private

Resided in Yadkin County where he enlisted at age 32, August 13, 1861. Mustered in as Private and was promoted to Corporal on October 30, 1861. Captured at Hanover Court House, Virginia, May 27, 1862. Confined at Fort Monroe, Virginia, and at Fort Columbus, New York Harbor. Paroled and transferred to Aiken's Landing, James River, Virginia, where he was received on July 12, 1862, for exchange. Declared exchanged at Aiken's Landing on August 5, 1862. Reduced to ranks prior to November 1, 1862. Reported absent without leave in January-February, 1863. Reported present for duty during September-December, 1864. Deserted on January 11, 1865.

COOK, ALVIN, Private
Previously served in Company G, 44th Regiment N.C. Troops. Transferred to this company on October 1, 1864. Present or accounted for through February, 1865.

DANNER, JOSHUA G., Private
Resided in Yadkin County where he enlisted at age 19, March 8, 1862. Wounded at Gettysburg, Pennsylvania, on or about July 3, 1863. Died on July 4, 1863, of wounds. Place of death not reported.

DAVIS, SAMUEL L., Private
Born in Mecklenburg County and resided in Yadkin County where he was by occupation a farmer prior to enlisting in Yadkin County at age 23, September 3, 1861. Discharged on February 3, 1862, by reason of "chronic rheumatism of the lower extremities."

DAVIS, WILLIAM A., Private
Company records indicate he enlisted at Camp Holmes on August 20, 1862, for the war; however, he was not listed on the rolls of this company until September-October, 1864. Present or accounted for through February, 1865.

DICKENSON, ISAAC D., Private
Resided in Yadkin County where he enlisted at age 23, August 13, 1861. Captured at Hanover Court House, Virginia, May 27, 1862. Confined at Fort Monroe, Virginia, and at Fort Columbus, New York Harbor. Paroled and transferred to Aiken's Landing, James River, Virginia, where he was received on July 12, 1862, for exchange. Declared exchanged at Aiken's Landing on August 5, 1862. Returned to duty prior to November 1, 1862. Wounded at Chancellorsville, Virginia, May 2-3, 1863. Detailed as a shoemaker at Richmond, Virginia, in February, 1864. Reported absent on detail at Richmond through February, 1865.

DICKERSON, DAVID A., Private
Resided in Yadkin County where he enlisted at age 23, March 8, 1862. Captured by the enemy on an unspecified date. Paroled and transferred to Aiken's Landing, James River, Virginia, where he was received on September 7, 1862, for exchange. Declared exchanged at Aiken's Landing on September 21, 1862. Returned to duty prior to November 1, 1862. Reported present for duty during September-December, 1864. Hospitalized at Richmond, Virginia, January 10, 1865, with "diarrhoea" and died on January 24, 1865.

DICKSON, HENRY, Private
Enlisted at Petersburg, Virginia, September 22, 1864, for the war. Reported absent without leave on December 15, 1864.

DOBBINS, JAMES, Private
Resided in Yadkin County where he enlisted at age 20, September 20, 1862, for the war. Died in hospital at Richmond, Virginia, May 27, 1863, of "fever."

DOBBINS, LEVI, Private
Born in Yadkin County* where he resided as a farmer prior to enlisting in Yadkin County at age 20, March 8, 1862. Captured at or near Winchester, Virginia, on or about December 2-3, 1862. Paroled at Winchester on December 4, 1862. Discharged on May 1, 1863, by reason of gunshot wounds of the left arm and right hip. Place and date wounded not reported.

DOBBINS, MILAS, Private
Resided in Yadkin County where he enlisted at age 19, August 13, 1861. Captured at Hanover Court House, Virginia, May 27, 1862. Confined at Fort Monroe, Virginia, and at Fort Columbus, New York Harbor. Paroled and transferred to Aiken's Landing, James River, Virginia, where he was received on July 12, 1862, for exchange. Declared exchanged at Aiken's Landing on August 5, 1862. Deserted in October, 1862.

DOBBINS, WILLIAM, Private
Resided in Yadkin County where he enlisted at age 19, March 8, 1862. Captured at or near Pickett's Farm, Virginia, on or about July 21, 1864. Confined at Point Lookout, Maryland. Paroled and transferred to Boulware's Wharf, James River, Virginia, where he was received on March 16, 1865, for exchange.

DOZIER, NATHAN C., Private
Resided in Yadkin County and enlisted in New Hanover County at age 18, October 1, 1861. Captured by the enemy on an unspecified date. Paroled and transferred to Aiken's Landing, James River, Virginia, where he was received on September 7, 1862, for exchange. Declared exchanged at Aiken's Landing on September 21, 1862. Returned to duty prior to November 1, 1862. Wounded at Gettysburg, Pennsylvania, July 1-3, 1863. Returned to duty on an unspecified date. Wounded in the right foot at Jericho Mills, Virginia, May 23, 1864. Reported absent wounded through October, 1864. Returned to duty in November-December, 1864. Retired to the Invalid Corps on February 18, 1865, by reason of disability.

DOZIER, SMITH W., Corporal
Born in Yadkin County* where he resided as a farmer prior to enlisting in Yadkin County at age 19, August 13, 1861. Mustered in as Private. Captured at Hanover Court House, Virginia, May 27, 1862. Confined at Fort Monroe, Virginia, and at Fort Columbus, New York Harbor. Paroled and transferred to Aiken's Landing, James River, Virginia, where he was received on July 12, 1862, for exchange. Declared exchanged at Aiken's Landing on August 5, 1862. Promoted to Corporal on August 29, 1862. Returned to duty prior to November 1, 1862. Transferred to the C.S. Navy on April 3, 1864.

DRAPER, JESSE, Private
Resided in Yadkin County where he enlisted at age 23, August 13, 1861. Died in hospital at Richmond, Virginia, July 4, 1862, of "typhoid fever."

DULL, A. N., Private
Resided in Yadkin County where he enlisted at age 24, March 8, 1862. Killed at or near Gaines' Mill, Virginia, on or about June 27, 1862.

ELLER, HENRY P., Private
Born in [Yadkin County*] where he resided as a farmer prior to enlisting in Yadkin County at age 18, August 13, 1861. Captured at Hanover Court House, Virginia, on or about May 27, 1862. Confined at Fort Monroe, Virginia, and at Fort Columbus, New York Harbor. Paroled and transferred to Aiken's Landing, James River, Virginia, where he was received on July 12, 1862, for exchange. Declared exchanged at Aiken's Landing on August 5, 1862. Returned to duty prior to November 1, 1862. Captured at or near Gettysburg, Pennsylvania,

on or about July 3, 1863. Confined at Fort Delaware, Delaware. Transferred to Point Lookout, Maryland, October 15-18, 1863. Released at Point Lookout on January 25, 1864, after taking the Oath of Allegiance and joining the U.S. Army. Assigned to Company G, 1st Regiment U.S. Volunteer Infantry.

EVANS, IREDELL C., Private
Resided in Yadkin County where he enlisted at age 18, August 13, 1861. Present or accounted for through February, 1865.

EVANS, J. C., Private
Resided in Catawba County. North Carolina pension records indicate he enlisted on August 13, 1861; however, he was first listed in the records of this company in July, 1863. Captured near Petersburg, Virginia, July 30, 1864. Confined at Point Lookout, Maryland. Transferred to Elmira, New York, August 8, 1864. Released on May 19, 1865, after taking the Oath of Allegiance.

EVERAGE, JOSEPH, Private
Resided in Yadkin County where he enlisted at age 27, August 13, 1861. Captured at Hanover Court House, Virginia, May 27, 1862. Confined at Fort Monroe, Virginia, and at Fort Columbus, New York Harbor. Paroled and transferred to Aiken's Landing, James River, Virginia, where he was received on July 12, 1862, for exchange. Declared exchanged at Aiken's Landing on August 5, 1862. Returned to duty on an unspecified date. Wounded at Chancellorsville, Virginia, May 2-3, 1863. Deserted on July 15, 1863. Hospitalized at Richmond, Virginia, May 18, 1864, with a gunshot wound of the right leg. Place and date wounded not reported. Returned to duty prior to November 1, 1864. Present or accounted for through February, 1865. Hospitalized at Richmond on March 10, 1865, with a gunshot wound of the right leg. Place and date wounded not reported. Captured in hospital at Richmond on April 3, 1865. Transferred to Newport News, Virginia, April 23, 1865. Released on June 30, 1865, after taking the Oath of Allegiance.

FARRINGTON, NATHAN H., Private
Born in Surry County and resided in Yadkin County where he was by occupation a farmer prior to enlisting in Yadkin County at age 22, March 8, 1862. Discharged on July 18, 1862, by reason of "scrotal hernia of the left side."

FARRIS, ENOCH H., Private
Born in Yadkin County* where he resided prior to enlisting in Yadkin County at age 18, August 13, 1861. Captured at Hanover Court House, Virginia, on or about May 27, 1862. Confined at Fort Wool, Virginia. Paroled at Fort Wool and transferred to Aiken's Landing, James River, Virginia, where he was received on August 26, 1862, for exchange. Declared exchanged at Aiken's Landing on November 10, 1862. Returned to duty on an unspecified date. Hospitalized at Danville, Virginia, January 1, 1863, with a gunshot wound. Place and date wounded not reported. Returned to duty on January 17, 1863. Killed at or near Wilderness, Virginia, May 5, 1864.

FARRIS, JOSEPH, Private
Resided in Yadkin County where he enlisted at age 19, August 13, 1861. Wounded at Sharpsburg, Maryland,

September 17, 1862. Died of wounds. Place and date of death not reported.

FARRIS, PRESTON T., Private
Resided in Yadkin County and enlisted at Liberty Mills, Virginia, at age 18, September 8, 1863, for the war. Captured at Spotsylvania Court House, Virginia, May 12, 1864. Confined at Point Lookout, Maryland. Transferred to Elmira, New York, August 10, 1864. Released at Elmira on July 11, 1865, after taking the Oath of Allegiance.

FARRIS, WILLIAM D., Sergeant
Resided in Yadkin County where he enlisted at age 33, August 13, 1861. Mustered in as Corporal. Promoted to Sergeant subsequent to December 31, 1861. Killed at or near Gaines' Mill, Virginia, on or about June 27, 1862.

FRASIER, LEANDER, Private
Resided in Yadkin County where he enlisted at age 22, August 13, 1861. Died in hospital at Richmond, Virginia, on or about December 20, 1862, of "pneumonia typhoides."

FREEMAN, JESSE, Private
Resided in Yadkin County where he enlisted at age 22, August 13, 1861. Deserted on September 21, 1861.

GENTRY, F. L., ———
North Carolina pension records indicate that he served in this company.

GENTRY, ROBERT W., Private
Enlisted in Yadkin County on August 13, 1861. Present or accounted for through February, 1863. No further records.

GENTRY, WILLIAM R., Private
Resided in Yadkin County where he enlisted at age 26, August 13, 1861. Mustered in as Sergeant but was reduced to ranks in November, 1861-October, 1862. Reported absent without leave from September 27, 1864, through February, 1865.

GROSS, W., Private
Born in Yadkin County* and enlisted on or about February 14, 1862. Died in hospital at Richmond, Virginia, June 29, 1864, of "rubeola."

HALL, DANIEL C., Private
Resided in Yadkin County where he enlisted at age 18, March 8, 1862. Wounded and captured at Gettysburg, Pennsylvania, July 1-5, 1863. Hospitalized at Davids Island, New York Harbor, on or about July 17, 1863. Paroled at Davids Island and transferred to City Point, Virginia, where he was received on September 8, 1863, for exchange.

HALL, LEWIS, Private
Previously served in Company G, 18th Regiment N.C. Troops (8th Regiment N.C. Volunteers). Transferred to this company on or about September 1, 1864. Present or accounted for through February, 1865.

HALL, RICHMOND, Private
Enlisted at Camp Holmes on November 30, 1863, for the war. Deserted on an unspecified date. Returned to duty on September 9, 1864. Transferred to Company G, 44th Regiment N.C. Troops, on or about October 1,

1864.

HARDING, GREEN BERRY, Sergeant

Resided in Yadkin County where he enlisted at age 18, March 8, 1862. Mustered in as Private. Wounded at Gaines' Mill, Virginia, on or about June 27, 1862. Returned to duty on an unspecified date. Wounded at Fredericksburg, Virginia, on or about December 13, 1862. Returned to duty prior to March 1, 1863. Promoted to Sergeant in March, 1863-October, 1864. Wounded at Gettysburg, Pennsylvania, July 1-3, 1863. Returned to duty on an unspecified date. Wounded at Gravel Hill, Virginia, July 28, 1864. Retired from service on December 28, 1864, by reason of disability.

HARDING, SAMUEL S., Sergeant

Born in Yadkin County* where he resided prior to enlisting in Yadkin County at age 23, August 31, 1861. Mustered in as Private and was promoted to Sergeant on April 12, 1862. Killed at Reams' Station, Virginia, August 25, 1864.

HARPER, THOMAS A., ———

Records of the United Daughters of the Confederacy indicate he was killed at Reams' Station, Virginia, August 25, 1864. No further records.

HARVILL, JOHN, Private

Born in Yadkin County* where he resided prior to enlisting in Yadkin County at age 35, March 8, 1862. Deserted on April 5, 1863. Returned to duty on an unspecified date. Wounded in the thigh near Petersburg, Virginia, on or about August 22, 1864. Died of wounds. Place and date of death not reported.

HAYNES, ANDERSON H., Private

Resided in Yadkin County where he enlisted at age 23, August 13, 1861. Captured at Hanover Court House, Virginia, May 27, 1862. Confined at Fort Monroe, Virginia, and at Fort Columbus, New York Harbor. Paroled and transferred to Aiken's Landing, James River, Virginia, where he was received on July 12, 1862, for exchange. Declared exchanged at Aiken's Landing on August 5, 1862. Returned to duty prior to November 1, 1862. Hospitalized at Richmond, Virginia, May 18, 1864, with a gunshot wound of the left arm. Place and date wounded not reported. Company records do not indicate whether he returned to duty. Reported absent without leave from November, 1864, through February, 1865.

HAYNES, GEORGE W., Private

Enlisted at Camp Holmes on February 7, 1864, for the war. Company records indicate he was captured on May 12, 1864; however, records of the Federal Provost Marshal do not substantiate that report. No further records.

HAYNES, THOMAS F., Private

Resided in Yadkin County where he enlisted at age 25, August 13, 1861. Present or accounted for until he surrendered at Appomattox Court House, Virginia, April 9, 1865.

HENDRICKS, CLEOPHUS D., 1st Sergeant

Resided in Yadkin County where he enlisted at age 30, August 13, 1861. Mustered in as Musician but was reduced to ranks in January-October, 1862. Captured at Hanover Court House, Virginia, May 27, 1862.

Confined at Fort Monroe, Virginia, and at Fort Columbus, New York Harbor. Paroled and transferred to Aiken's Landing, James River, Virginia, where he was received on July 12, 1862, for exchange. Declared exchanged at Aiken's Landing on August 5, 1862. Returned to duty prior to November 1, 1862. Promoted to Sergeant in November, 1862-February, 1863, and was promoted to 1st Sergeant in March, 1863-October, 1864. Wounded in the left leg and captured at Gettysburg, Pennsylvania, July 3-5, 1863. Hospitalized at Gettysburg. Transferred to hospital at Chester, Pennsylvania, where he arrived on July 15, 1863. Transferred to Point Lookout, Maryland, October 2, 1863. Paroled at Point Lookout and transferred to City Point, Virginia, where he was received on March 6, 1864, for exchange. Retired to the Invalid Corps on September 19, 1864, by reason of disability.

HILL, HARRISON H., Private

Born in Surry County and was by occupation a farmer prior to enlisting in Yadkin County at age 16, August 13, 1861. Discharged on November 18, 1862, by reason of being underage.

HINSHAW, JAMES, Private

Enlisted at Liberty Mills, Virginia, March 1, 1864, for the war. Paroled at Burkeville Junction, Virginia, April 14-17, 1865.

HOBSON, DAVID T., Corporal

Resided in Yadkin County where he enlisted at age 21, September 3, 1861. Mustered in as Private and was promoted to Corporal in March, 1863-July, 1864. Wounded at or near Chancellorsville, Virginia, on or about May 1-4, 1863. Returned to duty on an unspecified date. Present or accounted for through February, 1865.

HOBSON, JESSE F., Private

Enlisted in Yadkin County on October 8, 1863, for the war. Present or accounted for through February, 1865.

HOBSON, JOHN E., Private

Resided in Yadkin County where he enlisted at age 24, September 3, 1861. Retired to the Invalid Corps on December 7, 1864, by reason of disability.

HOLCOMB, BLOOM VIRGIL, Sergeant

Born in Yadkin County* where he resided prior to enlisting in Yadkin County at age 18, February 28, 1863, for the war. Mustered in as Private. Wounded at or near Gravel Hill, Virginia, on or about July 28, 1864. Returned to duty prior to November 1, 1864. Promoted to Sergeant on November 21, 1864. Captured near Petersburg, Virginia, April 2, 1865. Confined at Fort Delaware, Delaware, until released on June 19, 1865, after taking the Oath of Allegiance.

HOLCOMB, CALVIN M., Sergeant

Resided in Yadkin County where he enlisted at age 20, August 13, 1861. Mustered in as Private. Reported absent wounded in May-October, 1862. Place and date wounded not reported. Returned to duty prior to March 1, 1863. Wounded at Chancellorsville, Virginia, on or about May 1-4, 1863. Returned to duty on an unspecified date. Reported present for duty during September-December, 1864. Promoted to Sergeant in January, 1865. Retired to the Invalid Corps on January 28, 1865. [Roll of Honor indicates he was wounded in the foot "near the Rappahannock" River on an unspecified date.]

HOLCOMB, DANIEL F., Private

Previously served as 1st Lieutenant of this company. Defeated for reelection when the regiment was reorganized on April 12, 1862. Continued to serve in the company with the rank of Private. Died in hospital at Richmond, Virginia, December 8, 1863, of "smallpox." [For additional information see page 207 of this volume.]

HOLCOMB, JAMES, Private

Resided in Yadkin County and enlisted at Camp Holmes on November 14, 1863, for the war. Captured near Petersburg, Virginia, April 2, 1865. Confined at Fort Delaware, Delaware, until released on June 19, 1865, after taking the Oath of Allegiance.

HOLCOMB, JOHN T., Private

Previously served as 3rd Lieutenant of this company. Defeated for reelection when the regiment was reorganized on April 12, 1862. Continued to serve in the company with the rank of Private. Captured at Gettysburg, Pennsylvania, July 1-5, 1863. Confined at Davids Island, New York Harbor. Paroled and transferred to City Point, Virginia, where he was received on September 16, 1863, for exchange. Company records do not indicate whether he returned to duty. Died in hospital at Lynchburg, Virginia, April 29, 1864, of "hepatitis acuta." [For additional information see page 207 of this volume.]

HOLCOMB, JONES, Private

Resided in Yadkin County where he enlisted at age 19, August 13, 1861. Killed at Gettysburg, Pennsylvania, July 3, 1863.

HOLCOMB, LEANDER, Private

Resided in Yadkin County where he enlisted at age 23, August 13, 1861. Deserted on June 18, 1863. Returned to duty on an unspecified date. Transferred to Company G, 44th Regiment N.C. Troops, in January-February, 1864.

HOLCOMB, WILLIAM M., Private

Resided in Yadkin County and enlisted at Camp Holmes on November 14, 1863, for the war. Captured at Richmond, Virginia, April 3, 1865. Confined at Newport News, Virginia, April 24, 1865. Released on June 30, 1865, after taking the Oath of Allegiance. [North Carolina pension records indicate he was wounded "in battle of Horse Shoe" in 1863.]

HUDSPEATH, L. D., Private

Resided in Yadkin County where he enlisted at age 22, March 8, 1862. Died in hospital at Richmond, Virginia, January 5, 1863, of "febris typhoides."

HUDSPETH, DIRIT D., Private

Resided in Yadkin County where he enlisted at age 42, August 13, 1861. Died at Wilmington on or about October 31, 1861, of "fever."

HUDSPETH, JAMES, Private

Resided in Yadkin County where he enlisted at age 24, August 13, 1861. Captured at Hanover Court House, Virginia, May 27, 1862. Confined at Fort Monroe, Virginia, and at Fort Columbus, New York Harbor.

Paroled and transferred to Aiken's Landing, James River, Virginia, where he was received on July 12, 1862, for exchange. Declared exchanged at Aiken's Landing on August 5, 1862. Died "at home" on September 6, 1862, of disease.

HUTCHENS, COLUMBUS V., Private

Resided in Yadkin County where he enlisted at age 21, August 13, 1861. Captured at New Bern on March 14, 1862. Confined at Fort Columbus, New York Harbor. Paroled and transferred to Aiken's Landing, James River, Virginia, where he was received on July 12, 1862, for exchange. Declared exchanged at Aiken's Landing on August 5, 1862. Returned to duty prior to November 1, 1862. Present or accounted for through February, 1863. No further records.

HUTCHENS, ISAAC, Private

Resided in Yadkin County where he enlisted at age 18, March 8, 1862, as a substitute. Present or accounted for until he surrendered at Appomattox Court House, Virginia, April 9, 1865.

HUTCHENS, VESTOL C., Private

Enlisted in Yadkin County on September 7, 1861. Present or accounted for through December, 1861. No further records.

JARVIS, LUCKET C., Private

Resided in Yadkin County where he enlisted at age 25, March 8, 1862. Captured at Hanover Court House, Virginia, May 27, 1862. Confined at Fort Monroe, Virginia, and at Fort Columbus, New York Harbor. Paroled and transferred to Aiken's Landing, James River, Virginia, where he was received on July 12, 1862, for exchange. Declared exchanged at Aiken's Landing on August 5, 1862. Returned to duty prior to November 1, 1862. Died in hospital at Richmond, Virginia, June 24, 1863, of "febris typhoides."

JARVIS, WILLIE L., Private

Resided in Yadkin County where he enlisted at age 25, August 13, 1861. Mustered in as Corporal but was reduced to ranks in November-December, 1861. Captured at New Bern on March 14, 1862. Confined at Fort Columbus, New York Harbor. Paroled and transferred to Aiken's Landing, James River, Virginia, where he was received on July 12, 1862, for exchange. Declared exchanged at Aiken's Landing on August 5, 1862. Returned to duty prior to November 1, 1862. Captured near Petersburg, Virginia, April 2, 1865. Confined at Fort Delaware, Delaware. Released on June 19, 1865, after taking the Oath of Allegiance.

JAYNES, ABRAHAM, Private

Enlisted at Camp Holmes on October 14, 1863, for the war. Reported absent without leave in December, 1864.

JEFFERSON, ZACHARIAH M., Private

Previously served in Company H, 54th Regiment N.C. Troops. Transferred to this company on October 30, 1863. Paroled at Lynchburg, Virginia, April 15, 1865.

JENKINS, LODEWICK, Private

Born in Surry County and was by occupation a farmer prior to enlisting in Yadkin County on August 13, 1861. Discharged on March 15, 1863, by reason of being overage. Discharge certificate gives his age as 60.

JENKINS, ROBERT M., Private
Resided in Yadkin County where he enlisted at age 22, March 8, 1862. Wounded at Chancellorsville, Virginia, May 2-3, 1863. Transferred to Company H, 9th Regiment N.C. State Troops (1st Regiment N.C. Cavalry), October 31, 1863. [May have served previously in Company D, 21st Regiment N.C. Troops (11th Regiment N.C. Volunteers).]

JENNINGS, DAVID H., Private
Resided in Yadkin County where he enlisted at age 21, September 3, 1861. Wounded at Frayser's Farm, Virginia, June 30, 1862. Reported absent without leave in January-February, 1863. No further records.

JENNINGS, JOHN W., Private
Resided in Yadkin County where he enlisted at age 18, March 8, 1862. Wounded in the leg at Chancellorsville, Virginia, May 2-3, 1863. Hospitalized at Richmond, Virginia, where he died on November 24, 1863, of wounds.

JENNINGS, S. W., Private
Resided in Yadkin County where he enlisted at age 30, March 8, 1862. Captured at Hanover Court House, Virginia, on or about May 27, 1862. Confined at Fort Monroe, Virginia, and at Fort Columbus, New York Harbor. Died at Davids Island, New York Harbor, June 28-30, 1862, of "fever."

JOHN, JAMES P., Private
Place and date of enlistment not reported. Captured at Hanover Court House, Virginia, May 27, 1862. Exchanged at Aiken's Landing, James River, Virginia, August 5, 1862. Died at Richmond, Virginia, December 7, 1862, of "pneumonia."

JOHNSON, LEWIS W., Corporal
Resided in Yadkin County where he enlisted at age 21, August 13, 1861. Mustered in as Corporal but was reduced to ranks in January-October, 1862. Captured at New Bern on March 14, 1862. Confined at Fort Columbus, New York Harbor. Paroled and transferred to Aiken's Landing, James River, Virginia, where he was received on July 12, 1862, for exchange. Declared exchanged at Aiken's Landing on August 5, 1862. Returned to duty in January-February, 1863, after being absent without leave for four months. Promoted to Corporal in March, 1863-October, 1864. Wounded at Gettysburg, Pennsylvania, July 1-3, 1863. Company records do not indicate whether he returned to duty. Hospitalized at Richmond, Virginia, May 18, 1864, with a gunshot wound. Place and date wounded not reported. Reported absent sick during September, 1864-February, 1865. Captured in hospital at Richmond on April 3, 1865, and was paroled on April 24, 1865.

JOYCE, ABNER R., Private
Resided in Yadkin County and enlisted in New Hanover County at age 19, October 8, 1861. Wounded at Chancellorsville, Virginia, May 3, 1863. Returned to duty prior to July 2, 1863, when he was wounded at Gettysburg, Pennsylvania. Returned to duty on an unspecified date. Reported present for duty during September, 1864-February, 1865. Surrendered at Appomattox Court House, Virginia, April 9, 1865.

JOYCE, ROBERT H., Private
Resided in Yadkin County where he enlisted at age 25, September 3, 1861. Captured at Hanover Court House, Virginia, on or about May 27, 1862. Confined at Fort Columbus, New York Harbor. Exchanged on an unspecified date. Transferred to Company B, 38th

Regiment N.C. Troops, March 25, 1863.

LADD, MILES W., Private
Resided in Yadkin County and enlisted at age 19, August 13, 1861. Died near Hamptonville on September 25, 1861, of "typhoid fever." ["A young man of excellent qualities, strictly moral and pious in the fullest sense of the word. . . . In his death the State has lost a brave and efficient soldier—his parents a kind and obedient son."]

LEAGANS, ANANIAS, Private
Resided in Yadkin County where he enlisted at age 41, March 8, 1862. Captured at Hanover Court House, Virginia, May 27, 1862. Confined at Fort Monroe, Virginia, and at Fort Columbus, New York Harbor. Paroled and transferred to Aiken's Landing, James River, Virginia, where he was received on July 12, 1862, for exchange. Declared exchanged at Aiken's Landing on August 5, 1862. Detailed as a shoemaker at Salisbury in February, 1863. Reported absent on detail through February, 1865.

LEAGANS, JAMES M., Private
Enlisted in Yadkin County on August 13, 1861. Captured at Hanover Court House, Virginia, May 27, 1862. Confined at Fort Monroe, Virginia, and at Fort Columbus, New York Harbor. Paroled and transferred to Aiken's Landing, James River, Virginia, where he was received on July 12, 1862, for exchange. Declared exchanged at Aiken's Landing on August 5, 1862. Returned to duty on an unspecified date. Wounded in the neck and shoulder at Fredericksburg, Virginia, December 13, 1862. Returned to duty on February 10, 1863. Reported absent without leave from July 1, 1863, until January 5, 1864. Reported present for duty during November, 1864-February, 1865.

LEAGANS, MATTHEW, Private
Resided in Yadkin County where he enlisted at age 19, August 13, 1861. Deserted on July 15, 1863.

LONG, ELLIS, Private
Resided in Yadkin County where he enlisted at age 20, August 13, 1861. Captured at Fredericksburg, Virginia, on December 13, 1862. Exchanged on or about December 17, 1862. Deserted on July 23, 1863. Returned to duty on an unspecified date. Reported present for duty from September, 1864, through February, 1865. Captured near Petersburg, Virginia, April 2, 1865. Confined at Fort Delaware, Delaware. Released on June 19, 1865, after taking the Oath of Allegiance.

LONG, FRANCIS, Private
Resided in Yadkin County where he enlisted at age 18, August 13, 1861. Died on or about July 20, 1862, of "dip[h]theria." Place of death not reported.

LONG, NATHAN, Private
Resided in Yadkin County and enlisted at Camp Vance on April 17, 1864, for the war. Hospitalized at Richmond, Virginia, April 2, 1865, with a gunshot wound. Place and date wounded not reported. Captured in hospital at Richmond on April 3, 1865. Transferred to Newport News, Virginia, April 23, 1865. Released on June 30, 1865, after taking the Oath of Allegiance.

McBRIDE, DANIEL B., Private
Resided in Yadkin County where he enlisted at age 20, August 13, 1861. Wounded in the abdomen at Frayser's Farm, Virginia, or at Malvern Hill, Virginia, June 30-July 1, 1862. Hospitalized at Richmond, Virginia, where

he died on July 3, 1862, of wounds.

McBRIDE, JOHN G., Sergeant
Resided in Yadkin County where he enlisted at age 25, August 13, 1861. Mustered in as Private. Captured at Hanover Court House, Virginia, May 27, 1862. Confined at Fort Monroe, Virginia, and at Fort Columbus, New York Harbor. Paroled and transferred to Aiken's Landing, James River, Virginia, where he was received on July 12, 1862, for exchange. Declared exchanged at Aiken's Landing on August 5, 1862. Returned to duty prior to March 1, 1863. Promoted to Sergeant in March, 1863-June, 1864. Reported absent sick in September-October, 1864, and was reported absent without leave in November-December, 1864. Returned to duty in January-February, 1865. Captured near Petersburg, Virginia, April 2, 1865. Confined at Fort Delaware, Delaware. Released on June 19, 1865, after taking the Oath of Allegiance.

McKAUGHN, B. TEMPLE, Private
Resided in Yadkin County where he enlisted at age 18, March 8, 1862. Captured by the enemy on an unspecified date. Confined at Fort Monroe, Virginia, August 26, 1862. Paroled on September 1, 1862. Exchanged on or about September 21, 1862. Returned to duty prior to March 1, 1863. Wounded at Gettysburg, Pennsylvania, July 1-3, 1863. No further records.

MACKIE, JONAS, Private
Resided in Caldwell County and enlisted at age 19, April 13, 1863, for the war. Killed at Gettysburg, Pennsylvania, July 3, 1863.

MACKIE, ROBERT ALEXANDER, Private
Resided in Caldwell County and enlisted at age 23, August 28, 1862, for the war. Wounded in the right thigh and captured at Spotsylvania Court House, Virginia, May 12, 1864. Hospitalized at Washington, D.C. Transferred to Elmira, New York, December 16, 1864. Released on June 12, 1865, after taking the Oath of Allegiance.

MACY, THOMAS E., Private
Resided in Yadkin County where he enlisted at age 19, November 12, 1861. Reported absent without leave in May-October, 1862. Returned to duty subsequent to February 28, 1863. Hospitalized at Richmond, Virginia, May 18, 1864, with a gunshot wound. Place and date wounded not reported. Reported on duty as a prison guard at Salisbury during September, 1864-February, 1865.

MACY, WILLIAM L., Private
Resided in Yadkin County and enlisted in Yadkin or New Hanover County at age 24, November 12, 1861. Captured at Hanover Court House, Virginia, May 27, 1862. Confined at Fort Monroe, Virginia, and at Fort Columbus, New York Harbor. Paroled and transferred to Aiken's Landing, James River, Virginia, where he was received on July 12, 1862, for exchange. Declared exchanged at Aiken's Landing on August 5, 1862. Returned to duty prior to March 1, 1863. Hospitalized at Richmond, Virginia, April 21, 1864, with a gunshot wound of the left thigh. Place and date wounded not reported. Reported absent sick in September-October, 1864. Reported present for duty during November, 1864-February, 1865. Captured near Petersburg, Virginia, April 2, 1865. Confined at Fort Delaware, Delaware. Released on June 19, 1865, after taking the Oath of Allegiance.

MARTIN, ALFRED W., Private
Resided in Yadkin County where he enlisted at age 21, August 13, 1861. Deserted on August 5, 1862.

MARTIN, JOHN H., Jr., Private
Resided in Yadkin County where he enlisted at age 18, August 13, 1861. Captured at Hanover Court House, Virginia, May 27, 1862. Confined at Fort Monroe, Virginia, and at Fort Columbus, New York Harbor. Paroled and transferred to Aiken's Landing, James River, Virginia, where he was received on July 12, 1862, for exchange. Declared exchanged at Aiken's Landing on August 5, 1862. Returned to duty prior to November 1, 1862. Captured at Wilderness, Virginia, May 6, 1864. Confined at Point Lookout, Maryland. Paroled and transferred to Boulware's Wharf, James River, Virginia, where he was received on February 20-21, 1865, for exchange.

MARTIN, JOHN H., Sr., Private
Resided in Forsyth County and enlisted at Camp Holmes on October 20, 1862, for the war. Captured at Fussell's Mill, Virginia, August 16, 1864. Confined at Point Lookout, Maryland. Released on June 29, 1865, after taking the Oath of Allegiance.

MELTON, R. G., Private
Resided in Yadkin County where he enlisted at age 35, March 8, 1862. Died in hospital at Richmond, Virginia, July 27, 1862, or August 9, 1862, of "diarrhoea chronica" or "erysipelas."

MELTON, ZACHARIAH, Private
Resided in Yadkin County where he enlisted at age 23, March 8, 1862. Captured at Hanover Court House, Virginia, May 27, 1862. Confined at Fort Monroe, Virginia, and at Fort Columbus, New York Harbor. Paroled and transferred to Aiken's Landing, James River, Virginia, where he was received on July 12, 1862, for exchange. Declared exchanged at Aiken's Landing on August 5, 1862. Reported absent without leave in January-February, 1863. Returned from desertion on September 22, 1864. Transferred to Company G, 52nd Regiment N.C. Troops, the same date.

MOCK, JOHN, Private
Born in England and resided in Yadkin County where he enlisted at age 38, March 8, 1862. Captured at Hanover Court House, Virginia, May 27, 1862. Confined at Fort Monroe, Virginia, and at Fort Columbus, New York Harbor. Paroled and transferred to Aiken's Landing, James River, Virginia, where he was received on August 5, 1862, for exchange. Hospitalized at Richmond, Virginia, August 7, 1862, with "phthisis" and died on August 11, 1862.

MOORE, ISAAC, Private
Resided in Yadkin County where he enlisted at age 37, March 8, 1862. Captured near Petersburg, Virginia, April 2, 1865. Confined at Fort Delaware, Delaware. Released on June 19, 1865, after taking the Oath of Allegiance.

MYRES, JOHN, Private
Resided in Yadkin County where he enlisted at age 23, March 8, 1862. Died in hospital at Lynchburg, Virginia, on or about December 18, 1862, of "pneumonia."

NICHOLS, JESSE, Private

Resided in Yadkin County where he enlisted at age 23, August 13, 1861. Present or accounted for through December, 1861. Discharged on an unspecified date after providing a substitute.

NICHOLS, WILLIAM, Private

Enlisted in Yadkin County on August 13, 186[1]. Killed at Frayser's Farm, Virginia, June 30, 1862.

NORMAN, THOMAS, Private

Previously served in Company A, 44th Regiment N.C. Troops. Transferred to this company in July, 1863-May, 1864. Captured at Wilderness, Virginia, May 12, 1864. Confined at Point Lookout, Maryland. Transferred to Elmira, New York, August 10, 1864. Released on June 12, 1865, after taking the Oath of Allegiance.

PEARSON, JOHN W., Private

Resided in Yadkin County and enlisted at age 18, August 13, 1861. Mustered in as 1st Sergeant but was reduced to ranks on October 8, 1861. Records of this company indicate he was appointed Drillmaster and transferred to the 31st Regiment N.C. Troops in December, 1861; however, records of the 31st Regiment do not indicate that he served therein. No further records.

PENDRY, ROBY, Private

Resided in Yadkin County where he enlisted at age 21, August 13, 1861. Died at Wilmington on February 4, 1862, of ''measles.''

PENDRY, WILSON S., Private

Resided in Yadkin County where he enlisted at age 23, August 13, 1861. Died at Wilmington on November 6, 1861, of ''measles.''

PEOPLES, ALBERT, Private

Enlisted at Camp Holmes on November 30, 1863, for the war. Deserted on an unspecified date. Returned to duty on September 9, 1864. Transferred to Company G of this regiment subsequent to October 31, 1864.

PEOPLES, WILLIAM, Private

Enlisted at Camp Holmes on November 30, 1863, for the war. Deserted on or about April 1, 1864.

PETTY, ELIJAH, Private

Resided in Yadkin County where he enlisted at age 19, August 13, 1861. Reported absent without leave in May-October, 1862. Returned to duty subsequent to February 28, 1863. Deserted on August 5, 1863. Returned to duty on September 22, 1864. Deserted to the enemy on November 19, 1864. Confined at Washington, D.C. Released on or about November 23, 1864, after taking the Oath of Allegiance.

PETTY, MILES, Private

Resided in Yadkin County where he enlisted at age 25, August 13, 1861. Present or accounted for through February, 1863. Deserted on an unspecified date. Returned to duty on September 22, 1864. Deserted to the enemy on November 19, 1864. Confined at Washington, D.C. Released on or about November 25, 1864, after taking the Oath of Allegiance.

PETTYJOHN, JAMES, Private

Resided in Yadkin County where he enlisted at age 22, August 13, 1861. Captured at Hanover Court House,

Virginia, May 27, 1862. Confined at Fort Monroe, Virginia, and at Fort Columbus, New York Harbor. Exchanged on an unspecified date. Died in hospital at Richmond, Virginia, December 7, 1862, of ''pneumonia.''

PETTYJOHN, WILLIAM, Private

Resided in Yadkin County where he enlisted at age 22, August 13, 1861. Captured at Hanover Court House, Virginia, May 27, 1862. Confined at Fort Monroe, Virginia, and at Fort Columbus, New York Harbor. Paroled and transferred to Aiken's Landing, James River, Virginia, where he was received on July 12, 1862, for exchange. Declared exchanged at Aiken's Landing on August 5, 1862. Returned to duty prior to November 1, 1862. Killed at Fredericksburg, Virginia, December 13, 1862.

PILCHER, WILEY, Private

Resided in Yadkin County where he enlisted at age 22, September 1, 1861. Died at Wilmington on March 30 or April 1, 1862, of ''fever.''

PLOWMAN, HENRY, Private

Enlisted at Camp Holmes on November 30, 1863, for the war. Transferred to Company G, 18th Regiment N.C. Troops (8th Regiment N.C. Volunteers), September 1, 1864.

PLOWMAN, JAMES H., ———

North Carolina pension records indicate that he served in this company.

PLOWMAN, JOHN W., Private

Born in Surry County and resided in Yadkin County where he was by occupation a farmer prior to enlisting in Yadkin County at age 20, August 13, 1861. Discharged on December 24, 1861, by reason of ''the loss of motion of the left arm . . ., the cause in this case appears to be from an old fracture of the collar bone & rheumatism.''

PLOWMAN, WILLIAM, Private

Enlisted at Camp Holmes on November 30, 1863, for the war. Captured at or near Gravel Hill, Virginia, on or about July 28, 1864. Confined at Point Lookout, Maryland. Transferred to Elmira, New York, August 8, 1864. Released at Elmira on May 9, 1865, after taking the Oath of Allegiance.

POTTS, JOHN H., Private

Resided in Yadkin County where he enlisted at age 26, March 8, 1862. Mustered in as Private and was promoted to Musician prior to November 1, 1862. Reduced to ranks prior to March 1, 1863. Deserted on July 23, 1863.

REAVES, JAMES WASHINGTON, Private

Resided in Yadkin County where he enlisted at age 19, March 8, 1862. Reported absent without leave on February 8, 1865.

REAVIS, NATHAN, Private

Born in Yadkin County* where he resided prior to enlisting in Yadkin County at age 24, March 8, 1862. Died ''at home'' on November 17, 1864. Cause of death not reported.

REECE, ASBERRY H., Private
Resided in Yadkin County where he enlisted at age 21, September 10, 1862, for the war. Died in hospital at Montgomery White Sulphur Springs, Virginia, on or about March 9, 1863, of "smallpox."

REECE, EVAN H., Private
Resided in Yadkin County where he enlisted at age 19, March 8, 1862. Captured at Hanover Court House, Virginia, May 27, 1862. Confined at Fort Monroe, Virginia, and at Fort Columbus, New York Harbor. Paroled and transferred to Aiken's Landing, James River, Virginia, where he was received July 12, 1862, for exchange. Declared exchanged at Aiken's Landing on August 5, 1862. Returned to duty prior to November 1, 1862. Wounded at Gettysburg, Pennsylvania, July 1-3, 1863. Returned to duty on an unspecified date. Surrendered at Appomattox Court House, Virginia, April 9, 1865.

REYNOLDS, GEORGE T., Private
Resided in Yadkin County where he enlisted at age 18, March 8, 1862. Captured at Hanover Court House, Virginia, May 27, 1862. Confined at Fort Monroe, Virginia, and at Fort Columbus, New York Harbor. Paroled and transferred to Aiken's Landing, James River, Virginia, where he was received on July 12, 1862, for exchange. Declared exchanged at Aiken's Landing on August 5, 1862. Returned to duty prior to November 1, 1862. Reported missing at Gettysburg, Pennsylvania, July 1-3, 1863. No further records.

ROLEN, JOHN, Private
Resided in Wilkes County and was by occupation a farmer prior to enlisting in Yadkin County at age 52, September 20, 1862, for the war as a substitute. Present or accounted for through February, 1865.

ROSE, ISAAC W., Private
Resided in Yadkin County where he enlisted at age 22, August 13, 1861. Mustered in as Musician but was reduced to ranks in January-October, 1862. Captured at Hanover Court House, Virginia, May 27, 1862. Confined at Fort Monroe, Virginia, and at Fort Columbus, New York Harbor. Paroled and transferred to Aiken's Landing, James River, Virginia, where he was received on July 12, 1862, for exchange. Declared exchanged at Aiken's Landing on August 5, 1862. Returned to duty prior to November 1, 1862. Deserted on June 20, 1863. Returned to duty on an unspecified date. Reported absent without leave on September 22, 1864.

ROSE, THOMAS A., Private
Enlisted at Camp Holmes on October 14, 1862, for the war. Reported absent without leave on October 17, 186[4].

ROUGHTON, JAMES L., Private
Resided in Yadkin County where he enlisted at age 23, August 13, 1861. Wounded in the right shoulder near Richmond, Virginia, June 25-July 1, 1862. Returned to duty on an unspecified date. Captured by the enemy on an unspecified date. Paroled and transferred to Aiken's Landing, James River, Virginia, where he was received on September 7, 1862, for exchange. Declared exchanged at Aiken's Landing on September 21, 1862. Reported absent without leave but returned to duty prior to March 1, 1863. Deserted on June 20, 1863.

ROYAL, WILLIE D., Musician
Resided in Yadkin County where he enlisted at age 19, August 13, 1861. Mustered in as Private and was promoted to Musician (Drummer) in January-October, 1862. Captured at Hanover Court House, Virginia, May 27, 1862. Confined at Fort Monroe, Virginia, and at Fort Columbus, New York Harbor. Paroled and transferred to Aiken's Landing, James River, Virginia, where he was received on July 12, 1862, for exchange. Declared exchanged at Aiken's Landing on August 5, 1862. Returned to duty prior to March 1, 1863. Captured at Amelia Court House, Virginia, April 6, 1865. Confined at Point Lookout, Maryland. Released on June 19, 1865, after taking the Oath of Allegiance.

SCOTT, THOMAS G., Private
Born in Yadkin County* where he resided as a farmer prior to enlisting in Yadkin County at age 19, March 8, 1862. Present or accounted for until he surrendered at Appomattox Court House, Virginia, April 9, 1865.

SHORES, ALEXANDER F., Corporal
Resided in Yadkin County where he enlisted at age 21, August 13, 1861. Mustered in as Private and was promoted to Corporal in January-October, 1862. Captured at Hanover Court House, Virginia, May 27, 1862. Confined at Fort Monroe, Virginia, and at Fort Columbus, New York Harbor. Paroled and transferred to Aiken's Landing, James River, Virginia, where he was received on July 12, 1862, for exchange. Declared exchanged at Aiken's Landing on August 5, 1862. Returned to duty prior to August 28-30, 1862, when he was wounded at the Battle of Second Manassas, Virginia. Died on September 11, 1862, of wounds. Place of death not reported.

SHORES, ANDERSON, Private
Resided in Yadkin County where he enlisted at age 22, August 13, 1861. Killed at the Battle of Second Manassas, Virginia, August 28-30, 1862.

SHORES, DAVID, Private
Resided in Yadkin County and enlisted at age 19, August 13, 1861. [May have served later in Company A, 21st Regiment N.C. Troops (11th Regiment N.C. Volunteers).] No further records.

SHORES, HENRY, Private
Born in Surry County and resided in Yadkin County where he was by occupation a farmer prior to enlisting in Yadkin County at age 21, August 13, 1861. Discharged on April 14, 1862, by reason of "scrotal hernia."

SHORES, LEWIS W., Private
Resided in Yadkin County where he enlisted at age 18, August 13, 1861. Wounded at Chancellorsville, Virginia, May 2-3, 1863. Transferred to Company H, 54th Regiment N.C. Troops, prior to November 1, 1863.

SMITH, JOHN, Private
Resided in Yadkin County where he enlisted at age 18, January 6, 1862. Died in hospital at Lynchburg, Virginia, February 5, 1864, of a self-administered overdose of morphine.

SMITH, TAPLEY A., Private
Resided in Yadkin County where he enlisted at age 21, August 13, 1861. Reported absent wounded in May-

October, 1862. Place and date wounded not reported. Returned to duty prior to March 1, 1863. Present or accounted for through February, 1865. [North Carolina pension records indicate he was wounded in the forehead at "Cedar Mountain, Virginia, May 1, 1864"; Roll of Honor indicates he was wounded several times.]

SPRINKLE, JOHN S., Private
Born in Yadkin County.* Place and date of enlistment not reported. First listed in the records of this company in March, 1864. Killed at Wilderness, Virginia, May 5, 1864.

STINSON, ABRAHAM, Private
Enlisted in Yadkin County on November 1, 1862, for the war. Wounded in the head and leg at the Petersburg & Weldon Railroad, near Petersburg, Virginia, June 22, 1864. Returned to duty prior to November 1, 1864. Wounded in the right leg and captured near Petersburg on April 2, 1865. Right leg amputated. Reported in hospital at Fort Monroe, Virginia, through June 21, 1865. No further records.

STINSON, ELIAS, Private
Born in Yadkin County* where he resided prior to enlisting in Yadkin County at age 19, August 13, 1861. Present or accounted for through February, 1863. Died prior to December 17, 1864. Place, date, and cause of death not reported.

STOKES, JAMES, Private
Resided in Yadkin County and enlisted in New Hanover County at age 19, January 1, 186[2]. Reported absent without leave in May-October, 1862, and was listed as a deserter on May 27, 1863.

STRICKLAND, WILLIAM S., Private
Born in Yadkin County* and enlisted at Liberty Mills, Virginia, December 17, 186[3], for the war. Killed in battle at the Petersburg & Weldon Railroad, near Petersburg, Virginia, June 22, 1864.

SWAIM, LITTLE M., Corporal
Resided in Yadkin County where he enlisted at age 18, August 13, 1861. Mustered in as Private. Hospitalized at Richmond, Virginia, September 27, 1862, with gunshot wounds of the shoulder and hip. Place and date wounded not reported. Returned to duty on November 25, 1862. Promoted to Corporal on December 1, 1864. Captured near Petersburg, Virginia, April 2, 1865. Confined at Fort Delaware, Delaware. Released on June 19, 1865, after taking the Oath of Allegiance.

SWAIM, MILAS G., Private
Born in Yadkin County* where he resided as a farmer prior to enlisting in Yadkin County at age 18, March 8, 1862. Transferred to Company G, 44th Regiment N.C. Troops, in March-December, 1863. Transferred back to this company on October 1, 1864. Present or accounted for through February, 1865.

SWAIM, SOLOMON D., Private
Resided in Yadkin County and enlisted at age 33, July 19, 1862, for the war. Transferred to Company G, 44th Regiment N.C. Troops, in March-December, 1863.

SWAIM, WILLIAM, Private
Born in Surry County and resided in Yadkin County where he was by occupation a farmer prior to enlisting

in Yadkin County at age 37, September 1, 1861. Discharged on June 23, 1862, by reason of a heart condition following an attack of pneumonia.

TATE, LEWIS F., Private
Enlisted at Camp Holmes on October 8, 1863, for the war. Deserted on an unspecified date. Returned to duty on September 22, 1864. Reported absent wounded during September, 1864-February, 1865. Place and date wounded not reported.

TEASH, WILLIAM A., Corporal
Born in Yadkin County* where he resided prior to enlisting in Yadkin County at age 18, March 8, 1862. Mustered in as Private and was promoted to Corporal in November, 1862-February, 1863. Died "at home" or at Lynchburg, Virginia, May 4, 1864. Cause of death not reported.

THOMPSON, ALFRED R., Private
Resided in Lincoln County where he enlisted at age 18, August 14, 1863, for the war. Reported absent wounded in September-October, 1864. Place and date wounded not reported. Returned to duty in January-February, 1865. Present or accounted for through February, 1865.

THOMPSON, DANIEL G., Private
Previously served as Sergeant in Company G, 52nd Regiment N.C. Troops. Transferred to this company on November 1, 1864, with the rank of Private. Paroled at Greensboro on May 1, 1865.

VESTAL, J. M., Private
Resided in Yadkin County and enlisted at age 24, August 13, 1861. Discharged on an unspecified date by reason of disability.

VESTAL, JOHN B., Private
Born in Yadkin County* where he resided as a farmer prior to enlisting in New Hanover County at age 27, October 8, 1861. Transferred to Company B, 38th Regiment N.C. Troops, prior to April 1, 1862.

VESTAL, MARTIN V. B., Private
Resided in Yadkin County where he enlisted at age 24, March 8, 1862. Captured at Fredericksburg, Virginia, December 13, 1862. Exchanged on or about December 17, 1862. Returned to duty prior to March 1, 1863. Company records indicate he was captured at Spotsylvania Court House, Virginia, May 12, 1864; however, records of the Federal Provost Marshal do not substantiate that report. No further records.

VESTAL, MILES J., Sergeant
Born in Surry County and was by occupation a farmer prior to enlisting in New Hanover County on October 8, 1861. Mustered in as Sergeant. Discharged on February 15, 1862, by reason of "scrotal hernia of both sides." Discharge certificate gives his age as 24.

WAGGONER, CALVIN, Private
Resided in Yadkin County and was by occupation a farmer prior to enlisting in Yadkin County at age 21, August 13, 1861. Deserted on July 1, 1863. Returned to duty on an unspecified date. Wounded in the right elbow at or near Reams' Station, Virginia, on or about August 25, 1864. Reported absent wounded until December 1, 1864, when he was reported absent without leave.

WAGGONER, JACOB M., Private
Resided in Yadkin County where he enlisted at age 19, August 13, 1861. Captured by the enemy on an unspecified date. Confined at Fort Monroe, Virginia. Paroled and transferred to Aiken's Landing, James River, Virginia, where he was received on September 7, 1862, for exchange. Declared exchanged at Aiken's Landing on September 21, 1862. Reported absent without leave through February, 1863. Returned to duty on an unspecified date. Company records indicate he was captured by the enemy on July 21, 1864; however, records of the Federal Provost Marshal do not substantiate that report. [North Carolina pension records indicate he was wounded in the hip at "Wilderness, Virginia, October 16, 1863," and indicate that he survived the war.]

WAGGONER, JOHN W., Private
Resided in Yadkin County and enlisted in Orange County at age 21, September 20, 1863, for the war. Surrendered at Appomattox Court House, Virginia, April 9, 1865.

WARDEN, CARY W., Jr., Private
Resided in Yadkin County where he enlisted at age 21, August 13, 1861. Present or accounted for until transferred to Company B, 38th Regiment N.C. Troops, on an unspecified date.

WARNER, JOHN, ———
Place and date of enlistment not reported. Deserted to the enemy on or about February 1, 1865. Confined at Beverly, West Virginia, April 19, 1865. Released on an unspecified date after taking the Oath of Allegiance.

WEATHERMAN, BARTHOLOMEW W., Private
Resided in Yadkin County where he enlisted at age 20, August 13, 1861. Captured at or near Gravel Hill, Virginia, on or about July 28, 1864. Confined at Point Lookout, Maryland. Transferred to Elmira, New York, August 8, 1864. Died at Elmira on December 12, 1864, of "pneumonia."

WEATHERMAN, ROBERT W., 1st Sergeant
Resided in Yadkin County where he enlisted at age 21, August 13, 1861. Mustered in as Private and was promoted to Sergeant in November-December, 1861. Promoted to 1st Sergeant in January-October, 1862. Captured at Hanover Court House, Virginia, May 27, 1862. Confined at Fort Monroe, Virginia, and at Fort Columbus, New York Harbor. Paroled and transferred to Aiken's Landing, James River, Virginia, where he was received on July 12, 1862, for exchange. Declared exchanged at Aiken's Landing on August 5, 1862. Returned to duty prior to November 1, 1862. Died in hospital at Richmond, Virginia, on or about July 19, 1863, of "diarrhoea ch[ronic]."

WEAVER, JAMES M., Private
Resided in Yadkin County where he enlisted at age 23, August 13, 1861. Captured at Hanover Court House, Virginia, on or about May 27, 1862. Confined at Fort Monroe, Virginia. Paroled and transferred to Aiken's Landing, James River, Virginia, where he was received on July 12, 1862, for exchange. Declared exchanged at Aiken's Landing on August 5, 1862. Returned to duty prior to November 1, 1862. Present or accounted for through February, 1863. [North Carolina pension records indicate he was wounded at Fredericksburg, Virginia, and at Wilmington; North Carolina pension records indicate also that he survived the war.] No further records.

WHITEHEAD, CALVIN, Private
Enlisted at Camp Holmes on May 4, 1864, for the war. Deserted on January 11, 1865. No further records.

WHITEHEAD, HENRY W., Private
Resided in Yadkin County where he enlisted at age 23, March 8, 1862. Wounded at or near Gravel Hill, Virginia, July 28, 1864. Returned to duty prior to November 1, 1864. Captured near Petersburg, Virginia, April 2, 1865. Confined at Fort Delaware, Delaware. Released on June 19, 1865, after taking the Oath of Allegiance.

WHITEHEAD, JAMES S., Private
Resided in Yadkin County where he enlisted at age 20, August 13, 1861. Captured at Hanover Court House, Virginia, May 27, 1862. Confined at Fort Monroe, Virginia, and at Fort Columbus, New York Harbor. Paroled and transferred to Aiken's Landing, James River, Virginia, where he was received on July 12, 1862, for exchange. Declared exchanged at Aiken's Landing on August 5, 1862. Returned to duty prior to November 1, 1862. Died in hospital at Richmond, Virginia, on or about June 27, 1863, of a gunshot wound and/or "fever." Place and date wounded not reported.

WHITEHEAD, JOHN, ———
North Carolina pension records indicate that he served in this company.

WILLIAMS, LEWIS A., Corporal
Resided in Yadkin County where he enlisted at age 19, August 13, 1861. Mustered in as Corporal. Died in hospital at Wilmington on or about December 7, 1861, of "measles."

WISHON, JAMES T., Private
Born in Yadkin County* where he resided prior to enlisting in Yadkin County at age 19, August 13, 1861. Captured at New Bern on March 14, 1862. Confined at Fort Columbus, New York Harbor. Paroled and transferred to Aiken's Landing, James River, Virginia, where he was received on July 12, 1862, for exchange. Declared exchanged at Aiken's Landing on August 5, 1862. Returned to duty prior to November 1, 1862. Hospitalized at Danville, Virginia, June 16, 1864, with a gunshot wound of the neck. Place and date wounded not reported. Returned to duty prior to October 1, 1864, when he was killed in action at or near Jones' Farm, Virginia.

WISHON, SAMUEL A., Private
Resided in Yadkin County where he enlisted at age 27, March 8, 1862. Captured at Hanover Court House, Virginia, May 27, 1862. Confined at Fort Monroe, Virginia, and at Fort Columbus, New York Harbor. Paroled and transferred to Aiken's Landing, James River, Virginia, where he was received on July 12, 1862, for exchange. Declared exchanged at Aiken's Landing on August 5, 1862. Returned to duty prior to November 1, 1862. Deserted on July 15, 1863. Returned to duty on an unspecified date. Wounded in the left side and captured at or near Gravel Hill, Virginia, July 28, 1864. Hospitalized at City Point, Virginia. Transferred to

Point Lookout, Maryland, where he was confined on December 5, 1864. Paroled and transferred to Boulware's Wharf, James River, Virginia, where he was received on March 18, 1865, for exchange. Paroled at Salisbury in April-May, 1865.

WOODHOUSE, F. M., Private
Resided in Yadkin County where he enlisted at age 18, March 8, 1862. Died in camp near Richmond, Virginia, August 4, 1862, of "fever."

YOUNG, SOLOMON, ———
North Carolina pension records indicate that he served in this company.

YOUNG, WOODSON S., Private
Resided in Yadkin County where he enlisted at age 21, March 8, 1862. Deserted on August 1, 1862.

COMPANY K

This company, known as the "Stanly Guards," was raised in Stanly County and enlisted at Albemarle. It was mustered into service on September 7, 1861, and assigned to the 28th Regiment as Company K. After joining the regiment the company functioned as a part of the regiment, and its history for the war period is reported as a part of the regimental history.

The information contained in the following roster of the company was compiled principally from company muster rolls for September 7-December, 1861; March-April, 1862; November-December, 1862; and September, 1864-February, 1865. No company muster rolls were found for January-February, 1862; May-October, 1862; January, 1863-August, 1864; or for the period after February, 1865. Valuable information was obtained also from primary records such as the Roll of Honor, medical records, prisoner of war records, discharge certificates, and pension applications, and from secondary sources such as postwar rosters and histories, cemetery records, and records of the United Daughters of the Confederacy.

OFFICERS

CAPTAINS

MOODY, JOHN A.
Resided in Stanly County where he enlisted at age 33. Appointed Captain on September 7, 1861. Resigned on July 1, 1863, by reason of disability resulting from "pneumonia . . . typhoid fever, chronic diarrhoea, & rheumatism."

CROWELL, JAMES M.
Resided in Stanly County where he enlisted at age 31. Appointed 1st Lieutenant on September 7, 1861. Wounded at the Battle of Second Manassas, Virginia, August 28-30, 1862. Returned to duty prior to January 1, 1863. Promoted to Captain on July 8, 1863. Killed in battle near Petersburg, Virginia, June 24, 1864.

STONE, ADAM WHITMON
Resided in Stanly County where he enlisted at age 26. Appointed 3rd Lieutenant on September 7, 1861. Promoted to 2nd Lieutenant on April 12, 1862. Wounded at Gettysburg, Pennsylvania, July 1-3, 1863. Returned to duty on an unspecified date. Promoted to 1st Lieutenant July 8, 1863. Hospitalized at

Charlottesville, Virginia, May 12, 1864, with a gunshot wound of the chest. Place and date wounded not reported. Transferred to Salisbury on June 5, 1864. Promoted to Captain on June 24, 1864. Returned to duty in January-February, 1865. Surrendered at Appomattox Court House, Virginia, April 9, 1865.

LIEUTENANTS

BILES, ISAAC T., 2nd Lieutenant
Resided in Stanly County where he enlisted at age 21. Appointed 2nd Lieutenant on September 7, 1861. Wounded at Chancellorsville, Virginia, May 2-3, 1863. Returned to duty prior to July 3, 1863, when he was wounded in the right foot at Gettysburg, Pennsylvania. Resigned on December 10, 1863, by reason of disability.

BOST, DANIEL J., 2nd Lieutenant
Born in Cabarrus County where he resided prior to enlisting in Lenoir County at age 29, April 26, 1862, for the war. Mustered in as Private. Wounded at Ox Hill, Virginia, September 1, 1862. Returned to duty prior to January 1, 1863. Promoted to Sergeant in January, 1863-June, 1864. Appointed 2nd Lieutenant on July 1, 1864. Died in hospital at Richmond, Virginia, September 5, 1864, of wounds. Place and date wounded not reported.

TURNER, HENRY CLAY, 2nd Lieutenant
Previously served as Sergeant Major of the 52nd Regiment N.C. Troops. Transferred to this company upon election as 2nd Lieutenant on January 19, 1865. Surrendered at Appomattox Court House, Virginia, April 9, 1865.

TURNER, PRESTON H., 1st Lieutenant
Previously served as Sergeant Major of the 14th Regiment N.C. Troops (4th Regiment N.C. Volunteers). Transferred to this company upon appointment as 2nd Lieutenant on or about October 15, 1863. Captured at or near Spotsylvania Court House, Virginia, on or about May 12, 1864. Confined at Fort Delaware, Delaware. Promoted to 1st Lieutenant on June 24, 1864, while a prisoner of war. Confined at Fort Delaware until released on June 14, 1865, after taking the Oath of Allegiance.

NONCOMMISSIONED OFFICERS AND PRIVATES

ALDRIDGE, WILLIAM E., Private
Resided in Stanly County and enlisted at Liberty Mills, Virginia, March 1, 1864, for the war. Captured near Petersburg, Virginia, April 2, 1865. Confined at Point Lookout, Maryland. Released on June 23, 1865, after taking the Oath of Allegiance.

ALMOND, DANIEL, 1st Sergeant
Resided in Stanly County where he enlisted at age 23, September 7, 1861. Mustered in as 1st Sergeant. Wounded near Richmond, Virginia, June 25-July 1, 1862. Died at Richmond on July 25-28, 1862, of wounds.

ALMOND, DAVID, Private
Resided in Stanly County where he enlisted at age 20, March 15, 1862. Mustered in as Private and was promoted to Corporal in May-December, 1862. Captured at Fredericksburg, Virginia, December 13,

1862. Exchanged on or about December 17, 1862. Returned to duty on January 27, 1863. Wounded at Chancellorsville, Virginia, May 1-4, 1863. Returned to duty on an unspecified date. Promoted to Sergeant in November-December, 1864, but was reduced to ranks in January-February, 1865. Surrendered at Appomattox Court House, Virginia, April 9, 1865.

ALMOND, GREEN, Private
Resided in Stanly County where he enlisted at age 23, September 7, 1861. Wounded in the right foot at Chancellorsville, Virginia, May 3, 1863. Returned to duty on an unspecified date. Transferred to the C.S. Navy on April 10, 1864.

ALMOND, HARRIS, Private
Resided in Stanly County where he enlisted at age 17, March 27, 1862. Died at Richmond, Virginia, August 20, 1862, of "fever."

ALMOND, NATHAN, Private
Resided in Stanly County where he enlisted at age 27, March 15, 1862. Died on August 27, 1864, of disease. Place of death not reported.

AUSTIN, DALLAS P., Private
Enlisted at Liberty Mills, Virginia, February 1, 1864, for the war. Surrendered at Appomattox Court House, Virginia, April 9, 1865.

AUSTIN, SAMUEL D., Private
Resided in Stanly County where he enlisted at age 28, September 7, 1861. Captured at Fredericksburg, Virginia, December 13, 1862. Exchanged on or about December 17, 1862. Returned to duty on an unspecified date. Captured at Spotsylvania Court House, Virginia, May 12, 1864. Confined at Point Lookout, Maryland. Transferred to Elmira, New York, August 8, 1864. Died at Elmira on December 11, 1864, of "pneumonia."

BELL, BENJAMIN F., Private
Resided in Stanly County where he enlisted at age 20, September 7, 1861. Present or accounted for until he surrendered at Appomattox Court House, Virginia, April 9, 1865.

BILES, WILLIAM A. C., Corporal
Resided in Stanly County and was by occupation a farmer prior to enlisting in Stanly County at age 26, September 7, 1861. Mustered in as Private and was promoted to Corporal in May-December, 1862. Wounded in the head and side and captured at Gettysburg, Pennsylvania, July 2-3, 1863. Hospitalized at Gettysburg until transferred to hospital at Baltimore, Maryland, October 1, 1863. Transferred to Point Lookout, Maryland, January 10, 1864. Paroled at Point Lookout and transferred to City Point, Virginia, where he was received on March 20, 1864, for exchange. Reported absent wounded until December 21, 1864, when he was retired to the Invalid Corps.

BLACK, ROBERT S., Private
Resided in Cabarrus County and enlisted in Stanly County at age 24, March 12, 1862. Present or accounted for through February, 1865.

BOST, JAMES H., Private
Resided in Cabarrus County and enlisted at Liberty Mills, Virginia, February 1, 1862. Died in camp at Liberty Mills on April 23, 1862, of "typhoid fever."

BOST, WILLIAM A., Corporal
Resided in Cabarrus County and enlisted in New Hanover County at age 19, February 4, 1862. Mustered in as Private and was promoted to Corporal in January, 1863-October, 1864. Captured near Petersburg, Virginia, April 2, 1865. Confined at Hart's Island, New York Harbor, until released on June 18, 1865, after taking the Oath of Allegiance.

BOYSWORTH, JONATHAN, Private
Born in Stanly County where he resided prior to enlisting in Stanly County at age 17, September 7, 1861. Died in hospital at Wilmington on or about December 7, 1861, of "typhoid fever" and/or "measles."

BURLEYSON, EBEN, Private
Resided in Stanly County where he enlisted at age 22, March 15, 1862. Captured near Petersburg, Virginia, April 2, 1865. Confined at Point Lookout, Maryland. Released on June 23, 1865, after taking the Oath of Allegiance.

BURRIS, ADAM C., Private
Resided in Stanly County where he enlisted at age 16, September 7, 1861. Wounded at Chancellorsville, Virginia, May 2-3, 1863. Returned to duty prior to July 1-3, 1863, when he was wounded in the right thigh and captured at Gettysburg, Pennsylvania. Hospitalized at Gettysburg and at Baltimore, Maryland. Paroled and transferred to City Point, Virginia, where he was received on August 20, 1863, for exchange. Returned to duty on an unspecified date. Wounded in the right shoulder at or near Bethesda Church, Virginia, on or about May 31, 1864. Returned to duty prior to November 1, 1864. Reported on duty as an ambulance driver in November-December, 1864, and was reported on duty with the "ambulance train" in January-February, 1865.

BURRIS, LEVI P., Private
Resided in Stanly County where he enlisted at age 20, September 7, 1861. Wounded in the left leg and captured at Gettysburg, Pennsylvania, July 1-5, 1863. Hospitalized at Gettysburg. Transferred to Davids Island, New York Harbor, July 17-24, 1863. Transferred to Fort Wood, Bedloe's Island, New York Harbor, on or about October 15, 1863. Transferred to Point Lookout, Maryland, on or about January 8, 1864. Paroled and transferred to City Point, Virginia, where he was received on March 6, 1864, for exchange. Reported absent on furlough through February, 1865.

CAGLE, BENJAMIN, Private
Born in Stanly County* and resided in Cabarrus County where he was by occupation a farmer prior to enlisting in Stanly County at age 29, September 7, 1861. Discharged on February 3, 1862, by reason of "a loss of hearing."

CARKIER, WILEY, Private
Resided in Cabarrus County and enlisted in Stanly County at age 20, September 7, 1861. Present or accounted for until he surrendered at Appomattox Court House, Virginia, April 9, 1865.

CARKIER, WILLIAM M., Private
Born in Stanly County* and resided in Cabarrus

County prior to enlisting in Stanly County at age 23, September 7, 1861. Wounded in the right arm and captured at Gettysburg, Pennsylvania, July 1-3, 1863. Hospitalized at Chester, Pennsylvania. Paroled and transferred to City Point, Virginia, August 17, 1863, for exchange. Returned to duty on an unspecified date. Reported present for duty during September-December, 1864. Retired to the Invalid Corps on December 21, 1864, by reason of disability.

COLEY, JAMES F., Private
Resided in Stanly County and enlisted at Liberty Mills, Virginia, April 22, 1864, for the war. Captured near Petersburg, Virginia, April 2, 1865. Confined at Point Lookout, Maryland. Released on June 24, 1865, after taking the Oath of Allegiance.

COLEY, JESSE M., Private
Resided in Cabarrus County and enlisted in Stanly County at age 23, September 7, 1861. Captured at Hanover Court House, Virginia, May 27, 1862. Received at Aiken's Landing, James River, Virginia, July 12, 1862, for exchange. Declared exchanged at Aiken's Landing on August 5, 1862. Returned to duty prior to January 1, 1863. Wounded in the leg at Chancellorsville, Virginia, May 2-3, 1863. Returned to duty on an unspecified date. Wounded and captured at Spotsylvania Court House, Virginia, May 12, 1864. Confined at Point Lookout, Maryland. Transferred to Elmira, New York, July 8, 1864. Released at Elmira on May 29, 1865, after taking the Oath of Allegiance.

COLEY, JOHN M., Private
Born in Stanly County and resided in Cabarrus County prior to enlisting in Stanly County at age 17, March 2, 1863, for the war. Died on or about June 6, 1864. Place and cause of death not reported.

COLEY, WILLIAM M., Private
Resided in Cabarrus or Stanly County and enlisted in Stanly County at age 29, September 7, 1861. Captured near Petersburg, Virginia, April 2, 1865. Confined at Point Lookout, Maryland. Released on June 24, 1865, after taking the Oath of Allegiance. [Roll of Honor indicates he served as "Musician for the regiment."]

COOPER, NOAH, Sergeant
Resided in Cabarrus County and enlisted in Stanly County at age 30, September 7, 1861. Mustered in as Private and was promoted to Sergeant on December 2, 1861. Died in hospital at Staunton, Virginia, December 16, 1862, of "febris typhoides."

CROWELL, JAMES, Private
Resided in Cabarrus County and enlisted in Stanly County at age 36, March 2, 1863, for the war. Captured at Spotsylvania Court House, Virginia, May 12, 1864. Confined at Point Lookout, Maryland. Transferred to Elmira, New York, August 8, 1864. Released at Elmira on May 29, 1865, after taking the Oath of Allegiance.

CROWELL, WILLIAM FRANKLIN, Private
Born in Stanly County* and resided in Cabarrus County where he was by occupation a farmer prior to enlisting in Stanly County at age 36, March 2, 1863, for the war. Wounded in the right leg and captured at Gettysburg, Pennsylvania, July 1-5, 1863. Hospitalized at Davids Island, New York Harbor. Paroled and transferred to City Point, Virginia, where he was

received on September 16, 1863, for exchange. Retired from service on February 11, 1865, by reason of disability from wounds. Paroled at Salisbury on May 16, 1865.

DAVIS, DAVID D., Private
Previously served in Company D of this regiment. Transferred to this company in February, 1862. Wounded in the left leg and captured at Gettysburg, Pennsylvania, July 3, 1863. Left leg amputated. Confined at various Federal hospitals. Paroled at Point Lookout, Maryland, and transferred to City Point, Virginia, where he was received on March 20, 1864, for exchange. Reported absent wounded through February, 1865.

DAVIS, GEORGE W., Private
Previously served in Company D of this regiment. Transferred to this company in February, 1862. Captured at Spotsylvania Court House, Virginia, May 12, 1864. Confined at Point Lookout, Maryland. Transferred to Elmira, New York, August 15, 1864. Transferred back to Point Lookout on October 11, 1864. Paroled and transferred to Venus Point, Savannah River, Georgia, where he was received on November 15, 1864, for exchange. Returned to duty subsequent to February 28, 1865. Surrendered at Appomattox Court House, Virginia, April 9, 1865.

DRAKE, JEFFERSON, Private
Born in Stanly County* and resided in Cabarrus County where he was by occupation a farmer prior to enlisting in Stanly County at age 47, September 7, 1861. Discharged on March 6, 1862, by reason of "old age and a shortened leg from an old fracture of the thigh bone."

EARNHARDT, GEORGE R., Private
Resided in Stanly County where he enlisted at age 17, September 7, 1861. Died in hospital at Goldsboro on March 24, 1862, of "typhoid fever."

EFORD, DANIEL R. A., Private
Resided in Stanly County where he enlisted on November 29, 1864, for the war. Captured at Amelia Court House, Virginia, on or about April 5, 1865. Confined at Point Lookout, Maryland. Released on June 12, 1865, after taking the Oath of Allegiance.

ELLIOTT, WILLIAM A., Private
Resided in Stanly County where he enlisted at age 32, September 7, 1861. Present or accounted for through February, 1865.

EUDY, JACOB, Private
Enlisted in Stanly County on October 31, 1864, for the war. Surrendered at Appomattox Court House, Virginia, April 9, 1865.

EUDY, JACOB W., Private
Resided in Cabarrus County and enlisted in Stanly County at age 27, March 13, 1862. Records of this company indicate he was transferred to Company H, 8th Regiment N.C. State Troops, November 9, 1864; however, records of the 8th Regiment N.C. State Troops do not indicate that he served therein.

EUDY, JOHN C., Private
Resided in Stanly County where he enlisted at age 18,

September 7, 1861. Captured near Petersburg, Virginia, April 2, 1865. Confined at Point Lookout, Maryland. Released on June 12, 1865, after taking the Oath of Allegiance.

EUDY, WILLIAM, Private
Born in Stanly County* where he resided prior to enlisting in Stanly County at age 23, September 7, 1861. Captured at Hanover Court House, Virginia, May 27, 1862. Confined at Fort Monroe, Virginia, and at Fort Columbus, New York Harbor. Paroled and transferred to Aiken's Landing, James River, Virginia, where he was received on July 12, 1862, for exchange. Declared exchanged at Aiken's Landing on August 5, 1862. Died in hospital at Petersburg, Virginia, on or about August 16, 1862, of "diarrhoea."

EUDY, WILLIAM R., Private
Resided in Stanly County where he enlisted at age 25, March 14, 1862. Died in hospital at Richmond, Virginia, July 13, 1862, of "typhoid fever."

EURY, DAVID W., Private
Born in Stanly County* where he resided as a farmer prior to enlisting in Stanly County at age 22, September 7, 1861. Wounded and captured at Gettysburg, Pennsylvania, July 3, 1863. Hospitalized at Gettysburg. Paroled and transferred to City Point, Virginia, where he was received on August 20, 1863, for exchange. Discharged on January 18, 1864, by reason of disability from wounds.

FARMER, JOHN A., Private
Resided in Stanly County where he enlisted at age 21, September 7, 1861. Killed at Fredericksburg, Virginia, December 13, 1862.

FARMER, LEON R., Private
Resided in Stanly County where he enlisted at age 16, September 7, 1861. Captured at Hanover Court House, Virginia, May 27, 1862. Confined at Fort Monroe, Virginia, and at Fort Columbus, New York Harbor. Paroled and transferred to Aiken's Landing, James River, Virginia, where he was received on July 12, 1862, for exchange. Declared exchanged at Aiken's Landing on August 5, 1862. Returned to duty prior to January 1, 1863. Reported absent sick from May 1, 1864, through February, 1865.

FESPERMAN, JOHN E., Private
Resided in Stanly County where he enlisted at age 35, September 7, 1861. Wounded in the left thigh at Cold Harbor, Virginia, on or about May 31, 1864. Retired to the Invalid Corps on December 24, 1864, by reason of disability.

FORREST, SAMUEL P., Corporal
Resided in Stanly County where he enlisted at age 20, September 7, 1861. Mustered in as Private and was promoted to Corporal in January-April, 1862. Wounded in the right arm and captured at Gettysburg, Pennsylvania, July 1-2, 1863. Hospitalized at Gettysburg where he died on or about September 17, 1863, of wounds.

FORREST, THOMAS Y., Private
Resided in Stanly County where he enlisted at age 21, September 7, 1861. Died in hospital at Wilmington on December 23, 1861, of "fever."

FRY, DAVID A., Private
Enlisted at Liberty Mills, Virginia, March 15, 1864, for the war. Wounded at Spotsylvania Court House, Virginia, May 12, 1864. Returned to duty prior to November 1, 1864. Surrendered at Appomattox Court House, Virginia, April 9, 1865.

FURR, AARON, Private
Enlisted at Liberty Mills, Virginia, February 10, 1864, for the war. Captured near Petersburg, Virginia, April 2, 1865. Confined at Point Lookout, Maryland. Released on June 26, 1865, after taking the Oath of Allegiance.

FURR, CRITTENTON, Sergeant
Resided in Stanly County where he enlisted at age 21, September 7, 1861. Mustered in as Private. Wounded near Richmond, Virginia, June 25-July 1, 1862. Returned to duty prior to January 1, 1863. Promoted to Sergeant in January-July, 1863. Captured at Spotsylvania Court House, Virginia, May 12, 1864. Confined at Point Lookout, Maryland. Transferred to Elmira, New York, August 10, 1864. Released at Elmira on May 29, 1865, after taking the Oath of Allegiance.

FURR, FARRENTON, Private
Born in Cabarrus County and resided in Stanly County where he was by occupation a farmer prior to enlisting in Stanly County at age 26, September 7, 1861. Wounded in the side and right arm at Cedar Mountain, Virginia, August 9, 1862. Discharged on April 18, 1863, by reason of disability from wounds.

FURR, JAMES CHESLEY, Private
Resided in Cabarrus County and enlisted in Stanly County on October 31, 1864, for the war. Captured near Petersburg, Virginia, April 2, 1865. Confined at Point Lookout, Maryland, until released on June 26, 1865, after taking the Oath of Allegiance.

FURR, LAUSON ALEX, Private
Resided in Stanly County where he enlisted at age 28, March 17, 1862. Captured at Hanover Court House, Virginia, May 27, 1862. Confined at Fort Monroe, Virginia, and at Fort Columbus, New York Harbor. Paroled and transferred to Aiken's Landing, James River, Virginia, where he was received on July 12, 1862, for exchange. Declared exchanged at Aiken's Landing on August 5, 1862. Returned to duty prior to January 1, 1863. Wounded at Chancellorsville, Virginia, May 2-3, 1863. Returned to duty on an unspecified date. Captured at Spotsylvania Court House, Virginia, May 12, 1864. Confined at Point Lookout, Maryland. Transferred to Elmira, New York, August 10, 1864. Died at Elmira on December 6, 1864, of "pneumonia."

FURR, RUFUS, Private
Resided in Stanly County where he enlisted at age 24, September 7, 1861. Died at Richmond, Virginia, July 16, 1862, of "typhoid fever."

GILBERT, STEPHEN, Private
Resided in Stanly County and enlisted at age 16, September 7, 1861. Died in January, 1862. Place and cause of death not reported.

GRINDSTAFF, JACOB, ———
North Carolina pension records indicate that he served in this company.

HAGLER, McA., Private

Enlisted at Liberty Mills, Virginia, March 29, 1864, for the war. Hospitalized at Charlotte on November 1, 1864, with a gunshot wound of the right knee. Place and date wounded not reported. Reported absent or absent on furlough through February, 1865.

HARKEY, MARTIN A., Private

Resided in Stanly County where he enlisted at age 24, March 15, 1862. Hospitalized at Richmond, Virginia, May 27, 1864, with a gunshot wound of the left thigh. Place and date wounded not reported. Returned to duty on June 3, 1864. Hospitalized at Richmond on July 28, 1864, with gunshot wounds of the arm and right shoulder. Place and date wounded not reported. Furloughed from hospital at Richmond on March 31, 1865. [A pension application filed by his widow in 1885 indicates that Private Harkey died on an unspecified date of wounds received in June, 1864.]

HARKEY, SOLOMON, Private

Resided in Stanly County where he enlisted at age 34, March 27, 1862. Captured at Gettysburg, Pennsylvania, July 3, 1863. Confined at Fort Delaware, Delaware. Hospitalized at Chester, Pennsylvania, with "scurvy." Died at Chester on September 20, 1863.

HARKEY, WILSON, Private

Resided in Stanly County where he enlisted at age 20, September 7, 1861. Hospitalized at Charlottesville, Virginia, August 11, 1862, with a gunshot wound. Place and date wounded not reported. Returned to duty prior to January 1, 1863. Died at Hanover Junction, Virginia, June 10, 1863, of "fever."

HARWOOD, HOWELL, Private

Resided in Stanly County where he enlisted at age 20, March 15, 1862. Present or accounted for through February, 1865.

HARWOOD, REDDING, Private

Enlisted in Stanly County on November 17, 1863, for the war. Captured at Spotsylvania Court House, Virginia, May 12, 1864. Confined at Point Lookout, Maryland, where he died on June 2, 1864. Cause of death not reported. [A pension application filed by his widow in 1885 indicates he was wounded at Spotsylvania Court House on May 12, 1864.]

HARWOOD, WESLEY, Private

Born in Stanly County* where he resided prior to enlisting in Stanly County at age 22, March 15, 1862. Died in hospital at Richmond, Virginia, September 21-22, 1864, of "feb[ris] interm[ittent]."

HATHCOCK, EDNEY W., Private

Resided in Stanly County where he enlisted at age 17, September 7, 1861. Captured at Wilderness, Virginia, May 12, 1864. Confined at Point Lookout, Maryland. Transferred to Elmira, New York, August 10, 1864. Paroled at Elmira on February 9, 1865, and transferred to Boulware's Wharf, James River, Virginia, where he was received February 20, 1865, for exchange.

HATHCOCK, GEORGE W., Musician

Resided in Stanly County where he enlisted at age 26, September 7, 1861. Mustered in as Private and was promoted to Musician in March-April, 1862. Captured

at Hanover Court House, Virginia, on or about May 27, 1862. Confined at Fort Monroe, Virginia, and at Fort Columbus, New York Harbor. Paroled and transferred to Aiken's Landing, James River, Virginia, where he was received on July 12, 1862, for exchange. Declared exchanged at Aiken's Landing on August 5, 1862. Returned to duty prior to January 1, 1863. Died at Salisbury on September 3, 1863, of "fever" and/or "chronic diarrhoea."

HATHCOCK, GREEN L., Musician

Enlisted in Stanly County on March 15, 1862. Mustered in as Musician. Present or accounted for through February, 1865.

HATHCOCK, URIAH F., Corporal

Resided in Stanly County where he enlisted at age 20, March 15, 1862. Mustered in as Private. Wounded in the shoulder at Cedar Mountain, Virginia, August 9, 1862. Returned to duty prior to January 1, 1863. Promoted to Corporal in January, 1863-October, 1864. Surrendered at Appomattox Court House, Virginia, April 9, 1865.

HATLEY, DANIEL A., Private

Resided in Stanly County where he enlisted at age 17, September 7, 1861. Wounded near Richmond, Virginia, on an unspecified date. Wounded in the thigh and captured at Gettysburg, Pennsylvania, July 1-3, 1863. Leg amputated. Died in hospital at Gettysburg on July 24, 1863, of wounds.

HATLEY, EDMOND, Private

Resided in Stanly County where he enlisted at age 35, September 7, 1861. Died in camp near Brook Church, Virginia, June 19, 1862, of disease.

HATLEY, HASTINGS M., Private

Resided in Stanly County where he enlisted at age 33, September 7, 1861. Died in hospital at Richmond, Virginia, on or about May 30, 1862, of "pneumonia."

HATLEY, JOHN, Private

Resided in Stanly County where he enlisted at age 39, September 7, 1861. Captured at Hanover Court House, Virginia, May 27, 1862. Confined at Fort Monroe, Virginia, and at Fort Columbus, New York Harbor. Paroled and transferred to Aiken's Landing, James River, Virginia, where he was received on July 12, 1862, for exchange. Declared exchanged at Aiken's Landing on August 5, 1862. Discharged on or about September 23, 1862, by reason of being overage.

HATLY, J. F., Private

Enlisted in Stanly County on January 3, 1865, for the war. Present or accounted for through February, 1865.

HEARN, NEHEMIAH, ——

North Carolina pension records indicate that he served in this company.

HEARNE, WHITMAN F., Private

Resided in Stanly County where he enlisted at age 25, July 8, 1862, for the war. Captured near Petersburg, Virginia, April 2, 1865. Confined at Hart's Island, New York Harbor. Transferred to Davids Island, New York Harbor, July 1, 1865. Released on July 11, 1865, after taking the Oath of Allegiance.

HERRIN, ELI R., Sergeant
Born in Stanly County* where he resided as a farmer prior to enlisting in Stanly County at age 23, September 7, 1861. Mustered in as Sergeant. Wounded in the leg near Richmond, Virginia, in June, 1862. Leg amputated. Discharged on August 15, 1862, by reason of disability.

HINSON, ALFRED, Private
Resided in Stanly County where he enlisted at age 25, September 7, 1861. Captured by the enemy on an unspecified date. Paroled and transferred to Aiken's Landing, James River, Virginia, where he was received on September 7, 1862, for exchange. Declared exchanged at Aiken's Landing on September 21, 1862. Returned to duty prior to January 1, 1863. Wounded at Chancellorsville, Virginia, May 2-3, 1863. Died near Guinea Station, Virginia, June 6, 1863, of "t[y]phoid fever."

HINSON, JOHN, Private
Resided in Stanly County where he enlisted at age 28, March 24, 1862. Died in hospital at Richmond, Virginia, July 27, 1862, of "feb[ris] typh[oid]."

HINSON, JOSEPH M., Private
Resided in Stanly County where he enlisted at age 33, September 7, 1861. Wounded at Gettysburg, Pennsylvania, July 1-3, 1863. Returned to duty on an unspecified date. Reported present for duty during September, 1864-February, 1865. Captured near Petersburg, Virginia, April 2, 1865. Confined at Point Lookout, Maryland, until released on June 14, 1865, after taking the Oath of Allegiance.

HINSON, ROBERT, Private
Resided in Stanly County where he enlisted at age 18, March 2, 1863, for the war. Died in hospital at Richmond, Virginia, June 8, 1863, of "febris typhoides."

HINSON, WILLIAM, Private
Resided in Stanly County where he enlisted at age 28, March 10, 1862. Wounded and captured at Spotsylvania Court House, Virginia, May 12, 1864. Died on an unspecified date. Place and cause of death not reported.

HOLT, ALEXANDER, ———
North Carolina pension records indicate that he served in this company.

HOLT, BENJAMIN A., Private
Resided in Stanly County where he enlisted at age 33, September 7, 1861. Mustered in as Corporal but was reduced to ranks in January-April, 1862. Hospitalized at Richmond, Virginia, May 18, 1864, with a gunshot wound of the head. Place and date wounded not reported. Returned to duty prior to November 1, 1864. Surrendered at Appomattox Court House, Virginia, April 9, 1865.

HOLT, DAVID, Private
Resided in Stanly County where he enlisted at age 25, September 7, 1861. Killed at Gettysburg, Pennsylvania, July 3, 1863.

HOLT, JOHN A., Private
Resided in Stanly County where he enlisted at age 34,

February 26, 1863, for the war. Captured near Petersburg, Virginia, April 2, 1865. Confined at Point Lookout, Maryland. Released on June 27, 1865, after taking the Oath of Allegiance.

HOWELL, JOHN A., Private
Resided in Stanly County where he enlisted at age 22, September 7, 1861. Died at Wilmington on January 1, 1862. Cause of death not reported.

HOWELL, JOHN T., Private
Resided in Stanly County where he enlisted at age 22, September 7, 1861. Wounded in the pelvis and captured at Gettysburg, Pennsylvania, July 3, 1863. Died in hospital at Chester, Pennsylvania, July 28, 1863, of "exhaustion."

INGRAM, ANDREW, Private
Born in Davidson County and enlisted on November 20, 1863, for the war. Died in hospital at Lynchburg, Virginia, June 1, 1864, of "abscessus chron[ic]."

KENDALL, WILLIAM D., Private
Born in Stanly County* where he resided prior to enlisting in Stanly County at age 32, September 7, 1861. Killed at Reams' Station, Virginia, August 25, 1864.

KIMERY, LEONARD A., Private
Resided in Stanly County where he enlisted at age 30, March 27, 1862. Died at Richmond, Virginia, July 8, 1862, of disease.

KIRK, GEORGE E., Private
Resided in Stanly County where he enlisted at age 18, September 7, 1861. Reported missing and was "supposed to have been killed" at Gettysburg, Pennsylvania, July 3, 1863.

KIRK, LEWIS D. H., Private
Resided in Stanly County where he enlisted at age 20, April 3, 1862. Died in hospital at Danville, Virginia, July 25, 1862, of "phthisis pulmonalis."

KIRK, PARHAM, Private
Resided in Stanly County where he enlisted on October 31, 1864, for the war. Captured near Petersburg, Virginia, April 2, 1865. Confined at Point Lookout, Maryland, until released on June 28, 1865, after taking the Oath of Allegiance. [May have served previously in Company I, 52nd Regiment N.C. Troops.]

KIRK, WILLIAM A., Private
Enlisted in Stanly County on October 31, 1864, for the war. Surrendered at Appomattox Court House, Virginia, April 9, 1865. [May have served previously in Company I, 52nd Regiment N.C. Troops.]

KIRK, WILLIAM D., Private
Resided in Stanly County where he enlisted at age 26, September 7, 1861. Mustered in as Corporal but was reduced to ranks in January-April, 1862. Captured at Hanover Court House, Virginia, May 27, 1862. Confined at Fort Monroe, Virginia, and at Fort Columbus, New York Harbor. Exchanged on an unspecified date. Returned to duty prior to January 1, 1863. Wounded in the leg at Gettysburg, Pennsylvania, July 3, 1863. Returned to duty on an unspecified date. Reported present for duty during September, 1864-February, 1865. Captured near Petersburg, Virginia,

April 2, 1865. Confined at Point Lookout, Maryland. Released on June 28, 1865, after taking the Oath of Allegiance.

KIRK, WILLIAM G., Private
Resided in Stanly County where he enlisted at age 40, September 7, 1861. Captured at Hanover Court House, Virginia, May 27, 1862. Confined at Fort Monroe, Virginia, and at Fort Columbus, New York Harbor. Paroled and transferred to Aiken's Landing, James River, Virginia, where he was received on July 12, 1862, for exchange. Declared exchanged at Aiken's Landing on August 5, 1862. Returned to duty prior to January 1, 1863. Died "of sunstroke while on the march" in Virginia on June 18, 1863.

LAMBERT, C. WILEY, Private
Previously served in Company H, 8th Regiment N.C. State Troops. Transferred to this company on October 1, 1864. Captured at or near Jones' Farm, Virginia, on or about September 30, 1864. Confined at Point Lookout, Maryland, until paroled and transferred to Boulware's Wharf, James River, Virginia, where he was received March 19, 1865, for exchange.

LATON, CHRISTIAN GREEN, Private
Resided in Stanly County where he enlisted at age 38, October 31, 1864, for the war. Captured near Petersburg, Virginia, April 2, 1865. Confined at Point Lookout, Maryland. Released on June 28, 1865, after taking the Oath of Allegiance.

LEE, ROBERT B., Private
Resided in Stanly County and enlisted on April 20, 1863, for the war. Deserted on April 25, 1863.

LINKER, W. MONROE, Private
Enlisted at Camp Stokes on December 19, 1864, for the war. Hospitalized at Charlotte on March 19, 1865, with a gunshot wound of the "lower extremities left." Place and date wounded not reported. Paroled at Charlotte in May, 1865.

LOWDER, JOHN M., Private
Resided in Stanly County where he enlisted at age 31, March 25, 1862. Wounded at Ox Hill, Virginia, September 1, 1862. Returned to duty prior to January 1, 1863. Captured at Wilderness, Virginia, May 6, 1864. Confined at Point Lookout, Maryland. Transferred to Elmira, New York, August 10, 1864. Released on June 23, 1865, after taking the Oath of Allegiance.

LOWDER, LEE, Private
Resided in Stanly County where he enlisted at age 42, March 20, 1862. Captured at Fredericksburg, Virginia, December 13, 1862. Exchanged on or about December 17, 1862. Died in hospital at Lynchburg, Virginia, December 9, 1863, of "pneumonia."

McCLARTY, JOHN M., Private
Resided in Cabarrus County and enlisted in New Hanover County at age 22, February 4, 1862. Captured near Petersburg, Virginia, April 2, 1865. Confined at Hart's Island, New York Harbor. Released on June 17, 1865, after taking the Oath of Allegiance.

McCURDY, CALEB S., Private
Previously served in Company A, 20th Regiment N.C. Troops (10th Regiment N.C. Volunteers). Enlisted in

this company in Stanly County on April 26, 1862, for the war. Died in hospital at Richmond, Virginia, on or about November 25, 1863, of "phthisis pul[monalis]."

McINTYRE, ISAIAH, Private
Resided in Stanly County where he enlisted at age 22, September 7, 1861. Captured at Hanover Court House, Virginia, May 27, 1862. Confined at Fort Monroe, Virginia, and at Fort Columbus, New York Harbor. Paroled and transferred to Aiken's Landing, James River, Virginia, where he was received on July 12, 1862, for exchange. Declared exchanged at Aiken's Landing on August 5, 1862. Returned to duty prior to January 1, 1863. Captured at Spotsylvania Court House, Virginia, May 12, 1864. Confined at Point Lookout, Maryland. Transferred to Elmira, New York, August 10, 1864. Released at Elmira on July 7, 1865, after taking the Oath of Allegiance.

McINTYRE, JOHN F., Private
Resided in Stanly County where he enlisted at age 32, September 7, 1861. Captured at Hanover Court House, Virginia, May 27, 1862. Confined at Fort Monroe, Virginia, and at Fort Columbus, New York Harbor. Paroled and transferred to Aiken's Landing, James River, Virginia, where he was received July 12, 1862, for exchange. Declared exchanged at Aiken's Landing on August 5, 1862. Returned to duty prior to January 1, 1863. Hospitalized at Danville, Virginia, May 18, 1864, with a gunshot wound of the shoulder. Place and date wounded not reported. Retired to the Invalid Corps on November 9, 1864, by reason of disability.

McINTYRE, STOKES, Private
Born in Stanly County* where he resided as a farmer prior to enlisting in Stanly County at age 56, September 7, 1861. Discharged on March 6, 1862, by reason of "varicose veins of the legs."

McKINLEY, STEVEN C., Private
Born in Cabarrus County where he resided prior to enlisting in New Hanover County at age 19, February 4, 1862. Captured at or near Hanover Court House, Virginia, on or about May 28, 1862. Confined at Fort Monroe, Virginia, and at Fort Delaware, Delaware. Paroled and transferred to Aiken's Landing, James River, Virginia, where he was exchanged on August 5, 1862. Returned to duty on an unspecified date. Hospitalized at Richmond, Virginia, on or about August 26, 1864, with a gunshot wound of the chest. Place and date wounded not reported. Died "at his home" on November 23, 1864, of wounds.

McSWAIN, C. J., Private
Resided in Stanly County where he enlisted at age 37, September 7, 1861. Deserted on August 26, 1863. Apprehended on an unspecified date. Court-martialed on or about September 17, 1863. "Shot by order of court-martial" near Liberty Mills, Virginia, September 26, 1863.

MANN, WILLIAM C., Private
Resided in Stanly County where he enlisted at age 22, September 7, 1861. Transferred to Company C, 42nd Regiment N.C. Troops, on or about September 10, 1862.

MARBERRY, ARCHIBALD C., Private
Resided in Stanly County where he enlisted at age 23,

September 7, 1861. Wounded in the head near Richmond, Virginia, on or about May 9, 1864. Returned to duty in January-February, 1865. Surrendered at Appomattox Court House, Virginia, April 9, 1865.

MARBERRY, THOMAS F., Private
Resided in Stanly County and enlisted at age 18, March 2, 1863, for the war. Died in hospital at Richmond, Virginia, June 4-5, 1863, of "feb[ris] typhoides."

MAULDIN, JAMES, Private
Resided in Stanly County where he enlisted at age 30, March 15, 1862. Killed at Hanover Court House, Virginia, May 27, 1862.

MAULDIN, THOMAS, Private
Enlisted in Stanly County on September 10, 1863, for the war. Captured in hospital at Richmond, Virginia, April 3, 1865. Paroled at Richmond on May 3, 1865.

MILTON, ELISHA H., Private
Born in Stanly County where he resided as a wheelwright prior to enlisting in Stanly County at age 22, September 7, 1861. Captured at Falling Waters, Maryland, July 14, 1863. Confined at Fort McHenry, Maryland. Transferred to Point Lookout, Maryland, August 21-22, 1863. Released on January 24, 1864, after taking the Oath of Allegiance and joining the U.S. Army. Assigned to Company B, 1st Regiment U.S. Volunteer Infantry.

MILTON, GEORGE, Private
Resided in Stanly County where he enlisted at age 18, March 14, 1862. Captured at Hanover Court House, Virginia, May 27, 1862. Confined at Fort Columbus, New York Harbor. Paroled and transferred to Aiken's Landing, James River, Virginia, where he was received on July 12, 1862, for exchange. Declared exchanged at Aiken's Landing on August 5, 1862. Returned to duty prior to December 13, 1862, when he was wounded at Fredericksburg, Virginia, Returned to duty on an unspecified date. Present or accounted for through February, 1865.

MILTON, J., Private
Place and date of enlistment not reported. Surrendered at Appomattox Court House, Virginia, April 9, 1865.

MISENHIMER, JOHN A., Private
Resided in Stanly County where he enlisted at age 19, September 7, 1861. Died in hospital at or near Lynchburg, Virginia, June 23, 1862, of "typhoid fever."

MOODY, DANIEL W., Private
Born in Cabarrus County where he resided prior to enlisting in New Hanover County at age 19, February 4, 1862. Wounded in the left hand and captured at or near Gettysburg, Pennsylvania, on or about July 1-3, 1863. Middle finger amputated. Exchanged prior to August 1, 1863, when he was hospitalized at Petersburg, Virginia. Company records do not indicate whether he returned to duty. Died "at his home" on November 23, 1864. Cause of death not reported.

MOORE, LEMUEL, Private
Enlisted in Granville County on October 20, 1863, for the war. Captured at or near Spotsylvania Court House, Virginia, on or about May 12, 1864. Confined at Point Lookout, Maryland. Died at Point Lookout on July 20, 1864, of "dysentery acute."

MOOSE, DANIEL W., Private
Resided in Stanly County where he enlisted at age 20, March 15, 1862. Captured near Petersburg, Virginia, April 2, 1865. Confined at Hart's Island, New York Harbor. Transferred to Davids Island, New York Harbor, on or about July 1, 1865. Released at Davids Island on or about July 12, 1865, after taking the Oath of Allegiance.

MOOSE, JACOB A., Private
Resided in Stanly County where he enlisted on October 31, 1864, for the war. Captured near Petersburg, Virginia, April 2, 1865. Confined at Hart's Island, New York Harbor. Released on June 17, 1865, after taking the Oath of Allegiance.

MORTON, EZEKIEL R., Private
Resided in Stanly County where he enlisted at age 22, March 20, 1862. Hospitalized at Richmond, Virginia, on July 2, 1862, with a gunshot wound of the hand. Place and date wounded not reported. Died in hospital at Richmond on August 23, 1862, of "feb[ris] typhoides."

MORTON, JAMES, Musician
Resided in Stanly County where he enlisted at age 31, September 7, 1861. Mustered in as Musician. Hospitalized at Richmond, Virginia, October 2, 1864, with a gunshot wound of the right arm. Place and date wounded not reported. Returned to duty prior to November 1, 1864. Surrendered at Appomattox Court House, Virginia, April 9, 1865.

MORTON, JESSE A., Jr., Private
Resided in Stanly County where he enlisted at age 20, March 20, 1862. Killed in battle near Richmond, Virginia, in June, 1862.

MORTON, JESSE A., Sr., Private
Resided in Stanly County where he enlisted at age 23, September 7, 1861. Captured at Hanover Court House, Virginia, on or about May 27, 1862. Confined at Fort Monroe, Virginia, and at Fort Columbus, New York Harbor. Paroled and transferred to Aiken's Landing, James River, Virginia, where he was received on July 2, 1862, for exchange. Declared exchanged at Aiken's Landing on August 5, 1862. Returned to duty prior to January 1, 1863. Captured near Petersburg, Virginia, April 2, 1865. Confined at Point Lookout, Maryland, until released on June 29, 1865, after taking the Oath of Allegiance.

MORTON, LEMUEL, Private
Resided in Stanly County where he enlisted at age 21, September 7, 1861. Captured at Hanover Court House, Virginia, on or about May 27, 1862. Confined at Fort Monroe, Virginia, and at Fort Columbus, New York Harbor. Paroled and transferred to Aiken's Landing, James River, Virginia, where he was received on July 12, 1862, for exchange. Declared exchanged at Aiken's Landing on August 5, 1862. Returned to duty prior to January 1, 1863. Wounded at Chancellorsville, Virginia, May 1-4, 1863. Died at Guinea Station, Virginia, May 8, 1863, of wounds.

MORTON, WILLIAM G., Private
Resided in Stanly County where he enlisted at age 21, March 10, 1862. Captured at Hanover Court House,

Virginia, on or about May 27, 1862. Confined at Fort Monroe, Virginia, and at Fort Columbus, New York Harbor. Paroled and transferred to Aiken's Landing, James River, Virginia, where he was received on July 12, 1862, for exchange. Declared exchanged at Aiken's Landing on August 5, 1862. Returned to duty prior to January 1, 1863. Captured at Spotsylvania Court House, Virginia, May 12, 1864. Confined at Point Lookout, Maryland. Transferred to Elmira, New York, August 10, 1864. Paroled at Elmira and transferred to Boulware's Wharf, James River, Virginia, where he was received on March 18-21, 1865, for exchange.

MOTLEY, THOMAS, Private
Resided in Stanly County where he enlisted at age 30, March 17, 1862. Captured at Hanover Court House, Virginia, May 27, 1862. Confined at Fort Monroe, Virginia, and at Fort Columbus, New York Harbor. Paroled and transferred to Aiken's Landing, James River, Virginia, where he was received on July 12, 1862, for exchange. Declared exchanged at Aiken's Landing on August 5, 1862. Returned to duty on an unspecified date. Reported present for duty during September, 1864-February, 1865. Surrendered at Appomattox Court House, Virginia, April 9, 1865.

NASH, SIMPSON J., Private
Resided in Stanly County where he enlisted at age 18, September 7, 1861. Wounded and captured at Gettysburg, Pennsylvania, July 1-3, 1863. Hospitalized at Davids Island, New York Harbor. Exchanged on an unspecified date prior to September 28, 1863. Company records do not indicate whether he returned to duty. Retired to the Invalid Corps on September 28, 1864, by reason of disability.

NELSON, JOHN, Private
Resided in Cabarrus County and enlisted in Stanly County at age 31, September 27, 1862, for the war. Reported missing and was "supposed to be killed" at Gettysburg, Pennsylvania, July 3, 1863.

PAGE, HENRY C., Sergeant
Resided in Stanly County where he enlisted at age 19, September 7, 1861. Mustered in as Private and was promoted to Sergeant in May-December, 1862. Wounded in the scalp and captured at Hanover Court House, Virginia, May 27, 1862. Confined at various Federal hospitals until September 17, 1862, when he was transferred to Fort Monroe, Virginia. Paroled and transferred to Aiken's Landing, James River, Virginia, where he was declared exchanged on November 10; 1862. Returned to duty prior to January 1, 1863. Captured at Spotsylvania Court House, Virginia, May 12, 1864. Confined at Point Lookout, Maryland. Transferred to Elmira, New York, August 8, 1864. Released at Elmira on May 17, 1865, after taking the Oath of Allegiance.

PALMER, NAPOLEON B., Corporal
Resided in Stanly County where he enlisted at age 25, September 7, 1861. Mustered in as Corporal. Killed at Cedar Run, Virginia, August 9, 1862.

PARKER, DOCTOR F., Sergeant
Resided in Stanly County where he enlisted at age 26, September 7, 1861. Mustered in as Sergeant. Died at Wilmington on December 2, 1861, of "fever."

PARKER, WILEY, Private
Resided in Stanly County where he enlisted at age 23,

March 20, 1862. Died on July 13, 1862, of disease. Place of death not reported.

PARKS, BRITTON, Private
Resided in Stanly County where he enlisted at age 30, September 7, 1861. Wounded at Cedar Mountain, Virginia, August 9, 1862. Returned to duty prior to January 22, 1863. Wounded at Chancellorsville, Virginia, May 1-4, 1863. Returned to duty on an unspecified date. Captured at Spotsylvania Court House, Virginia, May 12, 1864. Confined at Point Lookout, Maryland. Transferred to Elmira, New York, August 10, 1864. Died at Elmira on April 1, 1865, of "chro[nic] val[vular] dis[ease] of heart."

PENNINGTON, JOHN S., Private
Resided in Stanly County where he enlisted on October 31, 1864, for the war. Captured at Petersburg, Virginia, April 2, 1865. Confined at Point Lookout, Maryland, until released on June 16, 1865, after taking the Oath of Allegiance.

POPLIN, DAVID, Private
Enlisted at Liberty Mills, Virginia, April 1, 1864, for the war. Surrendered at Appomattox Court House, Virginia, April 9, 1865.

POPLIN, NATHAN, Private
Born in Stanly County where he resided as a farmer prior to enlisting in Stanly County at age 18, September 7, 1861. Discharged on August 9, 1862, by reason of "phthisis pulmonalis."

RANDALL, ISAAC J., Private
Born in Stanly County* where he resided prior to enlisting in Stanly County at age 23, September 7, 1861. Killed at Spotsylvania Court House, Virginia, May 12, 1864.

RICHEY, EBEN, Private
Resided in Stanly County where he enlisted at age 18, March 10, 1862. Died in hospital at Staunton, Virginia, on or about November 17, 1862, of "febris typhoides."

ROGERS, AARON, Private
Resided in Stanly County where he enlisted at age 37, March 27, 1862. Captured at Hanover Court House, Virginia, May 27, 1862. Confined at Fort Monroe, Virginia, and at Fort Columbus, New York Harbor. Paroled and transferred to Aiken's Landing, James River, Virginia, where he was received on July 12, 1862, for exchange. Declared exchanged at Aiken's Landing on August 5, 1862. Returned to duty prior to December 13, 1862, when he was wounded in the elbow and captured at Fredericksburg, Virginia. Exchanged on or about December 17, 1862. Company records do not indicate whether he returned to duty. Paroled at Farmville, Virginia, April 11-21, 1865.

ROGERS, DAVID W., Private
Born in Stanly County* where he resided as a cabinet-maker prior to enlisting in Stanly County at age 25, September 7, 1861. Wounded at Gettysburg, Pennsylvania, July 1-3, 1863. Company records do not indicate whether he returned to duty. Hospitalized at Richmond, Virginia, May 18, 1864, with a gunshot wound of the right leg. Place and date wounded not reported. Returned to duty in January-February, 1865.

Paroled at Lynchburg, Virginia, April 15, 1865.

ROGERS, JOHN W., Sergeant
Resided in Stanly County where he enlisted at age 23, September 7, 1861. Mustered in as Sergeant. Captured at Hanover Court House, Virginia, May 27, 1862. Confined at Fort Monroe, Virginia, and at Fort Columbus, New York Harbor. Paroled and transferred to Aiken's Landing, James River, Virginia, where he was received on July 12, 1862, for exchange. Declared exchanged at Aiken's Landing on August 5, 1862. Returned to duty prior to December 13, 1862, when he was captured at Fredericksburg, Virginia. Exchanged on or about December 17, 1862. Died in hospital at Richmond, Virginia, June 8-9, 1863, of "typhoid fever."

ROSS, DOCTOR M., Sergeant
Resided in Stanly County where he enlisted at age 25, September 7, 1861. Mustered in as Private and was promoted to Sergeant in May-December, 1862. Captured at Hanover Court House, Virginia, May 27, 1862. Confined at Fort Monroe, Virginia, and at Fort Columbus, New York Harbor. Paroled and transferred to Aiken's Landing, James River, Virginia, where he was received on July 12, 1862, for exchange. Declared exchanged at Aiken's Landing on August 5, 1862. Returned to duty prior to January 1, 1863. Wounded in the right hip at Gettysburg, Pennsylvania, July 3, 1863. Returned to duty on an unspecified date. Reported present for duty during September, 1864-February, 1865. Surrendered at Appomattox Court House, Virginia, April 9, 1865.

ROSS, GEORGE P., Private
Resided in Stanly County where he enlisted at age 32, March 27, 1862. Captured at Hanover Court House, Virginia, on or about May 27, 1862. Confined at Fort Monroe, Virginia, and at Fort Columbus, New York Harbor. Paroled and transferred to Aiken's Landing, James River, Virginia, where he was received on July 12, 1862, for exchange. Declared exchanged at Aiken's Landing on August 5, 1862. Returned to duty prior to January 1, 1863. Wounded in the left hip and captured at Gettysburg, Pennsylvania, July 1-4, 1863. Hospitalized at Davids Island, New York Harbor. Paroled and transferred to City Point, Virginia, where he was received on October 28, 1863, for exchange. Returned to duty on an unspecified date. Reported present for duty during September, 1864-February, 1865. Surrendered at Appomattox Court House, Virginia, April 9, 1865.

ROSS, WILLIAM J., Sergeant
Resided in Stanly County where he enlisted at age 21, September 7, 1861. Mustered in as Sergeant. Wounded in the right arm at Gettysburg, Pennsylvania, July 3, 1863. Returned to duty on an unspecified date. Surrendered at Appomattox Court House, Virginia, April 9, 1865.

RUSSELL, ALEXANDER, ———
North Carolina pension records indicate that he served in this company.

RUSSELL, GABRIEL, Private
Resided in Stanly County where he enlisted at age 18, March 18, 1862. Wounded at Gettysburg, Pennsylvania, July 3, 1863. Company records indicate he was missing and presumed captured at Gettysburg on July 3, 1863;

however, records of the Federal Provost Marshal do not substantiate the report of his capture. No further records.

RUSSELL, HENRY, Private
Resided in Stanly County where he enlisted at age 32, September 7, 1861. Blinded in the left eye as a result of wounds received at Harpers Ferry, Virginia, on or about June 1, 1863. Returned to duty on an unspecified date. Reported present for duty during September, 1864-February, 1865. Captured near Petersburg, Virginia, April 2, 1865. Confined at Point Lookout, Maryland. Released on June 19, 1865, after taking the Oath of Allegiance.

RUSSELL, WILLIAM H., Private
Resided in Stanly County where he enlisted at age 17, September 7, 1861. Wounded in the right leg at Chancellorsville, Virginia, May 1-4, 1863. Company records do not indicate whether he returned to duty. Reported absent sick in hospital at Salisbury from August, 1864, through February, 1865. Paroled at Salisbury on May 2, 1865. Took the Oath of Allegiance at Salisbury on June 14, 1865.

SCOTT, B. FRANKLIN, Private
Resided in Stanly County. Place and date of enlistment not reported. First listed in the records of this company in January-February, 1865. Captured near Petersburg, Virginia, April 2, 1865. Confined at Point Lookout, Maryland. Released on June 20, 1865, after taking the Oath of Allegiance.

SHOE, REDDING, Private
Enlisted at Liberty Mills, Virginia, March 1, 1864, for the war. Surrendered at Appomattox Court House, Virginia, April 9, 1865.

SHOTTLE, CHRISTOPHER, Private
Resided in Stanly County where he enlisted at age 18, September 7, 1861. Company records indicate he was captured at Spotsylvania Court House, Virginia, May 12, 1864; however, records of the Federal Provost Marshal do not substantiate that report. No further records.

SIMPSON, ISAAC, Private
Resided in Stanly County where he enlisted at age 47, September 7, 1861. Died in hospital at Richmond, Virginia, on or about January 7, 1863, of "bronchitis ch[ronic]."

SMITH, BENJAMIN F., Private
Resided in Stanly County where he enlisted at age 28, September 7, 1861. Wounded in both knees and captured at Gettysburg, Pennsylvania, July 3, 1863. Confined at various Federal hospitals. Paroled and transferred to City Point, Virginia, where he was received on November 17, 1863, for exchange. Discharged on or about September 4, 1864, by reason of disability.

SMITH, DAVID D., Private
Resided in Stanly County where he enlisted at age 23, September 7, 1861. Present or accounted for through April 9, 1865.

SMITH, EDMUND R., Private
Resided in Stanly County where he enlisted at age 19, September 7, 1861. Captured near Richmond, Virginia,

June 28, 1862. Confined at Fort Columbus, New York Harbor. Transferred to Fort Delaware, Delaware, July 9, 1862. Paroled and transferred to Aiken's Landing, James River, Virginia, where he was received on July 12, 1862, for exchange. Declared exchanged at Aiken's Landing on August 5, 1862. Captured at Spotsylvania Court House, Virginia, May 12, 1864. Confined at Point Lookout, Maryland. Transferred to Elmira, New York, on or about August 10, 1864. Released on May 29, 1865, after taking the Oath of Allegiance.

SMITH, EVAN, Private
Resided in Stanly County where he enlisted at age 30, September 7, 1861. Captured at Hanover Court House, Virginia, May 27, 1862. Confined at Fort Monroe, Virginia, and at Fort Columbus, New York Harbor. Paroled and transferred to Aiken's Landing, James River, Virginia, where he was received on July 12, 1862, for exchange. Declared exchanged at Aiken's Landing on August 5, 1862. Returned to duty prior to January 1, 1863. Captured at Spotsylvania Court House, Virginia, May 12, 1864. Confined at Point Lookout, Maryland. Transferred to Elmira, New York, August 10, 1864. Died at Elmira on April 2, 1865, of "chro[nic] diarrhoea."

SMITH, GEORGE C., Private
Born in Stanly County* where he resided as a farmer prior to enlisting in Stanly County at age 33, September 7, 1861. Mustered in as Corporal and was promoted to Sergeant in January-April, 1862. Reduced to ranks in January, 1863-October, 1864. Surrendered at Appomattox Court House, Virginia, April 9, 1865.

SMITH, GEORGE L., Private
Resided in Stanly County where he enlisted at age 24, March 12, 1862. Died in hospital at Lovingston, Virginia, August 16, 1862, of "febris typhoides."

SMITH, JOHN D., Corporal
Resided in Stanly County where he enlisted at age 19, September 7, 1861. Mustered in as Private and was promoted to Corporal in January-April, 1862. Wounded in battle near Richmond, Virginia, on an unspecified date. Hospitalized at Richmond where he died on August 10, 1862, of wounds and/or disease.

SMITH, JOHN M., Private
Enlisted in Stanly County on October 15, 1863, for the war. Captured at Spotsylvania Court House, Virginia, May 12, 1864. Confined at Point Lookout, Maryland. Transferred to Elmira, New York, August 10, 1864. Died at Elmira on or about April 9, 1865, of "hospital gangrene."

SOLOMON, JAMES A., Private
Resided in Stanly County where he enlisted at age 20, September 7, 1861. Court-martialed and "drummed out of camp [on November 24, 1861,] by reason of conduct unbecoming a soldier or a gentleman."

STOKER, EVAN A., Private
Resided in Stanly County where he enlisted at age 41, September 7, 1861. Mustered in as Private. Promoted to Commissary prior to November 1, 1861, but was reduced to ranks prior to December 29, 1861. Died at Wilmington on December 29, 1861, of disease.

SWARINGEN, HENRY C., Private
Resided in Cabarrus County and enlisted in New

Hanover County at age 18, February 4, 1862. Captured at Fredericksburg, Virginia, December 13, 1862. Exchanged on or about December 17, 1862. Returned to duty on an unspecified date. Killed at Gettysburg, Pennsylvania, July 3, 1863.

SWARINGEN, JOHN, Private
Resided in Stanly County and enlisted at age 18, September 7, 1861. Discharged prior to October 1, 1861. Reason discharged not reported.

SWARINGEN, WILBER F., Private
Resided in Cabarrus County and enlisted in New Hanover County at age 19, February 4, 1862. Wounded in the neck and captured at Gettysburg, Pennsylvania, July 3-4, 1863. Confined at Fort Delaware, Delaware. Paroled and transferred to City Point, Virginia, where he was received on August 1, 1863, for exchange. Returned to duty on August 26, 1863. Wounded and captured at or near Wilderness, Virginia, on or about May 12, 1864. Confined at Point Lookout, Maryland. Paroled and transferred to Cox's Wharf, James River, Virginia, where he was received on October 15, 1864, for exchange. Returned to duty prior to January 1, 1865. Surrendered at Appomattox Court House, Virginia, April 9, 1865.

THOMPSON, CALVIN C., Private
Resided in Stanly County where he enlisted at age 21, September 7, 1861. Captured at Hanover Court House, Virginia, May 27, 1862. Confined at Fort Monroe, Virginia, and at Fort Columbus, New York Harbor. Paroled and transferred to Aiken's Landing, James River, Virginia, where he was received on July 12, 1862, for exchange. Declared exchanged at Aiken's Landing on August 5, 1862. Returned to duty prior to January 1, 1863. Died "at his home" on January 13, 1865. Cause of death not reported.

THOMPSON, EDMUND R., Private
Resided in Stanly County where he enlisted at age 31, September 7, 1861. Captured at Hanover Court House, Virginia, on or about May 27, 1862. Confined at Fort Monroe, Virginia, and at Fort Columbus, New York Harbor. Paroled and transferred to Aiken's Landing, James River, Virginia, where he was received on July 12, 1862, for exchange. Declared exchanged at Aiken's Landing on August 5, 1862. Returned to duty prior to December 13, 1862, when he was killed at Fredericksburg, Virginia.

TOLBERT, JOSIAH P., Private
Resided in Stanly County where he enlisted at age 26, September 7, 1861. Captured at Hanover Court House, Virginia, May 27, 1862. Confined at Fort Monroe, Virginia, and at Fort Columbus, New York Harbor. Paroled and transferred to Aiken's Landing, James River, Virginia, where he was received on July 12, 1862, for exchange. Declared exchanged at Aiken's Landing on August 5, 1862. Returned to duty prior to January 1, 1863. Captured at or near Gravel Hill, Virginia, on or about July 28, 1864. Confined at Point Lookout, Maryland. Transferred to Elmira, New York, August 8, 1864. Released at Elmira on July 3, 1865, after taking the Oath of Allegiance.

TURNER, ENOCH, Private
Resided in Stanly County where he enlisted at age 26,

September 7, 1861. Captured at Hanover Court House, Virginia, May 27, 1862. Confined at Fort Monroe, Virginia, and at Fort Columbus, New York Harbor. Paroled and transferred to Aiken's Landing, James River, Virginia, where he was received on July 12, 1862, for exchange. Declared exchanged at Aiken's Landing on August 5, 1862. Died in hospital at Richmond, Virginia, December 13, 1862, of "typhoid fever."

VANHOY, AMOS, Private
Resided in Stanly County where he enlisted at age 18, September 7, 1861. Present or accounted for until he surrendered at Appomattox Court House, Virginia, April 9, 1865.

WHITE, CHARLES MALONE, Corporal
Resided in Cabarrus County and enlisted in New Hanover County at age 18, February 4, 1862. Mustered in as Private and was promoted to Corporal on September 5, 1864. Captured near Petersburg, Virginia, April 2, 1865. Confined at Point Lookout, Maryland. Released on June 21, 1865, after taking the Oath of Allegiance.

WHITLEY, GEORGE, 1st Sergeant
Born in Stanly County* where he resided as a farmer prior to enlisting in Stanly County at age 45, September 7, 1861. Mustered in as Private. Captured at Hanover Court House, Virginia, May 27, 1862. Confined at Fort Monroe, Virginia, and at Fort Columbus, New York Harbor. Paroled and transferred to Aiken's Landing, James River, Virginia, where he was received on July 12, 1862, for exchange. Declared exchanged at Aiken's Landing on August 5, 1862. Returned to duty and was promoted to 1st Sergeant on an unspecified date. Discharged on September 23, 1862, by reason of being overage. Paroled at Salisbury on May 19, 1865.

WHITLEY, JESSE J., Private
Resided in Stanly County where he enlisted on November 17, 1863, for the war. Captured near Petersburg, Virginia, April 2, 1865. Confined at Point Lookout, Maryland. Released on June 21, 1865, after taking the Oath of Allegiance.

WHITLEY, MONROE, Private
Enlisted at Liberty Mills, Virginia, April 1, 1864, for the war. Surrendered at Appomattox Court House, Virginia, April 9, 1865.

WHITLEY, THOMAS W., Private
Resided in Stanly County where he enlisted at age 27, March 20, 1862. Wounded at Chancellorsville, Virginia, May 2-3, 1863. Company records do not indicate whether he returned to duty. Hospitalized at Richmond, Virginia, July 20, 1864, with a gunshot wound. Place and date wounded not reported. Reported absent on furlough in September-October, 1864. Returned to duty in November-December, 1864. Surrendered at Appomattox Court House, Virginia, April 9, 1865.

WOOD, JOSHUA, Private
Born in Stanly County* where he resided as a farmer prior to enlisting in Stanly County at age 32, March 15, 1862. Discharged on August 23, 1862, by reason of "deafness in both ears, chronic rheumatism and general debility."

MISCELLANEOUS

The following list of names was compiled from primary records which indicate that these men served in the 28th Regiment N.C. Troops but do not indicate the companies to which they belonged.

BURNS, M. T., Private
Records of Company G, 63rd Regiment N.C. Troops (5th Regiment N.C. Cavalry) indicate he was transferred to the 28th Regiment N.C. Troops on March 8, 1865. No further records.

BURRIS, A. A., ———
North Carolina pension records indicate that he served in this regiment.

HYATT, MARTIN, Private
Resided in Wake County. Place and date of enlistment not reported. Deserted to the enemy on or about July 10, 1864. Confined at Bermuda Hundred, Virginia. Transferred to Fort Monroe, Virginia, on or about July 11, 1864. Released on or about July 17, 1864, after taking the Oath of Allegiance.

This regiment was composed of mountain-county companies and was organized at Camp Patton, Asheville, on September 24, 1861; it was then ordered to Camp Vance, near Sulphur Springs in Buncombe County, where it began training. On October 28 the regiment broke camp and moved to Raleigh, where it arrived on November 6 and was issued arms, equipment, and uniforms. The regiment left Raleigh on November 25 under orders to proceed to Jonesboro, Tennessee; it arrived at Haynesville Depot, near Jonesboro on the East Tennessee & Virginia Railroad, on November 30.

Because of the activities of the large pro-Union faction in eastern Tennessee, the situation in that region was, and remained, a source of grave concern to Confederate and North Carolina authorities. On December 3 the 29th Regiment, with three companies of the 3rd Battalion Georgia Infantry, was dispatched to Cocke County, Tennessee, to engage a band of Unionists reported gathering at or near the bend of the Chucky River in the vicinity of Parrottsville and Newport. The four-day expedition met with little success because the Unionists retired to the hills and offered only token resistance to the advancing Confederates. In an effort to establish Confederate authority in the region, three companies of the regiment were then stationed at Parrottsville and three were sent to Warrensburg. Shortly thereafter the entire regiment was detailed for duty at various posts and bridges between Haynesville Depot and Chattanooga, on the East Tennessee & Virginia and the East Tennessee & Georgia railroads. Colonel Robert Vance, commander of the 29th Regiment, established regimental headquarters at Knoxville; Companies A and E were stationed at Loudon; Companies B and C were at Chattanooga; Company D was detailed at Charleston; Company F was sent to Lick Creek Bridge; Company G was at Midway; Company H was at Strawberry Plains; Company I was at Morristown; and Company K was at Flat Creek Bridge.

The companies remained on detached service until February 20, 1862, when the 29th Regiment was ordered to Cumberland Gap and was assigned to the garrison commanded by Colonel James E. Rains. At Cumberland Gap in late March the regiment was under fire during a skirmish with a Federal force. When General Carter L. Stevenson assumed command of the Cumberland Gap defenses on or about April 1, the 29th Regiment was assigned to his brigade along with the 30th Regiment Alabama Infantry, 3rd Battalion Georgia Infantry, 42nd Regiment Georgia Infantry, 4th Regiment Tennessee Infantry, 11th Regiment Tennessee Infantry, several unattached infantry companies, the 3rd Battalion Tennessee Cavalry, and three batteries of artillery.

On April 29 a second Federal attack against Cumberland Gap was turned back. The Federal commander, General George W. Morgan, then moved his men through gaps to the south, flanked the Confederate defenses, and forced the Confederates to abandon their position. Following the evacuation of Cumberland Gap on June 18, General Stevenson fell back to Bean's Station, ten miles northwest of Morristown. The Confederate forces in East Tennessee, now under the overall command of General E. Kirby Smith, were then reorganized, and the recently promoted General James E. Rains assumed command of Stevenson's brigade after Stevenson was promoted to division commander. On July 3, 1862, the 29th Regiment was officially reported as a part of the Second Brigade (Rains) of the First Division (Stevenson) of the Department of East Tennessee. In addition to this regiment, Rains's brigade was composed of the 4th Regiment Tennessee Infantry, 11th Regiment Tennessee

Infantry, 42nd Regiment Georgia Infantry, 3rd Battalion Georgia Infantry, and a battery of artillery.

Early in August, 1862, General Smith, acting in cooperation with the army of General Braxton Bragg at Chattanooga, began to move his force of about 18,000 men against the Federal force at Cumberland Gap. On August 5 the 29th Regiment was involved in a skirmish at Tazewell; it was then detached from the main force and sent with several other units to Baptist Gap, about five miles south of Cumberland Gap.

General Smith, in the meantime, had found the Federal garrison at Cumberland Gap too strong to attack; and, leaving Stevenson's division to contain the Federals, he moved northward with 9,000 men on August 24 to support Bragg's invasion of Kentucky. On August 30 Smith routed a force of green Federal troops at Richmond, Kentucky, and on September 1 he entered Lexington. The Federals evacuated Cumberland Gap on September 17, and Stevenson's division, now rejoined by the 29th Regiment, occupied the position the next day. On September 19 the division marched to join Smith in Kentucky, and on October 2 Smith's reunited force encamped at Frankfort.

General Bragg's defeat by a greatly superior Federal army at Perryville on October 8 brought his and Smith's invasion of Kentucky to an abrupt end, and the two commanders retired with their forces into Tennessee. Rains's brigade retreated with Stevenson's division through Cumberland Gap and encamped at Bean's Station on October 25. After a few days' rest, the 29th Regiment moved to Lenoir Station, twenty miles southwest of Knoxville on the East Tennessee & Georgia Railroad; it remained there until ordered to Normandy Station, ten miles east of Shelbyville on the Nashville & Chattanooga Railroad, on November 15. Moving by rail, the regiment, with the rest of Rains's brigade, arrived at Normandy Station on November 18. On November 28 the brigade was moved ten miles east to Manchester, and on December 7 it was sent north to Readyville, near Murfreesboro, where it arrived three days later.

Early in December, 1862, General Smith was reassigned, and Rains's brigade was transferred to General John P. McCown's division of General William J. Hardee's corps of General Bragg's Army of Tennessee. The 29th Regiment was detached on December 18 and sent to McMinnville; on December 25 it was ordered to Murfreesboro, where it rejoined the brigade.

After their success against Bragg at Perryville the Federals took the offensive in Tennessee; and in late December, 1862, a Federal army of approximately 41,000 men under General William Rosecrans moved south from Nashville against Bragg's 35,000-man army at Murfreesboro. There Bragg had taken a position astride the shallow waters of Stones River with Hardee's corps on the east bank (the right of Bragg's line) and the corps of General Leonidas Polk on the west bank. After waiting in vain for an expected Federal attack on December 30, Bragg decided to attack the Federal right the next day and moved the divisions of McCown and General Patrick R. Cleburn west of the river. At the same time, Rosecrans was making plans of this own for an assault on the Confederate right.

Bragg struck first on the morning of December 31 and, after hard fighting, forced the Federal right wing back to a position perpendicular to the Federal center and parallel to the river. Rosecrans then cancelled his scheduled attack, called up reinforcements, and by early afternoon had fought the Confederates to a standstill. Two more determined Confederate assaults in the late afternoon were repulsed with heavy casualties to the attackers.

The next day, January 1, 1863, Rosecrans pushed a force across to the east bank of Stones River, and inconclusive fighting continued at other points along the lines. On January 2 Bragg suffered heavy casualties in attacking the Federals on the east bank; he abandoned the battlefield on January 3 and withdrew in the direction of Shelbyville. During the Battle of Murfreesboro (known also as Stones River) the 29th Regiment lost about sixty men killed and wounded. General Rains was killed in the assault of December 31, and Colonel Vance of the 29th Regiment was assigned to temporary command of the brigade.

At Shelbyville, Bragg's army established a defensive position and began reorganizing. Several regiments were transferred from Rains's (Vance's) brigade and several new units were added, so that the brigade was now composed of the 29th Regiment N.C. Troops, 39th Regiment N.C. Troops, 3rd Battalion Georgia Infantry, and the 9th Regiment Georgia Infantry. At the same time, General W. B. Bate was assigned to command the brigade, and General Alexander P. Stewart replaced McCown as commander of the division.

The 29th Regiment remained at Shelbyville until May 12, 1863, when it and the 39th Regiment were ordered to Mississippi. The regiment arrived at Jackson on May 18 and marched thirty miles to Canton, where General Joseph E. Johnston was organizing an army to move against the Federals besieging Vicksburg. After moving by rail to Vaughan's Station, forty miles north of Jackson, the regiment was assigned to Colonel Claudius C. Wilson's brigade of General W. H. T. Walker's division of Johnston's army. On June 1 the regiment moved to Yazoo City, where it remained on garrison duty until it was forced to evacuate, after the fall of Vicksburg, on July 13. The regiment rejoined Johnston's army at Morton on July 23 and was ordered to Meridian on July 27. It remained there until August 24, when it was incorporated into General Matthew Ector's brigade of Walker's division. In addition to the 29th Regiment, Ector's brigade was composed of Stone's Battalion Alabama Sharpshooters, Pound's Battalion Mississippi Sharpshooters, the 9th Regiment Texas Infantry, and the 10th, 14th, and 32nd Regiments Texas Cavalry (serving as infantry). Ector's brigade was ordered to join Bragg's army at Chattanooga and reached Chickamauga Station, south of Chattanooga, on August 30.

General Bragg, having been repeatedly outmaneuvered by Rosecrans during the latter's offensive in the summer of 1863, retired from Chattanooga on September 7-8. Rosecrans then pushed three widely separated columns into the rugged north Georgia mountains, where a major Federal disaster probably was averted during the second week of September thanks to the ineptness and timidity of several of Bragg's lieutenants. On the morning of September 19, by which time Rosecrans had succeeded in reuniting most of his command behind the west branch of Chickamauga Creek, heavy and extremely confused fighting broke out between the two armies and lasted the rest of the day. Neither side was able to gain a clear advantage. The next day a Confederate attack on the Federal left, in which Ector's brigade took part, was stalemated with heavy casualties, but an attack by General James Longstreet on the right struck a gap in the enemy lines and precipitated a near rout of the Federal army. Only the stubborn and courageous defense of General George H. Thomas's corps against furious Confederate attacks prevented a debacle and permitted Rosecrans to escape with his army into the Chattanooga fortifications.

During the battle the 29th Regiment lost about eighty men killed and wounded and thirty missing.

On September 22, 1863, Ector's brigade was ordered to rejoin General Joseph E. Johnston's army in Mississippi. The brigade traveled by rail to Meridian, where it arrived on October 2, and was assigned to General Samuel G. French's division. The division moved to Brandon, Mississippi, on December 5. On December 16 General Johnston was ordered to take command of the Army of Tennessee at Dalton, Georgia, and General Leonidas Polk replaced Johnston as commander of the Department of Mississippi, Alabama, and East Louisiana.

Ector's brigade remained at Brandon until early January, 1864; it then moved to Meridian, where Polk was concentrating his command against a Federal force under General William T. Sherman. When Sherman advanced on Meridian, Polk retired to Demopolis, Alabama. Sherman's men occupied Meridian on February 14 and destroyed the town before retiring on February 20. Polk's infantry remained at Demopolis until ordered to Georgia in early May.

The Federal army in the Chattanooga area, under the direction of General Sherman, advanced against Johnston's position at Dalton, Georgia, on May 5, and Polk was ordered to move his force to Rome in support of Johnston. From Rome, Polk moved one of his divisions, commanded by General W. W. Loring, north to Resaca, just south of Johnston's position at Dalton. When it became evident that the main Federal thrust would be against Resaca, Johnston retired there and joined Loring. Ector's brigade, which was still a part of French's division, remained temporarily at Rome.

On the night of May 15 Johnston, dissatisfied with his position at Resaca, retreated to Calhoun, where he was joined by Polk's command; Johnston then fell back to Adairsville, Cassville, and Allatoona Pass. Declining to attack the strong Confederate position at Allatoona Pass, Sherman then cut loose from the Western & Atlantic Railroad, whose tracks he had been following, and marched south toward Dallas. Johnston followed, and on May 25 the two armies were engaged at New Hope Church. (At about this time the 39th Regiment N.C. Troops was assigned to Ector's brigade.) Skirmishing continued on May 26, and on May 27 new fighting broke out at Pickett's Mill. With his left flank in danger of being turned, Johnston retreated southeastward toward Marietta. Skirmishing between the two armies continued on a daily basis, and the 29th Regiment lost 2 men killed, 24 wounded, and 28 missing in fighting at or near Lattimer's Mills.

On June 8 Johnston fell back again to a strong position at Kennesaw Mountain, just northwest of Marietta. One division was left at Pine Mountain, several miles in advance of the Kennesaw Mountain line, and it was while observing the enemy from Pine Mountain that General Polk was killed on June 14. General Loring was appointed temporary commander of Polk's corps, and the division at Pine Mountain was pulled back to Kennesaw Mountain. Loring's corps held the right of the defensive line while Johnston's other two corps, commanded by Generals William J. Hardee and John B. Hood, held the center and left respectively. On June 27 two Federal assaults against the Confederate position were repulsed with heavy casualties to the attackers.

Sherman then reverted to his previous tactic of extending his line beyond the flank of the outnumbered Confederates, and Johnston retired during the darkness on July 2 to a prepared position along a ridge behind Nickjack Creek, which crossed the Western & Atlantic Railroad at

Smyrna, about six miles south of Marietta. Loring's corps was on the right of the line near Smyrna and received the brunt of an attack launched by the Federals on July 4. The 29th Regiment was actively engaged and lost 2 men killed, 8 wounded, and 27 missing. Johnston then withdrew to a position on the Chattahoochee River, which he occupied on July 5. On July 7 the corps previously commanded by Polk and Loring was assigned to General Alexander P. Stewart. Thus the 29th Regiment was now a part of Ector's brigade of French's division of Stewart's corps.

Sherman quickly moved up his army on the track of Johnston, and on July 8 he began fording the Chattahoochee upstream from the Confederate position. Johnston fell back to a defensive position on Peachtree Creek, north of Atlanta. By July 10 Johnston was in position on a line which began at the Western & Atlantic Railroad (about two miles south of the Chattahoochee River) on the left (west), extended six miles east to the confluence of Peachtree and Pea Vine creeks, and then turned south until it crossed the Georgia Railroad between Atlanta and Decatur. Stewart's corps was on the left on Peachtree Creek.

Johnston's withdrawals through north Georgia during the summer of 1864, although skillful, were both unproductive and self-defeating in the view of Confederate President Jefferson Davis, and on July 17 he replaced Johnston with one of the latter's corps commanders, General John B. Hood. Having no option other than to take the offensive, Hood launched a furious but poorly conducted, costly, and unsuccessful attack in which Stewart's corps took part. During the Battle of Peachtree Creek on July 20 the 29th Regiment lost twenty-eight men missing.

Hood then fell back to the fortifications of Atlanta and prepared to defend the city. Heavy fighting broke out on July 22 and, at Ezra Church, just west of Atlanta, on July 27. (General Ector was wounded on the latter date and was succeeded temporarily by Colonel William H. Young of the 9th Regiment Texas Infantry.) During August Sherman pursued a strategy of extending his lines west and south of Atlanta in order to cut Hood's railroad communications. Hood sought to match the Federal extensions, and by August 25 the lines had reached a point near the railroad junction at East Point. The brigade's activities during the period were described by Colonel Young as follows (*Official Records*, Series I, Vol. XXXVIII, pt. 3, p. 911):

From the 5th [of August] to the 27th the daily routine of service in the brigade was almost unvaried. From one to two regiments constantly occupied the picket-line; they successfully prevented the further advance of the enemy, and were constantly exposed to heavy fire of small-arms and occasionally from artillery. The other regiments lay behind the main works.

On August 26 Sherman made a new and powerful thrust to the south which quickly resulted in the severing of both the West Point and the Macon & Western railroads. While Stewart's corps remained behind to hold the Atlanta fortifications, Hood's other two corps, under Hardee and Stephen D. Lee, moved south to attempt to dislodge the Federals from the Macon & Western Railroad at Jonesboro. After an unsuccessful two-day battle during which two brigades of Hardee's corps were virtually destroyed, the Confederate force retreated from Jonesboro to Lovejoy's Station, just south of Jonesboro. There it was joined by Stewart's corps and Hood, who had evacuated

Atlanta on September 1. During the Atlanta campaign the 29th Regiment lost 1 man killed, 20 wounded, and 4 missing.

Following Sherman's occupation of Atlanta, the two armies maintained their respective positions until September 21 when Hood shifted his forces to Palmetto, about twenty-two miles northeast of Lovejoy's Station. Convinced that Sherman had relinquished the initiative and intended to rest on his laurels in Atlanta, Hood moved his army northward on October 1 to strike the Federal supply line on the Western & Atlantic Railroad. On October 4 General Stewart's corps captured the Federal garrisons at Acworth and Big Shanty, on the railroad just north of Marietta, and tore up fifteen miles of track. The next day French's division of Stewart's corps was sent to capture a major Federal supply depot at Allatoona, about five miles north of Acworth. French's men succeeded in driving the determined Federal defenders from two of their three redoubts but broke off the attack when a false report was received that Federal reinforcements were at hand. French then ordered his men to withdraw. Major E. H. Hampton reported the 29th Regiment's part in the Battle of Allatoona as follows (*Official Records*, Series I, Vol. XXXIX, pt. 1, pp. 820-821):

My regiment was formed on the left of Young's brigade on the 5th of October, at 9 a.m., ready for the action at Allatoona. At 10 a.m. we were ordered forward upon the enemy. My regiment moved forward as a unit through the timber, which was very thick. The enemy were meanwhile pouring a heavy fire into our ranks. My regiment had to advance through the forest farther than the other regiments of the brigade, and not being able to see the brigade got separated from and in advance of the brigade. Upon arriving to where the timber was all felled I saw my regiment was separated from the other regiments, and being exposed to a heavy fire from the enemy, and supposing the remainder of the brigade to be in advance, I ordered my regiment forward at a double-quick to within forty feet of the enemy's outer works, where I halted, ordered my men to lie down, rest, and load. After resting from three to five minutes, I ordered my regiment forward. The order was promptly obeyed. They moved into the enemy's works, where they had a hand-to-hand encounter with sword, bayonet, butt of muskets, rocks, &c., killing a good many and capturing 25 or 30 prisoners and the enemy's intrenchments; thence the regiment moved forward to within twenty yards of the foe's last and strong fort, where they remained contending with the enemy until withdrawn by order of Major-General French, when they fell back in good order.

I took 138 aggregate into the action and came out minus 12 killed, 39 wounded, and 3 missing.

Following the battle at Allatocna, Hood moved his army to the northwest and crossed the Coosa River west of Rome on October 10. Sherman, unable to come to grips with the elusive Hood, moved toward Rome and ordered General George H. Thomas, who had been sent back to Tennessee with his corps in September, to guard against a Confederate crossing of the Tennessee River west of Chattanooga. Hood then turned back to the northeast, struck the Western & Atlantic Railroad again at Resaca, and moved to Dalton, where he captured the garrison on October 13. After tearing up twenty miles of track between Resaca and Tunnel Hill, Hood marched west to Gadsden, Alabama. On October 22 he moved to Tuscumbia,

Alabama, where he awaited the arrival of supplies before crossing the Tennessee River. Sherman, convinced that Thomas would be able to deal with Hood, moved his army back to Atlanta and made preparations for his march to the sea.

Hood's men began fording the Tennessee on November 2 but were delayed by bad weather and high water, and it was not until three weeks later that the crossing was completed. Hood then moved against Columbia, hoping to seize the Duck River bridges there and cut off a large Federal force under General John Schofield south of the Duck at Pulaski. After a difficult march during which they encountered rain, sleet, and snow, Hood's men arrived at Columbia to find Schofield's force awaiting them. Hood then attempted to flank the Federals by crossing the Duck east of Columbia, whereupon Schofield, narrowly escaping entrapment, withdrew to Franklin.

Closely followed by Hood, who blamed the Federals' narrow escape on the lethargy of two of his corps commanders, Schofield arrived at Franklin on the morning of November 30 and, finding his crossing of the Harpeth River would be delayed until bridge repairs had been completed, formed a defensive line. Hood, still furious over Schofield's escape at Columbia, ordered his men forward in a frontal assault which produced some of the bloodiest and most desperate fighting of the war. After some initial gains, the frantic attackers were driven back with murderous losses. Hood's army of approximately 24,000 men suffered about 6,000 casualties while Schofield, with about the same number of men, lost 2,000. No casualties were suffered by the 29th Regiment, which was on detached service.

Schofield then withdrew to Nashville and united his command with that of Thomas while Hood, bloodied but still advancing, moved in behind Schofield and began entrenching in the hills south of Nashville. Now outnumbered by a margin of better than two to one, Hood hoped to entice Thomas into attacking him in a defensive position.

On December 15 Thomas launched a massive attack against the Confederate left, which was held by Stewart's corps, drove Ector's brigade (now commanded by Colonel David Coleman of the 39th Regiment N.C. Troops) from the field, and forced Hood to fall back to a new defensive line. The next day a new Federal assault smashed into the corps of General Benjamin F. Cheatham and sent it fleeing in confusion. Stewart's men also fell back in great disarray, and only a stubborn rear-guard action by the corps of General Stephen D. Lee and a heavy rain permitted the Confederates to escape down the road to Franklin.

Although Hood had managed to save a part of his army, the Battle of Nashville was an irredeemable catastrophe for the South because the Army of Tennessee, demoralized and decimated, was destroyed as an effective fighting force. The casualties of the 29th Regiment at Nashville were not reported.

Hood recrossed the Tennessee near Florence with what remained of his army on December 25 and 26, moved through Tuscumbia to Iuka, Mississippi, and from there proceeded to Corinth and Tupelo, where he went into camp on January 10, 1865. Soon after reaching Tupelo, French's division was sent to Mobile to reinforce the garrison commanded by General Dabney H. Maury. Ector's brigade was stationed at Spanish Fort on Mobile Bay and was under siege by Federal forces under General Edward Canby from March 27 until April 8, when the fort was evacuated. Some members of the garrison then retired to nearby Fort Blakely and some moved to Mobile. When Fort Blakely fell on April 9, General Maury evacuated

Mobile and retired with his command to Meridian, Mississippi, where he awaited word on the negotiations to surrender the troops of the Department of Mississippi, Alabama, and East Louisiana. On May 8, 1865, General Richard Taylor, commander of the department, surrendered all of his forces, including the remnants of the 29th Regiment N.C. Troops.

FIELD AND STAFF

COLONELS

VANCE, ROBERT BRANK

Resided in Buncombe County and enlisted at age 33. Appointed Colonel on September 11, 1861. Promoted to Brigadier General on March 16, 1863, and transferred.

CREASMAN, WILLIAM B.

Previously served as Captain of Company B of this regiment. Appointed Major on June 26, 1862, and transferred to the Field and Staff. Promoted to Lieutenant Colonel on March 16, 1863. Promoted to Colonel on September 8, 1863. Resigned on or about December 29, 1864. Reason he resigned not reported.

LIEUTENANT COLONELS

WALKER, WILLIAM C.

Previously served as Captain of Company A of this regiment. Appointed Lieutenant Colonel on September 24, 1861, and transferred to the Field and Staff. Declined to stand for reelection when the regiment was reorganized on May 2, 1862.

LOWRY, JAMES MARION

Previously served as Captain of Company C of this regiment. Appointed Lieutenant Colonel on May 2, 1862, and transferred to the Field and Staff. Resigned on June 6, 1862, by reason of "a severe case of typhoid fever." Resignation accepted on June 26, 1862.

GARDNER, THOMAS F.

Previously served as 2nd Lieutenant in Company B of this regiment. Appointed Major on September 24, 1861, and transferred to the Field and Staff. Promoted to Lieutenant Colonel on June 26, 1862. Captured by the enemy in the autumn of 1862. Exchanged at or near Vicksburg, Mississippi, on or about December 4, 1862. Resigned on March 2, 1863, by reason of "chronic diarrhoea of five months' standing consequent on an attack of pneumonia, with which he was attacked in Kentucky [and] in consequence of which he fell into the hands of the Yankees and the exposure he suffered while in their hands greatly ag[g]r[a]vated his disease." Resignation accepted on March 16, 1863.

PROFFITT, BACCHUS S.

Previously served as Captain of Company K of this regiment. Appointed Major on October 29, 1863, to rank from March 16, 1863, and transferred to the Field and Staff. Promoted to Lieutenant Colonel on March 7, 1864. Died near Demopolis, Alabama, March 21, 1865.

MAJOR

HAMPTON, EZEKIEL H.

Previously served as Captain of Company G of this regiment. Appointed Major on August 15, 1864, to rank from March 16, 1863, and transferred to the Field and

Staff. No further records.

ADJUTANTS

HOEY, JOHN E.

Previously served as Sergeant in Company E, 12th Regiment N.C. Troops (2nd Regiment N.C. Volunteers). Appointed Adjutant (1st Lieutenant) of this regiment on November 6, 1861. Wounded at Murfreesboro, Tennessee, on or about December 31, 1862. Wounded in the left ankle at Chickamauga, Georgia, September 19, 1863. Transferred to North Carolina for light duty as an enrolling officer prior to March 1, 1864. ["The conduct of Adjutant Hoey (at the battle of Murfreesboro) was the subject of general admiration, he having borne himself throughout the conflict with most daring gallantry."]

ROBERTS, ERVIN F.

Served as 2nd Lieutenant in Company D of this regiment. Reported on duty as acting Adjutant of this regiment during January-March, 1864.

ASSISTANT QUARTERMASTERS

NEILL, JAMES R.

Previously served as 1st Sergeant of Company K of this regiment. Appointed Assistant Quartermaster (Captain) on November 26, 1861, to rank from September 25, 1861. Resigned on June 2, 1862, by reason of being "physically unable to discharge the arduous duties devolving upon me." Resignation accepted on June 12, 1862. Later served as Quartermaster of the 111th Regiment N.C. Militia.

HERNDON, EDWARD W.

Previously served as 1st Lieutenant of Company F, 14th Regiment N.C. Troops (4th Regiment N.C. Volunteers). Appointed Assistant Quartermaster (Captain) of this regiment on October 4, 1862, to rank from June 12, 1862. Promoted to Quartermaster (Major) of Brigadier General Robert B. Vance's brigade on July 23, 1863, to rank from July 8, 1863, and transferred.

WEAVER, WILLIAM ELBERT

Previously served as Color Sergeant of this regiment. [See Ensigns and Color Sergeants' section below.] Appointed Assistant Quartermaster (Captain) on July 23, 1863, to rank from July 2, 1863. Paroled at Meridian, Mississippi, May 9, 1865.

ASSISTANT COMMISSARIES OF SUBSISTENCE

McKEE, ROBERT FIDELIO

Previously served as 1st Lieutenant of Company C of this regiment. Appointed Assistant Commissary of Subsistence (Captain) on December 24, 1861, and transferred to the Field and Staff. "Dropped" on August 2, 1862. Reason he was dropped not reported.

PLEMMONS, DAVID S.

Previously served as Private in Company C of this regiment. Appointed Assistant Commissary of Subsistence (Captain) on October 4, 1862, to rank from August 2, 1862, and transferred to the Field and Staff. Last reported in the records of this regiment on April 15, 1863.

SURGEONS

YANCEY, JOHN

Resided in Buncombe County. Appointed Surgeon of this regiment on October 4, 1861. Resigned on May 23, 1862, by reason of "decline of health, my age (55 years) & constitution. . . ."

NEILSON, MORGAN L.

Appointed Surgeon of this regiment on July 11, 1862, to rank from May 20, 1862. Resigned on or about March 4, 1863, by reason of disability.

MURDOCH, WILLIAM HENRY

Previously served as Assistant Surgeon of the 39th Regiment N.C. Troops. Appointed Surgeon of this regiment on March 4, 1863; however, his appointment was disapproved by the Surgeon General and he resigned. Later served as Chief Surgeon, District of Western North Carolina, and as Assistant Surgeon of the 69th Regiment N.C. Troops (7th Regiment N.C. Cavalry).

GORDON, GILBERT EUGENE

Previously served as Surgeon of the 29th Regiment Tennessee Infantry and the 9th Regiment Texas Cavalry. Appointed Surgeon of this regiment on or about August 1, 1863. Took the Oath of Allegiance at Meridian, Mississippi, May 9, 1865.

ASSISTANT SURGEONS

SHAFFNER, JOHN F.

Previously served as Assistant Surgeon of the 21st Regiment N.C. Troops (11th Regiment N.C. Volunteers). Reported on duty as Assistant Surgeon of this regiment in October, 1861. Later served as Surgeon of the 33rd Regiment N.C. Troops.

LOVE, WILLIAM

Resided in Haywood County and was by occupation a lawyer. Appointed Assistant Surgeon of this regiment on or about October 29, 1861. Resigned on September 10, 1863, by reason of having been elected solicitor of Transylvania County.

MAYO, ALBERT S.

Resided in Powhatan County, Virginia, and enlisted at age 22. Appointed Assistant Surgeon on November 10, 1863. Last reported in the records of this regiment on April 28, 1865.

CHAPLAINS

CHASTAIN, ABNER

Previously served as Corporal in Company E of this regiment. Appointed Chaplain on October 11, 1861, and transferred to the Field and Staff. Resigned on January 11, 1862, by reason of "his age (59 years) & feeble health."

TAYLOR, GREENFIELD

Appointed Chaplain on July 11, 1862, to rank from May 20, 1862, but declined the appointment.

WILSON, GEORGE W.

Previously served as Private in Company K of this regiment. Appointed Chaplain on July 8, 1863, to rank from June 29, 1863. Resigned on September 2, 1864, by reason of "being called on by the denomination to which I belong to labor in another field."

COLLIS, S. M.

Clark's *Regiments* indicates he served as Chaplain of this regiment. No further records.

WEXLER, E. C.

Clark's *Regiments* indicates he served as Chaplain of this regiment. No further records.

ENSIGNS AND COLOR SERGEANTS

WEAVER, WILLIAM ELBERT

Previously served as 1st Sergeant of Company H of this regiment. Promoted to Color Sergeant on an unspecified date and transferred to the Field and Staff. Appointed Assistant Quartermaster (Captain) of this regiment on July 23, 1863, to rank from July 2, 1863. [See Assistant Quartermasters' section above.]

RICH, JOHN R.

Born in Buncombe County where he resided prior to enlisting at age 19, August 6, 1861. Mustered in as Color Sergeant. Appointed Ensign (1st Lieutenant) on October 28, 1864, to rank from September 24, 1864. Took the Oath of Allegiance at Waynesville on March 1, 1865.

SERGEANTS MAJOR

ROLLINS, WALLACE W.

Previously served as 1st Sergeant of Company D of this regiment. Promoted to Sergeant Major on an unspecified date and transferred to the Field and Staff. Appointed Captain on May 2, 1862, and transferred back to Company D.

McELROY, JAMES G.

Previously served as Private in Company H of this regiment. Appointed Sergeant Major in 1862 and transferred to the Field and Staff. Appointed Assistant Commissary of Subsistence (Captain) to rank from December 13, 1862, and transferred to the Field and Staff, 16th Regiment N.C. Troops (6th Regiment N.C. Volunteers).

PATTON, HENRY C.

Previously served as Corporal in Company H of this regiment. Promoted to Sergeant Major on March 23, 1863, and transferred to the Field and Staff. Wounded at Chickamauga, Georgia, September 19-20, 1863. Last reported in the records of this regiment on June 27, 1864.

ELLIOTT, K. C.

Previously served as Private in Company G of this regiment. Promoted to Sergeant Major prior to April 8, 1865, and transferred to the Field and Staff. Captured at Spanish Fort, Mobile, Alabama, April 8, 1865. Confined at Ship Island, Mississippi, April 10, 1865. Transferred to Vicksburg, Mississippi, May 1, 1865. No further records.

QUARTERMASTER SERGEANTS

ENLOE, J. W.

Born in Jackson County* where he resided as a clerk

prior to enlisting in Jackson County at age 24, October 15, 1861. Mustered in as Quartermaster Sergeant. Discharged on April 8, 1862, by reason of "phthisis pulmonalis." Later served as "Lieutenant" of Company F of this regiment.

BROWN, WILLIAM ALBERT GALLATIN

Previously served as Private in Company D of this regiment. Promoted to Quartermaster Sergeant and transferred to the Field and Staff on October 1, 1863. Surrendered at Citronelle, Alabama, May 4, 1865. Paroled at Meridian, Mississippi, May 9, 1865.

COMMISSARY SERGEANTS

WELLS, WILLIAM F.

Previously served as Private in Company C of this regiment. Promoted to Commissary Sergeant in November, 1861, and transferred to the Field and Staff. Appointed 2nd Lieutenant on May 2, 1862, and transferred back to Company C.

PLEMMONS, LEVI

Previously served as Private in Company C of this regiment. Promoted to Commissary Sergeant on May 2, 1862, and transferred to the Field and Staff. Surrendered at Citronelle, Alabama, May 4, 1865. Paroled at Meridian, Mississippi, May 9, 1865.

ORDNANCE SERGEANTS

SMITH, LUCIUS H.

Previously served as Private in Company H of this regiment. Promoted to Ordnance Sergeant on an unspecified date and transferred to the Field and Staff. Appointed Adjutant (1st Lieutenant) on January 3, 1863, to rank from August 1, 1862, and transferred to the 64th Regiment N.C. Troops.

McGREGOR, DOUGALD

Previously served as Private in Company H of this regiment. Promoted to Ordnance Sergeant on July 20, 1863, and transferred to the Field and Staff. Last reported in the records of this regiment on October 13, 1863.

DRILLMASTER

ROULHAC, THOMAS R.

Place and date of enlistment not reported. Served as Drillmaster of this regiment from September 30, 1861, through January 1, 1862. No further records.

HOSPITAL STEWARDS

SMITH, JOSEPH H.

Previously served as Private in Company H of this regiment. Promoted to Hospital Steward on March 17, 1862, and transferred to the Field and Staff. No further records.

WELLS, JACOB W.

Previously served in Company C of this regiment. Promoted to Hospital Steward and transferred to the Field and Staff on an unspecified date subsequent to September 30, 1863. Surrendered at Citronelle, Alabama, May 4, 1865. Paroled at Meridian, Mississippi, May 9, 1865.

COMPANY A

This company, known as the "Cherokee Guards," was raised in Cherokee County and enlisted on June 17, 1861. It was then assigned to the 29th Regiment and designated Company A. After joining the regiment the company functioned as a part of the regiment, and its history for the war period is reported as a part of the regimental history.

The following company roster is based primarily on the North Carolina Roll of Honor, prisoner of war records, pension applications, and a variety of miscellaneous records. Information was obtained also from secondary sources such as postwar histories, cemetery records, and records of the United Daughters of the Confederacy. No muster rolls were located for the company.

OFFICERS

CAPTAINS

WALKER, WILLIAM C.

Resided in Cherokee County and enlisted at age 40. Appointed Captain on June 17, 1861. Promoted to Lieutenant Colonel on September 24, 1861, and transferred to the Field and Staff of this regiment.

ANDERSON, JAMES STANHOPE

Resided in Cherokee County and enlisted at age 26. Appointed 1st Lieutenant on June 17, 1861. Promoted to Captain on September 24, 1861. Resigned on February 16, 1863, by reason of "inguinal hernia."

SHEARER, JAMES M.

Resided in Cherokee County or in Berrien County, Georgia, and enlisted at age 26, June 17, 1861. Mustered in as 1st Sergeant and was appointed 2nd Lieutenant on September 24, 1861. Promoted to 1st Lieutenant on May 2, 1862, and was promoted to Captain on February 16, 1863. Captured at Chickamauga, Georgia, September 19-20, 1863. Confined at Louisville, Kentucky. Transferred to Johnson's Island, Ohio, where he arrived on October 7, 1863. Transferred to Point Lookout, Maryland, March 21, 1865. Confined at Fort Delaware, Delaware, April 28, 1865. Released on June 12, 1865, after taking the Oath of Allegiance.

LIEUTENANTS

HILL, ABEL S., 2nd Lieutenant

Resided in Cherokee County and enlisted at age 24, February, 1862, as a substitute. Mustered in as Private. Appointed 2nd Lieutenant on March 12, 1863. Company records indicate he was captured on April 25, 1864; however, records of the Federal Provost Marshal do not substantiate that report. Dropped from the rolls of the company on February 17, 1865.

HILL, NAPOLEON B., 1st Lieutenant

Resided in Cherokee County and enlisted at age 29, June 17, 1861. Mustered in as Private and was promoted to 3rd Lieutenant on November 4, 1861. Promoted to 1st Lieutenant on February 16, 1863. Reported absent without leave on or about May 17, 1864. Failed to return to duty and was dropped from the rolls of the company on February 17, 1865.

JOHNSON, JOHN J., 2nd Lieutenant

Resided in Cherokee County and enlisted at age 23, June 17, 1861. Mustered in as Private and was appointed 2nd Lieutenant on May 2, 1862. Resigned on September 17, 1862. Reason he resigned not reported.

LOUDERMILK, GEORGE M., 2nd Lieutenant

Resided in Cherokee County and enlisted at age 41. Appointed 2nd Lieutenant on June 17, 1861. Resigned on November 8, 1861. Reason he resigned not reported.

NELSON, WILLIAM B., 1st Lieutenant

Born in Hall County, Georgia, and resided in Cherokee County where he was by occupation a farmer prior to enlisting at age 39. Appointed 2nd Lieutenant on June 17, 1861, and was promoted to 1st Lieutenant on September 24, 1861. Defeated for reelection when the regiment was reorganized on or about May 2, 1862. Later served as Captain of Company B, Walker's Battalion, Thomas Legion.

PLYLER, M. A., 2nd Lieutenant

Place and date of enlistment not reported. Promotion record not reported. Name appears as signature to a parole datelined Meridian, Mississippi, May 9, 1865.

NONCOMMISSIONED OFFICERS AND PRIVATES

ADAMS, ASAPH L., Private

Resided in Cherokee County and enlisted at age 18, June 17, 1861. Discharged in May, 1862, "for dishonorable conduct." Took the Oath of Allegiance in eastern Tennessee in January, 1864.

ADAMS, DAVID P., Private

Resided in Cherokee County and enlisted at age 20, June 17, 1861. No further records.

ALLEN, BENTON C., Private

Enlisted on April 1, 1864, for the war. Captured at Allatoona, Georgia, October 5, 1864. Confined at Nashville, Tennessee, and at Louisville, Kentucky. Transferred to Camp Douglas, Chicago, Illinois, where he arrived on November 26, 1864. Died at Camp Douglas on or about February 9, 1865, of "typhoid fever."

ALLEN, WILLIAM E., Private

Resided in Cherokee or Yancey County and enlisted at age 26, June 17, 1861. Deserted in September, 1863. Later served in Company G of this regiment.

ANDERSON, J. H., Private

Resided in Alamance County. Place and date of enlistment not reported. Surrendered at Citronelle, Alabama, May 4, 1865, and was paroled at Meridian, Mississippi, May 9, 1865.

BELL, SAMUEL, Private

Resided in Cherokee County and enlisted at age 19, June 17, 1861. Deserted in April, 1862.

BLACKWELL, ELISHA, Private

Resided in Cherokee County and enlisted at age 24, June 17, 1861. Deserted in June, 1863.

BOONE, WILLIAM S., Private

Resided in Cherokee County and enlisted at age 28, June 17, 1861. Present or accounted for through August

8, 1863. No further records.

BOWERS, GEORGE W., Private
Resided in Cherokee County and enlisted at age 23, February, 1863, for the war. Deserted in September, 1863. Went over to the enemy on an unspecified date. Took the Oath of Allegiance at Chattanooga, Tennessee, on or about February 18, 1864.

BOWERS, JAMES L., Private
Resided in Cherokee County and enlisted at age 20, June 17, 1861. Deserted in May, 1863.

BOWMAN, ABEL, Private
Resided in Alexander County and enlisted at age 22, August 9, 1862, for the war. Captured near Marietta, Georgia, July 3, 1864. Sent to Knoxville, Tennessee. Confined at Louisville, Kentucky, July 14, 1864. Transferred to Camp Douglas, Chicago, Illinois, where he arrived on July 18, 1864. Released on May 13, 1865, after taking the Oath of Allegiance.

BRADLEY, B. G., Private
Previously served in Company D, Mallett's N.C. Battalion (Camp Guard). Place and date of enlistment in this company not reported. Captured at Spanish Fort, Mobile, Alabama, April 8, 1865. Confined at Ship Island, Mississippi. Transferred to Vicksburg, Mississippi, where he arrived on May 6, 1865. No further records.

BROWN, JAMES M., Private
Resided in Buncombe or Rowan County and enlisted at age 17, August 6, 1861. Captured at Allatoona, Georgia, October 5, 1864. Sent to Nashville, Tennessee. Transferred to Louisville, Kentucky, where he arrived November 22, 1864. Transferred to Camp Douglas, Chicago, Illinois, where he arrived on November 26, 1864. Released on July 17, 1865, after taking the Oath of Allegiance.

BROWN, JOHN, ———
North Carolina pension records indicate that he served in this company.

CABE, LUCIUS H., Private
Resided in Cherokee County and enlisted at age 18, July 17, 1861. Discharged in May, 1862, by reason of "dishonorable conduct."

CANUP, EPPIE M., Private
Born in Haywood County and resided in Cherokee County where he was by occupation a farmer prior to enlisting at age 19, June 17, 1861. Deserted in July, 1862. Later served in Company I, Infantry Regiment, Thomas Legion.

CANUP, FRANCIS M., Private
Born in Haywood County and resided in Cherokee County where he was by occupation a farmer prior to enlisting at age 26, June 17, 1861. Deserted in July, 1862. Later served in Company I, Infantry Regiment, Thomas Legion.

CARRINGER, JOHN B., Private
Resided in Cherokee County and enlisted at age 29, June 17, 1861. Deserted in February, 1862. Went over to the enemy on an unspecified date and took the Oath of Allegiance in Blount County, Tennessee, January 28,

1864.

CARRINGER, WILLIAM H., Private
Born in Cherokee County* where he resided as a farmer prior to enlisting at age 32, June 17, 1861. Discharged in October, 1861. Reason discharged not reported. Later served in Company F, Walker's Battalion, Thomas Legion.

CARTER, BENJAMIN F., Private
Born in Yadkin County* and resided in Cherokee County where he was by occupation a farmer prior to enlisting at age 22, June 17, 1861. Discharged in October, 1861. Reason discharged not reported. Later served in Company B, Walker's Battalion, Thomas Legion.

CARTER, ISAAC, Commissary
Resided in Cherokee County and enlisted at age 39, June 17, 1861. Promotion record not reported. Discharged on September 16, 1862. Reason discharged not reported.

CASE, JOHN J., Private
Resided in Cherokee County and enlisted at age 32, June 17, 1861. Transferred to Company E, 25th Regiment N.C. Troops, August 24, 1861, in exchange for Private George W. Fisher.

CHASTAIN, JOHN G., Private
Resided in Cherokee County and enlisted at age 31, June 17, 1861. Present or accounted for through April 29, 1863, when he was reported on duty at or near Shelbyville, Tennessee, as a teamster. No further records.

COFFEE, NOAH R., Private
Resided in Cherokee County and enlisted at age 21, January, 1863, for the war. Wounded at Chickamauga, Georgia, September 19-20, 1863. Hospitalized at Augusta, Georgia, where he died on October 16, 1863, of wounds.

COFFEE, RICE, Private
Born in Wilkes County and resided in Cherokee County where he was by occupation a farmer prior to enlisting in Cherokee County at age 59, June 17, 1861. Discharged on June 28, 1862, by reason of "advanced age" and "a shattered constitution."

COFFEE, ROBERT A., Private
Resided in Cherokee or Clay County and enlisted at age 20, June 17, 1861. Deserted to the enemy on an unspecified date. Confined at Nashville, Tennessee. Transferred to Louisville, Kentucky. Released on or about December 22, 1863, after taking the Oath of Allegiance.

COFFEY, JAMES M., Private
Resided in Cherokee or Clay County and enlisted at age 17, June 17, 1861. Captured in hospital at Grenada, Mississippi, August 17, 1863. Sent to Nashville, Tennessee. Transferred to Louisville, Kentucky, where he arrived on or about December 24, 1863. Released prior to January 1, 1864, after taking the Oath of Allegiance.

COFFEY, JOHN R., Sergeant
Resided in Cherokee County and enlisted at age 20,

June 17, 1861. Mustered in as Private and was promoted to Sergeant prior to September 19, 1863. Captured near Chickamauga, Georgia, September 19, 1863. Sent to Nashville, Tennessee. Confined at Louisville, Kentucky, September 30, 1863. Transferred to Camp Douglas, Chicago, Illinois, where he arrived on October 4, 1863. Released on June 16, 1865, after taking the Oath of Allegiance.

CROMWELL, WILLIAM O., Private
Born in Surry County and resided in Cherokee County where he was by occupation a farmer prior to enlisting at age 55, June 17, 1861. Discharged in February, 1862. Reason discharged not reported. Later served in Company E, Walker's Battalion, Thomas Legion.

DAGENHART, JULIUS, Private
Born in Alexander County and was by occupation a farmer. Place and date of enlistment not reported. Captured near Marietta, Georgia, July 3-5, 1864. Sent to Nashville, Tennessee. Confined at Louisville, Kentucky, July 14, 1864. Transferred to Camp Douglas, Chicago, Illinois, where he arrived on July 18, 1864. Released on March 24, 1865, after joining the U.S. Army. Assigned to Company D, 6th Regiment U.S. Volunteer Infantry.

DAMERON, HENRY W., Sergeant
Resided in Cherokee County and enlisted at age 27, June 17, 1861. Mustered in as Private. Promoted to Sergeant on an unspecified date. Present or accounted for through June 30, 1864. No further records.

DAVIS, BENJAMIN F., Private
Resided in Cherokee County and enlisted on June 17, 1861. Deserted in May, 1863. Went over to the enemy on an unspecified date. Took the Oath of Allegiance at Knoxville, Tennessee, January 23, 1864.

DAVIS, WILLIAM L., Corporal
Resided in Cherokee County and enlisted at age 21, June 17, 1861. Promotion record not reported. Died in March, 1863. Place and cause of death not reported.

DENTON, MOSES R., Private
Resided in Cherokee County and enlisted at age 32, June 17, 1861. Deserted on September 1, 1863.

DERR, JOHN H., Private
Previously served in Company D, Mallett's N.C. Battalion (Camp Guard). Place and date of enlistment in this company not reported. Captured at Egypt Station, Mississippi, December 28, 1864. Confined at Alton, Illinois, January 17, 1865. Paroled on February 21, 1865, and transferred for exchange. Received at Boulware's Wharf, James River, Virginia, March 6-9, 1865, for exchange.

DOCKERY, JACOB, Private
Previously served in Company A, Walker's Battalion, Thomas Legion. Transferred to this company in November, 1862. Deserted in September, 1863.

DOCKERY, JOHN, Private
Resided in Cherokee County and enlisted at age 23, June 17, 1861. Deserted near Chickamauga, Georgia, September 25, 1863. Went over to the enemy on an unspecified date. Took the Oath of Allegiance at Knoxville, Tennessee, April 8, 1865.

EDISON, JOSEPH G., Private
Resided in Iredell County and enlisted at age 21, May, 1864, for the war. Surrendered at Citronelle, Alabama, May 4, 1865. Paroled at Meridian, Mississippi, May 9, 1865.

EFLER, W., Private
Place and date of enlistment not reported. Captured at "Yazoo City, Mississippi, May 15, 1864." Confined at Fort Delaware, Delaware. Paroled on September 14, 1864, and transferred to Varina, Virginia, where he was received on September 22, 1864, for exchange.

ELY, ROBERT G., Private
Resided in Cherokee County and enlisted at age 22, June 17, 1861. Deserted in June, 1862. [May have served later in Company A, Walker's Battalion, Thomas Legion.]

EYRONS, ELBERT A., Private
Resided in Cherokee County and enlisted at age 16, January, 1862. Discharged in September, 1862. Reason discharged not reported.

FAUCETT, H. C., Private
Previously served in Company E, Mallett's N.C. Battalion (Camp Guard). Place and date of enlistment in this company not reported; however, he was first listed in the records of this company on July 20, 1864. Surrendered at Citronelle, Alabama, May 4, 1865. Paroled at Meridian, Mississippi, May 9, 1865.

FISHER, GEORGE W., Private
Previously served in Company E, 25th Regiment N.C. Troops. Transferred to this company on August 24, 1861, in exchange for Private John J. Case. Hospitalized at Macon, Georgia, June 17, 1864, with an unspecified wound. Place and date wounded not reported. Surrendered at Citronelle, Alabama, May 4, 1865. Paroled at Meridian, Mississippi, on or about May 9, 1865.

FORD, THOMAS G., ———
North Carolina pension records indicate that he served in this company.

FORESTER, EDWARD, Private
Resided in Cherokee County and enlisted at age 23, June 17, 1861. Company records indicate he was transferred to the Thomas Legion in March, 1863; however, records of the Thomas Legion do not indicate that he served therein. No further records.

FORESTER, JOHN C., Private
Resided in Cherokee County and enlisted at age 22, June 17, 1861. Deserted in July, 1862.

FREEMAN, ABNER B., Corporal
Resided in Cherokee County and enlisted at age 21, June 17, 1861. Mustered in as Private and was promoted to Corporal prior to December 31, 1862. Wounded in the left leg and captured at Murfreesboro, Tennessee, on or about December 31, 1862. Hospitalized at Nashville, Tennessee. [Commended for gallantry at Murfreesboro.] No further records.

FREEMAN, LAZARUS, Private
Resided in Cherokee County and enlisted at age 17,

June 17, 1861. Captured at Murfreesboro, Tennessee, on or about December 31, 1862. Confined at Camp Morton, Indianapolis, Indiana, where he died on April 17, 1863. Cause of death not reported.

FURR, CHARLES, Private
Resided in Georgia or in Cherokee County, North Carolina, and enlisted at age 18, June 17, 1861. Captured at Chickamauga, Georgia, September 19-20, 1863. Sent to Nashville, Tennessee. Confined at Louisville, Kentucky, October 1, 1863. Transferred to Camp Douglas, Chicago, Illinois, where he arrived on October 4, 1863. Released on June 16, 1865, after taking the Oath of Allegiance.

GARRINGE, DANIEL W., Private
Resided in Cherokee County and enlisted at age 24, June 17, 1861. Discharged in October, 1861. Reason discharged not reported.

GOODIN, WILLIAM, Private
Born in Knox County, Kentucky, and resided in Cherokee County where he was by occupation a physician prior to enlisting in Cherokee County at age 47, June 17, 1861. Discharged on July 14, 1862. "While reconnoitering the movement of the enemy [in Kentucky on an unspecified date] he encountered two of their scouts and after a combat escaped and in escaping received a wound in the hip from a fall."

GREEN, JAMES JEFFERSON, Sergeant
Resided in Cherokee County and enlisted at age 20, June 17, 1861. Mustered in as Private. Captured by the enemy on an unspecified date. Paroled at Camp Dick Robinson, Kentucky, October 25, 1862. Promoted to Corporal prior to November 1, 1862. Hospitalized at Macon, Georgia, September 27, 1863, with an unspecified wound. Place and date wounded not reported. Furloughed for thirty days on September 28, 1863. Promoted to Sergeant prior to October 1, 1863. Present or accounted for through December 31, 1863.

GREEN, JOHN V., Private
Resided in Cherokee County and enlisted at age 20, June 17, 1861. Captured at Chickamauga, Georgia, September 19-20, 1863. Sent to Nashville, Tennessee. Confined at Louisville, Kentucky, September 30, 1863. Transferred to Camp Douglas, Chicago, Illinois, where he arrived on October 4, 1863. Released on June 16, 1865, after taking the Oath of Allegiance.

GREEN, MARVILLE, Private
Previously served in Company B, Walker's Battalion, Thomas Legion. Transferred to this company on March 1, 1863. Deserted in September, 1863.

GRIBBLE, WILLIAM N. C., Private
Resided in Georgia or in Cherokee County, North Carolina, and enlisted at age 21, June 17, 1861. Captured at Chickamauga, Georgia, September 19-20, 1863. Sent to Nashville, Tennessee. Confined at Louisville, Kentucky, September 30, 1863. Transferred to Camp Douglas, Chicago, Illinois, where he arrived on October 4, 1863. Released on June 16, 1865, after taking the Oath of Allegiance.

HAGIN, WILLIAM H., Private
Resided in Cherokee County and enlisted at age 25, June 17, 1861. Died in May, 1863. Place and cause of death not reported.

HARPER, DAVID G., Private
Resided in Cherokee County and enlisted at age 29, June 17, 1861. Present or accounted for through April, 1863. No further records.

HARRIS, BENNETT SIDNEY, Private
Resided in Cherokee County and enlisted at age 24, June 17, 1861. Captured at Chickamauga, Georgia, September 20, 1863. Sent to Nashville, Tennessee. Confined at Louisville, Kentucky, October 1, 1863. Transferred to Camp Douglas, Chicago, Illinois, where he arrived on October 4, 1863. Released on June 16, 1865, after taking the Oath of Allegiance.

HARRIS, McCARNEY W., Private
Resided in Cherokee County and enlisted at age 21, June 17, 1861. Captured at Chickamauga, Georgia, September 19-20, 1863. Sent to Nashville, Tennessee. Confined at Louisville, Kentucky, October 1, 1863. Transferred to Camp Douglas, Chicago, Illinois, where he arrived on October 4, 1863. Released on June 16, 1865, after taking the Oath of Allegiance.

HARRIS, WILLIAM Y., Corporal
Resided in Cherokee County and enlisted at age 27, June 17, 1861. Promotion record not reported. Deserted in April, 1862.

HENRY, GEORGE H., Private
Resided in Iredell County. Place and date of enlistment not reported. Captured at or near Kennesaw Mountain, Georgia, July 3, 1864. Sent to Nashville, Tennessee. Confined at Louisville, Kentucky, July 13, 1864. Transferred to Camp Douglas, Chicago, Illinois, where he arrived on July 18, 1864. Released on June 16, 1865, after taking the Oath of Allegiance.

HIBBERT, JOHN, Sergeant
Born in Haywood County and resided in Cherokee County where he was by occupation a farmer prior to enlisting in Cherokee County at age 25, June 17, 1861. Mustered in as Sergeant. Discharged on March 13, 1862, by reason of "fever leg."

HILL, CHARLES L., Private
Resided in Cherokee County and enlisted at age 22, June 17, 1861. Discharged in May, 1862. Reason discharged not reported. [May have served later in Company B, 7th Battalion N.C. Cavalry.]

INGLE, J. S., Private
Enlisted at age 16, October, 1862, for the war. Wounded and captured at Spanish Fort, Mobile, Alabama, April 8, 1865. Confined at Ship Island, Mississippi, April 10, 1865. Released on an unspecified date.

JENKINS, JOHN K., Private
Resided in Cherokee County and enlisted at age 18, June 17, 1861. Deserted in June, 1862. Returned to duty prior to March 1, 1863. Present or accounted for through May 15, 1863. No further records.

JOHNSON, JOHN J., Private
Resided in Cherokee County and enlisted at age 41, June 17, 1861. Deserted in June, 1862.

JOHNSON, WILBORN, Private
Born in Rutherford County and resided in Cherokee

County where he was by occupation a farmer prior to enlisting at age 17, June 17, 1861. Discharged in May, 1862. Reason discharged not reported. Later served in Company F, Walker's Battalion, Thomas Legion.

JOHNSON, WILLIAM R., Private
Resided in Cherokee County and enlisted at age 23, January, 1862. Deserted in September, 1863.

JOHNSON, WILLIS M., Private
Resided in Cherokee County and enlisted at age 22, June 17, 1861. Present or accounted for through May 2, 1863. No further records.

JOHNSTON, M. W., Corporal
Resided in Cherokee County. Place and date of enlistment not reported. Promotion record not reported. Surrendered at Citronelle, Alabama, May 4, 1865. Paroled at Meridian, Mississippi, May 9, 1865.

JONES, JACOB, Private
Resided in Cherokee County and enlisted at age 38, June 17, 1861. Discharged in September, 1862. Reason discharged not reported.

JONES, THOMAS M., Private
Resided in Cherokee County and enlisted at age 27, June 17, 1861. Mustered in as Corporal but was reduced to ranks prior to September 19, 1863. Captured at Chickamauga, Georgia, September 19-20, 1863. Sent to Nashville, Tennessee. Confined at Louisville, Kentucky, October 1, 1863. Transferred to Camp Douglas, Chicago, Illinois, where he arrived on October 4, 1863. Released on June 16, 1865, after taking the Oath of Allegiance.

JONES, WILLIAM A., Private
Resided in Cherokee County and enlisted at age 18, June 17, 1861. Discharged in May, 1862, "for dishonorable conduct."

JONES, WILLIAM M., Private
Resided in Cherokee County and enlisted at age 17, June 17, 1861. Died at Loudon, Tennessee, February 18, 1862. Cause of death not reported.

KILPATRICK, MADISON, Private
Resided in Cherokee County and enlisted at age 16, June 17, 1861. No further records.

KING, WILLIAM D., Private
Place and date of enlistment not reported. Captured at or near Smyrna, Georgia, July 4, 1864. Sent to Nashville, Tennessee. Confined at Louisville, Kentucky, July 13, 1864. Transferred to Camp Douglas, Chicago, Illinois, where he arrived on July 16, 1864. Died at Camp Douglas on July 26, 1864, of "chronic diarrhoea."

KIRKPATRICK, J. T., Private
Records of the United Daughters of the Confederacy indicate he enlisted in April, 1863, for the war and was discharged on April 9, 1865. No further records.

KIRKPATRICK, JOSEPH, Private
Records of the United Daughters of the Confederacy indicate he enlisted on May 31, 1861. No further records.

LEDFORD, I. KETRON, Private
Resided in Cherokee County and enlisted at age 19, June 17, 1861. Deserted in September, 1862.

LEDFORD, JACKSON, Musician
Resided in Cherokee County and enlisted at age 18, June 17, 1861. Mustered in as Musician (Fifer). No further records. [May have served also in Company G, 39th Regiment N.C. Troops.]

LENTZ, JACOB, Private
Previously served in Company D, Mallett's N.C. Battalion (Camp Guard). Enlisted in this company on June 22, 1864, for the war. Captured at or near Smyrna, Georgia, July 4, 1864. Sent to Nashville, Tennessee. Confined at Louisville, Kentucky, July 13, 1864. Transferred to Camp Douglas, Chicago, Illinois, where he arrived on July 16, 1864. Released on January 31, 1865, after taking the Oath of Allegiance.

LIVINGSTON, THOMAS, ———
Previously served in Company D, Mallett's N.C. Battalion (Camp Guard). Place and date of enlistment in this company not reported. Wounded in the right arm at or near Atlanta, Georgia, on or about September 15, 1864. No further records.

LOUDERMILK, DANIEL, Private
Resided in Cherokee County and enlisted at age 34, June 17, 1861. Discharged on September 16, 1862. Reason discharged not reported.

LOUDERMILK, DAVID, Sergeant
Resided in Cherokee County and enlisted at age 21, June 17, 1861. Mustered in as Private and was promoted to Sergeant on an unspecified date. Present or accounted for through December, 1863. No further records.

LOUDERMILK, GEORGE W., Private
Born in Cherokee County where he resided as a farmer prior to enlisting at age 19, June 17, 1861. Deserted in June, 1862. Later served as Corporal in Company I, Infantry Regiment, Thomas Legion.

LOUDERMILK, JAMES R., Corporal
Born in Cherokee County where he resided as a farmer prior to enlisting in Cherokee County at age 21, June 17, 1861. Mustered in as Corporal. Discharged on May 29, 1862, by reason of a prewar injury caused by "a wagon wheel rolling over his ankle."

LOUDERMILK, MADISON, Private
Born in Cherokee County where he resided as a farmer prior to enlisting at age 17, June 17, 1861. Deserted in June, 1862. Later served in Company I, Infantry Regiment, Thomas Legion.

LUNSFORD, DAVID, Private
Resided in Cherokee County and enlisted at age 20, June 17, 1861. Deserted in November, 1862. Company records do not indicate whether he returned to duty. Captured by the enemy in Cherokee County on February 18, 1864. Sent to Nashville, Tennessee. Confined at Louisville, Kentucky, February 27, 1864. Transferred to Fort Delaware, Delaware, where he arrived on March 4-7, 1864. Paroled at Fort Delaware on October 30-31, 1864. Transferred to Venus Point, Savannah River, Georgia, where he was received on

November 15, 1864, for exchange.

LUNSFORD, JOHN, Private
Resided in Cherokee County and enlisted at age 30, June 17, 1861. No further records.

LUNSFORD, MICHAEL, Private
Resided in Cherokee or Macon County and enlisted at age 26, June 17, 1861. Deserted in September, 1863. Company records do not indicate whether he returned to duty. Captured by the enemy in Cherokee County on February 18, 1864. Sent to Nashville, Tennessee. Confined at Louisville, Kentucky, February 27, 1864. Transferred to Fort Delaware, Delaware, where he arrived on March 7, 1864. Released on June 8, 1865, after taking the Oath of Allegiance.

LUNSFORD, THOMAS, Private
Resided in Cherokee County and enlisted at age 32, June 17, 1861. Discharged in September, 1862. Reason discharged not reported.

McCLINE, A. J., ——
North Carolina pension records indicate that he served in this company.

McCLURE, ANDREW J., Private
Resided in Cherokee County and enlisted at age 22, June 17, 1861. Wounded at Chickamauga, Georgia, on or about September 19-20, 1863. No further records.

McCLURE, WILLIAM S., Private
Resided in Cherokee County and enlisted at age 24, June 17, 1861. Captured by the enemy on an unspecified date. Paroled at Lancaster, Kentucky, October 15, 1862. Returned to duty prior to December 31, 1862, when he was wounded in the left leg at Murfreesboro, Tennessee. Returned to duty on an unspecified date. Captured at Yazoo City, Mississippi, July 13, 1863. Paroled on or about the same date. No further records.

McCODAMS, A. M., Sergeant
Resided in Alamance County. Place and date of enlistment not reported. Promotion record not reported. Surrendered at Citronelle, Alabama, May 4, 1865. Paroled at Meridian, Mississippi, May 9, 1865. [May have served previously in Company E, Mallett's N.C. Battalion (Camp Guard).]

McDONALD, JEPTHA M., Private
Resided in Cherokee County and enlisted at age 29, June 17, 1861. Captured at Chickamauga, Georgia, September 19-20, 1863. Sent to Nashville, Tennessee. Confined at Louisville, Kentucky, October 1, 1863. Transferred to Camp Douglas, Chicago, Illinois, October 2, 1863. Died at Camp Douglas on December 13, 1864, of "smallpox."

MANCHESTER, WILLIAM M., Private
Resided in Cherokee County and enlisted at age 16, June 17, 1861. Discharged in September, 1862. Reason discharged not reported. [May have served later in Company B, 7th Battalion N.C. Cavalry.]

MARTIN, JOHN M., Jr., Private
Resided in Cherokee County and enlisted at age 27, June 17, 1861. Captured at Yazoo City, Mississippi, July 13, 1863. Paroled on or about the same date. No further

records.

MASON, JESSE, Sergeant
Resided in Cherokee County and enlisted at age 30, June 17, 1861. Mustered in as Sergeant. Wounded in the face at Murfreesboro, Tennessee, December 31, 1862. Company records do not indicate whether he returned to duty. Took the Oath of Allegiance at Chattanooga, Tennessee, May 21, 1865.

MASON, JOHN L., Private
Resided in Cherokee County and enlisted at age 21, June 17, 1861. Captured at Chickamauga, Georgia, September 20, 1863. Confined at Louisville, Kentucky, October 1, 1863. Transferred to Camp Douglas, Chicago, Illinois, where he arrived on October 4, 1863. Released on June 16, 1865, after taking the Oath of Allegiance.

MASON, WILLIAM, Private
Resided in Cherokee County and enlisted at age 18, June 17, 1861. Present or accounted for through May 18, 1863. No further records.

MONTGOMERY, ALFRED, Sergeant
Resided in Cherokee County and enlisted at age 25, June 17, 1861. Mustered in as Sergeant. No further records.

MOORE, J. A., Private
Resided in Iredell County. Place and date of enlistment not reported. Captured at Citronelle, Alabama, May 4, 1865. Paroled at Meridian, Mississippi, May 9, 1865.

MOORE, JAMES W., Private
Resided in Guilford County. Place and date of enlistment not reported. Captured near the Chattahoochee River, Georgia, July 10, 1864. Sent to Nashville, Tennessee. Confined at Louisville, Kentucky, July 25, 1864. Transferred to Camp Douglas, Chicago, Illinois, where he arrived on July 28, 1864. Released on July 12, 1865, after taking the Oath of Allegiance.

MOORE, T. F., Private
Previously served in Company D, Mallett's N.C. Battalion (Camp Guard). Place and date of enlistment in this company not reported. Captured at Spanish Fort, Mobile, Alabama, April 8, 1865. Confined at Ship Island, Mississippi, April 10, 1865. Transferred to Vicksburg, Mississippi, May 1, 1865. No further records.

MOORE, WILLIAM A., Sergeant
Resided in Giles County, Tennessee. Place and date of enlistment not reported. Promotion record not reported. Captured at or near Kennesaw Mountain, Georgia, July 3, 1864. Sent to Nashville, Tennessee. Confined at Louisville, Kentucky, July 14, 1864. Transferred to Camp Douglas, Chicago, Illinois, where he arrived on July 16, 1864. Released on May 13, 1865, after taking the Oath of Allegiance.

MORRISON, ANDREW J., Private
Resided in Iredell County. Place and date of enlistment not reported. Captured near the Chattahoochee River, Georgia, July 10, 1864. Sent to Nashville, Tennessee. Confined at Louisville, Kentucky, July 25, 1864. Transferred to Camp Douglas, Chicago, Illinois, where

he arrived on July 28, 1864. Discharged on May 15, 1865, after taking the Oath of Allegiance.

MORRISON, JOSEPH H., Private
Previously served in Company D, Mallett's N.C. Battalion (Camp Guard). Place and date of enlistment in this company not reported. Captured near the Chattahoochee River, Georgia, July 10, 1864. Sent to Nashville, Tennessee. Confined at Louisville, Kentucky, July 25, 1864. Transferred to Camp Douglas, Chicago, Illinois, where he arrived on July 28, 1864. Died at Camp Douglas on January 24, 1865, of "bronchitis."

NICHOLS, CHRISTOPHER C., Private
Resided in Georgia and enlisted at age 20, June 17, 1861. No further records.

OAR, JAMES D., Private
Resided in Cherokee County and enlisted at age 16, June 17, 1861. Discharged in September, 1862. Reason discharged not reported.

PACK, THOMAS, Private
Born in Cherokee County where he resided as a farmer prior to enlisting at age 21, June 17, 1861. Deserted in June, 1862. Later served in Company I, Infantry Regiment, Thomas Legion.

PALMER, ELI, ———
North Carolina pension records indicate that he served in this company.

PALMER, FRANCIS M., Private
Resided in Cherokee County and enlisted at age 22, June 17, 1861. Deserted in September, 1863.

PALMER, JOHN W., Private
Resided in Cherokee County and enlisted at age 19, June 17, 1861. Present or accounted for through October 13, 1863. No further records.

PASSMORE, NORMAN, Private
Resided in Cherokee County and enlisted at age 18, June 17, 1861. Deserted in September, 1863.

PASSMORE, WARREN, Private
Resided in Cherokee County and enlisted at age 23, June 17, 1861. No further records.

PASSMORE, WILLIAM, Private
Place and date of enlistment not reported. Captured "in Kentucky" in September-October, 1862. Confined at Chattanooga, Tennessee. Exchanged on January 11, 1863. Captured at Yazoo City, Mississippi, July 13, 1863. Paroled on or about the same date. No further records.

PATE, ELIJAH, Private
Resided in Cherokee County and enlisted at age 17, June 17, 1861, for the war. Died in October, 1862. Place and cause of death not reported.

PATE, JESSE, Private
Born in Buncombe County and resided in Cherokee County where he was by occupation a farmer prior to enlisting in Cherokee County at age 46, June 17, 1861. Discharged on April 16, 1862, by reason of "chronic rheumatism."

PATE, JOHN, Private
Resided in Cherokee County and enlisted at age 75, June 17, 1861. Discharged in September, 1861. Reason discharged not reported.

PATTERSON, NICHOLAS M., Private
Previously served in Company D, Mallett's N.C. Battalion (Camp Guard). Place and date of enlistment in this company not reported. Captured at or near Marietta, Georgia, July 3, 1864. Sent to Nashville, Tennessee. Confined at Louisville, Kentucky, July 14, 1864. Transferred to Camp Douglas, Chicago, Illinois, where he arrived on July 18, 1864. Released on May 18, 1865, after taking the Oath of Allegiance.

PATTERSON, RUFUS R., Private
Previously served in Company D, Mallett's N.C. Battalion (Camp Guard). Place and date of enlistment in this company not reported. Captured at or near Kennesaw Mountain, Georgia, July 3, 1864. Sent to Nashville, Tennessee. Confined at Louisville, Kentucky, July 14, 1864. Transferred to Camp Douglas, Chicago, Illinois, July 16, 1864. Released on May 18, 1865, after taking the Oath of Allegiance.

PAYNE, JACOB A., Private
Born in Alexander County and was by occupation a farmer. Place and date of enlistment not reported. Captured at Allatoona, Georgia, October 5, 1864. Sent to Nashville, Tennessee. Confined at Louisville, Kentucky, November 22, 1864. Transferred to Camp Douglas, Chicago, Illinois, where he arrived on November 26, 1864. Released on April 6, 1865, after joining the U.S. Army. Assigned to Company F, 5th Regiment U.S. Volunteer Infantry.

PAYNE, WILLIAM G., Private
Resided in Cherokee County and enlisted at age 15, June 17, 1861. Discharged on September 16, 1862. Reason discharged not reported.

PAYNE, WILLIAM P., Musician
Resided in Cherokee County and enlisted at age 23, June 17, 1861. Mustered in as Musician (Drummer). Deserted in April, 1862.

PEGRAM, DANIEL A., Private
Previously served in Company E, Mallett's N.C. Battalion (Camp Guard). Place and date of enlistment in this company not reported. Captured at or near Smyrna, Georgia, July 4, 1864. Sent to Nashville, Tennessee. Confined at Louisville, Kentucky, July 14, 1864. Transferred to Camp Douglas, Chicago, Illinois, where he arrived on July 18, 1864. Died at Camp Douglas on November 14, 1864, of "diarrhoea."

PETTIGREW, G. W., Private
Resided in Alamance County and enlisted on November 1, 1862, for the war. Captured at Spanish Fort, Mobile, Alabama, April 8, 1865. Sent to Ship Island, Mississippi. Transferred to Vicksburg, Mississippi, May 1, 1865. [May have served also in Company E, Mallett's N.C. Battalion (Camp Guard).]

PRINCE, MARTIN V., Private
Born in Cherokee County where he resided as a farmer prior to enlisting at age 21, June 17, 1861. Deserted in June, 1862. Later served in Company I, Infantry Regiment, Thomas Legion.

RANDOLPH, JOHN M., Private
Born in Yancey County* and resided in Cherokee County where he was by occupation a farmer prior to enlisting in Cherokee County at age 42, June 17, 1861. Discharged on June 1, 1862, by reason of "chronic rheumatism."

REYNOLDS, HIRAM C., Corporal
Resided in Cherokee County and enlisted at age 21, June 17, 1861. Mustered in as Private and was promoted to Corporal prior to September 19-20, 1863, when he was captured at Chickamauga, Georgia. Sent to Nashville, Tennessee. Confined at Louisville, Kentucky, October 1, 1863. Transferred to Camp Douglas, Chicago, Illinois, where he arrived on October 4, 1863. Died at Camp Douglas on February 11, 1865, of "erysipelas."

REYNOLDS, SIMON H., Private
Previously served in Company B, Walker's Battalion, Thomas Legion. Enlisted in this company in November, 1862, for the war. Killed at Chickamauga, Georgia, September 19, 1863.

RICKS, WILLIAM HENRY, Private
Resided in Cherokee County and enlisted at age 22, June 17, 1861. Deserted in September, 1863. Died "in North Carolina" on July 27, 1864. Cause of death not reported.

ROGERS, HOUSTEN, Private
Resided in Cherokee County and enlisted at age 22, June 17, 1861. Deserted in September, 1862. Transferred to Company B, Walker's Battalion, Thomas Legion, in March-April, 1863.

ROGERS, JOHN T., Private
Resided in Cherokee or Haywood County and enlisted at age 36, June 17, 1861. Transferred to Company B, Walker's Battalion, Thomas Legion, in November, 1862.

ROGERS, JONATHAN, Private
Resided in Cherokee County and enlisted at age 19, June 17, 1861. Discharged in September, 1862. Reason discharged not reported. [May have served later in Company B, Walker's Battalion, Thomas Legion.]

ROGERS, WILLIAM, Private
Resided in Cherokee County and enlisted at age 20, January, 1862, as a substitute. Wounded at Chickamauga, Georgia, September 19-20, 1863. Present or accounted for through October 19, 1863. No further records.

SHIELDS, ENOS D., Private
Born in Buncombe County and was by occupation a farmer prior to enlisting in Cherokee County on June 17, 1861. Discharged on June 10, 1862, by reason of "chronic rheumatism." Discharge certificate gives his age as 45.

SMITH, JOHN A., Corporal
Resided in Coosa County, Alabama. Place and date of enlistment not reported. Promotion record not reported. Captured at Chickamauga, Georgia, September 19-20, 1863. Sent to Nashville, Tennessee. Confined at Louisville, Kentucky, October 1, 1863. Transferred to

Camp Douglas, Chicago, Illinois, where he arrived on October 4, 1863. Released on June 16, 1865, after taking the Oath of Allegiance.

SMITH, JOHN E., Private
Resided in Alexander County and enlisted at age 36, June 20, 1864, for the war. Wounded in the right thigh at or near the Chattahoochee River, Georgia, July 1, 1864. Returned to duty on an unspecified date. Captured at Nashville, Tennessee, December 16, 1864. Confined at Nashville. Transferred to Louisville, Kentucky, where he arrived on February 25, 1865. Transferred to Camp Chase, Ohio, where he arrived on March 5, 1865. Released on June 13, 1865, after taking the Oath of Allegiance.

SMITH, JOHN R., Private
Resided in Cherokee County and enlisted at age 20, March, 1862. No further records.

SNEAD, ISAAC F., Private
Resided in Cherokee County and enlisted at age 17, June 17, 1861. Present or accounted for through September 30, 1863. [North Carolina pension records indicate that he survived the war.] No further records.

SNEAD, JOHN G., Private
Resided in Cherokee County and enlisted at age 29, June 17, 1861. No further records.

SNEED, JOHN R., Private
Born in Burke County and resided in Cherokee County where he enlisted at age 24, June 17, 1861. Died "at home" in December, 1861, or on February 8, 1862, of "fever."

SNEED, JOHN S., Private
Enlisted on September 5, 1861. Captured in hospital at Grenada, Mississippi, August 17, 1863, and was paroled on August 18, 1863. No further records.

STANDRIDGE, ELISHA A., Private
Resided in Cherokee County and enlisted at age 26, June 17, 1861. Roll of Honor indicates he died in October, 1862, of "fever"; however, records of the Federal Provost Marshal indicate he was captured on an unspecified date and died at Lexington, Kentucky, December 31, 1862. No further records.

STANDRIDGE, LUCIUS D., Private
Resided in Cherokee County and enlisted at age 29, June 17, 1861. Deserted in December, 1862. Returned to duty prior to March 1, 1863. Present or accounted for through May 8, 1863. No further records.

STILES, JAMES, Private
Place and date of enlistment not reported. Discharged on September 16, 1862. Reason discharged not reported. [May have served later in Company H, Walker's Battalion, Thomas Legion.]

SUTTON, WILLIAM, Private
Resided in Cherokee County and enlisted at age 15, June 17, 1861. Discharged on September 16, 1862. Reason discharged not reported.

TAYLOR, EARLES J., Private
Resided in Cherokee County and enlisted at age 34, June 17, 1861. Discharged on September 16, 1862.

Reason discharged not reported.

TAYLOR, ISAIAH, Private
Resided in Cherokee County and enlisted at age 39, June 17, 1861. Discharged on September 16, 1862. Reason discharged not reported.

TAYLOR, WALTER C., Private
Born in Monroe County, Tennessee, and was by occupation a farmer prior to enlisting on June 17, 1861. Discharged on September 16, 1862. Reason discharged not reported. Discharge certificate gives his age as 40.

WALKER, XENOPHEN L., Sergeant
Born in Cherokee County where he resided prior to enlisting at age 22, June 17, 1861. Mustered in as Sergeant. Died at Cumberland Gap, Tennessee, March 18, 1862, of "fever."

WALLACE, JOSEPH H., Corporal
Resided in Cherokee County and enlisted at age 20, June 17, 1861. Mustered in as Private and was promoted to Corporal prior to September 19, 1863. Wounded in the neck and/or head and captured at Chickamauga, Georgia, September 19, 1863. Hospitalized at Chattanooga, Tennessee. Transferred to hospital at Nashville, Tennessee, on or about November 16, 1863. Transferred to Louisville, Kentucky, where he arrived on December 3, 1863. Transferred to Rock Island, Illinois, December 16, 1863. Released at Rock Island on or about February 9, 1865, after taking the Oath of Allegiance.

WALLACE, WILLIAM C., Private
Previously served in Company E of this regiment. Transferred to this company on June 20, 1863. Wounded at Chickamauga, Georgia, September 19-20, 1863. Hospitalized at Macon, Georgia. Furloughed from hospital on September 28, 1863. No further records.

WEST, M. C., Private
Resided in Lenoir County. Place and date of enlistment not reported. Surrendered at Citronelle, Alabama, May 4, 1865. Paroled at Meridian, Mississippi, May 12, 1865.

WEST, WILLIAM P., Private
Resided in Cherokee County and enlisted at age 24, June 17, 1861. Deserted in December, 1862.

WHISENHUNT, M. E., Private
Previously served in Company D, Mallett's N.C. Battalion (Camp Guard). Place and date of enlistment in this company not reported. Surrendered at Citronelle, Alabama, May 4, 1865. Paroled at Meridian, Mississippi, May 9, 1865.

WHITE, W. P., Private
Previously served in Company D, Mallett's N.C. Battalion (Camp Guard). Place and date of enlistment in this company not reported. Surrendered at Citronelle, Alabama, May 4, 1865. Paroled at Meridian, Mississippi, May 9, 1865.

WILLIAMS, BARCLAY M., Private
Resided in Cherokee County and enlisted at age 18, June 17, 1861. Deserted in September, 1863.

WILLIAMS, GEORGE, Private
Resided in Cherokee County and enlisted at age 27, June 17, 1861. Deserted to the enemy on an unspecified date. Took the Oath of Allegiance in Blount County, Tennessee, January 28, 1864.

WILLIAMS, MARION M., Private
Resided in Cherokee County and enlisted at age 16, June 17, 1861. Discharged in October, 1861. Reason discharged not reported.

WILLIAMS, WILLIAM, Private
Resided in Cherokee County and enlisted at age 25, June 17, 1861. Roll of Honor indicates he was discharged in January, 1862; however, company records indicate he was present or accounted for through May 13, 1863. No further records.

WILSON, BENJAMIN F., Private
Resided in Cherokee or Caldwell County and enlisted at age 25, June 17, 1861. Surrendered at Citronelle, Alabama, May 4, 1865. Paroled at Meridian, Mississippi, May 9, 1865.

WILSON, JACOB, Private
Resided in Caldwell County and enlisted at age 42, August, 1861. Surrendered at Citronelle, Alabama, May 4, 1865. Paroled at Meridian, Mississippi, May 9, 1865.

WOODWARD, WILLIAM F., Private
Resided in Alexander County. Place and date of enlistment not reported. Hospitalized at Mobile, Alabama, April 3, 1865, with a gunshot wound of the back. Place and date wounded not reported. Transferred to Meridian, Mississippi, April 9, 1865. Paroled at Meridian on May 11, 1865.

YOUNGBLOOD, C. W., Private
Place and date of enlistment not reported. Paroled at Greensboro on May 23, 1865.

COMPANY B

This company was raised in Yancey County and enlisted on July 3, 1861. It was then assigned to the 29th Regiment and designated Company B. After joining the regiment the company functioned as a part of the regiment, and its history for the war period is reported as a part of the regimental history.

The following company roster is based primarily on the North Carolina Roll of Honor, prisoner of war records, pension applications, and a variety of miscellaneous records. Information was obtained also from secondary sources such as postwar histories, cemetery records, and records of the United Daughters of the Confederacy. No muster rolls were located for the company.

OFFICERS

CAPTAINS

CREASMAN, WILLIAM B.
Resided in Yancey County and enlisted at age 36. Appointed Captain on July 3, 1861. Appointed Major on June 26, 1862, and transferred to the Field and Staff of this regiment. Later served as Colonel of this regiment.

RAY, DAVID M.
Resided in Yancey County and enlisted at age 22, July 3, 1861. Mustered in as Sergeant and was appointed 2nd Lieutenant on September 25, 1861. Promoted to 1st Lieutenant on May 2, 1862, and was promoted to Captain on June 26, 1862. Wounded in the left arm at Murfreesboro, Tennessee, December 31, 1862. Resigned on March 23, 1863, by reason of "disease of the kidneys of a chronic character" and "chronic diarrhoea."

ANGEL, DANIEL W.
Resided in Yancey County and enlisted at age 23, July 3, 1861. Mustered in as Corporal and was appointed 3rd Lieutenant on May 2, 1862. Promoted to Captain on April 25, 1863. Wounded in the hand at Chickamauga, Georgia, September 19, 1863. Captured at Spanish Fort, Mobile, Alabama, April 8, 1865. Confined at Ship Island, Mississippi, April 10, 1865. Transferred to New Orleans, Louisiana. Confined at Vicksburg, Mississippi, May 6, 1865. Released on or about May 9, 1865.

LIEUTENANTS

ANGEL, DANIEL A., 2nd Lieutenant
Resided in Yancey County and enlisted at age 22, July 3, 1861. Mustered in as Private and was promoted to Corporal on September 16, 1861. Appointed 2nd Lieutenant on July 4, 1863. Wounded in the head at or near Chickamauga, Georgia, on or about September 19-20, 1863. Resigned on August 24, 1864, by reason of disability from wounds.

BLANKENSHIP, PRESLEY D., "Lieutenant"
Resided in Yancey County and enlisted at age 20, July 3, 1861. Mustered in as Private and was promoted to Sergeant on May 2, 1862. Appointed "Lieutenant" prior to December, 1863. Present or accounted for through August 20, 1864. No further records.

CREASMAN, B. C., 2nd Lieutenant
Place and date of enlistment not reported. Promotion record not reported. Resigned on April 27, 1863, by reason of "chronic neuralgia of the stomach."

GARDNER, THOMAS F., 2nd Lieutenant
Resided in Yancey County and enlisted at age 21. Appointed 2nd Lieutenant on July 3, 1861. Appointed Major on September 24, 1861, and transferred to the Field and Staff of this regiment. Later served as Lieutenant Colonel of this regiment.

HENSLEY, JOHN, 1st Lieutenant
Resided in Yancey County and enlisted at age 28, July 3, 1861. Mustered in as Sergeant and was appointed 2nd Lieutenant on May 2, 1862. Promoted to 1st Lieutenant on June 26, 1862. Furloughed for thirty days on November 15, 1862. Failed to return to duty and was listed as absent without leave. Resigned on November 9, 1863. Reason he resigned not reported.

HORTON, NATHAN Y., 3rd Lieutenant
Resided in Yancey County and enlisted at age 30. Appointed 3rd Lieutenant on July 3, 1861. Declined to stand for reelection when the regiment was reorganized on May 2, 1862, and was dropped from the rolls of the company. Later served as 2nd Lieutenant of Company D, 69th Regiment N.C. Troops (7th Regiment N.C. Cavalry).

RAY, WILLIAM A., 1st Lieutenant
Resided in Yancey County and enlisted at age 24. Appointed 1st Lieutenant on July 3, 1861. Declined to stand for reelection when the regiment was reorganized on May 2, 1862, and was dropped from the rolls of the company.

NONCOMMISSIONED OFFICERS AND PRIVATES

ADKINSON, H., Private
Resided in Wilson County. Place and date of enlistment not reported. Paroled at Goldsboro in 1865.

ALLEN, ADONIRAM, Private
Resided in Yancey County and enlisted at age 39, July 3, 1861. Transferred to Company K of this regiment on or about September 16, 1861. Transferred back to this company on an unspecified date. Discharged on October 4, 1862. Reason discharged not reported.

ALLEN, JACKSON, Private
Resided in Yancey County and enlisted at age 17, July 3, 1861. Deserted on September 6, 1863.

ALLEN, NATHAN O., Corporal
Born in Yancey County* where he resided as a farmer prior to enlisting in Yancey County at age 43, July 3, 1861. Mustered in as Corporal. Discharged on April 11, 1862, by reason of "nephritis of long standing."

ANGEL, DAVID M., Private
Resided in Yancey County and enlisted on October 20, 1863, for the war. Wounded in the jaw and right leg at Nashville, Tennessee, on or about December 15-16, 1864. Surrendered at Citronelle, Alabama, on or about May 4, 1865. Paroled at Meridian, Mississippi, May 11, 1865.

ANGEL, JAMES G., Private
Previously served in Company C, 58th Regiment N.C. Troops. Transferred to this company in October, 1862. Present or accounted for through December 19, 1864. [North Carolina pension records indicate that he survived the war.]

ANGEL, WILLIAM G., Private
Resided in Yancey County and enlisted at age 19, July 3, 1861. Last reported in the records of this company on December 19, 1864.

ARROWOOD, JOSHUA L., Private
Resided in Yancey County and enlisted at age 29, July 3, 1861. Captured near Marietta, Georgia, June 18, 1864. Confined at Louisville, Kentucky. Transferred to Camp Morton, Indianapolis, Indiana, where he arrived on June 28, 1864. Died at Camp Morton on February 23, 1865, of "chronic diarrhoea."

AUSTIN, CHARLES, Private
Place and date of enlistment not reported. Captured at or near Yazoo City, Mississippi, July 14, 1863. Confined at Fort Delaware, Delaware. Paroled and transferred to Venus Point, Savannah River, Georgia, where he was received on November 15, 1864, for exchange.

AUSTIN, CLINGMAN, Private
Resided in Yancey County and enlisted at age 19, June 9, 1862, for the war. Captured at Yazoo City, Mississippi, on or about July 13, 1863. Sent to Memphis, Tennessee. Confined at Camp Morton, Indianapolis, Indiana, August 14, 1863. Transferred to Fort Delaware, Delaware, where he arrived on March 22, 1864. No further records.

AUSTIN, EDWARD C., Private
Born in Yancey County where he resided as a farmer prior to enlisting in Yancey County at age 18, July 3, 1861. Discharged on January 30, 1862, by reason of "white swelling which has almost deprived him of the use of one leg."

AUSTIN, JAMES, Private
Resided in Yancey County and enlisted at age 19, July 3, 1861. Captured at Yazoo City, Mississippi, on or about July 13, 1863. Sent to Memphis, Tennessee. Confined at Camp Morton, Indianapolis, Indiana, August 14, 1863. Transferred to Fort Delaware, Delaware, where he arrived on March 22, 1864. Released on June 19, 1865, after taking the Oath of Allegiance.

AUSTIN, SAMUEL, Private
Previously served in Company C, 16th Regiment N.C. Troops (6th Regiment N.C. Volunteers). Enlisted in this company in Yancey County on July 3, 1861. Discharged on April 11, 1862, by reason of disability.

BAIN, WILLIAM M., Private
Resided in Yancey County and enlisted at age 29, July 3, 1861. Transferred to Company K of this regiment on September 16, 1861.

BAKER, WILLIAM S., ———
North Carolina pension records indicate that he served in this company.

BANKS, FRANCIS MARION, Private
Resided in Yancey County and enlisted at age 28, July 3, 1861. Died "at home" on September 21, 1861. Cause of death not reported.

BARKER, R. H. W., Private
Place and date of enlistment not reported. First listed in the records of this company on September 6, 1864. Age reported at that time as 20. [North Carolina pension records indicate that he survived the war.] No further records.

BEAVER, GEORGE L., Private
Previously served in Company G, 58th Regiment N.C. Troops. Enlisted in this company in September, 1863, for the war. [North Carolina pension records indicate that he survived the war.] No further records.

BENFIELD, J. H., Private
Records of the Federal Provost Marshal indicate he was captured near Jackson, Mississippi, and was sent to Snyder's Bluff, Mississippi, July 30, 1863. No further records.

BERGER, GEORGE, Private
Place and date of enlistment not reported. Deserted to the enemy on an unspecified date. Confined at Knoxville, Tennessee. Released on February 15, 1864, after taking the Oath of Allegiance.

BIGGS, JAMES, Private
Previously served in Company K of this regiment. Transferred to this company on March 11, 1863. Last reported in the records of this company on September 28, 1864.

BIGGS, WILLIAM B., Private
Resided in Yancey County and enlisted at age 29, July 3, 1861. Transferred to Company K of this regiment on September 16, 1861. Transferred back to this company on March 11, 1863. Last reported in the records of this company in November, 1864.

BLANKENSHIP, GEORGE A., Private
Resided in Yancey County and enlisted at age 17, July 3, 1861. Died at Stone Dam, Tennessee, January 2, 1862. Cause of death not reported.

BLANKENSHIP, JAMES, Private
Resided in Yancey County and enlisted at age 16, July 3, 1861. Discharged on October 4, 1862. Reason discharged not reported.

BLANKENSHIP, JOHN B., Private
Born in Yancey County where he resided as a farmer prior to enlisting in Yancey County at age 20, July 3, 1861. Discharged on October 18, 1862, by reason of "enlargement and anchylosis of the ankle joint."

BOON, JOHN W., Private
Resided in Yancey County and enlisted at age 17, July 3, 1861. Last reported in the records of this company on April 15, 1863. No further records.

BOONE, BACUS S., Private
Resided in Yancey County and enlisted at age 19, July 3, 1861. Captured at Yazoo City, Mississippi, on or about July 13, 1863. Sent to Memphis, Tennessee. Confined at Camp Morton, Indianapolis, Indiana, August 14, 1863. Died at Camp Morton on March 1, 1864, of "typhoid fever."

BRADFORD, SAMUEL, Private
Resided in Yancey County and enlisted at age 20, July 3, 1861. Roll of Honor indicates he died at Jonesboro, Tennessee, in February, 1862; however, company records indicate he was discharged on April 29, 1863. [May have served also in Company G of this regiment.] No further records.

BRADFORD, THOMAS, Private
Born in Yancey County where he resided prior to enlisting at age 24, July 3, 1861. Killed at Murfreesboro, Tennessee, December 31, 1862.

BROWN, JEREMIAH, ———
North Carolina pension records indicate that he served in this company.

BYRD, GEORGE W., Private
Resided in Yancey County and enlisted at age 20, July 3, 1861. Wounded in the hand at Murfreesboro, Tennessee, December 31, 1862. Surrendered at Citronelle, Alabama, May 4, 1865. Paroled at Meridian, Mississippi, May 9, 1865.

BYRD, M. T., ———
North Carolina pension records indicate that he served

in this company.

BYRD, SAMUEL, Private
Place and date of enlistment not reported. Name appears on a company record dated December 19, 1864. No further records.

CALLOWAY, THOMAS, Private
Resided in Yancey County and enlisted at age 36, July 3, 1861. Deserted on September 6, 1863.

CASE, JOHN L., Private
Resided in Yancey or Henderson County and enlisted in Yancey County at age 21, July 3, 1861. Transferred to Company K of this regiment on September 16, 1861.

CHUNN, JOSEPH S., ——
North Carolina pension records indicate that he served in this company.

CODY, WILLIAM A., Private
Resided in Yancey County and enlisted at age 26, July 3, 1861. Deserted on November 13, 1861. Returned to duty on an unspecified date. Captured at Spanish Fort, Mobile, Alabama, April 8, 1865. Confined at Ship Island, Mississippi. Transferred to Vicksburg, Mississippi, where he arrived on May 6, 1865. Released on an unspecified date. [North Carolina pension records indicate he was wounded on October 4, 1864.]

CROW, JOSEPH, ——
North Carolina pension records indicate that he served in this company.

DANIEL, A. W., ——
North Carolina pension records indicate that he served in this company.

DAVIS, HENRY, ——
Place and date of enlistment not reported. Died at or near Macon, Georgia, on or about June 27, 1864. Cause of death not reported.

EDWARDS, CORNELIUS W., Sergeant
Resided in Yancey County and enlisted at age 23, July 3, 1861. Mustered in as Private. Wounded in the left thigh and captured at Murfreesboro, Tennessee, December 31, 1862. Confined at Nashville, Tennessee, and at Camp Morton, Indianapolis, Indiana. Paroled and transferred to City Point, Virginia, where he was received on April 12, 1863, for exchange. Returned to duty on an unspecified date. Promoted to Sergeant prior to July 3, 1864, when he was captured at Marietta, Georgia. Sent to Nashville. Confined at Louisville, Kentucky, July 14, 1864. Transferred to Camp Douglas, Chicago, Illinois, where he arrived on July 18, 1864. Released on June 16, 1865, after taking the Oath of Allegiance.

EDWARDS, JOHN, Private
Resided in Yancey County and enlisted at age 26, July 3, 1861. Transferred to Company K of this regiment on September 16, 1861.

ELKINS, THOMAS, Private
Resided in Yancey County and enlisted at age 28, July 3, 1861. Nominated for the Badge of Distinction for gallantry at Murfreesboro, Tennessee, December 31, 1862. Wounded at Chickamauga, Georgia, September

20, 1863. [North Carolina pension records indicate that he survived the war.]

ENGLAND, MARK, ——
Alias of Mark Roberson of this company, q.v.

FENDER, ALLEN, Private
Resided in Yancey County and enlisted at age 31, July 3, 1861. Transferred to Company K of this regiment on September 16, 1861.

FENDER, ISHAM, Private
Resided in Yancey County and enlisted at age 37, July 3, 1861. Transferred to Company K of this regiment on September 16, 1861.

FERGUSON, JEREMIAH M., Private
North Carolina pension records indicate that he served in this company.

FERGUSON, MARION, Private
Resided in Yancey County and enlisted at age 19, July 3, 1861. Last reported in the records of this company on January 15, 1865.

FRADY, N. L., ——
North Carolina pension records indicate that he served in this company.

FRANKLIN, GAITHER, Private
Resided in Yancey County and enlisted at age 17, July 3, 1861. Died in hospital at Chattanooga, Tennessee, January 13, 1862. Cause of death not reported.

GADDIS, BAXTER, Private
Resided in Yancey County and enlisted at age 18, July 3, 1861. Wounded in the side and left arm and captured at Murfreesboro, Tennessee, December 31, 1862. Hospitalized at Louisville, Kentucky, where he died on April 11, 1863, of wounds.

GARDNER, GEORGE W., Private
Resided in Yancey County and enlisted at age 17, July 3, 1861. Died at Jonesboro, Tennessee, June 7 or June 18, 1862, of disease.

GARDNER, THOMAS J., Private
Resided in Yancey County and enlisted at age 20, July 3, 1861. Discharged on September 11, 1861, or April 10, 1862, by reason of disability.

GOFORTH, DAVID C., Private
Born in Washington County, Tennessee, and resided in Yancey County where he was by occupation a farmer prior to enlisting in Yancey County at age 35, July 3, 1861. Transferred to Company K of this regiment on September 16, 1861.

GRANT, SAMUEL S., Private
Resided in Yancey County and enlisted at age 22, July 3, 1861. Discharged on February 3 or March 1, 1862. Reason discharged not reported.

GREENE, JAMES, ——
North Carolina pension records indicate that he served in this company.

HARRIS, JAMES W., Private
Resided in Yancey County and enlisted at age 25, July 3,

1861. Deserted on September 6, 1863. Returned to duty on an unspecified date. Captured at Spanish Fort, Mobile, Alabama, April 8, 1865. Sent to Ship Island, Mississippi. Transferred to Vicksburg, Mississippi, May 1, 1865. Released on an unspecified date. [North Carolina pension records indicate he was wounded at "Nashville, Tennessee, in January, 1864."]

HARRIS, McWILLIAM, Sergeant
Resided in Yancey County and enlisted at age 22, July 3, 1861. Mustered in as Private. Deserted on September 6, 1863. Returned to duty on an unspecified date. Promoted to Sergeant prior to June 18, 1864. Captured at or near Marietta, Georgia, on or about June 18-19, 1864. Sent to Nashville, Tennessee. Confined at Louisville, Kentucky, June 26, 1864. Transferred to Camp Morton, Indianapolis, Indiana, where he arrived on June 28, 1864. Released on June 12, 1865, after taking the Oath of Allegiance.

HARRIS, NATHAN M., Private
Resided in Yancey County and enlisted at age 30, July 3, 1861. Deserted in March, 1863.

HARRIS, NELSON, Private
Resided in Yancey County and enlisted at age 19, July 3, 1861. Captured at Spanish Fort, Mobile, Alabama, April 8, 1865. Confined at Ship Island, Mississippi, April 10, 1865. Transferred to Vicksburg, Mississippi, where he arrived on May 6, 1865. No further records.

HARRIS, SOLOMON E., Private
Resided in Yancey County and enlisted at age 23, July 3, 1861. Hospitalized at Macon, Georgia, October 23, 1864, with a gunshot wound of the "trunk." Returned to duty on an unspecified date. Surrendered at Citronelle, Alabama, May 4, 1865. Paroled at Meridian, Mississippi, May 9, 1865.

HARRIS, THOMAS D., Private
Resided in Yancey County. Place and date of enlistment not reported. Surrendered at Citronelle, Alabama, May 4, 1865. Paroled at Meridian, Mississippi, May 9, 1865. [North Carolina pension records indicate he was wounded at Mobile, Alabama, on an unspecified date.]

HARRIS, W. A., Private
Resided in Yancey County and enlisted at age 17, May 15, 1862, for the war. Surrendered at Citronelle, Alabama, May 4, 1865. Paroled at Meridian, Mississippi, May 9, 1865.

HENSLEY, ABRAM, Private
Resided in Yancey County and enlisted at age 25, July 3, 1861. Deserted on September 6, 1863. Returned to duty on or about December 2, 1863. Present or accounted for through February 3, 1864. No further records.

HENSLEY, ANDREW J., Private
Resided in Yancey County and enlisted at age 26, July 3, 1861. Deserted in March, 1862. Reported on duty as a herdsman during September, 1862-April, 1863. Listed as a deserter on May 26, 1863.

HENSLEY, BACCHUS S., Private
Resided in Yancey County and enlisted at age 19, July 3, 1861. Promoted to Sergeant and transferred to Company K of this regiment on September 16, 1861. Later served as 2nd Lieutenant of Company K.

HENSLEY, EASON H., Corporal
Resided in Yancey County and enlisted at age 22, July 3, 1861. Mustered in as Corporal. Promoted to Sergeant and transferred to Company K of this regiment on September 16, 1861. Later served as 2nd Lieutenant of Company K.

HENSLEY, G. M., Private
Resided in Yancey County and enlisted at age 17, August 31, 1862, for the war. Records of the Federal Provost Marshal indicate he was captured in hospital at Grenada, Mississippi, August 17, 1863, and was paroled on August 18, 1863. No further records.

HENSLEY, HOWARD, ——
North Carolina pension records indicate that he served in this company.

HENSLEY, JAMES B., Private
Resided in Yancey County and enlisted at age 23, July 3, 1861. Deserted on September 6, 1863. Went over to the enemy on an unspecified date. Confined at Knoxville, Tennessee, May 20, 1864. Transferred to Louisville, Kentucky, where he arrived on May 29, 1864. Released on May 31, 1864, after taking the Oath of Allegiance.

HENSLEY, JESSE, Private
Born in Yancey County* where he resided as a farmer prior to enlisting at age 34, July 4, 1861. Captured at Chickamauga, Georgia, September 19-20, 1863. Sent to Nashville, Tennessee. Confined at Louisville, Kentucky, September 30, 1863. Transferred to Camp Douglas, Chicago, Illinois, where he arrived on October 4, 1863. Released on March 24, 1865, after joining the U.S. Army. Assigned to Company D, 6th Regiment U.S. Volunteer Infantry. [May have served also in Company K of this regiment.]

HENSLEY, JOEL, ——
North Carolina pension records indicate that he served in this company.

HENSLEY, JOHN A., Private
Born in Madison County* and resided in Yancey County where he was by occupation a farmer prior to enlisting in Yancey County at age 32, July 3, 1861. Discharged on January 30, 1862, by reason of "diseased lungs." [May have served later in Company G, 18th Regiment N.C. Troops (8th Regiment N.C. Volunteers).]

HENSLEY, LEWIS W., Private
Resided in Yancey County and enlisted at age 21, July 3, 1861. Transferred to Company K of this regiment on September 16, 1861.

HENSLEY, SILAS, Private
Born in Yancey County where he resided as a farmer prior to enlisting in Yancey County at age 20, July 3, 1861. Discharged on January 30, 1862, by reason of injuries suffered prior to the war. These injuries included "a severe cut across the arm, a fracture of the ulna, & dislocation of the wrist which almost entirely deprives him of the use of the right arm."

HICKS, W. M., Private
Place and date of enlistment not reported. Captured at Spanish Fort, Mobile, Alabama, April 8, 1865. Sent to

Ship Island, Mississippi. Transferred to Vicksburg, Mississippi, where he was received on May 6, 1865. No further records.

HIGGINS, SANDERS, ———
North Carolina pension records indicate that he served in this company.

HONEYCUTT, EDWARD, Private
Resided in Yancey County and enlisted at age 17, July 3, 1861. Deserted on December 28, 1862. Returned to duty on an unspecified date. Captured at Yazoo City, Mississippi, on or about July 13, 1863. Sent to Memphis, Tennessee. Confined at Camp Morton, Indianapolis, Indiana, on or about August 14, 1863. Paroled and transferred to Boulware's Wharf, James River, Virginia, where he was received on March 10-12, 1865, for exchange.

HONEYCUTT, JOSEPH, Private
Resided in Yancey County and enlisted at age 22, July 3, 1861. Deserted on December 28, 1862. Apprehended on an unspecified date and was reported in confinement on January 20, 1863. [North Carolina pension records indicate that he survived the war.] No further records.

HORTON, JESSE, 1st Sergeant
Resided in Yancey County and enlisted at age 32, July 3, 1861. Mustered in as 1st Sergeant. Dropped from the rolls of the company "by order of General Bragg" on an unspecified date.

HORTON, JOSHUA, ———
North Carolina pension records indicate that he served in this company.

HUBBARD, WILLIAM, Private
Resided in Yancey County and enlisted at age 24, July 3, 1861. Transferred to Company K of this regiment in February, 1863.

HUNTER, D. V., Private
Enlisted at age 19, January 2, 1863, for the war. Captured at Spanish Fort, Mobile, Alabama, April 8, 1865. Sent to Ship Island, Mississippi. Transferred to Vicksburg, Mississippi, where he was received on May 6, 1865. [North Carolina pension records indicate he was wounded at Kennesaw Mountain, Georgia, July 2, 1864.]

HUNTER, JAMES J., Private
Resided in Yancey County and enlisted at age 22, July 3, 1861. Wounded at Chickamauga, Georgia, on or about September 19-20, 1863. Last reported in the records of this company on December 19, 1864. [North Carolina pension records indicate that he survived the war.]

INGLE, D. M., Private
Place and date of enlistment not reported. Captured at Spanish Fort, Mobile, Alabama, April 8, 1865. Confined at Ship Island, Mississippi, April 10, 1865. Transferred to Vicksburg, Mississippi, where he arrived on May 6, 1865. No further records.

JOHNSON, A. L., Private
Place and date of enlistment not reported. Captured at Spanish Fort, Mobile, Alabama, April 8, 1865. Confined at Ship Island, Mississippi, April 10, 1865. Transferred to Vicksburg, Mississippi, where he arrived on May 6, 1865. No further records.

JONES, EMORY, Private
Resided in Yancey County and enlisted at age 23, July 3, 1861. Captured at Yazoo City, Mississippi, on or about July 13, 1863. Sent to Memphis, Tennessee. Confined at Camp Morton, Indianapolis, Indiana, August 14, 1863. Paroled and transferred to Boulware's Wharf, James River, Virginia, where he was received on March 23, 1865, for exchange.

JONES, JARRETT, Private
Place and date of enlistment not reported. Captured by the enemy on an unspecified date. Died in hospital at St. Louis, Missouri, February 25, 1863, of "bronchitis."

JONES, M. M., Private
Place and date of enlistment not reported. Captured by the enemy on an unspecified date. Died in hospital at St. Louis, Missouri, December 25, 1862, of "pneumonia."

JONES, NOAH, Private
Born in Yancey County where he resided prior to enlisting at age 19, July 3, 1861. Died at Cumberland Gap, Tennessee, March 18-19, 1862, of disease.

KAISER, JAMES B., Private
Resided in Yancey County and enlisted at age 25, July 3, 1861. Wounded in the thigh at Murfreesboro, Tennessee, December 31, 1862. Returned to duty on an unspecified date. Captured at Yazoo City, Mississippi, on or about July 13, 1863. Sent to Memphis, Tennessee. Confined at Camp Morton, Indianapolis, Indiana, August 14, 1863. Paroled and transferred to City Point, Virginia, February 26, 1865, for exchange.

KENDRICK, JAMES W., ———
North Carolina pension records indicate that he served in this company.

KING, ROBERT E., Private
Resided in Yancey County and enlisted at age 24, July 3, 1861. Transferred to Company K of this regiment on September 16, 1861.

McCAULES, WILLIAM W., Private
Resided in Yancey County and enlisted at age 21, July 3, 1861. No further records.

McINTOSH, BARNETT, Private
Resided in Yancey County and enlisted at age 21, July 3, 1861. Transferred to Company K of this regiment on September 16, 1861.

McINTOSH, NEWTON A., Private
Resided in Yancey County and enlisted at age 23, July 3, 1861. Transferred to Company K of this regiment on September 16, 1861.

McINTYRE, J., Private
Place and date of enlistment not reported. Captured at Spanish Fort, Mobile, Alabama, April 8, 1865. Confined at Ship Island, Mississippi, April 10, 1865. Transferred to Vicksburg, Mississippi, where he arrived on May 6, 1865. No further records.

McLAUGHLIN, WILLIAM A., ———
North Carolina pension records indicate that he served in this company.

McMAHAN, EDWARD, Private

Resided in Yancey County and enlisted at age 37, July 3, 1861. Deserted in March, 1862.

McMAHAN, HOWARD M., Private

Born in Yancey County where he resided prior to enlisting in Yancey County at age 20, July 3, 1861. Mustered in as Private. Promoted to Sergeant on September 25, 1861. Reduced to ranks on an unspecified date. Died at Knoxville, Tennessee, November 5, 1862. Cause of death not reported.

McMAHAN, JACKSON, Private

Resided in Yancey County where he enlisted at age 19, July 3, 1861. Captured at Spanish Fort, Mobile, Alabama, April 8, 1865. Confined at Ship Island, Mississippi, April 10, 1865. Transferred to Vicksburg, Mississippi, where he arrived on May 6, 1865. No further records.

McMAHAN, JOHN, Private

Resided in Yancey County and enlisted at age 29, July 3, 1861. Died at Knoxville, Tennessee, in November, 1862. Cause of death not reported.

McMAHAN, JOHN Y., Private

Resided in Yancey County and enlisted at age 24, July 3, 1861. Deserted in March, 1862. Reported on duty as a nurse on April 29, 1863. No further records.

McMAHAN, RILEY A., Corporal

Born in Yancey County* where he resided as a farmer prior to enlisting in Yancey County at age 31, July 3, 1861. Mustered in as Private. Promoted to Corporal on an unspecified date. Discharged on October 24, 1862, by reason of "loss of use of right hand & severe injury of left." Place and date injured not reported.

McMAHAN, ROBERT, ———

North Carolina pension records indicate that he served in this company.

McMAHAN, SAMUEL, Private

Born in Yancey County where he resided prior to enlisting at age 25, July 3, 1861. Died in hospital at Atlanta, Georgia, March 10-12, 1863, of "diarrhoea" and/or "fever."

McMAHAN, WILLIAM B., Private

Resided in Yancey County and enlisted at age 33, July 3, 1861. Mustered in as Sergeant. Deserted in March, 1863. Returned to duty on an unspecified date. Reduced to ranks prior to June 18, 1864. Captured at or near Marietta, Georgia, on or about June 18, 1864. Sent to Nashville, Tennessee. Confined at Louisville, Kentucky, June 26, 1864. Transferred to Camp Morton, Indianapolis, Indiana, where he arrived on June 28, 1864. Released on June 12, 1865, after taking the Oath of Allegiance.

McMAHAN, WILSON, Private

Resided in Yancey County and enlisted at age 27, July 3, 1861. Deserted on September 17, 1862. Reported absent without leave in Yancey County in September-October, 1864. Went over to the enemy on an unspecified date. Took the Oath of Allegiance at Chattanooga, Tennessee, November 24, 1864.

McMAHON, ROBERT, Private

Resided in Yancey County and enlisted at age 27, July 3, 1861. Mustered in as Musician (Drummer) but was reduced to ranks on an unspecified date. Reported absent without leave in September-October, 1864. Took the Oath of Allegiance at Chattanooga, Tennessee, November 24, 1864. Reported in a Federal hospital at Chattanooga on January 4, 1865. No further records.

METCALF, ENOS, Private

Resided in Yancey County and enlisted at age 23, July 3, 1861. Transferred to Company K of this regiment on September 16, 1861.

METCALF, WILLIAM J., Private

Resided in Yancey or Madison County and enlisted at age 27, July 3, 1861. Transferred to Company D of this regiment on May 1, 1862.

MORSE, JOHN R., Private

Enlisted at age 18, April 2, 1864, for the war. Captured at or near Marietta, Georgia, on or about June 19, 1864. Sent to Nashville, Tennessee. Confined at Louisville, Kentucky, June 26, 1864. Transferred to Camp Morton, Indianapolis, Indiana, where he arrived on June 28, 1864. Paroled and transferred to Boulware's Wharf, James River, Virginia, where he was received March 10-12, 1865, for exchange.

NANEY, ANDREW J., Private

Resided in Yancey County and enlisted at age 17, July 3, 1861. No further records.

NORTON, BALIS, Private

Resided in Yancey County and enlisted at age 18, July 3, 1861. Transferred to Company K of this regiment on September 16, 1861.

OGLE, LUCIUS H., Private

Resided in Yancey County and enlisted at age 18, July 3, 1861. Deserted on September 17, 1862. [North Carolina pension records indicate he was wounded at "Cuniklan Mountain," Tennessee, in 1864.]

PARROTT, ROBERT, Private

Resided in Yancey County and enlisted at age 17, July 3, 1861. No further records.

PATE, DOCTOR A., Private

Resided in Yancey County and enlisted at age 24, July 3, 1861. Transferred to Company K of this regiment on September 16, 1861.

PATE, GEORGE W., Private

Born in Yancey County* where he resided as a farmer prior to enlisting in Yancey County at age 36, July 3, 1861. Discharged on August 16, 1862, by reason of "chronic rheumatism." Died at Cumberland Gap, Tennessee, August 28, 1862. Cause of death not reported. [May have served also in Company G of this regiment.]

PATE, JOHN OLIVER, Private

Resided in Yancey County and enlisted at age 19, July 3, 1861. Transferred to Company K of this regiment on

September 16, 1861.

PATE, MARCELLUS S., Private
Resided in Yancey County and enlisted at age 22, July 3, 1861. Transferred to Company K of this regiment on September 16, 1861.

PEAK, HIRAM R., Private
Enlisted at age 18, February 20, 1864, for the war. Captured at or near Marietta, Georgia, on or about June 18, 1864. Sent to Nashville, Tennessee. Confined at Louisville, Kentucky, June 26, 1864. Transferred to Camp Morton, Indianapolis, Indiana, where he arrived on June 28, 1864. Paroled and transferred to City Point, Virginia, February 26, 1865, for exchange. Reported in hospital at Richmond, Virginia, March 13, 1865.

PHILLIPS, A. E., Private
Place and date of enlistment not reported. Captured at Spanish Fort, Mobile, Alabama, April 8, 1865. Confined at Ship Island, Mississippi, April 10, 1865. Transferred to Vicksburg, Mississippi, where he arrived on May 6, 1865. No further records.

PHILLIPS, JAMES, ———
North Carolina pension records indicate that he served in this company.

PHIPPS, ANDREW ERVIN, ———
Enlisted in 1863. Last reported in the records of this company on October 14, 1864. [North Carolina pension records indicate that he survived the war.]

PHIPPS, JACOB N., Sergeant
Resided in Yancey County and enlisted at age 22, July 3, 1861. Mustered in as Private and was promoted to Sergeant prior to December 31, 1862. Captured at or near Murfreesboro, Tennessee, on or about December 31, 1862-January 1, 1863. Sent to Nashville, Tennessee. Confined at Camp Douglas, Chicago, Illinois, February 11, 1863. Paroled and transferred to City Point, Virginia, where he was received on April 4, 1863, for exchange. Last reported in the records of this company on December 19, 1864.

PRICE, ISAIAH, Private
Born in Wilkes County and resided in Yancey County where he was by occupation a farmer prior to enlisting in Yancey County at age 45, July 3, 1861. Transferred to Company K of this regiment on September 16, 1861.

PROFFITT, BACCHUS S., Sergeant
Resided in Yancey County and enlisted at age 20, July 3, 1861. Mustered in as Sergeant. Appointed Captain on September 16, 1861, and transferred to Company K of this regiment.

RADFORD, JOHN, Private
Born in Yancey County where he resided prior to enlisting at age 20, July 3, 1861. Transferred to Company K of this regiment on September 16, 1861.

RANDOLPH, ANANIAS, Private
Resided in Buncombe or Yancey County and enlisted at age 21, July 3, 1861. Captured at Murfreesboro, Tennessee, January 1-5, 1863, apparently while serving as a nurse for the wounded. Sent to Nashville, Tennessee. Confined at Louisville, Kentucky, May 16, 1863. Transferred to Baltimore, Maryland, May 19,

1863. Paroled at Baltimore and transferred to City Point, Virginia, where he was received on May 26, 1863, for exchange. Wounded and captured at Spanish Fort, Mobile, Alabama, April 8, 1865. Paroled at Meridian, Mississippi, May 11, 1865.

RANDOLPH, JAMES, Private
Resided in Yancey County and enlisted at age 21, July 3, 1861. No further records.

RANDOLPH, ROBERT, Private
Born in Buncombe County and resided in Yancey County prior to enlisting at age 19, July 3, 1861. Wounded at Murfreesboro, Tennessee, December 31, 1862. Died on January 3, 1863, of wounds. Place of death not reported.

RANDOLPH, SAMUEL W., Private
Resided in Yancey County and enlisted at age 16, July 3, 1861. Discharged on October 4, 1862. Reason discharged not reported.

RAY, ALBERT, Private
Previously served in Company D of this regiment. Transferred to this company on February 20, 1863. Captured at Yazoo City, Mississippi, July 14, 1863. Confined at Camp Morton, Indianapolis, Indiana, August 14, 1863. Released prior to September 1, 1863, after joining the U.S. Army. Assigned to the 7th Regiment U.S. Cavalry.

RAY, HENRY B., Private
Resided in Yancey County and enlisted at age 20, July 3, 1861. Died at Jonesboro, Tennessee, December 26, 1861. Cause of death not reported.

RAY, ISICHA B., Private
Born in Yancey County* and was by occupation a farmer prior to enlisting in Yancey County on July 3, 1861. Discharged on July 23, 1862, by reason of disability resulting from rubeola. Discharge certificate gives his age as 34.

RAY, J. B., Private
Resided in Yancey County and enlisted at age 34, July 3, 1861. Discharged on July 24, 1862. Reason discharged not reported.

RAY, JAMES B., Private
Resided in Yancey County and enlisted at age 26, July 3, 1861. Died on December 21, 1861. Place and cause of death not reported.

RAY, JAMES M., Private
Born in Yancey County where he resided prior to enlisting at age 16, July 3, 1861. Died at Cumberland Gap, Tennessee, May 28 or July 3, 1862, of disease.

RAY, JOHN BAILUS, Private
Resided in Yancey County and enlisted at age 36, July 3, 1861. Transferred to Company D of this regiment on May 1, 1862. [North Carolina pension records indicate he was wounded at "Jonesboro, Tennessee, November 1, 1861."]

RAY, KELSIE, Private
Born in Yancey County where he resided prior to enlisting at age 20, July 3, 1861. Died at Pearl River, Mississippi, August 15, 1863, of wounds received "by

accident" on August 1, 1863.

RAY, WILLIAM B., Private
Resided in Yancey County and enlisted at age 19, July 3, 1861. Deserted on September 6, 1863.

REYNOLDS, JAMES H., Private
Place and date of enlistment not reported. Captured at or near Smyrna, Georgia, on or about July 4, 1864. Sent to Nashville, Tennessee. Confined at Louisville, Kentucky, July 14, 1864. Transferred to Camp Douglas, Chicago, Illinois, where he arrived on July 18, 1864. Released on March 15, 1865.

RIDDLE, ANDREW JACKSON, Private
Resided in Yancey County and enlisted at age 31, July 3, 1861. Died on December 25, 1861. Place and cause of death not reported.

RIDDLE, JAMES H., Musician
Resided in Yancey County and enlisted at age 29, July 3, 1861. Mustered in as Musician (Fifer). Deserted to the enemy on December 20, 1864. Took the Oath of Allegiance at Nashville, Tennessee, January 13, 1865.

RIDDLE, SAMUEL, Private
Resided in Yancey County and enlisted at age 22, July 3, 1861. Transferred to Company C, 58th Regiment N.C. Troops, November 7, 1862.

ROBERSON, JOHN, Private
Resided in Yancey County and enlisted at age 24, July 3, 1861. Wounded in the right knee at Chickamauga, Georgia, September 19-20, 1863. Reported absent wounded through January 29, 1864. Last reported in the records of this company on December 19, 1864.

ROBERSON, MARK, ———
North Carolina pension records indicate that he served in this company. [Alias Mark England.]

ROBERSON, WILLIAM L., Private
Resided in Yancey County and enlisted at age 20, July 3, 1861. Transferred to Company K of this regiment on September 16, 1861.

ROBERSON, WYATT, Private
Born in Buncombe County and resided in Yancey County where he was by occupation a farmer prior to enlisting in Yancey County at age 41, July 3, 1861. Transferred to Company K of this regiment on September 16, 1861.

ROBERSON, YOUNG, Private
Resided in Yancey County and enlisted at age 20, July 3, 1861. Deserted on September 6, 1863.

ROBERTSON, M., Private
Place and date of enlistment not reported. Captured at Spanish Fort, Mobile, Alabama, April 8, 1865. Confined at Ship Island, Mississippi, April 10, 1865. Transferred to Vicksburg, Mississippi, where he arrived on May 6, 1865. [North Carolina pension records indicate that he survived the war.]

ROGERS, JAMES B., Private
Born in Wilkes County and resided in Yancey County prior to enlisting at age 22, July 3, 1861. Died at Cumberland Gap, Tennessee, May 12, 1862, of disease.

[May have served also in Company G of this regiment.]

ROGERS, JOHN W., Private
Born in Surry County and resided in Yancey County where he was by occupation a farmer prior to enlisting in Yancey County at age 30, July 3, 1861. Discharged on August 5, 1862, by reason of "anasarca which greatly debilitates him & which renders him total[l]y unfit for the duties of a soldier."

ROLAND, RAYBURN, Private
Resided in Yancey County and enlisted at age 20, July 3, 1861. Deserted on September 17, 1862.

RUMPLES, ROBERT A., Private
Resided in Yancey County where he enlisted at age 28, July 3, 1861. Mustered in as Private and was promoted to Sergeant on May 2, 1862. Reduced to ranks subsequent to March 31, 1864. Last reported in the records of this company on December 19, 1864.

SHELTON, RODERICK, Private
Resided in Yancey County and enlisted at age 19, July 3, 1861. Transferred to Company K of this regiment on September 16, 1861.

SHEPHERD, MITCHELL G., Private
Resided in Yancey County and enlisted at age 18, July 3, 1861. Mustered in as Private. Promoted to Corporal on May 2, 1862. Captured in hospital at Grenada, Mississippi, August 17, 1863. Paroled at Grenada on August 18, 1863. Reduced to ranks on an unspecified date. Last reported in the records of this company on December 19, 1864.

SHEPHERD, THOMAS ERWIN, Private
Born in Yancey County where he resided as a farmer prior to enlisting at age 15, July 3, 1861. "Rejected by the mustering officer." Later served in Company C, 58th Regiment N.C. Troops.

SHEPHERD, WESLEY, Corporal
Resided in Yancey County and enlisted at age 18, July 3, 1861. Mustered in as Private. Promoted to Corporal on May 2, 1862. Last reported in the records of this company on August 22, 1864.

SHOOK, W. RILEY, Private
Resided in Yancey County and enlisted at age 34, July 4, 1862, for the war. Surrendered at Citronelle, Alabama, May 4, 1865. Paroled at Meridian, Mississippi, May 9, 1865.

SHURRETT, JAMES B., Private
Place and date of enlistment not reported. Captured and paroled at or near Yazoo City, Mississippi, on or about July 13, 1863. Captured at or near the Chattahoochie River, Georgia, July 21, 1864. Sent to Nashville, Tennessee. Confined at Louisville, Kentucky, August 3, 1864. Transferred to Camp Chase, Ohio, August 3, 1864. No further records.

SILVER, THOMAS D., Private
Resided in Yancey County and enlisted at age 17, July 3, 1861. Wounded in the left shoulder at Murfreesboro, Tennessee, on or about December 31, 1862. Returned to duty on an unspecified date. Captured at Spanish Fort, Mobile, Alabama, April 8, 1865. Confined at Ship Island, Mississippi, April 10, 1865. Transferred to

Vicksburg, Mississippi, where he arrived on May 6, 1865. No further records.

TAFFER, IREDELL, Private
Resided in Ashe County and enlisted at age 21, May 13, 1862, for the war. Transferred to Company K of this regiment on August 1, 1863.

TAFFER, JOHN S., Private
Resided in Yancey County and enlisted at age 51, July 3, 1861. Transferred to Company K of this regiment on or about September 16, 1861.

TIPTON, J. M., ———
North Carolina pension records indicate that he served in this company.

TOWNSAND, E. W., ———
North Carolina pension records indicate that he served in this company.

VEST, SILAS, Private
Resided in Buncombe or Henderson County and enlisted at age 17, July 3, 1861. Transferred to Company K of this regiment on September 16, 1861.

WESTALL, JOHN B., Musician
Resided in Yancey County and enlisted at age 19, July 3, 1861. Mustered in as Private and was promoted to Musician (Fifer) on an unspecified date. Surrendered at Citronelle, Alabama, May 4, 1865. Paroled at Meridian, Mississippi, May 9, 1865. [North Carolina pension records indicate he was wounded in the left hand at "Atlanta, Georgia, July 3, 1863."]

WESTALL, SAMUEL J., Private
Resided in Yancey County and enlisted at age 33, July 3, 1861. Dropped from the rolls of the company on an unspecified date. Reason he was dropped not reported.

WHEELER, JOHN, Private
Born in Washington County, Virginia, and resided in Yancey County where he was by occupation a "minister of the Gospel" prior to enlisting in Yancey County at age 68, July 3, 1861. Discharged on May 15, 1862, by reason of "age and a diseas[e] of the liver."

WHEELER, JOHN H., Private
Resided in Yancey County and enlisted at age 24, July 3, 1861. No further records.

WILLIAMS, JOHN, Private
Resided in Yancey County and enlisted at age 33, July 3, 1861. Deserted on an unspecified date. [May have served also in Company K of this regiment.]

WILSON, AMOS K., Private
Resided in Yancey County and enlisted at age 19, July 3, 1861. Wounded at Chickamauga, Georgia, September 19-20, 1863. No further records.

WILSON, E. W., Private
Resided in Yancey County. Place and date of enlistment not reported. Surrendered at Citronelle, Alabama, May 4, 1865. Paroled at Meridian, Mississippi, May 9, 1865.

WILSON, EDWARD, Private
Resided in Yancey County and enlisted at age 16, July 3, 1861. Transferred to Company K of this regiment on

September 16, 1861.

WILSON, HAMELTON, Private
Place and date of enlistment not reported. Reported in records of this company on December 19, 1864. No further records.

WILSON, JAMES, Private
Born in Yancey County where he resided as a farmer prior to enlisting in Yancey County at age 24, July 3, 1861. Transferred to Company K of this regiment on September 16, 1861.

WILSON, JOHN, Private
Resided in Yancey County and enlisted at age 23, July 3, 1861. Transferred to Company K of this regiment on September 16, 1861.

WILSON, THOMAS, Private
Resided in Yancey County and enlisted at age 18, July 3, 1861. Transferred to Company K of this regiment on September 16, 1861.

WILSON, WILLIAM, Private
Resided in Yancey County and enlisted at age 22, July 3, 1861. Transferred to Company K of this regiment on September 16, 1861.

WOODY, ARTHUR, ———
North Carolina pension records indicate that he served in this company.

WRIGHT, JOHN, Private
Resided in Yancey County and enlisted at age 22, July 3, 1861. Transferred to Company K of this regiment on September 16, 1861. Later served as Captain of Company K.

COMPANY C

This company, known as the "Bold Mountain Tigers," was raised in Buncombe County and enlisted on August 6, 1861. It was then assigned to the 29th Regiment N.C. Troops and designated Company C. After joining the regiment the company functioned as a part of the regiment, and its history for the war period is reported as a part of the regimental history.

The following company roster is based primarily on the North Carolina Roll of Honor, prisoner of war records, pension applications, and a variety of miscellaneous records. Information was obtained also from secondary sources such as postwar histories, cemetery records, and records of the United Daughters of the Confederacy. No muster rolls were located for the company.

OFFICERS

CAPTAINS

LOWRY, JAMES MARION
Resided in Buncombe County and enlisted at age 41. Appointed Captain on August 6, 1861. Appointed Lieutenant Colonel on May 2, 1862, and transferred to the Field and Staff of this regiment.

GUDGER, JOHN W.
Resided in Buncombe County and enlisted at age 22. Appointed 2nd Lieutenant on August 6, 1861. Promoted to Captain on May 2, 1862. Paroled at Meridian,

Mississippi, May 9, 1865.

LIEUTENANTS

ALEXANDER, ERASMUS B., 1st Lieutenant
Previously served as 2nd Lieutenant of Company F, 16th Regiment N.C. Troops (6th Regiment N.C. Volunteers). Enlisted in this company on September 12, 1862. Mustered in as Private. Accidentally wounded in the left toe on January 2, 1863. Returned to duty on an unspecified date. Appointed 2nd Lieutenant on August 1, 1863, and was promoted to 1st Lieutenant on September 23, 1863. Killed at Allatoona, Georgia, October 5, 1864.

McKEE, ROBERT FIDELIO, 1st Lieutenant
Resided in Buncombe or Haywood County and enlisted at age 30, August 6, 1861. Mustered in as Private. Appointed 1st Lieutenant on November 7, 1861. Appointed Assistant Commissary of Subsistence (Captain) on December 24, 1861, and transferred to the Field and Staff of this regiment.

RATCLIFF, MARION ISAAC, 2nd Lieutenant
Resided in Buncombe County and enlisted at age 35. Appointed 2nd Lieutenant on August 6, 1861. Resigned on April 10, 1862, by reason of "chronic rheumatism."

REEVES, JOHN A., 2nd Lieutenant
Resided in Madison County and enlisted at age 18, August 6, 1861. Mustered in as Private and was promoted to Sergeant on May 2, 1862. Elected 2nd Lieutenant on November 4, 1863. Present or accounted for through March 1, 1864. No further records.

REEVES, MALACHI W., 1st Lieutenant
Resided in Madison County and enlisted at age 38. Appointed 1st Lieutenant on August 6, 1861. Resigned on November 8, 1861, or April 23, 1862. Reason he resigned not reported.

ROBERSON, W. H., 2nd Lieutenant
Resided in Buncombe County where he enlisted at age 20, August 6, 1861. Mustered in as Sergeant and was promoted to 1st Sergeant on May 2, 1862. Appointed 2nd Lieutenant prior to August 1, 1864. Present or accounted for through December 3, 1864. No further records.

WELLS, WILLIAM F., 2nd Lieutenant
Born in Buncombe County where he resided as a farmer prior to enlisting at age 32, August 6, 1861. Mustered in as Private. Promoted to Commissary Sergeant in November, 1861, and transferred to the Field and Staff of this regiment. Appointed 2nd Lieutenant on May 2, 1862, and transferred back to this company. Died in hospital at Chattanooga, Tennessee, February 8, 1863. Cause of death not reported.

WILLIAMS, HENRY W., 1st Lieutenant
Resided in Buncombe County and enlisted at age 31, August 6, 1861. Mustered in as 1st Sergeant. Appointed 1st Lieutenant on May 2, 1862. Resigned on January 12, 1863, by reason of "chronic orchitis."

WORLEY, WILLIAM J., 2nd Lieutenant
Resided in Buncombe County and enlisted at age 22, August 6, 1861. Mustered in as Sergeant. Promoted to 2nd Lieutenant on May 2, 1862. Killed at

Chickamauga, Georgia, September 20, 1863.

NONCOMMISSIONED OFFICERS AND PRIVATES

ALDRED, ELKANA, Private
Born in Randolph County and resided in Buncombe County prior to enlisting at age 16, August 6, 1861. Died at Raleigh on December 13, 1861, of "fever."

ALEXANDER, JAMES E., Private
Born in Rabun County, Georgia, and resided in Buncombe County where he was by occupation a farmer prior to enlisting at age 16, August 6, 1861. Wounded at Chickamauga, Georgia, September 19-20, 1863. Returned to duty on an unspecified date. Captured at Nashville, Tennessee, December 15, 1864. Sent to Louisville, Kentucky. Transferred to Camp Douglas, Chicago, Illinois, where he arrived on December 22, 1864. Released on April 15, 1865, after joining the U.S. Army. Assigned to Company I, 5th Regiment U.S. Volunteer Infantry.

ALEXANDER, MARTIN S., Private
Resided in Buncombe County and enlisted at age 19, May 15, 1862, for the war. Present or accounted for through September 18, 1863. No further records.

ALLEN, LEONIDAS O., Private
Resided in Buncombe County and enlisted at age 21, August 6, 1861. Captured near Marietta, Georgia, June 18, 1864. Sent to Nashville, Tennessee. Confined at Louisville, Kentucky, June 26, 1864. Transferred to Camp Morton, Indianapolis, Indiana, where he arrived on June 28, 1864. Paroled and transferred to City Point, Virginia, February 26, 1865, for exchange.

ALLEN, NATHANIEL, Private
Place and date of enlistment not reported. Deserted to the enemy on an unspecified date. Confined at Knoxville, Tennessee, May 20, 1864. Transferred to Louisville, Kentucky, where he arrived on May 29, 1864. Released on May 31, 1864, after taking the Oath of Allegiance.

ALLEN, PHILANDER C., Corporal
Resided in Buncombe County and enlisted at age 23, August 6, 1861. Mustered in as Private. Wounded at Murfreesboro, Tennessee, December 31, 1862. Returned to duty on an unspecified date. Wounded at Chickamauga, Georgia, September 19-20, 1863. Returned to duty on an unspecified date. Promoted to Corporal prior to June 18, 1864. Captured near Marietta, Georgia, June 18, 1864. Sent to Nashville, Tennessee. Confined at Louisville, Kentucky, June 26, 1864. Transferred to Camp Morton, Indianapolis, Indiana, where he arrived on June 28, 1864. Paroled and transferred to City Point, Virginia, February 26, 1865, for exchange.

AUSTIN, BENJAMIN, Private
Resided in Madison County and enlisted at age 18, September 17, 1863, for the war. Died at Lockhart, Mississippi, December 4, 1863, of disease.

AUSTIN, JOSEPH W., Private
Resided in Madison County and enlisted at age 18, September 20, 1863, for the war. Reported absent without leave during September, 1864-February, 1865.

BALLEW, JOHN W., Private
Resided in Buncombe County and enlisted at age 17, August 6, 1861. Died at Chattanooga, Tennessee, April 9, 1863, of "pneumonia" and/or "fever."

BEACHBOARD, GEORGE W., Private
Resided in Buncombe County and enlisted at age 17, August 6, 1861. Captured near Marietta, Georgia, June 18, 1864. Sent to Nashville, Tennessee. Confined at Louisville, Kentucky, June 26, 1864. Transferred to Camp Morton, Indianapolis, Indiana, where he arrived on June 28, 1864. Paroled and transferred to City Point, Virginia, February 26, 1865. Died at Aiken's Landing, James River, Virginia, on an unspecified date. Cause of death not reported.

BLACK, ANDREW J., Private
Born in Buncombe County where he resided prior to enlisting at age 28, August 6, 1861. Died at Yazoo City, Mississippi, July 10, 1863. Cause of death not reported.

BLACK, JESSE L., Private
Resided in Buncombe County and enlisted at age 21, March 11, 1862. Reported absent without leave during September, 1864-February, 1865. [Roll of Honor indicates that he "deserted twice."]

BLACK, JOHN, Private
Born in Buncombe County where he resided prior to enlisting at age 22, April 8, 1862. Died at Tazewell, Tennessee, November 7, 1862, of "fever."

BLACK, JOHN L., Private
Resided in Buncombe County and enlisted at age 38, August 6, 1861. Discharged on or about May 26, 1862, under the provisions of the Conscription Act.

BLACK, JOSEPH, Private
Resided in Buncombe County and enlisted at age 18. Roll of Honor indicates he enlisted on August 6, 1861; however, North Carolina pension records indicate he enlisted on August 7, 1864. No further records.

BLACK, W. D., Private
Place and date of enlistment not reported. First listed in the records of this company on October 29, 1864. Captured at Spanish Fort, Mobile, Alabama, April 8, 1865. Confined at Ship Island, Mississippi, April 10, 1865. No further records.

BRIDGES, CALVIN W., Private
Resided in Buncombe County and enlisted at age 22, August 6, 1861. Reported absent without leave during September, 1864-February, 1865.

BROOKSHER, JOHN C., Private
Resided in Buncombe County and enlisted at age 22, August 6, 1861. Captured at Nashville, Tennessee, December 15, 1864. Confined at Louisville, Kentucky, December 19, 1864. Transferred to Camp Douglas, Chicago, Illinois, where he arrived on December 22, 1864. Died at Camp Douglas on May 9, 1865, of "pneumonia."

BROOKSHER, LARKIN H., Private
Born in Buncombe County where he resided as a farmer prior to enlisting in Buncombe County at age 26, August 6, 1861. Wounded in the right side at Baptist

Gap Tennessee, September 15, 1862, "while on picket duty." Discharged on April 4, 1863, by reason of wounds. Reenlisted in the company on an unspecified date. Captured near Atlanta, Georgia, July 21, 1864. Sent to Nashville, Tennessee. Confined at Louisville, Kentucky, August 3, 1864. Transferred to Camp Chase, Ohio, where he arrived on August 4, 1864. Paroled and transferred to Boulware's Wharf, James River, Virginia, where he was received on March 10-12, 1865, for exchange.

BROWN, JOHN E., Private
Resided in Buncombe County and enlisted at age 18, August 6, 1861. Captured near Marietta, Georgia, June 18, 1864. Sent to Nashville, Tennessee. Confined at Louisville, Kentucky, June 26, 1864. Transferred to Camp Morton, Indianapolis, Indiana, where he arrived on June 28, 1864. Paroled and transferred to City Point, Virginia, February 26, 1865, for exchange.

BROWN, WILLIAM J., Private
Born in Buncombe County where he resided as a farmer prior to enlisting in Buncombe County at age 24, August 6, 1861. Discharged on November 22, 1862, by reason of "epileptic fits."

BRUCE, JAMES I., ———
North Carolina pension records indicate that he served in this company.

BUCKNER, M. A., ———
North Carolina pension records indicate that he served in this company.

CAIN, JOSHUA PERRY, Private
Place and date of enlistment not reported. Captured at Richmond, Kentucky, September 15, 1862. Paroled and transferred to Camp Chase, Ohio, February 25, 1863. No further records.

CAPPS, ELISHA L., Private
Resided in Buncombe County and enlisted at age 20, August 6, 1861. Deserted on September 7, 1863.

CARLILE, LEVI, ———
North Carolina pension records indicate that he served in this company.

CARVER, JACOB A., Private
Resided in Madison County and enlisted at age 28, August 6, 1861. No further records.

CASADA, NATHANIEL V., Private
Resided in Buncombe County and enlisted at age 23, August 6, 1861. Deserted on July 17, 1863.

CASH, SHADRACH, Private
Resided in Madison or Buncombe County and enlisted at age 29, August 6, 1861. Transferred to Company H of this regiment on or about September 11, 1861. Transferred back to this company prior to December 31, 1862, when he was wounded in the left thigh at Murfreesboro, Tennessee. Reported absent without leave during September, 1864-February, 1865.

CASSADA, G. D., Private
Resided in Buncombe County and enlisted on June 15, 1861. Reported on duty as a blacksmith from December 10, 1863, through March 13, 1864. Surrendered at

Citronelle, Alabama, May 4, 1865. Paroled at Meridian, Mississippi, May 9, 1865. [North Carolina pension records indicate he was wounded at Kennesaw Mountain, Georgia, in 1864.]

CASSADA, GARRETT, Musician
Resided in Buncombe County and enlisted at age 29, August 6, 1861. Mustered in as Musician (Fifer). Detailed for duty as a blacksmith on or about May 1, 1863. Deserted on July 17, 1863. Returned to duty prior to September 30, 1863. No further records.

CASSADA, GEORGE C., Private
Born in Buncombe County where he resided prior to enlisting at age 18, August 6, 1861. Died at Morristown, Tennessee, December 12, 1862, of "fever."

CLARK, ABSALOM E., Private
Resided in Buncombe County and enlisted at age 17, August 6, 1861. Present or accounted for through February 16, 1864. No further records.

CLARK, J. M., ———
North Carolina pension records indicate that he served in this company.

CLARK, JOSEPH W., Private
Resided in Buncombe County and enlisted at age 22, August 6, 1861. Reported absent without leave during September, 1864-February, 1865. Returned to duty on an unspecified date. Surrendered at Citronelle, Alabama, May 4, 1865. Paroled at Meridian, Mississippi, May 9, 1865.

CLARK, M. T., Private
Place and date of enlistment not reported. Captured by the enemy on an unspecified date. Confined at Camp Chase, Ohio, where he died on May 13, 1865. Cause of death not reported.

CLARK, MARCUS F., Private
Place and date of enlistment not reported. Captured near Atlanta, Georgia, July 21, 1864. Sent to Nashville, Tennessee. Confined at Louisville, Kentucky, August 3, 1864. Transferred to Camp Chase, Ohio, where he arrived on August 4, 1864. Died at Camp Chase on May 13, 1865, of "remit[tent] fever."

CLARK, MITCHELL, Private
Resided in Buncombe County and enlisted at age 23, August 6, 1861. No further records.

COGGINS, ENOCH C., Private
Born in Davidson County and resided in Buncombe County prior to enlisting at age 30, August 6, 1861. Transferred to Company H of this regiment on or about September 11, 1861. Transferred back to this company prior to April 5, 1862, when he died at Tazewell, Tennessee, of "fever."

COGGINS, HENRY A., Private
Born in Davidson County and resided in Buncombe County where he was by occupation a farmer prior to enlisting at age 19, August 6, 1861. Wounded in the left thigh at Murfreesboro, Tennessee, December 31, 1862. Returned to duty on an unspecified date. Captured at Franklin, Tennessee, December 16, 1864. Sent to Nashville, Tennessee. Confined at Louisville, Kentucky, December 20, 1864. Transferred to Camp Douglas,

Chicago, Illinois, where he arrived on December 22, 1864. Released on March 24, 1865, after joining the U.S. Army. Assigned to Company D, 6th Regiment U.S. Volunteer Infantry.

COLE, J. HARDY, Private
Resided in Buncombe County and enlisted at age 33, May 1, 1863, for the war. Wounded at Chickamauga, Georgia, September 19-20, 1863. Retired to the Invalid Corps on October 10, 1864, by reason of disability.

COLE, WILLIAM H., Private
Born in Buncombe County where he resided as a farmer prior to enlisting at age 18, August 6, 1861. Transferred to Company H of this regiment on or about September 11, 1861. Transferred back to this company on an unspecified date. Captured at Chickamauga, Georgia, September 19-20, 1863. Sent to Nashville, Tennessee. Confined at Louisville, Kentucky, September 30, 1863. Transferred to Camp Douglas, Chicago, Illinois, where he arrived on October 4, 1863. Released on April 6, 1865, after joining the U.S. Army. Assigned to Company F, 5th Regiment U.S. Volunteer Infantry.

CRANE, ANDREW, Private
Resided in Yancey County. Place and date of enlistment not reported. First listed in the records of this company on June 1, 1863. Surrendered at Citronelle, Alabama, on or about May 4, 1865. Paroled at Meridian, Mississippi, on an unspecified date.

CREASMAN, RAUZ, ———
North Carolina pension records indicate that he served in this company.

CROOK, WILLIAM JASPER, Private
North Carolina pension records indicate that he served in this company.

DEAVER, JOHN, Private
Resided in Buncombe County and enlisted at age 30, August 6, 1861. Deserted on August 29, 1863. Captured by the enemy on an unspecified date. Confined at Camp Morton, Indianapolis, Indiana, where he died on January 26, 1865. Cause of death not reported.

DEBARD, THOMAS C., Sergeant
Born in Buncombe County where he resided as a farmer prior to enlisting in Buncombe County at age 36, August 6, 1861. Mustered in as Sergeant. Discharged on May 8, 1862, by reason of "general debility and severe cough."

DOCKERY, ELIJAH, Private
Resided in Buncombe County and enlisted at age 23, August 6, 1861. Reported absent without leave during September, 1864-February, 1865.

DOVER, JOHN D., Private
Place and date of enlistment not reported. First listed in the records of this company on February 27, 1864. Captured near Marietta, Georgia, June 18, 1864. Sent to Nashville, Tennessee. Confined at Louisville, Kentucky, June 26, 1864. Transferred to Camp Morton, Indianapolis, Indiana, where he arrived on June 28, 1864. Died at Camp Morton on January 26, 1865, of "inflammation of the lungs."

DUCKETT, DAVID M., Private
Resided in Buncombe County and enlisted at age 41,

August 6, 1861. Discharged on November 6, 1862, by reason of being overage.

DUCKETT, JESSE A., Private
Resided in Buncombe County and enlisted at age 21, August 6, 1861. Wounded at Chickamauga, Georgia, September 19-20, 1863. Reported absent without leave during September, 1864-February, 1865.

DUCKETT, THOMAS B., Private
Resided in Buncombe County and enlisted at age 17, April 1, 1862. Reported absent without leave during September, 1864-February, 1865.

DUCKETT, THOMAS O., Ensign
Born in Buncombe County where he resided as a farmer prior to enlisting in Buncombe County at age 42, August 6, 1861. Mustered in as Ensign. Discharged on May 26, 1862, by reason of "a dropsical effusion in both legs tending to anasarca from a long & serious attack of fever."

DUCKETT, WESLEY, Private
Born in Buncombe County where he resided as a farmer prior to enlisting in Buncombe County at age 45, August 6, 1861. Discharged on May 23, 1862, by reason of "general weakness & rheumatism of the hips (sciatica) from a long attack of fever last fall."

EMBLER, JACKSON, Private
Resided in Buncombe County and enlisted at age 29, August 6, 1861. No further records.

EMBLER, POSEY, Private
Resided in Buncombe County and enlisted at age 23, August 6, 1861. Captured near Atlanta, Georgia, July 21, 1864. Sent to Nashville, Tennessee. Confined at Louisville, Kentucky, August 2, 1864. Transferred to Camp Chase, Ohio, where he arrived on August 4, 1864. Died at Camp Chase on January 24, 1865, of "pneumonia."

EMBLER, WILLIAM, Private
Resided in Buncombe County where he enlisted at age 31, August 6, 1861. Captured near Atlanta, Georgia, July 21, 1864. Sent to Nashville, Tennessee. Confined at Louisville, Kentucky, August 3, 1864. Transferred to Camp Chase, Ohio, where he arrived on August 4, 1864. Paroled and transferred to Boulware's Wharf, James River, Virginia, where he was received March 10-12, 1865, for exchange.

ENDSLEY, JOHN, Private
Resided in Buncombe County and enlisted at age 35, August 6, 1861. Deserted on February 22, 1862. No further records.

FORE, JOSEPH, Private
Born in Buncombe County and was by occupation a farmer prior to enlisting in Buncombe County at age 36, August 6, 1861. Discharged on June 17, 1863, by reason of "old age, weak, and the Conscript Law." [North Carolina pension records indicate he was wounded at "Chickamauga, Georgia, in the spring of 1863."]

FOSTER, ALFRED M., Private
Resided in Buncombe County and enlisted at age 19, August 6, 1861. Killed at Chickamauga, Georgia, September 20, 1863.

FOSTER, JAMES, Private
Resided in Buncombe County and enlisted at age 21, August 6, 1861. Captured at Spanish Fort, Mobile, Alabama, April 8, 1865. Confined at Ship Island, Mississippi, April 10, 1865. Transferred to Vicksburg, Mississippi, May 1, 1865.

FOSTER, THOMAS FRANKLIN, Corporal
Born in Buncombe County where he resided as a farmer prior to enlisting in Buncombe County at age 26, August 6, 1861. Mustered in as Corporal. Retired from service on March 1, 1865, by reason of "chronic rheumatism."

FRISBEE, ALFRED, Private
Resided in Buncombe County and enlisted at age 36, May 1, 1863, for the war. Died in hospital at Meridian, Mississippi, January 29, 1864, of "chr[onic] diarrhoea."

FRISBEE, ANDREW J., Private
Resided in Buncombe County and enlisted at age 21, August 6, 1861. Died at Chattanooga, Tennessee, March 9, 1863, of "fever."

FRISBEE, M. FRANK, Private
Place and date of enlistment not reported. Captured near Atlanta, Georgia, July 21, 1864. Sent to Nashville, Tennessee. Confined at Louisville, Kentucky, August 3, 1864. Transferred to Camp Chase, Ohio, where he arrived on August 4, 1864. Died at Camp Chase on February 12, 1865, of "pneumonia."

FRISBEE, THOMAS, Private
Born in Buncombe County and resided in Madison County where he was by occupation a farmer prior to enlisting in Buncombe County at age 36, August 6, 1861. Discharged on June 27, 1862, by reason of "general paralysis."

FRISBEE, WILLIAM R., Sergeant
Born in Buncombe County where he resided as a farmer prior to enlisting in Buncombe County at age 22, August 6, 1861. Mustered in as Sergeant. Died at Cleveland, Tennessee, March 13, 1863, of disease.

GARMAN, ISAAC M., Private
Resided in Buncombe County and enlisted at age 15 in May, 1863, for the war. Surrendered at Citronelle, Alabama, May 4, 1865. Paroled at Meridian, Mississippi, May 9, 1865.

GARMAN, MARCUS D. L., Private
Born in Buncombe County where he resided as a farmer prior to enlisting in Buncombe County at age 35, August 6, 1861. Died at "home" on June 24-25, 1862, of "fever."

GLANCE, JACOB M., Corporal
Born in Buncombe County where he resided as a farmer prior to enlisting in Buncombe County at age 20, August 6, 1861. Mustered in as Corporal. Accidentally wounded in the left leg at Shelbyville, Tennessee,

January 5, 1863. Retired from service on February 20, 1865, by reason of wounds received at Shelbyville.

GUDGER, BENJAMIN GATTING, Private
Enlisted in 1863 for the war. Captured at Nashville, Tennessee, December 15-16, 1864. Confined at Louisville, Kentucky. Transferred to Camp Douglas, Chicago, Illinois, where he arrived on December 23, 1864. Released on June 19, 1865.

GUDGER, HUGH L., Private
Born in Buncombe County where he resided prior to enlisting at age 19, May 15, 1862, for the war. Died at Knoxville, Tennessee, July 15, 1862/63, of "fever."

GUDGER, WILLIAM J., Private
Resided in Buncombe County and enlisted at age 18, September 17, 1863. [North Carolina pension records indicate he was wounded at Allatoona, Georgia, on or about October 5, 1864.] No further records.

HALL, THOMAS, ———
North Carolina pension records indicate that he served in this company.

HANEY, JOSEPH A., Private
Resided in Buncombe County and enlisted at age 19, August 6, 1861. Captured at Chickamauga, Georgia, September 19-20, 1863. Sent to Nashville, Tennessee. Confined at Louisville, Kentucky, September 30, 1863. Transferred to Camp Douglas, Chicago, Illinois, October 2, 1863. Died at Camp Douglas on February 20, 1864, of "inflam[mation] of lungs."

HARBIN, JASPER M., Private
Resided in Buncombe County and enlisted at age 20, August 6, 1861. Wounded at Chickamauga, Georgia, September 19-20, 1863. Surrendered at Citronelle, Alabama, May 4, 1865. Paroled at Meridian, Mississippi, May 9, 1865.

HARBIN, JOSEPH D., Private
Resided in Buncombe County and enlisted at age 17, August 6, 1861. Transferred to Company H of this regiment on or about September 11, 1861. Transferred back to this company on an unspecified date. [North Carolina pension records indicate he was wounded in the right shoulder near Waynesboro on January 17, 1864.] No further records.

HAWKINS, THOMAS N., Private
Resided in Buncombe County and enlisted at age 19, May 15, 1862, for the war. No further records.

HAYES, RANSOM H., Private
Resided in Buncombe County and enlisted at age 21, August 6, 1861. Wounded in the right shoulder at Murfreesboro, Tennessee, December 31, 1862. Wounded at Chickamauga, Georgia, September 19-20, 1863. Dropped from the rolls of the company on an unspecified date for "not reporting."

HEMBREE, ABRAHAM A., Private
Resided in Buncombe County and enlisted at age 18, September 17, 1863, for the war. No further records.

HILL, HENRY, Private
Born in Newberry District, South Carolina, and resided in Buncombe County where he was by occupation a farmer prior to enlisting in Buncombe County at age 43, August 6, 1861. Discharged on May 23, 1862, by reason of "chronic rheaumatism [sic] in his hips & back."

INGLE, ANDREW E., Private
Resided in Buncombe County where he enlisted at age 27, August 6, 1861. Transferred to Company H of this regiment on January 19, 1863.

INGLE, E. S., Private
Place and date of enlistment not reported. Captured at Spanish Fort, Mobile, Alabama, April 8, 1865. Confined at Ship Island, Mississippi, April 10, 1865. Transferred to Vicksburg, Mississippi, May 1, 1865. No further records.

INGLE, MITCHELL A., Private
Resided in Buncombe County and enlisted at age 38, August 6, 1861. Discharged on November 6, 1862, by reason of being overage.

JAMES, JOHN, Private
Resided in Buncombe County and enlisted at age 39, May 1, 1863, for the war. Last reported in the records of this company on February 27, 1864.

JONES, ALLEN, Private
Born in Buncombe County where he resided as a farmer prior to enlisting in Buncombe County at age 51, August 6, 1861. Discharged on May 23, 1862, by reason of "chronic rheaumatism [sic] in his back & hips caused by an attack of fever."

KING, ANDREW J., Private
Resided in Buncombe County and enlisted at age 17, April 1, 1862. Discharged on November 6, 1862, by reason of being underage.

KING, DANIEL E., Private
Resided in Buncombe County and enlisted at age 30, August 6, 1861. Last reported in the records of this company on May 8, 1863. [North Carolina pension records indicate he was wounded near Atlanta, Georgia, September 25, 1864.]

KING, JAMES, Private
Resided in Buncombe County. Place and date of enlistment not reported. Captured in Buncombe County on an unspecified date. Confined at Chattanooga, Tennessee. Transferred to Louisville, Kentucky, where he arrived on July 28, 1864. Released on July 31, 1864, after taking the Oath of Allegiance.

KING, JONATHAN W., Private
Resided in Buncombe County and enlisted at age 20, August 6, 1861. Wounded at Chickamauga, Georgia, September 19-20, 1863. Hospitalized at Augusta, Georgia, where he died on October 21, 1863, of wounds.

KING, JOSEPH H., Private
Previously served in Company K, 60th Regiment N.C. Troops. Transferred to this company on August 1, 1863. Wounded at Chickamauga, Georgia, September 19-20, 1863. No further records.

KING, JOSHUA P., Private
Resided in Buncombe County and enlisted at age 27, August 6, 1861. Captured "in Kentucky" in September-

October, 1862. Confined at Louisville, Kentucky. Transferred to Camp Chase, Ohio, where he arrived on February 26, 1863. Paroled and transferred to City Point, Virginia, where he was received April 1-2, 1863, for exchange. No further records.

KING, WILEY C., Private
Resided in Buncombe County and enlisted at age 17, August 6, 1861. No further records.

KING, WILLIAM, Private
Place and date of enlistment not reported. Captured near Atlanta, Georgia, July 21, 1864. Sent to Nashville, Tennessee. Confined at Louisville, Kentucky, August 3, 1864. Transferred to Camp Chase, Ohio, where he arrived on August 4, 1864. Paroled and transferred to Boulware's Wharf, James River, Virginia, where he was received March 10-12, 1865, for exchange.

KING, WILLIAMSON E., Private
Resided in Buncombe County and enlisted at age 19, August 6, 1861. No further records.

KIRKPATRICK, JAMES TAYLOR, Private
Records of the United Daughters of the Confederacy indicate he enlisted in this company at age 17, April 30, 1862, for the war. No further records.

LANKFORD, W. L., ———
North Carolina pension records indicate that he served in this company.

LANNING, JAMES R., Private
Previously served in Company E, 1st Regiment N.C. Infantry (6 months, 1861). Enlisted in this company on January 27, 1862. Captured at Spanish Fort, Mobile, Alabama, April 8, 1865. Confined at Ship Island, Mississippi, April 10, 1865. Transferred to Vicksburg, Mississippi, May 1, 1865.

LANNING, JOHN W., Private
Resided in Buncombe County and enlisted at age 24, August 6, 1861. Died at Shelbyville, Tennessee, April 13, 1863, of "fever."

LITTERAL, THOMAS, Private
Resided in Buncombe County and enlisted at age 37, August 6, 1861. Discharged on November 6, 1862, by reason of being overage.

LUNSFORD, AMOS, Private
Resided in Madison County and enlisted at age 30, August 6, 1861. Captured "in Kentucky" in September-October, 1862. Confined at Cincinnati, Ohio. Transferred to Camp Chase, Ohio, where he arrived on April 18, 1863. Paroled and transferred to City Point, Virginia, where he was received on May 17, 1863, for exchange. Declared exchanged on May 23, 1863. No further records.

LUNSFORD, EZEKIEL, Private
Resided in Madison County and enlisted at age 25, August 6, 1861. Deserted on September 6, 1863. Went over to the enemy on an unspecified date. Took the Oath of Allegiance at Nashville, Tennessee, December 31, 1864.

LUNSFORD, SIDNEY, Private
Resided in Madison County and enlisted at age 27,

August 6, 1861. Deserted on September 6, 1863. Returned to duty on an unspecified date. Captured near Franklin, Tennessee, December 17, 1864. Sent to Nashville, Tennessee. Confined at Louisville, Kentucky, December 20, 1864. Transferred to Camp Douglas, Chicago, Illinois, where he arrived on December 22, 1864. Released on May 11, 1865, after taking the Oath of Allegiance.

LUSK, JOHN R., Private
Previously served in Company E, 1st Regiment N.C. Infantry (6 months, 1861). Enlisted in this company on February 1, 1862. Reported absent without leave during September, 1864-February, 1865.

McENTIRE, JOSEPH M., Private
Resided in Buncombe County and enlisted at age 19, May 1, 1863, for the war. Surrendered at Citronelle, Alabama, May 4, 1865. Paroled at Meridian, Mississippi, May 9, 1865.

McFALLS, DANIEL A., Private
Resided in Buncombe County and enlisted at age 19, January 21, 1862. Captured at Chickamauga, Georgia, September 19-20, 1863. Sent to Nashville, Tennessee. Confined at Louisville, Kentucky, October 1, 1863. Transferred to Camp Douglas, Chicago, Illinois, October 2, 1863. Released at Camp Douglas on December 26, 1863, after joining the U.S. Navy.

McFALLS, WILLIAM J., Private
Resided in Haywood County and enlisted at age 32, May 2, 1862, for the war. Transferred to Company E of this regiment on February 1, 1863.

McINTYRE, JAMES M., Corporal
Resided in Buncombe County and enlisted at age 16, October 27, 1861. Mustered in as Private and was promoted to Corporal prior to July 21, 1864. Captured near Atlanta, Georgia, July 21, 1864. Sent to Nashville, Tennessee. Confined at Louisville, Kentucky, August 3, 1864. Transferred to Camp Chase, Ohio, where he arrived on August 4, 1864. Paroled and transferred to Boulware's Wharf, James River, Virginia, where he was received on March 10-12, 1865, for exchange. Hospitalized at Meridian, Mississippi, April 11, 1865, with a wound. Place and date wounded not reported.

MANN, ISAAC, Private
Resided in Buncombe County and enlisted at age 20, August 6, 1861. Captured at Chickamauga, Georgia, September 19, 1863. Sent to Nashville, Tennessee. Confined at Louisville, Kentucky, September 30, 1864. Transferred to Camp Douglas, Chicago, Illinois, where he arrived on October 4, 1863. Died at Camp Douglas on May 9, 1865. Cause of death not reported.

MILES, ANDREW J., Private
Born in Buncombe County where he resided as a farmer prior to enlisting in Buncombe County at age 25, August 6, 1861. Discharged on May 1, 1862, by reason of "phthisis pulmonalis of long standing."

MILES, HENRY B., Private
Resided in Buncombe County and enlisted at age 21, August 6, 1861. Mustered in as Private and was promoted to Sergeant on August 20, 1863. Reduced to ranks on an unspecified date. Deserted to the enemy on an unspecified date. Confined at Louisville, Kentucky,

August 5, 1864. Released on or about August 10, 1864, after taking the Oath of Allegiance.

MILES, HUMPHREY P., Private
Enlisted in March, 1863, for the war. Captured near Atlanta, Georgia, July 21, 1864. Sent to Nashville, Tennessee. Confined at Louisville, Kentucky, August 3, 1864. Transferred to Camp Chase, Ohio, where he arrived on August 4, 1864. Died at Camp Chase on February 6, 1865, of "pneumonia."

MILES, LEWIS P., Private
Resided in Buncombe County and enlisted at age 25, August 6, 1861. Captured near Atlanta, Georgia, July 21, 1864. Sent to Nashville, Tennessee. Confined at Louisville, Kentucky, August 3, 1864. Transferred to Camp Chase, Ohio, where he arrived on August 4, 1864. Paroled and transferred to Boulware's Wharf, James River, Virginia, where he was received on March 10-12, 1865, for exchange.

MILLER, JAMES L., Private
Resided in Buncombe County and enlisted at age 36, August 6, 1861. Hospitalized at Macon, Georgia, on or about October 26, 1864, with a fracture of the left forearm. Place and date injured not reported. No further records.

MILLER, JAMES P., Private
Resided in Madison or Buncombe County and enlisted at age 21, August 6, 1861. Captured by the enemy (or deserted) on an unspecified date. Confined at Nashville, Tennessee, where he was released on January 4, 1864, after taking the Oath of Allegiance.

MOODY, J. W. D., Private
Resided in Haywood County. Place and date of enlistment not reported. Deserted to the enemy on an unspecified date. Confined at Louisville, Kentucky, April 2, 1865. Released on or about April 8, 1865, after taking the Oath of Allegiance.

NASH, ROBERT, Private
Born in Buncombe County where he resided prior to enlisting at age 18, May 1, 1863, for the war. Died in hospital at Lauderdale Springs, Mississippi, August 22, 1863, of disease.

NASH, THOMAS M., Private
Resided in Buncombe County and enlisted at age 20, August 6, 1861. Captured near Atlanta, Georgia, July 21, 1864. Sent to Nashville, Tennessee. Confined at Louisville, Kentucky, August 3, 1864. Transferred to Camp Chase, Ohio, where he arrived on August 4, 1864. Died at Camp Chase on October 21, 1864, of "smallpox."

NEILL, J. S., Private
Place and date of enlistment not reported. Died in hospital at Griffin, Georgia, July 12, 1864. Cause of death not reported.

NETHERTON, JAMES M., Private
Resided in Buncombe County and enlisted at age 19, August 6, 1861. Wounded in the left leg at Murfreesboro, Tennessee, December 31, 1862. Discharged on July 26, 1864, by reason of having been elected 2nd Lieutenant of Company C, 64th Regiment N.C. Troops.

NETHERTON, THOMAS J., Sergeant
Resided in Buncombe County and enlisted at age 23, August 6, 1861. Mustered in as Private and was promoted to Sergeant on May 2, 1862. Wounded in the left thumb at Murfreesboro, Tennessee, December 31, 1862. Returned to duty on an unspecified date. Captured at Yazoo City, Mississippi, July 13, 1863. Died at Yazoo City on July 20, 1863. Cause of death not reported.

PARHAM, PHILIP, Private
Resided in Buncombe County where he enlisted at age 39, May 1, 1863, for the war. Surrendered at Citronelle, Alabama, May 4, 1865. Paroled at Meridian, Mississippi, May 9, 1865.

PARRIS, DAVID M., Private
Resided in Buncombe County and enlisted at age 18, August 6, 1861. Captured near Atlanta, Georgia, July 21, 1864. Sent to Nashville, Tennessee. Confined at Louisville, Kentucky, August 3, 1864. Transferred to Camp Chase, Ohio, where he arrived on August 4, 1864. Paroled and transferred to Boulware's Wharf, James River, Virginia, where he was received on March 10-12, 1865, for exchange.

PENLAND, WILLIAM M., Private
Born in Buncombe County and was by occupation a farmer prior to enlisting in Buncombe County at age 44, April 4, 1864, for the war. Captured by the enemy on an unspecified date. Paroled at Catawba Bridge, South Carolina, May 5, 1865. [May have served previously as Sergeant Major of the 109th Regiment N.C. Militia.]

PHILLIPS, J. C., ———
North Carolina pension records indicate that he served in this company.

PLEMMONS, ANDREW J., Private
Born in Buncombe County and resided in Buncombe or Madison County where he was by occupation a farmer prior to enlisting in Buncombe County at age 36, August 6, 1861. Discharged on June 26, 1862, by reason of "an attack of fever." Reenlisted in the company on an unspecified date. Surrendered at Citronelle, Alabama, May 4, 1865. Paroled at Meridian, Mississippi, May 9, 1865. [North Carolina pension records indicate he was wounded in the shoulder at Mobile, Alabama, April 1, 1865.]

PLEMMONS, DAVID S., Private
Resided in Buncombe County and enlisted at age 31, August 6, 1861. Appointed Assistant Commissary of Subsistence (Captain) on October 4, 1862, to rank from August 2, 1862, and transferred to the Field and Staff of this regiment.

PLEMMONS, LEVI, Private
Resided in Buncombe County and enlisted at age 26, August 6, 1861. Promoted to Commissary Sergeant on May 2, 1862, and transferred to the Field and Staff of this regiment.

PLEMMONS, MERRIT, Private
Born in Buncombe County where he resided as a farmer prior to enlisting in Buncombe County at age 20, August 6, 1861. Died at or near Haynesville, Tennessee, January 8-9, 1862. Cause of death not reported.

RANDALL, ABRAM E., Musician
Resided in Buncombe County and enlisted at age 22, August 6, 1861. Mustered in as Musician (Drummer). Reported absent without leave during September, 1864-February, 1865.

RATCLIFF, THOMAS J., Private
Resided in Buncombe County where he enlisted at age 30, August 6, 1861. Died at Marion Station, Mississippi, in November, 1863. Cause of death not reported.

REDMON, DANIEL M., Private
Resided in Buncombe County and enlisted at age 44, August 6, 1861. Discharged on November 6, 1862. Reason discharged not reported.

REEVES, ANDERSON P., Corporal
Resided in Buncombe County and enlisted at age 33, August 6, 1861. Mustered in as Corporal. Deserted on September 6, 1863.

REEVES, JAMES M., Private
Resided in Madison County and enlisted at age 18, October 27, 1861. Wounded in the left arm at Murfreesboro, Tennessee, December 31, 1862. Reported absent without leave during September, 1864-February, 1865.

REEVES, WILLIAM H., 1st Sergeant
Resided in Madison County and enlisted at age 18, August 6, 1861. Mustered in as Private. Promoted to Sergeant on May 2, 1862. Promoted to 1st Sergeant on an unspecified date. Reported absent without leave during September, 1864-February, 1865.

REEVES, WILLS, Private
Born in Buncombe County and resided in Madison County where he was by occupation a farmer prior to enlisting in Buncombe County at age 62, August 6, 1861. Discharged on June 6, 1862, by reason of "fever contracted in camp & followed by rheumatism & general debility & being 63 years of age."

REYNOLDS, DANIEL C., Private
Resided in Buncombe County and enlisted at age 22, August 6, 1861. Reported absent without leave during September, 1861-February, 1865.

RICH, JOHN R., Private
Resided in Buncombe County and enlisted at age 18, June 27, 1862, for the war. Clark's *Regiments* gives the following information concerning Rich: "[He] was so small and so young that he was not allowed to enlist regularly, but like many other boys . . ., would not be deterred by little obstacles of that kind, but followed along with the battle [at Murfreesboro, Tennessee, December 31, 1862], without [a] gun, and when the first man in ranks fell he grabbed his gun and went to shooting. A little later the color-bearer being killed, he voluntarily caught up the flag and carried it almost continuously to the end." No further records.

ROBERSON, DAVID H., Private
Resided in Buncombe County and enlisted at age 23, August 6, 1861. Reported absent without leave during September, 1864-February, 1865.

ROBERSON, GEORGE C., Private
Resided in Buncombe County and enlisted at age 18,

May 1, 1863, for the war. Reported absent without leave during September, 1864-February, 1865.

ROBERSON, JAMES D., Sergeant
Resided in Buncombe County and enlisted at age 19, August 6, 1861. Mustered in as Private and was promoted to Corporal on August 20, 1863. Wounded at Chickamauga, Georgia, September 19-20, 1863. Promoted to Sergeant on an unspecified date. Reported absent without leave during September, 1864-February, 1865.

ROBERSON, WILLIAM N., Private
Born in Buncombe County where he resided as a farmer prior to enlisting in Buncombe County at age 20, August 6, 1861. Died at Tazewell, Tennessee, March 29, 1862, of "fever."

ROBERTS, MARQUIS L., Private
Resided in Buncombe County and enlisted at age 17, August 6, 1861. Wounded at Chickamauga, Georgia, September 19-20, 1863. Present or accounted for through October 17, 1863. No further records.

ROBINSON, JESSE A., Private
Resided in Buncombe County and enlisted at age 21, August 6, 1861. Reported absent without leave in September, 1864-February, 1865.

RODGERS, JOHN W., Private
Born in Buncombe County where he resided prior to enlisting at age 16, August 6, 1861. Died at Morristown, Tennessee, July 14, 1862, of "fever."

SAMS, ANSON M., Private
Resided in Buncombe County and enlisted at age 21, August 6, 1861. Last reported in the records of this company on September 26, 1863.

SELLERS, T. L., Private
Records of the United Daughters of the Confederacy indicate he enlisted in this company on March 14, 1862. No further records.

SLUDER, FEDILLA, Corporal
Resided in Buncombe County and enlisted at age 17, August 6, 1861. Mustered in as Private. Promoted to Corporal on May 2, 1862. Wounded at Chickamauga, Georgia, September 19-20, 1863. [North Carolina pension records indicate that he survived the war.] No further records.

SLUDER, J. E., ———
North Carolina pension records indicate that he served in this company.

SLUDER, MERRIT J., Private
Born in Buncombe County where he resided prior to enlisting at age 24, August 6, 1861. Died at Shelbyville, Tennessee, January 30-31, 1863, of "smallpox."

SLUDER, W. M., Private
Place and date of enlistment not reported. Captured at Spanish Fort, Mobile, Alabama, April 8, 1865. Confined at Ship Island, Mississippi, April 10, 1865. Transferred to Vicksburg, Mississippi, May 1, 1865. No further records.

SMATHERS, CHARLES L., Corporal
Records of the United Daughters of the Confederacy

indicate he enlisted on June 3, 1862, for the war. [May have served later in Company C, Infantry Regiment, Thomas Legion.] No further records.

SMATHERS, JAMES HENRY, Private

Records of the United Daughters of the Confederacy indicate he was born in Haywood County and enlisted on May 2, 1862, for the war. [May have served later in Company C, Infantry Regiment, Thomas Legion.] No further records.

SMITH, SILAS, ———

North Carolina pension records indicate that he served in this company.

SNELSON, T. E., ———

North Carolina pension records indicate that he served in this company.

SNELSON, WILLIAM, Private

Resided in Buncombe County and enlisted at age 18, March 1, 1863, for the war. Captured near Marietta, Georgia, June 18-19, 1864. Sent to Nashville, Tennessee. Confined at Louisville, Kentucky, June 26, 1864. Transferred to Camp Morton, Indianapolis, Indiana, where he arrived on June 28, 1864. Died at Camp Morton on February 10, 1865, of "inflammation of the lungs." [May have served previously in Company B, 16th Regiment N.C. Troops (6th Regiment N.C. Volunteers).]

SPIREY, BENJAMIN F., Private

Resided in Buncombe County and enlisted at age 37, May 1, 1863, for the war. Captured at Spanish Fort, Mobile, Alabama, April 8, 1865. Confined at Ship Island, Mississippi, April 10, 1865. Transferred to Vicksburg, Mississippi, May 1, 1865. No further records.

SPURLING, JAMES C., Private

Resided in Buncombe County and enlisted at age 36, May 1, 1863, for the war. Wounded at Chickamauga, Georgia, September 19-20, 1863. Surrendered at Citronelle, Alabama, May 4, 1865. Paroled at Meridian, Mississippi, May 9, 1865.

STARNES, GEORGE H., Private

Born in Burke County and resided in Buncombe County where he was by occupation a farmer prior to enlisting in Buncombe County at age 52, August 6, 1861. Discharged on June 5, 1862, by reason of "a worn out constitution (being 54 years old) & c[hronic] [rhe]umatism."

STARNES, JOHN H., Private

Resided in Buncombe County and enlisted at age 18, August 6, 1861. Captured near Atlanta, Georgia, July 21, 1864. Sent to Nashville, Tennessee. Confined at Louisville, Kentucky, August 3, 1864. Transferred to Camp Chase, Ohio, where he arrived on August 4, 1864. Paroled and transferred to Boulware's Wharf, James River, Virginia, where he was received on March 10-12, 1865, for exchange.

SURRETT, JAMES B., Private

Resided in Buncombe County and enlisted at age 29, August 6, 1861. Captured near Atlanta, Georgia, July 21, 1864. Sent to Nashville, Tennessee. Confined at Louisville, Kentucky, on or about August 3, 1864.

Transferred to Camp Chase, Ohio, where he arrived on August 4, 1864. Released on June 11, 1865, after taking the Oath of Allegiance.

TEAGUE, ADOLPHUS H., Corporal

Resided in Buncombe County and enlisted at age 18, August 6, 1861. Mustered in as Private and was promoted to Corporal on May 2, 1862. Captured "in Kentucky" in September-November, 1862. Confined at Chattanooga, Tennessee. Exchanged on January 11, 1863. Wounded at Chickamauga, Georgia, September 19-20, 1863. Returned to duty on an unspecified date. Captured in Cherokee County, Alabama, October 21, 1864. Sent to Nashville, Tennessee. Confined at Louisville, Kentucky, November 22, 1864. Transferred to Camp Douglas, Chicago, Illinois, where he arrived on November 26, 1864. Paroled and transferred to Boulware's Wharf, James River, Virginia, where he was received on March 18-21, 1865, for exchange.

TEAGUE, J. A., ———

North Carolina pension records indicate that he served in this company.

TREADAWAY, ERWIN N., Private

Resided in Buncombe County and enlisted at age 21, August 6, 1861. Wounded at Chickamauga, Georgia, September 19-20, 1863. Returned to duty on an unspecified date. Present or accounted for through June 30, 1864. No further records.

TREADAWAY, MADISON M., Sergeant

Resided in Buncombe County and enlisted at age 24, August 6, 1861. Mustered in as Private and was promoted to Sergeant on May 2, 1862. Surrendered at Citronelle, Alabama, May 4, 1865. Paroled at Meridian, Mississippi, May 9, 1865. [North Carolina pension records indicate he was wounded in two places at Kennesaw Mountain, Georgia.]

WARLEY, JOSEPH D., Private

Resided in Madison County and enlisted at age 19, August 6, 1861. Deserted on June 27, 1862.

WELLS, J. D., Private

Place and date of enlistment not reported. Captured and paroled at Yazoo City, Mississippi, July 13, 1863. Returned to duty on an unspecified date. Captured at Spanish Fort, Mobile, Alabama, April 8, 1865. Confined at Ship Island, Mississippi, April 10, 1865. Transferred to Vicksburg, Mississippi, May 1, 1865. No further records.

WELLS, JACOB W., Private

Resided in Buncombe County and enlisted at age 22, August 6, 1861. Transferred to Company H of this regiment on September 11, 1861. Discharged on May 22, 1862, while a member of Company H. Reenlisted in this company on an unspecified date. Present or accounted for from April 13 through September 30, 1863. Appointed Hospital Steward and transferred to the Field and Staff of this regiment on an unspecified date.

WELLS, JASON HENRY, Private

Resided in Buncombe County and enlisted at age 32, August 6, 1861. Deserted on an unspecified date. Enlisted in Company A, 5th Battalion N.C. Cavalry, October 25, 1862.

WELLS, JULIUS D., Private
Resided in Buncombe County and enlisted at age 18, August 6, 1861. Transferred to Company H of this regiment on September 11, 1861.

WHITEHEAD, JAMES, Private
Born in Chester District, South Carolina, and resided in Buncombe County where he was by occupation a farmer prior to enlisting in Buncombe County at age 34, August 6, 1861. Transferred to Company H of this regiment on or about September 11, 1861. Transferred back to this company on an unspecified date. Discharged on June 17, 1863, by reason of being overage.

WILLIAMS, EDMUND R., Private
Resided in Buncombe County and enlisted at age 20, August 6, 1861. Captured near Marietta, Georgia, June 18, 1864. Sent to Nashville, Tennessee. Confined at Louisville, Kentucky, June 26, 1864. Transferred to Camp Morton, Indianapolis, Indiana, where he arrived on June 28, 1864. Paroled and transferred to Boulware's Wharf, James River, Virginia, where he was received on March 10-12, 1865, for exchange. Hospitalized at Richmond, Virginia, March 11, 1865. Furloughed for sixty days on March 15, 1865.

WILLS, ADOLPHUS E., Corporal
Resided in Buncombe County and enlisted at age 27, August 1, 1861. Mustered in as Corporal. Deserted on September 6, 1863.

WRIGHT, JAMES M., Private
Resided in Buncombe County and enlisted at age 23, August 6, 1861. Deserted on September 6, 1863.

WRIGHT, THOMAS S., Private
Previously served in Company A, 60th Regiment N.C. Troops. Transferred to this company in July-August, 1863. Died at Lauderdale Springs, Mississippi, August 9, 1863. Cause of death not reported.

COMPANY D

This company was raised in Madison County and enlisted on August 13, 1861. It was then assigned to the 29th Regiment and designated Company D. After joining the regiment the company functioned as a part of the regiment, and its history for the war period is reported as a part of the regimental history.

The following company roster is based primarily on the North Carolina Roll of Honor, prisoner of war records, pension applications, and a variety of miscellaneous records. Information was obtained also from secondary sources such as postwar histories, cemetery records, and records of the United Daughters of the Confederacy. No muster rolls were located for the company.

OFFICERS

CAPTAINS

JARVIS, JOHN A.
Resided in Madison County and enlisted at age 33. Appointed Captain on August 13, 1861. Defeated for reelection when the regiment was reorganized on May 2, 1862.

ROLLINS, WALLACE W.
Resided in Madison County and enlisted at age 23,

August 13, 1861. Mustered in as 1st Sergeant. Promoted to Sergeant Major on an unspecified date and transferred to the Field and Staff of this regiment. Appointed Captain on May 2, 1862, and transferred back to this company. Deserted from hospital at Augusta, Georgia, August 12, 1864. "Went to the enemy & took . . . twenty men with him and is now [January 17, 1865] commanding troops in the enemy's lines in east Tennessee." Dropped from the rolls of the company on February 17, 1865.

LIEUTENANTS

BROWN, WILLIAM H., 2nd Lieutenant
Resided in Madison County prior to enlisting at age 30. Appointed 2nd Lieutenant on August 13, 1861. Resigned on August 13, 1862, by reason of "a broken down constitution" resulting from "frequent attacks of fever and diarrhoea."

DEWEES, ARTHUR A., 1st Lieutenant
Resided in Madison County and enlisted at age 29. Appointed 1st Lieutenant on August 13, 1861. Defeated for reelection when the regiment was reorganized on May 2, 1862. Later served as Captain of Company D, 64th Regiment N.C. Troops.

HALL, JOHN W., 1st Lieutenant
Resided in Madison County and enlisted at age 29. Appointed 2nd Lieutenant on August 13, 1861. Promoted to 1st Lieutenant on May 2, 1862. Wounded in the left thigh at Murfreesboro, Tennessee, December 31, 1862. Deserted to the enemy on or about June 3, 1864. Confined at Knoxville, Tennessee. Released on or about June 24, 1864, after taking the Oath of Allegiance.

McLEAN, HENRY L., 2nd Lieutenant
Resided in Madison County and enlisted at age 35. Appointed 3rd Lieutenant on August 13, 1861. Promoted to 2nd Lieutenant on May 2, 1862. Paroled at Meridian, Mississippi, May 9, 1865.

RAMSAY, JAMES A., 2nd Lieutenant
Resided in Madison County and enlisted at age 21, August 13, 1861. Mustered in as Corporal and was appointed 2nd Lieutenant on November 20, 1862. Resigned on February 23, 1863, by reason of "chronic diarrhoea" and "chronic rheumatism of both hips." Resignation accepted on or about March 11, 1863.

ROBERTS, ERVIN F., 3rd Lieutenant
Resided in Madison County and enlisted at age 22, August 13, 1861. Mustered in as Sergeant. Appointed 3rd Lieutenant on June 24, 1863. Deserted to the enemy on or about May 25, 1864. Confined at Knoxville, Tennessee. Released on or about June 24, 1864, after taking the Oath of Allegiance. [Nominated for the Badge of Distinction for gallantry at Murfreesboro, Tennessee, December 31, 1862. Reported on duty as acting Adjutant with the Field and Staff of this regiment during January-March, 1864.]

NONCOMMISSIONED OFFICERS AND PRIVATES

ALLEN, A. C., Private
Resided in Yancey County. Place and date of enlistment not reported. Surrendered at Citronelle, Alabama, May

4, 1865. Paroled at Meridian, Mississippi, May 9, 1865.

AMMONS, ALLEN, Private
Resided in Madison County and enlisted at age 32, August 13, 1861. Captured at Murfreesboro, Tennessee, December 31, 1862. Confined at Camp Douglas, Chicago, Illinois. Paroled and transferred to City Point, Virginia, where he was received on April 4, 1863, for exchange. Deserted to the enemy on an unspecified date. Confined at Knoxville, Tennessee, March 3, 1865. Transferred to Louisville, Kentucky, where he arrived on March 18, 1865. Released on March 21, 1865, after taking the Oath of Allegiance.

AMMONS, HIRAM D., Private
Resided in Madison County and enlisted at age 24, August 13, 1861. Captured at Yazoo City, Mississippi, July 13, 1863. Sent to Memphis, Tennessee. Confined at St. Louis, Missouri, August 3, 1863. Transferred to Camp Morton, Indianapolis, Indiana, where he arrived on August 27, 1863. Paroled and transferred to City Point, Virginia, where he was received on February 26, 1865, for exchange.

AUSTIN, WILLIAM A., Private
Resided in Madison County and enlisted at age 29, August 13, 1861. Discharged in November, 1861, after providing a substitute.

BLANKENSHIP, JOHN O., Private
Resided in Madison County and enlisted at age 37, August 13, 1861. Discharged on November 6, 1862. Reason discharged not reported.

BOON, GEORGE W., Private
Born in Yancey County and resided in Madison County prior to enlisting at age 21, August 13, 1861. Died at Cleveland, Tennessee, February 17, 1863, of "smallpox."

BOON, JAMES E., Private
Resided in Madison County and enlisted at age 27, August 13, 1861. Deserted on September 7, 1863. [North Carolina pension records indicate he was wounded in 1863.]

BOONE, W. RILEY, Private
Resided in Madison County and enlisted at age 17, August 13, 1861. Last reported in the records of this company on November 30, 1863. [North Carolina pension records indicate he was wounded at Murfreesboro, Tennessee, in 1863.]

BRADLEY, JERE W., Private
Resided in Madison County and enlisted at age 20, August 13, 1861. Captured at Spanish Fort, Mobile, Alabama, April 8, 1865. Confined at Ship Island, Mississippi, April 10, 1865. Transferred to Vicksburg, Mississippi, May 1, 1865. [North Carolina pension records indicate he was wounded in 1863.]

BRADLEY, JOSEPH D., Private
Resided in Madison County and enlisted at age 28, August 13, 1861. No further records.

BRIGGS, HENRY, Private
Place and date of enlistment not reported. Captured at or near Jonesboro, Georgia, on or about October 19, 1864. Sent to Nashville, Tennessee. Confined at

Louisville, Kentucky, November 22, 1864. Transferred to Camp Chase, Ohio, where he arrived on January 2, 1865. Died at Camp Chase on February 14, 1865, of "variola."

BROWN, ANDREW J., Private
Resided in Madison County and enlisted at age 25, April 7, 1862. Appointed 3rd Lieutenant and transferred to Company F, 64th Regiment N.C. Troops, on or about November 5, 1862.

BROWN, WILLIAM ALBERT GALLATIN, Private
Born in Blount County, Tennessee, and resided in Jefferson County, Tennessee, prior to enlisting at age 32, May 1, 1862, for the war. Wounded at Chickamauga, Georgia, September 19-20, 1863. Promoted to Quartermaster Sergeant and transferred to the Field and Staff of this regiment on October 1, 1863.

BUCKNER, ALBERT, Private
Resided in Madison County and enlisted at age 27, August 13, 1861. Died at Atlanta, Georgia, April 15 or May 15-19, 1863, of "fever."

BUCKNER, ELIJAH, Private
Previously served in Company K of this regiment. Transferred to this company on June 1, 1862. No further records.

BUGMON, MAY, Private
Resided in Madison County and enlisted at age 21, August 13, 1861. Company records indicate he was transferred to the 64th Regiment N.C. Troops on November 7, 1862; however, records of the 64th Regiment do not indicate that he served therein. No further records.

CALAHAN, JAMES W., Private
Born in Yancey County and resided in Madison County where he was by occupation a farmer prior to enlisting in Madison County at age 23, August 13, 1861. Died at Cumberland Gap, Tennessee, April 27, 1862, of "fever."

CALAHAN, JOEL, Private
Born in Yancey County and resided in Madison County where he enlisted at age 24, August 13, 1861. Discharged on or about January 29, 1862, after "accidently cutting off four of his fingers on the left hand."

CARTER, WILLIAM G., Private
Place and date of enlistment not reported. Captured near Atlanta, Georgia, July 21, 1864. Confined at Louisville, Kentucky. Transferred to Camp Chase, Ohio, where he arrived on August 4, 1864. Died at Camp Chase on January 28, 1865, of "typhoid fever."

CHAMBERS, GARRET S., 1st Sergeant
Resided in Madison County and enlisted at age 17, August 13, 1861. Mustered in as Private and was promoted to 1st Sergeant on June 24, 1863. Captured by the enemy (or deserted) in Madison County on an unspecified date. Confined at Knoxville, Tennessee, June 21, 1864. Transferred to Louisville, Kentucky, where he arrived on June 29, 1864. Released on July 1, 1864, after taking the Oath of Allegiance.

CHAMBERS, STEPHEN M., Private
Resided in Madison County and enlisted at age 22,

August 13, 1861. Wounded at Chickamauga, Georgia, September 19-20, 1863. Took the Oath of Allegiance at Cumberland Gap, Tennessee, January 30, 1865.

CHANDLER, TIMOTHY, Private
Resided in Madison County and enlisted at age 18, August 13, 1861. Deserted on September 5, 1863.

CLARK, LEWIS, Private
Born in Yancey County and resided in Madison County prior to enlisting at age 20, August 13, 1861. Died at Shelbyville, Tennessee, February 17, 1863. Cause of death not reported.

COATS, GARRET D., Private
Resided in Madison County and enlisted at age 25, August 13, 1861. Last reported in the records of this company on April 30, 1863.

COPENING, E. H., Private
Resided in McDowell County. Place and date of enlistment not reported. Surrendered at Citronelle, Alabama, May 4, 1865. Paroled at Meridian, Mississippi, May 16, 1865.

CROWDER, JAMES A., Corporal
Resided in Madison County and enlisted at age 32, August 13, 1861. Mustered in as Corporal. Deserted on September 26, 1863.

CROWDER, JOHN W., Private
Born in Yancey County and resided in Madison County where he was by occupation a farmer prior to enlisting in Madison County at age 22, August 13, 1861. Died in hospital at Chattanooga, Tennessee, February 17, 1863, of ''fever.''

CRYSEL, J. A., Private
Resided in Wilkes County. Place and date of enlistment not reported. Captured at Citronelle, Alabama, May 4, 1865. Paroled at Meridian, Mississippi, May 9, 1865.

DANIEL, JOHN H., Private
Resided in Madison County and enlisted at age 20, August 13, 1861. Mustered in as Private and was promoted to Sergeant on June 30, 1863. Reduced to ranks on an unspecified date. Deserted on March 4, 1864. Went over to the enemy on an unspecified date. Sent to Knoxville, Tennessee. Transferred to Louisville, Kentucky, where he arrived on July 16, 1864. Released on or about July 18, 1864, after taking the Oath of Allegiance.

DANIEL, WILLIAM, Private
Resided in Madison County and enlisted at age 22, August 13, 1861. Mustered in as Private and was promoted to Corporal on August 3, 1863. Reduced to ranks on an unspecified date. Deserted on March 4, 1864. Went over to the enemy on an unspecified date. Confined at Knoxville, Tennessee. Transferred to Louisville, Kentucky, where he arrived on July 16, 1864. Released on or about July 18, 1864, after taking the Oath of Allegiance.

DEAVER, HARRY B., Private
Resided in Madison County and enlisted at age 17, August 13, 1861. Deserted on September 7, 1863.

DEAVER, WILLIAM H., Private
Resided in Madison County and enlisted at age 16, July 7, 1862, for the war. No further records.

DRAKE, F., Private
Place and date of enlistment not reported. Captured at Spanish Fort, Mobile, Alabama, April 8, 1865. Confined at Ship Island, Mississippi, April 10, 1865. Transferred to Vicksburg, Mississippi, May 1, 1865. No further records.

DRAKE, JOHN, Private
Place and date of enlistment not reported. Captured at Spanish Fort, Mobile, Alabama, April 8, 1865. Confined at Ship Island, Mississippi, April 10, 1865. Transferred to Vicksburg, Mississippi, May 1, 1865. No further records.

EDWARDS, WILLIAM E. N., Private
Resided in Madison County and enlisted at age 17, August 13, 1861. Mustered in as Private. Promoted to Corporal on November 21, 1862. Reduced to ranks prior to July 21, 1864. Captured near Atlanta, Georgia, July 21, 1864. Sent to Nashville, Tennessee. Confined at Louisville, Kentucky, August 3, 1864. Transferred to Camp Chase, Ohio, where he arrived on August 4, 1864. Released on May 15, 1865, after taking the Oath of Allegiance.

FISHER, HUMPHREY P., Private
Resided in Madison County and enlisted at age 27, October 28, 1861. Deserted to the enemy on an unspecified date. Confined at Knoxville, Tennessee, June 21, 1864. Transferred to Louisville, Kentucky, where he arrived on June 29, 1864. Released on or about June 30, 1864, after taking the Oath of Allegiance.

FITTS, WILLIAM A., Private
Resided at Tuscaloosa, Alabama. Place and date of enlistment not reported. Surrendered at Citronelle, Alabama, May 4, 1865. Paroled at Columbus, Mississippi, May 16, 1865.

FOSTER, ISAAC, Private
Resided in Madison County and enlisted at age 40, August 13, 1861. Discharged on May 20, 1862. Reason discharged not reported.

GENTRY, JOHN B., Corporal
Resided in Madison County and enlisted at age 42, August 13, 1861. Mustered in as Corporal. Discharged on November 26, 1862. Reason discharged not reported.

GILLIS, LEVI, Private
Resided in Madison County and enlisted at age 34, April 7, 1862. No further records.

GONGS, EDMOND, ———
North Carolina pension records indicate that he served in this company.

GUTHRIE, ERVIN, Private
Resided in Madison County and enlisted at age 16, August 13, 1861. Captured at Spanish Fort, Mobile, Alabama, April 8, 1865. Confined at Ship Island, Mississippi, April 10, 1865. Transferred to Vicksburg, Mississippi, May 1, 1865. [North Carolina pension records indicate he was wounded near Atlanta, Georgia, in August, 1864.] No further records.

HAMLIN, JOHN, Private

Resided in Madison County and enlisted at age 25, August 13, 1861. Wounded at Chickamauga, Georgia, September 19-20, 1863. Reported absent without leave during September, 1864-February, 1865.

HAMLIN, LEVI, Sergeant

Resided in Madison County and enlisted at age 27, August 13, 1861. Mustered in as Private. Promoted to Sergeant on November 3, 1863. No further records.

HAMLIN, WILLIAM A., 1st Sergeant

Resided in Madison County and enlisted at age 20, August 13, 1861. Mustered in as Private. Wounded in the left thumb at Murfreesboro, Tennessee, December 31, 1862. Promoted to 1st Sergeant prior to July 13, 1863. Captured at Yazoo City, Mississippi, July 13, 1863. Sent to Memphis, Tennessee. Confined at St. Louis, Missouri, August 3, 1863. Transferred to Camp Morton, Indianapolis, Indiana, where he arrived on August 14, 1863. Died at Camp Morton on January 1, 1864, of "chronic diarrhoea."

HAMPTON, JASON W., Private

Resided in Madison County and enlisted at age 25, August 13, 1861. Deserted on February 1, 1862.

HOLCOMBE, E. R., Private

Resided in Madison County where he enlisted at age 23, August 13, 1861. Captured "in Kentucky" in September-November, 1862. Confined at Chattanooga, Tennessee. Exchanged on January 11, 1863. Captured and paroled at Yazoo City, Mississippi, July 13, 1863. Hospitalized at Marion, Alabama, February 24, 1864. No further records.

HOLCOMBE, JOHN, Private

Born in Buncombe County and resided in Madison County where he was by occupation a farmer prior to enlisting in Madison County at age 22, August 13, 1861. Discharged on May 11, 1862, by reason of "deafness & inflam[m]ation of the lungs occasioned by relapse of measles."

HOLLYFIELD, D. M., Private

Resided in Madison County and enlisted at age 19, August 13, 1861. Wounded in the right arm at Chickamauga, Georgia, September 19, 1863. Present or accounted for through November 27, 1863. No further records.

HOLYFIELD, WILLIAM REECE, Private

Resided in Madison County and enlisted at age 22, August 13, 1861. Captured in Madison County on an unspecified date. Confined at Louisville, Kentucky, August 3, 1864. Released on August 4, 1864, after taking the Oath of Allegiance.

HOOKER, JOHN A., Private

Resided in Madison County and enlisted at age 19, August 13, 1861. Wounded in the back at Murfreesboro, Tennessee, December 31, 1862. No further records.

INGLE, ROBERT H., Private

Resided in Madison County and enlisted at age 19, August 13, 1861. No further records.

JENKINS, ALFRED J., Private

Resided in Buncombe County and enlisted at age 29, April 13, 1862. Captured near Marietta, Georgia, June 19, 1864. Sent to Nashville, Tennessee. Confined at Louisville, Kentucky, June 26, 1864. Transferred to Camp Morton, Indianapolis, Indiana, where he arrived on June 28, 1864. Paroled and transferred to City Point, Virginia, February 26, 1865, for exchange.

JENKINS, JAMES M., Sergeant

Resided in Madison County and enlisted at age 24, October 28, 1861. Mustered in as Private. Promoted to Sergeant on November 3, 1863. Deserted to the enemy on an unspecified date. Confined at Knoxville, Tennessee, June 21, 1864. Transferred to Louisville, Kentucky, where he arrived on June 29, 1864. Released on July 1, 1864, after taking the Oath of Allegiance.

JERVIS, JAMES A., Sergeant

Resided in Madison County and enlisted at age 29, August 13, 1861. Mustered in as Sergeant. Appointed 2nd Lieutenant on or about September 11, 1862, and transferred to Company F, 64th Regiment N.C. Troops.

JERVIS, JOHN A., Jr., Private

Resided in Tennessee and enlisted at age 22, April 7, 1862. Reported in confinement at Louisville, Kentucky, on an unspecified date. No further records.

KEETER, HENRY, ———

North Carolina pension records indicate that he served in this company.

KEITH, JAMES GRAHAM, Private

Resided in Madison County and enlisted at age 21, August 13, 1861. Last reported in the records of this company on September 30, 1863.

KEITH, ROBERT, Private

Resided in Madison County and enlisted at age 18, August 13, 1861. Paroled at Vicksburg, Mississippi, May 10, 1865. Took the Oath of Allegiance at Nashville, Tennessee, August 14, 1865.

KEITH, W. B., ———

North Carolina pension records indicate that he served in this company.

LEDFORD, THOMAS, Private

Resided in Mitchell County and enlisted at age 30, June 11, 1861. Deserted on September 7, 1863.

LEWIS, JAMES W., Private

Resided in Madison County and enlisted at age 18, August 13, 1861. Wounded at Chickamauga, Georgia, September 19-20, 1863. Last reported in the records of this company on October 1, 1863.

LEWIS, MARION, Private

Resided in Madison County and enlisted at age 17, April 13, 1861. Wounded at Chickamauga, Georgia, September 19-20, 1863. Last reported in the records of this company in November, 1863.

LIPPARD, MARCUS, ———

North Carolina pension records indicate that he served in this company.

McELROY, HOWARD J., Private

Resided in Madison County and enlisted at age 18, May

4, 1863, for the war. Wounded at Chickamauga, Georgia, September 19-20, 1863. Died September 26, 1863, of wounds. Place of death not reported.

McELROY, JOHN W., Sergeant
Resided in Madison County and enlisted at age 19, August 13, 1861. Mustered in as Corporal and was promoted to Sergeant on an unspecified date. Wounded at Chickamauga, Georgia, September 19, 1863. No further records.

McLEAN, JOHN L., Sutler
Resided in Madison County and enlisted at age 31, April 7, 1862, as a substitute. Captured at Yazoo City, Mississippi, July 13, 1863. Sent to Memphis, Tennessee. Confined at St. Louis, Missouri, August 3, 1863. Transferred to Camp Morton, Indianapolis, Indiana, where he arrived on August 14, 1863. Released "on parole" on October 28, 1864.

McLEAN, QUINCY CLAY, Sergeant
Resided in Madison County and enlisted at age 18, August 13, 1861. Mustered in as Private and was promoted to Sergeant on November 20, 1862. Captured at Chickamauga, Georgia, September 19-20, 1863. Sent to Nashville, Tennessee. Confined at Louisville, Kentucky, September 30, 1863. Transferred to Camp Douglas, Chicago, Illinois, where he arrived on October 4, 1863. Released on May 18, 1865, after taking the Oath of Allegiance.

McLEAN, SIDNEY S., Private
Born in Yancey County and resided in Madison County where he was by occupation a farmer prior to enlisting in Madison County at age 26, August 13, 1861. Discharged on May 14, 1862, by reason of "chronic rheumatism and disease of kidnies [sic]" and/or "syphilis."

McLEAN, W. A., Private
Resided in Madison County and enlisted at age 26. Enlistment date reported as May 5, 1861; however, that date is erroneous. Deserted on September 2, 1863. No further records.

McLEAN, YANCEY C., Sergeant
Resided in Madison County and enlisted at age 19, August 13, 1861. Mustered in as Private and was promoted to Sergeant prior to September 19-20, 1863. Captured at Chickamauga, Georgia, September 19-20, 1863. Sent to Nashville, Tennessee. Confined at Louisville, Kentucky, September 30, 1863. Transferred to Camp Douglas, Chicago, Illinois, where he arrived on October 4, 1863. Released on June 16, 1865, after taking the Oath of Allegiance.

McMAHAN, JAMES B., Private
Resided in Madison County and enlisted at age 65, August 13, 1861. Discharged on November 25, 1861. Reason discharged not reported.

MATTHEWS, E. K., Private
Resided in Buncombe County. Place and date of enlistment not reported. Captured at Spanish Fort, Mobile, Alabama, April 8, 1865. Confined at Ship Island, Mississippi, April 10, 1865. Transferred to Vicksburg, Mississippi, May 1, 1865. No further records.

METCALF, WILLIAM J., Private
Previously served in Company B of this regiment. Transferred to this company on May 1, 1862. Captured at or near Yazoo City, Mississippi, on or about July 16, 1863. Sent to Snyder's Bluff, Mississippi. Transferred to Camp Morton, Indianapolis, Indiana, where he arrived on August 7, 1863. Paroled and transferred to Boulware's Wharf, James River, Virginia, where he was received on March 23, 1865, for exchange.

MORRIS, J. A., Private
Resided in Burke County and enlisted at age 31, December 14, 1864, for the war. Surrendered at Citronelle, Alabama, May 4, 1865. Paroled at Meridian, Mississippi, May 9, 1865.

NELSON, DANIEL J., Private
Resided in Madison County and enlisted at age 16, August 13, 1861. Discharged on November 6, 1862. Reason discharged not reported.

NEWSON, JAMES C., Private
Place and date of enlistment not reported. Captured near Atlanta, Georgia, July 22, 1864. Sent to Louisville, Kentucky. Transferred to Camp Chase, Ohio, July 31, 1864. No further records.

OLIVER, ALLISON W., Musician
Born in Yancey County and resided in Madison County where he enlisted at age 20, August 13, 1861. Mustered in as Musician (Drummer). Died at McMinnville, Tennessee, December 27-28, 1862, of "fever."

OLIVER, JABEZ B., Private
Born in Yancey County and resided in Madison County where he was by occupation a farmer prior to enlisting in Madison County at age 23, August 13, 1862. Captured near Jackson, Mississippi, in July, 1863. Sent to Snyder's Bluff, Mississippi. Transferred to Camp Morton, Indianapolis, Indiana, where he arrived on August 7, 1863. Died at Camp Morton on August 23, 1863. Cause of death not reported.

OLIVER, JOSEPH M., Private
Resided in Madison County and enlisted at age 22, August 13, 1861. Captured at or near Jackson, Mississippi, on or about July 4, 1863. Sent to Snyder's Bluff, Mississippi. Transferred to Camp Morton, Indianapolis, Indiana, where he arrived on August 7, 1863. Transferred to Fort Delaware, Delaware, March 19, 1864. Released on June 19, 1865, after taking the Oath of Allegiance.

PAINE, JOEL A., Private
Resided in Madison County and enlisted at age 22, August 13, 1861. Deserted on February 7, 1862.

PHILLIPS, W. W., Private
Resided in Madison County and enlisted at age 20, April 7, 1862. Surrendered at Citronelle, Alabama, May 4, 1865. Paroled at Meridian, Mississippi, May 9, 1865.

PONDER, JOHN H., Private
Born in Yancey County and resided in Madison County where he was by occupation a farmer prior to enlisting in Madison County at age 25, August 13, 1861. Died in hospital at Knoxville, Tennessee, September 8, 1862, of "fever."

PONDER, JOSEPH F., Private
Resided in Madison County where he enlisted at age 24, August 13, 1861. Mustered in as Sergeant but was reduced to ranks on June 24, 1863. Reported in hospital at Marion, Alabama, in January-February, 1864. No further records.

RAMSAY, ROBERT, Private
Resided in Madison County and enlisted at age 21, August 13, 1861. Deserted on September 5, 1863.

RAY, ALBERT, Private
Resided in Madison County and enlisted at age 25, August 13, 1861. Transferred to Company B of this regiment on February 20, 1863.

RAY, JAMES A., Private
Resided in Madison County and enlisted at age 31, August 13, 1861. Last reported in the records of this company on April 29, 1863.

RAY, JOHN B., Private
Resided in Madison County and enlisted at age 22, August 13, 1861. No further records.

RAY, JOHN BAILUS, Private
Previously served in Company B of this regiment. Transferred to this company on May 1, 1862. No further records.

RAY, JOHN P., Private
Born in Yancey County and resided in Madison County prior to enlisting at age 26, August 13, 1861. Died at Loudon, Tennessee, November 27 or December 7, 1862, of "fever."

RAY, JOSEPH M., Private
Resided in Madison or Yancey County and enlisted at age 18, August 13, 1861. Captured at Yazoo City, Mississippi, July 13, 1863. Sent to Memphis, Tennessee. Transferred to St. Louis, Missouri, where he arrived on August 3, 1863. Transferred to Camp Morton, Indianapolis, Indiana, on or about August 26, 1863. Paroled and transferred on or about February 14, 1865, for exchange. Hospitalized at Richmond, Virginia, February 28, 1865, with an unspecified complaint. Returned to duty on an unspecified date. Surrendered at Citronelle, Alabama, May 4, 1865. Paroled at Meridian, Mississippi, May 9, 1865.

RAY, SAMUEL C., Private
Resided in Madison County and enlisted at age 33, August 13, 1861. Captured "in Kentucky" in September-November, 1862. Confined at Chattanooga, Tennessee. Declared exchanged on January 11, 1863. Last reported in the records of this company on August 5, 1863.

RAY, THOMAS W., Private
Place and date of enlistment not reported. Captured near Atlanta, Georgia, July 21, 1864. Sent to Nashville, Tennessee. Confined at Louisville, Kentucky, August 2, 1864. Transferred to Camp Chase, Ohio, where he arrived on August 4, 1864. Died at Camp Chase on February 24, 1865, of "diarrhoea chronic."

RAY, WILLIAM H., Private
Born in Yancey County and resided in Madison County

where he was by occupation a farmer prior to enlisting in Madison County at age 21, August 13, 1861. Discharged on March 11, 1863, by reason of "an abs[c]ess . . . which has now assumed a malignant character."

RAY, WILLIAM M., Private
Resided in Madison County and enlisted at age 25, August 13, 1861. Mustered in as Color Sergeant but was reduced to ranks prior to July 13, 1863. Captured at Yazoo City, Mississippi, on or about July 13, 1863. Sent to Memphis, Tennessee. Confined at St. Louis, Missouri, August 3, 1863. Transferred to Camp Morton, Indianapolis, Indiana, on or about August 26, 1863. Paroled and transferred to City Point, Virginia, where he was received on or about February 26, 1865, for exchange.

RICE, JOHN, Private
Resided in Madison County and enlisted at age 23, August 13, 1861. Deserted on March 2, 1862.

ROBERTS, ALBERT F., Private
Resided in Buncombe County and enlisted at age 18, May 12, 1863, for the war. Deserted on September 10, 1863. Went over to the enemy on an unspecified date. Confined at Knoxville, Tennessee, June 1, 1864. Transferred to Louisville, Kentucky, where he arrived on June 6, 1864. Released on June 8, 1864, after taking the Oath of Allegiance.

ROBERTS, H. C., Private
Resided in Buncombe County and enlisted at age 18, May 12, 1863, for the war. Deserted on September 10, 1863.

ROBERTS, JAMES B., Private
Resided in Madison County and enlisted at age 25, August 13, 1861. Discharged on May 20, 1862. Reason discharged not reported.

ROBERTS, JAMES G., Private
Resided in Madison or Buncombe County and enlisted at age 26, August 13, 1861. Mustered in as Private. Promoted to Corporal on February 5, 1862. Wounded at Chickamauga, Georgia, September 19-20, 1863. Reduced to ranks subsequent to October 30, 1863. Deserted to the enemy on an unspecified date. Confined at Knoxville, Tennessee, June 1, 1864. Transferred to Louisville, Kentucky, where he arrived on June 6, 1864. Released on June 8, 1864, after taking the Oath of Allegiance.

ROBERTS, JOHN H., Private
Born in Buncombe County where he resided prior to enlisting at age 18, August 13, 1861. Died at Jonesboro, Tennessee, January 19, 1862, of "fever."

ROBERTS, JOSHUA J., Private
Resided in Madison County and enlisted at age 20, August 13, 1861. Wounded at Chickamauga, Georgia, September 19-20, 1863. Deserted to the enemy on an unspecified date. Confined at Knoxville, Tennessee, June 1, 1864. Transferred to Louisville, Kentucky, where he arrived on June 6, 1864. Released on June 8, 1864, after taking the Oath of Allegiance.

ROBERTS, MARTIN, Private
Resided in Madison County and enlisted at age 18,

August 13, 1861. Wounded at Chickamauga, Georgia, September 19-20, 1863. Hospitalized at Macon, Georgia. Furloughed for thirty days on September 28, 1863. No further records.

ROBERTS, MOSES, ——
North Carolina pension records indicate that he served in this company.

ROBERTS, TILFORD J., Private
Resided in Madison County and enlisted at age 22, August 13, 1861. Killed at Chickamauga, Georgia, September 19, 1863.

ROBERTS, WILEY S., Private
Born in Buncombe County where he resided as a farmer prior to enlisting in Madison County at age 21, August 13, 1861. Discharged in August, 1862, by reason of "phthisis pulmonalis."

ROBERTS, WILLIAM J., Private
Resided in Madison County and enlisted at age 18, August 13, 1861. Captured at Yazoo City, Mississippi, July 13, 1863. Paroled on or about the same date. No further records.

ROBINSON, MITCHELL E., Private
Resided in Madison County and enlisted at age 25, August 13, 1861. Deserted on September 7, 1863.

ROLAND, SILAS, Private
Resided in Yancey County. Place and date of enlistment not reported. Captured near Atlanta, Georgia, July 21, 1864. Sent to Nashville, Tennessee. Confined at Louisville, Kentucky, August 3, 1864. Transferred to Camp Chase, Ohio, where he arrived on August 4, 1864. Released on June 11, 1865, after taking the Oath of Allegiance. [Oath of Allegiance gives his age as 30.]

ROUECHE, RICHARD F., Private
Born in Rowan County and was by occupation a farmer. Place and date of enlistment not reported. Captured at Nashville, Tennessee, December 16, 1864. Confined at Louisville, Kentucky, December 21, 1864. Transferred to Camp Douglas, Chicago, Illinois, where he arrived on December 24, 1864. Released on or about April 14, 1865, after joining the U.S. Army. Assigned to Company H, 5th Regiment U.S. Volunteer Infantry.

RUNYAN, JAMES H., Private
Resided in Madison County and enlisted at age 20, August 13, 1861. Captured near Marietta, Georgia, July 4, 1864. Confined at Camp Douglas, Chicago, Illinois, on an unspecified date. Released on June 12, 1865, after taking the Oath of Allegiance.

RUSSELL, JAMES R., Private
Born in Wythe County, Virginia, and resided in Madison County where he was by occupation a farmer prior to enlisting in Madison County at age 38, August 13, 1861. Died at Cumberland Gap, Tennessee, May 7, 1862, of "fever."

SAMS, JOSEPH L., Private
Resided in Madison County and enlisted at age 31, August 13, 1861. Captured at Yazoo City, Mississippi, on or about July 13, 1863. Sent to Memphis, Tennessee. Confined at St. Louis, Missouri, August 3, 1863. Transferred to Camp Morton, Indianapolis, Indiana,

where he arrived on August 14, 1863. Died at Camp Morton on or about January 6, 1864, of "pneumonia."

SAMS, ROBERT R., Private
Resided in Madison County and enlisted at age 25, August 13, 1861. Captured near Atlanta, Georgia, July 21, 1864. Sent to Nashville, Tennessee. Confined at Louisville, Kentucky, August 3, 1864. Transferred to Camp Chase, Ohio, where he arrived on August 4, 1864. Paroled and transferred to Boulware's Wharf, James River, Virginia, where he was received on March 10-12, 1865, for exchange.

SCOTT, JOHN L., Private
Born in Burke County and resided in Madison County prior to enlisting at age 27, August 13, 1861. Died at Grenada, Mississippi, August 12, 1863, of "fever."

SCOTT, MARCUS L., Private
Resided in Madison County and enlisted at age 21, August 13, 1861. Captured near Atlanta, Georgia, July 21, 1864. Sent to Nashville, Tennessee. Confined at Louisville, Kentucky, August 3, 1864. Transferred to Camp Chase, Ohio, where he arrived on August 4, 1864. Released on May 15, 1865, after taking the Oath of Allegiance.

SCOTT, THOMAS J., Sergeant
Resided in Madison County and enlisted at age 17, August 13, 1861. Mustered in as Private. Wounded in the leg at Murfreesboro, Tennessee, December 31, 1862. Promoted to Corporal on May 5, 1863. Promoted to Sergeant on an unspecified date. Wounded in the breast at Chickamauga, Georgia, September 19-20, 1863. Wounded in the arm at Atlanta, Georgia, on an unspecified date. Wounded in the head at Nashville, Tennessee, on or about December 15-16, 1864. Wounded in the shoulder at Spanish Fort, Mobile, Alabama, on or about April 8, 1865.

SIGMON, JOHN J., Private
Place and date of enlistment not reported. Deserted to the enemy at or near Marietta, Georgia, on or about July 3, 1864. Sent to Nashville, Tennessee. Confined at Louisville, Kentucky, July 14, 1864. Transferred to Camp Douglas, Chicago, Illinois, where he arrived on July 18, 1864. Released on May 16, 1865.

SMITH, JOHN A., Private
Resided in Madison County. Place and date of enlistment not reported. Captured at Spanish Fort, Mobile, Alabama, April 8, 1865. Confined at Ship Island, Mississippi, April 10, 1865. Transferred to Vicksburg, Mississippi, May 1, 1865. No further records.

SWANEY, ISHAM H., Private
Born in Henderson County and resided in Madison County where he was by occupation a farmer prior to enlisting in Buncombe County at age 17, August 13, 1861. Captured at Nashville, Tennessee, December 15, 1864. Confined at Louisville, Kentucky, December 20, 1864. Transferred to Camp Douglas, Chicago, Illinois, where he arrived on December 22, 1864. Released on March 24, 1865, after joining the U.S. Army. Assigned to Company D, 6th Regiment U.S. Volunteer Infantry.

THOMPSON, ISAAC, Private
Born in Yancey County and resided in Madison County

where he was by occupation a farmer prior to enlisting in Madison County at age 24, August 13, 1861. Died at Tazewell, Tennessee, or at Cumberland Gap, Tennessee, May 10, 1862, of "fever."

VARNER, W. A., Private
Place and date of enlistment not reported. Captured at Spanish Fort, Mobile, Alabama, April 8, 1865. Confined at Ship Island, Mississippi, April 10, 1865. Transferred to Vicksburg, Mississippi, where he arrived on May 1, 1865. No further records.

WALDREP, JAMES H., Private
Born in Yancey County and resided in Madison County where he was by occupation a farmer prior to enlisting at Cumberland Gap, Tennessee, at age 23, April 7, 1862. Killed "on the first fire" at Murfreesboro, Tennessee, December 31, 1862.

WARDREP, WILLIAM, Private
Resided in Madison County and enlisted at age 33, April 7, 1862. Deserted on September 19, 1863.

WATTS, WILLIAM R., Private
Resided in Madison County and enlisted at age 17, August 13, 1861. Last reported in the records of this company on November 7, 1863.

WEBB, BURTON G., Musician
Born in Buncombe County and resided in Madison County where he was by occupation a farmer prior to enlisting in Madison County at age 45, August 13, 1861. Mustered in as Musician (Fifer). Discharged on July 2, 1862, by reason of "chronic rheumatism."

WEBB, JAMES, Private
Resided in Madison County and enlisted at age 16, August 13, 1861. Wounded in the hip "by shell fragment" at Murfreesboro, Tennessee, December 31, 1862. Returned to duty on an unspecified date. Captured at or near Yazoo City, Mississippi, on or about July 14-19, 1863. Sent to Snyder's Bluff, Mississippi. Confined at Camp Morton, Indianapolis, Indiana, August 7, 1863. Transferred to Fort Delaware, Delaware, March 19, 1864. Released on June 19, 1865, after taking the Oath of Allegiance.

WHITE, WILLIAM, Private
Resided in Madison County and enlisted at age 21, August 13, 1861. Last reported in the records of this company on May 7, 1863.

YOUNG, LUKE B., Sergeant
Born in Yancey County* and resided in Madison County where he was by occupation a farmer prior to enlisting in Madison County at age 32, August 13, 1861. Mustered in as Sergeant. Discharged on November 13, 1862, by reason of "dropsical affection."

COMPANY E

This company was raised in Haywood County and enlisted on August 17, 1861. It was then assigned to the 29th Regiment and designated Company E. After joining the regiment the company functioned as a part of the regiment, and its history for the war period is reported as a part of the regimental history.

The following company roster is based primarily on the North Carolina Roll of Honor, prisoner of war records, pension applications, and a variety of miscellaneous records. Information was obtained also from secondary sources such as postwar histories, cemetery records, and records of the United Daughters of the Confederacy. No muster rolls were located for the company.

OFFICERS

CAPTAINS

ROGERS, HIRAM CYRUS
Resided in Haywood County and enlisted at age 36. Appointed Captain on August 17, 1861. Declined to stand for reelection when the regiment was reorganized on May 2, 1862.

TEAGUE, JOHN A.
Resided in Haywood County and enlisted at age 33. Appointed 2nd Lieutenant on August 17, 1861. Promoted to Captain on May 2, 1862. Wounded at Chickamauga, Georgia, September 19-20, 1863. Reported absent without leave during September, 1864-February, 1865.

LIEUTENANTS

FERGUSON, WILLIAM BURDER, 1st Lieutenant
Resided in Haywood County and enlisted at age 23. Appointed 1st Lieutenant on August 17, 1861. Last reported in the records of this company in January-March, 1864.

HENRY, JAMES S., 2nd Lieutenant
Resided in Haywood County and enlisted at age 20, August 17, 1861. Mustered in as Corporal. Promoted to 2nd Lieutenant on May 1, 1862. Died at Augusta, Georgia, October 17, 1863, of a wound of the shoulder. Place and date wounded not reported.

MURRAY, JAMES F., 2nd Lieutenant
Resided in Buncombe County and enlisted at age 31, August 17, 1861. Mustered in as Private. Appointed 2nd Lieutenant on May 1, 1862. Paroled at Meridian, Mississippi, May 9, 1865.

PLOTT, HENRY B., 2nd Lieutenant
Resided in Clay County and enlisted at age 50. Appointed 2nd Lieutenant on August 17, 1861. A regimental record dated January, 1862, indicates he had not reported for duty. Apparently declined to stand for reelection when the regiment was reorganized on May 2, 1862. [May have served later as 1st Lieutenant of Company E, 5th Regiment N.C. Senior Reserves.]

NONCOMMISSIONED OFFICERS AND PRIVATES

ADAMS, CHARLES, Private
Resided in Clay or Cherokee County and enlisted at age 18, August 17, 1861. Wounded in the hand at Murfreesboro, Tennessee, December 31, 1862. Deserted to the enemy on an unspecified date. Confined at Louisville, Kentucky, May 29, 1864. Released on May 31, 1864, after taking the Oath of Allegiance.

ALLEN, HENRY H., Private
Enlisted on October 25, 1864, for the war. Captured at Spanish Fort, Mobile, Alabama, April 8, 1865. Sent to

Ship Island, Mississippi, where he arrived on April 10, 1865. Released on May 6, 1865.

ALLEN, THOMAS O., Private
Resided in South Carolina and enlisted at age 24, August 17, 1861. Reported absent without leave in September, 1864-February, 1865.

ALLISON, ASEPH W., Private
Born in Haywood County where he resided prior to enlisting in Haywood County at age 18, August 17, 1861. Mortally wounded at Allatoona, Georgia, October 5, 1864. Place and date of death not reported.

ARRINGTON, ELBERT S., Corporal
Resided in Haywood County and enlisted at age 20, August 17, 1861. Mustered in as Private. Wounded at Chickamauga, Georgia, on or about September 20, 1863. Promoted to Corporal on September 20, 1863. Reported absent without leave during September, 1864-February, 1865.

ARRINGTON, GEORGE W., Private
Resided in Tennessee and enlisted at age 24, August 17, 1861. Last reported in the records of this company on September 10, 1863.

ASKEW, C. M., ———
North Carolina pension records indicate that he served in this company.

BARNES, HENRY H., Private
Resided in Haywood County and enlisted at age 33, August 17, 1861. Discharged on November 18, 1862. Reason discharged not reported.

BEASLEY, JAMES B., Private
Resided in Haywood County and enlisted at age 18, August 17, 1861. Reported absent without leave during September, 1864-February, 1865.

BEASLEY, REUBEN, Private
Resided in Haywood County and enlisted at age 25, August 17, 1861. Last reported in the records of this company on October 3, 1864.

BENNETT, ARCHER L., Sergeant
Resided in Haywood County and enlisted at age 26, August 17, 1861. Mustered in as Sergeant. Wounded in the left leg and captured at Murfreesboro, Tennessee, December 31, 1862. Hospitalized at Murfreesboro where he died on January 22-23, 1863, of wounds.

BENNETT, SILVANDES C., Private
Resided in Haywood County and enlisted at age 20, August 17, 1861. Killed at Chickamauga, Georgia, September 19, 1863.

BENNETT, WASHINGTON GEORGE, Private
Resided in Haywood County and enlisted at age 21, August 17, 1861. Mustered in as Sergeant. Captured at or near Murfreesboro, Tennessee, on or about December 31, 1862. Paroled and transferred to City Point, Virginia, where he was received on April 12, 1863, for exchange. Reduced to ranks prior to September, 1863. Captured at Chickamauga, Georgia, September 19-20, 1863. Sent to Nashville, Tennessee. Confined at Louisville, Kentucky, September 30, 1863.

Transferred to Camp Douglas, Chicago, Illinois, where he arrived on October 4, 1863. Paroled at Camp Douglas on March 14, 1865, and transferred to Boulware's Wharf, James River, Virginia, where he was received on March 18-21, 1865, for exchange.

BENNETT, YOUNG A., Private
Place and date of enlistment not reported. Captured at Elk Creek, Tennessee, June 20-21, 1864. Confined at Nashville, Tennessee. Transferred to Louisville, Kentucky, where he arrived on July 14, 1864. Transferred to Camp Chase, Ohio, where he arrived on August 23, 1864. Transferred to Point Lookout, Maryland, March 18, 1865. Paroled and transferred to Boulware's Wharf, James River, Virginia, where he was received on March 27, 1865, for exchange. [Federal hospital records dated July-August, 1864, give his age as 18.]

BRANSON, GREENBURY, Private
Place and date of enlistment not reported. Captured in hospital at Richmond, Virginia, April 3, 1865. Transferred to Newport News, Virginia, April 23, 1865. No further records.

BRIGHT, D. A., Private
Enlisted at age 17, October 1, 1864, for the war. No further records.

BRINDLE, JAMES F., Private
Born in Haywood County where he resided as a farmer prior to enlisting in Haywood County at age 19, August 17, 1861. Died at Chattanooga, Tennessee, April 14, 1863. Cause of death not reported.

BROWN, A. E., ———
North Carolina pension records indicate that he served in this company.

BROWN, ROBERT G., Private
Resided in Haywood County and enlisted at age 18, December 15, 1861. No further records.

CARVER, GILSON, Private
Resided in Haywood County and enlisted at age 38, February 25, 1863, for the war. [North Carolina pension records indicate he was wounded at Chickamauga, Georgia, September 19, 1863.] No further records.

CARVER, JOHN, Private
Resided in Haywood County and enlisted at age 21, August 17, 1861. No further records.

CHASTAIN, ABNER, Corporal
Resided in Haywood County and enlisted at age 57, August 17, 1861. Mustered in as Corporal. Appointed Chaplain on October 11, 1861, and transferred to the Field and Staff of this regiment.

CHASTAIN, BENJAMIN S., Private
Resided in Haywood County and enlisted at age 22, August 17, 1861. Transferred to Company B, 6th Regiment Georgia Cavalry, August 11, 1863. [North Carolina pension records indicate he was wounded in an unspecified battle.]

CHASTAIN, JOHN P., Private
Resided in Clay County and enlisted at age 27, August

17, 1861. Mustered in as Sergeant. Defeated for reelection when the regiment was reorganized on May 2, 1862, and was reduced to the rank of Private. Last reported in the records of this company on February 16, 1864.

CHASTAIN, SIMPSON B., Private
Resided in Haywood County and enlisted at age 19, August 17, 1861. No further records.

CLARK, ALFRED S., Private
Resided in Haywood County and enlisted at age 29, August 17, 1861. Captured at Citronelle, Alabama, May 4, 1865. Paroled at Meridian, Mississippi, May 9, 1865.

CLARK, DALLAS P., Private
Born in Haywood County where he resided as a farmer prior to enlisting in Haywood County at age 15, August 17, 1861. Discharged on April 25, 1862, by reason of being underage and because of "very weak lungs with a tendancy to pulmonary consumption."

COFFEY, COLTON, Musician
Resided in Tennessee and enlisted at age 34, August 17, 1861. Mustered in as Musician (Drummer). Reported absent without leave during September, 1864-February, 1865.

COLWELL, JAMES M., ———
North Carolina pension records indicate that he served in this company.

COLWELL, R. A., ———
North Carolina pension records indicate that he served in this company.

COOK, JAMES R., Private
Resided in Tennessee and enlisted at age 23, August 17, 1861. Deserted on July 5, 1862.

CRUMP, EDWARD G., Private
Resided in Montgomery County and enlisted at age 39, August 17, 1861. Appointed Assistant Surgeon of Smith's Legion (Partisan Rangers) on August 5, 1862, and transferred.

DAVIS, GEORGE W., Sergeant
Born in Haywood County where he resided prior to enlisting at age 23, August 17, 1861. Mustered in as Sergeant. Died at Parrottsville, Tennessee, December 30, 1861, of "typhoid fever."

DAVIS, J. C., ———
North Carolina pension records indicate that he served in this company.

DOTSON, JAMES A., ———
North Carolina pension records indicate that he served in this company.

ENDY, W. R., Private
Place and date of enlistment not reported. Captured at Spanish Fort, Mobile, Alabama, April 8, 1865. Sent to Ship Island, Mississippi. Transferred to Vicksburg, Mississippi, May 1, 1865. No further records.

FERGUSON, ANDREW J., 1st Sergeant
Resided in Haywood County and enlisted at age 23, August 17, 1861. Mustered in as Private. Promoted to

1st Sergeant on May 1, 1862. Died at Atlanta, Georgia, May 29, 1863. Cause of death not reported.

FERGUSON, JAMES W., Private
Resided in Haywood County and enlisted at age 19, August 17, 1861. No further records.

FERGUSON, ROBERT M., Corporal
Resided in Haywood County and enlisted at age 35, August 17, 1861. Mustered in as Corporal. Reported absent without leave during September, 1864-February, 1865.

FERGUSON, WILLIAM J., Private
Born in Haywood County where he resided as a farmer prior to enlisting in Haywood County at age 24, August 17, 1861. Died at Parrottsville, Tennessee, December 29, 1861, of "typhoid fever."

FINGER, SOLOMON, Private
Resided in Haywood County and enlisted in August, 1863, for the war. Captured near Atlanta, Georgia, July 22, 1864. Sent to Nashville, Tennessee. Confined at Louisville, Kentucky, July 30, 1864. Transferred to Camp Chase, Ohio, where he arrived on August 2, 1864. Released on or about May 15, 1865, after taking the Oath of Allegiance.

FISH, JOHN L., Private
Resided in Burke County and enlisted in Buncombe County at age 21, August 17, 1861. Wounded at Chickamauga, Georgia, September 19-20, 1863. Surrendered at Citronelle, Alabama, May 4, 1865. Paroled at Meridian, Mississippi, May 9, 1865.

FISHER, J. J., ———
North Carolina pension records indicate that he served in this company.

FRANCIS, W., Private
Place and date of enlistment not reported. Captured at Spanish Fort, Mobile, Alabama, April 8, 1865. Confined at Ship Island, Mississippi, April 10, 1865. Transferred to Vicksburg, Mississippi, where he arrived on May 1, 1865. No further records.

FRANKLIN, JAMES, Private
Resided in Haywood County and enlisted at age 19, October 15, 1861. Deserted on June 20, 1862.

FRISBY, WESLEY W., Private
Resided in Buncombe County and enlisted at age 18, November 1, 1862, for the war. Last reported in the records of this company on May 7, 1863.

GOWAN, JAMES H., ———
North Carolina pension records indicate that he served in this company.

GRAHL, JOHN L., Private
Resided in Haywood County and enlisted at age 18, August 12, 1862, for the war. Last reported in the records of this company on January 8, 1863.

GREEN, JOHN, Private
Resided in Haywood County and enlisted at age 40, April 6, 1863, for the war. Captured at Yazoo City, Mississippi, July 13, 1863. Died at Yazoo City on July 19, 1863. Cause of death not reported.

GROOMS, ADOLPHUS, Private
Resided in Burke County and enlisted at age 24, August 17, 1861. Deserted on January 6, 1863.

HAMMONDS, M. F., ———
North Carolina pension records indicate that he served in this company.

HANNAH, ALEXANDER, Private
Resided in Haywood County and enlisted at age 25, August 12, 1862, for the war. Died at Hillsboro, Mississippi, July 27, 1863. Cause of death not reported.

HANNAH, JEREMIAH, Private
Born in Haywood County where he resided prior to enlisting at age 31, August 17, 1861. Died at Normandy, Tennessee, November 19, 1862. Cause of death not reported.

HARRIS, JAMES B., Private
Resided in Haywood County and enlisted at age 21, August 17, 1861. Last reported in the records of this company on August 11, 1863.

HARRIS, WILLIAM H., Private
Resided in Haywood or Polk County and enlisted at age 17, August 17, 1861. Wounded near Atlanta, Georgia, September 15, 1864. Returned to duty on an unspecified date. Captured at Columbia, South Carolina, February 18, 1865. Confined at Hart's Island, New York Harbor, April 10, 1865. Released on June 18, 1865, after taking the Oath of Allegiance.

HAWKINS, ADOLPHUS, ———
North Carolina pension records indicate that he served in this company.

HAYNES, JOHN H., Private
Resided in Haywood County and enlisted at age 34, August 17, 1861. Reported absent without leave in September, 1864-February, 1865.

HAYNES, JUDSON P., Private
Born in Missouri and resided in Washington County where he was by occupation a farmer prior to enlisting in Haywood County at age 42, August 17, 1861. Discharged on February 24, 1862, by reason of "chronic rh[e]umatism."

HENRY, HARVEY M., Private
Resided in Haywood County and enlisted at age 18, November 6, 1862, for the war. Wounded in the breast at Murfreesboro, Tennessee, December 31, 1862. Captured at Spanish Fort, Mobile, Alabama, April 8, 1865. Confined at Ship Island, Mississippi, April 10, 1865. Transferred to Vicksburg, Mississippi, May 1, 1865. No further records.

HENRY, ROBERT P., Private
Resided in Cherokee County and enlisted at age 17, August 17, 1861. Discharged on November 7, 1862. Reason discharged not reported.

HIPP, LEVI C., Private
Resided in Buncombe County and enlisted at age 17, August 17, 1861. [North Carolina pension records indicate he was wounded at "Red Banks of Chuck," Tennessee, in 1864.] No further records.

HIPPS, DAN R., ———
North Carolina pension records indicate that he served in this company.

HIPPS, J. M., ———
North Carolina pension records indicate that he served in this company.

HIPPS, W. G. B., ———
North Carolina pension records indicate that he served in this company.

HOPKINS, WILLIAM M., 1st Sergeant
Resided in Tennessee and enlisted at age 24, August 17, 1861. Mustered in as 1st Sergeant. Defeated for reelection when the regiment was reorganized on or about May 2, 1862, and dropped from the rolls of the company.

JACKSON, WILLIAM Y., Private
Enlisted in Buncombe County on October 14, 1861. Captured and paroled at Yazoo City, Mississippi, July 13, 1863. No further records.

JENKINS, ELIJAH J., Private
Resided in Tennessee and enlisted at age 33, August 17, 1861. No further records.

JUSTICE, MOSES N., Private
Born in Buncombe County where he resided as a farmer prior to enlisting in Haywood County at age 21, August 17, 1861. Discharged on April 10, 1862, by reason of "chronic rheumatism." Later served in Company A, 62nd Regiment N.C. Troops.

KERR, ANAMANDER, Private
Resided in Rutherford County and enlisted at age 18, August 17, 1861. Died at Raleigh on December 24, 1861. Cause of death not reported.

KIRKPATRICK, J. M., ———
North Carolina pension records indicate that he served in this company.

LINER, LEANDER, Jr., ———
North Carolina pension records indicate that he served in this company.

LINER, WILLIAM M., Private
Resided in Haywood County and enlisted at age 20, August 17, 1861. Captured and paroled at Yazoo City, Mississippi, July 13, 1863. Reported absent without leave during September, 1864-February, 1865.

McCRACKEN, DEALY L., Private
Resided in Haywood County and enlisted at age 24, August 17, 1861. Captured near Smyrna, Georgia, July 3, 1864. Sent to Nashville, Tennessee. Confined at Louisville, Kentucky, July 13, 1864. Transferred to Camp Douglas, Chicago, Illinois, where he arrived on July 16, 1864. Released on June 16, 1865, after taking the Oath of Allegiance.

McCRACKEN, GREEN V., Private
Born in Haywood County where he resided prior to enlisting at age 27, August 17, 1861. Died at Jonesboro, Tennessee, December 24, 1861, of "typhoid fever."

McCRACKEN, W. L., Private
Place and date of enlistment not reported. Captured at Spanish Fort, Mobile, Alabama, April 8, 1865. Confined at Ship Island, Mississippi, April 10, 1865. Transferred to Vicksburg, Mississippi, May 1, 1865. No further records.

McDANIEL, S. L., Private
Place and date of enlistment not reported. Captured at Spanish Fort, Mobile, Alabama, April 8, 1865. Confined at Ship Island, Mississippi, April 10, 1865. Transferred to Vicksburg, Mississippi, May 1, 1865. No further records.

McELROY, ABLE, Private
Resided in Haywood County. Place and date of enlistment not reported. Captured near Smyrna, Georgia, July 3, 1864. Sent to Nashville, Tennessee. Confined at Louisville, Kentucky, July 13, 1864. Transferred to Camp Douglas, Chicago, Illinois, where he arrived on July 16, 1864. Discharged on June 16, 1865, after taking the Oath of Allegiance.

McFALLS, WILLIAM J., Private
Previously served in Company C of this regiment. Transferred to this company on February 1, 1863. No further records.

McGEE, JESSE, Private
Resided in Haywood County and enlisted at age 40, April 6, 1863, for the war. Reported absent without leave in September, 1864-February, 1865. Took the Oath of Allegiance at Chattanooga, Tennessee, June 8, 1865.

McMILLEN, GRIFFITH, Sergeant
Resided in Haywood County and enlisted at age 42, August 17, 1861. Mustered in as Private. Promoted to Sergeant on an unspecified date. Captured "in Kentucky" in September-November, 1862. Confined at Chattanooga, Tennessee. Exchanged on January 11, 1863. Died "at home" on an unspecified date prior to October 13, 1864. Cause of death not reported.

MANNEY, WILLIAM H., Sergeant
Born in Catawba County. Place and date of enlistment not reported. Promotion record not reported. Wounded in the right leg at Murfreesboro, Tennessee, December 31, 1862. Died in hospital at Lauderdale Springs, Mississippi, August 12, 1863. Cause of death not reported.

MEDFORD, ELIAS, Private
Born in Haywood County where he resided prior to enlisting at age 18, August 17, 1861. Died in hospital at Loudon, Tennessee, November 14, 1862. Cause of death not reported.

MEECE, BURGESS H., Private
Resided in Haywood County and enlisted at age 30, August 17, 1861. Wounded in the left hip and captured at Murfreesboro, Tennessee, December 31, 1862. Sent to Nashville, Tennessee. Transferred to Camp Morton, Indianapolis, Indiana. Paroled and transferred to City Point, Virginia, where he was received on April 12, 1863, for exchange. Furloughed on April 18, 1863.

MELTON, A. E., ———
North Carolina pension records indicate that he served in this company.

MELTON, WILLIAM R., Private
Resided in Haywood County and enlisted at age 32, September 17, 1863, for the war. No further records.

MESSER, COONROD, Musician
Born in Haywood County where he resided prior to enlisting at age 23, August 17, 1861. Mustered in as Musician (Fifer). Died "on the march in Kentucky" on October 18, 1862. Cause of death not reported.

MESSER, HENRY, Private
Resided in Haywood County and enlisted at age 26, August 17, 1861. Surrendered at Citronelle, Alabama, May 4, 1865. Paroled at Meridian, Mississippi, May 9, 1865.

MESSER, LAWSON, Private
Place and date of enlistment not reported. First listed in the records of this company on September 1, 1862. Captured at Spanish Fort, Mobile, Alabama, April 8, 1865. Confined at Ship Island, Mississippi, April 10, 1865. Transferred to Vicksburg, Mississippi, May 1, 1865. [North Carolina pension records indicate he was wounded in the side at Sugar Creek, Tennessee, in 1865.] No further records.

MESSER, WILLIAM O., Private
Resided in Haywood County and enlisted at age 40, February 15, 1863, for the war. Surrendered at Citronelle, Alabama, May 4, 1865. Paroled at Meridian, Mississippi, May 9, 1865.

MORROW, FRANCIS M., Private
Born in Haywood County where he enlisted on February 15, 1864, for the war. Died at Montgomery, Alabama, July 31, 1864. Cause of death not reported. [May have served previously in Company C, 62nd Regiment N.C. Troops.]

MORROW, ROBERT V., Private
Resided in Haywood County and enlisted at age 18, August 17, 1861. Captured near Smyrna, Georgia, July 3, 1864. Sent to Nashville, Tennessee. Confined at Louisville, Kentucky, July 13, 1864. Transferred to Camp Douglas, Chicago, Illinois, where he arrived on July 16, 1864. Died at Camp Douglas on December 26, 1864, of "smallpox."

MOUNEY, WALLACE H. H., Sergeant
Resided in Catawba County and enlisted at age 21, August 17, 1861. Mustered in as Private. Promoted to Sergeant on an unspecified date. Died on August 12, 1863. Place and cause of death not reported.

NOLAND, JOHN, Private
Born in Haywood County where he enlisted on February 15, 1864, for the war. Died at Montgomery, Alabama, July 9, 1864. Cause of death not reported.

NOLAND, JOSEPH S., Private
Resided in Haywood County and enlisted at age 23, August 17, 1861. Killed at Chickamauga, Georgia, September 19, 1863.

NOLAND, ROBERT WILBURN, Private
Resided in Haywood County and enlisted on August 17, 1861. Reported absent without leave during September, 1864-February, 1865.

PALMER, HENRY C., Private
Born in Buncombe County where he resided prior to enlisting at age 17, August 17, 1861. Died at Parrottsville, Tennessee, December 23, 1861, of "typhoid fever."

PARKS, HIRAM, ———
North Carolina pension records indicate that he served in this company.

PENLAND, GUSS, ———
North Carolina pension records indicate that he served in this company.

PLATT, HENRY B., Corporal
Resided in Haywood County and enlisted at age 21, August 17, 1861. Mustered in as Private. Captured "in Kentucky" in September-November, 1862. Confined at Chattanooga, Tennessee. Exchanged on January 11, 1863. Promoted to Corporal on an unspecified date. Died at Catoosa Springs, Georgia, January 22, 1863. Cause of death not reported.

PLATT, WILLIAM F., Sergeant
Resided in Haywood County and enlisted at age 18, August 17, 1861. Mustered in as Private and was promoted to Sergeant on September 20, 1863. No further records.

PLEMMONS, D. P., ———
North Carolina pension records indicate that he served in this company.

PLEMMONS, T. L., ———
North Carolina pension records indicate that he served in this company.

PLOTT, HENRY F., Private
Resided in Haywood County and enlisted at age 18, March 31, 1862. Died in hospital at Catoosa Springs, Georgia, January 22, 1863. Cause of death not reported.

PRICE, JAMES H., Private
Resided in Haywood County and enlisted at age 21, August 17, 1861. Reported absent without leave during September, 1864-February, 1865.

PRICE, JOHN J., Private
Born in Haywood County where he resided as a farmer prior to enlisting in Buncombe County at age 24, August 17, 1861. Discharged on February 25, 1862, by reason of "tuberculosis." [May have served later in Company A, 62nd Regiment N.C. Troops.]

PRICE, JOSIAH, Private
Born in Buncombe County where he resided prior to enlisting at age 23, August 17, 1861. Died in hospital at Morristown, Tennessee, June 22, 1862. Cause of death not reported.

RAINES, ALLEN, Private
Enlisted in 1861. Captured at Yazoo City, Mississippi, July 13, 1863. Sent to Memphis, Tennessee. Confined at St. Louis, Missouri, August 3, 1863. Transferred to Camp Morton, Indianapolis, Indiana, where he arrived August 14, 1863. Enlisted in the 7th Regiment U.S. Cavalry prior to September 1, 1863.

RALPH, M., Private
Place and date of enlistment not reported. Captured at Yazoo City, Mississippi, on or about July 13, 1863. Sent to Indianapolis, Indiana. Transferred to Fort Delaware, Delaware, where he arrived on March 22, 1864. Died at Fort Delaware on an unspecified date. Cause of death not reported.

RATHBONE, JACOB M., Private
Resided in Haywood County and enlisted at age 37, February 25, 1863, for the war. Last reported in the records of this company on October 1, 1863.

RATHBONE, JOHN HIRAM, Private
Born in Haywood County where he resided prior to enlisting at age 19, [August] 17, 1861. Died at Raleigh on November 28-29, 1861, of "pneumonia."

RATHBONE, JOSEPH, Private
Resided in Haywood County and enlisted at age 42, August 16, 1863, for the war. Reported absent without leave during September, 1864-February, 1865.

RATHBONE, WILLIAM H., Private
Resided in Haywood County and enlisted at age 16, August 17, 1861. Wounded at Chickamauga, Georgia, September 19, 1863. Reported absent without leave during September, 1864-February, 1865.

REDMAN, JACOB, Private
Born in Buncombe County where he resided prior to enlisting at age 16, August 17, 1861. Killed at Chickamauga, Georgia, September 19, 1863.

REYNOLDS, JOHN, ———
North Carolina pension records indicate that he served in this company.

RODER, J. T., Sergeant
Place and date of enlistment not reported. Promotion record not reported. Captured "in Kentucky" in September-November, 1862. Confined at Chattanooga, Tennessee. Exchanged on January 11, 1863. No further records.

RODGERS, JAMES M., Private
Place and date of enlistment not reported. Captured near Atlanta, Georgia, July 22, 1864. Sent to Nashville, Tennessee. Confined at Louisville, Kentucky, July 30, 1864. Transferred to Camp Chase, Ohio, where he arrived on August 2, 1864. Died at Camp Chase on February 28, 1865, of "congestion of lungs."

ROGERS, ALLEN THADDEUS, Corporal
Resided in Haywood County and enlisted at age 22, August 17, 1861. Mustered in as Private. Promoted to Corporal on April 25, 1863. Captured and paroled at Yazoo City, Mississippi, July 13, 1863. Reported absent without leave during September, 1864-February, 1865.

ROGERS, C. MELVIN, ———
North Carolina pension records indicate that he served in this company.

ROGERS, GEORGE N., 1st Sergeant
Born in Haywood County where he resided prior to enlisting at age 23, August 17, 1861. Mustered in as Corporal. Promoted to 1st Sergeant on June 20, 1863. Killed at Chickamauga, Georgia, September 19, 1863.

ROGERS, JAMES R., Private

Born in Haywood County where he resided prior to enlisting at age 20, July 25, 1862, for the war. Died at Chattanooga, Tennessee, January 25 or February 4, 1863. Cause of death not reported.

ROGERS, JESSE F., Private

Born in Haywood County where he resided as a farmer prior to enlisting in Haywood County at age 18, August 17, 1861. Wounded in the left arm at Murfreesboro, Tennessee, December 31, 1862. Retired from service on March 6, 1865, by reason of disability from wounds received at Murfreesboro.

ROGERS, JESSE R., Private

Resided in Haywood County and enlisted at age 19, August 17, 1861. Deserted to the enemy on an unspecified date. Sent to Chattanooga, Tennessee. Confined at Louisville, Kentucky, August 5, 1864. Released on or about August 10, 1864, after taking the Oath of Allegiance.

ROGERS, JOSEPH T., Private

Born in Haywood County where he resided prior to enlisting at age 20, August 17, 1861. Killed at Chickamauga, Georgia, September 19, 1863.

ROGERS, ROBERT W., Private

Resided in Haywood County and enlisted at age 23, August 17, 1861. Wounded in the left hand at Murfreesboro, Tennessee, December 31, 1862. Reported absent without leave during September, 1864-February, 1865.

ROGERS, THOMAS J., Private

Resided in Haywood County and enlisted at age 19, August 17, 1861. Mustered in as Private. Promoted to Sergeant on September 20, 1863. Reduced to ranks on an unspecified date. Deserted to the enemy on an unspecified date. Confined at Knoxville, Tennessee, March 10, 1865. Transferred to Louisville, Kentucky, where he arrived on March 18, 1865. Released on March 21, 1865, after taking the Oath of Allegiance.

ROGERS, WILLIAM A., Private

Born in Haywood County where he resided prior to enlisting at age 33, July 30, 1862, for the war. Died at Bean's Station, Tennessee, November 8, 1862. Cause of death not reported.

RUFF, GEORGE, ———

North Carolina pension records indicate that he served in this company.

RUFF, MINOR, Private

Resided in Haywood County and enlisted at age 25, August 12, 1863, for the war. Captured at Yazoo City, Mississippi, on or about July 13, 1863. Sent to Memphis, Tennessee. Confined at St. Louis, Missouri, August 3, 1863. Transferred to Camp Morton, Indianapolis, Indiana, where he arrived on August 14, 1863. Transferred to Fort Delaware, Delaware, March 19, 1864. Died in hospital at Fort Delaware on May 9, 1864, of "inflam[mation] of lungs."

RUSSELL, GEORGE W., Private

Resided in Haywood County and enlisted at age 20, August 17, 1861. Last reported in the records of this company on September 26, 1863.

RUSSELL, JOSEPH HASCUE, Private

Resided in Haywood County and enlisted at age 30, February 25, 1863, for the war. Last reported in the records of this company on October 3, 1863.

RUSSELL, WILLIAM H., Private

Resided in Haywood County and enlisted at age 18, August 17, 1861. Reported absent without leave during September, 1864-February, 1865.

SENSABAUGH, JOHN S., Private

Resided in Haywood County and enlisted at age 19, February 13, 1863, for the war. Captured near Atlanta, Georgia, July 22, 1864. Sent to Nashville, Tennessee. Confined at Louisville, Kentucky, July 30, 1864. Transferred to Camp Chase, Ohio, where he arrived on August 2, 1864. Died at Camp Chase on February 8, 1865, of "pneumonia."

SHELSON, JOSEPH, Private

Resided in Buncombe County and enlisted at age 24, August 17, 1861. No further records.

SMITH, JESSE BURTON, Private

Resided in Haywood County and enlisted at age 34, July 30, 1862, for the war. Wounded in the left hand at Chickamauga, Georgia, September 19, 1863. Reported absent without leave during September, 1864-February, 1865.

SMITH, THOMAS, Private

Resided in Surry County and enlisted at age 22, August 17, 1861. Captured "in Kentucky" in September-November, 1862. Confined at Chattanooga, Tennessee. Exchanged on January 11, 1863. Captured at Yazoo City, Mississippi, July 14, 1863. Sent to Memphis, Tennessee. Transferred to St. Louis, Missouri. Confined at Camp Morton, Indianapolis, Indiana, August 27, 1863. Transferred to Fort Delaware, Delaware, where he arrived on March 22, 1864. Exchanged prior to February 28, 1865, when he was hospitalized at Richmond, Virginia. Furloughed from hospital at Richmond on March 9, 1865.

SMITH, THOMAS W., Private

Resided in Haywood County and enlisted at age 18, August 17, 1861. Captured at Yazoo City, Mississippi, on or about July 13, 1863. Sent to Memphis, Tennessee. Confined at St. Louis, Missouri, August 3, 1863. Transferred to Camp Morton, Indianapolis, Indiana, where he arrived on August 14, 1863. Transferred to Fort Delaware, Delaware, February 19, 1865. Transferred to Cairo, Illinois, April 10, 1865. Transferred to New Orleans, Louisiana, where he arrived on April 22, 1865. Transferred to the mouth of the Red River, Louisiana, May 2, 1865, for exchange.

SMITH, WILBURN S., Private

Resided in Surry County and enlisted at age 28, [August] 17, 1861. Nominated for the Badge of Distinction for gallantry at Murfreesboro, Tennessee, December 31, 1862. No further records.

SNELSON, JOSEPH Y., Private

North Carolina pension records indicate that he served in this company.

SUMMEY, WILLIAM F., Private
Records of the United Daughters of the Confederacy indicate he enlisted at age 32, August 17, 1861. No further records.

SUMNER, JAMES, Private
Resided in Haywood County and enlisted at age 43, September 17, 1863, for the war. No further records.

TATE, JOHN MANSON, Private
Born in Haywood County and resided in Haywood or Buncombe County prior to enlisting in Haywood County at age 26, August 17, 1861. Captured at Chickamauga, Georgia, September 19-20, 1863. Sent to Nashville, Tennessee. Confined at Louisville, Kentucky, September 30, 1863. Transferred to Camp Douglas, Chicago, Illinois, where he arrived on October 4, 1863. Paroled at Camp Douglas and transferred to Point Lookout, Maryland, February 20-21, 1865. Exchanged on an unspecified date. Hospitalized at Richmond, Virginia, March 2, 1865. Reported in hospital at Richmond through March 6, 1865. No further records.

TEAGUE, GEORGE W., Private
Born in Iredell County and resided in Iredell or Haywood County where he was by occupation a farmer prior to enlisting in Haywood County at age 31, August 17, 1861. Discharged on April 4, 1862, by reason of "a lame leg occasioned by a fall from a horse 'several years' ago." Reenlisted in the company prior to April 6, 1863. Captured near Smyrna, Georgia, July 5, 1864. Sent to Nashville, Tennessee. Confined at Louisville, Kentucky, July 18, 1864. Transferred to Camp Douglas, Chicago, Illinois. Released on June 16, 1865, after taking the Oath of Allegiance.

TEEM, LEANDER, Private
Resided in Burke County and enlisted at age 34, August 17, 1861. Apparently captured in Kentucky in September-October, 1862. Sent to Camp Dick Robinson, Kentucky. Reported in confinement at Gallatin, Tennessee, November 18, 1862. Company records do not indicate whether he returned to duty. Deserted on October 8, 1863.

THOMPSON, PINKY A., ———
Records of the United Daughters of the Confederacy indicate he enlisted at age 18, July 29, 1862, for the war. No further records.

VESS, JAMES M., Private
Resided in South Carolina and enlisted at age 20, August 17, 1861. Captured and paroled at Yazoo City, Mississippi, July 13, 1863. No further records.

WADE, WALTER P., Private
Born in Anson County where he resided prior to enlisting at age 24, August 17, 1861. Died at Loudon, Tennessee, January 31, 1862, of "ty[phoid] fever."

WALLACE, JOHN O., Private
Resided in Rutherford County and enlisted at age 18, August 17, 1861. Mustered in as Private. Promoted to Corporal on January 31, 1863. Reduced to ranks on an unspecified date. Captured and paroled at Yazoo City, Mississippi, July 13, 1863. No further records.

WALLACE, WILLIAM C., Private
Resided in Rutherford or Cherokee County and enlisted

at age 21, August 17, 1861. Transferred to Company A of this regiment on June 20, 1863.

WARREN, JOHN, ———
North Carolina pension records indicate that he served in this company.

WHITEHEAD, WILLIAM M., ———
North Carolina pension records indicate that he served in this company.

WILLIAMSON, ALEXANDER M.,Sergeant
Resided in Tennessee and enlisted at age 32, August 17, 1861. Mustered in as Private. Promoted to Sergeant on May 1, 1862. Captured at or near Richmond, Kentucky, on or about October 27, 1862. Sent to Louisville, Kentucky. Transferred to Vicksburg, Mississippi, where he arrived on December 22, 1862. Exchanged on an unspecified date. Last reported in the records of this company on September 26, 1863.

WILSON, HARRISON, Private
Born in Buncombe County and was by occupation a farmer. Place and date of enlistment not reported. Captured in Cherokee County, Alabama, October 21, 1864. Sent to Nashville, Tennessee. Confined at Louisville, Kentucky, November 22, 1864. Transferred to Camp Douglas, Chicago, Illinois, November 23-24, 1864. Released on March 24, 1865, after joining the U.S. Army. Assigned to Company D, 6th Regiment U.S. Volunteer Infantry.

WILSON, WILLIAM L., 1st Sergeant
Resided in Buncombe County and enlisted at age 30, August 17, 1861. Mustered in with an unspecified rank and was promoted to 1st Sergeant on September 20, 1863. Died "in North Carolina" in April, 1865, of wounds. Place and date wounded not reported.

WINCHESTER, WILLIAM R., Private
Resided in Haywood County and enlisted at age 16, August 17, 1861. Captured at Yazoo City, Mississippi, on or about July 14, 1863. Confined at St. Louis, Missouri, August 3, 1863. Transferred to Camp Morton, Indianapolis, Indiana, where he arrived on August 14, 1863. Died at Camp Morton on January 28, 1864, of "typhoid pneumonia."

WOODY, M. L., ———
North Carolina pension records indicate that he served in this company.

WYATT, JAMES B., Corporal
Records of the United Daughters of the Confederacy indicate he enlisted at age 20, July 19, 1862, for the war. No further records.

YATES, JAMES, Private
Resided in Clay County or in Tennessee and enlisted at age 17, November 10, 1863, for the war. Captured by the enemy (or deserted) on an unspecified date. Took the Oath of Allegiance at Chattanooga, Tennessee, March 22, 1864.

COMPANY F

This company was raised in Jackson County and enlisted on August 31, 1861. It was then assigned to the 29th Regiment and designated Company F. After joining the regiment the company functioned as a part of the regiment, and its history for the war period is reported as a part of the regimental history.

The following company roster is based primarily on the North Carolina Roll of Honor, prisoner of war records, pension applications, and a variety of miscellaneous records. Information was obtained also from secondary sources such as postwar histories, cemetery records, and records of the United Daughters of the Confederacy. No muster rolls were located for the company.

OFFICERS

CAPTAINS

ENLOE, WILLIAM ALFRED
Resided in Jackson County and enlisted at age 29. Appointed Captain on August 31, 1861. Resigned on April 20, 1863, by reason of "chronic affection of the kidneys from which he had suffered for ten years [and] also from chronic diarrhoea from which he had suffered for the five or six months past."

CONLEY, JAMES L.
Resided in Jackson County and enlisted at age 32, August 31, 1861. Mustered in as 1st Sergeant. Appointed 2nd Lieutenant on May 2, 1862. Promoted to 1st Lieutenant on August 2, 1862, and was promoted to Captain on April 20, 1863. Killed at Allatoona, Georgia, October 5, 1864.

LIEUTENANTS

CONLEY, JAMES, 2nd Lieutenant
Born in Jackson County* where he resided as a farmer prior to enlisting at age 23. Appointed 2nd Lieutenant on August 31, 1861. Defeated for reelection when the regiment was reorganized on or about May 2, 1862. Later served as Private in Company F, Infantry Regiment, Thomas Legion.

ENLOE, ABRAM M., 3rd Lieutenant
Born in Jackson County* where he resided prior to enlisting at age 34, January 1, 1862. Mustered in as Private. Appointed 3rd Lieutenant on May 2, 1862. Died "in North Carolina" on April 8, 1863, of disease.

ENLOE, J. W., "Lieutenant"
Previously served as Quartermaster Sergeant on the Field and Staff of this regiment. Appointed "Lieutenant" in this company on May 2, 1862. No further records.

MILLER, STEPHEN H., 2nd Lieutenant
Resided in Jackson County and enlisted at age 31. Appointed 2nd Lieutenant on August 31, 1861. Shot through the thigh by a "bushwhacker" in a skirmish at Cumberland Gap, Tennessee, on or about March 21-23, 1862. Defeated for reelection when the regiment was reorganized on or about May 2, 1862.

MILLSAPS, ANDREW K., 2nd Lieutenant
Resided in Jackson County and enlisted at age 25, August 31, 1861. Mustered in as Private. Promoted to 1st Sergeant prior to February 4, 1864. Appointed 2nd Lieutenant prior to May 9, 1865. Paroled at [Meridian], Mississippi, May 9, 1865.

MORRIS, WILLIAM L., 1st Lieutenant
Resided in Jackson County and enlisted at age 25,

August 31, 1861. Mustered in as Corporal. Appointed 2nd Lieutenant on November 13, 1862. Promoted to 1st Lieutenant on April 20, 1863. Wounded in the left leg at Allatoona, Georgia, October 5, 1864. [North Carolina pension records indicate that he survived the war.]

PARKER, DEVANIA, 2nd Lieutenant
Resided in Jackson County and enlisted at age 25, August 31, 1861. Mustered in as Sergeant. Appointed 2nd Lieutenant on June 20, 1863. Wounded "by a cannon ball carrying off his right arm making amputation necessary" at Chickamauga, Georgia, September 19, 1863. [North Carolina pension records indicate that he survived the war.]

THOMPSON, JAMES A., 1st Lieutenant
Resided in Jackson County and enlisted at age 32. Appointed 1st Lieutenant on August 31, 1861. Resigned on August 31, 1862, by reason of "hemor[r]hage of the lungs."

NONCOMMISSIONED OFFICERS AND PRIVATES

ALLISON, JOHN B., Jr., Corporal
Born in Jackson County* where he resided as a farmer prior to enlisting in Jackson County on August 31, 1861, or April 1, 1862. Mustered in as Private. Promoted to Corporal on an unspecified date. Discharged on November 11, 1862, by reason of the expiration of his term of service. Discharge certificate gives his age as 17.

BARKER, JOHN, Private
Resided in Jackson County and enlisted at age 30, August 31, 1861. Last reported in the records of this company on February 4, 1864.

BARKER, SHADRACH, Private
Resided in Jackson County and enlisted at age 20, August 31, 1861. Captured and paroled at Yazoo City, Mississippi, July 13, 1863. No further records.

BENSON, ALEXANDER C., Private
Resided in Jackson County and enlisted at age 16, August 31, 1861. Captured near Jackson, Mississippi, July 13, 1863. Sent to Snyder's Bluff, Mississippi, July 30, 1863. Transferred to Camp Morton, Indianapolis, Indiana, where he arrived on August 7, 1863. Enlisted in Company F, 6th Regiment Indiana Cavalry, prior to September 1, 1863.

BOWERS, A. J., Private
Enlisted in July, 1861, at age 18. Wounded at Chickamauga, Georgia, September 19, 1863. Captured by the enemy on February 7, 1864. Confined at Knoxville, Tennessee. Released on February 20, 1864, after taking the Oath of Allegiance.

BOWERS, JAMES A., Corporal
Resided in Jackson County and enlisted at age 25, August 31, 1861. Promotion record not reported. Deserted on September 25, 1863.

BOWERS, JASPER J., Private
Resided in Cherokee County and enlisted at age 18, March, 1863, for the war. Deserted on an unspecified date. [May have served also in Company H, Walker's Battalion, Thomas Legion.]

BOWERS, LEWIS, Corporal
Born in Chester District, South Carolina, and resided in Jackson County where he was by occupation a farmer prior to enlisting in Jackson County at age 47, August 31, 1861. Mustered in as Corporal. Discharged on May 21, 1862, by reason of ''chronic inflammation of the pleura.''

BOWERS, P. J., Private
Place and date of enlistment not reported. Captured and paroled at Yazoo City, Mississippi, July 13, 1863.

BOWERS, RICHARD J., Private
Resided in Jackson County and enlisted at age 21, August 31, 1861. Wounded in the face at Murfreesboro, Tennessee, December 31, 1862. Captured by the enemy on an unspecified date. Confined at Knoxville, Tennessee, February 7, 1864. Released on or about February 20, 1864, after taking the Oath of Allegiance.

BOYD, JAMES E., Private
Previously served in Company K, 39th Regiment N.C. Troops. Transferred to this company on September 25, 1863. Died on January 18, 1864. Place and cause of death not reported.

BOYD, R. W., Private
Resided in Macon County and enlisted at age 18, September 1, 1861. Surrendered at Citronelle, Alabama, May 4, 1865. Paroled at Meridian, Mississippi, May 9, 1865. [North Carolina pension records indicate he was wounded in the head on November 1, 1864.]

BOYD, ROBERT A., Private
Resided in Jackson County and enlisted at age 21, August 31, 1861. No further records.

BOYD, SAMUEL M., Private
Resided in Jackson County and enlisted at age 24, August 31, 1861. Captured at Spanish Fort, Mobile, Alabama, April 8, 1865. Confined at Ship Island, Mississippi. Transferred to Vicksburg, Mississippi, May 1, 1865. Paroled at Meridian, Mississippi, May 11, 1865.

BRADLEY, JAMES, Private
Place and date of enlistment not reported. Captured and paroled at Yazoo City, Mississippi, July 13, 1863. No further records.

BRADLEY, JOHN, Private
Resided in Jackson County and enlisted at age 19, August 31, 1861. No further records.

BROOKS, J. S., ———
North Carolina pension records indicate that he served in this company.

BROWN, HUGH R., Private
Resided in Jackson County and enlisted at age 19, August 31, 1861. Last reported in the records of this company on February 4, 1864.

BUCHANAN, F. B., Private
Place and date of enlistment not reported. Captured in hospital at Grenada, Mississippi, August 17, 1863. Paroled at Grenada on August 18, 1863. No further records.

BUCHANAN, JULIUS W., Private
Resided in Jackson County and enlisted at age 19, December 1, 1861. Captured near Smyrna, Georgia, July 3-4, 1864. Sent to Nashville, Tennessee. Confined at Louisville, Kentucky, July 13, 1864. Transferred to Camp Morton, Indianapolis, Indiana, where he arrived on July 14, 1864. Paroled and transferred to Boulware's Wharf, James River, Virginia, where he was received on March 23, 1865, for exchange.

BUCHANNAN, PATTON, Private
Resided in Jackson County and enlisted at age 19, August 31, 1861. No further records.

BUMGARNER, ANTHONY, Private
Resided in Jackson County and enlisted at age 18, August 31, 1861. Last reported in the records of this company on February 4, 1864.

BUMGARNER, ENOS S., Private
Resided in Jackson County and enlisted at age 21, August 31, 1861. Deserted on May 19, 1863. Returned to duty prior to July 13, 1863, when he was captured by the enemy near Jackson, Mississippi. Sent to Louisville, Kentucky. Confined at Camp Morton, Indianapolis, Indiana, August 7, 1863. Released prior to September 1, 1863, after joining the U.S. Army. Assigned to Company F, 6th Regiment Indiana Cavalry.

CARTER, J. T., Private
Place and date of enlistment not reported. Paroled at Farmville, Virginia, April 11-21, 1865.

CHASTEEN, JOHN, Private
Resided in Jackson County and enlisted at age 18, August 31, 1861. No further records.

COLLINS, DANIEL, Private
Resided in Jackson County and enlisted at age 46, August 31, 1861. Discharged on November 8, 1862, by reason of being overage.

CONLEY, JOHN H., 1st Sergeant
Born in Macon County and resided in Jackson County prior to enlisting at age 20, August 31, 1861. Mustered in as Corporal. Promoted to 1st Sergeant on November 13, 1862. Died in hospital at Shelbyville, Tennessee, March 28, 1863, of disease.

CONLEY, SAMUEL C., Private
Born in Macon County* and resided in Jackson County where he enlisted at age 34, August 31, 1861. Killed ''by the accidental discharge of a gun'' at Grassy Branch, Tennessee, December 5, 1861.

CONNER, SAMUEL P., Private
Resided in Jackson County and enlisted at age 18, August 31, 1861. Captured at Spanish Fort, Mobile, Alabama, April 8, 1865. Confined at Ship Island, Mississippi, April 10, 1865. Transferred to Vicksburg, Mississippi, May 1, 1865. No further records.

CONNER, WILLIAM, Private
Resided in Jackson County and enlisted at age 32, August 31, 1861. Wounded at Cumberland Gap, Tennessee, on an unspecified date. Discharged on an unspecified date by reason of disability from wounds.

COOK, WILLIAM J., Private
Resided in Jackson County and enlisted on August 31, 1861. Transferred to Company I, 25th Regiment N.C. Troops (15th Regiment N.C. Volunteers), prior to September 8, 1861.

CUNNINGHAM, GEORGE R., Private
Born in Jackson County* where he resided as a farmer prior to enlisting in Jackson County on August 31, 1861. Discharged on May 19, 1862, by reason of "general debility from effects of disease [including typhoid fever]." Discharge certificate gives his age as 17.

DILLS, JOHN RAMSAY, Private
Resided in Jackson County and enlisted at age 30, August 31, 1861. Appointed 1st Lieutenant on or about July 11, 1862, and transferred to Company H, 62nd Regiment N.C. Troops.

DURHAM, HIRAM, Private
Resided in Jackson County and enlisted on August 31, 1861. Discharged on an unspecified date under the provisions of the Conscription Act.

ENDY, R., Private
Place and date of enlistment not reported. Captured at Spanish Fort, Mobile, Alabama, April 8, 1865. Confined at Ship Island, Mississippi, April 10, 1865. Transferred to Vicksburg, Mississippi, May 1, 1865. No further records.

ENSLOE, SAMUEL W., Private
Resided in Jackson County and enlisted at age 24, August 31, 1861. Discharged on an unspecified date by reason of disability.

EUDY, MALICHI, ———
North Carolina pension records indicate that he served in this company.

EVANS, COONROD, Private
Resided in Jackson County and enlisted on August 31, 1861. Discharged on an unspecified date by reason of disability.

FELTS, CASWELL G., Private
Resided in Wake County. Place and date of enlistment not reported. First reported in the records of this company on September 30, 1864. Took the Oath of Allegiance at Raleigh on May 24, 1865.

FORD, HORATIO, Private
Resided in Jackson County and enlisted at age 30, August 31, 1861. Discharged on an unspecified date by reason of disability.

FOUNTAIN, P. F., Private
Resided in New Hanover County and enlisted on June 15, 1863, for the war. Surrendered at Citronelle, Alabama, May 4, 1865. Paroled at Meridian, Mississippi, May 9, 1865. [North Carolina pension records indicate he was wounded at Spanish Fort, Mobile, Alabama, on or about April 10, 1865.]

FOX, W. A., ———
North Carolina pension records indicate that he served in this company.

FRANKLIN, W. R., Private
Resided in Jackson County. Place and date of enlistment

not reported. Captured at Spanish Fort, Mobile, Alabama, April 8, 1865. Confined at Ship Island, Mississippi, April 10, 1865. Transferred to Vicksburg, Mississippi, May 1, 1865. Paroled at Meridian, Mississippi, May 11, 1865.

FREEMAN, JOHN A., Private
Place and date of enlistment not reported. Reported missing at Murfreesboro, Tennessee, December 31, 1862. Returned to duty on an unspecified date. Captured at Yazoo City, Mississippi, on or about July 14, 1863. Confined at St. Louis, Missouri, August 3, 1863. Transferred to Camp Morton, Indianapolis, Indiana, August 13, 1863. Released prior to September 1, 1863, after joining the U.S. Army. Assigned to Company F, 6th Regiment Indiana Cavalry.

FRIZZLE, SAMUEL M., Private
Resided in Jackson County and enlisted at age 19, August 31, 1861. Captured at Chickamauga, Georgia, September 19, 1863. Sent to Nashville, Tennessee. Confined at Louisville, Kentucky, September 30, 1863. Transferred to Camp Douglas, Chicago, Illinois, where he arrived on October 4, 1863. Released on June 16, 1865, after taking the Oath of Allegiance. [North Carolina pension records indicate he was wounded on January 1, 1862.]

GIBSON, STEPHEN, Private
Resided in Jackson County and enlisted at age 34, August 31, 1861. Discharged on November 8, 1862. Reason discharged not reported.

GRIFFIN, EDWARD A., Private
Place and date of enlistment not reported. Captured at or near Franklin, Tennessee, December 17, 1864. Sent to Nashville, Tennessee. Confined at Louisville, Kentucky, December 20, 1864. Transferred to Camp Douglas, Chicago, Illinois, where he arrived on December 22, 1864. Died at Camp Douglas on January 4, 1865, of "pneumonia." [May have served previously in Company E, Mallett's N.C. Battalion (Camp Guard).]

GUNTER, ENOS, Private
Resided in Jackson County and enlisted at age 18, August 31, 1861. Last reported in the records of this company on February 4, 1864.

HALL, KINSEY J., Private
Resided in Jackson County and enlisted on August 31, 1861. Failed to report for duty with the company.

HATLEY, ISAAC W., Private
Resided in Stanly County. Place and date of enlistment not reported. Captured near Smyrna, Georgia, July 4, 1864. Sent to Nashville, Tennessee. Confined at Louisville, Kentucky, July 13, 1864. Transferred to Camp Douglas, Chicago, Illinois, where he arrived on July 16-18, 1864. Released on June 16, 1865, after taking the Oath of Allegiance.

HOLCOMBE, OBADIAH, ———
North Carolina pension records indicate that he served in this company.

HOLT, J. H., Sergeant
Place and date of enlistment not reported. Promotion record not reported. First reported in the records of this

company on September 6, 1864. Surrendered at Citronelle, Alabama, May 4, 1865. Paroled at Meridian, Mississippi, May 16, 1865.

HUTCHINGS, R., Private
Place and date of enlistment not reported. Captured and paroled at Yazoo City, Mississippi, July 13, 1863. No further records.

HYDE, ADOLPHUS E., Private
Resided in Jackson County and enlisted at age 23, August 31, 1861. Deserted in June, 1863.

HYDE, NATHAN F., Musician
Resided in Jackson County and enlisted at age 20, August 31, 1861. Mustered in as Musician (Fifer). Deserted on an unspecified date.

HYDE, WILLIAM H., Private
Resided in Jackson County and enlisted at age 25, August 31, 1861. Deserted on an unspecified date.

JENKINS, CHARLES DOCK, Sergeant
Born in Haywood County and resided in Jackson County prior to enlisting at age 41, August 31, 1861. Wounded in an unspecified battle. [North Carolina pension records indicate that he survived the war.]

JENKINS, FRANCIS M., Private
Resided in Jackson County and enlisted at age 17, August 31, 1861. Deserted in June, 1862. Later served in Captain Levi's Light Artillery Battery, Thomas Legion.

JENKINS, JONAS, Private
Resided in Jackson County and enlisted on August 31, 1861. Failed to report for duty with the company. [May have served later in Company F, Infantry Regiment, Thomas Legion.]

JENKINS, MITCHELL, Private
Born in Jackson County* where he resided prior to enlisting at age 25, August 31, 1861. Died at Cumberland Gap, Tennessee, May 12, 1862, of "typhoid fever."

JENKINS, THOMAS, Private
Resided in Jackson County and enlisted at age 18, August 31, 1861. Deserted on an unspecified date.

JOB, WILLIAM F., Private
Born in Guilford County and was by occupation a farmer. Place and date of enlistment not reported. Captured near Jonesboro, Georgia, September 5, 1864. Sent to Nashville, Tennessee. Confined at Louisville, Kentucky, October 28, 1864. Transferred to Camp Douglas, Chicago, Illinois, where he arrived on November 1, 1864. Released on April 6, 1865, after joining the U.S. Army. Assigned to Company F, 5th Regiment U.S. Volunteer Infantry. [May have served previously in Company E, Mallett's N.C. Battalion (Camp Guard).]

JOHNSON, WILLIS, Private
Resided in Jackson County and enlisted at age 18, December, 1861. Died at Morristown, Tennessee, April 21, 1862, of "inflam[mation] of lungs."

JONES, THOMAS J., Private
Resided in Jackson County where he enlisted at age 21,

August 31, 1861. Last reported in the records of this company on February 4, 1864.

KING, H. WESLEY, ———
North Carolina pension records indicate that he served in this company.

KIRKLAND, JAMES, Musician
Resided in Jackson County and enlisted on August 31, 1861. Mustered in as Musician (Drummer). Failed to report for duty with the company.

LITTLE, TILMAN, Private
Enlisted on July 29, 1863, for the war. Captured near Smyrna, Georgia, July 4, 1864. Sent to Nashville, Tennessee. Confined at Louisville, Kentucky, July 13, 1864. Transferred to Camp Douglas, Chicago, Illinois, where he arrived on July 16, 1864. Died at Camp Douglas on November 27, 1864, of "smallpox."

LONG, JAMES R., Private
Resided in Jackson County and enlisted at age 17, October, 1861. Discharged on November 8, 1862, under the provisions of the Conscription Act.

LOVE, WILLIAM L., Private
Resided in Jackson County and enlisted at age 31, August 31, 1861. Hospitalized at Macon, Georgia, August 10, 1864, with a gunshot wound of the back or leg. Place and date wounded not reported. Furloughed on August 20, 1864. Hospitalized at Meridian, Mississippi, April 11, 1865, with a wound. Place and date wounded not reported. Surrendered at Citronelle, Alabama, May 4, 1865. Paroled at Meridian on May 9, 1865.

McHARG, WILLIAM P., Private
Born in Rowan County and resided in Jackson County prior to enlisting at age 34, August 31, 1861. Died at Tazewell, Tennessee, September 18, 1862, of disease.

McHARGE, JAMES L., Private
Born in Mississippi and resided in Jackson County prior to enlisting at age 22, January, 1862. Died at Morristown, Tennessee, March 4, 1862, of "typhoid fever."

MARSHALL, JAMES H., Private
Resided in Forsyth County and enlisted at age 26, August 29, 1862, for the war. Wounded in the left thigh at Nashville, Tennessee, December 15-16, 1864. Captured at Columbia, Tennessee, December 22, 1864. Sent to Nashville. Confined at Louisville, Kentucky, February 25, 1865. Transferred to Camp Chase, Ohio, where he arrived on March 5, 1865. Released on June 13, 1865, after taking the Oath of Allegiance.

MARTIN, JAMES, Private
Place and date of enlistment not reported. Captured at Spanish Fort, Mobile, Alabama, April 8, 1865. Confined at Ship Island, Mississippi, April 10, 1865. Transferred to Vicksburg, Mississippi, May 1, 1865. No further records.

MARTIN, W. A., Sergeant
Place and date of enlistment not reported. Promotion record not reported. Captured at Spanish Fort, Mobile, Alabama, April 8, 1865. Confined at Ship Island, Mississippi, April 10, 1865. Transferred to Vicksburg,

Mississippi, May 1, 1865. No further records. [May have served previously in Company C, Mallett's N.C. Battalion (Camp Guard).]

MATHIS, JAMES H., Private
Resided in Jackson County and enlisted at age 22, August 31, 1861. Last reported in the records of this company on February 4, 1864.

MEDLIN, JAMES, Private
Born in Jackson County* where he resided prior to enlisting at age 18, January, 1862. Died at Cumberland Gap, Tennessee, May 7-12, 1862, of "typhoid fever."

MIDDLETON, NATHANIEL, Private
Resided in Jackson County and enlisted at age 36, August 31, 1861. Killed at Chickamauga, Georgia, September 19-20, 1863.

MILLSAPS, DEVANIA, Private
Born in Jackson County* where he resided prior to enlisting at age 19, August 31, 1861. Killed at Murfreesboro, Tennessee, December 31, 1862. Nominated for the Badge of Distinction for gallantry at Murfreesboro.

MILLSAPS, JASPER, Private
Born in Jackson County* where he resided prior to enlisting at age 22, August 31, 1861. Died at Bean's Station, Tennessee, April 18, 1862, of disease.

MILLSAPS, LAFAYETTE, Private
Resided in Jackson County and enlisted at age 26, August 31, 1861. Deserted on September 25, 1863.

MILLSAPS, M. S., Private
Place and date of enlistment not reported. First listed in the records of this company on November 1, 1863. "Mentioned for gallantry" at Shelbyville, Tennessee, in 1863. No further records.

MOTHAS, M. S., Private
Resided in Jackson County. Place and date of enlistment not reported. Surrendered at Citronelle, Alabama, May 4, 1865. Paroled at Meridian, Mississippi, May 9, 1865.

NATIONS, ARATH C., Private
Resided in Jackson County and enlisted at age 19, August 31, 1861. No further records

PARKER, JEREMIAH M., Private
Resided in Jackson County and enlisted at age 16, August 31, 1861. Discharged on April 8 or November 13, 1862. Reason discharged not reported.

PARKER, WILLIAM J., Sergeant
Resided in Jackson County and enlisted at age 18, August 31, 1861. Mustered in as Private. Wounded at Allatoona, Georgia, on or about October 5, 1864. Returned to duty on an unspecified date. Promoted to Sergeant prior to December 16, 1864, when he was wounded in the chest and/or head and captured at Nashville, Tennessee. Hospitalized at Nashville. Transferred to Louisville, Kentucky, January 27, 1865. Transferred to Camp Chase, Ohio, where he arrived on February 3, 1865. Released at Camp Chase on June 13, 1865, after taking the Oath of Allegiance.

PEGG, R. A., Corporal
Resided in Guilford County. Place and date of

enlistment not reported. Promotion record not reported. Surrendered at Citronelle, Alabama, May 4, 1865. Paroled at Meridian, Mississippi, May 9, 1865.

PHILLIPS, ANDREW J., Private
Resided in Jackson County and enlisted at age 29, August 31, 1861. Present or accounted for through July 28, 1862. Deserted on an unspecified date.

PHILLIPS, JOHN W., Private
Resided in Jackson County and enlisted at age 18, August 31, 1861. Wounded in the left shoulder at Murfreesboro, Tennessee, December 31, 1862. Returned to duty on an unspecified date. Captured near Smyrna, Georgia, July 4, 1864. Sent to Nashville, Tennessee. Confined at Louisville, Kentucky, July 14, 1864. Transferred to Camp Douglas, Chicago, Illinois, where he arrived on July 18, 1864. Died at Camp Douglas on August 13, 1864, of "dysentery."

PHIPPS, JOHN, ———
North Carolina pension records indicate that he served in this company.

PINION, ELBERT S., Private
Resided in Jackson County and enlisted at age 18, August 31, 1861. Deserted on an unspecified date.

PLOUGHMAN, W., Private
Resided in Rowan County. Place and date of enlistment not reported. Captured by the enemy on an unspecified date. Confined at Elmira, New York. Released on or about May 29, 1865, after taking the Oath of Allegiance.

PRICE, ARCHIBALD N., Private
Resided in Jackson County and enlisted at age 31, August 31, 1861. Wounded in the right leg at Chickamauga, Georgia, September 19-20, 1863. [North Carolina pension records indicate that he survived the war.]

PUGH, THOMAS, Private
Resided in Randolph County. Place and date of enlistment not reported. Captured at Nashville, Tennessee, December 16, 1864. Sent to Louisville, Kentucky. Transferred to Camp Chase, Ohio, where he arrived on January 6, 1865. Released at Camp Chase on May 15, 1865, after taking the Oath of Allegiance

RABEY, ALFRED B., Private
Resided in Jackson County and enlisted at age 19, August 31, 1861. Captured at Murfreesboro, Tennessee, December 31, 1862. Confined at Camp Douglas, Chicago, Illinois, February 11, 1863. Paroled and transferred to City Point, Virginia, where he was received on April 4, 1863, for exchange. Hospitalized at Jackson, Mississippi, February 17, 1864, with debilitas and returned to duty on February 29, 1864. No further records.

REEVES, J. S., Private
Resided in Surry County. Place and date of enlistment not reported. Surrendered at Citronelle, Alabama, May 4, 1865. Paroled at Meridian, Mississippi, May 9, 1865.

ROBINSON, ISRAEL L., Private
Resided in Jackson County and enlisted at age 35, August 31, 1861. Deserted on an unspecified date.

ROSE, QUILLAN L., Private
Resided in Jackson County and enlisted at age 18, August 31, 1861. Deserted on an unspecified date. Later served in Captain Levi's Light Artillery Battery, Thomas Legion.

SENSEBAUGH, E. G., Private
Records of the United Daughters of the Confederacy indicate he enlisted at age 47, February 13, 1863, for the war. No further records.

SHERRILL, JASON KEENER, Sergeant
Resided in Jackson County and enlisted at age 33, August 31, 1861. Mustered in as Sergeant. Last reported in the records of this company on February 4, 1864.

SHULAR, DAVID, Private
Resided in Jackson County and enlisted at age 18, March, 1862. Deserted on an unspecified date.

SHULAR, WILLIAM M., Private
Resided in Jackson County and enlisted at age 31, August 31, 1861. Hospitalized at Meridian, Mississippi, April 11, 1865, with a wound. Place and date wounded not reported. Surrendered at Citronelle, Alabama, May 4, 1865. Paroled at Meridian on May 9, 1865.

SHULER, D. M., Private
North Carolina pension records indicate that he served in this company. [May have served later in Captain Levi's Light Artillery Battery, Thomas Legion.]

SHULER, J. M., Private
Resided in Jackson County and enlisted at age 17, September 1, 1864, for the war. Captured at Spanish Fort, Mobile, Alabama, April 8, 1865. Confined at Ship Island, Mississippi, April 10, 1865. Transferred to Vicksburg, Mississippi, May 1, 1865. Paroled at Meridian, Mississippi, May 11, 1865.

SHULER, JAMES, Sergeant
Resided in Jackson County and enlisted at age 23, August 31, 1861. Mustered in as Sergeant. Deserted in June, 1862.

SHULER, JOHN F., Private
Resided in Jackson County and enlisted at age 36, August 31, 1861. Deserted in June, 1862. Transferred to Company H, Walker's Battalion, Thomas Legion, March 1, 1863. Reenlisted in this company in October, 1864-January, 1865. Hospitalized at Meridian, Mississippi, February 2, 1865, with an unspecified wound. Place and date wounded not reported. Transferred to Marion, Alabama, on an unspecified date. No further records.

SHULER, THOMAS J., Private
Resided in Jackson County and enlisted at age 21, August 31, 1861. Deserted in June, 1862. Later served in Captain Levi's Light Artillery Battery, Thomas Legion.

SHULER, WILLIAM P., Private
Resided in Jackson County or in Jefferson County, Tennessee, and enlisted at age 19, August 31, 1861. Deserted in June, 1862. Later served in Captain Levi's Light Artillery Battery, Thomas Legion.

STANBERRY, WILLIAM P., Private
Resided in Jackson County and enlisted at age 22,

August 31, 1861. Deserted on an unspecified date.

STEAPLETON, WILLIAM S., Private
Born in Guilford County and was by occupation a laborer. Place and date of enlistment not reported. Captured at or near Nashville, Tennessee, on or about December 17, 1864. Confined at Nashville. Transferred to Louisville, Kentucky, where he arrived on December 22, 1864. Transferred to Camp Chase, Ohio, where he arrived on January 6, 1865. Released on April 22, 1865, after joining the U.S. Army. Assigned to Company E, 5th Regiment U.S. Volunteer Infantry.

STEPLETON, S. B., Private
Place and date of enlistment not reported. Captured at Spanish Fort, Mobile, Alabama, April 8, 1865. Confined at Ship Island, Mississippi, April 10, 1865. Transferred to Vicksburg, Mississippi, May 1, 1865. No further records. [May have served previously in Company C, Mallett's N.C. Battalion (Camp Guard).]

STILLWELL, IRIS E., Private
Born in Jackson County* where he resided as a carpenter prior to enlisting in Jackson County at age 21, August 31, 1861. Died at Loudon, Tennessee, on or about December 26, 1862, of disease.

STRATTON, DANIEL C., Sergeant
Resided in Jackson County and enlisted at age 19, August 31, 1861. Mustered in as Private. Promoted to Sergeant on an unspecified date. Hospitalized at Meridian, Mississippi, January 16, 1865, with an unspecified wound. Place and date wounded not reported. Surrendered at Citronelle, Alabama, May 4, 1865. Paroled at Meridian on May 9, 1865.

STRATTON, JOSEPH, Private
Resided in Jackson County and enlisted at age 49, December, 1861. Discharged on November 8, 1862, by reason of being overage.

STROUP, JOHN E., Private
Resided in Jackson or Buncombe County and enlisted at age 17, August 31, 1861. Captured near Marietta, Georgia, June 19, 1864. Sent to Nashville, Tennessee. Confined at Louisville, Kentucky, June 26, 1864. Transferred to Camp Morton, Indianapolis, Indiana, where he arrived on June 28, 1864. Released on June 12, 1865, after taking the Oath of Allegiance.

THOMPSON, WILLIAM, ———
Place and date of enlistment not reported. Died at Griffin, Georgia, July 13, 1864, of disease.

VANHOY, CALVIN, Private
Enlisted at age 25, July 2, 1862, for the war. Hospitalized at Meridian, Mississippi, January 29, 1865, with an unspecified wound. Paroled at Charlotte on May 11, 1865.

WARREN, WILLIAM K., Private
Born in Buncombe County and resided in Jackson County where he was by occupation a carpenter prior to enlisting in Jackson County at age 24, August 31, 1861. Last reported in the records of this company on September 19, 1864.

WATSON, DANIEL, Private
Resided in Jackson County and enlisted at age 26,

August 31, 1861. Last reported in the records of this company on February 4, 1864.

WEST, JAMES, Private

Born in Buncombe County and resided in Jackson County where he was by occupation a mechanic prior to enlisting at age 34, August 31, 1861. Transferred to Company A, 16th Regiment N.C. Troops (6th Regiment N.C. Volunteers), on or about March 8, 1862. Later served as 2nd Lieutenant of that company.

WHITAKER, A. L., Private

Resided in Surry County. Place and date of enlistment not reported. Surrendered at Citronelle, Alabama, May 4, 1865. Paroled at Meridian, Mississippi, May 9, 1865.

WIGGINS, ANDREW C., Private

Resided in Jackson County and enlisted at age 18, August 31, 1861. Deserted in June, 1862.

WIGGINS, MOSES L., Private

Resided in Jackson County and enlisted at age 23, August 31, 1861. Deserted in June, 1862.

WILSON, JAMES, Private

Resided in Jackson County and enlisted on August 31, 1861. Hospitalized at Marion, Alabama, April 25, 1864. No further records.

WILSON, JOHN G., Private

Resided in Jackson County and enlisted on August 31, 1861. Last reported in the records of this company on March 7, 1864.

WOOD, ICEM, Private

Resided in Halifax County. Place and date of enlistment not reported. Died on April 16, 1865, of a gunshot wound of the shoulder and spine. Place and date wounded not reported.

WOOD, LEVI M., Private

Born in Jackson County* where he resided prior to enlisting at age 36, August 31, 1861. Died in hospital at Jonesboro, Tennessee, November 22, 1861, or January 3, 1862, of disease.

ZACKARY, COLUMBUS C., Sergeant

Resided in Jackson County and enlisted at age 30, January, 1862. Mustered in as Private. Promoted to Sergeant on an unspecified date. Deserted on an unspecified date.

COMPANY G

This company was raised in Yancey County and enlisted on July 26, 1861. It was then assigned to the 29th Regiment and designated Company G. After joining the regiment the company functioned as a part of the regiment, and its history for the war period is reported as a part of the regimental history.

The following company roster is based primarily on the North Carolina Roll of Honor, prisoner of war records, pension applications, and a variety of miscellaneous records. Information was obtained also from secondary sources such as postwar histories, cemetery records, and records of the United Daughters of the Confederacy. No muster rolls were located for the company.

OFFICERS

CAPTAINS

CHANDLER, MELCHISADIC

Resided in Yancey County and was by occupation a farmer prior to enlisting at age 41. Appointed Captain on July 26, 1861. Defeated for reelection when the regiment was reorganized on May 2, 1862. Later served as 3rd Lieutenant of Company H, 4th Regiment N.C. Senior Reserves.

HAMPTON, EZEKIEL H.

Resided in Yancey County and enlisted at age 27. Appointed 2nd Lieutenant on July 26, 1861. Promoted to Captain on May 2, 1862. Appointed Major on August 15, 1864, to rank from March 16, 1863, and transferred to the Field and Staff of this regiment. He was "an officer of sober, steady habits, prompt in discharge of his duties and [of] excellent moral character." [North Carolina pension records indicate he was wounded at Atlanta, Georgia, on an unspecified date.]

LIEUTENANTS

ADKINS, DAVID W., 2nd Lieutenant

Resided in Yancey County and enlisted at age 22, July 26, 1861. Mustered in as 1st Sergeant. Appointed 2nd Lieutenant on May 2, 1862. Company records indicate he was captured on February 27, 1864; however, records of the Federal Provost Marshal do not substantiate that report. Dropped from the rolls of the company on September 2, 1864.

ADKINS, WILSON, 2nd Lieutenant

Resided in Yancey County. Appointed 3rd Lieutenant on July 26, 1861. Promoted to 2nd Lieutenant on May 2, 1862. Company records indicate he was captured by the enemy on or about August 26, 1863; however, records of the Federal Provost Marshal do not substantiate that report. Dropped from the rolls of the company on February 17, 1864.

ALEXANDER, LEWIS, 3rd Lieutenant

Resided in Yancey County and enlisted at age 27, July 26, 1861. Mustered in as Musician (Drummer). Appointed 3rd Lieutenant on March 8, 1862. Defeated for reelection when the regiment was reorganized on May 2, 1862.

HONEYCUTT, WAIGHTSTELL T., 2nd Lieutenant

Resided in Yancey County and enlisted at age 18, July 26, 1861. Mustered in as Sergeant. Captured near Atlanta, Georgia, July 7, 1864. Exchanged on September 19-22, 1864. Appointed 2nd Lieutenant on an unspecified date. Paroled at Meridian Mississippi, May 9, 1865.

LEWIS, ALEXANDER M., 2nd Lieutenant

Resided in Yancey County and enlisted at age 27. Appointed 2nd Lieutenant on July 26, 1861. Not reelected when the regiment was reorganized on May 2, 1862.

PATTERSON, JAMES W., 2nd Lieutenant

Born in Yancey County where he resided as a farmer prior to enlisting at age 23. Appointed 2nd Lieutenant on July 26, 1861. Died at Parrottsville, Tennessee, December 17-25, 1861, of "pneumonia."

WILLIAMS, WILLIAM D., 1st Lieutenant
Resided in Yancey County and enlisted at age 25. Appointed 1st Lieutenant on July 26, 1861. Wounded at or near Ezra Church, Georgia, on or about July 28, 1864. No further records.

NONCOMMISSIONED OFFICERS AND PRIVATES

ADKINS, ISAAC, Private
Resided in Yancey County and enlisted at age 27, July 26, 1861. Wounded at Chickamauga, Georgia, September 19-20, 1863. [North Carolina pension records indicate that he survived the war.]

ADKINS, J. A., Private
North Carolina pension records indicate that he served in this company.

ADKINS, JASON, Private
Resided in Yancey County and enlisted at age 25, July 26, 1861. Wounded in the left thigh at Murfreesboro, Tennessee, December 31, 1862. Captured at Yazoo City, Mississippi, on or about July 13, 1863. Sent to Memphis, Tennessee. Confined at St. Louis, Missouri, August 3, 1863. Transferred to Camp Morton, Indianapolis, Indiana, where he arrived on August 14, 1863. Transferred to Fort Delaware, Delaware, March 19, 1864. Released on or about June 7, 1865, after taking the Oath of Allegiance.

ALLEN, ASA M., Corporal
Resided in Yancey County and enlisted at age 19, July 26, 1861. Mustered in as Private. Promoted to Corporal prior to July 13-14, 1863, when he was captured at Yazoo City, Mississippi. Sent to Memphis, Tennessee. Confined at St. Louis, Missouri, August 3, 1864. Transferred to Camp Morton, Indianapolis, Indiana, where he arrived on August 27, 1863. Died at Camp Morton on March 5, 1864, of "inflammation of brain."

ALLEN, JOSEPH, Private
Resided in Yancey County and enlisted at age 18, July 26, 1861. No further records.

ALLEN, JOSEPH G., Private
Place and date of enlistment not reported. First listed in the records of this company on March 1, 1863. Last reported in the records of this company on July 23, 1863. [North Carolina pension records indicate he was wounded at New Hope Church, Georgia, in 1863 or 1864.]

ALLEN, PHILIP M., Private
Resided in Yancey County and enlisted at age 27, July 26, 1861. Mustered in as Musician (Fifer). Reduced to ranks "from choice" on an unspecified date. Surrendered at Citronelle, Alabama, May 4, 1865. Paroled at Meridian, Mississippi, May 9, 1865.

ALLEN, SAMUEL, Private
Place and date of enlistment not reported. Captured by the enemy on an unspecified date. Died in a Federal hospital at Louisville, Kentucky, August 3, 1864, of "chronic valvular disease of the heart."

ALLEN, WILLIAM E., Private
Previously served in Company A of this regiment.

Enlisted in this company on March 1, 1864. Surrendered at Citronelle, Alabama, May 4, 1865. Paroled at Meridian, Mississippi, May 9, 1865.

ARROWOOD, ELIJAH W., Sergeant
Resided in Yancey County and enlisted at age 34, July 26, 1861. Mustered in as Private. Promoted to Sergeant on January 13, 1862. Captured in Yancey County on an unspecified date. Confined at Louisville, Kentucky. Released on July 31, 1864, after taking the Oath of Allegiance.

AUSTIN, EDWARD, Private
Resided in Yancey County and enlisted at age 18, July 26, 1861. No further records.

AYERS, BAKER, Private
Resided in Yancey County and enlisted at age 34, July 26, 1861. [North Carolina pension records indicate he was wounded near Atlanta, Georgia, in July, 1864.] No further records.

AYERS, JEREMIAH, Private
Resided in Yancey County and enlisted at age 44, July 26, 1861. Discharged at Cumberland Gap, Tennessee, on an unspecified date. [North Carolina pension records indicate he was wounded at Cumberland Gap on October 15, 1862.]

AYRES, JAMES W., Private
Born in Yancey County* where he resided as a farmer prior to enlisting in Yancey County at age 49, July 26, 1861. Failed to report for duty. Discharged on May 16, 1862, by reason of dislocated left shoulder suffered prior to his enlistment.

AYRES, MESHACK, Private
Born in Yancey County* where he resided as a farmer prior to enlisting in Yancey County at age 32, July 26, 1861. Died at Parrottsville, Tennessee, February 5-7, 1862, of "typhoid fever."

BAILEY, ANSEL, ———
Place and date of enlistment not reported. Reported on duty with this company on June 29, 1864. No further records.

BAILEY, EZEKIEL, Private
Resided in Yancey County and enlisted at age 19, July 26, 1861. No further records. [May have served later in Company G, 58th Regiment N.C. Troops.]

BAILEY, HARVEY, ———
Place and date of enlistment not reported. Wounded in the left hand at or near Kennesaw Mountain, Georgia, June 18, 1864. Died at Covington, Georgia, July 9, 1864, of wounds.

BAILEY, JAMES W., ———
Place and date of enlistment not reported. Reported on duty with this company on June 29, 1864. No further records.

BATSON, J. W., Private
Place and date of enlistment not reported. Reported on duty with this company from July 1, 1863, through September 30, 1863. No further records.

BENNETT, ALLEN H., 1st Sergeant
Place and date of enlistment not reported. Promotion

record not reported. Captured at Yazoo City, Mississippi, on or about July 13, 1863. Sent to Memphis, Tennessee. Confined at St. Louis, Missouri, August 3, 1863. Transferred to Camp Morton, Indianapolis, Indiana, where he arrived on August 14, 1863. Paroled and transferred to City Point, Virginia, February 26, 1865, for exchange.

BENNETT, HENRY, Private
Resided in Yancey County and enlisted at age 18, November 2, 186[2], for the war. Killed at Murfreesboro, Tennessee, December 31, 1862.

BENNETT, HONELY A., Private
Resided in Yancey County and enlisted at age 22, July 26, 1861. No further records.

BENNETT, JAMES H., Private
Born in Yancey County. Place and date of enlistment not reported. Killed at Murfreesboro, Tennessee, December 31, 1862.

BENNETT, SAMUEL M., Private
Resided in Yancey County and enlisted at age 23, July 26, 1861. Captured and paroled at Yazoo City, Mississippi, July 13, 1863. No further records.

BENTLEY, WILLIAM R., Private
Resided in Yancey County and enlisted at age 22, July 26, 1861. Deserted on July 19, 1863. Returned to duty on an unspecified date. Surrendered at Citronelle, Alabama, May. 4, 1865. Paroled at Meridian, Mississippi, May 13, 1865.

BRACKIN, THOMAS, Private
Resided in Yancey County and enlisted at age 18, July 26, 1861. Captured and paroled at Yazoo City, Mississippi, July 13, 1863. Deserted to the enemy on an unspecified date. Confined at Knoxville, Tennessee, May 20, 186[4]. Released on an unspecified date after taking the Oath of Allegiance.

BRADFORD, ERWIN, Private
Resided in Yancey County and enlisted at age 26, July 26, 1861. No further records.

BRADFORD, JOHN, Private
Resided in Yancey County and enlisted at age 25, July 26, 1861. No further records.

BRADFORD, SAMUEL, Private
Served in Company B of this regiment; however, he may have served briefly in this company during 1861. No further records.

BRANCH, STANHOPE, Private
Resided in Yancey County and enlisted at age 40, July 26, 1861. Discharged on September 22, 1862. Reason discharged not reported.

BRYANT, ALLEN M., Private
Resided in Yancey County and enlisted at age 18, March 11, 1862. Captured and paroled at Yazoo City, Mississippi, July 13, 1863. No further records.

BRYANT, DAVID, Private
Resided in Yancey County. Place and date of enlistment not reported. Surrendered at Citronelle, Alabama, May 4, 1865. Paroled at Meridian, Mississippi, May 9, 1865.

BYRD, E. R., Private
Place and date of enlistment not reported. Captured and paroled at Yazoo City, Mississippi, July 13, 1863. No further records.

BYRD, EZEKIEL K., Corporal
Resided in Yancey County and enlisted at age 21, July 26, 1861. Mustered in as Corporal. Last reported in the records of this company on September 24, 1862.

BYRD, I. N., Sergeant
Resided in Yancey County. Place and date of enlistment not reported. Promotion record not reported. Surrendered at Citronelle, Alabama, May 4, 1865. Paroled at Meridian, Mississippi, May 9, 1865. [May have served previously in Company C, 16th Regiment N.C. Troops (6th Regiment N.C. Volunteers).]

BYRD, MARCUS C., Corporal
Born in Yancey County where he resided as a farmer prior to enlisting in Yancey County at age 18, July 26, 1861. Mustered in as Corporal. Discharged on March 29, 1863, by reason of "chronic pleurisy."

BYRD, MOSES J., Private
Born in Yancey County where he resided as a farmer prior to enlisting at age 18, July 26, 1861. Discharged on an unspecified date under the provisions of the Conscription Act. Later served in Company G, 58th Regiment N.C. Troops.

BYRD, W. A., Private
Resided in Yancey County. Place and date of enlistment not reported. First reported in the records of this company on November 14, 1864. Captured at Spanish Fort, Mobile, Alabama, April 8, 1865. Confined at Ship Island, Mississippi, April 10, 1865. Transferred to Vicksburg, Mississippi, May 1, 1865. Paroled at Meridian, Mississippi, May 11, 1865. [North Carolina pension records indicate he was wounded on June 24, 1864.]

COX, ELI, Private
Resided in Yancey County and enlisted at age 40, July 26, 1861. Deserted on September 10, 1863.

CRAIN, A. J., Private
Enlisted on September 5, 1861. Captured at Spanish Fort, Mobile, Alabama, April 8, 1865. Confined at Ship Island, Mississippi, April 10, 1865. Transferred to Vicksburg, Mississippi, May 1, 1865. No further records.

CRANE, ANDREW, Private
Resided in Yancey County and enlisted at age 32, July 26, 1861. Deserted on July 19, 1863.

DEYTON, JACKSON, Private
Resided in Yancey County where he enlisted at age 20, July 26, 1861. Captured at Spanish Fort, Mobile, Alabama, April 8, 1865. Confined at Ship Island, Mississippi, April 10, 1865. Transferred to Vicksburg, Mississippi, May 1, 1865. No further records.

DUNCAN, GEORGE W., Private
Born in Ashe County and resided in Yancey County where he was by occupation a farmer prior to enlisting in Yancey County at age 29, July 26, 1861. Died in hospital at Knoxville, Tennessee, June 20-27, 1862, of "diarrhoea."

EDWARDS, CORNELIUS W., Corporal
Born in Yancey County where he resided as a farmer prior to enlisting in Yancey County at age 21, July 26, 1861. Mustered in as Corporal. Wounded in the right hip at Murfreesboro, Tennessee, December 31, 1862. Discharged on November 12, 1863, by reason of disability from wounds.

EDWARDS, ROBERT, Private
Resided in Yancey County and enlisted at age 27, July 26, 1861. Roll of Honor indicates he was dropped from the rolls on an unspecified date for absence without leave; however, a pension application filed by his widow indicates he was killed in battle at Allatoona, Georgia, on or about October 5, 1864. No further records.

EDWARDS, RUBEN, Private
Resided in Yancey County and enlisted at age 26, July 26, 1861. Deserted at Atlanta, Georgia, on an unspecified date.

EDWARDS, WILLIAM, Private
Resided in Yancey County and enlisted at age 32, July 26, 1861. "Stabbed by F.M." on September 16, 1861. Died on November 5, 1861, of wounds. Place of death not reported.

ELLIOTT, K. C., Private
Resided in Yancey County and enlisted on July 26, 1861, as a substitute. Promoted to Sergeant Major prior to April 8, 1865, and transferred to the Field and Staff of this regiment.

FRANKLIN, GABRIEL L., Private
Resided in Yancey County and enlisted at age 21, July 26, 1861. Surrendered at Citronelle, Alabama, May 4, 1865. Paroled at Meridian, Mississippi, May 9, 1865.

HAMPTON, OLIVER S., Ordnance Sergeant
Resided in Yancey County and enlisted at age 18, July 26, 1861. Mustered in as Sergeant. Wounded in the right thigh at Murfreesboro, Tennessee, December 31, 1862. Promoted to Ordnance Sergeant prior to July 13, 1863, when he was captured and paroled at Yazoo City, Mississippi. No further records.

HAMPTON, SAMUEL D., Sergeant
Born in Buncombe County and resided in Yancey County where he was by occupation a farmer prior to enlisting in Yancey County at age 29, July 26, 1861. Mustered in as Sergeant. Discharged on April 20, 1863, by reason of "general weakness induced by a long spell of fever," "rheumatism," and "chronic disease of the left lung."

HEADRICK, MACK, ———
North Carolina pension records indicate that he served in this company.

HEATH, JOHN B., Private
Resided in Lenoir County. Place and date of enlistment

not reported. Captured at Allatoona, Georgia, October 5, 1864. Sent to Nashville, Tennessee. Confined at Louisville, Kentucky, October 21, 1864. Transferred to Camp Chase, Ohio, where he arrived on October 24, 1864. Released on May 16, 1865, after taking the Oath of Allegiance.

HEDRICK, ABRAHAM H., Private
Born in Yancey County where he resided as a farmer prior to enlisting in Yancey County at age 19, July 26, 1861. Wounded in the left breast and captured at Murfreesboro, Tennessee, December 31, 1862. Died at Murfreesboro on January 7, 1863, of wounds. [Nominated for the Badge of Distinction for gallantry at Murfreesboro.]

HENSLEY, GARRISON, Private
Resided in Yancey County and enlisted at age 18, July 26, 1861. Died in Yancey County on June 16, 1863. Cause of death not reported.

HENSLEY, GEORGE W., Private
Resided in Yancey County and enlisted at age 41, July 26, 1861. Discharged on October 25-26, 1862. Reason discharged not reported.

HIGGINS, GEORGE W., Private
Resided in Yancey County and enlisted at age 19, July 26, 1861. Captured and paroled at Yazoo City, Mississippi, July 13, 1863. No further records.

HIGGINS, HOSEA J., Private
Resided in Yancey County and enlisted at age 37, July 26, 1861. Company records indicate he was discharged on October 26, 1862; however, Roll of Honor indicates he was discharged on October 26, 1863. North Carolina pension records indicate he was mortally wounded "in North Carolina" on October 26, 1863. No further records.

HIGGINS, JOHN, Private
Resided in Yancey County and enlisted at age 19, July 26, 1861. Captured and paroled at Yazoo City, Mississippi, July 13, 1863. No further records. [May have served later in Company G, 58th Regiment N.C. Troops.]

HIGGINS, MARION, Private
Resided in Yancey County and enlisted at age 23, July 26, 1861. Last reported in the records of this company on July 11, 1863. No further records.

HONEYCUTT, ANSEL, Sergeant
Born in Yancey County where he resided as a farmer prior to enlisting in Yancey County at age 19, July 26, 1861. Mustered in as Sergeant. Died at Tazewell, Tennessee, May 15 or September 16-17, 1862, of "inflam[m]ation of kidneys."

HONEYCUTT, AUSTIN, Private
Born in Yancey County where he resided as a farmer prior to enlisting in Yancey County at age 27, July 26, 1861. Died "at home" on August 17, 1862, of "dropsy."

HONEYCUTT, CHARLES M., Private
Born in Yancey County where he resided prior to enlisting at age 18, July 26, 1861. Died at Bean's Station, Tennessee, October 25, 1862. Cause of death not reported.

HONEYCUTT, NOAH, Private

Born in Yancey County* where he resided as a farmer prior to enlisting in Yancey County at age 32, July 26, 1861. Discharged on August 5, 1862, by reason of "chronic dysentery."

HONEYCUTT, PINKNEY A., Private

Born in Yancey County where he resided as a farmer prior to enlisting in Buncombe County at age 19, July 26, 1861. Captured at or near Richmond, Kentucky, on or about October 27, 1862. Sent to Louisville, Kentucky. Transferred to Vicksburg, Mississippi, where he arrived on or about December 4, 1862. Exchanged on an unspecified date. Discharged on December 24, 1862, by reason of "tubercular disease of the lungs with hemoptysis."

HOWARD, HENRY H., Private

Born in Lincoln County and resided in Yancey County where he was by occupation a carpenter prior to enlisting in Yancey County at age 28, July 26, 1861. Discharged on April 8, 1862, by reason of "disease of the heart."

HOWELL, JAMES, Private

Resided in Yancey County and enlisted at age 20, July 26, 1861. Discharged on October 26, 1862. Reason discharged not reported.

HOWELL, THOMAS, Private

Born in Yancey County where he resided as a farmer prior to enlisting at age 22, July 26, 1861. No further records. Later served in Company G, 58th Regiment N.C. Troops.

HUGHES, DAVID, Corporal

Resided in Yancey County and enlisted at age 24, July 26, 1861. Mustered in as Private. Promoted to Corporal on September 8, 1862. Captured at or near Nashville, Tennessee, on or about December 17, 1864. Confined at Louisville, Kentucky, December 20, 1864. Transferred to Camp Douglas, Chicago, Illinois, where he arrived on December 22, 1864. Released on May 11, 1865, after taking the Oath of Allegiance.

HUGHES, JEREMIAH, Private

Resided in Yancey County and enlisted at age 25, July 26, 1861. Wounded in the left breast and captured at Murfreesboro, Tennessee, December 31, 1862. Died at Murfreesboro on January 13, 1863, of wounds.

HUGHES, JEREMIAH, Private

Resided in Yancey County and enlisted at age 18, November 2, 1863, for the war. Captured and paroled at Yazoo City, Mississippi, July 13, 1863. No further records.

JONES, HIRAM, Private

Enlisted at age 26, May 1, 1862, for the war. Captured at Spanish Fort, Mobile, Alabama, April 8, 1865. Confined at Ship Island, Mississippi, April 10, 1865. Transferred to Vicksburg, Mississippi, May 1, 1865. No further records.

LEDFORD, JOHN, Private

Resided in Yancey County and enlisted at age 22, July 26, 1861. Captured at Yazoo City, Mississippi, on or about July 13, 1863. Sent to Memphis, Tennessee.

Confined at St. Louis, Missouri, August 3, 1863. Transferred to Camp Morton, Indianapolis, Indiana, where he arrived on August 14, 1863. Transferred to Fort Delaware, Delaware, March 19, 1864. Released at Fort Delaware on June 19, 1865, after taking the Oath of Allegiance.

LETTERMAN, JOSEPH, Private

Resided in Yancey County. Place and date of enlistment not reported. Deserted to the enemy at or near Atlanta, Georgia, August 9, 1864. Confined at Chattanooga, Tennessee. Transferred to Louisville, Kentucky, where he arrived on August 15, 1864. Released on or about August 27, 1864, after taking the Oath of Allegiance. [May have served previously in Company C, 58th Regiment N.C. Troops.]

LEWIS, N. PALMER, Private

Resided in Yancey County and enlisted at age 26, July 26, 1861. No further records.

McCOURY, FRANKLIN, Private

Born in Yancey County where he resided as a farmer prior to enlisting in Yancey County at age 18, July 26, 1861. Captured "in Kentucky" in September-November, 1862. Confined at Chattanooga, Tennessee. Exchanged on January 11, 1863. Died in Yancey County on July 20, 1863, of "chronic diarr[ho]ea."

McCOURY, SEWELL, Private

Born in Yancey County where he resided as a farmer prior to enlisting in Yancey County at age 22, July 26, 1861. Died in hospital at Knoxville, Tennessee, June 27-July 2, 1862, of "flux."

McCOURY, ZEPHANIAH, Private

Born in Yancey County where he resided as a farmer prior to enlisting in Yancey County at age 26, July 26, 1861. Discharged on April 10, 1862, by reason of "hemorrhage of the lungs of several years' standing." Died at Cumberland Gap, Tennessee, April 13, 1862.

McCRACKEN, WILLIAM H., Private

Born in Virginia. Place and date of enlistment not reported. Died at Cumberland Gap, Tennessee, March 11, 1862. Cause of death not reported.

McCRACKIN, ROBERT, Private

Resided in Yancey County and enlisted at age 25, July 26, 1861. Last reported in the records of this company on September 24, 1864.

McDONALD, HEDRICK, Private

Resided in Yancey County and enlisted at age 21, July 26, 1861. No further records.

PATE, GEORGE W., Private

Served in Company B of this regiment; however, he may have served briefly in this company during 1861.

PATTERSON, REUBEN M., Private

Resided in Yancey County and enlisted at age 30, July 26, 1861. Captured at Yazoo City, Mississippi, July 13, 1863. Sent to Memphis, Tennessee. Confined at St. Louis, Missouri, August 3, 1863. Transferred to Camp Morton, Indianapolis, Indiana, where he arrived on August 14, 1863. Transferred to Fort Delaware, Delaware, March 19, 1864. Released at Fort Delaware on June 19, 1865, after taking the Oath of Allegiance.

PEEK, SAMUEL J., Corporal
Born in Yancey County where he resided as a farmer prior to enlisting in Yancey County at age 19, July 26, 1861. Mustered in as Corporal. Discharged on April 3, 1863, by reason of "white swelling . . . [of] the left knee & leg producing considerable deformity and lameness."

PETERSON, ALMA, Private
Resided in Yancey County and enlisted at age 26, July 26, 1861. Wounded in the left thigh and captured at Franklin, Tennessee, November 30, 1864. Left leg amputated. Hospitalized at Nashville, Tennessee, where he died on May 18, 1865, of "exhaustion."

PHILLIPS, JOHN D., Private
Resided in Yancey County and enlisted at age 22, July 26, 1861. Captured "in Kentucky" in September-November, 1862. Confined at Chattanooga, Tennessee. Exchanged on January 11, 1863. Returned to duty on an unspecified date. Captured at Yazoo City, Mississippi, July 13, 1863. Sent to Memphis, Tennessee. Confined at St. Louis, Missouri, August 3, 1863. Transferred to Camp Morton, Indianapolis, Indiana, where he arrived on August 14, 1863. Paroled and transferred for exchange on February 19, 1865. Hospitalized at Richmond, Virginia, March 2, 1865, and was transferred on March 5, 1865. [North Carolina pension records indicate he was wounded in both legs at Murfreesboro, Tennessee, in December, 1862.]

PHILLIPS, LAZARUS, Private
Resided in Yancey County and enlisted at age 18, July 26, 1861. Deserted at Chattanooga, Tennessee, September 15, 1863. Returned to duty on an unspecified date. Last reported in the records of this company on June 28, 1864.

PHILLIPS, MOSES, Private
Born in Yancey County where he resided as a farmer prior to enlisting in Yancey County at age 28, July 26, 1861. Discharged on May 12, 1863, by reason of "scrofula."

PHILLIPS, WILLIS G., Private
Resided in Yancey County and enlisted at age 33, July 26, 1861. Deserted on September 10, 1863.

PRESNELL, JAMES P., Private
Resided in Yancey County and enlisted at age 18, July 26, 1861. [North Carolina pension records indicate he was wounded in the left side at Kennesaw Mountain, Georgia, in July, 186(4).] No further records.

RANDOLPH, POSEY, ———
North Carolina pension records indicate that he served in this company.

ROBERSON, GILBERT, Private
Born in Rutherford County and resided in Yancey County where he was by occupation a farmer prior to enlisting in Yancey County at age 28, July 26, 1861. Killed at Murfreesboro, Tennessee, December 31, 1862.

ROGERS, JAMES B., Private
Served in Company B of this regiment; however, he may have served briefly in this company during 1861.

ROSE, FRANKLIN, Private
Born in Yancey County where he resided as a farmer

prior to enlisting at age 26, July 26, 1861. Died at Midway, Tennessee, February 5 or February 16, 1862, of "typhoid fever."

SCISK, JOHN, Private
Resided in McDowell County. Place and date of enlistment not reported. Surrendered at Citronelle, Alabama, May 4, 1865. Paroled at Meridian, Mississippi, May 9, 1865.

TAYLOR, EDWIN, Private
Enlisted at "Rolla" on September 10, 1863, for the war. Captured at Kinston on March 14, 1865. Sent to New Bern. Transferred to Point Lookout, Maryland, where he arrived on March 30, 1865. Released on June 8, 1865, after taking the Oath of Allegiance.

TAYLOR, WESLEY, Private
Resided in Yancey County and enlisted at age 35, July 26, 1861. Discharged on October 26, 1862. Reason discharged not reported.

TIPTON, C. C., ———
North Carolina pension records indicate that he served in this company.

TIPTON, DAVID, Private
Born in Yancey County* and was by occupation a farmer prior to enlisting in Yancey County on July 26, 1861. Discharged on April 6, 1862, by reason of "an injury of the left shoulder received before he entered the service." Discharge certificate gives his age as 44.

TIPTON, SEBRON, Private
Resided in Yancey County and enlisted at age 30, July 26, 1861. Captured at Chickamauga, Georgia, September 19, 1863. Sent to Nashville, Tennessee. Confined at Louisville, Kentucky, September 30, 1863. Transferred to Camp Douglas, Chicago, Illinois, October 2, 1863. Released at Camp Douglas in January, 1864, after joining the U.S. Navy.

WHITSON, JOEL, Private
Born in Yancey County* where he resided as a farmer prior to enlisting in Yancey County at age 32, July 26, 1861. Discharged on November 6, 1862, by reason of "deafness which resulted from an attac[k] of fever." [Roll of Honor indicates he died at Chattanooga, Tennessee, December 20, 1863. Cause of death not reported.]

WILLIAMS, PITTMAN, Private
Born in Montgomery County and resided in Yancey County where he was by occupation a farmer prior to enlisting in Yancey County at age 51, July 26, 1861. Discharged on July 23, 1862, by reason of "chronic rheumatism."

WILLIAMS, SAMUEL, Private
Resided in Yancey County and enlisted at age 21, July 26, 1861. Wounded in the right shoulder at Murfreesboro, Tennessee, December 31, 1862. Deserted on July 15, 1863.

WILLIAMS, WILLIAM, Private
Resided in Yancey County and enlisted at age 24, July 26, 1861. Last reported in the records of this company on May 13, 1863. • Roll of Honor indicates he was

reported absent without leave on an unspecified date and was later dropped from the rolls of the company.

WILSON, ALFORD, Private
Resided in Yancey County and enlisted at age 21, July 26, 1861. Deserted prior to May 26, 1863. Apparently returned to duty but deserted again on September 10, 1863.

WILSON, GEORGE, Private
Resided in Yancey County and enlisted at age 23, July 26, 1861. Reported absent without leave on an unspecified date. Court-martialed on February 27, 1864. No further records.

WILSON, LEVI, Private
Resided in Yancey County and enlisted at age 16, July 26, 1861. Discharged on an unspecified date by reason of being underage. Later served in Company G, 58th Regiment N.C. Troops.

COMPANY H

This company was raised in Buncombe County and enlisted on September 11, 1861. It was then assigned to the 29th Regiment and designated Company H. After joining the regiment the company functioned as a part of the regiment, and its history for the war period is reported as a part of the regimental history.

The following company roster is based primarily on the North Carolina Roll of Honor, prisoner of war records, pension applications, and a variety of miscellaneous records. Information was obtained also from secondary sources such as postwar histories, cemetery records, and records of the United Daughters of the Confederacy. No muster rolls were located for the company.

OFFICERS

CAPTAINS

ROBINSON, JOHN H.
Resided in Buncombe County and enlisted at age 41. Appointed Captain on September 11, 1861. Declined to stand for reelection when the regiment was reorganized on May 2, 1862.

PARKER, WILEY F.
Resided in Buncombe County and enlisted at age 32. Appointed 2nd Lieutenant on September 11, 1861. Promoted to Captain on May 2, 1862. Resigned on November 4, 1862, by reason of being ''[a minister] of the Gospel'' and because of ''a severe attack of chronic diarrhoea.'' Resignation accepted on or about December 23, 1862. Later served as Captain of Company F, 69th Regiment N.C. Troops (7th Regiment N.C. Cavalry).

BREVARD, JOSEPH A.
Resided in Buncombe County and enlisted at age 31, September 11, 1861. Mustered in as Private and was appointed 1st Lieutenant on May 2, 1862. Promoted to Captain on December 23, 1862. Died on July 20, 1864, of disease. Place of death not reported.

LIEUTENANTS

PENLAND, PETER H., 2nd Lieutenant
Resided in Buncombe County and enlisted at age 22. Appointed 2nd Lieutenant on September 11, 1861.

Defeated for reelection when the regiment was reorganized on May 2, 1862.

PINKERTON, ALFRED H., 2nd Lieutenant
Resided in Buncombe County and enlisted at age 28, September 11, 1861. Mustered in as Sergeant. Wounded in the wrist at Murfreesboro, Tennessee, December 31, 1862. Returned to duty on an unspecified date. Appointed 2nd Lieutenant on or about September 16, 1864. Wounded in the left arm at Nashville, Tennessee, December 15, 1864. Captured at Columbia, Tennessee, December 17-22, 1864. Sent to Nashville. Confined at Louisville, Kentucky, January 24, 1865. Transferred to Fort Delaware, Delaware, where he arrived on February 1, 1865. Paroled and transferred to City Point, Virginia, February 27, 1865, for exchange. Hospitalized at Richmond, Virginia, March 2, 1865, and was transferred the next day.

REEVES, JOHN A., 2nd Lieutenant
Resided in Buncombe County and enlisted at age 18, September 11, 1861. Promotion record not reported. No further records.

ROBERTS, WILLIAM McB., 1st Lieutenant
Resided in Buncombe County and enlisted at age 25. Appointed 1st Lieutenant on September 11, 1861. Defeated for reelection when the regiment was reorganized on May 2, 1862.

SHERRILL, FRANCIS M., 1st Lieutenant
Resided in Buncombe County and enlisted at age 20, September 11, 1861. Mustered in as Sergeant. Appointed 2nd Lieutenant on May 2, 1862. Promoted to 1st Lieutenant on December 23, 1863. Killed near Smyrna, Georgia, July 4, 1864.

STRADLEY, JOSEPH H., 2nd Lieutenant
Resided in Buncombe County and enlisted at age 26, September 11, 1861. Mustered in as Private. Appointed 3rd Lieutenant on May 2, 1862, and was promoted to 2nd Lieutenant on December 23, 1862. Wounded in the head at or near Kennesaw Mountain, Georgia, on or about June 29, 1864. Retired to Invalid Corps on March 28, 1865, by reason of disability from wounds.

NONCOMMISSIONED OFFICERS AND PRIVATES

AIKENS, THOMAS J., Private
Resided in Buncombe County and enlisted at age 22, September 11, 1861. Last reported in the records of this company on December 11, 1864.

ARMSTRONG, W. D., Private
Place and date of enlistment not reported. Captured at Nashville, Tennessee, December 15, 1864. Confined at Camp Douglas, Chicago, Illinois. No further records.

ARMSTRONG, WILLIAM B., Private
Place and date of enlistment not reported. Captured at Nashville, Tennessee, December 16, 1864. Confined at Louisville, Kentucky, December 21, 1864. Transferred to Camp Douglas, Chicago, Illinois, where he arrived on December 24, 1864. Released on May 18, 1865.

ASHWORTH, JOHN, Private
Resided in Buncombe County and enlisted at age 17, September 11, 1861. Accidentally wounded in the head

near Murfreesboro, Tennessee, January 2, 1863. Captured near Murfreesboro on January 2-5, 1863. Sent to Nashville, Tennessee. Transferred to Louisville, Kentucky, where he arrived on April 20, 1863. Transferred to Fort McHenry, Maryland. Paroled at Fort McHenry on April 30, 1863, and transferred to City Point, Virginia, where he was received on May 2, 1863, for exchange. Returned to duty on an unspecified date. Captured at Spanish Fort, Mobile, Alabama, April 8, 1865. Confined at Ship Island, Mississippi, April 10, 1865. Transferred to Vicksburg, Mississippi, May 1, 1865. No further records.

BAKER, JAMES, Private
Place and date of enlistment not reported. Captured near Smyrna, Georgia, July 3-4, 1864. Sent to Nashville, Tennessee. Confined at Louisville, Kentucky, July 13, 1864. Transferred to Camp Morton, Indianapolis, Indiana, where he arrived on July 14, 1864. Paroled and transferred to Boulware's Wharf, James River, Virginia, where he was received on March 10-12, 1865, for exchange.

BALLARD, GEORGE H., Private
Resided in Buncombe County and enlisted at age 41, September 15, 1863, for the war. Last reported in the records of this company on September 3, 1864.

BARRETT, CHRISTOPHER, Musician
Born in Buncombe County where he resided as a farmer prior to enlisting in Buncombe County at age 20, September 11, 1861. Mustered in as Musician (Fifer). Discharged on April 23, 1862, by reason of "an accidental gunshot wound in the right hand impairing the use of the forefinger and destroying the use of the middle one."

BARRETT, JOHN E., Musician
Resided in Buncombe County and enlisted at age 33, September 11, 1861. Mustered in as Musician (Drummer). Deserted on July 20, 1863.

BLACK, MONTRAVALE, Private
Resided in Buncombe County and enlisted at age 25, September 11, 1861. Last reported in the records of this company on December 16, 1863.

BREVARD, ZEBULON P., Private
Place and date of enlistment not reported. Captured near Smyrna, Georgia, July 4, 1864. Sent to Nashville, Tennessee. Confined at Louisville, Kentucky, July 13, 1864. Transferred to Camp Morton, Indianapolis, Indiana, where he arrived on July 14, 1864. Paroled and transferred to Boulware's Wharf, James River, Virginia, where he was received on March 10-12, 1865, for exchange.

BRITTAIN, ISAAC W., Private
Resided in Buncombe County and enlisted at age 26, September 11, 1861. Died at Greenville, Tennessee, June 23, 1863. Cause of death not reported.

BROWN, JAMES K., Private
Resided in Buncombe County. Place and date of enlistment not reported. Deserted to the enemy on an unspecified date. Confined at Knoxville, Tennessee, June 1, 1864. Transferred to Louisville, Kentucky, where he arrived on June 7, 1864. Released on June 8, 1864, after taking the Oath of Allegiance.

BROWN, WILLIAM H., Private
Born in Buncombe County where he resided prior to enlisting at age 21, September 11, 1861. Died at Jonesboro, Tennessee, December 16 or December 28, 1861, of "typhoid fever."

BROWN, WILLIAM J., Private
Resided in Buncombe County and enlisted at age 25, September 11, 1861. No further records.

BUTLER, THOMAS O., Private
Resided in Buncombe County and enlisted at age 17, September 27, 1862, for the war. Wounded in the left hip at or near Spanish Fort, Mobile, Alabama, on or about March 30, 1865. Surrendered at Citronelle, Alabama, May 4, 1865. Paroled at Meridian, Mississippi, May 9, 1865.

CAPPS, ALFRED, Private
Resided in Buncombe County and enlisted at age 18, September 11, 1861. Deserted on September 26, 1863.

CAPPS, MANLY W., Musician
Resided in Buncombe County and enlisted at age 19, September 11, 1861. Mustered in as Private. Promoted to Musician (Bugler) on August 1, 1862. Promoted to Musician (Drummer) on an unspecified date. Last reported in the records of this company on November 4, 1863.

CASADY, NATHANIEL B., Private
Resided in Buncombe County and enlisted at age 23, September 11, 1861. No further records. [May have served later in Company B, 69th Regiment N.C. Troops (7th Regiment N.C. Cavalry).]

CASH, SHADRACH, Private
Previously served in Company C of this regiment. Transferred to this company on or about September 11, 1861. Transferred back to Company C prior to December 31, 1862.

CLARK, JAMES H., Private
Resided in Buncombe County and enlisted at age 17, September 11, 1861. Deserted on September 26, 1863.

COGGINS, ENOCH C., Private
Previously served in Company C of this regiment. Transferred to this company on or about September 11, 1861. Transferred back to Company C prior to April 5, 1862.

COLE, WILLIAM H., Private
Previously served in Company C of this regiment. Transferred to this company on or about September 11, 1861. Transferred back to Company C prior to September 19-20, 1863.

COON, JOHN, Private
Resided in Buncombe County. Place and date of enlistment not reported. Captured at Spanish Fort, Mobile, Alabama, April 8, 1865. Confined at Ship Island, Mississippi, April 10, 1865. Paroled at Meridian, Mississippi, May 11, 1865.

CORDELL, JOSEPH W., Private
Born in Buncombe County where he resided as a farmer prior to enlisting in Buncombe County at age 20,

September 11, 1861. Died in hospital at Raleigh on November 12, 1861. Cause of death not reported.

CORDELL, LUCIUS B., Private
Place and date of enlistment not reported. Captured near Smyrna, Georgia, July 3, 1864. Sent to Nashville, Tennessee. Confined at Louisville, Kentucky, July 13, 1864. Transferred to Camp Morton, Indianapolis, Indiana, where he arrived on July 14, 1864. Died at Camp Morton on July 21, 1864, of "measles."

CORDELL, SOLOMON, Private
Born in Buncombe County where he resided as a farmer prior to enlisting at age 22, September 11, 1861. Wounded in the left leg at Murfreesboro, Tennessee, December 31, 1862. Returned to duty on an unspecified date. Captured at Chickamauga, Georgia, September 19, 1863. Sent to Nashville, Tennessee. Confined at Louisville, Kentucky, September 30, 1863. Transferred to Camp Douglas, Chicago, Illinois, where he arrived on October 4, 1863. Released on April 6, 1865, after joining the U.S. Army. Assigned to Company F, 5th Regiment U.S. Volunteer Infantry.

CORDELL, WILLIAM B., Private
Resided in Buncombe County where he enlisted at age 24, September 11, 1861. Died at Bean's Station, Tennessee, September 4 or November 4, 1862. Cause of death not reported.

CORN, HUGH B., Private
Resided in Buncombe County and enlisted at age 18. Date of enlistment not reported. Furloughed for sixty days on or about August 4, 1864. No further records.

DANIEL, ELIAS F., Private
Resided in Buncombe County and enlisted at age 26, September 11, 1861. Captured at Chickamauga, Georgia, September 19-20, 1863. Sent to Nashville, Tennessee. Confined at Louisville, Kentucky, October 9, 1863. Transferred to Camp Morton, Indianapolis, Indiana, where he arrived on October 22, 1863. Paroled at Camp Morton on March 4, 1865, and transferred to Boulware's Wharf, James River, Virginia, where he was received on March 10-12, 1865, for exchange.

DAVIS, ABEL, Private
Born in Buncombe County where he resided prior to enlisting at age 17, September 11, 1861. Died at Bean's Station, Tennessee, July 26-August 1, 1862. Cause of death not reported.

DAVIS, JOHN B., Private
Resided in Buncombe County and enlisted at age 21, March 24, 1862. Died at Swannanoa on August 19, 1863. Cause of death not reported.

DILLARD, STEWART, Private
Resided in Buncombe County and enlisted at age 53, September 11, 1861. Died at Jonesboro, Tennessee, January 20, 1862, of "fever."

EARWOOD, BARTIS J., Private
Resided in Buncombe County and enlisted at age 18, September 11, 1861. Deserted on September 10, 1863. Hospitalized at Macon, Georgia, July 5, 1864. Returned to duty on July 14, 1864. [North Carolina pension records indicate he was wounded. Place and date wounded not reported.] No further records.

EARWOOD, JOSHUA, Private
Resided in Buncombe County and enlisted at age 18. Date of enlistment not reported. Deserted on September 10, 1863.

EDMONDS, JOSEPH M., Private
Resided in Buncombe County and enlisted at age 22, September 11, 1861. Captured and paroled at Yazoo City, Mississippi, July 13, 1863. No further records.

EDNEY, HENRY C., Private
Previously served in Company A, 5th Battalion N.C. Cavalry. Transferred to this company in July, 1862. Transferred to Company A, 25th Regiment N.C. Troops (15th Regiment N.C. Volunteers), on or about January 1, 1863.

ELLISON, BENJAMIN, Private
Resided in Buncombe County and enlisted at age 21, September 11, 1861. Deserted on December 25, 1861.

FOX, THOMAS, Private
Resided in Buncombe County and enlisted at age 18, March 14, 1862. Captured (or deserted to the enemy) at Yazoo City, Mississippi, on or about July 13, 1863. Confined at St. Louis, Missouri, where he died on August 4, 1863, of "typhoid fever."

FRANKLIN, MELGER W., Private
Resided in Buncombe County where he enlisted on May 1, 1863, for the war. Last reported in the records of this company in October, 1863.

FREEMAN, LEANDER, Private
Resided in Buncombe County and enlisted at age 26, September 11, 1861. Deserted on September 10, 1863.

GARREN, JOSEPH BENJAMIN, Private
Resided in Buncombe County and enlisted at age 16, April 14, 1862. Discharged on November 6, 1862. Reason discharged not reported. [May have served later in Company A, 1st Battalion N.C. Junior Reserves.]

GARRON, ELI, Sergeant
Resided in Buncombe County and enlisted at age 20, September 11, 1861. Mustered in as Private. Promoted to Sergeant on June 20, 1863. Captured at Yazoo City, Mississippi, July 13, 1863. Died at Yazoo City on July 22, 1863. Cause of death not reported.

GILLESPIE, JAMES A., Sergeant
Resided in Buncombe County and enlisted at age 28, September 11, 1861. Mustered in as Private. Promoted to Sergeant on an unspecified date. Captured at Spanish Fort, Mobile, Alabama, April 8, 1865. Confined at Ship Island, Mississippi, April 10, 1865. Transferred to Vicksburg, Mississippi, May 1, 1865. [Nominated for the Badge of Distinction for gallantry at Murfreesboro, Tennessee, December 31, 1862.] No further records.

GILLESPIE, JOHN D., Private
Born in Buncombe County where he resided as a farmer prior to enlisting in Buncombe County at age 37, September 11, 1861. Discharged on May 9, 1862, by reason of "general debility involving his liver." Reenlisted in the company on September 15, 1863. No further records.

GILLESPIE, WILLIAM A., Private
Born in Buncombe County where he resided as a farmer prior to enlisting in Buncombe County at age 36, September 11, 1861. Discharged on May 19, 1862, by reason of "a stoppage in his speech" and because "he is of a feeble habit and unfit for any kind of army duty."

GRANT, HENRY, Private
Resided in Buncombe County and enlisted at age 18, May 13, 1862, for the war. Captured at Spanish Fort, Mobile, Alabama, April 8, 1865. Confined at Ship Island, Mississippi, April 10, 1865. Transferred to Vicksburg, Mississippi, May 1, 1865. [North Carolina pension records indicate he was wounded at "Kennesaw Mountain, Georgia, April 25, 1863."] No further records.

GRANT, JAMES S., Private
Resided in Buncombe County and enlisted at age 23, September 11, 1861. Captured and paroled at Yazoo City, Mississippi, July 13, 1863. Reported absent without leave during September, 1864-February, 1865.

GRANT, THOMAS, Private
Resided in Buncombe County and enlisted at age 25, September 11, 1861. Captured and paroled at Yazoo City, Mississippi, July 13, 1863. Returned to duty on an unspecified date. Captured at Spanish Fort, Mobile, Alabama, April 8, 1865. Confined at Ship Island, Mississippi, April 10, 1865. Transferred to Vicksburg, Mississippi, May 1, 1865. [North Carolina pension records indicate he was wounded on October 10, 1862.] No further records.

HALL, BENJAMIN M., Sergeant
Resided in Buncombe County and enlisted at age 22, September 11, 1861. Mustered in as Private. Promoted to Corporal prior to December 31, 1862, when he was wounded in the head at Murfreesboro, Tennessee. Promoted to Sergeant on June 20, 1863. Killed at Chickamauga, Georgia, September 19, 1863.

HAMPER, F. C., Private
Place and date of enlistment not reported. Captured at Spanish Fort, Mobile, Alabama, April 8, 1865. Confined at Ship Island, Mississippi, April 10, 1865. Transferred to Vicksburg, Mississippi, May 1, 1865. No further records.

HANEY, GEORGE C., Private
Resided in Madison County and enlisted at age 27, September 11, 1861. Deserted on December 20, 1862.

HANEY, WILLIAM G., Private
Resided in Madison County and enlisted at age 19, September 11, 1861. Deserted on December 20, 1862.

HARBIN, JOSEPH D., Private
Previously served in Company C of this regiment. Transferred to this company on or about September 11, 1861. Transferred back to Company C on an unspecified date.

HARPER, FOSTER C., Private
Resided in Buncombe County and enlisted at age 19, September 11, 1861. Last reported in the records of this company on April 10, 1863.

HAYES, JAMES M., Private
Resided in Buncombe County and enlisted at age 26, September 11, 1861. Deserted on September 6, 1863. Captured by the enemy in Buncombe County on an unspecified date. Sent to Chattanooga, Tennessee. Confined at Louisville, Kentucky, on or about June 6, 1864. Released on June 8, 1864, after taking the Oath of Allegiance.

HUGHES, GEORGE A., ———
North Carolina pension records indicate that he served in this company.

HUGHES, JOHN B., Private
Resided in Buncombe County and enlisted at age 33, September 11, 1861. Surrendered at Citronelle, Alabama, May 4, 1865. Paroled at Meridian, Mississippi, May 9, 1865.

HUMPHREYS, JAMES, Private
Resided in Buncombe County and enlisted at age 18, September 11, 1861. No further records.

HUMPHREYS, JOHN P., Private
Resided in Buncombe County and enlisted at age 22, September 11, 1861. Deserted on September 27, 1862.

HUNTER, ANDREW J., Private
Resided in Buncombe County and enlisted at age 25, September 11, 1861. No further records.

INGLE, ANDREW E., Private
Previously served in Company C of this regiment. Transferred to this company on January 19, 1863. Wounded at Chickamauga, Georgia, September 19-20, 1863. Hospitalized at Meridian, Mississippi, April 11, 1865, with a "fracture." Place and date injured not reported. Surrendered at Citronelle, Alabama, May 4, 1865. Paroled at Meridian on May 9, 1865.

JENKINS, GEORGE W., Private
Resided in Buncombe County and enlisted at age 29, September 11, 1861. Captured and paroled at Yazoo City, Mississippi, July 13, 1863. No further records.

JENKINS, JOHN S., Private
Resided in Buncombe County and enlisted at age 18. Date of enlistment not reported. Captured and paroled at Yazoo City, Mississippi, July 13, 1863.

JENKINS, THOMAS M., Private
Resided in Buncombe County and enlisted at age 22, September 11, 1861. Captured and paroled at Yazoo City, Mississippi, July 13, 1863. No further records.

JOHNSON, THOMPSON, ———
North Carolina pension records indicate that he served in this company.

JOHNSTON, JAMES A., Private
Resided in Buncombe County where he enlisted at age 21, September 11, 1861. Mustered in as Corporal. Reduced to ranks prior to November 15, 1864. Deserted to the enemy on December 20, 1864. Took the Oath of Allegiance at Nashville, Tennessee, January 13, 1865.

JONES, WILLIAM W., Private
Resided in Buncombe County and enlisted at age 28, September 11, 1861. Wounded at Murfreesboro, Tennessee, December 31, 1862. Captured and paroled

at Yazoo City, Mississippi, July 13, 1863.

JUSTICE, NICHOLAS H., Private
Born in Buncombe County where he resided as a farmer prior to enlisting in Buncombe County at age 25, September 11, 1861. Discharged on March 24, 1863, by reason of "chronic . . . rheumatism" and "phthisis pulmonalis."

KERLEE, MOSES C., Private
Resided in Buncombe County and enlisted at age 18, September 11, 1861. Died at Loudon, Tennessee, November 14, 1862. Cause of death not reported.

KERLEY, S. P., Private
Resided in Alexander County and enlisted at age 25, September 11, 1861. No further records.

LANNING, MITCHELL A., Private
Resided in Buncombe County and enlisted at age 27, September 11, 1861. Mustered in as Private. Promoted to Corporal prior to December 31, 1862, when he was wounded in the left hand at Murfreesboro, Tennessee. Reduced to ranks on an unspecified date. Deserted on September 10, 1863. Reported absent without leave during September, 1864-February, 1865.

LAUGHTER, B. J., ———
North Carolina pension records indicate that he served in this company.

McDOWELL, GEORGE M., 1st Sergeant
Resided in Madison County and enlisted at age 26, September 11, 1861. Mustered in as 1st Sergeant. Deserted on September 1, 1863.

McELROY, JAMES G., Private
Resided in Buncombe County and enlisted on September 11, 1861. Appointed Sergeant Major in 1862 and transferred to the Field and Staff of this regiment.

McGREGOR, DOUGALD, Private
Resided in Buncombe County and enlisted at age 28, September 11, 1861. Mustered in as Private. Promoted to Ordnance Sergeant on July 20, 1863, and transferred to the Field and Staff of this regiment.

McGREGOR, GREGER K., Sergeant
Resided in Cumberland County and enlisted at age 20, September 11, 1861. Mustered in as Private. Wounded at Chickamauga, Georgia, September 19-20, 1863. Returned to duty on an unspecified date. Promoted to Sergeant prior to April 8, 1865, when he was captured at Spanish Fort, Mobile, Alabama. Confined at Ship Island, Mississippi, April 10, 1865. Transferred to Vicksburg, Mississippi, May 1, 1865. Paroled at Augusta, Georgia, May 20, 1865.

MARSHALL, WILLIAM, Private
Enlisted at Camp Vance on October 8, 1863, for the war. Captured at Spanish Fort, Mobile, Alabama, April 8, 1865. Confined at Ship Island, Mississippi, April 10, 1865. Transferred to Vicksburg, Mississippi, May 1, 1865. No further records.

MEECE, GEORGE W., Private
Place and date of enlistment not reported. Captured at or near Oxford, Georgia, on or about July 22, 1864. Sent to Nashville, Tennessee. Confined at Louisville, Kentucky, August 3, 1864. Transferred to Camp Chase, Ohio, where he arrived on August 4, 1864. Paroled and transferred to Boulware's Wharf, James River, Virginia,

where he was received on or about March 10, 1865, for exchange. Hospitalized at Richmond, Virginia, March 11, 1865, and was transferred the next day.

MILLER, C. C., Private
North Carolina pension records indicate that he served in this company.

MILLER, GEORGE WILLIAM, Private
Resided in Buncombe or Haywood County and enlisted at age 32, August 6, 1861. Surrendered at Citronelle, Alabama, May 4, 1865. Paroled at Meridian, Mississippi, May 9, 1865.

MILLER, JOHN H., Private
Born in Haywood County and resided in Buncombe County where he was by occupation a farmer prior to enlisting at age 20, September 11, 1861. Captured near Smyrna, Georgia, July 5, 1864. Sent to Nashville, Tennessee. Confined at Louisville, Kentucky, July 13, 1864. Transferred to Camp Douglas, Chicago, Illinois, where he arrived on July 16, 1864. Released on or about March 26, 1865, after joining the U.S. Army. Assigned to Company F, 6th Regiment U.S. Volunteer Infantry.

MILLER, SAMUEL, Private
Resided in Madison County and enlisted at age 23, September 11, 1861. Deserted on September 6, 1863.

MILLER, THOMAS A., Private
Resided in Buncombe County and enlisted at age 25, September 11, 1861. Discharged in 1863. Reason discharged not reported.

MILLER, W. A. P., Private
Resided in Buncombe County and enlisted at age 30, September 11, 1861. Discharged on November 6, 1862. Reason discharged not reported.

MILLER, WILLIAM, Private
Born in Jefferson County, Tennessee, and resided in Buncombe County where he was by occupation a farmer prior to enlisting at Cumberland Gap, Tennessee, March 20, 1862. Discharged on March 20, 1862, by reason of "pain in the breast [resulting from an injury received five years ago and] amounting to chronic inflam[m]ation." Discharge certificate gives his age as 35.

MINCE, J. Z., Private
Place and date of enlistment not reported. Captured at Spanish Fort, Mobile, Alabama, April 8, 1865. Confined at Ship Island, Mississippi, April 10, 1865. Transferred to Vicksburg, Mississippi, May 1, 1865. No further records. [May have served previously in Company E, McRae's Battalion N.C. Cavalry.]

MINCE, JOHN M., Private
Place and date of enlistment not reported. Captured at Spanish Fort, Mobile, Alabama, April 8, 1865. Confined at Ship Island, Mississippi, April 10, 1865. Transferred to Vicksburg, Mississippi, May 1, 1865. No further records. [May have served previously in Company E, McRae's Battalion N.C. Cavalry.]

MIRCE, GEORGE W., Private
Place and date of enlistment not reported. Hospitalized at Richmond, Virginia, March 8, 1865, with scorbutus and was furloughed for sixty days on March 15, 1865.

OWNBY, OLIVER DEATON, Private
Resided in Buncombe County and enlisted at age 32, September 11, 1861. Deserted on September 10, 1863. Returned to duty on an unspecified date. Deserted to the enemy on an unspecified date. Confined at Chattanooga, Tennessee, on or about August 1, 1864. Transferred to Louisville, Kentucky. Released on or about August 6, 1864, after taking the Oath of Allegiance.

PADGET, JAMES, Private
Resided in Buncombe County and enlisted at age 25, September 11, 1861. Captured at Spanish Fort, Mobile, Alabama, April 8, 1865. Confined at Ship Island, Mississippi, April 10, 1865. Transferred to Vicksburg, Mississippi, May 1, 1865. No further records.

PARRIS, HENRY, Private
Resided in Buncombe County and enlisted at age 19, September 11, 1861. Deserted on March 10, 1863.

PARRIS, RUBEN, Private
Resided in Buncombe County and enlisted at age 20, September 11, 1861. Discharged on November 27, 1862. Reason discharged not reported. Reenlisted in the company on September 15, 1863. No further records.

PATTON, DAVID H., Private
Resided in Buncombe County and enlisted at age 21, September 11, 1861. Wounded at Murfreesboro, Tennessee, December 31, 1862. Died at Murfreesboro on February 8, 1863, of wounds.

PATTON, HENRY C., Corporal
Resided in Buncombe County and enlisted at age 18, September 11, 1861. Mustered in as Corporal. Promoted to Sergeant Major on March 23, 1863, and transferred to the Field and Staff of this regiment.

PATTON, JOHN A., Private
Resided in Buncombe County and enlisted at age 41, September 11, 1861. No further records.

PATTON, ROBERT H., Private
Previously served in Company E, 1st Regiment N.C. Infantry (6 months, 1861). Enlisted in this company at Cumberland Gap, Tennessee, April 8, 1862. Discharged on July 11, 1862, by reason of "rheumatism" and "general inflam[m]atory pains through his whole system." Later served as 2nd Lieutenant of Company I, 65th Regiment N.C. Troops (6th Regiment N.C. Cavalry).

PATTON, SAMUEL ALEXANDER, Sergeant
Resided in Buncombe County and enlisted at age 27, September 11, 1861. Mustered in as Private. Promoted to Sergeant on July 10, 1862. Wounded in the right thigh at Murfreesboro, Tennessee, December 31, 1862. Died at Murfreesboro on January 15, 1863, of wounds.

PLEMMONS, JESSE, ——
North Carolina pension records indicate that he served in this company.

PORTER, ROBERT W., Private
Resided in Buncombe County and enlisted at age 16, September 11, 1861. Discharged on November 6, 1862. Reason discharged not reported.

PRICE, JOHN, Private
Place and date of enlistment not reported. Captured near Smyrna, Georgia, July 3, 1864. Sent to Nashville, Tennessee. Confined at Louisville, Kentucky, July 14, 1864. Transferred to Camp Douglas, Chicago, Illinois, where he arrived on July 18, 1864. Died at Camp Douglas on or about July 29, 1864, of "typhoid fever."

RANDOLPH, WILLIAM M., ——
North Carolina pension records indicate that he served in this company.

RAY, SILAS M., Private
Born in Buncombe County where he resided prior to enlisting at age 20, September 11, 1861. Died at Cumberland Gap, Tennessee, April 27, 1862. Cause of death not reported.

REED, CHARLES, Private
Born in Buncombe County where he resided prior to enlisting in Buncombe County at age 19, September 11, 1861. Died at Camp Mangum, near Raleigh, November 17, 1861. Cause of death not reported.

REVIS, THOMAS F., Private
Resided in Buncombe County and enlisted in Tennessee on February 1, 1862. Captured by the enemy on an unspecified date. Exchanged at or near Vicksburg, Mississippi, on or about December 4, 1862. Wounded in the arm and captured at Chickamauga, Georgia, September 19-20, 1863. Sent to Nashville, Tennessee. Confined at Louisville, Kentucky, October 9, 1863. Transferred to Camp Morton, Indianapolis, Indiana, where he arrived on October 11, 1863. Paroled and transferred to City Point, Virginia, on or about February 26, 1865, for exchange. Hospitalized at Richmond, Virginia, March 10, 1865, with debilitas and was transferred the same day.

RHOADES, DAVID, Private
Place and date of enlistment not reported. Captured at Spanish Fort, Mobile, Alabama, April 8, 1865. Confined at Ship Island, Mississippi, April 10, 1865. Transferred to Vicksburg, Mississippi, May 1, 1865. No further records. [May have served previously in McRae's Battalion N.C. Cavalry.]

RICKERMAN, MILES, Sergeant
Resided in Buncombe County and enlisted at age 27, September 11, 1861. Mustered in as Corporal. Promoted to Sergeant prior to March 1, 1863. Last reported in the records of this company on May 5, 1863.

ROBERTS, MARCUS Q., Corporal
Resided in Buncombe County and enlisted at age 17, September 11, 1861. Mustered in as Private. Promoted to Corporal prior to August 1, 1864. Deserted to the enemy on an unspecified date. Confined at Chattanooga, Tennessee, on or about August 1, 1864. Transferred to Louisville, Kentucky, where he arrived on August 5, 1864. Released on or about August 10, 1864, after taking the Oath of Allegiance.

ROBINSON, CALVIN, Private
Place and date of enlistment not reported. Captured by the enemy on or about October 5, 1864. Confined at Louisville, Kentucky, October 21, 1864. Transferred to Camp Chase, Ohio, on an unspecified date. No further

records.

RODERICK, ELISHA, Private

Place and date of enlistment not reported. Records of the Federal Provost Marshal indicate he died at Rock Island, Illinois, December 19, 1863. Cause of death not reported.

RYMES, CANADA J., Private

Resided in Buncombe County and enlisted at age 20, September 11, 1861. Last reported in the records of this company on September 21, 1864.

SMITH, ALFRED A., Private

Born in Buncombe County where he resided prior to enlisting at age 20, September 11, 1861. Died in hospital at Jonesboro, Tennessee, December 19-20, 1861, of "fever."

SMITH, DAVID V., Private

Resided in Buncombe County and enlisted at age 16, September 11, 1861. Discharged on November 6, 1862. Reason discharged not reported. Later served as 3rd Lieutenant of Company I, 65th Regiment N.C. Troops (6th Regiment N.C. Cavalry).

SMITH, JOSEPH H., Private

Resided in Madison County and enlisted on September 11, 1861. Promoted to Hospital Steward on March 17, 1862, and transferred to the Field and Staff of this regiment.

SMITH, LUCIUS H., Private

Resided in Buncombe County and enlisted on September 11, 1861. Promoted to Ordnance Sergeant on an unspecified date and transferred to the Field and Staff of this regiment.

SMITH, RANSOM S., Private

Resided in Buncombe County and enlisted at age 27, September 11, 1861. Discharged on February 3 or February 12, 1862. Reason discharged not reported.

SMITH, THOMAS, Private

Born in Buncombe County where he resided as a farmer prior to enlisting in Buncombe County at age 18, September 11, 1861. Died in hospital at Jonesboro, Tennessee, December 18 or December 27, 1861. Cause of death not reported.

SPARKS, WILLIAM, Private

Resided in Buncombe County and enlisted at age 20, September 11, 1861. Died on July 6, 1862. Place and cause of death not reported.

STARNES, FRANCIS M., Private

Born in Buncombe County where he resided as a farmer prior to enlisting in Buncombe County on September 11, 1861. Discharged prior to May 17, 1862. Later served in Company I, 60th Regiment N.C. Troops.

STEPP, JOHN M., Private

Born in Buncombe County where he resided as a farmer prior to enlisting in Buncombe County at age 18, September 11, 1861. Died at Chattanooga, Tennessee, November 22, 1862. Cause of death not reported.

STEWART, DILLARD, Private

Born in Haywood County and resided in Buncombe

County prior to enlisting at age 53, September 11, 1861. Died at Jonesboro, Tennessee, December 10, 1861, or January 20, 1862, of "fever."

STRADLEY, EBENEZAR W., 1st Sergeant

Born in Buncombe County where he resided as a painter prior to enlisting at age 20, September 11, 1861. Mustered in as Corporal. Promoted to 1st Sergeant on July 10, 1862. Captured near Marietta, Georgia, June 19, 1864. Sent to Nashville, Tennessee. Confined at Louisville, Kentucky, June 26, 1864. Transferred to Camp Morton, Indianapolis, Indiana, where he arrived on June 28, 1864. Released on or about March 24, 1865, after joining the U.S. Army. Assigned to Company G, 6th Regiment U.S. Volunteer Infantry. [Roll of Honor indicates he was wounded slightly in an unspecified battle.]

STROUP, JOHN M., Private

Resided in Buncombe County and enlisted at age 17, September 11, 1861. Wounded in the foot at Murfreesboro, Tennessee, December 31, 1862. Transferred to Company C, 14th Battalion N.C. Cavalry, June 16, 1864. [See the roster for Company C, 69th Regiment N.C. Troops (7th Regiment N.C. Cavalry), in Volume II of this series.] Transferred back to this company subsequent to September 20, 1864. Captured at Spanish Fort, Mobile, Alabama, April 8, 1865. Confined at Ship Island, Mississippi, April 10, 1865. Transferred to Vicksburg, Mississippi, May 1, 1865. No further records.

STROUPE, RUFUS L., Private

Born in Buncombe County where he resided prior to enlisting at age 20, May 13, 1862, for the war. Died at Loudon, Tennessee, November 12, 1862. Cause of death not reported.

SWISI, D., Private

Place and date of enlistment not reported. Captured by the enemy on an unspecified date. Reported in confinement at Louisville, Kentucky, November 3, 1862. No further records.

TEAGUE, JOHN, Private

Resided in Buncombe County and enlisted on September 11, 1861. No further records.

TRANTHAM, DAVID A., Private

Resided in Buncombe County and enlisted on May 12, 1862, for the war. Died at Bean's Station, Tennessee, November 1, 1862. Cause of death not reported.

TRANTHAM, JAMES, ———

North Carolina pension records indicate that he served in this company.

TRANTHAM, MERRITT C., Private

Born in Buncombe County where he resided as a farmer prior to enlisting at age 17, February 28, 1862. Captured near Smyrna, Georgia, July 3-5, 1864. Sent to Nashville, Tennessee. Confined at Louisville, Kentucky, July 14, 1864. Transferred to Camp Douglas, Chicago, Illinois, where he arrived on July 18, 1864. Released on or about April 6, 1865, after joining the U.S. Army. Assigned to Company F, 5th Regiment U.S. Volunteer Infantry.

TRIGG, ALEXANDER, Private

Resided in Virginia and enlisted at age 22, December

25, 1861. Wounded at Chickamauga, Georgia, September 19-20, 1863. No further records.

TRIPLETT, EDWARD W., Private
Place and date of enlistment not reported. Captured near Marietta, Georgia, June 19, 1864. Sent to Nashville, Tennessee. Confined at Louisville, Kentucky, June 26, 1864. Transferred to Camp Morton, Indianapolis, Indiana, where he arrived on June 28, 1864. Died at Camp Morton on July 31, 1864, of "typho[id] malarial fever."

VAUGHN, W. W., ——
North Carolina pension records indicate that he served in this company.

WALTON, TISDELL M., Private
Resided in Buncombe County and enlisted at age 29, September 11, 1861. Captured "in Kentucky" in September-November, 1862. Confined at Chattanooga, Tennessee. Exchanged on January 11, 1863. Hospitalized at Mobile, Alabama, March 30, 1865, with a gunshot wound. Place and date wounded not reported. Surrendered at Citronelle, Alabama, May 4, 1865. Paroled at Meridian, Mississippi, May 16, 1865. [North Carolina pension records indicate he was wounded in the head near Atlanta, Georgia, in July, 1864, and that the wound resulted in "blindness."]

WEAVER, WILLIAM ELBERT, 1st Sergeant
Resided in Buncombe County and enlisted at age 19, September 11, 1861. Mustered in as Sergeant. Promoted to 1st Sergeant on an unspecified date. Promoted to Color Sergeant on an unspecified date and transferred to the Field and Staff of this regiment.

WELCH, JOSEPH, ——
North Carolina pension records indicate that he served in this company.

WELLS, J. FRANK, Private
Records of the United Daughters of the Confederacy indicate he enlisted on September 1, 1864, for the war and was "mustered out" on April 1, 1865. No further records.

WELLS, JACOB W., Private
Previously served in Company C of this regiment. Transferred to this company on September 11, 1861. Discharged on May 22, 1862. Reason discharged not reported. Later reenlisted in Company C of this regiment.

WELLS, JULIUS D., Private
Previously served in Company C of this regiment. Transferred to this company on September 11, 1861. No further records.

WELLS, JULIUS M., Sergeant
Born in Buncombe County where he resided as a farmer prior to enlisting at age 38, September 11, 1861. Mustered in as Sergeant. Discharged on May 19, 1862, by reason of "a paralytic predisposition rendering him unfit for any kind of service in the army."

WELLS, ROBERT CHRISTY, Corporal
Resided in Buncombe County and enlisted at age 21, September 11, 1861. Mustered in as Private. Promoted to Corporal on August 1, 1863. Wounded at

Chickamauga, Georgia, September 19-20, 1863. Last reported in the records of this company on September 26, 1863. [Records of the United Daughters of the Confederacy indicate that he survived the war.]

WELLS, WILLIAM F., Jr., Private
Resided in Buncombe County and enlisted at age 16, September 11, 1861. Surrendered at Citronelle, Alabama, May 4, 1865. Paroled at Meridian, Mississippi, May 9, 1865. [North Carolina pension records indicate he was wounded in the arm, chest, and right leg at "Murfreesboro, Tennessee, in 1864."]

WHITEHEAD, JAMES, Private
Previously served in Company C of this regiment. Transferred to this company on or about September 11, 1861. Transferred back to Company C prior to June 17, 1863.

WHITESIDE, JAMES A., Private
Place and date of enlistment not reported. Hospitalized at Meridian, Mississippi, January 29, 1865, with a wound. Place and date wounded not reported. Paroled at Montgomery, Alabama, June 20, 1865.

WHITLOW, MATTHEW C., Private
Enlisted on October 24 or December 11, 1864, for the war. Captured near Nashville, Tennessee, December 15, 1864. Confined at Louisville, Kentucky, December 20, 1864. Transferred to Camp Douglas, Chicago, Illinois, where he arrived on December 22, 1864. Died at Camp Douglas on April 3, 1865, of "pleurisy."

WILSON, HARRISON, Private
Resided in Madison County and enlisted at age 27, September 11, 1861. Deserted on September 6, 1863.

WILSON, ISAIAH, Private
Resided in Buncombe County and enlisted at age 42, September 15, 1863, for the war. No further records.

WILSON, ISRAEL, Private
Born in Buncombe County where he resided as a farmer prior to enlisting in Buncombe County at age 39, September 11, 1861. Discharged on May 20, 1862, by reason of "chronic rh[e]umatism and general debility, the result of successive attacks of parotitis, dysentery, and icterus."

WILSON, JEREMIAH L., Private
Place and date of enlistment not reported. Captured in Cherokee County on October 17, 1864. Sent to Nashville, Tennessee. Confined at Louisville, Kentucky, November 22, 1864. Transferred to Camp Douglas, Chicago, Illinois, where he arrived on November 26, 1864. Released on June 20, 1865.

WISE, ANDREW J., Private
Resided in Buncombe County and enlisted at age 18, November 16, 1862, for the war. Captured near Marietta, Georgia, June 19, 1864. Sent to Nashville, Tennessee. Confined at Louisville, Kentucky, June 26, 1864. Transferred to Camp Morton, Indianapolis, Indiana, where he arrived on June 28, 1864. Paroled and transferred to Boulware's Wharf, James River, Virginia, for exchange. Hospitalized at Richmond, Virginia, March 5, 1865, with frostbitten feet. No further records.

WISE, HENRY, Private

Resided in Buncombe County and enlisted at age 18, September 11, 1861. Captured near Marietta, Georgia, June 19, 1864. Sent to Nashville, Tennessee. Confined at Louisville, Kentucky, June 26, 1864. Transferred to Camp Morton, Indianapolis, Indiana, where he arrived on June 28, 1864. Paroled and transferred to City Point, Virginia, February 26, 1865, for exchange.

WRIGHT, HENDERSON, Private

Previously served in Company A, 60th Regiment N.C. Troops. Transferred to this company in July-October, 1863. Last reported in the records of this company on May 4, 1864.

WRIGHT, JAMES M., Private

Born in Buncombe County where he resided as a farmer prior to enlisting at age 23, September 11, 1861. Captured near Smyrna, Georgia, July 3, 1864. Sent to Nashville, Tennessee. Confined at Louisville, Kentucky, July 14, 1864. Transferred to Camp Douglas, Chicago, Illinois, where he arrived on July 18, 1864. Released on or about March 29, 1865, after joining the U.S. Army. Assigned to Company H, 6th Regiment U.S. Volunteer Infantry.

WRIGHT, JEFFERSON, Private

Resided in Buncombe County and enlisted at age 16, September 11, 1861. Discharged on November 6, 1862. Reason discharged not reported.

YELTON, CHARLES, Private

Resided in Buncombe County. Enlistment date not reported. Deserted on September 24, 1863.

COMPANY I

This company was raised in Mitchell County and enlisted on July 11, 1861. It was then assigned to the 29th Regiment and designated Company I. After joining the regiment the company functioned as a part of the regiment, and its history for the war period is reported as a part of the regimental history.

The following company roster is based primarily on the North Carolina Roll of Honor, prisoner of war records, pension applications, and a variety of miscellaneous records. Information was obtained also from secondary sources such as postwar histories, cemetery records, and records of the United Daughters of the Confederacy. No muster rolls were located for the company.

OFFICERS

CAPTAIN

BLALOCK, JOHN C.

Resided in Mitchell County and enlisted at age 32. Appointed Captain on July 11, 1861. Resigned on March 16, 1863, by reason of "chronic rheumatism."

LIEUTENANTS

BAKER, ELIJAH W., 2nd Lieutenant

Appointed 2nd Lieutenant on July 11, 1861. Not reelected when the regiment was reorganized on May 2, 1862. Later served as 1st Sergeant of Company B, 58th Regiment N.C. Troops.

GARLAND, ELIJAH W., 2nd Lieutenant

Resided in Mitchell County and enlisted at age 22.

Appointed 2nd Lieutenant on July 11, 1861. Defeated for reelection when the regiment was reorganized on May 2, 1862.

GARLAND, JOSEPH E., 2nd Lieutenant

Resided in Mitchell County and enlisted at age 19, July 11, 1861. Mustered in as Private. Appointed 2nd Lieutenant on June 24, 1863. Last reported in the records of this company on August 24, 1863.

GARLAND, JUNIUS S., 1st Lieutenant

Resided in Mitchell County and enlisted at age 45. Appointed 1st Lieutenant on July 11, 1861. Resigned in February, 1862. Reason he resigned not reported.

McKINNEY, CHARLES C., 2nd Lieutenant

Resided in Mitchell County and enlisted at age 22, July 11, 1861. Mustered in as Private. Appointed 2nd Lieutenant on May 2, 1862. Resigned on May 9, 1863, by reason of physical disability. Resignation accepted on or about May 27, 1863.

WILSON, HENRY T., 2nd Lieutenant

Resided in Mitchell County and enlisted at age 23, July 11, 1861. Mustered in as 1st Sergeant. Appointed 2nd Lieutenant on May 2, 1862. Wounded in the head at Murfreesboro, Tennessee, December 31, 1862. Returned to duty on an unspecified date. Wounded in the right arm near Atlanta, Georgia, August 8, 1864. Reported absent in hospital through August 20, 1864. [North Carolina pension records indicate that he survived the war.] No further records.

YOUNG, DAVID M., 1st Lieutenant

Resided in Mitchell County and enlisted at age 28. Elected 2nd Lieutenant on July 11, 1861. Promoted to 1st Lieutenant on May 2, 1862. Resigned on or about August 31, 1862, after being elected to the North Carolina House of Commons as a representative from Yancey County.

NONCOMMISSIONED OFFICERS AND PRIVATES

ALLEN, R., Private

Place and date of enlistment not reported. Discharged on May 1, 1862. Reason discharged not reported.

BAKER, JOHN F., Private

Resided in Mitchell County and enlisted at age 20, July 11, 1861. Died at Bakersville on June 10, 1863, of "fever."

BAKER, THEODORE P., ———

North Carolina pension records indicate that he served in this company.

BARKER, ROBERT F., Corporal

Born in Grayson County, Virginia, and resided in Mitchell County prior to enlisting at age 21, July 11, 1861. Mustered in as Corporal. Transferred to Company B, 58th Regiment N.C. Troops, in July, 1862.

BEASLEY, JOSEPH, Private

Place and date of enlistment not reported. Captured near Smyrna, Georgia, July 5, 1864. Confined at Louisville, Kentucky. Transferred to Camp Douglas, Chicago, Illinois, July 26, 1864. No further records.

BOWMAN, WILLIAM G., ———
North Carolina pension records indicate that he served in this company.

BUCHANAN, ARTHUR, Private
Resided in Mitchell County and enlisted at age 24, July 11, 1861. Deserted in February, 1863. Returned to duty on an unspecified date. Last reported in the records of this company on May 2, 1863.

BUCHANAN, DAVID, Private
Resided in Mitchell County and enlisted at age 20, July 11, 1861. Captured at or near Lancaster, Kentucky, on or about October 15, 1862. Exchanged on January 11, 1863. No further records.

BUCHANAN, EDMUND, Private
Born in Mitchell County* where he resided prior to enlisting at age 24, July 11, 1861. Died at Chattanooga, Tennessee, or at Marietta, Georgia, July 18-19, 1863, of "fever."

BUCHANAN, GEORGE, Private
Born in Mitchell County* where he resided prior to enlisting at age 28, July 11, 1861. Discharged in October, 1861, after providing a substitute. Died at Pleasant Garden on November 1, 1861. Cause of death not reported. He was "found dead in the public road."

BUCHANAN, JOHN V. Y., Private
Resided in Mitchell County and enlisted at age 32, July 11, 1861. Discharged on or about May 1, 1862. Reason discharged not reported.

BUCHANAN, NEWTON, Private
Resided in Mitchell County and enlisted at age 19, July 11, 1861. Reported absent without leave during September, 1864-February, 1865.

BUCHANAN, WILLIAM G., 1st Sergeant
Resided in Mitchell County and enlisted at age 17, July 11, 1861. Mustered in as Private. Promoted to 1st Sergeant on August 1, 1863. Wounded in the leg near Atlanta, Georgia, on or about August 19, 1864. Hospitalized at Macon, Georgia, August 26, 1864, and was transferred to Augusta, Georgia, the next day. [North Carolina pension records indicate that he survived the war.] No further records.

BUCHANAN, WILLIAM S., Corporal
Resided in Mitchell County and enlisted at age 28, July 11, 1861. Mustered in as Corporal. Last reported in the records of this company on April 15, 1863.

BURLESON, CHARLES, Private
Resided in Mitchell County and enlisted at age 35, July 17, 1861. Discharged on or about May 1, 1862. Reason discharged not reported.

BURLESON, ISAAC C., Private
Resided in Mitchell County and enlisted at age 17, January 4, 1862. Discharged in October, 1862. Reason discharged not reported.

BURLESON, REUBEN, ———
North Carolina pension records indicate that he served in this company. [May have served also in Company B, 58th Regiment N.C. Troops.]

BYRD, CHARLES, ———
North Carolina pension records indicate that he served in this company.

COOK, ALBERT B., Private
Resided in Mitchell County and enlisted at age 21, July 11, 1861. Transferred to Company E, 58th Regiment N.C. Troops, in July, 1862.

COOK, WILLIAM, Private
Born in Mitchell County* where he resided prior to enlisting at age 19, July 11, 1861. Died at Morristown, Tennessee, February 27, 1862, of "typhoid fever."

DAVIS, ALLEN, Private
Resided in Mitchell County and enlisted at age 31, July 11, 1861. Discharged in October, 1862. Reason discharged not reported.

DAVIS, JAMES H., Private
Resided in Mitchell County and enlisted at age 25, July 11, 1861. Deserted on September 7, 1863.

DAYTON, WILLIAM HARVEY, Private
Resided in Mitchell County and enlisted at age 25, February 17, 1862. Deserted on September 7, 1863. [North Carolina pension records indicate he was wounded on September 10, 1864.] No further records.

DEAN, JOHN K., Private
Resided in Mitchell County and enlisted at age 24, July 11, 1861. Deserted in October, 1862.

DUNCAN, WILLIAM, Sergeant
Resided in Mitchell County and enlisted at age 21, July 11, 1861. Mustered in as Private. Promoted to Sergeant prior to December 31, 1862, when he was wounded in the left thigh and captured at Murfreesboro, Tennessee. Confined at Camp Morton, Indianapolis, Indiana. Transferred to City Point, Virginia, where he was received on or about April 22, 1863, for exchange. Returned to duty on an unspecified date. Captured at Spanish Fort, Mobile, Alabama, April 8, 1865. Confined at Ship Island, Mississippi, April 10, 1865. Transferred to Vicksburg, Mississippi, May 1, 1865. No further records.

FORTNER, WILLIAM B., Private
Resided in Mitchell County and enlisted at age 19, July 11, 1861. Wounded in the right arm at Murfreesboro, Tennessee, January 2, 1863. Deserted on September 7, 1863. Returned to duty on an unspecified date. Killed at Nashville, Tennessee, December 15-16, 1864.

FREEMAN, JOSEPH, Private
Resided in Mitchell County and enlisted at age 21, July 11, 1861. Deserted on September 7, 1863.

GARLAND, CHARLES, Private
Resided in Mitchell County and enlisted at age 16, July 11, 1861. Discharged in October, 1862. Reason discharged not reported.

GARLAND, CRESENBERRY, Private
Resided in Mitchell County and enlisted at age 16, July 11, 1861. Discharged in October, 1862. Reason discharged not reported.

GARLAND, ELISHA, Private
Resided in Mitchell County and enlisted at age 16, October, 1861. Discharged in October, 1862. Reason discharged not reported.

GARLAND, GUTRIDGE, Musician
Born in Mitchell County* where he resided prior to enlisting at age 23, July 11, 1861. Mustered in as Musician (Drummer). Died at Morristown, Tennessee, February 27, 1862, of ''typhoid fever.''

GARLAND, SAMUEL, Private
Resided in Mitchell County and enlisted at age 25, July 11, 1861. Discharged in July, 1863. Reason discharged not reported.

GARLAND, WILLIAM McD., Sergeant
Resided in Mitchell County and enlisted at age 30, July 11, 1861. Mustered in as Sergeant. Deserted in November, 1862.

GOUGE, CARSON, Private
Resided in Mitchell County and enlisted at age 18, July 11, 1861. No further records.

GOUGE, EDMUND, Private
Born in Mitchell County* where he resided as a farmer prior to enlisting in Mitchell County at age 23, July 11, 1861. Discharged on February 7, 1862, by reason of ''an incurable cutaneous eruption which has followed him from childhood.''

GOUGE, LEONARD, Private
Resided in Mitchell County and enlisted at age 17, July, 1862, for the war as a substitute. Court-martialed on or about February 24, 1864. No further records.

GREEN, STEPHEN M., Sergeant
Born in Mitchell County* where he resided as a farmer prior to enlisting in Mitchell County at age 23, July 11, 1861. Mustered in as Sergeant. Discharged on July 22, 1862, by reason of ''chronic hepatitis [and] a recent spell of camp fever.''

GRINDSTAFF, ISAAC, Private
Resided in Mitchell or Yancey County and enlisted at age 17, June 13, 1862, for the war as a substitute. Wounded in the knee and captured at Murfreesboro, Tennessee, December 31, 1862-January 5, 1863. Sent to Nashville, Tennessee. Confined at Camp Morton, Indianapolis, Indiana. Transferred to City Point, Virginia, April 22, 1863, for exchange. Captured at Spanish Fort, Mobile, Alabama, April 8, 1865. Confined at Ship Island, Mississippi, April 10, 1865. Transferred to Vicksburg, Mississippi, May 1, 1865. Paroled at Meridian, Mississippi, May 11, 1865.

GRINDSTAFF, LAWRENCE E., Private
Resided in Mitchell County and enlisted at age 20, July 11, 1861. Discharged on January 31, 1863, by reason of ''ascites.''

GRINDSTAFF, MACK, ———
North Carolina pension records indicate that he served in this company.

GRINDSTAFF, PETER, Private
Resided in Mitchell County and enlisted at age 22, July 11, 1861. Deserted on September 23, 1863. Reported

absent without leave during September, 1864-February, 1865. [North Carolina pension records indicate he was wounded at Murfreesboro, Tennessee, on or about December 31, 1862.]

HILLMAN, THOMAS, Private
Resided in Mitchell County and enlisted at age 17, January 4, 1862. Captured near Smyrna, Georgia, July 4, 1864. Sent to Nashville, Tennessee. Confined at Louisville, Kentucky, July 13, 1864. Transferred to Camp Douglas, Chicago, Illinois, where he arrived on July 16, 1864. Released on or about June 16, 1865, after taking the Oath of Allegiance.

HOBSON, BENJAMIN, ———
North Carolina pension records indicate that he served in this company.

HOBSON, ISAAC, Private
Resided in Mitchell County and enlisted at age 22, July 11, 1861. Deserted in February, 1863.

HODGE, FRANKLIN, Private
Resided in Mitchell County and enlisted at age 35, July 11, 1861. Deserted in October, 1861.

HUSKINS, JAMES R., ———
North Carolina pension records indicate that he served in this company.

HUTCHINS, WRIGHT, Private
Resided in Mitchell County and enlisted at age 18, July 11, 1861. No further records. [May have served also in Company F, 58th Regiment N.C. Troops.]

JOHNSON, LINDSAY, Private
Place and date of enlistment not reported. Paroled at Troy on May 23, 1865.

KINNY, GEORGE H., Private
Place and date of enlistment not reported. Deserted to the enemy on July 3, 1864. Confined at Camp Douglas, Chicago, Illinois. No further records.

KNIFE, JAMES M., Private
Resided in Mitchell County and enlisted at age 18, July 11, 1861. Died on March 3, 1862, of ''fever.'' Place of death not reported.

LEDFORD, CURTIS, Private
Resided in Mitchell County and enlisted at age 35, July 11, 1861. Discharged on or about May 1, 1862. Reason discharged not reported. [May have served later in Company K, 58th Regiment N.C. Troops.]

LEDFORD, ISAAC, Sergeant
Resided in Mitchell County and enlisted at age 20, July 11, 1861. Mustered in as Private. Promoted to Sergeant on May 2, 1862. No further records.

LEDFORD, REUBEN, Private
Resided in Mitchell County and enlisted at age 19, July 11, 1861. Discharged in January, 1862, or on March 10, 186[3]. Reason discharged not reported.

LEDFORD, THOMAS, ———
North Carolina pension records indicate that he served in this company.

McKINNEY, CHARLES, Private

Resided in Mitchell County and enlisted at age 22, July 11, 1861. Discharged in August, 1862. Reason discharged not reported.

McKINNEY, MOSES, Musician

Born in Mitchell County* where he resided prior to enlisting at age 32, July 11, 1861. Mustered in as Musician (Fifer). Died at Morristown, Tennessee, February 20, 1862, of "typhoid fever."

McKINNEY, THOMAS J., Corporal

Born in Mitchell County* where he resided prior to enlisting at age 27, July 11, 1861. Mustered in as Corporal. Died at Morristown, Tennessee, February 20 or March 6, 1862, of "typhoid fever."

McKINNEY, WILLIAM, ———

Place and date of enlistment not reported. Died at La Grange, Georgia, June 1, 1864. Cause of death not reported.

McPRICHARD, BENJAMIN, Private

Resided in Mitchell County and enlisted at age 32, July 11, 1861. Discharged in October, 1862. Reason discharged not reported.

MARSHALL, ASA M., Private

Resided in Forsyth County. Place and date of enlistment not reported. First reported in the records of this company on September 3, 1863. Deserted to the enemy on an unspecified date. Confined at Chattanooga, Tennessee. Transferred to Louisville, Kentucky. Released on or about July 18, 1864, after taking the Oath of Allegiance.

MASHBURN, A. M., Private

Place and date of enlistment not reported. Company records indicate he was absent on sick furlough during October, 1863. No further records.

MILLER, SAMUEL, Private

Born in Washington County, Tennessee, and resided in Mitchell County where he was by occupation a farmer prior to enlisting in Mitchell County at age 18, July 11, 1861. Discharged on February 7, 1862, by reason of "chronic gastritis." [May have served later in Company B, 58th Regiment N.C. Troops.]

MURPHY, JOSEPH, Private

Born in McDowell County* and resided in Mitchell County where he enlisted at age 31, July 11, 1861. Discharged on July 23, 1862, by reason of "injury . . . of the right hip and lower part of the spinal column . . . received by a log rolling over his body in the spring of 1860."

PATTON, LEWIS E., Private

Resided in Mitchell County and enlisted at age 18, July 11, 1861. Last reported in the records of this company on March 2, 1864. [North Carolina pension records indicate he was wounded in the right side at "Atlanta, Georgia, in April, 1863," and was wounded in the right hand at Pine Mountain, Tennessee, July 4, 1863.]

PATTON, MONTERRILE, Private

Resided in Mitchell County and enlisted at age 22, July 11, 1861. Captured "in Kentucky" in September-November, 1862. Confined at Chattanooga, Tennessee.

Exchanged on January 11, 1863. Deserted on September 1, 1863.

PETERSON, JOSHUA, ———

North Carolina pension records indicate that he served in this company.

PHILLIPS, JAMES O., ———

North Carolina pension records indicate that he served in this company.

PHILLIPS, WILLIAM L., ———

North Carolina pension records indicate that he served in this company.

PITTMAN, JOSIAH, Private

Resided in Mitchell County and enlisted at age 32, July 11, 1861. Company records indicate he was discharged on or about May 1, 1862; however, North Carolina pension records indicate he died of wounds received near Atlanta, Georgia, "near close of war."

PITTMAN, ROBERT MILTON, Private

Resided in Mitchell County and enlisted at age 39, July 11, 1861. Discharged in October, 1861. Reason discharged not reported.

PITTMAN, SOLOMON, Private

Resided in Mitchell County and enlisted at age 17, October, 1861, as a substitute. Surrendered at Citronelle, Alabama, May 4, 1865. Paroled at Meridian, Mississippi, May 9, 1865.

PITTMAN, WILSON, Private

Resided in Mitchell County and enlisted at age 28, July 11, 1861. Discharged in October, 1861. Reason discharged not reported.

PRITCHARD, AZOR M., Sergeant

Resided in Mitchell County and enlisted at age 30, July 11, 1861. Mustered in as Sergeant. Transferred to Company B, 58th Regiment N.C. Troops, in July, 1862. Later served as 3rd Lieutenant of that unit.

RENFRO, M. G., ———

North Carolina pension records indicate that he served in this company.

RENFRO, THOMAS, Private

Resided in Mitchell County and enlisted at age 18, July 11, 1861. Deserted on September 7, 1863.

RENFRO, WILLIAM G., Private

Resided in Mitchell County and enlisted at age 16, June 30, 1862, for the war. Discharged in October, 1862. Reason discharged not reported. [North Carolina pension records indicate he was wounded in the hip "by piece of shell" at "Nashville, Tennessee, September, 1865."]

ROSE, EMANUEL M., Private

Resided in Mitchell County and enlisted at age 21, July 11, 1861. Deserted on September 7, 1863. Reported absent without leave during September, 1864-February, 1865. [North Carolina pension records indicate he was wounded in the right thigh at Allatoona, Georgia, in October, 1864.]

ROSE, FRANKLIN, Private

Born in Mitchell County* where he resided as a farmer

prior to enlisting in Mitchell County at age 48, July 11, 1861. Discharged on July 22, 1862, by reason of "advanced age & general constitutional debility."

SILVER, JOHN, Private
Resided in Mitchell County and enlisted at age 17, July 11, 1861. Captured near Atlanta, Georgia, July 22, 1864. Sent to Nashville, Tennessee. Confined at Louisville, Kentucky, July 29, 1864. Transferred to Camp Chase, Ohio, where he arrived on August 2, 1864. Paroled and transferred to Boulware's Wharf, James River, Virginia, where he was received on March 10-12, 1865, for exchange.

SILVER, LEWIS·P., Private
Resided in Mitchell County where he enlisted at age 22, July 11, 1861. Captured "in Kentucky" in September-November, 1862. Confined at Chattanooga, Tennessee. Exchanged on January 11, 1863. Captured near Atlanta, Georgia, July 22, 1864. Sent to Nashville, Tennessee. Confined at Louisville, Kentucky, July 30, 1864. Transferred to Camp Chase, Ohio, where he arrived on August 2, 1864. Died at Camp Chase on November 8-9, 1864, of "typhoid fever."

SLAGLE, WILLIAM, Private
Resided in Mitchell County and enlisted at age 21, July 11, 1861. Last reported in the records of this company on October 6, 1863.

SMITH, R. W., Private
Resided in Mitchell County. Place and date of enlistment not reported. Surrendered at Citronelle, Alabama, May 4, 1865. Paroled at Meridian, Mississippi, May 9, 1865.

SORRELLS, RICHARD, Private
Resided in Mitchell County and enlisted at age 48, July 11, 1861. Discharged on or about May 1, 1862. Reason discharged not reported. [North Carolina pension records indicate he was wounded near Cumberland Gap, Tennessee, in the fall of 1862.]

SPARKS, CHARLES, Private
Resided in Mitchell County and enlisted at age 24, July 11, 1861. Deserted on September 7, 1863.

SPARKS, REUBEN, Corporal
Resided in Mitchell County and enlisted at age 24, July 11, 1861. Mustered in as Corporal. Deserted on September 1, 1863.

SPARKS, WHITFIELD, Private
Resided in Mitchell County and enlisted at age 18, July 11, 1861. Deserted on September 7, 1863.

STEWARD, ISAAC, Private
Resided in Mitchell County and enlisted at age 16, October, 1861. Discharged on or about May 1, 1862. Reason discharged not reported.

THOMAS, HENRY, ——
North Carolina pension records indicate that he served in this company.

THOMAS, JAMES H., Private
Resided in Yancey County and enlisted at age 21, July 11, 1861. Wounded in the left hip at Murfreesboro,

Tennessee, December 31, 1862. Deserted on September 7, 1863. Company records indicate he was transferred to Company K, 58th Regiment N.C. Troops, August 27, 1864; however, records of the 58th Regiment do not indicate that he served therein. [North Carolina pension records indicate he was wounded in Mitchell County and at Marietta, Georgia, and was wounded at Little Rock, Arkansas, October 14, 1864.]

WHITSON, JOHN W., Private
Resided in Mitchell County and enlisted at age 23, July 11, 1861. Captured and paroled at Yazoo City, Mississippi, July 13, 1863. No further records.

WIKLE, THOMAS L., ——
North Carolina pension records indicate that he served in this company.

WILLIS, HENRY, Private
Resided in Mitchell County and enlisted at age 25, July 11, 1861. Captured at Yazoo City, Mississippi, on or about July 13, 1863. Sent to Memphis, Tennessee. Confined at St. Louis, Missouri, August 3, 1863. Transferred to Camp Morton, Indianapolis, Indiana, where he arrived on August 14, 1863. Paroled and transferred to Boulware's Wharf, James River, Virginia, where he was received on March 10-12, 1865, for exchange.

WILLIS, JOHN, Private
Resided in Mitchell County and enlisted at age 21, July 11, 1861. Captured at Yazoo City, Mississippi, on or about July 13, 1863. Sent to Memphis, Tennessee. Confined at St. Louis, Missouri, August 3, 1863. Transferred to Camp Morton, Indianapolis, Indiana, where he arrived on August 13, 1863. Paroled at Camp Morton and transferred for exchange on or about February 26, 1865.

WILLIS, JOSEPH W., Private
Born in Mitchell County* where he resided prior to enlisting at age 19, July 11, 1861. Died at Bristol, Virginia, November 21, 1861, of "ty[phoid] fever."

WILLIS, S. M., Private
Enlisted at age 18, April 10, 1862. Captured at Spanish Fort, Mobile, Alabama, April 8, 1865. Confined at Ship Island, Mississippi, April 10, 1865. Transferred to Vicksburg, Mississippi, May 1, 1865. No further records.

WILLIS, THOMAS, Private
Resided in Mitchell County and enlisted at age 25, July 11, 1861. Wounded in the right side at Murfreesboro, Tennessee, December 31, 1862. Captured at Yazoo City, Mississippi, on or about July 13, 1863. Sent to Memphis, Tennessee. Confined at St. Louis, Missouri, August 3, 1863. Transferred to Camp Morton, Indianapolis, Indiana, where he arrived on August 13, 1863. Paroled and transferred to City Point, Virginia, on or about February 26, 1865, for exchange. [Nominated for the Badge of Distinction for gallantry at Murfreesboro.]

WILLIS, WILLIAM M., Private
Resided in Mitchell County and enlisted at age 23, July 11, 1861. Deserted on September 7, 1863. [North Carolina pension records indicate he was wounded in the left leg at Spanish Fort, Mobile, Alabama, March

10, 1865.]

WILSON, MADISON D., Sergeant
Resided in Mitchell County and enlisted at age 19, July 11, 1861. Mustered in as Sergeant. Deserted on September 27, 1862. Returned to duty on an unspecified date. Captured at Spanish Fort, Mobile, Alabama, April 8, 1865. Confined at Ship Island, Mississippi, April 10, 1865. Transferred to Vicksburg, Mississippi, May 1, 1865. [North Carolina pension records indicate he was wounded in the knee at Nashville, Tennessee, in December, 1864.] No further records.

WILSON, MILTON, ———
North Carolina pension records indicate that he served in this company.

WILSON, PHILLIP H., Private
Resided in Mitchell County and enlisted at age 17, May 1, 1863, for the war. Surrendered at Citronelle, Alabama, May 4, 1865. Paroled at Meridian, Mississippi, May 9, 1865. [North Carolina pension records indicate he was wounded in the head and left shoulder near Corinth, Mississippi, in 1864, and was wounded in the face (resulting in loss of left eye) at Spanish Fort, Mobile, Alabama, March 29, 1865.]

WILSON, SIDNEY L., ———
North Carolina pension records indicate that he served in this company.

WILSON, THOMAS I., Private
Resided in Mitchell County and enlisted at age 28, July 11, 1861. Last reported in the records of this company on July 15, 1863.

WILSON, WILBURN, Private
Resided in Mitchell County and enlisted at age 28, July 11, 1861. Deserted on September 7, 1863.

WILSON, WILLIAM, Private
Resided in Mitchell or Yancey County and enlisted at age 30, June 11, 1862, for the war. Captured at Yazoo City, Mississippi, on or about July 13, 1863. Sent to Memphis, Tennessee. Confined at St. Louis, Missouri, August 3, 1863. Transferred to Camp Morton, Indianapolis, Indiana, where he arrived on August 14, 1863. Released on June 19, 1865, after taking the Oath of Allegiance.

WOODY, WILLIE G., Private
Resided in Mitchell County and enlisted at age 28, July 11, 1861. Died prior to April 21, 1864. Place and cause of death not reported.

YOUND, WILLIAM M., Private
Place and date of enlistment not reported. Captured and paroled at Yazoo City, Mississippi, July 13, 1863. No further records.

YOUNG, GEORGE WASHINGTON, Private
Previously served in Company K of this regiment. Transferred to this company on May 1, 1862. Died at Shelbyville, Tennessee, February 13, 1863. Cause of death not reported.

YOUNG, J. T., ———
North Carolina pension records indicate that he served in this company.

YOUNG, JAMES G., ———
North Carolina pension records indicate that he served in this company.

YOUNG, PATTERSON, Private
Resided in Mitchell County and enlisted at age 18, July 11, 1861. Captured "in Kentucky" in September-November, 1862. Confined at Chattanooga, Tennessee. Exchanged on January 11, 1863. No further records.

YOUNG, REUBEN J., Jr., ———
North Carolina pension records indicate that he served in this company.

YOUNG, SAMUEL F., Private
Enlisted at age 19 in 1862. Captured "in Kentucky" in September-November, 1862. Confined at Chattanooga, Tennessee. Exchanged on January 11, 1863. Wounded in the chest and captured at Murfreesboro, Tennessee, December 31, 1862-January 1, 1863. Hospitalized at Nashville, Tennessee. Transferred to Louisville, Kentucky, where he arrived on May 23, 1863. Transferred to Baltimore, Maryland, May 25-29, 1863. Paroled at Fort McHenry, Maryland, June 3, 1863. Transferred to City Point, Virginia, where he was received on June 5, 1863, for exchange. No further records.

YOUNG, SAMUEL N., ———
North Carolina pension records indicate that he served in this company.

YOUNG, STRAWBRIDGE, Private
Resided in Mitchell County and enlisted at age 23, July 11, 1861. Captured by the enemy on an unspecified date. Paroled at Lancaster, Kentucky, October 15, 1862.

YOUNG, W. M., ———
North Carolina pension records indicate that he served in this company.

YOUNG, W. P., ———
North Carolina pension records indicate that he served in this company.

YOUNG, WILLIAM, Private
Resided in Mitchell County and enlisted at age 20, July 11, 1861. Deserted on September 7, 1863. Returned to duty on an unspecified date. Hospitalized at Macon, Georgia, August 15, 1864, with a gunshot wound of the left leg. Place and date wounded not reported. Last reported in the records of this company on October 19, 1864. [North Carolina pension records indicate he was wounded in the right shoulder near Atlanta, Georgia, in August, 1864, and was wounded in the right arm at Allatoona, Georgia, October 5, 1864.]

COMPANY K

This company was raised in Yancey County and enlisted on September 16, 1861. It was then assigned to the 29th Regiment and designated Company K. After joining the regiment the company functioned as a part of the regiment, and its history for the war period is reported as a part of the regimental history.

The following company roster is based primarily on the North Carolina Roll of Honor, prisoner of war records, pension applications, and a variety of miscellaneous records. Information was obtained also from secondary sources such as postwar histories, cemetery records, and records of the United Daughters of the Confederacy. No muster rolls were located for the company.

OFFICERS

CAPTAINS

PROFFITT, BACCHUS S.
Previously served as Sergeant of Company B of this regiment. Appointed Captain on September 16, 1861, and transferred to this company. Appointed Major on October 29, 1863, to rank from March 16, 1863, and transferred to the Field and Staff of this regiment. Later served as Lieutenant Colonel of this regiment.

WRIGHT, JOHN
Previously served in Company B of this regiment. Transferred to this company on September 16, 1861, with the rank of Private. Promoted to Corporal on an unspecified date. Appointed 2nd Lieutenant on May 1, 1862. Promoted to Captain on or about October 29, 1863, to rank from March 16, 1863. Deserted on March 12 or April 22, 1864. Went over to the enemy on an unspecified date. Confined at Knoxville, Tennessee. Transferred to Louisville, Kentucky, where he arrived on July 25, 1864. Released on July 27, 1864, after taking the Oath of Allegiance.

LIEUTENANTS

HENSLEY, BACCHUS S., 2nd Lieutenant
Previously served as Private in Company B of this regiment. Transferred to this company with the rank of Sergeant on September 16, 1861. Captured "in Kentucky" in September-November, 1862. Confined at Chattanooga, Tennessee. Exchanged on January 11, 1863. Appointed 2nd Lieutenant on July 13, 1863. Captured at or near Kennesaw Mountain, Georgia, on or about July 3, 1864. Sent to Nashville, Tennessee. Confined at Louisville, Kentucky, July 14, 1864. Transferred to Johnson's Island, Ohio, where he arrived on July 16, 1864. Released on June 14, 1865, after taking the Oath of Allegiance.

HENSLEY, EASON H., 2nd Lieutenant
Previously served as Corporal in Company B of this regiment. Promoted to Sergeant and transferred to this company on September 16, 1861. Appointed 2nd Lieutenant on May 1, 1862. Died at Loudon, Tennessee, November 11, 1862, of disease.

PENLAND, NOBLE Z., 2nd Lieutenant
Resided in Yancey County and enlisted at age 19, September 16, 1861. Mustered in as Corporal. Promoted to 1st Sergeant on June 13, 1863. Appointed 2nd Lieutenant on an unspecified date. Captured at Spanish Fort, Mobile, Alabama, April 8, 1865. Confined at Ship Island, Mississippi, April 10, 1865. Transferred to Vicksburg, Mississippi, April 28, 1865. No further records.

PROFFITT, BENAJAH A., 1st Lieutenant
Resided in Yancey County and enlisted at age 33. Appointed 2nd Lieutenant on September 16, 1861. Promoted to 1st Lieutenant on May 2, 1862. Resigned on July 29, 1863, by reason of "chronic diarrhoea" and "chronic affection of the kidneys."

PROFFITT, JAMES C., 2nd Lieutenant
Resided in Yancey County and enlisted at age 30. Appointed 2nd Lieutenant on September 16, 1861. "Declined reelection" when the regiment was reorganized on May 2, 1862.

WHITTINGTON, BENJAMIN BEVERLY,
1st Lieutenant
Resided in Yancey County and enlisted at age 39. Appointed 1st Lieutenant on September 16, 1861. Declined to stand for reelection when the regiment was reorganized on May 2, 1862.

NONCOMMISSIONED OFFICERS AND PRIVATES

ALLEN, ADONIRAM, Private
Previously served in Company B of this regiment. Transferred to this company on or about September 16, 1861. Transferred back to Company B on an unspecified date.

ALLISON, N. H., ——
North Carolina pension records indicate that he served in this company.

ANGEL, DANIEL W., Private
Resided in Yancey County and enlisted at age 22, September 16, 1861. No further records.

BAILEY, GEORGE M., Private
Born in Yancey County where he resided as a farmer prior to enlisting in Yancey County at age 23, September 16, 1861. Discharged on April 15, 1862, by reason of "hereditary phthisis pulmonalis."

BAIN, WILLIAM M., Private
Previously served in Company B of this regiment. Transferred to this company on September 16, 1861. Died at Lauderdale Springs, Mississippi, August 11, 1863. Cause of death not reported.

BALLEW, ROBERT A., ——
North Carolina pension records indicate that he served in this company.

BARTLETT, JOHN ROBERT, ——
North Carolina pension records indicate that he served in this company.

BIGGS, JAMES, Private
Resided in Yancey County where he enlisted at age 25, September 16, 1861. Transferred to Company B of this regiment on March 11, 1863.

BIGGS, WILLIAM B., Private
Previously served in Company B of this regiment. Transferred to this company on September 16, 1861. Transferred back to Company B on March 11, 1863.

BRIGGS, A. WESLEY, Private
Resided in Yancey County and enlisted at age 21, September 16, 1861. Captured at Yazoo City, Mississippi, on or about July 13, 1863. Sent to Memphis, Tennessee. Confined at St. Louis, Missouri, August 3, 1863. Transferred to Camp Morton, Indianapolis, Indiana, where he arrived on August 14, 1863. Paroled and transferred to City Point, Virginia, February 25, 1865, for exchange.

BRIGGS, BURTON, Private
Resided in Tennessee and enlisted at age 36, September 16, 1861. Captured and paroled at Yazoo City, Mississippi, July 13, 1863. No further records.

BRIGGS, MELVIN W., Private
Resided in Yancey County and enlisted at age 23, September 16, 1861. Appointed 2nd Lieutenant on November 13, 1863, and transferred to Company C, 58th Regiment N.C. Troops.

BRIGGS, RUFUS S., Private
Resided in Yancey County and enlisted on May 13, 1862, for the war. No further records.

BRIGGS, SOLOMON R., Private
Place and date of enlistment not reported. Captured at Yazoo City, Mississippi, on or about July 13, 1863. Sent to Memphis, Tennessee. Confined at St. Louis, Missouri, August 3, 1863. Transferred to Camp Morton, Indianapolis, Indiana, where he arrived on August 14, 1863. Paroled and transferred to City Point, Virginia, February 26, 1865, for exchange.

BROWN, LEE, ———
North Carolina pension records indicate that he served in this company.

BROWN, W. E., Sergeant
Place and date of enlistment not reported. Promotion record not reported. Captured at Spanish Fort, Mobile, Alabama, April 8, 1865. Confined at Ship Island, Mississippi, April 10, 1865. Transferred to Vicksburg, Mississippi, May 1, 1865. No further records.

BUCKNER, ELIJAH, Private
Resided in Madison County and enlisted at age 25, September 16, 1861. Transferred to Company D of this regiment on June 1, 1862.

BYRD, FRANK, ———
North Carolina pension records indicate that he served in this company.

BYRD, J. C., ———
North Carolina pension records indicate that he served in this company.

CASE, A. P., ———
North Carolina pension records indicate that he served in this company.

CASE, JOHN L., Private
Previously served in Company B of this regiment. Transferred to this company on September 16, 1861. Hospitalized at Macon, Georgia, July 11, 1864, with a gunshot wound of the left foot. Place and date wounded not reported. Furloughed for thirty days on an unspecified date. No further records.

COUSINS, CLARK, Private
Previously served in Company K, 65th Regiment N.C. Troops (6th Regiment N.C. Cavalry). Enlisted in this company on an unspecified date subsequent to September 2, 1863. Deserted on March 4, 1864. Went over to the enemy on an unspecified date. Confined at Knoxville, Tennessee, on or about July 7, 1864. Transferred to Louisville, Kentucky. Released at

Louisville on July 18, 1864, after taking the Oath of Allegiance.

DUNCAN, DAVID W., Private
Resided in Yancey County and enlisted at age 17, August 15 or September 14, 1864, for the war. Captured at Spanish Fort, Mobile, Alabama, April 8, 1865. Confined at Ship Island, Mississippi, April 10, 1865. Transferred to Vicksburg, Mississippi, May 1, 1865. No further records.

EDWARDS, CORNELIUS W., Private
Resided in Yancey County and enlisted at age 23, September 16, 1861. No further records.

EDWARDS, J. W., Private
Place and date of enlistment not reported. Captured at Richmond, Kentucky, on an unspecified date. Confined at Lexington, Kentucky, on or about November 3, 1862. Transferred to Louisville, Kentucky, on or about the same date. Last reported in records of the Federal Provost Marshal on January 25, 1863. No further records.

EDWARDS, JOHN, Private
Previously served in Company B of this regiment. Transferred to this company on September 16, 1861. Captured at Yazoo City, Mississippi, on or about July 13, 1863. Sent to Memphis, Tennessee. Confined at St. Louis, Missouri, August 3, 1863. Transferred to Camp Morton, Indianapolis, Indiana, where he arrived on August 14, 1863. Released prior to September 1, 1863, **after joining the U.S. Army. Assigned to the 7th Regiment U.S. Cavalry.**

EDWARDS, JOHN J., Private
Resided in Yancey County or at Jonesboro, Tennessee, and enlisted at age 23, May 13, 1862, for the war. Deserted on May 14, 1863. Returned to duty on an unspecified date. Captured by the enemy near Marietta, Georgia, June 18, 1864. Sent to Nashville, Tennessee. Confined at Louisville, Kentucky, June 26, 1864. Transferred to Camp Morton, Indianapolis, Indiana, where he arrived on June 28, 1864. Released on or about May 20, 1865, after taking the Oath of Allegiance.

EDWARDS, JOHN W., Private
Resided in Yancey County and enlisted at age 20, May 13, 1862, for the war. Died on December 16, 1862, of "fever." Place of death not reported.

EDWARDS, ROBERT, Private
Resided in Yancey County and enlisted at age 21, May 13, 1862, for the war. No further records.

EDWARDS, WILLIAM SILAS, Private
Born in Yancey County where he resided prior to enlisting at age 20, September 16, 1861. Captured "in Kentucky" in September-November, 1862. Exchanged on January 11, 1863. Died at Dalton, Georgia, January 21, 1863, of "febris typhoides."

FENDER, ALLEN, Private
Previously served in Company B of this regiment. Transferred to this company on September 16, 1861. Dropped from the rolls of the company on an unspecified date for absence without leave.

FENDER, ISHAM, Private
Previously served in Company B of this regiment.

Transferred to this company on September 16, 1861. Dropped from the rolls of the company on an unspecified date for absence without leave.

GIBBS, JAMES N., ——
Resided in Yancey County and enlisted at age 27, September 16, 1861. Captured at or near Marietta, Georgia, July 3, 1864. Sent to Nashville, Tennessee. Confined at Louisville, Kentucky, July 14, 1864. Transferred to Camp Douglas, Chicago, Illinois, where he arrived on July 18, 1864. Released on June 16, 1865, after taking the Oath of Allegiance.

GIBBS, THOMAS C., Private
Resided in Yancey County where he enlisted at age 32, September 16, 1861. Last reported in the records of this company in October, 1863.

GOFORTH, DAVID C., Private
Previously served in Company B of this regiment. Transferred to this company on September 16, 1861. Discharged on May 8, 1862, by reason of "his age" and disability resulting from "typhoid fever."

GOFORTH, JOHN W., Private
Enlisted at age 19 in 1864 for the war. Captured at Spanish Fort, Mobile, Alabama, April 8, 1865. Confined at Ship Island, Mississippi, April 10, 1865. Transferred to Vicksburg, Mississippi, May 1, 1865. No further records.

GORVIS, JAMES, Private
Resided in Yancey County and enlisted at age 21, November 20, 186-. Deserted at Atlanta, Georgia, on an unspecified date.

HALL, IRA, Private
Resided in Yancey County and enlisted at age 19, September 16, 1861. Captured at Yazoo City, Mississippi, on or about July 13, 1863. Sent to Memphis, Tennessee. Confined at St. Louis, Missouri, August 3, 1863. Transferred to Camp Morton, Indianapolis, Indiana, where he arrived on August 27, 1863. Transferred to Fort Delaware, Delaware, on an unspecified date. Released at Fort Delaware on June 19, 1865, after taking the Oath of Allegiance.

HARRIS, JAMES J., Corporal
Born in Yancey County* where he resided prior to enlisting at age 44, September 16, 1861. Mustered in as Corporal. Died at Cumberland Gap, Tennessee, June 1, 1862, of "typhoid fever."

HAYDOCK, JAMES M., Private
Previously served in Company K, 10th Regiment N.C. State Troops (1st Regiment N.C. Artillery). Place and date of enlistment in this company not reported. Captured at Nashville, Tennessee, December 15, 1864. Confined at Louisville, Kentucky, December 19, 1864. Transferred to Camp Douglas, Chicago, Illinois, where he arrived on December 23, 1864. Released on May 12, 1865, after taking the Oath of Allegiance.

HENSLEY, GEORGE, Private
Resided in Yancey County and enlisted at age 26, September 16, 1861. No further records.

HENSLEY, JESSE, Private
Served in Company B of this regiment. [May have served briefly in this company.]

HENSLEY, LEWIS W., Private
Previously served in Company B of this regiment. Transferred to this company on September 16, 1861. Last reported in the records of this company on December 1, 1864.

HENSLEY, WILLIAM M. P., Private
Resided in Yancey County and enlisted at age 22, September 16, 1861. Mustered in as Sergeant. Deserted on September 6, 1863. Reduced to ranks prior to December 17, 1864. Captured at or near Nashville, Tennessee, on or about December 17, 1864. Confined at Louisville, Kentucky, December 18, 1864. Transferred to Camp Douglas, Chicago, Illinois, where he arrived on December 22, 1864. Released on March 25, 1865, after joining the U.S. Army. Assigned to the 6th Regiment U.S. Volunteer Infantry.

HENSLEY, WILLIAM MALCOMBE, Private
Born in Yancey County where he resided prior to enlisting at age 17, September 16, 1861. Died at Cumberland Gap, Tennessee, April 26, 1862, of "typhoid fever." "He was a good soldier—brave and true."

HENSLEY, WILLIS, Private
Resided in Yancey County and enlisted at age 20, May 13, 1862, for the war. Killed at Chickamauga, Georgia, September 19-20, 1863.

HOLLAWAY, DANIEL, Private
Born in Ashe County and resided in Yancey County where he was by occupation a farmer prior to enlisting in Yancey County at age 36, September 16, 1861. Discharged on February 27, 1863, by reason of "chronic diarrhoea."

HORTON, DAVID M., Private
Resided in Yancey County and enlisted at age 17, September 16, 1861. Captured "in Kentucky" in September-November, 1862. Exchanged on January 11, 1863. Last reported in the records of this company on May 23, 1863. [North Carolina pension records indicate that he survived the war.]

HUBBARD, WILLIAM, Private
Previously served in Company B of this regiment. Transferred to this company in February, 1863. Captured at Yazoo City, Mississippi, on or about July 13, 1863. Sent to Memphis, Tennessee. Confined at St. Louis, Missouri, August 3, 1863. Transferred to Camp Morton, Indianapolis, Indiana, where he arrived on August 14, 1863. Released on June 19, 1865, after taking the Oath of Allegiance.

KING, ROBERT E., Private
Previously served in Company B of this regiment. Transferred to this company on September 16, 1861. Captured at Yazoo City, Mississippi, on or about July 13, 1863. Sent to Memphis, Tennessee. Confined at St. Louis, Missouri, August 3, 1863. Transferred to Camp Morton, Indianapolis, Indiana, where he arrived on August 14, 1863. Died at Camp Morton on January 1, 1864, of "pneumonia." [Nominated for the Badge of Distinction for gallantry at Murfreesboro, Tennessee.]

LUTHER, ALLEN, Private
Resided in Randolph County. Place and date of enlistment not reported. Captured at Nashville, Tennessee, December 16, 1864. Confined at Louisville, Kentucky, December 21, 1864. Transferred to Camp Douglas, Chicago, Illinois, where he arrived on December 24, 1864. Died at Camp Douglas on March 9, 1865, of "typhoid fever."

LUTHER, JAMES, Private
Place and date of enlistment not reported. Deserted to the enemy at Nashville, Tennessee, December 15, 1864. Confined at Louisville, Kentucky, December 19, 1864. Transferred to Camp Douglas, Chicago, Illinois, where he arrived on December 23, 1864. Discharged on May 12, 1865, after taking the Oath of Allegiance.

McINTOSH, ALBERT, Private
Resided in Yancey County. Place and date of enlistment not reported. Captured at Allatoona, Georgia, October 5, 1864. Sent to Nashville, Tennessee. Confined at Louisville, Kentucky, November 22, 1864. Transferred to Camp Douglas, Chicago, Illinois, where he arrived on November 26, 1864. Released on June 17, 1865, after taking the Oath of Allegiance.

McINTOSH, ANDREW, Private
Resided in Yancey County. Place and date of enlistment not reported. Surrendered at Citronelle, Alabama, May 4, 1865. Paroled at Meridian, Mississippi, May 9, 1865.

McINTOSH, BARNETT, Private
Previously served in Company B of this regiment. Transferred to this company on September 16, 1861. Died at Cumberland Gap, Tennessee, April 1, 1862, of "pneumonia."

McINTOSH, NEWTON A., Sergeant
Previously served in Company B of this regiment. Transferred to this company on September 16, 1861, with the rank of Private. Promoted to Sergeant on May 1, 1862. Wounded in the shoulder and breast at Allatoona, Georgia, October 5, 1864. [Survived the war.]

METCALF, ABSALOM, Private
Resided in Yancey County and enlisted at age 29, September 16, 1861. Last reported in the records of this company on May 6, 1863.

METCALF, ENOS, Private
Previously served in Company B of this regiment. Transferred to this company on September 16, 1861. "Lost off the steam boat on the Alabama River May 16, 1863."

METCALF, JOHN, Private
Resided in Yancey County and enlisted at age 19, September 16, 1861. Deserted on May 14, 1863.

METCALF, WILLIAM J., Private
Resided in Yancey County and enlisted at age 31, September 16, 1861. No further records.

METCALF, WILLIAM J., 1st Sergeant
Resided in Yancey County and enlisted at age 28, September 16, 1861. Mustered in as Private. Promoted to 1st Sergeant prior to July 13, 1863. Captured at Yazoo City, Mississippi, on or about July 13, 1863. Sent to Memphis, Tennessee. Confined at St. Louis, Missouri,

August 3, 1863. Transferred to Camp Morton, Indianapolis, Indiana, where he arrived on August 14, 1863. Transferred to Fort Delaware, Delaware, March 19, 1864. Released at Fort Delaware on June 19, 1865, after taking the Oath of Allegiance.

NEILL, JAMES R., 1st Sergeant
Resided in Yancey County and enlisted at age 37, September 16, 1861. Mustered in as 1st Sergeant. Appointed Assistant Quartermaster (Captain) on November 26, 1861, to rank from September 25, 1861, and transferred to the Field and Staff of this regiment.

NORTON, BALIS, Private
Previously served in Company B of this regiment. Transferred to this company on September 16, 1861. No further records.

PACKER, STEPHEN, Private
Place and date of enlistment not reported. Captured at or near Nashville, Tennessee, on or about December 17, 1864. Confined at Louisville, Kentucky, January 3, 1865. Transferred to Camp Chase, Ohio, where he arrived on January 11, 1865. Enlisted in the U.S. service on March 20, 1865. Unit to which assigned not reported.

PARKER, FRANCIS M., Private
Resided in Yancey County and enlisted at age 22, September 16, 1861. Mustered in as Musician (Drummer). Reduced to ranks on an unspecified date. Surrendered at Citronelle, Alabama, May 4, 1865. Paroled at Meridian, Mississippi, May 9, 1865.

PARKER, GEORGE W., Private
Resided in Yancey County and enlisted at age 19, September 16, 1861. Captured "in Kentucky" in September-November, 1862. Exchanged on January 11, 1863. Last reported in the records of this company on September 18, 1864. [North Carolina pension records indicate that he survived the war.]

PARKER, SILAS, Private
Resided in Yancey County and enlisted at age 18, September 16, 1861. Deserted on September 24, 1863. Returned to duty on an unspecified date. Captured at Spanish Fort, Mobile, Alabama, April 8, 1865. Confined at Ship Island, Mississippi, April 10, 1865. Transferred to Vicksburg, Mississippi, May 1, 1865. No further records.

PARKER, STEPHEN, Private
Resided in Yancey County and enlisted at age 17, September 16, 1861. Discharged on December 18, 1862. Reason discharged not reported.

PARKER, WILLIAM, Sergeant
Born in Yancey County where he resided prior to enlisting at age 26, September 16, 1861. Mustered in as Private. Promoted to Sergeant on May 1, 1862. Died at Shelbyville, Tennessee, January 15, 1863, of disease.

PATE, DOCTOR A., Private
Previously served in Company B of this regiment. Transferred to this company on September 16, 1861. Deserted on May 14, 1863. Returned to duty on an unspecified date. Deserted to the enemy on an unspecified date. Confined at Chattanooga, Tennessee. Transferred to Louisville, Kentucky, where he arrived

on July 25, 1864. Released on July 27, 1864, after taking the Oath of Allegiance. [North Carolina pension records indicate he was wounded in the knee on August 10, 1862.]

PATE, JAMES M., Private

Born in Yancey County where he resided as a farmer prior to enlisting at Cumberland Gap, Tennessee, at age 18, May 13, 1862, for the war. Discharged on August 25, 1862, by reason of "general debility resulting from the scrofulous diathesis. He is now and has been for some time suffering from a severe cough and expectoration which seems to portend the approach of phthisis."

PATE, JOHN OLIVER, Private

Previously served in Company B of this regiment. Transferred to this company on September 16, 1861. Name appears on a court-martial record dated February 27, 1864. Reason he was court-martialed not reported. Deserted at Atlanta, Georgia, on an unspecified date.

PATE, MARCELLUS S., Private

Previously served in Company B of this regiment. Transferred to this company on September 16, 1861, with the rank of Private. Promoted to Corporal on an unspecified date. Reduced to ranks on an unspecified date. Deserted on September 6, 1863.

PATE, MORRIS S., Private

Place and date of enlistment not reported. Captured at or near Kennesaw Mountain, Georgia, on or about July 3, 1864. Sent to Nashville, Tennessee. Confined at Louisville, Kentucky, July 14, 1864. Transferred to Camp Douglas, Chicago, Illinois, where he arrived on July 18, 1864. Released on June 16, 1865, after taking the Oath of Allegiance.

PATE, SAMUEL F., Private

Resided in Yancey County. Place and date of enlistment not reported. Deserted to the enemy on an unspecified date. Confined at Chattanooga, Tennessee, on or about July 31, 1864. Transferred to Louisville, Kentucky, where he arrived on August 3, 1864. Released on August 4, 1864, after taking the Oath of Allegiance.

PHILLIPS, ANDREW G., Sergeant

Resided in Yancey County and enlisted at age 20, September 16, 1861. Mustered in as Private. Promoted to Sergeant on an unspecified date. Last reported in the records of this company on December 19, 1864.

PHILLIPS, EPHRAIM, Private

Resided in Yancey County and enlisted at age 46, September 16, 1861. Died "at home" on or about January 7, 1862, of "fever."

PIKE, J. W., ———

North Carolina pension records indicate that he served in this company.

PRICE, ISAIAH, Private

Previously served in Company B of this regiment. Transferred to this company on September 16, 1861. Discharged on July 23, 1862, by reason of "chronic rheumatism" and "chronic inflam[m]ation of the kidneys. . . ."

PROFFITT, DAVID S., Private

Resided in Yancey County and enlisted at age 21,

September 16, 1861. Mustered in as Private. Promoted to Sergeant on an unspecified date. Reduced to ranks on an unspecified date. Last reported in the records of this company on January 30, 1864.

PROFFITT, JAMES MADISON, Private

North Carolina pension records indicate that he served in this company.

RADFORD, JOHN, Corporal

Previously served in Company B of this regiment. Transferred to this company on September 16, 1861, with the rank of Private. Promoted to Corporal on May 1, 1862. Died at Bean's Station, Tennessee, November 3, 1862, of disease.

RADFORD, ROBERT P., Private

Resided in Yancey County and enlisted at age 23, September 16, 1861. Captured at Chickamauga, Georgia, September 19, 1863. Sent to Nashville, Tennessee. Confined at Louisville, Kentucky, October 1, 1863. Transferred to Camp Douglas, Chicago, Illinois, October 2, 1863. Died at Camp Douglas on April 1, 1864, of "inflam[mation] of lungs."

RAY, THOMAS B., Private

Resided in Yancey County and enlisted at age 19, September 16, 1861. Mustered in as Sergeant. Reduced to ranks prior to July 13, 1863. Captured at Yazoo City, Mississippi, on or about July 13, 1863. Sent to Memphis, Tennessee. Confined at St. Louis, Missouri, August 3, 1863. Transferred to Camp Morton, Indianapolis, Indiana, where he arrived on August 14, 1863. Paroled at Camp Morton and transferred to City Point, Virginia, February 26, 1865, for exchange. Hospitalized at Richmond, Virginia, March 13, 1865, and was furloughed for thirty days the next day.

ROBERSON, J. C., ———

North Carolina pension records indicate that he served in this company.

ROBERSON, WILLIAM L., Private

Previously served in Company B of this regiment. Transferred to this company on September 16, 1861. Wounded in the face at Chickamauga, Georgia, September 19-20, 1863. Last reported in the records of this company on December 1, 1864. [North Carolina pension records indicate that he survived the war.]

ROBERSON, WYATT, Private

Previously served in Company B of this regiment. Transferred to this company on September 16, 1861. Discharged on April 29, 1862, by reason of "chronic inflam[m]ation of the pleura, general debility, & a worn out constitution."

SEAGRAVES, JOHN, ———

Place and date of enlistment not reported. Died in hospital at Asheville on June 2, 1864. Cause of death not reported.

SHELTON, JOSEPH, Private

Born in Yancey County where he resided as a farmer prior to enlisting in Yancey County at age 24, September 16, 1861. Discharged on April 15, 1862, by reason of "a fall at Jonesborough, Tennessee, hospital . . . [resulting in] a spinal injury."

SHELTON, RODERICK, Private
Previously served in Company B of this regiment. Transferred to this company on September 16, 1861. Undated records of the Federal Provost Marshal indicate he was confined at or near Louisville, Kentucky. No further records.

SPALDING, FIELDER S., Private
Resided in Yancey County or at Jonesboro, Tennessee, and enlisted at age 18, September 16, 1861. Captured "in Kentucky" in September-November, 1862. Exchanged on January 11, 1863. Captured near Marietta, Georgia, June 18, 1864. Sent to Nashville, Tennessee. Confined at Louisville, Kentucky, June 26, 1864. Transferred to Camp Morton, Indianapolis, Indiana, where he arrived June 28, 1864. Released on May 23, 1865, after taking the Oath of Allegiance.

TAFFER, IREDELL, Private
Previously served in Company B of this regiment. Transferred to this company on August 1, 1863. No further records.

TAFFER, JOHN S., Private
Previously served in Company B of this regiment. Transferred to this company on or about September 16, 1861. Discharged on October 4, 1862. Reason discharged not reported.

VEST, SILAS, Private
Previously served in Company B of this regiment. Transferred to this company on September 16, 1861. Captured and paroled at Yazoo City, Mississippi, July 13, 1863.

WATTS, ANDERSON, Private
Resided in Yancey or Mitchell County and enlisted at age 16, May 13, 1862, for the war. Surrendered at Citronelle, Alabama, May 4, 1865. Paroled at Meridian, Mississippi, May 9, 1865.

WATTS, JAMES A., Private
Resided in Yancey County and enlisted on May 13, 1862, for the war. Deserted to the enemy on an unspecified date. Confined · at Knoxville, Tennessee, May 20, 1864. Transferred to Louisville, Kentucky, where he arrived on May 29, 1864. Released on May 31, 1864, after taking the Oath of Allegiance. Returned to duty with this company on an unspecified date. Wounded in the left breast at Spanish Fort, Mobile, Alabama, in April, 1865. [North Carolina pension records indicate that he survived the war.]

WESTALL, JOHN D., Private
Resided in Yancey County and enlisted at age 19, September 16, 1861. No further records.

WILLIAMS, JOHN, Private
Served in Company B of this regiment. [May have served briefly in this company.]

WILSON, EDWARD, Private
Previously served in Company B of this regiment. Transferred to this company on September 16, 1861. Discharged on October 3, 1862. Reason discharged not reported.

WILSON, GEORGE W., Private
Resided in Yancey County and enlisted at age 24, September 16, 1861. Appointed Chaplain on July 8, 1863, to rank from June 29, 1863, and transferred to the Field and Staff of this regiment.

WILSON, JAMES, Private
Previously served in Company B of this regiment. Transferred to this company on September 16, 1861. Discharged on June 8, 1862, by reason of "epileptic spasms with paralysis of the left arm."

WILSON, JOHN, Private
Previously served in Company B of this regiment. Transferred to this company on September 16, 1861. Died at Rome, Georgia, June 4, 1863, of "chr[onic] diarr[hoea]."

WILSON, JOHN CAL, Private
Resided in Yancey County and enlisted at age 25, September 16, 1861. Deserted on May 14, 1863.

WILSON, THOMAS, Private
Previously served in Company B of this regiment. Transferred to this company on September 16, 1861. Captured at Yazoo City, Mississippi, on or about July 13, 1863. Sent to Memphis, Tennessee. Confined at St. Louis, Missouri, August 3, 1863. Transferred to Camp Morton, Indianapolis, Indiana, where he arrived on August 14, 1863. Released on or about September 23, 1863, after joining the U.S. Army.

WILSON, THOMAS D., Private
Resided in Yancey County and enlisted at age 38, September 16, 1861. Mustered in as Musician (Fifer). Reduced to ranks on an unspecified date. Discharged on December 2, 1862, by reason of being overage.

WILSON, WILLIAM, Private
Previously served in Company B of this regiment. Transferred to this company on September 16, 1861. Captured "in Kentucky" in September-November, 1862. Exchanged on January 11, 1863. Captured (or deserted to the enemy) on an unspecified date. Took the Oath of Allegiance at Knoxville, Tennessee, October 31, 1864.

WILSON, WILLIAM S., Private
Born in Yancey County* where he resided as a farmer prior to enlisting in Yancey County at age 44, September 16, 1861. Discharged on August 21, 1862, by reason of "occasional but positive insanity of several years' standing."

YOUNG, GEORGE, Private
Resided in Yancey County and enlisted at age 22, September 16, 1861. Captured at Yazoo City, Mississippi, on or about July 14, 1863. Confined at St. Louis, Missouri, August 3, 1863. Died in hospital at St. Louis on September 5, 1863, of "erysipelas."

YOUNG, GEORGE WASHINGTON, Private
Resided in Yancey County and enlisted at age 30, September 16, 1861. Transferred to Company I of this regiment on May 1, 1862.

YOUNG, I. J., Private
Place and date of enlistment not reported. Captured and paroled at Yazoo City, Mississippi, July 13, 1863. No further records.

YOUNG, JOSHUA, Private
Resided in Yancey County and enlisted at age 20, September 16, 1861. Captured at Yazoo City, Mississippi, July 13, 1863. Sent to Stevenson, Alabama. Transferred to Nashville, Tennessee, where he arrived on or about September 23, 1863. Transferred to Louisville, Kentucky, where he arrived on October 28, 1863. Transferred to Camp Morton, Indianapolis, Indiana, October 28, 1863. Paroled at Camp Morton and transferred to Boulware's Wharf, James River, Virginia, where he was received on March 10-12, 1865, for exchange. Hospitalized at Richmond, Virginia, March 11, 1865. Furloughed for sixty days on March 15, 1865.

YOUNG, McWILLIAM, Private
Resided in Yancey County and enlisted on September 16, 1861. Captured at or near Vicksburg, Mississippi, on or about July 4, 1863. Sent to Stevenson, Alabama. Transferred to Nashville, Tennessee, where he arrived on or about September 23, 1863. Transferred to Louisville, Kentucky, where he arrived on October 28, 1863. Transferred to Camp Morton, Indianapolis, Indiana, October 28, 1863. Released on January 3, 1865, after taking the Oath of Allegiance.

MISCELLANEOUS

Civil War records indicate that the following soldiers served in the 29th Regiment N.C. Troops; however, the companies in which they served are not reported.

ALLEN, A. A., Private
Place and date of enlistment not reported. Captured at Spanish Fort, Mobile, Alabama, April 8, 1865. Sent to Ship Island, Mississippi. Transferred to Vicksburg, Mississippi, May 1, 1865. No further records.

ALLEN, H. C., ———
Place and date of enlistment not reported. Died prior to March 15, 1864. Place and cause of death not reported.

ALLISON, NATHAN H., ———
North Carolina pension records indicate that he served in this regiment.

BLOCK, W. H., Private
Place and date of enlistment not reported. Captured at Spanish Fort, Mobile, Alabama, April 8, 1865. Sent to Ship Island, Mississippi. Transferred to Vicksburg, Mississippi, May 1, 1865. No further records.

BOVIM, R. J., Private
Place and date of enlistment not reported. Captured at Spanish Fort, Mobile, Alabama, April 8, 1865. Sent to Ship Island, Mississippi. Transferred to Vicksburg, Mississippi, May 1, 1865. No further records.

BOYD, E. K., Private
Place and date of enlistment not reported. Mentioned in the records of this regiment on April 23, 1863. No further records.

BUCHANNON, FIDELA P., Private
Resided in Jackson County. Place and date of enlistment not reported. Captured in Jackson County on an unspecified date. Confined at Chattanooga, Tennessee, on or about July 14, 1864. Transferred to Louisville, Kentucky. Released on or about July 18, 1864, after

taking the Oath of Allegiance.

BUMGARNER, H., Private
Place and date of enlistment not reported. Mentioned in the records of this regiment on November 15, 1862. No further records.

CARLTON, C. B., Private
Place and date of enlistment not reported. Captured at Spanish Fort, Mobile, Alabama, April 8, 1865. Sent to Ship Island, Mississippi. Transferred to Vicksburg, Mississippi, May 1, 1865. No further records.

CEBOLT, F. L., Private
Resided in Cherokee County. Place and date of enlistment not reported. Captured by the enemy on an unspecified date. Confined at Fort Delaware, Delaware. Released on June 19, 1865, after taking the Oath of Allegiance.

CROCKETT, B. F., Private
Place and date of enlistment not reported. Captured at Spanish Fort, Mobile, Alabama, April 8, 1865. Confined at Ship Island, Mississippi. Transferred to Vicksburg, Mississippi, May 1, 1865. No further records.

DENNIS, DANIEL, Private
Resided in Guilford County. Place and date of enlistment not reported. Deserted to the enemy on an unspecified date. Confined at Chattanooga, Tennessee, on or about July 11, 1864. Transferred to Louisville, Kentucky. Released at Louisville on July 16, 1864, after taking the Oath of Allegiance.

DENNIS, JOHN L., Private
Resided in Union County. Place and date of enlistment not reported. Deserted to the enemy on or about December 18, 1864. Confined at Nashville, Tennessee. Released on or about January 15, 1865, after taking the Oath of Allegiance.

DENNIS, ROBERT, Private
Resided in Guilford County. Place and date of enlistment not reported. Deserted to the enemy on an unspecified date. Confined at Chattanooga, Tennessee. Transferred to Louisville, Kentucky. Released on July 16, 1864, after taking the Oath of Allegiance.

GORMAN, W. H., ———
North Carolina pension records indicate that he served in this regiment.

GREEN, JAMES S., Sergeant
Resided in Cherokee County. Place and date of enlistment not reported. Promotion record not reported. Captured by the enemy on an unspecified date. Took the Oath of Allegiance at Chattanooga, Tennessee, May 21, 1865.

HOWARD, JOHN H., Private
Place and date of enlistment not reported. Deserted to the enemy on an unspecified date. Confined at Knoxville, Tennessee, September 18, 1864. Took the Oath of Allegiance on September 20, 1864.

JOHNSON, WILLIAM, Private
Resided in Cherokee County. Place and date of enlistment not reported. Captured by the enemy on an

unspecified date. Took the Oath of Allegiance at Chattanooga, Tennessee, February 25, 1864.

JORDAN, SOLOMON A., Private
Resided in Mecklenburg County and enlisted on or about October 27, 1864, for the war. Deserted on November 1, 1864. Went over to the enemy on an unspecified date. Confined at Nashville, Tennessee. Transferred to Louisville, Kentucky, where he arrived on January 29, 1865. Released on January 31, 1865, after taking the Oath of Allegiance.

JORDAN, SOLOMON I., Private
Resided in Mecklenburg County and enlisted on or about October 27, 1864, for the war. Deserted on November 1, 1864. Went over to the enemy on an unspecified date. Confined at Nashville, Tennessee. Transferred to Louisville, Kentucky, where he arrived on January 29, 1865. Released on January 31, 1865, after taking the Oath of Allegiance.

KEITH, WILLIAM M., 1st Lieutenant
Promotion record not reported. Captured by the enemy on an unspecified date. Paroled at Vicksburg, Mississippi, May 10, 1865. Took the Oath of Allegiance at Nashville, Tennessee, August 14, 1865.

LUNSFORD, LOGAN, Private
Resided in Madison County and enlisted in Buncombe County in April, 1864, for the war. Captured by the enemy on an unspecified date. Confined at Nashville, Tennessee. Released on or about December 31, 1864, after taking the Oath of Allegiance.

LUNSFORD, W. L., Private
Records of the United Daughters of the Confederacy indicate he enlisted on April 2, 1863, for the war. No further records.

McGINNIS, B., Private
Place and date of enlistment not reported. Deserted to the enemy on an unspecified date. Confined at Louisville, Kentucky. Released on July 16, 1864, after taking the Oath of Allegiance.

MARSHALL, JOSEPH W., Private
Resided in Forsyth County. Place and date of enlistment not reported. Captured by the enemy on an unspecified date. Confined at Chattanooga, Tennessee. Transferred to Louisville, Kentucky. Released on or about July 16, 1864, after taking the Oath of Allegiance.

MILLER, HENRY, Private
Resided in Surry County and enlisted on or about November 13, 1864, for the war. Deserted on December 5, 1864. Went over to the enemy on an unspecified date. Confined at Nashville, Tennessee. Transferred to Louisville, Kentucky, where he arrived on January 29, 1865. Released on January 31, 1865, after taking the Oath of Allegiance.

MOORE, J. O., ———
North Carolina pension records indicate that he served in this regiment.

MORGAN, NEWELL R., Private
Resided in Guilford County. Place and date of

enlistment not reported. Deserted to the enemy on an unspecified date. Confined at Chattanooga, Tennessee, on or about July 11, 1864. Transferred to Louisville, Kentucky, where he arrived on July 14, 1864. Released on July 16, 1864, after taking the Oath of Allegiance.

PEGRAM, JOHN L., Private
Resided in Guilford County. Place and date of enlistment not reported. Deserted to the enemy on an unspecified date. Confined at Chattanooga, Tennessee, on or about July 11, 1864. Transferred to Louisville, Kentucky. Released at Louisville on July 16, 1864, after taking the Oath of Allegiance.

PRIDGEN, ROBERT WILLIAM, ———
North Carolina pension records indicate that he served in this regiment.

RICH, ALFRED, Private
Resided in Randolph County and enlisted on or about November 13, 1864, for the war. Deserted to the enemy on December 5, 1864. Sent to Nashville, Tennessee. Transferred to Louisville, Kentucky, where he arrived on January 29, 1865. Released on January 31, 1865, after taking the Oath of Allegiance.

ROBERTS, ROBERT N., Private
Resided in Jackson County. Place and date of enlistment not reported. Captured by the enemy on an unspecified date. Confined at Camp Douglas, Chicago, Illinois. Released on June 16, 1865, after taking the Oath of Allegiance.

SHELTON, B., Private
Place and date of enlistment not reported. Captured by the enemy on an unspecified date. Reported in confinement at Cairo, Illinois, October 25, 1862. Transferred to Vicksburg, Mississippi, where he arrived on November 1, 1862. No further records.

SLOAN, JAMES H., Private
Enlisted on or about August 8, 1862, for the war. Deserted to the enemy on or about December 15, 1864. Sent to Nashville, Tennessee. Transferred to Louisville, Kentucky, where he arrived on January 29, 1865. Released on January 31, 1865, after taking the Oath of Allegiance.

TENEPURGH, W. D., Private
Place and date of enlistment not reported. Paroled at Charlotte on May 24, 1865.

WILSON, WILLIAM JACKSON, ———
North Carolina pension records indicate that he served in this regiment.

WITHERS, WALTER C., Private
Resided in Gaston County and enlisted on November 13, 1864, for the war. Deserted to the enemy on an unspecified date. Confined at Nashville, Tennessee. Transferred to Louisville, Kentucky, where he arrived on January 29, 1865. Released on January 31, 1865, after taking the Oath of Allegiance.

YOUNG, JOSEPH, ———
North Carolina pension records indicate that he served in this regiment.

This regiment was organized at Camp Mangum, near Raleigh, on September 26, 1861. Two days later it left for Wilmington under orders to report to General Joseph R. Anderson, Commander of the District of Cape Fear. After arriving at Wilmington on September 29, the regiment camped at Camp Lamb. On October 8 it was mustered into Confederate service for twelve months; the next day it moved by steamboat to Smithville (now Southport) and encamped at Camp Walker, on the outskirts of the town. There the regiment underwent training while serving as a support unit for the coastal defenses.

On November 1, 1861, orders were received to move to Charleston, South Carolina, but these were quickly cancelled, and on November 6 the regiment was sent to relieve the 18th Regiment N.C. Troops (8th Regiment N.C. Volunteers) at Camp Wyatt, near Fort Fisher. A detachment of the regiment was engaged during an artillery exchange with the enemy at Anderson's Battery on November 15. After that action winter quarters were established at Camp Wyatt, where the regiment remained until March, 1862.

Up the coast from Wilmington a Federal force under General Ambrose E. Burnside captured Roanoke Island on February 8, 1862, and then moved against New Bern. On March 14 the 30th Regiment was ordered to the relief of New Bern and moved by steamer to its former base at Camp Lamb, where its orders were cancelled. Company K was detached to do picket duty in Wilmington on March 26, and on that day the remainder of the regiment moved about three miles to a new base at Camp French. Five days later the regiment was sent to Camp Holmes, near Masonboro Sound.

Companies A, D, and H were detached from the regiment on April 18, 1862, and ordered to Onslow County to defend against Federal raiding parties; on April 20 the rest of the companies, with the exception of Company E, were ordered to follow. Company E was sent to Wilmington to replace Company K on picket duty, and Company K rejoined the regiment on April 23. On that day, Companies B, C, F, G, I, and K left Camp Holmes for Onslow County. In the meantime, Companies A, D, and H had arrived at Jacksonville on April 21 and moved to Hatchels Mills on April 24; there they were joined by the other six companies on April 28. Still minus Company E, the regiment moved to the White Oak River and set up Camp Sanders; on May 1 the regiment was reorganized to serve for the duration of the war (rather than twelve months).

On May 8 Companies D and H, supported by a company of cavalry and a detachment of artillery, were sent on a scouting mission to Swansboro. The next day orders were received directing the regiment to return to Wilmington, and it departed on the evening of May 12. Three days later the regiment moved to Wrightsville Sound, where it remained until May 21; it then moved to Masonboro Sound. On May 27 the men moved back to Wilmington and went into camp at Camp Lamb. Company E had already rejoined the regiment on a previous but unknown date.

In June, 1862, the situation in Virginia, where a Federal army under General George B. McClellan had inched its way up the peninsula between the James and York rivers and was threatening Richmond, became so ominous that troops were transferred there from North Carolina. The 30th Regiment was ordered north to the Confederate capital and left Wilmington on June 13. Upon its arrival on June 16, the regiment was assigned to General George B. Anderson's brigade which, in addition to the 30th Regiment, was composed of the 2nd Regiment N.C. State Troops, 4th Regiment N.C. State Troops, and the 14th Regiment N.C. Troops (4th Regiment N.C. Volunteers). Anderson's brigade was assigned to the division of General D. H. Hill.

On June 23, 1862, the Confederate commander, General Robert E. Lee, and his principal lieutenants made plans to attack and, if possible, destroy the Federal army. Fighting broke out at King's School House on June 25, and on the morning of June 26 Lee made dispositions to attack the Federal right at Mechanicsville. Anderson's brigade was moved from its camp near the Williamsburg road, about five miles from Richmond, to the Chickahominy bridge on the Mechanicsville Turnpike. At 4:00 P.M. Brigadier General Roswell S. Ripley's brigade of D. H. Hill's division crossed the bridge to aid General A. P. Hill's troops engaged at Mechanicsville. The remainder of the division followed but did not take part in the fighting. During the night the Federals fell back to a defensive position at Gaines' Mill and then retired to Cold Harbor.

Early on the morning of June 27 the divisions of A. P. Hill and General James Longstreet moved against the center of the new enemy position while D. H. Hill's and General Thomas J. Jackson's divisions advanced against the Federal right. Finding his route blocked by the enemy, D. H. Hill sent Anderson's and Samuel Garland's brigades to turn the Federal left flank. The Federals then abandoned their position, and Hill's division moved on toward Cold Harbor.

In the meantime, Jackson had been forced to change his route and was proceeding by a road that would bring his troops in behind and to the right of D. H. Hill's division. Hill advanced his troops to Cold Harbor and deployed them along the edge of Powhite Swamp. To his right, Jackson's troops came into position, and on Jackson's right the men of A. P. Hill's and Longstreet's divisions engaged the enemy at Gaines' Mill. D. H. Hill's and Jackson's troops were then ordered forward to the support of A. P. Hill and Longstreet. Anderson's brigade, including the 30th Regiment, was second from the end on the left of the line and met the enemy in a woods on the edge of the swamp. After a short but bloody contest, the woods was cleared of the enemy. A general attack was ordered, and the Federals withdrew under pressure from the front and the threat posed by the attacks on their right. Night brought an end to the contest, and the Federals made good their escape.

From Gaines' Mill the Confederate left wing, now under the command of General Jackson, moved to cross the Chickahominy at Grapevine Bridge. The bridge had been destroyed by the enemy in his retreat, and the position was lightly defended to delay any attempted crossing. There Jackson's and Hill's men went into bivouac while the bridge was rebuilt on June 28-29. The next day the two divisions advanced over Grapevine Bridge and marched to White Oak Bridge. That bridge, which crossed White Oak Swamp, also had been destroyed by the enemy and was strongly defended, and there the Confederate left wing was kept at bay while the Battle of Frayser's Farm was raging. Following the battle the bridge was rebuilt, and Jackson and Hill joined forces with the right wing of the army and moved to meet the enemy at Malvern Hill.

Late on the afternoon of July 1 a general assault was launched against the Federal position at Malvern Hill. D. H. Hill's division, in the center, advanced across an open field against enemy batteries some 700-800 yards distant and was repulsed with devastating casualties. During the night the Federals retired to their base at Harrison's Landing, on the James River. The Battle of Malvern Hill was the last of the Seven Days' battles around Richmond, June 25-July 1, 1862; during that campaign the 30th Regiment lost 30 men killed and 137 wounded.

The brigade remained in bivouac near Malvern Hill until it was marched back to its original camp near Richmond on July 9-10. D. H. Hill's division was then left at Richmond to watch McClellan's army at Harrison's Landing while Jackson and then Longstreet moved to confront General John Pope's Federal army in middle Virginia. In mid-August General Anderson's brigade was sent with two other brigades of D. H. Hill's division to Hanover Junction, about forty-five miles north of Richmond. On August 26 the brigades at Hanover Junction marched to join the remainder of the division at Orange Court House, and on August 28 the entire division moved to join the Army of Northern Virginia. Hill's division rejoined the army at Chantilly on September 2, after the Battle of Second Manassas. General Lee's first invasion of the North began on September 4-5, 1862, when the Confederate army crossed into Maryland.

Upon reaching Frederick, Maryland, the army halted, and Jackson was dispatched to capture Harpers Ferry while Longstreet moved northwest to Hagerstown. On September 10 D. H. Hill's division moved out of Frederick as the rear guard of Longstreet's column. Mounting pressure from the Federals, plus the necessity of protecting Jackson at Harpers Ferry, resulted in the deployment of Hill's division along the South Mountain gaps below Boonsboro on September 13. Anderson's brigade, together with the brigade of General Samuel Garland, saw action at Fox's Gap on September 14, but the 30th Regiment took little part in the fighting. The regiment's activities were reported by Major William W. Sillers as follows (*Official Records*, Series I, Vol. XIX, pt. 1, pp. 1050-1051):

The regiment, except as to its skirmishers, was not actually engaged with any visible portion of the enemy's forces at any time during the battle. Late in the forenoon our skirmishers exchanged a few shots with those of the enemy near the point where General Garland's brigade engaged the enemy, by which we lost 1 captain and 3 privates wounded; total, 4.

A few minutes before night the regiment was under fire from an unseen foe. The fire was replied to; with what effect is not known, as it soon became dark and the brigade moved down the mountain. We changed position several times during the day, marching up and down the mountain. In these movements, made very rapidly and in the heat of the day, some of the men became exhausted and fell out of the ranks. Others were, no doubt, wounded, in the random firing late in the afternoon, causing a loss, in missing, of 15 privates, and making a total of wounded and missing, during the day, of 19.

The next day General Hill withdrew his troops from South Mountain under orders to concentrate at Sharpsburg. Anderson's brigade arrived on September 15 and went into position on the heights east of Antietam Creek. The brigade was moved later, with the rest of Hill's division, to a position in front of Sharpsburg between the troops of Jackson (on the left) and Longstreet (on the right).

On the morning of September 17 the Confederate left was vigorously assaulted, and three brigades of Hill's division were ordered to go to the support of Jackson. Anderson's brigade was ordered to extend its line to cover the vacated area. When the Federal attack shifted to the Confederate center, Anderson's and General Robert E.

Rodes's brigades were in the sunken road later known as Bloody Lane. Several determined assaults were repulsed, but the Federals succeeded in enfilading the right of Rodes's brigade. An order for the regiment on Rodes's right flank to form a line perpendicular to the road was misconstrued as an order for a general withdrawal; Rodes's brigade then retired, while Anderson's brigade continued to hold its position. The enemy moved in on Anderson's front and flank, Anderson was mortally wounded, and his brigade was routed. During the battle Colonel Francis M. Parker was wounded and Major Sillers assumed command of the 30th Regiment. He reported the regiment's part in the fighting as follows (*Official Records*, Series I, Vol. XIX, pt. 1, pp. 1051-1052):

Supposing that the main road which leads from the bridge across Antietam Creek through the center of Sharpsburg to run north and south, our brigade took position northwest and about half a mile from the town, and the Thirtieth Regiment was on the right of the brigade. Our line was formed in a road which, by the wear of travel, had been let down to the depth of a foot or more into the earth. In front of the right wing of our regiment, and at a distance of not more than 50 paces, there was a ravine which, extending diagonally to the left, gradually narrowed down the level space in front until in front of the extreme left of the Thirtieth there was not more than 30 paces of level ground. Our position was taken, I suppose, about 8.30 a.m. In the space of half or three-quarters of an hour the enemy made his appearance, crossed the ravine, and began his advance up the hill. A well-directed fire broke his line and drove him back. Up to this time, as far as the eye could reach to the right (300 yards), there was no support to our brigade; but about this time Brigadier-General [Ambrose R.] Wright's brigade came up. The enemy continued to make his appearance, first on one hill, then another, but always at long range. The line was ordered to advance, and halted on the edge of the ravine. Here a hot fire was kept up for a few minutes. Soon the line was ordered to take its first position, and did so. In a very short time Colonel Parker passed me, retiring, seriously wounded, from the field. From this time, about 11.30 a.m., the regiment was under my command. A desultory fire was kept up for some time, the enemy making demonstrations in front of the brigade on our right. Our fire at this point was not very effective, the range being too great and a fence intervening. Soon my attention was called to our right, which was again unsupported. Almost immediately my attention was called to the opposite flank (the left), which was uncovered as far as I could see. I sent a captain to the left to see if any one was there, and he reported no one. I then gave the order to fall back. We retired about 300 yards. Here we made a stand. Twice we advanced from this point, and twice we fell back to it. A short time before sunset the enemy advanced. We joined in a charge against them, and drove them so effectually that they did not appear again. In our last position we were under a pretty severe fire from artillery, playing on the front and flank. Here we remained until after nightfall, when we were withdrawn by order of Maj. Gen. D. H. Hill.

The regiment before the fight numbered about 250, all told. We lost in killed, 10, in wounded, 62, and in missing, 1, making a total of 76[*sic*]. I brought off from the fight 159.

After the Confederates rallied, General Hill led about 200 men in an unsuccessful assault on the Federal position. Serious fighting on that part of the line then came to an end. The two armies rested on the field the next day, and during the night of September 18 the Army of Northern Virginia retired across the Potomac.

General Anderson died of his wound on October 16, 1862, and on November 7 Colonel Stephen D. Ramseur of the 49th Regiment N.C. Troops was promoted to brigadier general and assigned to command Anderson's brigade. Ramseur was himself absent wounded at that time and did not assume command until March, 1863. In the interim, Colonel Bryan Grimes of the 4th Regiment N.C. State Troops commanded the brigade, which remained a part of D. H. Hill's division.

The Army of Northern Virginia remained in the Shenandoah Valley until the Army of the Potomac began crossing the Blue Ridge Mountains on October 26, 1862. On October 28 Lee ordered Longstreet's corps to move east of the mountains to Culpeper Court House and Jackson's corps, of which D. H. Hill's division was technically a part, to move closer to Winchester. Hill's division was posted at the forks of the Shenandoah River to guard the mountain passes.

When it became apparent that the Federal army, now commanded by General Ambrose E. Burnside, was concentrating on the Rappahannock River across from Fredericksburg, Lee ordered Longstreet's corps to take position on the heights overlooking the town while Jackson's men went into line on Longstreet's right. Hill's division was pulled back from the Shenandoah to Strasburg; it moved to Gordonsville on November 21 and then to Fredericksburg. On December 3 the division was sent to Port Royal, below Fredericksburg, to prevent any crossing of the Rappahannock at or near that point. On the morning of December 13 Hill's men returned to Fredericksburg and were placed in the third defensive line. During the battle of that day the division was subjected to heavy artillery fire but saw little action. After the battle it was advanced to the second line, where it remained throughout December 14. The next day it went into the first line and remained there for two days. While on the battlefield the 30th Regiment was never actually engaged but suffered the loss of nine men wounded from the artillery fire. The regiment then went into camp near Hamilton's Crossing, near Fredericksburg, and remained there during the winter doing picket duty and throwing up breastworks along the Rappahannock.

In January, 1863, General D. H. Hill was ordered to report to Richmond for reassignment, and his division was placed under the command of General Edward Johnson. As Johnson was absent wounded, General Robert E. Rodes, the senior brigadier, assumed temporary command of the division. In March General Ramseur, who had recovered from his wounds, reported for duty and relieved Colonel Grimes as commander of the brigade. Thus the 30th Regiment was then a part of Ramseur's brigade of Johnson's (Rodes's) division of Jackson's corps.

Early on the morning of April 28, 1863, the Army of the Potomac, commanded by General Joseph Hooker, began crossing the Rappahannock River in the Wilderness area upstream from Fredericksburg; at the same time, a large Federal force at Fredericksburg under General John Sedgwick began to make apparent preparations for a crossing. Lee, temporarily baffled as to where the main Federal thrust would come, retained the bulk of his army at Fredericksburg while keeping a sharp watch on Hooker. On April 29 Johnson's (Rodes's) division was moved to a position on the right of the Fredericksburg entrenchments

and extended the line to Massaponax Creek. Ramseur's brigade was placed on the south side of the creek to guard the ford near its mouth. On April 29 and 30 the brigade was subjected to occasional shelling, but no general action occurred. Concluding that the Federal activity at Fredericksburg was a feint, Lee began moving the bulk of his army upstream to oppose Hooker. A small force under General Jubal Early was left behind at Fredericksburg to contain Sedgwick.

Jackson's corps, including Ramseur's brigade, moved down the Orange Plank Road in the direction of Chancellorsville on May 1. After advancing about seven miles, Ramseur's brigade was detached and ordered to report to Major General Richard H. Anderson, whose division was engaged to the right of Jackson's column. Ramseur's men assisted Anderson in driving the enemy back and rejoined Jackson the next morning.

Early on the morning of May 2 Jackson's corps was dispatched by Lee to turn the exposed right wing of Hooker's army; and, after hard marching, Jackson succeeded in reaching a point about four miles west of Chancellorsville on Hooker's flank. As his troops moved up, Jackson deployed them in three lines for the attack. Four brigades of Johnson's (Rodes's) divison were placed in the first line; Ramseur's brigade was in the second line in a position to secure the right flank of the brigades to its front.

The attack began about 5:15 P.M., and the Federal troops, caught by surprise, fell back in disorder toward Chancellorsville. During the advance the brigade in front of Ramseur's failed to maintain the pace, and the Confederate right thus was unable to bring its full weight against the enemy. The second line then began to overtake the first, and the two became one as they drove in Hooker's right flank. The advance continued until darkness and strong resistance forced a halt. The Confederate lines were then re-formed, and Ramseur's brigade was placed on the right side of the Plank Road in the third line. The activities of the brigade on the following day, May 3, were reported by General Ramseur as follows (*Official Records*, Series I, Vol. XXV, pt. 1, pp. 995-996):

> Saturday night our division occupied the last line of battle within the intrenchments from which the routed corps of [Franz] Sigel had fled in terror. My brigade was placed perpendicular to the Plank road, the left resting on the road, General [George P.] Doles on my right and Colonel [E. A.] O'Neal, commanding Rodes' brigade, on my left. I placed Colonel [F. M.] Parker, Thirtieth North Carolina, on the right of my brigade; Colonel [R. T.] Bennett, Fourteenth North Carolina, on right center; Colonel [W. R.] Cox, Second North Carolina, left center, and Colonel [Bryan] Grimes, Fourth North Carolina, on left.

> Sunday, May 3, the division being, as stated, in the third line of battle, advanced about 9 o'clock in the support of the second line. After proceeding about one-fourth of a mile, I was applied to by Major [W. J.] Pegram for a support to his battery, when I detached Colonel Parker, Thirtieth North Carolina, for this purpose, with orders to advance obliquely to his front and left, and rejoin me after his support should be no longer needed, or to fight his regiment as circumstances might require. I continued to advance to the first line of breastworks, from which the enemy had been driven, and behind which I found a small portion of [Elisha F.] Paxton's brigade and [John R.] Jones' brigade, of [Isaac R.] Trimble's division.

Knowing that a general advance had been ordered, I told these troops to move forward. Not a man moved. I then reported this state of things to Major-General [J. E. B.] Stuart, who directed me to assume command of these troops and compel them to advance. This I essayed to do; and, after fruitless efforts, ascertaining that General Jones was not on the field, and that Colonel [T. S.] Garnett had been killed, I reported again to General Stuart, who was near, and requested permission to run over the troops in my front, which was cheerfully granted. At the command "Forward," my brigade, with a shout, cleared the breastworks, and charged the enemy. The Fourth North Carolina (Colonel Grimes) and seven companies of the Second North Carolina (Colonel Cox) drove the enemy before them until they had taken the last line of his works, which they held under a severe, direct, and enfilading fire, repulsing several assaults on this portion of our front. The Fourteenth North Carolina (Colonel Bennett) and three companies of the Second were compelled to halt some 150 or 200 yards in rear of the troops just mentioned, for the reason that the troops on my right had failed to come up, and the enemy was in heavy force on my right flank. Had Colonel Bennett advanced, the enemy could easily have turned my right. As it was, my line was subjected to a horrible enfilade fire, by which I lost severely. I saw the danger threatening my right, and sent several times to Jones' brigade to come to my assistance; and I also went back twice myself and exhorted and ordered it (officers and men) to fill up the gap (some 500 or 600 yards) on my right, but all in vain. I then reported to General Rodes that unless support was sent to drive the enemy from my right, I would have to fall back.

In the meantime Colonel Parker, of the Thirtieth [North Carolina], approaching my position from the battery on the right, suddenly fell upon the flank and handsomely repulsed a heavy column of the enemy who were moving to get in my rear by my right flank, some 300 or 400 of them surrendering to him as prisoners of war. The enemy still held his strong position in the ravine on my right, so that the Fourteenth [North Carolina] and the three companies of the Second [North Carolina] could not advance. The enemy discovered this situation of affairs, and pushed a brigade to the right and rear of Colonel Grimes, and seven companies of Colonel Cox's (Second [North Carolina]), with the intention of capturing their commands. This advance was made under a terrible direct fire of musketry and artillery. The move necessitated a retrograde movement on the part of Colonels Grimes and Cox, which was executed in order, but with the loss of some prisoners, who did not hear the command to retire. Colonel Bennett held his position until ordered to fall back, and, in common with all the others, to replenish his empty cartridge-boxes. The enemy did not halt at this position, but retired to his battery, from which he was quickly driven, Colonel Parker, of the Thirtieth [North Carolina], sweeping over it with the troops on my right.

After refilling cartridge boxes, the brigade was ordered to the left to meet an expected enemy attack. The entire Confederate line then converged on Chancellorsville and forced the Federals to retire. Once Chancellorsville was occupied, Johnson's (Rodes's) division was ordered to entrench along the Orange Plank Road. It occupied that position until Hooker recrossed the Rappahannock. Lee then moved his army back to Fredericksburg, and on May 6 Ramseur's brigade encamped at Hamilton's Crossing. During the Battle of Chancellorsville the 30th Regiment lost 26 men killed, 99 wounded, and 1 missing.

Following the Chancellorsville campaign and the death of Jackson, the Army of Northern Virginia was reorganized into three corps under Generals James Longstreet, Richard S. Ewell, and A. P. Hill. Rodes was appointed permanent commander of the division originally intended for Edward Johnson, and the 30th Regiment became a part of Ramseur's brigade of Rodes's division of Lieutenant General Ewell's 2nd Corps. The composition of the brigade remained the same.

On June 3, 1863, General Lee put his army in motion toward the Shenandoah Valley to begin the campaign that would end at Gettysburg. Ewell's corps, with Rodes's division in the lead, reached a point just beyond Culpeper Courthouse on June 7; the division then moved to Brandy Station, where a major cavalry battle was in progress, on June 9. After arriving too late to take part in the battle, the division resumed its march toward the Shenandoah Valley.

On June 12 Rodes's division received orders to proceed by way of Chester Gap to Cedarville in advance of the other two divisions of the corps, commanded by Generals Edward Johnson and Jubal Early. At Cedarville, Rodes was ordered to move to Berryville and Martinsburg and into Maryland while Johnson and Early advanced against Winchester. Berryville was occupied on June 13 after its defenders withdrew, and on June 14 Rodes's division deployed before the defenses of Martinsburg. Fearing the defenders might escape, Rodes ordered a charge and, with Ramseur's brigade in the lead, drove the enemy at almost a run for two miles beyond the town. However, the Federal infantry escaped by taking the Shepherdstown road while the Confederates were concentrating on the Federal cavalry and artillery on the Williamsport road.

On June 15 Rodes, having learned of the Confederate victory at Winchester, moved his men to Williamsport, where Ramseur's brigade and two other brigades from the division crossed the Potomac River before nightfall. After waiting three days for the arrival of the remainder of the corps, Rodes's division resumed its advance on June 19 and marched to Hagerstown, where it remained for two days. The division advanced again on June 22, crossed into Pennsylvania, and bivouacked at Greencastle. The next day Rodes moved toward Chambersburg, where he was joined by Johnson's division; the two divisions then moved to Carlisle, arriving there on June 27.

On the night of June 30 Rodes's division, at Heidlersburg, received orders to proceed the next day to either Cashtown, where two divisions of A. P. Hill's corps were located, or to Gettysburg, where Federal troops had been reported. Rodes marched toward Cashtown on the morning of July 1 but was redirected to Gettysburg when word came that Hill was moving against the latter town. When Rodes's division arrived on the field, Hill's men were already engaged; Rodes then moved into position on Hill's left, placing four brigades on the line and Ramseur's brigade in reserve. The timely arrival of Early's division, combined with assaults launched by Hill and Rodes, drove the Federal infantry through the streets of Gettysburg to Cemetery Hill south of the town. General Ramseur reported the activities of his brigade on that day as follows (*Official Records*, Series I, Vol. XXVII, pt. 2, p. 587):

July 1, in rear of the division train, as a guard on the march from Heidlersburg to Gettysburg. My brigade arrived on the field after the division had formed line of battle. I was then held in reserve to support General [George P.] Doles, on the left; Colonel [E. A.] O'Neal, left center, or General [Alfred] Iverson, on the right center, according to circumstances.

After resting about fifteen minutes, I received orders to send two regiments to the support of Colonel O'Neal, and with the remaining two to support Iverson. I immediately detached the Second and Fourth North Carolina troops to support O'Neal, and with the Fourteenth and Thirtieth hastened to the support of Iverson. I found three regiments of Iverson's command almost annihilated, and the Third Alabama Regiment coming out of the fight from Iverson's right. I requested Colonel [C. A.] Battle, Third Alabama, to join me, which he cheerfully did. With these regiments (Third Alabama, Fourteenth and Thirtieth North Carolina), I turned the enemy's strong position in a body of woods, surrounded by a stone fence, by attacking *en masse* on his right flank, driving him back, and getting in his rear. At the time of my advance on the enemy's right, I sent to the commanding officer of the Twelfth North Carolina, of Iverson's brigade, to push the enemy in front. This was done. The enemy seeing his right flank turned, made but feeble resistance to the front attack, but ran off the field in confusion, leaving his killed and wounded and between 800 and 900 prisoners in our hands. The enemy was pushed through Gettysburg to the heights beyond, when I received an order to halt, and form line of battle in a street in Gettysburg running east and west.

Ramseur's brigade took no major part in the fighting at Gettysburg on July 2 and 3. Ramseur's report continued as follows (*Official Records*, Series I, Volume XXVII, pt. 2, pp. 587-588):

July 2, remained in line of battle all day, with very heavy skirmishing in front. At dark, I received an order from Major-General Rodes to move by the right flank until Brigadier-General Doles' troops cleared the town, and then to advance in line of battle on the enemy's position on the Cemetery Hill. Was told that the remaining brigades of the division would be governed by my movements. Obeyed this order until within 200 yards of the enemy's position where batteries were discovered in position to pour upon our lines direct, cross, and enfilade fires. Two lines of infantry behind stone walls and breastworks were supporting these batteries. The strength and position of the enemy's batteries and their supports induced me to halt and confer with General Doles, and, with him, to make representation of the character of the enemy's position, and ask further instructions.

In answer, received an order to retire quietly to a deep road some 300 yards in rear, and be in readiness to attack at daylight; withdrew accordingly.

July 3, remained in line all day, with severe and damaging skirmishing in front, exposed to the artillery of the enemy and our own short-range guns, by the careless use or imperfect ammunition of which I lost 7 men killed and wounded. Withdrew at night, and formed line of battle near Gettysburg, where we remained on July 4. Commenced retreat with the army on the night of the 4th instant.

Major William W. Sillers, who commanded the 30th Regiment at Gettysburg after Colonel Francis M. Parker

was wound on July 1, reported the activities of the regiment during the three-day battle as follows (*Official Records*, Series I, Volume XXVII, pt. 2, p. 591):

The regiment (excepting as to its sharpshooters) was actively engaged only during the early part of the afternoon of Wednesday, July 1. It participated in the charge upon the enemy which resulted in driving him from a strong position behind a stone wall on elevated ground to the plain below in front of Gettysburg. After this, the enemy made but faint show of resistance until safe behind stone walls and intrenchments on the heights above the town. We sustained some losses during Thursday and Friday, chiefly among sharpshooters. . . . We neither lost nor captured a flag during the engagement.

Our losses were 6 killed, 36 wounded, and 5 missing, making a total of 47.

Following the failure of the Pickett-Pettigrew Charge on July 3, Lee held his army in position to receive an expected attack. On the night of July 4 the army fell back toward Hagerstown by way of Fairfield. Rodes's division became the rear guard on the morning of July 6 and was engaged in several brief skirmishes. Upon reaching Hagerstown on July 7 a line of battle was established but no general engagement occurred. On the night of July 14 the division recrossed the Potomac and marched to near Darkesville.

When the Federal army crossed into Virginia in mid-July, Lee moved his army east of the Blue Ridge Mountains to interpose it between the enemy and Richmond. By August 4 the Army of Northern Virginia occupied the Rapidan River line, and the Army of the Potomac had taken position on the Rappahannock.

In October, 1863, Lee learned that the Army of the Potomac had been weakened in order to send additional forces to take part in the Chattanooga campaign, and, although still heavily outnumbered, he moved west and then north in an attempt to turn the Federal right flank. Lee's advance compelled the Federal commander, General George G. Meade, to retire toward Centreville, and on October 14 the Federal rear guard was intercepted at Bristoe Station. Failure to coordinate the ensuing attack resulted in severe casualties to troops of A. P. Hill's corps and in the escape of the Federals. Although it was not engaged in the fighting at Bristoe Station, the 30th Regiment was involved in skirmishes near Warrenton Springs and Warrenton Court House on October 12 and 14. Casualties during those engagements were not reported, but the casualty report for the period October 10-21 indicates that the regiment lost five men wounded.

After the escape of the Federal army at Centreville and Bristoe Station, Lee fell back to the Rappahannock. Rodes's division was positioned in the vicinity of Kelly's Ford, where the 2nd Regiment N.C. State Troops of Ramseur's brigade was on picket duty on November 7 when the Federals delivered a heavy assault. The 30th Regiment was ordered forward to support the 2nd Regiment, and the two units sustained severe casualties before retiring on the reserves and leaving the ford in Federal hands. Regimental adjutant Peter W. Arrington reported the activities of the 30th Regiment at Kelly's Ford as follows (North Carolina Roll of Honor):

The Regiment . . . advanced about 1/4 mile through an open field under a heavy fire of the Enemies Infantry and Artillery attempting to take a position on the banks of the river. In advancing we had to cross a fence that ran obliquely to our line of battle which kept the Regt very much broken and together with the fact of there being a residence immediately in our front, encircled by pailings [sic] with a garden fence of the same kind, which while it necessarily scattered the men, afforded them but little protection. The Lt. Colonel [William W. Sillers] after passing the obstruction found it necessary to halt and reform, but before he had time to accomplish his purpose he received orders to withdraw. He ordered the fall back and though wounded and lame made every effort to get all the men to the rear as there were a number of buildings on the premises into some of which men had been sent to annoy the enemy, by discharging their pieces from the windows &c. while behind others they had sought protection. The Regt fell back from this position with considerable loss, the most of whom were captured.

General Rodes's commented unfavorably upon the 30th Regiment's conduct at Kelly's Ford as follows (*Official Records*, Series I, Vol. XXIX, pt. 1, pp. 632-633):

The Thirtieth North Carolina, going to the assistance of the Second, was speedily broken and demoralized under the concentrated artillery fire which swept the ground over which it had to march.

. . . .

The Thirtieth did not sustain its reputation. It arrived at the mills [*i.e.*, the scene of the battle] in great confusion and became uncontrollable. Its leader, Lieutenant-Colonel Sillers, behaved gallantly and did his duty, but many of his men refused utterly to leave the shelter of the houses when he ordered the regiment to fall back. All who refused were of course captured, and hence the large number of prisoners from this regiment.

The precise number of casualties sustained by the 30th Regiment was not reported, but the 30th and 2nd Regiments appear to have lost a combined total of 5 men killed, 59 wounded, and 295 captured or missing. Between one third and one half of the members of the 30th Regiment would appear to have been casualties at Kelly's Ford.

Lee withdrew his army south across the upper Rapidan River toward Orange Court House, where the men went into camp. Ramseur's brigade encamped at Morton's Ford. On November 26 Meade began moving the Army of the Potomac across the lower Rapidan below Lee's position, and Lee shifted his forces eastward to intercept the Federals. By November 29 Lee's men were strongly entrenched at Mine Run, and Meade, unable to locate a vulnerable point against which to launch an attack, also began entrenching. On the morning of December 2 Lee sent an attack force composed of two divisions from A. P. Hill's corps against what he believed to be an exposed Federal flank; however, when the Confederates moved out they discovered that the Federals had retreated. The activities of Ramseur's brigade at Mine Run were described in Ramseur's report as follows (*Official Records*, Series I, Vol. XXIX, pt. 1, pp 886-887):

[M]y brigade moved with the division about 3 o'clock on the morning of November 27. Formed line of battle along ridge road leading by Zoar Church; remained here several hours, right resting near the church, left near right of Major-General [Edward] Johnson's intrenchments, and then took up line of march toward Locust Grove. Met the enemy in heavy

force near and this side of Locust Grove. Division was again formed in line of battle and advanced a short distance, developing the enemy in strong force; then halted, and my brigade, on the right, was thrown forward so as to connect with the left to Major-General [Jubal A.] Early's division, Brigadier-General [John B.] Gordon's brigade. Remained thus in line of battle, with sharp skirmishing in front, until dark. My brigade was then moved from the right to the left of the division, partially covering a wide gap between Major-General Rodes and Major-General Johnson.

About 12 o'clock at night the division fell back from its advanced position near Locust Grove, and took up line of battle again on Mine Run. My brigade was left to cover this movement. This line was strongly and rapidly fortified, and here we awaited the onset of the enemy, November 28, 29, and 30, and December 1. This he declined to make, and during the night of the 1st retreated to the north bank of the Rapidan.

At daylight Wednesday morning, December 2, advanced with my brigade and followed the retreating enemy as far as the river, picking up some 50 or 60 stragglers. Returned to camp at Morton's Ford December 3.

Both armies then went into winter quarters, and Ramseur's brigade built quarters near Orange Court House. During the winter of 1863-1864 the regiment served on picket duty at Morton's Ford and engaged the enemy there in a heavy skirmish on February 6, 1864.

On the morning of May 4, 1864, the Army of the Potomac, under the strategic direction of General U.S. Grant, began crossing the lower Rapidan and entered a thicket- and vine-choked woods of dense scrub oak and pine known as the Wilderness. While the remainder of Rodes's division moved to oppose the Federal advance, Ramseur's brigade remained behind to guard the river crossings from Rapidan Station to Mitchell's Ford. The brigade remained in position on May 5, the first day of the Battle of the Wilderness, but rejoined the division on the evening of May 6 and was placed on the extreme left of the Confederate line to protect the flank. On the morning of May 7 it was moved to the rear as a reserve. When a Federal force appeared to be moving into a gap between Ewell's and A. P. Hill's corps on that day, Ramseur's brigade closed the gap and halted the Federal advance.

Late on the evening of May 7 it became apparent that Grant's army was on the march southeastward toward Spotsylvania Court House, and throughout the night Lee's men pushed in the same direction in a race with the Federals to that vital crossroad. The race was narrowly won by the Confederates on the morning of May 8, and a strong defensive line was quickly constructed. Ramseur's brigade launched a successful attack on a Federal force threatening the flank of a brigade of General Joseph B. Kershaw's division and then went into position to the left of the so-called "Mule Shoe," a convex, U-shaped salient in the center of the Confederate line. Heavy skirmishing with the enemy occurred on May 9, 10, and 11.

On the morning of May 12 a violent Federal assault broke through the Confederate line at the Mule Shoe, and Ramseur's brigade was ordered forward with other units to throw back the attackers. After driving the enemy out of the captured works, the Confederates held the line from about 7:30 P.M. on May 12 until 3:00 A.M. on May 13, when they were withdrawn to a newly constructed line in the rear.

On May 15, 1864, the 1st and 3rd Regiments N.C. State Troops, or rather the remnants of those units, were assigned to Ramseur's brigade. Those two regiments, formerly components of George H. Steuart's brigade of Edward Johnson's division of Ewell's corps, had been at the Mule Shoe on the morning of May 12 and had been overrun by the Federal attack. Only a few of their members had escaped death or capture and, at the time they joined Ramseur's brigade, the two regiments mustered about thirty men each.

About two weeks later, on May 27, Ramseur was promoted to Major General and assigned to command a division; Colonel William R. Cox of the 2nd Regiment N.C. Troops was then promoted to brigadier general and assigned to command Ramseur's former brigade. Thus the 30th Regiment was now a part of Cox's brigade of Rodes's division of Ewell's 2nd Corps.

After several more unsuccessful attempts at the Confederate line, Grant began quietly shifting his army eastward, and Lee, suspecting that the Federals were once more attempting to flank him on the right, ordered Ewell to launch a probing attack and attempt to discover the enemy's intentions. With Cox's brigade leading, Ewell's corps moved out of the entrenchments on May 19 and found itself engaged in battle with the rear guard of the Federal army. The Confederate attack was repulsed, and, as Federal reinforcements came up, the enemy began to press Ewell's men. Night brought an end to the fighting, and the Confederates retired to their lines.

Lee then moved his army to the North Anna River to a point just north of Hanover Junction, where he once again blocked the Federal route of advance. Fighting broke out at the North Anna on May 24-25, but the 2nd Corps, under the command of General Jubal Early following the disabling of Ewell at Spotsylvania, was not engaged.

Grant began moving eastward on the night of May 26-27, and Lee quickly followed. On May 27 Early's corps marched some twenty-four miles and entrenched between Beaver Dam Creek and Pole Green Church. Longstreet's corps, temporarily commanded by General Richard H. Anderson, came up on Early's right, and Hill's corps extended the left of Early's line. On May 30, under orders from Lee, Early moved to attack the Federal left at Bethesda Church. The attack failed to turn the Federal left but revealed that the enemy was once again moving to the Confederate right.

The two armies began concentrating at Cold Harbor, where new fighting broke out on June 1. An attack by Early's corps, with Rodes's division in the lead, achieved initial success on June 2 but was then driven back by Federal reinforcements. On June 3 Grant launched a massive and murderously unsuccessful assault against the six-mile-long Confederate position. During the battle the Federals lost around 7,000 men killed and wounded in considerably less time than an hour. Early's corps, on the left of the line at Cold Harbor, remained in its position until June 12, when it was dispatched to Lynchburg to defend that city against an anticipated attack by troops under General David Hunter.

Early's troops, including the 30th Regiment (which was still in Cox's brigade of Rodes's division), began arriving at Lynchburg on June 17, and by the next day the entire command was there. Hunter retired after a brief skirmish, and Early, after attempting unsuccessfully to overtake the retreating Federals, proceeded into the Shenandoah Valley. On July 6 Early's command crossed into Maryland and advanced on Washington, D.C. At the Battle of the Monocacy River on July 9 Rodes's division operated on the Baltimore road while the main fighting occurred on the Washington road to the division's right. Driving the Federals before them, Early's troops, with

Rodes's division in the vanguard, moved toward Washington, which they reached on July 11. After finding the defenses heavily manned on the morning of July 12, Early called off a planned assault, and that night he began to retire toward Virginia. Early's men were engaged at Snicker's Gap on July 18, at Stephenson's Depot on July 20, and at Kernstown on July 24; Early then fell back to Martinsburg.

In August, 1864, the Federals began concentrating a large force at Harpers Ferry under General Phil Sheridan with the intention of driving the Confederates out of the Shenandoah Valley once and for all. On August 10 Early, aware of the decisive numerical inferiority of his command, began a series of maneuvers designed to create the impression that his force was a match for that of the enemy. Early's men were northeast of Winchester when Sheridan began to move. On September 19 contact was made between the two armies, and Early concentrated his force to receive the Federal attack. During the initial stages of the battle General Rodes was killed as he deployed his division between those of Ramseur and John B. Gordon. The three divisions held their positions against repeated assaults, and only when their left flank appeared to be turned did they begin to retire to a defensive line close to Winchester. Again the Federals assaulted the center and left of the Confederate line. Word of a Federal column turning the right flank then caused Early to issue orders for a general withdrawal; however, upon finding that the troops moving on the right were his own men adjusting the alignment, Early tried to countermand the order. It was too late. The troops continued to the rear through Winchester and rallied south of the town. From there they retired to Fisher's Hill, near Strasburg.

At Fisher's Hill General Ramseur was placed in command of Rodes's division, and General John Pegram was assigned to command Ramseur's old division. On September 22 Sheridan struck Early's left and center at Fisher's Hill and forced a general retreat. Early regrouped at Waynesboro on September 28. There he received reinforcements and again began moving down the Valley. On October 7 his troops occupied New Market. After moving to Fisher's Hill on October 12-13, Early found the enemy on the north bank of Cedar Creek. On October 19 Early launched a surprise attack on the Federal camp and succeeded in driving the Federals from two defensive lines; but, believing the enemy was beaten and would abandon the field, Early then assumed the defensive. Sheridan took advantage of this respite to rally his troops; he then launched a devastating counterattack that routed Early's army. General Ramseur was wounded mortally and captured while attempting to rally his men.

The 2nd Corps regrouped at New Market after the Cedar Creek disaster and went into camp. General Bryan Grimes, as senior brigadier, was assigned to command Ramseur's division; thus the 30th Regiment was a part of Cox's brigade of Grimes's division of Early's corps. Except for minor skirmishing and the repulse of a Federal cavalry force on November 22, the army remained inactive.

Early in December, 1864, the 2nd Corps was ordered to return to Richmond and rejoin the Army of Northern Virginia. Gordon's and Pegram's divisions moved on December 6, and Grimes's followed a few days later. Cox's brigade arrived on December 16 and went into winter quarters with the division at Swift Creek, about three miles north of Petersburg.

The division remained at Swift Creek until February 17, 1865, when three of its brigades were moved to Sutherland's Depot on the right of the Confederate line.

Cox's brigade covered the division front at Swift Creek during the transfer and then rejoined the division at Sutherland's Depot. In mid-March the division was ordered into the trenches in front of Petersburg. There it remained until the night of March 24 when the 2nd Corps, then under the command of General Gordon, was massed for an assault on Fort Stedman, a key Federal fortification whose capture would help relieve the intensifying pressure on the Richmond-Petersburg defenses. Early on the morning of March 25 Gordon launched an assault which, after some initial success, was shattered by a Federal counterattack. Many Confederate units were cut off or forced to retreat over open ground raked by Federal artillery. Casualties were severe, and many prisoners were taken by the enemy.

The remnants of the 30th Regiment returned to the trenches with the rest of Grimes's division and occupied a portion of the line near Fort Mahone. On April 2, 1865, General Grant, following up on a major victory at Five Forks the previous day that rendered Lee's position at Richmond untenable, launched a massive attack. Grimes's division lost and then reoccupied its trenches, but other portions of the line were overrun and, on the evening of April 2, Lee ordered the evacuation of the Richmond-Petersburg fortifications and a retreat to the west.

The Army of Northern Virginia, reduced to a shadow of its former self, began its withdrawal that night, and the 2nd Corps, still commanded by Gordon, acted as rear guard as the men marched toward Amelia Court House. The army camped near Amelia Court House on the night of April 4; the retreat resumed the next day and continued through the night of April 5-6. As the rear guard, Gordon's corps was subjected to attacks by Federal cavalry and infantry. At a crossing of Sayler's Creek on April 6, Gordon's men made a stand and repulsed an assault on their front. To the south of Gordon's position, Confederate units under Generals Richard S. Ewell and Richard H. Anderson were defeated and captured. The Federals then moved against Gordon's right and broke his line, but Gordon's men rallied west of the creek and rejoined the army. At Farmville on April 7 Gordon's corps went to the relief of General Mahone's division. The Federal attackers were held, and the army continued its retreat.

On the night of April 7-8 Gordon's corps moved to the advance of the army. Its lead elements reached Appomattox Court House in the late afternoon of April 8 and halted. Later that evening Gordon's men discovered Federal cavalry in their front, and it was decided that an attack should be made the next day to cut through the enemy. Gordon's men moved into position west of the town during the night. At 5:00 A.M. the advance began, and the Federal cavalry was driven from the crossroads. The Confederates then took up a defensive position and came under attack by Federal infantry and cavalry. Gordon held his line until word came of a truce. A cease-fire was arranged, and Gordon began to withdraw; however, Cox's brigade did not receive the cease-fire order, and as the men fell back they turned and fired on an advancing Federal cavalry force. These shots were, according to some reports, the last fired by the Army of Northern Virginia. Colonel Francis M. Parker of the 30th Regiment N.C. Troops claimed later that the last shots were fired by Company D of his regiment.

The Army of Northern Virginia surrendered on April 9, 1865; on April 12, 153 members of the 30th Regiment N.C. Troops were paroled.

FIELD AND STAFF
COLONEL

PARKER, FRANCIS MARION
Previously served as Captain of Company I, 1st Regiment N.C. Infantry (6 months, 1861). Elected Colonel of this regiment on October 7, 1861. Wounded in the head at Sharpsburg, Maryland, September 17, 1862. Returned to duty on an unspecified date. Wounded in the face at Gettysburg, Pennsylvania, July 1, 1863. Returned to duty on May 4, 1864. Wounded in the abdomen at Spotsylvania Court House, Virginia, May 19, 1864. Retired to the Invalid Corps on January 17, 1865, by reason of disability from wounds.

LIEUTENANT COLONELS

DRAUGHAN, WALTER F.
Resided in Cumberland County and enlisted at age 40. Appointed Lieutenant Colonel on September 26, 1861. Defeated for reelection when the regiment was reorganized on May 1, 1862.

KELL, JAMES T.
Previously served as Captain of Company K of this regiment. Elected Major on September 26, 1861, and transferred to the Field and Staff. Promoted to Lieutenant Colonel on May 1, 1862. Wounded in the hand, leg, and side at Gaines' Mill, Virginia, June 27, 1862. Resigned on August 18, 1863, by reason of disability from wounds. Resignation accepted on or about September 1, 1863.

SILLERS, WILLIAM W.
Previously served as 1st Lieutenant of Company A of this regiment. Elected Major on May 1, 1862, and transferred to the Field and Staff. Wounded in the arm at Malvern Hill, Virginia, July 1, 1862. Returned to duty on an unspecified date. Promoted to Lieutenant Colonel on or about September 3, 1863. Wounded at Kelly's Ford, Virginia, November 7, 1863. Died at Gordonsville, Virginia, on November 9, 1863, of wounds.

MAJOR

HOLMES, JAMES C.
Previously served as Captain of Company A of this regiment. Appointed Major on September 3, 1863, and transferred to the Field and Staff. Medical records dated April 26, 1864, indicate he was "unfit for duty in the field on account of partial paralysis on the left side, principally affecting the arm, and chronic diarrhoea and general debility." Retired to the Invalid Corps on August 19. 1864.

ADJUTANTS

CARTER, ROBERT M.
Resided in Davidson County and enlisted at age 23. Appointed Adjutant (1st Lieutenant) on February 25, 1862, to rank from October 16, 1861. "Retired" when the regiment was reorganized on May 1, 1862.

PHILLIPS, FREDERICK
Previously served as 2nd Lieutenant of Company I, 15th Regiment N.C. Troops (5th Regiment N.C. Volunteers). Appointed Adjutant on June 5, 1862. Wounded in the head at Sharpsburg, Maryland,

September 17, 1862. Returned to duty on an unspecified date. Wounded in the left thigh at Kelly's Ford, Virginia, November 7, 1863. Appointed Assistant Quartermaster (Captain) of this regiment on March 12, 1864, to rank from January 22, 1864. [See Assistant Quartermasters' section below.]

ARRINGTON, PETER W.

Previously served as Sergeant Major of this regiment. [See Sergeants Major's section below.] Appointed Adjutant (1st Lieutenant) to rank from April 2, 1864. Captured at or near Spotsylvania Court House, Virginia, May 10-12, 1864. Confined at Fort Delaware, Delaware. Released on June 16, 1865, after taking the Oath of Allegiance.

ASSISTANT QUARTERMASTERS

WILLIAMS, BUCKNER D.

Previously served as 1st Lieutenant of Company B of this regiment. Appointed Assistant Quartermaster (Captain) on September 26, 1861, and transferred to the Field and Staff. Promoted to Brigade Quartermaster on or about November 20, 1863, and transferred.

PHILLIPS, FREDERICK

Previously served as Adjutant of this regiment. [See Adjutants' section above.] Appointed Assistant Quartermaster (Captain) on March 12, 1864, to rank from January 22, 1864 "Vacated" his position on an unspecified date by reason of "nonconfirmation." Appointed Assistant Quartermaster (Captain) on March 15, 1865, to rank from March 8, 1865, and assigned to duty with Cox's brigade.

ASSISTANT COMMISSARY OF SUBSISTENCE

COLLINS, JOHN

Previously served as Private in Company B of this regiment. Appointed Assistant Commissary of Subsistence (Captain) on or about August 25, 1861, and transferred to the Field and Staff. Dropped from the rolls of the regiment on or about August 2, 1862, because "his official bond [had not] been filed." Returned to duty on or about February 10, 1863. Dropped from the rolls of the regiment on an unspecified date in 1863 after his office was abolished by an act of the Confederate Congress. "He is a most faithful officer in the discharge of his many duties, has served his regiment well, and has given general satisfaction."

SURGEONS

JOYNER, HENRY

Resided in Halifax County and enlisted at age 36. Appointed Surgeon on or about October 21, 1861. Resigned on May 1, 1862. [Served in the North Carolina House of Commons during 1862-1865.]

GARRETT, FRANCIS M.

Resided in Halifax County and enlisted at age 37. Appointed Surgeon on September 26, 1862, to rank from July 10, 1862. Resigned on April 1, 1863, by reason of disability.

BRIGGS, GEORGE W.

Previously served as Surgeon of the 15th Regiment Alabama Infantry and of the 44th Regiment Virginia Infantry. Appointed Surgeon of this regiment on or about April 1, 1863. Present or accounted for until he surrendered at Appomattox Court House, Virginia,

April 9, 1865.

ASSISTANT SURGEONS

DRAKE, N. T.

Appointed Assistant Surgeon on October 27, 1861. Resigned on January 13, 1862. Reason he resigned not reported.

GREGORY, CHARLES G.

Previously served as Private in Company I, 1st Regiment N.C. Infantry (6 months, 1861). Appointed Assistant Surgeon of this regiment on February 17, 1862, to rank from January 20, 1862. Resigned on December 31, 1863. Reason he resigned not reported.

LAWSON, JOHN M.

Resided in Virginia and enlisted at age 27. Appointed Assistant Surgeon on June 1, 1863. No further records.

COKE, LUCIUS C.

Previously served as Assistant Surgeon of the 1st Regiment N.C. State Troops. Assigned to temporary duty as Assistant Surgeon of this regiment in August, 1864. Permanently transferred to this regiment in February, 1865. Surrendered at Appomattox Court House, Virginia, April 9, 1865.

CHAPLAIN

BETTS, ALEXANDER DAVIS

Resided in Harnett County and enlisted at age 31. Appointed Chaplain on October 26, 1861. Present or accounted for through January 20, 1865. "Very attentive to his duties."

SERGEANTS MAJOR

WHITE, LALLISTER M.

Previously served as Private in Company A of this regiment. Promoted to Sergeant Major on October 10, 1861, and transferred to the Field and Staff. Elected 3rd Lieutenant on May 1, 1862, and transferred back to Company A.

LAWHON, ARCHIBALD FRANCIS

Previously served as Sergeant in Company A of this regiment. Promoted to Sergeant Major on or about May 1, 1862, and transferred to the Field and Staff. Appointed 2nd Lieutenant on or about March 12, 1863, and transferred to Company F, 20th Regiment N.C. Troops (10th Regiment N.C. Volunteers).

ARRINGTON, PETER W.

Previously served as Corporal in Company I of this regiment. Promoted to Sergeant Major in June, 1863-March, 1864, and transferred to the Field and Staff. Appointed Adjutant (1st Lieutenant) of this regiment to rank from April 2, 1864. [See Adjutants' section above.]

FITTS, FRANCIS MICHAEL

Previously served as Private in Company B of this regiment. Promoted to Sergeant Major in January-July, 1864, and transferred to the Field and Staff. Wounded in the head and left side at Snicker's Gap, Virginia, July 18, 1864. Returned to duty on September 14, 1864. Hospitalized at Richmond, Virginia, October 23, 1864, with a gunshot wound of the arm. Place and date wounded not reported. Furloughed on October 29,

1864. Returned to duty on an unspecified date. Surrendered at Appomattox Court House, Virginia, April 9, 1865.

QUARTERMASTER SERGEANT

STALLINGS, THEOPHILUS

Previously served as Private in Company B of this regiment. Promoted to Quartermaster Sergeant on Ocotber 16, 1861, and transferred to the Field and Staff. Present or accounted for until he surrendered at Appomattox Court House, Virginia, April 9, 1865.

COMMISSARY SERGEANTS

DAVIS, ALEXANDER L.

Previously served as Sergeant in Company D of this regiment. Promoted to Commissary Sergeant in January-March, 1862, and transferred to the Field and Staff. Discharged on April 20, 1862, by reason of "rheumatism, general debility and the los[s] of the use of the right arm."

SMITH, LEMUEL H.

Previously served as Sergeant in Company F of this regiment. Promoted to Commissary Sergeant on or about July 20, 1863, and transferred to the Field and Staff. Present or accounted for through August, 1864.

ORDNANCE SERGEANT

ELLIS, JOHN W.

Previously served as Private in Company E of this regiment. Promoted to Ordnance Sergeant on October 17, 1861, and transferred to the Field and Staff. Elected 3rd Lieutenant on February 27, 1863, and transferred back to Company E.

HOSPITAL STEWARD

LAWRENCE, JOHN J.

Previously served as Private in Company F of this regiment. Promoted to Hospital Steward on November 10, 1863, and transferred to the Field and Staff. Hospitalized at Farmville, Virginia, April 7, 1865, with chronic rheumatism. Captured in hospital at Farmville on an unspecified date. Released on or about June 15, 1865.

COMPANY A

This company, known as the "Sampson Rangers," was raised in Sampson County and enlisted on April 20, 1861. The company was mustered into state service on June 18, 1861, and assigned to the 20th Regiment N.C. Troops (10th Regiment N.C. Volunteers); however, as that unit was composed of eleven companies, one more than the officially permissible number, the "Sampson Rangers" was reassigned to the 30th Regiment N.C. Troops. The company was mustered into the 30th Regiment on October 8, 1861, and was designated Company A. After joining the regiment the company functioned as a part of the regiment, and its history for the war period is reported as a part of the regimental history.

The information contained in the following roster of the company was compiled principally from a company muster-in and descriptive roll dated October 8, 1861, and from company muster rolls for April 20, 1861-April, 1862;

November-December, 1862; May-August, 1863; and November, 1863-August, 1864. No company muster rolls were found for May-October, 1862; January-April, 1863; September-October, 1863; or for the period after August, 1864. Valuable information was obtained from primary records such as the Roll of Honor, discharge certificates, medical records, prisoner of war records, and pension applications. Secondary sources such as postwar rosters and histories, cemetery records, and records of the United Daughters of the Confederacy also provided useful information.

OFFICERS

CAPTAINS

FAISON, FRANKLIN J.

Born in Sampson County where he resided as a farmer prior to enlisting in Sampson County at age 36. Appointed Captain on or about April 20, 1861. Elected Lieutenant Colonel of the 20th Regiment N.C. Troops (10th Regiment N.C. Volunteers) on June 18, 1861, and transferred to the Field and Staff of that regiment.

HOLMES, JAMES C.

Born in Sampson County where he resided as a farmer prior to enlisting in Sampson County at age 35. Elected 2nd Lieutenant on or about April 20, 1861. Elected Captain on August 3, 1861. Present or accounted for until appointed Major on September 3, 1863, and transferred to the Field and Staff of this regiment.

WILLIAMS, GARY F.

Born in Sampson County where he resided as a farmer prior to enlisting at age 20, April 20, 1861. Mustered in as Corporal. Promoted to 1st Sergeant on August 3, 1861. Elected 1st Lieutenant on May 1, 1862. Promoted to Captain on September 3, 1863. Captured at or near Spotsylvania Court House, Virginia, May 10-12, 1864. Confined at Fort Delaware, Delaware. Released on June 8, 1865, after taking the Oath of Allegiance.

LIEUTENANTS

BLALOCK, WILLIAM A., 2nd Lieutenant

Records of Company E, 31st Regiment N.C. Troops, indicate he was appointed 2nd Lieutenant and transferred to this company in March, 1863; however, records of the 30th Regiment do not indicate that he served herein.

MARSH, GEORGE WASHINGTON, 3rd Lieutenant

Born in Cumberland County and resided in Sampson County where he was by occupation a merchant prior to enlisting in Sampson County at age 32. Appointed 3rd Lieutenant of this company on or about April 20, 1861. Promoted to 1st Lieutenant and transferred to Company A, 61st Regiment N.C. Troops, on or about June 26, 1861.

MOSELEY, ROBERT A., 1st Lieutenant

Born in Sampson County and was by occupation a merchant prior to enlisting in Sampson County at age 28. Appointed 1st Lieutenant on April 20, 1861. No further records.

PATRICK, CORNELIUS, 2nd Lieutenant

Born in Putnam County, New York, and resided in Sampson County where he was by occupation a merchant prior to enlisting at age 24, April 20, 1861. Mustered in as Private. Elected 2nd Lieutenant on August 3, 1861. Present or accounted for until he was defeated for reelection when the regiment was reorganized on May 1, 1862.

SILLERS, WILLIAM W., 1st Lieutenant
Born in Sampson County where he resided as a farmer prior to enlisting in Sampson County at age 22, April 20, 1861. Mustered in as Private. Elected 1st Lieutenant on August 3, 1861. Present or accounted for until elected Major on May 1, 1862, and transferred to the Field and Staff of this regiment. Later served as Lieutenant Colonel of this regiment.

STEVENS, CHARLES T., 2nd Lieutenant
Born in Sampson County where he resided as a farmer prior to enlisting in Sampson County at age 31, April 20, 1861. Mustered in as Corporal. Elected 3rd Lieutenant on August 3, 1861. Elected 2nd Lieutenant on May 1, 1862. "Accidentally shot himself in the foot" on January 18, 1863. Reported on duty as Enrolling Officer of Sampson County during November-December, 1863. Reported on duty as Enrolling Officer of Duplin County during January-August, 1864. No further records.

WHITE, LALLISTER M., 1st Lieutenant
Born in Sampson County where he resided as a farmer prior to enlisting in Sampson County at age 28, April 20, 1861. Mustered in as Private. Promoted to Sergeant Major on October 10, 1861, and transferred to the Field and Staff of this regiment. Elected 3rd Lieutenant and transferred back to this company on May 1, 1862. Promoted to 1st Lieutenant on September 3, 1863. Killed at or near Spotsylvania Court House, Virginia, May 12, 1864.

NONCOMMISSIONED OFFICERS AND PRIVATES

ALLMAN, GIDEON, Private
Resided in Cabarrus County where he enlisted at age 44, September 22, 1863, for the war. Captured near Spotsylvania Court House, Virginia, May 12, 1864. Confined at Point Lookout, Maryland, May 18, 1864. Transferred to Elmira, New York, August 10, 1864. Released at Elmira on June 12, 1865, after taking the Oath of Allegiance.

ALSBROOK, S. C., Private
Resided in Halifax County where he enlisted at age 33, June 24, 1863, for the war. Captured at Kelly's Ford, Virginia, November 7, 1863. Confined at Point Lookout, Maryland, November 11, 1863. Died at Point Lookout on February 8, 1864, of "chr[onic] dysentery."

ARMSTRONG, JOHN O., Private
Born in Sampson County and was by occupation a trader prior to enlisting in Brunswick County at age 24, June 1, 1861. No further records.

AUTRY, WILLIAM, Private
Born in Sampson County where he resided as a farmer prior to enlisting at age 21, September 1, 1861. Captured and paroled at Warrenton, Virginia, September 29, 1862. Died in hospital at Gordonsville, Virginia, December 18, 1862, of "pneumonia."

BAGGOT, JAMES W., Private
Born in Sampson County where he resided prior to

enlisting in Sampson County at age 17, September 1, 1861. Present or accounted for until killed at Malvern Hill, Virginia, July 1, 1862.

BASS, WILLIAM E., Corporal
Resided in Duplin County and enlisted in Sampson County at age 24, April 20, 1861. Mustered in as Private. Promoted to Corporal in January-June, 1863. Captured at or near Spotsylvania Court House, Virginia, on or about May 8, 1864. Confined at Point Lookout, Maryland, May 17, 1864. Transferred to Elmira, New York, August 10, 1864. Released at Elmira on May 29, 1865, after taking the Oath of Allegiance.

BELL, ROBERT, Private
Resided in New Hanover County and enlisted at Camp Holmes at age 37, July 28, 1863, for the war. Captured near Spotsylvania Court House, Virginia, May 12, 1864. Confined at Point Lookout, Maryland, May 18, 1864. Transferred to Elmira, New York, August 10, 1864. Paroled at Elmira on October 11, 1864. Received at Venus Point, Savannah River, Georgia, November 15, 1864, for exchange.

BENTON, BRADLEY C., Private
Born in Baker County, Georgia, and resided in Sampson County where he was by occupation a farmer prior to enlisting at age 25, April 20, 1861. Reported absent wounded in November-December, 1862. Place and date wounded not reported. Discharged on or about July 11, 1863, by reason of "paraplegia."

BIZZELL, AGIFFE, ———
North Carolina pension records indicate that he served in this company.

BOON, STEPHEN, Corporal
Resided in Sampson County and enlisted in New Hanover County at age 28, April 14, 1862. Mustered in as Private. Wounded and captured at Malvern Hill, Virginia, July 1, 1862. Paroled and transferred to Aiken's Landing, James River, Virginia, where he was received on July 16, 1862, for exchange. Declared exchanged at Aiken's Landing on August 5, 1862. Returned to duty prior to January 1, 1863. Promoted to Corporal in January-June, 1863. Captured at Spotsylvania Court House, Virginia, May 12, 1864. Confined at Point Lookout, Maryland, May 18, 1864. Transferred to Elmira, New York, August 10, 1864. Released on May 29, 1865, after taking the Oath of Allegiance. [May have served previously in 1st Company D, 12th Regiment N.C. Troops (2nd Regiment N.C. Volunteers).]

BOON, SYLVESTER, Private
Born in Sampson County where he resided as a farmer prior to enlisting in Sampson County at age 20, April 20, 1861. Hospitalized at Wilmington on or about May 4, 1862, with catarrhus. Returned to duty on May 5, 1862. No further records.

BOONE, NICHOLAS, Private
Resided in Sampson County and enlisted at age 20, September 1, 1861. Captured at Spotsylvania Court House, Virginia, May 12, 1864. Confined at Point Lookout, Maryland, May 18, 1864. Transferred to Elmira, New York, August 10, 1864. Released on June 30, 1865, after taking the Oath of Allegiance.

BOSWELL, WILLIAM H., Private

Born in Bertie County where he resided prior to enlisting in Halifax County at age 50, June 24, 1863, for the war as a substitute. Present or accounted for until killed at Kelly's Ford, Virginia, November 7, 1863.

BRADSHAW, OWEN K., Private

Resided in Sampson County where he enlisted at age 27, September 1, 1861. Deserted on April 26, 1862. Returned to duty on an unspecified date. Deserted on August 25, 1862. Arrested and was confined at Clinton but "broke jail" prior to July 1, 1863. No further records.

BRADSHAW, ROBERT M., Private

Born in Sampson County where he resided as a farmer prior to enlisting in Sampson County at age 21, April 20, 1861. Present or accounted for until he died in hospital at Palmyra, Virginia, March 17, 1863, of "variola."

BRADSHAW, WILLIAM K., Private

Born in Sampson County where he resided prior to enlisting in Sampson County at age 22, September 1, 1861. Present or accounted for until he deserted on or about September 12, 1862. Returned to duty prior to January 1, 1863. Wounded at Chancellorsville, Virginia, May 3, 1863. Died on May 5, 1863, of wounds. Place of death not reported.

BREWER, ABRAHAM H., Corporal

Born in Sampson County where he resided as a farmer prior to enlisting in Sampson County at age 34, April 20, 1861. Mustered in as Private. Wounded in the left hand and captured at or near Gettysburg, Pennsylvania, on or about July 3-4, 1863. Sent to Fort McHenry, Maryland. Confined at Fort Delaware, Delaware, July 7-12, 1863. Transferred to Point Lookout, Maryland, October 15-18, 1863. Paroled at Point Lookout and transferred to City Point, Virginia, where he was received on March 6, 1864, for exchange. Returned to duty and was promoted to Corporal subsequent to August 31, 1864. Surrendered at Appomattox Court House, Virginia, April 9, 1865.

BRIDGES, JOSEPH, Private

Resided in Halifax County and enlisted in Franklin County at age 52, June 11, 1863, for the war as a substitute. Present or accounted for until he was paroled at Lynchburg, Virginia, in April, 1865.

BROWN, GEORGE E., Private

Born in Sampson County where he resided as a farmer prior to enlisting at age 23, May 17, 1862, for the war. Wounded at Malvern Hill, Virginia, July 1, 1862. Returned to duty prior to September 17, 1862, when he was killed at Sharpsburg, Maryland.

BUNTING, THOMAS OWEN, Corporal

Born in Sampson County where he resided as a student prior to enlisting in Sampson County at age 15, April 20, 1861. Mustered in as Corporal. "Withdrew" in July, 1861. Later served in Company C, 63rd Regiment N.C. Troops (5th Regiment N.C. Cavalry).

BURKHARDT, FRED, Private

Resided in Sampson County and was by occupation a laborer prior to enlisting at age 27, April 20, 1861. Present or accounted for through January 21, 1863. No further records.

BUTLER, EDWARD N., Private

Resided in Sampson County and enlisted at Camp Wyatt at age 18, January 1, 1862. Wounded in both thighs at Chancellorsville, Virginia, May 3-4, 1863. Reported absent wounded through August, 1864. Paroled at Burkeville Junction, Virginia, April 14-17, 1865.

BUTLER, GEORGE C., Private

Born in Sampson County where he resided as a farmer prior to enlisting in Sampson County at age 19, April 20, 1861. Present or accounted for until November-December, 1862, when he was reported absent without leave. Reported absent on sick furlough from March 22, 1863, through August 31, 1864.

BUTLER, HARTWELL, Private

Resided in Sampson County where he enlisted at age 20, September 1, 1861. Present or accounted for until November-December, 1862, when he was reported absent without leave. Returned to duty in July-August, 1863. Captured at Kelly's Ford, Virginia, November 7, 1863. Confined at Point Lookout, Maryland. Exchanged on September 30, 1864.

BUTLER, JAMES R., Private

Resided in Sampson County and enlisted at age 17, September 1, 1861. Died at Lynchburg, Virginia, January 2, 1863. Cause of death not reported.

BUTLER, JOSEPH, Private

Resided in Sampson County where he enlisted at age 27, September 1, 1861. Wounded in the left leg at or near Spotsylvania Court House, Virginia, on or about May 8-9, 1864. Left leg amputated. Died in a field hospital near Spotsylvania Court House on May 9, 1864, of wounds.

BUTLER, RAIFORD D., Private

Resided in Sampson County where he enlisted at age 16, September 1, 1861. Captured near Spotsylvania Court House, Virginia, May 12, 1864. Confined at Point Lookout, Maryland, May 18, 1864. Transferred to Elmira, New York, August 10, 1864. Released at Elmira on June 30, 1865, after taking the Oath of Allegiance.

CLARKSON, THOMAS M., Musician

Born on the "Rock of Gibraltar" and resided in Sampson County where he was by occupation a painter prior to enlisting in Sampson County at age 49, April 20, 1861. Mustered in as Musician (Drummer). Present or accounted for until wounded at Sharpsburg, Maryland, September 17, 1862. Reported absent wounded or absent sick through December, 1862. Detailed for light duty on March 24, 1863. Company records do not indicate that he rejoined the company. Paroled at Greensboro on May 1, 1865.

CLARKSON, THOMAS N., Private

Born in Sampson County where he resided as a painter prior to enlisting in Sampson County at age 22, September 1, 1861. Present or accounted for until he died in hospital at Mount Jackson, Virginia, November 14, 1862, of "pneumonia."

COBB, OBED B., Private

Born in Sampson County where he resided as a farmer prior to enlisting in Sampson County at age 17, April 20,

1861. Present or accounted for until wounded at Kelly's Ford, Virginia, November 7, 1863. Reported absent wounded through December, 1863. Reported absent on detached service during January-August, 1864. Paroled at Raleigh on or about April 19, 1865.

COX, ROBERT GASTON, Private
Born in Sampson County where he resided as a student prior to enlisting in Sampson County at age 16, June 12, 1861. Present or accounted for until wounded in the head at Malvern Hill, Virginia, July 1, 1862. Returned to duty on an unspecified date. Wounded in the left thigh at Winchester, Virginia, September 19, 1864. Captured at Harrisonburg, Virginia, September 25, 1864. Hospitalized at Baltimore, Maryland. Confined at Point Lookout, Maryland, October 29, 1864. Paroled and transferred to Venus Point, Savannah River, Georgia, where he was received on November 15, 1864, for exchange. Captured in hospital at Richmond, Virginia, April 3, 1865. Paroled on April 18, 1865.

CRUMPLER, JAMES M., Corporal
Born in Sampson County where he resided as a farmer prior to enlisting in Sampson County at age 20, April 20, 1861. Mustered in as Private. Promoted to Corporal in May-December, 1862. Wounded in the jaw at Chancellorsville, Virginia, May 3, 1863. Returned to duty in January-August, 1864. Captured at Burkeville, Virginia, or at Farmville, Virginia, April 6, 1865. Confined at Newport News, Virginia, April 14, 1865. Released on June 14, 1865, after taking the Oath of Allegiance.

CRUMPLER, ROBERT MATHEW, Sr., 1st Sergeant
Resided in Sampson County where he enlisted at age 20, September 1, 1861. Mustered in as Private. Promoted to 1st Sergeant on May 1, 1862. Wounded in the thigh at Gaines' Mill, Virginia, June 27, 1862. Returned to duty prior to January 1, 1863. Wounded at Chancellorsville, Virginia, May 3, 1863. Returned to duty subsequent to August 31, 1863. Wounded at Kelly's Ford, Virginia, November 7, 1863. Returned to duty on an unspecified date. Wounded on July 12, 1864. Returned to duty subsequent to August 31, 1864. Surrendered at Appomattox Court House, Virginia, April 9, 1865. [North Carolina pension records indicate he was wounded at Mechanicsville, Virginia, and at Washington, D.C., on unspecified dates.]

CURRIE, JOHN BETHUNE, Private
Born in Moore County and resided in Sampson County where he was by occupation a trader prior to enlisting in Sampson County at age 22, April 20, 1861. Present or accounted for until he surrendered at Appomattox Court House, Virginia, April 9, 1865.

DIXON, J. M., ———
North Carolina pension records indicate that he served in this company.

DOVE, MONROE, Private
Resided in Cabarrus County where he enlisted at age 42, September 12, 1863, for the war. Wounded in the left thigh at Kelly's Ford, Virginia, November 7, 1863. Reported absent on furlough or absent in hospital at Richmond, Virginia, through August 31, 1864. Captured in hospital at Richmond on April 3, 1865. Paroled on April 18, 1865.

DRAUGHON, GEORGE H., Corporal
Born in Sampson County or in Marlboro District, South Carolina, and resided in Sampson County where he was by occupation a student prior to enlisting in Sampson County at age 18, April 20, 1861. Mustered in as Private. Promoted to Corporal in March-December, 1862. Present or accounted for until he died at Clinton on December 26, 1862. Cause of death not reported.

DRAUGHON, MILES S., Sergeant
Born in Sampson County where he resided as a farmer prior to enlisting in Sampson County at age 21, April 20, 1861. Mustered in as Private. Promoted to Sergeant on August 3, 1861. Captured at Kelly's Ford, Virginia, November 7, 1863. Confined at Point Lookout, Maryland, November 11, 1863. Paroled at Point Lookout on or about February 13, 1865, and transferred to Cox's Wharf, James River, Virginia, where he was received on February 14-15, 1865, for exchange.

DRAUGHON, WILLIAM BRIGHT, Sergeant
Resided in Sampson County where he enlisted at age 21, April 20, 1861. Mustered in as Private. Promoted to Sergeant on August 3, 1861. Present or accounted for through May, 1862. Discharged on an unspecified date after providing a substitute.

DUDLEY, MICHAEL S., Private
Resided in Sampson County where he enlisted at age 20, September 1, 1861. Present or accounted for until he died at Wilmington on January 5 or January 15, 1862, of "typhoid fever."

DUDLEY, WILLIAM W., Private
Resided in Sampson County where he enlisted at age 18, September 1, 1861. Present or accounted for until July, 1862, when he was discharged. Reason discharged not reported. [May have served later in Captain George L. Giddins's N.C. Company (Detailed and Petitioned Men).]

DUNCAN, CHARLES W., Private
Born in Sampson County where he resided prior to enlisting in Sampson County at age 18, September 1, 1861. Present or accounted for until wounded at Chancellorsville, Virginia, May 3, 1863. Hospitalized at Richmond, Virginia, where he died on May 5, May 26, or May 29, 1863, of wounds.

DUNCAN, JAMES D., Private
Born in Sampson County where he resided as a mechanic prior to enlisting in Sampson County at age 21, April 20, 1861. Present or accounted for until captured at Kelly's Ford, Virginia, November 7, 1863. Confined at Point Lookout, Maryland, November 11, 1863. Paroled at Point Lookout on or about February 24, 1865, and transferred to Aiken's Landing, James River, Virginia, where he was received on February 25-March 3, 1865, for exchange.

DUNN, DAVID W., Private
Resided in Halifax County where he enlisted at age 41, June 24, 1863, for the war. Present or accounted for until he died in camp near Orange Court House, Virginia, April 5, 1864, of disease.

FAIRCLOTH, JOHN, Private
Resided in Sampson County where he enlisted at age 26, September 1, 1861. Present or accounted for until he

died in camp near Fredericksburg, Virginia, February 10, 1863, of "pneumonia."

FAIRCLOTH, JOHN L., Private
Resided in Sampson County where he enlisted at age 22, September 1, 1861. Present or accounted for until he died in hospital at Richmond, Virginia, January 15, 1863, of "smallpox" and/or "plueropneumonia."

FRIZELAND, JACOB, Private
Resided in Cabarrus County where he enlisted at age 41, September 12, 1863, for the war. Present or accounted for until wounded at Kelly's Ford, Virginia, November 7, 1863. Returned to duty on an unspecified date. Hospitalized at Richmond, Virginia, May 19, 1864, with a gunshot wound of the head. Place and date wounded not reported. Returned to duty prior to September 1, 1864. Captured at Burkeville, Virginia, April 6, 1865. Confined at Newport News, Virginia, April 14, 1865. Died in hospital at Newport News on June 14, 1865, of "diarrhoea chron[ic]."

GILBERT, WILLIS, Private
Born in Sampson County where he resided as a farmer prior to enlisting in Sampson County at age 21, September 1, 1861. Present or accounted for until he died in hospital at Lynchburg, Virginia, October 12, 1862, of "febris typhoides."

GODWIN, NATHAN H., Private
Resided in Sampson County where he enlisted at age 19, September 1, 1861. Present or accounted for until captured at Kelly's Ford, Virginia, November 7, 1863. Confined at Point Lookout, Maryland, November 11, 1863. Paroled at Point Lookout on or about February 24, 1865, and transferred to Aiken's Landing, James River, Virginia, where he was received on February 25-March 3, 1865, for exchange. [North Carolina pension records indicate he was wounded at "Malvern Hill, Virginia, June 25, 1862."]

GOODRICH, JAMES T., Private
Born in Sampson County where he resided prior to enlisting in Sampson County at age 18, September 1, 1861. Present or accounted for until killed at Gaines' Mill, Virginia, June 27, 1862.

HAGLER, JOHN, Private
Resided in Cabarrus County where he enlisted at age 44, September 12, 1863, for the war. Present or accounted for until he "died suddenly" on May 13, 1864. Place and cause of death not reported.

HALL, WILLIAM G., Private
Resided in Sampson County where he enlisted at age 21, May 22, 1861. Present or accounted for until captured at Kelly's Ford, Virginia, November 7, 1863. Confined at Point Lookout, Maryland, November 11, 1863. Paroled on or about October 30, 1864, and transferred to Venus Point, Savannah River, Georgia, where he was received on November 15, 1864, for exchange. Returned to duty on an unspecified date. Surrendered at Appomattox Court House, Virginia, April 9, 1865.

HERRING, TIMOTHY J., Corporal
Resided in Sampson County where he enlisted at age 23, September 1, 1861. Mustered in as Private. Promoted to Corporal in January-June, 1863. Present or accounted for until he was reportedly captured at or near

Spotsylvania Court House, Virginia, May 12, 1864. Records of the Federal Provost Marshal do not substantiate the report of his capture. No further records.

HOBBS, ABRAHAM, Private
Resided in Sampson County where he enlisted at age 25, April 20, 1861. Mustered in as Private. Promoted to Corporal on August 3, 1861. Promoted to Sergeant in May-December, 1862. Present or accounted for until wounded at Sharpsburg, Maryland, September 17, 1862. Returned to duty in January-June, 1863. Reduced to ranks in July-August, 1863. Present or accounted for through August, 1864.

HOBBS, JUDSON, Sergeant
Resided in Sampson County where he enlisted at age 17, April 20, 1861. Mustered in as Private. Promoted to Sergeant on June 1, 1864. Captured at Winchester, Virginia, October 19, 1864. Confined at Point Lookout, Maryland, October 25, 1864. Released on June 27, 1865, after taking the Oath of Allegiance. [North Carolina pension records indicate he was wounded at Martinsburg, West Virginia, "in 1862 and 1863."]

HOLLAND, JAMES F., Musician
Resided in Sampson County where he enlisted at age 19, September 1, 1861. Mustered in as Private and was promoted to Musician (Fifer) in March-April, 1862. Present or accounted for until he surrendered at Appomattox Court House, Virginia, April 9, 1865. [North Carolina pension records indicate he was wounded at Fort Caswell on September 15, 1861.]

HOLLAND, JOHN R., Private
Resided in Sampson County where he enlisted at age 21, September 1, 1861. Present or accounted for until hospitalized at Richmond, Virginia, October 3, 1862, with a wound of the head. Place and date wounded not reported. Returned to duty on an unspecified date. Killed at Chancellorsville, Virginia, May 3, 1863. Nominated for the Badge of Distinction for gallantry at Chancellorsville.

HOLMES, MILTON, ———
North Carolina pension records indicate that he served in this company.

HOLSHOUSER, AMBROSE N., Private
Resided in Cabarrus County where he enlisted at age 41, September 12, 1863, for the war. Captured at Kelly's Ford, Virginia, November 7, 1863. Confined at Point Lookout, Maryland, November 11, 1863. Paroled at Point Lookout on or about February 24, 1865, and transferred to Aiken's Landing, James River, Virginia, where he was received on February 25-March 3, 1865, for exchange.

HONEYCUTT, MILES C., Private
Resided in Sampson County where he enlisted at age 23, September 1, 1861. Present or accounted for until captured at Fisher's Hill, Virginia, September 22, 1864. Confined at Washington, D.C., November 11, 1864. Transferred to Elmira, New York, February 3, 1865. Released on May 29, 1865, after taking the Oath of Allegiance.

HOWARD, FLEET HIRAM, Private
Resided in Sampson County where he enlisted at age 19,

September 1, 1861. Present or accounted for until wounded at Sharpsburg, Maryland, September 17, 1862. Returned to duty in January-June, 1863. Present or accounted for until captured near Spotsylvania Court House, Virginia, on or about May 12, 1864. Confined at Point Lookout, Maryland, May 18, 1864. Transferred to Elmira, New York, August 10, 1864. Paroled at Elmira on October 11, 1864, and transferred to Venus Point, Savannah River, Georgia, where he was received on November 15, 1864, for exchange.

HOWARD, JOSEPH C., Private
Resided in Sampson County where he enlisted at age 19, September 1, 1861. Present or accounted for until paroled at Farmville, Virginia, April 11-21, 1865.

HOWARD, THOMAS M., Sergeant
Resided in Sampson County where he enlisted at age 30, May 1, 1862, for the war. Mustered in as Private. Present or accounted for until wounded in the head at Malvern Hill, Virginia, July 1, 1862. Returned to duty prior to September 1, 1863. Promoted to Sergeant in September-December, 1863. Present or accounted for until killed at or near Spotsylvania Court House, Virginia, May 12, 1864.

HOWARD, WILLIAM S., Private
Resided in Sampson County where he enlisted at age 17, September 1, 1861. Present or accounted for until wounded in the right thigh and captured at Winchester, Virginia, September 19, 1864. Hospitalized at Frederick, Maryland, and at Baltimore, Maryland. Confined at Fort McHenry, Maryland, February 10, 1865. Transferred to Point Lookout, Maryland, February 20, 1865. Paroled and exchanged prior to February 25, 1865, when he was hospitalized at Richmond, Virginia. Furloughed for sixty days on March 6, 1865.

HUTCHINSON, ANDREW JACKSON, Private
Resided in Cabarrus County where he enlisted at age 45, September 12, 1863, for the war. Present or accounted for until captured at Spotsylvania Court House, Virginia, May 12, 1864. Confined at Point Lookout, Maryland, May 18, 1864. Transferred to Elmira, New York, where he arrived on August 14, 1864. Died at Elmira on or about February 28, 1865, of "variola."

INGRAM, WILLIAM W., Private
Born in Sampson County where he resided as a farmer prior to enlisting in Sampson County at age 31, April 20, 1861. Present or accounted for until discharged on July 16, 1862. Reason discharged not reported.

IVEY, W. L., Private
Resided in Halifax County where he enlisted at age 38, June 23, 1863, for the war. Present or accounted for until captured at Kelly's Ford, Virginia, November 7, 1863. Confined at Point Lookout, Maryland, November 11, 1863. Died at Point Lookout on January 26, 1865. Cause of death not reported.

JACKSON, JAMES W., Private
Born in Cumberland County and resided in Sampson County where he enlisted at age 20, September 1, 1861. Present or accounted for until he died in hospital at Richmond, Virginia, on or about December 26, 1862, of "anasarca."

JACKSON, MARTIN G. B., Private
Resided in Sampson County where he enlisted at age 22, September 1, 1861. Present or accounted for until captured near Spotsylvania Court House, Virginia, May 12, 1864. Confined at Point Lookout, Maryland, May 18, 1864. No further records.

JOHNSON, L. W., Private
Resided in Halifax County where he enlisted at age 36, June 23, 1863, for the war. Present or accounted for until captured at or near Spotsylvania Court House, Virginia, May 8-12, 1864. Confined at Point Lookout, Maryland, May 17, 1864. Paroled at Point Lookout on or about March 14, 1865, and transferred to Boulware's Wharf, James River, Virginia, where he was received on March 16, 1865, for exchange.

JOHNSON, WILLIAM H., Sergeant
Resided in Sampson County where he enlisted at age 22, April 20, 1861. Mustered in as Private. Promoted to Corporal in May-December, 1862. Present or accounted for until wounded at Malvern Hill, Virginia, July 1, 1862. Returned to duty prior to January 1, 1863. Promoted to Sergeant on June 1, 1863. Present or accounted for until captured near Spotsylvania Court House, Virginia, May 12, 1864. Confined at Point Lookout, Maryland, May 18, 1864. Transferred to Elmira, New York, August 10, 1864. Released at Elmira on June 19, 1865, after taking the Oath of Allegiance.

KELLY, CHESTER, Musician
Born in Sampson County where he resided as a mechanic prior to enlisting in Sampson County at age 18, April 20, 1861. Mustered in as Private. Promoted to Musician (Drummer) in January-June, 1863. Present or accounted for through August, 1864. Captured at Clinton on an unspecified date. Paroled at Raleigh on or about April 22, 1865.

KELLY, JAMES M., Private
Born in Sampson County where he resided as a farmer prior to enlisting in Sampson County at age 21, April 20, 1861. Present or accounted for until wounded at Chancellorsville, Virginia, May 3, 1863. Returned to duty in September-December, 1863. Reported absent wounded during January-August, 1864. Place and date wounded not reported. No further records.

KING, LEWIS D., Private
Born in Sampson County where he resided as a farmer prior to enlisting in Sampson County at age 21, April 20, 1861. Present or accounted for until wounded at or near Snicker's Gap, Virginia, on or about July 18, 1864. Reported absent wounded or absent on furlough through November 1, 1864. Returned to duty on an unspecified date. Surrendered at Appomattox Court House, Virginia, April 9, 1865. "Acted gallantly at Mine Run, [Virginia,] as a skirmisher."

KING, STEPHEN J., Private
Resided in Sampson County where he enlisted at age 24, September 1, 1861. Present or accounted for until hospitalized at Richmond, Virginia, June 3, 1864, with a gunshot wound of the right heel. Place and date wounded not reported. Reported absent wounded through August, 1864. Returned to duty on an unspecified date. Surrendered at Appomattox Court House, Virginia, April 9, 1865.

LAWHON, ARCHIBALD FRANCIS, Sergeant
Born in Moore County and resided in Sampson County where he enlisted at age 24, April 20, 1861. Mustered in as Private. Promoted to Sergeant on August 3, 1861. Promoted to Sergeant Major on or about May 1, 1862, and transferred to the Field and Staff of this regiment.

LEE, THOMAS J., Private
Born in Sampson County and was by occupation a merchant prior to enlisting in Sampson County at age 24, April 20, 1861. Discharged on December 26, 1861, by reason of disability.

LEE, WILLIS, Private
Resided in Harnett County and enlisted in Sampson County at age 20, September 1, 1861. Present or accounted for until he deserted on or about September 20, 1862. Apprehended on or about February 26, 1864, and was sent to Camp Holmes. Deserted again on an unspecified date.

LEWIS, ARCHIBALD A., Private
Born in Sampson County where he resided as a mechanic prior to enlisting in Sampson County at age 22, April 20, 1861. Present or accounted for until wounded in the arm in a skirmish near Richmond, Virginia, June 22, 1862. Reported absent wounded through August, 1863. Reported absent on duty as a provost guard at Gordonsville, Virginia, from November, 1863, through August, 1864.

LEWIS, CORNELIUS, Private
Born in Sampson County where he resided as a farmer prior to enlisting in Sampson County at age 16, September 27, 1861, as a substitute. Died at Richmond, Virginia, August 25, 1862. Cause of death not reported.

LEWIS, PRIOR, ———
North Carolina pension records indicate that he served in this company.

McKENZIE, REDDIN, Private
Born in Sampson County where he resided as a farmer prior to enlisting at age 23, April 20, 1861. Present or accounted for until captured at or near Spotsylvania Court House, Virginia, on or about May 8-12, 1864. Confined at Point Lookout, Maryland, May 17, 1864. Paroled at Point Lookout on or about March 14, 1865, and transferred to Boulware's Wharf, James River, Virginia, where he was received on March 16, 1865, for exchange.

McLAMORE, TOBIAS, Private
Resided in Sampson County where he enlisted at age 23, September 1, 1861. Present or accounted for until he was "sent to hospital" at Lynchburg, Virginia, in August, 1862. Failed to rejoin the company and was "supposed to be dead."

McLAMORE, WILLIAM S., Private
Resided in Sampson County where he enlisted at age 19, September 1, 1861. Captured by the enemy on an unspecified date. Paroled at Leesburg, Virginia, October 2, 1862. Returned to duty prior to January 1, 1863. Present or accounted for through December, 1863. Died in hospital at Richmond, Virginia, May 27, 1864, of a gunshot wound. Place and date wounded not reported.

MAYNOR, WILLIAM R., ———
North Carolina pension records indicate that he served in this company.

MERRITT, ISAAC W., Private
Born in Sampson County where he resided as a farmer prior to enlisting in Sampson County at age 27, April 20, 1861. Mustered in as Private. Promoted to Corporal in May-December, 1862. Promoted to Sergeant in January-June, 1863. Wounded in the side and/or left arm and captured at Gettysburg, Pennsylvania, July 1-3, 1863. Confined at Fort Delaware, Delaware, on or about July 9, 1863. Transferred to Point Lookout, Maryland, October 15-18, 1863. Reduced to ranks on November 1, 1863, while a prisoner of war. Paroled at Point Lookout on or about February 13, 1865, and transferred to Cox's Wharf, James River, Virginia, where he was received on February 14-15, 1865, for exchange.

MEWBORN, PARROTT, Private
Resided in Greene County where he enlisted at age 27, June 19, 1863, for the war. Present or accounted for through August, 1864.

MILES, JOHN, Private
Resided in Halifax County where he enlisted at age 40, June 23, 1863, for the war. Present or accounted for through December, 1863. Reported absent wounded during January-August, 1864. Place and date wounded not reported. No further records.

MITCHEL, HENRY, Private
Resided in Sampson County where he enlisted at age 30, September 1, 1861. Present or accounted for until he died in camp near Fredericksburg, Virginia, February 14, 1863, of "pneumonia."

MOORE, WALTER J., Private
Born in Sampson County and was by occupation a farmer prior to enlisting in Sampson County at age 21, April 20, 1861. Present or accounted for until discharged on January 30, 1862, by reason of "a spinal disease which renders him totally unfit for military duty." Reenlisted in the company on August 30, 1863. Present or accounted for through December, 1863. No further records.

NAYLOR, RANSOM, Private
Born in Sampson County where he resided prior to enlisting in Sampson County at age 21, September 1, 1861. Present or accounted for until killed at Chancellorsville, Virginia, May 3, 1863.

NORWOOD, R. W., ———
North Carolina pension records indicate that he served in this company.

NOWLES, WILLIAM R., Private
Resided in Sampson County where he enlisted at age 34, September 1, 1861. Present or accounted for until discharged on July 16, 1862. Reason discharged not reported.

OGBURN, N. S., Private
Resided in Guilford County and enlisted at age 17, April, 1864, for the war. Captured at Petersburg, Virginia, April 3, 1865. Confined at Hart's Island, New York Harbor, until released on June 17, 1865, after taking the Oath of Allegiance.

PAGE, JACOB S., Private
Resided in Sampson County where he enlisted at age 20, September 1, 1861. Present or accounted for until killed at Spotsylvania Court House, Virginia, May 12, 1864.

PAGE, OWEN, Private
Born in Sampson County where he resided as a mechanic prior to enlisting in Sampson County at age 23, April 20, 1861. Present or accounted for until he died in hospital at Richmond, Virginia, December 29, 1862, of "varioloid."

PARKER, JAMES M., Private
Resided in Sampson County where he enlisted at age 24, September 1, 1861. Present or accounted for until wounded at Chancellorsville, Virginia, May 3, 1863. Returned to duty prior to September 1, 1863. Present or accounted for until he surrendered at Appomattox Court House, Virginia, April 9, 1865.

PARTING, HENRY A., Private
Resided in Halifax County where he enlisted at age 18, June 23, 1863, for the war. Present or accounted for until captured at Kelly's Ford, Virginia, November 7, 1863. Confined at Point Lookout, Maryland. Died in the smallpox hospital at Point Lookout on December 28, 1863.

PENNINGTON, HENRY, Private
Resided in Wayne County and enlisted at Orange Court House, Virginia, at age 17, February 17, 1864, for the war. Present or accounted for until captured at Fisher's Hill, Virginia, September 22, 1864. Sent to Harpers Ferry, West Virginia. Confined at Point Lookout, Maryland, November 27, 1864. No further records.

PENNINGTON, JOHN, Private
Resided in Wayne County and enlisted in Sampson County at age 18, May 1, 1862, for the war. Present or accounted for until killed on August 12, 1864. Place of death not reported.

PENNINGTON, WILLIAM, Color Sergeant
Born in Sampson County where he resided as a farmer prior to enlisting in Sampson County at age 21, April 20, 1861. Mustered in as Private. Promoted to Color Sergeant in July-August, 1863. Present or accounted for until January-August, 1864, when he was reported absent wounded. Place and date wounded not reported. [North Carolina pension records indicate he was wounded in the head at "Chancellorsville, Virginia, April, 1862," and also indicate that he survived the war.]

PIPKIN, LEWIS H., Corporal
Born in Sampson or Wayne County and resided in Sampson County where he was by occupation a shoemaker prior to enlisting in Sampson County at age 29, April 20, 1861. Mustered in as Private. Promoted to Corporal on May 1, 1862. Present or accounted for until killed at Malvern Hill, Virginia, July 1, 1862. "A most excellent soldier."

POPE, ALEXANDER, Private
Resided in Sampson County where he enlisted at age 34, September 1, 1861. Present or accounted for until wounded in the chest at Malvern Hill, Virginia, July 1, 1862. Discharged in July, 1862.

POPE, STEPHEN, Private
Resided in Sampson County where he enlisted at age 36, September 1, 1861. Present or accounted for until discharged in July, 1862. Reason discharged not reported. [May have served later in 1st Company I, 36th Regiment N.C. Troops (2nd Regiment N.C. Artillery).]

POPE, WILEY, Private
Resided in Sampson County where he enlisted at age 24, September 1, 1861. Present or accounted for until wounded in the hand and knee at Malvern Hill, Virginia, on or about July 1, 1862. Returned to duty prior to January 1, 1863. Present or accounted for until captured at Spotsylvania Court House, Virginia, May 12, 1864. Confined at Point Lookout, Maryland, May 18, 1864. Paroled at Point Lookout on or about March 14, 1865, and transferred to Boulware's Wharf, James River, Virginia, where he was received on March 16, 1865, for exchange.

POPE, WILLIAM BRIGHT, Private
Resided in Sampson or Harnett County and enlisted in Sampson County at age 21, September 1, 1861. Present or accounted for until captured at Mine Run, Virginia, November 28, 1863. Confined at Old Capitol Prison, Washington, D.C., December 5, 1863. Transferred to Point Lookout, Maryland, February 3, 1864. Released at Point Lookout on June 17, 1865, after taking the Oath of Allegiance. [North Carolina pension records indicate he was wounded in the head and left hand in Virginia in 1864.]

PRIDGEN, WILLIAM E., Private
Resided in Sampson County where he enlisted at age 26, September 1, 1861. Present or accounted for until discharged in July, 1862. Reason discharged not reported.

PUGH, JAMES H., Sergeant
Born in Sampson County where he resided as a student prior to enlisting in Sampson County at age 22, April 20, 1861. Mustered in as Sergeant. Present or accounted for until transferred to Company I, 20th Regiment N.C. Troops (10th Regiment N.C. Volunteers), June 29, 1861.

RACKLEY, GEORGE W., Sergeant
Born in Sampson County where he resided as a farmer prior to enlisting in Sampson County at age 22, April 20, 1861. Mustered in as Private. Present or accounted for until wounded at Chancellorsville, Virginia, May 1-4, 1863. Returned to duty prior to September 1, 1863. Promoted to Sergeant in September-December, 1863. Present or accounted for until captured near Spotsylvania Court House, Virginia, May 12, 1864. Confined at Point Lookout, Maryland. Transferred to Elmira, New York, August 10, 1864. Released at Elmira on June 19, 1865, after taking the Oath of Allegiance.

REED, M. D., Private
Enlisted in Halifax County on June 23, 1863, for the war. Present or accounted for until discharged on September 3, 1863. Reason discharged not reported.

REGISTER, EDWARD M., Private
Resided in Sampson County where he enlisted at age 18, September 27, 1861. Present or accounted for until wounded at Malvern Hill, Virginia, July 1, 1862. Returned to duty prior to January 1, 1863. Died in camp

near Fredericksburg, Virginia, February 16, 1863, of "pneumonia."

REGISTER, HARMON H., Private
Born in Sampson County and was by occupation a merchant prior to enlisting in Sampson County at age 24, April 20, 1861. Discharged prior to November 1, 1861. Reason discharged not reported. [May have served later in Company C, 63rd Regiment N.C. Troops (5th Regiment N.C. Cavalry).]

REYNOLDS, CHARLES H., Private
Born in Sampson County where he resided prior to enlisting in Sampson County at age 18, September 1, 1861. Present or accounted for until he died at Guinea Station, Virginia, January 11, 1863, of "smallpox."

REYNOLDS, JOHN R., Private
Resided in Sampson County where he enlisted at age 20, September 1, 1861. Present or accounted for until captured at Spotsylvania Court House, Virginia, May 12, 1864. Confined at Point Lookout, Maryland, May 18, 1864. Transferred to Elmira, New York, August 10, 1864. Died at Elmira on March 29, 1865, of "typh[oid] fever."

RICH, JAMES O., Private
Resided in Sampson County where he enlisted at age 21, September 1, 1861. Present or accounted for through April, 1862. Discharged on an unspecified date after providing a substitute.

RICH, L. M., Private
Enlisted in Brunswick County on October 20, 1861. "Name cancelled" on an unspecified date and he was dropped from the rolls of the company. Reason he was dropped not reported.

ROBINSON, HARMON R., Private
Born in Sampson County where he resided as a farmer prior to enlisting in Sampson County at age 21, April 20, 1861. Present or accounted for until he died at Martinsburg, Virginia, June 19, 1863. Cause of death not reported.

ROBINSON, THOMAS M., Private
Born in Sampson County where he resided as a farmer prior to enlisting in Sampson County at age 32, April 20, 1861. Present or accounted for until discharged on July 16, 1862. Reason discharged not reported.

ROBINSON, W. J., ———
North Carolina pension records indicate that he served in this company.

ROGERS, WILLIAM, Private
Resided in Halifax County where he enlisted at age 27, June 24, 1863, for the war. Present or accounted for until captured at Petersburg, Virginia, April 3, 1865. Confined at Hart's Island, New York Harbor, April 7, 1865. Released on June 17, 1865, after taking the Oath of Allegiance.

ROGISTER, JAMES, Private
Resided in Halifax County and enlisted at Camp Holmes at age 28, July 11, 1863, for the war. Present or accounted for until captured at Kelly's Ford, Virginia, November 7, 1863. Confined at Point Lookout, Maryland, November 11, 1863. Paroled at Point

Lookout on or about February 24, 1865, and transferred to Aiken's Landing, James River, Virginia, where he was received on February 25-March 3, 1865, for exchange.

ROYAL, ALEXANDER, ———
North Carolina pension records indicate that he served in this company.

ROYAL, HARDY S., Private
Born in Sampson County where he resided as a farmer prior to enlisting in Sampson County at age 24, April 20, 1861. Mustered in with an unspecified rank. Promoted to Sergeant on August 3, 1861. Promoted to Color Sergeant in May-December, 1862. Wounded at Gaines' Mill, Virginia, June 27, 1862. Returned to duty prior to January 1, 1863. Wounded in the knee and/or thigh at Chancellorsville, Virginia, May 3, 1863. Leg amputated. Reduced to ranks in July-August, 1863. Reported absent wounded until September 21, 1864, when he was retired to the Invalid Corps.

ROYAL, MARSHALL, Private
Resided in Sampson County where he enlisted at age 22, September 1, 1861. Present or accounted for until he died in Sampson County on January 21, 1862. Cause of death not reported.

ROYAL, MARTIN, Private
Born in Sampson County where he resided as a farmer prior to enlisting in Sampson County at age 18, September 1, 1861. Reported absent without leave in November-December, 1862. Died in hospital at Weldon on March 8, 1863, of "acute dysentery."

ROYAL, NEVIL, Private
Born in Sampson County where he resided prior to enlisting in Sampson County at age 26, September 1, 1861. Present or accounted for until wounded at Gaines' Mill, Virginia, June 27, 1862. Returned to duty in July-December, 1862. Transferred to Company E, 35th Regiment Georgia Infantry, January 1, 1863.

ROYAL, SHERMAN, Corporal
Born in Sampson County where he resided prior to enlisting in Sampson County at age 18, September 1, 1861. Mustered in as Private. Promoted to Corporal on May 1, 1862. Wounded in the head at Malvern Hill, Virginia, July 1, 1862. Hospitalized at Richmond, Virginia, where he died on or about July 5, 1862, of wounds.

SESSOMS, CALTON, Private
Resided in Sampson County where he enlisted at age 29, September 1, 1861. Present or accounted for until discharged in July, 1862. Reason discharged not reported. Company records do not indicate whether he reenlisted in this company; however, he was captured by the enemy in Sampson County on March 16, 1865. Confined at Hart's Island, New York Harbor, April 10, 1865. Released on June 19, 1865.

SMITH, RICHARD P., Private
Resided in Virginia and enlisted in Sampson County at age 26, September 27, 1861. Reported absent without leave in November-December, 1862, and was listed as a deserter on February 7, 1863.

SPELL, GASTON, Private
Resided in Sampson County where he enlisted at age 28,

March 27, 1862. Present or accounted for until he surrendered at Appomattox Court House, Virginia, April 9, 1865. [May have served previously in Company F, 20th Regiment N.C. Troops (10th Regiment N.C. Volunteers).]

SPELL, HARDY L., Private
Born in Sampson County where he resided as a farmer prior to enlisting in Sampson County at age 28, April 20, 1861. Present or accounted for until discharged in July, 1862. Reason discharged not reported.

STEELE, JAMES H., Private
Resided in Cabarrus County where he enlisted at age 40, September 12, 1863, for the war. Present or accounted for until captured at Kelly's Ford, Virginia, November 7, 1863. Confined at Point Lookout, Maryland, November 11, 1863. Paroled and transferred to Varina, Virginia, where he was received on September 22, 1864, for exchange. Returned to duty on an unspecified date. Surrendered at Appomattox Court House, Virginia, April 9, 1865.

STRICKLAND, WALTER D., Private
Born in Sampson County where he resided prior to enlisting in Sampson County at age 22, September 1, 1861. Present or accounted for until he died at Guinea Station, Virginia, January 9, 1863. Cause of death not reported.

SUTTON, JOHN J., Private
Enlisted in Sampson County at age 21, September 1, 1861; however, his name was cancelled and he was dropped from the rolls of the company. No further records.

SUTTON, MICHAEL, Private
Born in Sampson County where he resided as a farmer prior to enlisting in Sampson County at age 17, April 20, 1861. Present or accounted for until discharged on December 20, 1861, by reason of "caxalgia." [May have served later in Company B, 51st Regiment N.C. Troops.]

TATOM, LOVE A., Private
Born in Sampson County where he resided as a farmer prior to enlisting in Sampson County at age 56, July 10, 1862, for the war as a substitute. Discharged on September 15, 1862, by reason of "old age & general debility."

TAYLOR, T. J., Private
Born in Halifax County where he resided as a farmer prior to enlisting in Halifax County at age 18, June 24, 1863, for the war. Present or accounted for through December, 1863; however, he was reported absent sick during most of that period. Discharged on January 20, 1864, by reason of "organic disease of the heart." [North Carolina pension records indicate he was wounded at Fredericksburg, Chancellorsville, and Spotsylvania Court House and was discharged in 1864 by reason of wounds.]

TAYLOR, WILLIAM J., Private
Resided in Harnett County and enlisted in Sampson County at age 17, September 1, 1861. Reported absent without leave in November-December, 1862. Returned to duty prior to May 3, 1863, when he was wounded in the back and left shoulder at Chancellorsville, Virginia. Returned to duty prior to January 1, 1864. Captured at Spotsylvania Court House, Virginia, in May, 1864. Confined at Elmira, New York. Released at Elmira on May 29, 1865, after taking the Oath of Allegiance.

TEW, BLACKMAN, Private
Born in Sampson County where he resided as a farmer prior to enlisting in Sampson County at age 22, September 1, 1861. Present or accounted for until killed at Gaines' Mill, Virginia, June 27, 1862.

TEW, WILEY, Private
Resided in Sampson County where he enlisted at age 17, September 1, 1861. Present or accounted for until he died in hospital at Scottsville, Virginia, January 19, 1863, of "typhoid pneumonia."

THRAILKILL, JOSEPH M., Sergeant
Born in Harnett County* and resided in Sampson County where he was by occupation a painter prior to enlisting in Sampson County at age 34, April 20, 1861. Mustered in as Private. Promoted to Corporal on August 3, 1861. Promoted to Sergeant in May-December, 1862. Present or accounted for until he died in camp near Fredericksburg, Virginia, February 21, 1863, of "chr[onic] diarr[hoea]."

TINDELL, DAVID, Private
Resided in Sampson County where he enlisted at age 22, September 1, 1861. Discharged prior to January 1, 1862. Reason discharged not reported.

TINDELL, MILES S., Private
Resided in Sampson County where he enlisted at age 18, September 1, 1861. Present or accounted for until captured at Spotsylvania Court House, Virginia, May 8-12, 1864. Confined at Point Lookout, Maryland, May 18, 1864. Transferred to Elmira, New York, August 10, 1864. Paroled at Elmira on March 14, 1865, and transferred to Boulware's Wharf, James River, Virginia, where he was received on March 18-21, 1865, for exchange.

TURNER, CICERO, Musician
Born in Sampson County where he resided as a mechanic prior to enlisting in Sampson County at age 16, April 20, 1861. Mustered in as Musician (Fifer). Appointed Musician (Drummer) in January-February, 1862. Present or accounted for until discharged on July 16, 1862. Reason discharged not reported. [May have served later in Company B, 2nd Battalion N.C. Local Defense Troops.]

UNDERWOOD, DANIEL R., Private
Born in Sampson County where he resided prior to enlisting in Sampson County at age 17, September 1, 1861. Present or accounted for until killed at Chancellorsville, Virginia, May 3, 1863.

WALKER, JAMES C., Private
Resided in Sampson County where he enlisted at age 38, September 1, 1861. Present or accounted for until wounded at Chancellorsville, Virginia, May 3, 1863. Returned to duty prior to January 1, 1864. Present or accounted for through August, 1864.

WAMMACK, LEVI T., Private
Previously served in Company F, 43rd Regiment N.C.

Troops. Enlisted in this company in Halifax County on June 24, 1863, for the war. Present or accounted for through March, 1865; however, he was reported absent on hospital duty during much of that period. Captured in hospital at Richmond, Virginia, April 3, 1865, and was paroled on April 20, 1865.

WARRICK, T. J., Private
Resided in Sampson County and enlisted at Camp Holmes at age 18, July 10, 1863, for the war. Present or accounted for until wounded at Kelly's Ford, Virginia, November 7, 1863. Reported absent in hospital or absent on guard duty through June, 1864. Died in hospital at Richmond, Virginia, July 7, 1864, of "typhoid fever."

WEEKS, JOHN A., Private
Born in Sampson County where he resided as a farmer prior to enlisting in Sampson County at age 21, April 20, 1861. Present or accounted for until wounded at Chancellorsville, Virginia, May 3, 1863. Hospitalized at Richmond, Virginia, where he died on or about May 11, 1863, of wounds.

WHITFIELD, J. E., Private
Place and date of enlistment not reported. Paroled at Raleigh on April 19, 1865.

WILLIAMS, CLABRAM, ———
North Carolina pension records indicate that he served in this company.

WILLIAMS, JOHN C., Private
Resided in Sampson County where he enlisted at age 18, April 20, 1861. Mustered in as Private. Promoted to Corporal on August 3, 1861. Reduced to ranks in May-December, 1862. Present or accounted for until he died at Wilmington on June 23, 1863, of "typhoid fever."

WILLIAMSON, DAVID, Private
Resided in Sampson County where he enlisted at age 20, September 1, 1861. Present or accounted for until captured at Kelly's Ford, Virginia, November 7, 1863. Confined at Point Lookout, Maryland, November 11, 1863. Paroled at Point Lookout on or about February 24, 1865, and transferred to Aiken's Landing, James River, Virginia, where he was received February 25-March 3, 1865, for exchange.

WILLIAMSON, HENRY, Private
Born in Sampson County where he resided as a mechanic prior to enlisting in Sampson County at age 23, April 20, 1861. Mustered in as Private. Promoted to Corporal on August 3, 1861. Promoted to Sergeant in May-December, 1862. Present or accounted for until wounded at Chancellorsville, Virginia, May 3, 1863. Reduced to ranks in September-December, 1863. Reported on duty as a provost guard at Gordonsville, Virginia, during November, 1863-August, 1864. Rejoined the company on an unspecified date. Surrendered at Appomattox Court House, Virginia, April 9, 1865.

WILLIAMSON, JAMES, Private
Resided in Sampson County where he enlisted at age 22, September 1, 1861. Present or accounted for until wounded in the right hip at Gaines' Mill, Virginia, on or about June 27, 1862. Returned to duty prior to January 1, 1863. Wounded in the arm at or near

Fredericksburg, Virginia, on or about April 30, 1863. Returned to duty subsequent to August 31, 1863. Wounded in the right arm at Kelly's Ford, Virginia, November 7, 1863. Returned to duty subsequent to December 31, 1863. Captured at Spotsylvania Court House, Virginia, May 12, 1864. Confined at Point Lookout, Maryland. Transferred to Elmira, New York, where he arrived on August 14, 1864. Released on June 23, 1865, after taking the Oath of Allegiance.

WINSCOFF, GEORGE W., Private
Resided in Cabarrus County where he enlisted at age 40, September 12, 1863, for the war. Present or accounted for until captured at Kelly's Ford, Virginia, November 7, 1863. Confined at Point Lookout, Maryland, November 11, 1863. Paroled at Point Lookout on or about February 24, 1865, and transferred to Aiken's Landing, James River, Virginia, where he was received February 25-March 3, 1865, for exchange.

COMPANY B

This company, known as the "Nat Macon Guards," was raised in Warren County and enlisted there on August 16, 1861. The company was then assigned to the 30th Regiment N.C. Troops and was designated Company B. After joining the regiment the company functioned as a part of the regiment, and its history for the war period is reported as a part of the regimental history.

The information contained in the following roster of the company was compiled principally from a company muster-in and descriptive roll dated October 8, 1861, and from company muster rolls for August 16, 1861-April, 1862; November-December, 1862; May-August, 1863; and November, 1863-August, 1864. No company muster rolls were found for May-October, 1862; January-April, 1863; September-October, 1863; or for the period after August, 1864. Valuable information was obtained from primary records such as the Roll of Honor, discharge certificates, medical records, prisoner of war records, and pension applications. Secondary sources such as postwar rosters and histories, cemetery records, and records of the United Daughters of the Confederacy also provided useful information.

OFFICERS

CAPTAINS

DRAKE, WILLIAM CASWELL
Resided in Warren County where he enlisted at age 29. Elected Captain on August 16, 1861. Present or accounted for until he resigned on December 10, 1862, by reason of "chronic hepatitis." Resignation accepted on January 5, 1863.

DAVIS, WELDON EDWARDS
Resided in Warren County where he enlisted at age 23. Appointed 3rd Lieutenant on August 16, 1861. Promoted to 2nd Lieutenant on September 26, 1861. Promoted to 1st Lieutenant on May 1, 1862. Promoted to Captain on June 13, 1863. Wounded in the right thigh and captured at Kelly's Ford, Virginia, November 7, 1863. Hospitalized at Washington, D.C. Right leg amputated on November 10, 1863. Died in hospital at Washington on November 22, 1863, of wounds.

LIEUTENANTS

BRAME, JOHN M., 1st Lieutenant
Resided in Warren County where he enlisted at age 37.

Elected 2nd Lieutenant on August 16, 1861. Promoted to 1st Lieutenant on September 26, 1861. Present or accounted for until he was defeated for reelection when the regiment was reorganized on May 1, 1862.

FOOTE, JAMES S., 2nd Lieutenant
Previously served as Sergeant of Company F, 12th Regiment N.C. Troops (2nd Regiment N.C. Volunteers). Appointed 2nd Lieutenant on May 1, 1862; however, he was not listed in the records of this company until July 31, 1863. Name appears on a surgeon's certificate dated November 4, 1864, which recommends that he be "honorably retired."

LOUGHLIN, JAMES J., 3rd Lieutenant
Born at Manchester, England, and resided at Norfolk, Virginia, and in Warren County where he enlisted at age 21, August 16, 1861. Mustered in as 1st Sergeant. Captured at Malvern Hill, Virginia, on or about July 1, 1862. Paroled and transferred to Aiken's Landing, James River, Virginia, where he was received on July 16, 1862, for exchange. Declared exchanged at Aiken's Landing on August 5, 1862. Returned to duty prior to January 1, 1863. Elected 3rd Lieutenant on or about January 8, 1863. Captured at Manassas Gap, Virginia, July 21, 1863. Confined at Old Capitol Prison, Washington, D.C. Transferred to Johnson's Island, Ohio, August 8, 1863. Released at Johnson's Island on June 11, 1865, after taking the Oath of Allegiance.

NICHOLSON, JOHN HIRAM, 1st Lieutenant
Resided in Warren County where he enlisted at age 29, August 16, 1861. Mustered in as Sergeant. Elected 3rd Lieutenant on September 26, 1861. Elected 2nd Lieutenant on May 1, 1862. Promoted to 1st Lieutenant on January 13, 1863. Present or accounted for until captured at Kelly's Ford, Virginia, November 7, 1863. Confined at Old Capitol Prison, Washington, D.C. Transferred to Johnson's Island, Ohio, November 11, 1863. Released at Johnson's Island on or about June 13, 1865, after taking the Oath of Allegiance.

WILLIAMS, BUCKNER D., 1st Lieutenant
Resided in Warren County where he enlisted at age 28. Appointed 1st Lieutenant on or about August 16, 1861. Appointed Assistant Quartermaster (Captain) on September 26, 1861, and transferred to the Field and Staff of this regiment.

NONCOMMISSIONED OFFICERS AND PRIVATES

ABBOTT, MACON, Private
Born in Warren County and resided in Franklin County prior to enlisting in Warren County at age 27, August 16, 1861. Present or accounted for until he died at Richmond, Virginia, January 1 or January 8, 1863. Cause of death not reported.

ARRINGTON, JAMES L., Private
Resided in Warren County and was by occupation a farmer prior to enlisting in Warren County at age 33, August 16, 1861. Present or accounted for until wounded in the thigh and left hand at Chancellorsville, Virginia, May 3, 1863. Reported absent wounded until September 15, 1863, when he was reported absent without leave. Returned to duty on or about November

24, 1863. Captured at Spotsylvania Court House, Virginia, May 20, 1864. Confined at Point Lookout, Maryland, May 23, 1864. Transferred to Elmira, New York, July 3, 1864. Died at Elmira on February 7, 1865, of "variola."

ASKEW, JOHN, Private
Resided in Warren County where he enlisted at age 19, August 16, 1861. Present or accounted for until captured at Kelly's Ford, Virginia, November 7, 1863. Confined at Washington, D.C. Transferred to Point Lookout, Maryland, where he arrived on November 11, 1863. Died at Point Lookout on August 25, 1864. Cause of death not reported.

AYCOCK, EDWARD S., Private
Resided in Virginia and enlisted in Warren County at age 21, August 16, 1861. Present or accounted for until he surrendered at Appomattox Court House, Virginia, April 9, 1865.

AYCOCK, GEORGE G., Private
Resided in Virginia and enlisted in Warren County at age 22, August 16, 1861. Present or accounted for through August, 1864. Hospitalized at Farmville, Virginia, on an unspecified date with a gunshot wound of the left thigh. Place and date wounded not reported. Captured in hospital at Farmville in April, 1865. "Discharged from service" on June 9, 1865.

AYCOCK, SAMUEL, Private
Resided in Warren County where he enlisted at age 24, August 16, 1861. Present or accounted for until killed at Kelly's Ford, Virginia, November 7, 1863.

BELL, ROBERT M., Private
Resided in Sampson County and enlisted in Wake County at age 37, July 28, 1863, for the war. Deserted on August 1, 1863.

BELL, WILLIAM S., Corporal
Resided in Warren County where he enlisted at age 24, August 16, 1861. Mustered in as Corporal. Present or accounted for until wounded at Gaines' Mill, Virginia, June 27, 1862. Reported absent without leave from October 1, 1862, through December, 1862. "Sent to hospital" on June 7, 1863. Returned to duty in September-December, 1863. Present or accounted for through August, 1864.

BISHOP, ALFRED, Private
Resided in Warren County where he enlisted at age 26, August 16, 1861. Present or accounted for until wounded in the right shoulder at or near Malvern Hill, Virginia, on or about July 1, 1862. Transferred to Company C, 46th Regiment N.C. Troops, September 25, 1862.

BISHOP, SAMUEL D., Private
Born in Warren County where he resided prior to enlisting in Warren County at age 19, August 16, 1861. Present or accounted for until killed at Chancellorsville, Virginia, May 3, 1863.

BOBBITT, BURWELL B., Private
Resided in Warren County and was by occupation a farmer prior to enlisting in Warren County at age 17, August 16, 1861. Present or accounted for until wounded at Gaines' Mill, Virginia, June 27, 1862.

Reported absent on detail in hospital at Richmond, Virginia, during November-December, 1862. Returned to duty prior to May 3, 1863, when he was wounded in the left hip at Chancellorsville, Virginia. Reported absent wounded through August, 1863. Returned to duty in November-December, 1863. Detailed for hospital duty at Salisbury on January 23, 1864. Reported absent on detail until he was paroled at Salisbury on May 2, 1865.

BOBBITT, E. FLETCHER, Private
Born in Warren County where he resided prior to enlisting at age 33, April 28, 1862, for the war. Died in hospital at Richmond, Virginia, October 23, 1862, of "typhoid fever."

BORGUS, REUBEN, Private
Resided in Wilkes County and enlisted in Wake County at age 28, September 21, 1862, for the war. Present or accounted for until captured at Kelly's Ford, Virginia, November 7, 1863. Confined at Point Lookout, Maryland, November 11, 1863. Paroled at Point Lookout and transferred to City Point, Virginia, April 27, 1864, for exchange. Hospitalized at Richmond, Virginia, May 1, 1864, and was furloughed for thirty days on May 6, 1864. No further records.

BRACK, B. BAKER, Private
Born in Warren County where he resided prior to enlisting in Warren County at age 24, August 16, 1861. Present or accounted for until killed at Chancellorsville, Virginia, May 3, 1863.

BRACK, GEORGE W., Private
Born in Warren County where he resided prior to enlisting in Warren County at age 26, August 16, 1861. Present or accounted for until killed at Chancellorsville, Virginia, May 3, 1863.

BRINKLY, THOMAS H., Private
Resided in Wake County where he enlisted at age 28, July 1, 1863, for the war. Deserted on August 1, 1863.

BROWN, D. M., Private
Place and date of enlistment not reported. Surrendered at Appomattox Court House, Virginia, April 9, 1865.

BROWN, WILLIAM E., Private
Resided in Warren County and enlisted in Wake County at age 38, July 16, 1863, for the war. Present or accounted for until he surrendered at Appomattox Court House, Virginia, April 9, 1865.

BUFF, PETER, Private
Resided in Cleveland County and enlisted in Wake County at age 24, September 21, 1862, for the war. Captured near Paris, Virginia, November 4, 1862. Paroled on November 9, 1862. Returned to duty on an unspecified date. Wounded at Chancellorsville, Virginia, May 3, 1863. Returned to duty in September-December, 1863. Reported absent on furlough during January-August, 1864. No further records.

BUFF, WILLIAM, Private
Resided in Cleveland County and enlisted in Wake County at age 31, September 1, 1862, for the war. Present or accounted for until he deserted on June 11, 1863. Company records do not indicate whether he returned to duty. Discharged on April 1, 1864. Reason

discharged not reported.

CARROLL, WILLIAM HENRY, Private
Resided in Warren County where he enlisted at age 17, August 16, 1861. Present or accounted for until wounded in the right arm and captured on or about April 7, 1865. Hospitalized at Farmville, Virginia. [North Carolina pension records indicate that he survived the war.] No further records.

CARTER, JOHN, Private
Born in Warren County where he resided as a farmer prior to enlisting in Warren County at age 25, August 16, 1861. Present or accounted for until discharged on March 5, 1862, by reason of "cancer of the stomach."

CARTER, WILLIAM J., Private
Resided in Warren County where he enlisted at age 35, August 16, 1861. Reported absent without leave on July 1, 1862. Returned to duty in January-June, 1863. Captured at Kelly's Ford, Virginia, November 7, 1863. Confined at Point Lookout, Maryland, November 11, 1863. Released on January 30, 1864, after joining the U.S. Army. Assigned to Company E, 1st Regiment U.S. Volunteer Infantry.

CLANTON, ROBERT K., Private
Resided in Warren County and enlisted in Brunswick County at age 26, August 16, 1861. Present or accounted for until discharged on March 3-5, 1863, after providing a substitute.

CLOYD, J. M., Private
Place and date of enlistment not reported. Captured at or near Harrisonburg, Virginia, October 9-19, 1864. Confined at Point Lookout, Maryland, October 20, 1864. Paroled and transferred to Boulware's Wharf, James River, Virginia, where he was received on March 30, 1865, for exchange.

COCKERHAM, JAMES B., Private
Resided in Wilkes County and enlisted in Wake County at age 24, September 21, 1862, for the war. "Sent to hospital" on November 7, 1862, and was not heard from again. No further records.

COLLINS, DAVID, Private
Previously served in Company C, 46th Regiment N.C. Troops. Transferred to this company on October 8, 1862. Present or accounted for until captured at Kelly's Ford, Virginia, November 7, 1863. Confined at Point Lookout, Maryland, November 11, 1863. Paroled at Point Lookout on or about March 15, 1865, and transferred to Boulware's Wharf, James River, Virginia, where he was received on March 18, 1865, for exchange.

COLLINS, JOHN, Private
Resided in Warren County where he enlisted at age 30, August 16, 1861. Appointed Assistant Commissary of Subsistence (Captain) on or about August 25, 1861, and transferred to the Field and Staff of this regiment.

COLLINS, STOGDON, Private
Born in Philadelphia, Pennsylvania, and resided in Warren County prior to enlisting at Hamilton's Crossing, Virginia, at age 53, March 5, 1863, for the war as a substitute. Died in camp near Hamilton's Crossing on or about June 3, 1863. Cause of death not reported.

COOK, DAVID, Private
Resided in Cleveland County and enlisted in Wake County at age 23, September 21, 1862, for the war. Present or accounted for until he died in hospital at Richmond, Virginia, on or about March 31, 1863, of disease.

DARNELL, JAMES R., Private
Resided in Warren County where he enlisted at age 19, August 16, 1861. Present or accounted for until captured at Kelly's Ford, Virginia, November 7, 1863. Confined at Point Lookout, Maryland, November 11, 1863. Paroled at Point Lookout on January 17, 1865, and transferred to Boulware's Wharf, James River, Virginia, where he was received on January 21, 1865, for exchange.

DAVIS, BENJAMIN P., Sergeant
Resided in Warren County where he enlisted at age 26, August 16, 1861. Mustered in as Sergeant. Reduced to ranks in May-December, 1862. Promoted to Sergeant on July 15, 1864. Present or accounted for through August, 1864.

DAVIS, BURWELL P., Private
Resided in Warren County where he enlisted at age 28, August 16, 1861. Mustered in as Sergeant. Present or accounted for until wounded at Malvern Hill, Virginia, July 1, 1862. Detailed for hospital duty at Richmond, Virginia, on April 26, 1863. Reported absent on detail at Richmond through December, 1863. Reduced to ranks in January-August, 1864. Reported absent on detail at Raleigh during January-August, 1864.

DAVIS, ISHAM H., Private
Born in Warren County where he resided prior to enlisting in Warren County at age 29, August 16, 1861. Present or accounted for until discharged on March 10, 1864, by reason of "general debility from chron[ic] diarrhoea with predisposition to & . . . symptoms of phthisis pulmonalis."

DAVIS, JOHN S., Jr., Private
Resided in Warren County where he enlisted at age 21, August 16, 1861. Present or accounted for through February, 1862. Suffered an attack of yellow fever in March, 1862, and was sent home on March 18, 1862. Never returned to duty. [Roll of Honor indicates he was "a lunatic caused by fever in March, 1862."]

DICKERSON, GEORGE, Private
Resided in Franklin County and enlisted in Wake County at age 40, September 2, 1863, for the war. Present or accounted for through August, 1864; however, he was reported absent in hospital or absent on furlough during most of that period.

DUKE, GEORGE J., Private
Resided in Warren County where he enlisted at age 25, August 16, 1861. Present or accounted for until wounded at Malvern Hill, Virginia, July 1, 1862. Returned to duty subsequent to December 31, 1862. Wounded in the arm and side at Chancellorsville, Virginia, May 3, 1863. Reported absent wounded through December, 1863. Detailed for hospital duty at Lynchburg, Virginia, April 15, 1864. Reported absent on detail through October, 1864.

DUKE, ROBERT W., Private
Born in Wayne County and resided in Warren County

where he enlisted at age 27, August 16, 1861. Present or accounted for until wounded at Malvern Hill, Virginia, July 1, 1862. Hospitalized at Richmond, Virginia, where he died on August 1, 1862, of wounds and/or "diarrhoea."

FINCH, IRA J., Private
Resided in Warren County and enlisted in Wake County at age 36, July 16, 1863, for the war. Present or accounted for until captured at or near Winchester, Virginia, on or about August 10, 1864. Confined at Old Capitol Prison, Washington, D.C., August 17, 1864. Transferred to Elmira, New York, August 28, 1864. Paroled at Elmira on or about February 20, 1865, and transferred to the James River, Virginia, for exchange. Reported in hospital at Richmond, Virginia, March 5, 1865.

FITTS, FRANCIS MICHAEL, Private
Previously served in 2nd Company C, 12th Regiment N.C. Troops (2nd Regiment N.C. Volunteers). Transferred to this company on March 24, 1863, in exchange for Private Wyatt A. Floyd. Present or accounted for until promoted to Sergeant Major in January-July, 1864, and transferred to the Field and Staff of this regiment.

FLOYD, WYATT A., Private
Resided in Warren County where he enlisted at age 27, August 16, 1861. Present or accounted for until transferred to 2nd Company C, 12th Regiment N.C. Troops (2nd Regiment N.C. Volunteers), March 24, 1863, in exchange for Private Francis Michael Fitts.

GHOLSON, ABRAHAM, Private
Born in Mecklenburg County, [Virginia,] and resided in Virginia prior to enlisting in Warren County at age 19, August 16, 1861. Present or accounted for until hospitalized at Richmond, Virginia, July 30, 1862, with "typhoid fever." Died in hospital at Richmond on August 4-5, 1862.

GILL, PHILIP P., Private
Born in Warren County where he resided as a farmer prior to enlisting in Warren County at age 29, August 16, 1861. Present or accounted for until wounded in the face at Malvern Hill, Virginia, July 1, 1862. Discharged on September 20, 1862, by reason of "the total loss of vision of one eye (the left) from the explosion of a shell & consequent impairment of vision of the other."

GLADSTONE, D. S., Private
Enlisted in Wake County on July 11, 1863, for the war. Present or accounted for until discharged on April 26, 1864. Reason discharged not reported.

GOEBEL, CHARLES L., Private
Resided in Warren County where he enlisted at age 31, August 16, 1861. Present or accounted for until he was detailed to work in the armory at Richmond, Virginia, March 28, 1862, and was assigned to duty with Company A, 1st Battalion Virginia Infantry (Local Defense). Reported absent on detail through June, 1863. Reported absent without leave from July-August, 1863, through August, 1864.

GREGORY, LAWRENCE B., Private
Previously served in Company G, 12th Regiment N.C.

Troops (2nd Regiment N.C. Volunteers). Transferred to this company on December 19, 1861. Discharged on July 26, 1862, by reason of being underage. Later served in Company F, 36th Regiment N.C. Troops (2nd Regiment N.C. Artillery).

HAITHCOCK, ALFRED LOFTIN, Private
Resided in Warren County where he enlisted at age 22, August 16, 1861. Present or accounted for until captured at Kelly's Ford, Virginia, November 7, 1863. Confined at Point Lookout, Maryland, November 11, 1863. Paroled at Point Lookout on or about March 14, 1865, and transferred to Boulware's Wharf, James River, Virginia, where he was received on March 16, 1865, for exchange.

HAITHCOCK, WILLIAM G., Private
Resided in Warren County where he enlisted at age 47, August 16, 1861. Present or accounted for until discharged on December 2, 1862, by reason of being overage.

HARDY, FRANCIS M., Private
Resided in Warren County where he enlisted at age 19, August 16, 1861. Present or accounted for until captured at or near Frederick, Maryland, September 12-13, 1862. Confined at Fort Delaware, Delaware. Paroled and transferred to City Point, Virginia, where he was received on December 18, 1862, for exchange. Returned to duty prior to May 1-4, 1863, when he was wounded at Chancellorsville, Virginia. Returned to duty in July-August, 1863. Present or accounted for until wounded in both forearms and captured at or near Silver Spring, Maryland, July 12-13, 1864. Hospitalized at Washington, D.C., where he died on August 17, 1864, of wounds.

HARDY, HENRY, Private
Born in Warren County where he resided prior to enlisting in Warren County at age 27, August 16, 1861. Present or accounted for until he died at Guinea Station, Virginia, February 17, 1863, of "smallpox."

HARDY, THOMAS WILLIAM, Private
Born in Warren County where he resided as a farmer prior to enlisting in Warren County at age 24, August 16, 1861. Present or accounted for until discharged on March 19, 1862, by reason of "inflammation of the bladder" and "hemorrhoids." Reenlisted in the company on February 20, 1863, for the war. Detailed for light duty on or about May 30, 1863. Reported absent on detail through February, 1865. Hospitalized at Richmond, Virginia, March 13, 1865, with intermittent fever and returned to duty on March 23, 1865.

HARRIS, JOHN N., Private
Resided in Warren County where he enlisted at age 28, August 16, 1861. Reported absent without leave until November 18, 1861. Present or accounted for until captured at Kelly's Ford, Virginia, November 7, 1863. Confined at Point Lookout, Maryland, November 11, 1863. Died at Point Lookout on August 12, 1864. Cause of death not reported.

HARRISS, DAVID W., Private
Born in Warren County where he resided as a farmer prior to enlisting in Warren County at age 50, August 16, 1861. Present or accounted for until discharged on January 14, 1862, by reason of "chronic rheumatism."

HARRISS, GEORGE W., Private
Resided in Warren County and enlisted at Camp Wyatt at age 29, January 4, 1862. Present or accounted for until May 2, 1863, when he was reported absent without leave. Returned to duty on September 29, 1863. Reported under arrest through December, 1863. Reported in hospital at Richmond, Virginia, from May 13, 1864, through December, 1864. Paroled at Richmond on April 18, 1865.

HARRISS, JOHN AMOS, Sergeant
Resided in Warren County where he enlisted at age 18, August 16, 1861. Mustered in as Corporal. Promoted to Sergeant in January-February, 1862. Present or accounted for until wounded at Malvern Hill, Virginia, July 1, 1862. Returned to duty prior to January 1, 1863. Present or accounted for until captured at Kelly's Ford, Virginia, November 7, 1863. Confined at Point Lookout, Maryland, November 11, 1863. Paroled at Point Lookout on February 18, 1865, and transferred to Boulware's Wharf, James River, Virginia, where he was received February 20-21, 1865, for exchange.

HARRISS, JOHN W., Private
Resided in Warren County and enlisted in New Hanover County at age 30, April 28, 1862, for the war. Reported absent sick from October 10, 1862, through June, 1863. Returned to duty on or about September 12, 1863. Present or accounted for until he surrendered at Appomattox Court House, Virginia, April 9, 1865.

HARRISS, JOSEPH J., Jr., Private
Born in Warren County where he resided as a farmer prior to enlisting in Warren County at age 37, August 16, 1861. Present or accounted for until discharged on May 19, 1862, by reason of "chronic rheumatism."

HARRISS, WILLIAM L., Private
Resided in Warren County and enlisted at Camp Saunders at age 15, April 28, 1862, for the war. Present or accounted for until captured at Bunker Hill, Virginia, August 9-10, 1864. Confined at Old Capitol Prison, Washington, D.C., August 17, 1864. Transferred to Elmira, New York, August 28, 1864. Released at Elmira on July 7, 1865, after taking the Oath of Allegiance.

HENDRICK, ALEXANDER W., Private
Resided in Granville County and enlisted in Warren County at age 21, August 16, 1861. Mustered in as Corporal. Reduced to ranks in May-December, 1862. Detailed for duty as a hospital nurse at Richmond, Virginia, on or about July 20, 1862. Reported absent on detail at Richmond through August, 1863. Detailed as a provost guard at Raleigh on October 17, 1863, by reason of disability from wounds. Place and date wounded not reported. Reported absent on detail at Raleigh through December, 1864.

HOBBS, M. V., Private
Born in Guilford County where he resided as a farmer prior to enlisting in Wake County at age 36, July 11, 1863, for the war. Present or accounted for until captured in hospital at Richmond, Virginia, April 3, 1865. Transferred to Newport News, Virginia, April 23, 1865. Released on June 16, 1865, after taking the Oath of Allegiance.

HUNDLEY, GEORGE W., Corporal
Resided in Warren County where he enlisted at age 18,

August 16, 1861. Mustered in as Private. Promoted to Corporal in January-June, 1863. Hospitalized at Richmond, Virginia, May 8, 1863, with a gunshot wound. Place and date wounded not reported. Returned to duty prior to September 1, 1863. Captured at Kelly's Ford, Virginia, November 7, 1863. Confined at Point Lookout, Maryland, November 11, 1863. Paroled at Point Lookout on or about February 24, 1865, and transferred to Aiken's Landing, James River, Virginia, where he was received February 25-March 3, 1865, for exchange.

INSCOE, WILLIAM, Private
Resided in Franklin County and enlisted in Wake County at age 44, September 30, 1863, for the war. Captured at Kelly's Ford, Virginia, November 7, 1863. Confined at Point Lookout, Maryland, November 11, 1863. Paroled at Point Lookout on or about February 24, 1865, and transferred to Aiken's Landing, James River, Virginia, where he was received on February 25-March 3, 1865, for exchange. No further records.

JACKSON, MARION J., Private
Resided in Warren County and enlisted in Wake County at age 41, September 4, 1863, for the war. Wounded in the left foot on October 22, 1863. Left toe amputated. Reported absent wounded or absent on furlough through August, 1864.

JOHNSTON, WILLIAM H., Private
Resided in Warren County where he enlisted at age 30, August 16, 1861. Present or accounted for through August, 1864. Paroled at Richmond, Virginia, on or about June 3, 1865.

KIMBALL, NATHANIEL, Private
Resided in Warren County where he enlisted at age 34, August 16, 1861. Present or accounted for until wounded at Sharpsburg, Maryland, September 17, 1862. Reported absent wounded through December, 1862. Returned to duty prior to May 3, 1863, when he was wounded in the right foot at Chancellorsville, Virginia. Returned to duty in September-November, 1863. Captured at Kelly's Ford, Virginia, November 7, 1863. Confined at Point Lookout, Maryland, November 11, 1863. Paroled at Point Lookout on or about February 24, 1865, and transferred to Aiken's Landing, James River, Virginia, where he was received February 25-March 3, 1865, for exchange.

KING, JOHN F., Private
Resided in Warren County where he enlisted at age 19, August 16, 1861. Present or accounted for through August, 1864.

KING, WILLIAM A., Private
Resided in Warren County where he enlisted at age 21, August 16, 1861. Present or accounted for until he died in hospital at Richmond, Virginia, September 8, 1862, of "typhoid fever."

KIRKLAND, STEPHEN H., Private
Resided in Warren County where he enlisted at age 18, August 16, 1861. Present or accounted for until captured at Kelly's Ford, Virginia, November 7, 1863. Confined at Point Lookout, Maryland, November 11, 1863. Died at Point Lookout on August 11, 1864. Cause of death not reported.

LOUGHLIN, CHARLES, Musician
Resided in Warren County where he enlisted at age 17, August 16, 1861. Mustered in as Musician (Drummer). Present or accounted for until transferred to the C.S. Navy on or about April 10, 1862.

LOUGHLIN, JOHN, Private
Resided in Warren County where he enlisted at age 27, August 16, 1861. Present or accounted for until wounded at Malvern Hill, Virginia, July 1, 1862. Returned to duty prior to January 1, 1863. Wounded at Gettysburg, Pennsylvania, July 1, 1863. Failed to rejoin the company. Company muster roll dated January 1-August 31, 1864, indicates he deserted to the enemy in July, 1863; however, he is not listed in the records of the Federal Provost Marshal. No further records.

MILAM, H. D., Private
Resided in Warren County and enlisted at age 27, August 16, 1861. Discharged on September 20, 1861. Reason discharged not reported. [May have served later in Mallett's N.C. Battalion (Camp Guard).]

MILES, JAMES, Private
Resided in Guilford County. Place and date of enlistment not reported. Captured at or near High Branch, Virginia, April 6, 1865. Confined at Point Lookout, Maryland, April 14, 1865. Released on June 29, 1865, after taking the Oath of Allegiance.

MYRICK, WILLIAM W., Private
Resided in Warren County and enlisted at Camp Saunders at age 38, April 24, 1862, for the war. Present or accounted for until wounded at Sharpsburg, Maryland, September 17, 1862. Reported absent without leave in November-December, 1862. Returned to duty on an unspecified date. Captured at or near Gettysburg, Pennsylvania, on or about July 3, 1863. Confined at Fort Delaware, Delaware, on or about July 7, 1863. Transferred to Point Lookout, Maryland, October 15-18, 1863. Died in the smallpox hospital at Point Lookout on or about February 7, 1864.

NEAL, DUDLEY H., Private
Born in Warren County where he resided as a farmer prior to enlisting in Warren County at age 24, August 16, 1861. Present or accounted for until wounded in the leg at Malvern Hill, Virginia, July 1, 1862. Returned to duty in July-August, 1863. Present or accounted for until wounded in both legs at Spotsylvania Court House, Virginia, May 16, 1864. Reported absent wounded through August, 1864. Retired from service on March 14, 1865, by reason of disability from wounds.

NEWSOM, JOHN GILHAM, 1st Sergeant
Resided in Warren County where he enlisted at age 16, August 16, 1861. Mustered in as Private. Promoted to Corporal in May-December, 1862. Wounded in the right thigh at Malvern Hill, Virginia, July 1, 1862. Returned to duty prior to January 1, 1863. Wounded in the right side at Chancellorsville, Virginia, May 1-4, 1863. Promoted to 1st Sergeant in January-June, 1863. Returned to duty prior to July 1, 1863. Wounded in the head and captured at Kelly's Ford, Virginia, November 7, 1863. Hospitalized at Washington, D.C. Confined at Old Capitol Prison, Washington, December 7, 1863. Transferred to Point Lookout, Maryland, February 3, 1864. Paroled at Point Lookout on or about November

1, 1864, and transferred to Venus Point, Savannah River, Georgia, where he was received on November 15, 1864, for exchange. Returned to duty on an unspecified date. Surrendered at Appomattox Court House, Virginia, April 9, 1865.

NORTH, JOSHUA, Private
Born in Rockingham County where he resided as a farmer prior to enlisting in Wake County at age 38, May 23, 1863, for the war. Present or accounted for until he surrendered at Appomattox Court House, Virginia, April 9, 1865.

PASCHALL, SAMUEL A., Corporal
Resided in Warren County where he enlisted at age 25, August 16, 1861. Mustered in as Private. Promoted to Corporal in May-December, 1862. Present or accounted for until captured at Kelly's Ford, Virginia, November 7, 1863. Confined at Point Lookout, Maryland, November 11, 1863. Paroled at Point Lookout on or about February 24, 1865, and transferred to Aiken's Landing, James River, Virginia, where he was received on February 25-March 3, 1865, for exchange.

PATTERSON, GREEN R., Private
Resided in Warren County where he enlisted at age 36, August 16, 1861. Present or accounted for until wounded at Chancellorsville, Virginia, May 3, 1863. Hospitalized at Richmond, Virginia, where he died on or about June 4, 1863, of wounds and/or disease.

AYNTER, THOMAS P., Private
Born in Warren County where he resided as a farmer prior to enlisting in Warren County at age 24, August 16, 1861. Present or accounted for until discharged on January 14, 1862, by reason of "a wound received on the scalp about five years ago" while a civilian. Reenlisted in the company on July 16, 1863, for the war. Detailed as a shoemaker on September 17, 1863. Reported absent on detail through August, 1864. Hospitalized at Richmond, Virginia, February 24, 1865, with "nostalgia." Captured in hospital at Richmond on April 3, 1865. Paroled at Richmond on or about April 21, 1865.

PEGRAM, GEORGE W., Private
Born in Warren County where he resided prior to enlisting at age 30, April 19, 1862, for the war. Died in hospital at Lynchburg, Virginia, on or about August 29, 1862, of "tonsillitis."

PEGRAM, JAMES B., Private
Resided in Warren County and enlisted at Camp Wyatt at age 23, January 28, 1862. Present or accounted for until wounded at Gaines' Mill, Virginia, June 27, 1862. Reported absent without leave on October 21, 1862. "Sent to hospital" on May 15, 1863. Reported absent without leave on June 30, 1863. Died at Orange Court House, Virginia, December 25, 1863, of "hemorrhage of the bowells [sic]."

PEGRAM, JOHN J., Private
Resided in Warren County and enlisted at Camp Lamb at age 18, March 21, 1862. Present or accounted for until captured at Frederick, Maryland, September 12-13, 1862. Confined at Fort Delaware, Delaware. Paroled and transferred to Aiken's Landing, James River, Virginia, October 2, 1862, for exchange. Declared exchanged at Aiken's Landing on November

10, 1862. Returned to duty in July-August, 1863. Captured at Kelly's Ford, Virginia, November 7, 1863. Confined at Point Lookout, Maryland, November 11, 1863. Paroled at Point Lookout on or about April 27, 1864, and transferred to City Point, Virginia, where he was received on April 30, 1864, for exchange. Returned to duty subsequent to August 31, 1864. Wounded in the left arm at Petersburg, Virginia, in January, 1865. Hospitalized at Richmond, Virginia. Furloughed from hospital on February 11, 1865.

PEGRAM, MITCHELL S., Private
Born in Warren County where he resided as a farmer prior to enlisting in Warren County at age 17, February 19, 1863, for the war. Present or accounted for until wounded in the left foot and right knee at Spotsylvania Court House, Virginia, May 12, 1864. Retired from service on March 14, 1865, by reason of "gunshot wound of the left foot with complete destruction of all the metatarsal bones."

PEGRAM, ROBERT B., Private
Resided in Warren County where he enlisted at age 22, August 16, 1861. Present or accounted for until wounded in the left thigh at Mechanicsville, Virginia, June 26, 1862. Returned to duty on January 2, 1863. Wounded in the shoulder at Chancellorsville, Virginia, on or about May 5, 1863. Returned to duty prior to July 1, 1863. Present or accounted for until he surrendered at Appomattox Court House, Virginia, April 9, 1865.

RIGGAN, CHARLES D., Private
Resided in Warren County where he enlisted at age 25, August 16, 1861. Present or accounted for until he surrendered at Appomattox Court House, Virginia, April 9, 1865.

RIGGAN, CHARLES S., Private
Resided in Warren County where he enlisted at age 18, August 16, 1861. Present or accounted for until wounded in the right arm at Spotsylvania Court House, Virginia, May 12, 1864. Returned to duty prior to October 19, 1864, when he was wounded in the left shoulder at Cedar Creek, Virginia. Returned to duty on an unspecified date. Surrendered at Appomattox Court House, Virginia, April 9, 1865.

RIGGAN, ISHAM S., Private
Resided in Warren County and enlisted in Wake County at age 35, July 16, 1863, for the war. Present or accounted for until captured at or near Spotsylvania Court House, Virginia, on or about May 12, 1864. Confined at Point Lookout, Maryland, May 17, 1864. Transferred to Elmira, New York, August 10, 1864. Died at Elmira on September 27, 1864, of "typhoid pneumonia."

RIGGAN, MINGA E., Private
Born in Warren County where he resided as an engineer prior to enlisting in Warren County at age 24, August 16, 1861. Present or accounted for until discharged on December 14, 1861, by reason of "a fractured arm."

RIGGAN, SUGAR A., Private
Resided in Warren County and enlisted at Camp Saunders at age 41, April 14, 1862. Present or accounted for until captured at Spotsylvania Court House, Virginia, May 12, 1864. Confined at Point Lookout, Maryland, May 18, 1864. Transferred to Elmira, New

York, August 10, 1864. Died at Elmira on November 29, 1864, of "chronic diarrhoea."

ROBERTSON, PETER E., Corporal
Born in Warren County where he resided prior to enlisting in Warren County at age 25, August 16, 1861. Mustered in as Private. Promoted to Corporal in January-February, 1862. Present or accounted for until wounded at Sharpsburg, Maryland, September 17, 1862. Discharged on December 1, 1862. Reason discharged not reported.

ROSE, LEWIS D., Private
Born in Warren County where he resided as a farmer prior to enlisting in Warren County at age 20, August 16, 1861. Present or accounted for until discharged on May 19, 1862, by reason of "disease of the lungs." [May have served later in 2nd Company C, 12th Regiment N.C. Troops (2nd Regiment N.C. Volunteers).]

SAINTSING, JOHN A., Private
Resided in Warren County where he enlisted at age 22, August 16, 1861. Present or accounted for until wounded in the right shoulder at Spotsylvania Court House, Virginia, May 12, 1864. Returned to duty subsequent to August 31, 1864. Surrendered at Appomattox Court House, Virginia, April 9, 1865.

SALMON, HENRY, Private
Resided in Warren County where he enlisted at age 40, August 16, 1861. Present or accounted for until discharged on December 2, 1862, by reason of being overage.

SHEARIN, E. C., Private
Resided in Warren County and enlisted at age 24, April 17, 1862, for the war. Present or accounted for until he died in hospital at Richmond, Virginia, November 4, 1862, of "febris typhoides."

SHEARIN, GARDINER E., Private
Born in Warren County where he resided prior to enlisting in Warren County at age 23, August 16, 1861. Present or accounted for until September 1, 1862, when he was reported absent without leave. Returned to duty in January-June, 1863. Present or accounted for until captured at Kelly's Ford, Virginia, November 7, 1863. Confined at Point Lookout, Maryland, November 11, 1863. Paroled at Point Lookout on or about February 18, 1865, and transferred to Boulware's Wharf, James River, Virginia, where he was received February 20-21, 1865, for exchange.

SHEARIN, JACOB J., Private
Born in Warren County where he resided as a farmer prior to enlisting in Warren County at age 32, August 16, 1861. Present or accounted for until discharged on January 22, 1863, by reason of "irreduceable [sic] ventral hernia."

SHEARIN, JOHN D., Sergeant
Resided in Warren County and enlisted at age 25, August 16, 1861. Mustered in as Sergeant. Present or accounted for until captured at or near Spotsylvania Court House, Virginia, on or about May 8, 1864. Confined at Point Lookout, Maryland, May 17, 1864. Transferred to Elmira, New York, August 10, 1864. Died at Elmira on October 4, 1864, of "chronic diarrhoea."

SHEARIN, JOHN L., Private
Born in Warren County where he resided as a farmer prior to enlisting in Warren County at age 19, August 16, 1861. Present or accounted for until discharged on May 22, 1862, by reason of "general constitutional debility." Reenlisted in the company on July 16, 1863, for the war. Present or accounted for until captured at Kelly's Ford, Virginia, November 7, 1863. Confined at Point Lookout, Maryland, November 11, 1863. Paroled at Point Lookout on May 3, 1864, and transferred to Aiken's Landing, James River, Virginia, where he was received on May 8, 1864, for exchange. Returned to duty prior to September 1, 1864. Wounded in the right foot at Winchester, Virginia, September 19, 1864. Returned to duty on an unspecified date. Wounded in the face at Appomattox, Virginia, "in 1865." Captured by the enemy on an unspecified date and was paroled at Farmville, Virginia, April 11-21, 1865.

SHEARIN, JOHN R., Private
Resided in Warren County where he enlisted at age 31, August 16, 1861. Present or accounted for through April 8, 1865.

SHEARIN, JOSEPH W., Private
Enlisted at Hamilton's Crossing, Virginia, at age 17, April 18, 1863, for the war. Discharged on June 1, 1863, after providing a substitute.

SHEARIN, LANDON T., Private
Resided in Warren County and enlisted at Camp Wyatt at age 19, January 8, 1862. Present or accounted for until captured at or near Gettysburg, Pennsylvania, on or about July 3, 1863. Confined at Fort Delaware, Delaware, on or about July 7, 1863. Transferred to Point Lookout, Maryland, October 15-18, 1863. Died at Point Lookout on or about February 25, 1865, of "pneumonia." [Roll of Honor indicates that he was "a lunatic."]

SHEARIN, MOSES T., Private
Resided in Halifax County and enlisted in Warren County at age 22, August 16, 1861. Present or accounted for until June 13, 1863, when he was reported absent without leave. Returned to duty subsequent to August 31, 1863. Detailed for duty at Staunton, Virginia, on or about March 17, 1864. Reported absent on detail through August, 1864. Paroled at Ashland, Virginia, April 23, 1865.

SHEARIN, NICHOLAS L., Private
Born in Warren County where he resided prior to enlisting at Camp Wyatt at age 34, December 6, 1861. Present or accounted for until killed at Malvern Hill, Virginia, July 1, 1862.

SHEARIN, RICHARD E., Private
Resided in Warren County and enlisted at Camp Saunders at age 30, April 14, 1862. Present or accounted for until captured near Mine Run, Virginia, November 26-December 2, 1863. Confined at Old Capitol Prison, Washington, D.C., December 5, 1863. Transferred to Point Lookout, Maryland, February 3, 1864. Released at Point Lookout on February 20, 1864, after joining the U.S. Army. Unit to which assigned not reported.

SHEARIN, RICHARD R., Private
Born in Warren County where he resided prior to

enlisting in Warren County at age 35, August 16, 1861. Present or accounted for until killed at Gaines' Mill, Virginia, June 27, 1862.

SHEARIN, THOMAS G., Sergeant
Resided in Warren County where he enlisted at age 22, August 16, 1861. Mustered in as Private. Present or accounted for until wounded at Sharpsburg, Maryland, September 17, 1862. Returned to duty prior to May 3, 1863, when he was wounded at Chancellorsville, Virginia. Returned to duty in November-December, 1863. Promoted to Sergeant in January-June, 1864. Killed near Washington, D.C., July 12, 1864.

SHEARIN, THOMAS W., Corporal
Resided in Warren County where he enlisted at age 19, August 16, 1861. Mustered in as Private. Promoted to Corporal in May-December, 1862. Present or accounted for until wounded in the right thigh at Spotsylvania Court House, Virginia, May 12, 1864. Returned to duty subsequent to August 31, 1864. Surrendered at Appomattox Court House, Virginia, April 9, 1865.

SMITH, GEORGE W., Private
Born in Warren County where he resided prior to enlisting in Warren County at age 44, August 16, 1861. Present or accounted for until he died in hospital at Richmond, Virginia, January 16, 1863, of "pneumonia" and/or "chr[onic] diar[rhoea]."

STALLINGS, ELISHA B., Private
Resided in Edgecombe County and enlisted in Wake County at age 38, July 1, 1863, for the war. Present or accounted for until September 9, 1863, when he was detailed for hospital duty. Reported absent on duty as a nurse at Richmond, Virginia, through December, 1864.

STALLINGS, JOHN A., Private
Born in Warren County where he resided prior to enlisting in New Hanover County at age 26, April 28, 1862, for the war. Present or accounted for until he died in hospital at Staunton, Virginia, November 13, 1862, of "febris typhoides."

STALLINGS, THEOPHILUS, Private
Resided in Warren County and enlisted in Brunswick County at age 28, September 26, 1861. Promoted to Quartermaster Sergeant on October 16, 1861, and transferred to the Field and Staff of this regiment.

TALLEY, BENJAMIN T., Private
Born in Warren County where he resided prior to enlisting in Warren County at age 19, August 16, 1861. Present or accounted for until he died in hospital at Lynchburg, Virginia, or at Liberty, Virginia, February 23, 1863, of "diarrhoea chronic."

THOMAS, GEORGE L., Private
Born in Warren County where he resided prior to enlisting in Warren County at age 19, August 16, 1861. Present or accounted for until he died at Leesburg, Virginia, September 25, 1862. Cause of death not reported.

THOMAS, WILLIAM H., Private
Resided in Warren County where he enlisted at age 22, August 16, 1861. Present or accounted for until June 26, 1862, when he was reported absent without leave. Reported absent without leave through December, 1862.

Returned to duty on an unspecified date. Wounded near Hamilton's Crossing, Virginia, April 30, 1863. Reported absent wounded through December, 1863. Reported on detail at Richmond, Virginia, from February 13, 1864, through December, 1864. [Roll of Honor indicates he was wounded near Frederick, Maryland, on an unspecified date.]

THOMPSON, JOHN A., Private
Born in Warren County where he resided prior to enlisting in Warren County at age 25, August 16, 1861. Present or accounted for until hospitalized at Richmond, Virginia, June 30, 1862, with a gunshot wound of the arm. Place and date wounded not reported. Died at Richmond on July 20 or July 30, 1862. Cause of death not reported.

TURNER, HENRY, Private
Resided in Warren County and enlisted at age 38, August 16, 1861. Discharged on September 28, 1861. Reason discharged not reported.

VERSER, JOHN, Private
Resided in Warren County and enlisted in Wake County at age 40, September 1, 1863, for the war. Died in hospital at Richmond, Virginia, on or about December 22, 1863, of "diarrhoea ch[ronic]."

WALKER, CHRISTOPHER N., Private
Resided in Warren County where he enlisted at age 21, August 16, 1861. Present or accounted for until he surrendered at Appomattox Court House, Virginia, April 9, 1865.

WALKER, LEVI, Private
Born in Warren County where he resided prior to enlisting in Warren County at age 25, August 16, 1861. Present or accounted for until he died in hospital at Petersburg, Virginia, October 31-November 1, 1862, of "ty[phoid] fever."

WALKER, W. H., Private
Resided in Warren County and enlisted at age 33, August 16, 1861. Discharged on or about August 16, 1861, by reason of having "failed to pass the inspection of the mustering officer."

WHITE, JAMES J., Private
Born in Warren County where he resided prior to enlisting in Warren County at age 20, August 16, 1861. Present or accounted for until wounded at Malvern Hill, Virginia, July 1, 1862. Hospitalized at Richmond, Virginia, where he died on July 6 or August 1, 1862, of wounds.

WILLIAMS, ROBERT D., Sergeant
Resided in Warren County where he enlisted at age 20, August 16, 1861. Mustered in as Corporal. Promoted to Sergeant in May-December, 1862. Present or accounted for until wounded in the scalp at Gettysburg, Pennsylvania, July 1, 1863. Returned to duty prior to September 1, 1863. Captured at Kelly's Ford, Virginia, November 7, 1863. Confined at Point Lookout, Maryland, November 11, 1863. Paroled at Point Lookout on or about November 1, 1864, and transferred to Venus Point, Savannah River, Georgia, where he was received on November 15, 1864, for exchange.

WILLIAMS, WILLIAM A., Private
Resided in Warren County and enlisted "at camp" at

age 18, November 3, 1862, for the war. Present or accounted for until captured at Kelly's Ford, Virginia, November 7, 1863. Confined at Point Lookout, Maryland, November 11, 1863. Paroled at Point Lookout on May 3, 1864, and transferred to Aiken's Landing, James River, Virginia, where he was received on May 8, 1864, for exchange. Returned to duty on an unspecified date. Killed on August 21, 1864. Place of death not reported.

WILLIAMS, WILLIAM ALSTON, Private
Resided in Warren County where he enlisted at age 23, August 16, 1861. Present or accounted for until discharged on August 20, 1862, by reason of "rheumatism & disease of the heart."

WIMBERLY, MATTHEW, Private
Resided in Wake County where he enlisted at age 24, July 23, 1863, for the war. Deserted on or about August 15, 1863.

COMPANY C

This company, known as the "Brunswick Double Quicks," was raised in Brunswick County and enlisted at Camp Howard on July 18, 1861. The company was then assigned to the 30th Regiment N.C. Troops and was designated Company C. After joining the regiment the company functioned as a part of the regiment, and its history for the war period is reported as a part of the regimental history.

The information contained in the following roster of the company was compiled principally from a company muster-in and descriptive roll dated October 8, 1861, and from company muster rolls for October-December, 1861; March-April, 1862; November-December, 1862; May-August, 1863; and November, 1863-August, 1864. No company muster rolls were found for July 18-September, 1861; January-February, 1862; May-October, 1862; January-April, 1863; September-October, 1863; or for the period after August, 1864. Valuable information was obtained from primary records such as the Roll of Honor, discharge certificates, medical records, prisoner of war records, and pension applications. Secondary sources such as postwar rosters and histories, cemetery records, and records of the United Daughters of the Confederacy also provided useful information.

OFFICERS

CAPTAINS

GREEN, JOSEPH
Resided in Brunswick County and enlisted at age 46. Elected Captain on July 18, 1861. Present or accounted for until he was defeated for reelection when the regiment was reorganized on May 1, 1862.

ALLEN, DAVID CHARLES
Resided in Brunswick County and enlisted at Camp Howard at age 25. Appointed 1st Lieutenant on September 26, 1861, and was elected Captain on May 2, 1862. Present or accounted for until wounded at Winchester, Virginia, September 19, 1864. Returned to duty on an unspecified date. Surrendered at Appomattox Court House, Virginia, April 9, 1865. "As gallant a man as ever drew a blade."

LIEUTENANTS

BENNETT, SOLOMON W., 1st Lieutenant
Resided in Brunswick County and enlisted at Camp Howard at age 29, July 18, 1861. Mustered in as Private. Elected 2nd Lieutenant on May 1, 1862. Promoted to 1st Lieutenant on August 1, 1862. Present or accounted for until wounded at Chancellorsville, Virginia, May 3, 1863. Reported on detail as Assistant Enrolling Officer of Brunswick County in November-December, 1863. Reported on duty as an enrolling officer in North Carolina in January-August, 1864. Reported on duty as Enrolling Officer of Robeson County on April 3, 1865.

CAIN, LORENZO DOW, 3rd Lieutenant
Resided in Brunswick County and was by occupation a teacher prior to enlisting at Camp Howard at age 31. Elected 3rd Lieutenant on September 26, 1861. Present or accounted for until wounded in the shoulder at Gaines' Mill, Virginia, June 27, 1862. Died in hospital at Richmond, Virginia, August 3, 1862, of "typhoid fever." He was "a bright [and] amiable young man."

DOSHIER, JAMES HENRY, 3rd Lieutenant
Resided in Brunswick County where he enlisted at age 18, July 18, 1861. Mustered in as Sergeant. Present or accounted for until wounded at Sharpsburg, Maryland, September 17, 1862. Returned to duty prior to January 1, 1863. Elected 3rd Lieutenant on January 14, 1863. Present or accounted for until promoted to 1st Lieutenant on February 4, 1864, and transferred to Company G, 20th Regiment N.C. Troops (10th Regiment N.C. Volunteers).

GREER, EPHRAIM J., 1st Lieutenant
Resided in Brunswick County where he enlisted at age 29, September 2, 1861. Mustered in as Private. Elected 1st Lieutenant on May 1, 1862. Present or accounted for until wounded at or near Malvern Hill, Virginia, on or about July 1, 1862. Hospitalized at Richmond, Virginia, where he died on or about July 26, 1862, of wounds.

RUARK, EDWARD R., 3rd Lieutenant
Resided in Brunswick County where he enlisted at age 23, July 18, 1861. Mustered in as Private. Promoted to Sergeant in May, 1862. Elected 3rd Lieutenant on September 23, 1862. Present or accounted for until he died at Smithville (Southport) on or about December 9, 1862. "He went home and died of smallpox, spreading it and killing his mother and others." He was "gallant, brave, and ambitious."

SWAIN, JOHN R., Jr., 2nd Lieutenant
Resided in Brunswick County and enlisted at Camp Holmes at age 22, July 18, 1861. Mustered in as 1st Sergeant. Elected 2nd Lieutenant on September 23, 1862. Appointed 2nd Lieutenant of Company D, 10th Regiment N.C. State Troops (1st Regiment N.C. Artillery) to rank from October 31, 1862; however, he declined the appointment and remained with this company. Present or accounted for until wounded at Chancellorsville, Virginia, May 3, 1863. Returned to duty prior to July 1, 1863. Present or accounted for until captured at or near Spotsylvania Court House, Virginia, May 10-12, 1864. Confined at Fort Delaware, Delaware, May 17, 1864. Released at Fort Delaware on June 16, 1865, after taking the Oath of Allegiance.

THARP, SAMUEL P., 2nd Lieutenant
Resided in Brunswick County where he enlisted at age

23. Elected 2nd Lieutenant on July 18, 1861. Present or accounted for until he was defeated for reelection when the regiment was reorganized on May 1, 1862. Later served in Captain John W. Galloway's Company (Coast Guards), North Carolina Troops.

NONCOMMISSIONED OFFICERS AND PRIVATES

ALLEN, CHARLES W., Private
Previously served in Company B, 18th Regiment N.C. Troops (8th Regiment N.C. Volunteers). Enlisted in this company at Camp Holmes on July 13, 1863, for the war. Present or accounted for through August, 1864.

ARMFIELD, JOHN J., Private
Place and date of enlistment not reported. First reported in the records of this company in October-December, 1864. Captured at Farmville, Virginia, April 6, 1865. Confined at Point Lookout, Maryland, April 14, 1865. Died at Point Lookout on June 8, 1865, of "dia[rrhoea] acuta."

BALLENTON, J. N., Private
Born in New Hanover County where he resided as a cooper prior to enlisting at Camp Holmes at age 38, June 14, 1863, for the war. "Was taken from his shop by a file of men without being allowed an opportunity of seeing his family. Never fired a gun in the rebellion and took the first opportunity of deserting and came into the Union lines at Kelly's Ford," Virginia, November 8, 1863. Confined at Old Capitol Prison, Washington, D.C., on or about November 10, 1863. Died in hospital at Washington on March 13, 1864, of "variola confluenta."

BELL, JOHN, Private
Resided in Brunswick County where he enlisted at age 48, September 2, 1861. Present or accounted for until November-December, 1862, when he was reported absent without leave. Returned to duty prior to July 1, 1863. Present or accounted for through August, 1864.

BENNETT, DANIEL K., Private
Previously served as Captain of Company K, 36th Regiment N.C. Troops (2nd Regiment N.C. Artillery). Enlisted in this company with the rank of Private on July 11, 1863. Present or accounted for until elected 2nd Lieutenant of Company G, 20th Regiment N.C. Troops (10th Regiment N.C. Volunteers), July 31, 1863, and transferred to that unit. Later served as Captain of Company G, 20th Regiment N.C. Troops (10th Regiment N.C. Volunteers).

BENTON, THOMAS A., Private
Enlisted on September 2, 1861. Discharged prior to January 1, 1862, after providing a substitute.

BICKNELL, BENJAMIN E., Private
Resided in Wilkes County and enlisted at Camp Holmes at age 30, September 23, 1862. Detailed at the government shoeshops at Richmond, Virginia, prior to January 1, 1863. Assigned to Company B, 2nd Battalion Virginia Infantry (Local Defense), on an unspecified date. Reported on hospital duty during May-August, 1863. Transferred to the government shops at Salisbury on or about August 1, 1863. Reported absent with leave in North Carolina in January-August, 1864. [North

Carolina pension records indicate he was wounded at "Fredericksburg, Virginia, November 1, 1863."]

BLACKWELDER, W., Private
Resided in Cabarrus County and enlisted at Camp Holmes at age 40, September 2, 1863, for the war. Present or accounted for until captured at Kelly's Ford, Virginia, November 7, 1863. Confined at Old Capitol Prison, Washington, D.C., November 8, 1863. Transferred to Point Lookout, Maryland, February 3, 1864. Died at Point Lookout on April 16, 1864, of "congestive chill."

BOWERS, JOHN, Private
Resided in Pitt County and enlisted in Brunswick County at age 45, September 2, 1861. Present or accounted for until discharged on March 21, 1862, "for larceny."

BURNS, OTTOWAY J., Corporal
Resided in Brunswick County and enlisted at Camp Howard at age 20, July 18, 1861. Mustered in as Private. Promoted to Corporal on December 23, 1861. Present or accounted for until transferred to Company A, 41st Regiment N.C. Troops (3rd Regiment N.C. Cavalry), June 1, 1862.

BUTLER, BENJAMIN L., Sergeant
Born in Brunswick County and enlisted at Camp Howard at age 25, July 18, 1861. Mustered in as Sergeant. Present or accounted for until wounded in the foot at Malvern Hill, Virginia, July 1, 1862. Reported absent wounded or absent on detail through June, 1863. Returned to duty in July-August, 1863. Present or accounted for until he surrendered at Appomattox Court House, Virginia, April 9, 1865.

BUTLER, JOHN C., Private
Resided in Brunswick County and enlisted at Camp Howard at age 21, July 18, 1861. Present or accounted for until wounded in the face at Fredericksburg, Virginia, on or about December 13, 1862. Returned to duty on March 10, 1863. Present or accounted for until captured at Spotsylvania Court House, Virginia, May 12, 1864. Confined at Point Lookout, Maryland, May 18, 1864. Transferred to Elmira, New York, August 10, 1864. Died at Elmira on January 4, 1865, of "variola."

BYRD, JOHN, Private
Born in Brunswick County where he resided prior to enlisting in Brunswick County at age 17, September 2, 1861. Present or accounted for until he died in hospital at Richmond, Virginia, April 21, 1863, of "typhoid fever" and/or "pneumonia."

CHIMIS, MICHAEL H., Private
Resided in Brunswick County and enlisted at Camp Howard at age 17, July 18, 1861. Present or accounted for until he died at Smithville (Southport) on October 13, 1861, of "brain fever."

CLIFF, EDWARD, Private
Resided in Brunswick County where he enlisted at age 44, September 2, 1861. Present or accounted for until he died at Camp Wyatt on December 30, 1861, of "brain fever."

CLIFF, JOHN, Private
Born in Brunswick County where he resided prior to

enlisting at Camp Howard at age 15, July 18, 1861. Present or accounted for until he died in hospital at Richmond, Virginia, in April, 1863, of "typhoid pneumonia."

COLEMAN, ETHELDRED, Private
Resided in Brunswick County where he enlisted at age 23, September 2, 1861. Present or accounted for until he surrendered at Appomattox Court House, Virginia, April 9, 1865.

COLEMAN, GEORGE W., Private
Resided in Brunswick County where he enlisted at age 27, September 2, 1861. Present or accounted for until wounded in the hip and captured at Sharpsburg, Maryland, September 17, 1862. No further records.

COLEMAN, JAMES, Private
Resided in Brunswick County and enlisted at Camp Howard at age 27, September 2, 1861. Reported absent without leave on October 31, 1861. Returned to duty prior to January 1, 1862. Present or accounted for through August, 1863. Deserted prior to January 1, 1864. Apprehended on an unspecified date. Court-martialed on or about February 12, 1864. Returned to duty prior to May 12, 1864, when he was captured at Spotsylvania Court House, Virginia. Confined at Point Lookout, Maryland, May 18, 1864. Transferred to Elmira, New York, August 10, 1864. Paroled at Elmira on October 11, 1864, and transferred to Venus Point, Savannah River, Georgia, where he was received on November 15, 1864, for exchange.

COLEMAN, JOHN C., Private
Resided in Brunswick County where he enlisted at age 25, September 2, 1861. Present or accounted for until he died at Richmond, Virginia, August 20, 1862, of "fever."

CORBETT, WESLEY, Private
Born in New Hanover County where he resided as a farmer prior to enlisting in Brunswick County at age 19, September 2, 1861. Present or accounted for until discharged on February 7, 1862, by reason of "constitutional debility and chronic diarrhoea."

COSTNER, JACOB B., Private
Resided in Gaston County and enlisted at Camp Holmes at age 34, August 24, 1863, for the war. Present or accounted for until captured at Kelly's Ford, Virginia, November 7, 1863. Confined at Point Lookout, Maryland, November 11, 1863. Released on January 25, 1864, after joining the U.S. service. Unit to which assigned not reported.

CRISS, WILEY, Private
Resided in Cabarrus County and enlisted at Camp Holmes at age 40, September 1, 1863, for the war. Present or accounted for until wounded in the right thigh at or near Spotsylvania Court House, Virginia, May 19, 1864. Reported absent wounded through February 26, 1865.

DAIL, BENJAMIN, Private
Resided in Brunswick County where he enlisted at age 18, September 2, 1861. Present or accounted for until he died in hospital at Gordonsville, Virginia, August 12, 1863, of "febris remittens."

DANFORD, ABRAM, Private
Resided in Brunswick County and enlisted at Camp Howard at age 21, July 18, 1861. Present or accounted for until wounded in the face at Gaines' Mill, Virginia, June 27, 1862. Reported absent without leave in November-December, 1862. Reported on detail as a hospital nurse at Weldon from March 1, 1863, through August, 1864. Returned to duty on an unspecified date. Surrendered at Appomattox Court House, Virginia, April 9, 1865.

DANFORD, JOHN WILLIAM, Private
Resided in Brunswick County where he enlisted at age 24, September 2, 1861. Present or accounted for until captured at Kelly's Ford, Virginia, November 7, 1863. Confined at Point Lookout, Maryland, November 11, 1863. Paroled at Point Lookout on or about February 13, 1865, and transferred to Cox's Wharf, James River, Virginia, where he was received February 14-15, 1865, for exchange. [North Carolina pension records indicate he was wounded on June 10, 1864.]

DANIEL, MADISON, Private
Place and date of enlistment not reported. Deserted on August 11, 1861.

DEW, DAVID C., Private
Resided in Brunswick County and enlisted at Camp Howard at age 21, July 18, 1861. Mustered in as Corporal. Reduced to ranks on December 25, 1861. Present or accounted for until wounded at Malvern Hill, Virginia, July 1, 1862. Detailed for duty as a hospital nurse at Richmond, Virginia, during November, 1862-February, 1863. Returned to duty prior to July 1, 1863. Captured at Kelly's Ford, Virginia, November 7, 1863. Confined at Point Lookout, Maryland, November 11, 1863. Paroled at Point Lookout on or about March 14, 1865, and transferred to Boulware's Wharf, James River, Virginia, where he was received on March 16, 1865, for exchange.

DICKENS, ANDREW J., Private
Resided in Chatham County and enlisted at Camp Holmes at age 36, July 3, 1863, for the war. Present or accounted for until wounded at Spotsylvania Court House, Virginia, in May, 1864. Hospitalized at Richmond, Virginia, May 22, 1864. Furloughed for sixty days on June 7, 1864. Reported absent without leave on August 4, 1864.

DIRDIN, W. M., Private
Resided in Guilford County and enlisted at Camp Holmes at age 30, August 29, 1863, for the war. Present or accounted for through December, 1863. Reported absent without leave in January-August, 1864.

DREW, JOHN T., Private
Resided in Brunswick County where he enlisted at age 22, September 5, 1861. Present or accounted for through April, 1862. Discharged on an unspecified date by reason of "insanity."

EDWARDS, WILLIAM H., Sergeant
Resided in Brunswick County and enlisted at Camp Howard at age 21, July 18, 1861. Mustered in as Sergeant. Present or accounted for until killed at Sharpsburg, Maryland, September 17, 1862.

ELLER, W. W., Private
Resided in Wilkes County and enlisted at Camp

Holmes at age 38, September 23, 1862, for the war. Present or accounted for until he died in hospital at Richmond, Virginia, February 25, 1863, of "pneumonia."

EUSLEY, JOHN, Private

Resided in Jackson County. Place and date of enlistment not reported. Deserted to the enemy on February 7, 1862. Confined at Knoxville, Tennessee, until released on an unspecified date.

EVERHART, JACOB, Private

Born in Davidson County where he resided as a farmer prior to enlisting at age 22, July 11, 1863, for the war. Captured (or deserted to the enemy) at Flint Hill, Virginia, July 22-24, 1863. Confined at Point Lookout, Maryland, July 31, 1863. Released on January 26, 1864, after taking the Oath of Allegiance and joining the U.S. Army. Assigned to Company D, 1st Regiment U.S. Volunteer Infantry.

FILE, J. N., Private

Resided in Cabarrus County and enlisted at Camp Holmes at age 33, June 30, 1863, for the war. Present or accounted for until paroled at Lynchburg, Virginia, April 13, 1865. [May have served previously as 1st Lieutenant of Company H, 8th Regiment N.C. State Troops.]

FLYNN, JAMES WASHINGTON, Private

Resided in New Hanover County and enlisted in Brunswick County at age 18, September 2, 1861. Present or accounted for until wounded at Malvern Hill, Virginia, July 1, 1862. Returned to duty prior to January 1, 1863. Present or accounted for through August, 1864.

GALLIMORE, RANSOM, Private

Resided in Randolph County and enlisted at Camp Holmes at age 29, July 13, 1863, for the war. Present or accounted for until captured at Kelly's Ford, Virginia, November 7, 1863. Confined at Point Lookout, Maryland, November 11, 1863. Paroled at Point Lookout on or about September 18, 1864, and transferred to Varina, Virginia, where he was received on September 22, 1864, for exchange. Hospitalized at Richmond, Virginia, September 23, 1864, with phthisis pulmonalis and was furloughed for sixty days on October 4, 1864.

GORE, JOHN, Private

Born in Brunswick County where he resided prior to enlisting at Camp Howard at age 35, July 18, 1861. Present or accounted for until December, 1862, when he was reported absent without leave. Returned to duty on an unspecified date. Killed at Chancellorsville, Virginia, May 3, 1863.

GREEN, WILLIAM B., Private

Resided in Brunswick County and enlisted at Camp Howard at age 19, July 18, 1861. Present or accounted for until transferred to Company A, 41st Regiment N.C. Troops (3rd Regiment N.C. Cavalry), June 1, 1862.

GREER, LEWIS T., Corporal

Born in Brunswick County where he resided prior to enlisting in Brunswick County at age 22, September 2, 1861. Mustered in as Private. Promoted to Corporal on February 16, 1863. Present or accounted for until killed at Chancellorsville, Virginia, on or about May 3, 1863.

HARRIS, GEORGE W., Private

Resided in Brunswick County and enlisted at Camp Howard at age 17, July 18, 1861. Present or accounted for until wounded in the knee at Malvern Hill, Virginia, July 1, 1862. Hospitalized at Richmond, Virginia, where he died on July 19, 1862, of wounds.

HART, OBEDIAH, Private

Resided in Brunswick County and enlisted at Camp Howard at age 45, July 18, 1861. Present or accounted for until December, 1862, when he was reported absent without leave. Returned to duty prior to July 1, 1863. Died at or near Richmond, Virginia, September 27-28, 1863, of "febris typh[oid]."

HARVELL, JAMES M., Private

Resided in Brunswick County where he enlisted at age 18, September 2, 1861. Present or accounted for until captured at Kelly's Ford, Virginia, November 7, 1863. Confined at Point Lookout, Maryland, November 11, 1863. Paroled at Point Lookout on or about February 24, 1865, and transferred to Aiken's Landing, James River, Virginia, where he was received on February 25-March 2, 1865, for exchange. Furloughed for thirty days on March 14, 1865.

HARVELL, JOHN V., Private

Resided in Brunswick County where he enlisted at age 21, September 2, 1861. Present or accounted for until wounded at Sharpsburg, Maryland, September 17, 1862. Hospitalized at Staunton, Virginia, where he died on October 7, 1862, of wounds and/or "febris typhoides." "He was a brave and gallant soldier."

HAYWOOD, RICHARD, Private

Resided in Guilford County. Place and date of enlistment not reported. Captured at Farmville, Virginia, April 6, 1865. Confined at Point Lookout, Maryland, April 14, 1865. Released on June 28, 1865, after taking the Oath of Allegiance.

HENDRON, SOLOMON R., Private

Resided in Wilkes County and enlisted at Camp Holmes at age 19, September 23, 1862, for the war. Present or accounted for until wounded and captured at Spotsylvania Court House, Virginia, May 12, 1864. Confined at Point Lookout, Maryland, May 18, 1864. Paroled on or about March 11, 1865, and transferred to Boulware's Wharf, James River, Virginia, where he was received on March 16, 1865, for exchange.

HEWETT, LORENZO D., Private

Resided in Brunswick County where he enlisted at age 18, September 2, 1861. Present or accounted for until captured at Kelly's Ford, Virginia, November 7, 1863. Confined at Point Lookout, Maryland, November 11, 1863. Exchanged on September 30, 1864. Furloughed for sixty days on or about October 11, 1864.

HEWETT, SAMUEL M., Private

Resided in Brunswick County where he enlisted at age 22, September 2, 1861. Present or accounted for until killed at Gettysburg, Pennsylvania, July 1, 1863.

HEWETT, URIAH, Private

Resided in Brunswick County where he enlisted at age 23, September 12, 1861. Present or accounted for until wounded at Malvern Hill, Virginia, July 1, 1862. Died at Richmond, Virginia, July 12, 1862, of wounds.

HICKMAN, BENJAMIN R., Private
Born in Brunswick County where he resided prior to enlisting in Brunswick County at age 30, July 18, 1861. Deserted on August 11, 1861. Returned to duty prior to January 1, 1862. Present or accounted for until hospitalized at Richmond, Virginia, May 3, 1863, with "pneumonia." Died in hospital at Richmond on May 12, 1863.

HICKMAN, ROBERT, Private
Resided in Brunswick County where he enlisted at age 33, September 2, 1861. Present or accounted for until wounded at Malvern Hill, Virginia, July 1, 1862. Returned to duty prior to January 1, 1863. Present or accounted for until captured at or near Spotsylvania Court House, Virginia, May 8-9, 1864. Confined at Point Lookout, Maryland, May 18, 1864. Transferred to Elmira, New York, August 10, 1864. Died at Elmira on December 6, 1864, of "pneumonia."

HOWARD, GEORGE W., Sergeant
Resided in Buncombe County and enlisted at Camp Howard at age 20, July 18, 1861. Mustered in as Private. Promoted to Corporal in May-June, 1862. Present or accounted for until wounded at Gaines' Mill, Virginia, June 27, 1862. Returned to duty prior to January 1, 1863. Promoted to Sergeant in January-July, 1864. Present or accounted for until hospitalized at Charlottesville, Virginia, July 26, 1864, with a gunshot wound of the right thigh. Place and date wounded not reported. Returned to duty prior to September 1, 1864. No further records.

HOWARD, JOHN J., Private
Resided in Brunswick County where he enlisted at age 22, September 2, 1861. Present or accounted for until captured at or near Sharpsburg, Maryland, on or about September 17, 1862. Paroled on September 21, 1862. Paroled again on October 4, 1862. No further records.

HUGHES, JOSEPH, Private
Resided in Brunswick County and enlisted at Camp Holmes at age 39, September 23, 1863, for the war. Present or accounted for until he died at Orange Court House, Virginia, February 4, 186[4]. Cause of death not reported.

HYATT, JESSE, Private
Place and date of enlistment not reported. Deserted to the enemy on an unspecified date. Confined at Bermuda Hundred, Virginia, January 26, 1865. Transferred to Washington, D.C., where he arrived on February 1, 1865. Released on or about February 1, 1865, after taking the Oath of Allegiance.

INSCORE, JAMES, Private
Resided in Wilkes County and enlisted at Camp Holmes at age 31, April 12, 1863, for the war. Wounded at Chancellorsville, Virginia, May 1-4, 1863. Reported absent without leave in November-December, 1863. Reported absent without leave in Wilkes County on August 14, 1864.

JARVIS, LEVI, Private
Resided in Wilkes County and enlisted at Camp Holmes at age 32, September 23, 1862, for the war. Present or accounted for until hospitalized at

Richmond, Virginia, April 1, 1863, with "pleurisy." Died in hospital at Richmond on April 20, 1863.

JARVIS, WILEY, Private
Resided in Wilkes County and enlisted at Camp Holmes at age 34, September 23, 1862, for the war. Present or accounted for until he died at Front Royal, Virginia, in July-August, 1863. Cause of death not reported.

JENKINS, JOSEPH S., Private
Resided in Brunswick County and enlisted at Camp Howard at age 18, July 18, 1861. Present or accounted for until April 5, 1864, when he was transferred to the C.S. Navy.

JOHNSON, A. L., Private
Resided in Wilkes County and enlisted at Camp Holmes at age 35, September 23, 1862, for the war. Present or accounted for until captured near Spotsylvania Court House, Virginia, May 12, 1864. Confined at Point Lookout, Maryland, May 18, 1864. Transferred to Elmira, New York, August 10, 1864. Released at Elmira on June 23, 1865.

JOHNSON, A. MARION, Private
Resided in Wilkes County and enlisted at Camp Holmes at age 28, September 23, 1862, for the war. Present or accounted for until he was reported absent without leave for two months in the autumn of 1863. Returned to duty on an unspecified date. Captured near Spotsylvania Court House, Virginia, May 12, 1864. Confined at Point Lookout, Maryland, May 18, 1864. Transferred to Elmira, New York, August 10, 1864. Paroled at Elmira on October 11, 1864, and transferred to Venus Point, Savannah River, Georgia, where he was received on November 15, 1864, for exchange.

JOHNSON, CALVIN, Private
Born in Wilkes County where he resided as a shoemaker prior to enlisting at Camp Holmes at age 23, September 23, 1862, for the war. Present or accounted for until he died at Richmond, Virginia, April 22-23, 1863. Cause of death not reported.

JOHNSON, JOHN, Private
Resided in Wilkes County and enlisted at Camp Holmes at age 26, September 23, 1862, for the war. Present or accounted for until he deserted on January 10, 1863. Returned to duty prior to July 1, 1863. Present or accounted for until he was reported absent without leave in January-August, 1864. [North Carolina pension records indicate he was wounded at Spotsylvania Court House, Virginia, May 12, 1864.]

KIMEL, DANIEL A., Private
Resided in Davidson County and enlisted at Camp Howard at age 18, June 20, 1863, for the war. Present or accounted for until captured at Farmville, Virginia, April 6, 1865. Confined at Newport News, Virginia, April 14, 1865. Released on June 27, 1865, after taking the Oath of Allegiance.

KLUTTS, TOBIAS, Private
Resided in Cabarrus County and enlisted at Camp Holmes at age 41, September 2, 1863, for the war. Present or accounted for until hospitalized at Richmond, Virginia, May 19, 1864, with a gunshot wound of the mouth. Place and date wounded not

reported. Died in hospital at Richmond on June 18, 1864, of "gangrene."

LAMB, ITHAMER, Private
Place and date of enlistment not reported. First listed in the records of this company in the autumn of 1864. Surrendered at Appomattox Court House, Virginia, April 9, 1865.

LAMBETH, WILLIAM, Private
Resided in Davidson County and enlisted at age 36. Place and date of enlistment not reported. Mustered in as Private. Promoted to Corporal on May 1, 1862. Wounded at Malvern Hill, Virginia, July 1, 1862. Discharged on February 4, 1863, by reason of disability from wounds. Reenlisted in the company at Camp Holmes on July 1, 1863, for the war. Mustered in as Private. Present or accounted for through August, 1864.

LARKINS, ROBERT S., Private
Resided in Brunswick County and enlisted at Camp Howard at age 23, July 18, 1861. Present or accounted for until wounded at Malvern Hill, Virginia, July 1, 1862. Returned to duty prior to January 1, 1863. Present or accounted for until he surrendered at Appomattox Court House, Virginia, April 9, 1865. [North Carolina pension records indicate he was wounded at "Wilderness, Virginia, in 1863."]

LAWRENCE, J. S., Private
Place and date of enlistment not reported. Paroled at Farmville, Virginia, April 11-21, 1865.

LEONARD, SAMUEL B., Corporal
Resided in Brunswick County and enlisted at Camp Howard at age 17, July 18, 1861. Mustered in as Private. Promoted to Corporal in May-June, 1862. Present or accounted for until wounded in the chest at Malvern Hill, Virginia, July 1, 1862. Was apparently discharged on an unspecified date by reason of disability from wounds.

LUNSFORD, JAMES R., Private
Resided in Wilkes County and was by occupation a farmer prior to enlisting at Camp Holmes at age 27, September 23, 1862, for the war. Present or accounted for until he deserted from hospital at Danville, Virginia, March 24, 1863. Returned to duty prior to January 1, 1864. Captured near Spotsylvania Court House, Virginia, May 10-12, 1864. Confined at Point Lookout, Maryland, May 18, 1864. Transferred to Elmira, New York, August 10, 1864. Released at Elmira on May 29, 1865, after taking the Oath of Allegiance.

LUNSFORD, JOEL, Private
Resided in Wilkes County and enlisted at Camp Holmes at age 20, September 23, 1862, for the war. Present or accounted for until he died in hospital at Liberty, Virginia, on or about February 16, 1863, of "diarrhoea chron[ic]."

McCALL, JOHN W., Private
Resided in Brunswick County where he enlisted at age 32, September 2, 1861. Present or accounted for until killed at Gaines' Mill, Virginia, June 27, 1862. He was "a good soldier and very brave in action."

McCALL, PAUL S., Private
Resided in Brunswick County and enlisted at Camp

Howard at age 24, July 18, 1861. Present or accounted for until wounded at Malvern Hill, Virginia, July 1, 1862. Returned to duty prior to January 1, 1863. Present or accounted for until captured at Kelly's Ford, Virginia, November 7, 1863. Confined at Point Lookout, Maryland, November 11, 1863. Paroled at Point Lookout on or about February 24, 1865, and transferred to Aiken's Landing, James River, Virginia, where he was received February 25-March 3, 1865, for exchange.

McDOWELL, WILLIAM J., Corporal
Born in Brunswick County where he resided as a farmer prior to enlisting at Camp Howard at age 18, July 18, 1861. Mustered in as Private. Promoted to Corporal in January-August, 1864. Present or accounted for until wounded in both feet on August 21, 1864. Three toes amputated. Reported absent wounded until March 14, 1865, when he was retired from service by reason of disability. [Nominated for the Badge of Distinction for gallantry at Chancellorsville, Virginia, May 1-4, 1863.]

McMICHAEL, JESSE, Private
Place and date of enlistment not reported. Surrendered at Black and White, Virginia, April 17, 1865.

MALTSBY, WILLIAM A., Private
Resided in Brunswick County where he enlisted at age 22, September 2, 1861. Died in hospital at Wilmington on or about October 11, 1861, of "pneumonia."

MARSHALL, WILLIAM D., Corporal
Resided in New Hanover County and was by occupation a blacksmith prior to enlisting at Camp Howard at age 16, July 18, 1861. Mustered in as Private. Promoted to Corporal in May-December, 1862. Present or accounted for until captured near Spotsylvania Court House, Virginia, May 12, 1864. Confined at Point Lookout, Maryland, May 18, 1864. Transferred to Elmira, New York, August 10, 1864. Released at Elmira on June 23, 1865, after taking the Oath of Allegiance.

MILLER, ALEXANDER B., Private
Resided in Wilkes County and enlisted at Camp Holmes at age 24, September 23, 1862, for the war. Present or accounted for until he deserted on November 25, 1862. Returned to duty in November-December, 1863. Captured at Spotsylvania Court House, Virginia, May 12, 1864. Confined at Point Lookout, Maryland, May 18, 1864. Transferred to Elmira, New York, August 10, 1864. Died at Elmira on April 12, 1865, of "pneumonia."

MILLER, H. C., Private
Resided in Wilkes County and enlisted at Camp Holmes at age 26, September 23, 1862, for the war. Present or accounted for until he deserted on November 25, 1862.

MILLER, JOHN L., Private
Resided in Wilkes County and enlisted at Camp Holmes at age 27, September 23, 1862, for the war. Present or accounted for until wounded in the right leg and captured at Manassas Gap, Virginia, July 23, 1863. Right leg amputated. Confined at Point Lookout, Maryland, July 31, 1863. Transferred on May 8, 1864. No further records.

MILLIKEN, ISAAC, 1st Sergeant
Resided in Brunswick County where he enlisted at age

23, September 12, 1861. Mustered in as Private. Present or accounted for until wounded in the left hand at Malvern Hill, Virginia, July 1, 1862. One finger amputated. Returned to duty on an unspecified date. Promoted to Sergeant on September 23, 1862, "for good conduct at Sharpsburg," Maryland. Promoted to 1st Sergeant in January-June, 1863. Present or accounted for until captured near Spotsylvania Court House, Virginia, May 12, 1864. Confined at Point Lookout, Maryland, May 18, 1864. Transferred to Elmira, New York, August 10, 1864. Released at Elmira on June 23, 1865, after taking the Oath of Allegiance.

MINTS, JESSE O., Private
Resided in Brunswick County and enlisted at Camp Howard at age 25, July 18, 1861. Present or accounted for through April, 1862. Reported absent without leave from December, 1862, through August, 1863.

MOORE, ROBERT, Private
Born in Wilkes County where he resided prior to enlisting at Camp Holmes at age 34, September 23, 1862, for the war. Present or accounted for until hospitalized at Richmond, Virginia, May 2, 1863, with "typhoid pneumonia." Died on May 9-11, 1863.

MOORE, THEOPHILUS, Private
Born in Edgecombe County where he resided as a farmer prior to enlisting at Camp Holmes at age 43, August 31, 1863, for the war. Hospitalized at Richmond, Virginia, May 17, 1864, with a gunshot wound. Place and date wounded not reported. Furloughed for sixty days on June 3, 1864. Reported absent without leave on or about August 1, 1864. Returned to duty on an unspecified date. Paroled at Burkeville Junction, Virginia, April 14-17, 1865.

MOTT, JOHN, Private
Resided in Brunswick County where he enlisted at age 17, October 15, 1861. Present or accounted for until wounded at Malvern Hill, Virginia, July 1, 1862. Returned to duty prior to January 1, 1863. Present or accounted for until he was reported missing at Gettysburg, Pennsylvania, July 1-3, 1863.

OAKLEY, DAVID, Private
Place and date of enlistment not reported. First reported in the records of this company in the autumn of 1864. Surrendered at Appomattox Court House, Virginia, April 9, 1865.

PARKER, BENJAMIN T., Private
Previously served in 1st Company D, 12th Regiment N.C. Troops (2nd Regiment N.C. Volunteers). Enlisted in this company at Camp Holmes at age 18, July 11, 1863, for the war. Present or accounted for through August, 1864.

PARKER, GEORGE, Private
Resided in Wilkes County and enlisted at Camp Holmes at age 34, September 23, 1862, for the war. Present or accounted for until he died at Strasburg, Virginia, in November, 1862. Cause of death not reported.

PARKER, J. C., Private
Resided in Randolph County and enlisted at Camp Holmes at age 33, July 1, 1863, for the war. Present or

accounted for through November 4, 1863. Died prior to September 1, 1864. Place and cause of death not reported.

PATTERSON, JOHN J., Private
Born in Cabarrus County where he resided as a farmer prior to enlisting at Camp Holmes at age 37, September 2, 1863, for the war. Present or accounted for until wounded in the right wrist at Kelly's Ford, Virginia, November 7, 1863. Discharged on March 22, 1865, by reason of disability from wounds.

PENDERGRASS, ELIJAH, Private
Resided in Wilkes County and enlisted at Camp Holmes at age 18, September 23, 1862, for the war. Died at Strasburg, Virginia, in November, 1862. Cause of death not reported.

PENDERGRASS, J. R., Private
Resided in Wilkes County and enlisted at Camp Holmes at age 28, September 23, 1862, for the war. Present or accounted for until captured at Kelly's Ford, Virginia, November 7, 1863. Confined at Point Lookout, Maryland, November 11, 1863. Died at Point Lookout on August 29, 1864. Cause of death not reported.

PENDERGRASS, WILLIAM M., Private
Resided in Wilkes County and enlisted at Camp Holmes at age 22, September 23, 1862, for the war. Present or accounted for through December, 1863. Reported absent without leave in January-August, 1864.

PENINGER, MOSES, Private
Resided in Cabarrus County and enlisted at Camp Holmes at age 39, September 11, 1863, for the war. Present or accounted for until he died in hospital at Richmond, Virginia, February 24, 1864, of "pyaemia."

PENNY, BENJAMIN F., Musician
Resided in Brunswick County and enlisted at Camp Howard at age 18, July 18, 1861. Mustered in as Musician (Drummer). Reported absent without leave in December, 1862. Returned to duty prior to July 1, 1863. Transferred to the C.S. Navy on September 3, 1863.

PILGRIM, McGILBERT, Private
Resided in Brunswick County and enlisted at Camp Holmes at age 18, July 18, 1861. Present or accounted for until reported missing at Fredericksburg, Virginia, December 13, 1862. Returned to duty on an unspecified date. Died near Summerville Ford, Virginia, June 20, 1863. Cause of death not reported.

PILGRIM, WILLIAM H. H., Private
Resided in Brunswick County where he enlisted at age 19, September 2, 1861. Present or accounted for until killed near Spotsylvania Court House, Virginia, May 12, 1864.

POTTER, HENRY G., Private
Resided in New Hanover County and enlisted in Brunswick County at age 17, September 2, 1861. Present or accounted for until wounded at Malvern Hill, Virginia, July 1, 1862. Died in hospital at Staunton, Virginia, November 10, 1862, of "febris typhoides."

POTTER, WILLIAM M., Private
Resided in New Hanover County and enlisted in

Brunswick County at age 17, September 2, 1861. Discharged prior to January 1, 1862, by reason of disability.

PRIDGEON, ALEXANDER S., Private
Resided in Nash County and enlisted in Brunswick County at age 36, September 2, 1861. Deserted prior to January 1, 1862.

REGISTER, THOMAS, Private
Resided in Brunswick County and enlisted at Camp Howard at age 27, July 18, 1861. Present or accounted for until "sent to hospital" on November 24, 1862. Died in the smallpox hospital at Staunton, Virginia, on an unspecified date. "A true man and brave soldier."

RIDDLING, WILLIAM A., Private
Resided in Cabarrus County and enlisted at Camp Holmes at age 45, September 2, 1863, for the war. Captured at Kelly's Ford, Virginia, November 7, 1863. Confined at Point Lookout, Maryland, November 11, 1863. Released on January 25, 1864, after taking the Oath of Allegiance and joining the U.S. Army. [May have been assigned to the 1st Regiment U.S. Volunteer Infantry.]

ROACH, ARCHIBALD, Private
Resided in Randolph County and enlisted at Camp Holmes at age 35, September 2, 1863, for the war. Present or accounted for until he died at Orange Court House, Virginia, January 24, 1864. Cause of death not reported.

ROBBINS, JOHN, Private
Enlisted at Camp Holmes on May 28, 1863, for the war. Present or accounted for through October 3, 1864. No further records.

ROBBINS, JONATHAN, Private
Resided in Randolph County and enlisted at Camp Holmes at age 36, August 30, 1863, for the war. Reported absent without leave in January-August, 1864. Returned to duty on an unspecified date. Surrendered at Appomattox Court House, Virginia, April 9, 1865. [North Carolina pension records indicate he was wounded in the left side at "Fisher's Hill, Virginia, 1865."]

ROBINSON, ALEXANDER S., Corporal
Resided in Brunswick County and enlisted at Camp Howard at age 21, July 18, 1861. Mustered in as Private. Present or accounted for until December, 1862, when he was reported absent without leave. Returned to duty prior to July 3, 1863, when he was wounded in the face and captured at Gettysburg, Pennsylvania. Confined at Fort Delaware, Delaware, on or about July 9, 1863. Transferred to Point Lookout, Maryland, October 15-18, 1863. Paroled at Point Lookout and transferred to City Point, Virginia, where he was received on March 6, 1864, for exchange. Promoted to Corporal on June 1, 1864. Returned to duty prior to September 1, 1864. Surrendered at Appomattox Court House, Virginia, April 9, 1865.

RUSS, STEWART, Sergeant
Resided in Brunswick County where he enlisted at age 27, September 2, 1861. Mustered in as Private. Wounded at Gaines' Mill, Virginia, June 27, 1862. Returned to duty and was promoted to Corporal prior to January 1, 1863. Promoted to Sergeant in February,

1863. Present or accounted for until captured at Kelly's Ford, Virginia, November 7, 1863. Confined at Point Lookout, Maryland, November 11, 1863. Paroled at Point Lookout on February 24, 1865, and transferred to Aiken's Landing, James River, Virginia, where he was received on February 25-March 3, 1865, for exchange.

SELLERS, RAYMOND G., Private
Resided in Brunswick County where he enlisted at age 18, July 18, 1861. Died at Smithville (Southport) on August 18, 1861, of "fever."

SELLERS, SAMUEL H., Private
Resided in Brunswick County and enlisted at Camp Howard at age 57, July 18, 1861. Present or accounted for until he died "at home" on January 28, 1862, of "mumps."

SHEW, JACOB W., Private
Resided in Wilkes County and enlisted at Camp Holmes at age 18, September 23, 1862, for the war. Present or accounted for until wounded in the right leg at Chancellorsville, Virginia, on or about May 2, 1863. Reported absent without leave in November-December, 1863. Detailed as a hospital nurse at Raleigh on July 25, 1864. Reported absent on detail through November, 1864.

SHEW, JOEL, Private
Born in Wilkes County where he resided prior to enlisting at Camp Holmes at age 34, September 23, 1862, for the war. Present or accounted for until wounded at Chancellorsville, Virginia, on or about May 3, 1863. Died at Chancellorsville, Virginia, May 5, 1863, of wounds.

SIMMONS, DANIEL, Private
Resided in Brunswick County and enlisted at Camp Howard at age 21, July 18, 1861. Present or accounted for through August, 1864.

SIMMONS, DANIEL F., Private
Resided in Brunswick County where he enlisted at age 18, July 18, 1861. Present or accounted for until he died in hospital at Wilmington on June 25, 1862, of "erysipelas."

SIMMONS, JAMES A., Private
Resided in Brunswick County and enlisted at Camp Howard at age 26, July 18, 1861. Present or accounted for until he deserted from hospital at Richmond, Virginia, in January-August, 1863. Apprehended on an unspecified date but "escaped from [the] provost guard" on or about December 15, 1863. No further records.

SIMMONS, JOHN B., Private
Born in Brunswick County where he resided prior to enlisting at Camp Howard at age 26, July 18, 1861. Present or accounted for until killed at Chancellorsville, Virginia, May 3, 1863.

SIMMONS, JOHN C., Private
Resided in Brunswick County and enlisted at Camp Howard at age 22, July 18, 1861. Present or accounted for until he died in hospital at Wilmington on October 11, 1861, of "pneumonia."

SIMMONS, LEWIS, Private
Resided in Brunswick County and enlisted at Camp

Holmes at age 36, September 5, 1863, for the war Present or accounted for until captured at Cedar Creek, Virginia, October 19, 1864. Confined at Point Lookout, Maryland, October 25, 1864. Released on June 20, 1865, after taking the Oath of Allegiance.

SKIPPER, WESLEY W., Private
Resided in Bladen County and enlisted near Orange Court House, Virginia, at age 17, February 2, 1864, for the war. Wounded in the neck and/or head and captured near Spotsylvania Court House, Virginia, May 12, 1864. Hospitalized at Alexandria, Virginia, where he died on May 27-29, 1864, of wounds.

SMITH, BENJAMIN, Corporal
Resided in Brunswick County and enlisted at Camp Howard at age 24, July 18, 1861. Mustered in as Private. Promoted to Corporal in January-June, 1863. Wounded in the jaw and captured at Gettysburg, Pennsylvania, July 1-4, 1863. Hospitalized at Davids Island, New York Harbor, on or about July 17, 1863. Paroled and transferred to City Point, Virginia, where he was received on September 8, 1863, for exchange. Returned to duty subsequent to December 31, 1863. Captured at Fisher's Hill, Virginia, September 22, 1864. Sent to Harpers Ferry, West Virginia. Confined at Point Lookout, Maryland, January 3, 1865. Released on June 3, 1865, after taking the Oath of Allegiance. [North Carolina pension records indicate he was wounded at "Wilderness, Virginia, in 1863."]

SMITH, REUBEN, Private
Previously served in 1st Company D, 12th Regiment N.C. Troops (2nd Regiment N.C. Volunteers). Enlisted in this company at Camp Holmes on July 13, 1863, for the war. Present or accounted for until captured near Spotsylvania Court House, Virginia, May 12, 1864. Confined at Point Lookout, Maryland, May 18, 1864. Transferred to Elmira, New York, August 10, 1864. Released on June 12, 1865, after taking the Oath of Allegiance.

SPRINKLE, HUGH, Private
Resided in Yadkin County and enlisted at Camp Holmes at age 31, November 22, 1863, for the war. Present or accounted for until captured at Winchester, Virginia, September 19, 1864. Confined at Point Lookout, Maryland, September 26, 1864. Released on June 20, 1865, after taking the Oath of Allegiance.

STALEY, ENOCH, Private
Resided in Wilkes County and enlisted at Camp Holmes at age 33, September 23, 1862, for the war. Present or accounted for until wounded at Chancellorsville, Virginia, May 3, 1863. Reported absent wounded through August, 1863. Reported absent without leave in November-December, 1863. Returned to duty on an unspecified date. Reported absent without leave on August 7, 1864. Detailed for unspecified duty on February 18, 1865.

STALVEY, BENJAMIN L., Private
Resided in Brunswick County where he enlisted at age 18, July 18, 1861. Present or accounted for until he died "at home" on August 29 or September 29, 1861, of "pneumonia."

STANLY, EDWARD W., Private
Resided in Brunswick County and enlisted at Camp

Howard at age 32, July 18, 1861. Died "at home" on November 22-24, 1861, of "pneumonia" or "fever."

STANLY, PETER, Private
Born in Brunswick County where he resided prior to enlisting in Brunswick County at age 32, July 18, 1861. Present or accounted for until wounded at Chancellorsville, Virginia, May 3, 1863. Died on May 5-7, 1863, of wounds. Place of death not reported.

STANLY, SAMUEL V., Private
Resided in Brunswick County where he enlisted at age 25, July 18, 1861. Present or accounted for until he died in Brunswick County on March 9, 1862, of "consumption."

STANLY, STEWART, Private
Resided in Brunswick County and enlisted at Camp Howard at age 21, July 18, 1861. Present or accounted for until wounded at Gaines' Mill, Virginia, June 27, 1862. Died at or near Port Royal, Virginia, December 14, 1862, of "brain fever."

STANLY, WILLIAM F., Private
Resided in Brunswick County and enlisted at Camp Howard at age 22, July 18, 1861. Present or accounted for until transferred to the 20th Regiment N.C. Troops (10th Regiment N.C. Volunteers), in October, 1861. [This soldier apparently served in Company G, 20th Regiment N.C. Troops, under the name of William F. Stanland; see Volume VI, page 500 of this series.]

SWAIN, BENJAMIN F., Corporal
Resided in Brunswick County and enlisted at Camp Howard at age 18, July 18, 1861. Mustered in as Sergeant. Reduced to ranks in May-December, 1862. Wounded in the left arm at Gaines' Mill, Virginia, on or about June 27, 1862. Returned to duty prior to January 1, 1863. Promoted to Corporal in January-June, 1863. Present or accounted for until transferred to the C.S. Navy on April 5, 1864.

SWAIN, GEORGE T., Private
Resided in Brunswick County and enlisted at Camp Howard at age 19, July 18, 1861. Mustered in as Corporal. Reduced to ranks in May-December, 1862. Present or accounted for until wounded at Gettysburg, Pennsylvania, July 1-2, 1863. Died at Gettysburg on July 3, 1863, of wounds. "Acted very gallantly at Gettysburg."

THARP, JOHN L., Private
Resided in Brunswick County where he enlisted at age 21, July 18, 1861. Mustered in as Private. Promoted to Sergeant on May 1, 1862. Wounded in the hand at Malvern Hill, Virginia, July 1, 1862. Three fingers amputated. Reduced to ranks on an unspecified date. Reported absent on light duty from March 7, 1863, through November 18, 1864.

THARP, WILLIAM H., Private
Born in Brunswick County where he resided prior to enlisting in Brunswick County at age 18, July 18, 1861. Present or accounted for until wounded at Malvern Hill, Virginia, July 1, 1862. Returned to duty prior to January 1, 1863. Died in hospital at Richmond, Virginia, May 3, 1863, of "typhoid pneumonia" and/or "diarrhoea chro[nic]."

THOMPSON, A., Private
Resided in Stanly County and enlisted at Camp Holmes at age 37, August 24, 1863, for the war. Present or accounted for through August, 1864.

VINES, WILLIAM T., Private
Resided in Brunswick County where he enlisted at age 18, October 15, 1861. Present or accounted for until wounded in the right hand at Chancellorsville, Virginia, May 3, 1863. Returned to duty prior to September 1, 1863. Present or accounted for until he surrendered at Appomattox Court House, Virginia, April 9, 1865.

VUNCANNON, J. P., Private
Resided in Randolph County and enlisted at Camp Holmes at age 34, July 1, 1863, for the war. Present or accounted for until captured at Kelly's Ford, Virginia, November 7, 1863. Confined at Point Lookout, Maryland, November 11, 1863. Exchanged on March 3, 1864. Returned to duty prior to September 1, 1864. Hospitalized at Richmond, Virginia, January 17, 1865, with dropsy and was furloughed for sixty days on January 28, 1865. [North Carolina pension records indicate he was wounded in the chest, hip, and hand in an unspecified battle.]

WANETT, WILLIAM A., Private
Resided in Brunswick County and enlisted at Camp Howard at age 29, July 18, 1861. Present or accounted for until killed near Spotsylvania Court House, Virginia, May 12, 1864.

WESCOTT, HENRY A., Sergeant
Resided in Brunswick County where he enlisted at age 20, July 18, 1861. Mustered in as Musician (Fifer). Present or accounted for until reported absent without leave in December, 1862. Returned to duty on an unspecified date. Promoted to Sergeant in March, 1863. Present or accounted for until transferred to the C.S. Navy on April 5, 1864.

WESCOTT, JOHN W., Sergeant
Resided in Brunswick County where he enlisted at age 27, July 18, 1861. Mustered in as Corporal. Promoted to Sergeant on May 1, 1862. Present or accounted for until captured at or near Sharpsburg, Maryland, on or about September 17, 1862. Confined at Fort Delaware, Delaware. Paroled and transferred to Aiken's Landing, James River, Virginia, October 2, 1862, for exchange. Declared exchanged at Aiken's Landing on November 10, 1862. Returned to duty in January-April, 1863. Present or accounted for until captured at or near Winchester, Virginia, on or about September 19, 1864. Confined at Point Lookout, Maryland, October 25, 1864. Died at Point Lookout on January 25, 1865. Cause of death not reported.

WESCOTT, SAMUEL W., Private
Born in Brunswick County where he resided prior to enlisting in Brunswick County at age 23, July 18, 1861. Present or accounted for until wounded at Malvern Hill, Virginia, July 1, 1862. Returned to duty prior to January 1, 1863. Died in hospital at Richmond, Virginia, on or about April 3, 1863, of "pneumonia."

WESCOTT, WILLIAM H., 1st Sergeant
Resided in Brunswick County where he enlisted at age 20, September 2, 1861. Mustered in as Private. Promoted to 1st Sergeant on September 23, 1862. Present or accounted for until he died at Wilmington on February 28-March 1, 1863, of "consumption" and/or "chronic diarrhoea."

WHITE, ELI M., Private
Resided in Brunswick County where he enlisted at age 18, September 2, 1861. Present or accounted for until captured at Kelly's Ford, Virginia, November 7, 1863. Confined at Point Lookout, Maryland, November 11, 1863. Paroled at Point Lookout on May 3, 1864, and transferred to Aiken's Landing, James River, Virginia, where he was received on May 8, 1864, for exchange. Reported absent without leave through August, 1864. [North Carolina pension records indicate he was wounded at "Fort Fisher in March, 1863."]

WILLIAMS, JAMES B., Private
Resided in New Hanover County and enlisted at Camp Howard at age 22, July 18, 1861. Present or accounted for until he died at or near Guinea Station, Virginia, January 16, 1863, of "brain fever."

WILLIAMS, JOSEPH, Private
Resided in New Hanover County and enlisted in Brunswick County at age 25, July 18, 1861. Present or accounted for until December, 1862, when he was reported absent without leave. Returned to duty prior to July 1, 1863, when he was wounded in the hand and captured at Gettysburg, Pennsylvania. Confined at various Federal hospitals until paroled at Baltimore, Maryland, August 23, 1863. Received at City Point, Virginia, August 24, 1863, for exchange. Returned to duty prior to January 1, 1864. Died at Orange Court House, Virginia, March 17, 1864. Cause of death not reported.

WILLIAMSON, JOHN, Private
Resided in Randolph County and enlisted at Camp Holmes at age 36, January 10, 1864, for the war. Killed near Spotsylvania Court House, Virginia, May 12, 1864.

COMPANY D

This company was raised in Wake and Granville counties and enlisted on August 10, 1861. It was then assigned to the 30th Regiment N.C. Troops and was designated Company D. After joining the regiment the company functioned as a part of the regiment, and its history for the war period is reported as a part of the regimental history.

The information contained in the following roster of the company was compiled principally from a company muster-in and descriptive roll dated October 8, 1861, and from company muster rolls for October 31, 1861-April 30, 1862; August 31-December 31, 1862; May-August, 1863; and November, 1863-August, 1864. No company muster rolls were found for August 10-October 30, 1861; May 1-August 30, 1862; January-April, 1863; September-October, 1863; or for the period after August, 1864. Valuable information was obtained from primary records such as the Roll of Honor, discharge certificates, medical records, prisoner of war records, and pension applications. Secondary sources such as postwar rosters and histories, cemetery records, and records of the United Daughters of the Confederacy also provided useful information.

OFFICERS

CAPTAINS

GRISSOM, EUGENE

Born in Granville County where he resided prior to enlisting at age 35. Appointed Captain on August 10, 1861. Present or accounted for until wounded in the right shoulder in a skirmish near Richmond, Virginia, June 22, 1862. Served for an unspecified period in 1862 on the staff of North Carolina Surgeon General Edward Warren. Resigned on February 10, 1863, by reason of disability from wounds and because he had been elected to a seat in the North Carolina House of Commons. Resignation accepted on or about April 1, 1863.

ALLEN, CHARLES N.

Resided in Wake County where he enlisted at age 22, August 10, 1861. Mustered in as 1st Sergeant. Appointed 2nd Lieutenant on December 10, 1861. Promoted to 1st Lieutenant on March 10, 1862. Promoted to Captain on or about April 2, 1863. Present or accounted for until wounded in the right arm at Gettysburg, Pennsylvania, July 1, 1863. Right arm amputated. Reported absent wounded or absent on detached service until December 29, 1864, when he was retired to the Invalid Corps.

LIEUTENANTS

ABERNATHY, SIDNEY S., 1st Lieutenant

Resided in Wake County and enlisted at age 28. Elected 3rd Lieutenant on August 10, 1861. Defeated for reelection when the regiment was reorganized on May 1, 1862. Enlisted as a Private in Company I, 55th Regiment N.C. Troops, on or about May 12, 1862. Elected 2nd Lieutenant on September 27, 1862, and transferred back to this company. Promoted to 1st Lieutenant on April 12, 1863. Present or accounted for until captured at Kelly's Ford, Virginia, November 7, 1863. Confined at Old Capitol Prison, Washington, D.C., November 8, 1863. Transferred to Johnson's Island, Ohio, November 11, 1863. Transferred to Point Lookout, Maryland, February 9, 1864. Transferred to Fort Delaware, Delaware, June 23, 1864. Transferred to Hilton Head, South Carolina, August 20, 1864. Confined at Fort Pulaski, Georgia, on or about October 20, 1864. Reported in confinement at Fort Pulaski on December 26, 1864. Transferred back to Fort Delaware where he arrived on March 12, 1865. Released on June 12, 1865.

ALLEN, SOLOMON J., 1st Lieutenant

Resided in Wake County where he enlisted at age 30. Appointed 1st Lieutenant on August 10, 1861. Present or accounted for until he resigned on March 10, 1862. Reason he resigned not reported.

BAILEY, ALLEN, 2nd Lieutenant

Resided in Wake County where he enlisted at age 30. Elected 2nd Lieutenant on August 10, 1861. Resigned on or about December 10, 1861, by reason of disability.

FERRELL, JAMES E., 2nd Lieutenant

Resided in Wake County where he enlisted at age 24, August 10, 1861. Mustered in as Private. Promoted to Color Corporal on November 1, 1861. Present or

accounted for until wounded at Malvern Hill, Virginia, July 1, 1862. Returned to duty prior to September 24, 1862, when he was elected 3rd Lieutenant. Promoted to 2nd Lieutenant on April 12, 1863. Wounded at Chancellorsville, Virginia, May 3, 1863. Returned to duty prior to July 1, 1863. Captured at Kelly's Ford, Virginia, November 7, 1863. Confined at Old Capitol Prison, Washington, D.C., November 8, 1863. Transferred to Johnson's Island, Ohio, November 11, 1863. Released at Johnson's Island on June 13, 1865, after taking the Oath of Allegiance.

GILL, WILLIAM J., 3rd Lieutenant

Born in Wake County where he resided prior to enlisting in Wake County at age 24, August 10, 1861. Mustered in as Sergeant. Elected 3rd Lieutenant on March 10, 1862. Present or accounted for until wounded and captured at or near Sharpsburg, Maryland, on or about September 17, 1862. Hospitalized at Frederick, Maryland, where he died on October 13, 1862, of wounds. "He was a good man [and a] kind and generous officer."

NEWTON, SAMUEL B., 2nd Lieutenant

Served as 2nd Lieutenant of Company E of this regiment; however, he was reported in command of this company during January-August, 1864.

ROGERS, CHARLES M., 2nd Lieutenant

Born in Wake County where he resided prior to enlisting in Wake County at age 22, August 10, 1861. Mustered in as Sergeant. Promoted to 1st Sergeant in November-December, 1861. Elected 2nd Lieutenant on March 10, 1862. Present or accounted for until killed at Sharpsburg, Maryland, September 17, 1862. "He was a gallant and efficient officer."

ROGERS, MARTIN L. V., 3rd Lieutenant

Resided in Wake County where he enlisted at age 19, August 10, 1861. Mustered in as Private. Promoted to Corporal in November-December, 1861. Promoted to Sergeant in May-December, 1862. Elected 3rd Lieutenant on or about April 2, 1863. Present or accounted for until wounded at Snicker's Gap, Virginia, July 18, 1864. Reported absent wounded through November 28, 1864.

NONCOMMISSIONED OFFICERS AND PRIVATES

ALLEN, ELIAS G., Color Corporal

Born in Pitt County and resided in Granville County where he was by occupation a farmer prior to enlisting in Granville County at age 22, February 13, 1862. Mustered in as Private. Present or accounted for until wounded in both thighs at Fredericksburg, Virginia, December 13, 1862. Returned to duty prior to July 1, 1863. Promoted to Color Corporal on July 17, 1863. Present or accounted for until wounded in the left lung and captured at Kelly's Ford, Virginia, November 7, 1863. Confined at Point Lookout, Maryland, November 11, 1863. Released on February 9, 1864, after joining the U.S. Army. Assigned to Company D, 1st Regiment U.S. Volunteer Infantry.

ALLEN, HENRY C., Sergeant

Resided in Alabama or in Wake County and enlisted in Wake County at age 19, April 20, 1862, for the war. Mustered in as Private. Promoted to Sergeant on April

1, 1863. Present or accounted for until wounded at Chancellorsville, Virginia, May 3, 1863. Reported absent wounded through August, 1863. Reported absent on detached service at Raleigh from November-December, 1863, through December, 1864. Took the Oath of Allegiance at Raleigh on April 21, 1865.

ALLEN, JAMES P., Corporal
Born in Wake County and resided in Granville County where he was by occupation a farmer prior to enlisting in Granville County at age 25, August 10, 1861. Mustered in as Private. Promoted to Corporal on May 1, 1862. Present or accounted for until killed at Malvern Hill, Virginia, July 1, 1862.

ALLEN, MARION FRANCIS, Private
Resided in Granville County where he enlisted at age 24, August 10, 1861. Present or accounted for until captured at or near Sharpsburg, Maryland, on or about September 17, 1862. Paroled on September 21, 1862. Returned to duty prior to July 1, 1863. Present or accounted for until captured at Gettysburg, Pennsylvania, July 3-4, 1863. Confined at Fort Delaware, Delaware, July 7, 1863. Transferred to Point Lookout, Maryland, October 15-18, 1863. Released at Point Lookout on June 4, 1865, after taking the Oath of Allegiance.

ALLEN, WYATT M., Private
Resided in Wake County where he enlisted at age 39, March 2, 1863, for the war. Present or accounted for until he died "at home" on November 12, 1863. Cause of death not reported.

BAILEY, JEREMIAH, Private
Resided in Granville County and was by occupation a tanner prior to enlisting in Granville County at age 18, August 10, 1861. Present or accounted for through January 15, 1864. Died in hospital at Mount Jackson, Virginia, October 26, 1864, of a gunshot wound of the left side. Place and date wounded not reported.

BAILEY, JONES F., Private
Resided in Granville County where he enlisted at age 18, August 10, 1861. Present or accounted for until he died "at home" on September 20, 1862. Cause of death not reported.

BAILEY, WILLIAM M. H., Private
Born in Wake County where he resided as a farmer prior to enlisting in Wake County at age 18, August 10, 1861. Present or accounted for until he died at Richmond, Virginia, July 17 or August 15, 1862. Cause of death not reported.

BAILEY, YOUNG F., Private
Resided in Granville County where he enlisted at age 36, August 10, 1861. Present or accounted for through April, 1862. Reported absent without leave in September-December, 1862. Reported absent sick during May-August, 1863. Returned to duty in November-December, 1863. Killed at or near Spotsylvania Court House, Virginia, May 12, 1864.

BARKER, JOHN W., Private
Resided in Wake County where he enlisted at age 29, August 10, 1861. Present or accounted for until wounded in the hand and/or right arm at Gettysburg, Pennsylvania, on or about July 1, 1863. Returned to duty prior to September 1, 1863. Captured at Kelly's

Ford, Virginia, November 7, 1863. Confined at Point Lookout, Maryland, November 11, 1863. Paroled on or about February 24, 1865, and transferred to Aiken's Landing, James River, Virginia, where he was received on February 25-March 3, 1865, for exchange.

BLEDSOE, GILES, Private
Resided in Orange County and enlisted in Wake County at age 35, March 30, 1862, as a substitute. Present or accounted for until September-December, 1862, when he was reported absent without leave. Returned to duty prior to July 1, 1863. Reported absent sick from September 14, 1863, through August, 1864. Returned to duty on an unspecified date. Surrendered at Appomattox Court House, Virginia, April 9, 1865.

BOWLES, DAVID A., Private
Born in Person County and resided in Wake County where he was by occupation a carpenter prior to enlisting in Wake County at age 30, March 23, 1862. Present or accounted for through June, 1864; however, he was reported absent sick or absent on detached service during most of that period. Discharged on July 25, 1864, by reason of "chronic rheumatism of 3 years' standing, contraction of muscles of left leg, paralysis of left arm . . . with atrophy of muscles."

BOWLIN, WILLIS N., Private
Born in Orange County and resided in Granville County where he enlisted at age 18, March 30, 1862. Reported absent without leave during September-December, 1862. Returned to duty on an unspecified date. Hospitalized at Richmond, Virginia, January 19, 1863, with a gunshot wound of the shoulder. Place and date wounded not reported. Returned to duty on January 21, 1863. Wounded in the right arm at Chancellorsville, Virginia, on or about May 3, 1863. Right arm amputated. Died in hospital at Richmond on May 5 or May 29, 1863, of wounds.

BRANTON, CHARLES E., Private
Resided in Wake County where he enlisted at age 18, April 14, 1862. Present or accounted for until wounded at Chancellorsville, Virginia, May 1-4, 1863. Returned to duty prior to November 7, 1863, when he was captured at Kelly's Ford, Virginia. Confined at Point Lookout, Maryland, November 11, 1863. Paroled at Point Lookout on or about February 24, 1865, and transferred to Aiken's Landing, James River, Virginia, where he was received on or about February 25, 1865, for exchange.

BRANTON, LEWIS O., Private
Resided in Wake County. Place and date of enlistment not reported. Hospitalized at Richmond, Virginia, March 25, 1865, with typhoid fever. Captured in hospital at Richmond on April 3, 1865. Transferred to Newport News, Virginia, April 23, 1865. Released on July 3, 1865, after taking the Oath of Allegiance.

BRASSFIELD, JAMES W., Private
Resided in Orange County and enlisted in Wake County at age 32, February 13, 1862. Present or accounted for until captured at Gettysburg, Pennsylvania, July 3, 1863. Confined at Fort Delaware, Delaware, July 7-12, 1863. Transferred to Point Lookout, Maryland, October 15-18, 1863. Died at Point Lookout on February 12, 1864, of "chro[nic] diarrhoea."

BRIDGES, GEORGE W., Private
Born in Wake County where he resided prior to enlisting in Wake County at age 18, August 10, 1861. Present or accounted for until he died at Forrestville on or about January 20, 1863, of ''rheumatism.''

BROWN, JOHN W., Private
Place and date of enlistment not reported. Captured at or near Gettysburg, Pennsylvania, on or about July 4, 1863. Died at Gettysburg on July 15, 1863. Cause of death not reported.

CANADY, FRANCIS R., Private
Resided in Wake County where he enlisted at age 43, September 10, 1863, for the war. Present or accounted for until captured at Fisher's Hill, Virginia, September 22, 1864. Confined at Point Lookout, Maryland, October 3, 1864. Paroled at Point Lookout on January 17, 1865, and transferred to Boulware's Wharf, James River, Virginia, where he was received on January 21, 1865, for exchange.

CAWTHON, ARCHER L., Private
Resided in Wake County where he enlisted at age 42, February 13, 1862, as a substitute. Mustered in as Private. Promoted to Corporal in May-December, 1862. Reduced to ranks prior to July 1, 1863. Present or accounted for through August 31, 1864; however, he was reported absent sick or absent on detail during much of that period.

CHAMPION, JERRY M., Private
Resided in Granville County where he enlisted at age 20, August 10, 1861. Present or accounted for until captured at Kelly's Ford, Virginia, November 7, 1863. Confined at Point Lookout, Maryland, November 11, 1863. Paroled at Point Lookout on or about February 13, 1865, and transferred to Cox's Wharf, James River, Virginia, where he was received February 14-15, 1865, for exchange.

CLAY, ROBERT L., Private
Resided in Granville County where he enlisted at age 22, August 10, 1861. Mustered in as Private. Promoted to Corporal prior to October 31, 1861. Reduced to ranks in May, 1862. Present or accounted for until transferred to Company G, 41st Regiment N.C. Troops (3rd Regiment N.C. Cavalry), May 28, 1862.

COOPER, WILLIAM W., Private
Resided in Wake County where he enlisted at age 20, August 10, 1861. Present or accounted for until wounded in the right arm at Sharpsburg, Maryland, September 17, 1862. Returned to duty on or about December 4, 1862. Present or accounted for until wounded in the head at Winchester, Virginia, September 19, 1864. Reported absent wounded through November 9, 1864. Returned to duty on an unspecified date. Captured at High Bridge, Virginia, April 6, 1865. Confined at Point Lookout, Maryland, April 14, 1865. Released on June 26, 1865, after taking the Oath of Allegiance.

COUSINS, JOHN A., Sergeant
Resided in Granville County where he enlisted at age 20, August 10, 1861. Mustered in as Private. Promoted to Sergeant on April 1, 1862. Present or accounted for until wounded at Gettysburg, Pennsylvania, July 1-3,

1863. Returned to duty prior to September 1, 1863. Captured at Kelly's Ford, Virginia, November 7, 1863. Confined at Point Lookout, Maryland, November 11, 1863. Paroled at Point Lookout on or about February 24, 1865, and transferred to Aiken's Landing, James River, Virginia, where he was received February 25-March 3, 1865, for exchange. Returned to duty on an unspecified date. Captured at Farmville, Virginia, April 6, 1865. Confined at Point Lookout on April 14, 1865. Released on June 26, 1865.

CRENSHAW, FREDERICK B., Private
Born in Wake County where he resided as a mechanic prior to enlisting in Granville County at age 55, August 10, 1861. Present or accounted for until discharged on July 23, 1862, by reason of ''old age and general debility.'' Later served in Company C, 8th Regiment N.C. State Troops.

DANIEL, JOHN B., Private
Resided in Orange County where he enlisted at age 40, July 9, 1863, for the war. Reported absent on detached service at Richmond, Virginia, from September 13, 1863, through August 31, 1864. Paroled at Greensboro on May 10, 1865.

DAVIS, ALEXANDER L., Sergeant
Born in Wake County and resided in Granville County where he was by occupation a farmer prior to enlisting in Granville County at age 38, August 10, 1861. Mustered in as Sergeant. Present or accounted for until January-March, 1862, when he was promoted to Commissary Sergeant and transferred to the Field and Staff of this regiment.

DAVIS, ARRINGTON J., Private
Resided in Wake County and enlisted at age 19, August 10, 1861. Killed at Malvern Hill, Virginia, July 1, 1862.

DAVIS, BURTON, Private
Resided in Wake County where he enlisted at age 37, November 19, 1863, for the war. Died at Orange Court House, Virginia, January 14, 1864. Cause of death not reported.

DAVIS, J. A., Private
Born in Granville County and enlisted in Granville or Wake County at age 18, August 10, 1861. Present or accounted for until killed at Malvern Hill, Virginia, July 1, 1862.

DAVIS, JAMES T., Private
Resided in Wake County where he enlisted at age 18, August 10, 1861. Wounded at Gaines' Mill, Virginia, June 27, 1862. Reported absent without leave during September-December, 1862. Listed as a deserter on March 28, 1863. Returned to duty in January-August, 1864. Captured at Fisher's Hill, Virginia, September 22, 1864. Confined at Point Lookout, Maryland, October 3, 1864. Released on June 12, 1865, after taking the Oath of Allegiance.

DAVIS, JESSE A., Private
Resided in Wake County where he enlisted at age 24, January 28, 1864, for the war. Present or accounted for until wounded in the right leg at Spotsylvania Court House, Virginia, May 12, 1864. Reported absent wounded through August, 1864.

DAVIS, JOHN R., Private
Born in Granville County and resided in Wake County prior to enlisting in Granville or Wake County at age 29, August 10, 1861. Reported absent without leave in September-December, 1862. Died "at home" on January 4 or January 31, 1863, of "dysentery."

DAVIS, JOSEPH CHARLES, Private
Previously served in Company E, 23rd Regiment N.C. Troops (13th Regiment N.C. Volunteers). Transferred to this company on August 10, 1862. Died in hospital at Richmond, Virginia, December 25, 1862, of "disease of heart."

DAVIS, JOSEPH E., Private
Resided in Wake County and enlisted at age 22, [on or about August 10], 1861. Died at Richmond, Virginia, July 20, 1862. Cause of death not reported.

DAVIS, RICHARD S., ———
North Carolina pension records indicate that he served in this company.

DAVIS, SAMUEL R., Musician
Born in Granville County and was by occupation a minor prior to enlisting in Granville County at age 15, August 10, 1861. Mustered in as Musician (Drummer). Discharged on January 25, 1862, by reason of "his youth, small size & delicate health."

DAVIS, WILLIAM E., Private
Resided in Wake County where he enlisted at age 25, August 10, 1861. Present or accounted for until he deserted on March 28, 1863. Returned to duty in January-August, 1864. Captured at Cedar Creek, Virginia, October 19, 1864. Confined at Point Lookout, Maryland. Released on June 12, 1865, after taking the Oath of Allegiance.

DICKEY, ZACHARIAH T., Private
Resided in Orange County where he enlisted at age 18, July 5, 1863, for the war. Present or accounted for until he surrendered at Appomattox Court House, Virginia, April 9, 1865.

DILLARD, WILLIAM SAMUEL, Private
Born in Wake County and resided in Granville County where he enlisted at age 16, August 10, 1861. Present or accounted for until he died "at home" on September 20 or October 23, 1862. Cause of death not reported.

EDWARDS, WALTER, Private
Resided in Orange County where he enlisted at age 18, July 30, 1863, for the war. Present or accounted for until captured near Spotsylvania Court House, Virginia, May 12, 1864. Cofined at Point Lookout, Maryland, May 18, 1864. Transferred to Elmira, New York, August 10, 1864. Died at Elmira on October 14, 1864, of "chronic diarrhoea."

ELLEN, JAMES B., Sergeant
Resided in Wake County where he enlisted at age 17, September 2, 1861. Mustered in as Private. Promoted to Sergeant on August 20, 1862. Present or accounted for until wounded in the right lung and captured at Kelly's Ford, Virginia, November 7, 1863. Hospitalized at Washington, D.C., where he died on December 9, 1863, of wounds.

EMERY, SIMEON, Private
Resided in Wake County and enlisted in Wake or Granville County at age 20, August 10, 1861. Present or accounted for until discharged on May 30, 1862. Reason discharged not reported.

ESTIS, JOHN W., Private
Resided in Granville County where he enlisted at age 40, August 10, 1861. Reported absent without leave during September-December, 1862. Returned to duty prior to July 1, 1863. Discharged on August 10, 1864. Reason discharged not reported.

EVANS, ABSALOM F., Private
Resided in Wake County where he enlisted at age 36, August 10, 1861. Present or accounted for until discharged on September 29 or November 10, 1862, under the provisions of the Conscription Act.

EVANS, ISAIAH H., Private
Born in Wake County where he resided as a farmer prior to enlisting in Wake County at age 30, August 30, 1861. Died "at home" May 20-June 3, 1862. Cause of death not reported.

EVANS, JOSEPH E., Private
Born in Wake County where he resided as a farmer prior to enlisting in Wake County at age 18, March 23, 1862. Died in hospital at Richmond, Virginia, July 6 or July 20, 1862. Cause of death not reported.

EVANS, WILLIAM A., Private
Resided in Wake County where he enlisted at age 22, August 30, 1861. Present or accounted for until December 10, 1862, when he was detailed for duty as a shoemaker at Richmond, Virginia. Assigned to Company K, 2nd Regiment Virginia Infantry (Local Defense). Reported absent on detail through October, 1864.

FERRELL, A. L., Private
Enlisted in Wake County on July 23, 1864, for the war. Captured at Winchester, Virginia, September 19, 1864. Hospitalized at Winchester on September 20, 1864, with typhoid fever. Hospitalized at Frederick, Maryland, December 23, 1864. Transferred to Baltimore, Maryland, December 30, 1864. Transferred to Fort McHenry, Maryland, February 16, 1865, for exchange. [Federal medical records dated December, 1864, give his age as 19.]

FERRELL, FRANCIS M., Private
Resided in Wake County where he enlisted at age 18, April 20, 1862, for the war. Present or accounted for until wounded in the arm at Chancellorsville, Virginia, May 3, 1863. Arm amputated. Reported absent wounded until December 29, 1864, when he was retired to the Invalid Corps.

FERRELL, JOHN C., 1st Sergeant
Resided in Wake County where he enlisted at age 18, August 10, 1861. Mustered in as Private. Promoted to Corporal on July 2, 1862. Wounded at Chancellorsville, Virginia, May 1-4, 1863. Returned to duty prior to July 1, 1863. Promoted to 1st Sergeant on November 12, 1863. Present or accounted for until captured near Spotsylvania Court House, Virginia, May 12, 1864. Confined at Point Lookout, Maryland, May 18, 1864. Transferred to Elmira, New York, August 10, 1864.

Paroled at Elmira on February 20, 1865, and transferred for exchange. [North Carolina pension records indicate he was wounded in June, 1862.]

FERRELL, SAMUEL B., Private
Resided in Wake County where he enlisted at age 18, July 9, 1863, for the war. Present or accounted for until June 6, 1864, when he was reported absent wounded. Reported absent wounded through August, 1864. Returned to duty on an unspecified date. Surrendered at Appomattox Court House, Virginia, April 9, 1865.

FORSYTH, JAMES R., Corporal
Resided in Granville County where he enlisted at age 21, February 13, 1862. Mustered in as Private. Present or accounted for until wounded at Chancellorsville, Virginia, May 1-4, 1863. Promoted to Corporal on June 1, 1863. Returned to duty prior to July 1, 1863. Present or accounted for until killed at or near Charles Town, West Virginia, August 21, 1864.

GARNER, JOHN T., Private
Resided in Wake County where he enlisted at age 19, February 13, 1862. Present or accounted for until wounded at Malvern Hill, Virginia, July 1, 1862. Returned to duty on August 2, 1862. Present or accounted for through August, 1864.

GILBERT, THADDEUS, Private
Resided in Orange County where he enlisted at age 18, July 5, 1863, for the war. Present or accounted for until paroled at Burkeville Junction, Virginia, April 14-17, 1865.

GOODIN, JOHN C., Private
Born in Wake County where he resided prior to enlisting in Wake County at age 18, September 2, 1861. Present or accounted for until killed at Gettysburg, Pennsylvania, on or about July 1, 1863.

GOODIN, JOSEPH J., Private
Resided in Wake County where he enlisted at age 19, March 20, 1864, for the war. Surrendered at Appomattox Court House, Virginia, April 9, 1865.

GOODIN, WILLIS N., Private
Born in Wake County where he resided prior to enlisting in Wake County at age 20, September 2, 1861. Present or accounted for until he died in hospital at Richmond, Virginia, August 30, 1862, of "feb[ris] typhoides" and/or "dys[entery] ch[ronic]."

GRADY, JOHN H., Private
Born in Wake County where he resided as a farmer prior to enlisting in Wake County at age 18, August 10, 1861. Present or accounted for until he died in hospital at Wilmington on December 1-4, 1861, or January 4-14, 1862, of "typhoid fever."

GRISSOM, LOUIS T., Private
Born in Granville County and was by occupation a farmer prior to enlisting in Granville or Wake County at age 31, September 25, 1861. Present or accounted for until discharged on May 29, 1862, by reason of "incipient phthisis."

HARRIS, HENRY, Private
Resided in Granville County where he enlisted at age 24, August 10, 1861. Present or accounted for until wounded at or near Snicker's Gap, Virginia, on or about July 18, 1864. Returned to duty subsequent to August 31, 1864. Surrendered at Appomattox Court House, Virginia, April 9, 1865.

HARRIS, THOMAS PETER, Private
Resided in Granville County where he enlisted at age 21, August 10, 1861. Reported absent without leave during September-December, 1862. Returned to duty prior to July 1, 1863. Present or accounted for until he surrendered at Appomattox Court House, Virginia, April 9, 1865.

HINSHAW, DANIEL, Private
Enlisted in Chatham County on July 15, 1863, for the war. Discharged on November 24, 1863, by reason of being a member of the Society of Friends.

HOLLOWAY, ALBERT W., Private
Resided in Wake County where he enlisted at age 21, August 10, 1861. Present or accounted for until transferred in September-December, 1862. Unit to which transferred not reported.

HUSKETH, WILLIAM R., Private
Resided in Granville County where he enlisted at age 44, August 10, 1861. Present or accounted for until discharged on September 30, 1862, under the provisions of the Conscription Act. [May have served later in Company E, 4th Regiment N.C. State Troops.]

JONES, ISHAM F., Private
Born in Wake County where he resided as a farmer prior to enlisting in Wake County at age 20, August 10, 1861. Present or accounted for until killed at Malvern Hill, Virginia, July 1, 1862.

JONES, WILLIAM H., Private
Resided in Wake County where he enlisted at age 38, April 1, 1864, for the war. Present or accounted for until captured in Amelia County, Virginia, April 6, 1865. Confined at Newport News, Virginia, May 17, 1865. Died at Newport News on June 23, 1865, of "chronic dysentery."

JOPLIN, WILLIAM Y., Private
Born in Wake County where he enlisted at age 26, August 10, 1861. Present or accounted for until he died in hospital at Liberty, Virginia, January 29, 1863, of "smallpox."

JOYNER, JOHN L., Musician
Resided in Granville County and enlisted at age 19, August 10, 1861. Mustered in as Private. Wounded at Gaines' Mill, Virginia, June 27, 1862. Returned to duty prior to September 14, 1862, when he was captured at South Mountain, Maryland. Confined at Fort Delaware, Delaware. Paroled and transferred to Aiken's Landing, James River, Virginia, October 2, 1862, for exchange. Declared exchanged at Aiken's Landing on November 10, 1862. Returned to duty and was promoted to Musician in January-June, 1863. Present or accounted for until he surrendered at Appomattox Court House, Virginia, April 9, 1865.

KEITH, C. C., Private
Enlisted in Wake County on February 9, 1863, for the war. Deserted on March 28, 1863.

KING, ALLEN F., Private
Resided in Wake County where he enlisted at age 22, April 1, 1864, for the war. Captured at Spotsylvania Court House, Virginia, May 12-20, 1864. Confined at Point Lookout, Maryland, May 23, 1864. Transferred to Elmira, New York, July 3, 1864. Paroled at Elmira on October 11, 1864, and transferred back to Point Lookout. Transferred to Venus Point, Savannah River, Georgia, where he was received on November 15, 1864, for exchange. Returned to duty on an unspecified date. Hospitalized at Raleigh on March 6, 1865, with a gunshot wound of the right thumb. Place and date wounded not reported. "Transferred" on March 20, 1865.

KING, CASWELL, Private
Resided in Wake County where he enlisted at age 39, April 1, 1864, for the war. Captured near Spotsylvania Court House, Virginia, May 12, 1864. Confined at Point Lookout, Maryland, May 18, 1864. Transferred to Elmira, New York, August 10, 1864. Died at Elmira on March 6, 1865, of "diarrhoea."

KING, JOHN, Private
Resided in Wake County where he enlisted at age 28, April 1, 1864, for the war. Hospitalized at Raleigh on October 15, 1864, with a gunshot wound. Place and date wounded not reported. Returned to duty on December 2, 1864. Captured at Farmville, Virginia, April 6, 1865. Confined at Point Lookout, Maryland, where he died on or about May 29, 1865, of "chro[nic] diarrhoea."

LAWRENCE, JOHN, Private
Resided in Wake County and enlisted at age 18, August 10, 1861. Discharged on August 30, 1861. Reason discharged not reported.

LAWRENCE, WILLIAM H., Private
Resided in Granville County where he enlisted at age 21, August 10, 1861. Reported absent without leave during September-December, 1862. Returned to duty prior to July 1, 1863. Captured at Gettysburg, Pennsylvania, on or about July 3, 1863. Confined at Fort Delaware, Delaware, on or about July 7, 1863. Transferred to Point Lookout, Maryland, October 15-18, 1863. Paroled at Point Lookout on February 18, 1865, and transferred to Boulware's Wharf, James River, Virginia, where he was received February 20-21, 1865, for exchange.

LLOYD, GEORGE E., Private
Resided in Granville County and was by occupation a farmer prior to enlisting in Granville County at age 20, August 10, 1861. Present or accounted for until hospitalized at Richmond, Virginia, October 13, 1862, with a gunshot wound. Place and date wounded not reported. Reported absent without leave during November-December, 1862. Reported absent sick from April 16, 1863, through December, 1863. Returned to duty in January-August, 1864. Surrendered at Appomattox Court House, Virginia, April 9, 1865.

LONG, ALEXANDER V., Private
Resided in Granville or Wake County and enlisted in Granville County at age 25, August 10, 1861. Present or accounted for until wounded in both hips and captured at Gettysburg, Pennsylvania, July 3, 1863. Confined at Fort Delaware, Delaware, on or about July 9, 1863.

Released at Fort Delaware on June 19, 1865, after taking the Oath of Allegiance.

LUMBLEY, WILLIAM L., Private
Resided in Wake County where he enlisted at age 24, August 10, 1861. Present or accounted for until wounded at Fredericksburg, Virginia, December 13, 1862. Returned to duty prior to January 1, 1863. Present or accounted for until captured at or near Spotsylvania Court House, Virginia, on or about May 20, 1864. Confined at Point Lookout, Maryland, May 23, 1864. Transferred to Elmira, New York, July 3, 1864. Released at Elmira on June 19, 1865, after taking the Oath of Allegiance.

LYNAM, EMELIOUS J. T., Private
Born in Granville County where he resided as a farmer prior to enlisting in Granville County at age 19, August 10, 1861. Died at Camp Wyatt on October 15 or November 14-15, 1861, of "typhoid fever."

LYNAM, WILLIAM, Private
Born in Franklin County and resided in Granville County where he was by occupation a mechanic or farmer prior to enlisting in Wake County at age 44, August 10, 1861. Present or accounted for until discharged on February 5, 1862, by reason of "inability from a stiffened & deformed hand."

MANGUM, CALVIN T., Private
Resided in Wake County and enlisted in Granville County at age 16, August 10, 1861. Present or accounted for until wounded in the left hip and big toe of right foot at or near Malvern Hill, Virginia, on or about July 1, 1862. Returned to duty in January-June, 1863. Present or accounted for until captured at Kelly's Ford, Virginia, November 7, 1863. Confined at Point Lookout, Maryland, November 11, 1863. Paroled at Point Lookout on February 18, 1865, and transferred to Boulware's Wharf, James River, Virginia, where he was received February 20-21, 1865, for exchange.

MANGUM, JOHN E., Private
Born in Granville County and resided in Wake County where he was by occupation a farmer prior to enlisting in Wake or Granville County at age 24, August 10, 1861. Present or accounted for until he died at Richmond, Virginia, June 30 or July 29, 1862, of disease.

MANGUM, ORASTUS P., Private
Resided in Wake County where he enlisted at age 25, February 13, 1862. Present or accounted for until he surrendered at Appomattox Court House, Virginia, April 9, 1865. [North Carolina pension records indicate he was wounded in the foot near Richmond, Virginia, in 1864.]

MANGUM, PATON G., Private
Born in Granville County and resided in Wake County where he was by occupation a farmer prior to enlisting in Granville County at age 42, August 10, 1861. Present or accounted for until discharged on April 20, 1862, by reason of "chronic rheumatism."

MANGUM, THEOPHILUS P., Private
Resided in Wake County where he enlisted at age 20, August 10, 1861. Reported absent without leave during September-December, 1862. Reported absent on

detached service at Raleigh from April 2 through August 31, 1863. Rejoined the company prior to January 1, 1864. Present or accounted for until he surrendered at Appomattox Court House, Virginia, April 9, 1865.

MANUS, FRANCIS, Private
Resided in Moore County. Place and date of enlistment not reported. Captured at Williamsport, Maryland, July 7, 1863. Confined at Fort Delaware, Delaware, July 23, 1863. Released at Fort Delaware on May 3, 1865, after taking the Oath of Allegiance. [May have served in Company I rather than Company D of this regiment.]

MARCOM, JAMES A., Private
Resided in Wake County where he enlisted at age 21, February 13, 1862. Present or accounted for until captured at Kelly's Ford, Virginia, November 7, 1863. Confined at Point Lookout, Maryland, November 11, 1863. Paroled at Point Lookout on or about February 24, 1865, and transferred to Aiken's Landing, James River, Virginia, where he was received February 25-March 3, 1865, for exchange.

MARCOM, WILLIAM A., Private
Resided in Wake County and enlisted in Orange County at age 18, September 10, 1863, for the war. Captured at Kelly's Ford, Virginia, November 7, 1863. Confined at Point Lookout, Maryland, November 11, 1863. Paroled at Point Lookout on or about February 24, 1865, and transferred to Aiken's Landing, James River, Virginia, where he was received February 25-March 3, 1865, for exchange.

MARTIN, JESSE B., Private
Born in Wake County where he resided as a farmer prior to enlisting in Wake County at age 20, August 10, 1861. Died "at home" on September 28, October 2, or November 1, 1861, of "phthisis."

MASON, ISRAEL H., Private
Previously served in Company F, 47th Regiment N.C. Troops. Transferred to this company in March-April, 1862. Present or accounted for until wounded and captured at Gettysburg, Pennsylvania, on or about July 1, 1863. Died at or near Gettysburg prior to July 16, 1863, of wounds.

MASON, JOSEPH, Private
Born in Wake County where he resided as a farmer prior to enlisting in Granville County at age 18, August 10, 1861. Present or accounted for until wounded in the left leg at Malvern Hill, Virginia, July 1, 1862. Left leg amputated. Died on July 7, 1862, of wounds. Place of death not reported.

MASSEY, MARION M., Private
Resided in Wake County where he enlisted at age 39, August 10, 1861. Mustered in as Private. Promoted to Corporal in January-February, 1862. Promoted to Sergeant in May-November, 1862. Reduced to ranks on December 1, 1862. Present or accounted for until he surrendered at Appomattox Court House, Virginia, April 9, 1865.

MOORE, WILLIAM HENRY H., Private
Resided in Granville County where he enlisted at age 20, August 10, 1861. Present or accounted for until wounded at or near Spotsylvania Court House, Virginia, on or about May 5-9, 1864. Reported absent

wounded through August, 1864. Hospitalized at Raleigh on March 2, 1865, with a gunshot wound of the left shoulder. Place and date wounded not reported. Returned to duty on March 8, 1865.

MORRIS, ALFRED J., Private
Born in Granville County and resided in Wake County prior to enlisting in Granville County at age 40, August 10, 1861. Present or accounted for until he died in hospital at Petersburg, Virginia, on or about January 2, 1863, of "typhoid pneumonia" and/or "dysentery."

NICHOLS, JOHN T., Private
Resided in Wake County where he enlisted at age 20, August 10, 1861. Mustered in as Sergeant. Promoted to 1st Sergeant on April 1, 1862. Reduced to ranks on December 1, 1863. Present or accounted for through May, 1864. Company records indicate he was captured on June 3, 1864; however, records of the Federal Provost Marshal do not substantiate that report. No further records.

OAKLEY, J. W., ———
North Carolina pension records indicate he served in this company.

O'NEAL, HARDY, Private
Resided in Wake County where he enlisted at age 27, August 10, 1861. Present or accounted for until hospitalized at Richmond, Virginia, July 2, 1862, with a gunshot wound of the arm. Place and date wounded not reported. Returned to duty in January-June, 1863. Present or accounted for until captured at Kelly's Ford, Virginia, November 7, 1863. Confined at Point Lookout, Maryland, November 11, 1863. Paroled at Point Lookout on or about February 13, 1865, and transferred to Cox's Wharf, James River, Virginia, where he was received February 14-15, 1865, for exchange.

O'NEAL, LOFTIN M., Private
Resided in Wake County where he enlisted at age 18, August 10, 1861. Present or accounted for until November 7, 1863, when he was reportedly captured at Kelly's Ford, Virginia; however, records of the Federal Provost Marshal do not substantiate that report. No further records.

PEED, WILLIAM C., Private
Resided in Granville County where he enlisted at age 21, November 1, 1861. Mustered in as Private. Promoted to Corporal on April 20, 1862. Reduced to ranks prior to January 1, 1863. Present or accounted for until wounded in the left hand at Chancellorsville, Virginia, May 3, 1863. Returned to duty in July-August, 1863. Present or accounted for until captured at Winchester, Virginia, September 19, 1864. Confined at Point Lookout, Maryland, September 26, 1864. Released at Point Lookout on June 16, 1865, after taking the Oath of Allegiance. [North Carolina pension records indicate he was wounded in the left side at Gaines' Mill, Virginia, on or about June 27, 1862.]

PEED, WILLIAM H., Private
Resided in Granville County where he enlisted at age 19, November 1, 1861. Present or accounted for until wounded at Chancellorsville, Virginia, May 1-4, 1863. Returned to duty prior to September 1, 1863. Captured at Kelly's Ford, Virginia, November 7, 1863. Confined

at Point Lookout, Maryland, November 11, 1863. Paroled at Point Lookout on February 18, 1865, and transferred to Boulware's Wharf, James River, Virginia, where he was received February 20-21, 1865, for exchange.

PENNY, SOLOMON W., Private
Resided in Wake County where he enlisted at age 18, August 10, 1861. Present or accounted for until wounded at Sharpsburg, Maryland, September 17, 1862. Returned to duty prior to January 1, 1863. Present or accounted for until killed at or near Washington, D.C., July 12, 1864.

PIERCE, GEORGE W., Private
Resided in Wake County where he enlisted at age 18, February 13, 1862. Present or accounted for until wounded in the right knee at Malvern Hill, Virginia, July 1, 1862. Returned to duty in January-June, 1863. Captured at Kelly's Ford, Virginia, November 7, 1863. Confined at Point Lookout, Maryland, November 11, 1863. Paroled at Point Lookout on or about September 18, 1864, and transferred for exchange. Hospitalized at Richmond, Virginia, September 21, 1864, and was transferred to another hospital the next day. No further records.

PIERCE, JAMES T., Private
Resided in Wake County where he enlisted at age 23, August 10, 1861. Present or accounted for until wounded at Malvern Hill, Virginia, July 1, 1862. Returned to duty prior to September 15, 1862, when he was captured at South Mountain, Maryland. Confined at Fort Delaware, Delaware. Paroled and transferred to Aiken's Landing, James River, Virginia, where he was received on October 2, 1862, for exchange. Declared exchanged at Aiken's Landing on November 10, 1862. Returned to duty subsequent to December 31, 1862. Deserted on March 28, 1863. Returned to duty subsequent to December 31, 1863. Wounded in the index finger of the right hand at or near Cold Harbor, Virginia, on or about June 1, 1864. Reported absent wounded or absent sick until March 20, 1865, when he returned to duty.

PIPER, WESLEY Y., Private
Resided in Wake County where he enlisted at age 24, April 20, 1862, for the war. Present or accounted for until wounded at Malvern Hill, Virginia, July 1, 1862. Reported absent wounded until May 1, 1863, when he was detailed for light duty. Reported absent on detail through August, 1864. Returned to duty on an unspecified date. Hospitalized at Charlotte on March 14, 1865, with a gunshot wound of the "lower extremities right." Furloughed on March 24, 1865. Paroled at Raleigh on May 29, 1865.

POLLARD, JOSHUA H., Private
Born in Wake County where he resided as a farmer prior to enlisting in Wake County at age 23, August 23, 1861. Present or accounted for until he deserted on March 28, 1863. Returned to duty subsequent to August 31, 1863. Captured at Kelly's Ford, Virginia, November 7, 1863. Confined at Point Lookout, Maryland, November 11, 1863. Released on January 26, 1864, after taking the Oath of Allegiance and joining the U.S. Army. Assigned to Company E, 1st Regiment U.S. Volunteer Infantry.

POLLARD, SAMUEL R., Private
Born in Wake County where he resided as a powdermaker prior to enlisting in Wake County at age 27, August 10, 1863, for the war. Present or accounted for until captured at Kelly's Ford, Virginia, November 7, 1863. Confined at Point Lookout, Maryland, November 11, 1863. Released on January 26, 1864, after taking the Oath of Allegiance and joining the U.S. Army. Assigned to Company E, 1st Regiment U.S. Volunteer Infantry.

POLLARD, WILLIAM H. H., Private
Born in Wake County where he resided prior to enlisting in Wake County at age 17, August 10, 1861. Present or accounted for until wounded at Gaines' Mill, Virginia, June 27, 1862. Died "at home" on December 3 or December 15, 1862. Cause of death not reported.

POLLARD, WILLIE G., Private
Resided in Wake County where he enlisted at age 18, August 10, 1861. Present or accounted for until wounded at Gettysburg, Pennsylvania, July 1-3, 1863. Returned to duty on an unspecified date. Captured at Kelly's Ford, Virginia, November 7, 1863. Confined at Point Lookout, Maryland, November 11, 1863. Paroled at Point Lookout on or about February 24, 1865, and transferred to Aiken's Landing, James River, Virginia, where he was received February 25-March 3, 1865, for exchange.

RAY, CASWELL, Private
Resided in Wake County and enlisted at age 23, February 9, 1863, for the war. Deserted on March 28, 1863.

RAY, DAVID A., Private
Resided in Wake County where he enlisted at age 28, August 10, 1861. Mustered in as Corporal. Promoted to Sergeant in November-December, 1861. Reduced to ranks in May-December, 1862. Present or accounted for until he deserted on March 28, 1863. Returned to duty on an unspecified date. Captured at Kelly's Ford, Virginia, November 7, 1863. Confined at Point Lookout, Maryland, November 11, 1863. Paroled at Point Lookout on or about February 13, 1865, and transferred to Cox's Wharf, James River, Virginia, where he was received February 14-15, 1865, for exchange.

RAY, HENRY C., Private
Enlisted in Wake County on February 9, 1863, for the war. Deserted on March 28, 1863. Returned to duty on an unspecified date. Captured at Kelly's Ford, Virginia, November 7, 1863. Confined at Point Lookout, Maryland, November 11, 1863. Paroled at Point Lookout on or about March 14, 1865, and transferred to Boulware's Wharf, James River, Virginia, where he was received March 16, 1865, for exchange.

RAY, WILLIAM B., Private
Resided in Wake County where he enlisted at age 19, August 10, 1861. Mustered in as Musician but was reduced to ranks in November-December, 1861. Present or accounted for until he deserted on March 28, 1863. Returned to duty on an unspecified date. Captured at Kelly's Ford, Virginia, November 7, 1863. Confined at Point Lookout, Maryland, November 11, 1863. Paroled at Point Lookout on or about February 13, 1865, and transferred to Cox's Wharf, James River, Virginia,

where he was received February 14-15, 1865, for exchange.

RAY, ZEDDOCK D., Sergeant

Resided in Wake County where he enlisted at age 20, August 10, 1861. Mustered in as Corporal. Promoted to Sergeant in January-February, 1862. Present or accounted for until wounded at Gaines' Mill, Virginia, June 27, 1862. Returned to duty prior to January 1, 1863. Present or accounted for until captured at Kelly's Ford, Virginia, November 7, 1863. Confined at Point Lookout, Maryland, November 11, 1863. Released at Point Lookout on June 17, 1865, after taking the Oath of Allegiance.

REAVIS, JOSEPH H., Private

Resided in Wake County where he enlisted at age 29, August 10, 1861. Present or accounted for until June 13, 1863, when he was sent on detached service. Assigned to Company K, 2nd Regiment Virginia Infantry (Local Defense). Reported absent on detached service through December 18, 1864. [North Carolina pension records indicate he was wounded by a shell at Gettysburg, Pennsylvania, on or about July 1-3, 1863.]

ROGERS, JOHN HENRY, Private

Resided in Wake County where he enlisted at age 22, April 20, 1862, for the war. Present or accounted for until captured at or near Spotsylvania Court House, Virginia, on or about May 12, 1864. Confined at Point Lookout, Maryland, May 17, 1864. Transferred to Elmira, New York, August 10, 1864. Died at Elmira on January 22, 1865, of "variola."

ROSS, RICHARD S., Private

Resided in Wake County where he enlisted at age 42, September 10, 1863, for the war. Present or accounted for through August, 1864.

SMITH, LOUIS TURNER, ———

Records of the United Daughters of the Confederacy indicate that he served in this company.

SMITH, THOMAS G., Private

Resided in Wake County where he enlisted at age 27, August 10, 1861. Reported absent without leave in October-December, 1862. Returned to duty prior to July 1, 1863. Captured at Kelly's Ford, Virginia, November 7, 1863. Confined at Point Lookout, Maryland, November 11, 1863. Released on June 19, 1865, after taking the Oath of Allegiance.

SYKES, WESLEY, ———

North Carolina pension records indicate that he served in this company.

THOMAS, ROBERT H. B., Corporal

Resided in Wake County where he enlisted at age 18, March 4, 1863, for the war. Mustered in as Private. Promoted to Corporal on November 30, 1863. Present or accounted for until captured at Wilderness, Virginia, May 8, 1864. Confined at Point Lookout, Maryland, May 17, 1864. Transferred to Elmira, New York, August 10, 1864. Died at Elmira on October 16, 1864, of "chronic diarrhoea."

THOMPSON, SOLOMON, Private

Resided in Orange or Wake County and enlisted in Wake County at age 37, March 30, 1862, as a substitute.

Reported absent without leave in September-December, 1862. Returned to duty on an unspecified date. Reported absent without leave from August 29 until September 28, 1863. Reported absent sick from November 2, 1863, through August, 1864. Captured in hospital at Richmond, Virginia, April 3, 1865. Transferred to Newport News, Virginia, April 23, 1865. Released at Newport News on June 15, 1865, after taking the Oath of Allegiance.

TILLEY, JOHN R., Private

Resided in Wake County where he enlisted at age 19, February 10, 1862. Present or accounted for until captured at South Mountain, Maryland, September 15, 1862. Confined at Fort Delaware, Delaware. Paroled and transferred to Aiken's Landing, James River, Virginia, where he was received on October 6, 1862, for exchange. Declared exchanged at Aiken's Landing on November 10, 1862. Returned to duty prior to January 1, 1863. Present or accounted for until captured at Kelly's Ford, Virginia, November 7, 1863. Confined at Point Lookout, Maryland, November 11, 1863. Died in hospital at Point Lookout on February 8, 1865, of "chro[nic] diarr[hoea] and scurvy."

TILLY, WILLIAM BEDFORD, Private

Resided in Orange County where he enlisted at age 18, July 30, 1863, for the war. Present or accounted for through December, 1863. Wounded in action on an unspecified date subsequent to December 31, 1863. Reported absent wounded through August, 1864.

TILLY, WILLIAM H. L., Private

Resided in Wake County where he enlisted at age 18, April 20, 1862, for the war. Present or accounted for until captured at Kelly's Ford, Virginia, November 7, 1863. Confined at Point Lookout, Maryland, November 11, 1863. Paroled at Point Lookout and transferred to City Point, Virginia, where he was received on April 30, 1864, for exchange. Reported absent sick through August, 1864.

TILLY, WILLIAM L., Private

Born in Wake County where he resided as a farmer prior to enlisting in Wake County at age 21, August 10, 1861. Present or accounted for until he died at Richmond, Virginia, August 10 or August 31, 1862. Cause of death not reported.

VAUGHAN, JOHN G., Private

Resided in Granville County and enlisted in Granville or Wake County at age 17, August 10, 1861. Present or accounted for through December, 1862. Reported absent sick from May-June, 1863, through August, 1864. Captured at High Bridge, Virginia, April 6, 1865. Confined at Point Lookout, Maryland, April 14, 1865. Released on June 21, 1865, after taking the Oath of Allegiance.

WADFORD, ALEXANDER, Private

Resided in Wake County and enlisted in Granville County at age 22, March 21, 1862. Present or accounted for until captured at or near Gettysburg, Pennsylvania, July 3-4, 1863. Confined at Fort Delaware, Delaware, on or about July 9, 1863. Transferred to Point Lookout, Maryland, October 15-18, 1863. Paroled at Point Lookout and transferred to City Point, Virginia, where he was received on April 30, 1864, for exchange. Reported absent sick through August, 1864. Returned to duty on an unspecified date. Surrendered at Appomattox Court House, Virginia, April 9, 1865.

WALKER, JARRETT, Private
Resided in Granville County and was by occupation a farmer prior to enlisting in Granville County at age 23, November 1, 1861. Present or accounted for until discharged on September 19, 1862, by reason of "disease of the heart."

WALKER, WILLIS S., Private
Resided in Granville County where he enlisted at age 24, March 13, 1862. Reported absent sick from July 1, 1862, through August, 1864.

WALLER, P. H., Private
Born in Granville County where he resided prior to enlisting in Granville County at age 20, February 13, 1862. Present or accounted for until he died in hospital at Richmond, Virginia, on or about December 22, 1862, of "pneumonia."

WARD, ISAAC B., Private
Resided in Wake County where he enlisted at age 31, August 10, 1861. Present or accounted for until captured at Burkeville, Virginia, April 6, 1865. Confined at Point Lookout, Maryland, April 14, 1865. Released on June 21, 1865, after taking the Oath of Allegiance.

WARD, WILLIAM, Private
Enlisted in Wake County at age 17, August 10, 1861. Present or accounted for until captured at Kelly's Ford, Virginia, November 7, 1863. Confined at Point Lookout, Maryland, November 11, 1863. Paroled at Point Lookout on February 18, 1865, and transferred to Boulware's Wharf, James River, Virginia, where he was received February 20-21, 1865, for exchange.

WARE, WILLIAM J., Corporal
Resided in Wake County where he enlisted at age 19, August 10, 1861. Mustered in as Private. Promoted to Corporal in May-December, 1862. Present or accounted for until captured at Kelly's Ford, Virginia, November 7, 1863. Confined at Point Lookout, Maryland, November 11, 1863. Paroled at Point Lookout on or about February 13, 1865, and transferred to Cox's Wharf, James River, Virginia, where he was received February 14-15, 1865, for exchange. Returned to duty on an unspecified date. Captured at Burkeville, Virginia, April 6, 1865. Confined at Point Lookout on April 14, 1865. Released on June 21, 1865, after taking the Oath of Allegiance.

WHEELONS, JAMES, Private
Born in Granville County where he resided as a farmer prior to enlisting in Granville County at age 46, March 21, 1862, as a substitute. Present or accounted for until killed at Malvern Hill, Virginia, July 1, 1862.

WHEELONS, JOHN WESLEY, Private
Resided in Granville County where he enlisted at age 36, August 10, 1861. Present or accounted for until killed at Chancellorsville, Virginia, May 3, 1863.

WHITE, ALMON W., Private
Born in Wake County and resided in Granville County where he was by occupation a farmer prior to enlisting in Wake County at age 27, August 10, 1861. Present or accounted for until killed at Malvern Hill, Virginia, July

1, 1862.

WHITE, JAMES, Private
Born in Wake County and resided in Granville County where he was by occupation a farmer prior to enlisting at Camp McRae at age 20, May 2, 1862, for the war. Present or accounted for until wounded in the stomach at Malvern Hill, Virginia, on or about July 2, 1862. Discharged on July 23, 1862, by reason of "double hernia."

WHITE, JAMES D., Private
Resided in Wake County where he enlisted at age 27, August 10, 1861. Mustered in as Corporal. Reduced to ranks in May-December, 1862. Present or accounted for until he deserted on March 28, 1863. "Killed by the guard while resisting arrest in the woods" on January 10, 1864.

WHITE, JOHN E., Private
Resided in Wake County where he enlisted at age 20, August 10, 1861. Present or accounted for until he deserted on March 28, 1863.

WHITE, MASON, Private
Born in Granville County and resided in Franklin County where he was by occupation a farmer prior to enlisting in Wake County at age 43, August 10, 1861. Present or accounted for until discharged on December 26, 1861, by reason of "inguinal hernia." Later served in Company F, 47th Regiment N.C. Troops.

WILKINS, ELIJAH, Private
Resided in Granville County and enlisted in Wake or Granville County at age 21, September 22, 1861. Present or accounted for until hospitalized at Richmond, Virginia, July 2, 1862, with a gunshot wound. Place and date wounded not reported. Returned to duty on August 2, 1862. Wounded at Fredericksburg, Virginia, December 13, 1862. Returned to duty prior to January 1, 1863. Wounded at Chancellorsville, Virginia, May 3, 1863. Returned to duty subsequent to December 31, 1863. Killed at or near Charles Town, West Virginia, August 21, 1864.

WILKINS, HINTON, Private
Resided in Granville County where he enlisted at age 19, February 19, 1862. Present or accounted for until he died "at home" on April 14 or April 25, 1863, of "chronic diarrhoea."

WILKINS, JAMES A., Private
Born in Wake County where he resided as a farmer prior to enlisting in Wake County at age 26, August 10, 1861. Present or accounted for until wounded at Gaines' Mill, Virginia, June 27, 1862. Died at Camp Winder, Virginia, on July 25-August 1, 1862. Cause of death not reported.

WILKINS, WILLIAM, Private
Resided in Orange County where he enlisted at age 18, July 30, 1863, for the war. Present or accounted for until captured at Kelly's Ford, Virginia, November 7, 1863. Confined at Point Lookout, Maryland, November 11, 1863. Paroled on or about February 24, 1865, and transferred to Aiken's Landing, James River, Virginia, where he was received February 25-March 3, 1865, for exchange.

WILLIAMS, SAMUEL S. D., Private
Born in Franklin County and resided in Granville County where he was by occupation a mechanic prior to enlisting in Granville County at age 27, September 2, 1861. Present or accounted for until wounded at Gaines' Mill, Virginia, June 27, 1862. Discharged on or about January 16, 1863, by reason of "deafness, congenital in the right ear and caused in the left ear by explosion of shell during the battle near Richmond," Virginia.

WILLIAMS, SIMON P., Private
Born in Granville County where he resided prior to enlisting in Wake or Granville County at age 25, August 10, 1861. Present or accounted for until transferred to Company E, 23rd Regiment N.C. Troops (13th Regiment N.C. Volunteers), June 20, 1862.

YEARBY, ALLEN, Private
Enlisted in Wake County at age 40, August 10, 1861. Reported absent without leave prior to October 9, 1861.

COMPANY E

This company, known as the "Duplin Turpentine Boys," was raised in Duplin County and enlisted at Teachey on August 28, 1861. It was then assigned to the 30th Regiment N.C. Troops and designated Company E. After joining the regiment the company functioned as a part of the regiment, and its history for the war period is reported as a part of the regimental history.

The information contained in the following roster of the company was compiled principally from a company muster-in and descriptive roll dated October 8, 1861, and from company muster rolls for November, 1861-February, 1862; August 31-December 31, 1862; April 30, 1863; July-August, 1863; and November, 1863-August, 1864. No company muster rolls were found for August 28-October, 1861; March-August 30, 1862; January-April 29, 1863; May-June, 1863; September-October, 1863; or for the period after August, 1864. Valuable information was obtained from primary records such as the Roll of Honor, discharge certificates, medical records, prisoner of war records, and pension applications. Secondary sources such as postwar rosters and histories, cemetery records, and records of the United Daughters of the Confederacy also provided useful information.

OFFICERS

CAPTAIN

McMILLAN, JOHN CORNELIUS
Resided in Duplin County where he enlisted at age 23. Elected Captain on August 28, 1861. Court-martialed on or about October 28, 1862, and found guilty of conduct unbecoming an officer. Publicly reprimanded in the presence of his regiment and suspended from his command for one month. Returned to duty on an unspecified date. Wounded in the wrist and hip at Chancellorsville, Virginia, May 1-4, 1863. Returned to duty prior to September 1, 1863. Present or accounted for until hospitalized at Wilmington on June 5, 1864, with a gunshot wound. Place and date wounded not reported. Returned to duty prior to September 1, 1864. Present or accounted for until wounded in the right side on or about April 6, 1865. Surrendered at Appomattox Court House, Virginia, April 9, 1865. Confined at various Federal hospitals until confined at Fort McHenry, Maryland, May 9, 1865. Released on June

10, 1865.

LIEUTENANTS

BONEY, WILLIAM J., 2nd Lieutenant
Resided in Duplin County where he enlisted at age 21. Appointed 2nd Lieutenant on August 28, 1861. Present or accounted for until he was defeated for reelection when the regiment was reorganized on March 27, 1862.

CARR, JACOB O., 3rd Lieutenant
Resided in Duplin County where he enlisted at age 21, August 28, 1861. Mustered in as Sergeant. Elected 3rd Lieutenant on March 27, 1862. Present or accounted for until he was "relieved of command by gen[era]l court-martial" on or about October 28, 1862.

ELLIS, JOHN W., 3rd Lieutenant
Resided in Columbus County and enlisted in Duplin County at age 28, August 28, 1861. Mustered in as Private. Promoted to Ordnance Sergeant on October 17, 1861, and transferred to the Field and Staff of this regiment. Elected 3rd Lieutenant and transferred back to this company on February 27, 1863. Present or accounted for until wounded at Chancellorsville, Virginia, May 3, 1863. Resigned on August 18, 1863, by reason of disability from wounds.

JOHNSON, CORNELIUS, 1st Lieutenant
Resided in Duplin County where he enlisted at age 21. Appointed 1st Lieutenant on August 28, 1861. Present or accounted for until he was defeated for reelection when the regiment was reorganized on March 27, 1862.

JOHNSON, IRA J., 1st Lieutenant
Resided in Duplin County where he enlisted at age 19, August 28, 1861. Mustered in as 1st Sergeant. Elected 3rd Lieutenant on January 24, 1862. Elected 1st Lieutenant on March 27, 1862. Present or accounted for until wounded at Kelly's Ford, Virginia, November 7, 1863. Returned to duty on December 9, 1863. Present or accounted for until wounded at or near Snicker's Gap, Virginia, July 18, 1864. Reported absent wounded through August, 1864. Returned to duty on an unspecified date. Surrendered at Appomattox Court House, Virginia, April 9, 1865.

McMILLAN, DANIEL T., 2nd Lieutenant
Resided in Duplin County and enlisted at age 26. Elected 2nd Lieutenant on March 27, 1862. Present or accounted for until he resigned on January 18, 1863, by reason of "bronchial irritation & incipient phthisis." Resignation accepted on or about February 14, 1863.

NEWTON, SAMUEL B., 2nd Lieutenant
Resided in Duplin County where he enlisted at age 18, August 28, 1861. Mustered in as Private. Promoted to Corporal prior to October 8, 1861. Promoted to Sergeant on October 14, 1861, and was promoted to 1st Sergeant on March 27, 1862. Appointed 3rd Lieutenant on January 14, 1863, and was promoted to 2nd Lieutenant on February 27, 1863. Present or accounted for until captured at Sayler's Creek, Virginia, April 6, 1865. Confined at Old Capitol Prison, Washington, D.C., April 14, 1865. Transferred to Johnson's Island, Ohio, April 17, 1865. Released on June 19, 1865, after taking the Oath of Allegiance.

TEACHEY, DANIEL, Jr., 3rd Lieutenant
Resided in Duplin County where he enlisted at age 22.

Elected 3rd Lieutenant on August 28, 1861. Present or accounted for until he resigned on January 14, 1862, by reason of "ill health." Resignation accepted on or about January 24, 1862.

NONCOMMISSIONED OFFICERS AND PRIVATES

BALKCUM, LEMUEL, Private
Resided in Sampson County and enlisted at Camp Holmes at age 40, September 4, 1863, for the war. Present or accounted for until he died in hospital at Richmond, Virginia, on or about December 24, 1863, of "typhoid fever."

BEASLEY, CALVIN, Private
Resided in Duplin County where he enlisted at age 21, August 28, 1861. Present or accounted for until he died at Wilmington on November 26, 1861, of "typhoid fever."

BEASLEY, EDWARD, Private
Resided in Duplin County where he enlisted at age 23, August 28, 1861. Present or accounted for until wounded in action in May, 1864. Reported absent wounded through September, 1864. Company records do not indicate whether he returned to duty; however, he was hospitalized at Danville, Virginia, April 7, 1865, with a gunshot wound of the scalp. Place and date wounded not reported. Furloughed for thirty days on April 9, 1865.

BENTON, ELLIS A., Corporal
Enlisted in Duplin County at age 18, August 28, 1861. Mustered in as Private. Promoted to Corporal in January-February, 1862. Present or accounted for until captured at Burkeville, Virginia, April 6, 1865. Confined at Newport News, Virginia, April 14, 1865. Date of release not reported.

BEST, JOHN B., Sergeant
Resided in Duplin County and was by occupation a farmer prior to enlisting in Duplin County at age 18, August 28, 1861. Mustered in as Private. Present or accounted for until hospitalized at Richmond, Virginia, September 26, 1862, with a gunshot wound. Place and date wounded not reported. Returned to duty subsequent to December 31, 1862. Wounded in the leg at Gettysburg, Pennsylvania, July 1-2, 1863. Returned to duty subsequent to December 31, 1863. Promoted to Sergeant on July 18, 1864. Present or accounted for until wounded in the right leg and/or right ankle and captured at or near Burkeville, Virginia, April 9, 1865. Hospitalized at Washington, D.C., April 19, 1865. Released on or about June 14, 1865, after taking the Oath of Allegiance.

BEST, ROWLAND J., Private
Born in Duplin County where he resided as a farmer prior to enlisting in Duplin County at age 21, August 28, 1861. Discharged on March 9, 1862, by reason of "chronic phthisis."

BLAND, DAVID, Private
Resided in Duplin County where he enlisted at age 21, August 28, 1861. Hospitalized at Wilmington on an unspecified date with typhoid fever. Died at Wilmington on March 9, 1862, and was "carried home by his father."

BLAND, JOHN J., Private
Resided in Duplin County where he enlisted at age 24, August 28, 1861. Present or accounted for until wounded and captured at Malvern Hill, Virginia, July 1, 1862. Exchanged at Aiken's Landing, James River, Virginia, August 5, 1862. Returned to duty in January-April, 1863. Present or accounted for until wounded in the arm at or near Charles Town, West Virginia, August 21, 1864. No further records.

BLANTON, MORRIS, Private
Resided in Duplin County and enlisted at Camp Wyatt at age 18, January 1, 1862. Killed at Gaines' Mill, Virginia, June 27, 1862.

BLANTON, THOMAS, Private
Resided in Duplin County where he enlisted at age 19, August 28, 1861. Present or accounted for through August, 1864.

BONEY, HIRAM S., Private
Resided in Duplin County and enlisted in New Hanover County at age 23, March 3, 1862. Company muster roll dated August 31-December 31, 1862, indicates he was captured by the enemy on an unspecified date; however, records of the Federal Provost Marshal do not substantiate that report. Reported absent without leave in September-December, 1862. Returned to duty prior to May 1, 1863. Present or accounted for until captured at Fisher's Hill, Virginia, September 22, 1864. Confined at Point Lookout, Maryland, October 3, 1864. Paroled and transferred to Cox's Wharf, James River, Virginia, where he was received February 14-15, 1865, for exchange. [North Carolina pension records indicate he was wounded near Richmond, Virginia, July 2, 1862.]

BONEY, J. K., Private
Resided in Duplin County and enlisted in New Hanover County at age 24, March 3, 1862. Died at Richmond, Virginia, August 21 or August 31, 1862. Cause of death not reported.

BONEY, JAMES T., Private
Resided in Duplin County where he enlisted at age 22, August 28, 1861. Killed at Gaines' Mill, Virginia, June 27, 1862.

BOSTICK, BRYANT W., Private
Born in Duplin County where he resided as a farmer prior to enlisting in New Hanover County at age 25, March 3, 1862. Present or accounted for until wounded in the left leg at Wilderness, Virginia, on or about May 6, 1864. Retired from service on February 18, 1865, by reason of "fracture upper third left tibia result of a gunshot wound received . . . at the Wilderness. . . . He requires the use of two crutches."

BOSTICK, D. R., Private
Born in Duplin County where he resided as a student prior to enlisting in New Hanover County on March 3, 1862. Discharged on September 15, 1862, by reason of "anemia & a feeble constitution" and also because he was under 16 years of age.

BOWEN, JOHN R., Private
Resided in Duplin County where he enlisted at age 35, August 28, 1861. Wounded in the side at Gaines' Mill,

Virginia, June 27, 1862. Hospitalized at Richmond, Virginia, where he died on July 18, 1862, of wounds.

BRADSHAW, B. D., Private
Resided in Duplin County and enlisted in New Hanover County at age 17, March 3, 1862, as a substitute. Present or accounted for until he surrendered at Appomattox Court House, Virginia, April 9, 1865.

BRADSHAW, JACOB B., ———
North Carolina pension records indicate that he served in this company.

BRADSHAW, JAMES B., Private
Resided in Duplin County and enlisted in Duplin or New Hanover County at age 18, October 8, 1861. Present or accounted for until wounded in the right leg at or near Bristoe Station, Virginia, on or about October 14, 1863. Returned to duty subsequent to December 31, 1863. Present or accounted for until captured at Fisher's Hill, Virginia, September 22, 1864. Confined at Point Lookout, Maryland, October 3, 1864. Paroled at Point Lookout on or about March 17, 1865, and transferred to Boulware's Wharf, James River, Virginia, where he was received on March 19, 1865, for exchange.

BRADSHAW, OBED, Private
Born in Duplin County where he resided prior to enlisting in New Hanover County at age 25, March 3, 1862. Present or accounted for until killed at Chancellorsville, Virginia, May 3, 1863.

BRADSHAW, SAMUEL W., Private
Born in Duplin County where he resided as a farmer prior to enlisting at Camp Wyatt at age 18, November 10, 1861. Discharged on September 9, 1862, by reason of "a helpless condition of the right foot following a compound fracture of the tarsal bones."

BRAY, J. W., Private
Resided in Randolph County and enlisted at Camp Holmes at age 21, July 1, 1862, for the war. Failed to report to his company and "remained at home concealed in the woods until December 2, 1863, when he was arrested and sent to his reg[imen]t where he was kept in close confinement for five months." Deserted to the enemy on May 8, 1864. Confined at Point Lookout, Maryland, May 17, 1864. Transferred to Elmira, New York, July 25, 1864. Released at Elmira on May 29, 1865, after taking the Oath of Allegiance.

BREWER, ———, ———
Regimental records dated May, 1862, indicate he was on duty as a company cook.

BRIGMAN, JOHN, Private
Resided in Union County where he enlisted at age 44, September 16, 1863, for the war. Present or accounted for until captured at or near Old Church, Virginia, on or about May 31, 1864. Confined at Point Lookout, Maryland, June 8, 1864. Transferred to Elmira, New York, July 8, 1864. Died at Elmira on October 24, 1864, of "chronic diarrhoea."

BROWN, FELIX, Private
Resided in Duplin County and enlisted in New Hanover County at age 29, March 3, 1862. Present or accounted for until captured at or near Cold Harbor, Virginia, on or about May 31, 1864. Confined at Point Lookout,

Maryland, June 8, 1864. Paroled at Point Lookout on or about October 29, 1864, and transferred to Venus Point, Savannah River, Georgia, where he was received on November 15, 1864, for exchange.

BROWN, H., Private
Place and date of enlistment not reported. Surrendered at Appomattox Court House, Virginia, April 9, 1865.

BROWN, JESSE, Private
Resided in Duplin County and enlisted in Brunswick County at age 27, October 14, 1861. Present or accounted for until hospitalized at Charlottesville, Virginia, June 16, 1864, with an unspecified complaint. Reported in hospital at Charlottesville until April 20, 1865. Paroled at Richmond, Virginia, April 23, 1865.

BROWN, JOHN, Private
Resided in Duplin County where he enlisted at age 32, August 28, 1861. Died at Camp Wyatt on March 2, 1862, of "pneumonia typh[oid]."

BROWN, JOHN, Private
Resided in Duplin County and enlisted in New Hanover County at age 40, August 31, 1863, for the war. Present or accounted for until wounded in the face at or near Spotsylvania Court House, Virginia, May 12, 1864. Hospitalized at Richmond, Virginia, where he died on or about May 24, 1864, of wounds.

BUTLER, BEN AGE, Private
Resided in Duplin County where he enlisted at age 20, August 28, 1861. Wounded and captured at Sharpsburg, Maryland, September 17, 1862. Died at "Stone House Hospital" on October 1, 1862, of wounds.

BUTLER, H. G., Private
Resided in Duplin County and enlisted in New Hanover County at age 30, March 3, 1862. Present or accounted for until killed at or near Cold Harbor, Virginia, June 3, 1864.

BUTLER, J. C., Private
Resided in Johnston County. Place and date of enlistment not reported. Deserted to the enemy on January 9, 1865. Sent to Hilton Head, South Carolina. Transferred to New York City where he arrived on or about January 17, 1865. No further records.

CARR, JOHN JAMES, Private
Resided in Duplin County where he enlisted at age 20, August 28, 1861. Present or accounted for until captured at or near Farmville, Virginia, April 6, 1865. Confined at Newport News, Virginia, April 14, 1865. Released on June 27, 1865, after taking the Oath of Allegiance.

CARR, OBED, Private
Resided in Duplin County where he enlisted at age 44, August 28, 1861. Died at Camp Wyatt on or about November 16, 1861, of "typhoid pneumonia."

CARTER, JAMES, Private
Resided in Duplin County where he enlisted at age 19, August 28, 1861. Mustered in as Corporal. Reduced to ranks on October 14, 1861. Died "at home" on March 6, 1863, of "pneumonia."

CARTER, LINTON, Private
Resided in Duplin County where he enlisted at age 22,

August 28, 1861. Present or accounted for until wounded in the leg near Shepherdstown, West Virginia, on or about August 26, 1864. Died of wounds. Place and date of death not reported.

CAVENAUGH, GEORGE W., Private
Resided in Duplin County and enlisted in New Hanover County at age 21, March 3, 1862. Wounded in the right eye at or near Warrenton, Virginia, on or about October 14, 1863. Captured at Warrenton on or about October 20, 1863. Confined at various Federal hospitals until confined at Old Capitol Prison, Washington, D.C., December 3, 1863. Transferred to Point Lookout, Maryland, February 3, 1864. Died at Point Lookout on February 5, 1865, of "chronic diarrhoea."

CAVENAUGH, JACOB W., Private
Resided in Duplin County where he enlisted at age 20, August 28, 1861. Mustered in as Private. Promoted to Corporal in March-June, 1862. Wounded at Malvern Hill, Virginia, July 1, 1862. Returned to duty prior to January 1, 1863. Reduced to ranks on August 1, 1863. Hospitalized at Richmond, Virginia, May 9, 1864, with a gunshot wound. Place and date wounded not reported. Returned to duty prior to August 21, 1864, when he was wounded in the leg at or near Charles Town, West Virginia. Returned to duty on an unspecified date. Captured at High Bridge, Virginia, April 6, 1865. Confined at Point Lookout, Maryland, April 15, 1865. Released at Point Lookout on June 26, 1865, after taking the Oath of Allegiance.

CAVENAUGH, JAMES DAVID, Private
Resided in Duplin County and enlisted in New Hanover County at age 25, March 3, 1862. Present or accounted for until wounded in the foot at Malvern Hill, Virginia, July 1, 1862. Returned to duty in January-April, 1863. Present or accounted for until captured at Kelly's Ford, Virginia, November 7, 1863. Confined at Point Lookout, Maryland, November 11, 1863. Paroled at Point Lookout on or about February 24, 1865, and transferred to Aiken's Landing, James River, Virginia, where he was received February 25-March 3, 1865, for exchange.

CAVENAUGH, JAMES H., Private
Resided in Duplin County and enlisted in New Hanover County at age 18, March 3, 1862. Present or accounted for until he died at Orange Court House, Virginia, December 17, 1863. Cause of death not reported.

CAVENAUGH, OBED E., Private
Resided in Duplin County and enlisted at age 28, March 3, 1862. Killed at Malvern Hill, Virginia, July 1, 1862.

COLE, J. T., Private
Resided in Duplin County and enlisted at age 18, March 3, 1862. Present or accounted for until he died in hospital at Richmond, Virginia, January 10 or June 10, 1863, of "variola confl[luen]t."

COLE, JESSE, Private
Born in Duplin County where he resided as a farmer prior to enlisting in New Hanover County at age 30, March 3, 1862. Present or accounted for until discharged on September 28, 1862, by reason of "gen[era]l nervousness."

COTTLE, FREDERICK, Private
Resided in Duplin County where he enlisted at age 22, August 28, 1861. Mustered in as Sergeant but was reduced to ranks on October 14, 1861. Present or accounted for until he died in hospital at or near Gordonsville, Virginia, on or about February 7, 1863, of "pneumonia."

COTTLE, W. D., Private
Resided in Duplin County and enlisted at age 23, March 3, 1862, as a substitute. Present or accounted for until he died in hospital at Richmond, Virginia, March 11, 1863, of "pneumonia" or "chron[ic] bronchitis."

CROUCH, A., Private
Place and date of enlistment not reported. Captured in hospital at Richmond, Virginia, April 3, 1865. Transferred to the Federal Provost Marshal on April 14, 1865. No further records.

DAVIS, SIMPSON, Private
Resided in Union County where he enlisted at age 40, September 16, 1863, for the war. Present or accounted for until he surrendered at Appomattox Court House, Virginia, April 9, 1865.

DEMPSEY, KINCHEN H., Sergeant
Resided in Duplin County where he enlisted at age 18, August 28, 1861. Mustered in as Private. Promoted to Corporal on July 20, 1863. Promoted to Sergeant on August 21, 1864. Present or accounted for until captured at Fisher's Hill, Virginia, September 22, 1864. Confined at Point Lookout, Maryland, October 1, 1864. Paroled at Point Lookout on or about February 13, 1865, and transferred to Cox's Wharf, James River, Virginia, where he was received February 14-15, 1865, for exchange.

DICKSON, HARRELL, Private
Resided in Duplin County and enlisted in New Hanover County at age 25, March 3, 1862. Present or accounted for until wounded in the head at Gaines' Mill, Virginia, June 27, 1862. Reported absent wounded until April 12, 1864, when he was retired to the Invalid Corps by reason of disability. [North Carolina pension records indicate that his mind was impaired as a result of wounds received at Gaines' Mill.]

DICKSON, JAMES, Private
Resided in Duplin County where he enlisted at age 17, August 28, 1861. Present or accounted for until wounded at Gaines' Mill, Virginia, June 27, 1862. Reported absent wounded or absent sick until April, 1864, when he was retired from service. Reason he was retired not reported.

DICKSON, RIOL, Private
Resided in Duplin County where he enlisted at age 18, August 28, 1861. Present or accounted for until wounded at Sharpsburg, Maryland, on or about September 17, 1862. Returned to duty on July 13, 1863. Present or accounted for until wounded in the spine and leg and captured at Winchester, Virginia, September 19, 1864. Hospitalized at Winchester where he died on October 3, 1864, of "exhaustion, paralysis, & general debility."

DICKSON, ROBERT L., Private
Born in Duplin County where he resided as a farmer

prior to enlisting in Duplin County at age 20, August 28, 1861. Present or accounted for until discharged on February 3, 1862. Reason discharged not reported.

DUFF, JOHN T., Private
Resided in Duplin County and enlisted at Orange Court House, Virginia, at age 17, March 19, 1864, for the war. Present or accounted for until he surrendered at Appomattox Court House, Virginia, April 9, 1865.

EDWARDS, ISAAC N., Private
Resided in Duplin County where he enlisted at age 30, August 28, 1861. Present or accounted for until captured near Spotsylvania Court House, Virginia, May 12, 1864. Confined at Point Lookout, Maryland, May 18, 1864. Transferred to Elmira, New York, August 10, 1864. Released at Elmira on June 23, 1865, after taking the Oath of Allegiance.

EVANS, ADIN, Private
Resided in Duplin County and enlisted in New Hanover County at age 35, March 3, 1862. Present or accounted for until wounded at Gaines' Mill, Virginia, or at Malvern Hill, Virginia, June 27-July 1, 1862. Returned to duty in January-April, 1863. Present or accounted for through August, 1864.

EZZEL, WILLIAM W., Private
Born in Duplin County where he resided as a shoemaker prior to enlisting in Duplin County at age 22, August 28, 1861. Present or accounted for until discharged on January 21, 1862, by reason of "chronic disease of the bones of the leg."

FUSSELL, ANDREW GRAYHAM, Private
Resided in Duplin County where he enlisted at age 18, August 28, 1861. Mustered in as Private. Promoted to Corporal in March, 1862. Present or accounted for until wounded in the hip at Gaines' Mill, Virginia, June 27, 1862. Returned to duty in March, 1863, and was detailed for hospital duty. Reduced to ranks on August 1, 1863. Reported absent on detail until December 7, 1864, when he was retired to the Invalid Corps.

GRADY, JOHN W., Private
Resided in Duplin County where he enlisted at age 20, August 28, 1861. Present or accounted for until wounded in the thigh at or near Auburn, Virginia, on or about October 13, 1863. Leg amputated. Hospitalized at Richmond, Virginia, where he died on October 25, 1863, of wounds.

HAMILTON, W. S., Private
Resided in Union County where he enlisted at age 44, September 16, 1863, for the war. Present or accounted for until captured at Spotsylvania Court House, Virginia, May 20, 1864. Confined at Point Lookout, Maryland, May 23, 1864. Transferred to Elmira, New York, July 3, 1864. Paroled at Elmira on October 11, 1864, and transferred to Venus Point, Savannah River, Georgia, where he was received on November 15, 1864, for exchange.

HAMLET, C. C., Private
Resided in Union County where he enlisted at age 20, September 24, 1863, for the war. Present or accounted for through August, 1864.

HANCHEY, BRYANT W., Private
Resided in Duplin County and enlisted at age 22, March 3, 1862. Present or accounted for until he died at Richmond, Virginia, or at Fredericksburg, Virginia, February 18, 1863, of "pneumonia."

HANCHEY, JOHN WILLIAM, Sergeant
Resided in Duplin County where he enlisted at age 22, August 28, 1861. Mustered in as Private. Present or accounted for until wounded at Sharpsburg, Maryland, on or about September 17, 1862. Hospitalized at Richmond, Virginia, December 16, 1862, with a gunshot wound. Place and date wounded not reported. Returned to duty in January-April, 1863. Promoted to Corporal on August 1, 1863, and was promoted to Sergeant on May 19, 1864. Present or accounted for until he surrendered at Appomattox Court House, Virginia, April 9, 1865.

HANCHEY, OWEN, ———
North Carolina pension records indicate that he served in this company.

HARRELL, JOHN O., Private
Resided in Duplin County and enlisted in New Hanover County at age 35, March 3, 1862. Present or accounted for until July-August, 1863, when he was reported absent without leave. Died at Orange Court House, Virginia, December 17, 1863, of disease.

HELMS, A. M., Private
Resided in Union County where he enlisted at age 35, October 3, 1863, for the war. Present or accounted for until he surrendered at Appomattox Court House, Virginia, April 9, 1865.

HELMS, ARCHEY, Private
Resided in Union County where he enlisted at age 33, September 24, 1863, for the war. Present or accounted for until captured at Burkeville, Virginia, or at Farmville, Virginia, April 6, 1865. Confined at Newport News, Virginia, April 14, 1865. Released on June 27, 1865, after taking the Oath of Allegiance.

HENDERSON, ABRAHAM, Private
Resided in Duplin County where he enlisted at age 22, August 28, 1861. Present or accounted for until he died in hospital at Richmond, Virginia, on June 10-11, 1863, of "pneumonia."

HENDERSON, BRANTLY B., Sergeant
Resided in Duplin County and enlisted in New Hanover County at age 22, March 3, 1862. Mustered in as Private. Promoted to Sergeant on March 27, 1862. Present or accounted for until wounded in the left leg and captured near Hagerstown, Maryland, September 21, 1862. Confined at Fort Delaware, Delaware. Transferred to Fort Monroe, Virginia, December 15, 1862. Paroled and transferred to City Point, Virginia, where he was received on December 18, 1862, for exchange. Returned to duty prior to May 1, 1863. Present or accounted for until killed at or near Spotsylvania Court House, Virginia, May 12, 1864.

HENDERSON, JAMES W., Private
Resided in Duplin County where he enlisted at age 19, August 28, 1861. Present or accounted for until hospitalized at Wilmington on or about April 26, 1863, with a gunshot wound. Place and date wounded not

reported. Returned to duty prior to July 3, 1863, when he was captured at Gettysburg, Pennsylvania. Died at Waynesboro, Pennsylvania, August 27, 1863, of disease and/or wounds received at Gettysburg.

HENDERSON, JESSE R., Private
Born in Duplin County where he resided prior to enlisting in New Hanover County at age 24, March 3, 1862. Present or accounted for until wounded at Malvern Hill, Virginia, July 1, 1862. Company records do not indicate whether he returned to duty. Died in hospital at Gordonsville, Virginia, March 28, 1863, of "pneumonia."

HENDERSON, RILEY N., ———
North Carolina pension records indicate that he served in this company.

HUNTER, MARTIN, Private
Resided in Duplin County and enlisted in New Hanover County at age 28, March 3, 1862. Present or accounted for until captured near Spotsylvania Court House, Virginia, May 12, 1864. Confined at Point Lookout, Maryland, May 18, 1864. Transferred to Elmira, New York, August 10, 1864. Released at Elmira on June 23, 1865, after taking the Oath of Allegiance.

JOHNSON, EZRA W., Private
Resided in Duplin County where he enlisted at age 22, August 28, 1861. Present or accounted for until he was reported absent without leave for two months in the spring of 1863. Returned to duty prior to May 1, 1863. Present or accounted for until he surrendered at Appomattox Court House, Virginia, April 9, 1865.

JOHNSON, JAMES C., Private
Born in Duplin County where he resided prior to enlisting in Duplin County at age 20, August 28, 1861. Mustered in as Sergeant. Reduced to ranks at his own request on October 14, 1861. Present or accounted for until wounded at Gaines' Mill, Virginia, June 27, 1862. Reported absent wounded or absent sick until he died in New Hanover County in March, 1863, or on May 2, 1863. Cause of death not reported.

JOHNSON, JOSIAH, Private
Resided in New Hanover County where he enlisted at age 27, August 28, 1861. Present or accounted for until he died at Smithville (Southport) on or about November 13, 1861, of "typhoid fever."

JOHNSON, MAJOR O., Musician
Resided in Duplin County where he enlisted at age 18, August 28, 1861. Mustered in as Private. Promoted to Musician (Drummer) in January-April, 1863. Present or accounted for until he surrendered at Appomattox Court House, Virginia, April 9, 1865.

JONES, ISAAC, Private
Resided in Duplin County and enlisted in Brunswick County at age 40, November 5, 1861. Medical records indicate he was "suffering from gonorrhea" and was discharged on February 10, 1862.

JONES, J. K., Sergeant
Resided in Duplin County and enlisted at Camp Holmes at age 24, June 29, 1863, for the war. Mustered in as Private. Promoted to Sergeant on May 19, 1864. Present or accounted for until he surrendered at

Appomattox Court House, Virginia, April 9, 1865.

JONES, JAMES W., Private
Resided in New Hanover County and enlisted in Duplin County at age 19, August 28, 1861. Present or accounted for until wounded in the shoulder at Chancellorsville, Virginia, May 3, 1863. Discharged on August 20, 1863, by reason of disability from wounds.

JONES, JOHN J., Private
Resided in Duplin County and was by occupation a carpenter prior to enlisting in Duplin or New Hanover County at age 25, October 2, 1861. Present or accounted for until May, 1862, when he was "detailed to work on gunboats at Wilmington." Reported absent on detail at Wilmington through August, 1864. Took the Oath of Allegiance on April 1, 1865.

KNIGHT, THOMAS H., Private
Resided in Halifax County where he enlisted at age 18, June 29, 1863, for the war. Detailed as a shoemaker at Richmond, Virginia, August 5, 1863. Reported absent on detail through August, 1864. Rejoined the company on an unspecified date. Captured at Clover Hill, Virginia, April 4, 1865. Confined at Hart's Island, New York Harbor, where he died on June 5, 1865, of "scurvy."

LANEY, LEWIS C., Private
Resided in Union County where he enlisted at age 38, September 24, 1863, for the war. Captured near Kelly's Ford, Virginia, November 7, 1863. Confined at Point Lookout, Maryland, November 11, 1863. Paroled on October 11, 1864, and transferred to Cox's Wharf, James River, Virginia, where he was received on October 15, 1864, for exchange.

LANIER, BRANTLEY, Private
Resided in Duplin County and enlisted in New Hanover County at age 35, March 3, 1862. Present or accounted for until November 3, 1863, when he was detailed for guard duty at Gordonsville, Virginia. Reported absent on light duty at Gordonsville through August, 1864. Rejoined the company prior to October 19, 1864, when he was captured at Cedar Creek, Virginia. Confined at Point Lookout, Maryland, October 23, 1864. Paroled at Point Lookout on an unspecified date. Transferred to Cox's Wharf, James River, Virginia, where he was received February 14-15, 1865, for exchange.

LANIER, JACOB W., Private
Resided in Duplin County where he enlisted at age 19, August 28, 1861. Present or accounted for until wounded in the head (skull fractured) at Gettysburg, Pennsylvania, July 1-3, 1863. Returned to duty in November-December, 1863. Present or accounted for until wounded in the "bladder & bowels" at or near Cold Harbor, Virginia, June 1, 1864. Hospitalized at Richmond, Virginia, where he died on June 4, 1864, of wounds.

LANIER, JAMES P., Private
Resided in Duplin County and enlisted at age 23, March 3, 1862. Present or accounted for until he died in Duplin County on February 27, 1863, of "pneumonia."

LANIER, LOUIS W., Private
Resided in Duplin County and enlisted in New Hanover County at age 22, March 3, 1862. Present or accounted

for until he died in hospital at Richmond, Virginia, December 4-6, 1862, of "variola confluent."

McNELLIS, JOHN, Private
Resided in Duplin County where he enlisted at age 28, August 28, 1861. Present or accounted for until wounded at Chancellorsville, Virginia, May 3, 1863. Returned to duty in September-December, 1863. Present or accounted for through August, 1864.

MALLARD, JOHN W., Private
Resided in Duplin County where he enlisted at age 18, August 28, 1861. Present or accounted for until captured near Spotsylvania Court House, Virginia, May 12, 1864. Confined at Point Lookout, Maryland, May 18, 1864. Transferred to Elmira, New York, August 10, 1864. Paroled at Elmira on March 14, 1865, and transferred to Boulware's Wharf, James River, Virginia, where he was received March 18-21, 1865, for exchange.

MALLARD, WILLIAM W., Private
Resided in Duplin County where he enlisted at age 25, August 28, 1861. Present or accounted for until wounded in the left leg at Chancellorsville, Virginia, May 3, 1863. Left leg amputated below the knee. Retired to the Invalid Corps on May 24, 1864.

MALPASS, CARLETON, Private
Resided in New Hanover County and enlisted in Duplin County at age 20, August 28, 1861. Present or accounted for until wounded at Gaines' Mill, Virginia, June 27, 1862. Returned to duty in May-August, 1863. Present or accounted for until wounded in the right hip at or near Spotsylvania Court House, Virginia, May 12, 1864. Reported absent wounded through January 11, 1865.

MANELLIS, JOHN, Private
Enlisted in Duplin County on August 28, 1861. Present or accounted for until wounded in the right side (rib fractured) at Chancellorsville, Virginia, May 3, 1863. Company records do not indicate that he returned to duty; however, he was paroled at Burkeville Junction, Virginia, April 14-17, 1865.

MERRIT, LEVI J., Private
Resided in Duplin County where he enlisted at age 22, August 28, 1861. Present or accounted for until he died "at home" on September 27, 1862. Cause of death not reported.

MOBLEY, W. V., Private
Resided in Duplin County and enlisted in New Hanover County at age 27, March 3, 1862. Present or accounted for until wounded at Gaines' Mill, Virginia, June 27, 1862. Returned to duty in September-December, 1862. Present or accounted for until captured at Winchester, Virginia, September 19, 1864. Confined at Point Lookout, Maryland. Died at Point Lookout on February 12, 1865, of "consumption."

MOBLEY, W. W., Private
Born in Duplin County where he resided prior to enlisting in New Hanover County at age 27, March 3, 1862. Present or accounted for until he died "at home" on May 19, 1863. Cause of death not reported.

MURPHY, TIMOTHY C., Private
Born in Duplin County where he resided as a farmer prior to enlisting in Duplin County at age 43, August 28, 1861. Present or accounted for until discharged on December 26, 1861, by reason of "opthalmia." Took the Oath of Allegiance on April 2, 1865.

MURRAY, THOMAS M., Private
Resided in Duplin County and enlisted in New Hanover County at age 30, March 3, 1862. Deserted in May, 1862. Returned to duty in January-April, 1863. Present or accounted for until paroled at Burkeville Junction, Virginia, April 14-17, 1865. [North Carolina pension records indicate he was wounded in the hand at "Spotsylvania Court House, Virginia, in June, 1863."]

NEWKIRK, GEORGE B., Sergeant
Resided in Duplin County where he enlisted at age 19, August 28, 1861. Mustered in as Private. Promoted to Sergeant on October 24, 1862. Present or accounted for until killed at or near Charles Town, West Virginia, August 21, 1864.

NEWTON, JAMES O., Private
Resided in Duplin County where he enlisted at age 18, August 28, 1861. Present or accounted for until he "was left near Charles Town, [West] Virginia," in October, 1862. Died on an unspecified date. Place and cause of death not reported.

NORRIS, JAMES, Private
Born in Duplin County where he resided prior to enlisting at Fredericksburg, Virginia, at age 28, November 1, 1862, for the war. Present or accounted for until he died "at home" on or about July 2, 1863. Cause of death not reported.

NORRIS, JOSEPH, Private
Born in Duplin County where he resided as a farmer prior to enlisting in Duplin County at age 45, August 28, 1861. Present or accounted for until discharged on September 27, 1862, by reason of "chronic rheumatism."

NORRIS, REUBEN, Private
Born in Duplin County where he resided as a farmer prior to enlisting in New Hanover County at age 35, March 3, 1862. Present or accounted for until discharged on July 1, 1863, by reason of "ascites."

NORRIS, TIMOTHY, Private
Born in Duplin County where he resided as a farmer prior to enlisting in New Hanover County at age 30, March 3, 1862. Discharged on June 3, 1862, by reason of "chronic rheumatism."

NORRISS, WILLIAM W., Private
Resided in Duplin County and enlisted in New Hanover County at age 20, March 3, 1862. Present or accounted for until wounded at Gaines' Mill, Virginia, June 27, 1862. Returned to duty in January-April, 1863. Present or accounted for until he surrendered at Appomattox Court House, Virginia, April 9, 1865.

PARKER, JACOB W., Private
Resided in Duplin County and enlisted in New Hanover County at age 25, March 3, 1862. Present or accounted for until captured at Spotsylvania Court House, Virginia, May 19-20, 1864. Confined at Point Lookout, Maryland, May 23, 1864. Transferred to Elmira, New

York, July 3, 1864. Paroled at Elmira on March 2, 1865, and transferred to the James River, Virginia, for exchange.

PICKETT, JOHN L., Private
Resided in Duplin County and enlisted in New Hanover County at age 23, March 3, 1862. Present or accounted for until wounded at Fredericksburg, Virginia, December 13, 1862. Returned to duty in January-April, 1863. Present or accounted for until captured at Kelly's Ford, Virginia, November 7, 1863. Confined at Point Lookout, Maryland, November 11, 1863. Paroled at Point Lookout on or about February 24, 1865, and transferred to Aiken's Landing, James River, Virginia, where he was received February 25-March 3, 1865, for exchange.

PICKETT, WILLIAM D., Private
Resided in Duplin County where he enlisted at age 25, August 28, 1861. Present or accounted for until hospitalized at Richmond, Virginia, July 4, 1862, with a gunshot wound. Place and date wounded not reported. Returned to duty on July 5, 1862. Present or accounted for until captured in an unspecified battle in September-October, 1864. Paroled on an unspecified date. Hospitalized at Richmond on October 24, 1864, with an unspecified complaint and was furloughed on October 30, 1864.

PIERCE, NIXON, Corporal
Resided in Duplin County and enlisted in New Hanover County at age 40, March 3, 1862. Mustered in as Private. Promoted to Corporal on August 1, 1863. Present or accounted for until captured near Spotsylvania Court House, Virginia, May 12, 1864. Confined at Point Lookout, Maryland, May 18, 1864. Transferred to Elmira, New York, where he arrived on August 14, 1864. Released on June 23, 1865, after taking the Oath of Allegiance.

PINER, JAMES J., Private
Resided in New Hanover County where he enlisted at age 27, August 21, 1863, for the war. Present or accounted for until captured at Spotsylvania Court House, Virginia, May 19-20, 1864. Confined at Point Lookout, Maryland, May 23, 1864. Transferred to Elmira, New York, July 3, 1864. Died at Elmira on March 4, 1865, of "variola."

PRUITT, TELL M., Private
Resided in Wilkes County and was by occupation a farmer. Place and date of enlistment not reported. Deserted to the enemy on an unspecified date. Took the Oath of Allegiance at Charleston, West Virginia, February 6, 1865. Oath of Allegiance gives his age as 34.

PULLY, DANIEL, ——
North Carolina pension records indicate that he served in this company.

RACKLEY, JAMES S., Private
Resided in Duplin County where he enlisted at age 20, August 28, 1861. Present or accounted for through August, 1864.

RAYNER, JOHN C., Private
Born in Duplin County where he resided as a farmer prior to enlisting in Duplin County at age 25, August 28, 1861. Present or accounted for until discharged on

March 27, 1862, by reason of "chronic consumption."

REGISTER, SAMUEL C., Private
Resided in Duplin County where he enlisted at age 22, August 28, 1861. Present or accounted for until captured at Kelly's Ford, Virginia, November 7, 1863. Confined at Point Lookout, Maryland, November 11, 1863. Paroled at Point Lookout on or about February 24, 1865, and transferred to Aiken's Landing, James River, Virginia, where he was received on February 25-March 3, 1865, for exchange.

RICH, CHRISTOPHER C., Private
Resided in Duplin County where he enlisted at age 17, August 28, 1861. Present or accounted for until captured at Kelly's Ford, Virginia, on or about November 7, 1863. Confined at Old Capitol Prison, Washington, D.C., November 8, 1863. Transferred to Point Lookout, .Maryland, February 3, 1864. Paroled at Point Lookout on or about February 13, 1865, and transferred to Cox's Wharf, James River, Virginia, where he was received February 14-15, 1865, for exchange.

RIVENBARK, JAMES T., Private
Born in Duplin County where he resided as a student prior to enlisting in Duplin County at age 18, August 28, 1861. Mustered in as Private. Promoted to Corporal on October 14, 1861. Reduced to ranks on July 20, 1863. Present or accounted for until captured at or near Front Royal, Virginia, July 23-24, 1863. Confined at Point Lookout, Maryland, July 31, 1863. Released on February 23, 1864, after taking the Oath of Allegiance and joining the U.S. Army. Assigned to Company F, 1st Regiment U.S. Volunteer Infantry.

RIVENBARK, JOSEPH, Private
Resided in Duplin County and enlisted at age 17, August 28, 1861. Present or accounted for until wounded at Gaines' Mill, Virginia, June 27, 1862. Died at Richmond, Virginia, of wounds. Date of death not reported.

RIVENBARK, TEACHEY, 1st Sergeant
Resided in Duplin County where he enlisted at age 18, August 28, 1861. Mustered in as Private. Present or accounted for until wounded at Gaines' Mill, Virginia, June 27, 1862. Returned to duty in September-December, 1862, and was promoted to Sergeant on October 24, 1862. Present or accounted for until wounded in the thigh at Kelly's Ford, Virginia, November 7, 1863. Returned to duty in January-August, 1864, and was promoted to 1st Sergeant on August 21, 1864. No further records.

RIVENBARK, WILLIAM, Corporal
Resided in Duplin County where he enlisted at age 19, August 28, 1861. Mustered in as Corporal. Present or accounted for until killed at Malvern Hill, Virginia, July 1, 1862.

ROGERS, JOBE B., Private
Resided in Union County where he enlisted at age 45, September 16, 1863, for the war. Present or accounted for until captured at Old Church, Virginia, May 31, 1864. Confined at Point Lookout, Maryland, June 8, 1864. Transferred to Elmira, New York, July 8, 1864. Died at Elmira on January 28, 1865, of "chronic diarrhoea."

ROUSE, BARNET, Private

Resided in Duplin County where he enlisted at age 25, August 28, 1861. Present or accounted for until wounded at Gaines' Mill, Virginia, June 27, 1862. Died of wounds. Place and date of death not reported.

SALMON, KILBY, Private

Born in Duplin County where he resided prior to enlisting in New Hanover County on March 3, 1862. Discharged on May 29, 1862, by reason of "old age, chronic rheumatism and physical weakness." Discharge certificate gives his age as 45.

SAVAGE, CORNELIUS, Sergeant

Born in Duplin County where he resided as a farmer prior to enlisting in Duplin County at age 20, August 28, 1861. Mustered in as Private. Promoted to Sergeant in March-October, 1862. Died near Winchester, Virginia, October 20, 1862. Cause of death not reported.

SAVAGE, JOHN, Private

Resided in Duplin County where he enlisted at age 19, March 3, 1862. Present or accounted for until captured at or near Gettysburg, Pennsylvania, on or about July 3, 1863. Confined at Fort Delaware, Delaware, on or about July 9, 1863. Transferred to Point Lookout, Maryland, October 15-18, 1863. Paroled at Point Lookout on or about February 13, 1865, and transferred to Cox's Wharf, James River, Virginia, where he was received on February 14-15, 1865, for exchange.

SHOLAR, JAMES H., Private

Resided in Duplin County and enlisted in New Hanover County at age 30, March 3, 1862. Present or accounted for until captured and paroled at or near Warrenton, Virginia, on or about September 29, 1862. Reported absent without leave through August, 1864. Returned to duty on an unspecified date. Captured at or near Farmville, Virginia, on or about April 6, 1865. Confined at Newport News, Virginia, April 14, 1865. Released on June 27, 1865, after taking the Oath of Allegiance. [North Carolina pension records indicate he "lost sight in left eye" at Richmond, Virginia, in 1864.]

SHUTE, HENRY BLAKNEY, Private

Resided in Union County where he enlisted at age 19, September 24, 1863, for the war. Present or accounted for until captured at Cedar Creek, Virginia, October 19, 1864. Confined at Point Lookout, Maryland, October 25, 1864. Released at Point Lookout on June 20, 1865, after taking the Oath of Allegiance.

SOUTHERLAND, JAMES, Private

Resided in Duplin County and enlisted in New Hanover County at age 35, March 3, 1862. Present or accounted for until wounded in the thigh at Gettysburg, Pennsylvania, July 1-3, 1863. Returned to duty prior to November 7, 1863, when he was captured at Kelly's Ford, Virginia. Confined at Point Lookout, Maryland, November 11, 1863. Released on January 25, 1864, after taking the Oath of Allegiance and joining the U.S. Army. [May have been assigned to duty with the 1st Regiment U.S. Volunteer Infantry.]

STEEL, ROBERT, Private

Resided in Union County where he enlisted at age 30, September 24, 1863, for the war. Present or accounted for until captured at or near Old Church, Virginia, on or about May 31, 1864. Confined at Point Lookout,

Maryland, June 8, 1864. Transferred to Elmira, New York, July 9, 1864. Paroled at Elmira on March 14, 1865, and transferred to Boulware's Wharf, James River, Virginia, where he was received March 18-21, 1865, for exchange.

STREETS, WIMBERT, Private

Resided in Duplin County and enlisted at Camp Wyatt at age 45, November 27, 1861. Present or accounted for until he died in hospital at Staunton, Virginia, March 19-20, 1863, of "pneumonia."

STRICKLAND, DAVID R., Private

Resided in Duplin County and enlisted in New Hanover County at age 21, March 3, 1862. Present or accounted for until captured and paroled at or near Warrenton, Virginia, on or about September 29, 1862. Reported absent without leave through December, 1862. Returned to duty prior to May 1, 1863. Present or accounted for until captured at Spotsylvania Court House, Virginia, in May, 1864. Confined at Point Lookout, Maryland, May 23, 1864. Transferred to Elmira, New York, August 10, 1864. Released at Elmira on June 27, 1865, after taking the Oath of Allegiance.

STRICKLAND, ISAAC J., Ordnance Sergeant

Resided in Duplin County where he enlisted at age 23, August 28, 1861. Mustered in as Private. Promoted to Corporal on October 14, 1861. Promoted to Sergeant in January-February, 1862. Appointed Acting Ordnance Sergeant in January-December, 1862, and was permanently promoted to the rank of Ordnance Sergeant on May 1, 1863. Present or accounted for through February 28, 1865.

STRICKLAND, JACOB, Private

Place and date of enlistment not reported. Records of the Federal Provost Marshal indicate he died at Elmira, New York, May 16, 1865. Cause of death not reported.

STRICKLAND, WILLIAM H., Private

Born in Duplin County where he resided as a farmer prior to enlisting in Duplin County at age 20, August 28, 1861. Mustered in as Corporal. Reduced to ranks at his own request on October 14, 1861. Present or accounted for until discharged on March 9, 1862, by reason of "chronic rheumatism."

STRICKLAND, WILLIAM W., Private

Resided in Duplin County where he enlisted at age 24, August 28, 1861. Present or accounted for until killed at Gaines' Mill, Virginia, June 27, 1862.

STYLES, JOHN M. D., Private

Enlisted in Duplin County at age 28, August 28, 1861. Present or accounted for until he died at Guinea Station, Virginia, January 14, 1863, of "brain fever."

TADLOCK, S. D., Private

Resided in Union County where he enlisted at age 19, September 16, 1863, for the war. Present or accounted for until captured at or near Farmville, Virginia, on or about April 6, 1865. Confined at Newport News, Virginia, April 14, 1865. Released on June 27, 1865, after taking the Oath of Allegiance.

TEACHEY, ATLAS, Private

Resided in Duplin County where he enlisted at age 19, February, 1862. Present or accounted for through

August, 1864; however, he was reported absent sick or absent on light duty during much of that period. Paroled at Lynchburg, Virginia, April 13, 1865.

TEACHEY, JACOB T., Private
Born in Duplin County where he resided as a farmer prior to enlisting in New Hanover County at age 19, March 3, 1862. Present or accounted for until "wound[ed] through the bowels" at Snicker's Gap, Virginia, July 18, 1864. Reported absent wounded until January 17, 1865, when he was retired from service by reason of disability from wounds.

TEACHEY, JAMES W., Sergeant
Resided in Duplin County where he enlisted at age 23, August 28, 1861. Mustered in as Private. Promoted to Sergeant in June, 1863. Present or accounted for until killed at or near Snicker's Gap, Virginia, July 18, 1864.

TEACHEY, MARSHALL, Sergeant
Resided in Duplin County where he enlisted at age 23, August 28, 1861. Mustered in as Sergeant. Present or accounted for until he died in hospital at Richmond, Virginia, August 14, 1862, of "febris typhoides."

TEACHEY, W. B., Corporal
Resided in Duplin County and enlisted in New Hanover County at age 29, March 3, 1862. Mustered in as Private. Promoted to Corporal on August 21, 1864. Present or accounted for until captured at Cedar Creek, Virginia, October 19, 1864. Confined at Point Lookout, Maryland, October 23, 1864. Paroled at Point Lookout on or about February 10, 1865, and transferred to Cox's Wharf, James River, Virginia, where he was received February 14-15, 1865, for exchange. [North Carolina pension records indicate he was "wounded at Spotsylvania Court House, Virginia, October 1, 1864."]

THOMPSON, ANDREW J., Private
Resided in Duplin County where he enlisted at age 37, August 28, 1861. Present or accounted for until killed at Kelly's Ford, Virginia, November 7, 1863.

TUCKER, OWEN, Private
Resided in Duplin County and enlisted at Camp Wyatt at age 21, January 1, 1862. Present or accounted for until he died in hospital at Mount Jackson, Virginia, November 22, 1862, of "dysenteria chronica."

TUCKER, WILLIAM, Private
Resided in Duplin County where he enlisted at age 18, August 28, 1861. Present or accounted for until captured at Spotsylvania Court House, Virginia, May 19-20, 1864. Confined at Point Lookout, Maryland, May 23, 1864. Transferred to Elmira, New York, July 3, 1864. Paroled at Elmira on February 9, 1865, and transferred to Boulware's Wharf, James River, Virginia, where he was received February 20-21, 1865, for exchange.

TURNER, DAVID W., Private
Resided in Duplin County and enlisted in New Hanover County at age 27, August 31, 1863, for the war. Present or accounted for until wounded at Kelly's Ford, Virginia, November 7, 1863. Returned to duty on an unspecified date. Wounded in the head at or near Charles Town, West Virginia, August 21, 1864. Returned to duty on an unspecified date. Surrendered at Appomattox Court House, Virginia, April 9, 1865.

UNDERWOOD, R. H., Private
Place and date of enlistment not reported. Died at Camp Draughon on May 8, 1862. Cause of death not reported.

WALLACE, ROBERT CHASTEN, Private
Resided in Duplin County where he enlisted at age 22, April 28, 1861. Mustered in as Private. Promoted to Sergeant on October 14, 1861. Promoted to 1st Sergeant prior to March 1, 1862. Reduced to ranks prior to January 1, 1863. Present or accounted for until he died at Hamilton's Crossing, Virginia, on or about March 11, 1863, of "pneumonia."

WALLACE, WILLIAM THOMAS, Private
Resided in Duplin County where he enlisted at age 18, August 28, 1861. Present or accounted for until wounded at Gaines' Mill, Virginia, June 27, 1862. Returned to duty prior to January 1, 1863. Present or accounted for until killed at Chancellorsville, Virginia, on or about May 3, 1863.

WARD, JOHN F., Corporal
Resided in Duplin or Wake County and enlisted in Duplin County at age 23, August 28, 1861. Mustered in as Corporal. Reduced to ranks on October 14, 1861. Promoted to Corporal on May 19, 1864. Present or accounted for through August, 1864.

WELLS, JAMES W., 1st Sergeant
Resided in Duplin County where he enlisted at age 22, August 28, 1861. Mustered in as Private. Promoted to Sergeant in January-December, 1862. Present or accounted for until wounded at Sharpsburg, Maryland, September 17, 1862. Reported absent wounded through December, 1862. Promoted to 1st Sergeant in January, 1863. Returned to duty in January-April, 1863. Present or accounted for until killed at or near Spotsylvania Court House, Virginia, May 18, 1864.

WELLS, JOHN H., Sergeant
Born in Duplin County where he resided prior to enlisting in Duplin County at age 24, August 28, 1861. Mustered in as Private. Promoted to Corporal on October 14, 1861. Present or accounted for until wounded at Gaines' Mill, Virginia, June 27, 1862. Returned to duty on an unspecified date. Promoted to Sergeant on October 1, 1862. Died near Fredericksburg, Virginia, December 22-23, 1862. Cause of death not reported.

WILSON, J. L., Private
Resided in Robeson County. Date of enlistment not reported. Died in hospital at Gordonsville, Virginia, October 31, 1863, of "febris typhoides."

WOOD, MARLEY, Private
Resided in Duplin County where he enlisted at age 30, August 28, 1861. Present or accounted for until he died in hospital at Gordonsville, Virginia, on or about January 21, 1863, of "pneumonia."

WOOD, UZZELL T., Private
Resided in Duplin County where he enlisted at age 33, August 28, 1861. Present or accounted for until he surrendered at Appomattox Court House, Virginia, April 9, 1865.

COMPANY F

This company, known as the "Sparta Band," was raised in Edgecombe County and enlisted at Sparta on August 31, 1861. It was then assigned to the 30th Regiment N.C. Troops and designated Company F. After joining the regiment the company functioned as a part of the regiment, and its history for the war period is reported as a part of the regimental history.

The information contained in the following roster of the company was compiled principally from a company muster-in and descriptive roll dated October 8, 1861, and from company muster rolls for September, 1861-April, 1862; November-December, 1862; May-August, 1863; and November, 1863-August, 1864. No company muster rolls were found for May-October, 1862; January-April, 1863; September-October, 1863; or for the period after August, 1864. Valuable information was obtained from primary records such as the Roll of Honor, discharge certificates, medical records, prisoner of war records, and pension applications. Secondary sources such as postwar rosters and histories, cemetery records, and records of the United Daughters of the Confederacy also provided useful information.

OFFICERS

CAPTAINS

PITT, FRANKLIN G.
Resided in Edgecombe County where he enlisted at age 35. Elected Captain on August 31, 1861. Present or accounted for until he was defeated for reelection when the regiment was reorganized on March 10, 1862.

MOORE, WILLIAM M. B.
Resided in Edgecombe County where he enlisted at age 25. Elected 1st Lieutenant on August 31, 1861. Promoted to Captain on March 10, 1862. Present or accounted for until wounded in the left breast near Spotsylvania Court House, Virginia, May 8, 1864. Returned to duty on September 23, 1864. Killed at or near Cedar Creek, Virginia, October 19, 1864. "There was not a more gallant soldier left in the Army of Northern Virginia."

MOORE, SAMUEL RUFUS
Resided in Edgecombe County where he enlisted at age 20, August 31, 1861. Mustered in as Private. Appointed 1st Sergeant on March 10, 1862. Elected 3rd Lieutenant on January 20, 1863. Captured by the enemy on July 26, 1863, and was paroled on August 2, 1863. Returned to duty prior to January 1, 1864. Promoted to Captain on October 19, 1864. Present or accounted for until he surrendered at Appomattox Court House, Virginia, April 9, 1865.

LIEUTENANTS

EAGLES, LORENZO DOW, 2nd Lieutenant
Resided in Edgecombe County and was by occupation a teacher prior to enlisting in Edgecombe County at age 24, August 31, 1861. Mustered in as Sergeant. Elected 3rd Lieutenant on March 10, 1862. Wounded at Gaines' Mill, Virginia, June 27, 1862. Returned to duty prior to January 1, 1863. Promoted to 2nd Lieutenant on January 20, 1863. Present or accounted for until wounded at or near Spotsylvania Court House, Virginia, May 12, 1864. Died on May 24, 1864, of wounds. Place of death not reported.

HARRELL, GEORGE K., 1st Lieutenant
Resided in Edgecombe County where he enlisted at age 19, August 31, 1861. Mustered in as 1st Sergeant. Elected 1st Lieutenant on March 10, 1862. Present or accounted for until wounded at Sharpsburg, Maryland, September 17, 1862. Returned to duty in January-June, 1863. Present or accounted for until killed at Spotsylvania Court House, Virginia, May 12, 1864.

HOUSE, JAMES W. J., 2nd Lieutenant
Resided in Edgecombe County where he enlisted at age 26, August 31, 1861. Mustered in as Private. Promoted to Sergeant on March 10, 1862. Present or accounted for until wounded at Kelly's Ford, Virginia, on or about November 7, 1863. Returned to duty prior to January 1, 1864. Elected 2nd Lieutenant on May 24, 1864. Present or accounted for until wounded in the right foot and captured at Appomattox Court House, Virginia, April 9, 1865. Confined at various Federal hospitals until confined at Fort McHenry, Maryland, May 9, 1865. Released on June 10, 1865, after taking the Oath of Allegiance. Nominated for the Badge of Distinction for gallantry at Chancellorsville, Virginia, May 1-4, 1863.

PITT, JAMES W., 2nd Lieutenant
Resided in Edgecombe County where he enlisted at age 19. Elected 3rd Lieutenant on or about August 31, 1861, and was elected 2nd Lieutenant on March 10, 1862. Present or accounted for until he died in hospital at Richmond, Virginia, on or about August 3, 1862, of "feb[ris] typh[oid]."

VINES, CHARLES, 3rd Lieutenant
Resided in Edgecombe County where he enlisted at age 19. Elected 3rd Lieutenant on or about August 31, 1861. Present or accounted for until he was defeated for reelection [or resigned] when the regiment was reorganized in March, 1862. Later served as 1st Lieutenant of Company E, 43rd Regiment N.C. Troops.

NONCOMMISSIONED OFFICERS AND PRIVATES

ABRAMS, JOHN, Private
Place and date of enlistment not reported. "Failed to pass the inspection of the mustering officer and [was] honorably discharged" on or about September 23, 1861.

BAILEY, BENJAMIN, Private
Resided in Greene County and enlisted in Edgecombe County at age 20, August 31, 1861. Present or accounted for until he surrendered at Appomattox Court House, Virginia, April 9, 1865.

BARNES, SPENCER, Private
Resided in Wilson County and enlisted in Wake County at age 28, January 20, 1862. Present or accounted for until wounded at Kelly's Ford, Virginia, on or about November 7, 1863. Reported absent wounded through December, 1863. Detailed "to guard ordnance stores" in March, 1864. Reported absent on detail through August, 1864. Surrendered at Appomattox Court House, Virginia, April 9, 1865.

BELL, BENNETT, Private
Resided in Edgecombe County where he enlisted at age 30, August 31, 1861. Present or accounted for until hospitalized at Charlottesville, Virginia, October 24, 1864, with a gunshot wound of the left knee. Place and

date wounded not reported. Company records do not indicate whether he returned to duty. Paroled at Farmville, Virginia, April 11-21, 1865.

BOLSTER, R., Private
Resided in Wilson County. Place and date of enlistment not reported. Paroled at Goldsboro on May 9, 1865.

BOYCE, WILLIAM, Private
Resided in Edgecombe County and enlisted in Wake County at age 34, August 31, 1861. Present or accounted for until wounded at Malvern Hill, Virginia, July 1, 1862. Reported absent wounded through December, 1862. Discharged on May 15, 1863, by reason of disability from wounds received at Malvern Hill.

BRADLEY, OLIVER, Corporal
Resided in Edgecombe County where he enlisted at age 20, August 31, 1861. Mustered in as Private. Promoted to Corporal on March 10, 1862. Present or accounted for until he died at or near Richmond, Virginia, December 16-17, 1862, of "variola."

BRASWELL, JAMES B., Private
Resided in Edgecombe County where he enlisted at age 19, August 31, 1861. Present or accounted for until he surrendered at Appomattox Court House, Virginia, April 9, 1865. [North Carolina pension records indicate he was wounded at Spotsylvania Court House, Virginia, and at Petersburg, Virginia, on unspecified dates.]

BREWER, WARREN, Private
Born in Edgecombe County and resided in Edgecombe or Pitt County prior to enlisting in Edgecombe County at age 32, August 31; 1861. Present or accounted for until he died in hospital at Wilmington, April 20-26, 1862. Cause of death not reported.

BROWN, HENRY, Corporal
Resided in Edgecombe County where he enlisted at age 26, August 31, 1861. Mustered in as Private. Promoted to Corporal on March 10, 1862. Present or accounted for through April, 1862.

BROWN, J., Private
Place and date of enlistment not reported. Paroled at Burkeville Junction, Virginia, April 14-17, 1865.

BROWN, LEVI, ——
North Carolina pension records indicate that he served in this company.

BROWN, W. H., Corporal
Born in Edgecombe County and was by occupation a farmer prior to enlisting in Wake County on August 31, 1861. Mustered in as Private. Promoted to Corporal in March-December, 1862. Present or accounted for until captured at or near Sharpsburg, Maryland, on or about September 17, 1862. Paroled on September 30, 1862. Returned to duty prior to January 1, 1863. Present or accounted for until captured at Kelly's Ford, Virginia, November 7, 1863. Confined at Point Lookout, Maryland, November 11, 1863. Paroled at Point Lookout on or about February 24, 1865, and transferred to Aiken's Landing, James River, Virginia, where he was received February 25-March 3, 1865, for exchange. [Company records dated November, 1862, give his age as 26.]

BRYANT, CHARLES, Private
Resided in Edgecombe County and enlisted in Wake County at age 18, August 31, 1861. Present or accounted for through August, 1862. Roll of Honor indicates he was reported missing at Sharpsburg, Maryland, on or about September 17, 1862; however, company records dated November-December, 1862, indicate he was absent sick in hospital at Richmond, Virginia, since September 26, 1862. No further records.

BRYANT, JOHN, Private
Resided in Edgecombe County and enlisted at Camp Wyatt at age 18, March 10, 1862. Present or accounted for until killed at Gaines' Mill, Virginia, June 27, 1862.

BURGESS, H. B., ——
North Carolina pension records indicate that he served in this company.

BURGESS, HARDY, Private
Resided in Edgecombe County where he enlisted at age 23, August 31, 1861. Present or accounted for until wounded at Spotsylvania Court House, Virginia, May 12, 1864. Reported absent wounded through August, 1864. Returned to duty on an unspecified date. Surrendered at Appomattox Court House, Virginia, April 9, 1865.

CARNEY, JAMES, Private
Born in Pitt County and resided in Edgecombe County where he was by occupation a farmer prior to enlisting in Edgecombe County at age 28, August 31, 1861. Mustered in as Corporal. Present or accounted for until discharged on March 19, 1862, by reason of "chronic rheumatism." Reenlisted in the company with the rank of Private on June 11, 1863. Present or accounted for until December 1, 1863, when he was detailed for hospital duty at Orange Court House, Virginia. Reported absent on detail until October 18, 1864, when he rejoined the company. No further records.

CHERRY, SPENCER, Sergeant
Resided in Edgecombe County where he enlisted at age 28, August 31, 1861. Mustered in as Corporal. Reduced to ranks in March-April, 1862. Promoted to Sergeant in May-December, 1862. Present or accounted for until wounded at Malvern Hill, Virginia, July 1, 1862. Returned to duty prior to July 1, 1863. Present or accounted for until wounded at or near Spotsylvania Court House, Virginia, May 12, 1864. Hospitalized at Richmond, Virginia, where he died on May 21-22, 1864, of wounds.

CHRISP, S. E., Private
Resided in Edgecombe County where he enlisted at age 28, May 1, 1862, for the war. Present or accounted for until hospitalized at Danville, Virginia, on or about June 4, 1864, with a gunshot wound of the arm. Place and date wounded not reported. Reported absent in hospital through August, 1864.

CHRISP, W. S., Private
Resided in Edgecombe County where he enlisted at age 25, May 1, 1862, for the war. Present or accounted for until captured at or near Spotsylvania Court House, Virginia, May 8, 1864. Confined at Point Lookout, Maryland, May 17, 1864. Transferred to Elmira, New York, August 10, 1864. Released at Elmira on June 30,

1865, after taking the Oath of Allegiance.

CHRISP, WILLIAM G., Private

Resided in Greene County and enlisted in Edgecombe County at age 20, August 31, 1861. Present or accounted for until wounded at or near Spotsylvania Court House, Virginia, May 12, 1864. Died on May 20, 1864, of wounds. Place of death not reported.

CLINE, J., Private

Place and date of enlistment not reported. Captured at or near the Appomattox River, Virginia, April 3, 1865. Confined at Point Lookout, Maryland, April 16, 1865. Released on June 4, 1865, after taking the Oath of Allegiance.

COBB, JOHN B., Private

Resided in Edgecombe County where he enlisted at age 20, August 31, 1861. Mustered in as Sergeant. Reduced to ranks in March, 1862. Present or accounted for until hospitalized at Richmond, Virginia, March 19, 1863, with a "puncture" wound. Place and date injured not reported. Returned to duty on March 27, 1863. Present or accounted for until he surrendered at Appomattox Court House, Virginia, April 9, 1865.

COBB, JOHN R., Private

Resided in Edgecombe County where he enlisted at age 23, August 31, 1861. Mustered in as Sergeant. Reduced to ranks in January, 1862. Present or accounted for until he died at Tarboro on January 25, 1862, of "bilious fever."

COBB, WILLIAM E., Private

Resided in Pitt County and enlisted in Wake County at age 18, August 31, 1861. Present or accounted for until discharged on July 10, 1862, by reason of disability.

CORBETT, DEMPSEY, Private

Resided in Edgecombe County where he enlisted at age 20, August 31, 1861. Present or accounted for until wounded at Spotsylvania Court House, Virginia, May 12, 1864. Reported absent wounded through August, 1864. Hospitalized at Farmville, Virginia, April 7, 1865, with a gunshot wound. Place and date wounded not reported. Paroled at Farmville on April 11-21, 1865. [North Carolina pension records indicate he was wounded at Culpeper Court House, Virginia, on an unspecified date.]

CORBETT, HENRY, Private

Resided in Edgecombe County where he enlisted at age 20, August 31, 1861. Present or accounted for through August, 1864.

CORBITT, JAMES, Private

Resided in Edgecombe County where he enlisted at age 16, August 31, 1861. Present or accounted for until he died at Smithville (Southport) on November 10, 1861, of "typhoid fever."

CORBITT, WILLIAM W., Private

Resided in Edgecombe County where he enlisted at age 23, August 31, 1861. Present or accounted for until captured at or near Gettysburg, Pennsylvania, July 1-5, 1863. Confined at Fort Delaware, Delaware, on or about July 7, 1863. Transferred to hospital at Chester, Pennsylvania, on or about July 19, 1863. Paroled and transferred to City Point, Virginia, where he was

received on August 20, 1863, for exchange. Returned to duty prior to January 1, 1864. Present or accounted for until captured at or near Spotsylvania Court House, Virginia, May 8, 1864. Confined at Point Lookout, Maryland, May 17, 1864. Transferred to Elmira, New York, August 10, 1864. Paroled at Elmira on March 14, 1865, and transferred to Boulware's Wharf, James River, Virginia, where he was received March 18-21, 1865, for exchange.

CRISP, AMOS, Private

Resided in Greene County and enlisted at Camp Wyatt at age 19, March 10, 1862. Present or accounted for until he died "in camp" on or about February 13, 1863, of "pneumonia."

CRISP, EASON, Private

Born in Edgecombe County where he resided prior to enlisting in Edgecombe County at age 20, August 31, 1861. Present or accounted for until wounded at Malvern Hill, Virginia, July 1, 1862. Hospitalized at Richmond, Virginia, where he died July 25-27, 1862, of wounds.

CRISP, LEVI, Private

Resided in Edgecombe County where he enlisted at age 38, August 31, 1861. Present or accounted for until wounded in the mouth at Gettysburg, Pennsylvania, July 1-3, 1863. Returned to duty prior to September 1, 1863. Present or accounted for through August, 1864. Company records indicate he was discharged on September 8, 1864; however, records of the Federal Provost Marshal indicate he surrendered at Appomattox Court House, Virginia, April 9, 1865.

DEAL, REUBEN, Private

Resided in Edgecombe County where he enlisted at age 23, August 31, 1861. Present or accounted for through August, 1864.

DENTON, LEVI, Private

Born in Edgecombe County where he resided as a farmer prior to enlisting in Edgecombe County at age 21, August 31, 1861. Present or accounted for until wounded at Malvern Hill, Virginia, July 1, 1862. Reported absent wounded or absent sick until December 28, 1863, when he was discharged by reason of "serious impairment of use of right leg the result of white swelling of over two years standing."

DEW, LEWIS, Private

Resided in Edgecombe County where he enlisted at age 30, August 31, 1861. Present or accounted for until captured at or near Gettysburg, Pennsylvania, July 3-5, 1863. Confined at Fort Delaware, Delaware, August 10, 1863. Died at Fort Delaware on November 12, 1863, of "scurvy."

DEW, WILLIAM, Private

Resided in Edgecombe County where he enlisted at age 17, August 31, 1861. Present or accounted for until wounded in the head and/or lungs at Gaines' Mill, Virginia, June 27, 1862. Hospitalized at Richmond, Virginia, where he died on July 2-3, 1862, of wounds.

DICKENS, EPHRAIM, Private

Resided in Edgecombe County where he enlisted at age 19, August 31, 1861. Present or accounted for until wounded at Sharpsburg, Maryland, September 17,

1862. Returned to duty in January-June, 1863. Hospitalized at Richmond, Virginia, June 5, 1863, with a gunshot wound of the left thigh. Place and date wounded not reported. Returned to duty on or about July 11, 1863. Present or accounted for until killed at or near Spotsylvania Court House, Virginia, May 19, 1864.

DIXON, HENRY O., Private
Resided in Edgecombe County where he enlisted at age 20, August 31, 1861. Present or accounted for until wounded in the left leg and captured at Kelly's Ford, Virginia, November 7, 1863. Confined at Point Lookout, Maryland, November 11, 1863. Released at Point Lookout on June 12, 1865, after taking the Oath of Allegiance.

EAGLES, T. R., Private
Resided in Edgecombe County where he enlisted at age 20, May 1, 1862, for the war. Present or accounted for until he surrendered at Appomattox Court House, Virginia, April 9, 1865.

EASON, JAMES SCARBOROUGH, Private
Born in Edgecombe County where he resided as a farmer prior to enlisting in Edgecombe County at age 35, August 31, 1861. Present or accounted for until discharged on March 5, 1862, by reason of "chronic rheumatism." Later served in Company H of this regiment.

EDWARDS, ELSBERRY B., Private
Resided in Edgecombe County where he enlisted at age 28, August 31, 1861. Present or accounted for until wounded at South Mountain, Maryland, in September, 1862. Returned to duty prior to January 1, 1863. Present or accounted for until he surrendered at Appomattox Court House, Virginia, April 9, 1865.

EDWARDS, HARDY, Private
Enlisted on or about September 1, 1861. "Failed to pass the inspection of the mustering officer" and was honorably discharged on or about September 23, 1861. [May have served later in Company E, 43rd Regiment N.C. Troops.]

EDWARDS, MONTGOMERY, Private
Born in Edgecombe County where he resided prior to enlisting in Edgecombe County at age 20, August 31, 1861. Present or accounted for until wounded in the side at Gaines' Mill, Virginia, June 27, 1862. Returned to duty on July 18, 1862. Present or accounted for until he died in hospital at Richmond, Virginia, on or about April 18-19, 1863, of disease.

EDWARDS, THOMAS, Private
Resided in Edgecombe County and enlisted at age 35, May 1, 1862, for the war. Present or accounted for until he died in hospital at Wilmington on June 15, 1862, of "typhoid fever."

EDWARDS, W. B., Private
Resided in Edgecombe County and enlisted at age 29, May 1, 1862, for the war. Discharged on August 5, 1862, after providing a substitute.

ELLIS, JAMES, Corporal
Resided in Edgecombe County where he enlisted at age 19, May 1, 1862, for the war. Mustered in as Private.

Promoted to Corporal subsequent to August 31, 1864. Present or accounted for until he surrendered at Appomattox Court House, Virginia, April 9, 1865.

ELLIS, WILLIE, Private
Resided in Edgecombe County where he enlisted at age 21, May 1, 1862, for the war. Mustered in as Private. Promoted to Musician prior to January 1, 1863. Reduced to ranks in July-August, 1863. Present or accounted for through March 15, 1865; however, he was reported absent sick during most of that period.

EVERETT, JOSEPH, Private
Resided in Edgecombe County where he enlisted at age 29, May 1, 1862, for the war. Present or accounted for until he died near Woodstock, Virginia, July 23, 1864, of disease.

EVERETT, WILLIAM, Private
Resided in Edgecombe County where he enlisted at age 32, August 31, 1861. Present or accounted for until killed at Gaines' Mill, Virginia, June 27, 1862.

FELTON, ELI, Private
Resided in Edgecombe County where he enlisted at age 27, May 1, 1862, for the war. Present or accounted for until wounded at or near the Appomattox River, Virginia, April 6, 1865. Surrendered at Appomattox Court House, Virginia, April 9, 1865.

FELTON, RICHARD, Corporal
Resided in Edgecombe County where he enlisted at age 29, August 31, 1861. Mustered in as Private. Promoted to Corporal on March 10, 1862. Present or accounted for until wounded at Malvern Hill, Virginia, July 1, 1862. Returned to duty in January-June, 1863. Present or accounted for until killed at Snicker's Gap, Virginia, July 18, 1864.

FORBES, ARTHUR, Sergeant
Resided in Edgecombe County where he enlisted at age 20, August 31, 1861. Mustered in as Private. Present or accounted for until hospitalized at Richmond, Virginia, June 29, 1862, with a gunshot wound of the side. Place and date wounded not reported. Returned to duty in January-April, 1863. Wounded at Chancellorsville, Virginia, May 1-4, 1863. Returned to duty on May 26, 1863. Present or accounted for until wounded at Kelly's Ford, Virginia, on or about November 7, 1863. Returned to duty prior to January 1, 1864. Promoted to Sergeant subsequent to August 31, 1864. Present or accounted for until he surrendered at Appomattox Court House, Virginia, April 9, 1865.

FORBES, JAMES, Private
Resided in Edgecombe County where he enlisted at age 18, May 1, 1862, for the war. Present or accounted for until wounded at Gaines' Mill, Virginia, June 27, 1862. Returned to duty in July-August, 1863. Present or accounted for until wounded at Snicker's Gap, Virginia, July 18, 1864. Returned to duty subsequent to August 31, 1864. Surrendered at Appomattox Court House, Virginia, April 9, 1865.

FORBES, RANDOLPH, Private
Resided in Edgecombe or Wilson County and enlisted in Brunswick County at age 17, October 10, 1861. Mustered in as Private. Promoted to Corporal in January-June, 1863. Reduced to ranks in September-

December, 1863. Present or accounted for until hospitalized at Charlottesville, Virginia, October 18, 1863, with a gunshot wound. Place and date wounded not reported. Reported absent in hospital through August, 1864. Paroled at Goldsboro on May 15, 1865. [Roll of Honor indicates he was wounded at Warrenton Springs, Virginia, on an unspecified date.]

FOUNTAIN, ALMON L., Private
Born in Edgecombe County where he resided prior to enlisting in Edgecombe County at age 20, August 31, 1861. Present or accounted for until captured at Kelly's Ford, Virginia, November 7, 1863. Confined at Point Lookout, Maryland. Paroled at Point Lookout on an unspecified date and transferred to Cox's Wharf, James River, Virginia, where he was received February 14-15, 1865, for exchange.

GAY, HENRY, Private
Resided in Greene County and enlisted in Edgecombe County at age 18, May 1, 1862, for the war. Present or accounted for until he died in hospital at or near Guinea Station, Virginia, on or about February 1 or February 23, 1863, of "ty[phoid] fever" and/or "pneumonia."

HAGINS, LEWIS W., Private
Resided in Edgecombe County where he enlisted at age 18, May 1, 1862, for the war. Present or accounted for until he died in hospital at or near Charlottesville, Virginia, November 14, 1863, of "pneumonia."

HARPER, J. DAVID, Private
Resided in Edgecombe County where he enlisted at age 24, August 31, 1861. Died "at home" in September, 1861, of "typhoid fever."

HARRELL, DAVID, Private
Resided in Edgecombe County where he enlisted at age 18, August 31, 1861. Present or accounted for until wounded at Malvern Hill, Virginia, July 1, 1862. Returned to duty prior to September 17, 1862, when he was killed at Sharpsburg, Maryland.

HARRELL, E. T., Private
Resided in Edgecombe County where he enlisted at age 22, May 1, 1862, for the war. Present or accounted for until wounded at Spotsylvania Court House, Virginia, May 12, 1864. Hospitalized at Richmond, Virginia, where he died on May 26-29, 1864, of "compressio cerebri."

HARRELL, JACKSON, Private
Place and date of enlistment not reported. "Failed to pass the inspection of the mustering officer and [was] honorably discharged" on or about September 23, 1861.

HARRELL, PETER, Private
Resided in Edgecombe County where he enlisted at age 20, August 31, 1861. Present or accounted for until wounded in the foot and right leg at Chancellorsville, Virginia, May 3, 1863. Reported absent wounded or absent on furlough until April 15, 1864, when he was detailed for light duty. Reported absent on detail at Lynchburg, Virginia, through December, 1864.

HARRELL, WATSON, Private
Resided in Edgecombe County where he enlisted at age 19, August 31, 1861. Present or accounted for until he surrendered at Appomattox Court House, Virginia,

April 9, 1865.

HARRELL, WILLIAM, Musician
Resided in Edgecombe County where he enlisted at age 18, August 31, 1861. Mustered in as Musician (Drummer). Present or accounted for until he died "at home" on November 25, 1862. Cause of death not reported.

HARRIS, GEORGE, Private
Place and date of enlistment not reported. "Failed to pass the inspection of the mustering officer and [was] honorably discharged" on or about September 23, 1861.

HARRISS, WILLIAM J., Private
Resided in Edgecombe County where he enlisted at age 21, August 31, 1861. Present or accounted for until he died in hospital at Richmond, Virginia, on or about August 7, 1862, of "feb[ris] typhoides."

HATHAWAY, AUGUSTUS, Private
Resided in Edgecombe County and enlisted in Wake County at age 35, January 21, 1862. Present or accounted for until wounded in the shoulder at Sharpsburg, Maryland, September 17, 1862. Reported absent wounded until May 15, 1863, when he was discharged by reason of disability from wounds.

HATHAWAY, HENRY, Private
Resided in Edgecombe County where he enlisted at age 19, August 31, 1861. Present or accounted for until wounded at Malvern Hill, Virginia, July 1, 1862. Returned to duty prior to January 1, 1863. Present or accounted for until wounded in the jaw and shoulder and captured at Gettysburg, Pennsylvania, July 1-3, 1863. Died at Gettysburg on July 10, 1863, of wounds.

HATHAWAY, JAMES J., Private
Resided in Edgecombe County where he enlisted at age 18, May 1, 1862, for the war. Present or accounted for until captured near Spotsylvania Court House, Virginia, May 8, 1864. Confined at Point Lookout, Maryland, May 17, 1864. Transferred to Elmira, New York, August 10, 1864. Released at Elmira on June 27, 1865, after taking the Oath of Allegiance.

HATHAWAY, RICHARD, Private
Resided in Edgecombe County where he enlisted at age 18, August 31, 1861. Present or accounted for until he surrendered at Appomattox Court House, Virginia, April 9, 1865.

HEARN, AMOS, Private
Resided in Edgecombe County and enlisted at age 25, May 1, 1862, for the war. Present or accounted for until he died at Wilmington on June 22, 1862. Cause of death not reported.

HOWARD, WILEY, ———
North Carolina pension records indicate that he served in this company.

JOHNSON, A. C. J., Private
Resided in Edgecombe County where he enlisted at age 32, May 1, 1862, for the war. Present or accounted for until wounded in the right arm at Snicker's Gap, Virginia, July 18, 1864. Reported absent wounded through August, 1864. [North Carolina pension records indicate he was wounded at "Fredericksburg, Virginia,

in 1863."]

JOHNSON, ELLIS, Private

Born in Edgecombe County where he resided as a farmer prior to enlisting in Edgecombe County at age 18, August 31, 1861. Present or accounted for until wounded in the head at Chancellorsville, Virginia, May 3, 1863. Hospitalized at Petersburg, Virginia, where he died on or about May 24, 1863, of wounds.

JONES, LEVI, Private

Resided in Edgecombe County where he enlisted at age 23, May 1, 1862, for the war. Present or accounted for until wounded at Sharpsburg, Maryland, September 17, 1862. Returned to duty in January-June, 1863. Present or accounted for through August, 1864.

KEELE, WILLIAM, Private

Resided in Edgecombe County where he enlisted at age 28, August 31, 1861. Present or accounted for through April, 1864. Detailed for guard duty at Richmond, Virginia, May 20, 1864, by reason of a gunshot wound of the left shoulder. Place and date wounded not reported. Reported on duty at Richmond through August, 1864.

LANGLEY, MORRISON, Private

Resided in Edgecombe County where he enlisted at age 26, May 1, 1862, for the war. Present or accounted for until killed at or near Bethesda Church, Virginia, May 31, 1864.

LANGLY, R., Private

Place and date of enlistment not reported. Discharged on or about September 23, 1861, after he "failed to pass the inspection of the mustering officer." [May have served later in Company E, 43rd Regiment N.C. Troops.]

LAWRENCE, JOHN J., Private

Resided in Edgecombe County where he enlisted at age 23, May 1, 1862, for the war. Captured at or near Sharpsburg, Maryland, on or about September 17, 1862. Exchanged on or about December 1, 1862. Returned to duty prior to July 1, 1863. Promoted to Hospital Steward on November 10, 1863, and transferred to the Field and Staff of this regiment. [May have served previously in Company A, 1st Regiment N.C. Infantry (6 months, 1861).]

LAWRENCE, PETER, Private

Place and date of enlistment not reported. Discharged on or about September 23, 1861, after he "failed to pass the inspection of the mustering officer."

LEIGH, JOSEPH, Private

Resided in Edgecombe County where he enlisted at age 21, August 31, 1861. Present or accounted for until hospitalized at Wilmington on or about April 2, 1862, with "typhoid fever." Died in hospital at Wilmington on April 20-26, 1862.

LEIGH, THEOPHILUS, Private

Resided in Edgecombe County where he enlisted at age 20, August 31, 1861. Present or accounted for until wounded at Kelly's Ford, Virginia, November 7, 1863. Returned to duty prior to September 1, 1864. Paroled at Burkeville, Virginia, April 14-17, 1865.

LEWIS, JOHN D., Private

Resided in Edgecombe or Wilson County and enlisted in Edgecombe County at age 34, May 1, 1862, for the war. Present or accounted for until he surrendered at Appomattox Court House, Virginia, April 9, 1865. Apparently served as a butcher during much of the war.

LEWIS, JOHN I., Private

Resided in Edgecombe County where he enlisted at age 18, August 31, 1861. Present or accounted for until wounded in the right arm at Kelly's Ford, Virginia, November 7, 1863. Right arm amputated. Reported absent wounded until April 1, 1864, when he was retired from service.

LITTLE, JESSE, Private

Resided in Edgecombe County where he enlisted at age 18, August 31, 1861. Present or accounted for until wounded at Fredericksburg, Virginia, December 13, 1862. Returned to duty prior to January 1, 1863. Present or accounted for until wounded in the left thigh and captured at Cedar Creek, Virginia, October 19, 1864. Hospitalized at Baltimore, Maryland. Paroled at Baltimore on an unspecified date and transferred on February 16, 1865, for exchange. Furloughed for thirty days from hospital at Richmond, Virginia, March 9, 1865.

LITTLE, JESSE C., Private

Resided in Edgecombe County where he enlisted at age 24, August 31, 1861. Present or accounted for until wounded at Sharpsburg, Maryland, on or about September 17, 1862. Returned to duty in January-June, 1863. Present or accounted for until he surrendered at Appomattox Court House, Virginia, April 9, 1865.

LITTLE, LORENZO, Private

Born in Pitt County and resided in Edgecombe County where he enlisted at age 34, May 1, 1862, for the war. Present or accounted for until he died in hospital at Richmond, Virginia, April 13, 1863, of "pneumonia."

LITTLE, WILLIS, Private

Resided in Edgecombe County where he enlisted at age 25, August 31, 1861. Present or accounted for until he died in hospital at Richmond, Virginia, September 7-20, 1862, of "febris typhoides."

MADRA, ANDREW J., Private

Resided in Edgecombe County where he enlisted at age 18, August 31, 1861. Present or accounted for until captured at South Mountain, Maryland, September 14, 1862. Confined at Fort Delaware, Delaware. Paroled and transferred to Aiken's Landing, James River, Virginia, October 2, 1862, for exchange. Declared exchanged at Aiken's Landing on November 10, 1862. Returned to duty prior to January 1, 1863. Present or accounted for until wounded in the face at Chancellorsville, Virginia, May 1-4, 1863. Returned to duty prior to July 1, 1863. Wounded in the hand and knee at Gettysburg, Pennsylvania, July 1-3, 1863. Returned to duty prior to September 1, 1863. Present or accounted for until captured at Spotsylvania Court House, Virginia, May 19-20, 1864. Confined at Point Lookout, Maryland, May 23, 1864. Transferred to Elmira, New York, July 3, 1864. Released at Elmira on June 19, 1865, after taking the Oath of Allegiance.

MARLEY, W. H., ———

North Carolina pension records indicate that he served in this company.

MARLOW, NATHAN, Private

Resided in Edgecombe County and enlisted at Richmond, Virginia, at age 58, August 5, 1862, for the war as a substitute. Present or accounted for until he died in hospital at or near Richmond on or about February 5, 1863, of "pneumonia."

MATHEWS, RODERICK, Private

Resided in Pitt County and enlisted in Wake County at age 44, August 22, 1863, for the war. Present or accounted for until captured at Farmville, Virginia, April 6, 1865. Confined at Point Lookout, Maryland, April 14, 1865. Released at Point Lookout on June 29, 1865, after taking the Oath of Allegiance.

MAYO, JAMES, Private

Resided in Edgecombe County where he enlisted at age 19, August 31, 1861. Present or accounted for until wounded at Fredericksburg, Virginia, December 13, 1862. Returned to duty on or about January 23, 1863. Died in hospital at Richmond, Virginia, February 21, 1863, of "typhoid pneumonia."

MERCER, JACOB J., Private

Resided in Edgecombe County where he enlisted at age 22, August 31, 1861. Present or accounted for until wounded in the left arm and captured at Gettysburg, Pennsylvania, July 1-3, 1863. Left arm amputated. Hospitalized at Gettysburg until transferred to hospital at Baltimore, Maryland, October 6, 1863. Paroled on November 12, 1863, and transferred for exchange. Exchanged on an unspecified date. Reported absent wounded until January 12, 1865, when he was retired to the Invalid Corps.

MOORE, JOHN J., Private

Resided in Edgecombe County and enlisted at Camp Wyatt at age 24, March 10, 1862. Present or accounted for until wounded at Malvern Hill, Virginia, July 1, 1862. Reported absent wounded until March 17, 1863, when he was discharged by reason of disability from wounds.

MOORE, THOMAS J., Private

Resided in Pitt County where he enlisted at age 21, August 31, 1861. Mustered in as Corporal. Promoted to Sergeant on an unspecified date. Reduced to ranks on an unspecified date. Present or accounted for until wounded in the arm at Gaines' Mill, Virginia, June 27, 1862. Furloughed from hospital at Danville, Virginia, July 18, 1862. No further records.

MORGAN, JAMES B., Private

Resided in Edgecombe County where he enlisted at age 22, August 31, 1861. Present or accounted for until wounded in the shoulder at Malvern Hill, Virginia, July 1, 1862. Returned to duty prior to January 1, 1863. Present or accounted for until captured at Kelly's Ford, Virginia, November 7, 1863. Confined at Point Lookout, Maryland, November 11, 1863. Paroled at Point Lookout on or about February 24, 1865, and transferred to Aiken's Landing, James River, Virginia, where he was received February 25-March 3, 1865, for exchange.

MORGAN, THOMAS, Private

Resided in Edgecombe County and enlisted at Orange Court House, Virginia, at age 17, February 10, 1864, for the war. Present or accounted for until wounded in the right leg at Snicker's Gap, Virginia, July 18, 1864. Reported absent wounded until December 29, 1864, when he was furloughed for sixty days.

MORGAN, WILLIAM GRAY, Private

Resided in Edgecombe County and was by occupation a farmer prior to enlisting in Edgecombe County at age 20, August 31, 1861. Present or accounted for until wounded at South Mountain, Maryland, in September, 1862. Returned to duty prior to January 1, 1863. Present or accounted for until he surrendered at Appomattox Court House, Virginia, April 9, 1865.

MORTON, ISAAC, Private

Resided in Onslow County where he enlisted at age 18, May 9, 1862. Present or accounted for until captured at South Mountain, Maryland, September 15, 1862. Confined at Fort Delaware, Delaware. Paroled and transferred to Aiken's Landing, James River, Virginia, October 2, 1862, for exchange. Declared exchanged at Aiken's Landing on November 10, 1862. Died at Richmond, Virginia, December 30, 1862. Cause of death not reported.

MOSELEY, ALLEN, Private

Born in Pitt County where he resided prior to enlisting at age 18, January 20, 186[3], for the war. Killed at Chancellorsville, Virginia, May 3, 1863. [May have served previously in Company E, 43rd Regiment N.C. Troops.]

MOSELEY, ELISHA, Private

Resided in Pitt County and enlisted in Edgecombe County at age 18, August 31, 1861. Present or accounted for until he died in hospital at Wilmington on June 1-7, 1862, of "typhoid fever."

NORVILLE, JAMES, Private

Resided in Edgecombe County where he enlisted at age 27, May 1, 1862, for the war. Present or accounted for until he surrendered at Appomattox Court House, Virginia, April 9, 1865.

O'NEAL, JOHN, Private

Resided in Edgecombe County where he enlisted at age 23, August 31, 1861. Present or accounted for until killed at Malvern Hill, Virginia, July 1, 1862.

OWENS, JAMES, Private

Resided in Edgecombe County and enlisted at Camp Holmes at age 27, July 11, 1863, for the war. Detailed for hospital duty at Richmond, Virginia, August 11, 1863. Reported absent on detail through August, 1864.

OWENS, ROBERT, Private

Place and date of enlistment not reported. Discharged on or about September 23, 1861, after he "failed to pass the inspection of the mustering officer."

PHILLIPS, DAVID J., Private

Resided in Edgecombe County and enlisted in Wake County at age 21, August 31, 1861. Present or accounted for until killed at Malvern Hill, Virginia, July 1, 1862.

PHILLIPS, JAMES, Private
Enlisted in Edgecombe County at age 21, August 31, 1861. Present or accounted for through October, 1861.

PHILLIPS, RICHARD, Private
Resided in Edgecombe County where he enlisted at age 18, May 1, 1862, for the war. Present or accounted for until hospitalized at Charlottesville, Virginia, September 27, 1864, with a gunshot wound of the right knee. Place and date wounded not reported. Furloughed on October 9, 1864. Returned to duty on an unspecified date. Surrendered at Appomattox Court House, Virginia, April 9, 1865.

PITT, THEOPHILUS, Private
Resided in Edgecombe County where he enlisted at age 22, May 1, 1862, for the war. Present or accounted for until captured at Kelly's Ford, Virginia, November 7, 1863. Confined at Point Lookout, Maryland, November 11, 1863. Paroled at Point Lookout on or about February 24, 1865, and transferred to the James River, Virginia, where he was received February 25-March 3, 1865, for exchange.

PITTMAN, GEORGE W., Private
Resided in Greene County and enlisted in Edgecombe or Wake County at age 30, August 31, 1861. Present or accounted for until wounded in the right thigh at Sharpsburg, Maryland, September 17, 1862. Returned to duty prior to July 3-5, 1863, when he was captured at or near Gettysburg, Pennsylvania. Confined at Fort Delaware, Delaware, on or about July 9, 1863. Transferred to Point Lookout, Maryland, October 15-18, 1863. Paroled at Point Lookout on February 18, 1865, and transferred to Boulware's Wharf, James River, Virginia, where he was received February 20-21, 1865, for exchange.

PITTMAN, REDDIN E., Corporal
Resided in Edgecombe County and enlisted in Edgecombe or Wake County at age 19, August 31, 1861. Mustered in as Private. Present or accounted for until wounded at Gaines' Mill, Virginia, June 27, 1862. Returned to duty prior to January 1, 1863. Promoted to Corporal on November 1, 1863. Present or accounted for until he surrendered at Appomattox Court House, Virginia, April 9, 1865.

POLLARD, JAMES, Private
Resided in Edgecombe County and enlisted in Edgecombe or Wake County at age 20, August 31, 1861. Present or accounted for until he died in hospital at Richmond, Virginia, September 13 or September 21, 1862, of "febris typhoides."

PRICE, THOMAS, Private
Resided in Edgecombe County and enlisted in Edgecombe or Wake County at age 20, August 31, 1861. Present or accounted for until killed at or near Spotsylvania Court House, Virginia, May 12, 1864.

REDICK, EPINETUS, Private
Resided in Edgecombe County and enlisted in Edgecombe or Wake County at age 17, August 31, 1861. Present or accounted for until wounded at Kelly's Ford, Virginia, November 7, 1863. Returned to duty prior to January 1, 1864. Present or accounted for until wounded in the ear and left eye and captured at Silver Spring, Maryland, July 12, 1864. Hospitalized at Washington, D.C. Transferred to Old Capitol Prison,

Washington, on an unspecified date. Transferred to Elmira, New York, where he arrived on August 29, 1864. Died at Elmira on February 7, 1865, of "pneumonia."

ROBERSON, JAMES, Private
Resided in Edgecombe County and enlisted in Edgecombe or Wake County at age 18, August 31, 1861. Present or accounted for until wounded at Chancellorsville, Virginia, May 1-4, 1863. Returned to duty prior to July 1, 1863. Present or accounted for until captured at Kelly's Ford, Virginia, November 7, 1863. Confined at Point Lookout, Maryland, November 11, 1863. Paroled at Point Lookout on or about February 24, 1865, and transferred to Aiken's Landing, James River, Virginia, where he was received February 25-March 3, 1865, for exchange.

ROBISON, WILLIAM, Private
Resided in Edgecombe County and enlisted in Edgecombe or Wake County at age 23, August 31, 1861. Present or accounted for until killed at Gaines' Mill, Virginia, June 27, 1862.

SMITH, LEMUEL H., Sergeant
Resided in Edgecombe County and enlisted in Edgecombe or Wake County at age 33, August 31, 1861. Mustered in as Sergeant. Present or accounted for until promoted to Commissary Sergeant on or about July 20, 1863, and transferred to the Field and Staff of this regiment.

STALLINGS, EDWIN, Private
Resided in Edgecombe County and enlisted in Edgecombe or Wake County at age 19, August 31, 1861. Present or accounted for until he surrendered at Appomattox Court House, Virginia, April 9, 1865.

STALLINGS, RUFUS, Private
Resided in Edgecombe County where he enlisted at age 24, May 13, 1862, for the war. Present or accounted for until he surrendered at Appomattox Court House, Virginia, April 9, 1865.

STEELE, H. A., Private
Place and date of enlistment not reported. Paroled at Burkeville Junction, Virginia, April 14-17, 1865.

SUMMERLIN, GEORGE, Private
Resided in Edgecombe County and enlisted in Edgecombe or Wake County at age 30, August 31, 1861. Present or accounted for until wounded near Spotsylvania Court House, Virginia, May 19, 1864. Reported absent wounded through August, 1864. Paroled at Goldsboro in 1865.

TILMAN, A. B., Private
Place and date of enlistment not reported. Paroled at Farmville, Virginia, April 11-21, 1865.

VICK, LORENZO, Private
Resided in Edgecombe County and enlisted in Edgecombe or Wake County at age 21, August 31, 1861. Present or accounted for until killed at Sharpsburg, Maryland, September 17, 1862.

VICK, WILLIAM, Private
Resided in Edgecombe County and enlisted in Edgecombe or Wake County at age 19, August 31,

1861. Present or accounted for until wounded at Malvern Hill, Virginia, July 1, 1862. Returned to duty prior to January 1, 1863. Present or accounted for through August, 1864.

WALSTON, FRANKLIN, Corporal
Resided in Edgecombe County and enlisted in Edgecombe or Wake County at age 19, August 31, 1861. Mustered in as Private. Promoted to Corporal on March 10, 1862. Present or accounted for until wounded at Sharpsburg, Maryland, September 17, 1862. Returned to duty prior to January 1, 1863. Present or accounted for until captured at Kelly's Ford, Virginia, November 7, 1863. Confined at Point Lookout, Maryland, November 11, 1863. Paroled at Point Lookout on or about February 24, 1865, and transferred to Aiken's Landing, James River, Virginia, where he was received February 25-March 3, 1865, for exchange.

WALSTON, JAMES, Private
Resided in Edgecombe County and enlisted in Edgecombe or Wake County at age 21, August 31, 1861. Present or accounted for until killed at Malvern Hill, Virginia, July 1, 1862.

WALSTON, JOHN, 1st Sergeant
Resided in Edgecombe County where he enlisted at age 21, May 1, 1862, for the war. Mustered in as Private. Promoted to Sergeant in January, 1863. Promoted to 1st Sergeant subsequent to August 31, 1864. Present or accounted for until he surrendered at Appomattox Court House, Virginia, April 9, 1865.

WALSTON, KINCHEN, Private
Resided in Edgecombe County and enlisted in Edgecombe or Wake County at age 21, August 31, 1861. Roll of Honor indicates he was discharged on September 26, 1861; however, company muster rolls dated September, 1861-February, 1862, indicate he was present and company muster rolls dated March-April, 1862, indicate he was absent sick at Camp Holmes. No further records.

WALSTON, LEVI, Private
Resided in Edgecombe County where he enlisted at age 23, May 1, 1862, for the war. Present or accounted for until captured at High Bridge, Virginia, April 6, 1865. Confined at Point Lookout, Maryland, until released on June 21, 1865, after taking the Oath of Allegiance. [North Carolina pension records indicate he was wounded in the collarbone in Virginia in 1863.]

WALSTON, RAIFORD, ——
North Carolina pension records indicate that he served in this company.

WALSTON, RALPH, Private
Enlisted at Orange Court House, Virginia, April 24, 1864, for the war. Present or accounted for until he surrendered at Appomattox Court House, Virginia. April 9, 1865.

WALSTON, RUFUS, Private
Resided in Edgecombe County where he enlisted at age 18, May 1, 1862, for the war. Present or accounted for until captured at Kelly's Ford, Virginia, November 7, 1863. Confined at Point Lookout, Maryland, November 11, 1863. Paroled at Point Lookout on or about

February 13, 1865, and transferred to Cox's Wharf, James River, Virginia, where he was received February 14-15, 1865, for exchange.

WALSTON, WILLIAM FRANKLIN, Private
Resided in Edgecombe County and enlisted in Edgecombe or Wake County at age 24, August 31, 1861. Present or accounted for until captured at South Mountain, Maryland, September 14, 1862. Confined at Fort Delaware, Delaware. Paroled and transferred to Aiken's Landing, James River, Virginia, October 2, 1862, for exchange. Declared exchanged at Aiken's Landing on November 10, 1862. Returned to duty prior to January 1, 1863. Present or accounted for until wounded at or near Charles Town, West Virginia, August 21, 1864. [North Carolina pension records indicate he was wounded at Chancellorsville, Virginia, in May, 1863, and died at Staunton, Virginia, March 10, 1865. Cause of death not reported.]

WAMACK, WILLIAM D., Private
Resided in Edgecombe County and enlisted at Camp Holmes at age 30, July 11, 1863, for the war. Present or accounted for until wounded at or near Spotsylvania Court House, Virginia, May 12, 1864. Died on May 14, 1864, of wounds. Place of death not reported.

WARREN, LEMUEL, Private
Resided in Edgecombe County where he enlisted at age 20, May 1, 1862, for the war. Present or accounted for until wounded in the head and left side at Sharpsburg, Maryland, September 17, 1862. Returned to duty prior to July 1, 1863. Present or accounted for until wounded at or near Charles Town, West Virginia, August 21, 1864. Returned to duty on an unspecified date. Captured at High Bridge, Virginia, April 6, 1865. Confined at Point Lookout, Maryland, April 14, 1865. Released on June 22, 1865, after taking the Oath of Allegiance.

WATSON, K., Private
Resided in Wilson County. Place and date of enlistment not reported. Paroled at Goldsboro on May 9, 1865.

WEBB, BENNETT, Private
Resided in Wilson County and enlisted at Orange Court House, Virginia, at age 17, February 20, 1864, for the war. Present or accounted for until wounded in the right leg at Cold Harbor, Virginia, June 1, 186[4]. Hospitalized at Richmond, Virginia. Furloughed for sixty days on November 4, 1864.

WEBB, HARDY, Private
Resided in Edgecombe County and enlisted at age 36, May 12, 1862, for the war. Present or accounted for until killed at Malvern Hill, Virginia, July 1, 1862.

WEBB, JOHN N., Private
Resided in Wilson County and enlisted at Orange Court House, Virginia, at age 18, February 20, 1864, for the war. Present or accounted for until he surrendered at Appomattox Court House, Virginia, April 9, 1865.

WEBB, MORRISON, Private
Resided in Edgecombe County and enlisted in Edgecombe or Wake County at age 25, August 31, 1861. Present or accounted for until wounded at Warrenton, Virginia, October 11, 1863. Died on November 2, 1863, of wounds. Place of death not

reported.

WEBB, NEWETT, Musician
Resided in Edgecombe County and enlisted in Wake County at age 22, August 31, 1861. Mustered in as Private. Present or accounted for until wounded at Sharpsburg, Maryland, September 17, 1862. Returned to duty and was promoted to Musician (Drummer) in January-June, 1863. Present or accounted for until he surrendered at Appomattox Court House, Virginia, April 9, 1865.

WELLS, LOUIS REDMON, Private
Resided in Edgecombe County and enlisted in Edgecombe or Wake County at age 38, August 31, 1861. Mustered in as Corporal. Promoted to Sergeant on March 10, 1862. Reduced to ranks in January-June, 1863. Present or accounted for until wounded in the breast at Snicker's Gap, Virginia, July 18, 1864. Hospitalized at Winchester, Virginia, where he died on July 20-21, 1864, of wounds.

WETHERSBEE, JOSEPH, Private
Resided in Halifax County where he enlisted at age 36, June 24, 1863, for the war. Present or accounted for through August, 1864.

WHITEHURST, W. THOMAS, 1st Sergeant
Resided in Edgecombe County and enlisted in Edgecombe or Wake County at age 29, August 31, 1861. Mustered in as Private. Promoted to Sergeant on March 10, 1862. Promoted to 1st Sergeant in January-June, 1863. Present or accounted for until killed at or near Spotsylvania Court House, Virginia, May 8, 1864.

WIGGINS, MARTIN W., Sergeant
Born in Edgecombe County where he resided as a farmer prior to enlisting in Edgecombe or Wake County at age 19, August 31, 1861. Mustered in as Private. Present or accounted for until wounded in the thigh at Gaines' Mill, Virginia, June 27, 1862. Returned to duty prior to January 1, 1863. Promoted to Sergeant on January 1, 1863. Present or accounted for until wounded in the right arm at Chancellorsville, Virginia, May 1-4, 1863. Right arm amputated. Died in hospital at Petersburg, Virginia, June 1 or June 8, 1863, of wounds.

WILLIFORD, S. T., Sergeant
Resided in Edgecombe County and enlisted in Edgecombe or Wake County at age 22, August 31, 1861. Mustered in as Private. Promoted to Sergeant on March 10, 1862. Present or accounted for until killed at Malvern Hill, Virginia, July 1, 1862.

WOOTEN, JOHN S., Private
Resided in Pitt County and enlisted in Edgecombe or Wake County at age 24, August 31, 1861. Present or accounted for until he died "at home" on July 28, 1862. Cause of death not reported.

COMPANY G

This company, known as the "Granville Rangers," was raised in Granville County and enlisted at Oxford on September 7, 1861. It was then assigned to the 30th Regiment N.C. Troops and designated Company G. After joining the regiment the company functioned as a part of the regiment, and its history for the war period is reported as a part of the regimental history.

The information contained in the following roster of the company was compiled principally from a company muster-in and descriptive roll dated October 8, 1861, and from company muster rolls for September 7, 1861-April, 1862; August 31-December 31, 1862; May-August, 1863; and November, 1863-August, 1864. No company muster rolls were found for May-August 30, 1862; January-April, 1863; September-October, 1863; and for the period after August, 1864. Valuable information was obtained from primary records such as the Roll of Honor, discharge certificates, medical records, prisoner of war records, and pension applications. Secondary sources such as postwar rosters and histories, cemetery records, and records of the United Daughters of the Confederacy also provided useful information.

OFFICERS

CAPTAINS

TAYLOR, RICHARD P.
Resided in Granville County where he enlisted at age 49. Elected Captain on September 7, 1861. Present or accounted for until he was defeated for reelection when the regiment was reorganized on May 1, 1862.

BARNETT, JAMES A.
Resided in Granville County where he enlisted at age 20. Elected 2nd Lieutenant on September 7, 1861. Elected Captain on May 1, 1862. Present or accounted for until wounded in the left thigh at Sharpsburg, Maryland, September 17, 1862. Reported absent wounded through December, 1862. Assigned to duty as an enrolling officer in January-June, 1863, and was reported absent on detail as an enrolling officer through August, 1864. Retired from service on March 21, 1865, by reason of disability from wounds. Took the Oath of Allegiance at Raleigh on May 24, 1865.

BADGETT, JAMES W.
Resided in Granville County where he enlisted at age 19, September 7, 1861. Mustered in as Sergeant. Elected 1st Lieutenant on May 1, 1862. Hospitalized at Williamsburg, Virginia, May 15, 1863, with a gunshot wound. Place and date wounded not reported. Returned to duty prior to July 1, 1863. Present or accounted for until wounded at or near Spotsylvania Court House, Virginia, May 19, 1864. Reported absent wounded through August, 1864. Returned to duty on an unspecified date. Promoted to Captain on September 20, 1864. Surrendered at Appomattox Court House, Virginia, April 9, 1865.

LIEUTENANTS

BROOKS, WILLIAM A., 3rd Lieutenant
Resided in Granville County where he enlisted at age 20. Elected 3rd Lieutenant on September 7, 1861. Present or accounted for until he was defeated for reelection when the regiment was reorganized on May 1, 1862.

CLIBORNE, ROBERT F., 2nd Lieutenant
Resided in Granville County where he enlisted at age 22, September 7, 1861. Mustered in as Private. Appointed 2nd Lieutenant on May 1, 1862. Present or accounted for until wounded at Malvern Hill, Virginia, July 1, 1862. Company records do not indicate whether he returned to duty. Resigned on May 11, 1863, by reason of "rheumatism with cardiac disease." Resignation accepted May 26, 1863.

CONNELL, IRA T., 3rd Lieutenant

Resided in Granville County where he enlisted at age 17, September 7, 1861. Mustered in as Private. Promoted to Sergeant on May 1, 1862. Promoted to 1st Sergeant in May-June, 1863, and was elected 3rd Lieutenant on or about June 26, 1863. Present or accounted for until killed at Gettysburg, Pennsylvania, on or about July 3, 1863.

CREWS, ALEXANDER, 2nd Lieutenant

Resided in Granville County where he enlisted at age 20, September 7, 1861. Mustered in as Sergeant. Elected 3rd Lieutenant on May 1, 1862. Present or accounted for until wounded in the chest at Sharpsburg, Maryland, September 17, 1862. Captured at or near Shepherdstown, Virginia, on or about September 30, 1862. Paroled the same date. Promoted to 2nd Lieutenant on May 26, 1863. Appointed Assistant Enrolling Officer of the 5th Congressional District of North Carolina in July-August, 1863. Rejoined the company in September-December, 1863. Reported on duty at Gordonsville, Virginia, during January-August, 1864. Retired to the Invalid Corps on November 15, 1864. Surrendered at Appomattox Court House, Virginia, April 9, 1865.

FULFORD, JOHN T., 3rd Lieutenant

Resided in Granville County where he enlisted at age 19, September 7, 1861. Mustered in as Private. Promoted to Corporal in May, 1862. Promoted to Sergeant on February 23, 1863, and was elected 3rd Lieutenant on August 3, 1863. Present or accounted for until he surrendered at Appomattox Court House, Virginia, April 9, 1865.

MITCHELL, RUSH J., 1st Lieutenant

Resided in Granville County where he enlisted at age 41. Elected 1st Lieutenant on September 7, 1861. Present or accounted for until he was defeated for reelection when the regiment was reorganized on May 1, 1862. Later served as Major of the 46th Regiment N.C. Troops.

NONCOMMISSIONED OFFICERS AND PRIVATES

ABSHER, EDMOND, Private

Enlisted in Wake County on September 21, 1862, for the war. Present or accounted for until he died in hospital at Mount Jackson, Virginia, November 28, 1862, of "diarrhoea chronica."

ADAMS, H. M., ———

Place and date of enlistment not reported. Died on August 31, 1862. Place and cause of death not reported.

ADAMS, JOHN P., Private

Enlisted in Wake County on September 21, 1862, for the war. Present or accounted for until he was "sent to hospital" on June 7, 1863. Reported absent without leave in January-February, 1864.

BADGETT, JOHN D., Private

Resided in Granville County where he enlisted at age 16, March 4, 1862. Present or accounted for until wounded at Gaines' Mill, Virginia, June 27, 1862. Returned to duty prior to January 1, 1863. Present or accounted for until he surrendered at Appomattox Court House, Virginia, April 9, 1865.

BADGETT, SANDY H., Sergeant

Resided in Granville County where he enlisted at age 21, September 7, 1861. Mustered in as Private. Promoted to Sergeant on May 1, 1862. Present or accounted for until he surrendered at Appomattox Court House, Virginia, April 9, 1865.

BADGETT, WILLIAM J., Sergeant

Resided in Granville County where he enlisted at age 19, September 7, 1861. Mustered in as Private. Promoted to Sergeant on May 1, 1862. Present or accounted for until wounded at Chancellorsville, Virginia, May 3, 1863. Returned to duty in September-December, 1863. Present or accounted for until wounded at or near Spotsylvania Court House, Virginia, May 19, 1864. Reported absent wounded through August, 1864. Returned to duty on an unspecified date. Surrendered at Appomattox Court House, Virginia, April 9, 1865.

BARKER, AMBROSE, Private

Enlisted in Granville County on September 7, 1861. Discharged prior to November 1, 1861, "without entering the service."

BARNES, HILLMOND, Private

Resided in Granville County and enlisted at Camp Holmes on or about October 14, 1863, for the war. Present or accounted for until captured at Burkeville, Virginia, April 6, 1865. Confined at Newport News, Virginia, April 14, 1865. Released on June 15, 1865, after taking the Oath of Allegiance.

BARNETT, GEORGE P., Private

Resided in Granville County where he enlisted at age 17, March 4, 1862. Present or accounted for until wounded at Malvern Hill, Virginia, July 1, 1862. Returned to duty in July-August, 1863. Present or accounted for until he surrendered at Appomattox Court House, Virginia, April 9, 1865.

BARNETT, JAMES P., 1st Sergeant

Resided in Granville County where he enlisted at age 30, September 7, 1861. Mustered in as 1st Sergeant. Present or accounted for until he was promoted to Sutler on May 1, 1862, and transferred.

BARNETT, WILLIAM S., Private

Born in Granville County and was by occupation a farmer prior to enlisting in Granville County at age 19, September 7, 1861. Present or accounted for until discharged on December 28, 1861, by reason of "diseased lungs."

BLACKNALL, THOMAS B., Private

Resided in Granville County where he enlisted at age 21, September 7, 1861. Mustered in as Sergeant. Reduced to ranks in May-December, 1862. Present or accounted for until he died in hospital at Richmond, Virginia, August 10-11, 1864, of "hernia right side."

BLACKWELL, JOHN, Private

Resided in Person County and enlisted at age 20, May 1, 1862, for the war. Present or accounted for until wounded at Malvern Hill, Virginia, July 1, 1862. Hospitalized at Richmond, Virginia, where he died on July 10 or July 30, 1862, of wounds.

BLEVINS, ANDREW, Private

Born in Smyth County, Virginia, and resided in Wilkes County prior to enlisting in Wake County at age 21, September 21, 1862, for the war. Present or accounted for until wounded in the right lung at Chancellorsville,

Virginia, May 1-4, 1863. Hospitalized at Richmond, Virginia, where he died on June 18-19, 1863, of wounds.

BLEVINS, HARVEY, Private
Resided in Wilkes County or in Smyth County, Virginia, and enlisted in Wake County at age 19, September 21, 1862, for the war. Present or accounted for until captured at Burkeville, Virginia, April 6, 1865. Confined at Newport News, Virginia, April 14, 1865. Released on June 27, 1865, after taking the Oath of Allegiance.

BLEVINS, JOHN, Private
Born in Wilkes County where he resided prior to enlisting in Wake County at age 24, September 21, 1862, for the war. Present or accounted for until killed at Chancellorsville, Virginia, May 3, 1863.

BLEVINS, SHADRACH, Private
Resided in Virginia and enlisted at Orange Court House, Virginia, at age 17, March 17, 1864, for the war. Present or accounted for until wounded in the left arm at Cold Harbor, Virginia, June 2-3, 1864. Reported absent wounded through August, 1864.

BLIZZARD, WILLIAM H., Private
Resided in Bladen County and enlisted in Granville County at age 28, March 24, 1862. Present or accounted for until he died on December 19, 1862. Place and cause of death not reported.

BOBBITT, ALEXANDER G., Corporal
Resided in Granville County where he enlisted at age 22, September 7, 1861. Mustered in as Private. Promoted to Corporal on an unspecified date. Present or accounted for until he died in Granville County on August 15, 1862. Cause of death not reported.

BOBBITT, ISHAM C., Private
Resided in Granville County where he enlisted at age 18, September 7, 1861. Present or accounted for until captured at or near Washington, D.C., July 12-13, 1864. Confined at Old Capitol Prison, Washington. Transferred to Elmira, New York, July 23, 1864. Paroled at Elmira on March 14, 1865, and transferred to Boulware's Wharf, James River, Virginia, where he was received March 18-21, 1865, for exchange.

BORROUGHS, EATON, Private
Enlisted in Granville County on September 7, 1861. Discharged prior to November 1, 1861, "without entering the service." Reason discharged not reported.

BOYD, JAMES A., Private
Resided in Granville County where he enlisted at age 23, March 3, 1862. Deserted on June 22, 1862. Returned to duty on April 4, 1864. Discharged on April 16, 1864. Reason discharged not reported.

BRADFORD, WILLIAM H., Private
Born in Granville County where he resided prior to enlisting in Granville County at age 31, September 7, 1861. Died at Raleigh on October 18, 1861, of "typhoid fever."

BREEDLOVE, JOHN H., Private
Enlisted in Granville County on September 7, 1861. Discharged on September 14, 1861, "in consequence [of] broken collar bone."

BROOKS, HENRY R., Private
Resided in Person County and enlisted in Granville County at age 33, March 4, 1862. Present or accounted

for until captured at or near Sharpsburg, Maryland, on or about September 17, 1862. Paroled on September 21, 1862. Returned to duty prior to May 3, 1863, when he was wounded at Chancellorsville, Virginia. Reported absent without leave in July-August and November-December, 1863. Reported absent in hospital in January-August, 1864. Hospitalized at Danville, Virginia, on or about June 16, 1864, with a gunshot wound of the leg. Place and date wounded not reported. Company records do not indicate whether he returned to duty. Paroled at Lynchburg, Virginia, on or about April 15, 1865.

BROOKS, JAMES L., 1st Sergeant
Enlisted in Granville County on March 3, 1862. Mustered in as Private. Promoted to 1st Sergeant in May-September, 1862. Present or accounted for until captured at Sharpsburg, Maryland, September 17, 1862. Paroled on or about September 21, 1862. Hospitalized at Richmond, Virginia, October 19, 1862, with rheumatism. No further records.

BROOKS, RICHARD D., Corporal
Resided in Person County and enlisted in Granville County at age 20, March 4, 1862. Mustered in as Private. Present or accounted for until wounded at Chancellorsville, Virginia, May 1-4, 1863. Returned to duty prior to July 1, 1863. Promoted to Corporal subsequent to August 31, 1864. Present or accounted for until he surrendered at Appomattox Court House, Virginia, April 9, 1865.

BROWN, ALFRED, Private
Resided in Wilkes County and enlisted in Wake County at age 25, September 27, 1862, for the war. Present or accounted for until he died in hospital at Mount Jackson, Virginia, on or about January 11, 1863, of "abs[cess] lung."

BROWN, WESLEY, Private
Resided in Wilkes County and enlisted in Wake County at age 30, September 27, 1862, for the war. Present or accounted for until he died in hospital at Mount Jackson, Virginia, December 24, 1862, of "rubeola."

BROWN, WILLIAM, Private
Resided in Wilkes County and enlisted in Wake County at age 28, September 27, 1862, for the war. Present or accounted for through September 17, 1863; however, he was reported absent sick during most of that period. Company muster roll dated January 1-August 31, 1864, states that he was "supposed to be dead." No further records.

BRUCE, G. C., ———
Place and date of enlistment not reported. Died at Richmond, Virginia, on or about July 8, 1864. Cause of death not reported.

BURROUGHS, WILLIAM A., Corporal
Resided in Granville County where he enlisted at age 17, September 7, 1861. Mustered in as Private. Promoted to Corporal on May 20, 1863. Present or accounted for until wounded in the hip at or near Bethesda Church, Virginia, on or about May 30, 1864. Hospitalized at Richmond, Virginia, where he died on June 8, 1864, of wounds.

BURTON, ROBERT W., Private
Resided in Granville County where he enlisted at age 35, September 7, 1861. Present or accounted for until transferred to Company K, 54th Regiment N.C. Troops, January 16, 1863, in exchange for Private William D. King.

CAWTHORN, JOHN W., Corporal
Resided in Granville or Wake County and enlisted in Granville County at age 17, September 7, 1861. Mustered in as Private. Present or accounted for until he was "sent to hospital" on January 28, 1863. Reported absent without leave from May-June, 1863, through December, 1863. Returned to duty in January-August, 1864. Promoted to Corporal subsequent to August 31, 1864. Captured at Fisher's Hill, Virginia, September 22, 1864. Confined at Harpers Ferry, West Virginia. Transferred to Point Lookout, Maryland, where he arrived January 3, 1865. Released on June 24, 1865, after taking the Oath of Allegiance.

CHALKLEY, BENJAMIN T., Private
Resided in Granville County where he enlisted at age 23, September 7, 1861. Present or accounted for until killed at Malvern Hill, Virginia, July 1, 1862.

CHALKLEY, EDWARD E., Private
Born in Granville County where he resided as a cooper prior to enlisting in Granville County at age 20, September 7, 1861. Present or accounted for until discharged on March 5, 1862, by reason of "scroffulous affection of the throat."

CHEATHAM, DAVID T., Corporal
Resided in Granville County where he enlisted at age 22, September 7, 1861. Mustered in as Corporal. Present or accounted for through April, 1862. Discharged on an unspecified date after providing a substitute. [Confederate medical records indicate he was wounded in the thigh at Gettysburg, Pennsylvania, July 2-3, 1863.]

CHEATHAM, JAMES T., Private
Resided in Granville County where he enlisted at age 17, July 25, 1862, for the war as a substitute. Present or accounted for until wounded and captured at Gettysburg, Pennsylvania, July 1-4, 1863. Hospitalized at Davids Island, New York Harbor, on or about July 17, 1863. Paroled at Davids Island and transferred to City Point, Virginia, where he was received on September 8, 1863, for exchange. Returned to duty subsequent to December 31, 1863. Captured near Washington, D.C., July 12-13, 1864. Confined at Old Capitol Prison, Washington, July 13, 1864. Transferred to Elmira, New York, July 23, 1864. Released at Elmira on June 12, 1865, after taking the Oath of Allegiance.

CHEATHAM, WILLIAM A., Private
Resided in Granville County where he enlisted at age 25, September 7, 1861. Present or accounted for until wounded at Malvern Hill, Virginia, July 1, 1862. Returned to duty prior to August 18, 1862. Present or accounted for until captured at Fisher's Hill, Virginia, September 22, 1864. Confined at Point Lookout, Maryland, October 3, 1864. Paroled at Point Lookout on or about February 13, 1865, and transferred to Cox's Wharf, James River, Virginia, where he was received February 14-15, 1865, for exchange.

CHURCH, CALTON, Private
Resided in Wilkes County and enlisted in Wake County at age 18, September 21, 1862, for the war. Present or accounted for until wounded at Chancellorsville, Virginia, May 1-4, 1863. Returned to duty prior to July 1, 1863. Present or accounted for until captured at

Spotsylvania Court House, Virginia, May 12, 1864. Confined at Point Lookout, Maryland, May 18, 1864. Transferred to Elmira, New York, August 10, 1864. Died at Elmira on December 9, 1864, of "pneumonia."

CHURCH, JOHN, Private
Resided in Wilkes County and enlisted in Wake County at age 20, September 21, 1862, for the war. Present or accounted for until he deserted to the enemy in September-December, 1864. Took the Oath of Allegiance on December 27, 1864. [North Carolina pension records indicate he was wounded in 1863.]

CLIBORN, JOHN W., Private
Enlisted in Granville County on July 26, 1863, for the war. Present or accounted for through August, 1863. Dropped from the rolls of the company in November-December, 1863. Reason he was dropped not reported.

CLOPTON, GEORGE, Private
Enlisted at Orange Court House, Virginia, January 15, 1864, for the war. Died in hospital at Richmond, Virginia, February 17, 1864, of "typhoid fever" and/or "variola conf[luen]t."

COLLINS, SAMUEL A., Private
Resided in Halifax County and enlisted in Granville County at age 29, September 7, 1861. Present or accounted for until wounded at or near Spotsylvania Court House, Virginia, May 12, 1864. Reported absent wounded through August, 1864. Returned to duty on an unspecified date. Surrendered at Appomattox Court House, Virginia, April 9, 1865.

CONNELL, WYATT G., Private
Resided in Granville County where he enlisted at age 26, September 7, 1861. Present or accounted for until wounded in the right elbow and captured at Spotsylvania Court House, Virginia, May 12, 1864. Confined at various Federal hospitals until confined at Old Capitol Prison, Washington, D.C., November 1, 1864. Transferred to Elmira, New York, December 16, 1864. Paroled at Elmira on February 9, 1865, and transferred to Boulware's Wharf, James River, Virginia, where he was received February 20-21, 1865, for exchange.

COTTRELL, SOLOMON, Private
Enlisted in Granville County on September 7, 1861. Discharged on September 14, 1861, by reason of "rheumatism."

CRAWFORD, JAMES S., Private
Resided in Gaston County where he enlisted at age 38, September 4, 1863, for the war. Present or accounted for until killed at or near Spotsylvania Court House, Virginia, May 12, 1864.

CREWS, EDWARD W., Private
Enlisted in Granville County on September 7, 1861. Discharged prior to November 1, 1861, "without entering service."

CREWS, THOMAS, Private
Enlisted in Granville County on September 7, 1861. Discharged prior to November 1, 1861, "without entering service."

CREWS, WILLIAM F., Private
Resided in Granville County where he enlisted at age

18, May 1, 1862, for the war. Present or accounted for until hospitalized at Danville, Virginia, on or about November 14, 1864, with a gunshot wound of the left leg. Place and date wounded not reported. Returned to duty on or about January 24, 1865. Surrendered at Appomattox Court House, Virginia, April 9, 1865. [North Carolina pension records indicate he was wounded at "South Mountain, Virginia, October 19, 1862."]

CRITCHER, WILLIAM H., Private
Resided in Granville County where he enlisted at age 36, June 26, 1863, for the war. Present or accounted for until captured at Winchester, Virginia, September 19, 1864. Confined at Point Lookout, Maryland, September 26, 1864. Paroled at Point Lookout on or about March 15, 1865, and transferred to Boulware's Wharf, James River, Virginia, where he was received on March 18, 1865, for exchange.

CURRAN, W. S., Private
Place and date of enlistment not reported. Paroled at Burkeville Junction, Virginia, April 14-17, 1865.

CURRIN, GEORGE W., Private
Enlisted in Granville County at age 29, September 7, 1861. Discharged on October 22, 1861, by reason of "hernia."

CURRIN, J. C., ——
North Carolina pension records indicate that he served in this company.

CURRIN, RALPH, Private
Resided in Granville County where he enlisted at age 18, May 1, 1862, for the war. Present or accounted for until he deserted on June 22, 1862. Was reportedly "lurking in the woods in Granville County" during September-December, 1862. Returned to duty on December 13, 1863. Furloughed for sixty days from hospital at Richmond, Virginia, February 11, 1864. Sent to hospital at Raleigh prior to September 1, 1864. No further records.

CURRIN, WILLIAM R., Private
Resided in Granville County where he enlisted at age 21, May 1, 1862, for the war. Deserted on June 22, 1862. Was reportedly "lurking in the woods in Granville County" during September-December, 1862. Returned to duty on December 13, 1863. Present or accounted for until paroled at Burkeville Junction, Virginia, April 14-17, 1865.

DANIEL, JAMES R., Private
Resided in Granville County where he enlisted at age 18, September 7, 1861. Present or accounted for until he died on July 22, 1862, of disease. Place of death not reported.

DANIEL, ROBERT M., Private
Resided in Granville County where he enlisted at age 24, March 3, 1862. Present or accounted for until captured at Kelly's Ford, Virginia, November 7, 1863. Confined at Point Lookout, Maryland, November 11, 1863. Paroled at Point Lookout on or about February 13, 1865, and transferred to Cox's Wharf, James River, Virginia, where he was received February 14-15, 1865, for exchange.

DANIEL, RUFUS, Private
Enlisted at Camp Holmes on October 14, 1863, for the war. "Assigned to this co[mpany]" on June 10, 1864. Present or accounted for through August, 1864. Paroled on May 15, 1865.

DANIEL, WESLEY, Private
Place and date of enlistment not reported. Transferred to this company in November-December, 1861, but failed to report for duty. No further records.

DANIEL, WILLIAM H., Private
Resided in Granville County where he enlisted at age 25, September 7, 1861. Present or accounted for until captured at or near Sharpsburg, Maryland, on or about September 17, 1862. Paroled on September 27, 1862. Returned to duty in January-June, 1863. Present or accounted for until wounded in the left thigh or left side and captured at Kelly's Ford, Virginia, November 7, 1863. Confined at various Federal hospitals until confined at Old Capitol Prison, Washington, D.C., on or about January 16, 1864. Transferred to Point Lookout, Maryland, February 3, 1864. Paroled at Point Lookout on February 24, 1865, and transferred to Aiken's Landing, James River, Virginia, where he was received February 25-March 3, 1865, for exchange.

DANIELL, JAMES W., Private
Previously served in an unspecified unit. Transferred to this company on January 10, 1862. Present or accounted for until he died at Grace Church, Virginia, February 22, 1863, of "fever."

DEAN, JESSE, Private
Resided in Granville County where he enlisted at age 22, March 4, 1862. Present or accounted for until October 22, 1863, when he was reported absent without leave. Returned to duty in January-May, 1864. Wounded in the head at or near Cold Harbor, Virginia, June 1, 1864. Reported absent wounded or absent sick through November 20, 1864.

DEAN, SIMPSON, Sergeant
Resided in [Granville County] where he enlisted at age 21, September 7, 1861. Mustered in as Private. Promoted to Corporal in May-December, 1862. Promoted to Sergeant on July 1, 1863. Present or accounted for until captured near Spotsylvania Court House, Virginia, May 12, 1864. Confined at Point Lookout, Maryland, May 18, 1864. Transferred to Elmira, New York, August 10, 1864. Released at Elmira on June 21, 1865, after taking the Oath of Allegiance.

DEMENT, HENRY F., Private
Resided in Granville County where he enlisted at age 21, September 7, 1861. Present or accounted for until wounded and captured at Shepherdstown, Virginia, September 30, 1862. Confined at Fort McHenry, Maryland. Paroled and transferred to Fort Monroe, Virginia, April 23, 1863, for exchange. Returned to duty prior to July 1, 1863. Present or accounted for until wounded at or near Silver Spring, Maryland, July 12, 1864, and "left in the enemies [sic] lines."

DICKERSON, MARTIN, Private
Resided in Granville County and enlisted at age 48, August 26, 1862, for the war. Present or accounted for until captured near Spotsylvania Court House, Virginia,

May 12, 1864. Confined at Point Lookout, Maryland, May 18, 1864. Transferred to Elmira, New York, August 10, 1864. Paroled at Elmira on March 14, 1865, and transferred to Boulware's Wharf, James River, Virginia, where he was received March 18-21, 1865, for exchange. [North Carolina pension records indicate he died at Elmira in 1865.]

DUKE, JOHN Y., Private
Resided in Granville County where he enlisted at age 50, March 6, 1862. Present or accounted for until he died in hospital at Richmond, Virginia, July 8-9, 1862, of "typh[oid] fever."

DUNCAN, JOHN B., Private
Resided in Granville County where he enlisted at age 28, March 4, 1862. Present or accounted for until hospitalized at Richmond, Virginia, August 18, 1862, with "typhoid fever." Died in hospital at Richmond on August 25 or August 30, 1862.

ELLIOTT, GREEN B., Private
Enlisted at Camp Holmes on August 18, 1863, for the war. Assigned to this company on June 9, 1864. Present or accounted for until killed at Cedar Creek, Virginia, October 19, 1864.

ELLIS, ANDREW J., Private
Enlisted in Granville County on September 7, 1861. Discharged prior to November 1, 1861, "without entering service."

FORREST, WILLIAM L., Private
Resided in Virginia and enlisted near Orange Court House, Virginia, at age 17, March 11, 1864, for the war. Present or accounted for through August, 1864. Deserted to the enemy on an unspecified date. Reported in confinement in a Federal prison at Richmond, Virginia, April 10, 1865.

FRANKLIN, THOMAS F., Private
Resided in Granville County where he enlisted at age 28, September 7, 1861. Present or accounted for until captured near Spotsylvania Court House, Virginia, May 12, 1864. Confined at Point Lookout, Maryland, May 18, 1864. Paroled at Point Lookout on or about September 18, 1864, and transferred to Varina, Virginia, where he was received September 22, 1864, for exchange. Returned to duty on or about December 4, 1864. Paroled at Burkeville Junction, Virginia, April 14-17, 1865.

FRAZIER, A. S., Private
Resided in Granville County where he enlisted at age 17, March 3, 1862. Present or accounted for until wounded in the knee at Malvern Hill, Virginia, July 1, 1862. Hospitalized at Richmond, Virginia, where he died on July 6, 1862, of wounds.

FRAZIER, ELISHA T., Private
Resided in Granville County where he enlisted at age 18, September 7, 1861. Present or accounted for until paroled at Burkeville Junction, Virginia, April 14-17, 1865.

FRAZIER, JAMES H., Private
Enlisted in Granville County on March 2, 1862. Present or accounted for until wounded at Sharpsburg, Maryland, September 17, 1862. Returned to duty in January-June, 1863. Present or accounted for until wounded at or near Charles Town, West Virginia, August 21, 1864. Returned to duty on an unspecified date. Surrendered at Appomattox Court House, Virginia, April 9, 1865.

FRAZIER, PUMFRED B., Private
Resided in Granville County where he enlisted at age 17, May 1, 1862, for the war. Present or accounted for until wounded in the foot at Gaines' Mill, Virginia, June 27, 1862. Furloughed on July 8, 1862. Company records do not indicate whether he rejoined the company. Died in hospital at Staunton, Virginia, November 14-18, 1862, of "smallpox" and/or "carditis."

FRAZIER, RANSOM P., Private
Resided in Granville County where he enlisted at age 20, September 7, 1861. Present or accounted for through August, 1864.

FULLER, JAMES N., Sergeant
Resided in Granville County where he enlisted at age 18, September 7, 1861. Mustered in as Private. Promoted to Corporal on September 22, 1862. Promoted to Sergeant on August 8, 1863. Present or accounted for until wounded in the right leg at or near Charles Town, West Virginia, August 21, 1864. Reported absent wounded until February 14, 1865, when he was retired to the Invalid Corps.

GORDON, JOHN W., Private
Resided in Granville County where he enlisted at age 20, September 7, 1861. Present or accounted for until discharged on July 22, 1862. Reason discharged not reported.

GREENWAY, SAMUEL, Private
Resided in Granville County where he enlisted at age 40, August 26, 1863, for the war. Present or accounted for until captured at Kelly's Ford, Virginia, on or about November 7, 1863. Confined at Old Capitol Prison, Washington, D.C., November 14, 1863. Died in hospital at Washington, December 28, 1863-January 1, 1864, of "variola confluent."

HALL, JAMES C., Private
Resided in Wilkes County and enlisted in Wake County at age 36, September 27, 1862, for the war. Present or accounted for until October 13, 1863, when he was reported absent without leave. [North Carolina pension records indicate he was wounded at Chancellorsville, Virginia, in May, 1863.]

HAMMIE, RICHARD F., Private
Resided in Granville County where he enlisted at age 16, September 7, 1861. Present or accounted for until wounded at Malvern Hill, Virginia, July 1, 1862. Returned to duty prior to January 1, 1863. Present or accounted for until captured at or near Gettysburg, Pennsylvania, July 4, 1863. Confined at Fort Delaware, Delaware, July 24, 1863. Transferred to Point Lookout, Maryland, October 15-18, 1863. Paroled at Point Lookout on December 24, 1863, and transferred to City Point, Virginia, where he was received on December 28, 1863, for exchange. Returned to duty subsequent to December 31, 1863. Captured at or near Spotsylvania Court House, Virginia, May 19, 1864. Confined at Elmira, New York. Released at Elmira on June 30, 1865, after taking the Oath of Allegiance.

HANCOCK, THOMAS C., Private
Enlisted in Granville County on September 7, 1861; however, having enlisted in 2nd Company D, 12th Regiment N.C. Troops (2nd Regiment N.C. Volunteers), on August 9, 1861, he elected to serve in

the latter unit.

HARRIS, RICHARD P., Private
Resided in Granville County where he enlisted at age 17, September 7, 1861. Present or accounted for until wounded in the left thigh at Warrenton Springs, Virginia, October 12, 1863. Returned to duty subsequent to December 31, 1863. Captured near Spotsylvania Court House, Virginia, May 12, 1864. Confined at Point Lookout, Maryland, May 18, 1864. Transferred to Elmira, New York, August 10, 1864. Released at Elmira on June 19, 1865, after taking the Oath of Allegiance.

HARRIS, WILLIAM H., Private
Resided in Granville County where he enlisted at age 22, September 7, 1861. Present or accounted for until wounded at Chancellorsville, Virginia, May 3, 1863. Returned to duty in July-August, 1863. Present or accounted for until killed at or near Spotsylvania Court House, Virginia, May 12, 1864.

HART, JAMES R., Sergeant
Resided in Granville County where he enlisted at age 24, September 7, 1861. Mustered in as Sergeant. Present or accounted for through April, 1862. Discharged on an unspecified date after providing a substitute.

HART, WILLIAM H., Private
Enlisted in Granville County on September 7, 1861. Discharged on September 26, 1861, by reason of "heart disease."

HARTWICK, CHRISTOPHER, Private
Resided in Cabarrus County and enlisted at Camp Holmes at age 39, September 30, 1863, for the war. Present or accounted for until he deserted to the enemy on or about February 25, 1864.

HARTWICK, JOHN, Private
Resided in Cabarrus County and enlisted at Camp Holmes at age 36, September 30, 1863, for the war. Present or accounted for until he deserted to the enemy on or about February 25, 1864.

HESTER, GEORGE W., Private
Resided in Granville County where he enlisted at age 19, March 17, 1862. Present or accounted for until captured at Kelly's Ford, Virginia, November 7, 1863. Confined at Point Lookout, Maryland, November 11, 1863. Paroled at Point Lookout on or about February 24, 1865, and transferred to Aiken's Landing, James River, Virginia, where he was received February 25-March 3, 1865, for exchange.

HIGHT, HARBIRD H., Private
Resided in Granville County where he enlisted at age 30, September 7, 1861. Present or accounted for through December, 1863; however, he was reported absent sick during much of that period. Dropped from the rolls of the company in January-August, 1864. Reason he was dropped not reported.

HOBGOOD, ISAAC N., Private
Resided in Granville County where he enlisted at age 17, May 1, 1862, for the war. Present or accounted for until discharged on March 8, 1864. Reason discharged not reported.

HOBGOOD, JAMES M., Private
Resided in Granville County and was by occupation a farmer prior to enlisting in Granville County at age 18, September 7, 1861. Present or accounted for until wounded at Malvern Hill, Virginia, July 1, 1862. Returned to duty prior to January 1, 1863. Wounded at Chancellorsville, Virginia, May 1-4, 1863. Returned to duty in September-December, 1863. Present or accounted for through April, 1864. Company records indicate he was captured at Spotsylvania Court House, Virginia, in May, 1864; however, records of the Federal Provost Marshal do not substantiate that report. Reported "at home" through August, 1864. No further records.

HOBGOOD, WILLIAM P., Corporal
Born in Granville County where he resided as a farmer prior to enlisting in Granville County at age 19, September 7, 1861. Mustered in as Private. Promoted to Corporal on September 22, 1862. Present or accounted for until wounded at Chancellorsville, Virginia, May 2-3, 1863. Died on May 14, 1863, of wounds. Place of death not reported.

HOLBROOK, PATERSON B., Private
Resided in Wilkes County and enlisted in Wake County at age 25, September 21, 1862, for the war. Present or accounted for until wounded at Fredericksburg, Virginia, December 13, 1862. Returned to duty prior to January 1, 1863. Present or accounted for until captured at Kelly's Ford, Virginia, November 7, 1863. Confined at Point Lookout, Maryland, November 11, 1863. Paroled at Point Lookout on or about February 24, 1865, and transferred to Aiken's Landing, James River, Virginia, where he was received February 25-March 3, 1865, for exchange.

HOLBROOKS, WILLIAM P., Private
Resided in Wilkes County and enlisted in Wake County at age 23, September 27, 1862, for the war. Present or accounted for through August, 1864.

HOWARD, JOSEPH M., Private
Resided in Granville County where he enlisted at age 18, September 7, 1861. Present or accounted for until captured at Kelly's Ford, Virginia, November 7, 1863. Confined at Point Lookout, Maryland, November 11, 1863. Transferred to Elmira, New York, July 27, 1864. Died at Elmira on February 18, 1865, of "chro[nic] diarrhoea."

HUNT, ALFRED H., Private
Born in Granville County where he resided as a farmer prior to enlisting in Granville County at age 18, September 7, 1861. Present or accounted for until he died on July 13-14, 1862, of "fever." Place of death not reported.

HUNT, DAVID Z., Private
Resided in Granville County where he enlisted at age 18, May 1, 1862, for the war. Present or accounted for until wounded at or near Charles Town, West Virginia, August 21, 1864. [North Carolina pension records indicate that he survived the war.]

HUNT, ISAAC B., Private
Resided in Granville County where he enlisted at age 20, September 7, 1861. Present or accounted for until wounded at Gaines' Mill, Virginia, June 27, 1862. Died

at Richmond, Virginia, of wounds. Date of death not reported.

HUNT, JAMES A., Corporal
Resided in Granville County where he enlisted at age 18, September 7, 1861. Mustered in as Corporal. Present or accounted for until wounded in the leg at or near Gaines' Mill, Virginia, on or about June 27, 1862. Leg amputated. Died in hospital at Richmond, Virginia, on or about July 2, 1862, of wounds.

HUNT, JOHN O., Private
Born in Granville County where he resided as a farmer prior to enlisting in Granville County at age 22, September 7, 1861. Present or accounted for until discharged on September 9, 1862, by reason of "phthisis pulmonalis." [North Carolina pension records indicate he was wounded at Malvern Hill, Virginia, July 2, 1862.]

INCORE, JAMES F., Private
Resided in Granville County where he enlisted at age 16, March 4, 1862. Present or accounted for until he died in hospital at Wilmington on May 29-30, 1862, of disease.

JENKINS, JOHN T., Private
Born in Granville County where he resided as a farmer prior to enlisting in Granville County at age 35, September 7, 1861. Present or accounted for until discharged on June 3, 1862, by reason of "typhoid fever."

JENKINS, W. H. P., ———
North Carolina pension records indicate that he served in this company.

JENKINS, WILLIAM T., Private
Born in Granville County where he resided as a farmer prior to enlisting in Granville County at age 19, September 7, 1861. Present or accounted for until discharged on March 27, 1862, by reason of "dislocation of the arm."

KING, JAMES D., Private
Resided in Granville County and was by occupation a farmer prior to enlisting in Granville County at age 18, March 4, 1862. Reported absent without leave during May-August, 1863. Returned to duty prior to November 7, 1863, when he was captured at Kelly's Ford, Virginia. Confined at Point Lookout, Maryland, November 11, 1863. Paroled at Point Lookout and transferred to City Point, Virginia, March 16-17, 1864, for exchange. Returned to duty prior to September 1, 1864. Captured in hospital at Richmond, Virginia, April 3, 1865. Transferred to Newport News, Virginia, April 23, 1865. Released on June 30, 1865, after taking the Oath of Allegiance. [North Carolina pension records indicate that he was wounded at Winchester, Virginia, in 1863.]

KING, WILLIAM D., Private
Previously served in Company K, 54th Regiment N.C. Troops. Transferred to this company on January 16, 1863, in exchange for Private Robert W. Burton. "Failed to appear" and was listed as a deserter in July-August, 1863.

KITTRELL, HARVEY W., Private
Previously served in an unspecified unit. Transferred to

this company on June 10, 1864. Present or accounted for through August, 1864.

KITTRELL, WILLIAM H., Private
Resided in Granville County where he enlisted at age 36, September 7, 1861. Mustered in as Corporal. Present or accounted for until wounded at Malvern Hill, Virginia, July 1, 1862. Reduced to ranks prior to January 1, 1863. Reported absent wounded through June, 1863. Dropped from the rolls of the company on an unspecified date.

KNOTT, JAMES W., Private
Resided in Granville County where he enlisted on September 7, 1861. Failed to report for duty. Enlisted in Company B, 12th Regiment N.C. Troops (2nd Regiment N.C. Volunteers), November 26, 1861.

KNOTT, LAWSON, Corporal
Resided in Granville County where he enlisted at age 20, September 7, 1861. Mustered in as Private. Promoted to Corporal in January-June, 1863. Present or accounted for until captured at Kelly's Ford, Virginia, November 7, 1863. Confined at Point Lookout, Maryland, November 11, 1863. Paroled on or about February 24, 1865, and transferred to Aiken's Landing, James River, Virginia, where he was received February 25-March 3, 1865, for exchange.

LOFTICE, WILLIAM A., Private
Resided in Virginia and enlisted in Granville County at age 32, March 8, 1862. Present or accounted for until wounded at Chancellorsville, Virginia, May 3, 1863. Reported absent wounded through August, 1864. Paroled on May 15, 1865.

LOVETT, AARON F., Private
Resided in Wilkes County and enlisted in Wake County at age 28, September 27, 1862, for the war. Died in hospital at Charlottesville, Virginia, March 4, 1864, of "phthisis" and/or "measles."

LUMPKINS, JAMES R. T., Private
Born in Granville County where he resided as a farmer prior to enlisting in Granville County at age 24, September 7, 1861. Present or accounted for until discharged on February 28, 1864, by reason of "general disability."

MERRITT, BENJAMIN H., Private
Resided in Granville County and enlisted at Camp Wyatt at age 20, February 4, 1862. Present or accounted for until captured at Spotsylvania Court House, Virginia, May 12-13, 1864. Confined at Point Lookout, Maryland, May 23, 1864. Transferred to Elmira, New York, July 3, 1864. Paroled at Elmira on October 11, 1864, and transferred to Venus Point, Savannah River, Georgia, where he was received on November 15, 1864, for exchange. Returned to duty on an unspecified date. Surrendered at Appomattox Court House, Virginia, April 9, 1865.

MORRIS, ALEXANDER H., Private
Previously served in Company E, 23rd Regiment N.C. Troops (13th Regiment N.C. Volunteers). Transferred to this company on June 1, 1862. Present or accounted for until he deserted on June 10, 1863. Took the Oath of Allegiance at Charleston, West Virginia, February 6, 1865.

MORRIS, JOHN W., Private

Resided in Granville County where he enlisted at age 17, September 7, 1861. Mustered in as Private. Promoted to Musician (Drummer) on May 1, 1863. Present or accounted for until captured at Kelly's Ford, Virginia, November 7, 1863. Confined at Point Lookout, Maryland, November 11, 1863. Reduced to ranks while a prisoner of war. Paroled at Point Lookout on February 18, 1865, and transferred to Boulware's Wharf, James River, Virginia, where he was received February 20-21, 1865, for exchange.

MOSS, THOMAS, Private

Born in Mecklenburg County, Virginia, and was by occupation a farmer prior to enlisting in Granville County at age 36, September 7, 1861. Present or accounted for until discharged on March 27, 1862, by reason of "scrotal hernia."

NORWOOD, DAVID, Private

Enlisted in Granville County on September 7, 1861. Reported absent without leave through December, 1861. Dropped from the rolls of the company on an unspecified date.

NORWOOD, FRANCIS M., Private

Enlisted in Granville County on September 7, 1861. "Rejected" on September 25, 1861. Reason he was rejected not reported.

OAKLEY, WILLIAM LEWIS, Private

Resided in Granville County and enlisted in Wake County at age 18, June 10, 1863, for the war. Present or accounted for until captured near Martinsburg, West Virginia, September 2, 1864. Confined at Fort Delaware, Delaware, September 6, 1864. Released at Fort Delaware on June 19, 1865, after taking the Oath of Allegiance.

O'BRIAN, ALEXANDER P., Corporal

Resided in Granville County where he enlisted at age 17, September 7, 1861. Mustered in as Musician (Drummer). Promoted to Corporal on July 1, 1863. Present or accounted for until captured at Kelly's Ford, Virginia, November 7, 1863. Confined at Point Lookout, Maryland, November 11, 1863. Paroled at Point Lookout on February 18, 1865, and transferred to Boulware's Wharf, James River, Virginia, where he was received February 20-21, 1865, for exchange.

O'BRIANT, WILLIAM G., Private

Born in Granville County where he resided prior to enlisting in Granville County at age 17, March 3, 1862. Present or accounted for until killed at Chancellorsville, Virginia, May 3, 1863.

O'BRIEN, ALFRED D., Sergeant

Resided in Granville County where he enlisted at age 19, September 7, 1861. Mustered in as Private. Promoted to Sergeant on May 1, 1862. Present or accounted for until captured at Kelly's Ford, Virginia, November 7, 1863. Confined at Point Lookout, Maryland, November 11, 1863. Paroled at Point Lookout on or about February 24, 1865, and transferred to Aiken's Landing, James River, Virginia, where he was received on February 25-March 3, 1865, for exchange.

OTTAWAY, JOHN, Private

Resided in Granville County and was by occupation a mechanic prior to enlisting in New Hanover County at age 37, August 22, 1863, for the war. Present or accounted for until captured at Kelly's Ford, Virginia, November 7, 1863. Confined at Point Lookout, Maryland, November 11, 1863. Released on May 14, 1865, after taking the Oath of Allegiance.

PARHAM, WILLIAM A., Private

Resided in Granville County where he enlisted at age 20, September 7, 1861. Mustered in as Corporal. Reduced to ranks in May-December, 1862. Present or accounted for until he surrendered at Appomattox Court House, Virginia, April 9, 1865.

PARKER, ARCHIBALD D., Private

Resided in Onslow County where he enlisted at age 38, June 3, 1863, for the war. Present or accounted for until captured at Kelly's Ford, Virginia, November 7, 1863. Confined at Point Lookout, Maryland, November 11, 1863. Paroled at Point Lookout on September 18, 1864, and transferred to Varina, Virginia, where he was received on September 22, 1864, for exchange.

PARRISH, MATHEW, Private

Resided in Granville County where he enlisted at age 17, September 7, 1861. Present or accounted for until killed at Gaines' Mill, Virginia, June 27, 1862.

PRUITT, HAMPTON, Private

Resided in Wilkes County and enlisted in Wake County at age 24, September 27, 1862, for the war. Present or accounted for until he died on December 15, 1863. Place of death not reported. [North Carolina pension records indicate he died of wounds and "fever."]

RAGLAND, WILLIAM GEORGE, Private

Resided in Granville County and enlisted at "Grace Church" at age 52, April 4, 1863, for the war as a substitute. Present or accounted for until he died in hospital near Orange Court House, Virginia, January 8-10, 1864, of disease.

READ, DAVID K., Private

Born in Caswell County and resided in Halifax County where he was by occupation a farmer prior to enlisting in Granville County at age 18, September 7, 1861. Present or accounted for until discharged on March 5, 1862, by reason of "epileptic fits." Reenlisted in the company on June 24, 1863. Discharged in September, 1863. Reason discharged not reported.

REAMES, GEORGE W., Private

Resided in Granville County where he enlisted at age 25, September 7, 1861. Present or accounted for until hospitalized at Richmond, Virginia, July 4, 1862, with a gunshot wound. Place and date wounded not reported. Discharged prior to January 1, 1863, after providing a substitute.

ROBERSON, CHARLES H., Private

Resided in Granville County where he enlisted at age 20, March 1, 1862. Present or accounted for through August, 1864.

ROBERSON, Z. R., Private

Enlisted at Camp Holmes on an unspecified date. Assigned to duty with this company on June 10, 1864.

Present or accounted for until captured at or near Harrisonburg, Virginia, on or about September 25, 1864. Hospitalized at Baltimore, Maryland, October 13, 1864. Died in hospital at Baltimore on December 15, 1864, of "chronic diarrhoea."

ROSS, JAMES P., Private
Resided in Granville County where he enlisted at age 28, March 4, 1862. Present or accounted for through December, 1862. Discharged prior to July 1, 1863. Reason discharged not reported.

SIZEMORE, WILLIAM P., Corporal
Resided in Granville County where he enlisted at age 24, September 7, 1861. Mustered in as Private. Present or accounted for until wounded at Gaines' Mill, Virginia, June 27, 1862. Returned to duty in January-June, 1863. Promoted to Corporal on August 8, 1863. Present or accounted for until killed at or near Wilderness, Virginia, May 6-7, 1864.

SLAUGHTER, JAMES H., Private
Resided in Granville County and enlisted at Camp Holmes at age 48, September 4, 1863, for the war. Discharged on October 21, 1863. Reason discharged not reported. Died in hospital at Richmond, Virginia, November 15, 1863, of "febris typhoid."

SLAUGHTER, THOMAS D., Private
Resided in Granville County where he enlisted at age 22, September 7, 1861. Present or accounted for until he surrendered at Appomattox Court House, Virginia, April 9, 1865.

SLAUGHTER, WILLIAM P., Private
Resided in Granville County and was by occupation a farmer prior to enlisting in Granville County at age 24, March 3, 1862. Present or accounted for until killed at or near Spotsylvania Court House, Virginia, May 12, 1864.

SOLLICE, D. VAUGHN, Private
Resided in Sampson County and enlisted at Camp Holmes at age 36, September 4, 1863, for the war. Present or accounted for until captured at Kelly's Ford, Virginia, November 7, 1863. Confined at Point Lookout, Maryland, November 11, 1863. Died at Point Lookout on January 23, 1864. Cause of death not reported.

STANTON, JAMES R., Private
Resided in Granville County where he enlisted at age 21, September 7, 1861. Present or accounted for through April, 1864. Company records indicate he was captured and paroled near Spotsylvania Court House, Virginia, in May, 1864; however, records of the Federal Provost Marshal do not substantiate that report. Returned to duty subsequent to August 31, 1864. Surrendered at Appomattox Court House, Virginia, April 9, 1865.

STONE, DANIEL B., Private
Resided in Granville County where he enlisted at age 20, September 7, 1861. Present or accounted for until transferred to Company E, 23rd Regiment N.C. Troops (13th Regiment N.C. Volunteers), June 18-20, 1862.

STRANGE, ALBERT, Private
Resided in Granville County where he enlisted at age 24, March 3, 1862. Present or accounted for until he

died on June 10, 1862, of disease. Place of death not reported.

TAYLOR, RICHARD D., Private
Resided in Granville County where he enlisted at age 17, March 2, 1862. Present or accounted for until discharged on or about July 17, 1862, by reason of being underage.

TRAYLOR, A. M., Private
Resided in Granville County and enlisted at age 18, May 1, 1862, for the war. Present or accounted for until wounded at Malvern Hill, Virginia, July 1, 1862. Died at Richmond, Virginia, prior to July 22, 1862, of wounds.

TRAYLOR, CHARLES L., Private
Born in Granville County and was by occupation a farmer prior to enlisting in Granville County at age 40, September 7, 1861. Present or accounted for until discharged on March 27, 1862, by reason of "pulmonary disease."

WAIN, THOMAS, Private
Resided in Virginia and enlisted at age 36, in July, 1862, for the war. "Died suddenly" at Richmond, Virginia, August 10, 1862. Cause of death not reported.

WAINWRIGHT, JOHN K., Private
Resided in Granville County where he enlisted at age 20, September 7, 1861. Present or accounted for until he died on August 25, 1862, of disease. Place of death not reported.

WALLS, WILLIAM B., Private
Resided in Wilkes County and enlisted in Wake County at age 36, September 21, 1862, for the war. Present or accounted for until he deserted on June 4, 1863. Returned to duty on November 10, 1863. Court-martialed on or about December 26, 1863, and was sentenced to "work [for three] years on division fortifications." Died in hospital at Richmond, Virginia, January 15, 1864, of "congestion of the lungs."

WATKINS, JOHN W., Private
Born in Halifax County, Virginia, and resided in Virginia prior to enlisting in Granville County at age 28, March 10, 1862. Present or accounted for until he deserted on June 4, 1863. Returned to duty on December 16, 1863. Transferred to 2nd Company G, 14th Regiment Virginia Infantry, April 26, 1864.

WERTMAN, DAVID D., Private
Resided in Cleveland County and enlisted in Wake County at age 28, September 21, 1862, for the war. Present or accounted for through November 9, 1864; however, he was reported absent sick or absent on duty as a nurse during much of that period. [North Carolina pension records indicate he was wounded in the right thigh at Moulton's Ford, Virginia, in November, 1863.]

WERTMAN, SIMEON, Private
Resided in Cleveland County and enlisted in Wake County at age 38, September 21, 1862, for the war. Died on November 18, 1862, of disease. Place of death not reported.

WILES, JAMES N., Private
Was by occupation a farmer prior to enlisting in Wake

County on September 21, 1862, for the war. Present or accounted for until he deserted on December 6, 1862.

WILKERSON, JAMES W., Private

Resided in Person County and enlisted in Granville County at age 21, March 5, 1862. Present or accounted for until captured at Kelly's Ford, Virginia, November 7, 1863. Confined at Point Lookout, Maryland, November 11, 1863. Paroled at Point Lookout on or about February 13, 1865, and transferred to Cox's Wharf, James River, Virginia, where he was received on February 14-15, 1865, for exchange.

WILSON, SAMUEL R., Private

Resided in Person County and enlisted at Hamilton's Crossing, Virginia, at age 54, February 23, 1863, for the war as a substitute. Present or accounted for until killed at or near Spotsylvania Court House, Virginia, May 12, 1864.

COMPANY H

This company was raised in Moore County (probably in that part of the county that was ceded in 1907 to Lee County) and enlisted at Jonesboro on August 15, 1861. It was then assigned to the 30th Regiment N.C. Troops and designated Company H. After joining the regiment the company functioned as a part of the regiment, and its history for the war period is reported as a part of the regimental history.

The information contained in the following roster of the company was compiled principally from a company muster-in and descriptive roll dated October 8, 1861, and from company muster rolls for August 15, 1861-April, 1862; November-December, 1862; May-August, 1863; and November, 1863-August, 1864. No company muster rolls were found for May-October, 1862; January-April, 1863; September-October, 1863; or for the period after August, 1864. Valuable information was obtained from primary records such as the Roll of Honor, discharge certificates, medical records, prisoner of war records, and pension applications. Secondary sources such as postwar rosters and histories, cemetery records, and records of the United Daughters of the Confederacy also provided useful information.

OFFICERS

CAPTAINS

SWANN, WILLIAM M.

Resided in Moore County where he enlisted at age 27. Elected Captain on August 15, 1861. Present or accounted for until he was defeated for reelection when the regiment was reorganized on May 1, 1862.

WICKER, JESSE JOHNSON

Resided in Moore County where he enlisted at age 22, August 15, 1861. Mustered in as Sergeant. Appointed 2nd Lieutenant in February, 1862. Elected Captain on May 1, 1862. Present or accounted for until wounded at or near Boonsboro, Maryland, September 14, 1862. Returned to duty prior to January 1, 1863. Present or accounted for until captured at or near Spotsylvania Court House, Virginia, on or about May 12, 1864. Confined at Fort Delaware, Delaware, May 17, 1864. Released on June 16, 1865, after taking the Oath of Allegiance.

LIEUTENANTS

BROWN, ALEXANDER H., 3rd Lieutenant

Resided in Moore or Chatham County and enlisted in Moore County at age 19, August 15, 1861. Mustered in as Private. Promoted to Sergeant in May, 1862. Elected 3rd Lieutenant on March 19, 1863. Present or accounted for until wounded in the left thigh at Gettysburg, Pennsylvania, July 1, 1863. Returned to duty subsequent to August 31, 1863. Captured at Kelly's Ford, Virginia, November 7, 1863. Confined at Old Capitol Prison, Washington, D.C., November 8, 1863. Transferred to Johnson's Island, Ohio, November 11, 1863. Transferred to Baltimore, Maryland, February 9, 1864. Confined at Point Lookout, Maryland, February 14, 1864. Transferred to Fort Delaware, Delaware, June 23, 1864. Transferred to Hilton Head, South Carolina, August 20, 1864. Confined at Fort Pulaski, Georgia, October 20, 1864. Transferred to Hilton Head on an unspecified date. Transferred to Fort Delaware where he arrived on March 12, 1865. Released on June 12, 1865, after taking the Oath of Allegiance.

JACKSON, ARCHIBALD A., 2nd Lieutenant

Resided in Moore County where he enlisted at age 26, August 15, 1861. Mustered in as Corporal. Promoted to Sergeant in February, 1862. Elected 2nd Lieutenant on May 1, 1862. Present or accounted for until wounded at Gettysburg, Pennsylvania, July 1, 1863. Returned to duty the same date. Present or accounted for until wounded at or near Spotsylvania Court House, Virginia, May 12, 1864. Died on May 19, 1864, of wounds. Place of death not reported.

McINTOSH, ARCHIBALD, 1st Lieutenant

Born in Moore County where he resided as a "soldier" prior to enlisting in Moore County at age 24. Elected 1st Lieutenant on August 15, 1861. Present or accounted for until he was defeated for reelection when the regiment was reorganized on May 1, 1862. Later served as Sergeant in Company A, 63rd Regiment N.C. Troops (5th Regiment N.C. Cavalry).

McINTOSH, DANIEL W., 2nd Lieutenant

Resided in Moore County where he enlisted at age 22. Elected 2nd Lieutenant on August 15, 1861. Present or accounted for until he was defeated for reelection when the regiment was reorganized on May 1, 1862.

McLEOD, LOUIS H., 2nd Lieutenant

Born in Moore County where he resided prior to enlisting in Moore County at age 32, August 15, 1861. Mustered in as Corporal. Elected 2nd Lieutenant on May 1, 1862. Present or accounted for until wounded at or near Malvern Hill, Virginia, July 1, 1862. Company records do not indicate whether he returned to duty. Died "at home" on or about March 19, 1863, of "dropsy."

McNEILL, HENRY J., 1st Lieutenant

Resided in Moore County where he enlisted at age 22, August 15, 1861. Mustered in as Corporal. Elected 1st Lieutenant on May 1, 1862. Present or accounted for until wounded at Gettysburg, Pennsylvania, July 1, 1863. Returned to duty on or about the same date. Present or accounted for until wounded in the right leg at or near Spotsylvania Court House, Virginia, May 19, 1864. Reported absent wounded through August, 1864. Resigned on March 27, 1865. Reason he resigned not reported.

MOORE, FRANCIS M., 2nd Lieutenant

Resided in Moore County where he enlisted at age 21. Elected 2nd Lieutenant on August 15, 1861. Present or accounted for until he resigned on February 13, 1862, by reason of "pulmonary consumption." Resignation accepted on or about February 27, 1862.

NONCOMMISSIONED OFFICERS AND PRIVATES

BAKER, HENRY C., Private

Born in Moore County where he resided prior to enlisting in Moore County at age 18, April 26, 1862, for the war. Present or accounted for until wounded in the jaw at South Mountain, Maryland, September 14, 1862. Captured by the enemy on an unspecified date. Hospitalized at Frederick, Maryland, where he died on December 17, 1862, of wounds.

BAKER, JAMES, Private

Resided in Moore County where he enlisted at age 23, August 15, 1861. Present or accounted for until discharged on February 15, 1862, after providing Private John Lawrence as a substitute.

BLACK, ALFRED, Private

Resided in Johnston or Cumberland County and enlisted in Moore County at age 29, August 15, 1861. Mustered in as Private. Promoted to Corporal on an unspecified date. Reduced to ranks on October 9, 1861. Present or accounted for until wounded at Gaines' Mill, Virginia, June 27, 1862. Reported absent without leave on September 1, 1862. Enlisted in 2nd Company B, 36th Regiment N.C. Troops (2nd Regiment N.C. Artillery), January 29, 1863, while absent without leave from this company. Transferred to Company B, 13th Battalion N.C. Light Artillery, November 4, 1863. Transferred back to this company on February 26, 1864. Wounded and captured at Spotsylvania Court House, Virginia, May 12, 1864. Confined at Point Lookout, Maryland, May 18, 1864. Transferred to Elmira, New York, July 23, 1864. Released at Elmira on May 19, 1865, after taking the Oath of Allegiance.

BLALOCK, F. M., Private

Resided in Moore County where he enlisted at age 24, August 15, 1861. Present or accounted for until hospitalized at Richmond, Virginia, August 26, 1862, with a gunshot wound. Place and date wounded not reported. Reported absent wounded or absent sick until he returned to duty in September-December, 1863. Detailed for duty as a shoemaker at Richmond on or about December 28, 1863. Assigned to duty with the 2nd Battalion Virginia Infantry (Local Defense). Listed as a deserter on a record for that unit dated August 2, 1864. Hospitalized at Raleigh on August 3, 1864, with a gunshot wound of the left knee. Place and date wounded not reported. Furloughed for sixty days on December 19, 1864.

BRAFFORD, ELI, Private

Resided in Chatham County and enlisted in Moore County at age 18, August 15, 1861. Present or accounted for until wounded at Gaines' Mill, Virginia, June 27, 1862. Reported absent wounded until February 9, 1863, when he was assigned to detached service in North Carolina. Reported absent on detached service through August, 1864. Retired to the Invalid Corps on February 14, 1865.

BRANCH, A. L., Private

Resided in Harnett County where he enlisted at age 43, September 28, 1863, for the war. Present or accounted for until he deserted to the enemy on February 25-26, 1864.

BROWN, ANDREW S., Corporal

Resided in Moore County where he enlisted at age 23, August 15, 1861. Mustered in as Private. Promoted to Corporal in April, 1863. Present or accounted for until he was reported missing at Gettysburg, Pennsylvania, July 1-3, 1863. Listed as a deserter on July 10, 1863. Reduced to ranks on December 1, 1863.

BROWN, G. M., Private

Place and date of enlistment not reported. Captured at or near Richmond, Virginia, on or about April 3, 1865. Paroled on April 20, 1865.

BROWN, JAMES, Private

Born in Moore County where he resided prior to enlisting in Moore County at age 24, August 15, 1861. Present or accounted for until wounded at Gaines' Mill, Virginia, June 27, 1862. Returned to duty prior to September 17, 1862, when he was killed at Sharpsburg, Maryland.

BUCHANAN, C. B., Private

Resided in Harnett County and enlisted in Moore County at age 21, August 15, 1861. Present or accounted for until he died in hospital at Lynchburg, Virginia, on or about August 11, 1863, of "febris."

BUCHANAN, JOSEPH, Private

Resided in Chatham County and enlisted at Camp Holmes on March 1, 1862, as a substitute for Private W. T. Yarborough. Present or accounted for until he died in hospital at Lynchburg, Virginia, October 15, 1864, of "diarrhoea acute."

BUCHANAN, THOMAS, Private

Born in Chatham County where he resided prior to enlisting in Moore County at age 22, August 15, 1861. Present or accounted for until he died in hospital at Staunton, Virginia, December 8, 1862, of "scarlatina."

BUCHANAN, WILLIAM MAY, Private

Resided in Chatham County and enlisted in Moore County at age 19, August 15, 1861. Present or accounted for until wounded and reported missing at Gaines' Mill, Virginia, June 27, 1862. Failed to rejoin the company and was dropped from the rolls in July-August, 1863.

BUIE, DANIEL, Private

Born in Moore County where he resided prior to enlisting in Moore County at age 25, August 15, 1861. Present or accounted for until wounded at Gaines' Mill, Virginia, June 27, 1862. Died at Drewry's Bluff, Virginia, July 14, 1862, of wounds.

BUIE, JOHN, Sergeant

Resided in Moore County where he enlisted at age 30, August 15, 1861. Mustered in as Private. Promoted to Sergeant on May 1, 1862. Present or accounted for until captured at Boonsboro, Maryland, September 16, 1862. Confined at Fort Delaware, Delaware. Paroled and transferred to Aiken's Landing, James River, Virginia, October 2, 1862, for exchange. Declared exchanged at Aiken's Landing on November 10, 1862. Returned to duty prior to January 1, 1863. Present or accounted for until captured at Kelly's Ford, Virginia, November 7, 1863. Confined at Point Lookout, Maryland, November 11, 1863. Paroled at Point Lookout on or about March 14, 1865, and transferred to Boulware's Wharf, James River, Virginia, where he was received on March 18, 1865, for exchange.

BURGESS, W. H., Private
Resided in Cumberland County where he enlisted at age 42, October 27, 1863, for the war. Present or accounted for until killed at Spotsylvania Court House, Virginia, May 12, 1864.

CAMPBELL, A. T., Private
Resided in Moore County where he enlisted at age 32, August 15, 1861. Present or accounted for until captured at or near Gettysburg, Pennsylvania, July 1-5, 1863. Confined at Davids Island, New York Harbor, on or about July 17, 1863. Paroled at Davids Island on August 24, 1863, and transferred to City Point, Virginia, where he was received on August 28, 1863, for exchange. Returned to duty prior to January 1, 1864. Present or accounted for until captured near Spotsylvania Court House, Virginia, May 12, 1864. Confined at Point Lookout, Maryland, May 18, 1864. Transferred to Elmira, New York, August 10, 1864. Died at Elmira on March 22, 1865, of "pneumonia."

CAMPBELL, DANIEL, Private
Resided in Moore County where he enlisted at age 28, August 15, 1861. Present or accounted for until September 6, 1862, when he was "left on the march" near Leesburg, Virginia. Company muster roll dated May-June, 1863, states that he was "supposed to be dead." Dropped from the rolls of the company in July-August, 1863.

CAMPBELL, GEORGE W., Private
Resided in Moore County where he enlisted at age 20, August 15, 1861. Present or accounted for until captured at Gettysburg, Pennsylvania, July 3, 1863. Confined at Fort Delaware, Delaware, July 30, 1863. Transferred to Point Lookout, Maryland, October 15-18, 1863. Paroled at Point Lookout on or about March 16, 1864, and transferred to City Point, Virginia, where he was received on March 20, 1864, for exchange. Returned to duty prior to September 1, 1864. Surrendered at Appomattox Court House, Virginia, April 9, 1865.

CAMPBELL, J. M., Private
Resided in Moore County where he enlisted at age 27, August 15, 1861. Present or accounted for until discharged on August 18, 1862, after providing a substitute.

CARR, DENNIS, Private
Born in Ireland and resided in Chatham County prior to enlisting in Moore County at age 20, August 15, 1861. Present or accounted for until wounded at Gaines' Mill, Virginia, June 27, 1862. Returned to duty on or about July 14, 1862. Discharged on September 22, 1862, by reason of "being an alien."

CENTER, CHARLES H., Private
Resided in Harnett County where he enlisted at age 40, September 28, 1863, for the war. Present or accounted for until wounded in the head and captured at Spotsylvania Court House, Virginia, May 12, 1864. Hospitalized at Washington, D.C., where he died on

May 31, 1864, of "exhaustion."

COLE, ANDREW, Private
Born in Moore County where he resided prior to enlisting in Moore County at age 21, April 24, 1862, for the war. Present or accounted for until captured by the enemy on an unspecified date. Paroled at Leesburg, Virginia, October 2, 1862. Returned to duty prior to January 1, 1863. Died in hospital at Richmond, Virginia, April 2, 1863, of "pneumonia."

COLE, GEORGE C., Private
Resided in Moore County where he enlisted at age 23, August 15, 1861. Present or accounted for until killed at Malvern Hill, Virginia, July 1, 1862.

COLE, GEORGE W., Private
Resided in Moore County where he enlisted at age 20, August 15, 1861. Present or accounted for until wounded at or near Wilderness, Virginia, May 6, 1864. Reported absent wounded through August, 1864.

COLE, GREEN B., 1st Sergeant
Resided in Moore County where he enlisted at age 26, August 15, 1861. Mustered in as 1st Sergeant. Present or accounted for until wounded at Chancellorsville, Virginia, May 3, 1863. Returned to duty in September-December, 1863. Present or accounted for until he surrendered at Appomattox Court House, Virginia, April 9, 1865.

COLE, NEILL M. N., Private
Resided in Moore County where he enlisted at age 23, August 15, 1861. Present or accounted for until he died near Richmond, Virginia, August 16, 1862, of "typhoid fever."

COLE, R. T., Private
Place and date of enlistment not reported. Surrendered at Appomattox Court House, Virginia, April 9, 1865.

COOK, ANDERSON, Private
Resided in Alamance County where he enlisted at age 43, September 19, 1863, for the war. Died at Gordonsville, Virginia, November 29, 1863, of disease.

COX, JOHN LOUIS, Private
Resided in Moore County where he enlisted at age 21, August 15, 1861. Mustered in as Sergeant. Reduced to ranks in May-June, 1862. Present or accounted for until wounded in the right arm at Malvern Hill, Virginia, July 1, 1862. Reported absent wounded or absent on detached service until June 21, 1864, when he was retired to the Invalid Corps.

COX, WILLIAM O., Private
Resided in Moore County where he enlisted at age 30, April 24, 1862, for the war. Present or accounted for until wounded at Gaines' Mill, Virginia, June 27, 1862. Returned to duty in September-December, 1863. Present or accounted for until captured at or near Spotsylvania Court House, Virginia, May 8, 1864. Confined at Point Lookout, Maryland, May 17, 1864. [North Carolina pension records indicate that he survived the war.]

COX, WILLIAM W., Private
Resided in Chatham County and enlisted in Moore County at age 19, August 15, 1861. Died at Camp Wyatt

on or about November 17, 1861, of "pneumonia."

CROTTS, ELIJAH, Private
Resided in Cleveland County where he enlisted at age 42, August 27, 1863, for the war. Present or accounted for until killed at or near Snicker's Gap or Snake Ferry, Virginia, July 18, 1864.

DEATON, JAMES P., Private
Resided in Chatham County and enlisted in Moore County at age 24, August 15, 1861. Mustered in as Private. Promoted to Musician prior to November 1, 1861. Promoted to Sergeant in May, 1862. Present or accounted for until wounded in the hand at Gaines' Mill, Virginia, June 27, 1862. Reported absent wounded until February 9, 1863, when he was assigned to detached service. Reduced to ranks in January-June, 1863. Reported absent on detached service through August, 1864.

DUDLEY, LABAN, Private
Resided in Harnett County where he enlisted at age 40, September 28, 1863, for the war. Present or accounted for until captured at or near Bethel Church, Virginia, May 22-23, 1864. Confined at Point Lookout, Maryland, May 30, 1864. Paroled at Point Lookout on or about March 14, 1865, and transferred to Boulware's Wharf, James River, Virginia, where he was received on March 16, 1865, for exchange.

EASON, JAMES SCARBOROUGH, Private
Previously served in Company F of this regiment. Enlisted in this company on October 5, 1863, for the war. Present or accounted for until captured "in Maryland" on June 10, 1864. Hospitalized at Frederick, Maryland, July 10, 1864. Died in hospital at Frederick on July 18, 1864, of "febris typhoides."

FIELDS, A., Private
Resided in Guilford County where he enlisted at age 33, September 12, 1863, for the war. Deserted on November 20, 1863. Never rejoined the company; however, he was reported in hospital at Richmond, Virginia, from December 30, 1864, through February 13, 1865.

FREEMAN, WILLIAM M., Private
Resided in Moore County where he enlisted at age 23, August 15, 1861. Present or accounted for through August, 1864.

GASTER, JOHN C., Private
Resided in Moore County where he enlisted at age 21, October 3, 1862, for the war. Present or accounted for until he died in hospital at Richmond, Virginia, on or about May 9, 1863, of disease.

GOINS, DUNCAN, Private
Resided in Chatham County and enlisted in Moore County at age 24, August 15, 1861. Present or accounted for until he died in hospital at Wilmington on March 10, 1862, of "typh[oi]d fever."

GOINS, EDWARD, Private
Resided in Chatham County and enlisted in Moore County at age 21, August 15, 1861. Present or accounted for until he surrendered at Appomattox Court House, Virginia, April 9, 1865.

GRAHAM, JARRATT B., Private
Resided in Moore County where he enlisted at age 35,

August 15, 1861. Present or accounted for until wounded at Gaines' Mill, Virginia, June 27, 1862. "Fell overboard" and was "drowned in Cape Fear River" on or about July 4, 1862, "on the passage of the *Hurt* from Wilmington to [Fayetteville]."

GRAHAM, SAMUEL W., Private
Born in Ireland and resided in Chatham County prior to enlisting in Moore County at age 45, August 15, 1861. Present or accounted for until he died in hospital at Richmond, Virginia, August 11-14, 1862, of "p[h]thisis pulmonalis."

GREEN, JAMES L., Private
Resided in Cleveland County and enlisted at age 42, August 28, 1863, for the war. Present or accounted for until captured near Spotsylvania Court House, Virginia, May 12, 1864. Confined at Point Lookout, Maryland, May 18, 1864. Transferred to Elmira, New York, August 10, 1864. Died at Elmira on October 4, 1864, of "chronic diarrhoea."

HAGLER, HIRAM, Private
Enlisted at Camp Holmes on September 24, 1863, for the war. Present or accounted for until wounded in the back and left side and captured at Silver Spring, Maryland, July 12, 1864. Hospitalized at Washington, D.C., where he died on August 3, 1864, of "gangrene." Federal medical records dated July-August, 1864, give his age as 43 and 50.

HARRINGTON, A. F., Sergeant
Resided in Moore County where he enlisted at age 31, August 15, 1861. Mustered in as Private. Promoted to Sergeant on May 1, 1863. Present or accounted for until he surrendered at Appomattox Court House, Virginia, April 9, 1865.

HEARTLEY, GEORGE, Private
Resided in Wayne County. Place and date of enlistment not reported. Paroled at Goldsboro in 1865.

HENDRICKS, E., Private
Resided in Cleveland County where he enlisted at age 42, August 25, 1863, for the war. Present or accounted for until captured at Winchester, Virginia, September 19, 1864. Confined at Point Lookout, Maryland. Paroled at Point Lookout on January 17, 1865, and transferred to Boulware's Wharf, James River, Virginia, where he was received on January 21, 1865, for exchange.

HIGHT, JOSEPH J., Corporal
Resided in Moore County where he enlisted at age 22, August 15, 1861. Mustered in as Private. Promoted to Corporal in May, 1862. Present or accounted for until wounded in the thigh and captured at or near Gettysburg, Pennsylvania, July 1-5, 1863. Hospitalized at Davids Island, New York Harbor, on or about July 17, 1863. Paroled at Davids Island on August 24, 1863, and transferred to City Point, Virginia, where he was received on August 28, 1863, for exchange. Returned to duty in November-December, 1863. Present or accounted for through August, 1864.

HORNADAY, LOUIS D., Private
Resided in Moore County where he enlisted at age 31, August 28, 1862, for the war. Present or accounted for until captured at Spotsylvania Court House, Virginia,

May 12, 1864. Confined at Point Lookout, Maryland, May 18, 1864. Transferred to Elmira, New York, August 10, 1864. Released at Elmira on June 27, 1865, after taking the Oath of Allegiance.

HORNE, PLEASANT, Private
Resided in Anson County and enlisted at Camp Holmes at age 41, September 13, 1863, for the war. Captured near Spotsylvania Court House, Virginia, May 12, 1864. Confined at Point Lookout, Maryland, May 18, 1864. Transferred to Elmira, New York, August 10, 1864. Died at Elmira on September 25, 1864, of "scorbutus."

HOYLE, NICHOLAS, Private
Resided in Cleveland County where he enlisted at age 42, September 22, 1863, for the war. Present or accounted for through October 25, 1864.

HUGHES, DOCTOR, Private
Born in Moore County where he resided prior to enlisting in Moore County at age 24, August 15, 1861. Present or accounted for until he died near Hamilton's Crossing, Virginia, May 13, 1863.

HUGHES, H., Private
Resided in Union County and enlisted at age 38, September 24, 1863, for the war. No further records.

HUNTER, CHARLES A., Corporal
Resided in Moore County and enlisted at Camp Wyatt at age 19, February 12, 1862. Mustered in as Private. Present or accounted for until wounded at Malvern Hill, Virginia, July 1, 1862. Returned to duty prior to January 1, 1863. Present or accounted for until wounded at Chancellorsville, Virginia, May 1-4, 1863. Returned to duty prior to July 1, 1863. Promoted to Corporal subsequent to August 31, 1864. Present or accounted for until he surrendered at Appomattox Court House, Virginia, April 9, 1865.

HUNTER, J. R., Sr., Private
Resided in Union County and enlisted at Camp Holmes at age 40, September 24, 1863, for the war. Present or accounted for until he deserted to the enemy on February 28, 1864.

HUNTER, JOHN REAVES, Jr., Private
Resided in Moore or Chatham County and enlisted in Moore County at age 18, August 15, 1861. Present or accounted for until wounded at Malvern Hill, Virginia, July 1, 1862. Returned to duty prior to December 15, 1862. Present or accounted for until captured at Kelly's Ford, Virginia, on or about November 7, 1863. Confined at Old Capitol Prison. Washington, D.C. Took the Oath of Allegiance at Washington on or about March 18, 1864.

HUNTER, STANFORD, Private
Resided in Moore County where he enlisted at age 20, August 15, 1861. Present or accounted for until he died at Richmond, Virginia, July 22, 1862. Cause of death not reported.

JACKSON, B. C., Private
Resided in Harnett County and enlisted in New Hanover County at age 23, May 10, 1862, for the war. Present or accounted for until wounded in the right knee at Gettysburg, Pennsylvania, July 1-3, 1863. Returned to duty prior to September 1, 1863. Present or accounted for until killed at Spotsylvania Court House, Virginia,

May 12, 1864.

JOHNSON, JOHN, Private
Born in Moore County where he resided as a cooper prior to enlisting in Moore County at age 21, August 15, 1861. Present or accounted for until discharged on August 8, 1863, by reason of "dropsy palsy."

KELLY, ALEX D., Private
Resided in Chatham County and enlisted in Moore County at age 19, August 15, 1861. Present or accounted for through August, 1864.

KELLY, ARCHIBALD, Jr., Private
Resided in Chatham County and enlisted in Moore County at age 19, August 15, 1861. Present or accounted for until discharged on July 30, 1862. Reason discharged not reported.

KELLY, ARCHIBALD, Sr., Private
Born in Moore County where he resided as a wheelwright prior to enlisting in Moore County at age 42, August 15, 1861. Present or accounted for until discharged on July 25, 1862, by reason of "inguinal hernia."

KELLY, DAVID W., Private
Resided in Chatham County and enlisted at Camp Lamb on March 1, 1862. Present or accounted for until captured at or near Chambersburg, Pennsylvania, on or about July 5, 1863. Confined at Harrisburg, Pennsylvania, on or about August 17, 1863. Transferred to Fort McHenry, Maryland, on an unspecified date. Transferred to Point Lookout, Maryland, where he arrived on September 15, 1863. Died at Point Lookout on July 13, 1864. Cause of death not reported.

KELLY, SANDY, ———
North Carolina pension records indicate that he served in this company.

KELLY, WILLIAM A., Private
Resided in Moore or Chatham County and enlisted in Moore County at age 41, August 15, 1861. Present or accounted for until captured at or near Kelly's Ford, Virginia, on or about November 7, 1863. Confined at Old Capitol Prison, Washington, D.C., November 14, 1863. Released on March 15, 1864, after taking the Oath of Allegiance.

KING, W. H., Private
Resided in Wake County and enlisted at Camp Holmes at age 41, September 14, 1863, for the war. Present or accounted for until captured near Spotsylvania Court House, Virginia, May 12, 1864. Confined at Point Lookout, Maryland, May 18, 1864. Died at Point Lookout on June 30, 1864. Cause of death not reported.

KNIGHT, BENJAMIN, Private
Resided in Moore County where he enlisted at age 30, August 15, 1861. Present or accounted for until wounded in the left hand at Cold Harbor, Virginia, June 27, 1862. Reported absent wounded through December, 1862. Assigned to detached service in North Carolina on February 9, 1863. Reported absent on detached service through August, 1864.

LAWRENCE, BENNETT, Private
Born in Chatham County where he resided as a farmer

prior to enlisting at Camp Wyatt at age 21, February 15, 1862, as a substitute for Private Marshall G. Thomas. Present or accounted for until wounded and captured at Sharpsburg, Maryland, September 17, 1862. Died in hospital near Antietam, Maryland, September 24, 1862, of wounds.

LAWRENCE, JOHN, Corporal
Resided in Chatham County and enlisted at Camp Wyatt at age 22, February 15, 1862, as a substitute for Private James Baker. Mustered in as Private. Present or accounted for until wounded at Gaines' Mill, Virginia, June 27, 1862. Returned to duty prior to November 1, 1862. Present or accounted for until wounded in the hip at Gettysburg, Pennsylvania, July 1-3, 1863. Returned to duty prior to January 1, 1864. Present or accounted for until wounded in the face at Cold Harbor, Virginia, June 3, 1864. Returned to duty and was promoted to Corporal subsequent to August 31, 1864. Surrendered at Appomattox Court House, Virginia, April 9, 1865.

LLOYD, MANLEY C., Private
Resided in Orange County where he enlisted at age 40, September 6, 1863, for the war. Present or accounted for until wounded at or near Wilderness, Virginia, May 6, 1864. Reported absent wounded through August, 1864.

LOGAN, PHILIP, Private
Resided in Cleveland County where he enlisted at age 43, September 22, 1863, for the war. Present or accounted for until he died "in Virginia" on November 1, 1864, of disease.

LYNN, WILLIAM, Private
Resided in Orange County where he enlisted at age 44, September 16, 1863, for the war. Present or accounted for until hospitalized at Richmond, Virginia, February 24, 1865, with a gunshot wound of the right thigh. Place and date wounded not reported. No further records.

McAULAY, WILLIAM, Private
Resided in Moore County where he enlisted at age 27, August 15, 1861. Present or accounted for until wounded and captured at Malvern Hill, Virginia, July 1, 1862. Confined at Fort Monroe, Virginia. Transferred to Fort Delaware, Delaware, July 15, 1862. Paroled and transferred to Aiken's Landing, James River, Virginia, where he was received on July 16, 1862, for exchange. Declared exchanged at Aiken's Landing on August 5, 1862. Returned to duty prior to January 1, 1863. Present or accounted for until wounded in the neck and captured at Gettysburg, Pennsylvania, July 1-4, 1863. Hospitalized at Davids Island, New York Harbor, on or about July 17, 1863. Paroled at Davids Island and transferred to City Point, Virginia, where he was received on September 27, 1863, for exchange. Retired to the Invalid Corps on May 15, 1864. Nominated for the Badge of Distinction for gallantry at Chancellorsville, Virginia, May 1-4, 1863.

McCULLOCH, WILLIAM, Private
Born in Scotland and resided in Chatham County prior to enlisting in Brunswick County at age 37, October 20, 1861. Present or accounted for until wounded at Malvern Hill, Virginia, July 1, 1862. Died on July 3, 1862, of wounds. Place of death not reported.

McDONALD, JAMES S., Private
Resided in Moore County where he enlisted at age 23, August 15, 1861. Present or accounted for until captured at or near Sharpsburg, Maryland, on or about September 17, 1862. Confined at Fort McHenry, Maryland. Paroled and transferred to Aiken's Landing, James River, Virginia, where he was received on October 25, 1862, for exchange. Declared exchanged at Aiken's Landing on November 10, 1862. Returned to duty prior to January 1, 1863. Present or accounted for until captured at Kelly's Ford, Virginia, November 7, 1863. Confined at Point Lookout, Maryland, November 11, 1863. Paroled at Point Lookout on or about February 24, 1865, and transferred to Aiken's Landing where he was received on February 25-March 3, 1865, for exchange.

McDONALD, JOHN A., Private
Resided in Harnett County where he enlisted at age 40, September 28, 1863, for the war. Present or accounted for until captured in hospital at Richmond, Virginia, April 3, 1865. Transferred to Newport News, Virginia, April 23, 1865. Released on June 30, 1865, after taking the Oath of Allegiance.

McDONALD, NEILL, Private
Resided in Moore County where he enlisted at age 28, August 15, 1861. Present or accounted for until wounded in the shoulder at Sharpsburg, Maryland, September 17, 1862. Died "at home" on December 25, 1862, of disease.

McDOUGALD, DUNCAN, Private
Resided in Moore County where he enlisted at age 24, August 15, 1861. Present or accounted for until captured at Boonsboro, Maryland, September 15, 1862. Confined at Fort Delaware, Delaware. Paroled and transferred to Aiken's Landing, James River, Virginia, October 2, 1862, for exchange. Declared exchanged at Aiken's Landing on November 10, 1862. Returned to duty prior to December 12-13, 1862, when he was wounded in both legs at Fredericksburg, Virginia. One leg amputated. Died prior to January 1, 1863, of wounds. Place of death not reported.

McFARLAND, ANDREW, Private
Born in Ireland and resided in Moore County where he enlisted at age 28, August 15, 1861. Present or accounted for until wounded at Sharpsburg, Maryland, September 17, 1862. Returned to duty prior to January 1, 1863. Present or accounted for through April, 1864. Company records indicate he was captured at or near Spotsylvania Court House, Virginia, May 12, 1864; however, records of the Federal Provost Marshal do not substantiate that report. No further records.

McFARLAND, JOHN A., Private
Resided in Moore County where he enlisted at age 19, August 15, 1861. Present or accounted for until captured at Sharpsburg, Maryland, September 17, 1862. Confined at Fort Delaware, Delaware. Paroled and transferred to Aiken's Landing, James River, Virginia, October 2, 1862, for exchange. Declared exchanged at Aiken's Landing on November 10, 1862. Returned to duty prior to January 1, 1863. Present or accounted for until he surrendered at Appomattox Court House, Virginia, April 9, 1865.

McFATTER, ALEXANDER, Private
Resided in Moore County where he enlisted at age 48, August 15, 1861. Present or accounted for until captured

at Malvern Hill, Virginia, July 1, 1862. Confined at Fort Monroe, Virginia. Transferred to Fort Delaware, Delaware, July 15, 1862. Paroled and transferred to Aiken's Landing, James River, Virginia, where he was received on July 16, 1862, for exchange. Declared exchanged at Aiken's Landing on August 5, 1862. Returned to duty prior to July 1, 1863. Present or accounted for until wounded in the shoulder and back at Kelly's Ford, Virginia, November 7, 1863. Hospitalized at Richmond, Virginia, where he died on November 28, 1863, of wounds.

McGILL, A. D., Corporal
Born in Scotland and resided in Cumberland County prior to enlisting at Camp Wyatt at age 19, January 16, 1862. Mustered in as Private. Promoted to Corporal in January-June, 1863. Present or accounted for until he surrendered at Appomattox Court House, Virginia, April 9, 1865.

McINTOSH, DAVID G., Sergeant
Resided in Moore County where he enlisted at age 26, August 15, 1861. Mustered in as Sergeant. Reduced to ranks on or about May 1, 1862. Promoted to Corporal in July, 1862, and was promoted to Sergeant in April, 1863. Present or accounted for until captured at Spotsylvania Court House, Virginia, May 20, 1864. Confined at Point Lookout, Maryland, May 23, 1864. Transferred to Elmira, New York, July 3, 1864. Released at Elmira on June 30, 1865, after taking the Oath of Allegiance.

McINTOSH, FRANCIS M., Private
Previously served as Corporal in Company H, 26th Regiment N.C. Troops. Transferred to this company on August 20, 1861, with the rank of Private. Present or accounted for until wounded at or near Snicker's Gap, Virginia, July 18, 1864. Reported absent wounded through August, 1864. Returned to duty on an unspecified date. Present or accounted for through March 16, 1865.

McIVER, D. M., Private
Resided in Moore County where he enlisted at age 26, April 24, 1862, for the war. Present or accounted for until he surrendered at Appomattox Court House, Virginia, April 9, 1865.

McIVER, D. N., Private
Resided in Moore County where he enlisted at age 29, April 24, 1862, for the war. Present or accounted for until wounded at or near Spotsylvania Court House, Virginia, May 19, 1864. Reported absent wounded through August, 1864. Returned to duty on an unspecified date. Surrendered at Appomattox Court House, Virginia, April 9, 1865.

McIVER, DAN W., Private
Resided in Moore County and enlisted at Camp Wyatt at age 33, January 9, 1862. Present or accounted for until discharged on July 22, 1862, by reason of disability.

McIVER, EDWARD, Private
Born in Moore County where he resided prior to enlisting in Moore County at age 23, April 24, 1862, for the war. Present or accounted for until he died near Front Royal, Virginia, December 13, 1862, of "pneumonia."

McIVER, JOHN W., Private
Born in Moore County where he resided prior to enlisting in Moore County at age 24, August 15, 1861. Present or accounted for until he died in hospital at Smithville (Southport) on or about November 8, 1861, of "measles" or "pneumonia."

McIVER, K. H., Private
Born in Moore County where he resided prior to enlisting in Moore County at age 18, April 24, 1862, for the war. Present or accounted for until wounded at Chancellorsville, Virginia, May 1-4, 1863. Hospitalized at Richmond, Virginia, where he died on June 6, 1863, of wounds.

McIVER, MURDOCK A., Private
Born in Moore County where he resided prior to enlisting in Moore County at age 19, August 15, 1861. Present or accounted for until he died in hospital at Richmond, Virginia, September 20-22, 1862, of "febris typhoides."

McNEILL, LAUGHLIN, Private
Born in Moore County where he resided as a carpenter prior to enlisting in Moore County at age 37, August 15, 1861. Present or accounted for until wounded in the right arm at Malvern Hill, Virginia, July 1, 1862. Right arm amputated. Discharged on August 3, 1862.

McPHERSON, A. DUGALL, Private
Born in Moore County where he resided prior to enlisting in Moore County at age 21, August 15, 1861. Present or accounted for until he died near Richmond, Virginia, July 22, 1862. Cause of death not reported.

McPHERSON, D. K., Private
Born in Moore County where he resided prior to enlisting at age 19, April 28, 1862, for the war. Present or accounted for until he died in hospital at Lynchburg, Virginia, November 25, 1862, of "rubeola" or "dropsy."

MASHBURN, ALFRED ISLEY, Private
Resided in Moore County where he enlisted at age 21, August 15, 1861. Present or accounted for until hospitalized at Richmond, Virginia, September 25, 1862, with an unspecified wound. Place and date wounded not reported. Returned to duty on an unspecified date. Present or accounted for through August, 1864; however, he was reported absent sick or absent on detached service during much of that period.

MASHBURN, J. D., Private
Born in Moore County where he resided prior to enlisting in Moore County at age 30, August 15, 1861. Present or accounted for until wounded at Malvern Hill, Virginia, July 1, 1862. Died on or about July 3, 1862, of wounds. Place of death not reported.

MATTHEWS, HARDIE, Corporal
Resided in Moore County where he enlisted at age 21, August 15, 1861. Mustered in as Private. Promoted to Corporal in May, 1862. Present or accounted for until wounded in the leg and left arm at Spotsylvania Court House, Virginia, May 12, 1864. Hospitalized at Richmond, Virginia. Returned to duty on or about July 25, 1864. Present or accounted for until wounded in the right leg and captured at Winchester, Virginia, September 19, 1864. Confined at Fort McHenry,

Maryland, January 5, 1865. Transferred to Point Lookout, Maryland, February 20, 1865. Exchanged prior to March 4, 1865.

MATTHEWS, JOHN B., Musician
Resided in Moore County where he enlisted at age 25, April 20, 1862, for the war. Mustered in as Musician (Drummer). Present or accounted for until wounded at Sharpsburg, Maryland, September 17, 1862. Captured at or near Sharpsburg on an unspecified date and was paroled on September 27, 1862. Reported absent on detached service on March 15, 1863. Rejoined the company in July-August, 1863. Present or accounted for until April 26, 1864, when he was retired to the Invalid Corps.

MATTHEWS, NATHAN, Private
Resided in Moore County where he enlisted at age 19, August 15, 1861. Present or accounted for until captured at Gettysburg, Pennsylvania, July 3, 1863. Confined at Fort Delaware, Delaware, on or about July 7, 1863. Transferred to Point Lookout, Maryland, October 15-18, 1863. Died at Point Lookout on September 16, 1864. Cause of death not reported.

MONROE, J. P., Private
Resided in Moore County where he enlisted at age 18, April 26, 1862, for the war. Present or accounted for until captured at Kelly's Ford, Virginia, November 7, 1863. Confined at Point Lookout, Maryland, November 11, 1863. Paroled at Point Lookout on or about February 13, 1865, and transferred to Cox's Wharf, James River, Virginia, where he was received on February 14-15, 1865, for exchange.

MONROE, JAMES A., Private
Resided in Moore County where he enlisted at age 19, August 15, 1861. Present or accounted for until wounded at Sharpsburg, Maryland, September 17, 1862. Returned to duty in January-June, 1863. Present or accounted for until captured at Kelly's Ford, Virginia, November 7, 1863. Confined at Point Lookout, Maryland, November 11, 1863. Paroled at Point Lookout on or about February 24, 1865, and transferred to Aiken's Landing, James River, Virginia, where he was received February 25-March 3, 1865, for exchange.

MORRIS, DAVID P., Private
Resided in Moore County where he enlisted at age 42, August 15, 1861. Present or accounted for until wounded in the right shoulder and captured at Gettysburg, Pennsylvania, July 1-4, 1863. Hospitalized at Gettysburg. Transferred to hospital at Baltimore, Maryland, September 16, 1863. Paroled at Baltimore on September 25, 1863, and transferred to City Point, Virginia, where he was received on September 27, 1863, for exchange. Reported absent wounded through August, 1864. Returned to duty on an unspecified date. Captured at High Bridge, Virginia, April 6, 1865. Confined at Point Lookout, Maryland, April 14, 1865. Died at Point Lookout on or about May 3, 1865, of ''chronic diarrhoea.''

MORRIS, JOHN D., Private
Born in Moore County where he resided prior to enlisting in Moore County at age 24, August 15, 1861. Present or accounted for until he died at Richmond, Virginia, July 16, 1862. Cause of death not reported.

MORRISON, HORACE, Sergeant
Resided in Moore County where he enlisted at age 23, August 15, 1861. Mustered in as Private. Promoted to Corporal on October 1, 1861. Present or accounted for until wounded at Malvern Hill, Virginia, July 1, 1862. Returned to duty in January-June, 1863. Promoted to Sergeant in April, 1863. Present or accounted for until killed at Spotsylvania Court House, Virginia, May 8, 1864.

NASON, ALBERT, Private
Resided in Moore County where he enlisted at age 28, August 15, 1861. Present or accounted for until he surrendered at Appomattox Court House, Virginia, April 9, 1865.

O'NEAL, DANIEL, Private
Resided in Virginia and enlisted at Richmond, Virginia, at age 46, August 18, 1862, for the war as a substitute. ''Deserted same day he enlisted.''

PHILLIPS, JOHN H., Private
Resided in Moore County where he enlisted at age 18, August 15, 1861. Present or accounted for until hospitalized at Richmond, Virginia, October 5, 1862, with a gunshot wound of the left knee. Place and date wounded not reported. Returned to duty in January-June, 1863. Wounded in the left hip at Bunker Hill, West Virginia, in June, 1863. Returned to duty prior to July 1-3, 1863, when he was wounded in the left arm at Gettysburg, Pennsylvania. Returned to duty prior to September 1, 1863. Present or accounted for until captured at Kelly's Ford, Virginia, November 7, 1863. Confined at Point Lookout, Maryland, November 11, 1863. Paroled at Point Lookout on or about February 24, 1865, and transferred to Aiken's Landing, James River, Virginia, where he was received February 25-March 3, 1865, for exchange.

POOL, THOMAS, Private
Born in Orange County where he resided prior to enlisting in Orange County at age 18, September 4, 1863, for the war. Present or accounted for until he died ''in camp'' on or about February 8-9, 1864. Cause of death not reported.

RAPE, J. S., Private
Resided in Union County where he enlisted at age 44, September 21, 1863, for the war. Present or accounted for through August, 1864.

RIDDLE, GEORGE W., Private
Resided in Moore County where he enlisted at age 24, August 15, 1861. Present or accounted for until wounded in the left hand and left ankle at Malvern Hill, Virginia, July 1, 1862. Returned to duty in January-June, 1863. Present or accounted for until captured at Kelly's Ford, Virginia, November 7, 1863. Confined at Point Lookout, Maryland, November 11, 1863. Paroled at Point Lookout on or about October 30, 1864, and transferred to Venus Point, Savannah River, Georgia, where he was received on November 15, 1864, for exchange.

RODES, WILEY, Private
Born in Orange County where he resided as a farmer prior to enlisting in Orange County at age 43, September 4, 1863, for the war. Present or accounted for

until paroled at Greensboro on May 3, 1865.

ROGERS, JAMES, Private
Born in Ayrshire, Scotland, and resided in Chatham County where he was by occupation a miner prior to enlisting in Moore County at age 22, August 15, 1861. Present or accounted for until captured near Spotsylvania Court House, Virginia, May 12, 1864. Confined at Point Lookout, Maryland, May 18, 1864. Released on June 18, 1864, after joining the U.S. Army. Assigned to Company I, 1st Regiment U.S. Volunteer Infantry.

ROSE, HENRY B., Sergeant
Resided in Cumberland County. Place and date of enlistment not reported. Promotion record not reported. Captured at Spotsylvania Court House, Virginia, May 12, 1864. Confined at Point Lookout, Maryland. Transferred to Elmira, New York, where he was received on July 11, 1864. Released at Elmira on May 29, 1865, after taking the Oath of Allegiance.

SHAW, D. C., Private
Resided in Moore County where he enlisted at age 22, August 15, 1861. Present or accounted for until captured at or near Sharpsburg, Maryland, on or about September 17, 1862. Confined at Fort McHenry, Maryland. Paroled and transferred to Fort Monroe, Virginia, October 13, 1862. Transferred to Aiken's Landing, James River, Virginia, where he was received on October 17, 1862, for exchange. Declared exchanged at Aiken's Landing on November 10, 1862. Returned to duty in January-June, 1863. Present or accounted for until wounded in the left foot and captured at Kelly's Ford, Virginia, November 7, 1863. Confined at various Federal hospitals until confined at Old Capitol Prison, Washington, D.C., on or about February 8, 1864. Transferred to Fort Delaware, Delaware, June 15, 1864. Released at Fort Delaware on or about June 7-8, 1865, after taking the Oath of Allegiance. [North Carolina pension records indicate he suffered a fractured skull at "Warrenton, Virginia, May 3, 1863."]

SHORT, WILLIAM F., Private
Resided in Union County where he enlisted at age 18, September 24, 1863, for the war. Present or accounted for until he surrendered at Appomattox Court House, Virginia, April 9, 1865.

SINCLAIR, JOHN D., Private
Resided in Moore County and enlisted at Camp Wyatt at age 17, January 16, 1862. Present or accounted for until he surrendered at Appomattox Court House, Virginia, April 9, 1865.

SLOAN, DAVID H., Private
Resided in Moore County and enlisted at Camp Wyatt at age 19, January 9, 1862. Present or accounted for until wounded in the right elbow at Sharpsburg, Maryland, September 17, 1862. Returned to duty prior to January 1, 1863. Present or accounted for until wounded in the left hand at Chancellorsville, Virginia, May 1-4, 1863. Returned to duty in September-November, 1863. Wounded in the right knee and captured at or near Kelly's Ford, Virginia, on or about November 7, 1863. Confined at Old Capitol Prison, Washington, D.C., November 14, 1863. Transferred to Fort Delaware, Delaware, June 15, 1864. Released at Fort Delaware on or about June 19, 1865, after taking

the Oath of Allegiance.

SLOAN, JOHN A., Private
Born in Moore County where he resided prior to enlisting at Camp Wyatt at age 18, January 9, 1862. Present or accounted for until he died in hospital at Staunton, Virginia, November 4, 1862, of "pneumonia."

STARNES, D. A., Private
Resided in Union County where he enlisted at age 42, September 24, 1863, for the war. Present or accounted for until wounded in the right leg at Snicker's Gap, Virginia, July 18, 1864. Reported absent wounded through August, 1864.

STARNES, EPHRAIM, Private
Resided in Union County where he enlisted at age 43, September 24, 1863, for the war. Present or accounted for until captured near Spotsylvania Court House, Virginia, May 12, 1864. Confined at Point Lookout, Maryland, May 18, 1864. Transferred to Elmira, New York, August 10, 1864. Died at Elmira on January 12, 1865, of "congestion of the brain."

STARNES, THOMAS, Private
Resided in Union County where he enlisted at age 42, September 24, 1863, for the war. Present or accounted for until wounded at or near Warrenton, Virginia, on or about October 17, 1863. Returned to duty subsequent to December 31, 1863. Present or accounted for until he surrendered at Appomattox Court House, Virginia, April 9, 1865.

STEDMAN, DAVID B., Private
Resided in Chatham County and enlisted in Moore County at age 21, August 15, 1861. Present or accounted for until he died in hospital at Richmond, Virginia, April 15, 1863, of "typhoid pneumonia."

TAYLOR, JACKSON, Private
Resided in Harnett County and enlisted in Moore County at age 35, August 15, 1861. Present or accounted for until wounded in the foot at Wilderness, Virginia, May 6, 1864. Reported absent wounded through October 9, 1864.

THOMAS, HENRY TILMAN, Private
Resided in Moore County and enlisted at Camp Wyatt at age 18, February 12, 1862. Present or accounted for until he surrendered at Appomattox Court House, Virginia, April 9, 1865.

THOMAS, JEFFERSON, Private
Born in Moore County where he resided as a shoemaker prior to enlisting in Moore County at age 26, August 15, 1861. Present or accounted for until discharged on February 15, 1862, by reason of "dislocation of left arm and fracture of the clavicle." Place and date injured not reported. [North Carolina pension records indicate he was wounded at Wilmington on October 30, 1861.]

THOMAS, JOHN WEST, Private
Born in Moore County where he resided prior to enlisting in Moore County at age 23, August 15, 1861. Present or accounted for until he died in hospital at Richmond, Virginia, August 7, 1862, of "typhoid fever."

THOMAS, MARSHALL G., Private
Resided in Chatham County and enlisted in Moore County at age 25, August 15, 1861. Present or accounted for until discharged on February 15, 1862, after providing Private Bennett Lawrence as a substitute.

THOMAS, MURPHY J., Private
Resided in Chatham County and enlisted in Moore County at age 18, August 15, 1861. Present or accounted for through April, 1864. Company records indicate he was captured at or near Spotsylvania Court House, Virginia, May 18, 1864; however, records of the Federal Provost Marshal do not substantiate that report. No further records.

THOMAS, WILLIAM A., Private
Born in Chatham County where he resided prior to enlisting in Moore County at age 21, August 15, 1861. Present or accounted for until he died "at home" on or about November 26, 1861, of "typhoid fever" and/or "pneumonia."

UNDERWOOD, JOHN A., Corporal
Resided in Moore County where he enlisted at age 18, August 15, 1861. Mustered in as Private. Promoted to Corporal in December, 1863. Present or accounted for until wounded in the right ankle at Spotsylvania Court House, Virginia, May 12, 1864. Reported absent wounded through August, 1864. Returned to duty on an unspecified date. Surrendered at Appomattox Court House, Virginia, April 9, 1865. [Roll of Honor indicates he was wounded at Warrenton, Virginia, on an unspecified date.]

UTLEY, JOHN WILLIAM, Private
Born in Chatham County where he resided as a farmer prior to enlisting at Camp Wyatt at age 19, January 26, 1862. Present or accounted for until captured at Gettysburg, Pennsylvania, July 1-3, 1863, after he "skulked off somewhere." Confined at Fort Delaware, Delaware, on or about July 7, 1863. Transferred to Point Lookout, Maryland, October 15-18, 1863. Released at Point Lookout on February 9, 1864, after taking the Oath of Allegiance and joining the U.S. Army. Assigned to Company D, 1st Regiment U.S. Volunteer Infantry.

WALKER, TANDY, Private
Resided in Moore County where he enlisted at age 24, August 15, 1861. Present or accounted for through August, 1864. Captured at Raleigh on an unspecified date and was paroled at Raleigh on April 20, 1865.

WATKINS, B., Private
Enlisted at Camp Holmes on August 1, 1864, for the war. Paroled at Burkeville Junction, Virginia, April 14-17, 1865.

WATSON, ANDREW J., Private
Born in Chatham County and resided in Moore County where he enlisted at age 37, August 15, 1861. Present or accounted for until he died "at home" on or about February 11, 1863, of disease.

WICKER, ALVIS, Private
Resided in Moore County and enlisted at Richmond, Virginia, at age 17, July 12, 1862, for the war as a substitute. Died at Staunton, Virginia, December 17, 1862, of disease.

WICKER, CHARLES B., Private
Resided in Moore County where he enlisted at age 47, October 9, 1862, for the war as a substitute. Present or accounted for until captured at High Bridge, Virginia, April 6, 1865. Confined at Point Lookout, Maryland, April 14, 1865. Released on or about July 19, 1865, after taking the Oath of Allegiance.

WICKER, JOHN J., Private
Born in Moore County where he resided prior to enlisting in Moore County at age 26, August 15, 1861. Present or accounted for until he died at Richmond, Virginia, on or about July 19, 1862, of "fever."

WICKER, K. W., Private
Born in Moore County where he resided prior to enlisting at age 26, April 24, 1862, for the war. Present or accounted for until wounded at Malvern Hill, Virginia, July 1, 1862. Hospitalized at Richmond, Virginia, where he died on July 11, 1862, of wounds.

WICKER, LOUIS M., Private
Resided in Moore County where he enlisted at age 30, August 15, 1861. Mustered in as Sergeant. Reduced to ranks in May-December, 1862. Present or accounted for until killed at Gettysburg, Pennsylvania, July 1, 1863.

WICKER, O. R., Private
Born in Moore County where he resided prior to enlisting in Moore County at age 21, August 15, 1861. Present or accounted for until he died "at home" on May 5 or May 30, 1863, of disease.

WICKER, THOMAS, Private
Resided in Moore County where he enlisted at age 37, August 15, 1861. Present or accounted for until wounded at Sharpsburg, Maryland, September 17, 1862. Returned to duty in January-June, 1863. Wounded in the arm and/or wrist at Gettysburg, Pennsylvania, July 1-3, 1863. Reported absent wounded until February 15, 1865, when he was retired to the Invalid Corps.

WICKER, WILLIAM FORDHAM, Private
Resided in Moore County and was by occupation a farmer prior to enlisting in Moore County at age 20, April 25, 1862, for the war. Present or accounted for until wounded in the right forearm at Sharpsburg, Maryland, September 17, 1862. Reported absent wounded until December 25, 1863, when he was discharged by reason of disability.

WICKER, WILLIAM M., Private
Born in Moore County and resided in Chatham County prior to enlisting in Moore County at age 25, August 15, 1861. Present or accounted for until killed at Gaines' Mill, Virginia, June 27, 1862.

WOMACK, JAMES RUFUS, Private
Resided in Chatham County and enlisted in Moore County at age 19, August 15, 1861. Present or accounted for until captured at Kelly's Ford, Virginia, November 7, 1863. Confined at Point Lookout, Maryland, November 11, 1863. Died at Point Lookout on May 3, 1865, of "chronic diarrhoea."

YANCY, THOMAS A., Private
Resided in Cumberland County and enlisted in Moore County at age 17, August 15, 1861. Present or

accounted for until wounded at Malvern Hill, Virginia, July 1, 1862. Returned to duty prior to December 14, 1862. Present or accounted for until captured at Kelly's Ford, Virginia, November 7, 1863. Confined at Point Lookout, Maryland, November 11, 1863. Paroled at Point Lookout on or about February 24, 1865, and transferred to Aiken's Landing, James River, Virginia, where he was received February 25-March 3, 1865, for exchange. Captured in hospital at Richmond, Virginia, April 3, 1865. Paroled at Richmond on April 22, 1865.

YARBOROUGH, W. T., Private
Resided in Moore County where he enlisted at age 22, August 15, 1861. Present or accounted for until discharged on or about March 1, 1862, after providing Private Joseph Buchanan as a substitute.

COMPANY I

This company was raised in Nash County and enlisted there on September 10, 1861. It was then assigned to the 30th Regiment N.C. Troops and designated Company I. After joining the regiment the company functioned as a part of the regiment, and its history for the war period is reported as a part of the regimental history.

The information contained in the following roster of the company was compiled principally from a company muster-in and descriptive roll dated October 8, 1861, and from company muster rolls for September 10, 1861-April, 1862; August 31-December 31, 1862; May-June, 1863; and November, 1863-August, 1864. No company muster rolls were found for May-August 30, 1862; January-April, 1863; July-October, 1863; or for the period after August, 1864. Valuable information was obtained from primary records such as the Roll of Honor, discharge certificates, medical records, prisoner of war records, and pension applications. Secondary sources such as postwar rosters and histories, cemetery records, and records of the United Daughters of the Confederacy also provided useful information.

OFFICERS

CAPTAINS

ARRINGTON, WILLIAM T.
Resided in Nash County or in Georgia and enlisted in Nash County at age 40. Appointed Captain on September 10, 1861. Present or accounted for until killed at Malvern Hill, Virginia, July 1, 1862.

HARRIS, JAMES J.
Resided in Nash or Jones County and enlisted in Nash County at age 27. Elected 2nd Lieutenant on September 10, 1861. Elected 1st Lieutenant on April 1, 1862, and was promoted to Captain on July 1, 1862. Present or accounted for until killed at Spotsylvania Court House, Virginia, May 12, 1864.

LIEUTENANTS

ARRINGTON, KEARNEY W., 1st Lieutenant
Previously served as Sergeant in Company E, 19th Regiment N.C. Troops (2nd Regiment N.C. Cavalry). Transferred to this company upon appointment as 2nd Lieutenant to rank from February 22, 1863. Promoted to 1st Lieutenant on or about December 14, 1863. Present or accounted for until wounded in the left leg and captured at Spotsylvania Court House, Virginia, May

12, 1864. Hospitalized at Washington, D.C., May 27, 1864. Transferred to Old Capitol Prison, Washington, August 11, 1864. Transferred to Fort Delaware, Delaware, August 27, 1864. Transferred to Point Lookout, Maryland, where he arrived on October 8, 1864. Transferred to Washington on November 2, 1864. Transferred to Fort Delaware on December 16, 1864. Paroled at Fort Delaware and transferred to City Point, Virginia, February 27, 1865, for exchange.

BUNN, ELIAS, 1st Lieutenant
Resided in Edgecombe County and enlisted in Nash County at age 19. Elected 1st Lieutenant on September 10, 1861. Present or accounted for until he was defeated for reelection when the regiment was reorganized on April 1, 1862. Later served as Adjutant on the staff of General Lawrence O'B. Branch.

PERRY, SIDNEY R., 3rd Lieutenant
Resided in Nash County where he enlisted at age 18, September 10, 1861. Mustered in as Private. Promoted to 1st Sergeant on April 1, 1862. Elected 3rd Lieutenant on March 17, 1863. Present or accounted for until wounded in the left foot and left thigh at Chancellorsville, Virginia, May 3, 1863. Returned to duty subsequent to June 30, 1863. Wounded in the ankle at Snicker's Gap, Virginia, July 18, 1864. Reported absent wounded through August, 1864. Retired from service on February 17, 1865, by reason of disability from wounds.

TISDALE, THOMAS B., Jr., 3rd Lieutenant
Resided in Nash County where he enlisted at age 23, September 10, 1861. Mustered in as Private. Promoted to Sergeant prior to November 1, 1861. Elected 3rd Lieutenant on March 27, 1862. Resigned on February 23, 1863, by reason of "the feeble condition of my health." Discharged on February 26, 1863, by reason of "phthisis."

WILLIFORD, BURTON B., 1st Lieutenant
Resided in Nash County where he enlisted at age 18, September 10, 1861. Mustered in as Private. Promoted to Sergeant prior to November 1, 1861. Elected 2nd Lieutenant on March 27, 1862, and was promoted to 1st Lieutenant on July 2, 1862. Present or accounted for until wounded in the groin and right thigh at Chancellorsville, Virginia, May 3, 1863. Resigned on December 11, 1863, by reason of "lameness." Resignation accepted on December 14, 1863.

WOODARD, COLEMAN W. W., 3rd Lieutenant
Resided in Nash County where he enlisted at age 25. Elected 3rd Lieutenant on or about September 10, 1861. Present or accounted for until he resigned on April 1, 1862. Reason he resigned not reported.

NONCOMMISSIONED OFFICERS AND PRIVATES

ABERNATHY, EDWARD, ——
Enlisted in Nash County at age 19, September 10, 1861. Rejected for service. Reason he was rejected not reported.

ADDISON, QUINCY E., Private
Resided in Wake County where he enlisted at age 18, September 1, 1863, for the war. Present or accounted for until discharged on May 3, 1864. Reason discharged not

reported.

ANDERSON, THOMAS J., Private
Resided in Edgecombe County and enlisted in Wake County at age 22, July 8, 1863, for the war. Present or accounted for until captured at High Bridge, Virginia, April 6, 1865. Confined at Point Lookout, Maryland, April 14, 1865. Released on June 28, 1865. [May have served previously in Company C, 8th Regiment N.C. State Troops.]

ARMSTRONG, GRAY, Private
Resided in Nash County and enlisted in Wake County at age 25, September 1, 1863, for the war. Present or accounted for until captured at Petersburg, Virginia, April 3, 1865. Confined at Hart's Island, New York Harbor, April 7, 1865. Released on June 17, 1865, after taking the Oath of Allegiance.

ARRINGTON, PETER W., Corporal
Previously served as Corporal in Company G, 6th Regiment Virginia Infantry. Transferred to this company on May 28, 1863. Promoted to Sergeant Major prior to April 1, 1864, and transferred to the Field and Staff of this regiment.

BARKLEY, JAMES H., Corporal
Resided in Nash County where he enlisted at age 21, September 10, 1861. Mustered in as Corporal. Reduced to ranks on April 1, 1862. Promoted to Corporal on June 1, 1863. Present or accounted for until captured at Kelly's Ford, Virginia, November 7, 1863. Confined at Point Lookout, Maryland, November 11, 1863. Paroled at Point Lookout on or about February 24, 1865, and transferred to Aiken's Landing, James River, Virginia, where he was received on February 25-March 3, 1865, for exchange.

BARNES, BRYANT B., Private
Resided in Nash County where he enlisted at age 22, September 10, 1861. Died in Wilson County on or about October 28, 1861, of "typhoid fever" and/or "pneumonia."

BASS, JOHN S., Private
Born in Madison County* where he resided prior to enlisting in Nash County at age 18, September 10, 1861. Present or accounted for until wounded at Malvern Hill, Virginia, July 1, 1862. Returned to duty prior to January 1, 1863. Present or accounted for until wounded at Chancellorsville, Virginia, May 3, 1863. Died on May 5, 1863, of wounds. Place of death not reported.

BASS, RICHARD H., Private
Resided in Nash County where he enlisted at age 18, September 10, 1861. Present or accounted for until wounded mortally at Gaines' Mill, Virginia, June 27, 1862. Place and date of death not reported.

BASS, WILLIAM, Private
Born in Nash County where he resided prior to enlisting at age 52, December 4, 1862, for the war as a substitute. Died in hospital at Richmond, Virginia, March 12-18, 1863, of "pneumonia." [Company records indicate that Private Bass's "five little children" were left in the care of the soldier for whom Bass enlisted as a substitute.]

BATCHELOR, ANDREW J., Private
Resided in Nash County and enlisted at Camp Wyatt at age 19, January 28, 1862. Present or accounted for until wounded at Chancellorsville, Virginia, May 3, 1863. Reported present for duty in November-December, 1863. Present or accounted for until paroled at

Burkeville Junction, Virginia, April 14-17, 1865. He was "noted for coolness in battle."

BATCHELOR, ELKANAH, Private
Resided in Nash County and enlisted in Nash County or at Camp Wyatt at age 28, September 10, 1861. Present or accounted for until paroled at Greensboro on May 1-2, 1865.

BATCHELOR, HENRY H., Private
Resided in Nash County and was by occupation a farmer prior to enlisting in Nash County at age 22, March 4, 1862. Present or accounted for until wounded at Malvern Hill, Virginia, July 1, 1862. Returned to duty prior to January 1, 1863. Present or accounted for until wounded in the right arm at Chancellorsville, Virginia, May 3, 1863. Right arm amputated. Reported absent wounded until January 17, 1865, when he was retired to the Invalid Corps.

BATCHELOR, JOHN W., Private
Resided in Nash County where he enlisted at age 22, March 4, 1862. Present or accounted for until November-December, 1862, when he was reported absent without leave. Returned to duty in November-December, 1863. Present or accounted for through June 7, 1864. No further records.

BATCHELOR, NEVERSON A., Private
Resided in Nash County where he enlisted at age 23, September 10, 1861. Present or accounted for until he was reported absent without leave on or about November 10, 1862. Returned to duty subsequent to December 31, 1862. Captured at Kelly's Ford, Virginia, November 7, 1863. Confined at Point Lookout, Maryland, November 11, 1863. Died in the smallpox hospital at Point Lookout on February 7-9, 1864.

BATCHELOR, REDMUN W., Private
Resided in Nash County where he enlisted at age 18, May 1, 1862, for the war. Reported absent without leave in September-December, 1862. Returned to duty prior to May 1-4, 1863, when he was wounded at Chancellorsville, Virginia. Returned to duty prior to July 1, 1863. Present or accounted for until paroled at Burkeville Junction, Virginia, April 14-17, 1865.

BATCHELOR, RUFFIN L., Private
Previously served in Company A, 47th Regiment N.C. Troops. Transferred to this company on January 22, 1864. Wounded at or near Snicker's Gap, Virginia, July 18, 1864. Reported absent wounded through August, 1864. Captured at Petersburg, Virginia, April 3, 1865. Confined at Hart's Island, New York Harbor, April 7, 1865. Released on June 17, 1865, after taking the Oath of Allegiance.

BATCHELOR, SAMUEL Mc., Private
Resided in Nash County where he enlisted at age 19, March 4, 1862. Present or accounted for until he died in hospital at Richmond, Virginia, on or about September 22, 1862, of "diarrhoea acuta."

BATCHELOR, THOMAS R., Private
Resided in Nash or New Hanover County and enlisted in Nash County at age 30, March 4, 1862. Present or accounted for until September-December, 1862, when he was reported absent without leave. Returned to duty on an unspecified date. Deserted to the enemy in Perry County, Pennsylvania, on or about June 28, 1863. Confined at Fort Mifflin, Pennsylvania, on or about July 2, 1863. Released on or about January 1, 1864, after

taking the Oath of Allegiance.

BATCHELOR, VAN BUREN, Sergeant
Resided in Nash County where he enlisted at age 28, September 10, 1861. Mustered in as Corporal. Promoted to Sergeant on April 1, 1862. Present or accounted for until wounded and captured at or near Sharpsburg, Maryland, on or about September 17, 1862. Paroled on or about September 20, 1862. Returned to duty in January-June, 1863. Present or accounted for until captured at Kelly's Ford, Virginia, November 7, 1863. Confined at Point Lookout, Maryland, November 11, 1863. Paroled at Point Lookout on or about February 24, 1865, and transferred to Aiken's Landing, James River, Virginia, where he was received February 25-March 3, 1865, for exchange.

BATCHELOR, WILLIAM D., Corporal
Resided in Nash County where he enlisted at age 20, September 10, 1861. Mustered in as Private. Promoted to Corporal on May 1, 1863. Present or accounted for until killed at Kelly's Ford, Virginia, November 7, 1863.

BATTLE, LAWRENCE F., Private
Resided in Nash County and enlisted at Camp Holmes at age 24, January 5, 1862. Present or accounted for until discharged on September 1, 1862, after providing a substitute. Later was appointed Drillmaster (2nd Lieutenant) and assigned the task of clearing Nash County of deserters. He was a soldier "of strict probity, unbiased by either fear or favor in the discharge of his duties."

BATTS, WILLIAM J., Private
Resided in Nash County where he enlisted at age 30, May 1, 1862, for the war. Present or accounted for until hospitalized at Charlottesville, Virginia, September 23, 1864, with a gunshot wound of the head. Place and date wounded not reported. Returned to duty on an unspecified date. Surrendered at Appomattox Court House, Virginia, April 9, 1865.

BELL, ARKIN B., Private
Resided in Nash County and enlisted in Wilson County at age 25, March 10, 1862. Present or accounted for until killed in battle in July, 1864. Place of death not reported.

BISSETT, PAYTON, Private
Resided in Nash County and enlisted in camp near Richmond, Virginia, August 5, 1862, for the war. Present or accounted for until captured at South Mountain, Maryland, September 15, 1862. Confined at Fort Delaware, Delaware. Transferred to Fort Monroe, Virginia, December 15, 1862. Paroled and transferred to City Point, Virginia, where he was received on December 18, 1862, for exchange. Present or accounted for until transferred to Company A, 47th Regiment N.C. Troops, January 22, 1864.

BONE, HARDY H., Private
Resided in Nash County where he enlisted at age 29, September 10, 1861. Present or accounted for until he died in hospital at Richmond, Virginia, November 18, 1862, of "pneumonia."

BONE, JOHN WESLEY, Private
Resided in Nash County where he enlisted at age 18, September 10, 1861. Present or accounted for until

hospitalized at Richmond, Virginia, July 2, 1862, with a gunshot wound of the hand. Place and date wounded not reported. Returned to duty prior to January 1, 1863. Present or accounted for until he surrendered at Appomattox Court House, Virginia, April 9, 1865.

BONE, JOSEPH H., Private
Born in Nash County where he enlisted on March 4, 1862. Present or accounted for until he died at Lynchburg, Virginia, on or about January 10, 1863, of "epilepsy."

BORROWS, JAMES, Private
Enlisted on or about July 30, 186[3], for the war. Deserted on August 7, 1863.

BRANTLEY, J. REDMOND, Private
Resided in Nash County where he enlisted at age 23, September 10, 1861. Present or accounted for until wounded at Malvern Hill, Virginia, July 1, 1862. Returned to duty on an unspecified date. Wounded in the abdomen and/or left hip and captured at Kelly's Ford, Virginia, November 7, 1863. Hospitalized at Washington, D.C. Confined at Old Capitol Prison, Washington, December 5, 1864. Transferred to Elmira, New York, December 16, 1864. Paroled at Elmira on February 9, 1865, and transferred to Boulware's Wharf, James River, Virginia, where he was received February 20-21, 1865, for exchange.

BRYAN, JAMES H., Private
Resided in Nash County where he enlisted at age 18, September 10, 1861. Mustered in as Private. Promoted to Corporal on April 1, 1862. Present or accounted for until wounded at Malvern Hill, Virginia, July 1, 1862. Returned to duty prior to January 1, 1863. Promoted to Sergeant on May 1, 1863. Present or accounted for until wounded in the neck and/or scalp and captured at Kelly's Ford, Virginia, November 7, 1863. Confined at various Federal hospitals until confined at Old Capitol Prison, Washington, D.C., December 15, 1863. Transferred to Point Lookout, Maryland, February 3, 1864. Paroled at Point Lookout on October 11, 1864, and transferred to Cox's Wharf, James River, Virginia, where he was received on October 15, 1864, for exchange. Returned to duty on an unspecified date. Reduced to ranks subsequent to October 20, 1864. Surrendered at Appomattox Court House, Virginia, April 9, 1865.

BUNN, BENJAMIN HICKMAN, Private
Born in Nash County where he resided prior to enlisting at age 17, September 10, 1861. Mustered in as Private. Promoted to 1st Sergeant prior to November 1, 1861. Reduced to ranks on April 1, 1862. Present or accounted for until appointed 3rd Lieutenant and transferred to Company A, 47th Regiment N.C. Troops, on or about September 24, 1862. [He was the brother of Adjutant Elias Bunn of the 12th Regiment N.C. Troops (2nd Regiment N.C. Volunteers) and of Captain William H. Bunn of 1st Company H, 12th Regiment N.C. Troops (2nd Regiment N.C. Volunteers).]

BUNN, JAMES D. A., Private
Resided in Nash County where he enlisted at age 18, March 4, 1862. Present or accounted for until he surrendered at Appomattox Court House, Virginia, April 9, 1865.

CAPPS, WILLIAM HENRY, Private

Resided in Nash County where he enlisted at age 28, September 10, 1861. Present or accounted for until captured at or near Farmville, Virginia, April 6, 1865. Confined at Newport News, Virginia, April 14, 1865. Released on June 27, 1865, after taking the Oath of Allegiance.

COBB, JEFFERSON, Sergeant

Resided in Nash County and enlisted at Camp Wyatt at age 20, December 19, 1861. Mustered in as Private. Promoted to Corporal on April 1, 1862. Present or accounted for until captured at Frederick, Maryland, September 12, 1862. Confined at Fort Delaware, Delaware. Paroled and transferred to Aiken's Landing, James River, Virginia, October 2, 1862, for exchange. Declared exchanged at Aiken's Landing on November 10, 1862. Reported absent without leave on December 31, 1862. Returned to duty prior to June 1, 1863, when he was promoted to Sergeant. Present or accounted for until he surrendered at Appomattox Court House, Virginia, April 9, 1865.

COLEY, JAMES J., Private

Born in Nash County where he resided as a farmer prior to enlisting in Nash County at age 25, September 10, 1861. Present or accounted for until discharged on April 18, 1862. Reason discharged not reported.

COOK, RANSOM L., Private

Born in Nash County where he resided as a farmer prior to enlisting in Edgecombe County at age 21, September 10, 1861. Present or accounted for until discharged on December 14, 1861, by reason of "general anemic condition."

CRICKMAN, JOSIAH GORDON, Private

Born in Franklin County and resided in Nash County where he enlisted at age 17, September 10, 1861. Present or accounted for until wounded at Chancellorsville, Virginia, May 3, 1863. Returned to duty prior to January 1, 1864. Captured at Spotsylvania Court House, Virginia, May 12-19, 1864. Confined at Point Lookout, Maryland. Transferred to Elmira, New York, July 3, 1864. Released at Elmira on June 27, 1865, after taking the Oath of Allegiance.

CROWELL, JONAS W., 1st Sergeant

Previously served as Private in Company D, 5th Regiment Alabama Infantry. Transferred to this company on April 5, 1863. Mustered in as Private. Promoted to 1st Sergeant on May 1, 1863. Present or accounted for until hospitalized at Richmond, Virginia, June 3, 1864, with a gunshot wound of the left thigh. Place and date wounded not reported. Returned to duty subsequent to October 5, 1864. Surrendered at Appomattox Court House, Virginia, April 9, 1865.

CRUMP, SAMUEL W., Private

Resided in Nash County where he enlisted at age 30, September 10, 1861. Present or accounted for until he died at Camp Wyatt on February 5-6, 1862, of "typhoid pneumonia."

CRUMPLER, BENNETT, Private

Resided in Nash County where he enlisted at age 35, May 1, 1862, for the war. Reported absent without leave on December 31, 1862. Apprehended on or about October 29, 1863. Deserted on December 22, 1863. Court-martialed, apparently in absentia, on or about

January 8, 1864.

CULPEPPER, JETHRO D., Private

Previously served in 2nd Company H, 32nd Regiment N.C. Troops. Transferred to this company on February 16, 1864. No further records.

CULPEPPER, JOHN, Private

Resided in Nash County where he enlisted at age 25, May 1, 1862, for the war. Present or accounted for until wounded at Chancellorsville, Virginia, May 3, 1863. Returned to duty prior to July 1, 1863. Present or accounted for until captured at Cedar Creek, Virginia, October 19, 1864. Confined at Point Lookout, Maryland, October 25, 1864. Paroled at Point Lookout on or about March 17, 1865, and transferred to Boulware's Wharf, James River, Virginia, where he was received on March 19, 1865, for exchange. Returned to duty on an unspecified date. Surrendered at Appomattox Court House, Virginia, April 9, 1865.

CULPEPPER, WILLIAM J., Corporal

Previously served as Corporal in 1st Company H, 12th Regiment N.C. Troops (2nd Regiment N.C. Volunteers). Transferred to this company on October 1, 1863. Company records indicate he was captured at Kelly's Ford, Virginia, November 7, 1863; however, records of the Federal Provost Marshal do not substantiate that report. No further records.

DAVIS, BILL, ——

North Carolina pension records indicate that he served in this company.

DAVIS, MILES, Private

Resided in Nash County where he enlisted at age 19, May 1, 1862, for the war. Reported absent without leave during September-December, 1862. Returned to duty prior to July 1, 1863. Company records indicate he was captured at Kelly's Ford, Virginia, November 7, 1863; however, records of the Federal Provost Marshal do not substantiate that report. No further records.

DEANS, WILLIAM, Private

Resided in Nash County and enlisted in Wake County at age 44, September 1, 1863, for the war. Captured at Kelly's Ford, Virginia, November 7, 1863. Confined at Point Lookout, Maryland, November 11, 1863. Exchanged on April 27, 1864. Reported absent without leave through August, 1864.

DENSON, ALEXANDER, Private

Resided in Nash County where he enlisted at age 19, September 10, 1861. Present or accounted for until captured at Kelly's Ford, Virginia, November 7, 1863. Confined at Point Lookout, Maryland, November 11, 1863. Paroled at Point Lookout on or about February 24, 1865, and transferred to Aiken's Landing, James River, Virginia, where he was received on February 25-March 3, 1865, for exchange.

DENSON, BENJAMIN E., Private

Resided in Nash County where he enlisted at age 22, September 10, 1861. Present or accounted for until discharged on February 14 or March 1, 1862. Reason discharged not reported.

DORTRIDGE, RICHARD J., Private

Resided in Nash County where he enlisted at age 18,

March 2, 1863, for the war. Present or accounted for until killed at or near Spotsylvania Court House, Virginia, May 12, 1864.

DOZIER, JAMES W., Sergeant
Born in Nash County where he resided prior to enlisting in Nash County at age 25, September 10, 1861. Mustered in as Private. Promoted to Corporal prior to November 1, 1861. Promoted to Sergeant on April 1, 1862. Present or accounted for until hospitalized at Richmond, Virginia, April 10, 1863, with "typhoid pneumonia." Died in hospital at Richmond on April 18, 1863.

EASON, HAYWOOD, Private
Born in Nash County where he enlisted on May 1, 1862, for the war. Present or accounted for until he died "in camp" on May 18, 1863, of disease.

EASON, WILLIAM, Private
Resided in Nash County where he enlisted at age 18, May 1, 1862, for the war. Present or accounted for through August, 1864.

EDWARDS, EDWIN, Private
Resided in Nash County and enlisted in Wake County at age 43, September 20, 1863, for the war. Present or accounted for through August, 1864.

EDWARDS, JAMES, Private
Resided in Nash County where he enlisted at age 20, September 10, 1861. Present or accounted for through October, 1863. Company records indicate he was captured at Kelly's Ford, Virginia, November 7, 1863; however, records of the Federal Provost Marshal do not substantiate that report.

EDWARDS, ROBERT C., Private
Resided in Nash County where he enlisted at age 22, September 10, 1861. Present or accounted for until discharged on or about February 14, 1862. Reason discharged not reported. [May have served later in 2nd Company H, 32nd Regiment N.C. Troops.]

EDWARDS, SOLOMON, Private
Resided in Nash County where he enlisted at age 18, November 10, 1863, for the war. Present or accounted for through January 8, 1865.

EDWARDS, WILLIE, Private
Enlisted in Nash County on March 18, 1864, for the war. Present or accounted for until paroled at Farmville, Virginia, April 11-21, 1865.

EVANS, WILLIAM M., Corporal
Resided in Wilson County where he enlisted at age 23, May 10, 1862, for the war. Mustered in as Private. Promoted to Corporal subsequent to August 31, 1864. Surrendered at Appomattox Court House, Virginia, April 9, 1865.

FOX, REDDEN P., Private
Resided in Nash County where he enlisted at age 16, September 10, 1861. Present or accounted for until he surrendered at Appomattox Court House, Virginia, April 9, 1865.

FRYER, LAWRENCE D., Private
Resided in Nash County where he enlisted at age 19,

September 10, 1861. Present or accounted for through April, 1862. Reported absent without leave in September-December, 1862. Returned to duty prior to January 1, 1864. Hospitalized at Richmond, Virginia, June 3, 1864, with a gunshot wound of the left leg. Place and date wounded not reported. Reported absent in hospital through August, 1864.

GAY, GEORGE W., Corporal
Resided in Nash County where he enlisted at age 21, March 4, 1862. Mustered in as Private. Promoted to Corporal on May 1, 1863. Present or accounted for until wounded at Chancellorsville, Virginia, May 1-4, 1863. Returned to duty prior to January 1, 1864. Present or accounted for until he surrendered at Appomattox Court House, Virginia, April 9, 1865.

GRIFFIN, ARCHIBALD CALHOUN, Private
Resided in Nash County where he enlisted at age 19, March 4, 1862. Present or accounted for until captured at Kelly's Ford, Virginia, November 7, 1863. Confined at Point Lookout, Maryland, November 11, 1863. Paroled at Point Lookout on February 18, 1865, and transferred to Boulware's Wharf, James River, Virginia, where he was received February 20-21, 1865, for exchange.

GRIFFIN, JAMES D., Private
Resided in Nash County where he enlisted at age 22, September 10, 1861. Present or accounted for until wounded at Sharpsburg, Maryland, September 17, 1862. Reported absent wounded through December, 1862. Company records do not indicate whether he rejoined the company. Reported on duty as a hospital nurse at Richmond, Virginia, from November-December, 1863, through August, 1864. Captured in hospital at Richmond on April 3, 1865. Paroled at Richmond on April 21, 1865.

GRIFFIN, JESSE R., Private
Resided in Nash County where he enlisted at age 24, September 10, 1861. Mustered in as Private. Promoted to Sergeant on April 1, 1862. Reduced to ranks in January-June, 1863. Present or accounted for until he deserted on June 4, 1863. Returned to duty prior to November 7, 1863, when he was captured at Kelly's Ford, Virginia. Confined at Point Lookout, Maryland, November 11, 1863. Paroled at Point Lookout on February 18, 1865, and transferred to Boulware's Wharf, James River, Virginia, where he was received on February 20-21, 1865, for exchange.

GRIFFIN, JOHN B., Private
Born in Nash County where he resided prior to enlisting in "camp" at age 33, March 1, 1863, for the war. Killed at Chancellorsville, Virginia, May 3, 1863.

GRIFFIN, MARK S., Private
Resided in Nash County and enlisted in "camp" at age 18, February 15, 1864, for the war. Present or accounted for until he surrendered at Appomattox Court House, Virginia, April 9, 1865.

GRIFFIN, WILLIAM B., Private
Resided in Nash County and enlisted in "camp" at age 27, March 1, 1863, for the war. Present or accounted for until captured at or near Spotsylvania Court House, Virginia, on or about May 8, 1864. Confined at Point Lookout, Maryland, May 17, 1864. Paroled on or about March 15, 1865, and transferred to Boulware's Wharf,

James River, Virginia, where he was received on March 18, 1865, for exchange.

GRIMMER, ELIAS G., Private
Resided in Edgecombe County and enlisted in Wake County at age 38, July 8, 1863, for the war. Present or accounted for until captured at or near Farmville, Virginia, April 6, 1865. Confined at Newport News, Virginia, April 14, 1865. Released on June 27, 1865, after taking the Oath of Allegiance.

GRIMMER, LAWRENCE, ———
North Carolina pension records indicate that he served in this company.

GUPTON, THOMAS, Private
Resided in Franklin County and enlisted in Nash County at age 21, September 10, 1861. Present or accounted for through April, 1862. Reported absent without leave in September-December, 1862. Reported absent sick in May-June, 1863. Returned to duty subsequent to December 31, 1863. Killed at or near Snicker's Gap, Virginia, July 18, 1864.

HARPER, JOHN H., Private
Born in Nash County where he resided prior to enlisting in Nash County at age 25, March 4, 1862. Present or accounted for until he died in hospital at Richmond, Virginia, February 9, 1863, of "variola conf[luen]t."

HARRIS, ELBERT H., Private
Resided in Warren County and enlisted in Nash County at age 40, September 10, 1861. Present or accounted for until June 25, 1862, when he was dropped from the rolls of the company. Reason he was dropped not reported.

HEDGEPETH, ELIAS G., Private
Resided in Nash County where he enlisted at age 26, September 10, 1861. Present or accounted for until he died at Orange Court House, Virginia, March 20 or March 30, 1864, of disease.

HUNEYCUTT, A. E., ———
North Carolina pension records indicate that he served in this company.

HUNT, JAMES A. F., Private
Born in Nash County where he resided as a farmer prior to enlisting in Nash County at age 28, September 10, 1861. Present or accounted for until captured at Kelly's Ford, Virginia, November 7, 1863. Confined at Point Lookout, Maryland, November 11, 1863. Released on January 30, 1864, after joining the U.S. Army. Assigned to Company C, 1st Regiment U.S. Volunteer Infantry.

JOHNSON, CHRISTOPHER B., Private
Resided in Nash County and enlisted in Wake County at age 36, September 1, 1863, for the war. Present or accounted for until paroled at Burkeville, Virginia, April 14-17, 1865.

JOHNSON, HENRY, Private
Resided in Wake County where he enlisted at age 40, September 1, 1863, for the war. Captured at Kelly's Ford, Virginia, November 7, 1863. Confined at Point Lookout, Maryland, November 11, 1863. Paroled at Point Lookout on or about March 15, 1865, and transferred to Boulware's Wharf, James River, Virginia, where he was received on March 18, 1865, for exchange.

JONES, CALVIN F., Private
Resided in Nash County where he enlisted at age 49, March 15, 1862. Present or accounted for through April, 1862. Reported absent without leave in September-December, 1862. Listed as a deserter on June 4, 1863. Returned to duty prior to January 1, 1864. Present or accounted for through August, 1864. [North Carolina pension records indicate he was wounded at Spotsylvania Court House, Virginia, May 12, 1864.]

JONES, JOHN R., Private
Resided in Nash County where he enlisted at age 16, September 10, 1861. Present or accounted for through April, 1862. Reported absent without leave in September-December, 1862. Returned to duty prior to July 1-5, 1863, when he was wounded in the foot and captured at Gettysburg, Pennsylvania. Confined at Fort Delaware, Delaware, on or about July 7, 1863. Transferred to Point Lookout, Maryland, October 15-18, 1863. Paroled at Point Lookout on or about February 18, 1865, and transferred to Boulware's Wharf, James River, Virginia, where he was received on February 20-21, 1865, for exchange.

JOYNER, ALSEY M., Private
Resided in Nash County where he enlisted at age 26, September 10, 1861. Present or accounted for until wounded at Fredericksburg, Virginia, December 13, 1862. Returned to duty prior to January 1, 1863. Present or accounted for until killed at or near Spotsylvania Court House, Virginia, May 12, 1864.

JOYNER, ASHLEY G., Private
Resided in Nash County where he enlisted at age 18, September 10, 1861. Present or accounted for until hospitalized at Richmond, Virginia, November 28, 1862, with "rheum[atism] ac[ute] & congestion of lungs." Died in hospital at Richmond on December 13, 1862.

JOYNER, CALVIN M., Private
Resided in Nash County where he enlisted at age 30, May 1, 1862, for the war. Present or accounted for until he died in hospital at Richmond, Virginia, on or about January 20, 1862, of "variola conf[luen]t."

JOYNER, GEORGE WASHINGTON, Private
Resided in Nash County and enlisted in "camp" at age 18, March 10, 1863, for the war. Present or accounted for until wounded at Chancellorsville, Virginia, May 3, 1863. Returned to duty on an unspecified date. Captured at or near Gettysburg, Pennsylvania, July 3-5, 1863, after he was "left to nurse wounded." Confined at Fort Delaware, Delaware, on or about July 7, 1863. Transferred to Point Lookout, Maryland, on an unspecified date. Paroled at Point Lookout and transferred to Venus Point, Savannah River, Georgia, where he was received on November 15, 1864, for exchange.

JOYNER, IRA E., Private
Resided in Nash County where he enlisted at age 28, May 1, 1862, for the war. Reported absent without leave in September-December, 1862. Returned to duty prior to July 3, 1863, when he was captured at Gettysburg, Pennsylvania. Confined at Fort Delaware, Delaware. Transferred to Point Lookout, Maryland, where he

arrived on October 15, 1863. Exchanged on November 1, 1864.

JOYNER, JAMES A., Private
Resided in Nash County where he enlisted at age 24, September 10, 1861. Present or accounted for until he deserted in November, 1862.

JOYNER, JONAS A., Private
Resided in Nash County where he enlisted at age 21, September 10, 1861. Present or accounted for until captured at Kelly's Ford, Virginia, November 7, 1863. Confined at Point Lookout, Maryland, November 11, 1863. Paroled at Point Lookout on or about February 24, 1865, and transferred to Aiken's Landing, James River, Virginia, where he was received on February 25-March 3, 1865, for exchange.

JOYNER, LITTLE BERRY, Private
Resided in Nash County where he enlisted at age 25, May 1, 1862, for the war. Present or accounted for until he died in hospital at Richmond, Virginia, August 10, 1862, of "febris typhoides."

JOYNER, NATHAN T., Private
Born in Nash County where he resided as a farmer prior to enlisting in Nash County at age 24, September 10, 1861. Present or accounted for until discharged on April 25, 1862, by reason of "mental and physical debility."

JOYNER, NELSON V., Private
Born in Nash County where he resided as a farmer prior to enlisting in Nash County at age 20, September 10, 1861. Present or accounted for until September-December, 1862, when he was reported absent without leave. Returned to duty prior to July 3, 1863, when he was wounded in the right wrist at Gettysburg, Pennsylvania. Reported absent wounded, absent without leave, or absent on detail through February 13, 1865.

JOYNER, WILLIAM B., Private
Resided in Nash County where he enlisted at age 38, September 10, 1861. Present or accounted for until he surrendered at Appomattox Court House, Virginia, April 9, 1865.

LAMM, JACOB, Private
Enlisted in Nash County at age 29, September 10, 1861. No further records.

LANGLEY, SINGLETON, Private
Resided in Nash County where he enlisted at age 40, September 10, 1861. Present or accounted for until wounded in the hip at Malvern Hill, Virginia, July 1, 1862. Hospitalized at Richmond, Virginia, where he died on July 7, 1862, of wounds.

LEWIS, ARNOLD L., Private
Resided in Nash County where he enlisted at age 16, March 15, 1862. Present or accounted for until wounded at Malvern Hill, Virginia, July 1, 1862. Returned to duty subsequent to December 31, 1862. Present or accounted for until captured at Kelly's Ford, Virginia, November 7, 1863. Confined at Point Lookout, Maryland, November 11, 1863. Paroled at Point Lookout on or about February 24, 1865, and transferred to Aiken's Landing, James River, Virginia, where he was received February 25-March 3, 1865, for

exchange. Returned to duty on an unspecified date. Surrendered at Appomattox Court House, Virginia, April 9, 1865.

LEWIS, EDWARD W., Private
Resided in Nash County where he enlisted at age 18, September 10, 1861. Present or accounted for until killed at Sharpsburg, Maryland, September 17, 1862.

LEWIS, JOHN A., Private
Resided in Nash County and enlisted in Wake County at age 35, February 23, 1864, for the war. Present or accounted for until hospitalized at Charlottesville, Virginia, June 16, 1864, with "diarrhoea." Died in hospital at Charlottesville on July 28, 1864.

LINDSEY, NEVERSON A., Private
Resided in Nash County where he enlisted at age 17, September 10, 1861. Present or accounted for until discharged on or about February 14, 1862. Reason discharged not reported. [May have served later in Company D, 47th Regiment N.C. Troops.]

LINDSEY, RICHARD, Private
Resided in Nash County where he enlisted at age 30, September 10, 1861. Present or accounted for through April, 1862. Reported absent without leave in September-December, 1862. Returned to duty on an unspecified date. Captured at or near Kelly's Ford, Virginia, on or about November 8, 1863. Confined at Old Capitol Prison, Washington, D.C., November 14, 1863. Died in hospital at Washington on January 16, 1864, of "variola conf[luent]."

LINDSEY, WILLIAM A., Private
Born in Nash County where he resided prior to enlisting at age 20, March 15, 1863, for the war. Present or accounted for until he died at Hamilton's Crossing, Virginia, March 22 or April 10, 1863, of "brain fever." [May have served previously in Company A, 47th Regiment N.C. Troops.]

MANNING, JAMES D., ——
North Carolina pension records indicate that he served in this company.

MANNING, JEREMIAH D., Private
Resided in Nash County where he enlisted at age 20, May 1, 1862, for the war. Present or accounted for until he surrendered at Appomattox Court House, Virginia, April 9, 1865.

MANNING, JOHN E., Musician
Resided in Nash County where he enlisted at age 23, September 10, 1861. Mustered in as Private. Appointed Musician on November 1, 1861. Present or accounted for until he died in hospital at Richmond, Virginia, August 20 or August 31, 1862. Cause of death not reported.

MANNING, MOSES V. B., Private
Resided in Nash County where he enlisted at age 27, May 1, 1862, for the war. Present or accounted for until wounded at Sharpsburg, Maryland, September 17, 1862. Died "at home" on September 28, 1862, of wounds.

MANNING, RICHARD M., Private
Resided in Nash County where he enlisted at age 28,

May 1, 1862, for the war. Present or accounted for until he died at Winchester, Virginia, November 10, 1862. Cause of death not reported.

MANUS, FRANCIS, Private
[See page 358 of this volume.]

MATTHEWS, HILLIARD, Private
Resided in Nash County and enlisted in "camp" at age 17, March 10, 1864, for the war. Present or accounted for through September 26, 1864.

MORGAN, MOSES B., Private
Resided in Nash County where he enlisted at age 39, September 10, 1861. Present or accounted for until he died at Camp Wyatt on December 2, 1861, or February 15, 1862. Cause of death not reported.

ODOM, DAVID M., Private
Resided in Nash County where he enlisted at age 26, September 10, 1861. Mustered in as Private. Promoted to Corporal on April 1, 1862. Reduced to ranks in July-December, 1863. Present or accounted for until he deserted on or about July 5, 1863. Returned to duty prior to January 1, 1864. Transferred to 2nd Company H, 32nd Regiment N.C. Troops, February 16, 1864.

ODOM, JACOB E., Private
Born in Nash County where he resided prior to enlisting in Nash County at age 19, September 10, 1861. Present or accounted for until killed at Chancellorsville, Virginia, May 3, 1863.

PARKER, JOSIAH, Corporal
Resided in Nash County where he enlisted at age 31, September 10, 1861. Mustered in as Private. Promoted to Corporal December 14, 1861. Present or accounted for until he died in hospital at Wilmington on or about January 4, 1862, of "typ[hoid] pneum[onia]."

PENDER, JOHN, Private
Resided in Nash County and enlisted in Wake County at age 18, July 8, 1863, for the war. Present or accounted for until wounded in the left thigh and captured at or near Kelly's Ford, Virginia, on or about November 7, 1863. Confined at Old Capitol Prison, Washington, D.C., January 27, 1864. Transferred to Point Lookout, Maryland, February 3, 1864. Paroled at Point Lookout on or about February 24, 1865, and transferred to Aiken's Landing, James River, Virginia, where he was received February 25-March 3, 1865, for exchange. Hospitalized at Richmond, Virginia, March 5, 1865, and was furloughed for thirty days the next day.

PITT, FREDERICK C., Private
Resided in Nash County where he enlisted at age 20, September 10, 1861. Present or accounted for until he died in hospital at Salisbury on February 2, 1864, of "variola."

PITT, JAMES W., Private
Resided in Nash County where he enlisted at age 18, September 10, 1861. Present or accounted for until wounded in the left leg at Spotsylvania Court House, Virginia, May 12, 1864. Reported absent wounded through August, 1864. Returned to duty on an unspecified date. Surrendered at Appomattox Court House, Virginia, April 9, 1865.

PITT, JOHN W., Private
Previously served in Company K, 15th Regiment N.C. Troops (5th Regiment N.C. Volunteers). Transferred to this company on June 21, 1862. Present or accounted for until he died at Richmond, Virginia, January 28, 1864. Cause of death not reported.

PITT, WILLIAM M., Private
Previously served in Company K, 15th Regiment N.C. Troops (5th Regiment N.C. Volunteers). Transferred to this company on June 21, 1862. Present or accounted for until captured at Burkeville, Virginia, April 6, 1865. Confined at Newport News, Virginia, April 14, 1865. Released on June 15, 1865, after taking the Oath of Allegiance.

PITTMAN, WILLIAM B., Private
Resided in Nash County where he enlisted at age 38, March 4, 1862. Reported absent without leave in September-December, 1862. Reported absent sick from May-June, 1863, through August, 1864. No further records.

POLAND, ALFORD, Private
Resided in Nash County where he enlisted at age 39, September 10, 1861. Present or accounted for until he died "at home" on December 16, 1862. Cause of death not reported.

POLAND, SIMEON H., Private
Resided in Nash County where he enlisted at age 27, May 1, 1862, for the war. Reported absent without leave in September-December, 1862. Reported absent without leave and unfit for duty in May-June, 1863. Returned to duty prior to January 1, 1864. Died in hospital at Charlottesville, Virginia, July 23, 1864. Cause of death not reported.

PRICE, JOEL L., Private
Resided in Nash County where he enlisted at age 26, September 10, 1861. Present or accounted for until wounded in the head at Malvern Hill, Virginia, July 1, 1862. Returned to duty prior to January 1, 1863. Reported absent without leave for four months and eighteen days during 1863. Court-martialed on or about December 26, 1863. Reported "at Saulsbury [sic] . . . under sentence of Gen. Court Martial" in company records dated December 31, 1863-August 31, 1864.

PRIDGEN, ALEXANDER, Private
Resided in Nash County where he enlisted at age 30, September 10, 1861. Present or accounted for until he deserted on November 15, 1862.

PRIDGEN, DREWRY, Private
Resided in Nash County where he enlisted at age 27, May 1, 1862, for the war. Present or accounted for until wounded in the arm at Kelly's Ford, Virginia, on or about November 7, 1863. Arm amputated. Retired to the Invalid Corps on April 16, 1864.

PRIDGEN, HENRY H., Private
Resided in Nash County and was by occupation a farmer prior to enlisting at age 29, May 1, 1862, for the war. Present or accounted for until captured at Kelly's Ford, Virginia, November 7, 1863. Confined at Point Lookout, Maryland, November 11, 1863. Released on January 30, 1864, after taking the Oath of Allegiance and joining the U.S. Army. Assigned to Company G, 1st

Regiment U.S. Volunteer Infantry.

PRIDGEN, JOSIAH J., Private

Resided in Nash County where he enlisted at age 25, May 1, 1862, for the war. Present or accounted for until captured at Kelly's Ford, Virginia, November 7, 1863. Confined at Point Lookout, Maryland, November 11, 1863. Died at Point Lookout on November 26, 1863. Cause of death not reported.

RACKLEY, JAMES M., Private

Resided in Nash County where he enlisted at age 22, September 10, 1861. Present or accounted for until captured at the Monocacy River, Maryland, July 9, 1864. Reported in confinement at Fort McHenry, Maryland, May 9, 1865. Released on or about May 13, 1865, after taking the Oath of Allegiance.

RACKLEY, PARSON N., Private

Resided in Nash County and enlisted at Camp Wyatt at age 20, February 5, 1862. Present or accounted for until he "dropped out on battlefield" and was captured at or near Gettysburg, Pennsylvania, July 1-5, 1863. Confined at Fort Delaware, Delaware, on or about July 10, 1863. Transferred to hospital at Chester, Pennsylvania, August 10, 1863. Died in hospital at Chester on August 20, 1863, of "typhoid fever."

RENFROW, PERRY V. B., Sergeant

Resided in Johnston County and enlisted in Nash County at age 21, September 10, 1861. Mustered in as Private. Promoted to Corporal on January 6, 1862. Promoted to Sergeant on April 1, 1862. Present or accounted for until wounded in the hip at or near Sharpsburg, Maryland, on or about September 15, 1862. Reported absent without leave through December, 1862. Returned to duty prior to July 1, 1863. Present or accounted for until captured at Kelly's Ford, Virginia, November 7, 1863. Confined at Point Lookout, Maryland, November 11, 1863. Paroled at Point Lookout on or about February 24, 1865, and transferred to Aiken's Landing, James River, Virginia, where he was received February 25-March 3, 1865, for exchange.

RICKS, JOHN A., Private

Resided in Nash County where he enlisted at age 22, September 10, 1861. Mustered in as Private. Promoted to Sergeant prior to November 1, 1861. Reduced to ranks on April 1, 1862. Present or accounted for until discharged in July, 1862, after providing a substitute.

RIGSBEE, WILLIAM C., Private

Resided in Wake County where he enlisted at age 37, September 1, 1863, for the war. Present or accounted for until wounded in the shoulder and/or right lung at or near Spotsylvania Court House, Virginia, May 12, 1864. Hospitalized at Richmond, Virginia, where he died on May 21, 1864, of wounds.

ROBBINS, EDWARD J. M. C., Private

Resided in Nash County where he enlisted at age 36, September 10, 1861. Present or accounted for until March 9, 1862, when he was reported absent sick. No further records.

ROBBINS, WILLIE H., Private

Resided in Edgecombe County and enlisted in Nash County at age 32, September 10, 1861. Mustered in as Corporal. Reported absent on sick furlough on October

9, 1861. Reduced to ranks on December 14, 1861. Failed to return from furlough and was reported absent without leave in May, 1862. Dropped from the rolls of the company subsequent to December 31, 1862.

ROBERTSON, ROBERT, Private

Resided in Caswell County and enlisted in Wake County at age 39, September 1, 1863, for the war. Present or accounted for until he died in hospital at Lynchburg, Virginia, on or about November 27, 1863, of "febris typhoides."

RUFFIN, CHARLES H., Private

Resided in Nash County and enlisted at Camp Wyatt at age 18, September 10, 1861. Present or accounted for until killed in a skirmish near Warrenton, Virginia, October 14-15, 1863.

SHERWOOD, EDWIN, Private

Born in Nash County where he resided prior to enlisting in Nash County at age 23, May 1, 1862, for the war. Present or accounted for until wounded at Malvern Hill, Virginia, July 1, 1862. Returned to duty prior to January 1, 1863. Killed at Chancellorsville, Virginia, May 3, 1863.

SHERWOOD, GEORGE A., Private

Resided in Nash County where he enlisted at age 21, May 1, 1862, for the war. Present or accounted for until wounded in the shoulder and/or jaw at Malvern Hill, Virginia, July 1, 1862. Returned to duty prior to January 1, 1863. Present or accounted for until wounded in the shoulder at Chancellorsville, Virginia, May 3, 1863. Returned to duty prior to November 7, 1863, when he was captured at Kelly's Ford, Virginia. Confined at Point Lookout, Maryland, November 11, 1863. Paroled at Point Lookout on or about February 24, 1865, and transferred to Aiken's Landing, James River, Virginia, where he was received February 25-March 3, 1865, for exchange.

SMITH, ALBERT, Private

Born in Nash County where he enlisted on May 1, 1862, for the war. Present or accounted for until killed at Chancellorsville, Virginia, May 3, 1863.

STALLINGS, FRANKLIN, Private

Born in Nash County where he resided prior to enlisting in Nash County at age 27, May 1, 1862, for the war. Present or accounted for until killed at Chancellorsville, Virginia, May 3, 1863.

STALLINGS, WILLIE, Private

Resided in Nash County where he enlisted at age 25, May 1, 1862, for the war. Present or accounted for until November 24, 1863, when he was reported absent without leave. Reported "at home on retired list" in company records dated December 31, 1863-August 31, 1864. Retired to the Invalid Corps on January 9, 1865.

STRICKLAND, HENRY Q., Private

Born in Nash County where he resided prior to enlisting in Wake County at age 28, July 8, 1863, for the war. Present or accounted for until he surrendered at Appomattox Court House, Virginia, April 9, 1865.

SYKES, WILLIAM JORDAN, Private

Resided in Nash County where he enlisted at age 18, September 10, 1861. Present or accounted for through

April, 1862. Reported absent without leave in September-December, 1862. Reported absent sick in May-June, 1863. Returned to duty prior to January 1, 1864. Hospitalized at Richmond, Virginia, June 3, 1864, with a gunshot wound of the right arm. Place and date wounded not reported. Returned to duty prior to September 1, 1864. No further records.

TAYLOR, BOLLING, Private
Resided in Nash County where he enlisted at age 18, September 10, 1861. Present or accounted for until he died "at home" on November 3 or November 13, 1861, of "pneumonia."

TAYLOR, CALVIN, Private
Born in Nash County where he resided as a farmer prior to enlisting in Nash County at age 25, September 10, 1861. Present or accounted for until discharged on May 18, 1862, by reason of "chest disease of a pulmonary character."

TAYLOR, EGBERT H., Private
Resided in Nash County where he enlisted at age 35, September 10, 1861. Present or accounted for until he deserted on February 10, 1863.

THORN, WILLIAM A., Private
Resided in Nash County where he enlisted at age 21, September 10, 1861. Present or accounted for until he died in Nash County on November 10 or November 18, 1861, of "diarrhoea."

TUCKER, LEMUEL D., Private
Resided in Nash County where he enlisted at age 16, September 10, 1861. "Rejected" for service on or about October 8, 1861, by reason of disability.

TURNER, WALTER S., Musician
Was by occupation a clerk prior to enlisting in Nash County at age 13, September 10, 1861. Mustered in as Private. Appointed Musician prior to November 1, 1861. Present or accounted for until discharged on September 29, 1862, by reason of being underage.

VICK, BENJAMIN H., Private
Resided in Nash County where he enlisted at age 23, September 10, 1861. Present or accounted for until discharged in February, 1862. Reason discharged not reported.

VICK, EXUM R., Private
Resided in Nash County where he enlisted at age 23, September 10, 1861. Mustered in as Private. Promoted to Corporal on April 1, 1862. Present or accounted for until wounded in the right thigh at Malvern Hill, Virginia, July 1, 1862. Right leg amputated. Reduced to ranks on May 1, 1863. Retired to the Invalid Corps on April 27, 1864.

VICK, JAMES F., Private
Born in Nash County where he resided as a farmer prior to enlisting in Nash County at age 37, September 10, 1861. Present or accounted for until September-December, 1862, when he was reported absent without leave. Returned to duty on an unspecified date. Captured at Kelly's Ford, Virginia, November 7, 1863. Confined at Point Lookout, Maryland, November 11, 1863. Released on January 30, 1864, after taking the Oath of Allegiance and joining the U.S. Army. Assigned

to Company I, 1st Regiment U.S. Volunteer Infantry.

VICK, JOSEPH J., Private
Resided in Nash County where he enlisted at age 32, September 10, 1861. Present or accounted for until September-December, 1862, when he was reported absent without leave. Returned to duty prior to January 1, 1864. Deserted on June 20, 1864. Returned to duty prior to September 25, 1864, when he was captured at Harrisonburg, Virginia. Confined at Point Lookout, Maryland, October 4, 1864. Paroled at Point Lookout on or about March 17, 1865, and transferred to Boulware's Wharf, James River, Virginia, where he was received on March 19, 1865, for exchange.

VICK, WILLIAM H., Private
Resided in Nash County where he enlisted at age 25, March 10, 1862. Present or accounted for until he died in hospital "in North Carolina" on May 11, 1862, of disease.

VICK, WILLIE R., Private
Resided in Nash County and enlisted at Camp Wyatt at age 18, January 28, 1862. Present or accounted for until wounded and captured at or near Gettysburg, Pennsylvania, July 1-4, 1863. Confined at Fort Delaware, Delaware, on or about July 7, 1863. Transferred to Point Lookout, Maryland, October 15-18, 1863. Paroled at Point Lookout on or about February 18, 1865, and transferred to Boulware's Wharf, James River, Virginia, where he was received February 20-21, 1865, for exchange.

WALKER, BENJAMIN F., ———
Resided in Nash County. Place and date of enlistment not reported. Wounded at or near Gettysburg, Pennsylvania, on or about July 1-3, 1863. Died at Gettysburg on August 12, 1863.

WALKER, BERRYMAN, Private
Resided in Nash County where he enlisted at age 21, March 4, 1862. Present or accounted for until July 1, 1862, when he was reported missing at Malvern Hill, Virginia. No further records.

WALKER, JOHN BLOUNT, Private
Resided in Nash County where he enlisted at age 24, April 25, 1862, for the war. Present or accounted for until wounded in the right shoulder "in the skirmish line" at Gettysburg, Pennsylvania, July 3-4, 1863. Hospitalized at Gettysburg where he died on or about August 13, 1863, of wounds.

WALKER, RICHMOND D., Private
Born in Nash County where he resided as a farmer prior to enlisting in Nash County at age 21, September 10, 1861. Present or accounted for until captured at Kelly's Ford, Virginia, November 7, 1863. Confined at Point Lookout, Maryland, November 11, 1863. Released on January 30, 1864, after taking the Oath of Allegiance and joining the U.S. Army. Assigned to Company C, 1st Regiment U.S. Volunteer Infantry.

WALKER, WORRELL P., Private
Resided in Nash County where he enlisted at age 33, September 10, 1861. Mustered in as Private. Promoted to Sergeant prior to November 1, 1861. Reduced to ranks on or about March 6, 1862. Promoted to Corporal on May 1, 1863, but was reduced to ranks on June 1,

1863. Present or accounted for until captured at Kelly's Ford, Virginia, November 7, 1863. Confined at Point Lookout, Maryland, November 11, 1863. Paroled at Point Lookout on or about March 17, 1864, and transferred to City Point, Virginia, where he was received on March 20, 1864, for exchange. Reported absent without leave during June-August, 1864. Returned to duty on an unspecified date. Captured at or near Farmville, Virginia, April 6, 1865. Confined at Newport News, Virginia, April 14, 1865. Released on June 15, 1865, after taking the Oath of Allegiance.

WESTRAY, ARCHIBALD H., Private
Resided in Franklin County and enlisted in Nash County at age 23, March 1, 1862. Present or accounted for until wounded in the right leg and captured at Gettysburg, Pennsylvania, July 3, 1863. Right leg amputated below the knee. Hospitalized at Gettysburg and at Baltimore, Maryland. Paroled at Baltimore on September 25, 1863, and transferred for exchange. Reported absent wounded until July 12, 1864, when he was retired to the Invalid Corps.

WHITFIELD, JOHN W., Private
Resided in Nash County where he enlisted at age 28, May 1, 1862, for the war. Reported absent without leave in September-December, 1862. Returned to duty prior to July 1, 1863. Captured at Kelly's Ford, Virginia, November 7, 1863. Confined at Point Lookout, Maryland, November 11, 1863. Paroled at Point Lookout on or about November 1, 1864, and transferred to Venus Point, Savannah River, Georgia, where he was received on November 15, 1864, for exchange.

WHITFIELD, PATRICK L., Private
Resided in Nash County where he enlisted at age 30, March 4, 1862. Present or accounted for until March 1, 1864, when he was assigned to duty as a hospital nurse at Wilson. Reported absent on detail at Wilson through December, 1864.

WHITLEY, JOHN S., Private
Resided in Nash County where he enlisted at age 30, September 10, 1861. Present or accounted for until hospitalized at Wilmington on or about March 21, 1862, with "typhoid fever" and/or "anasarca." Died in hospital at Wilmington on or about April 30, 1862.

WHITLEY, JOLLEY B., Private
Resided in Nash County where he enlisted at age 25, March 4, 1862. Present or accounted for until captured at or near Sharpsburg, Maryland, on or about September 17, 1862. Paroled on September 21, 1862. Reported absent without leave through December, 1862. Returned to duty on an unspecified date. Killed at Gettysburg, Pennsylvania, July 1-3, 1863.

WILLIAMS, HENRY H., Private
Resided in Nash County where he enlisted at age 24, September 10, 1861. Present or accounted for until wounded at Malvern Hill, Virginia, July 1, 1862. Reported absent wounded or absent sick through June, 1863. Returned to duty prior to November 7, 1863, when he was captured at Kelly's Ford, Virginia. Confined at Point Lookout, Maryland, November 11, 1863. Released on January 30, 1864, after taking the Oath of Allegiance and joining the U.S. service. Unit to which assigned not reported.

WILLIAMS, JOSEPH J., Private
Resided in Nash County where he enlisted at age 29, September 10, 1861. Present or accounted for until captured at South Mountain, Maryland, September 14, 1862. Confined at Fort Delaware, Delaware. Paroled and transferred to Aiken's Landing, James River, Virginia, October 2, 1862, for exchange. Declared exchanged at Aiken's Landing on November 10, 1862. Returned to duty prior to July 1, 1863. Present or accounted for until captured at or near Hanover Court House, Virginia, May 22, 1864. Confined at Point Lookout, Maryland, May 30, 1864. Paroled at Point Lookout on or about March 15, 1865, and transferred to Boulware's Wharf, James River, Virginia, where he was received on March 18, 1865, for exchange.

WILLIAMS, MICAJAH THOMAS, Corporal
Resided in Nash County where he enlisted at age 18, May 1, 1862, for the war. Mustered in as Private. Wounded at Malvern Hill, Virginia, July 1, 1862. Returned to duty prior to January 1, 1863. Promoted to Corporal on June 1, 1863. Present or accounted for through June, 1863. No further records.

WILLIAMS, NATHAN C., Private
Enlisted in Wake County on September 1, 1863, for the war. Present or accounted for until captured at Kelly's Ford, Virginia, November 7, 1863. Confined at Point Lookout, Maryland, November 11, 1863. Died at Point Lookout on December 28, 1863. Cause of death not reported.

WILLIAMS, WRIGHT J., Private
Born in Edgecombe County and was by occupation a farmer prior to enlisting in Edgecombe County on March 13, 1862. Present or accounted for until discharged on July 23, 1862, by reason of "inguinal hernia."

WINBOURNE, RUFFIN F., Private
Resided in Nash County where he enlisted at age 29, September 10, 1861. Present or accounted for until wounded at Malvern Hill, Virginia, July 1, 1862. Died on July 3, 1862, of wounds. Place of death not reported.

WINSTEAD, G. J., Private
Enlisted in November, 1862, for the war. Wounded in the leg at Gettysburg, Pennsylvania, July 1-3, 1863. Leg amputated. No further records.

WINSTEAD, GEORGE T., Private
Resided in Nash County and enlisted at Camp Wyatt at age 18, November 20, 1861. Present or accounted for until wounded at Malvern Hill, Virginia, July 1, 1862. Reported absent without leave through December, 1862. Returned to duty prior to May 3, 1863, when he was killed at Chancellorsville, Virginia.

WINSTEAD, HILLIARD H., Corporal
Resided in Nash County and enlisted at Camp Wyatt at age 19, November 20, 1861. Mustered in as Private. Present or accounted for until captured at or near Sharpsburg, Maryland, on or about September 17, 1862. Paroled on September 24, 1862. Returned to duty prior to January 1, 1863. Promoted to Corporal on November 7, 1863. Present or accounted for through February 2, 1864. Wounded in an unspecified battle and died of wounds prior to September 1, 1864.

WINSTEAD, THEOPHILUS T., Private

Resided in Nash County where he enlisted at age 18, March 4, 1862. Present or accounted for until captured at Frederick, Maryland, September 12, 1862. Paroled and transferred to Aiken's Landing, James River, Virginia, where he was received on October 6, 1862, for exchange. Declared exchanged at Aiken's Landing on November 10, 1862. Returned to duty subsequent to December 31, 1862. Wounded in the right leg and captured at Gettysburg, Pennsylvania, July 1-5, 1863. Right leg amputated below the knee. Confined at various Federal hospitals until hospitalized at Baltimore, Maryland, October 1, 1863. Paroled at Baltimore on November 12, 1863, and transferred to City Point, Virginia, where he was received on November 17, 1863, for exchange. Retired to the Invalid Corps on July 8, 1864.

WINTERS, GEORGE, Private

Resided in Nash County where he enlisted at age 18, September 10, 1861. Present or accounted for until wounded at Chancellorsville, Virginia, May 3, 1863. Reported absent wounded through June, 1863. Reported on duty as a nurse in hospital at Richmond, Virginia, November-December, 1863. Rejoined the company prior to May 18, 1864, when he was captured at Spotsylvania Court House, Virginia. Confined at Point Lookout, Maryland. Transferred to Elmira, New York, where he arrived on July 6, 1864. Released at Elmira on June 30, 1865, after taking the Oath of Allegiance.

WOOD, JAMES, Private

Resided in Nash County where he enlisted at age 21, September 10, 1861. Present or accounted for until he died in hospital at Richmond, Virginia, on or about October 4, 1862, of "erysipelas."

WOOD, WILLIAM, Private

Resided in Nash County where he enlisted at age 21, September 10, 1861. Present or accounted for until wounded at Chancellorsville, Virginia, May 3, 1863. Died on May 10 or May 17, 1863, of wounds. Place of death not reported.

WOODARD, JOHN E., Private

Resided in Nash County where he enlisted at age 25, September 10, 1861. Present or accounted for until wounded at Malvern Hill, Virginia, July 1, 1862. Reported absent without leave in November-December, 1862. Returned to duty prior to July 1, 1863. Captured at Kelly's Ford, Virginia, November 7, 1863. Confined at Point Lookout, Maryland, November 11, 1863. Paroled at Point Lookout on or about February 24, 1865, and transferred to Aiken's Landing, James River, Virginia, where he was received February 25-March 3, 1865, for exchange.

COMPANY K

This company was raised in Mecklenburg County and enlisted there on September 13, 1861. It was then assigned to the 30th Regiment N.C. Troops and designated Company K. After joining the regiment the company functioned as a part of the regiment, and its history for the war period is reported as a part of the regimental history.

The information contained in the following roster of the company was compiled principally from a company muster-in and descriptive roll dated October 8, 1861, and from company muster rolls for November, 1861-April,

1862; August 31-December 31, 1862; May-August, 1863; and November, 1863-August, 1864. No company muster rolls were found for September 13-October, 1861; May-August 30, 1862; January-April, 1863; September-October, 1863; or for the period after August, 1864. Valuable information was obtained from primary records such as the Roll of Honor, discharge certificates, medical records, prisoner of war records, and pension applications. Secondary sources such as postwar rosters and histories, cemetery records, and records of the United Daughters of the Confederacy also provided useful information.

OFFICERS

CAPTAINS

KELL, JAMES T.

Resided in Mecklenburg County and enlisted at age 26. Appointed Captain on September 13, 1861. Elected Major on September 26, 1861, and transferred to the Field and Staff of this regiment. Later served as Lieutenant Colonel of this regiment.

MORROW, BENJAMIN F.

Resided in Mecklenburg County where he enlisted at age 28. Elected 1st Lieutenant on September 13, 1861. Elected Captain on September 26, 1861. Present or accounted for until he was defeated for reelection when the regiment was reorganized on May 1, 1862.

WITHERSPOON, JOHN G.

Resided in Cabarrus County and enlisted in Mecklenburg County at age 23, September 13, 1861. Mustered in as 1st Sergeant. Elected 3rd Lieutenant on September 27, 1861. Elected 2nd Lieutenant on April 8, 1862, and was promoted to Captain on May 1, 1862. Present or accounted for until killed at Kelly's Ford, Virginia, November 7, 1863. He was "shot through the breast . . . and died a prisoner on the spot a few hours afterwards. . . . He was a brave and gallant soldier."

ARDREY, WILLIAM ERSKINE

Previously served as Private in Company C, 1st Regiment N.C. Infantry (6 months, 1861). Enlisted in this company on February 10, 1862. Mustered in as Private. Elected 2nd Lieutenant on May 1, 1862. Promoted to 1st Lieutenant on September 1, 1863, and was promoted to Captain on November 7, 1863. Present or accounted for until hospitalized at Richmond, Virginia, June 3, 1864, with a gunshot wound of the head. Place and date wounded not reported. Returned to duty on July 7, 1864. Surrendered at Appomattox Court House, Virginia, April 9, 1865.

LIEUTENANTS

BELL, CHARLES EDWIN, 1st Lieutenant

Resided in Mecklenburg County where he enlisted at age 33. Appointed 2nd Lieutenant on September 13, 1861. Promoted to 1st Lieutenant on September 27, 1861. Present or accounted for until he resigned on or about March 14, 1862. Reason he resigned not reported.

DOWNS, JAMES THOMAS, 1st Lieutenant

Resided in Mecklenburg County where he enlisted at age 31. Elected 3rd Lieutenant on September 13, 1861. Promoted to 2nd Lieutenant on September 25, 1861, and was elected 1st Lieutenant on April 8, 1862. Present or accounted for until he was defeated for reelection when the regiment was reorganized on May 1, 1862. Later served as Private in Company F, 63rd Regiment N.C. Troops (5th Regiment N.C. Cavalry).

DOWNS, JOHN T., 1st Lieutenant
Resided in Mecklenburg County and enlisted at Camp Wyatt at age 22, September 13, 1861. Mustered in as Private. Elected 3rd Lieutenant on May 1, 1862. Present or accounted for until wounded at Malvern Hill, Virginia, July 1, 1862. Returned to duty prior to January 1, 1863. Promoted to 2nd Lieutenant in September, 1863, and was promoted to 1st Lieutenant on November 7, 1863. Present or accounted for until wounded in the wrist near Winchester, Virginia, September 19, 1864. Reported absent wounded through February 25, 1865.

ORR, NATHAN D., 1st Lieutenant
Previously served as Corporal in Company B, 20th Regiment N.C. Troops (10th Regiment N.C. Volunteers). Transferred to this company on or about September 13, 1861. Mustered in as Sergeant. Promoted to 1st Sergeant on September 27, 1861. Elected 3rd Lieutenant on April 8, 1862, and was promoted to 1st Lieutenant on May 1, 1862. Present or accounted for until he resigned on August 17, 1863, by reason of "phthisis pulmonalis." Resignation accepted on September 1, 1863.

NONCOMMISSIONED OFFICERS AND PRIVATES

ADAMS, WILLIAM, Private
Resided in Cumberland County and enlisted in Wake County at age 35, May 18, 1863, for the war. Present or accounted for until captured at Spotsylvania Court House, Virginia, May 19, 1864. Confined at Point Lookout, Maryland, May 23, 1864. Transferred to Elmira, New York, June 3, 1864. Died at Elmira on September 18, 1864, of "chronic diarrhoea."

ADKINS, WILLIAM H., Private
Resided in South Carolina and enlisted in Mecklenburg County at age 18, September 13, 1861. Present or accounted for until wounded at Kelly's Ford, Virginia, on or about November 7, 1863. Returned to duty prior to May 18-19, 1864, when he was captured at Spotsylvania Court House, Virginia. Confined at Point Lookout, Maryland, May 23, 1864. Transferred to Elmira, New York, July 3, 1864. Died at Elmira on January 15, 1865, of "chronic diarrhoea."

ALEXANDER, J. L., Private
Previously served as Private in Company I, 6th Regiment N.C. State Troops. Transferred to this company on April 10, 1863. Present or accounted for until captured at Kelly's Ford, Virginia, November 7, 1863. Confined at Point Lookout, Maryland, November 11, 1863. Paroled at Point Lookout on or about February 24, 1865, and transferred to Aiken's Landing, James River, Virginia, where he was received on February 25, 1865, for exchange. Hospitalized at Richmond, Virginia. Furloughed for thirty days from hospital at Richmond on March 1, 1865.

ALEXANDER, J. M., Private
Resided in Mecklenburg County and enlisted in Wake County at age 44, August 20, 1863, for the war. Present or accounted for until killed at Spotsylvania Court House, Virginia, May 12, 1864.

ALEXANDER, SAMUEL D., Private
Resided in Mecklenburg County where he enlisted at age 21, September 13, 1861. Present or accounted for until wounded at Kelly's Ford, Virginia, November 7, 1863. Returned to duty prior to January 1, 1864. Present or accounted for through November 22, 1864.

ALEXANDER, T. P., Private
Resided in Mecklenburg County where he enlisted at age 26, March 25, 1863, for the war. Present or accounted for until he was detailed for duty as a hospital nurse on or about November 1, 1863. Reported absent on hospital duty through December, 1864. Hospitalized at Richmond, Virginia, February 19, 1865, with "chronic conjunctivitis." No further records.

ALLEN, JAMES H., Private
Born in Johnston County where he resided prior to enlisting in Wake County at age 34, September 17, 1862, for the war. Present or accounted for until he died at Gordonsville, Virginia, December 5-7, 1862, of "pneumonia."

ANDERSON, M. J., Private
Place and date of enlistment not reported. Surrendered at Appomattox Court House, Virginia, April 9, 1865.

ANDERSON, WILLIAM, Private
Resided in Wilkes County and enlisted in Wake County at age 29, September 17, 1862, for the war. Present or accounted for until he deserted on or about September 1, 1863. Returned to duty on an unspecified date. Died at Orange Court House, Virginia, on or about January 1, 1864. Cause of death not reported.

BAILEY, ELIAS D., Private
Resided in Wake County where he enlisted at age 21, September 17, 1862, for the war. Present or accounted for until captured at or near Harpers Ferry, West Virginia, on or about July 8, 1864. Confined at Old Capitol Prison, Washington, D.C., July 17, 1864. Transferred to Elmira, New York, July 23, 1864. Died at Elmira on February 19, 1865, of "chro[nic] diarrhoea."

BAILEY, JAMES A., Private
Resided in Wake County where he enlisted at age 22, September 17, 1862, for the war. Present or accounted for until captured at Kelly's Ford, Virginia, November 7, 1863. Confined at Point Lookout, Maryland, November 11, 1863. Paroled at Point Lookout on or about March 16, 1864, and transferred to City Point, Virginia, where he was received on March 20, 1864, for exchange. Died on April 1, 1864, of disease. Place and cause of death not reported.

BAILEY, WILLIAM, Private
Resided in Wake County where he enlisted at age 41, October 20, 1863, for the war. Present or accounted for until wounded in the foot at or near Snicker's Gap, Virginia, July 18, 1864. Reported absent wounded through August, 1864. Returned to duty on an unspecified date. Paroled at Burkeville, Virginia, April 14-17, 1865.

BAKER, JEPTHA, Private
Resided in Mecklenburg County and was by occupation a "house carpenter" prior to enlisting in Mecklenburg County at age 27, September 13, 1861. Present or

accounted for until wounded in the left ear at Sharpsburg, Maryland, September 17, 1862. Hospitalized at Richmond, Virginia. Furloughed on October 3, 1862. Died on October 23, 1862, of wounds received at Sharpsburg. Place of death not reported.

BALES, ELIJAH M., Sergeant

Resided in Mecklenburg County where he enlisted at age 19, September 13, 1861. Mustered in as Private. Promoted to Corporal on May 3, 1863. Present or accounted for until wounded in the arm at Gettysburg, Pennsylvania, July 1, 1863. Reported absent wounded until December 10, 1863, when he was detailed for light duty at Charlotte. Reported absent on detail through August, 1864. Promoted to Sergeant on August 1, 1864. Rejoined the company on an unspecified date. Surrendered at Appomattox Court House, Virginia, April 9, 1865. Nominated for the Badge of Distinction for gallantry at Chancellorsville, Virginia, May 1-4, 1863.

BALES, JAMES PARKS, Private

Resided in South Carolina and enlisted in Mecklenburg County at age 24, September 13, 1861. Mustered in as Corporal. Reduced to ranks on May 1, 1862. Present or accounted for until wounded at or near Chancellorsville, Virginia, May 1-4, 1863. Returned to duty prior to July 1, 1863. Present or accounted for until he surrendered at Appomattox Court House, Virginia, April 9, 1865.

BAREFOOT, NOAH GIDEON, Private

Resided in Johnston County and enlisted in Wake County at age 27, September 17, 1862, for the war. Present or accounted for until wounded at or near Chancellorsville, Virginia, May 1-4, 1863. Returned to duty prior to July 1, 1863. Present or accounted for through August, 1864; however, he was reported absent on duty as a provost guard or absent sick in hospital during most of that period. Returned to duty on an unspecified date. Wounded in the hand at Cedar Creek, Virginia, October 19, 1864. No further records.

BARNETT, ROBERT C., Private

Previously served in Company B, 1st Regiment N.C. Infantry (6 months, 1861). Enlisted in this company at Camp Wyatt at age 22, February 10, 1862. Present or accounted for until killed at Chancellorsville, Virginia, May 3, 1863.

BELL, N. J., Private

Resided in Cumberland County and enlisted in Wake County at age 40, June 12, 1863, for the war. Present or accounted for until he died in hospital at Richmond, Virginia, November 12, 1863, of "typhoid pneumonia."

BENTLY, MOSES W. H., Private

Resided in Mecklenburg County where he enlisted at age 19, September 13, 1861. Present or accounted for until wounded at Malvern Hill, Virginia, July 1, 1862. Returned to duty prior to January 1, 1863. Present or accounted for until wounded in the "lower extremities right" at or near Charles Town, West Virginia, August 22, 1864. Returned to duty on November 25, 1864. Captured at Burkeville, Virginia, April 6, 1865. Confined at Newport News, Virginia, April 14, 1865. Released on June 14, 1865, after taking the Oath of Allegiance.

BLACK, JAMES H., Private

Resided in Mecklenburg County where he enlisted at

age 17, September 13, 1861. Present or accounted for until wounded in the left arm at Malvern Hill, Virginia, July 1, 1862. Returned to duty prior to September 17, 1862, when he was killed at Sharpsburg, Maryland. "Very gallant."

BLACK, JOHN N., Sergeant

Born in Mecklenburg County and resided in Cabarrus County prior to enlisting in Johnston County at age 26, October 15, 1861. Mustered in as Private. Promoted to Corporal in May-December, 1862. Promoted to Sergeant in January-June, 1863. Present or accounted for until killed at or near Snicker's Gap, Virginia, July 18, 1864.

BLACK, JOHN S., Private

Born in Mecklenburg County and resided in Cabarrus County prior to enlisting in Mecklenburg County at age 29, September 13, 1861. Present or accounted for until he died at Guinea Station, Virginia, on or about January 10, 1863, of "smallpox."

BLACK, THOMAS, Private

Resided in Mecklenburg County and enlisted in Wake County at age 43, October 1, 1863, for the war. Present or accounted for until he died in hospital at Orange Court House, Virginia, January 11, 1864. Cause of death not reported.

BOWMAN, R., Private

Resided in Randolph County and enlisted in Wake County at age 33, July 1, 1863, for the war. Present or accounted for until he deserted on November 20 or December 21, 1863. Paroled at Greensboro on May 10, 1865.

BOYCE, SAMUEL J., Sergeant

Resided in Mecklenburg County where he enlisted at age 18, September 13, 1861. Mustered in as Private. Promoted to Corporal in May-December, 1862. Promoted to Sergeant in January-June, 1863. Present or accounted for until wounded in the right thigh and captured at Kelly's Ford, Virginia, November 7, 1863. Right leg amputated above the knee. Hospitalized at Washington, D.C., where he died on November 11, 1863. "Noted for coolness and bravery in battle."

BRADSHAW, V. B., Private

Resided in Mecklenburg County and enlisted in Wake County at age 39, October 20, 1863, for the war. Present or accounted for until he died in hospital at Farmville, Virginia, May 4, 1864, of "febris typhoides."

BREWER, JAMES H., Private

Resided in Mecklenburg County and enlisted in Wake County at age 29, September 17, 1862, for the war. Present or accounted for until he died at Staunton, Virginia, February 9, 1863, of "febris typhoides."

BRINKLEY, HENRY, Private

Resided in Wake County where he enlisted at age 22, July 1, 1863, for the war. Present or accounted for until captured in hospital at Richmond, Virginia, April 3, 1865. Transferred to Newport News, Virginia, April 23, 1865. Released on June 30, 1865, after taking the Oath of Allegiance.

BRISTOW, J. C., Private

Resided in Orange County and enlisted at age 41, July

1, 1863, for the war. No further records.

BURTON, J. C., Private
Enlisted in Wake County on July 1, 1863, for the war. Present or accounted for until he surrendered at Appomattox Court House, Virginia, April 9, 1865.

CHURCH, ELI, Private
Resided in Ashe County and enlisted in Wake County at age 24, September 17, 1862, for the war. Present or accounted for until he deserted on April 15, 1863. Returned to duty subsequent to August 31, 1864. Captured at Amelia Court House, Virginia, April 6, 1865. Confined at Point Lookout, Maryland, April 14, 1865. Released on June 24, 1865, after taking the Oath of Allegiance.

CHURCH, MARTIN, Private
Resided in Ashe County and enlisted in Wake County at age 22, September 17, 1862, for the war. Present or accounted for until he deserted on April 15, 1863. Returned to duty subsequent to August 31, 1864. Present or accounted for until captured at Farmville, Virginia, April 6, 1865. Confined at Point Lookout, Maryland, April 14, 1865. Released on June 24, 1865, after taking the Oath of Allegiance.

COFFEY, ANDREW S., Private
Resided in Mecklenburg County where he enlisted at age 35, September 13, 1861. Present or accounted for through August, 1864.

COLTHARP, HENRY T., Private
Born in York District, South Carolina, and resided in Mecklenburg County where he was by occupation a farmer prior to enlisting in Mecklenburg County at age 33, September 13, 1861. Mustered in as Corporal. Reduced to ranks on April 8, 1862. Present or accounted for until discharged on September 10, 1862, by reason of ''disability of one hand.''

COWAN, JOHN D., Private
Enlisted in Mecklenburg County on September 13, 1861. Company records indicate that he ''never appeared [on a] plea [of] not being legally sworn.''

CRAIG, M. F., Private
Enlisted in Mecklenburg County on September 13, 1861. Company records indicate that he ''never appeared [on a] plea [of] not being legally sworn.''

CRAIN, M. C., Private
Place and date of enlistment not reported. Paroled at Burkeville, Virginia, April 14-17, 1865.

CROWELL, ISRAEL, Private
Resided in Mecklenburg County where he enlisted at age 31, September 13, 1861. Present or accounted for until May 1, 1862, when he was detailed ''to work on gunboats'' at Wilmington. Reported absent on detail at Wilmington through August, 1864.

CULP, ALEY A., Sergeant
Resided in Mecklenburg County and was by occupation a farmer prior to enlisting in Mecklenburg County at age 25, September 13, 1861. Mustered in as Private. Present or accounted for until wounded in the thigh and breast at Sharpsburg, Maryland, September 17, 1862.

Returned to duty prior to January 1, 1863. Promoted to Corporal in January-June, 1863. Present or accounted for until captured at Kelly's Ford, Virginia, November 7, 1863. Confined at Point Lookout, Maryland, November 11, 1863. Paroled on or about March 16, 1864, and transferred to City Point, Virginia, where he was received on March 20, 1864, for exchange. Returned to duty on an unspecified date. Promoted to Sergeant on July 1, 1864. Present or accounted for until wounded in both thighs and captured at or near Fisher's Hill, Virginia, on or about September 22, 1864. Hospitalized at Baltimore, Maryland. Transferred to Point Lookout where he arrived on October 18, 1864. Paroled at Point Lookout and transferred to Venus Point, Savannah River, Georgia, where he was received on November 15, 1864, for exchange.

DAVIS, GEORGE W., Private
Resided in Mecklenburg County where he enlisted at age 17, September 13, 1861. Present or accounted for until killed at Gaines' Mill, Virginia, June 27, 1862.

DeARMOND, AARON LEONIDAS, Sergeant
Born in Mecklenburg County where he resided prior to enlisting in Mecklenburg County at age 35, September 13, 1861. Mustered in as Sergeant. Reduced to ranks in May-September, 1862. Present or accounted for until captured at Sharpsburg, Maryland, September 17, 1862. Paroled on September 21, 1862. Present or accounted for until wounded in the arm at Fredericksburg, Virginia, December 13, 1862. Returned to duty and was promoted to Sergeant prior to July 1, 1863. Present or accounted for until captured at Kelly's Ford, Virginia, November 7, 1863. Confined at Point Lookout, Maryland, November 11, 1863. Paroled at Point Lookout on or about March 16, 1864, and transferred to City Point, Virginia, where he was received on March 20, 1864, for exchange. Returned to duty prior to July 18, 1864, when he was wounded at or near Snicker's Gap, Virginia. Died on August 19, 1864, of wounds. Place of death not reported.

DIXON, S. L., Private
Resided in Mecklenburg County and enlisted in Wake County at age 40, November 3, 1863, for the war. Present or accounted for until wounded at or near Spotsylvania Court House, Virginia, May 8, 1864. Reported absent wounded through August, 1864. Returned to duty on an unspecified date. Surrendered at Appomattox Court House, Virginia, April 9, 1865.

DOWNS, WILLIAM HENRY, Private
Born in Mecklenburg County where he resided as a student prior to enlisting in Mecklenburg County at age 17, September 13, 1861. Present or accounted for until discharged on January 21, 1862, by reason of ''general constitutional debility.''

DUCKWORTH, THOMAS P., Private
Born in Mecklenburg County where he resided prior to enlisting in Wake County at age 42, October 1, 1863, for the war. Present or accounted for until wounded ''through the bowels'' at or near Spotsylvania Court House, Virginia, May 12, 1864. Died ''at home'' on July 10, 1864, of wounds.

DUNN, ANDREW JACKSON, Private
Born in Mecklenburg County where he resided prior to enlisting in Mecklenburg County at age 32, September

13, 1861. Mustered in as Corporal. Reduced to ranks in May-September, 1862. Present or accounted for until killed at Sharpsburg, Maryland, September 17, 1862.

DUNN, ANDREW S., Private
Born in Union County* and resided in Mecklenburg County where he was by occupation a farmer prior to enlisting in Mecklenburg County at age 23, September 13, 1861. Present or accounted for until discharged on January 21, 1862. Reason discharged not reported.

DUNN, GEORGE, Private
Resided in Rowan County and enlisted in Wake County at age 43, July 1, 1863, for the war. Present or accounted for until captured at or near Spotsylvania Court House, Virginia, May 8, 1864. Confined at Point Lookout, Maryland, May 17, 1864. Transferred to Elmira, New York, August 10, 1864. Died at Elmira on December 1, 1864, of "pneumonia."

DUNN, SAMUEL W. T., Private
Resided in Union County and enlisted in Mecklenburg County at age 17, September 13, 1861. Present or accounted for until he died at Wilmington on December 1, 1861. Cause of death not reported.

EZZELL, MOSES F., Private
Resided in Mecklenburg County and was by occupation a farmer prior to enlisting at Camp Wyatt at age 18, January 20, 1862. Mustered in as Private. Promoted to Corporal on April 8, 1862. Present or accounted for until bruised in the back by a bomb at Sharpsburg, Maryland, September 17, 1862. Returned to duty on or about October 1, 1862. Reduced to ranks prior to November 10, 1862. Died at Strasburg, Virginia, November 10, 1862. Cause of death not reported.

FIELDS, ABSALOM F., Private
Resided in Guilford County. Place and date of enlistment not reported. Captured at Farmville, Virginia, April 6, 1865. Confined at Point Lookout, Maryland, April 14, 1865. Released on June 26, 1865, after taking the Oath of Allegiance.

GAMBLE, JAMES H., Private
Resided in Mecklenburg County and enlisted in Wake County at age 41, August 20, 1863, for the war. Present or accounted for until he died in hospital at Richmond, Virginia, January 19, 1864, of "febris typhoides."

GEORGE, EDWARD PAYSON, Private
Resided in Mecklenburg County where he enlisted at age 20, September 13, 1861. Mustered in as Private. Promoted to Sergeant on or about February 26, 1862. Reduced to ranks on or about April 8, 1862. Served as Drillmaster of this company for a brief period in March-April, 1862. Appointed Assistant Commissary of Subsistence (Captain) on May 1, 1862, and transferred to the 49th Regiment N.C. Troops.

GEORGE, PRESSLY, Private
Born in Wake County where he resided prior to enlisting in Wake County at age 30, September 17, 1862, for the war. Present or accounted for until he died in hospital at Richmond, Virginia, on or about January 8, 1863, of "pneumonia."

GLOVER, BENJAMIN C., Private
Resided in Mecklenburg County where he enlisted at

age 16, September 13, 1861. Present or accounted for until wounded in the left hip at Chancellorsville, Virginia, May 3, 1863. Reported absent wounded until November 17, 1864, when he was retired to the Invalid Corps.

GRAHAM, JOHN W., Private
Resided in Robeson County and enlisted in Wake County at age 27, May 15, 1863, for the war. Present or accounted for until captured at Kelly's Ford, Virginia, November 7, 1863. Confined at Point Lookout, Maryland, November 11, 1863. Paroled at Point Lookout on or about March 16, 1864, and transferred to City Point, Virginia, where he was received on March 20, 1864, for exchange. Returned to duty prior to September 1, 1864. Captured at Burkeville, Virginia, April 6, 1865. Confined at Newport News, Virginia, April 14, 1865. Released on June 27, 1865, after taking the Oath of Allegiance.

GRIFFIN, JOHN J., Private
Resided in Mecklenburg County where he enlisted at age 16, September 13, 1861. Present or accounted for until he died at or near Smithville (Southport) on or about October 23, 1861. Cause of death not reported.

GRIFFITH, AARON E., Private
Resided in Mecklenburg County where he enlisted at age 18, October 5, 1861. Present or accounted for until wounded in the hip at Gettysburg, Pennsylvania, July 3, 1863. Died on November 3, 1863, of wounds. Place of death not reported.

HALL, JOHN G., Private
Resided in Mecklenburg County where he enlisted at age 34, September 13, 1861. Present or accounted for until captured at Frederick, Maryland, September 12, 1862. Confined at Fort Delaware, Delaware. Paroled on an unspecified date and transferred to Aiken's Landing, James River, Virginia, October 2, 1862, for exchange. Declared exchanged at Aiken's Landing on November 10, 1862. Reported absent without leave through December, 1862. Returned to duty prior to July 1, 1863. Present or accounted for until wounded at or near Spotsylvania Court House, Virginia, May 8, 1864. Reported absent wounded through August, 1864. Company records do not indicate whether he returned to duty. Hospitalized at Charlotte on October 24, 1864, with a gunshot wound of the left hand. Place and date wounded not reported. Returned to duty on October 25, 1864. No further records.

HALL, JOSEPH F., Private
Resided in Mecklenburg County and enlisted in Wake County at age 28, August 10, 1863, for the war. Present or accounted for until captured at or near Farmville, Virginia, April 6, 1865. Confined at Newport News, Virginia, April 14, 1865. Released on June 14, 1865, after taking the Oath of Allegiance.

HALL, ROBERT B., Private
Born in Montgomery County and resided in Mecklenburg County where he was by occupation a farmer prior to enlisting in Mecklenburg County at age 30, September 13, 1861. Present or accounted for until discharged on January 6, 1863, by reason of "disease of the heart with general dropsy."

HARTIS, JOHN H., Private
Resided in Mecklenburg County where he enlisted at

age 35, September 13, 1861. Present or accounted for until captured at or near Boonsboro, Maryland, on or about September 17, 1862. Confined at Fort Delaware, Delaware. Transferred to Aiken's Landing, James River, Virginia, October 2, 1862, for exchange. Declared exchanged at Aiken's Landing on November 10, 1862. Died in hospital at Lynchburg, Virginia, January 13, 1863, of "diarrhoea chron[ic]."

HARTIS, WILSON L., Corporal
Previously served as Private in Company B, 1st Regiment N.C. Infantry (6 months, 1861). Enlisted in this company at Camp Wyatt on January 18, 1862. Mustered in as Private. Promoted to Corporal in January-April, 1863. Present or accounted for until killed at Chancellorsville, Virginia, May 3, 1863.

HARVEY, JOHN F., Private
Place and date of enlistment not reported. Captured at Farmville, Virginia, April 6, 1865. Confined at Point Lookout, Maryland, April 14, 1865. Released on June 1, 1865, after taking the Oath of Allegiance.

HENDERSON, WILLIAM, Private
Resided in Johnston County and enlisted in Wake County at age 33, September 17, 1862, for the war. Reported absent without leave through December, 1862. Reported absent sick in May-July, 1863. Died in hospital at Richmond, Virginia, August 12, 1863, of "ch[ronic] diarrhoea."

HENDERSON, WILLIAM TAYLOR, Private
Resided in Mecklenburg County where he enlisted at age 22, September 13, 1861. Present or accounted for until he died at Charlotte in May, 1862. Cause of death not reported.

HOLMES, BEN, Private
Resided in Johnston County and enlisted in Wake County at age 29, September 17, 1862, for the war. Died at Richmond, Virginia, prior to December 9, 1862. Cause of death not reported.

HOOD, ABNER B., Private
Resided in Mecklenburg County where he enlisted at age 23, September 13, 1861. Mustered in as Private. Promoted to Sergeant on October 1, 1861. Reduced to ranks in May-June, 1862. Present or accounted for until killed at Gaines' Mill, Virginia, June 27, 1862, by "a minie ball passing through his heart."

HOOD, WILLIAM L., Corporal
Resided in Mecklenburg County where he enlisted at age 17, September 13, 1861. Mustered in as Private. Present or accounted for until wounded in the arm at Gettysburg, Pennsylvania, July 3, 1863. Returned to duty prior to September 1, 1863. Present or accounted for until hospitalized at Richmond, Virginia, May 27, 1864, with a gunshot wound of the right hand. Place and dated wounded not reported. Returned to duty prior to September 1, 1864. Wounded in the thigh and captured at Cedar Creek, Virginia, October 19, 1864. Hospitalized at Baltimore, Maryland. Transferred to Point Lookout, Maryland, where he arrived on October 26, 1864. Paroled at Point Lookout on or about October 30, 1864. Transferred to Venus Point, Savannah River,

Georgia, where he was received on November 15, 1864, for exchange. Returned to duty and was promoted to Corporal on an unspecified date. Surrendered at Appomattox Court House, Virginia, April 9, 1865.

HOWEY, JOHN HOYLE, Private
Resided in Mecklenburg County where he enlisted at age 16, September 13, 1861. Present or accounted for until captured at or near Sharpsburg, Maryland, on or about September 17, 1862. Paroled on September 27, 1862. Returned to duty prior to January 1, 1863. Present or accounted for until wounded at Winchester, Virginia, on or about September 19, 1864. Returned to duty on an unspecified date. Surrendered at Appomattox Court House, Virginia, April 9, 1865.

HOWEY, WILLIAM, Private
Born in Mecklenburg County where he resided as a farmer prior to enlisting in Mecklenburg County at age 42, September 13, 1861. Present or accounted for until discharged on February 13, 1862, by reason of "dropsy."

JENNINGS, GEORGE W., Private
Born in York District, South Carolina, and resided in Mecklenburg County where he was by occupation a millwright prior to enlisting in Mecklenburg County at age 24, September 13, 1861. Present or accounted for until wounded in the right leg at Malvern Hill, Virginia, July 1, 1862. Right leg amputated. Discharged on September 25, 1862.

JOHNSON, G. W., Private
Resided in Wilkes County and was by occupation a farmer prior to enlisting in Wake County at age 23, September 17, 1862, for the war. Present or accounted for until he deserted on April 15, 1863.

JOHNSTON, DAVID E., Private
Born in Surry County and resided in Mecklenburg County where he was by occupation a farmer prior to enlisting in Mecklenburg County at age 35, September 13, 1861. Present or accounted for until wounded at Sharpsburg, Maryland, on or about September 17, 1862. Discharged on October 25, 1862, under the provisions of the Conscription Act.

JOHNSTON, JAMES HENRY, Private
Resided in Johnston County and enlisted in Wake County at age 28, September 17, 1862, for the war. Present or accounted for until wounded at Chancellorsville, Virginia, May 3, 1863. Returned to duty in September-December, 1863. Present or accounted for until wounded in the side at Winchester, Virginia, September 19, 1864. No further records.

JOHNSTON, S. A., Private
Born in Alleghany County* and resided in Wilkes County prior to enlisting in Wake County at age 24, September 17, 1862, for the war. Present or accounted for until wounded at Chancellorsville, Virginia, May 3, 1863. Returned to duty on or about August 6, 1863. Present or accounted for until wounded at or near Spotsylvania Court House, Virginia, May 8, 1864. Died on or about May 18, 1864, of wounds. Place of death not reported.

KIRKPATRICK, HUGH Y., Sergeant
Previously served as Private in Company B, 1st

Regiment N.C. Infantry (6 months, 1861). Enlisted in this company at Camp Wyatt at age 20, January 1, 1862. Mustered in as Private. Promoted to Sergeant on April 8, 1862. Present or accounted for until he died "in the house of Mrs. Davis" at or near Strasburg, Virginia, November 8, 1862. Cause of death not reported. "How tenderly a few of his comrades raked the snow, dug the grave and laid the noble youth away."

LEE, JAMES A., Private
Resided in Mecklenburg County where he enlisted at age 19, September 13, 1861. Present or accounted for until he died in hospital at Richmond, Virginia, March 25-28, 1863, of "pneumonia."

LEE, JAMES T., Sergeant
Born in Mecklenburg County where he resided prior to enlisting in Mecklenburg County at age 23, September 13, 1861. Mustered in as Sergeant. Reduced to ranks on February 26, 1862. Promoted to 1st Sergeant on April 8, 1862. Reduced to the rank of Sergeant prior to January 1, 1863. Present or accounted for until killed at or near Spotsylvania Court House, Virginia, May 12, 1864.

LEE, SAMUEL B., Private
Born in Mecklenburg County where he resided prior to enlisting in Mecklenburg County at age 19, September 13, 1861. Present or accounted for until wounded in the groin and/or right hip at or near Hanover Junction, Virginia, on or about May 24, 1864. Hospitalized at Richmond, Virginia, where he died June 21-22, 1864, of wounds.

LEWIS, W. H., Private
Resided in Halifax County and enlisted in Wake County at age 42, October 2, 1863, for the war. Present or accounted for until September 1, 1864, when he was reported absent without leave.

McKENNEY, JOHN W., Private
Resided in Mecklenburg County where he enlisted at age 40, September 13, 1861. Mustered in as Corporal. Promoted to Sergeant on November 1, 1861. Reduced to ranks in May-November, 1862. Present or accounted for until discharged on November 22, 1862, under the provisions of the Conscription Act.

McKINNEY, R. MUNROE, Private
Resided in Mecklenburg County where he enlisted at age 19, September 13, 1861. Present or accounted for through September 30, 1864. Reported on duty as a teamster during most of the war.

McLANE, THOMAS, Private
Resided in Johnston County and enlisted in Wake County at age 28, September 17, 1862, for the war. Present or accounted for until wounded in the right eye at Kelly's Ford, Virginia, November 7, 1863. Reported absent wounded or absent without leave through August, 1864. [North Carolina pension records dated 1909 indicate that he "lost an eye" as a result of his wounds and that the "ball . . . is still in his head causing great pain & swelling."]

McLURE, J. A., Private
Resided in Mecklenburg County and enlisted in Wake County at age 26, June 4, 1863, for the war. Present or accounted for until wounded in the right arm at or near Bethesda Church, Virginia, May 30, 1864. Right arm

amputated. Reported absent wounded until December 1, 1864, when he was retired to the Invalid Corps.

McMULLEN, JAMES H., Private
Resided in Mecklenburg County where he enlisted at age 24, September 13, 1861. Present or accounted for until wounded in the shoulder at Gaines' Mill, Virginia, June 27, 1862. Died of wounds. Place and date of death not reported.

McQUAY, JOSEPH F., Private
Resided in Mecklenburg County and enlisted in Wake County at age 29, August 20, 1863, for the war. Present or accounted for until captured at Burkeville, Virginia, April 6, 1865. Confined at Newport News, Virginia, April 14, 1865. Released on June 14, 1865, after taking the Oath of Allegiance.

MASSINGILL, R. S., Private
Resided in Johnston County and was by occupation a farmer prior to enlisting in Wake County at age 33, September 17, 1862, for the war. Present or accounted for until wounded in the side at Gaines' Mill, Virginia, on or about June 27, 1862. Returned to duty on an unspecified date. Reported absent sick from December 20, 1862, until June 15, 1863, when he was reported absent without leave. Reported absent without leave through December, 1863. Returned to duty prior to May 30, 1864, when he was captured at or near Bethesda Church, Virginia. Confined at Point Lookout, Maryland, June 8, 1864. Transferred to Elmira, New York, July 9, 1864. Released at Elmira on May 29, 1865, after taking the Oath of Allegiance.

MILLER, DAVID M., Private
Resided in Mecklenburg County and enlisted in Wake County at age 42, August 20, 1863, for the war. Present or accounted for until captured at High Bridge, Virginia, April 6, 1865. Confined at Point Lookout, Maryland, April 14, 1865. Released on June 29, 1865, after taking the Oath of Allegiance.

MILTON, JOSEPH G., Private
Resided in Mecklenburg County where he enlisted at age 17, September 13, 1861. Present or accounted for until he died in hospital at Culpeper, Virginia, October 19, 1862, of "chronic diarrhoea."

MORRIS, JAMES T., Private
Resided in Mecklenburg County where he enlisted at age 18, September 13, 1861. Present or accounted for until he was "left" at Leesburg, Virginia, "on the march into Maryland," on or about September 3, 1862. Died on an unspecified date. Place and cause of death not reported.

MORRIS, W. T., Private
Resided in Mecklenburg County and enlisted at age 17, January 12, 1863, for the war. Present or accounted for until he died at Richmond, Virginia, February 25, 1863. Cause of death not reported.

MYERS, JAMES, Private
Resided in Davie County and enlisted in Wake County at age 40, July 9, 1863, for the war. Present or accounted for until captured at Kelly's Ford, Virginia, November 7, 1863. Confined at Point Lookout, Maryland, November 11, 1863. Paroled at Point Lookout on or about February 24, 1865, and transferred to Aiken's

Landing, James River, Virginia, where he was received February 25-March 3, 1865, for exchange.

NELSON, JOHN H., Private
Resided in Pitt County and enlisted in Wake County at age 27, July 1, 1863, for the war. Present or accounted for until wounded in the left foot on or about October 25, 1863. Returned to duty in November-December, 1863. Present or accounted for until hospitalized at Richmond, Virginia, May 19, 1864, with a gunshot wound of the head. Place and date wounded not reported. Reported absent wounded through August, 1864. Returned to duty on an unspecified date. Captured at Burkeville, Virginia, April 6, 1865. Confined at Newport News, Virginia, April 14, 1865. Released on June 15, 1865, after taking the Oath of Allegiance.

NICHOLS, BURGES G., Sergeant
Resided in Mecklenburg County and enlisted at Camp Wyatt at age 20, February 10, 1862. Mustered in as Private. Promoted to Corporal in September-December, 1863. Present or accounted for until wounded in the right thigh at or near Spotsylvania Court House, Virginia, May 12, 1864. Returned to duty and was promoted to Sergeant on or about September 1, 1864. Surrendered at Appomattox Court House, Virginia, April 9, 1865.

NICHOLS, J., Private
Place and date of enlistment not reported. Captured at Spotsylvania Court House, Virginia, May 20, 1864. Confined at Point Lookout, Maryland, May 23, 1864. Transferred to Elmira, New York, July 3, 1864. Paroled at Elmira on March 14, 1865, and transferred to Boulware's Wharf, James River, Virginia, where he was received March 18-21, 1865, for exchange.

ORR, THOMAS J., Private
Previously served in Company B, 1st Regiment N.C. Infantry (6 months, 1861). Enlisted in this company at Camp Wyatt on February 10, 1862. Present or accounted for until he surrendered at Appomattox Court House, Virginia, April 9, 1865.

PATTERSON, WILLIAM S., Private
Resided in South Carolina and enlisted in Mecklenburg County at age 17, September 13, 1861. Died at Wilmington on January 1, 1862. Cause of death not reported.

PAXTON, JAMES L., Private
Enlisted in Mecklenburg County on September 13, 1861. Company records indicate that he "never appeared, plea not having been legally sworn."

PIERCE, JAMES M., Private
Resided in Mecklenburg County where he enlisted at age 22, September 13, 1861. Present or accounted for until May 19, 1864, when he was wounded at or near Spotsylvania Court House, Virginia. Company records indicate he was captured on May 19, 1864; however, records of the Federal Provost Marshal do not substantiate that report. No further records.

PIERCE, JAMES W., Private
Resided in Wake County where he enlisted at age 26, September 17, 1862, for the war. Present or accounted for until he deserted on or about March 29, 1863.

Returned to duty subsequent to December 31, 1863. Deserted on July 9, 1864.

PIERCE, ORREN L., Private
Resided in Mecklenburg County where he enlisted at age 20, September 13, 1861. Present or accounted for until captured at Frederick, Maryland, September 13, 1862. Confined at Fort Delaware, Delaware. Paroled and transferred to Aiken's Landing, James River, Virginia, October 2, 1862, for exchange. Declared exchanged at Aiken's Landing on November 10, 1862. Returned to duty subsequent to December 31, 1862. Present or accounted for until captured at Fisher's Hill, Virginia, September 22, 1864. Confined at Point Lookout, Maryland, October 3, 1864. Paroled at Point Lookout on or about March 17, 1865, and transferred to Boulware's Wharf, James River, Virginia, where he was received on March 19, 1865, for exchange.

POTTS, J. R., Private
Resided in Mecklenburg County and enlisted in Wake County at age 38, August 20, 1863, for the war. Present or accounted for until he died in hospital at Staunton, Virginia, November 4, 1863, of "typhoid fever."

RAYL, JOHN F., Private
Resided in Guilford County. Place and date of enlistment not reported. Captured at Burkeville, Virginia, April 6, 1865. Confined at Point Lookout, Maryland, April 14, 1865. Released on June 30, 1865, after taking the Oath of Allegiance.

RAYNER, LOVET, Private
Resided in Johnston County and enlisted in Wake County at age 33, September 17, 1862, for the war. Present or accounted for until wounded in the "bowels" and captured at Kelly's Ford, Virginia, November 7, 1863. Died of wounds. Place and date of death not reported.

REA, JAMES MILTON, Private
Resided in Mecklenburg County where he enlisted at age 24, September 13, 1861. Present or accounted for until killed at Chancellorsville, Virginia, May 3, 1863. "While in a desperate charge on the enemy's batteries, he was shot through the head, a minnie [sic] ball entering the left eye. . . . He was a faithful and good soldier."

RICHARDSON, WILLIAM W., Private
Resided in Mecklenburg County where he enlisted at age 17, September 13, 1861. Present or accounted for until captured at or near Farmville, Virginia, April 6, 1865. Confined at Newport News, Virginia, April 14, 1865. Released on June 27, 1865, after taking the Oath of Allegiance.

ROBINSON, JAMES R., Private
Resided in Union County and enlisted in Mecklenburg County at age 16, September 13, 1861. Present or accounted for until killed at Malvern Hill, Virginia, July 1, 1862.

ROBINSON, WILLIAM H., Private
Resided in Mecklenburg County where he enlisted at age 34, September 13, 1861. Present or accounted for until captured near Washington, D.C., July 12, 1864. Confined at Old Capitol Prison, Washington, July 13, 1864. Transferred to Elmira, New York, July 23, 1864.

Died at Elmira on January 30, 1865, of "acute bronchitis."

ROSS, J. N., Private
Born in Mecklenburg County where he resided prior to enlisting in Wake County at age 36, November 3, 1863, for the war. Present or accounted for until wounded at Spotsylvania Court House, Virginia, May 12, 1864. Died at Spotsylvania Court House on May 15, 1864, of wounds.

ROSS, WILLIAM J., Private
Resided in Mecklenburg County where he enlisted at age 33, September 13, 1861. Present or accounted for until he surrendered at Appomattox Court House, Virginia, April 9, 1865.

RUSSELL, WILLIAM D., Sergeant
Resided in Mecklenburg County where he enlisted at age 18, September 13, 1861. Mustered in as Private. Present or accounted for until wounded at Fredericksburg, Virginia, December 13, 1862. Returned to duty subsequent to December 31, 1862. Promoted to Corporal on May 3, 1863. Present or accounted for until wounded in the head and captured at Gettysburg, Pennsylvania, July 1-4, 1863. Confined at Fort Delaware, Delaware, on or about July 9, 1863. Paroled at Fort Delaware and transferred to City Point, Virginia, where he was received on August 1, 1863, for exchange. Returned to duty prior to January 1, 1864. Present or accounted for until hospitalized at Richmond, Virginia, May 18, 1864, with a gunshot wound of the left leg. Place and date wounded not reported. Promoted to Sergeant on August 1, 1864. Returned to duty subsequent to August 31, 1864. Captured at or near Farmville, Virginia, April 6, 1865. Confined at Newport News, Virginia, April 14, 1865. Released on June 27, 1865, after taking the Oath of Allegiance.

SAMPLE, WILLIAM, Private
Resided in Mecklenburg County and enlisted in Wake County at age 37, October 7, 1863, for the war. Present or accounted for until captured at Wilderness, Virginia, May 8, 1864. Confined at Point Lookout, Maryland, May 17, 1864. Paroled at Point Lookout on October 11, 1864, and transferred to Cox's Wharf, James River, Virginia, where he was received on October 15, 1864, for exchange. Company records do not indicate whether he returned to duty. Paroled at Burkeville, Virginia, April 14-17, 1865.

SAVILLE, JOHN CROCKETT, Corporal
Resided in Mecklenburg County and enlisted in Wake County at age 18, August 20, 1863, for the war. Mustered in as Private. Present or accounted for until wounded in the face at or near Snicker's Gap, Virginia, on or about July 18, 1864. Hospitalized at Charlottesville, Virginia. Returned to duty on August 9, 1864. Promoted to Corporal subsequent to August 31, 1864. Surrendered at Appomattox Court House, Virginia, April 9, 1865.

SHAW, ALEXANDER G., Private
Resided in Mecklenburg County where he enlisted at age 23, September 13, 1861. Present or accounted for until May, 1862, when he was detailed "to work on gunboats" at Wilmington. Reported absent on detail at Wilmington through August, 1864.

SHELBY, D. H., Private
Resided in Mecklenburg County and enlisted in Wake County at age 42, August 20, 1863, for the war. Present or accounted for until hospitalized at Richmond, Virginia, February 15, 1865, with typhoid fever. Furloughed for sixty days on March 10, 1865.

SIMMONS, ELISHA, Private
Resided in Caswell County and enlisted in Wake County at age 44, September 10, 1863, for the war. Present or accounted for until captured in hospital at Richmond, Virginia, April 3, 1865. Confined at Newport News, Virginia, April 24, 1865. No further records.

SIMPSON, JEFFERSON, Private
Born in Mecklenburg County where he resided as a farmer prior to enlisting in Mecklenburg County at age 43, September 13, 1861. Present or accounted for until discharged on October 15, 1862, under the provisions of the Conscription Act. Later served in Company G, 4th Regiment N.C. Senior Reserves.

SIMPSON, MARCUS L., Private
Previously served in Company F, 35th Regiment N.C. Troops. Enlisted in this company in New Hanover County at age 24, October 5, 1861. Present or accounted for until July 1, 1862, when he was reported absent without leave. Reported absent without leave through December, 1863. Returned to duty prior to May 12, 1864, when he was captured at Spotsylvania Court House, Virginia. Confined at Point Lookout, Maryland, May 18, 1864. Released on May 27, 1864, after joining the U.S. Army. Unit to which assigned not reported.

SMITH, J. D., Private
Resided in Cabarrus County and enlisted in Wake County at age 40, June 2, 1863, for the war. Present or accounted for until detailed as a hospital nurse at Raleigh on September 10, 1864. Captured in hospital at Raleigh on April 13, 1865. No further records.

SMITH, J. S., Private
Resided in Anson County and enlisted in Wake County at age 37, April 2, 1863, for the war. Present or accounted for until he deserted on November 15, 1863. Returned to duty prior to May 8, 1864, when he was captured at or near Spotsylvania Court House, Virginia. Confined at Point Lookout, Maryland, May 17, 1864. Died at Point Lookout on February 6-7, 1865, of "diarrhoea chr[onic]."

SMITH, S. BLACK, Corporal
Resided in Mecklenburg County and enlisted at Richmond, Virginia, at age 26, July 10, 1862, for the war. Mustered in as Private. Promoted to Corporal in January-June, 1863. Present or accounted for until he died in hospital at Charlotte on July 11, 1863. Cause of death not reported.

SMITH, WILLIAM STEWART, 1st Sergeant
Resided in Mecklenburg County where he enlisted at age 24, September 13, 1861. Mustered in as Private. Promoted to 1st Sergeant on May 1, 1862. Present or accounted for until he surrendered at Appomattox Court House, Virginia, April 9, 1865.

SQUIRES, JAMES W., Private
Born in Mecklenburg County where he resided prior to

enlisting in Mecklenburg County at age 25, September 13, 1861. Present or accounted for until killed at or near Spotsylvania Court House, Virginia, May 12, 1864.

SQUIRES, JOHN BROWN, Private
Previously served in Company B, 1st Regiment N.C. Infantry (6 months, 1861). Enlisted in this company at Camp Wyatt at age 23, January 25, 1862. Mustered in as Private. Present or accounted for until captured at Frederick, Maryland, September 12, 1862. Confined at Fort Delaware, Delaware. Paroled and transferred to Aiken's Landing, James River, Virginia, October 2, 1862, for exchange. Declared exchanged at Aiken's Landing on November 10, 1862. Returned to duty in January-June, 1863. Promoted to Ordnance Sergeant on May 10, 1864. Reduced to ranks subsequent to August 31, 1864. Present or accounted for until he surrendered at Appomattox Court House, Virginia, April 9, 1865.

STANCILL, ARTHUR G., Private
Resided in Mecklenburg County where he enlisted at age 23, September 13, 1861. Present or accounted for until he deserted on September 10, 1862. Discharged from service on February 12, 1863, by reason of disability.

STANFORD, MOSES T., Private
Resided in Mecklenburg County where he enlisted at age 39, September 13, 1861. Present or accounted for until discharged in October, 1862, under the provisions of the Conscription Act.

STEEL, ANDREW F., Sergeant
Born in Mecklenburg County where he resided prior to enlisting in Mecklenburg County at age 28, September 13, 1861. Mustered in as Private. Promoted to Corporal on November 1, 1861. Promoted to Sergeant in May-July, 1862. Present or accounted for until wounded at Gaines' Mill, Virginia, June 27, 1862. Died prior to July 22, 1862, of wounds. Place of death not reported.

STEPHENSON, JAMES R., Private
Born in Mecklenburg County where he resided prior to enlisting in Mecklenburg County at age 19, September 13, 1861. Present or accounted for until wounded at Sharpsburg, Maryland, September 17, 1862. Died in hospital at Staunton, Virginia, on or about December 12, 1862, of wounds.

TART, HENRY, Private
Resided in Harnett County and enlisted in Wake County at age 18, June 1, 1863, for the war. Present or accounted for until September 1, 1864, when he was reported absent without leave.

TEDDER, SIDNEY, Sergeant
Resided in Mecklenburg County where he enlisted at age 31, September 13, 1861. Mustered in as Private. Promoted to Sergeant in May-June, 1862. Present or accounted for until killed at Gaines' Mill, Virginia, June 27, 1862.

THOMAS, LEWIS R., Private
Resided in Montgomery County and enlisted in Wake County at age 30, August 20, 1863, for the war. Present or accounted for until detailed for duty as a hospital guard at Richmond, Virginia, on or about May 29, 1864. Reported absent on detail at Richmond through December, 1864. Returned to duty on an unspecified date. Captured at Harper's Farm, Virginia, April 6,

1865. Confined at Fort McHenry, Maryland, May 9, 1865. Released on or about May 31, 1865.

THOMAS, WILLIAM B., Corporal
Resided in Mecklenburg County and enlisted at Camp Wyatt at age 23, January 1, 1862. Mustered in as Private. Promoted to Corporal subsequent to August 31, 1864. Present or accounted for until he surrendered at Appomattox Court House, Virginia, April 9, 1865.

THOMASON, JOHN L., Private
Resided in Mecklenburg County where he enlisted at age 18, September 13, 1861. Present or accounted for until wounded at Gaines' Mill, Virginia, June 27, 1862. Died of wounds. Place and date of death not reported.

THOMPSON, JAMES, Private
Resided in Rowan County and enlisted in Wake County at age 37, June 26, 1863, for the war. Present or accounted for until he died at Morton's Ford, Virginia, December 12, 1863, of disease.

THOMPSON, LEE, Private
Resided in Mecklenburg County and was by occupation a farmer prior to enlisting in Mecklenburg County at age 28, September 13, 1861. Present or accounted for until wounded on or about August 14, 1862. Returned to duty on November 10, 1862. Present or accounted for until he died in hospital at Richmond, Virginia, on or about February 16, 1863, of "febris typhoides."

THOMPSON, LEWIS, Private
Resided in Mecklenburg County where he enlisted at age 34, September 13, 1861. Present or accounted for until September-December, 1862, when he was reported absent wounded. Place and date wounded not reported. Returned to duty prior to May 1-4, 1863, when he was wounded at Chancellorsville, Virginia. Detailed for light duty at Charlotte in December, 1863. Reported absent on detail at Charlotte through August, 1864. Hospitalized at Charlotte on September 23, 1864, with debilitas and returned to duty on September 27, 1864. No further records.

THROWER, THOMAS J., Private
Born in Mecklenburg County where he resided as a farmer prior to enlisting in Mecklenburg County at age 17, September 13, 1861. Present or accounted for until discharged on March 5, 1862, by reason of "an attack of rubeola" which threatened to develop into "tuberculor phthisis."

WALL, J. G., Private
Place and date of enlistment not reported. Paroled at Charlotte on May 18, 1865.

WALLACE, MARQUIS L., Private
Enlisted in Mecklenburg County on September 13, 1861. Discharged "without having served" on an unspecified date. Reason discharged not reported.

WALSTON, SILAS L., Private
Resided in Johnston County and enlisted in Wake County at age 28, September 17, 1862, for the war. Present or accounted for until he died at Staunton, Virginia, January 3, 1863, of "erysipelas."

WEBB, WILLIAM, Private
Resided in Johnston County and enlisted in Wake

County at age 37, September 17, 1862, for the war. Present or accounted for until he died at Richmond, Virginia, March 11 or March 18, 1863, of "pneumonia" and/or "chr[onic] diarr[hoea]."

WEEKS, RUFUS B., Sergeant
Born in Mecklenburg County where he resided as a farmer prior to enlisting at Camp Wyatt at age 19, February 10, 1862. Mustered in as Private. Present or accounted for until he was "bruised by bomb" and wounded in the left shoulder at or near Sharpsburg, Maryland, September 17, 1862. Returned to duty on October 5, 1862. Promoted to Sergeant subsequent to December 31, 1863. Present or accounted for until killed at or near Spotsylvania Court House, Virginia, May 19, 1864.

WEST, WILLIAM M., Private
Resided in Rowan County and enlisted in Wake County at age 40, June 7, 1863, for the war. Present or accounted for until captured at or near Fisher's Hill, Virginia, on or about September 22, 1864. Confined at Point Lookout, Maryland, October 3, 1864. Died at Point Lookout on April 26, 1865, of "pneumonia."

WILLIAMSON, WILLIAM E., Private
Resided in Mecklenburg County where he enlisted at age 17, September 13, 1861. Present or accounted for until captured at or near Sharpsburg, Maryland, on or about September 17, 1862. Paroled on September 27, 1862. Reported absent sick through December, 1862. Discharged on an unspecified date under the provisions of the Conscription Act.

WINGATE, WILLIAM C., Private
Enlisted in Mecklenburg County on September 13, 1861. "Never appeared, plea not having been legally sworn."

WITHERSPOON, M. J., Private
Resided in Cabarrus County and enlisted at Camp Drane at age 18, May 26, 1862, for the war. Present or accounted for until wounded at Chancellorsville, Virginia, May 3, 1863. Died on May 7, 1863, of wounds. Place of death not reported.

WOLF, THOMAS D., Private
Resided in Mecklenburg County and was by occupation a farmer prior to enlisting at Camp Wyatt at age 19, February 10, 1862. Present or accounted for until hospitalized at Richmond, Virginia, September 28, 1862, with a gunshot wound of the hand. Place and date wounded not reported. Reported absent on furlough through December, 1862. Died in hospital at Richmond on March 29-31, 1863, of "pneumonia" and/or "chr[onic] diarr[hoea]."

WOLFE, JOHN N., Private
Resided in Mecklenburg County where he enlisted at age 16, September 13, 1861. Present or accounted for until wounded at Gaines' Mill, Virginia, June 27, 1862. Discharged prior to January 1, 1863, under the provisions of the Conscription Act. [May have served later in Company C, 10th Battalion N.C. Heavy Artillery.]

WOLFE, ROBERT B., Private
Resided in Mecklenburg County where he enlisted at age 20, September 13, 1861. Present or accounted for

through April, 1862. Listed as a deserter in September-December, 1862. Returned to duty on an unspecified date. Reported absent without leave on May 1, 1863. Returned to duty on August 8, 1863. Captured at Kelly's Ford, Virginia, November 7, 1863. Confined at Point Lookout, Maryland, November 11, 1863. Died at Point Lookout on March 1, 1865, of "pneumonia."

YEARGEN, WYATT, Private
Resided in Mecklenburg County and enlisted in Wake County at age 28, September 17, 1862, for the war. Present or accounted for until transferred to Company I, 6th Regiment N.C. State Troops, April 10, 1863

YOUNG, SAMUEL T., Private
Resided in Johnston County and enlisted in Wake County at age 36, September 17, 1862, for the war. Present or accounted for until reported absent without leave on November 15, 1863. Reported absent without leave through August, 1864.

YOUNTS, JOHN A., Private
Resided in Mecklenburg County where he enlisted at age 16, September 13, 1861. Present or accounted for until wounded at Malvern Hill, Virginia, July 1, 1862. Returned to duty prior to January 1, 1863. Present or accounted for until wounded at Chancellorsville, Virginia, May 3, 1863. Reported absent in hospital through August, 1863. Discharged on an unspecified date under the provisions of the Conscription Act. Later served in Company F, 63rd Regiment N.C. Troops (5th Regiment N.C. Cavalry).

YOUNTS, SAMUEL, Sergeant
Enlisted in Mecklenburg County on September 13, 1861. Mustered in as Sergeant. Company records indicate he was "absent, never appeared, plea not being legally sworn."

MISCELLANEOUS

Civil War records indicate that the following soldiers served in the 30th Regiment N.C. Troops; however, the companies in which these soldiers served are not reported.

BALL, THOMAS, ———
North Carolina pension records indicate that he served in this regiment.

CASE, WILLIAM H., ———
North Carolina pension records indicate that he served in this regiment.

CRAVER, A. J., Private
Resided in Yadkin County. Place and date of enlistment not reported. Deserted to the enemy on an unspecified date. Took the Oath of Allegiance at City Point, Virginia, on or about October 15, 1864.

LEE, B. L., Private
Place and date of enlistment not reported. Paroled at Richmond, Virginia, April 30, 1865.

OUTEN, W. R., ———
North Carolina pension records indicate that he served in this regiment.

PITMAN, WILLIAM, Private
Place and date of enlistment not reported. Deserted to

the enemy on an unspecified date. Took the Oath of Allegiance at Bermuda Hundred, Virginia, March 18, 1865.

RUSH, J. H., ———
North Carolina pension records indicate that he served in this regiment.

SOUTHERLAND, I. R., ———
North Carolina pension records indicate that he served in this regiment.

WARDEN, NATHAN C., Private
Resided in Yadkin County. Place and date of enlistment

not reported. Deserted to the enemy on an unspecified date. Took the Oath of Allegiance at City Point, Virginia, October 15, 1864.

WATSON, THOMAS, Private
Place and date of enlistment not reported. Captured at Raleigh on or about April 13, 1865. Paroled at Raleigh on April 24, 1865.

WILSON, THOMAS, Private
Place and date of enlistment not reported. Deserted to the enemy on an unspecified date. Took the Oath of Allegiance on or about March 24, 1865.

31st REGIMENT N.C. TROOPS

This regiment was organized at Hill's Point, Beaufort County, on September 19, 1861, for twelve months' service. The regiment remained at Hill's Point as a supporting unit for Fort Hill until December 7, 1861, when it was ordered to Roanoke Island. The regiment arrived at Plymouth on December 9, boarded transports the next day, and landed at Roanoke Island on December 12. It then went into camp on the northern end of the island. For the next two months the men of the 31st Regiment were kept busy building barracks, constructing fortifications, filling schooners with sand to blockade the channel west of the island, and piling the sound. The island was strategically located and, if properly defended, could block the passage from Pamlico Sound to Albemarle Sound.

Toward the end of 1861 the Federals began making preparations for an expedition against Roanoke Island, and an amphibious force of approximately 7,500 men under General Ambrose E. Burnside was assembled at Fort Monroe, Virginia. The enemy fleet entered Pamlico Sound on January 13, 1862, moved against Roanoke Island on February 6, and, under cover of a heavy bombardment, succeeded in landing troops on the island on February 7. Colonel John V. Jordan reported the activities of the 31st Regiment during February 6 and 7 to Colonel Henry M. Shaw, who was in command of the 1,500-man Confederate defense force, as follows (*Official Records*, Series I, Vol. IX, pp. 175-177):

The first appearance of the enemy was on the morning of the 6th instant, about 8 o'clock, as seen from Ashby's Landing by the forces stationed there, consisting of two companies (B and F, infantry) of my regiment, under command of Captains [Edward R.] Liles and [Charles W.] Knight, with two pieces of artillery, one 24-pounder navy howitzer, and one 18-pounder field gun, the whole force, including the artillery, under Captain Liles, he being the senior officer present. Under an order from you to proceed to Ashby's Landing I arrived there at [noon] on the 6th, and discovered by aid of a glass a large number of the enemy's fleet, consisting of steam and sail vessels, then apparently lying at anchor at a point 10 miles below the southern point of the island. I left Ashby's at 2 p.m. and met you, in company with Captain [John S.] Taylor, of the Navy, and reported the information I had received.

Upon your return to the camp I received an order from you to prepare one day's rations for all the available forces under my command, with the exception of one company, which was to be left in charge of the camp, and that portion of Captain [Condary] Godwin's company which was then in quarters and which you ordered to be sent to the western side of the sound, at a point called Fort Forrest, then in charge of Captain [Joseph] Whitty, with instructions to Captain Godwin to support Captain Whitty in protecting that point. The remaining portion of my available forces, with one day's provisions, was ordered to take up the line of march to Ashby's Landing or that vicinity. On arriving at Suple's Hill, about a mile and a half above this landing, the forces were ordered to bivouac for the night.

At a very early hour on the morning of the 7th myself [*sic*], in company with Major [Jesse J.] Yeates, proceeded to the landing, leaving Lieutenant-Colonel [Daniel G.] Fowle in charge of the forces at Suple's Hill, with a view of making further preparation to meet the enemy should a landing be attempted at that point.

About 10 a. m. I perceived that the enemy's fleet was in motion, advancing up the sound, and at about 11.45 o'clock the leading steamer opened fire upon Fort Bartow. About 3 p. m. the engagement became general upon the part of the enemy's vessels against Fort Bartow. At about 4 p. m. a small boat, containing about 15 men, left one of the transports of the enemy, apparently with a view of taking soundings at Hammond's Landing, about half a mile above Ashby's. As the boat approached the land I detailed a force of 25, under command of Captain Liles, to intercept it. The party in the boat had effected a landing, when Captain Liles ordered the men under his command to fire upon them, by which fire it has since been ascertained that 3 of the enemy were killed and 1 wounded. The remainder immediately retreated to the vessel in the sound. About 5 o'clock a large steamer and a number of smaller boats, carrying a force estimated at 8,000 or 10,000 men, with several pieces of artillery, and under cover of the gunboats in the sound, was seen approaching Hammond's Landing, between which and the point occupied by my forces lay a large marsh impassable by artillery. Having no horses for our artillery, fearing that we might be cut off, or at least that the shells from the enemy's guns in the sound might confuse and disconcert the men under my command and cause the eventual loss of the field pieces, which you enjoined upon me at all hazards to save, I considered it judicious to order a retreat. The infantry, under command of Lieutenant-Colonel Fowle, was placed in rear of the artillery to protect it, and all the forces retired in good order to a redoubt thrown across the main road one mile and a quarter above Ashby's, where the guns were placed in battery, the 18-pounder on the left and the howitzer on the right, under command of Captain Schermerhorn and Lieutenant [T. C.] Kinney, and a 6-pounder occupying the center, under command of Lieutenant [W. B.] Selden. The gun detachments were immediately ordered to take position at their pieces. A picket guard was thrown out and a detail ordered from each company present, to mask the battery as effectually as the short time rendered practicable. Soon afterward you arrived and took command.

Late in the afternoon of February 7 the Confederate forces occupied a defensive position across the main road and awaited the Federal attack, which was delivered on the morning of February 8. Colonel Shaw reported the action to General Henry A. Wise, the district commander, as follows (*Official Records*, Series I, Vol. IX, pp. 171-173):

At 7 a. m. the battle commenced, and as soon as the enemy gathered in force, which was in a very few minutes thereafter, our battery opened fire. This battery was composed of three pieces—one 24-pounder howitzer, one 18-pounder field piece, and one 6-pounder. For the 18-pounder the only ammunition we had was 12-pounder ammunition. The artillery detachments may be said to have been almost totally uninstructed. Having in my command no officer acquainted with that practice save Major [G. H.] Hill, whose duties confined him to Pork Point Battery, I applied to Colonel [J. H.] Richardson, upon his arrival at Nag's Head, for some officers to instruct the men. He had none. Upon your reaching that place I made a like application to you. Captain

Schermerhorn and Lieutenant Kinney were sent. The former disclaimed any particular knowledge upon the subject. They were immediately sent to Ashby's; but the enemy made his appearance so soon, little time was allowed them to drill the men.

Captain Schermerhorn was placed in charge of the 18-pounder, Lieutenant Kinney of the 24-pounder, and Lieut. W. B. Selden, Engineer Department, who had patriotically volunteered his services in the line, was assigned to the 6-pounder, and, notwithstanding the men had received so little instruction, these pieces were handled in such a way as to produce immense havoc in the enemy's ranks; especially that of Lieutenant Selden, whose conduct elicited the unbounded admiration of all who witnessed it. Unhappily at about 11 o'clock that gallant officer received a rifle-ball in his head, and he fell without a groan, a willing sacrifice to a cause which he had espoused with all the ardor of his generous nature.

In the mean time [sic] the fire of the musketry had been kept up from the commencement of the action with unabated vigor by the following companies under cover of the breastwork: Company B, Captain [J. M.] Whitson, Eighth Regiment North Carolina State troops; Company B, Captain [E. R.] Liles, and Company F, Captain [C. W.] Knight, Thirty-first Regiment North Carolina troops; Company D, Captain [Hiram B.] Dickinson, and Company K, Lieutenant [Christopher C.] Roy, Fifty-ninth Virginia Volunteers; and Company E, Lieut. J. R. Murchison, Eighth Regiment North Carolina State troops, whose second lieutenant, N. G. Munro [Monroe], a promising young officer, fell on his approach near the redoubt.

By the gallant officers and brave men of the above-named companies an unceasing and effective fire was kept up from 7 a. m. until 12.20, when, our artillery ammunition having been exhausted and our right flank having been turned by an overwhelming force of the enemy, I was compelled to yield the place.

The entire available force of my command, exclusive of the companies on duty at the several batteries, amounted to 1,434, rank and file. Of these 568 were of the Eighth North Carolina State troops, 456 of the Thirty-first North Carolina troops, and the balance of the Forty-sixth and Fifty-ninth Virginia Volunteers, commanded by Lieutenant-Colonel [F. P.] Anderson, who, together with Major [John] Lawson, was at the redoubt during the most part of the action, and rendered efficient service. The enemy's force amounted to 15,000 men, with several pieces of artillery. With the very great disparity of forces, the moment the redoubt was flanked I considered the island lost. The struggle could have been protracted, and the small body of brave men which had been held in reserve might have been brought up into the open space to receive the fire of the overwhelming force on our flank, which was under cover of trees; but they would have been sacrificed without the smallest hope of a successful result.

The mules and horses attached to the artillery had been killed during the action; the pieces had to be abandoned, and believing it utterly impossible to make a successful stand against such an overwhelming force, I deemed it my duty to surrender.

During the Battle of Roanoke Island the 31st Regiment lost 2 men killed, 8 wounded, and 76 missing. Most of the remaining members of the regiment, except those belonging to Companies A and H, were captured. The captives were transported to Elizabeth City, where they were paroled and sent home. Under the parole agreement, the men could not return to duty until they were exchanged man-for-man for Federal prisoners or parolees.

The men of Company A blew up Fort Forrest on the evening of February 8 and made their escape, as did the men of Company H, who had been stationed at a battery at Midgett's Hommock. Members of other companies who evaded capture or were absent from the island during the battle were ordered to organize into two provisional companies until their comrades were exchanged.

The Roanoke Island captives remained on parole until August 21, 1862, when they were exchanged. They were then ordered to report to Camp Mangum, near Raleigh, where the 31st Regiment was reorganized on September 17 to serve for the duration of the war. The regiment remained at Camp Mangum until October 23, when it moved to Kinston. The activities of the regiment during the next three weeks were reported on the North Carolina Roll of Honor as follows:

The Regiment left Camp Mangum Oct. 23. 1862 for Kinston N. C. [and] arrived at that place Oct. 24: established our encampment on the plantation of John Tull Esq: one Mile North of Kinston and called it Camp Martin. Left Camp Martin Nov. 4th. in light marching order in Company with the whole force in and about Kinston under Command of Col. H. M. Shaw of the 8th N. C. T. for Greenville N. C.[,] it being reported that the Enemy were advancing in that direction. Arrived at Greenville on the 5th[,] distance twenty-five miles marched in twenty two [sic] hours, finding no enemy there or in its vicinity[.] On the 6th received orders to return to Kinston. This march was accomplished under a pitiless storm of snow and rain, the most of the men were without blankets or shoes and suffered terribly. On the evening of the 8th arrived at our Old Camp. On the morning of [the] 9th received orders to take up line of march for the vicinity of Newbern N. C. On the night of the 9th bivouacked at Shady Grove Church, Jones County N. C. On the night of the 10th [we bivouacked] opposite Trenton, Jones County N. C. On the 11th we marched to Rocky Run six miles from Newbern[.] [H]ere we met a Yankee force of Cavalry and Infantry supposed to be One Thousand strong[.] [T]hey were driven across the Run destroying the bridge in their retreat. On the night of the 11th we entered and encamped on Dardens Farm two miles west of Rocky Run[.] [R]eturned to the Run on the morning of the 12th and finding no Enemy we received orders to move towards Kinston[.] [A]rrived at that place on the evening of the 13th.

The regiment returned to Camp Martin shortly thereafter, and towards the end of November it was assigned to General Thomas L. Clingman's brigade. On December 7 the regiment left its camp near Kinston and traveled by train to Wilmington, where it joined the brigade the next day. In addition to this regiment the brigade was composed of the 8th Regiment N.C. State Troops, 51st Regiment N.C. Troops, and 61st Regiment N.C. Troops.

The regiment left Wilmington for Kinston on December 15 to reinforce the Confederate troops opposing an advancing Federal force under General John G. Foster.

At Falling Creek, seven miles west of Kinston, orders were received to retire to White Hall (now called Seven Springs) on the Neuse River. After arriving within one mile of White Hall at 4:00 A.M. on December 16, the regiment was halted. At 8:00 A.M. General Beverly H. Robertson, commander of the Confederate force, ordered the 31st Regiment to take a position on the north side of the Neuse, about a hundred yards from the riverbank, on the road leading from the burnt-out White Hall bridge to Goldsboro. General Robertson reported the ensuing engagement at White Hall as follows (*Official Records*, Series I, Vol. XVIII, pp. 121-122):

> About 9 a. m. on the 16th a brisk picket skirmish commenced. I visited the bridge, and after giving the necessary instructions went back to order up the Thirty-first North Carolina Regiment, Col. [John V.] Jordan, which had arrived during the night, and which I placed in position as much sheltered as circumstances would permit. I then posted the artillery as well as the nature of the ground would admit and ordered both shell and solid shot to be fired. For some time previous the enemy had been firing from 12 to 18 pounders, some of immense caliber. Owing to a range of hills on the White Hall side the enemy had the advantage of position. The point occupied by his troops being narrow, not more than one regiment at a time could advantageously engage him. I therefore held [Colonels Collett] Leventhorpe, [Dennis D.] Ferebee, and [Peter G.] Evans in reserve, leaving the artillery, Thirty-first Regiment, and two picket companies in front. The cannonading from the enemy's batteries became so terrific that the Thirty-first Regiment withdrew from their position without instructions but in good order. I immediately ordered Colonel Leventhorpe forward [with the 11th Regiment N.C. Troops]. The alacrity with which the order was obeyed by his men gave ample proof of their gallant bearing, which they so nobly sustained during the entire fight, which raged with intensity for several hours after they became engaged. No veteran soldiers ever fought better or inflicted more terrible loss upon an enemy considering the numbers engaged. It was with difficulty they could be withdrawn from the field. Three times did they drive the Yankee cannoneers from their guns and as often prevent their infantry regiments from forming line in their front. In spite of the four hostile regiments whose standards waved from the opposite bank did these brave men continue to hold their ground, and finally drove the enemy in confusion from the field.

During the fight the 31st Regiment lost two men killed and twenty-two wounded.

The engagement at White Hall, contrary to General Robertson's report, was something less than a Confederate victory, and Foster's force continued to advance up the south bank of the Neuse toward Goldsboro. The 31st Regiment was ordered to picket the north bank of the river, but those orders were canceled on the morning of December 17, and the regiment, minus a 200-man detail, was sent to Best Station. From there it moved to Spring Bank, eight miles from Goldsboro, where it arrived on the morning of December 18. In the meantime, the other three regiments of Clingman's brigade had been engaged on the previous day in an unsuccessful attempt to prevent Foster's men from burning the important railroad bridge at Goldsboro. Foster, regarding as accomplished his mission

to disrupt Confederate communications in eastern North Carolina, then retired to the defenses of New Bern.

The 31st Regiment remained on picket until it was relieved on December 19, 1862; it then went into camp one fourth of a mile from Spring Bank. On the morning of December 20 the 200-man detail left behind on December 17 rejoined the regiment, and that evening orders were received to proceed to Goldsboro. The regiment bivouacked one mile from the town on the Little River on December 20, and on December 21 it rejoined Clingman's brigade in the vicinity of the railroad bridge. The brigade remained in camp until December 29, when it departed for Wilmington. After a long and tedious march Clingman's men arrived at Wilmington on January 2, 1863, and the 31st Regiment went into camp at Camp Whiting.

In January, 1863, Federal naval activity along the coast of South Carolina and Georgia necessitated a call for reinforcements to that area, and on February 16 General Clingman's brigade was ordered to Charleston, South Carolina, where it arrived the next day. The 31st Regiment encamped in a woods near the Savannah & Charleston Railroad two miles from Charleston. On March 2 the brigade moved to Savannah, where it arrived on March 3; on March 8 it began the return trip to Charleston. At Charleston the 31st Regiment encamped on James Island until April 10, when it moved to Mt. Pleasant; it returned to James Island on April 19. Early in May the brigade was ordered back to Wilmington. After a brief respite at Camp Ashe, located near Old Topsail Sound about twelve miles from Wilmington, the brigade received orders on July 10 to return to Charleston.

On that date a combined naval and ground attack was launched by the Federals against the Confederate fortifications on Morris Island in Charleston Harbor. Federal ironclads under Admiral John A. Dahlgren began bombarding Fort Wagner, a key defensive work which controlled access to the northern tip of Morris Island (called Cumming's Point) and whose capture would provide the Federals with a platform from which to bombard Fort Sumter, a mile to the north in the mouth of the harbor. At the same time, General Q. A. Gillmore's Federal artillery on Folly Island, southwest of Morris Island, opened fire on Confederate infantry occupying the sand hills on the southern end of Morris Island. The Confederates in the sand hills retired to Fort Wagner, and Gillmore, having crossed his infantry to Morris Island on the heels of the retreating defenders, unsuccessfully attacked Fort Wagner on July 11.

Clingman's brigade arrived at Charleston the same day and was sent to James Island, west of Morris Island, on July 13. The 31st and 51st Regiments were then sent to reinforce the garrison at Fort Wagner. On July 18 the fort was subjected to an all-out attack by a combined force of infantry and artillery, supported by the Federal fleet. General William B. Taliaferro, commander of the garrison, reported the successful Confederate defense as follows (*Official Records*, Series I, Vol. XXVIII, pt. 1, pp. 417-419):

> On Saturday, the 18th instant, at 8.15 a. m., the enemy having disclosed his land batteries, brought up to their support his entire fleet, consisting of the Ironsides, flag-ship, five monitors, and a large number of wooden steam gunships. With this immense circle of fire by land and sea, he poured for eleven hours, without cessation or intermission, a storm of shot and shell upon Fort Wagner which is perhaps unequaled in history. My estimate is that not less than 9,000 solid shot and shell of all sizes, from 15-inch down ward [*sic*] were hurled during this

period at the work. The estimate of others is very much greater.

The garrison of the fort on this day consisted of the Charleston Battalion, Lieutenant-Colonel [P. C.] Gaillard, whose position extended from the sally-port in Light-House Inlet Creek, on the right, to the left, until it rested on Colonel [Hector] McKethan's regiment, Fifty-first North Carolina Troops, which extended to the gun-chamber opposite the bomb-proof door, at which point and extending along the face of the work to the left to the sally-port next Fort Gregg, the Thirty-first North Carolina Troops, Lieutenant-Colonel [C. W.] Knight, occupied the work. These positions for the infantry were verified by frequent inspections, and the several commands were required to sleep in position, and each man was instructed as to the exact point which he should occupy, and which in any moment of confusion he would be required to gain and hold. In addition to this, a small portion of the Thirty-first North Carolina Troops were held as a reserve in the parade, and a part occupied the parapet just to the right of the sally-port.

On the outside of the fort, two companies of the Charleston Battalion held the sand-hills along the beach and the face extending from the sally-port to the sea beach. The artillerists occupied the several gun-chambers, and two light field pieces were placed in battery outside of the fort, on the traverse near the sally-port. The artillery command consisted of Captains [W. T.] Tatom and [Warren] Adams, First South Carolina [Regular] Infantry [Third Artillery]; [J. T.] Buckner and [W. J.] Dixon, Sixty-third Georgia Heavy Artillery, and Captain [W. L.] De Pass, commanding light artillery, all under the general command of Lieutenant-Colonel [J. C.] Simkins, chief of artillery.

The infantry, excepting the Charleston Battalion, and the artillery, excepting the gun detachments, were placed, shortly after the shelling commenced, under cover of the bomb-proofs. The first-named battalion, with a heroic intrepidity never surpassed, animated by the splendid example of their field officers (Lieutenant-Colonel Gaillard and Major [David] Ramsay), had no protection except such as the parapet afforded them, yet maintained their position without flinching during the entire day. The 10-inch gun was fired at intervals of ten to fifteen minutes against the iron-clads, and the heavy guns on the land face whenever the working parties or cannoneers of the enemy on the land showed themselves within range. The mortar, in charge of Captain Tatom, was fired every half hour.

The casualties during the day of the bombardment did not exceed 8 killed and 20 wounded.

About 2 o'clock, the flag halyards were cut and the Confederate flag blew over into the fort. Instantly Major Ramsay, Charleston Battalion; Lieutenant [William E.] Readick, Sixty-third Georgia (artillery); Sergeant [William] Shelton and Private Flinn, Charleston Battalion, sprang forward and replaced it on the ramparts, while at the same time Captain [R. H.] Barnwell, of the engineers, dashed out, seized a battle-flag, and erected it by the side of the garrison flag. This flag was subsequently shot away, and replaced by Private [A.] Gilliland, Charleston Battalion.

As night approached, the increased severity of the bombardment plainly indicated that an assault would be made, and orders were issued to the commands to prepare to man the ramparts. At 7.45 o'clock the lines of the enemy were seen advancing, and the bombardment slackened to an occasional shell from the ships and the land batteries. As the enemy advanced, they were met by a shower of grape and canister from our guns, and a terrible fire of musketry from the Charleston Battalion and the Fifty-first North Carolina. These two commands gallantly maintained their position and drove the enemy back quickly from their front, with immense slaughter.

In the meantime, on the left of the work, the Thirty-first North Carolina could not be induced to occupy their position, and ingloriously deserted the ramparts, when, no resistance being offered at this point, the advance of the enemy, pushing forward, entered the ditch and ascended the work at the extreme left salient of the land face, and occupied it. I at once directed Lieutenant-Colonel Gaillard to keep up a severe enfilading fire to his left, and directed the field pieces on the left of the fort outside of the sally-port to direct their fire to the right, so as to sweep the ditch and exterior slope of that part of the work thus occupied, and thus, at the same time, prevented the enemy from being supported at that point, and cut off all hope of his escape. The main body of the enemy, after a brief attempt to pass over the field of fire, retreated under the fire of our artillery and the shells of Fort Sumter, and must have suffered heavily as long as they were within the range of our guns.

Lieutenant Colonel Charles W. Knight reported the 31st Regiment's part in the battle as follows (*Official Records*, Series I, Vol. XXVIII, pt. 1, p. 524):

> The line occupied by my regiment extended from the second gun from the bomb-proof to where the gun was dismounted, part of the line from the sally-port on the right to the right of Colonel McKethan's command [51st Regiment N.C. Troops]. The working parties from Cumming's Point were engaged outside the sally-port main entrance.
>
> Owing to not being able to get my men in position where the bursted gun was, we were repulsed; afterwards made a charge upon them and were again repulsed. The number of men that made the charge was 20. The working party from Cumming's Point got in position in time to repulse the enemy at the main entrance.

During the battle of July 18 the 31st Regiment lost 7 men killed, 31 wounded, and 1 missing.

Following the attack the regiment was moved to Sullivan's Island, whose fortifications guarded the northeastern (left) flank of Fort Sumter as those of Morris Island guarded the southern (right) flank. As the siege of Fort Wagner continued, its guns were silenced one by one, and the fort was evacuated on September 6. On September 7 the batteries on Sullivan's Island were shelled. After a Federal attempt to capture Fort Sumter was repulsed on the night of September 8, relative quiet settled in as both sides strengthened their positions. Clingman's brigade remained in the Charleston area until late November, when it was moved to Petersburg, Virginia.

At Petersburg the regiment went into camp on the outskirts of the city and set up winter quarters. On January 23, 1864, the regiment left Petersburg for Ivor Station, where it arrived the same day. Three companies of the regiment moved to the James River town of Smithfield on

February 1 and engaged a party of Federals landing from a gunboat. After a sharp skirmish the Federals surrendered and their gunboat was destroyed. The three companies then returned to Ivor Station and rejoined the regiment. On February 29 the regiment marched to Suffolk; it arrived there on March 1 and remained until March 6, when it returned to Ivor Station. On March 25 the regiment left Ivor Station for its old camp at Petersburg, arriving on March 26. There the regiment remained through the month of April.

On May 5, 1864, a Federal force of 30,000 men under the command of General Benjamin Butler began landing at City Point, Virginia, on the James River southeast of Richmond and northeast of Petersburg. After skirmishing with Federal pickets on the City Point road on May 9, Clingman's brigade was ordered to reinforce the Confederate defenders at Drewry's Bluff, a key position on the James whose loss would sever communications between Richmond and Petersburg and expose the Confederate capital to attack from the south. Clingman's brigade arrived during the night of May 10-11 and went into a reserve position behind the brigade of General Bushrod Johnson. After seeing action as skirmishers on May 13, 14, and 15, Clingman's men took part in driving Butler back toward Bermuda Hundred, a neck of land surrounded on three sides by the James River, on May 16. Skirmishing continued on May 17, 18, and 19 as Butler completed his withdrawal. On May 20 the Confederates attacked and captured a line of Federal entrenchments, thereby "sealing" Butler in the famous Bermuda Hundred "bottle."

Clingman's brigade, as a part of General Robert F. Hoke's division, remained on the Bermuda Hundred line until the division was ordered to Richmond, where the Army of Northern Virginia, commanded by General Robert E. Lee, was confronting the Army of the Potomac, under the strategic direction of General U. S. Grant. Hoke's division was ordered to Cold Harbor, on the Confederate right, and Clingman's brigade occupied the crossroads there on May 31. Late in the day Clingman's men were attacked on their left flank and driven from the field. The brigade then took up position with Hoke's division on the right of Lee's line. On June 1 an enemy force slipped into a gap between Clingman's brigade and the command to its left and moved against Clingman's left flank. The brigade was faced about to receive the attack, and a seesaw battle raged until the arrival of Confederate reinforcements forced the Federals to retire. June 2 was spent in fortifying the Confederate line. On June 3 Grant launched a massive but ill-conceived attack against the six-mile-long Confederate position and was repulsed with heavy losses.

The two armies settled down into defensive positions, where they remained until Grant began moving south toward the James River on June 12. Lee followed on June 13, and Hoke's divison marched to Chaffin's Bluff. It moved to Drewry's Bluff on June 15, to Bermuda Hundred on June 16, and to Petersburg that same evening. Hoke's brigades were sent into the trenches east and south of the city, where they repulsed Federal attackers after heavy fighting on June 17 and 18. Both Lee and Grant then began extending their lines westward around Petersburg, and Clingman's brigade was ordered into the trenches next to the Appomattox River. After taking part in an unsuccessful attack on a Federal position near Globe Tavern, on the Petersburg & Weldon Railroad, on August 19, the brigade returned to the trenches; it remained there until it was ordered to Richmond, with the remainder of Hoke's division, on September 29.

North of the James River the Federals captured Fort

Harrison, a key redoubt in the Richmond defense system, on September 29, and, after the arrival of Hoke's division and other troops from Petersburg, the Confederates attempted to recapture the fort the next day. Three successive attacks on Fort Harrison on September 30 were repulsed with heavy casualties, and the 31st Regiment was almost annihilated. On the night of September 30 the regiment was under the command of a 1st Lieutenant, and approximately sixty men were present for duty.

Following the unsuccessful Confederate assaults on Fort Harrison a new line was established, and Hoke's division was ordered to remain north of the James. On October 7 the regiment was in reserve and was not engaged in an attack on the enemy on the Darbytown road. The brigade then moved into position between the Darbytown and Charles City roads and was involved in frequent skirmishes with Federal pickets. The regiment remained north of the James until Hoke's division was ordered to Wilmington in late December to meet an anticipated Federal amphibious assault on Fort Fisher. The division entrained at Richmond on December 22 and moved to Danville. It then marched to Greensboro and proceeded by rail to Wilmington. The 31st Regiment arrived there on December 28, three days after a somewhat irresolute Federal attack on Fort Fisher had been repulsed.

On January 12, 1865, the Federal fleet returned, and the next day an assault force landed unopposed. Hoke's division was sent immediately to the Sugar Loaf defensive position just above Fort Fisher, but Hoke's superior, General Braxton Bragg, refused to authorize any effort by Hoke to go to the aid of the fort's garrison, and on January 15 Fort Fisher was stormed and captured.

Hoke's division held the line below Wilmington until February 19, when it was pulled back in the face of a Federal advance up the west bank of the Cape Fear River. The division then withdrew to Wilmington, crossed the Northeast Cape Fear River, and cut the bridges in an effort to slow the Federal advance. During the retreat the 31st Regiment served as rear guard and was frequently engaged in skirmishes with the Federals. After the fall of Wilmington on February 22, Bragg ordered Hoke's troops to Kinston to oppose a Federal column advancing on Goldsboro from New Bern. The two forces met at Wise's Forks on March 7, and Bragg brought up a division commanded by General D. H. Hill to reinforce Hoke. On March 8 Hoke's men crossed Southwest Creek and, after successfully flanking the Federal defenders, captured about 1,000 prisoners; however, the enemy refused to yield the field. Confederate attacks on March 8 and 9 were repulsed, and Bragg withdrew his command to Goldsboro and then to Smithfield, where it was united with General Joseph E. Johnston's Army of Tennessee.

From Smithfield, Johnston moved his army to Bentonville, where he hoped to ambush and defeat one of General William T. Sherman's two advancing columns. Hoke's division held the left of the Confederate line during the battle of March 19 and was actively engaged; however, the Federal army, although halted momentarily, was too powerful to be defeated. Sherman arrived with reinforcements the next day, and Johnston retired to Smithfield on March 21. During the next three weeks the army remained in camp at Smithfield, and Hoke's division was assigned to the corps of General William J. Hardee.

Johnston retreated from Smithfield on April 10 in the face of a new advance by Sherman. Raleigh was captured by the Federals on April 13, and the Confederates fell back to Chapel Hill and then to Bush Hill in Randolph County. While there, Johnston negotiated the surrender of his army, which occurred on April 26. The few survivors of the

31st Regiment N.C. Troops were paroled on May 2, 1865.

FIELD AND STAFF

COLONEL

JORDAN, JOHN V.
Resided in Craven County and enlisted at age 33. Appointed Colonel on September 19, 1861. Captured at Roanoke Island on February 8, 1862. Paroled at Elizabeth City on February 21, 1862. Returned to duty on or about September 15, 1862. Hospitalized at Richmond, Virginia, May 16, 1864, with gunshot wounds of the side and right leg. Place and date wounded not reported. Resigned on October 15, 1864. Reason he resigned not reported. Resignation accepted on November 5, 1864. "A faithful officer and fine disciplinarian."

LIEUTENANT COLONELS

FOWLE, DANIEL GOULD
Resided in Wake County and enlisted at age 31. Appointed Lieutenant Colonel on September 19, 1861. Captured at Roanoke Island on February 8, 1862. Paroled at Elizabeth City on February 21, 1862. Defeated for reelection when the regiment was reorganized on September 17, 1862. Later served as Adjutant General of North Carolina.

LILES, EDWARD R.
Previously served as Captain of Company B of this regiment. Appointed Lieutenant Colonel on September 17, 1862, and transferred to the Field and Staff. Resigned on April 3, 1863. Letter of resignation reads in part as follows: "Not only preferring to resign rather than be examined [i.e., appear before an officers' examining board] but conscientiously believing it to be my duty to do so, I hereby tender my resignation as Lieutenant Colonel of the regiment to take effect *immediately and unconditionally.*" Resignation accepted on April 22, 1863.

KNIGHT, CHARLES W.
Previously served as Captain of Company F of this regiment. Appointed Lieutenant Colonel on June 7, 1863, and transferred to the Field and Staff. Reported absent sick in hospital in November-December, 1864. Paroled subsequent to April 26, 1865.

MAJORS

YEATES, JESSE JOHNSTON
Resided in Hertford County and enlisted at age 32. Appointed Major on September 19, 1861. Captured at Roanoke Island on February 8, 1862. Paroled at Elizabeth City on February 21, 1862. Regimental records do not indicate whether he returned to duty. Resigned on November 8, 1862, by reason of "fistula in ano." Resignation accepted on December 15, 1862.

McKAY, JOHN A. D.
Previously served as Captain of Company I of this regiment. Appointed Major on June 7, 1863, and transferred to the Field and Staff. Resigned on July 11, 1864. Charged with cowardice in battles at Cold Harbor, Virginia, May 31-June 1, 1864, and near Petersburg, Virginia, June 16-17, 1864. There is no evidence either that he was court-martialed or that the charges against him were dropped. Resignation accepted on July 25, 1864.

ADJUTANTS

HOLDEN, JOSEPH W.
Previously served as 3rd Lieutenant of Company D of this regiment. Appointed Adjutant (2nd Lieutenant) on November 27, 1861, and transferred to the Field and Staff. Captured at Roanoke Island on February 8, 1862. Paroled at Elizabeth City on February 21, 1862. Defeated for reelection when the regiment was reorganized on September 17, 1862.

BRYAN, EDWARD K.
Previously served as 1st Lieutenant of Company I, 2nd Regiment N.C. State Troops. Appointed Adjutant (1st Lieutenant) of this company on December 20, 1862, to rank from October 20, 1862. Joined the company on or about January 22, 1863. Wounded in the stomach at Cold Harbor, Virginia, June 1, 1864. Reported absent wounded for "several months." Reported present for duty in November-December, 1864. Paroled subsequent to February 26, 1865.

ASSISTANT QUARTERMASTERS

STRAGAN, R.
Appointed Assistant Quartermaster (Captain) on February 13, 1862, to rank from November 27, 1861; however, his appointment was canceled. No further records.

COX, J. J.
Resided in Anson County and enlisted at age 36. Appointed Assistant Quartermaster (Captain) on November 27, 1862, to rank from October 16, 1862. Present or accounted for through September 19, 1864. Assigned to duty with the ordnance train of Hoke's division on September 20, 1864.

ASSISTANT COMMISSARIES OF SUBSISTENCE

STANLEY, JOHN A.
Appointed Assistant Commissary of Subsistence (Captain) on February 13, 1862, to rank from November 27, 1861. Dropped from the rolls of the regiment on August 2, 1862, because "he failed to give bond."

CLARK, CHARLES C.
Resided in Craven County and enlisted at age 35. Appointed Assistant Commissary of Subsistence (Captain) on October 14, 1862, to rank from September 22, 1862. Resigned on December 8, 1862, by reason of having been elected to the North Carolina General Assembly[?].

LANE, HARDY B.
Previously served as Sergeant in Company H, 9th Regiment N.C. State Troops (1st Regiment N.C. Cavalry). Appointed Assistant Commissary of Subsistence (Captain) on April 11, 1863, to rank from January 8, 1863, and transferred to this regiment. Transferred to the staff of General T.L. Clingman on or about July 31, 1863.

SURGEONS

CUSTIS, PETER BARTON

Resided in Craven County and enlisted at age 38. Appointed Surgeon on February 17, 1862, to rank from November 27, 1861. Assigned to duty as a hospital surgeon at Wilmington on April 10, 1862.

BATTLE, WILLIAM H.

Resided in Anson County. Appointed Surgeon on November 27, 1862, to rank from October 6, 1862. Present or accounted for through February, 1865.

ASSISTANT SURGEONS

BUSBEE, WILLIAM J.

Resided in Wake County and enlisted at age 36. Appointed Assistant Surgeon on February 17, 1862, to rank from November 27, 1861. Resigned on September 19, 1862.

POOL, WILLIAM E.

Previously served as Private in Company D, 17th Regiment N.C. Troops (1st Organization). Appointed Assistant Surgeon of this regiment on or about May 20, 1862. Reported absent without leave in November-December, 1864.

HUGHES, WILLIAM R.

Resided in Orange County. Appointed Assistant Surgeon on December 12, 1863. Reported absent sick in November-December, 1864. Took the Oath of Allegiance at Raleigh on June 6, 1865.

FEW, BENJAMIN F.

Previously served as Private in Company G, 16th Regiment South Carolina Infantry. Appointed Assistant Surgeon of this regiment on December 15, 1864. Reported on temporary duty as Assistant Surgeon of the 61st Regiment N.C. Troops in February, 1865. No further records.

CHAPLAIN

CHURCHILL, ORREN

Appointed Chaplain of this regiment on April 10, 1863, to rank from March 18, 1863. Had been "laboring with the regiment in a ministerial capacity for a number of months" prior to his appointment. No further records.

ENSIGN

PERRY, SIMON S.

Previously served in Company F of this regiment. Appointed Ensign (1st Lieutenant) on April 21, 1864, and transferred to the Field and Staff. Wounded in the chest and left arm at Cold Harbor, Virginia, June 1, 1864. Returned to duty subsequent to September 11, 1864. Present or accounted for through December, 1864. Paroled subsequent to April 26, 1865.

SERGEANTS MAJOR

GUION, JOHN

Resided in Craven County and enlisted in Wake County at age 18, October 20, 1862, for the war. Mustered in as Sergeant Major. Present or accounted for until reduced to ranks and transferred to Company A, 1st Battalion N.C. Local Defense Troops, July 25, 1863.

BEAL, CRISPIAN B.

Previously served as Sergeant in Company G of this regiment. Promoted to Sergeant Major on October 1, 1863, and transferred to the Field and Staff. Wounded in both legs at or near Fort Harrison, Virginia, September 30, 1864. Reported absent wounded through December, 1864.

QUARTERMASTER SERGEANTS

LINDSEY, JAMES B.

Previously served as 1st Sergeant in Company I, 43rd Regiment N.C. Troops. Appointed Quartermaster Sergeant on October 18, 1862, and transferred to this company. Appointed 3rd Lieutenant and transferred to Company B of this regiment on or about May 16, 1863.

ROBINSON, C. H.

Previously served as Private in Company B of this regiment. Appointed Quartermaster Sergeant and transferred to the Field and Staff in June, 1863. Paroled subsequent to April 26, 1865.

COMMISSARY SERGEANT

CLARKE, BENJAMIN F.

Previously served as 1st Sergeant of Company B of this regiment. Promoted to Commissary Sergeant on August 1, 1863, and transferred to the Field and Staff. Present or accounted for through December, 1864.

ORDNANCE SERGEANT

POOLE, NEEDHAM W.

Previously served in Company H of this regiment. Promoted to Ordnance Sergeant on or about September 17, 1862, and transferred to the Field and Staff. Present or accounted for through December, 1864. Paroled subsequent to April 26, 1865.

DRILLMASTERS

PERRY, JESSE A.

Previously served as 1st Lieutenant of Company D, 17th Regiment N.C. Troops (1st Organization). Served as Drillmaster of this regiment from November 20, 1861, through December 31, 1861. Later served as 1st Lieutenant of Company D, 3rd Battalion N.C. Light Artillery.

PEARSON, JOHN W.

Served as Private in Company I, 28th Regiment N.C. Troops. Records of the 28th Regiment indicate he was appointed Drillmaster and transferred to the 31st Regiment in December, 1861; however, records of the 31st Regiment do not indicate that he served herein. No further records.

HOSPITAL STEWARD

WORTHINGTON, GEORGE W.

Previously served as Private in Company G of this regiment. Detailed as Hospital Steward in September, 1862-February, 1863, and transferred to the Field and Staff. Promoted to Hospital Steward in May, 1863-April, 1864, and assigned to permanent duty with the Field and Staff. Present or accounted for through December, 1864. Paroled subsequent to April 26, 1865.

COMPANY A

This company was raised in Robeson County and enlisted at Lumberton on September 6, 1861. It was then assigned to the 31st Regiment N.C. Troops and designated Company A. After joining the regiment the company functioned as a part of the regiment, and its history for the war period is reported as a part of the regimental history.

The information contained in the following roster of the company was compiled principally from company muster rolls for September 6-December 31, 1861; May-June, 1862; January-April, 1863; March-April, 1864; and November-December, 1864. No company muster rolls were found for January-April, 1862; July-December, 1862; May, 1863-February, 1864; May-October, 1864; or for the period after December, 1864. Valuable information was obtained from primary records such as the Roll of Honor, discharge certificates, medical records, prisoner of war records, and pension applications. Secondary sources such as postwar rosters and histories, cemetery records, and records of the United Daughters of the Confederacy also provided useful information.

OFFICERS

CAPTAINS

GODWIN, CONDARY
Resided in Robeson County where he enlisted at age 28. Appointed Captain on or about September 6, 1861. Present or accounted for until he resigned on or about October 10, 1862.

COLLINS, SAMUEL P.
Previously served as 2nd Lieutenant in Company E of this regiment. Promoted to 1st Lieutenant and transferred to this company on May 3, 1862. Promoted to Captain on May 13, 1863. Present or accounted for until killed at Drewry's Bluff, Virginia, May 16, 1864.

FORTE, JOHN F.
Previously served as Private in Company B of this regiment. Appointed 2nd Lieutenant on May 3, 1862, and transferred to this company. Promoted to 1st Lieutenant on May 13, 1863, and was promoted to Captain in May-September, 1864. Present or accounted for through September 29, 1864. Company records indicate he was "supposed to have been killed" at Fort Harrison, Virginia, September 30, 1864; however, other company records indicate he was captured at Fort Harrison. Records of the Federal Provost Marshal do not substantiate the report of his capture. No further records.

LIEUTENANTS

BARNES, JOHN C., 2nd Lieutenant
Previously served as Private in Company F of this regiment. Transferred to this company with the rank of Private on or about January 14, 1862. Promoted to Corporal on February 9, 1863. Appointed 3rd Lieutenant on May 20, 1863, and was promoted to 2nd Lieutenant in May-December, 1864. Present or accounted for until wounded in the head and captured at Fort Harrison, Virginia, September 30, 1864. Confined at Old Capitol Prison, Washington, D.C., October 6, 1864. Transferred to Fort Delaware, Delaware, October 21, 1864. Released on June 10, 1865, after taking the Oath of Allegiance.

FREEMAN, WILLIAM R., 1st Lieutenant
Resided in Robeson County where he enlisted at age 17, September 6, 1861. Mustered in as Sergeant. Appointed 2nd Lieutenant on May 20, 1863. Promoted to 1st Lieutenant in May-December, 1864. Present or accounted for through December, 1864.

HARTMAN, WILLIAM H., 1st Lieutenant
Resided in Robeson County and enlisted at age 26. Appointed 1st Lieutenant on September 6, 1861. Present or accounted for until he was defeated for reelection when the regiment was reorganized on September 17, 1862.

SEALY, MOORE T., 3rd Lieutenant
Resided in Robeson County where he enlisted at age 37. Appointed 3rd Lieutenant on September 6, 1861. Present or accounted for until he was defeated for reelection when the regiment was reorganized on September 17, 1862.

STEAGALL, RAIBON, 2nd Lieutenant
Resided in Robeson County where he enlisted at age 30. Appointed 2nd Lieutenant on September 6, 1861. Present or accounted for until he was defeated for reelection when the regiment was reorganized on September 17, 1862.

THOMPSON, GEORGE W., 2nd Lieutenant
Previously served as Private in Company G of this regiment. Appointed 2nd Lieutenant and transferred to this company on May 1, 1862. Present or accounted for until he resigned on March 28, 1863, by reason of "chronic rheumatism of the feet & ankles." Resignation accepted on April 23, 1863.

NONCOMMISSIONED OFFICERS AND PRIVATES

ABBOTT, J. M., Private
Place and date of enlistment not reported. Paroled at Greensboro on or about April 29, 1865.

ALBIN, SYLVESTER, Private
Resided in New York and enlisted in Robeson County at age 25, September 6, 1861. Reported absent without leave in January-February, 1863. Reported absent sick in March-April, 1863. Reported absent on detached service at Wilmington in March-April, 1864. Deserted on December 28, 1864. [May have been captured at Roanoke Island on February 8, 1862, and paroled at Elizabeth City on February 21, 1862.]

ALLEN, GLENN, Private
Resided in Robeson County where he enlisted at age 19, September 6, 1861. Present or accounted for until he died in hospital at Washington, North Carolina, December 20 or December 27, 1861, of disease. "He was an orderly and obedient soldier, a warm friend, and much esteemed by his associates."

ALLEN, RICHARD, Private
Resided in Robeson County where he enlisted at age 16, September 6, 1861. Present or accounted for until he died in hospital at Washington, North Carolina, on or about December 27, 1861, of disease.

BAGGETT, BARTON, Private
Previously served in Company F of this regiment.

Transferred to this company on or about January 14, 1862. Present or accounted for through December, 1864.

BAGGETT, NEIL, Private
Previously served in Company F of this regiment. Transferred to this company on or about January 14, 1862. Present or accounted for until March-April, 1863, when he was reported absent without leave. Returned to duty prior to May 1, 1864. Deserted on September 29, 1864.

BAGGETT, WILLIAM J., Private
Resided in Robeson County where he enlisted at age 19, September 6, 1861. Present or accounted for until he deserted on September 29, 1864.

BARNES, JOHN D., Private
Resided in Robeson County where he enlisted at age 23, September 6, 1861. Reported absent without leave during January-April, 1863. Returned to duty prior to May 1, 1864. Reported absent sick during November-December, 1864. [May have been captured at Roanoke Island on February 8, 1862, and paroled at Elizabeth City on February 21, 1862. North Carolina pension records indicate he was wounded in the face at "Fort Harrison, Virginia, June 20, 1863."]

BASS, JEREMIAH, Private
Resided in Robeson County where he enlisted at age 35, September 6, 1861. Present or accounted for until he deserted on July 6, 1864.

BASS, MATTHEW, Private
Resided in Robeson County where he enlisted at age 25, September 6, 1861. Died in September, 1862, of disease. Place of death not reported.

BAXLEY, JOHN W., Private
Resided in Robeson County and enlisted at Charleston, South Carolina, at age 35, March 10, 1863, for the war. Present or accounted for until captured at or near Cold Harbor, Virginia, June 1, 1864. Confined at Point Lookout, Maryland, June 11, 1864. Transferred to Elmira, New York, July 12, 1864. Killed in a railroad accident at Shohola, Pennsylvania, July 15, 1864, while en route to Elmira.

BIGGS, RESDEN, Private
Resided in Robeson County where he enlisted at age 23, September 6, 1861. Present or accounted for until captured at or near Cold Harbor, Virginia, June 1, 1864. Confined at Point Lookout, Maryland, June 11, 1864. Transferred to Elmira, New York, July 12, 1864. Killed in a railroad accident at Shohola, Pennsylvania, July 15, 1864, while en route to Elmira.

BLANKS, JOHN, Private
Resided in Robeson County where he enlisted at age 41, September 6, 1861. Discharged on September 15, 1862. Reason discharged not reported.

BLOUNT, JAMES A., Private
Resided in Robeson County where he enlisted at age 21, September 6, 1861. Died in hospital at Wilmington on or about December 2, 1862, of "cerebritis."

BRITT, ALEXANDER S., Private
Resided in Robeson County and enlisted in New Hanover County at age 33, May 3, 1862, for the war. Reported absent without leave in March-April, 1863. Reported present but on "extra duty" in March-April, 1864. Deserted on July 6, 1864.

BRITT, FELIX, Private
Resided in Robeson County where he enlisted at age 26, September 6, 1861. Present or accounted for until he died at or near White House, Virginia, on or about June 9, 1864. Cause of death not reported.

BRITT, GILES, Private
Resided in Robeson County and enlisted in New Hanover County at age 25, April 15, 1862. Present or accounted for until he deserted on July 6, 1864.

BRITT, HENRY C., Private
Resided in Robeson County where he enlisted at age 23, September 6, 1861. Deserted on February 15, 1863. Apprehended on an unspecified date subsequent to April 30, 1863. Reported in prison at Petersburg, Virginia, in March-April, 1864. Returned to duty on an unspecified date. Deserted on July 6, 1864.

BRITT, WILLIAM, Private
Resided in Robeson County where he enlisted at age 24, September 6, 1861. Present or accounted for until captured at Fort Harrison, Virginia, September 30, 1864. Confined at Point Lookout, Maryland, October 5, 1864. Released on June 24, 1865, after taking the Oath of Allegiance.

BRUMBLE, ANDREW, Private
Enlisted at Ivor Station, Virginia, March 8, 1864, for the war. Reported absent without leave in November-December, 1864.

BRUMBLE, ORREL, Private
Resided in Robeson County and enlisted in New Hanover County at age 20, May 10, 1863, for the war. Present or accounted for through December, 1864.

BULLET, JESSIE N., Private
Place and date of enlistment not reported. Captured on the "White Hall Road" on March 14, 1865, and was transferred to Kinston on an unspecified date. No further records.

BYRD, JOHN, Corporal
Resided in Robeson County where he enlisted on September 6, 1861. Mustered in as Private. Promoted to Corporal subsequent to April 30, 1864. Present or accounted for until he deserted on December 28, 1864.

CAPPS, WILLIAM H., Private
Resided in Johnston County and enlisted in Robeson County at age 22, September 6, 1861. Present or accounted for until captured at Fort Harrison, Virginia, September 30, 1864. Confined at Point Lookout, Maryland, October 5, 1864. Released on May 13, 1865, after taking the Oath of Allegiance.

CARLISLE, JAMES S., Private
Resided in Robeson County where he enlisted at age 26, September 6, 1861. Died at Roanoke Island on December 26, 1861, of disease. "He was unassuming in his manners, punctual in the discharge of every duty as a soldier, and highly respected by his officers and companions in arms."

CARROLL, STEWART, Private
Resided in Robeson County where he enlisted at age 65, September 6, 1861. Discharged on September 15, 1862. Reason discharged not reported.

CATHEY, THOMAS H., Private
Place and date of enlistment not reported. Paroled on an unspecified date subsequent to April 26, 1865.

CHAMBERS, JOSEPH, Private
Place and date of enlistment not reported. Paroled on an unspecified date subsequent to April 26, 1865.

COBB, ALEXANDER, Cook
Negro. Joined the company at Kinston on October 23, 1862. Present or accounted for through December, 1864.

COLLINS, JOHN H., Private
Resided in Robeson County where he enlisted at age 25, September 6, 1861. Mustered in as Corporal. Reduced to ranks subsequent to June 30, 1862. Present or accounted for until transferred to Company B, 50th Regiment N.C. Troops, on or about January 16, 1863.

DAVIS, ALEXANDER, Private
Resided in Robeson County where he enlisted at age 30, September 6, 1861. Roll of Honor indicates he was discharged on September 15, 1862. Confederate medical records indicate he died in hospital at Wilmington on January 20, 1863, of ''pneumonia.''

DAVIS, JAMES, Private
Enlisted in Robeson County on September 6, 1861. Detailed for hospital duty at Wilmington on March 3, 1863, by reason of chronic rheumatism. Reported absent on detail at Wilmington through November, 1864. Rejoined the company in December, 1864. No further records.

DEESE, JONATHAN, Private
Previously served in Company B of this regiment. Transferred to this company on April 1, 1864. Hospitalized at Petersburg, Virginia, June 19, 1864, with a gunshot wound. Place and date wounded not reported. Company records do not indicate whether he returned to duty. Reported absent sick in November-December, 1864.

DENT, ELIAS J., Private
Resided in Robeson County where he enlisted on September 6, 1861. Present or accounted for through December, 1864. [May have been captured at Roanoke Island on February 8, 1862, and paroled at Elizabeth City on February 21, 1862.]

DENT, ISAIAH, Private
Resided in Robeson County where he enlisted on September 6, 1861. Discharged on or about November 22, 1861, by reason of disability. [May have served later in Company H, 58th Regiment N.C. Troops.]

DENT, JAMES, ——
North Carolina pension records indicate that he served in this company.

EDMUND, CALVIN, Private
Resided in Robeson County where he enlisted at age 32,

July 1, 1862, for the war. Deserted on December 1, 1863.

EDWARDS, ROWLAND, Private
Resided in Robeson County and enlisted at Sullivan's Island, Charleston, South Carolina, at age 18, July 25, 1863, for the war. Company records dated March-April, 1864, indicate he was in hospital at Petersburg, Virginia. Company records dated November-December, 1864, indicate he was a prisoner of war; however, records of the Federal Provost Marshal do not substantiate that report. No further records.

EVANS, MARSHAL, Private
Resided in Anson County and enlisted in New Hanover County at age 55, January 11, 1863, for the war as a substitute. Present or accounted for through December, 1864.

FLOYD, BUD M., Private
Resided in Robeson County where he enlisted at age 26, September 6, 1861. Mustered in as Sergeant. Reduced to the rank of Corporal in July, 1862-February, 1863. Reduced to ranks on February 19, 1863. Reported absent without leave in January-February, 1863. Reported absent on furlough in March-April, 1863. Reported absent without leave in March-April, 1864. Reported present for duty in November-December, 1864.

FREEMAN, JACKSON M., Private
Resided in Robeson County where he enlisted at age 23, September 6, 1861. Mustered in as Corporal. Reduced to ranks on September 15, 1863. Reported absent on detached service in March-April, 1863, and March-April, 1864. Reported present for duty in November-December, 1864.

GAUTIER, WILLIAM HENRY, Private
Resided in Robeson County where he enlisted at age 39, September 6, 1861. Discharged on or about September 19, 1862. Reason discharged not reported.

GLOVER, WILLIAM W., Sergeant
Resided in Robeson County where he enlisted at age 30, September 6, 1861. Mustered in as Sergeant. Present or accounted for through December, 1864. [May have been captured at Roanoke Island on February 8, 1862, and paroled at Elizabeth City on February 21, 1862.]

HARDEN, FELIX, Private
Resided in Robeson County where he enlisted at age 27, September 6, 1861. Present or accounted for until captured at Fort Harrison, Virginia, September 30, 1864. Confined at Point Lookout, Maryland, October 5, 1864. Paroled at Point Lookout on March 17, 1865, and transferred to Boulware's Wharf, James River, Virginia, where he was received on March 19, 1865, for exchange.

HARDIN, ALLEN, Private
Resided in Robeson County where he enlisted at age 25, September 6, 1861. Present or accounted for until he died at Wilmington on July 14 or July 20, 1863, of ''ty[phoid] fever.''

HAYNES, THOMAS L., Private
Enlisted in New Hanover County on May 10, 1863, for the war. Died in hospital at Petersburg, Virginia, March 11, 1864, of ''pneumonia.''

HEDGEPETH, JOHN THOMAS, Private

Born in Robeson County where he resided as a farmer prior to enlisting in Robeson County at age 23, September 6, 1861. Present or accounted for until wounded in the left leg at Drewry's Bluff, Virginia, May 16, 1864. Left leg amputated above the knee. Retired from service on February 10, 1865, by reason of disability.

HESTERS, JOHN T., Private

Previously served in Company F of this regiment. Transferred to this company on or about January 14, 1862. Died on February 26, 1862. Place and cause of death not reported.

HILL, H. G., ———

North Carolina pension records indicate that he served in this company.

HODGES, ANDREW, ———

North Carolina pension records indicate that he served in this company.

HOWELL, SHADRACH, Jr., ———

North Carolina pension records indicate that he served in this company.

IVEY, BRIGHT, Private

Resided in Robeson County and enlisted in New Hanover County at age 18, February 10, 1863, for the war. Present or accounted for until he deserted on July 14, 1864.

IVEY, DANIEL, Private

Enlisted in Robeson County on September 6, 1861. Present or accounted for through June, 1862.

IVEY, HENRY WILLIAM, Private

Resided in Robeson County where he enlisted at age 21, September 6, 1861. Present or accounted for until he deserted on July 6, 1864.

JOHNSON, ATLAS, Private

Resided in Robeson County where he enlisted at age 22, September 6, 1861. Present or accounted for until he died on August 29, 1863, of disease. Place of death not reported.

JOHNSON, CARRY, Private

Resided in Robeson County where he enlisted at age 30, September 6, 1861. Discharged on September 15, 1862. Reason discharged not reported.

JONES, ARTHUR, Private

Resided in Robeson County where he enlisted at age 26, September 6, 1861. Died in February, 1862, or on March 20, 1862, of disease. Place of death not reported.

JONES, DANIEL, Private

Resided in Robeson County where he enlisted at age 26, September 6, 1861. Present or accounted for through December, 1864. [May have been captured at Roanoke Island on February 8, 1862, and paroled at Elizabeth City on February 21, 1862.]

JONES, HENRY T., Private

Enlisted in New Hanover County on May 3, 1862, for the war. Reported present for duty in March-April,

1864. Company records dated November-December, 1864, indicate that he was a prisoner of war; however, records of the Federal Provost Marshal do not substantiate that report. No further records.

JONES, JACKSON, Private

Resided in Robeson County where he enlisted at age 23, September 6, 1861. Company records indicate he was discharged on January 22, 1864, by reason of being a member of the Society of Friends; however, other company records indicate he was present for duty in November-December, 1864. No further records.

JONES, JAMES D., Private

Resided in Robeson County where he enlisted at age 22, September 6, 1861. Present or accounted for through June, 1862. Discharged on an unspecified date by reason of disability.

JONES, THOMAS, Private

Resided in Robeson County where he enlisted at age 22, September 6, 1861. Wounded at or near Fort Wagner, Charleston, South Carolina, July 18, 1863. [May have been captured at Roanoke Island on February 8, 1862, and paroled at Elizabeth City on February 21, 1862.] No further records.

KING, JAMES, Private

Resided in Robeson County where he enlisted at age 21, September 6, 1861. Present or accounted for through April, 1864. Reported absent without leave in November-December, 1864. [North Carolina pension records indicate he was wounded at Richmond, Virginia, on an unspecified date.]

KING, JOHN H., Private

Resided in Robeson County where he enlisted at age 23, September 6, 1861. Present or accounted for through December, 1864.

KINLAW, ELI, Private

Resided in Robeson County where he enlisted at age 25, September 6, 1861. Present or accounted for through December, 1864.

KINLAW, HAYNES L., Private

Resided in Robeson County where he enlisted at age 19, September 6, 1861. Wounded at Drewry's Bluff, Virginia, in May, 1864. Hospitalized at Williamsburg, Virginia. Furloughed on May 29, 1864. Reported absent without leave in November-December, 1864. [May have been captured at Roanoke Island on February 8, 1862, and paroled at Elizabeth City on February 21, 1862.]

KINLAW, PINKNEY J., Private

Previously served in 1st Company D, 12th Regiment N.C. Troops (2nd Regiment N.C. Volunteers). Enlisted in this company in Robeson County at age 20, September 6, 1861. Transferred to Company D, 51st Regiment N.C. Troops, on or about March 20, 1862.

KINLAW, WILLIAM H., Private

Resided in Robeson County where he enlisted at age 18, September 6, 1861. Present or accounted for until he died at Roanoke Island on January 9-10, 1862, of disease. "He was modest and agreeable as a companion [and] prompt and obedient as a soldier. . . ."

KINLAW, WILLIS, Private

Resided in Robeson County where he enlisted at age 23,

September 6, 1861. Killed at Fort Wagner, Charleston, South Carolina, July 18, 1863.

LAMB, RICHARD C., Private
Resided in Robeson County where he enlisted at age 38, September 6, 1861. Discharged on September 15, 186[2]. Reason discharged not reported. [May have been captured at Roanoke Island on February 8, 1862, and paroled at Elizabeth City on February 21, 1862. May have served later in Company D, 18th Regiment N.C. Troops (8th Regiment N.C. Volunteers).]

LEWIS, COUNSIL, Private
Previously served in Company F of this regiment. Transferred to this company on or about January 14, 1862. Present or accounted for until transferred to Captain W. J. McDugald's Unattached Company, North Carolina Troops, in January-February, 1863, in exchange for Private Joseph Ratley.

LEWIS, DURHAM, Corporal
Resided in Robeson County where he enlisted on September 6, 1861. Mustered in as Corporal. Present or accounted for through June, 1862. Discharged on an unspecified date. Reason discharged not reported.

LEWIS, EDWARD S., Sergeant
Resided in Robeson County where he enlisted on September 6, 1861. Mustered in as Private. Promoted to Sergeant in July, 1862-February, 1863. Wounded at Fort Wagner, Charleston, South Carolina, on or about July 18, 1863. Returned to duty on an unspecified date. Captured at or near Cold Harbor, Virginia, June 1, 1864. Confined at Point Lookout, Maryland, June 11, 1864. Transferred to Elmira, New York, July 12, 1864. Died at Elmira on September 15, 1864, of "pneumonia."

McKAY, JAMES H., Corporal
Resided in Robeson County where he enlisted at age 22, September 6, 1861. Mustered in as Private. Promoted to Corporal on February 19, 1863. Present or accounted for through December, 1864.

McLAUCHLIN, JAMES W., Private
Records of Company E, 40th Regiment N.C. Troops (3rd Regiment N.C. Artillery) indicate that he served in that unit after prior service in Company A, 31st Regiment N.C. Troops; however, records of the latter unit do not indicate that he served therein. No further records.

McLEAN, DANIEL, Private
Resided in Robeson County where he enlisted on September 6, 1861. Discharged on February 15, 1863, by reason of disability.

McPHAIL, ANGUS, Private
Resided in Robeson County where he enlisted at age 45, September 6, 1861. Discharged on September 15, 1862. Reason discharged not reported. Later served in 2nd Company K, 40th Regiment N.C. Troops (3rd Regiment N.C. Artillery).

McPHATTER, JOHN, Private
Resided in Robeson County where he enlisted at age 26, September 6, 1861. Died at Roanoke Island on January 9 or February 1, 1862, of disease.

McQUEEN, EDMUND, 1st Sergeant
Resided in Robeson County where he enlisted at age 17, September 6, 1861. Mustered in as 1st Sergeant. Discharged on September 15, 186[2]. Reason discharged not reported. Later served as Private in 2nd Company K, 40th Regiment N.C. Troops (3rd Regiment N.C. Artillery).

MAYS, DENNIS, Private
Resided in Robeson County where he enlisted at age 17, September 6, 1861. Present or accounted for through April, 1864. Died prior to December 17, 1864. Place and cause of death not reported.

MERCER, HIRAM C., Private
Resided in Robeson County where he enlisted at age 20, September 6, 1861. Mustered in as Corporal. Reduced to ranks on September 15, 1863. Captured at Fort Harrison, Virginia, September 30, 1864. Confined at Point Lookout, Maryland, October 5, 1864. Paroled on or about March 17, 1865, and transferred to Boulware's Wharf, James River, Virginia, where he was received on March 19, 1865, for exchange. Furloughed for thirty days on March 24, 1865.

MERCER, STEPHEN C., Private
Enlisted at Petersburg, Virginia, May 4, 1864, for the war. Furloughed on October 21, 1864. Returned to duty on November 12, 1864. Reported absent without leave prior to January 1, 1865.

MERCER, TRAVIS, Private
Resided in Robeson County where he enlisted at age 24, September 6, 1861. Present or accounted for through April, 1864. [May have served previously in Company D, 18th Regiment N.C. Troops (8th Regiment N.C. Volunteers).]

MERCER, WILLIAM H., Private
Resided in Robeson County where he enlisted at age 23, September 6, 1861. Present or accounted for through December, 1864.

MISSHOE, ISAAC, Private
Resided in Robeson County where he enlisted at age 26, September 6, 1861. Died at Roanoke Island on February 6-7, 1862, of disease.

MOORE, JAMES H., Private
Previously served in Company B of this regiment. Transferred to this company in May, 1863-March, 1864. Transferred back to Company B on April 1, 1864.

MUSSLEWHITE, ALFRED, Private
Resided in Robeson County where he enlisted at age 52, September 6, 1861. Discharged on September 15, 1862. Reason discharged not reported.

MUSSLEWHITE, ARCHIBALD, Private
Born in Robeson County where he resided as a farmer prior to enlisting in Robeson County at age 23, September 6, 1861. Present or accounted for until transferred to Company D, 51st Regiment N.C. Troops, on or about March 7, 1862.

MUSSLEWHITE, HENRY J. M., Private
Resided in Robeson County where he enlisted at age 22, September 6, 1861. Present or accounted for through

April, 1864. Reported absent without leave in November-December, 1864.

MUSSLEWHITE, JAMES T., Private
Resided in Robeson County where he enlisted at age 18, September 6, 1861. Hospitalized at Richmond, Virginia, May 17, 1864, with a gunshot wound of the right thigh. Place and date wounded not reported. Returned to duty prior to May 31, 1864, when he was wounded in the right hip and captured at or near Cold Harbor, Virginia. Confined at Old Capitol Prison, Washington, D.C., August 16, 1864. Transferred to Elmira, New York, August 28, 1864. Paroled at Elmira on March 2, 1865, and transferred to the James River, Virginia, for exchange. Furloughed for thirty days on March 15, 1865. [May have been captured at Roanoke Island on February 8, 1862, and paroled at Elizabeth City on February 21, 1862.]

MUSSLEWHITE, JOHN W. M., Private
Resided in Robeson County where he enlisted at age 19, September 6, 1861. Present or accounted for through April, 1864. Reported absent without leave in November-December, 1864. [North Carolina pension records indicate he was wounded in the right leg at Drewry's Bluff, Virginia, May 16, 1864.]

MUSSLEWHITE, LEWIS, Private
Born in Robeson County where he resided as a farmer prior to enlisting in Robeson County at age 25, September 6, 1861. Present or accounted for until transferred to Company D, 51st Regiment N.C. Troops, on or about March 7, 1862.

MUSSLEWHITE, RANDALL, Private
Resided in Robeson County where he enlisted at age 21, September 6, 1861. Died at Roanoke Island on December 18-19, 1861, of disease.

PARNELL, BENJAMIN, Private
Resided in Robeson County where he enlisted at age 30, September 6, 1861. Died in hospital at Wilmington on or about March 11, 1863, of ''febris congestiva'' and/or ''pneumonia.''

PHILLIPS, EDMUND M., Private
Resided in Robeson County where he enlisted at age 23, September 6, 1861. Died in hospital at Charleston, South Carolina, March 21-22, 1863, of disease.

PHILLIPS, ORREN, Private
Resided in Robeson County where he enlisted at age 21, September 6, 1861. Present or accounted for through April, 1863. Reported absent without leave in March-April, 1864. Died prior to February 20, 1865. Place and cause of death not reported.

PITMAN, BENJAMIN F., Private
Resided in Robeson County where he enlisted at age 19, September 6, 1861. Died in hospital at Washington, North Carolina, on or about December 19, 1861, of disease. ''He was a good soldier, a general favorite in the company in which he belonged. . . . His gentle manners, his warm affections, his devoted friendship, his scrupulous sense of honor, all combined to make him the gentleman and soldier.''

POPE, JAMES W., Private
Resided in Robeson County where he enlisted on

September 6, 1861. Discharged on September 15, 1862. Reason discharged not reported.

POWERS, ELIAS, Private
Resided in Robeson County where he enlisted at age 22, September 6, 1861. Died in June, 1862, of disease. Place of death not reported.

PRICE, WILLIAM, Private
Resided in Robeson County where he enlisted on September 6, 1861. Listed as a deserter on September 15, 1862. [May have been captured at Roanoke Island on February 8, 1862, and paroled at Elizabeth City on February 21, 1862.]

RATLEY, JOSEPH, Private
Previously served in Captain W. J. McDugald's Unattached Company, North Carolina Troops. Transferred to this company in January-February, 1863, in exchange for Private Counsil Lewis. Present or accounted for through December, 1864.

RATLEY, RICHARD, Private
Enlisted in Robeson County on March 1, 1862. Present or accounted for through December 19, 1864. Reported absent without leave prior to January 1, 1865.

RATLEY, THOMAS, ———
North Carolina pension records indicate that he served in this company.

RATTLE, HINNANT, Private
Resided in Robeson County where he enlisted at age 37, September 6, 1861. Present or accounted for through June, 1862. No further records.

REGAN, DANIEL, Private
Resided in Robeson County where he enlisted at age 21, September 6, 1861. Present or accounted for until transferred to the Engineering Corps on August 3, 1863.

REGAN, HUGH BARTON, Sergeant
Resided in Robeson County where he enlisted at age 22, September 6, 1861. Mustered in as Sergeant. Present or accounted for until hospitalized at Danville, Virginia, June 4, 1864, with a gunshot wound of the arm. Place and date wounded not reported. Furloughed on June 7, 1864. Returned to duty prior to October 2, 1864, when he was hospitalized at Richmond, Virginia, with a gunshot wound of the right foot. Place and date wounded not reported. Reported absent wounded through December, 1864.

REVELS, HENRY, Private
Resided in Robeson County where he enlisted at age 21, September 6, 1861. Reported absent without leave during January-April, 1863. Reported present but under arrest in March-April, 1864. Returned to duty prior to June 1, 1864, when he was captured at or near Cold Harbor, Virginia. Confined at Point Lookout, Maryland, June 11, 1864. Transferred to Elmira, New York, July 12, 1864. Killed in a railroad accident at Shohola, Pennsylvania, July 15, 1864, while en route to Elmira. [May have been captured at Roanoke Island on February 8, 1862, and paroled at Elizabeth City on February 21, 1862.]

RHODES, WILLIAM A., Private
Resided in Robeson County where he enlisted at age 24, September 6, 1861. Present or accounted for through

April, 1863. Reported absent without leave in March-April, 1864. Returned to duty prior to June 1, 1864, when he was captured at or near Cold Harbor, Virginia. Confined at Point Lookout, Maryland, June 11, 1864. Transferred to Elmira, New York, July 12, 1864. Died at Elmira on October 29, 1864, of "pneumonia."

ROZIER, MILBY, Private
Resided in Robeson County where he enlisted at age 18, September 6, 1861. Discharged on November 22, 1861, or in January, 1862, by reason of disability.

RUSS, HAMDEN, Private
Resided in Robeson County where he enlisted at age 20, September 6, 1861. Present or accounted for through April, 1864. [May have been captured at Roanoke Island on February 8, 1862, and paroled at Elizabeth City on February 21, 1862.] No further records.

SEALEY, WILEY A., Private
Resided in Robeson County where he enlisted at age 39, September 6, 1861. Discharged on September 15, 1862. Reason discharged not reported. Later served in Captain W. J. McDugald's Unattached Company, North Carolina Troops.

SEALY, ALLEN H., Private
Resided in Robeson County where he enlisted at age 17, September 6, 1861. Present or accounted for until wounded at Fort Wagner, Charleston, South Carolina, July 18, 1863. Returned to duty on an unspecified date. Reported present for duty in March-April, 1864. Captured at or near Cold Harbor, Virginia, June 1, 1864. Confined at Point Lookout, Maryland, June 11, 1864. Transferred to Elmira, New York, July 12, 1864. Paroled at Elmira on October 11, 1864, and transferred to Venus Point, Savannah River, Georgia, where he was received on November 15, 1864, for exchange. Reported absent without leave in November-December, 1864.

STEAGALL, ISAAC H., 1st Sergeant
Resided in Granville County and enlisted in Robeson County at age 22, March 1, 1862. Mustered in as Private. Promoted to 1st Sergeant on September 15, 1862. Present or accounted for through December, 1864.

SULLIVAN, PATRICK, Private
Previously served in 2nd Company H, 40th Regiment N.C. Troops (3rd Regiment N.C. Artillery). Transferred to this company on July 1, 1863. Captured at or near Cold Harbor, Virginia, June 1, 1864. Confined at Point Lookout, Maryland, June 11, 1864. Transferred to Elmira, New York, July 12, 1864. Paroled at Elmira on October 11, 1864, and transferred to Venus Point, Savannah River, Georgia, where he was received on November 15, 1864, for exchange.

THOMPSON, JOHN L., Private
Resided in Robeson County where he enlisted at age 16, September 6, 1861. Wounded at Fort Wagner, Charleston, South Carolina, July 18, 1863. Returned to duty on an unspecified date. Reported present for duty in March-April, 1864. No further records.

TYSON, JOSEPH H., Private
Resided in Robeson County where he enlisted at age 22, September 6, 1861. Died on February 15, 186[2], of disease. Place of death not reported. [May have been

captured at Roanoke Island on February 8, 1862.]

VAUGHN, RICHARD, Private
Resided in Anson County and enlisted in New Hanover County at age 52, February 10, 1863, for the war as a substitute. Present or accounted for through December, 1864.

WALTERS, ARREN, Private
Resided in Robeson County where he enlisted at age 28, September 6, 1861. Mustered in as Private. Promoted to Corporal in May, 1863-April, 1864. Reduced to ranks subsequent to April 30, 1864. Reported absent without leave in March-April, 1864. Returned to duty prior to September 30, 1864, when he was wounded in the right wrist and captured at Fort Harrison, Virginia. Confined at Point Lookout, Maryland. Paroled at Point Lookout and transferred to Cox's Wharf, James River, Virginia, where he was received February 14-15, 1865, for exchange.

WALTERS, WILLIAM T., Private
Resided in Robeson County where he enlisted at age 21, September 6, 1861. Died in Robeson County in July, 1862-August, 1863, of disease. [May have been captured at Roanoke Island on February 8, 1862, and paroled at Elizabeth City on February 21, 1862.]

WATSON, ALEXANDER D., Sergeant
Previously served in Company F of this regiment. Transferred to this company with the rank of Private on or about January 14, 1862. Promoted to Corporal in July, 1862-February, 1863. Promoted to Sergeant in May, 1863-April, 1864. Present or accounted for through April, 1864. Company records dated November-December, 1864, indicate that he was a prisoner of war; however, records of the Federal Provost Marshal do not substantiate that report. No further records.

WATTS, DOCTOR T., Private
Resided in Robeson County where he enlisted at age 25, September 6, 1861. Present or accounted for through June, 1862. Reported absent without leave during January-April, 1863. Returned to duty on an unspecified date. Deserted on July 20, 1863. Reported under arrest in March-April, 1864. Reported absent without leave in November-December, 1864. [North Carolina pension records indicate he was shot through the head at Cold Harbor, Virginia, in the winter of 1864.]

WATTS, JOHN WILLIAM, Private
Resided in Robeson County where he enlisted at age 20, September 6, 1861. Present or accounted for until wounded in the groin and right thigh and captured at Fort Harrison, Virginia, September 30, 1864. Hospitalized at Fort Monroe, Virginia. Transferred to Point Lookout, Maryland, where he was confined on January 14, 1865. Paroled at Point Lookout and transferred to Cox's Wharf, James River, Virginia, where he was received February 14-15, 1865, for exchange. Furloughed for thirty days on March 2, 1865.

WEST, ARCHIBALD, Private
Resided in Robeson County where he enlisted at age 21, September 6, 1861. Captured at Cold Harbor, Virginia, June 1, 1864. Confined at Point Lookout, Maryland. Released on June 27, 1864, after joining the U.S. Army. Unit to which assigned not reported. [May have been

captured at Roanoke Island on February 8, 1862, and paroled at Elizabeth City on February 21, 1862.]

WEST, ELIAS, Corporal
Resided in Robeson County where he enlisted at age 24, September 6, 1861. Mustered in as Private. Promoted to Corporal in July-December, 1862. Reduced to ranks on February 19, 1863. Promoted to Corporal in May, 1863-April, 1864. Captured at or near Fort Harrison, Virginia, September 30, 1864. Confined at Point Lookout, Maryland, October 5, 1864. Paroled at Point Lookout on or about March 17, 1865, and transferred to Boulware's Wharf, James River, Virginia, where he was received on March 19, 1865, for exchange.

WEST, JOHN THOMAS, Private
Resided in Robeson County where he enlisted on September 6, 1861. Present or accounted for until he died at Washington, North Carolina, November 22, 1861, of disease.

WILLIS, RICHARD M., Private
Resided in Robeson County where he enlisted at age 35, September 6, 1861. Discharged on September 19, 1862. Reason discharged not reported.

WILLIS, WILLIAM J., Private
Born in Robeson County where he resided as a farmer prior to enlisting in Robeson County at age 18, September 6, 1861. Discharged on December 1, 1862, by reason of "hypertrophy of heart." [May have been captured at Roanoke Island on February 8, 1862, and paroled at Elizabeth City on February 21, 1862.]

WISHART, ALLADIN STRONG, Corporal
Resided in Robeson County where he enlisted at age 19, September 6, 1861. Mustered in as Private. Promoted to Corporal on February 19, 1863. Present or accounted for until wounded at Fort Harrison, Virginia, September 30, 1864. Returned to duty prior to January 1, 1865. No further records.

COMPANY B

This company was raised in Anson County and enlisted there on October 3, 1861. It was then assigned to the 31st Regiment N.C. Troops and designated Company B. After joining the regiment the company functioned as a part of the regiment, and its history for the war period is reported as a part of the regimental history. [A Beaufort County company, known as the "McMillan Artillery," was designated Company B, 31st Regiment N.C. Troops, on October 1, 1861; however, after what appears to have been a two-day career as such the unit was transferred. It was later designated Company B, 40th Regiment N.C. Troops (3rd Regiment N.C. Artillery). For the history of that company, see Volume I, pages 385-386, of this series.]

The information contained in the following roster of the company was compiled principally from company muster rolls for October 3-December 31, 1861; January-April, 1863; March-April, 1864; and November-December, 1864. No company muster rolls were found for January-December, 1862; May, 1863-February, 1864; May-October, 1864; or for the period after December, 1864. Valuable information was obtained from primary records such as the Roll of Honor, discharge certificates, medical records, prisoner of war records, and pension applications. Secondary sources such as postwar rosters and histories,

cemetery records, and records of the United Daughters of the Confederacy also provided useful information.

OFFICERS

CAPTAINS

LILES, EDWARD R.
Resided in Anson County where he enlisted at age 29. Appointed Captain on October 3, 1861. Present or accounted for until captured at Roanoke Island on February 8, 1862. Paroled at Elizabeth City on February 21, 1862. Appointed Lieutenant Colonel on September 17, 1862, and transferred to the Field and Staff of this regiment.

LINDSEY, CHARLES B.
Resided in Anson County where he enlisted at age 25. Appointed 2nd Lieutenant on October 3, 1861. Promoted to 1st Lieutenant on November 28, 1861. Present or accounted for until captured at Roanoke Island on February 8, 1862. Paroled at Elizabeth City on February 21, 1862. Promoted to Captain on September 17, 1862. Resigned on April 6, 1863, after refusing to appear before an officers' examining board. Resignation accepted on April 22, 1863.

BRADLEY, JAMES T.
Resided in Anson County where he enlisted at age 25, October 3, 1861. Mustered in as 1st Sergeant. Present or accounted for until captured at Roanoke Island on February 8, 1862. Paroled at Elizabeth City on February 21, 1862. Appointed 1st Lieutenant on September 17, 1862. Promoted to Captain on May 13, 1863. Hospitalized at Richmond, Virginia, May 14, 1864, with a gunshot wound of the neck. Place and date wounded not reported. Returned to duty prior to September 30, 1864, when he was captured at Fort Harrison, Virginia. Confined at Old Capitol Prison, Washington, D.C., October 6, 1864. Transferred to Fort Delaware, Delaware, October 21, 1864. Released at Fort Delaware on June 17, 1865, after taking the Oath of Allegiance.

LIEUTENANTS

ALLISON, JOSEPH W., 3rd Lieutenant
Served in Company E of this regiment. Reported in command of this company in November-December, 1864.

BALLARD, MATTHEW T., 2nd Lieutenant
Resided in Anson County where he enlisted at age 34, October 3, 1861. Mustered in as Private. Appointed 2nd Lieutenant on November 28, 1861. Resigned on June 6, 1862, by reason of being over 35 years of age and because "all the men of my command [are] paroled prisoners." Resignation accepted June 14, 1862. Later served as Private in Company C, 14th Regiment N.C. Troops (4th Regiment N.C. Volunteers).

BONNER, MACON, 1st Lieutenant
Born in Beaufort County where he resided prior to enlisting at age 25. Appointed 1st Lieutenant in September, 1861. Transferred to Company B, 40th Regiment N.C. Troops (3rd Regiment N.C. Artillery), on or about September 30, 1861.

CRUMP, STEPHEN, 2nd Lieutenant
Resided in Anson County where he enlisted at age 28.

Appointed 2nd Lieutenant on October 3, 1861. Present or accounted for until captured at Roanoke Island on February 8, 1862. Paroled at Elizabeth City on February 21, 1862. Defeated for reelection when the regiment was reorganized on September 17, 1862.

LILES, JUNIUS A., 2nd Lieutenant
Resided in Anson County where he enlisted at age 37, October 3, 1861. Mustered in as Private. Present or accounted for until captured at Roanoke Island on February 8, 1862. Paroled at Elizabeth City on February 21, 1862. Appointed 3rd Lieutenant on October 8, 1862. Promoted to 2nd Lieutenant on May 13, 1863. Hospitalized at Richmond, Virginia, May 16, 1864, with a gunshot wound of the left lung. Place and date wounded not reported. Died in hospital on May 24, 1864, of wounds.

LINDSEY, JAMES B., 3rd Lieutenant
Previously served as Quartermaster Sergeant of this regiment. Appointed 3rd Lieutenant and transferred to this company on or about May 16, 1863. Captured at or near Cold Harbor, Virginia, June 1, 1864. Confined at Point Lookout, Maryland, June 11, 1864. Transferred to Fort Delaware, Delaware, June 23, 1864. Transferred to Hilton Head, South Carolina, August 20, 1864. Confined at Fort Pulaski, Georgia, on or about October 21, 1864. Reported in confinement at Fort Pulaski on December 26, 1864. Transferred to Hilton Head on an unspecified date. Transferred to Fort Delaware where he arrived on March 12, 1865. Released on June 8, 1865.

STREATER, EDWARD H., 1st Lieutenant
Resided in Anson County where he enlisted at age 32, October 3, 1861. Mustered in as Private. Present or accounted for until captured at Roanoke Island on February 8, 1862. Paroled at Elizabeth City on February 21, 1862. Appointed 2nd Lieutenant on September 15, 1862. Promoted to 1st Lieutenant on May 13, 1863. Captured at or near Cold Harbor, Virginia, June 1, 1864. Confined at Point Lookout, Maryland, June 11, 1864. Transferred to Fort Delaware, Delaware, June 23, 1864. Released at Fort Delaware on June 17, 1865, after taking the Oath of Allegiance.

NONCOMMISSIONED OFFICERS AND PRIVATES

ADCOCK, ARCHY, Private
Resided in Anson County where he enlisted at age 16, October 3, 1861. Hospitalized at Richmond, Virginia, December 7, 1864, with a gunshot wound of the right leg. Place and date wounded not reported. Returned to duty on March 20, 1865. No further records.

ADCOCK, WILEY, Private
Resided in Anson County where he enlisted at age 32, October 3, 1861. Present or accounted for until captured at Roanoke Island on February 8, 1862. Paroled at Elizabeth City on February 21, 1862. Returned to duty on or about September 15, 1862. Wounded in the right buttock at or near Cold Harbor, Virginia, June 1, 1864. Furloughed on October 1, 1864. Reported absent without leave in November-December, 1864.

ALLEN, SOLOMON, Private
Resided in Anson County where he enlisted at age 19, October 3, 1861. Present or accounted for until captured at Roanoke Island on February 8, 1862. Paroled at Elizabeth City on February 21, 1862. Returned to duty on or about September 15, 1862. Present or accounted for through April, 1864. Reported absent without leave in November-December, 1864.

ALLEN, WILLIAM, Private
Resided in Anson County where he enlisted at age 17, October 3, 1861. Present or accounted for until captured at Roanoke Island on February 8, 1862. Paroled at Elizabeth City on February 21, 1862. Returned to duty on or about September 15, 1862. Discharged on April 7, 1863, by reason of being a minor on the date of his enlistment. [North Carolina pension records indicate he was wounded at Charleston, South Carolina, in 1863 or 1864.]

AYCOCK, THOMAS, Private
Resided in Anson County where he enlisted at age 31, October 3, 1861. Deserted on December 1, 1863.

BALLARD, SHERWOOD D., Private
Resided in Anson County where he enlisted on October 3, 1861. Present or accounted for until captured at Roanoke Island on February 8, 1862. Paroled at Elizabeth City on February 21, 1862. Returned to duty on or about September 15, 1862. Present or accounted for through April, 1864. Reported absent without leave in November-December, 1864.

BARNWELL, B. F., Private
Resided in Anson County and enlisted in Wake County at age 40, August 1, 1863, for the war. Present or accounted for through December, 1864.

BARTON, JOSEPH T., Private
Born in Lexington District, South Carolina, and resided in Anson County where he was by occupation a farmer prior to enlisting in Anson County at age 39, October 3, 1861. Discharged on April 22, 1862, by reason of "disability caused by peuperah."

BENNETT, JOHN G., Private
Resided in Anson County where he enlisted at age 24, October 3, 1861. Discharged on October 3, 1862, by reason of disability. Later served in Company A, 59th Regiment N.C. Troops (4th Regiment N.C. Cavalry).

BENNETT, SAMUEL PINES, Corporal
Resided in Anson County where he enlisted at age 19, October 3, 1861. Mustered in as Private. Discharged on July 30, 1862. Reason discharged not reported. Reenlisted in the company on January 28, 1863, for the war. Mustered in as Corporal. Present or accounted for through April, 1864. Company records dated November-December, 1864, indicate that he was a prisoner of war; however, records of the Federal Provost Marshal do not substantiate that report.

BERRY, A. B., ———
North Carolina pension records indicate that he served in this company.

BIRD, JAMES C., Corporal
Resided in Anson County where he enlisted at age 20, October 3, 1861. Mustered in as Private. Present or accounted for until captured at Roanoke Island on February 8, 1862. Paroled at Elizabeth City on February 21, 1862. Returned to duty on or about September 15,

1862. Wounded at White Hall on December 16, 1862. Promoted to Corporal subsequent to that date. Died "at home" on February 7-10, 1863. Cause ot death not reported.

CAPELL, T. C., Private
Enlisted in Wake County on August 14, 1863, for the war. Present or accounted for through December, 1864.

CLARK, MIAL, Private
Resided in Anson County where he enlisted at age 35, December 19, 1862, for the war. Present or accounted for through December, 1864.

CLARK, SAMUEL A., Private
Resided in Anson County where he enlisted at age 18, February 24, 1863, for the war. Captured at Cold Harbor, Virginia, June 1, 1864. Confined at Point Lookout, Maryland, June 11, 1864. Transferred to Elmira, New York, July 12, 1864. Paroled at Elmira on or about February 9, 1865, and transferred to Boulware's Wharf, James River, Virginia, where he was received on February 20, 1865, for exchange.

CLARKE, BENJAMIN F., 1st Sergeant
Resided in Anson County where he enlisted at age 25, October 3, 1861. Mustered in as Sergeant. Present or accounted for until captured at Roanoke Island on February 8, 1862. Paroled at Elizabeth City on February 21, 1862. Returned to duty on or about September 15, 1862. Promoted to 1st Sergeant on September 15, 1862. Promoted to Commissary Sergeant on August 1, 1863, and transferred to the Field and Staff of this regiment.

CLARKE, JOSEPH B., Private
Resided in Anson County where he enlisted at age 23, October 3, 1861. Present or accounted for until captured at Roanoke Island on February 8, 1862. Paroled at Elizabeth City on February 21, 1862. Returned to duty on or about September 15, 1862. Present or accounted for through December, 1864.

COLE, FRANCIS L., Private
Resided in Anson County where he enlisted at age 18, October 3, 1861. Present or accounted for until captured at Roanoke Island on February 8, 1862. Paroled at Elizabeth City on February 21, 1862. Returned to duty on or about September 15, 1862. Present or accounted for through December, 1864.

COX, CALVIN, Private
Resided in Anson County where he enlisted at age 19, October 3, 1861. Died in hospital at Washington, North Carolina, December 17-19, 1861. Cause of death not reported.

COX, JOHN, Private
Resided in Anson County where he enlisted at age 22, October 3, 1861. Died at Roanoke Island on February 3, 1862. Cause of death not reported.

COX, JULIUS M., Private
Previously served in Company K, 26th Regiment N.C. Troops. Enlisted in this company in Anson County on January 28, 1863, for the war. Captured at Cold Harbor, Virginia, June 1, 1864. Confined at Point Lookout, Maryland, June 11, 1864. Transferred to Elmira, New York, July 12, 1864. Paroled at Elmira on March 10, 1865, and transferred to Boulware's Wharf, James River,

Virginia, where he was received on March 15, 1865, for exchange.

COX, PETER B., Private
Resided in Anson County where he enlisted at age 23, October 3, 1861. Captured at Cold Harbor, Virginia, June 1, 1864. Confined at Point Lookout, Maryland, June 11, 1864. Transferred to Elmira, New York, July 12, 1864. Died at Elmira on April 16, 1865, of "chro[nic] diarr[hoea]."

COX, S. L., Private
Resided in Anson County where he enlisted at age 38, January 19, 186[3], for the war. Transferred to the Engineer Corps on July 1, 1863.

CRUMP, W. D., Private
Enlisted in Wake County on August 14, 1863, for the war. Present or accounted for through December, 1864.

De BERRY, JAMES N., Sergeant
Resided in Anson County where he enlisted at age 18, October 3, 1861. Mustered in as Private. Promoted to Corporal on September 15, 1862. Promoted to Sergeant on August 1, 1863. Present or accounted for through June 29, 1864.

De BERRY, WILLIAM G., Private
Resided in Anson County where he enlisted at age 18, February 23, 1863, for the war. Died at Charleston, South Carolina, August 31-September 1, 1863, of "remitt[e]nt fever."

DEESE, HENRY, Private
Resided in Anson County and enlisted at Charleston, South Carolina, at age 42, September 8, 1863, for the war. Captured at Cold Harbor, Virginia, on or about June 1, 1864. Confined at Point Lookout, Maryland, June 11, 1864. Transferred to Elmira, New York, July 12, 1864. Paroled at Elmira on March 14, 1865, and transferred to Boulware's Wharf, James River, Virginia, where he was received on or about March 18, 1865, for exchange. Hospitalized at Richmond, Virginia, where he was captured on April 3, 1865. Took the Oath of Allegiance on May 19, 1865.

DEESE, JOHN, Private
Resided in Anson County where he enlisted at age 22, October 3, 1861. Present or accounted for through December, 1864. [North Carolina pension records indicate he was wounded at Fort Harrison, Virginia, on an unspecified date.]

DEESE, JONATHAN, Private
Resided in Anson County and enlisted in New Hanover County at age 40, July 7, 1863, for the war. Wounded at Fort Wagner, Charleston, South Carolina, July 18, 1863. Returned to duty on an unspecified date. Transferred to Company A of this regiment on April 1, 1864.

DEESE, WILLIAM B., Private
Resided in Anson County where he enlisted at age 24, October 3, 1861. Died in hospital at Wilmington on or about September 3, 1863, of "pneumonia."

DIGGS, THOMAS E., 1st Sergeant
Resided in Anson County where he enlisted at age 28,

October 3, 1861. Mustered in as Corporal. Promoted to Sergeant in January, 1862-February, 1863. Present or accounted for until captured at Roanoke Island on February 8, 1862. Paroled at Elizabeth City on February 21, 1862. Returned to duty on or about September 15, 1862. Promoted to 1st Sergeant on August 1, 1863. Captured at or near Cold Harbor, Virginia, on or about May 31, 1864. Confined at Point Lookout, Maryland, June 11, 1864. Transferred to Elmira, New York, July 12, 1864. Paroled at Elmira on March 10, 1865, and transferred to Boulware's Wharf, James River, Virginia, where he was received on March 15, 1865, for exchange.

DIGGS, W. M., Private
Enlisted in Anson County on March 13, 1864, for the war. Died in hospital at Wilmington on September 14, 1864, of "diarrhoea chron[ic]."

DIGGS, WILLIAM RILEY, Private
Resided in Anson County where he enlisted at age 21, October 3, 1861. Present or accounted for until captured at Roanoke Island on February 8, 1862. Paroled at Elizabeth City on February 21, 1862. Returned to duty on or about September 15, 1862. Captured at Cold Harbor, Virginia, on or about June 1, 1864. Confined at Point Lookout, Maryland, June 11, 1864. Transferred to Elmira, New York, where he arrived on August 6, 1864. Died at Elmira on November 26, 1864, of "chronic diarrhoea."

DIGGS, WILLIAM S., Private
Resided in Anson County where he enlisted at age 33, October 3, 1861. Present or accounted for until captured at Roanoke Island on February 8, 1862. Paroled at Elizabeth City on February 21, 1862. Returned to duty on or about September 15, 1862. Captured at Cold Harbor, Virginia, May 31-June 1, 1864. Confined at Point Lookout, Maryland, June 11, 1864. Transferred to Elmira, New York, July 12, 1864. Paroled at Elmira on October 11, 1864, and transferred to Venus Point, Savannah River, Georgia, where he was received on November 15, 1864, for exchange. Reported absent sick through December, 1864.

DOWNER, W. P., Private
Enlisted at Camp Stokes on November 8, 1864, for the war. Present or accounted for through December, 1864.

DUMAS, JOSEPH P., Private
Born in [Richmond County] and resided in Anson County where he was by occupation a student prior to enlisting in Anson County at age 18, October 23, 1862, for the war. Wounded in the head and captured at or near Drewry's Bluff, Virginia, on or about May 16, 1864. Confined at Point Lookout, Maryland, May 24, 1864. Released on October 15, 1864, after joining the U.S. Army. Assigned to Company C, 4th Regiment U.S. Volunteer Infantry. [May have served previously in Company A, 14th Regiment N.C. Troops (4th Regiment N.C. Volunteers).]

EDWARDS, GEORGE T., Private
Resided in Anson County where he enlisted at age 28,

October 3, 1861. Present or accounted for through April, 1864. No further records.

FLAKE, HIRAM J., Private
Resided in Anson County where he enlisted at age 23, October 3, 1861. Mustered in as Corporal. Present or accounted for until captured at Roanoke Island on February 8, 1862. Paroled at Elizabeth City on February 21, 1862. Returned to duty on or about September 15, 1862. Reduced to ranks on September 15, 1863. Deserted on November 12, 1863.

FLOWERS, JAMES M., Sergeant
Resided in Anson County where he enlisted at age 19, October 3, 1861. Mustered in as Private. Present or accounted for until captured at Roanoke Island on February 8, 1862. Paroled at Elizabeth City on February 21, 1862. Returned to duty on or about September 15, 1862. Promoted to Sergeant on September 15, 1862. Discharged on May 23, 1863, after providing a substitute.

FORTE, JOHN, Private
Resided in Anson County where he enlisted at age 35, October 3, 1861. Discharged on October 3, 1862, under the provisions of the Conscription Act. [May have served later in Company I, 6th Regiment N.C. Senior Reserves.]

FORTE, JOHN F., Private
Resided in Anson County where he enlisted at age 25, October 3, 1861. Appointed 2nd Lieutenant on May 3, 1862, and transferred to Company A of this regiment.

GALLAGHER, NEIL, Private
Previously served in 2nd Company H, 40th Regiment N.C. Troops (3rd Regiment N.C. Artillery). Transferred to this company in July, 1863. Deserted to the enemy on or about February 16, 1864. Confined at Fort Monroe, Virginia. Released on or about February 24, 1864, after taking the Oath of Allegiance.

GILBERT, STEPHEN, Private
Resided in Anson County where he enlisted at age 16, October 3, 1861. Present or accounted for until the regiment was reorganized on September 17, 1862.

GILBERT, WILLIAM R., Private
Resided in Anson County where he enlisted at age 18, October 3, 1861. Present or accounted for until the regiment was reorganized on September 17, 1862.

GREGORY, JOHN V., Private
Born in Chesterfield District, South Carolina, and resided in Anson County where he was by occupation a farmer prior to enlisting in Anson County at age 31, October 3, 1861. Discharged on October 3, 1862, under the provisions of the Conscription Act. Later served in Company I, 43rd Regiment N.C. Troops.

HAIRE, GEORGE W., Private
Resided in Anson County where he enlisted at age 25, October 3, 1861. Present or accounted for until captured at Roanoke Island on February 8, 1862. Paroled at Elizabeth City on February 21, 1862. Returned to duty

on or about September 15, 1862. Transferred to Company H, 43rd Regiment N.C. Troops, on or about March 23, 1863.

HAMER, J. F., Private
Resided in Anson County and enlisted in New Hanover County at age 28, May 20, 1863, for the war. Present or accounted for through December, 1864.

HANCOCK, JOHN N., Sergeant
Resided in Anson County where he enlisted at age 29, October 3, 1861. Mustered in as Private. Present or accounted for until captured at Roanoke Island on February 8, 1862. Paroled at Elizabeth City on February 21, 1862. Returned to duty on or about September 15, 1862. Promoted to Sergeant on September 15, 1862. Present or accounted for through April, 1864. Died prior to March 9, 1865. Place and cause of death not reported.

HARBERT, CHARLES, Private
Resided in Anson County where he enlisted at age 43, October 3, 1861. Died at Plymouth on January 4, 1862. Cause of death not reported.

HARRIS, B. B., Private
Resided in Anson County where he enlisted at age 18, February 24, 1863, for the war. Killed at Fort Wagner, Charleston, South Carolina, July 18, 1863.

HATCHER, WILLIAM V., Private
Resided in Anson County and enlisted at Charleston, South Carolina, at age 44, September 8, 1863, for the war. Wounded in the head at or near Fort Harrison, Virginia, on or about September 30, 1864. Hospitalized at Richmond, Virginia, where he died on October 4, 1864, of wounds.

HENRY, ELYAH FRANK, Private
Resided in Anson County where he enlisted at age 16, October 3, 1861. Present or accounted for until captured at Roanoke Island on February 8, 1862. Paroled at Elizabeth City on February 21, 1862. Discharged on October 3, 1862, under the provisions of the Conscription Act. [May have served later in Company I, 43rd Regiment N.C. Troops.]

HENRY, REUBEN, Private
Resided in Anson County where he enlisted at age 59, October 5, 1862, for the war as a substitute. Present or accounted for through April, 1864. Reported absent without leave in November-December, 1864.

HENRY, WILLIAM, Private
Resided in Anson County where he enlisted at age 53, October 3, 1861. Present or accounted for until captured at Roanoke Island on February 8, 1862. Paroled at Elizabeth City on February 21, 1862. Discharged on October 3, 1862, under the provisions of the Conscription Act. Reenlisted in the company on May 1, 1863, for the war. Present or accounted for through April, 1864. Reported absent without leave in November-December, 1864.

HILL, DAVID K., Private
Resided in Anson County where he enlisted at age 18, October 3, 1861. Present or accounted for until captured at Roanoke Island on February 8, 1862. Paroled at Elizabeth City on February 21, 1862. Returned to duty on or about September 15, 1862. Wounded in the left thigh at or near Petersburg, Virginia, in June, 1864. Furloughed for sixty days on August 5, 1864. Reported absent without leave in November-December, 1864.

HILL, JAMES R., Private
Resided in Anson County where he enlisted at age 21, October 3, 1861. Present or accounted for until captured at Roanoke Island on February 8, 1862. Paroled at Elizabeth City on February 21, 1862. Died at Elizabeth City on February 23, 1862. Cause of death not reported.

HINSON, JOHN A., Private
Resided in Anson County where he enlisted at age 19, October 3, 1861. Present or accounted for until captured at Roanoke Island on February 8, 1862. Paroled at Elizabeth City on February 21, 1862. Died in Stanly County on April 5, 1862. Cause of death not reported.

HINSON, ROWAN, Private
Resided in Anson County where he enlisted at age 17, October 3, 1861. No further records.

HOWELL, JAMES E., Sergeant
Resided in Anson County where he enlisted at age 27, October 3, 1861. Mustered in as Private. Present or accounted for until captured at Roanoke Island on February 8, 1862. Paroled at Elizabeth City on February 21, 1862. Returned to duty on or about September 15, 1862. Promoted to Corporal on September 15, 1862. Promoted to Sergeant on May 23, 1863. Hospitalized at Raleigh on August 3, 1864, with a gunshot wound of the right hip. Place and date wounded not reported. Returned to duty on October 5, 1864. Present or accounted for through December, 1864.

JOHNSON, HUGH, Private
Resided in Anson County where he enlisted at age 30, July 8, 1862, for the war. Present or accounted for through January 7, 1865.

JOHNSON, JOHN D., Private
Resided in Anson County where he enlisted at age 24, October 3, 1861. Captured at Cold Harbor, Virginia, June 1, 1864. Confined at Point Lookout, Maryland, June 11, 1864. Transferred to Elmira, New York, July 12, 1864. Died on July 18, 1864, of injuries received in a railroad accident at Shohola, Pennsylvania, July 15, 1864, while en route to Elmira. Place of death not reported.

JOHNSON, R. T., Private
Resided in Anson County where he enlisted at age 18, February 23, 1863, for the war. Hospitalized at Richmond, Virginia, on or about May 17, 1864, with a gunshot wound of the left leg. Place and date wounded not reported. Furloughed for sixty days on August 7, 1864.

KINZEL, JOHN FRANCIS, Private
Resided in Anson County where he enlisted at age 37, October 16, 1861. Present or accounted for through December, 1861. Reported on duty as a baker with the 20th Regiment N.C. Troops in April, 1862. Apparently discharged on or about May 1, 1862. Reason discharged not reported. Enlisted in Company I, 43rd Regiment N.C. Troops, in the spring of 1862 but was rejected for service. Later served in 2nd Company D, 36th Regiment N.C. Troops (2nd Regiment N.C. Artillery).

LASSITER, GEORGE W., ———
North Carolina pension records indicate that he served in this company.

LILES, ARMSBERRY D., Private
Resided in Anson County where he enlisted at age 27, October 3, 1861. Present or accounted for through December, 1864.

LILES, BENJAMIN P., Private
Resided in Anson County where he enlisted at age 21, October 3, 1861. Present or accounted for through January 14, 1865.

LILES, J. C., Private
Resided in Anson County where he enlisted at age 18, February 23, 1863, for the war. Present or accounted for through December, 1864.

LILES, J. M., Private
Resided in Anson County and enlisted at Charleston, South Carolina, at age 38, September 8, 1863, for the war. Present or accounted for through December, 1864.

LILES, JOHN, ———
North Carolina pension records indicate that he served in this company.

LILES, JOSEPH E., Private
Resided in Anson County where he enlisted at age 20, October 3, 1861. Present or accounted for until killed at Roanoke Island on February 8, 1862.

LILES, JOSEPH W., Sergeant
Resided in Anson County where he enlisted at age 24, October 3, 1861. Mustered in as Corporal. Present or accounted for until captured at Roanoke Island on February 8, 1862. Paroled at Elizabeth City on February 21, 1862. Returned to duty on or about September 15, 1862. Promoted to Sergeant on September 15, 1862. Wounded at White Hall on December 16, 1862. Died at Camp Whiting, near Wilmington, January 27, 1863. Cause of death not reported.

LILES, NELSON P., Private
Resided in Anson County where he enlisted at age 17, October 3, 1861. Present or accounted for through December, 1864.

LILES, THOMAS H., Private
Resided in Anson County where he enlisted at age 27, October 22, 1862, for the war. Present or accounted for through December, 1864. [North Carolina pension records indicate he was wounded at "Goldsboro on October 1, 1863."]

LILES, WILLIAM H., Corporal
Resided in Anson County where he enlisted at age 21, October 3, 1861. Mustered in as Private. Present or accounted for until captured at Roanoke Island on February 8, 1862. Paroled at Elizabeth City on February 21, 1862. Returned to duty on or about September 15, 1862. Promoted to Corporal on September 15, 1862. "Killed instantly by the bursting of a shell" at White Hall on December 16, 1862.

LINDSEY, C. B., Private
Enlisted at Charleston, South Carolina, April 26, 1863, for the war. Present or accounted for through April,

1863.

LIVINGSTON, ALEXANDER L., Corporal
Resided in Anson County where he enlisted at age 32, October 3, 1861. Mustered in as Private. Promoted to Corporal in January, 1862-February, 1863. Present or accounted for until captured at Roanoke Island on February 8, 1862. Paroled at Elizabeth City on February 21, 1862. Returned to duty on or about September 15, 1862. Captured at Cold Harbor, Virginia, June 1, 1864. Confined at Point Lookout, Maryland, June 11, 1864. Transferred to Elmira, New York, July 12, 1864. Paroled at Elmira on an unspecified date and transferred to the James River, Virginia, where he was received on or about February 20, 1865, for exchange.

LONG, WILLIAM H., Private
Previously served in 2nd Company D, 36th Regiment N.C. Troops (2nd Regiment N.C. Artillery). Transferred to this company in April, 1862-April, 1864. Captured at Cold Harbor, Virginia, May 31, 1864. Confined at Point Lookout, Maryland, June 8, 1864. Released on June 8, 1864, after joining the U.S. Army. Assigned to Company C, 1st Regiment U.S. Volunteer Infantry. Deserted from the U.S. Army at Elizabeth City on August 2, 1864. Returned to duty with this company on an unspecified date. Present or accounted for through January 5, 1865.

McEACHERN, ALFRED H., Private
Resided in Anson County and enlisted at age 37, October 3, 1861. Present or accounted for until captured at Roanoke Island on February 8, 1862. Paroled at Elizabeth City on February 21, 1862. Discharged on October 3, 1862, under the provisions of the Conscription Act.

McQUAGE, ALEXANDER, Private
Resided in Anson County where he enlisted at age 18, February 27, 1863, for the war. Captured at Cold Harbor, Virginia, June 1, 1864. Confined at Point Lookout, Maryland, June 11, 1864. Transferred to Elmira, New York, July 12, 1864. Killed in a railroad accident at Shohola, Pennsylvania, July 15, 1864, while en route to Elmira.

McQUAGE, ELI W., Private
Resided in Anson County where he enlisted at age 19, October 3, 1861. Present or accounted for until captured at Roanoke Island on February 8, 1862. Paroled at Elizabeth City on February 21, 1862. Returned to duty on or about September 15, 1862. Present or accounted for through December, 1864.

McRAE, JAMES, Private
Resided in Anson County where he enlisted at age 18, October 3, 1861. Wounded in the left eye and captured at or near Cold Harbor, Virginia, on or about June 1, 1864. Confined at Point Lookout, Maryland, June 11, 1864. Transferred to Elmira, New York, July 12, 1864. Paroled at Elmira on March 10, 1865, and transferred to Boulware's Wharf, James River, Virginia, where he was received on March 15, 1865, for exchange. [North Carolina pension records indicate he "was also wounded slightly two other different times. . . ."]

MARTIN, JOHN A., Private
Resided in Anson County where he enlisted at age 23, October 3, 1861. Wounded at White Hall on December

16, 1862. Returned to duty prior to March 1, 1863. Present or accounted for through April, 1864. No further records.

MASK, J. HAMP, Private
Resided in Anson County where he enlisted at age 22, October 3, 1861. Present or accounted for until captured at Roanoke Island on February 8, 1862. Paroled at Elizabeth City on February 21, 1862. Returned to duty on or about September 15, 1862. Wounded at White Hall on December 16, 1862. Returned to duty prior to March 1, 1863. Present or accounted for through December, 1864.

MAY, HUGH McBINGIE, Corporal
Born in Anson County where he resided prior to enlisting in Anson County at age 35, October 3, 1861. Mustered in as Corporal. Present or accounted for until captured at Roanoke Island on February 8, 1862. Paroled at Elizabeth City on February 21, 1862. Discharged on October 3, 1862, under the provisions of the Conscription Act. Later served in 1st Company I, 36th Regiment N.C. Troops (2nd Regiment N.C. Artillery).

MEGGS, JAMES W., Private
Resided in Anson County where he enlisted at age 20, October 3, 1861. Wounded at White Hall on December 16, 1862. Returned to duty in January-February, 1863. Discharged on February 27 or March 15, 1863. Reason discharged not reported.

MOORE, JAMES H., Private
Born in Washington County and resided in Washington or Rowan County prior to enlisting in Anson County at age 35, December 7, 1861. Present or accounted for through April, 1863. Transferred to Company A of this regiment on an unspecified date. Transferred back to this company on April 1, 1864. Present or accounted for through January 24, 1865. Paroled at Salisbury on May 2, 1865. Took the Oath of Allegiance at Salisbury on June 17, 1865.

MORRIS, COLUMBUS W., Private
Resided in Anson County where he enlisted at age 17, October 3, 1861. Present or accounted for until captured at Roanoke Island on February 8, 1862. Paroled at Elizabeth City on February 21, 1862. Returned to duty on or about September 15, 1862. Captured at Cold Harbor, Virginia, June 1, 1864. Confined at Point Lookout, Maryland, June 11, 1864. Transferred to Elmira, New York, July 12, 1864. Died at Elmira on September 13, 1864, of "typhoid fever."

MORSE, JAMES B., Private
Resided in Anson County where he enlisted at age 39, February 28, 1863, for the war. Killed at or near Cold Harbor, Virginia, on or about June 1, 1864.

MUNNERLYN, JOHN, Private
Resided in Anson County where he enlisted at age 48, October 3, 1861. Present or accounted for until captured at Roanoke Island on February 8, 1862. Paroled at Elizabeth City on February 21, 1862. Discharged on October 3, 1862, under the provisions of the Conscription Act.

NEAL, FRANCIS M., Private
Resided in Anson County where he enlisted at age 31,

October 3, 1861. Present or accounted for until captured at Roanoke Island on February 8, 1862. Paroled at Elizabeth City on February 21, 1862. Died on April 17 or April 23, 1862. Place and cause of death not reported.

NEW, JAMES COLUMBUS, Private
Resided in Anson County where he enlisted at age 17, October 3, 1861. Present or accounted for until captured at Roanoke Island on February 8, 1862. Paroled at Elizabeth City on February 21, 1862. Returned to duty on or about September 15, 1862. Present or accounted for through December, 1864. [North Carolina pension records indicate he was wounded in the right arm at Kinston on or about March 1, 1865.]

NEW, ROBERT W., Private
Resided in Anson County where he enlisted at age 59, October 3, 1861. Present or accounted for until captured at Roanoke Island on February 8, 1862. Paroled at Elizabeth City on February 21, 1862. Returned to duty on or about September 15, 1863. Died in hospital at Charleston, South Carolina, November 18, 1863. Cause of death not reported.

NEWTON, JOHN A., Private
Resided in Anson County where he enlisted at age 29, September 4, 1862, for the war. Present or accounted for through December, 1864. [North Carolina pension records indicate he was wounded in the left arm at Drewry's Bluff, Virginia, in 1863.]

NEWTON, WILLIAM T., Private
Previously served in Company H, 43rd Regiment N.C. Troops. Transferred to this company on December 27, 1862. Died at Ivor Station, Virginia, March 4, 1864, of "fever."

PARKER, EDWARD, Private
Enlisted at Petersburg, Virginia, January 15, 1864, for the war. Present or accounted for through June 1, 1864. No further records.

PARKER, JOHN B., Private
Resided in Anson County where he enlisted at age 20, October 3, 1861. Present or accounted for through December, 1864.

PARKER, MUMFORD S., Corporal
Resided in Anson County where he enlisted at age 19, October 3, 1861. Mustered in as Private. Promoted to Corporal on August 1, 1863. Captured at Cold Harbor, Virginia, June 1, 1864. Confined at Point Lookout, Maryland, June 11, 1864. Transferred to Elmira, New York, July 12, 1864. Paroled at Elmira on March 14, 1865, and transferred to Boulware's Wharf, James River, Virginia, where he was received on or about March 18, 1865, for exchange.

PARKER, MYRICK N., Private
Resided in Anson County where he enlisted at age 23, October 3, 1861. Present or accounted for until captured at Roanoke Island on February 8, 1862. Paroled at Elizabeth City on February 21, 1862. Returned to duty on or about September 15, 1862. Captured at Cold Harbor, Virginia, June 1, 1864. Confined at Point Lookout, Maryland, June 11, 1864. Transferred to Elmira, New York, July 12, 1864. Died at Elmira on April 11, 1865, of "pneumonia."

PARKER, SYDNEY, Private
Resided in Anson County where he enlisted at age 27, October 3, 1861. Present or accounted for until captured at Roanoke Island on February 8, 1862. Paroled at Elizabeth City on February 21, 1862. Returned to duty on or about September 15, 1862. Killed at Fort Wagner Charleston, South Carolina, July 18, 1863.

PARKER, W. THOMAS, Private
Enlisted in Anson County on October 3, 1861. Died in hospital at Washington, North Carolina, December 20, 1861. Cause of death not reported.

PARKER, WILLIAM D., Private
Resided in Anson County where he enlisted at age 21, October 3, 1861. Present or accounted for through December, 1864.

PARKER, WILLIAM T., Private
Resided in Anson County where he enlisted at age 18, October 3, 1861. Died at Washington, North Carolina, December 10-15, 1861. Cause of death not reported.

POPLIN, THOMAS J., Private
Resided in Anson County where he enlisted at age 30, October 3, 1861. Present or accounted for until captured at Roanoke Island on February 8, 1862. Paroled at Elizabeth City on February 21, 1862. Returned to duty on or about September 15, 1862. Present or accounted for through December, 1864.

PORTER, JAMES T., Sergeant
Resided in Anson County where he enlisted at age 19, October 3, 1861. Mustered in as Private. Promoted to Corporal subsequent to December 31, 1861. Present or accounted for until captured at Roanoke Island on February 8, 1862. Paroled at Elizabeth City on February 21, 1862. Returned to duty on or about September 15, 1862. Promoted to Sergeant on January 28, 1863. Captured at Cold Harbor, Virginia, June 1, 1864. Confined at Point Lookout, Maryland, June 11, 1864. Transferred to Elmira, New York, July 12, 1864. Suffered an injury to his right thigh on July 15, 1864, presumably in a railroad accident at Shohola, Pennsylvania, Arrived at Elmira on July 17, 1864. Paroled at Elmira on October 11, 1864, and transferred to Venus Point, Savannah River, Georgia, where he was received on November 15, 1864, for exchange. Reported absent without leave in November-December, 1864.

PRATT, DANIEL M., Private
Resided in Anson County where he enlisted at age 22, October 3, 1861. Wounded in the right hip at Fort Harrison, Virginia, on or about September 30, 1864. Returned to duty on an unspecified date. Present or accounted for through December, 1864.

PRATT, S. M., Private
Enlisted in Anson County on March 13, 1864, for the war. Captured at Cold Harbor, Virginia, June 1, 1864. Confined at Point Lookout, Maryland, June 4, 1864. Transferred to Elmira, New York, July 12, 1864. Paroled at Elmira on October 11, 1864, and transferred to Venus Point, Savannah River, Georgia, where he was received on November 15, 1864, for exchange.

RATLIFF, CHARLES H., Private
Resided in Anson County where he enlisted at age 19, October 3, 1861. Present or accounted for until captured

at Roanoke Island on February 8, 1862. Paroled at Elizabeth City on February 21, 1862. Returned to duty on or about September 15, 1862. Captured at Cold Harbor, Virginia, June 1, 1864. Confined at Point Lookout, Maryland, June 11, 1864. Transferred to Elmira, New York, July 12, 1864. Released at Elmira on May 29, 1865, after taking the Oath of Allegiance.

RICHARDSON, HARDY H., Private
Resided in Anson County where he enlisted at age 19, October 3, 1861. Present or accounted for through June 3, 1864. Retired from service prior to January 1, 1865. Reason he was retired not reported.

ROBINSON, C. H., Private
Records of this company indicate he served previously in Company C, 61st Regiment N.C. Troops, and was transferred to this company on June 14, 1863; however, records of the 61st Regiment do not indicate that he served therein. Appointed Quartermaster Sergeant and transferred to the Field and Staff of this regiment prior to July 1, 1863.

SASSER, HENRY, Private
Enlisted at Camp Stokes on November 8, 1864, for the war. Present or accounted for through December, 1864.

SEAGO, PATRICK H., Private
Resided in Anson County where he enlisted at age 21, October 3, 1861. Captured at Cold Harbor, Virginia, June 1, 1864. Confined at Point Lookout, Maryland, June 11, 1864. Transferred to Elmira, New York, July 11, 1864. Killed in a railroad accident at Shohola, Pennsylvania, July 15, 1864, while en route to Elmira.

SEAGO, WILLIAM, Private
Resided in Anson County where he enlisted at age 21, August 15, 1862, for the war. Died in hospital at Petersburg, Virginia, May 9, 1864, of ''dysenteria c[hronic].''

SELLERS, JOHN, Private
Resided in Anson County and enlisted at Charleston, South Carolina, at age 39, September 8, 1863, for the war. Killed at or near Petersburg, Virginia, in May, 1864.

SMITH, JAMES, Private
Enlisted in Anson County on September 4, 1862, for the war. Hospitalized at Wilmington on February 16, 1863, with pneumonia. Died at Wilmington on or about February 23, 1863.

SMITH, JOHN W., Private
Resided in Anson County where he enlisted at age 23, October 3, 1861. Died on January 2, 1862. Place and cause of death not reported.

STATEN, JESSE B., Corporal
Resided in Anson County where he enlisted at age 20, October 3, 1861. Mustered in as Sergeant. Reduced to ranks on September 15, 1862. Promoted to Corporal on May 1, 1863. Died at Wilmington on July 15, 1863, of ''ty[phoid] fever.''

STATEN, WILLIAM C., Corporal
Resided in Anson County where he enlisted at age 25, October 3, 1861. Mustered in as Sergeant. Present or accounted for until captured at Roanoke Island on

February 8, 1862. Paroled at Elizabeth City on February 21, 1862. Returned to duty on or about September 15, 1862. Reduced to ranks on September 15, 1862. Promoted to Corporal on September 5, 1863. Captured at Cold Harbor, Virginia, May 31-June 1, 1864. Confined at Point Lookout, Maryland, June 11, 1864. Transferred to Elmira, New York, July 12, 1864. Released at Elmira on July 3, 1865, after taking the Oath of Allegiance.

STATON, JOHN S., Private
Resided in Anson County where he enlisted at age 19, October 3, 1861. Discharged prior to April 2, 1862. Reason discharged not reported. Enlisted in Company I, 43rd Regiment N.C. Troops, April 2, 1862. Reenlisted in this company in Wake County on September 15, 1862, for the war. Present or accounted for until wounded in the right hip and right leg at Fort Harrison, Virginia, on or about September 30, 1864. Returned to duty on an unspecified date. Present or accounted for through December, 1864.

STEPHENS, W. L., Private
Place and date of enlistment not reported. Captured in hospital at Raleigh on April 13, 1865. No further records.

STREATER, ELIJAH, Private
Resided in Anson County where he enlisted at age 27, October 3, 1861. Present or accounted for through December, 1864.

TYSON, HARVEY, Private
Resided in Anson County where he enlisted at age 47, October 3, 1861. Present or accounted for until captured at Roanoke Island on February 8, 1862. Paroled at Elizabeth City on February 21, 1862. Discharged on October 3, 1862, under the provisions of the Conscription Act.

TYSON, WILLIAM GREEN, Private
Resided in Anson County where he enlisted at age 22, October 3, 1861. Present or accounted for until captured at Roanoke Island on February 8, 1862. Paroled at Elizabeth City on February 21, 1862. Returned to duty on or about September 15, 1862. Present or accounted for through December, 1864. Paroled on an unspecified date subsequent to April 26, 1865.

WALKER, A. S., Private
Enlisted at Camp Stokes at age 20, October 25, 1864, for the war. Present or accounted for through March 28, 1865. Paroled at Salisbury on May 11, 1865.

WALKER, JOHN W., Private
Resided in Anson County where he enlisted at age 22, October 3, 1861. Present or accounted for until captured at Roanoke Island on February 8, 1862. Paroled at Elizabeth City on February 21, 1862. Returned to duty on or about September 15, 1862. Present or accounted for through December, 1864. Paroled at Salisbury on May 2, 1865. [The Charlotte *Western Democrat* of April 4, 1865, indicates he was wounded in the shoulder in an unspecified battle in North Carolina and was hospitalized at Raleigh.]

WALL, J. C., Private
Born in Anson County where he resided as a farmer prior to enlisting in New Hanover County at age 18,

May 20, 1863, for the war. Captured at Cold Harbor, Virginia, June 1, 1864. Confined at Point Lookout, Maryland, June 11, 1864. Transferred to Elmira, New York, July 12, 1864. Suffered a fractured left leg in a railroad accident at Shohola, Pennsylvania, July 15, 1864, while en route to Elmira. Arrived at Elmira on an unspecified date. Paroled at Elmira on October 11, 1864, and transferred to Venus Point, Savannah River, Georgia, where he was received on November 15, 1864, for exchange. Retired from service on February 20, 1865, by reason of injuries suffered at Shohola.

WILLIAMS, JAMES A., Private
Enlisted at Petersburg, Virginia, March 27, 1864, for the war. Captured at Cold Harbor, Virginia, June 1, 1864. Confined at Point Lookout, Maryland, June 11, 1864. Transferred to Elmira, New York, July 12, 1864. Died at Elmira on September 17, 1864, of "jaundice & chronic diarrhoea."

WILLIAMS, WILLIAM, Private
Enlisted at Charleston, South Carolina, April 26, 1863, for the war. Died in August-December, 1863. Place and cause of death not reported.

WILSON, WILLIAM, Private
Place and date of enlistment not reported. Paroled at Greensboro on May 19, 1865.

YATES, M. HARRISON, Private
Resided in Anson County where he enlisted at age 22, October 3, 1861. Present or accounted for until captured at Roanoke Island on February 8, 1862. Paroled at Elizabeth City on February 21, 1862. Returned to duty on or about September 15, 1862. Captured at Cold Harbor, Virginia, June 1, 1864. Confined at Point Lookout, Maryland, June 11, 1864. Transferred to Elmira, New York, July 12, 1864. Paroled at Elmira on October 11, 1864, and transferred to Venus Point, Savannah River, Georgia, where he was received on November 15, 1864, for exchange. Reported absent with leave through December, 1864.

COMPANY C

This company was raised in Harnett and Wake counties and enlisted in Wake County on October 4, 1861. It was then assigned to the 31st Regiment N.C. Troops and designated Company C. After joining the regiment the company functioned as a part of the regiment, and its history for the war period is reported as a part of the regimental history.

The information contained in the following roster of the company was compiled principally from company muster rolls for October 4-December 31, 1861; January-April, 1863; and December 31, 1863-April 30, 1864. No company muster rolls were found for January-December, 1862; May 1-December 30, 1863; or for the period after April 30, 1864. Valuable information was obtained from primary records such as the Roll of Honor, discharge certificates, medical records, prisoner of war records, and pension applications. Secondary sources such as postwar rosters and histories, cemetery records, and records of the United Daughters of the Confederacy also provided useful information.

OFFICERS

CAPTAINS

BETTS, ANDREW W.
Resided in Wake County where he enlisted at age 40.

Appointed Captain on October 4, 1861. Present or accounted for until captured at Roanoke Island on February 8, 1862. Paroled at Elizabeth City on February 21, 1862. Died "at home" on April 16, 1862, of disease.

LONG, WILLIAM J.

Resided in Harnett County and enlisted in Wake County at age 27, October 4, 1861. Mustered in as Sergeant. Present or accounted for until captured at Roanoke Island on February 8, 1862. Paroled at Elizabeth City on February 21, 1862. Appointed Captain on or about September 17, 1862. Present or accounted for through September 8, 1864.

LIEUTENANTS

BETTS, ANDERSON N., 2nd Lieutenant

Resided in Wake County where he enlisted at age 37. Appointed 2nd Lieutenant on October 4, 1861. Resigned on January 28, 1862. Reason he resigned not reported.

GODWIN, THOMAS H., 3rd Lieutenant

Resided in Wake County where he enlisted at age 30, October 4, 1861. Mustered in as Private. Appointed 3rd Lieutenant on or about September 17, 1862. Present or accounted for until August 19, 1864, when he was reported absent without leave. Hospitalized at Richmond, Virginia, September 19, 1864. Reported absent sick on November 26, 1864. Reported absent without leave on December 31, 1864.

UTLEY, QUINTON, 1st Lieutenant

Resided in Wake County where he enlisted at age 48. Appointed 1st Lieutenant on October 4, 1861. Present or accounted for until captured at Roanoke Island on February 8, 1862. Paroled at Elizabeth City on February 21, 1862. Defeated for reelection when the regiment was reorganized on September 17, 1862.

WILLIAMS, JACOB C., 2nd Lieutenant

Resided in Harnett County and enlisted in Wake County at age 26, October 4, 1861. Mustered in as Sergeant. Present or accounted for until captured at Roanoke Island on February 8, 1862. Paroled at Elizabeth City on February 21, 1862. Appointed 2nd Lieutenant on or about September 17, 1862. Captured at Fort Harrison, Virginia, September 30, 1864. Confined at Old Capitol Prison, Washington, D.C., October 6, 1864. Transferred to Fort Delaware, Delaware, October 21, 1864. Released on June 10, 1865, after taking the Oath of Allegiance.

NONCOMMISSIONED OFFICERS AND PRIVATES

ADAMS, J. A., Private

Resided in Wake County where he enlisted at age 19, July 15, 1862, for the war. Present or accounted for through September 19, 1864. [North Carolina pension records indicate that he survived the war.]

BAKER, JOHN B., Private

Resided in Wake County where he enlisted at age 38, October 4, 1861. Present or accounted for until captured at Roanoke Island on February 8, 1862. Paroled at Elizabeth City on February 21, 1862. Discharged on

October 4, 1862. Reason discharged not reported.

BALLENTINE, J. D., 1st Sergeant

Resided in Harnett County and enlisted in Wake County at age 20, October 4, 1861. Mustered in as Sergeant. Present or accounted for until captured at Roanoke Island on February 8, 1862. Paroled at Elizabeth City on February 21, 1862. Promoted to 1st Sergeant on September 15, 1862. Present or accounted for through April, 1864.

BALLENTINE, JOHN C., Sergeant

Resided in Harnett County and enlisted in Wake County at age 32, October 4, 1861. Mustered in as Sergeant. Present or accounted for until captured at Roanoke Island on February 8, 1862. Paroled at Elizabeth City on February 21, 1862. Returned to duty on or about September 15, 1862. Wounded in the lung at or near Drewry's Bluff, Virginia, May 16, 1864. Hospitalized at Richmond, Virginia. Furloughed for sixty days on June 9, 1864. [North Carolina pension records indicate that he survived the war.] No further records.

BARNHILL, M. A., Private

Resided in Bladen County and enlisted in Wake County at age 20, July 17, 1862, for the war. Present or accounted for through April, 1864.

BEASLEY, HINTON, Private

Resided in Wake County where he enlisted at age 25, September 8, 1862, for the war. Deserted on October 8, 1862. Returned to duty on March 10, 1863. Present or accounted for through April, 1864. No further records.

BEASLEY, JAMES K., ———

North Carolina pension records indicate that he served in this company.

BEASLEY, JASPER J., Private

Resided in Wake or Harnett County and enlisted in Wake County at age 24, October 4, 1861. Transferred to Company F, 15th Regiment N.C. Troops (5th Regiment N.C. Volunteers), on or about March 20, 1863.

BELL, BURWELL, Private

Resided in Wake County where he enlisted at age 34, September 20, 1862, for the war. Reported absent on hospital duty from January-February, 1863, through August, 1864. Paroled at Greensboro on May 1, 1865.

BETTS, ARCHIBALD B., Private

Resided in Wake County where he enlisted at age 25, October 4, 1861. Present or accounted for until captured at Roanoke Island on February 8, 1862. Paroled at Elizabeth City on February 21, 1862. Reported absent on duty as a shoemaker during January-April, 1863, and January-April, 1864. [North Carolina pension records indicate that he survived the war.] No further records.

BETTS, W. H., Sergeant

Resided in Wake County where he enlisted at age 16 September 8, 1862, for the war. Mustered in as Private. Promoted to Sergeant on September 15, 1862. Captured at Fort Harrison, Virginia, September 30, 1864. Confined at Point Lookout, Maryland, October 5, 1864. Died at Point Lookout on January 18, 1865, of "chronic diarrhoea."

BLALOCK, RICHARD A., Private
Resided in Wake County where he enlisted at age 18, October 4, 1861. Present or accounted for through April, 1863. Reported absent without leave on April 8, 1864. Hospitalized at Raleigh on September 19, 1864, with chronic bronchitis. Returned to duty on November 1, 1864. No further records.

BROOKS, JOEL, ———
North Carolina pension records indicate that he served in this company.

BROWN, W. W., Private
Resided in New Hanover County and enlisted in Wake County at age 23, July 20, 1862, for the war. Present or accounted for through May 31, 1864. [North Carolina pension records indicate that he survived the war.] No further records.

CAMPBELL, BARNEY C., Private
Resided in Wake County where he enlisted at age 26, October 4, 1861. Present or accounted for until captured at Roanoke Island on February 8, 1862. Paroled at Elizabeth City on February 21, 1862. Returned to duty on or about September 15, 1862. Captured at Fort Harrison, Virginia, September 30, 1864. Confined at Point Lookout, Maryland, October 5, 1864. Paroled at Point Lookout on or about February 10, 1865, and transferred to Cox's Wharf, James River, Virginia, where he was received on or about February 14, 1865, for exchange. Furloughed for sixty days on February 24, 1865.

CHAMPION, JAMES H., Private
Resided in Wake County where he enlisted at age 23, October 4, 1861. Present or accounted for until captured at Roanoke Island on February 8, 1862. Paroled at Elizabeth City on February 21, 1862. Returned to duty on or about September 15, 1862. Present or accounted for through April, 1864. [North Carolina pension records indicate that he survived the war.] No further records.

CHAMPION, LEVI, Private
Resided in Wake County where he enlisted at age 44, October 4, 1861. Present or accounted for until captured at Roanoke Island on February 8, 1862. Paroled at Elizabeth City on February 21, 1862. Discharged on October 4, 1862. Reason discharged not reported. [May have served later in Company G, 8th Regiment N.C. State Troops.]

CHURCHILL, J. R., Private
Resided in Wake County where he enlisted at age 18, October 12, 1862, for the war. Captured at Fort Harrison, Virginia, September 30, 1864. Confined at Point Lookout, Maryland, October 5, 1864. Paroled on or about February 10, 1865, and transferred to Cox's Wharf, James River, Virginia, where he was received on or about February 14, 1865, for exchange.

COLLINS, THOMAS, Private
Resided in Wake County where he enlisted at age 18, June 16, 1863, for the war. Present or accounted for through April, 1864. No further records.

CUTTS, JOSEPH F., 1st Sergeant
Resided in Harnett County and enlisted in Wake County at age 23, October 4, 1861. Mustered in as 1st Sergeant. Captured at Roanoke Island on February 8, 1862. Paroled at Elizabeth City on February 21, 1862. Died "at home" on April 5, 1862, of disease.

DIXON, B. A. J., Private
Resided in Johnston County and enlisted at age 34, October 15, 1862, for the war. Discharged on November 15, 1863, by reason of disability.

DORMAN, JAMES, Private
Resided in Johnston County and enlisted in Wake County at age 20, October 4, 1861. Present or accounted for until captured at Roanoke Island on February 8, 1862. Paroled at Elizabeth City on February 21, 1862. Died on November 30, 1862, of "disability." Place of death not reported.

DUPREE, J. G., Private
Resided in Johnston County and enlisted in Wake County at age 25, October 9, 1862, for the war. Reported absent without leave on April 18, 1864.

DUPREE, W. H., Private
Resided in Johnston County and enlisted at age 26, October 9, 1862, for the war. Died in hospital at Wilmington on January 5-6, 1863, of "febris congestiva."

DURHAM, LITTLETON, Private
Resided in Wake County where he enlisted at age 22, October 4, 1861. Mustered in as Private. Promoted to Corporal on September 15, 1862. Reduced to ranks in May, 1863-April, 1864. Reported absent without leave on March 30, 1864.

ELLER, RIGDEN H., Private
Resided in Wake County where he enlisted at age 32, February 13, 1863, for the war. Reported absent without leave on April 18, 1863. Returned to duty prior to July 18, 1863, when he was wounded at Fort Wagner, Charleston, South Carolina. Returned to duty on an unspecified date. Present or accounted for through April, 1864.

ENNIS, WILLIAM B., Private
Resided in Harnett County and enlisted in Wake County at age 18, October 4, 1861. Present or accounted for until captured at Roanoke Island on February 8, 1862. Paroled at Elizabeth City on February 21, 1862. Returned to duty on or about September 15, 1862. Present or accounted for through October 2, 1864. [North Carolina pension records indicate he was wounded on September 15, 1864.]

FUQUAY, DAVID, Private
Resided in Wake County where he enlisted at age 40, October 4, 1861. Mustered in as Musician. Reduced to ranks prior to February 8, 1862. Present or accounted for until captured at Roanoke Island on February 8, 1862. Paroled at Elizabeth City on February 21, 1862. Discharged on October 4, 1862. Reason discharged not reported.

FUQUAY, WILLIAM, Private
Resided in Wake County where he enlisted at age 53, October 4, 1861. Present or accounted for until captured at Roanoke Island on February 8, 1862. Paroled at Elizabeth City on February 21, 1862. Discharged on

October 4, 1862. Reason discharged not reported.

GARDNER, S. H., Private
Resided in Harnett County and enlisted in Wake County at age 19, July 17, 1862, for the war. Captured near Drewry's Bluff, Virginia, May 16, 1864. Confined at Point Lookout, Maryland, May 19, 1864. Transferred to Elmira, New York, August 16, 1864. Paroled at Elmira on October 11, 1864, and transferred to Venus Point, Savannah River, Georgia, where he was received on November 15, 1864, for exchange.

GOWER, JAMES, Private
Resided in Wake County where he enlisted at age 20, June 16, 1863, for the war. Wounded at Fort Wagner, Charleston, South Carolina, on or about July 16, 1863. Returned to duty prior to May 1, 1864. Present or accounted for through October 5, 1864.

GREGORY, JAMES R., Private
Resided in Wake County where he enlisted at age 26, October 4, 1861. Present or accounted for until captured at Roanoke Island on February 8, 1862. Paroled at Elizabeth City on February 21, 1862. Returned to duty on or about September 15, 1862. Present or accounted for through April, 1864. Later served as Sergeant in Company G, 2nd Regiment Confederate Engineering Troops.

GREGORY, JOHN A., Private
Resided in Wake County where he enlisted at age 28, October 4, 1861. Present or accounted for until captured at Roanoke Island on February 8, 1862. Paroled at Elizabeth City on February 21, 1862. Reported absent without leave on April 18, 1863. Wounded at Fort Wagner, Charleston, South Carolina, July 18, 1863. Reported present for duty during January-April, 1864. [Roll of Honor indicates that he "deserted three times."] No further records.

GRIFFIN, DARLIN, Private
Resided in Harnett County and enlisted in Wake County at age 35, October 1, 1862, for the war. Discharged on March 20, 1863, by reason of disability.

GRIFFIS, JAMES H., Private
Resided in Wake County where he enlisted at age 32, October 4, 1861. Present or accounted for until captured at Roanoke Island on February 8, 1862. Paroled at Elizabeth City on February 21, 1862. Died "at home" on April 7, 1862, of disease.

GRIFFIS, JOSHUA M., Corporal
Resided in Wake County where he enlisted at age 22, October 4, 1861. Mustered in as Private. Present or accounted for until captured at Roanoke Island on February 8, 1862. Paroled at Elizabeth City on February 21, 1862. Promoted to Corporal on September 15, 1862. Present or accounted for through April, 1864. No further records.

GRIFFITHS, JOHN M., ———
North Carolina pension records indicate that he served in this company.

HAMILTON, ASA G., Private
Resided in Harnett County and enlisted in Wake County at age 22, October 4, 1861. Present or accounted for through February 5, 1865.

HARVEL, JOHN, Private
Resided in Wake County where he enlisted at age 34, October 4, 1861. Died "at home" on January 14, 1862, of disease.

HOLLAND, TURNER T., Private
Resided in Wake County where he enlisted at age 33, October 4, 1862, for the war. Reported absent without leave on July 1, 1863. Returned to duty on an unspecified date. Reported present for duty during January-April, 1864. Hospitalized at Richmond, Virginia, August 20, 1864, and was transferred to another hospital the next day. No further records.

HOLLAND, W. H., Private
Resided in Wake County where he enlisted at age 27, October 4, 1862, for the war. Discharged on or about May 25, 1863, by reason of "hypert[rophy] heart."

JOHNSON, DAVID W., Private
Resided in Wake County where he enlisted at age 16, October 4, 1861. Present or accounted for until captured at Roanoke Island on February 8, 1862. Paroled at Elizabeth City on February 21, 1862. Discharged on October 4, 1862. Reason discharged not reported.

JOHNSON, GEORGE W., Private
Resided in Wake County where he enlisted at age 23, October 4, 1861. Present or accounted for until captured at Roanoke Island on February 8, 1862. Paroled at Elizabeth City on February 21, 1862. Reported absent without leave on December 5, 1863. [Roll of Honor indicates that he "deserted three times."]

JOHNSON, JOHN, Private
Resided in Wake or Johnston County and enlisted in Wake County at age 34, October 4, 1861. Discharged on October 4, 1862, under the provisions of the Conscription Act. Reenlisted in the company on February 28, 1863, for the war. Present or accounted for through May 23, 1864. No further records.

JOHNSON, JOHN L., Private
Resided in Harnett County and enlisted in Wake County at age 23, October 4, 1861. Died in Harnett County on May 20, 1863, of disease.

JOHNSON, WILLIAM, Private
Resided in Wake County where he enlisted at age 33, October 4, 1861. Present or accounted for until captured at Roanoke Island on February 8, 1862. Paroled at Elizabeth City on February 21, 1862. Discharged on October 4, 1862, under the provisions of the Conscription Act.

JOHNSON, WILLIAM, Sr., Private
Born in Wake County where he resided as a laborer prior to enlisting at Camp Mangum at age 37, October 1, 1862, for the war. Discharged on December 27, 1862, by reason of "loss of right eye & impairment of left."

JOHNSON, WILLIAM ALLEN, Private
Previously served in Company F, 15th Regiment N.C. Troops (5th Regiment N.C. Volunteers). Transferred to this company on March 20, 1863. Killed at or near Fort Wagner, Charleston, South Carolina, July 16, 1863.

JOHNSON, WILLIAM J., Private
Resided in Wake County where he enlisted at age 25,

October 4, 1862, for the war. Discharged on May 25-27, 1863, by reason of "phthisis pul[monalis]."

JONES, A. B., Private
Resided in Wake County where he enlisted at age 32, October 1, 1862, for the war. Discharged on March 20, 1863, by reason of disability.

JONES, ANDREW D., Private
Resided in Wake County where he enlisted at age 26, October 4, 1861. Present or accounted for until captured at Roanoke Island on February 8, 1862. Paroled at Elizabeth City on February 21, 1862. Returned to duty on or about September 15, 1862. Present or accounted for through April, 1864. [North Carolina pension records indicate that he survived the war.] No further records.

JONES, JOHN H., Private
Resided in Harnett County and enlisted in Wake County at age 34, October 4, 1861. Discharged on February 1, 1862, by reason of disability.

JONES, WILEY, Private
Resided in Wake County where he enlisted at age 23, October 4, 1861. Present or accounted for until captured at Roanoke Island on February 8, 1862. Paroled at Elizabeth City on February 21, 1862. Returned to duty on an unspecified date. Reported absent in hospital at Charleston, South Carolina, in March-April, 1863. Present or accounted for through October 3, 1864.

LEE, ELISHA ALLEN, Private
Resided in Wake County where he enlisted at age 22, October 4, 1861. Present or accounted for until captured at Roanoke Island on February 8, 1862. Paroled at Elizabeth City on February 21, 1862. Returned to duty on or about September 15, 1862. Wounded at or near Fort Wagner, Charleston, South Carolina, July 16, 1863. Returned to duty on an unspecified date. Present or accounted for through April, 1864. [North Carolina pension records indicate that he was wounded at Petersburg, Virginia, on an unspecified date.]

LEE, MATTHEW, Private
Resided in Wake County where he enlisted at age 26, September 20, 1862, for the war. Present or accounted for through April, 1864. No further records.

LEWIS, A., ———
Place and date of enlistment not reported. Records of the United Daughters of the Confederacy indicate he died on March 20, 1865, and was buried at Raleigh.

McKEE, JOSEPH, Private
Resided in Wake County where he enlisted at age 33, October 4, 1861. Discharged on October 4, 1862, under the provisions of the Conscription Act.

McKEY, JOSEPH, Private
Resided in Wake County where he enlisted at age 36, August 24, 1863, for the war. Captured at Fort Harrison, Virginia, September 30, 1864. Confined at Point Lookout, Maryland, October 5, 1864. Released at Point Lookout on June 29, 1865, after taking the Oath of Allegiance.

McLEAN, JOHN L., Private
Resided in Wake County where he enlisted at age 21,

October 4, 1861. Present or accounted for until captured at Roanoke Island on February 8, 1862. Paroled at Elizabeth City on February 21, 1862. Returned to duty on or about September 15, 1862. Present or accounted for through April, 1864. No further records.

McLEOD, JAMES B., Private
Enlisted in Wake County on October 4, 1861. Discharged on October 9, 1861. Reason discharged not reported.

McLEOD, NORMAN, Private
Resided in Wake County and enlisted at age 34, October 16, 1862, for the war. Died in hospital at Wilmington on January 9, 1863, of "febris typhoides."

MAINARD, RUFUS P., Corporal
Resided in Wake County where he enlisted at age 21, October 4, 1861. Mustered in as Private. Present or accounted for until captured at Roanoke Island on February 8, 1862. Paroled at Elizabeth City on February 21, 1862. Reported absent sick during January-April, 1863. Returned to duty on an unspecified date. Promoted to Corporal on March 31, 1864. Hospitalized at Richmond, Virginia, June 4, 1864, with a gunshot wound of the lung. Place and date wounded not reported. Died in hospital at Richmond on June 11, 1864, of wounds.

MALONEY, TIMOTHY, Private
Previously served in 2nd Company H, 40th Regiment N.C. Troops (3rd Regiment N.C. Artillery). Transferred to this company in July, 1863. Deserted to the enemy on or about February 1, 1864. Confined at Fort Monroe, Virginia. Released on or about February 10, 1864, after taking the Oath of Allegiance.

MASON, A. B., Private
Resided in Wake County where he enlisted at age 17, September 20, 1862, for the war. Wounded in the right arm at Drewry's Bluff, Virginia, on or about May 16, 1864. Reported in hospital at Danville, Virginia, May 23, 1864. [North Carolina pension records indicate that he survived the war.] No further records.

MASON, MANLY LAFAYETTE, Private
Resided in Wake County where he enlisted on October 4, 1861. Present or accounted for until captured at Roanoke Island on February 8, 1862. Paroled at Elizabeth City on February 21, 1862. Discharged on October 4, 1862. [May have served later in Company C, 2nd Regiment N.C. Junior Reserves.]

MASON, RICHARD, Private
Resided in Wake County where he enlisted at age 46, October 4, 1861. Died "at home" on August 13, 1862, of disease.

MATTHEWS, ICA, Private
Resided in Johnston County and enlisted in Wake County at age 31, October 4, 1861. Present or accounted for until captured at Roanoke Island on February 8, 1862. Paroled at Elizabeth City on February 21, 1862. Returned to duty on or about September 15, 1862. Present or accounted for through April, 1864. Paroled at or near Raleigh on or about May 24, 1865.

MATTHEWS, ROBERT, Private
Resided in Wake County where he enlisted at age 48,

October 4, 1861. Present or accounted for until captured at Roanoke Island on February 8, 1862. Paroled at Elizabeth City on February 21, 1862. Roll of Honor indicates he was discharged on October 4, 1862; however, company muster rolls indicate he was present or accounted for through April, 1863. No further records.

MATTHEWS, SIMON W., Private
Born in Harnett County* where he resided as a farmer prior to enlisting in Wake County at age 19, September 20, 1862, for the war. Discharged on December 12, 1863, by reason of disability.

MATTHEWS, THOMAS, Private
Born in Cumberland County where he resided as a farmer prior to enlisting in Wake County at age 42, October 24, 1861. Discharged on April 29, 1862, by reason of "deficiency of eyesight."

MATTHEWS, WILLIAM, Private
Resided in Wake County where he enlisted at age 36, October 17, 1862, for the war. Killed at or near Fort Wagner, Charleston, South Carolina, July 18, 1863.

NORRIS, C. F., Private
Resided in Wake County where he enlisted at age 18, June 16, 1863, for the war. Present or accounted for through April, 1864. [North Carolina pension records indicate that he survived the war.]

OGBURN, JOSEPH P., Sergeant
Resided in Johnston County and enlisted in Wake County at age 23, October 4, 1861. Mustered in as Private. Present or accounted for until captured at Roanoke Island on February 8, 1862. Paroled at Elizabeth City on February 21, 1862. Promoted to Sergeant on September 15, 1862. Captured at or near Cold Harbor, Virginia, June 1, 1864. Confined at Point Lookout, Maryland, June 11, 1864. Transferred to Elmira, New York, July 12, 1864. Released at Elmira on June 14, 1865, after taking the Oath of Allegiance.

OLIVE, L. T., Private
Resided in Wake County where he enlisted at age 19, October 4, 1862, for the war. Present or accounted for through May 31, 1864. No further records.

OLIVER, WILLIAM B., Corporal
Resided in Wake County where he enlisted at age 28, October 4, 1861. Mustered in as Corporal. Present or accounted for until captured at Roanoke Island on February 8, 1862. Paroled at Elizabeth City on February 21, 1862. Returned to duty on or about September 15, 1862. Present or accounted for until wounded in the right shoulder and captured at or near Fort Harrison, Virginia, September 30, 1864. Hospitalized at Fort Monroe, Virginia, October 4, 1864. Transferred to Camp Hamilton, Virginia, in March, 1865. Transferred to Point Lookout, Maryland, where he was confined on March 25, 1865. Released on June 29, 1865, after taking the Oath of Allegiance.

PAGE, J. H., Private
Resided in Wake County where he enlisted at age 22, July 16, 1862, for the war. Hospitalized at Richmond, Virginia, July 9, 1864, with a gunshot wound of the head (fractured skull). Place and date wounded not

reported. Died in hospital at Richmond on August 2-3, 1864, of wounds.

PATE, RANSOM, Private
Resided in Harnett County and enlisted in Wake County at age 43, October 4, 1861. Present or accounted for until captured at Roanoke Island on February 8, 1862. Paroled at Elizabeth City on February 21, 1862. Discharged on October 4, 1862. Reason discharged not reported.

POWELL, ALFRED, Musician
Resided in Wake County where he enlisted at age 24, October 4, 1861. Mustered in as Private. Present or accounted for until captured at Roanoke Island on February 8, 1862. Paroled at Elizabeth City on February 21, 1862. Promoted to Musician (Fifer) on September 15, 1862. Present or accounted for through April, 1864.

POWELL, DEMPSEY F., Private
Resided in Wake County where he enlisted at age 29, October 4, 1861. Present or accounted for until captured at Roanoke Island on February 8, 1862. Paroled at Elizabeth City on February 21, 1862. Returned to duty on or about September 15, 1862. "Stunned by shell" at or near Fort Wagner, Charleston, South Carolina, on or about July 18, 1863. Returned to duty on an unspecified date. Present or accounted for through April, 1864. [North Carolina pension records indicate that he survived the war.] No further records.

POWELL, WILEY, Private
Resided in Wake County where he enlisted at age 33, October 4, 1861. Present or accounted for until captured at Roanoke Island on February 8, 1862. Paroled at Elizabeth City on February 21, 1862. Returned to duty on or about September 15, 1862. Present or accounted for through April, 1864. Killed at or near Richmond, Virginia, on an unspecified date.

POWELL, WYATT H., Private
Resided in Johnston County and enlisted in Wake County at age 33, October 4, 1861. Present or accounted for until captured at Roanoke Island on February 8, 1862. Paroled at Elizabeth City on February 21, 1862. Returned to duty on or about September 15, 1862. Present or accounted for until captured at or near Cold Harbor, Virginia, May 31-June 1, 1864. Confined at Point Lookout, Maryland, June 11, 1864. Transferred to Elmira, New York, July 12, 1864. Released on June 19, 1865, after taking the Oath of Allegiance.

PRINCE, HENDERSON, Private
Resided in Wake County where he enlisted at age 45, October 4, 1861. Discharged on October 4, 1862. Reason discharged not reported.

PRINCE, JOHN, Private
Resided in Wake County where he enlisted at age 37, October 4, 1861. Present or accounted for until captured at Roanoke Island on February 8, 1862. Paroled at Elizabeth City on February 21, 1862. Discharged on October 4, 1862. Reason discharged not reported.

RAMBEAUT, HENRY L., Private
Resided in Wake County where he enlisted at age 36, October 4, 1861. Present or accounted for through December, 1861. Discharged on an unspecified date. Reenlisted in the company on February 13, 1863, for the

war. Died at Summerville, South Carolina, October 3, 1863, of disease.

REAVES, WILLIAM A., Private

Resided in Wake County where he enlisted at age 31, October 4, 1861. Present or accounted for until captured at Roanoke Island on February 8, 1862. Paroled at Elizabeth City on February 21, 1862. Returned to duty on or about September 15, 1862. Present or accounted for through February 28, 1865.

RHODES, W. C., Private

Resided in Wake County where he enlisted at age 23, September 13, 1862, for the war. Present or accounted for through January 8, 1865. Paroled at Raleigh on May 24, 1865. [North Carolina pension records indicate he was wounded near Richmond, Virginia, April 1, 1865.]

ROGERS, ALEXANDER, Private

Resided in Wake County where he enlisted at age 26, October 4, 1861. Present or accounted for until captured at Roanoke Island on February 8, 1862. Paroled at Elizabeth City on February 21, 1862. Returned to duty on or about September 15, 1862. Wounded at or near Fort Wagner, Charleston, South Carolina, July 18, 1863. Reported absent without leave from November 6, 1863, through April, 1864.

ROGERS, ELI, Private

Resided in Harnett County and enlisted in Wake County at age 25, October 4, 1861. Present or accounted for until captured at Roanoke Island on February 8, 1862. Paroled at Elizabeth City on February 21, 1862. Returned to duty on or about September 15, 1862. Present or accounted for through April, 1864.

ROGERS, EZEKIEL Z., Private

Resided in Harnett County and enlisted in Wake County at age 23, October 4, 1861. Present or accounted for through April, 1864. No further records.

ROGERS, J. W., Private

Resided in Harnett County and enlisted in Wake County at age 29, September 13, 1862, for the war. Present or accounted for through April, 1864. No further records.

ROLLS, HENRY, Private

Resided in Wake County where he enlisted at age 42, August 10, 1863, for the war. Present or accounted for through August 31, 1864. [North Carolina pension records indicate that he survived the war.] No further records.

SEGRAVES, SIDNEY C., Private

Resided in Wake County where he enlisted at age 29, September 20, 1862, for the war. Present or accounted for through April, 1864. [North Carolina pension records indicate he was wounded in the hip at Bentonville in March, 1865.]

SEXTON, ALSEY, Private

Resided in Harnett County and enlisted in Wake County at age 33, September 20, 1862, for the war. Captured at Cold Harbor, Virginia, June 1, 1864. Confined at Point Lookout, Maryland, June 11, 1864. Transferred to Elmira, New York, July 12, 1864. Died at Elmira on February 19, 1865, of "variola."

SEXTON, AUGUSTINE G., Private

Enlisted in Wake County on April 15, 1864, for the war. Captured at Cold Harbor, Virginia, June 1, 1864. Confined at Point Lookout, Maryland, June 11, 1864. Died at Point Lookout on or about July 13, 1864. Cause of death not reported.

SEXTON, RANDALL R., Private

Resided in Harnett County and enlisted in Wake County at age 19, October 4, 1861. Present or accounted for until captured at Roanoke Island on February 8, 1862. Paroled at Elizabeth City on February 21, 1862. Returned to duty prior to May 1, 1863. Present or accounted for through April, 1864. No further records.

SMITH, A. J., Corporal

Resided in Wake County where he enlisted at age 23, October 4, 1861. Mustered in as Corporal. Present or accounted for until captured at Roanoke Island on February 8, 1862. Paroled at Elizabeth City on February 21, 1862. Returned to duty on or about September 15, 1862. Present or accounted for through October 3, 1864.

SMITH, ALFRED A., Private

Resided in Harnett County and enlisted in Wake County at age 33, July 19, 1862, for the war. Died at Charleston, South Carolina, November 20, 1863, of disease.

SMITH, DAVID, Private

Resided in Harnett County and enlisted in Wake County at age 22, October 4, 1861. Present or accounted for until captured at Roanoke Island on February 8, 1862. Paroled at Elizabeth City on February 21, 1862. Returned to duty on or about September 15, 1862. Present or accounted for through April, 1864. [North Carolina pension records indicate that he survived the war.] No further records.

SMITH, DURHAM H., Private

Resided in Wake County where he enlisted at age 31, October 4, 1861. Present or accounted for until captured at Roanoke Island on February 8, 1862. Paroled at Elizabeth City on February 21, 1862. Returned to duty prior to May 1, 1863. Wounded in the "bowels" at or near Cold Harbor, Virginia, on or about June 1, 1864. Hospitalized at Richmond, Virginia. Returned to duty on or about August 21, 1864. Hospitalized at Raleigh on February 23, 1865, with a gunshot wound of the breast. Place and date wounded not reported. Furloughed for sixty days on March 8, 1865.

SMITH, JOHN J., Private

Resided in Harnett County and enlisted in Wake County at age 26, October 4, 1861. Present or accounted for until captured at Roanoke Island on February 8, 1862. Paroled at Elizabeth City on February 21, 1862. Returned to duty on or about September 15, 1862. Present or accounted for through April, 1864. [North Carolina pension records indicate that he survived the war.] No further records.

SMITH, SAMUEL, Private

Resided in Wake County where he enlisted at age 37, October 4, 1861. Mustered in as Corporal. Present or accounted for until captured at Roanoke Island on February 8, 1862. Paroled at Elizabeth City on February 21, 1862. Discharged on October 4, 1862. Reason discharged not reported. Reenlisted in the company on

August 10, 1863, for the war. Mustered in as Private. Hospitalized at Petersburg, Virginia, June 3, 1864, with a gunshot wound of the left hand. Place and date wounded not reported. Transferred to Raleigh on June 5, 1864. No further records.

SMITH, WILLIAM T., Sergeant
Resided in Wake County where he enlisted at age 25, October 4, 1861. Mustered in as Private. Present or accounted for until captured at Roanoke Island on February 8, 1862. Paroled at Elizabeth City on February 21, 1862. Promoted to Sergeant on September 15, 1862. Captured at Fort Harrison, Virginia, September 30, 1864. Confined at Point Lookout, Maryland, October 5, 1864. Released on June 20, 1865, after taking the Oath of Allegiance.

SPENCE, THEOPILAL D., Chief Musician
Resided in Wake County where he enlisted at age 19, October 4, 1861. Mustered in as Private. Promoted to Musician prior to January 1, 1862. Present or accounted for until captured at Roanoke Island on February 8, 1862. Paroled at Elizabeth City on February 21, 1862. Returned to duty on or about September 15, 1862. Promoted to Chief Musician (Drum Major) prior to March 1, 1863. Present or accounted for through April, 1864. No further records.

SPIVEY, GEORGE W., Private
Resided in Johnston County and enlisted in Wake County at age 36, February 13, 1863, for the war. Captured at Fort Harrison, Virginia, September 30, 1864. Confined at Point Lookout, Maryland, October 5, 1864. Paroled at Point Lookout on or about March 17, 1865, and transferred to Boulware's Wharf, James River, Virginia, where he was received on March 19, 1865, for exchange.

STEPHENSON, SIMON, Private
Enlisted in Wake County on October 4, 1861. Present or accounted for through December, 1861. No further records.

STUART, JAMES H., Private
Resided in Harnett County and enlisted in Wake County at age 18, March 30, 1863, for the war. Captured at or near Globe Tavern, Virginia, August 19, 1864. Confined at Point Lookout, Maryland, August 22, 1864. Paroled at Point Lookout on or about March 14, 1865, and transferred to Boulware's Wharf, James River, Virginia, where he was received on March 16, 1865, for exchange.

SWINSON, DANIEL, Private
Resided in Wake County where he enlisted at age 45, October 4, 1861. Discharged on October 4, 1862. Reason discharged not reported.

THAMES, J. W., ———
North Carolina pension records indicate that he served in this company.

UTLEY, ADDISON C., Private
Resided in Wake County where he enlisted at age 15, October 4, 1861. Discharged on October 4, 1862. Reason discharged not reported. Later served in Captain E. D. Snead's Unattached Local Defense Company, North Carolina Troops.

UTLEY, GASTON T., Private
Resided in Wake County where he enlisted at age 19, October 4, 1861. Present or accounted for until captured at Roanoke Island on February 8, 1862. Paroled at Elizabeth City on February 21, 1862. Returned to duty on or about September 15, 1862. Present or accounted for through April, 1864. No further records.

UTLEY, W. H., Private
Resided in Wake County where he enlisted at age 23, September 1, 1862, for the war. Present or accounted for through April, 1864. No further records.

WADDELL, GEORGE W., Private
Resided in Johnston County and enlisted in Wake County on October 4, 1861. Present or accounted for until captured at Roanoke Island on February 8, 1862. Paroled at Elizabeth City on February 21, 1862. Returned to duty on or about September 15, 1862. Present or accounted for through April, 1864. [North Carolina pension records indicate that he survived the war.] No further records.

WALLIS, JOHN J., Private
Resided in Wake County where he enlisted at age 32, October 4, 1861. Present or accounted for through November 7, 1864.

WHITE, SIDNEY, ———
Place and date of enlistment not reported. Name appears on a company record dated February 11, 1863. No further records.

WHITTENTON, J. P., Private
Resided in Johnston County and enlisted in Wake County at age 24, October 4, 1861. Mustered in as Corporal. Reduced to ranks on September 15, 1862. Hospitalized at Richmond, Virginia, October 2, 1864, with a gunshot wound of the right hip. Place and date wounded not reported. Died in hospital at Richmond on October 19, 1864, of wounds.

WILBORN, D. H., ———
North Carolina pension records indicate that he served in this company.

WILLIAMS, G. W., Private
Resided in Harnett County and enlisted in Wake County at age 18, October 1, 1862, for the war. Died at or near Charleston, South Carolina, May 1-2, 1863, of disease.

WOMACK, WILEY J., Private
Resided in Wake County where he enlisted at age 16, October 4, 1861. Discharged on October 4, 1862. Reason discharged not reported.

WOMBLE, THOMAS, ———
North Carolina pension records indicate that he served in this company.

WOOD, A. Q., Private
Resided in Wake County and enlisted at age 16, June 19, 1863, for the war. Discharged on November 10, 1863, by reason of being underage. [North Carolina pension records indicate he was wounded in the hip at Fort Wagner, Charleston, South Carolina; in the left knee at White Hall; and in the chest at Petersburg, Virginia. May have served later in Company D, 1st

Regiment N.C. Junior Reserves.]

WOOD, ALFRED, Private
Resided in Wake County where he enlisted at age 15, October 4, 1861. Rejected for service the same date.

WOOD, ARCHIBALD L., Private
Resided in Wake County where he enlisted at age 23, October 4, 1861. Present or accounted for until captured at Roanoke Island on February 8, 1862. Paroled at Elizabeth City on February 21, 1862. Returned to duty on or about September 15, 1862. Wounded at or near Fort Wagner, Charleston, South Carolina, July 18, 1863. Returned to duty on an unspecified date. Present or accounted for through September 19, 1864.

WOOD, JOHN W., Private
Resided in Wake County where he enlisted at age 32, October 4, 1861. Present or accounted for until captured at Roanoke Island on February 8, 1862. Paroled at Elizabeth City on February 21, 1862. Returned to duty on or about September 15, 1862. Wounded in the right leg at or near Goldsboro on or about November 15, 1862. Returned to duty in March-April, 1863. Reported on detached service as a cooper in January-April, 1864. [North Carolina pension records indicate that he survived the war.] No further records.

WOOD, L. H., Private
Resided in Wake County where he enlisted at age 30, October 1, 1862, for the war. Reported absent without leave on or about June 26, 1863.

WOOD, MACOM J., Private
Resided in Wake County where he enlisted at age 26, October 4, 1861. Present or accounted for until captured at Roanoke Island on February 8, 1862. Paroled at Elizabeth City on February 21, 1862. Returned to duty on or about September 15, 1862. Present or accounted for through October 5, 1864.

YATES, J. C., Private
Resided in Wake County and enlisted at age 18, June 19, 1863, for the war. No further records.

COMPANY D

This company was raised in Wake County and enlisted there on September 18, 1861. It was then assigned to the 31st Regiment N.C. Troops and designated Company D. After joining the regiment the company functioned as a part of the regiment, and its history for the war period is reported as a part of the regimental history.

The information contained in the following roster of the company was compiled principally from company muster rolls for September 18, 1861-April 30, 1862; January-April, 1863; March-April, 1864; and November-December, 1864. No company muster rolls were found for May-December, 1862; May, 1863-February, 1864; May-October, 1864; or for the period after December, 1864. Valuable information was obtained from primary records such as the Roll of Honor, discharge certificates, medical records, prisoner of war records, and pension applications. Secondary sources such as postwar rosters and histories, cemetery records, and records of the United Daughters of the Confederacy also provided useful information.

OFFICERS

CAPTAINS

MANLY, LANGDON CHEVES
Resided in Wake County where he enlisted at age 37. Appointed 1st Lieutenant on September 18, 1861. Promoted to Captain on October 4, 1861. Present or accounted for until captured at Roanoke Island on February 8, 1862. Paroled at Elizabeth City on February 21, 1862. Defeated for reelection when the regiment was reorganized on September 17, 1862.

BRYANT, RUFFIN L.
Resided in Wake County where he enlisted at age 33. Appointed 2nd Lieutenant on September 18, 1861. Promoted to Captain on or about September 17, 1862. Present or accounted for through December, 1864.

LIEUTENANTS

BRYAN, SAMUEL H., 2nd Lieutenant
Resided in Wake County where he enlisted at age 26, September 18, 1861. Mustered in as Sergeant. Present or accounted for until captured at Roanoke Island on February 8, 1862. Paroled at Elizabeth City on February 21, 1862. Appointed 2nd Lieutenant on or about September 17, 1862. Present or accounted for through April, 1864. No further records.

HOLDEN, JOSEPH W., 3rd Lieutenant
Resided in Wake County where he enlisted at age 17, September 18, 1861. Mustered in as 1st Sergeant. Appointed 3rd Lieutenant on October 4, 1861. Appointed Adjutant (2nd Lieutenant) on November 27, 1861, and transferred to the Field and Staff of this regiment.

JORDAN, HENRY B., 1st Lieutenant
Resided in Wake County where he enlisted at age 26. Appointed 2nd Lieutenant on September 18, 1861. Promoted to 1st Lieutenant on October 4, 1861. Present or accounted for until captured at Roanoke Island, February 8, 1862. Paroled at Elizabeth City on February 21, 1862. Defeated for reelection when the regiment was reorganized on September 17, 1862.

WALTON, BENJAMIN F., 1st Lieutenant
Resided in Wake County where he enlisted at age 33, September 18, 1861. Mustered in as Sergeant. Promoted to 1st Sergeant on October 4, 1861. Present or accounted for until captured at Roanoke Island on February 8, 1862. Paroled at Elizabeth City on February 21, 1862. Appointed 1st Lieutenant on or about September 17, 1862. Present or accounted for through December, 1864.

WILLIAMS, WILLIAM GASTON, 3rd Lieutenant
Resided in Wake County where he enlisted at age 19, September 18, 1861. Mustered in as Private. Present or accounted for until captured at Roanoke Island on February 8, 1862. Paroled at Elizabeth City on February 21, 1862. Appointed 3rd Lieutenant on or about September 17, 1862. Present or accounted for through December, 1864.

NONCOMMISSIONED OFFICERS AND PRIVATES

BAGWELL, ANDREW J., Private
Resided in Wake County where he enlisted at age 38,

September 18, 1861. Present or accounted for until captured at Roanoke Island on February 8, 1862. Paroled at Elizabeth City on February 21, 1862. Returned to duty on an unspecified date. Discharged on September 15, 1862, under the provisions of the Conscription Act. Reenlisted in the company at Camp Holmes on October 26, 1864, for the war. Deserted on January 29, 1865. Took the Oath of Allegiance at Raleigh on May 25, 1865.

BAGWELL, N. B., Private
Enlisted at Camp Holmes on October 26, 1864, for the war. Present or accounted for through December, 1864.

BAILEY, W. R., Private
Enlisted at Camp Holmes on October 26, 1864, for the war. Present or accounted for through December, 1864.

BAILEY, WILLIAM, Private
Resided in Wake County and was by occupation a farmer prior to enlisting in Wake County at age 19, September 18, 1861. Present or accounted for until captured at Roanoke Island on February 8, 1862. Paroled at Elizabeth City on February 21, 1862. Returned to duty on or about September 15, 1862. Wounded in the left thigh at or near Drewry's Bluff, Virginia, May 16, 1864. Left leg amputated. Hospitalized at Richmond, Virginia, where he died on June 4, 1864, of wounds.

BARBER, GEORGE W., Sergeant
Resided in Wake County where he enlisted at age 22, September 18, 1861. Mustered in as Private. Present or accounted for until captured at Roanoke Island on February 8, 1862. Paroled at Elizabeth City on February 21, 1862. Returned to duty on or about September 15, 1862. Promoted to Sergeant on January 20, 1863. Died on March 7-8, 1863, of disease.

BAUCOM, TROY, Private
Enlisted at Camp Holmes on October 26, 1864, for the war. Present or accounted for through December, 1864. Paroled subsequent to April 26, 1865.

BLINSON, GASTON W., Private
Enlisted at Camp Holmes on November 3, 1864, for the war. Deserted on December 27, 1864.

BLINSON, JAMES R., Private
Resided in Wake County where he enlisted at age 22, September 18, 1861. Present or accounted for until captured at Roanoke Island on February 8, 1862. Paroled at Elizabeth City on February 21, 1862. Returned to duty on or about September 15, 1862. Deserted on May 20, 1863. Returned to duty on March 9, 1864. Retired to the Invalid Corps on September 25, 1864. Reason he was retired not reported. Took the Oath of Allegiance at Raleigh on May 5, 1865.

BOON, DEMPSEY W., Private
Resided in Johnston County and was by occupation a farmer prior to enlisting in Wake County at age 26, September 18, 1861. Hospitalized at Danville, Virginia, June 4, 1864, with a gunshot wound of the head. Place and date wounded not reported. Reported absent sick through December, 1864. Returned to duty prior to February 19, 1865. Paroled at Raleigh on May 17, 1865.

BOON, JOHN C., Private
Resided in Johnston County and enlisted in Wake County at age 19, September 18, 1861. Died at Fort Hill on November 22-23, 1861, of disease.

BRANNUM, NEEDHAM, Private
Enlisted at Camp Holmes on October 26, 1864, for the war. Present or accounted for through December, 1864.

BRANUM, WILLIAM M., Private
Resided in Wake County where he enlisted at age 25, September 15, 1862, for the war. Deserted on October 25, 1862. Returned to duty on February 9, 1863. Deserted on December 4, 1863.

BROOKS, THOMAS J., Private
Resided in Wake County where he enlisted at age 16, September 18, 1861. Present or accounted for until captured at Roanoke Island on February 8, 1862. Paroled at Elizabeth City on February 21, 1862. Returned to duty on or about September 15, 1862. Present or accounted for through December, 1864.

BROUGHTON, JOSEPH T., Private
Resided in Wake County where he enlisted at age 18, August 10, 1863, for the war. Present or accounted for through December, 1864. Took the Oath of Allegiance at Raleigh on May 25, 1865.

BRYAN, HENRY, Private
Resided in Wake County and enlisted at age 18, November 5, 1863, for the war. Died in hospital at Petersburg, Virginia, January 13, 1864, of "febris typhoides."

BRYAN, LYNN W., Corporal
Resided in Wake County where he enlisted at age 21, September 18, 1861. Mustered in as Private. Present or accounted for until captured at Roanoke Island on February 8, 1862. Paroled at Elizabeth City on February 21, 1862. Returned to duty on or about September 15, 1862. Promoted to Corporal on May 4, 1863. Present or accounted for through December, 1864.

BRYANT, WILLIAM R., Private
Resided in Wake County where he enlisted at age 20, September 18, 1861. Present or accounted for until captured at Roanoke Island on February 8, 1862. Paroled at Elizabeth City on February 21, 1862. Returned to duty on or about September 15, 1862. Wounded at Fort Wagner, Charleston, South Carolina, July 18, 1863. Died at or near Charleston on July 20, 1863, of wounds.

BUSBEE, FRANCIS M., Private
Resided in Wake County where he enlisted at age 26, September 18, 1861. Reported absent without leave in January-April, 1862. Returned to duty prior to May 1, 1863. Reported absent without leave on August 29, 1864. Returned to duty on or about December 26, 1864. Confined at Castle Thunder Prison, Richmond, Virginia, January 3, 1865. [North Carolina pension records indicate he was wounded at Drewry's Bluff, Virginia, September 10, 1862.] No further records.

BUSBEE, LARKIN, Private
Resided in Wake County and enlisted at Camp Mangum at age 37, September 15, 1862, for the war. Died in hospital at Petersburg, Virginia, March 26,

1864, of "pneumonia."

CARROLL, HENRY, Private
Resided in Wake County where he enlisted at age 22, September 15, 1862, for the war. Died in hospital at Wilmington on or about August 22, 1863, of "febris congestiva."

CARROLL, WILLIAM, Private
Resided in Wake County where he enlisted at age 18, November 7, 1862, for the war. Wounded and captured at Cold Harbor, Virginia, May 31, 1864. Died at or near White House, Virginia, on or about June 9, 1864. Cause of death not reported.

CARTER, WASHINGTON M., Private
Resided in Wake County and enlisted at Camp Whiting at age 26, February 9, 1863, for the war. Present or accounted for through April, 1864. No further records.

COATS, THOMAS, Private
Enlisted at Camp Holmes on October 26, 1864, for the war. Deserted on December 27, 1864.

COGDELL, STEVEN, Private
Enlisted at Camp Holmes on November 8, 1864, for the war. Deserted on December 27, 1864.

COLLINS, DAVID, Private
Resided in Johnston County and enlisted in Wake County at age 17, September 18, 1861. Present or accounted for through December, 1861. Reported absent without leave in January-April, 1862.

COLLINS, URIAS, Private
Resided in Johnston County and enlisted in Wake County at age 19, September 18, 1861. Present or accounted for until captured at Roanoke Island on February 8, 1862. Paroled at Elizabeth City on February 21, 1862. Reported absent without leave from October 23, 1862, through April, 1863. Returned to duty on an unspecified date. Reported absent without leave on August 9, 1863.

DUKE, ROBERT, Private
Resided in Wake County where he enlisted at age 25, September 18, 1861. Present or accounted for until captured at Roanoke Island on February 8, 1862. Paroled at Elizabeth City on February 21, 1862. Returned to duty on or about September 15, 1862. Reported absent without leave from July 15, 1863, until February 18, 1865. No further records.

EVANS, LEWIS T., ———
North Carolina pension records indicate that he served in this company.

FAIRCLOTH, HARDY, Private
Resided in Johnston County and enlisted in Wake County at age 20, September 18, 1861. Present or accounted for until captured at Roanoke Island on February 8, 1862. Paroled at Elizabeth City on February 21, 1862. Discharged on an unspecified date by reason of disability.

FINCH, JOHN L., 1st Sergeant
Resided in Wake County where he enlisted at age 18, September 18, 1861. Mustered in as Private. Promoted to Sergeant on September 15, 1862. Promoted to 1st

Sergeant on May 1, 1863. Present or accounted for through December, 1864.

FLOWERS, JOEL J., Private
Resided in Wake County and enlisted at Camp Holmes at age 25, July 25, 1863, for the war. Present or accounted for through December, 1864.

GARRARD, DOCTOR C., Private
Resided in Orange County and enlisted at Camp Mangum at age 30, October 9, 1862, for the war. Died at Hillsborough on August 6, 1863, of disease.

GARRARD, JAMES L., Private
Previously enlisted in Company K, 63rd Regiment N.C. Troops (5th Regiment N.C. Cavalry). Never reported for duty with that company. Enlisted in this company at Camp Mangum at age 23, October 9, 1862, for the war. Hospitalized at Danville, Virginia, on or about June 4, 1864, with a gunshot wound of the arm. Place and date wounded not reported. Furloughed on June 21, 1864. Returned to duty on an unspecified date. Present or accounted for through December, 1864.

GARRARD, JOSEPH, Private
Resided in Orange County and was by occupation a carpenter prior to enlisting at Camp Holmes at age 29, April 4, 1863, for the war. Present or accounted for through December, 1864. Records of this company indicate he was transferred to Mallett's N.C. Battalion (Camp Guard) on an unspecified date; however, records of Mallett's Battalion do not indicate that he served therein.

GARRARD, SAMUEL, Private
Previously enlisted in Company K, 63rd Regiment N.C. Troops (5th Regiment N.C. Cavalry). Never reported for duty with that company. Enlisted in this company at Camp Mangum at age 27, September 15, 1862, for the war. Present or accounted for through December, 1864. [May have served also in the 2nd Regiment Confederate Engineering Troops.]

GILL, DAVID C., Private
Resided in Wake County where he enlisted at age 19, October 15, 1862, for the war. Transferred to Company D, 26th Regiment N.C. Troops, on or about January 20, 1863, in exchange for Private Henry Clay Hicks. [May have enlisted previously in Company I, 41st Regiment N.C. Troops (3rd Regiment N.C. Cavalry).]

GILL, L. T., Private
Resided in Wake County and enlisted at age 20, September 15, 1862, for the war. "Killed instantly by the bursting of a shell" at White Hall on December 16, 1862.

GOODWIN, HINTON, Private
Resided in Wake County and enlisted at James Island, Charleston, South Carolina, at age 42, November 2, 1863, for the war. Present or accounted for through December, 1864.

GOODWIN, JOSEPH P., Corporal
Resided in Wake County where he enlisted at age 18, October 15, 1862, for the war. Mustered in as Private. Promoted to Corporal on December 15, 1863. Wounded in the right arm at Fort Harrison, Virginia, on or about September 30, 1864. Right arm amputated on or about

October 7, 1864. Hospitalized at Richmond, Virginia. Furloughed for sixty days on November 8, 1864. Retired from service prior to January 1, 1865.

GREEN, WILLIAM, Private
Born in Johnston County and resided in Wake County where he was by occupation a farmer prior to enlisting in Wake County at age 24, September 18, 1861. Present or accounted for until captured at Roanoke Island on February 8, 1862. Paroled at Elizabeth City on February 21, 1862. Hospitalized at Wilmington on or about January 5, 1863, with pneumonia. Furloughed on January 7, 1863. Died on January 10, 1863. Place and cause of death not reported.

HAMILTON, GEORGE, Private
Resided in Wake County where he enlisted at age 28, September 18, 1861. Present or accounted for until captured at Roanoke Island on February 8, 1862. Paroled at Elizabeth City on February 21, 1862. Returned to duty on or about September 15, 1862. Present or accounted for through April, 1864. No further records.

HAMLET, DAVID B., Private
Resided in Wake County where he enlisted at age 27, September 18, 1861. Present or accounted for through December, 1864; however, he was reported absent on detached service or absent sick during much of that period.

HARRISS, HENRY C., Musician
Resided in Wake County where he enlisted at age 17, September 18, 1861. Mustered in as Private. Promoted to Musician (Drummer) prior to January 1, 1862. Present or accounted for through December, 1864.

HENTON, COSWELL, ——
Negro. Joined the company in Wake County on March 19, 1864, and served as a cook. Present or accounted for through December, 1864.

HICKS, HENRY CLAY, Sergeant
Previously served as Private in Company D, 26th Regiment N.C. Troops. Transferred to this company on or about January 20, 1863, in exchange for Private David C. Gill. Mustered in as Private. Promoted to Sergeant in May, 1863-April, 1864. Captured at Cold Harbor, Virginia, June 1, 1864. Confined at Point Lookout, Maryland, June 11, 1864. Transferred to Elmira, New York, July 12, 1864. Paroled at Elmira on March 2, 1865 and transferred to the James River, Virginia, for exchange.

HICKS, WILLIAM H., Private
Resided in Wake County where he enlisted at age 20, September 18, 1861. Present or accounted for until captured at Roanoke Island on February 8, 1862. Paroled at Elizabeth City on February 21, 1862. Returned to duty on or about September 15, 1862. Captured at Fort Harrison, Virginia, September 30, 1864. Confined at Point Lookout, Maryland, October 5, 1864. Paroled at Point Lookout on January 17, 1865, and transferred to Boulware's Wharf, James River, Virginia, where he was received on January 21, 1865, for exchange. [North Carolina pension records indicate he was wounded at Petersburg, Virginia, in the summer of 1864.]

HILL, WILLIAM L. D., Private
Resided in Wake County where he enlisted at age 33, September 18, 1861. Present or accounted for through January 18, 1865.

HOBBY, HENRY P., Private
Resided in Wake County where he enlisted at age 20, September 18, 1861. Present or accounted for until captured at Roanoke Island on February 8, 1862. Paroled at Elizabeth City on February 21, 1862. Returned to duty on or about September 15, 1862. Present or accounted for through December, 1864.

HOBBY, SIMEON, Private
Resided in Wake County where he enlisted at age 18, September 15, 1862, for the war. Discharged on January 28, 1863, by reason of disability.

HOLTSCLATH, ELIJAH, Private
Enlisted on November 3, 1864, for the war. Present or accounted for through December, 1864.

HONEYCUTT, BARTLET, Private
Enlisted in Wake County on February 27, 1862. Present or accounted for through April, 1863. No further records.

HONEYCUTT, RUFUS, Private
Resided in Wake County where he enlisted at age 25, September 18, 1861. Present or accounted for until captured at Roanoke Island on February 8, 1862. Paroled at Elizabeth City on February 21, 1862. Returned to duty on or about September 15, 1862. Deserted on December 4, 1863. Returned to duty on February 24, 1864. Deserted on August 13, 1864.

HUDDLESTON, SAMUEL, Private
Born in Granville County where he resided as a farmer prior to enlisting at James Island, Charleston, South Carolina, March 30, 1863, for the war as a substitute for Private John S. McCullers. Discharged on October 23, 1863, by reason of being "seventy years of age and very weak. . . ." [May have served previously in Company E, 46th Regiment N.C. Troops.]

HURST, J. W., Private
Place and date of enlistment not reported. Paroled at Greensboro on May 1, 1865.

JOHNS, THOMAS J., Private
Previously served in Company I, 41st Regiment N.C. Troops (3rd Regiment N.C. Cavalry). Transferred to this company on or about April 12, 1863. Present or accounted for through December, 1864.

JOHNSON, RICHARD, Private
Resided in Wake County where he enlisted at age 20, September 18, 1861. Present or accounted for until captured at Roanoke Island on February 8, 1862. Paroled at Elizabeth City on February 21, 1862. Returned to duty on or about September 15, 1862. Wounded at White Hall on December 16, 1862. Returned to duty prior to March 1, 1863. Hospitalized at Richmond, Virginia, May 17, 1864, with a gunshot wound. Place and date wounded not reported. Died in hospital at Richmond on May 21, 1864, of wounds.

JOHNSON, RIGDON, Private
Resided in Wake County where he enlisted at age 21,

November 13, 1862, for the war. Wounded at White Hall on December 16, 1862. Reported absent wounded through December, 1864. Took the Oath of Allegiance at Raleigh on June 3, 1865.

JONES, CLINTON, Private
Resided in Wake County where he enlisted at age 51, September 18, 1861. Present or accounted for through December, 1861. Discharged on an unspecified date under the provisions of the Conscription Act.

JONES, GASTON, Private
Enlisted at Camp Holmes on July 15, 1862, for the war. Present or accounted for through December, 1864.

JONES, JAMES, Private
Enlisted in Wake County on September 18, 1861. Present or accounted for through December, 1861. No further records.

JONES, JAMES A., Private
Resided in Wake County where he enlisted at age 22, September 15, 186[2]. Present or accounted for through December, 1864.

JORDAN, CORNELIUS, Sergeant
Resided in Wake County where he enlisted at age 25, September 18, 1861. Mustered in as Sergeant. Present or accounted for until captured at Roanoke Island on February 8, 1862. Paroled at Elizabeth City on February 21, 1862. Returned to duty on or about September 15, 1862. Reduced to ranks in May, 1862-February, 1863. Promoted to Sergeant on April 15, 1863. Died in hospital at Wilmington on July 8, 1863, of "typhoid fever."

KELLEY, WESLEY W., Private
Resided in Wake County where he enlisted at age 21, September 18, 1861. Deserted at James Island, Charleston, South Carolina, August 29, 1863.

KING, ADDISON, Private
Enlisted at Camp Holmes on September 15, 1862, for the war. Company records indicate he was captured on September 30, 1864; however, records of the Federal Provost Marshal do not substantiate that report. No further records.

LAMBERT, WILLIAM, Private
Resided in New Hanover County and enlisted at Camp Martin at age 46, November 15, 1862, for the war as a substitute for Private William H. Penny. Deserted on November 20 or December 1, 1862.

LANDERS, CHARLES L., Private
Resided in Craven County and enlisted at Camp Martin at age 17, December 5, 1862, for the war. Present or accounted for through January 5, 1865. [North Carolina pension records indicate he was wounded at "Bentonville on April 1, 1865."]

LASSITER, GASTON, Private
Resided in Wake County where he enlisted at age 21, September 18, 1861. Hospitalized at Richmond, Virginia, May 20, 1864, with a gunshot wound of the thigh. Place and date wounded not reported. Died in hospital at Richmond on June 23, 1864, of wounds.

LASSITER, H. L., ———
North Carolina pension records indicate that he served in this company.

LASSITER, LEONARD, Private
Resided in Wake County where he enlisted at age 29, September 15, 1862, for the war. Present or accounted for through December, 1864.

LASTER, H. L., Private
Place and date of enlistment not reported. Captured at Raleigh on or about April 14, 1865. No further records.

LILES, JAMES, Private
Resided in Wake County and enlisted at age 30, November 5, 1862, for the war. Discharged on August 7, 1863, by reason of disability.

LILES, JOSEPH R., Private
Enlisted in Wake County on September 15, 186[2]. Hospitalized at Farmville, Virginia, June 3, 1864, with a gunshot wound of the hand. Returned to duty on June 29, 1864. Reported present but under arrest in November-December, 1864. No further records.

LILES, SAMUEL, Private
Resided in Wake County and enlisted at Camp Whiting at age 32, February 9, 1863, for the war. Present or accounted for through December, 1864.

LILES, WRIGHT, Private
Resided in Wake County where he enlisted at age 24, September 18, 1861. Present or accounted for through February, 1863.

LITTLE, SAMUEL, Private
Enlisted at Petersburg, Virginia, April 28, 1864, for the war. Present or accounted for through December, 1864.

LYNCH, RUFUS N., Private
Resided in Wake County where he enlisted at age 33, September 18, 1861. Mustered in as Corporal. Present or accounted for until captured at Roanoke Island on February 8, 1862. Paroled at Elizabeth City on February 21, 1862. Returned to duty on or about September 15, 1862. Promoted to Sergeant on March 10, 1863. Reduced to ranks on February 21, 1864, "for disobedience." Paroled at Raleigh on April 20, 1865.

McCULLERS, JOHN S., Private
Resided in Wake County where he enlisted at age 28, September 18, 1861. Present or accounted for until captured at Roanoke Island on February 8, 1862. Paroled at Elizabeth City on February 21, 1862. Returned to duty on or about September 15, 1862. Discharged on March 30, 1863, after providing Private Samuel Huddleston as a substitute.

McNEIL, N. A., ———
North Carolina pension records indicate that he served in this company.

MILLER, GEORGE DEVEREUX, Private
Resided in Wake County where he enlisted at age 18, September 15, 1862, for the war. Transferred to Company K, 14th Regiment N.C. Troops (4th Regiment N.C. Volunteers), November 7, 1863.

MITCHENER, GEORGE J., Private
Resided in Wake County where he enlisted at age 18,

August 18, 1863, for the war. Mustered in as Private. Promoted to Corporal on March 9, 1864. Reduced to ranks on January 6, 1865. Captured at Raleigh on or about April 15, 1865. No further records.

MITCHENER, SAMUEL JOHN, Sergeant
Resided in Wake County where he enlisted at age 18, September 18, 1861. Mustered in as Private. Present or accounted for until captured at Roanoke Island on February 8, 1862. Paroled at Elizabeth City on February 21, 1862. Returned to duty on or about September 15, 1862. Promoted to Sergeant on May 1, 1863. Wounded at Fort Wagner, Charleston, South Carolina, July 18, 1863. Returned to duty prior to May 1, 1864. Hospitalized at Williamsburg, Virginia, May 20, 1864, with a gunshot wound. Place and date wounded not reported. Returned to duty prior to January 1, 1865. Captured at Raleigh on or about April 15, 1865. No further records.

MOORE, JAMES L., ——
North Carolina pension records indicate that he served in this company.

NOWELL, JAMES ALVIN, Private
Resided in Wake County and enlisted at Sullivan's Island, Charleston, South Carolina, at age 38, October 10, 1863, for the war. Deserted on December 4, 1863. Returned to duty on February 11, 1864. Reported present but under arrest in November-December, 1864. [North Carolina pension records indicate he was wounded in the left thigh "in Virginia" on May 19, 1864.] No further records.

PARRISH, J. C., Private
Enlisted at Camp Holmes on March 10, 1864, for the war. Reported absent sick in November-December, 1864. No further records.

PARRISH, JAMES M., Private
Resided in Johnston County and enlisted in Wake County at age 19, September 18, 1861. Mustered in as Private. Promoted to Musician (Fifer) prior to January 1, 1862. Present or accounted for until captured at Roanoke Island on February 8, 1862. Paroled at Elizabeth City on February 21, 1862. Returned to duty on or about September 15, 1862. Reduced to ranks on December 10, 1864. Present or accounted for through December, 1864.

PARRISH, JOHN, Private
Born in Johnston County where he resided as a farmer prior to enlisting in Johnston County at age 36, February 25, 1863, for the war. Died in hospital at Wilmington on or about May 18, 1863, of "feb[ris] typh[oid]."

PARRISH, JOHN F., Private
Resided in Wake County where he enlisted at age 23, September 18, 1861. Present or accounted for until captured at Roanoke Island on February 8, 1862. Paroled at Elizabeth City on February 21, 1862. Returned to duty prior to May 1, 1863. Captured at Cold Harbor, Virginia, June 1, 1864. Confined at Point Lookout, Maryland, June 11, 1864. Transferred to Elmira, New York, July 12, 1864. Paroled at Elmira on March 2, 1865, and transferred to the James River, Virginia, for exchange. Reported in hospital at Richmond, Virginia, March 9, 1865. [North Carolina pension records indicate that he survived the war.]

PARRISH, KINCHISS, Private
Resided in Wake County where he enlisted at age 34, September 18, 1861. Present or accounted for until captured at Roanoke Island on February 8, 1862. Paroled at Elizabeth City on February 21, 1862. Returned to duty on or about September 15, 1862. Deserted on January 15, 1863. Reported sick in hospital at Columbia, South Carolina, in March-April, 1863. Transferred to an unspecified unit on August 3, 1863.

PARRISH, MORDECAU, Private
Resided in Wake County and enlisted at age 32, September 15, 1862, for the war. Discharged on November 25, 1862, by reason of disability.

PARRISH, PARHAM P., Sergeant
Resided in Wake County where he enlisted at age 19, September 18, 1861. Mustered in as Private. Present or accounted for until captured at Roanoke Island on February 8, 1862. Paroled at Elizabeth City on February 21, 1862. Returned to duty prior to May 1, 1863. Promoted to Sergeant in May, 1863-April, 1864. Wounded in the right thigh and captured at Fort Harrison, Virginia, September 30, 1864. Right leg amputated. Hospitalized at Fort Monroe, Virginia, where he died on October 9, 1864, of "exhaustion."

PARRISH, PASCHAL, Private
Resided in Wake County where he enlisted at age 18, September 18, 1861. Present or accounted for until captured at Roanoke Island on February 8, 1862. Paroled at Elizabeth City on February 21, 1862. Returned to duty on or about September 15, 1862. Captured at Cold Harbor, Virginia, June 1, 1864. Confined at Point Lookout, Maryland, June 11, 1864. Transferred to Elmira, New York, July 12, 1864. Paroled at Elmira on March 14, 1865, and transferred to Boulware's Wharf, James River, Virginia, where he was received on or about March 18, 1865, for exchange.

PARRISH, PUTNEY, Private
Previously served in Company D, 41st Regiment N.C. Troops (3rd Regiment N.C. Cavalry). Transferred to this company on September 16, 1863. Deserted on July 1, 1864. Listed as a deserter in November-December, 1864. Captured by the enemy at "Harney" on March 17, 1865. Confined at Point Lookout, Maryland, March 30, 1865. Released on June 16, 1865, after taking the Oath of Allegiance.

PARRISH, WILLIS, Private
Resided in Wake County and enlisted at Camp Davis at age 36, June 1, 1863, for the war. Deserted on September 29, 1864.

PENNINGTON, JOHN, Private
Resided in Wake County where he enlisted at age 27, September 18, 1861. Present or accounted for until captured at Roanoke Island on February 8, 1862. Paroled at Elizabeth City on February 21, 1862. Returned to duty on or about September 15, 1862. Died in hospital at Wilmington on or about July 29, 1863, of "febris typh[oides]."

PENNY, WILLIAM H., Private
Resided in Wake County where he enlisted at age 30, September 18, 1861. Present or accounted for until captured at Roanoke Island on February 8, 1862.

Paroled at Elizabeth City on February 21, 1862. Discharged on or about November 15, 1862, after providing Private William Lambert as a substitute. Later served in Captain William D. Crowder's Company, 1st Regiment N.C. Militia.

PHILLIPS, JAMES H., Private
Resided in Wake County where he enlisted at age 27, September 18, 1861. Present or accounted for until captured at Roanoke Island on February 8, 1862. Paroled at Elizabeth City on February 21, 1862. Returned to duty on or about September 15, 1862. Paroled at Raleigh on April 20, 1865.

POOL, ALONZO, ——
North Carolina pension records indicate that he served in this company.

POOL, EDWIN, Private
Place and date of enlistment not reported. Hospitalized at Greensboro on February 22, 1865. Transferred the next day. No further records.

POOL, JOHN R., Private
Resided in Wake County where he enlisted at age 24, September 15, 1862, for the war. Discharged on or about May 25-27, 1863, by reason of "dropsy chest."

POOL, W. T., Private
Enlisted at Camp Holmes on October 26, 1864, for the war. Deserted on January 29, 1865.

POOLE, CALVIN, Private
Resided in Wake County where he enlisted at age 40, September 18, 1861. Discharged on or about October 28, 1861, by reason of disability. Later served in Captain William D. Crowder's Company, 1st Regiment N.C. Militia.

POOLE, ETHELBERT, Private
Resided in Wake County where he enlisted at age 38, August 18, 1863, for the war. Present or accounted for through December, 1864.

POOLE, GREEN, Private
Resided in Wake County where he enlisted at age 35, September 18, 1861. Discharged on or about October 28, 1861. Reason discharged not reported.

POOLE, HANSEL, Private
Resided in Wake County where he enlisted at age 19, September 18, 1861. Present or accounted for through February 25, 1865. Paroled at Raleigh on April 22, 1865. Took the Oath of Allegiance at Raleigh on May 27, 1865.

POOLE, HOWARD, Private
Resided in Wake County and enlisted at Camp Whiting at age 32, February 9, 1863, for the war. Present or accounted for until he was captured at Raleigh on or about April 14, 1865. No further records.

POOLE, IRVIN, Private
Resided in Wake County where he enlisted at age 18, September 18, 1861. Present or accounted for through April, 1864. Reported absent without leave in November-December, 1864.

POOLE, JAMES K., Private
Resided in Wake County where he enlisted at age 16,

September 18, 1861. Present or accounted for until captured at Roanoke Island on February 8, 1862. Paroled at Elizabeth City on February 21, 1862. Returned to duty on or about September 15, 1862. Present or accounted for through December, 1864. Captured at Raleigh on or about April 14, 1865. No further records.

POOLE, LANGDON, Private
Resided in Wake County where he enlisted at age 17, September 18, 1861. Died at Roanoke Island on January 12-15, 1862, of disease.

POOLE, QUINTON R., Private
Resided in Wake County and enlisted at Camp Davis at age 23, July 1, 1863, for the war. Captured at Cold Harbor, Virginia, May 31-June 1, 1864. Confined at Point Lookout, Maryland, June 11, 1864. Transferred to Elmira, New York, July 12, 1864. Died at Elmira on October 3, 1864, of "typhoid fever."

POOLE, SIDNEY, Private
Resided in Wake County where he enlisted at age 33, September 18, 1861. Present or accounted for through April, 1864. Reported absent on detached service in November-December, 1864. No further records.

POOLE, STANFORD, Private
Resided in Wake County where he enlisted at age 28, September 18, 1861. Present or accounted for until captured at Roanoke Island on February 8, 1862. Paroled at Elizabeth City on February 21, 1862. Reported absent sick during January-April, 1863. Reported present on extra duty in March-April, 1864. Reported present for duty in November-December, 1864. Took the Oath of Allegiance at Raleigh on June 3, 1865.

POOLE, WESLEY, Private
Resided in Wake County where he enlisted at age 33, September 18, 1861. Present or accounted for until captured at Roanoke Island on February 8, 1862. Paroled at Elizabeth City on February 21, 1862. Returned to duty on or about September 15, 1862. Transferred to an unspecified unit on August 3, 1863.

POOLE, WILLIAM, Private
Resided in Wake County where he enlisted at age 45, September 18, 1861. Discharged on September 15, 1862, under the provisions of the Conscription Act.

POWELL, JAMES, Private
Resided in Wake County where he enlisted at age 32, September 18, 1861. Present or accounted for until captured at Roanoke Island on February 8, 1862. Paroled at Elizabeth City on February 21, 1862. Reported absent sick during January-April, 1863. Died on September 19, 1863, of disease. Place of death not reported.

POWELL, KADER J., Private
Resided in Wake County where he enlisted at age 27, September 18, 1861. Deserted on August 1, 1863. Returned to duty subsequent to April 30, 1864. Deserted on December 27, 1864.

POWELL, LEONIDAS, Private
Resided in Wake County where he enlisted at age 33,

September 18, 1861. Present or accounted for until captured at Roanoke Island on February 8, 1862. Paroled at Elizabeth City on February 21, 1862. Returned to duty on or about September 15, 1862. Present or accounted for through February 4, 1865. Paroled at Raleigh on April 22, 1865.

POWELL, TAYLOR I., Private
Place and date of enlistment not reported. Captured at Roanoke Island on February 8, 1862. Paroled at Elizabeth City on February 21, 1862. No further records.

POWERS, HENRY T., ——
North Carolina pension records indicate that he served in this company.

RAND, GEORGE DALLAS, Sergeant
Enlisted in Wake County on May 5, 1864, for the war. Mustered in as Private. Promoted to Sergeant subsequent to January 2, 1865. Captured at or near Raleigh on or about April 17, 1865. No further records.

RICHARDSON, JAMES R., Corporal
Resided in Wake County where he enlisted at age 27, September 18, 1861. Mustered in as Corporal. Present or accounted for until captured at Roanoke Island on February 8, 1862. Paroled at Elizabeth City on February 21, 1862. Returned to duty on or about September 15, 1862. Died at or near Charleston, South Carolina, on or about May 4, 1863. Cause of death not reported.

ROBERTS, DAVID, Private
Resided in Johnston County and enlisted in Wake County at age 18, September 18, 1861. Present or accounted for until captured at Roanoke Island on February 8, 1862. Paroled at Elizabeth City on February 21, 1862. Returned to duty prior to March 1, 1863. Died at or near Charleston, South Carolina, on or about March 18, 1863, of disease.

SAULS, JAMES BURTON, Private
Resided in Wake County where he enlisted at age 37, September 18, 1861. Present or accounted for until captured at Roanoke Island on February 8, 1862. Paroled at Elizabeth City on February 21, 1862. Discharged on September 15, 1862, under the provisions of the Conscription Act.

SHERRON, WYATT Y., Private
Resided in Wake County where he enlisted at age 20, September 18, 1861. Died in camp at Fort Hill on November 15, 1861, of disease.

SIMPKINS, WILLIAM T., Private
Resided in Wake County where he enlisted at age 27, October 4, 1861. Present or accounted for through December, 1864.

SMITH, EDWIN J., Private
Resided in Wake County where he enlisted at age 21, September 18, 1861. Present or accounted for until captured at Roanoke Island on February 8, 1862. Paroled at Elizabeth City on February 21, 1862. Returned to duty on or about September 15, 1862. Present or accounted for through December, 1864.

SMITH, LARKIN, Private
Enlisted at Camp Holmes on October 26, 1864, for the war. Present or accounted for through December, 1864.

SMITH, MARCELLUS A., Corporal
Resided in Wake County where he enlisted at age 23, September 18, 1861. Mustered in as Private. Present or accounted for until captured at Roanoke Island on February 8, 1862. Paroled at Elizabeth City on February 21, 1862. Reported absent sick during January-April, 1863. Returned to duty on an unspecified date. Promoted to Corporal on May 4, 1863. Present or accounted for through April, 1864. Reported on the "retired list" in November-December, 1864.

SMITH, ORRIN A., Private
Resided in Wake County where he enlisted at age 16, September 18, 1861. Present or accounted for until captured at Roanoke Island on February 8, 1862. Paroled at Elizabeth City on February 21, 1862. Discharged on September 15, 1862, after providing a substitute. Later served as Corporal in Captain William D. Crowder's Company, 1st Regiment N.C. Militia.

SMITH, RICHARD A., Sergeant
Resided in Wake County where he enlisted at age 20, September 18, 1861. Mustered in as Private. Present or accounted for until captured at Roanoke Island on February 8, 1862. Paroled at Elizabeth City on February 21, 1862. Returned to duty on or about September 15, 1862. Promoted to Corporal prior to March 1, 1863. Promoted to Sergeant in March, 1863. Died in hospital at Savannah, Georgia, March 23, 1863, of "typhoid fever."

SMITH, RUFUS A., Sergeant
Resided in Wake County where he enlisted at age 27, September 18, 1861. Mustered in as Private. Present or accounted for until captured at Roanoke Island on February 8, 1862. Paroled at Elizabeth City on February 21, 1862. Returned to duty on or about September 15, 1862. Promoted to Corporal on May 1, 1863. Promoted to Sergeant on March 9, 1864. Present or accounted for through December, 1864.

SMITH, SAMUEL A., Private
Resided in Wake County where he enlisted at age 21, September 18, 1861. Present or accounted for until captured at Roanoke Island on February 8, 1862. Paroled at Elizabeth City on February 21, 1862. Returned to duty on or about September 15, 1862. Died on March 20-24, 1863, of disease. Place of death not reported.

SMITH, SIMEON, Private
Records of this company indicate that he served previously in Mallett's N.C. Battalion (Camp Guard); however, records of Mallett's Battalion do not indicate that he served therein. Enlisted in this company on or about April 4, 1863. Captured at Fort Harrison, Virginia, September 30, 1864. Confined at Point Lookout, Maryland, October 5, 1864. Paroled at Point Lookout and transferred to Boulware's Wharf, James River, Virginia, where he was received on March 19, 1865, for exchange. Paroled again at Raleigh on May 12, 1865.

SMITH, WILLIAM F., Private
Resided in Wake County where he enlisted at age 37, September 18, 1861. Present or accounted for until captured at Roanoke Island on February 8, 1862. Paroled at Elizabeth City on February 21, 1862.

Discharged on September 15, 1862. Reason discharged not reported.

SMITH, WILLIAM P., Private
Resided in Wake County where he enlisted at age 25, September 18, 1861. Present or accounted for until captured at Roanoke Island on February 8, 1862. Paroled at Elizabeth City on February 21, 1862. Reported absent sick during January-April, 1863, and was reported sick in camp in March-April, 1864. Reported present for duty in November-December, 1864.

STANLY, GIDEON, Private
Resided in Johnston County and enlisted in Wake County at age 37, September 18, 1861. Present or accounted for until captured at Roanoke Island on February 8, 1862. Paroled at Elizabeth City on February 21, 1862. Later served in Company D, 50th Regiment N.C. Troops.

STANLY, NICHOLAS, Private
Resided in Johnston County and enlisted in Wake County at age 35, September 18, 1861. Present or accounted for until captured at Roanoke Island on February 8, 1862. Paroled at Elizabeth City on February 21, 1862. Later served in Company D, 50th Regiment N.C. Troops.

STEPHENS, FESTUS A., Private
Resided in Wake County where he enlisted at age 22, September 18, 1861. Present or accounted for until captured at Roanoke Island on February 8, 1862. Paroled at Elizabeth City on February 21, 1862. Returned to duty on or about September 15, 1862. Present or accounted for through December 23, 1864. [North Carolina pension records indicate he was wounded in the back at Cold Harbor, Virginia, May 31, 1864.]

STEPHENSON, BYTHON, Private
Resided in Wake County where he enlisted at age 19, September 18, 1861. Present or accounted for until captured at Roanoke Island on February 8, 1862. Paroled at Elizabeth City on February 21, 1862. Returned to duty on or about September 15, 1862. Present or accounted for through December, 1864.

STEPHENSON, E. N., Private
Enlisted in Wake County on January 1, 1864, for the war. Reported absent sick at Petersburg, Virginia, in March-April, 1864. No further records.

STEVENS, WILLIAM H., Private
Resided in Wake County where he enlisted at age 18, September 15, 1862, for the war. Present or accounted for through December, 1864.

STEVENSON, AMOS, Private
Resided in Johnston County where he enlisted at age 39, February 25, 1863, for the war. Present or accounted for until captured at Cold Harbor, Virginia, May 31, 1864. Confined at Point Lookout, Maryland, June 11, 1864. Transferred to Elmira, New York, July 12, 1864. Released at Elmira on June 30, 1865, after taking the

Oath of Allegiance.

STURDEVANT, JOHN D., Private
Previously served in Company I, 41st Regiment N.C. Troops (3rd Regiment N.C. Cavalry). Transferred to this company on September 11, 1863. Hospitalized at Danville, Virginia, on or about June 4, 1864, with a gunshot wound of the arm. Place and date wounded not reported. Deserted on June 21, 1864.

STURDIVANT, ALBERT J., Private
Resided in Wake County where he enlisted at age 40, September 18, 1861. Present or accounted for until captured at Roanoke Island on February 8, 1862. Paroled at Elizabeth City on February 21, 1862. Discharged on September 15, 1862, under the provisions of the Conscription Act.

STURDIVANT, ALLEN, Private
Resided in Wake County where he enlisted at age 19, August 10, 1863, for the war. Present or accounted for through December, 1864.

STURDIVANT, J. B., Private
Resided in Wake County where he enlisted at age 23, September 18, 1861. Mustered in as Corporal. Present or accounted for until captured at Roanoke Island on February 8, 1862. Paroled at Elizabeth City on February 21, 1862. Returned to duty on or about September 15, 1862. Reduced to ranks prior to March 1, 1863. Discharged on March 16, 1863, by reason of disability.

STURDIVANT, THOMAS H., Private
Resided in Wake County and enlisted at Camp Mangum at age 26, September 15, 1862, for the war. Present or accounted for through January 5, 1865. [North Carolina pension records indicate he was wounded in the knee, thigh, and left ankle at Petersburg, Virginia, August 23, 1863.]

SUTTAN, MICHAEL, Private
Resided in Wake or New Hanover County and enlisted at age 25, July 1, 1862, for the war. Deserted to the enemy on or about February 16, 1864. Took the Oath of Allegiance at Fort Monroe, Virginia, February 24, 1864.

TODD, BERRY, Private
Resided in Johnston County and enlisted at James Island, Charleston, South Carolina, at age 38, March 13, 1863, for the war. Transferred to Company E of this regiment prior to May 1, 1863.

TODD, J. BRYANT, Private
Resided in Johnston County and enlisted at James Island, Charleston, South Carolina, at age 18, March 13, 1863, for the war. Wounded in the right thigh and captured at Fort Harrison, Virginia, September 30, 1864. Hospitalized at Fort Monroe, Virginia. Confined at Camp Hamilton, Virginia, February 15, 1865. Transferred to Point Lookout, Maryland, where he arrived on March 2, 1865. Released on June 3, 1865.

TURNER, GASTON, Private
Resided in Wake County where he enlisted at age 24, September 18, 1861. Present or accounted for until

captured at Roanoke Island on February 8, 1862. Paroled at Elizabeth City on February 21, 1862. Returned to duty on or about September 15, 1862. Present or accounted for through December, 1864.

TURNER, HENRY, Private
Previously served in Company A, Mallett's N.C. Battalion (Camp Guard). Transferred to this company on or about April 4, 1863. Present or accounted for through December, 1864. Paroled at Raleigh on May 25, 1865.

TURNER, JUNIUS D., 1st Sergeant
Resided in Wake County where he enlisted at age 24, September 18, 1861. Mustered in as Sergeant. Present or accounted for until captured at Roanoke Island on February 8, 1862. Paroled at Elizabeth City on February 21, 1862. Returned to duty on or about September 15, 1862. Promoted to 1st Sergeant on September 15, 1862. Died on May 1, 1863. Place and cause of death not reported.

TURNER, WILLIAM H., Private
Resided in Wake County where he enlisted at age 18, September 18, 1861. Captured at Cold Harbor, Virginia, May 31-June 1, 1864. Confined at Point Lookout, Maryland, June 11, 1864. Transferred to Elmira, New York, July 12, 1864. Died at Elmira on January 6, 1865, of "pleuritis."

UMPLES, JOHN W., Private
Place and date of enlistment not reported. Name appears on a company record dated April 25, 1864. No further records.

UTLEY, JOHN J., Private
Resided in Wake County where he enlisted at age 30, September 18, 1861. Present or accounted for until captured at Roanoke Island on February 8, 1862. Paroled at Elizabeth City on February 21, 1862. Returned to duty on or about September 15, 1862. Present or accounted for through February 26, 1865.

UTLEY, WILLIAM R., Private
Resided in Wake County where he enlisted at age 24, September 18, 1861. Present or accounted for until captured at Roanoke Island on February 8, 1862. Paroled at Elizabeth City on February 21, 1862. Returned to duty on or about September 15, 1862. Company records indicate he was captured at Fort Harrison on September 30, 1864; however, records of the Federal Provost Marshal do not substantiate that report. No further records.

WALTON, JOSEPH A., Private
Resided in Wake County where he enlisted at age 38, August 10, 1863, for the war. Company records dated March-April, 1864, state that he had two months' pay "deducted" by court-martial "for writing Sec[re]t[ar]y of War." Reported present for duty in November-December, 1864. Paroled at Raleigh on April 20, 1865.

WARREN, DANIEL, Private
Resided in Wake County where he enlisted at age 16, September 15, 1862, for the war as a substitute. Present or accounted for through December, 1864. Paroled subsequent to April 26, 1865.

WHEELER, JESSE, Private
Resided in Johnston County and enlisted in Wake

County at age 24, September 18, 1861. Mustered in as Corporal. Reduced to ranks in May, 1862-February, 1863. Captured at Cold Harbor, Virginia, May 31, 1864. Confined at Point Lookout, Maryland, June 11, 1864. Transferred to Elmira, New York, July 12, 1864. Released on May 19, 1865, after taking the Oath of Allegiance.

WHEELER, JOHN WESLEY, ——
North Carolina pension records indicate that he served in this company.

WHITE, JAMES, ——
North Carolina pension records indicate that he served in this company.

WHITLEY, JOHN B., Private
Resided in Wake County and enlisted at Camp Mangum at age 18, September 15, 1862, for the war. Died on March 17-19, 1863, of disease. Place of death not reported.

WHITLY, THOMAS, Private
Resided in Wake County where he enlisted at age 36, September 18, 1861. Present or accounted for until captured at Roanoke Island on February 8, 1862. Paroled at Elizabeth City on February 21, 1862. Discharged on September 15, 1862, under the provisions of the Conscription Act.

WILDER, ASHLEY, Private
Resided in Wake County and enlisted at Sullivan's Island, Charleston, South Carolina, at age 43, October 10, 1863, for the war. Present or accounted for through January 18, 1865.

WILDER, HENRY, Private
Born in Wake County where he resided prior to enlisting at age 18, November 5, 1863, for the war. Died in hospital at Petersburg, Virginia, March 26, 1864, of "rheumatismus."

WILDER, JAMES C., Private
Resided in Wake County and enlisted at Camp Mangum at age 20, September 15, 1862, for the war. Captured at Cold Harbor, Virginia, May 31-June 1, 1864. Confined at Point Lookout, Maryland, June 11, 1864. Transferred to Elmira, New York, July 12, 1864. Transferred for exchange on October 11, 1864. No further records.

WILDER, SAMUEL W., Private
Resided in Wake County where he enlisted at age 30, September 18, 1861. Present or accounted for until captured at Roanoke Island on February 8, 1862. Paroled at Elizabeth City on February 21, 1862. Returned to duty on or about September 15, 1862. Deserted on December 27, 1864.

WILLIAMS, JOSEPH R., Private
Resided in Wake County where he enlisted at age 23, September 18, 1861. Present or accounted for until captured at Roanoke Island on February 8, 1862. Paroled at Elizabeth City on February 21, 1862. Returned to duty on or about September 15, 1862. Wounded in the right arm at Drewry's Bluff, Virginia, May 16-18, 1864. Reported absent wounded or absent sick through December, 1864. Captured in hospital at

Raleigh on April 13, 1865.

WILSON, GEORGE S., Private
Resided in Wake County where he enlisted at age 19, September 18, 1861. Present or accounted for until captured at Roanoke Island on February 8, 1862. Paroled at Elizabeth City on February 21, 1862. Reported absent sick during January-April, 1863. Returned to duty prior to May 1, 1864. Present or accounted for through December, 1864. Paroled at Raleigh on April 22, 1865.

WILSON, WILLIS J. J., Private
Resided in Wake County where he enlisted at age 18, September 15, 1862, for the war. Died at or near Charleston, South Carolina, on or about March 8, 1863, of disease.

WOMBLES, JOHN W., Private
Resided in Wake County where he enlisted at age 25, September 18, 1861. Present or accounted for until captured at Roanoke Island on February 8, 1862. Paroled at Elizabeth City on February 21, 1862. Returned to duty on or about September 15, 1862. Wounded in the left arm at Drewry's Bluff, Virginia, May 16, 1864. Died of wounds. Place and date of death not reported.

COMPANY E

This company was raised in Orange County and enlisted there on October 6, 1861. It was then assigned to the 31st Regiment N.C. Troops and designated Company E. After joining the regiment the company functioned as a part of the regiment, and its history for the war period is reported as a part of the regimental history.

The information contained in the following roster of the company was compiled principally from company muster rolls for October 6-December 31, 1861; January-April, 1863; March-April, 1864; and November-December, 1864. No company muster rolls were found for January-December, 1862; May, 1863-February, 1864; May-October, 1864; or for the period after December, 1864. Valuable information was obtained from primary records such as the Roll of Honor, discharge certificates, medical records, prisoner of war records, and pension applications. Secondary sources such as postwar rosters and histories, cemetery records, and records of the United Daughters of the Confederacy also provided useful information.

OFFICERS

CAPTAINS

MILLER, JESSE
Resided in Orange County where he enlisted at age 27. Appointed Captain on October 6, 1861. Present or accounted for until captured at Roanoke Island on February 8, 1862. Paroled at Elizabeth City on February 21, 1862. Defeated for reelection when the regiment was reorganized on September 17, 1862.

ALLISON, JULIUS F.
Resided in Orange County where he enlisted at age 27, October 6, 1861. Mustered in as 1st Sergeant. Present or accounted for until captured at Roanoke Island on February 8, 1862. Paroled at Elizabeth City on February 21, 1862. Appointed Captain on or about September 17, 1862. Hospitalized at Richmond, Virginia, June 3,

1864, with a gunshot wound of the side. Place and date wounded not reported. Returned to duty prior to January 1, 1865. Paroled at Greensboro on May 22, 1865.

LIEUTENANTS

ALLISON, JOSEPH W., 3rd Lieutenant
Resided in Orange County where he enlisted at age 21, October 6, 1861. Mustered in as Private. Promoted to 3rd Lieutenant on or about September 17, 1862. Hospitalized at Richmond, Virginia, June 4, 1864, with a gunshot wound of the shoulder. Place and date wounded not reported. Returned to duty prior to January 1, 1865. Paroled at Greensboro on May 16, 1865.

BERRY, JOHN H., 2nd Lieutenant
Resided in Orange County where he enlisted at age 26, October 6, 1861. Mustered in as Corporal. Present or accounted for until captured at Roanoke Island on February 8, 1862. Paroled at Elizabeth City on February 21, 1862. Appointed 2nd Lieutenant on or about September 17, 1862. Hospitalized at Richmond, Virginia, May 16, 1864, with a gunshot wound of the right ankle. Place and date wounded not reported. Returned to duty on an unspecified date. Reported in command of Company K of this regiment during November-December, 1864. No further records.

COLLINS, SAMUEL P., 2nd Lieutenant
Resided in Orange County where he enlisted at age 29. Appointed 2nd Lieutenant on or about October 15, 1861. Promoted to 1st Lieutenant and transferred to Company A of this regiment on May 3, 1862.

HUGHES, JOHN H., 1st Lieutenant
Resided in Orange County and enlisted at age 24. Appointed 1st Lieutenant on October 6, 1861. Captured at Fort Harrison, Virginia, September 30, 1864. Confined at Old Capitol Prison, Washington, D.C., October 6, 1864. Transferred to Fort Delaware, Delaware, October 21, 1864. Released at Fort Delaware on June 17, 1865, after taking the Oath of Allegiance.

NONCOMMISSIONED OFFICERS AND PRIVATES

ALLISON, J. S., Private
Enlisted at Petersburg, Virginia, September 10, 1864, for the war. Present or accounted for through December, 1864. Paroled at Greensboro on May 14, 1865.

ALLISON, WILLIAM W., Sergeant
Resided in Orange County where he enlisted at age 22, October 6, 1861. Mustered in as Sergeant. Present or accounted for until captured at Roanoke Island on February 8, 1862. Paroled at Elizabeth City on February 21, 1862. Returned to duty on or about September 15, 1862. Present or accounted for through December, 1864. Paroled at Greensboro on May 14, 1865.

ANDERSON, JOSEPH J., Private
Resided in Orange County where he enlisted at age 16, October 6, 1861. Present or accounted for until captured at Roanoke Island on February 8, 1862. Paroled at Elizabeth City on February 21, 1862. Returned to duty on or about September 15, 1862. Present or accounted for through December, 1864. Paroled at Greensboro on May 11, 1865.

ANDERSON, LUCIAN J., Private
Resided in Orange County where he enlisted at age 21, October 6, 1861. Present or accounted for until captured at Roanoke Island on February 8, 1862. Paroled at Elizabeth City on February 21, 1862. Returned to duty prior to May 1, 1863. Present or accounted for through December, 1864. Paroled at Greensboro on May 16, 1865.

ANDERSON, MOSES G., Private
Enlisted at Sullivan's Island, Charleston, South Carolina, October 15, 1863, for the war. Hospitalized at Richmond, Virginia, October 1, 1864, with a gunshot wound of the abdomen and right arm. Place and date wounded not reported. Company records do not indicate whether he rejoined the company. Paroled at Greensboro on May 16, 1865.

ANDERSON, WILLIAM F., Corporal
Resided in Orange County where he enlisted at age 24, October 6, 1861. Mustered in as Corporal. Present or accounted for until captured at Roanoke Island on February 8, 1862. Paroled at Elizabeth City on February 21, 1862. Returned to duty on or about September 15, 1862. Died in hospital at Petersburg, Virginia, June 20, 1864, of wounds. Place and date wounded not reported.

ASHLEY, WILLIS, Private
Resided in Orange County where he enlisted at age 22, October 6, 1861. Present or accounted for until captured at Roanoke Island on February 8, 1862. Paroled at Elizabeth City on February 21, 1862. Returned to duty on or about September 15, 1862. Present or accounted for through December, 1864. Paroled at Greensboro on May 17, 1865.

BACON, WILLIAM T., Private
Resided in Orange County where he enlisted at age 17, October 6, 1861. Present or accounted for through April, 1864. Reported absent without leave in November-December, 1864.

BALDWIN, JOHN, Private
Resided in Orange County and enlisted in Wake County at age 20, September 26, 1862, for the war. Captured at Fort Harrison, Virginia, September 30, 1864. Confined at Point Lookout, Maryland, October 5, 1864. Paroled at Point Lookout on or about March 17, 1865, and transferred to Boulware's Wharf, James River, Virginia, where he was received on March 19, 1865, for exchange.

BERRY, J. P., Private
Enlisted at Sullivan's Island, Charleston, South Carolina, October 22, 1863, for the war. Captured in hospital at Raleigh on April 13, 1865. [North Carolina pension records indicate he was wounded in an unspecified battle but survived the war.] No further records.

BERRY, J. W., ——
North Carolina pension records indicate that he served in this company.

BERRY, JOHN R., Private
Resided in Orange County where he enlisted at age 19, October 6, 1861. Present or accounted for until captured at Roanoke Island on February 8, 1862. Paroled at Elizabeth City on February 21, 1862. Returned to duty

on or about September 15, 1862. Wounded in the hand and right shoulder and captured at Cold Harbor, Virginia, May 31-June 1, 1864. Hospitalized at Washington, D.C. Confined at Old Capitol Prison, Washington, August 16, 1864. Transferred to Elmira, New York, August 27, 1864. Released at Elmira on June 23, 1865, after taking the Oath of Allegiance.

BLACKWELL, JOHN H., Private
Resided in Orange County where he enlisted at age 20, October 6, 1861. Present or accounted for through April, 1863. Died at Summerville, South Carolina, prior to January 26, 1864. Cause of death not reported.

BLALOCK, JESSE, Private
Born in Orange County where he resided prior to enlisting in Orange County at age 25, October 6, 1861. Mustered in as Musician. Reduced to ranks in January, 1862-February, 1863. Died in hospital at Wilmington on June 27, 1863, of "feb[ris] typh[oi]d."

BLALOCK, WILLIAM A., Private
Resided in Orange County where he enlisted at age 19, October 6, 1861. Present or accounted for through December, 1861. Company records indicate he was appointed 2nd Lieutenant and transferred to Company A, 30th Regiment N.C. Troops, in March, 1863; however, records of the 30th Regiment do not indicate that he served therein. No further records.

BLALOCK, WILLIAM H., Private
Resided in Orange County where he enlisted at age 19, October 6, 1861. Died at Columbia, South Carolina, or at Charleston, South Carolina, May 28, 1863, of disease.

BOLDEN, WILLIAM D., Private
Born in Orange County where he resided as a farmer prior to enlisting in Wake County at age 33, September 18, 1862, for the war. Discharged on January 8, 1864, by reason of "inguinal hernia." Paroled at Greensboro on May 17, 1865.

BRADSHAW, THOMAS, Private
Resided in Orange County where he enlisted at age 24, October 6, 1861. Present or accounted for until captured at Roanoke Island on February 8, 1862. Paroled at Elizabeth City on February 21, 1862. Died on March 29 or April 7, 1862, of disease. Place of death not reported.

BROWN, WILSON, Private
Born in Duplin County and resided in Orange County where he was by occupation a blacksmith prior to enlisting in Orange County at age 47, October 6, 1861. Present or accounted for until captured at Roanoke Island on February 8, 1862. Paroled at Elizabeth City on February 21, 1862. Discharged on September 15, 1862. Reason discharged not reported. Later served in Company G, 27th Regiment N.C. Troops.

BURTON, JOHN A., Private
Resided in Orange County where he enlisted at age 24, October 6, 1861. Died on August 20, 1863, of disease. Place of death not reported.

BURTON, WILLIAM H., Private
Resided in Orange County where he enlisted at age 33, October 6, 1861. Present or accounted for through December, 1864. Paroled at Greensboro on May 1 or May 16, 1865.

CATES, NATHANIEL, Private
Resided in Person County and enlisted in Wake County at age 33, September 26, 1862, for the war. Present or accounted for through April, 1864.

CEARNAL, R. H., Private
Enlisted in Wake County on November 4, 1864, for the war. Present or accounted for through December, 1864.

CHEEK, ALEX M., Private
Enlisted in Orange County on May 9, 1864, for the war. Captured at Fort Harrison, Virginia, September 30, 1864. Confined at Point Lookout, Maryland, October 5, 1864. Paroled at Point Lookout on or about March 17, 1865, and transferred to Boulware's Wharf, James River, Virginia, where he was received on March 19, 1865, for exchange. Paroled at Greensboro on May 3, 1865.

CHEEK, F. M., Private
Enlisted in Orange County on May 9, 1864, for the war. Present or accounted for through December, 1864. Paroled at Greensboro on May 11, 1865.

CLARK, STEPHEN L., Private
Resided in Orange County and enlisted at Sullivan's Island, Charleston, South Carolina, at age 18, September 22, 1863, for the war. Present or accounted for through April, 1864. No further records.

CLARK, WILLIAM R., Sergeant
Resided in Orange County where he enlisted at age 20, October 6, 1861. Mustered in as Sergeant. Wounded in the thigh at Bermuda Hundred, Virginia, May 20, 1864. Furloughed for sixty days on June 1, 1864. Reported absent without leave in November-December, 1864. [North Carolina pension records indicate he was wounded on March 13, 1865, and survived the war.]

COLE, HENRY C., Private
Resided in Orange County where he enlisted at age 20, October 6, 1861. Died at Charleston, South Carolina, April 30-May 1, 1863, of disease.

COMPTON, INGRAM H., Private
Resided in Orange County and enlisted in Wake County at age 33, September 15, 1862, for the war. Captured at or near Globe Tavern, Virginia, August 19, 1864. Confined at Point Lookout, Maryland, August 22, 1864. Released at Point Lookout on June 24, 1865, after taking the Oath of Allegiance.

CORBIN, JACKSON B., 1st Sergeant
Resided in Orange County where he enlisted at age 20, October 6, 1861. Mustered in as Private. Promoted to 1st Sergeant on September 15, 1862. Present or accounted for through April, 1864. No further records.

CRABTREE, JOHN H., Private
Resided in Orange County and enlisted in Wake County at age 28, October 6, 1862, for the war. Reported absent without leave in March-April, 1863. Reported absent sick at Petersburg, Virginia, in March-April, 1864. Reported absent without leave in November-December, 1864.

DOUGLAS, JOHN H., Private
Resided in Alamance County and enlisted in Wake County at age 18, September 16, 1862, for the war. Died at Macon, Georgia, April 10-11, 1863, of "typhoid fever."

DUNN, WILLIAM P., Private
Resided in Orange County where he enlisted at age 42, October 6, 1861. Discharged on September 15, 1862. Reason discharged not reported. [May have served later in Captain Jackson Jones's Unattached Company (Supporting Force) North Carolina Troops.]

FAUCETTE, E. W., Private
Place and date of enlistment not reported. Paroled at Greensboro on May 22, 1865.

FAUCETTE, GEORGE C., 1st Sergeant
Resided in Alamance County and enlisted in Wake County at age 18, October 13, 1862, for the war. Mustered in as Private. Promoted to Sergeant on April 15, 1863. Promoted to 1st Sergeant in May-December, 1864. Present or accounted for through December, 1864. Reported under arrest in November-December, 1864. Paroled at Greensboro on May 24, 1865.

FAUCETTE, JOHN R., Private
Resided in Orange County where he enlisted at age 26, October 6, 1861. Present or accounted for until captured at Roanoke Island on February 8, 1862. Paroled at Elizabeth City on February 21, 1862. Returned to duty on or about September 15, 1862. Present or accounted for through October 5, 1863. No further records.

FAUCETTE, W. R., Private
Enlisted in Wake County on or about September 26, 1862, for the war. Transferred to the "Government Works" on March 2, 1863.

FAULKNER, FRANKLIN, Private
Resided in Orange County where he enlisted at age 25, October 6, 1861. Wounded at or near Fort Harrison, Virginia, September 30, 1864. Hospitalized at Richmond, Virginia. Reported absent wounded or absent sick through December, 1864.

FAULKNER, JAMES, Private
Enlisted at Petersburg, Virginia, January 9, 1864, for the war. Present or accounted for through December, 1864. Paroled at Greensboro on May 18, 1865.

FAULKNER, JOHN, Private
Resided in Orange County where he enlisted at age 27, October 6, 1861. Present or accounted for until captured at Roanoke Island on February 8, 1862. Paroled at Elizabeth City on February 21, 1862. Returned to duty on or about September 15, 1862. Wounded at Fort Wagner, Charleston, South Carolina, July 18, 1863. Company records do not indicate whether he returned to duty. Died on March 15, 1864. Place and cause of death not reported.

GAMBILL, FELIX, ———
North Carolina pension records indicate that he served in this company.

GARROTT, DEWAIN, Private
Resided in Orange County and enlisted in Wake County at age 23, October 4, 1862, for the war. Present or accounted for until wounded and captured at Fort Wagner, Charleston, South Carolina, July 18, 1863. Confined at Hilton Head, South Carolina, July 21,

1863. No further records.

GATES, PARSON, Private
Resided in Orange County and enlisted in Wake County at age 28, September 26, 1862, for the war. Present or accounted for through April, 1864. Died in Orange County prior to September 14, 1864. Cause of death not reported.

HALEY, WILLIAM J., Private
Resided in Orange County where he enlisted at age 22, October 6, 1861. Mustered in as Corporal. Present or accounted for until captured at Roanoke Island on February 8, 1862. Paroled at Elizabeth City on February 21, 1862. Returned to duty on or about September 15, 1862. Reduced to ranks prior to March 1, 1863. Present or accounted for through December, 1864. Paroled at Greensboro on May 18, 1865.

HALL, ALEXANDER RANKIN, Corporal
Resided in Orange County where he enlisted at age 29, October 6, 1861. Mustered in as Private. Present or accounted for until captured at Roanoke Island on February 8, 1862. Paroled at Elizabeth City on February 21, 1862. Promoted to Corporal on September 15, 1862. Captured near Kinston on March 10, 1865. Confined at Point Lookout, Maryland, March 16, 1865. Released on June 6, 1865, after taking the Oath of Allegiance.

HALL, JOSEPH W., Private
Born in Orange County where he resided prior to enlisting in Wake County at age 23, September 16, 1862, for the war. Hospitalized at Richmond, Virginia, May 16, 1864, with a gunshot wound of the finger. Place and date wounded not reported. Returned to duty on an unspecified date. Deserted to the enemy on or about August 27, 1864. No further records.

HOOD, ABEL T., Private
Resided in Orange County and enlisted in Wake County at age 24, October 13, 1862, for the war. Present or accounted for through April, 1864. Reported absent without leave in November-December, 1864. Paroled at Greensboro on May 16, 1865. [May have served previously in Company D, 13th Regiment N.C. Troops (3rd Regiment N.C. Volunteers).]

HUGHES, JOSEPH W., Private
Born in Orange County where he resided as a medical student prior to enlisting in Wake County at age 17, September 15, 1862, for the war. Died at Columbia, South Carolina, March 20, 1863, of disease.

JONES, JOHN T., Private
Resided in Alamance County and enlisted in Wake County at age 18, October 4, 1862, for the war. Transferred to Captain R. T. Beauregard's Company, South Carolina Light Artillery, on or about April 17, 1863.

JORDAN, A. D., Private
Enlisted in Orange County on May 9, 1864, for the war. Present or accounted for through December, 1864. Paroled subsequent to April 26, 1865.

JORDAN, DARIUS P., Private
Resided in Orange County where he enlisted at age 30, October 6, 1861. Present or accounted for until captured at Roanoke Island on February 8, 1862. Paroled at

Elizabeth City on February 21, 1862. Returned to duty on or about September 15, 1862. Hospitalized at Richmond, Virginia, October 2, 1864, with a gunshot wound of the thumb. Place and date wounded not reported. Returned to duty on October 20, 1864. Reported absent on furlough in November-December, 1864. Paroled at Greensboro on May 10, 1865.

JORDAN, JOHN W., Private
Born in Orange County where he resided as a farmer prior to enlisting in Orange County at age 20, October 6, 1861. Died in hospital at Goldsboro on December 27-30, 1862, after he was "attacked with diphtheria while on march."

JORDAN, THOMAS S., Corporal
Resided in Orange County where he enlisted at age 24, October 6, 1861. Mustered in as Private. Present or accounted for until captured at Roanoke Island on February 8, 1862. Paroled at Elizabeth City on February 21, 1862. Returned to duty on or about September 15, 1862. Promoted to Corporal in May-October, 1864. Hospitalized at Richmond, Virginia, October 2, 1864, with gunshot wounds of the knee and thigh. Place and date wounded not reported. Died in hospital at Richmond on or about October 19, 1864, of wounds.

KENION, JOSEPH S., Private
Resided in Orange County where he enlisted at age 27, October 6, 1861. Present or accounted for through December, 1864.

LINDSEY, JAMES C., Private
Resided in Orange County and enlisted at Sullivan's Island, Charleston, South Carolina, at age 43, September 22, 1863, for the war. Hospitalized at Richmond, Virginia, on or about October 4, 1864, with a gunshot wound of the left thigh. Place and date wounded not reported. Reported absent wounded or absent sick through December, 1864. Paroled at Greensboro on May 18, 1865.

LLOYD, ALVIS C., Private
Resided in Alamance County and enlisted in Wake County at age 25, October 14, 1862, for the war. Present or accounted for through April, 1864. Reported absent without leave in November-December, 1864. [North Carolina pension records indicate he was wounded near Petersburg, Virginia, May 16, 1864.]

McCAWLEY, ISAAC, Private
Enlisted in Orange County on May 9, 1864, for the war. Present or accounted for through December, 1864. Paroled at Greensboro on May 24, 1865.

McCAWLEY, THOMAS, Private
Was by occupation a farmer prior to enlisting in Orange County at age 17, May 9, 1864, for the war. Hospitalized at Danville, Virginia, on or about June 4, 1864, with a gunshot wound of the left elbow. Place and date wounded not reported. Furloughed on June 7, 1864. Returned to duty on an unspecified date. Present or accounted for through December, 1864.

McDADE, A. J., Private
Place and date of enlistment not reported. Paroled at Greensboro on May 16, 1865.

McDADE, JOSIAH, Private
Place and date of enlistment not reported. Paroled at

Greensboro on May 14, 1865.

McDADE, SAMUEL F., Private
Resided in Orange County where he enlisted at age 21, October 6, 1861. Present or accounted for until captured at Roanoke Island on February 8, 1862. Paroled at Elizabeth City on February 21, 1862. Returned to duty on or about September 15, 1862. Present or accounted for through December, 1864. Paroled at Greensboro on May 16, 1865.

McDADE, WILLIAM P., Private
Resided in Orange County where he enlisted at age 20, October 6, 1861. Present or accounted for until captured at Roanoke Island on February 8, 1862. Paroled at Elizabeth City on February 21, 1862. Returned to duty on or about September 15, 1862. Wounded in the left arm and left side at Drewry's Bluff, Virginia, May 16, 1864. Reported absent wounded or absent sick through December, 1864. Paroled at Greensboro on May 16, 1865.

McDADE, WILLIAM W., Private
Resided in Orange County where he enlisted at age 28, October 6, 1861. Present or accounted for until captured at Roanoke Island on February 8, 1862. Paroled at Elizabeth City on February 21, 1862. Died on March 18, 1862, of disease. Place of death not reported.

McKEE, GEORGE W., Private
Resided in Orange County where he enlisted at age 18, October 6, 1861. Present or accounted for until captured at Roanoke Island on February 8, 1862. Paroled at Elizabeth City on February 21, 1862. Returned to duty on or about September 15, 1862. Present or accounted for through April, 1864. Reported absent without leave in November-December, 1864.

McKEE, HENRY H., Sergeant
Resided in Orange County where he enlisted at age 23, October 6, 1861. Mustered in as Private. Present or accounted for until captured at Roanoke Island on February 8, 1862. Paroled at Elizabeth City on February 21, 1862. Promoted to Sergeant on September 15, 1862. Hospitalized at Williamsburg, Virginia, May 20, 1864, with a gunshot wound. Place and date wounded not reported. Retired to the Invalid Corps on November 29, 1864, by reason of disability.

McMINEMY, WILLIAM J., Private
Resided in Orange County and was by occupation a farmer prior to enlisting in Wake County at age 18, September 15, 1862, for the war. Hospitalized in Richmond, Virginia, June 3, 1864, with a gunshot wound of the right shoulder. Place and date wounded not reported. Returned to duty on July 14, 1864. Present or accounted for through December, 1864. Paroled at Greensboro on May 14, 1865.

MILLER, JAMES W., Private
Resided in Orange County where he enlisted at age 22, October 6, 1861. Present or accounted for until captured at Roanoke Island on February 8, 1862. Paroled at Elizabeth City on February 21, 1862. Returned to duty on or about September 15, 1862. Present or accounted for through December, 1864. [North Carolina pension records indicate he was wounded at Drewry's Bluff, Virginia, and at Petersburg, Virginia, in 1864.]

MOORE, JOHN M., Private
Resided in Orange County where he enlisted at age 18, October 6, 1861. Mustered in as Musician. Reduced to ranks prior to March 1, 1863. Captured at Fort Harrison, Virginia, September 30, 1864. Confined at Point Lookout, Maryland, October 5, 1864. Released on May 15, 1865, after taking the Oath of Allegiance.

MURRAY, HENRY G., Private
Resided in Orange County where he enlisted at age 20, October 6, 1861. Captured at or near Cold Harbor, Virginia, June 1, 1864. Confined at Point Lookout, Maryland, June 11, 1864. Transferred to Elmira, New York, July 12, 1864. Died at Elmira on September 18, 1864, of "chronic diarrhoea."

MURRAY, JOSIAH, Private
Enlisted at Sullivan's Island, Charleston, South Carolina, November 27, 1863, for the war. Present or accounted for through April, 1864. Died of wounds prior to January 1, 1865. Place and date wounded not reported. Place of death not reported.

NICHOLS, NELSON L., Private
Resided in Orange County where he enlisted at age 30, October 6, 1861. Present or accounted for until captured at Roanoke Island on February 8, 1862. Paroled at Elizabeth City on February 21, 1862. Returned to duty on or about September 15, 1862. Present or accounted for through April, 1864. Reported absent without leave in November-December, 1864. Paroled at Greensboro on May 3, 1865.

NICHOLS, STEPHEN, Private
Previously served in Company K, 19th Regiment N.C. Troops (2nd Regiment N.C. Cavalry). Enlisted in this company in Wayne County on December 20, 1862, for the war. Hospitalized at Richmond, Virginia, June 3, 1864, with a gunshot wound of the left hand. Place and date wounded not reported. Returned to duty on June 10, 1864. Captured at Fort Harrison, Virginia, September 30, 1864. Confined at Point Lookout, Maryland, October 5, 1864. Released on June 4, 1865, after taking the Oath of Allegiance.

NICHOLS, WILLIAM A., Private
Resided in Orange County and enlisted in Wake County at age 28, September 18, 1862, for the war. Present or accounted for through December, 1864.

O'DONNELL, JOHN, Private
Previously served in 2nd Company H, 40th Regiment N.C. Troops (3rd Regiment N.C. Artillery). Transferred to this company in July, 1863. Transferred to the C.S. Navy on April 6, 1864.

PENDER, ANDREW, Private
Resided in Orange County and enlisted in Wake County at age 28, September 26, 1862, for the war. Captured near Petersburg, Virginia, June 16, 1864. Confined at Point Lookout, Maryland, on or about June 22, 1864. Died at Point Lookout on or about February 15, 1865, of "chronic diarrhoea."

POPE, ABNER C., Sergeant
Born in Orange County where he resided prior to enlisting in Orange County at age 25, October 6, 1861. Mustered in as Sergeant. Present or accounted for until

captured at Roanoke Island on February 8, 1862. Paroled at Elizabeth City on February 21, 1862. Returned to duty on or about September 15, 1862. Died at Charleston, South Carolina, on or about April 3, 1863, of disease.

POPE, JOHN S., Private
Resided in Orange County and enlisted at age 25, October 6, 1861. Present or accounted for until captured at Roanoke Island on February 8, 1862. Paroled at Elizabeth City on February 21, 1862. Returned to duty on or about September 15, 1862. Present or accounted for through December, 1864. Paroled at Raleigh on May 17, 1865.

POPE, THOMAS, Sergeant
Resided in Orange County where he enlisted at age 32, October 6, 1861. Mustered in as Private. Present or accounted for until captured at Roanoke Island on February 8, 1862. Paroled at Elizabeth City on February 21, 1862. Returned to duty on or about September 15, 1862. Promoted to Sergeant on September 15, 1862. Wounded at Fort Wagner, Charleston, South Carolina, July 18, 1863. Returned to duty on an unspecified date. Died at Petersburg, Virginia, prior to September 14, 1864. Cause of death not reported.

PORTERFIELD, JAMES H., Private
Born in Orange County where he resided as a farmer prior to enlisting in Orange County at age 30, October 6, 1861. Present or accounted for until captured at Roanoke Island on February 8, 1862. Paroled at Elizabeth City on February 21, 1862. Returned to duty on an unspecified date. Died at Charleston, South Carolina, March 24, 1863, of disease.

PORTERFIELD, JOHN W., Private
Born in Orange County where he resided as a farmer prior to enlisting in Orange County at age 28, October 12, 1861. Present or accounted for until captured at Roanoke Island on February 8, 1862. Paroled at Elizabeth City on February 21, 1862. Returned to duty on an unspecified date. Died at Charleston, South Carolina, March 17-18, 1863, of disease.

PORTERFIELD, JOSEPH W., Private
Resided in Orange County and enlisted in Wake County at age 18, September 15, 1862, for the war. Present or accounted for through April, 1864. No further records.

RAY, GEORGE M., Private
Resided in Orange County where he enlisted at age 30, October 6, 1861. Present or accounted for until captured at Roanoke Island on February 8, 1862. Paroled at Elizabeth City on February 21, 1862. Returned to duty on an unspecified date. Died at Charleston, South Carolina, on or about April 3, 1863, of disease.

REGAN, SIDNEY M., Private
Enlisted at Ivor Station, Virginia, March 1, 1864, for the war. Present or accounted for through December, 1864. [North Carolina pension records indicate he was wounded in the hand and knee at "Petersburg, Virginia, July 1, 1863."]

RHEW, WALKER, Private
Born in Orange County where he resided as a farmer prior to enlisting in Wake County on September 26, 1862, for the war. Died in hospital at Wilmington on February 11, 1863, of disease.

RIGGAN, JAMES, Private
Resided in Orange County and enlisted in Wake County at age 19, September 26, 1862, for the war. Captured at Cold Harbor, Virginia, June 1, 1864. Confined at Point Lookout, Maryland, June 11, 1864. Transferred to Elmira, New York, July 12, 1864. Died at Elmira on or about November 14, 1864, of "pneumonia."

RILEY, DAVID W., Private
Resided in Orange County where he enlisted at age 28, October 6, 1861. Present or accounted for through November 26, 1864. Reported absent without leave prior to January 1, 1865.

ROBINSON, ALEXANDER, Private
Resided in Orange County where he enlisted at age 25, October 6,1861. Present or accounted for until captured at Roanoke Island on February 8, 1862. Paroled at Elizabeth City on February 21, 1862. Returned to duty prior to May 1, 1863. Hospitalized at Wilmington on May 13, 1863, with a gunshot wound. Place and date wounded not reported. Returned to duty on June 17, 1863. Present or accounted for through September 1, 1864.

SARTAIN, ZERA, Private
Resided in Orange County and enlisted in Wake County at age 20, October 10, 1862, for the war. Present or accounted for through April, 1864. No further records. [May have served previously in Company G, 11th Regiment N.C. Troops (1st Regiment N.C. Volunteers).]

SCOTT, GEORGE W., Private
Born in Orange County and was by occupation a farmer prior to enlisting at Petersburg, Virginia, April 1, 1864, for the war. Wounded in the left arm at or near Bermuda Hundred, Virginia, May 20, 1864. Left arm amputated. Retired to the Invalid Corps on or about January 9, 1865.

SHARP, ASHFORD, Private
Resided in Orange County where he enlisted at age 30, October 6, 1861. Present or accounted for until captured at Roanoke Island on February 8, 1862. Paroled at Elizabeth City on February 21, 1862. Returned to duty on an unspecified date. Hospitalized at Richmond, Virginia, May 18, 1864, with a gunshot wound of the right lung. Place and date wounded not reported. Died at Richmond on May 27, 1864, of wounds.

SHARP, PETER B., Private
Resided in Orange County where he enlisted at age 37, February 12, 1863, for the war. Captured at Cold Harbor, Virginia, June 1, 1864. Confined at Point Lookout, Maryland, June 11, 1864. Transferred to Elmira, New York, July 12, 1864. Died at Elmira on October 10, 1864, of "chronic diarrhoea."

SMITH, ANDREW H., Private
Resided in Orange County where he enlisted at age 39, February 12, 1863, for the war. Died "at home" on February 1, 1865. Cause of death not reported.

SMITH, JOHN H., Private
Born in Caswell County and resided in Orange County

where he was by occupation a farmer prior to enlisting in Orange County at age 41, October 6, 1861. Discharged on November 22, 1861, by reason of disability.

SMITH, LUCIAN C., Private
Resided in Orange County and enlisted in Wake County at age 23, October 19, 1862, for the war. Hospitalized at Richmond, Virginia, May 18, 1864, with a gunshot wound. Place and date wounded not reported. Returned to duty on October 1, 1864. Reported absent without leave in November-December, 1864.

SMITH, MURPHEY J., Private
Resided in Orange County and enlisted in Wake County at age 25, October 4, 1862, for the war. Reported absent without leave on November 18, 1862. Returned to duty on February 11, 1863. Transferred to the Engineering Corps at Wilmington on April 9, 1864.

SMITH, THOMAS W., ———
North Carolina pension records indicate that he served in this company.

SYKES, THOMAS, Private
Resided in Orange County and enlisted in Wake County at age 28, October 4, 1862, for the war. Deserted on November 18, 1862. Returned to duty on March 9, 1863. Died in hospital at Wilmington on May 23, 1863, of "pneumonia."

TAYLOR, GEORGE, Private
Resided in Orange County and enlisted at Sullivan's Island, Charleston, South Carolina, at age 18, September 22, 1863, for the war. Died at Petersburg, Virginia, prior to September 14, 1864. Cause of death not reported.

TAYLOR, JOHN H., Private
Resided in Orange County and enlisted at Sullivan's Island, Charleston, South Carolina, at age 18, September 22, 1863, for the war. Killed at Fort Harrison, Virginia, on or about September 30, 1864.

TAYLOR, JONATHAN J., Corporal
Resided in Orange County where he enlisted at age 24, October 6, 1861. Mustered in as Corporal. Present or accounted for until captured at Roanoke Island on February 8, 1862. Paroled at Elizabeth City on February 21, 1862. Returned to duty on or about September 15, 1862. Hospitalized at Richmond, Virginia, May 16, 1864, with a gunshot wound. Place and date wounded not reported. Returned to duty on an unspecified date. Present or accounted for through December, 1864. Paroled at Greensboro on May 16, 1865.

TERRY, JAMES F., Private
Resided in Orange County where he enlisted at age 18, October 6, 1861. Hospitalized at Richmond, Virginia, May 16, 1864, with a gunshot wound. Place and date wounded not reported. Returned to duty on an unspecified date. Present or accounted for through December, 1864.

THOMPSON, JOHN, Sergeant
Resided in Orange County and enlisted in Wake County at age 18, September 20, 1862, for the war. Mustered in as Private. Hospitalized at Richmond,

Virginia, May 16, 1864, with a gunshot wound. Returned to duty on an unspecified date. Promoted to Sergeant in May-December, 1864. Present or accounted for through December, 1864.

TILLEY, ROBERT C., Private
Resided in Orange County and enlisted in Wake County at age 18, October 6, 1862, for the war. Wounded in the foot and captured at or near Fort Harrison, Virginia, on or about September 30, 1864. Hospitalized at Fort Monroe, Virginia. Transferred from Fort Monroe to Camp Hamilton, Virginia, May 30, 1865. No further records.

TILLEY, WILLIAM B., Private
Resided in Orange County and enlisted in Wake County at age 32, September 29, 1862, for the war. Killed at Cold Harbor, Virginia, May 31, 1864.

TINNIN, JOSEPH A., Private
Resided in Orange County and enlisted in Wake County at age 26, September 15, 1862, for the war. Died at Charleston, South Carolina, on or about March 24, 1863, of disease.

TODD, BERRY, Private
Previously served in Company D of this regiment. Transferred to this company on or about April 1, 1863. Present or accounted for through April, 1863. No further records.

TURNER, JAMES F., Private
Resided in Orange County where he enlisted at age 20, October 6, 1861. Present or accounted for until captured at Roanoke Island on February 8, 1862. Paroled at Elizabeth City on February 21, 1862. Returned to duty on or about September 15, 1862. Present or accounted for through April, 1864. Reported absent without leave in November-December, 1864. Paroled at Greensboro on May 10, 1865.

TURNER, ROBERT, Private
Enlisted in Orange County on May 1, 1864, for the war. Company records dated November-December, 1864, indicate he was a prisoner of war; however, records of the Federal Provost Marshal do not substantiate that report. No further records.

WARD, JOHN H., Private
Resided in Orange County and was by occupation a farmer prior to enlisting in Orange County at age 20, October 6, 1861. Present or accounted for until captured at Roanoke Island on February 8, 1862. Paroled at Elizabeth City on February 21, 1862. Returned to duty on or about September 15, 1862. Present or accounted for through April, 1864. Reported absent without leave in November-December, 1864. Paroled at Greensboro on May 13, 1865. [North Carolina pension records indicate he was wounded in the head and knee at "Gaines' Mill, Virginia, May 15, 1862."]

WARD, SUTTON M., Private
Resided in Orange County where he enlisted at age 27, February 12, 1863, for the war. Present or accounted for through April, 1863. Died prior to February 21, 1865. Place and cause of death not reported.

WARREN, ALEXANDER, Private
Resided in Caswell County and enlisted in Orange

County at age 38, February 12, 1863, for the war. Retired to the Invalid Corps on August 11, 1864, by reason of disability. Paroled at Greensboro on May 18, 1865.

WARREN, JOHN B., Private
Resided in McDowell County and enlisted in Wake County at age 21, October 10, 1862, for the war. Present or accounted for through December, 1864. Paroled subsequent to April 26, 1865. [May have served previously in Company B, 22nd Regiment N.C. Troops (12th Regiment N.C. Volunteers).]

WATSON, DUDLEY, Private
Resided in Orange County where he enlisted at age 24, October 6, 1861. Present or accounted for through April, 1863. No further records.

WATSON, GEORGE W., Private
Resided in Orange County where he enlisted at age 20, October 6, 1861. Wounded in the neck at or near Bermuda Hundred, Virginia, on or about May 16, 1864. Reported absent wounded through August 1, 1864. Returned to duty on an unspecified date. Present or accounted for through December, 1864. Paroled at Greensboro on May 10, 1865.

WEBB, NELSON R., Private
Previously served in Captain R. T. Beauregard's Company, South Carolina Light Artillery. Transferred to this company on April 22, 1863. Captured at Cold Harbor, Virginia, June 1, 1864. Confined at Point Lookout, Maryland, June 11, 1864. Transferred to Elmira, New York, July 12, 1864. Paroled at Elmira on March 2, 1865, and transferred to the James River, Virginia, for exchange. Hospitalized at Richmond, Virginia, March 6, 1865, with varioloid. Furloughed for thirty days on March 27, 1865.

WEST, AVERY, Private
Resided in McDowell County and enlisted in Wake County at age 31, October 10, 1862, for the war. Captured at Cold Harbor, Virginia, June 1, 1864. Confined at Point Lookout, Maryland, June 11, 1864. No further records.

WILKINSON, DANIEL N., Private
Resided in Orange County where he enlisted at age 20, October 6, 1861. Present or accounted for until captured at Roanoke Island on February 8, 1862. Paroled at Elizabeth City on February 21, 1862. Returned to duty on or about September 15, 1862. Wounded in the right hand at Charleston, South Carolina, July 18, 1863. Returned to duty prior to May 1, 1864. Wounded in the head, arm, and/or left hand at Cold Harbor, Virginia, on or about June 1, 1864. Hospitalized at Richmond, Virginia. Furloughed on July 14, 1864. Discharged prior to January 1, 1865, by reason of disability.

WILKINSON, SAMUEL M., Private
Born in Orange County where he resided as an engineer prior to enlisting in Orange County at age 27, October 6, 1861. Discharged on November 22, 1861, by reason of disability.

WILSON, RICHARD J., Corporal
Resided in Orange County where he enlisted at age 20, October 6, 1861. Mustered in as Private. Present or accounted for until captured at Roanoke Island on

February 8, 1862. Paroled at Elizabeth City on February 21, 1862. Promoted to Corporal on September 15, 1862. Hospitalized at Richmond, Virginia, May 16, 1864, with a gunshot wound. Place and date wounded not reported. Reported absent wounded or absent sick through December, 1864. Paroled at Greensboro on May 16, 1865. [North Carolina pension records indicate he was wounded at Fort Harrison, Virginia, in September, 1864.]

WILSON, THOMAS, Private
Resided in Person County and enlisted in Orange County at age 18, July 20, 1863, for the war. Captured at Fort Harrison, Virginia, September 30, 1864. Confined at Point Lookout, Maryland, October 5, 1864. Died at Point Lookout on January 18, 1865, of "chronic diarrhoea."

WITHERSPOON, ASAGIL, Private
Resided in Orange County and enlisted in Wake County at age 27, September 16, 1862, for the war. Discharged on March 17-20, 1863, by reason of disability.

COMPANY F

This company was raised in Martin County and was enlisted at Williamston and at Hamilton on October 8, 1861. It was then assigned to the 31st Regiment N.C. Troops and designated Company F. After joining the regiment the company functioned as a part of the regiment, and its history for the war period is reported as a part of the regimental history.

The information contained in the following roster of the company was compiled principally from company muster rolls for October 8-December 31, 1861; January-April, 1863; March-April, 1864; and November-December, 1864. No company muster rolls were found for January-December, 1862; May, 1863-February, 1864; May-October, 1864; or for the period after December, 1864. Valuable information was obtained from primary records such as the Roll of Honor, discharge certificates, medical records, prisoner of war records, and pension applications. Secondary sources such as postwar rosters and histories, cemetery records, and records of the United Daughters of the Confederacy also provided useful information.

OFFICERS

CAPTAINS

KNIGHT, CHARLES W.
Previously served as 1st Lieutenant of Company F, 17th Regiment N.C. Troops (1st Organization). Promoted to Captain on or about October 8, 1861, and transferred to this company. Present or accounted for until captured at Roanoke Island on February 8, 1862. Paroled at Elizabeth City on February 21, 1862. Returned to duty on an unspecified date. Promoted to Lieutenant Colonel on June 7, 1863, and transferred to the Field and Staff of this regiment.

MORRISETT, STEPHEN W.
Previously served as Sergeant in Company G, 17th Regiment N.C. Troops (1st Organization). Appointed 2nd Lieutenant on October 8, 1861, and transferred to this company. Present or accounted for until captured at Roanoke Island on February 8, 1862. Paroled at Elizabeth City on February 21, 1862. Returned to duty

on or about September 15, 1862. Promoted to Captain on June 7, 1863. Reported missing and presumed killed at Fort Harrison, Virginia, September 30, 1864.

LIEUTENANTS

HYMAN, SAMUEL A., 1st Lieutenant
Previously served as Private in Company G, 17th Regiment N.C. Troops (1st Organization). Appointed 2nd Lieutenant on October 8, 1861, and transferred to this company. Present or accounted for until captured at Roanoke Island on February 8, 1862. Paroled at Elizabeth City on February 21, 1862. Returned to duty prior to May 1, 1863. Promoted to 1st Lieutenant on June 7, 1863. Captured at Globe Tavern, Virginia, August 19, 1864. Confined at Old Capitol Prison, Washington, D.C., August 22, 1864. Transferred to Fort Delaware, Delaware, August 27, 1864. Paroled at Fort Delaware on October 6, 1864. Received at Cox's Wharf, James River, Virginia, October 15, 1864, for exchange. Returned to duty on October 21, 1864. Present or accounted for through March 29, 1865. Paroled at High Point on or about May 1, 1865.

KNIGHT, ARTHUR B., 2nd Lieutenant
Previously served as Sergeant in Company F, 17th Regiment N.C. Troops (1st Organization). Transferred to this company on or about October 8, 1861, with the rank of Sergeant. Present or accounted for until captured at Roanoke Island on February 8, 1862. Paroled at Elizabeth City on February 21, 1862. Returned to duty on or about September 15, 1862. Appointed 3rd Lieutenant on January 8, 1863. Promoted to 2nd Lieutenant on June 7, 1863. Present or accounted for through March 1, 1865.

LATHAM, SIMON J., 1st Lieutenant
Born in Martin County where he resided prior to enlisting at age 44. Appointed 1st Lieutenant on October 8, 1861. Present or accounted for until captured at Roanoke Island on February 8, 1862. Paroled at Elizabeth City on February 21, 1862. Died in Martin County on March 13-15, 1862. Cause of death not reported.

PERKINS, JULIUS L., 2nd Lieutenant
Previously served as Private in Company G, 17th Regiment N.C. Troops (1st Organization). Transferred to this company on or about October 8, 1861. Mustered in as Private. Promoted to 1st Sergeant in January, 1862-February, 1863. Captured at Roanoke Island on February 8, 1862. Paroled at Elizabeth City on February 21, 1862. Returned to duty on or about September 15, 1862. Appointed 2nd Lieutenant on June 7, 1863. Killed near Smithfield, Virginia, on or about January 31, 1864.

WALDO, JOSEPH T., 1st Lieutenant
Resided in Martin County where he enlisted at age 22, October 8, 1861. Mustered in as 1st Sergeant. Present or accounted for until captured at Roanoke Island on February 8, 1862. Paroled at Elizabeth City on February 21, 1862. Appointed 1st Lieutenant on or about September 17, 1862. Resigned on November 15, 1862, by reason of "chronic diarrhoea." Resignation accepted on or about November 26, 1862.

NONCOMMISSIONED OFFICERS AND PRIVATES

ANDREWS, JOHN J. D., 1st Sergeant
Previously served as Private in Company G, 17th Regiment N.C. Troops (1st Organization). Transferred to this company on or about October 8, 1861. Mustered in as Corporal. Present or accounted for until captured at Roanoke Island on February 8, 1862. Paroled at Elizabeth City on February 21, 1862. Promoted to Sergeant in September, 1862. Promoted to 1st Sergeant on June 7, 1863. Captured at Cold Harbor, Virginia, June 1, 1864. Confined at Point Lookout, Maryland, June 11, 1864. Transferred to Elmira, New York, July 12, 1864. Died at Elmira on April 10, 1865, of "chro[nic] diarr[hoea]."

ANDREWS, SAMUEL A., Private
Resided in Martin County where he enlisted at age 31, October 8, 1862, for the war. Present or accounted for through December, 1864.

ANDREWS, WILLIAM W., Private
Previously served as Musician (Drummer) in Company G, 17th Regiment N.C. Troops (1st Organization). Transferred to this company on or about October 8, 1861. Mustered in as Private. Present or accounted for until captured at Roanoke Island on February 8, 1862. Paroled at Elizabeth City on February 21, 1862. Returned to duty on or about September 15, 1862. Captured at Cold Harbor, Virginia, June 1, 1864. Confined at Point Lookout, Maryland, June 11, 1864. Transferred to Elmira, New York, July 12, 1864. Paroled at Elmira on October 11, 1864, and transferred to Venus Point, Savannah River, Georgia, where he was received on November 15, 1864, for exchange.

BAGGETT, BARTON, Private
Previously served as Private in 1st Company D, 12th Regiment N.C. Troops (2nd Regiment N.C. Volunteers). Enlisted in this company on or about December 31, 1861. Transferred to Company A of this regiment on or about January 14, 1862.

BAGGETT, NEIL, Private
Resided in Robeson or Martin County and enlisted at Roanoke Island at age 30, December 31, 1861. Transferred to Company A of this regiment on or about January 14, 1862. [May have served previously in 1st Company D, 12th Regiment N.C. Troops (2nd Regiment N.C. Volunteers), under the name of Cornelius Baggett.]

BALLARD, JOSEPH R., Private
Previously served as Corporal in Company G, 17th Regiment N.C. Troops (1st Organization). Transferred to this company on or about October 8, 1861. Mustered in as Private. Discharged on October 8, 1862, after providing a substitute.

BARNES, JOHN C., Private
Previously served as Private in 1st Company D, 12th Regiment N.C. Troops (2nd Regiment N.C. Volunteers). Enlisted in this company on or about December 31, 1861. Transferred to Company A of this regiment on or about January 14, 1862.

BARNES, WILLIAM, Private
Resided in Martin County where he enlisted at age 55, October 8, 1861. Present or accounted for until captured at Roanoke Island on February 8, 1862. Paroled at

Elizabeth City on February 21, 1862. Died in North Carolina on March 7, 1862, of disease.

BAZEMORE, FRANKLIN PERRY, Sergeant

Previously served as Private in Company G, 17th Regiment N.C. Troops (1st Organization). Transferred to this company on or about October 8, 1861. Mustered in as Sergeant. Present or accounted for until captured at Roanoke Island on February 8, 1862. Paroled at Elizabeth City on February 21, 1862. Company records do not indicate whether he returned to duty. Discharged on October 8, 1862, by reason of being a justice of the peace.

BIGGS, JOHN D., Private

Resided in Martin County where he enlisted at age 22, October 8, 1861. Present or accounted for until captured at Roanoke Island on February 8, 1862. Paroled at Elizabeth City on February 21, 1862. Company records do not indicate whether he returned to duty. Transferred to Company A, 17th Regiment N.C. Troops (2nd Organization), January 1, 1863, in exchange for Private John R. Williams.

BLAND, ABNER, Private

Resided in Martin County where he enlisted at age 16, October 8, 1861. Present or accounted for until captured at Roanoke Island on February 8, 1862. Paroled at Elizabeth City on February 21, 1862. Company records do not indicate whether he returned to duty. Discharged on October 8, 1862, under the provisions of the Conscription Act. Later served in Company G, 17th Regiment N.C. Troops (2nd Organization).

BLAND, WILLIAM A., Private

Previously served in Company G, 17th Regiment N.C. Troops (1st Organization). Transferred to this company on or about October 8, 1861. Present or accounted for until captured at Roanoke Island on February 8, 1862. Paroled at Elizabeth City on February 21, 1862. Returned to duty prior to May 1, 1863. Present or accounted for through December, 1864. Hospitalized at Wilmington on February 17, 1865, with "amputation." Place and date injured not reported. Transferred on February 22, 1865. No further records.

BONDS, WILLIAM, Private

Previously served in Company F, 17th Regiment N.C. Troops (1st Organization). Enlisted in this company in Martin County at age 24, October 8, 1862, for the war. Captured (or deserted to the enemy) on October 21, 1864. Sent to Norfolk, Virginia, on or about October 22, 1864. No further records.

BOWEN, REUBEN, Private

Resided in Martin County where he enlisted at age 21, October 8, 1861. Present or accounted for until captured at Roanoke Island on February 8, 1862. Paroled at Elizabeth City on February 21, 1862. Returned to duty on or about September 15, 1862. Present or accounted for through December, 1864.

BOWERS, BENJAMIN A., Private

Previously served in Company G, 17th Regiment N.C. Troops (1st Organization). Transferred to this company on or about October 8, 1861. Present or accounted for until captured at Roanoke Island on February 8, 1862. Paroled at Elizabeth City on February 21, 1862. Returned to duty on or about September 15, 1862.

Present or accounted for through December, 1864.

BOWERS, LLEWELYN, Private

Resided in Martin County where he enlisted at age 28, October 8, 1861. Present or accounted for until captured at Roanoke Island on February 8, 1862. Paroled at Elizabeth City on February 21, 1862. Died on April 28, 1862. Place and cause of death not reported.

BREWER, ELI H., Private

Previously served in Company F, 17th Regiment N.C. Troops (1st Organization). Transferred to this company on or about October 8, 1861. Present or accounted for until captured at Roanoke Island on February 8, 1862. Paroled at Elizabeth City on February 21, 1862. Returned to duty on or about September 15, 1862. Hospitalized at Richmond, Virginia, in May, 1864, with a gunshot wound of the left nates. Furloughed for sixty days on May 27, 1864. Returned to duty on an unspecified date. Hospitalized at a Federal hospital at Point of Rocks, Virginia, October 2, 1864, with gunshot wounds of the leg and both shoulders. Place and date wounded and captured not reported. Died at Point of Rocks on October 13, 1864, of wounds.

BRITTON, JAMES L., Private

Resided in Pitt County and enlisted at Roanoke Island at age 30, December 31, 1861. Present or accounted for until captured at Roanoke Island on February 8, 1862. Paroled at Elizabeth City on February 21, 1862. Returned to duty on or about September 15, 1862. Reported absent on detached service at Wilmington in January-February, 1863. Furloughed on April 30, 1863. Returned to duty on an unspecified date. Reported present for duty in March-April, 1864. Died prior to December 18, 1864. Place and cause of death not reported.

BRITTON, WILLIAM H., Private

Resided in Pitt County and enlisted in Martin County at age 23, October 8, 1861. Present or accounted for until captured at Roanoke Island on February 8, 1862. Paroled at Elizabeth City on February 21, 1862. Reported absent on detached service at Wilmington in January-February, 1863. Rejoined the company prior to May 1, 1863. Captured at Cold Harbor, Virginia, June 1, 1864. Confined at Point Lookout, Maryland, June 11, 1864. No further records.

BRYAN, JOSEPH, ———

North Carolina pension records indicate that he served in this company.

BURNETT, T., Private

Enlisted at Petersburg, Virginia, May 10, 1864, for the war. Captured at Cold Harbor, Virginia, June 1, 1864. Confined at Point Lookout, Maryland, June 11, 1864. Transferred to Elmira, New York, July 12, 1864. Died at Elmira on November 7, 1864, of "dip[h]theria."

BURNETT, WILLIAM T., Private

Resided in Pitt County and enlisted at Roanoke Island at age 22, December 31, 1861. Present or accounted for until captured at Roanoke Island on February 8, 1862. Paroled at Elizabeth City on February 21, 1862. Returned to duty on or about September 15, 1862. Present or accounted for through December, 1864. [North Carolina pension records indicate he was wounded in March, 1865.]

CARSON, JESSE W., Private

Resided in Pitt County and enlisted in Martin County at age 32, October 8, 1862, for the war. Mustered in as Musician. Present or accounted for through April, 1863. Reduced to ranks on an unspecified date. Deserted prior to May 1, 1864.

CLARK, BENJAMIN, Private

Resided in Martin County where he enlisted at age 18, October 8, 1861. Present or accounted for until captured at Roanoke Island on February 8, 1862. Paroled at Elizabeth City on February 21, 1862. Returned to duty on or about September 15, 1862. Captured at Cold Harbor, Virginia, June 1, 1864. Confined at Elmira, New York, on an unspecified date. Died at Elmira on October 8, 1864, of "typhoid fever."

CLARY, RICHARD W., Private

Resided in Martin County where he enlisted at age 19, October 8, 1861. Transferred to Company A, 17th Regiment N.C. Troops (2nd Organization), October 6, 1862, in exchange for Private Josiah Williams.

COBERN, ALBERT, Private

Previously served in Company G, 17th Regiment N.C. Troops (1st Organization). Enlisted in this company in Martin County at age 43, July 21, 1863, for the war. Captured at Cold Harbor, Virginia, June 1, 1864. Confined at Point Lookout, Maryland, June 11, 1864. Transferred to Elmira, New York, July 12, 1864. Hospitalized at Baltimore, Maryland, February 15, 1865. Released on June 10, 1865, after taking the Oath of Allegiance.

COBURN, SETH, Private

Previously served in Company G, 17th Regiment N.C. Troops (1st Organization). Transferred to this company on or about October 8, 1861. Discharged on an unspecified date. Reason discharged not reported. Enlisted in Company E, 17th Regiment N.C. Troops (2nd Organization), March 10, 1862. Transferred back to this company in February, 1863. Reported absent on detail at Wilmington in March-April, 1864. Reported absent without leave in November-December, 1864.

COREY, JAMES E., Private

Previously served in Company G, 17th Regiment N.C. Troops (1st Organization). Transferred to this company at age 19 on or about October 8, 1861. Present or accounted for until captured at Roanoke Island on February 8, 1862. Paroled at Elizabeth City on February 21, 1862. Company records do not indicate whether he returned to duty. Died on March 16, 1863. Place and cause of death not reported.

CORY, JESSE E., Corporal

Previously served as Private in Company F, 17th Regiment N.C. Troops (1st Organization). Transferred to this company at age 26 on or about October 8, 1861. Mustered in as Musician (Drummer). Present or accounted for until captured at Roanoke Island on February 8, 1862. Paroled at Elizabeth City on February 21, 1862. Returned to duty on or about September 15, 1862. Promoted to Corporal in May, 1863-April, 1864. Present or accounted for through December, 1864.

CUSHING, FRILEY JOHN, Private

Previously served in Company G, 17th Regiment N.C.

Troops (1st Organization). Transferred to this company at age 35 on or about October 8, 1861. Discharged on or about December 31, 1861, by reason of disability. Later served in Company E, 17th Regiment N.C. Troops (2nd Organization).

DANIEL, ASA J., Sergeant

Previously served as Private in Company F, 17th Regiment N.C. Troops (1st Organization). Transferred to this company at age 28 on or about October 8, 1861. Mustered in as Sergeant. Wounded in both thighs at or near Drewry's Bluff, Virginia, May 16, 1864. Hospitalized at Richmond, Virginia, where he died on May 28, 1864, of "pyaemia."

DANIEL, KENNETH, Private

Resided in Martin County where he enlisted at age 34, October 8, 1861. Present or accounted for until captured at Roanoke Island on February 8, 1862. Paroled at Elizabeth City on February 21, 1862. Discharged on October 8, 1862. Reason discharged not reported.

EBORN, JOHN P., Sergeant

Resided in Martin County where he enlisted at age 18, October 8, 1861. Mustered in as Private. Present or accounted for until captured at Roanoke Island on February 8, 1862. Paroled at Elizabeth City on February 21, 1862. Returned to duty on or about September 15, 1862. Promoted to Corporal subsequent to April 30, 1863. Promoted to Sergeant prior to May 1, 1864. Captured at Fort Harrison, Virginia, September 30, 1864. Confined at Point Lookout, Maryland, October 5, 1864. Paroled at Point Lookout on or about March 17, 1865, and transferred to Boulware's Wharf, James River, Virginia, where he was received on March 19, 1865, for exchange.

EDMONDSON, LEVI, Private

Resided in Martin County where he enlisted at age 25, October 8, 1861. Present or accounted for until captured at Roanoke Island on February 8, 1862. Paroled at Elizabeth City on February 21, 1862. Returned to duty on or about September 15, 1862. Present or accounted for through December, 1864.

FAITHFUL, JOHN L., Private

Resided in Martin County and enlisted in Beaufort County at age 28, October 8, 1861. Present or accounted for through December, 1861. Enlisted in Company K, 41st Regiment N.C. Troops (3rd Regiment N.C. Cavalry), May 16, 1862.

GLISSON, WILLIAM D., Private

Born in Edgecombe County and resided in Martin County where he was by occupation a mechanic prior to enlisting in Martin County at age 25, October 8, 1861. Present or accounted for until captured at Roanoke Island on February 8, 1862. Paroled at Elizabeth City on February 21, 1862. Enlisted in Company F, 17th Regiment N.C. Troops (2nd Organization), May 1, 1862. [North Carolina pension records indicate he was wounded at "Bermuda Hundred, Virginia, March 8, 1862."]

GRAY, NIMPHUS H. L., Sergeant

Previously served as Private in Company G, 17th Regiment N.C. Troops (1st Organization). Transferred to this company at age 20 on or about October 8, 1861. Mustered in as Private. Present or accounted for until captured at Roanoke Island on February 8, 1862. Paroled at Elizabeth City on February 21, 1862. Returned to duty on or about September 15, 1862. Promoted to Corporal in May, 1863-April, 1864. Hospitalized at Richmond, Virginia, June 3, 1864, with a gunshot wound of the shoulder. Place and date wounded not reported. Furloughed on June 6, 1864. Returned to duty and was promoted to Sergeant prior to January 1, 1865. No further records.

GRIFFIN, ALEXANDER, Private
Previously served in Company G, 17th Regiment N.C. Troops (1st Organization). Transferred to this company at age 20 on or about October 8, 1861. Discharged prior to January 1, 1862, by reason of disability.

GRIFFIN, JOSHUA H., Corporal
Previously served as Private in Company F, 17th Regiment N.C. Troops (1st Organization). Enlisted in this company in Martin County at age 27, October 8, 1862, for the war. Mustered in as Private. Promoted to Corporal in May-December, 1864. Hospitalized at Danville, Virginia, on or about June 4, 1864, with a gunshot wound of the arm. Place and date wounded not reported. Furloughed on June 6, 1864. Returned to duty prior to January 1, 1865. No further records.

GRIFFIN, WILLIAM JACKSON, Private
Previously served in Company F, 17th Regiment N.C. Troops (1st Organization). Transferred to this company at age 20 on or about October 8, 1861. Present or accounted for until captured at Roanoke Island on February 8, 1862. Paroled at Elizabeth City on February 21, 1862. Returned to duty on or about September 15, 1862. Wounded in the right shoulder at Drewry's Bluff, Virginia, May 16, 1864. Furloughed for sixty days on July 20, 1864. Returned to duty prior to December 10, 1864, when he was captured at Jamesville, Virginia. Confined at Point Lookout, Maryland, December 27, 1864. Paroled on or about February 10, 1865, and transferred to Cox's Wharf, James River, Virginia, where he was received on February 14-15, 1865, for exchange. Discharged on March 14, 1865, by reason of "anchylosis of right shoulder joint" resulting from gunshot wounds received at Drewry's Bluff.

GURGANUS, MAJOR, Private
Previously served in Company G, 17th Regiment N.C. Troops (1st Organization). Transferred to this company at age 22 on or about October 8, 1861. Present or accounted for through April, 1864. Died prior to December 18, 1864. Place and cause of death not reported.

GURGANUS, OUTLAW, Private
Previously served in Company G, 17th Regiment N.C. Troops (1st Organization). Transferred to this company at age 30 on or about October 8, 1861. Present or accounted for until captured at Roanoke Island on February 8, 1862. Paroled at Elizabeth City on February 21, 1862. Returned to duty on or about September 15, 1862. Present or accounted for through December, 1864.

HARDISON, GEORGE W., Private
Resided in Martin County where he enlisted at age 28, October 8, 1861. Discharged on March 10, 1863, by reason of disability.

HARDY, WILLIAM R., Private
Born in Edgecombe County and resided in Martin County where he enlisted at age 18, October 8, 1861. Present or accounted for until captured at Roanoke Island on February 8, 1862. Paroled at Elizabeth City on February 21, 1862. Died at Elizabeth City on February 23, 1862. Cause of death not reported.

HARRELL, BENJAMIN T., Private
Previously served in Company G, 17th Regiment N.C. Troops (1st Organization). Transferred to this company at age 21, on or about October 8, 1861. Mustered in as Private. Present or accounted for until captured at Roanoke Island on February 8, 1862. Paroled at Elizabeth City on February 21, 1862. Promoted to Corporal on October 8, 1862. Reduced to ranks in May, 1863-April, 1864. Captured at or near Globe Tavern, Virginia, on or about August 19, 1864. Confined at Point Lookout, Maryland, August 22, 1864. Paroled and transferred to Boulware's Wharf, James River, Virginia, where he was received on March 16, 1865, for exchange.

HARRELL, GEORGE S., Private
Previously served in Company G, 17th Regiment N.C. Troops (1st Organization). Transferred to this company subsequent to March 20, 1862. First listed in the records of this company in January-February, 1863. Hospitalized at Richmond, Virginia, October 2, 1864, with a gunshot wound of the hand. Place and date wounded not reported. Furloughed for thirty days on October 13, 1864. Died on January 25, 1865, of wounds. Place of death not reported.

HARRELL, WILLIAM E., Corporal
Previously served as Private in Company G, 17th Regiment N.C. Troops (1st Organization). Transferred to this company at age 22 on or about October 8, 1861. Mustered in as Private. Present or accounted for until captured at Roanoke Island on February 8, 1862. Paroled at Elizabeth City on February 21, 1862. Returned to duty on or about September 15, 1862. Promoted to Corporal on October 8, 1862. Killed at Fort Wagner, Charleston, South Carolina, July 18, 1863.

HARRISON, GEORGE, Private
Resided in Martin County and enlisted at Roanoke Island on December 31, 1861. Present or accounted for until captured at Roanoke Island on February 8, 1862. Paroled at Elizabeth City on February 21, 1862. Returned to duty on or about September 15, 1862. Present or accounted for through March 13, 1865. Paroled at Charlotte on May 3, 1865.

HARRISON, RODMAN, Private
Previously served in Company G, 17th Regiment N.C. Troops (1st Organization). Transferred to this company at age 43 on or about October 8, 1861. Present or accounted for until captured at Roanoke Island on February 8, 1862. Paroled at Elizabeth City on February 21, 1862. Discharged on October 8, 1862, by reason of being overage. Later served in Company H, 17th Regiment N.C. Troops (2nd Organization).

HESTERS, JOHN T., Private
Previously served in 1st Company D, 12th Regiment N.C. Troops (2nd Regiment N.C. Volunteers). Enlisted in this company on December 31, 1861. Transferred to

Company A of this regiment on or about January 14, 1862.

HOARD, JAMES R., Corporal

Previously served as Private in Company G, 17th Regiment N.C. Troops (1st Organization). Transferred to this company at age 23 on or about October 8, 1861. Mustered in as Private. Promoted to Corporal on February 23, 1863. Captured at Cold Harbor, Virginia, June 1, 1864. Confined at Point Lookout, Maryland, June 11, 1864. Transferred to Elmira, New York, July 12, 1864. Paroled at Elmira on March 14, 1865, and transferred to Boulware's Wharf, James River, Virginia, where he was received March 18-21, 1865, for exchange.

HOARD, WYLIE J., Private

Resided in Martin County where he enlisted at age 17, October 8, 1861. Captured at Cold Harbor, Virginia, June 1, 1864. Confined at Point Lookout, Maryland, June 11, 1864. Transferred to Elmira, New York, July 12, 1864. Released at Elmira on July 11, 1865, after taking the Oath of Allegiance.

HOWE, P. T., Private

Place and date of enlistment not reported. Captured at or near Globe Tavern, Virginia, August 19, 1864. Sent to City Point, Virginia, August 20, 1864. No further records.

HUFF, SIMMONS B., Private

Previously served in Company G, 17th Regiment N.C. Troops (1st Organization). Transferred to this company at age 20 on or about October 8, 1861. Transferred to Company E, 17th Regiment N.C. Troops (2nd Organization), March 10, 1862.

HURST, JAMES, Private

Resided in Martin County where he enlisted at age 16, October 8, 1861. Present or accounted for until captured at Roanoke Island on February 8, 1862. Paroled at Elizabeth City on February 21, 1862. Died on March 27, 1862. Place and cause of death not reported.

HUTCHINS, JOSHUA H. T., Private

Previously served in Company G, 17th Regiment N.C. Troops (1st Organization). Transferred to this company at age 25 on or about October 8, 1861. Present or accounted for until captured at Roanoke Island on February 8, 1862. Paroled at Elizabeth City on February 21, 1862. Returned to duty on or about September 15, 1862. Hospitalized at Danville, Virginia, on or about June 4, 1864, with a gunshot wound of the hand. Place and date wounded not reported. Furloughed on June 6, 1864. Returned to duty prior to January 1, 1865. Hospitalized at Raleigh on March 11, 1865, with a gunshot wound of the head. Place and date wounded not reported.

JENKINS, J. L., Private

Enlisted in Martin County on February 29, 1864, for the war. Present or accounted for through March 26, 1865.

JENKINS, JAMES R., Private

Resided in Martin County where he enlisted at age 28, October 8, 1862, for the war. Present or accounted for through February 14, 1865.

JENKINS, JAMES W., Private

Resided in Martin County where he enlisted at age 19, October 8, 1862, for the war. Present or accounted for through December, 1864.

JOHNSON, MARTIN VAN BUREN, Private

Previously served in Company G, 17th Regiment N.C. Troops (1st Organization). Transferred to this company at age 21 on or about October 8, 1861. Present or accounted for until captured at Roanoke Island on February 8, 1862. Paroled at Elizabeth City on February 21, 1862. Returned to duty on or about September 15, 1862. Present or accounted for through December, 1864.

KNIGHT, WILLIAM B., Sergeant

Previously served as Private in Company F, 17th Regiment N.C. Troops (1st Organization). Transferred to this company at age 20 on or about October 8, 1861. Mustered in as Corporal. Present or accounted for until captured at Roanoke Island on February 8, 1862. Paroled at Elizabeth City on February 21, 1862. Returned to duty on or about September 15, 1862. Promoted to Sergeant in May, 1863-April, 1864. Hospitalized at Richmond, Virginia, October 1, 1864, with a gunshot wound of the left leg. Furloughed for forty days on October 19, 1864. Returned to duty prior to January 1, 1865. No further records.

LEE, THOMAS, Corporal

Resided in Martin County where he enlisted at age 40, October 8, 1861. Mustered in as Corporal. Present or accounted for until captured at Roanoke Island on February 8, 1862. Paroled at Elizabeth City on February 21, 1862. Discharged on October 8, 1862. Reason discharged not reported.

LEGGETT, STANLEY, Private

Previously served in Company G, 17th Regiment N.C. Troops (1st Organization). Transferred to this company at age 31 on or about October 8, 1861. Present or accounted for until captured at Roanoke Island on February 8, 1862. Paroled at Elizabeth City on February 21, 1862. Returned to duty on or about September 15, 1862. Present or accounted for through December, 1864.

LEWIS, COUNSIL, Private

Previously served in 1st Company D, 12th Regiment N.C. Troops (2nd Regiment N.C. Volunteers). Enlisted in this company at Roanoke Island on December 31, 1861. Transferred to Company A of this regiment on or about January 14, 1862.

LILLY, EBENEZER, Jr., Private

Previously served in Company F, 17th Regiment N.C. Troops (1st Organization). Transferred to this company at age 24 on or about October 8, 1861. Discharged on or about December 31, 1861, by reason of disability.

LILLY, HENRY F., Private

Previously served in Company F, 17th Regiment N.C. Troops (1st Organization). Transferred to this company at age 30 on or about October 8, 1861. Present or accounted for until captured at Roanoke Island on February 8, 1862. Paroled at Elizabeth City on February 21, 1862. Returned to duty on or about September 15, 1862. Present or accounted for through December, 1864.

LILLY, JOSEPH S., Private

Resided in Martin County where he enlisted at age 18, October 8, 1862, for the war. Captured at Cold Harbor, Virginia, June 1, 1864. Confined at Point Lookout, Maryland, June 11, 1864. Transferred to Elmira, New York, July 12, 1864. Died at Elmira on November 24, 1864, of "pneumonia."

LILLY, McGLORA, Private

Enlisted in Martin County on October 8, 1861. Present or accounted for through December, 1861. Died on an unspecified date. Place and cause of death not reported.

LYNCH, JAMES R., Private

Born in Martin County where he resided as a carpenter prior to enlisting in Martin County at age 33, October 8, 1861. Transferred to Company F, 17th Regiment N.C. Troops (2nd Organization), on or about May 1, 1862.

McFERRELL, ———, Private

Resided in New Hanover County where he enlisted at age 25, July 1, 1863, for the war. Transferred to the C.S. Navy prior to May 1, 1864.

MANNING, WALLACE, Private

Resided in Martin County where he enlisted at age 34, October 8, 1862, for the war. Captured at Cold Harbor, Virginia, June 1, 1864. Confined at Point Lookout, Maryland, June 11, 1864. Transferred to Elmira, New York, July 12, 1864. Killed in a railroad accident near Shohola, Pennsylvania, July 15, 1864, while en route to Elmira.

MARLET, WILLIAM, Private

Resided in Martin County and enlisted at age 18, December 29, 1863, for the war. No further records.

MARTIN, JESSE, Private

Resided in Martin County where he enlisted at age 54, October 8, 1861. Present or accounted for until captured at Roanoke Island on February 8, 1862. Paroled at Elizabeth City on February 21, 1862. Discharged on October 8, 1862. Reason discharged not reported.

MARTIN, WILLIAM G., Private

Previously served in Company G, 17th Regiment N.C. Troops (1st Organization). Transferred to this company at age 22 on or about October 8, 1861. Present or accounted for until captured at Roanoke Island on February 8, 1862. Paroled at Elizabeth City on February 21, 1862. Returned to duty on or about September 15, 1862. Died "in hospital" subsequent to April 30, 1864. Place and cause of death not reported.

MEEKS, MERRIMAN, Private

Previously served in Company G, 17th Regiment N.C. Troops (1st Organization). Transferred to this company at age 26 on or about October 8, 1861. Present or accounted for until captured at Roanoke Island on February 8, 1862. Paroled at Elizabeth City on February 21, 1862. Returned to duty on or about September 15, 1862. Present or accounted for through April, 1864. Died prior to December 18, 1864. Place and cause of death not reported.

MILLER, JESSE, Private

Resided in Orange County and enlisted at James Island, Charleston, South Carolina, at age 30, March 13, 1863, for the war. Hospitalized at Raleigh on January 18,

1865, with pneumonia and chronic diarrhoea. Furloughed for sixty days on February 20, 1865. Paroled at Greensboro on May 3, 1865.

MIZZELL, LUKE W., Musician

Born in Martin County where he resided as a farmer prior to enlisting in Martin County at age 22, October 8, 1861. Mustered in as Private. Promoted to Musician (Fifer) prior to January 1, 1862. Present or accounted for until captured at Roanoke Island on February 8, 1862. Paroled at Elizabeth City on February 21, 1862. Returned to duty on or about September 15, 1862. Reduced to ranks prior to March 1, 1863. Promoted to Musician in May, 1863-April, 1864. Captured at or near Globe Tavern, Virginia, August 19, 1864. Confined at Point Lookout, Maryland, August 22, 1864. Released at Point Lookout on October 15, 1864, after joining the U.S. Army. Assigned to Company B, 4th Regiment U.S. Volunteer Infantry.

MOORE, JOHN W., Private

Resided in Martin County where he enlisted at age 24, October 8, 1861. Present or accounted for until captured at Roanoke Island on February 8, 1862. Paroled at Elizabeth City on February 21, 1862. Company records do not indicate whether he returned to duty. Discharged on January 12, 1863, by reason of disability.

NELSON, GEORGE W., Private

Enlisted in Martin County on January 4, 1864, for the war. Present or accounted for through December, 1864.

NEWBERRY, ALPHRED L., Private

Resided in Martin County where he enlisted at age 27, October 8, 1861. Present or accounted for through July 8, 1862. Company records indicate he was transferred to the 17th Regiment N.C. Troops (2nd Organization) on an unspecified date; however, records of the 17th Regiment (2nd Organization) do not indicate that he served therein. No further records.

PAGE, DAWSON, Private

Previously served in Company G, 17th Regiment N.C. Troops (1st Organization). Transferred to this company at age 23 on or about October 8, 1861. Present or accounted for until captured at Roanoke Island on February 8, 1862. Paroled at Elizabeth City on February 21, 1862. Returned to duty on or about September 15, 1862. Present or accounted for through December, 1864.

PAGE, JAMES, Private

Resided in Martin County and enlisted at Roanoke Island on December 31, 1861. Captured at Roanoke Island on February 8, 1862. Paroled at Elizabeth City on February 21, 1862. Company records indicate he was transferred to the 17th Regiment N.C. Troops (2nd Organization) on an unspecified date. [May have served in Company F, 17th Regiment N.C. Troops (2nd Organization), under the name of Private James R. Page.]

PAGE, JOHN A., Private

Resided in Martin County where he enlisted at age 32, October 8, 1862, for the war. Died in hospital at Fayetteville on January 9, 1865, of "pneumonia typh[oid]."

PAGE, TURNER, Private

Resided in Martin County where he enlisted at age 45,

October 8, 1861. Died at Roanoke Island on or about December 30, 1861. Cause of death not reported.

PARKER, DAVID, Private

Previously served in Company G, 17th Regiment N.C. Troops (1st Organization). Transferred to this company at age 28 on or about October 8, 1861. Present or accounted for until captured at Roanoke Island on February 8, 1862. Paroled at Elizabeth City on February 21, 1862. Returned to duty on an unspecified date. Wounded in the left side and captured at Fort Harrison, Virginia, September 30, 1864. Hospitalized at Fort Monroe, Virginia. "Escaped" on January 6, 1865. Recaptured on an unspecified date and was confined at Fort Monroe on January 27, 1865. Transferred to Newport News, Virginia, where he arrived on May 1, 1865. Released on June 30, 1865, after taking the Oath of Allegiance.

PEEL, JOHN EDWARD, Private

Previously served as Private in Company F, 17th Regiment N.C. Troops (1st Organization). Transferred to this company on or about October 8, 1861. Mustered in as Sergeant. Reduced to ranks in May, 1863-April, 1864. Captured at Williamston on December 10, 1864. Confined at Point Lookout, Maryland, December 27, 1864. Released on June 16, 1865, after taking the Oath of Allegiance.

PERRY, JAMES R., Private

Previously served in Company F, 17th Regiment N.C. Troops (1st Organization). Transferred to this company at age 19 on or about October 8, 1861. Present or accounted for until captured at Roanoke Island on February 8, 1862. Paroled at Elizabeth City on February 21, 1862. Returned to duty on or about September 15, 1862. Present or accounted for through December, 1864.

PERRY, SIMON S., Sergeant

Resided in Martin County where he enlisted at age 31, October 8, 1861. Mustered in as Private. Present or accounted for until captured at Roanoke Island on February 8, 1862. Paroled at Elizabeth City on February 21, 1862. Returned to duty on or about September 15, 1862. Promoted to Sergeant on June 7, 1863. Wounded at Fort Wagner, Charleston, South Carolina, July 18, 1863. Returned to duty on an unspecified date. Appointed Ensign (1st Lieutenant) on April 21, 1864, and transferred to the Field and Staff of this regiment.

PRICE, JOHN D., Corporal

Resided in Martin County where he enlisted at age 29, October 8, 1861. Mustered in as Private. Present or accounted for until captured at Roanoke Island on February 8, 1862. Paroled at Elizabeth City on February 21, 1862. Returned to duty on or about September 15, 1862. Promoted to Corporal in May, 1863-April, 1864. Hospitalized at Richmond, Virginia, May 16, 1864, with a gunshot wound of the right foot. Place and date wounded not reported. Returned to duty prior to January 1, 1865. No further records.

PUGH, JOSIAH, Private

Resided in Martin County where he enlisted at age 43, October 8, 1861. Discharged on December 31, 1861. Reason discharged not reported.

RAWLS, JAMES HENRY, Private

Previously served in Company G, 17th Regiment N.C. Troops (1st Organization). Transferred to this company at age 20 on or about October 8, 1861. Present or accounted for until captured at Roanoke Island on February 8, 1862. Paroled at Elizabeth City on February 21, 1862. Returned to duty on or about September 15, 1862. Hospitalized at Williamsburg[?], Virginia, May 20, 1864, with a gunshot wound. Place and date wounded not reported. Furloughed on June 6, 1864. Returned to duty prior to January 1, 1865. No further records.

RAWLS, KENNETH J., Private

Resided in Martin County where he enlisted at age 27, October 8, 1861. Present or accounted for until captured at Roanoke Island on February 8, 1862. Paroled at Elizabeth City on February 21, 1862. No further records. [May have served later in Company F, 17th Regiment N.C. Troops (2nd Organization).]

RAWLS, WILLIAM, Private

Previously served in Company G, 17th Regiment N.C. Troops (1st Organization). Transferred to this company at age 24 on or about October 8, 1861. Present or accounted for until captured at Roanoke Island on February 8, 1862. Paroled at Elizabeth City on February 21, 1862. Returned to duty on or about September 15, 1862. Transferred to the Engineering Corps at Wilmington on or about August 3, 1863.

REDDICK, WILLIAM H., Private

Resided in Martin County where he enlisted at age 18, October 8, 1861. Present or accounted for until captured at Roanoke Island on February 8, 1862. Paroled at Elizabeth City on February 21, 1862. Died on February 25, 1862. Place and cause of death not reported.

ROBERSON, JESSE, Private

Enlisted in Martin County on March 8, 1864, for the war. Hospitalized at Raleigh on March 11, 1865, with a gunshot wound of the left arm (amputated). Place and date wounded not reported. Furloughed for sixty days on March 27, 1865.

ROBERSON, WYLIE, Private

Resided in Martin County where he enlisted at age 48, October 8, 1861. Captured at Fort Harrison, Virginia, September 30, 1864. Confined at Point Lookout, Maryland, October 5, 1864. Paroled at Point Lookout on or about February 13, 1865, and transferred to Cox's Wharf, James River, Virginia, where he was received February 14-15, 1865, for exchange.

ROBINSON, WILLIAM E., Private

Born in Martin County where he resided as a farmer prior to enlisting in Martin County at age 15, October 8, 1861. Present or accounted for until captured at Roanoke Island on February 8, 1862. Paroled at Elizabeth City on February 21, 1862. Discharged on October 8, 1862. Reason discharged not reported. Later served in Company K, 1st Regiment N.C. Junior Reserves.

ROGERSON, CALVIN, Private

Resided in Martin County where he enlisted at age 29, October 8, 1861. Died at Roanoke Island in January, 1862, of disease.

SCOTT, WILLIAM, Private
Previously served in Company G, 17th Regiment N.C. Troops (1st Organization). Transferred to this company at age 48 on or about October 8, 1861. Present or accounted for until captured at Roanoke Island on February 8, 1862. Paroled at Elizabeth City on February 21, 1862. Discharged on October 8, 1862. Reason discharged not reported. Died prior to November 18, 1863. Place and cause of death not reported.

STALLS, JOHN, Private
Resided in Martin County where he enlisted at age 41, October 8, 1861. Present or accounted for until captured at Roanoke Island on February 8, 1862. Paroled at Elizabeth City on February 21, 1862. Discharged on an unspecified date. Reason discharged not reported. Reenlisted in the company on July 21, 1863, for the war. Present or accounted for through December, 1864.

STATON, BAKER, Private,
Previously served in Company G, 17th Regiment N.C. Troops (1st Organization). Transferred to this company at age 23 on or about October 8, 1861. Present or accounted for until captured at Roanoke Island on February 8, 1862. Paroled at Elizabeth City on February 21, 1862. Died on March 10, 1862. Place and cause of death not reported.

STEPHENSON, JOHN B., Private
Resided in Martin County where he enlisted at age 19, October 8, 1861. Present or accounted for until captured at Roanoke Island on February 8, 1862. Paroled at Elizabeth City on February 21, 1862. Died on March 12, 1862, of disease. Place of death not reported.

TUNSTALL, PERCY R., Sergeant
Previously served as Private in Company G, 17th Regiment N.C. Troops (1st Organization). Transferred to this company at age 16 on or about October 8, 1861. Mustered in as Corporal. Reduced to ranks on February 23, 1863. Promoted to Sergeant in May-December, 1864. Captured at Cold Harbor, Virginia, June 1, 1864. Confined at Point Lookout, Maryland, June 11, 1864. Transferred to Elmira, New York, July 12, 1864. Paroled at Elmira on March 10, 1865, and transferred to Boulware's Wharf, James River, Virginia, where he was received on March 15, 1865, for exchange.

WADSWORTH, JAMES WILLIAM, Private
Previously served in Company G, 17th Regiment N.C. Troops (1st Organization). Transferred to this company at age 39 on or about October 8, 1861. Present or accounted for until wounded in the lungs and captured at Roanoke Island on February 8, 1862. Paroled at Elizabeth City on February 21, 1862. Died on February 24, 1862, of wounds. Place of death not reported.

WALTERS, E., Private
Place and date of enlistment not reported. Captured at Fort Harrison, Virginia, September 30, 1864. Sent to Fort Monroe, Virginia. Confined at Point Lookout, Maryland, January 14, 1865. Exchanged on February 10, 1865.

WARD, BENJAMIN C., Private
Born in Martin County where he resided as a farmer prior to enlisting in Martin County at age 31, October 8, 1861. Transferred to Company F, 17th Regiment N.C. Troops (2nd Organization), on or about May 5, 1862.

WARD, JAMES L., Private
Previously served in Company G, 17th Regiment N.C. Troops (1st Organization). Transferred to this company at age 23 on or about October 8, 1861. Present or accounted for until captured at Roanoke Island on February 8, 1862. Paroled at Elizabeth City on February 21, 1862. Returned to duty on or about September 15, 1862. Present or accounted for through December, 1864.

WARD, JOSEPH H., Private
Resided in Martin County where he enlisted at age 26, October 8, 1861. Present or accounted for until captured at Roanoke Island on February 8, 1862. Paroled at Elizabeth City on February 21, 1862. Returned to duty prior to May 1, 1863. Present or accounted for through December, 1864.

WARREN, HENRY W., Private
Previously served in Company G, 17th Regiment N.C. Troops (1st Organization). Transferred to this company at age 35 on or about October 8, 1861. Discharged on October 8, 1862. Reason discharged not reported.

WARREN, WILLIAM H., Private
Previously served in Company G, 17th Regiment N.C. Troops (1st Organization). Transferred to this company on or about October 8, 1861. Present or accounted for until captured at Roanoke Island on February 8, 1862. Paroled at Elizabeth City on February 21, 1862. No further records.

WATSON, ALEXANDER D., Private
Enlisted at Roanoke Island on December 31, 1861. Transferred to Company A of this regiment on or about January 14, 1862.

WEATHERSBEE, WILLIAM H., Private
Previously served in Company F, 17th Regiment N.C. Troops (1st Organization). Transferred to this company at age 21 on or about October 8, 1861. Discharged on November 22, 1862, by reason of "phthisis pulmonalis."

WEAVER, NOAH H., Private
Previously served in Company G, 17th Regiment N.C. Troops (1st Organization). Transferred to this company at age 27 on or about October 8, 1861. Present or accounted for until captured at Roanoke Island on February 8, 1862. Paroled at Elizabeth City on February 21, 1862. Returned to duty on or about September 15, 1862. Present or accounted for through April, 1864. Company records dated November-December, 1864, indicate that he was a prisoner of war; however, records of the Federal Provost Marshal do not substantiate that report. No further records.

WHICHARD, RANDOLPH, Private
Resided in Martin County where he enlisted at age 33, October 8, 1861. Present or accounted for until captured at Roanoke Island on February 8, 1862. Paroled at Elizabeth City on February 21, 1862. Reported present but sick in camp in January-February, 1863. Reported sick in hospital in March-April, 1863. Reported present for duty in March-April, 1864. Hospitalized at Richmond, Virginia, October 2, 1864, with remittent fever. Returned to duty on March 18, 1865. No further records.

WHITAKER, GREEN C., Private

Born in Beaufort County and resided in Martin County where he was by occupation a farmer prior to enlisting in Martin County at age 23, October 8, 1861. Present or accounted for until captured at Roanoke Island on February 8, 1862. Paroled at Elizabeth City on February 21, 1862. Discharged on November 22, 1862, by reason of "disease of the valves of the heart." [May have served later in Company F, 17th Regiment N.C. Troops (2nd Organization).]

WILLIAMS, HENRY R., Private

Previously served in Company G, 17th Regiment N.C. Troops (1st Organization). Transferred to this company at age 16, on or about October 8, 1861. Present or accounted for until captured at Roanoke Island on February 8, 1862. Paroled at Elizabeth City on February 21, 1862. Returned to duty on or about September 15, 1862. Present or accounted for through December, 1864.

WILLIAMS, JOHN R., Private

Previously served in Company A, 17th Regiment N.C. Troops (2nd Organization). Transferred to this company on January 1, 1863, in exchange for Private John D. Biggs. Hospitalized at Richmond, Virginia, May 16, 1864, with a gunshot wound. Place and date wounded not reported. Died in hospital at Richmond on May 20, 1864, of wounds.

WILLIAMS, JOSIAH, Private

Previously served in Company A, 17th Regiment N.C. Troops (2nd Organization). Transferred to this company on October 6, 1862, in exchange for Private Richard W. Clary. Present or accounted for through April, 1864. Company records dated November-December, 1864, indicate that he was a prisoner of war; however, records of the Federal Provost Marshal do not substantiate that report. No further records.

WILLIAMS, THOMAS, Private

Previously served in Company F, 17th Regiment N.C. Troops (1st Organization). Transferred to this company at age 22 on or about October 8, 1861. Present or accounted for until captured at Roanoke Island on February 8, 1862. Paroled at Elizabeth City on February 21, 1862. Returned to duty on or about September 15, 1862. Wounded in the right arm at or near Drewry's Bluff, Virginia, May 16, 1864. Hospitalized at Richmond, Virginia, where he died on June 14-15, 1864, of wounds.

COMPANY G

This company was raised in Hertford County and enlisted on September 12, 1861. It was then assigned to the 31st Regiment N.C. Troops and designated Company G. After joining the regiment the company functioned as a part of the regiment, and its history for the war period is reported as a part of the regimental history.

The information contained in the following roster of the company was compiled principally from company muster rolls for January-April, 1863; March-April, 1864; and November-December, 1864. No company muster rolls were found for September 12, 1861-December 31, 1862; May, 1863-February, 1864; May-October, 1864; or for the period after December, 1864. Valuable information was obtained from primary records such as the Roll of Honor,

discharge certificates, medical records, prisoner of war records, and pension applications. Secondary sources such as postwar rosters and histories, cemetery records, and records of the United Daughters of the Confederacy also provided useful information.

OFFICERS

CAPTAINS

PICOT, JULIAN

Resided in Hertford County and enlisted at age 30. Elected Captain on September 12, 1861. Captured at Roanoke Island on February 8, 1862. Paroled at Elizabeth City on February 21, 1862. Defeated for reelection when the regiment was reorganized on September 17, 1862.

PIPKIN, ISAAC

Resided in Hertford County and enlisted at age 26. Appointed 1st Lieutenant on September 12, 1861. Captured at Roanoke Island on February 8, 1862. Paroled at Elizabeth City on February 21, 1862. Promoted to Captain on or about September 17, 1862. Present or accounted for through December, 1864. Resigned on or about January 24, 1865. Reason he resigned not reported.

LIEUTENANTS

EVERETT, JOHN L., 3rd Lieutenant

Resided in Hertford County and enlisted at age 22, September 12, 1861. Mustered in as Private. Captured at Roanoke Island on February 8, 1862. Paroled at Elizabeth City on February 21, 1862. Appointed 3rd Lieutenant on or about September 17, 1862. Wounded at White Hall on December 16, 1862. Returned to duty prior to March 1, 1863. Captured at Fort Harrison, Virginia, September 30, 1864. Confined at Old Capitol Prison, Washington, D.C., October 6, 1864. Transferred to Fort Delaware, Delaware, October 21, 1864. Released on June 10, 1865, after taking the Oath of Allegiance.

GATLING, JOHN D., 2nd Lieutenant

Resided in Hertford County and enlisted at age 19, September 12, 1861. Mustered in as 1st Sergeant. Captured at Roanoke Island on February 8, 1862. Paroled at Elizabeth City on February 21, 1862. Appointed 2nd Lieutenant on or about September 17, 1862. Wounded in the arm at Drewry's Bluff, Virginia, May 16, 1864. Returned to duty on an unspecified date. Captured at Fort Harrison, Virginia, September 30, 1864. Confined at Old Capitol Prison, Washington, D.C., October 6, 1864. Transferred to Fort Delaware, Delaware, October 21, 1864. Released on June 17, 1865, after taking the Oath of Allegiance.

POOL, SIMON B., 1st Lieutenant

Resided in Hertford County and enlisted at age 29. Appointed 2nd Lieutenant on September 12, 1861. Captured at Roanoke Island on February 8, 1862. Paroled at Elizabeth City on February 21, 1862. Appointed 1st Lieutenant on or about September 17, 1862. Reported absent without leave in March-April, 1864. Dropped from the rolls of the company on June 6, 1864.

SLAUGHTER, JOHN A., 2nd Lieutenant

Resided in Hertford County and enlisted at age 25.

Appointed 2nd Lieutenant on September 12, 1861. Captured at Roanoke Island on February 8, 1862. Paroled at Elizabeth City on February 21, 1862. Defeated for reelection when the regiment was reorganized on September 17, 1862.

NONCOMMISSIONED OFFICERS AND PRIVATES

ADKINS, W. D., Corporal
Resided in Hertford County and enlisted at age 22, September 12, 1861. Mustered in as Corporal. Captured at Roanoke Island on February 8, 1862. Paroled at Elizabeth City on February 21, 1862. "Left the company at the reorganization" on September 17, 1862. [May have served later in Company A, 12th Battalion N.C. Cavalry.]

ASKEW, GEORGE W., Private
Resided in Hertford County and enlisted in Wake County at age 20, September 12, 1861. Captured at Roanoke Island on February 8, 1862. Paroled at Elizabeth City on February 21, 1862. Returned to duty on or about September 15, 1862. Present or accounted for through April, 1864. No further records.

BAILEY, JAMES A., Private
Resided in Hertford County and enlisted in Wake County at age 25, September 12, 1861. Captured at Roanoke Island on February 8, 1862. Paroled at Elizabeth City on February 21, 1862. Returned to duty on or about September 15, 1862. Present or accounted for through December, 1864.

BAKER, HENRY D., Private
Resided in Hertford County and enlisted in Wake County at age 20, September 12, 1861. Captured at Roanoke Island on February 8, 1862. Paroled at Elizabeth City on February 21, 1862. Returned to duty on or about September 15, 1862. Hospitalized at Richmond, Virginia, October 2, 1864, with a gunshot wound of the right shoulder. Place and date wounded not reported. Reported absent wounded or absent sick through December, 1864.

BAKER, JOHN W., Private
Resided in Hertford County and enlisted at Petersburg, Virginia, April 1, 1864, for the war. Captured at Cold Harbor, Virginia, on or about June 1, 1864. Confined at Point Lookout, Maryland, June 11, 1864. Transferred to Elmira, New York, July 12, 1864. Released at Elmira on July 11, 1865, after taking the Oath of Allegiance.

BAKER, RICHARD S., Corporal
Resided in Hertford County and enlisted in Wake County at age 18, September 12, 1861. Mustered in as Private. Captured at Roanoke Island on February 8, 1862. Paroled at Elizabeth City on February 21, 1862. Returned to duty on or about September 15, 1862. Promoted to Corporal in March, 1863-April, 1864. Wounded in the right cheek and captured at Cold Harbor, Virginia, on or about May 31, 1864. Hospitalized at Washington, D.C. Confined at Old Capitol Prison, Washington, February 5, 1865. Transferred to Elmira, New York, March 1, 1865. Released on June 30, 1865, after taking the Oath of Allegiance.

BARDEN, RICHARD H., Private
Resided in Hertford County and enlisted in Wake County at age 25, September 12, 1861. Captured at Roanoke Island on February 8, 1862. Paroled at Elizabeth City on February 21, 1862. Returned to duty on or about September 15, 1862. Present or accounted for through December, 1864.

BARNES, JOHN S., Private
Resided in Hertford County and enlisted in Wake County at age 16, September 15, 1862, for the war. Captured at Cold Harbor, Virginia, June 1, 1864. Confined at Point Lookout, Maryland, June 11, 1864. Transferred to Elmira, New York, July 12, 1864. Released at Elmira on July 7, 1865, after taking the Oath of Allegiance.

BARNES, SAMUEL, Private
Previously served in Company D, 17th Regiment N.C. Troops (1st Organization). Transferred to this company on October 18, 1861. Mustered in as Private. Captured at Roanoke Island on February 8, 1862. Paroled at Elizabeth City on February 21, 1862. Returned to duty on or about September 15, 1862. Appointed Musician prior to March 1, 1863. Reduced to ranks in May, 1863-April, 1864. Present or accounted for through December, 1864.

BARNES, WILLIAM H., Private
Previously served in Company C, 17th Regiment N.C. Troops (2nd Organization). Transferred to this company on or about February 1, 1863, in exchange for Private William H. Kiff. Hospitalized at Richmond, Virginia, May 16, 1864, with a gunshot wound of the left arm. Place and date wounded not reported. Returned to duty on an unspecified date. Captured at Fort Harrison, Virginia, September 30, 1864. Confined at Point Lookout, Maryland, October 5, 1864. Paroled at Point Lookout on or about March 17, 1865, and transferred to Boulware's Wharf, James River, Virginia, where he was received on March 19, 1865, for exchange.

BARRETTE, RICHARD A., Private
Resided in Hertford County and enlisted at age 22, September 12, 1861. Captured at Roanoke Island on February 8, 1862. Paroled at Elizabeth City on February 21, 1862. Returned to duty on or about September 15, 1862. Present or accounted for through December, 1864. Paroled subsequent to April 26, 1865.

BEAL, CRISPIAN B., Sergeant
Previously served as Private in Company D, 17th Regiment N.C. Troops (1st Organization). Transferred to this company on or about December 9, 1861. Mustered in as Private. Captured at Roanoke Island on February 8, 1862. Paroled at Elizabeth City on February 21, 1862. Promoted to Sergeant on September 15, 1862. Wounded at White Hall on December 16, 1862. Returned to duty prior to March 1, 1863. Promoted to Sergeant Major on October 1, 1863, and transferred to the Field and Staff of this regiment.

BEALE, ETHELRED W., Private
Resided in Hertford County where he enlisted at age 25, September 12, 1861. Captured at Roanoke Island on February 8, 1862. Paroled at Elizabeth City on February 21, 1862. Returned to duty on or about September 15, 1862. Present or accounted for through December,

1864.

BEALE, H. C., Private
Enlisted in Wake County on September 15, 1862, for the war. Hospitalized at Raleigh on February 23, 1865, with a gunshot wound of the left leg. Place and date wounded not reported. Returned to duty on March 6, 1865. No further records.

BLOW, BENJAMIN H., Private
Resided in Hertford County and enlisted at age 29, September 12, 1861. Captured at Roanoke Island on February 8, 1862. Paroled at Elizabeth City on February 21, 1862. Died at Norfolk, Virginia, March 5, 1862, of "pneumonia."

BLOW, RICHARD, Private
Resided in Hertford County and enlisted at age 24, September 12, 1861. Captured at Roanoke Island on February 8, 1862. Paroled at Elizabeth City on February 21, 1862. Returned to duty on or about September 15, 1862. Deserted on December 27, 1864. Captured by the enemy at Murfreesboro on April 5, 1865. Confined at Washington, D.C., April 12, 1865. Released on an unspecified date after taking the Oath of Allegiance.

BOGE, H., Private
Enlisted in Wake County on September 15, 1862, for the war. Reported absent without leave in January-February, 1863. Company records indicate he served as a cook. No further records.

BOWLES, JAMES, Private
Resided in Hertford County and enlisted at age 20, September 12, 1861. Captured at Roanoke Island on February 8, 1862. Paroled at Elizabeth City on February 21, 1862. Returned to duty on or about September 15, 1862. Present or accounted for through December, 1864.

BRETT, JOHN D., Private
Enlisted at Petersburg, Virginia, June 20, 1864, for the war. Captured at Fort Harrison, Virginia, September 30, 1864. Confined at Point Lookout, Maryland, October 5, 1864. Paroled on or about March 17, 1865, and transferred to Boulware's Wharf, James River, Virginia, where he was received on March 19, 1865, for exchange.

BRETT, M. C., Private
Enlisted at Petersburg, Virginia, June 20, 1864, for the war. Captured at Fort Harrison, Virginia, September 30, 1864. Confined at Point Lookout, Maryland, October 5, 1864. Paroled on or about March 17, 1865, and transferred to Boulware's Wharf, James River, Virginia, where he was received on March 19, 1865, for exchange.

BRETT, M. D., Private
Enlisted at Petersburg, Virginia, June 20, 1864, for the war. Captured at Fort Harrison, Virginia, September 30, 1864. Confined at Point Lookout, Maryland, October 5, 1864. Paroled at Point Lookout on or about March 17, 1865, and transferred to Boulware's Wharf, James River, Virginia, where he was received on March 19, 1865, for exchange.

BROWN, WILLIAM, Private
Resided in Hertford County and enlisted at age 23,

September 12, 1861. Captured at Roanoke Island on February 8, 1862. Paroled at Elizabeth City on February 21, 1862. Returned to duty on or about September 15, 1862. Captured at Fort Harrison, Virginia, September 30, 1864. Confined at Point Lookout, Maryland, October 5, 1864. Paroled at Point Lookout on or about March 17, 1865, and transferred to Boulware's Wharf, James River, Virginia, where he was received on March 19, 1865, for exchange.

CARROL, GEORGE WASHINGTON, Private
Enlisted at Petersburg, Virginia, May 20, 1864, for the war. Captured at Fort Harrison, Virginia, September 30, 1864. Confined at Point Lookout, Maryland, October 5, 1864. Paroled at Point Lookout on or about March 17, 1865, and transferred to Boulware's Wharf, James River, Virginia, where he was received on March 19, 1865, for exchange.

CARTER, JOHN, Private
Resided in Hertford County and enlisted at age 30, September 12, 1861. Discharged on or about September 17, 1862, "on account of age."

CHAPPELL, J. H., Private
Resided in Granville County and enlisted in Wake County at age 21, October 13, 1862, for the war. Deserted on December 27, 1864.

CHAPPELL, M. H., Private
Resided in Granville County and enlisted in Wake County at age 46, October 13, 1862, for the war as a substitute. Present or accounted for through December, 1864.

CLARK, J. J., Private
Previously served in Company K, 1st Regiment South Carolina Infantry (Butler's). Transferred to this company on November 25, 1863. Present or accounted for through April, 1864. No further records.

CLARK, JAMES D., Private
Resided in Hertford County and enlisted at age 19, September 12, 1861. Transferred to Company B, 3rd Battalion N.C. Light Artillery, April 12, 1862.

DARDAN, THOMAS, Private
Place and date of enlistment not reported. Captured at Roanoke Island on February 8, 1862. Paroled at Elizabeth City on February 21, 1862. No further records.

DARDEN, RICHARD F., Private
Born in Alabama and resided in Hertford County where he was by occupation a farmer prior to enlisting in Wake County at age 17, September 12, 1861. Captured at Roanoke Island on February 8, 1862. Paroled at Elizabeth City on February 21, 1862. Returned to duty on an unspecified date. Captured at Cold Harbor, Virginia, on or about May 31, 1864. Confined at Point Lookout, Maryland, June 11, 1864. Released on June 13, 1864, after joining the U.S. Army. Assigned to Company A, 1st Regiment U.S. Volunteer Infantry.

DOUGHTIE, JOHN, Private
Enlisted in Wake County on October 13, 1862, for the war. Present or accounted for through January 18, 1865.

DOUGHTIE, JOSEPH J., Private
Previously served in Company D, 17th Regiment N.C.

Troops (1st Organization). Transferred to this company on October 18, 1861. Captured at Roanoke Island on February 8, 1862. Paroled at Elizabeth City on February 21, 1862. Was apparently discharged on an unspecified date. Enlisted in Company A, 12th Battalion N.C. Cavalry, September 1, 1862. Reenlisted in this company on September 15, 1862, while listed as a deserter from the 12th Battalion N.C. Cavalry. Present or accounted for through June 20, 1864. No further records.

DOUGHTIE, THOMAS, Private
Resided in Hertford County and enlisted in Wake County at age 18, September 12, 1861. Captured at Roanoke Island on February 8, 1862. Paroled on an unspecified date. Returned to duty on or about September 15, 1862. Captured at Cold Harbor, Virginia, on or about June 1, 1864. Confined at Point Lookout, Maryland, June 11, 1864. Transferred to Elmira, New York, July 12, 1864. Paroled at Elmira on October 11, 1864, and transferred to Point Lookout. Died at Point Lookout on October 20, 1864, of "chronic diarrhoea."

DOUGHTIE, WILLIAM E., Private
Resided in Hertford County and enlisted in Wake County at age 18, September 12, 1861. Captured at Roanoke Island on February 8, 1862. Paroled at Elizabeth City on February 21, 1862. Returned to duty on or about September 15, 1862. Captured at Cold Harbor, Virginia, May 31-June 1, 1864. Confined at Point Lookout, Maryland, June 11, 1864. Transferred to Elmira, New York, July 12, 1864. Died at Elmira on March 12, 1865, of "chro[nic] diarr[hoea]."

DOWNING, STARKEY D., Private
Resided in Hertford County and enlisted at age 18, September 12, 1861. Transferred to Company D, 17th Regiment N.C. Troops (2nd Organization), April 12, 1862.

DRAKE, JAMES E., Private
Resided in Hertford County and enlisted at age 23, September 12, 1861. Captured at Roanoke Island on February 8, 1862. Paroled at Elizabeth City on February 21, 1862. Transferred to Company A, 13th Regiment Virginia Cavalry, September 19, 1862.

EDWARDS, J. R., Private
Enlisted in Wake County on September 15, 1862, for the war. Present or accounted for through February 23, 1865.

EDWARDS, JOHN, Private
Resided in Hertford County and enlisted at age 18, September 12, 1861. Died at Washington, North Carolina, November 27, 1861, of "typhoid fever."

EDWARDS, ROBERT J., Private
Resided in Hertford County and enlisted in Wake County at age 18, October 13, 1862, for the war. Present or accounted for through March 6, 1865.

EVANS, TROTMAN, Private
Resided in Hertford County and enlisted at age 18, September 12, 1861. Captured at Roanoke Island on February 8, 1862. Paroled at Elizabeth City on February 21, 1862. Returned to duty on or about September 15, 1862. Discharged on April 1, 1863, by reason of disability.

FERELL, JAMES P., Private
Enlisted in New Hanover County on July 21, 1863, for the war. Listed as a deserter in March-April, 1864, and dropped from the rolls of the company.

FLYTHE, A. M., Private
Resided in Hertford County and enlisted in Wake County at age 25, September 12, 1861. Captured at Roanoke Island on February 8, 1862. Paroled at Elizabeth City on February 21, 1862. Deserted on November 12, 1862.

FOWLER, BENJAMIN, Private
Resided in Hertford County and enlisted at age 17, October 13, 1862, for the war. Present or accounted for through December, 1864.

FOWLER, EVERETT, Private
Resided in Hertford County and enlisted at age 42, September 12, 1861. Discharged on November 18, 1862, by reason of being overage.

FRANCES, JOHN, Private
Enlisted at Richmond, Virginia, November 1, 1864, for the war. Present or accounted for through December, 1864.

FRANCIS, DAVIS, Private
Resided in Hertford County and enlisted at age 43, September 12, 1861. Present or accounted for through July 7, 1862. Discharged on an unspecified date by reason of being overage. Reenlisted in the company as a substitute on October 13, 1862, for the war. Hospitalized at Raleigh on March 10, 1865, with a gunshot wound of the left arm. Place and date wounded not reported. Transferred on March 20, 1865. No further records.

FURGASON, C. C., Sergeant
Resided in Hertford County and enlisted at age 18, September 12, 1861. Mustered in as Sergeant. Captured at Roanoke Island on February 8, 1862. Paroled at Elizabeth City on February 21, 1862. Returned to duty on or about September 15, 1862. Hospitalized at Danville, Virginia, June 4, 1864, with a gunshot wound of the face. Place and date wounded not reported. Returned to duty prior to January 1, 1865. Present or accounted for through February 25, 1865.

GRANT, JOHN A., Private
Resided in Hertford County and enlisted at age 19, September 12, 1861. Captured at Roanoke Island on February 8, 1862. Paroled at Elizabeth City on February 21, 1862. Returned to duty on or about September 15, 1862. Wounded at Fort Wagner, Charleston, South Carolina, July 18, 1863. Returned to duty prior to May 1, 1864. Present or accounted for through February 25, 1865.

HARRELL, A. C., Private
Resided in Hertford County and enlisted at age 17, September 12, 1861. Roll of Honor indicates that he never reported for duty; however, records of the Federal Provost Marshal indicate he was captured at Roanoke Island on February 8, 1862, and paroled at Elizabeth City on February 21, 1862. No further records.

HARRELL, GEORGE J., Private
Resided in Hertford County and enlisted at age 21,

September 12, 1861. Captured at Roanoke Island on February 8, 1862. Paroled at Elizabeth City on February 21, 1862. Returned to duty on or about September 15, 1862. Transferred to the C.S. Navy on December 30, 1863.

HARRELL, HENRY D., Corporal

Resided in Hertford County and enlisted in Wake County at age 18, September 12, 1861. Mustered in as Private. Captured at Roanoke Island on February 8, 1862. Paroled at Elizabeth City on February 21, 1862. Returned to duty on or about September 15, 1862. Promoted to Corporal on April 15, 1863. Hospitalized at Richmond, Virginia, May 17, 1864, with a gunshot wound of the right thigh. Place and date wounded not reported. Returned to duty prior to January 1, 1865. Present or accounted for through March 13, 1865. Paroled at Greensboro on April 28, 1865. [North Carolina pension records indicate he was wounded at Bermuda Hundred, Virginia, February 20, 1864.]

HARRELL, M. D., Private

Resided in Hertford County and enlisted at age 18, September 12, 1861. Wounded in the left shoulder and left leg and captured at Fort Harrison, Virginia, September 30, 1864. Left leg amputated. Hospitalized at Fort Monroe, Virginia, January 23, 1865. Confined at Camp Hamilton, Virginia, January 23, 1865. Confined at Point Lookout, Maryland, February 2, 1865. Paroled at Point Lookout on or about February 18, 1865, and transferred to Boulware's Wharf, James River, Virginia, where he was received February 20-21, 1865, for exchange.

HAYS, WILLIAM A., Sergeant

Resided in Hertford County and enlisted at age 18, September 12, 1861. Mustered in as Sergeant. Captured at Roanoke Island on February 8, 1862. Paroled at Elizabeth City on February 21, 1862. Returned to duty on or about September 15, 1862. Present or accounted for through January 20, 1865.

HOGGARD, T. W., Private

Resided in Hertford County and enlisted in Wake County at age 36, October 1, 1862, for the war. Hospitalized at Richmond, Virginia, June 3, 1864, with a gunshot wound of the face. Place and date wounded not reported. Furloughed on June 9, 1864. Reported absent without leave in November-December, 1864. [May have served previously in Company L, 1st Regiment N.C. Infantry (6 months, 1861).]

HOLLAND, G. J., Private

Enlisted at Petersburg, Virginia, June 20, 1864, for the war. Reported absent without leave in November-December, 1864.

HOLOMON, J. E., Corporal

Resided in Hertford County and enlisted at age 22, September 12, 1861. Mustered in as Corporal. Died on December 26, 1861, of "typhoid fever." Place of death not reported.

HOWELL, JAMES E., Private

Resided in Hertford County and enlisted at age 28, September 12, 1861. Present or accounted for through April, 1864. No further records.

HUSON, GEORGE W. C., Private

Previously served in Company D, 17th Regiment N.C.

Troops (1st Organization). Transferred to this company on December 9, 1861. Captured at Roanoke Island on February 8, 1862. Paroled at Elizabeth City on February 21, 1862. Returned to duty prior to March 8, 1863. Died at Charleston, South Carolina, April 10, 1863, of "typhoid fever."

JENKINS, J. E., Private

Resided in Hertford County and enlisted at age 19, September 12, 1861. Discharged on June 28, 1862, after providing a substitute.

JENKINS, THOMAS W., Sergeant

Resided in Hertford County and enlisted in Wake County at age 18, September 12, 1861. Mustered in as Private. Captured at Roanoke Island on February 8, 1862. Paroled at Elizabeth City on February 21, 1862. Promoted to Corporal on September 15, 1862. Promoted to Sergeant in May, 1863-April, 1864. Present or accounted for through February 24, 1865.

JOHNSON, JOSHUA, Private

Resided in Hertford County and enlisted at age 30, September 12, 1861. Captured at Roanoke Island on February 8, 1862. Paroled at Elizabeth City on February 21, 1862. Discharged on an unspecified date by reason of "old age."

JONES, JAMES F., Private

Resided in Hertford County and enlisted at age 20, September 12, 1861. Mustered in as Sergeant. Captured at Roanoke Island on February 8, 1862. Paroled at Elizabeth City on February 21, 1862. Returned to duty on or about September 15, 1862. Promoted to 1st Sergeant on April 1, 1863. Reduced to ranks prior to April 22, 1863, when he was transferred to an unspecified unit. [May have been transferred to a South Carolina unit.]

JONES, W. T., Private

Resided in Hertford County and enlisted at age 19, September 12, 1861. Died at Norfolk, Virginia, March 5, 1862, of "pneumonia."

JOYNER, R. T., Corporal

Resided in Hertford County and enlisted in Wake County at age 28, September 12, 1861. Mustered in as Private. Promoted to Corporal on September 15, 1862. Died on July 16, 1863. Place and cause of death not reported.

KIFF, WILLIAM H., Private

Resided in Hertford County and enlisted at age 26, October 1, 1862, for the war. Transferred to Company C, 17th Regiment N.C. Troops (2nd Organization), January 20, 1863, in exchange for Private William H. Barnes.

KNIGHT, J. J., Sergeant

Resided in Hertford County and enlisted at age 21, September 12, 1861. Mustered in as Corporal. Promoted to Sergeant in May, 1863-April, 1864. Present or accounted for through December, 1864. Paroled subsequent to April 26, 1865.

LANGLEY, H. P., Private

Resided in Edgecombe County and enlisted in Wake County at age 25, October 8, 1862, for the war. Captured at or near Globe Tavern, Virginia, August 19,

1864. Confined at Point Lookout, Maryland, August 22, 1864. Paroled at Point Lookout on January 17, 1865, and transferred to Boulware's Wharf, James River, Virginia, where he was received on January 21, 1865, for exchange.

LASSITER, B. B., Private
Resided in Hertford County and enlisted in Wake County at age 29, October 1, 1862, for the war. Present or accounted for through April, 1864. Reported absent without leave in November-December, 1864.

LAWRENCE, ANDREW, Private
Resided in Hertford County and enlisted at age 19, September 12, 1861. Captured at Roanoke Island on February 8, 1862. Paroled at Elizabeth City on February 21, 1862. Returned to duty on or about September 15, 1862. Wounded at Fort Wagner, Charleston, South Carolina, July 18, 1863. Died at or near Charleston on or about July 27, 1863, of wounds.

LEATHERWOOD, S., Private
Resided in Granville County and enlisted in Wake County at age 46, October 13, 1862, for the war as a substitute. Reported absent without leave in March-April, 1863. Listed as a deserter and dropped from the rolls of the company in March-April, 1864.

LIVERMAN, WILLIAM T., Private
Previously served in Company D, 17th Regiment N.C. Troops (1st Organization). Transferred to this company on November 20, 1861. Captured at Roanoke Island on February 8, 1862. Paroled at Elizabeth City on February 21, 1862. No further records.

LOYER, R. D., Private
Place and date of enlistment not reported. Captured at Roanoke Island on February 8, 1862. Paroled at Elizabeth City on February 21, 1862. No further records.

McFARLAND, WALTER, Musician
Resided in Hertford County and enlisted in Wake County at age 18, September 12, 1862. Mustered in as Private. Captured at Roanoke Island on February 8, 1862. Paroled at Elizabeth City on February 21, 1862. Returned to duty on or about September 15, 1862. Promoted to Musician prior to March 1, 1863. Present or accounted for through April, 1864. No further records.

MATTHEWS, SLADE B., Private
Resided in Hertford County and enlisted at age 40, September 12, 1861. Captured at Roanoke Island on February 8, 1862. Paroled at Elizabeth City on February 21, 1862. Discharged on September 15, 1862, under the provisions of the Conscription Act.

MERRITT, WILLIAM, Private
Resided in Granville County and enlisted in Wake County at age 46, October 13, 1862, for the war as a substitute. Captured at Cold Harbor, Virginia, June 1, 1864. Confined at Point Lookout, Maryland, June 11, 1864. Transferred to Elmira, New York, July 12, 1864. Died at Elmira on September 20, 1864, of "chronic diarrhoea."

MITCHELL, EDWARD D., Private
Previously served in Company D, 17th Regiment N.C. Troops (1st Organization). Transferred to this company

on or about December 9, 1861. Captured at Roanoke Island on February 8, 1862. Paroled at Elizabeth City on February 21, 1862. Returned to duty on or about September 15, 1862. Hospitalized at Raleigh on March 22, 1865, with a gunshot wound of the neck. Place and date wounded not reported. Died at Raleigh on March 26, 1865, of wounds.

MITCHELL, JAMES MADISON, Corporal
Previously served as Private in Company D, 17th Regiment N.C. Troops (1st Organization). Transferred to this company on November 20, 1861. Mustered in as Private. Captured at Roanoke Island on February 8, 1862. Paroled at Elizabeth City on February 21, 1862. Returned to duty on or about September 15, 1862. Promoted to Corporal in May, 1863-April, 1864. Hospitalized at Richmond, Virginia, June 13, 1864, with a gunshot wound of the back. Place and date wounded not reported. Furloughed for thirty days on June 29, 1864. Reported absent sick in November-December, 1864.

MITCHELL, W. JAMES, Private
Records of Company D, 17th Regiment N.C. Troops (1st Organization), indicate he was transferred to this company on December 9, 1861; however, records of this company do not indicate that he served herein. No further records.

MOLLOR, JOSEPH G., Private
Resided in Hertford County. Place and date of enlistment not reported. Paroled on April 30, 1865.

MUMFORD, JOHN, Private
Resided in Hertford County and enlisted at age 38, September 12, 1861. Discharged on September 15, 1862, under the provisions of the Conscription Act.

NETHERCUT, J. D., Private
Resided in Hertford County and enlisted at age 21, September 12, 1861. No further records.

NEWSOM, DAVID, Private
Resided in Hertford County and enlisted at age 19, September 12, 1861. Roll of Honor indicates he was wounded on an unspecified date. No further records.

NEWSOM, EDWARD D., Private
Enlisted in Wake County on October 13, 1862, for the war. Captured at Fort Harrison, Virginia, September 30, 1864. Confined at Point Lookout, Maryland, October 5, 1864. Paroled at Point Lookout on or about March 17, 1865, and transferred to Boulware's Wharf, James River, Virginia, where he was received on March 19, 1865, for exchange.

NEWSOM, LEANDER, Private
Resided in Hertford County and enlisted at age 18, September 12, 1861. Captured at Roanoke Island on February 8, 1862. Paroled at Elizabeth City on February 21, 1862. Returned to duty on or about September 15, 1862. Wounded at White Hall on December 16, 1862. Returned to duty prior to March 1, 1863. Hospitalized at Richmond, Virginia, on an unspecified date in 1864 with a gunshot wound of the shoulder. Place and date wounded not reported. Reported present for duty in March-April, 1864. Reported absent sick in November-December, 1864. No further records.

NOLLEY, EMMETT WOODVILLE, Private
Resided in Hertford County and enlisted at age 15, September 12, 1861. Captured at Roanoke Island on February 8, 1862. Paroled at Elizabeth City on February 21, 1862. Discharged on September 16, 1862, under the provisions of the Conscription Act. Enlisted in Company A, 15th Battalion N.C. Cavalry, September 8, 1863, for the war. Transferred to this company on March 29, 1864. Present or accounted for through December, 1864.

NOLLEY, MARCELLUS J., Sergeant
Previously served as Private in Company D, 17th Regiment N.C. Troops (1st Organization). Transferred to this company in November, 1861-March, 1862. Mustered in as Private. Captured at Roanoke Island on February 8, 1862. Paroled at Elizabeth City on February 21, 1862. Promoted to 1st Sergeant on September 15, 1862. Reduced to the rank of Sergeant on April 1, 1863. Present or accounted for through December, 1864. Paroled subsequent to April 26, 1865.

NORFLEET, CURL, Corporal
Resided in Hertford County and enlisted at age 28, September 12, 1861. Mustered in as Corporal. Roll of Honor indicates he was transferred to Company C, 17th Regiment N.C. Troops (2nd Organization), April 12, 1862; however, records of the 17th Regiment (2nd Organization) do not indicate that he served therein. No further records.

NORTHCUT, JAMES D., Private
Previously served in Company D, 17th Regiment N.C. Troops (1st Organization). Transferred to this company on December 9, 1861. Captured at Roanoke Island on February 8, 1862. Paroled at Elizabeth City on February 21, 1862. Returned to duty on or about September 15, 1862. Present or accounted for through December, 1864.

NOWELL, JONATHAN, Private
Previously served in Company B, 14th Regiment N.C. Troops (4th Regiment N.C. Volunteers). Enlisted in this company at Petersburg, Virginia, April 13, 1864, for the war. Present or accounted for through December, 1864.

OBERRY, H., Private
Enlisted at Petersburg, Virginia, June 20, 1864, for the war. Company records indicate he was captured at Fort Harrison, Virginia, September 30, 1864; however, records of the Federal Provost Marshal do not substantiate that report. No further records.

OUTLAW, WILLIAM R., Private
Previously served in Company D, 17th Regiment N.C. Troops (1st Organization). Transferred to this company on December 9, 1861. Deserted at White Hall on December 18, 1862.

OUTTAN, W. K., Private
Place and date of enlistment not reported. Captured at Roanoke Island on February 8, 1862. Paroled at Elizabeth City on February 21, 1862. No further records.

OVERMAN, BENJAMIN F., Private
Previously served in Company I, 17th Regiment N.C. Troops (1st Organization). Enlisted in this company subsequent to May 1, 1863, for the war. No further records.

PARKER, G. P., Private
Resided in Hertford County and enlisted in Wake County at age 40, September 12, 1861. Present or accounted for through December, 1864.

PARKER, GEORGE W., Private
Resided in Hertford County and enlisted at age 40, September 12, 1861. Captured at Roanoke Island on February 8, 1862. Paroled at Elizabeth City on February 21, 1862. Discharged on September 15, 1862, under the provisions of the Conscription Act.

PARRISH, CHARLTON, Private
Previously served in Company I, 17th Regiment N.C. Troops (1st Organization). Enlisted in this company on an unspecified date subsequent to May 1, 1863, for the war. No further records.

PEARCE, ISAAC T., Private
Previously served in Company D, 17th Regiment N.C. Troops (1st Organization). Transferred to this company in December, 1861-February, 1862. Captured at Roanoke Island on February 8, 1862. Paroled at Elizabeth City on February 21, 1862. Enlisted in Company C, 17th Regiment N.C. Troops (2nd Organization), March 24, 1862.

PERRY, JOHN A., Sergeant
Resided in Hertford County and enlisted at age 21, September 12, 1861. Mustered in as Sergeant. Captured at Roanoke Island on February 8, 1862. Paroled at Elizabeth City on February 21, 1862. Transferred to Company G, 19th Regiment N.C. Troops (2nd Regiment N.C. Cavalry), September 16, 1862.

PIERCE, RICHARD, Private
Resided in Hertford County and enlisted at age 18, September 12, 1861. Captured at Roanoke Island on February 8, 1862. Paroled at Elizabeth City on February 21, 1862. Returned to duty prior to May 1, 1863. Hospitalized at Richmond, Virginia, May 14, 1864, with a gunshot wound of the larynx. Place and date wounded not reported. Died in hospital at Richmond on May 16, 1864, of wounds.

PRUDEN, CHARLES, Private
Resided in Hertford County and enlisted at age 17, September 12, 1861. Discharged on September 15, 1862, under the provisions of the Conscription Act.

REID, JACOB, ———
Enlisted in Wake County on September 15, 1862, for the war. Reported on duty as a cook but also reported absent sick in January-February, 1863. Listed as a deserter and dropped from the rolls of the company in March-April, 1864.

REYNOLDS, THOMAS, ———
Free Negro. Enlisted at Ivor Station, Virginia, March 1, 1864, for the war. Served as a cook. Deserted on December 12, 1864.

RODGERSON, WILLIAM O., Private
Previously served in Company D, 17th Regiment N.C. Troops (1st Organization). Transferred to this company in November, 1861-March, 1862. Discharged on July 1, 1862. Reason discharged not reported. Later served in Company B, 12th Battalion N.C. Cavalry.

RONDTREE, JOHN, Private
Resided in Hertford County and enlisted at age 17, September 12, 1861. Discharged on November 25, 1862, by reason of disability.

SANDERFORD, EDWARD D., Private
Previously served in Company D, 17th Regiment N.C. Troops (1st Organization). Transferred to this company in November, 1861-February, 1862. Captured at Roanoke Island on February 8, 1862. Paroled at Elizabeth City on February 21, 1862. Returned to duty on an unspecified date. Wounded at Fort Wagner, Charleston, South Carolina, July 18, 1863. Returned to duty prior to May 1, 1864.

SEWELL, HENRY T., Private
Records of Company D, 17th Regiment N.C. Troops (1st Organization), indicate he was transferred to this company on an unspecified date; however, records of the 31st Regiment do not indicate that he served herein. No further records.

SEWELL, JOSEPH, Private
Resided in Hertford County and enlisted at age 18, September 12, 1861. Captured at Roanoke Island on February 8, 1862. Paroled at Elizabeth City on February 21, 1862. Died "at home" on June 12, 1863, of "typhoid fever."

SEWELL, WILLIAM J., Corporal
Previously served as Private in Company D, 17th Regiment N.C. Troops (1st Organization). Transferred to this company on November 20, 1861. Mustered in as Private. Captured at Roanoke Island on February 8, 1862. Paroled at Elizabeth City on February 21, 1862. Returned to duty on or about September 15, 1862. Promoted to Corporal in May, 1863-April, 1864. Hospitalized at Greensboro on March 6, 1865, with a gunshot wound. Place and date wounded not reported. No further records.

SHIPP, NATHANIEL M., Private
Previously served in Company I of this regiment. Transferred to this company on February 12, 1864. Transferred to Company I, 6th Regiment N.C. State Troops, in September-October, 1864.

STEWART, JOHN, ———
Free Negro. Enlisted in Wake County on September 15, 1862, for the war. Served as a cook. Present or accounted for through December, 1864.

STORY, JESSE, Private
Resided in Hertford County and enlisted at age 30, September 12, 1861. Captured at Roanoke Island on February 8, 1862. Paroled at Elizabeth City on February 21, 1862. Returned to duty on or about September 15, 1862. Present or accounted for through December, 1864.

TAYLOR, RICHARD J., Private
Enlisted at Petersburg, Virginia, April 1, 1864, for the war. Hospitalized at Richmond, Virginia, June 27, 1864, with a gunshot wound. Place and date wounded not reported. Furloughed for thirty days on July 30, 1864. Returned to duty on an unspecified date. Reported present for duty in November-December, 1864.

TAYLOR, W. F., Private
Resided in Hertford County and enlisted on September 12, 1861. No further records.

TAYLOR, WILLIAM EVERETT, Private
Resided in Hertford County and enlisted at age 20, September 12, 1861. Hospitalized at Richmond, Virginia, May 17, 1864, with a gunshot wound. Place and date wounded not reported. Furloughed for forty days on June 5, 1864. Returned to duty on an unspecified date. Reported present for duty in November-December, 1864.

TAYLOR, WILLIAM PATRICK, Corporal
Resided in Hertford County and enlisted at age 18, September 12, 1861. Mustered in as Corporal. Records of this company indicate he was appointed 2nd Lieutenant of Company A, 67th Regiment N.C. Troops, August 25, 1863; however, records of the 67th Regiment do not indicate that he served therein. No further records.

THOMPSON, GEORGE W., Private
Resided in Hertford or Chowan County and enlisted at age 25, September 12, 1861. Appointed 2nd Lieutenant on May 1, 1862, and transferred to Company A of this regiment.

TOULLER, B., Private
Place and date of enlistment not reported. Captured at Roanoke Island on February 8, 1862. Paroled at Elizabeth City on February 21, 1862. No further records.

TURNER, JOHN, Private
Resided in Gates County and enlisted at age 16, September 12, 1861. Captured at Roanoke Island on February 8, 1862. Paroled at Elizabeth City on February 21, 1862. Returned to duty on or about September 15, 1862. Wounded in the shoulder at or near Cold Harbor, Virginia, on or about June 1, 1864. Furloughed on June 6, 1864. Listed as a deserter on December 27, 1864. [North Carolina pension records indicate he was wounded at Fort Harrison, Virginia, and at Bentonville.]

VAUGHAN, H. THOMAS, Private
Resided in Hertford County and enlisted at age 19, September 12, 1861. Captured at Roanoke Island on February 8, 1862. Paroled at Elizabeth City on February 21, 1862. Returned to duty prior to May 1, 1863. Present or accounted for through December, 1864.

WALTERS, PHILIP, Private
Resided in Union County and enlisted at age 48, May 22, 1863, for the war as a substitute. Transferred to Company K, 1st Regiment South Carolina Infantry (Butler's), November 25, 1863.

WHITLEY, ELIJAH, Private
Resided in Hertford County and enlisted at age 35, September 12, 1861. Died at Wilmington on November 18, 1861, of "typhoid fever."

WHITLEY, EVERETT E., Private
Resided in Hertford County and enlisted in Wake County at age 32, September 12, 1861. Captured at Roanoke Island on February 8, 1862. Paroled at Elizabeth City on February 21, 1862. Discharged on January 10, 1863. Reason discharged not reported.

Reenlisted in the company on an unspecified date. Reported present for duty in November-December, 1864.

WIGGINS, BARTIMUS, Private

Previously served as Musician in Company D, 17th Regiment N.C. Troops (1st Organization). Transferred to this company on December 9, 1861. Mustered in as Private. Captured at Roanoke Island on February 8, 1862. Paroled at Elizabeth City on February 21, 1862. Discharged on September 18, 1862, by reason of the "expiration of his term of service."

WILLIAMS, BENJAMIN, Private

Previously served in Company D, 17th Regiment N.C. Troops (1st Organization). Transferred to this company in November-December, 1861. Died at Washington, North Carolina, December 24, 1861, of "typhoid fever."

WORTHINGTON, GEORGE W., Private

Previously served in Company D, 17th Regiment N.C. Troops (1st Organization). Transferred to this company on or about December 9, 1861. Captured at Roanoke Island on February 8, 1862. Paroled at Elizabeth City on February 21, 1862. Returned to duty on or about September 15, 1862. Detailed as a Hospital Steward prior to March 1, 1863, and transferred to the Field and Staff of this regiment. Promoted to Hospital Steward in May, 1863-April, 1864, and assigned to permanent duty with the Field and Staff.

COMPANY H

This company was raised in Wake County and enlisted at Raleigh on October 14, 1861. It was then assigned to the 31st Regiment N.C. Troops and designated Company H. After joining the regiment the company functioned as a part of the regiment, and its history for the war period is reported as a part of the regimental history.

The information contained in the following roster of the company was compiled principally from company muster rolls for October 14, 1861-February, 1862; January-April, 1863; March-April, 1864; and November-December, 1864. No company muster rolls were found for March-December, 1862; May, 1863-February, 1864; May-October, 1864; or for the period after December, 1864. Valuable information was obtained from primary records such as the Roll of Honor, discharge certificates, medical records, prisoner of war records, and pension applications. Secondary sources such as postwar rosters and histories, cemetery records, and records of the United Daughters of the Confederacy also provided useful information.

OFFICERS

CAPTAINS

JONES, WILLIS D.

Resided in Wake County where he enlisted at age 42. Appointed Captain on October 14, 1861. Present or accounted for until captured at Roanoke Island on February 8, 1862. Paroled at Elizabeth City on February 21, 1862. Defeated for reelection when the regiment was reorganized on September 17, 1862.

TODD, JAMES E.

Resided in Wake County where he enlisted at age 30, October 14, 1861. Mustered in as Corporal. Present or accounted for until captured at Roanoke Island on

February 8, 1862. Paroled at Elizabeth City on February 21, 1862. Appointed Captain on or about September 17, 1862. Resigned on December 15, 1863, by reason of "chronic hepatitis."

SMITH, JOHN W.

Resided in Wake County where he enlisted at age 21, October 14, 1861. Mustered in as 1st Sergeant. Present or accounted for until captured at Roanoke Island on February 8, 1862. Paroled at Elizabeth City on February 21, 1862. Appointed 1st Lieutenant on or about September 17, 1862. Wounded at White Hall on December 16, 1862. Returned to duty in March-April, 1863. Promoted to Captain on December 15, 1863. Wounded in the right arm at or near Fort Harrison, Virginia, September 30, 1864. Furloughed for sixty days on October 9, 1864. Returned to duty prior to January 1, 1865. Paroled subsequent to April 26, 1865.

LIEUTENANTS

DEBNAM, ROBERT W., 1st Lieutenant

Resided in Wake County where he enlisted at age 29, October 14, 1861. Mustered in as Sergeant. Appointed 2nd Lieutenant on or about September 17, 1862. Promoted to 1st Lieutenant in May, 1863-April, 1864. Present or accounted for through December, 1864.

DEBNAM, WALTER, 2nd Lieutenant

Born in Wake County where he resided as a farmer prior to enlisting at age 22. Appointed 2nd Lieutenant on October 14, 1861. Defeated for reelection when the regiment was reorganized on September 17, 1862. Later served as 1st Sergeant of Company D, McRae's Battalion N.C. Cavalry.

HORTON, ADONIRAM V., 3rd Lieutenant

Resided in Wake County where he enlisted at age 27, October 14, 1861. Mustered in as Corporal. Present or accounted for until captured at Roanoke Island on February 8, 1862. Paroled at Elizabeth City on February 21, 1862. Appointed 3rd Lieutenant on or about September 17, 1862. Hospitalized at Richmond, Virginia, May 15, 1864, with gunshot wounds of the neck and shoulder. Place and date wounded not reported. Died on May 30, 1864, of wounds.

NOWELL, J. R., 2nd Lieutenant

Resided in Wake County where he enlisted at age 20, October 14, 1861. Mustered in as Private. Promoted to 1st Sergeant on or about September 17, 1862. Appointed 2nd Lieutenant in May, 1863-September, 1864. Captured at Fort Harrison, Virginia, September 30, 1864. Confined at Old Capitol Prison, Washington, D.C., October 6, 1864. Transferred to Fort Delaware, Delaware, October 21, 1864. Released on June 17, 1865, after taking the Oath of Allegiance.

PERRY, FABIUS H., 1st Lieutenant

Resided in Wake County where he enlisted at age 28. Appointed 1st Lieutenant on October 14, 1861. Present or accounted for until captured at Roanoke Island on February 8, 1862. Paroled at Elizabeth City on February 21, 1862. Defeated for election as Captain on or about September 17, 1862, and was dropped from the rolls of the company.

PULLEY, WILLIAM, 3rd Lieutenant

Resided in Wake County where he enlisted at age 41.

Appointed 3rd Lieutenant on October 14, 1861. Defeated for reelection when the regiment was reorganized on September 17, 1862.

NONCOMMISSIONED OFFICERS AND PRIVATES

ALFORD, JOHN R., Private
Born in Franklin County and resided in Wake County where he was by occupation a farmer prior to enlisting in Wake County at age 46, October 14, 1861. Captured at Roanoke Island on February 8, 1862. Paroled at Elizabeth City on February 21, 1862. Discharged prior to March 1, 1863, by reason of being overage. Later served in Company A, 3rd Battalion N.C. Senior Reserves.

ALFORD, SIMON, Private
Born in Franklin County and resided in Wake County where he was by occupation a farmer prior to enlisting in Wake County at age 43, October 14, 1861. Captured at Roanoke Island on February 8, 1862. Paroled at Elizabeth City on February 21, 1862. Discharged prior to March 1, 1863, by reason of being overage. Later served in Company A, 3rd Battalion N.C. Senior Reserves.

ALLEN, JESSE, Private
Born in Wake County where he resided as a laborer prior to enlisting in Wake County at age 36, October 14, 1861. Captured at Roanoke Island on February 8, 1862. Paroled at Elizabeth City on February 21, 1862. Returned to duty on or about September 15, 1862. Killed at Fort Wagner, Charleston, South Carolina, July 18, 1863.

AMOS, RICHARD, Private
Enlisted at Camp Boyling. Enlistment date reported as April 30, 1861; however, he was not listed in the records of this company until August 31, 1864. Reported absent without leave in November-December, 1864. [May have served previously in Company A, 10th Regiment N.C. State Troops (1st Regiment N.C. Artillery).]

ANDERSON, HENRY H., 1st Sergeant
Resided in Wake County where he enlisted at age 19, October 14, 1861. Mustered in as Private. Captured at Roanoke Island on February 8, 1862. Paroled at Elizabeth City on February 21, 1862. Promoted to Sergeant on September 15, 1862. Wounded at White Hall on December 16, 1862. Returned to duty prior to March 1, 1863. Promoted to 1st Sergeant in May-December, 1864. Present or accounted for through December, 1864. Paroled at Greensboro on May 6, 1865.

ANDERSON, JAMES L., Private
Resided in Wake County where he enlisted on September 11, 1862, for the war. Wounded at White Hall on December 16, 1862. Returned to duty subsequent to April 30, 1863. Reported present for duty in March-April and November-December, 1864. Paroled at Greensboro on May 6, 1865.

ANDERSON, WILLIAM STATON, Private
Resided in Wake County where he enlisted at age 16,

October 14, 1861. Captured at Roanoke Island on February 8, 1862. Paroled at Elizabeth City on February 21, 1862. Discharged prior to March 1, 1863, under the provisions of the Conscription Act.

BARHAM, JASPER, Private
Resided in Wake County where he enlisted at age 35, October 14, 1861. Captured at Roanoke Island on February 8, 1862. Paroled at Elizabeth City on February 21, 1862. Discharged on September 15, 1862, by reason of being overage.

BARHAM, JOHN, Private
Resided in Wake County where he enlisted at age 24, October 14, 1861. Present or accounted for through April, 1863. Deserted prior to May 1, 1864.

BARHAM, T. J., Private
Resided in Wake or Johnston County and enlisted in Wake County at age 17, October 14, 1861. Captured at Roanoke Island on February 8, 1862. Paroled at Elizabeth City on February 21, 1862. Returned to duty on an unspecified date. Transferred to Company K of this regiment on June 13, 1863.

BEDDINGFIELD, A. R., Private
Resided in Wake County and enlisted at "High House" at age 25, October 14, 1861. Captured at Roanoke Island on February 8, 1862. Paroled at Elizabeth City on February 21, 1862. Returned to duty on or about September 15, 1862. Present or accounted for through December, 1864. Took the Oath of Allegiance at Raleigh on May 25, 1865.

BUNN, C. D., Corporal
Resided in Wake County where he enlisted at age 18, October 14, 1861. Mustered in as Private. Promoted to Corporal on September 16, 1863. Present or accounted for through December, 1864.

CHAMBLEE, A. T., Private
Resided in Wake County where he enlisted at age 16, October 14, 1861. Died in hospital at Washington, North Carolina, December 18-19, 1861. Cause of death not reported.

CHAMBLEE, ROBERT, Private
Resided in Wake County where he enlisted at age 23, October 14, 1861. Mustered in as Private. Captured at Roanoke Island on February 8, 1862. Paroled at Elizabeth City on February 21, 1862. Promoted to Corporal on September 15, 1862. Reduced to ranks on September 15, 1863. Captured at Cold Harbor, Virginia, June 1, 1864. Confined at Point Lookout, Maryland, June 11, 1864. Transferred to Elmira, New York, July 12, 1864. Released at Elmira on July 3, 1865, after taking the Oath of Allegiance.

CLIFTON, WILLIE, Private
Resided in Wake County where he enlisted at age 31, September 4, 1862, for the war. Present or accounted for through December, 1864.

CROWDER, ISAAC TURNER, Private
Resided in Wake County where he enlisted at age 26,

September 28, 1862, for the war. Deserted on December 27, 1864.

CROWDER, LUCANUS, Private
Resided in Wake County where he enlisted at age 20, October 13, 1862, for the war. Captured at Cold Harbor, Virginia, June 1, 1864. Confined at Point Lookout, Maryland, June 11, 1864. Transferred to Elmira, New York, July 12, 1864. Died at Elmira on or about October 4, 1864, of "chronic diarrhoea."

CROWDER, WILLIAM, Private
Resided in Wake County where he enlisted at age 37, October 13, 1862, for the war. Present or accounted for through April, 1864. No further records.

DAVIS, A. M., Private
Resided in Wake County where he enlisted at age 18, September 26, 1862, for the war. Died in hospital at Wilmington on or about January 20, 1863. Cause of death not reported.

DAVIS, HARDIE, Private
Resided in Wake County where he enlisted at age 18, September 25, 1862, for the war. Hospitalized at Wilmington on or about January 10, 1863, with pneumonia. Died in hospital at Wilmington on January 18-20, 1863.

DEBNAM, JOSEPH J., Private
Resided in Wake County where he enlisted at age 19, October 14, 1861. Captured at Roanoke Island on February 8, 1862. Paroled at Elizabeth City on February 21, 1862. Returned to duty on or about September 15, 1862. Present or accounted for through December, 1864. Name appears on a list of deserters datelined Greensboro, May 6, 1865, which states he was received at Raleigh on April 25, 1865.

DEBNAM, OMEGA T., Private
Resided in Wake County and was by occupation a farmer prior to enlisting in Wake County on November 20, 1864, for the war. Deserted on an unspecified date.

DEBNAM, THOMAS R., Private
Resided in Wake County where he enlisted at age 21, October 14, 1861. Mustered in as Private. Promoted to Sergeant on September 15, 1862. Reduced to ranks on July 1, 1863. No further records. [May have served later in Company E, 9th Regiment N.C. State Troops (1st Regiment N.C. Cavalry).]

EARP, Z. TAYLOR, ———
North Carolina pension records indicate that he served in this company.

EDDINS, SAM, ———
North Carolina pension records indicate that he served in this company.

ETHRIDGE, M., Private
Resided in Wake County where he enlisted at age 48, October 14, 1861. Discharged on September 15, 1862, by reason of being overage.

ETHRIDGE, MICHAEL, Private
Resided in Wake County where he enlisted at age 50,

October 14, 1861. Present or accounted for through April, 1864. No further records.

ETHRIDGE, MOSES A., Private
Resided in Wake County where he enlisted at age 29, September 4, 1862, for the war. Captured at Cold Harbor, Virginia, June 1, 1864. Confined at Point Lookout, Maryland, June 4, 1864. Transferred to Elmira, New York, July 12, 1864. Died at Elmira on March 13, 1865, of "pneumonia."

ETHRIDGE, WILLIAM H., Private
Resided in Wake County where he enlisted at age 27, October 4, 1862, for the war. Captured at Cold Harbor, Virginia, June 1, 1864. Confined at Point Lookout, Maryland, June 11, 1864. Transferred to Elmira, New York, July 12, 1864. Paroled at Elmira on October 11, 1864, and transferred to Venus Point, Savannah River, Georgia, where he was received on November 15, 1864, for exchange. Deserted on an unspecified date.

FAISON, JAMES W., Private
Resided in Wake County where he enlisted at age 29, January 3, 1863, for the war. Reported absent without leave in March-April, 1864.

FEENEY, PATRICK, Private
Previously served in 2nd Company H, 40th Regiment N.C. Troops (3rd Regiment N.C. Artillery). Transferred to this company in July, 1863. Deserted to the enemy on March 4, 1864. Took the Oath of Allegiance at Fort Monroe, Virginia, March 14, 1864. [Surname misspelled Feaney in Volume I of this series.]

FERRELL, HENRY, Private
Enlisted in Wake County on July 15, 1862, for the war. Deserted on November 15, 1864. [May have served also in Company F, Mallett's N.C. Battalion (Camp Guard).]

FERRELL, J. P., Private
Resided in Wake County where he enlisted at age 20, October 14, 1861. Captured at Roanoke Island on February 8, 1862. Paroled at Elizabeth City on February 21, 1862. Returned to duty on or about September 15, 1862. Died in hospital at Charleston, South Carolina, March 19, 1863. Cause of death not reported.

GARVER, S. H., Private
Place and date of enlistment not reported. Captured at Cold Harbor, Virginia, June 1, 1864. Confined at Point Lookout, Maryland, June 11, 1864. Transferred to Elmira, New York, July 12, 1864. Paroled at Elmira and transferred for exchange on October 11, 1864. No further records.

HAMILTON, ALDRIGE, Private
Resided in Wake County where he enlisted at age 37, October 14, 1861. Discharged on September 15, 1862, under the provisions of the Conscription Act.

HARP, C. T., Private
Place and date of enlistment not reported. Listed as a deserter in April, 1865.

HAYWOOD, J. T., Private
Resided in Wake County where he enlisted at age 18, October 14, 1861. Captured at Roanoke Island on

February 8, 1862. Paroled at Elizabeth City on February 21, 1862. Returned to duty on an unspecified date. Reported absent without leave from July 2, 1863, until February 1, 1864. Deserted on December 27, 1864.

HEARTSFIELD, F. J., Private
Enlisted in Wake County on September 20, 1864, for the war. Deserted on September 27, 1864.

HENDRICK, W. BADGER, Private
Enlisted at Charleston, South Carolina, November 15, 1863, for the war. Present or accounted for through December, 1864.

HERNDON, LESLIE, Private
Resided in Wake County where he enlisted at age 41, October 14, 1861. Captured at Roanoke Island on February 8, 1862. Paroled at Elizabeth City on February 21, 1862. Discharged on September 15, 1862, under the provisions of the Conscription Act.

HESTER, ABRAM, Private
Was by occupation a farmer prior to enlisting in Wake County on April 1, 1864, for the war. Reported absent without leave in November-December, 1864. Medical records dated June, 1864, give his age as 18. [North Carolina pension records indicate he was wounded in an unspecified battle.]

HESTER, T. H., Private
Enlisted in Wake County on January 18, 1864, for the war. Present or accounted for through February 18, 1865.

HICKS, BURTON, Private
Resided in Wake County where he enlisted at age 28, October 14, 1861. Captured at Roanoke Island on February 8, 1862. Paroled at Elizabeth City on February 21, 1862. Returned to duty on or about September 15, 1862. Deserted on or about May 15, 1863.

HICKS, H. B., Private
Resided in Wake County where he enlisted at age 20, October 14, 1861. Captured at Roanoke Island on February 8, 1862. Paroled at Elizabeth City on February 21, 1862. Died "at home" on April 22, 1862. Cause of death not reported.

HINDSBERRY, A., Private
Place and date of enlistment not reported. Captured at Roanoke Island on February 8, 1862. Paroled at Elizabeth City on February 21, 1862. No further records.

HODGE, H. C., Private
Enlisted in Wake County on June 20, 1864, for the war. Deserted on December 27, 1864.

HODGES, HENRY, Musician
Resided in Wake County where he enlisted at age 17, October 14, 1861. Mustered in as Private. Promoted to Musician (Drummer) in January-February, 1862. Discharged on September 15, 1862, under the provisions of the Conscription Act.

HOLDER, HARRIS W., Private
Resided in Wake County where he enlisted at age 18, November 15, 1862, for the war. Present or accounted for through April, 1864.

HONEYCUTT, BERT T., Corporal
Enlistment date reported as July 15, 1862; however, he was not listed in the records of this company until November-December, 1864. Promotion record not reported. Reported present for duty during November-December, 1864. [North Carolina pension records indicate that he survived the war. May have served also in Company F, Mallett's N.C. Battalion (Camp Guard).]

HONEYCUTT, W. S., Private
Resided in Wake County and enlisted at age 29, October 14, 1861. Company records indicate he was captured at Roanoke Island on February 8, 1862; however, records of the Federal Provost Marshal do not substantiate that report. Returned to duty prior to May 1, 1863. Reported absent without leave in November-December, 1864.

HONYCUTT, JACKSON, Private
Enlisted in Wake County on November 24, 1863, for the war. Reported under arrest in November-December, 1864. [May have served also in Company F, Mallett's N.C. Battalion (Camp Guard).]

HOPKINS, D. A., Private
Resided in Wake County where he enlisted at age 22, October 14, 1861. Present or accounted for until captured at Roanoke Island on February 8, 1862. Paroled at Elizabeth City on February 21, 1862. Returned to duty on or about September 15, 1862. Captured at Cold Harbor, Virginia, June 1, 1864. Confined at Point Lookout, Maryland, June 11, 1864. Transferred to Elmira, New York, July 12, 1864. Paroled at Elmira on March 10, 1865, and transferred to Boulware's Wharf, James River, Virginia, where he was received on March 15, 1865, for exchange.

HORTON, CURGUS, Private
Enlisted in Wake County on December 9, 1863, for the war. Present or accounted for through July 20, 1864. Died at or near Richmond, Virginia, on or about October 5, 1864. Cause of death not reported.

HORTON, H. W., Private
Enlisted in Wake County on an unspecified date. First listed in the records of this company in November-December, 1864, when he was reported absent sick in hospital. Returned to duty on January 9, 1865. [North Carolina pension records indicate that he survived the war.]

HORTON, JOSIAH, Private
Enlisted in Wake County on September 22, 1863, for the war. Present or accounted for through December, 1864. [May have served also in Company F, Mallett's N.C. Battalion (Camp Guard).]

HORTON, WILLIAM A., Private
Resided in Wake County where he enlisted at age 20, October 14, 1861. Died in hospital at Columbia, South Carolina, March 24, 1863. Cause of death not reported.

HURST, CASWELL, Private
Resided in Wake County where he enlisted at age 18, October 14, 1861. Present or accounted for until captured at Roanoke Island on February 8, 1862. Paroled at Elizabeth City on February 21, 1862. Returned to duty on or about September 15, 1862. Present or accounted for through April, 1864. Retired to

the Invalid Corps on December 3, 1864. Reason he was retired not reported.

JACKSON, G. J., Private

Enlisted in Wake County on May 1, 1864, for the war. Hospitalized at Danville, Virginia, on or about June 4, 1864, with a gunshot wound of the arm. Place and date wounded not reported. Returned to duty on June 15, 1864. Deserted on September 1, 1864. Paroled at Raleigh on or about May 25, 1865.

JOHNSON, JOHN W., Private

Resided in Wake County where he enlisted at age 21, October 4, 1862, for the war. Present or accounted for through April, 1864. Died prior to February 7, 1865. Place and cause of death not reported.

JOLLY, WILLIS, Private

Enlisted in Wake County on September 25, 1863, for the war. Deserted on December 27, 1864.

KEITH, R. B., Corporal

Resided in Wake County where he enlisted at age 18, October 14, 1862, for the war. Mustered in as Private. Wounded at Fort Wagner, Charleston, South Carolina, July 18, 1863. Returned to duty on an unspecified date. Promoted to Corporal in May-October, 1864. Hospitalized at Richmond, Virginia, May 16, 1864, with a gunshot wound of the right thigh. Place and date wounded not reported. Died in hospital at Richmond on October 15, 1864, of "pyaemia."

KELLEY, HENRY, Private

Resided in Wake County where he enlisted at age 34, October 14, 1861. Present or accounted for until captured at Roanoke Island on February 8, 1862. Paroled at Elizabeth City on February 21, 1862. Discharged on September 15, 1862, under the provisions of the Conscription Act.

KELLY, JAMES, Private

Resided in Wake County where he enlisted at age 21, October 14, 1861. Transferred to an unspecified unit on August 3, 1863.

LASSITER, JOHN S., Private

Resided in Wake County where he enlisted at age 43, October 14, 1861. Present or accounted for until captured at Roanoke Island on February 8, 1862. Paroled at Elizabeth City on February 21, 1862. Discharged on September 15, 1862, under the provisions of the Conscription Act.

LAUT, J. M., Private

Enlisted in Wake County on February 17, 1863, for the war. Reported absent without leave in November-December, 1864. No further records.

LEE, D. T., Sergeant

Resided in Wake County where he enlisted at age 24, October 14, 1861. Mustered in as Private. Present or accounted for until captured at Roanoke Island on February 8, 1862. Paroled at Elizabeth City on February 21, 1862. Returned to duty on or about September 15, 1862. Promoted to Corporal on July 1, 1863. Promoted to Sergeant in May-December, 1864. Hospitalized at Richmond, Virginia, June 13, 1864, with a gunshot wound of the left foot. Returned to duty on an unspecified date. Reported present for duty in November-December, 1864.

LEE, H. C., Private

Resided in Wake County where he enlisted at age 20, October 14, 1861. Mustered in as Private. Promoted to Corporal on June 22, 1863. Reduced to ranks in May-August, 1864. Company records indicate that he died in the hands of the enemy in August, 1864. Place and date captured not reported. Place and cause of death not reported.

LEE, WILLIAM H., Private

Resided in Wake County where he enlisted at age 30, October 14, 1861. Transferred to Company I, 1st Regiment N.C. State Troops, March 10, 1862.

LEWIS, MATTHEW, Private

Resided in Wake County where he enlisted at age 44, October 14, 1861. Discharged on September 15, 1862, under the provisions of the Conscription Act.

LILES, J. WRIGHT, Private

Resided in Wake County where he enlisted at age 43, August 15, 1863, for the war. Present or accounted for through December, 1864.

LOYD, W. R., Private

Enlisted in Wake County on October 1, 1864, for the war. Reported absent sick in November-December, 1864.

McALISTER, JOHN W., Private

Resided in Wake County where he enlisted at age 35, October 14, 1861. Discharged on September 15, 1862, under the provisions of the Conscription Act.

MARSHBORN, J. W., Private

Enlisted at Camp Holmes on July 13, 1862, for the war. Present or accounted for through December, 1864.

MARSHBURN, D. C., Private

Resided in Wake County where he enlisted on July 13, 1862, for the war. Captured near Kinston on March 8, 1865. Confined at Point Lookout, Maryland, March 16, 1865. Released at Point Lookout on June 29, 1865, after taking the Oath of Allegiance. [North Carolina pension records indicate he was wounded near Petersburg, Virginia, June 25, 1864. May have served also in Company F, Mallett's N.C. Battalion (Camp Guard).]

MARSHBURN, HENRY H., Private

Resided in Wake County where he enlisted at age 18, June 25, 1863, for the war. Present or accounted for through March 10, 1865.

MASSEY, A. H., Private

Resided in Wake County where he enlisted at age 21, September 16, 1862, for the war. Deserted on December 27, 1864.

MASSEY, ADOLOMUS, Private

Resided in Wake County where he enlisted at age 18, September 8, 1862, for the war. Died at Wilmington on February 19, 1863, of "angina pectoris."

MASSEY, T. H., Private

Resided in Wake County where he enlisted at age 27, September 8, 1862, for the war. Captured at Drewry's Bluff, Virginia, May 16, 1864. Confined at Point

Lookout, Maryland, May 21, 1864. Released on June 4, 1865, after taking the Oath of Allegiance.

MEDLIN, ARCHIBALD, Private
Resided in Wake County where he enlisted at age 38, October 14, 1861. Present or accounted for until captured at Roanoke Island on February 8, 1862. Paroled at Elizabeth City on February 21, 1862. Discharged on September 15, 1862, under the provisions of the Conscription Act.

MOONINGHAM, WILLIAM A., Private
Resided in Wake County where he enlisted at age 37, February 10, 1863, for the war. Deserted on May 15, 1863. Name appears on a casualty list dated October 4, 1863, which indicates that he was wounded slightly. Place and date wounded not reported. Reported present but under arrest in March-April, 1864. Company records indicate he deserted on December 27, 1864; however, North Carolina pension records indicate he was killed at Petersburg, Virginia, in 1864. No further records.

MOYER, JAMES, Private
Born in Franklin County and resided in Wake County where he was by occupation a cooper prior to enlisting in Wake County at age 29, October 14, 1861. Discharged on May 4, 1862, by reason of "inability to use his right arm."

NOWELL, A. J., Private
Enlistment date reported as July 15, 1862; however, he was not listed in the records of this company until November-December, 1864. Company records indicate that he deserted on November 27, 1864. [May have served also in Company A, Mallett's N.C. Battalion (Camp Guard).]

NOWELL, J. J., Private
Resided in Wake County where he enlisted at age 30, June 17, 1863, for the war. Deserted on November 27, 1864.

NOWELL, W. H., Private
Enlisted in Wake County on September 28, 1863, for the war. Captured at Cold Harbor, Virginia, June 1, 1864. Confined at Point Lookout, Maryland, June 11, 1864. Transferred to Elmira, New York, July 12, 1864. Died at Elmira on August 29, 1864, of "acute bronchitis."

PACE, W. W., Private
Enlisted in Wake County on July 17, 1862, for the war. Deserted on November 29, 1864. [May have served also in Company F, Mallett's N.C. Battalion (Camp Guard).]

PALL, J. G., Private
Enlisted in Wake County on September 17, 1863, for the war. Wounded at Fort Harrison, Virginia, on or about September 30, 1864. Reported absent wounded through December, 1864.

PARISH, CASWELL J., Musician
Resided in Wake County where he enlisted at age 40, October 14, 1861. Mustered in as Musician (Fifer). Present or accounted for until captured at Roanoke Island on February 8, 1862. Paroled at Elizabeth City on February 21, 1862. Died "at home" on March 12, 1862.

Cause of death not reported.

PARRISH, A. W., Private
Born in Wake County where he resided as a farmer prior to enlisting in Wake County at age 28, October 14, 1861. Mustered in as Musician (Drummer). Reduced to ranks in January-February, 1862. Discharged on June 14, 1862, by reason of "gravel."

PARRISH, JAMES, Private
Resided in Wake County where he enlisted at age 18, October 14, 1861. Present or accounted for until captured at Roanoke Island on February 8, 1862. Paroled at Elizabeth City on February 21, 1862. Returned to duty on or about September 15, 1862. Died in an unspecified North Carolina hospital on May 12-14, 1863, of "febris typhoides."

PARRISH, JAMES A., Private
Resided in Wake County where he enlisted at age 51, October 13, 1862, for the war as a substitute. Reported absent without leave from July 16, 1863, until February 1, 1864. Deserted on January 22, 1865.

PEEBLES, J. A., Private
Enlisted in Wake County on September 12, 1863, for the war. Present or accounted for through January 9, 1865.

PEEBLES, JOHN D., Private
Resided in Wake County where he enlisted at age 18, October 13, 1862, for the war. Captured at Cold Harbor, Virginia, June 1, 1864. Confined at Point Lookout, Maryland, June 11, 1864. Transferred to Elmira, New York, July 12, 1864. Released at Elmira on July 19, 1865, after taking the Oath of Allegiance.

PLEASANT, B. D., Private
Resided in Wake County where he enlisted at age 27, September 25, 1862, for the war. Deserted on or about October 23, 1862. Returned to duty on or about March 31, 1864. Deserted on December 27, 1864.

PLEASANT, R. H., Private
Resided in Wake County where he enlisted at age 21, October 14, 1861. Present or accounted for until captured at Roanoke Island on February 8, 1862. Paroled at Elizabeth City on February 21, 1862. Died on March 10-12, 1862. Place and cause of death not reported.

POOLE, NEEDHAM W., Private
Previously served in Company A, 40th Regiment N.C. Troops (3rd Regiment N.C. Artillery). Transferred to this company in September, 1861. Present or accounted for until captured at Roanoke Island on February 8, 1862. Paroled at Elizabeth City on February 21, 1862. Returned to duty on or about September 15, 1862. Promoted to Ordnance Sergeant on September 15, 1862, and transferred to the Field and Staff of this regiment.

PUGH, JOHN C., Private
Enlisted in Wake County on December 10, 1862, for the war. Captured at Fort Harrison, Virginia, September 30, 1864. Confined at Point Lookout, Maryland, October 2, 1864. Paroled at Point Lookout on or about November 1, 1864, and transferred to Venus Point, Savannah River, Georgia, where he was received on November 15,

1864, for exchange.

PULLEY, ADDISON, Private
Enlisted in Wake County on October 7, 1864, for the war. Present or accounted for through February 8, 1865.

PULLEY, JESSE, Private
Enlisted in Wake County on October 17, 1864, for the war. Present or accounted for through December, 1864.

PULLEY, ROBERT, Private
Resided in Wake County where he enlisted at age 30, October 14, 1861. Present or accounted for until captured at Roanoke Island on February 8, 1862. Paroled at Elizabeth City on February 21, 1862. Returned to duty prior to May 1, 1863. Deserted on November 27, 1864.

PULLEY, THOMAS P., Private
Resided in Wake County where he enlisted at age 40, October 14, 1861. Present or accounted for until captured at Roanoke Island on February 8, 1862. Paroled at Elizabeth City on February 21, 1862. Discharged on September 15, 1862, under the provisions of the Conscription Act.

RHODES, JAMES E., Sergeant
Resided in Wake County where he enlisted at age 16, October 14, 1861. Mustered in as Private. Present or accounted for until captured at Roanoke Island on February 8, 1862. Paroled at Elizabeth City on February 21, 1862. Discharged on September 15, 1862, under the provisions of the Conscription Act. Reenlisted in the company with the rank of Private in March, 1863, for the war. Present or accounted for through April, 1864. Promoted to Sergeant in May-December, 1864. Company records dated November-December, 1864, indicate that he was a prisoner of war; however, records of the Federal Provost Marshal do not substantiate that report. No further records.

RHODES, WILLIAM N., Private
Resided in Wake County where he enlisted at age 18, October 14, 1861. Discharged on March 3, 1863, after providing a substitute. Reenlisted in the company subsequent to December 31, 1864, for the war. Deserted in April, 1865.

RILEY, THOMAS, Private
Born at Belfast, Ireland, and resided in South Carolina prior to enlisting at Charleston, South Carolina, at age 50, November 1, 1863, for the war as a substitute. Reported present but under arrest in March-April, 1864. Deserted to the enemy on or about August 6, 1864.

ROBERTSON, JOHN T., Private
Resided in Wake County where he enlisted at age 20, October 14, 1861. Transferred to Company I, 1st Regiment N.C. State Troops, March 11, 1862.

SANDERFORD, J. J., Private
Enlisted in Wake County on September 16, 1862, for the war. Discharged on October 23, 1862. Reason discharged not reported.

SCARBOROUGH, A. C., Private
Resided in Wake County where he enlisted at age 19, October 14, 1861. Present or accounted for until captured at Roanoke Island on February 8, 1862.

Paroled at Elizabeth City on February 21, 1862. Returned to duty on or about September 15, 1862. Company records dated November-December, 1864, indicate that he was a prisoner of war; however, records of the Federal Provost Marshal do not substantiate that report. No further records.

SCARBOROUGH, A. J., Private
Resided in Wake County where he enlisted at age 24, September 16, 1862, for the war. Hospitalized at Richmond, Virginia, on or about June 3, 1864, with a gunshot wound of the hand. Place and date wounded not reported. Deserted on September 1 or November 29, 1864.

SCARBOROUGH, B. E., Private
Resided in Wake County where he enlisted at age 25, October 14, 1861. Hospitalized at Richmond, Virginia, May 17, 1864, with a gunshot wound. Place and date wounded not reported. Died on June 7, 1864, of wounds.

SCARBOROUGH, JASPER N., Private
Born in Wake County where he resided prior to enlisting in Wake County at age 26, October 14, 1861. Present or accounted for until captured at Roanoke Island on February 8, 1862. Paroled at Elizabeth City on February 21, 1862. Returned to duty on or about September 15, 1862. Died in hospital at Petersburg, Virginia, on or about March 26, 1864, of "pneumonia."

SCARBOROUGH, M. G., Private
Resided in Wake County where he enlisted at age 18, October 14, 1861. Present or accounted for until captured at Roanoke Island on February 8, 1862. Paroled at Elizabeth City on February 21, 1862. Returned to duty on or about September 15, 1862. Died in hospital at Wilmington on July 30, 1863, of "fever & hernia."

SCARBOROUGH, S. H., Private
Resided in Wake County where he enlisted at age 20, September 8, 1862, for the war. Reported absent without leave from July 3, 1863, until February 1, 1864. Captured at Cold Harbor, Virginia, June 1, 1864. Confined at Elmira, New York, on an unspecified date. Paroled at Elmira on October 11, 1864, and transferred to Venus Point, Savannah River, Georgia, where he was received on November 15, 1864, for exchange.

SHAMEL, JAMES, Private
Enlisted in Wake County on September 15, 1863, for the war. Present or accounted for through December, 1864.

STELL, A. B., Private
Resided in Wake County where he enlisted at age 29, September 25, 1862, for the war. Deserted on September 27, 1863.

STELL, H. H., Private
Resided in Wake County where he enlisted at age 25, September 15, 1862, for the war. Present or accounted for through December, 1864.

STELL, JOHN B., Private
Resided in Wake County and enlisted at "High House" at age 23, September 8, 1862, for the war. Deserted on or

about August 15, 1863.

STELL, LEMUEL, Private
Resided in Wake County where he enlisted at age 25, September 28, 1862, for the war. Deserted on or about May 15, 1863.

STRICKLAND, A. J., Private
Resided in Wake County and was by occupation a farmer prior to enlisting in Wake County at age 25, October 14, 1861. Wounded in the head and/or right arm at Cold Harbor, Virginia, June 1, 1864. Furloughed on or about June 7, 1864. Reported present for duty in November-December, 1864.

STRICKLAND, HENRY H., Private
Resided in Wake County where he enlisted at age 20, October 14, 1861. Present or accounted for until captured at Roanoke Island on February 8, 1862. Paroled at Elizabeth City on February 21, 1862. Returned to duty on or about September 15, 1862. Present or accounted for through December, 1864. Deserted on an unspecified date.

STRICKLAND, JAMES M., Private
Resided in Wake County where he enlisted at age 24, October 14, 1861. Present or accounted for until captured at Roanoke Island on February 8, 1862. Paroled at Elizabeth City on February 21, 1862. Returned to duty on or about September 15, 1862. Present or accounted for through December, 1864. Deserted on an unspecified date.

STRICKLAND, JOSEPH, Private
Place and date of enlistment not reported. Captured by the enemy on April 25, 1865. No further records.

STRICKLAND, SAMUEL, Private
Resided in Wake County where he enlisted at age 22, October 14, 1861. Present or accounted for until captured at Roanoke Island on February 8, 1862. Paroled at Elizabeth City on February 21, 1862. Returned to duty on or about September 15, 1862. Captured at Cold Harbor, Virginia, June 1, 1864. Confined at Point Lookout, Maryland, June 11, 1864. Transferred to Elmira, New York, July 12, 1864. Died at Elmira on August 4, 1864, of "chronic diarrhoea."

STRICKLAND, WILLIAM D., Corporal
Resided in Wake County and was by occupation a farmer prior to enlisting in Wake County at age 29, October 14, 1861. Mustered in as Private. Present or accounted for until captured at Roanoke Island on February 8, 1862. Paroled at Elizabeth City on February 21, 1862. Promoted to Corporal on September 15, 1862. Wounded in the left thigh at or near Cold Harbor, Virginia, on or about June 1, 1864. Left leg amputated. Reported absent wounded through December, 1864. Took the Oath of Allegiance at Raleigh on May 25, 1865.

STRICKLAND, WILLIE B., Private
Resided in Wake County where he enlisted at age 18, February 10, 1863, for the war. Deserted on July 17 1864. Listed as a deserter through December, 1864. Captured by the enemy on April 25, 1865. No further records.

TANT, J. M., Private
Resided in Wake County where he enlisted at age 31,

February 17, 1863, for the war. Hospitalized at Richmond, Virginia, October 1, 1864, with a gunshot wound of the chest. Place and date wounded not reported. Furloughed for sixty days on October 29, 1864.

TEMPLE, JAMES A., Sergeant
Resided in Wake County where he enlisted at age 34, October 14, 1861. Mustered in as Sergeant. Discharged on September 15, 1862, under the provisions of the Conscription Act.

THROWER, J. DALLAS, Private
Born in Wake County where he resided as a farmer prior to enlisting in Wake County at age 15, October 14, 1861. Present or accounted for until captured at Roanoke Island on February 8, 1862. Paroled at Elizabeth City on February 21, 1862. Discharged on September 15, 1862, under the provisions of the Conscription Act. Later served in Company D, 1st Regiment N.C. Junior Reserves.

TODD, HENRY R., Sergeant
Resided in Wake County where he enlisted at age 25, October 14, 1861. Mustered in as Private. Present or accounted for until captured at Roanoke Island on February 8, 1862. Paroled at Elizabeth City on February 21, 1862. Returned to duty on or about September 15, 1862. Promoted to Sergeant on September 15, 1862. Present or accounted for through April, 1864. No further records.

TODD, RUFUS, ———
North Carolina pension records indicate that he served in this company.

TODD, WILLIAM O., Private
Resided in Wake County where he enlisted at age 31, October 14, 1861. Mustered in as Sergeant. Present or accounted for until captured at Roanoke Island on February 8, 1862. Paroled at Elizabeth City on February 21, 1862. Returned to duty on or about September 15, 1862. Reduced to ranks prior to March 1, 1863. Present or accounted for through April, 1864. No further records.

TUCKER, ANDREW H., Sergeant
Resided in Wake County where he enlisted at age 19, October 14, 1861. Mustered in as Private. Present or accounted for until captured at Roanoke Island on February 8, 1862. Paroled at Elizabeth City on February 21, 1862. Returned to duty on or about September 15, 1862. Promoted to Corporal prior to March 1, 1863. Promoted to Sergeant in May, 1863-April, 1864. Present or accounted for through April, 1864. Reported absent without leave in November-December, 1864.

UNDERHILL, JAMES D., Private
Born in Wake County and was by occupation a farmer prior to enlisting in Wake County on December 3, 1863, for the war. Wounded in the left arm at Drewry's Bluff, Virginia, on or about May 15, 1864. Left arm amputated. Retired from service on March 4, 1865. Discharge certificate gives his age as 19.

UNDERWOOD, A. J., Private
Resided in Wake County where he enlisted at age 22, October 14, 1861. Present or accounted for through April, 1864. Reported under arrest in November-

December, 1864. No further records.

UNDERWOOD, WILLIAM H., Private
Resided in Wake County where he enlisted at age 36, April 6, 1863, for the war. Reported present but under arrest in March-April, 1864. Deserted on December 27, 1864.

UPCHURCH, DALLAS H., Private
Resided in Wake County where he enlisted at age 20, October 14, 1861. Mustered in as Corporal. Transferred to Company I, 1st Regiment N.C. State Troops, March 10, 1862. Reenlisted in this company with the rank of Private on or about June 20, 1863, for the war. Deserted on September 27, 1864.

WALKER, C. B., Private
Resided in Wake County where he enlisted at age 36, October 14, 1861. Present or accounted for until captured at Roanoke Island on February 8, 1862. Paroled at Elizabeth City on February 21, 1862. Discharged on September 15, 1862, under the provisions of the Conscription Act.

WALKER, HENDERSON H., Private
Resided in Wake County where he enlisted at age 19, October 14, 1861. Captured at Cold Harbor, Virginia, June 1, 1864. Confined at Point Lookout, Maryland, June 11, 1864. Transferred to Elmira, New York, July 12, 1864. Released at Elmira on July 3, 1865, after taking the Oath of Allegiance.

WALKER, JOEL H., Private
Resided in Wake County where he enlisted at age 56, October 1, 1862, for the war as a substitute. Captured at Cold Harbor, Virginia, June 1, 1864. Confined at Point Lookout, Maryland, June 11, 1864. Transferred to Elmira, New York, July 12, 1864. Died at Elmira on September 28, 1864, of ''pneumonia.''

WALKER, WILLIAM T., Private
Resided in Wake County where he enlisted at age 17, October 14, 1861. Present or accounted for until captured at Roanoke Island on February 8, 1862. Paroled at Elizabeth City on February 21, 1862. Returned to duty on or about September 15, 1862. Captured at Cold Harbor, Virginia, June 1, 1864. Confined at Point Lookout, Maryland, June 11, 1864. Transferred to Elmira, New York, July 12, 1864. Released at Elmira on July 3, 1865, after taking the Oath of Allegiance.

WALL, WILLIAM, Private
Resided in Wake County where he enlisted at age 21, October 14, 1861. Company records indicate he was captured at Roanoke Island on February 8, 1862; however, records of the Federal Provost Marshal do not substantiate that report. Returned to duty on an unspecified date. Deserted on or about May 15, 1863.

WARD, W. J., Sergeant
Place and date of enlistment not reported. Promotion record not reported. First listed in the records of this company on March 1, 1864. Last listed in the records of this company on September 1, 1864.

WATKINS, HUTSANIEL, Private
Resided in Wake County where he enlisted at age 24, September 25, 1862, for the war. Deserted on June 4, 1863.

WATKINS, STEPHEN, Private
Enlisted in Wake County on September 17, 1863, for the war. Deserted on January 22, 1865.

WATSON, FABIUS H., Private
Resided in Wake County where he enlisted at age 25, October 14, 1861. Present or accounted for through December, 1864; however, he was reported absent on detail in hospital at Wilmington during much of that period.

WATSON, J. LEONARD, Sergeant
Resided in Wake County where he enlisted at age 28, October 14, 1861. Mustered in as Private. Present or accounted for until captured at Roanoke Island on February 8, 1862. Paroled at Elizabeth City on February 21, 1862. Returned to duty on an unspecified date. Promoted to Sergeant in September, 1862-February, 1863. Present or accounted for through December, 1864.

WEATHERS, W. E., Private
Resided in Wake County where he enlisted at age 18, May 12, 1863, for the war. Present or accounted for through December, 1864.

WEATHERS, W. W., Private
Resided in Wake County where he enlisted at age 41, October 14, 1861. Discharged on September 15, 1862, under the provisions of the Conscription Act.

WHITLEY, DANIEL, Corporal
Resided in Wake County where he enlisted at age 30, October 14, 1861. Mustered in as Corporal. Present or accounted for until captured at Roanoke Island on February 8, 1862. Paroled at Elizabeth City on February 21, 1862. Company records do not indicate whether he returned to duty. Died on June 7, 1863. Place and cause of death not reported.

WILLIAMS, C. S., Private
Resided in Wake County where he enlisted at age 20, October 14, 1861. Mustered in as Sergeant. Reduced to ranks in March, 1862-February, 1863. Present or accounted for through December, 1864; however, he was reported absent sick or absent on detail during much of that period.

WILLIAMS, JOHN, Private
Resided in Wake County where he enlisted at age 19, September 8, 1862, for the war. Died in hospital at Wilmington on June 23, 1863, of ''typhoid fever.''

WILLIAMS, JOHN T., Private
Resided in Wake County where he enlisted at age 36, October 14, 1861. Present or accounted for until captured at Roanoke Island on February 8, 1862. Paroled at Elizabeth City on February 21, 1862. Returned to duty on or about September 15, 1862. Present or accounted for through December, 1864. [North Carolina pension records indicate he was wounded in the ankle at Taylor's Farm, Virginia, in 1863.]

COMPANY I

This company, known as the ''Cape Fear Boys,'' was

raised in Harnett County and enlisted there on October 30, 1861. It was then assigned to the 31st Regiment N.C. Troops and designated Company I. After joining the regiment the company functioned as a part of the regiment, and its history for the war period is reported as a part of the regimental history.

The information contained in the following roster of the company was compiled principally from company muster rolls for November 1, 1861-April 30, 1862; January-April, 1863; March-April, 1864; and November-December, 1864. No company muster rolls were found for May-December, 1862; May, 1863-February, 1864; May-October, 1864; or for the period after December, 1864. Valuable information was obtained from primary records such as the Roll of Honor, discharge certificates, medical records, prisoner of war records, and pension applications. Secondary sources such as postwar rosters and histories, cemetery records, and records of the United Daughters of the Confederacy also provided useful information.

OFFICERS

CAPTAINS

McKAY, JOHN A. D.

Resided in Harnett County where he enlisted at age 20. Appointed Captain on October 30, 1861. Captured at Roanoke Island on February 8, 1862. Paroled at Elizabeth City on February 21, 1862. Returned to duty on or about September 15, 1862. Wounded at White Hall on December 16, 1862. Appointed Major on June 7, 1863, and transferred to the Field and Staff of this regiment.

PARKER, ALLEN B.

Resided in Harnett County where he enlisted at age 25, October 30, 1861. Mustered in as Sergeant. Captured at Roanoke Island on February 8, 1862. Paroled at Elizabeth City on February 21, 1862. Returned to duty on or about September 15, 1862. Promoted to 1st Sergeant prior to February 11, 1863. Appointed 3rd Lieutenant on February 11, 1863, and was promoted to Captain on June 7, 1863. Wounded at Fort Wagner, Charleston, South Carolina, July 18, 1863. Died on July 22, 1863, of wounds. Place of death not reported.

DEWAR, WILLIAM A.

Resided in Harnett County where he enlisted at age 34, September 15, 1862, for the war. Mustered in as Private. Promoted to Sergeant on March 4, 1863. Appointed 1st Lieutenant on June 7, 1863, and was promoted to Captain on October 1, 1863. Captured at Cold Harbor, Virginia, June 1, 1864. Confined at Point Lookout, Maryland, June 4, 1864. Transferred to Fort Delaware, Delaware, June 23, 1864. Transferred to Hilton Head, South Carolina, August 20, 1864. Confined at Fort Pulaski, Georgia, on or about October 21, 1864. Transferred to Hilton Head on November 19, 1864. Transferred to Fort Delaware where he arrived on March 12, 1865. Released on June 10, 1865, after taking the Oath of Allegiance.

LIEUTENANTS

BETHEA, WILLIAM J., 3rd Lieutenant

Resided in Harnett County where he enlisted at age 17, October 30, 1861. Mustered in as Private. Captured at Roanoke Island on February 8, 1862. Paroled on an unspecified date. Reported absent sick in January-February, 1863. Promoted to Sergeant on February 11, 1863. Returned to duty on an unspecified date. Appointed 3rd Lieutenant on June 16, 1863. Captured at Cold Harbor, Virginia, June 1, 1864. Confined at Point Lookout, Maryland, June 11, 1864. Transferred to Fort Delaware, Delaware, June 23, 1864. Released on June 17, 1865, after taking the Oath of Allegiance.

COFFIELD, CORNELIUS H., 1st Lieutenant

Resided in Harnett County where he enlisted at age 41. Appointed 1st Lieutenant on October 30, 1861. Captured at Roanoke Island on February 8, 1862. Paroled at Elizabeth City on February 21, 1862. Resigned on September 15, 1862.

JONES, DANIEL McL., 2nd Lieutenant

Resided in Harnett County where he enlisted at age 18, October 30, 1861. Mustered in as Corporal. Captured at Roanoke Island on February 8, 1862. Paroled on an unspecified date. Returned to duty on or about September 15, 1862. Promoted to Sergeant on February 11, 1863. Appointed 2nd Lieutenant on June 8, 1863. Hospitalized at Richmond, Virginia, June 2, 1864, with a gunshot wound. Place and date wounded not reported. Furloughed for sixty days on June 6, 1864. No further records.

PEARSON, WILLIAM, 1st Lieutenant

Resided in Harnett County where he enlisted at age 27. Appointed 2nd Lieutenant on October 30, 1861. Captured at Roanoke Island on February 8, 1862. Paroled at Elizabeth City on February 21, 1862. Returned to duty on or about September 15, 1862. Promoted to 1st Lieutenant in March, 1863. Resigned on May 1, 1863, by reason of "phthisis pulmonalis." Resignation accepted on May 30, 1863.

PRINCE, WILLIAM A., 1st Lieutenant

Resided in Harnett County where he enlisted at age 33. Appointed 2nd Lieutenant on October 30, 1861. Captured at Roanoke Island on February 8, 1862. Paroled at Elizabeth City on February 21, 1862. Returned to duty on or about September 15, 1862. Promoted to 1st Lieutenant on September 15, 1862. Resigned on March 16, 1863, by reason of "phthisis pulmonalis." Resignation accepted on March 25, 1863.

TUTOR, WILLIAM O., 3rd Lieutenant

Resided in Harnett County and was by occupation a farmer prior to enlisting in Harnett County at age 22, October 30, 1861. Mustered in as Sergeant. Captured at Roanoke Island on February 8, 1862. Paroled at Elizabeth City on February 21, 1862. Returned to duty on or about September 15, 1862. Appointed 3rd Lieutenant on October 23, 1862. Died in hospital at Wilmington on or about January 29, 1863, of "febris typhoides" and/or "pneumonia."

WILLIAMS, EDMUND J., 1st Lieutenant

Previously served as Sergeant in Company A, 63rd Regiment N.C. Troops (5th Regiment N.C. Cavalry). Appointed 1st Lieutenant on October 13, 1863, to rank from October 9, 1863, and transferred to this company. Present or accounted for through December, 1864. Paroled subsequent to April 26, 1865.

WRAY, THOMAS H., 1st Lieutenant

Resided in Harnett County and enlisted in Wake County at age 31. Appointed 2nd Lieutenant on or about October 30, 1861. Present or accounted for until captured at Roanoke Island on February 8, 1862. Paroled at Elizabeth City on February 21, 1862. Returned to duty on or about September 15, 1862. Appointed 1st Lieutenant on or about September 17, 1862. Captured at or near Kinston on March 8, 1865. Confined at Point Lookout, Maryland, March 16, 1865. Transferred to Old Capitol Prison. Washington, D.C., where he was confined on March 19, 1865. Transferred to Fort Delaware, Delaware, March 24, 1865. Released at Fort Delaware on June 7, 1865, after taking the Oath of Allegiance.

NONCOMMISSIONED OFFICERS AND PRIVATES

ABBOT, JOHN, Private
Resided in Harnett County where he enlisted at age 45, October 30, 1861. Captured at Roanoke Island on February 8, 1862. Paroled on an unspecified date. "Mustered" at Richmond, Virginia, August 15, 1862. No further records.

ARNOLD, ABLE S., Private
Resided in Harnett County where he enlisted at age 23, October 30, 1861. Captured at Roanoke Island on February 8, 1862. Paroled at Elizabeth City on February 21, 1862. Returned to duty prior to May 1, 1863. Reported absent without leave on December 24, 1864.

ARNOLD, JAMES, Private
Resided in Harnett County where he enlisted at age 25, October 30, 1861. Captured at Roanoke Island on February 8, 1862. Paroled on an unspecified date. Discharged on May 20, 1862, by reason of disability.

ARNOLD, WILLIAM, Private
Resided in Harnett County where he enlisted at age 26, September 15, 1862, for the war. Wounded in the abdomen and/or hip and captured at Fort Harrison, Virginia, September 30, 1864. Hospitalized at Fort Monroe, Virginia, October 4, 1864. Confined at Point Lookout, Maryland, March 2, 1865. Released on June 3, 1865, after taking the Oath of Allegiance.

ARNOLD, WILLIAM S., Private
Born in Harnett County* where he resided prior to enlisting in Harnett County at age 27, September 15, 1862, for the war. Present or accounted for through December, 1864.

BALLARD, DAVID, Private
Resided in Harnett County where he enlisted at age 22, October 30, 1861. Captured at Roanoke Island on February 8, 1862. Paroled on an unspecified date. Returned to duty prior to May 1, 1863. Died in hospital at Wilmington on June 24, 1863, of "febris typhoides."

BARRY, HENRY, Private
Enlisted in Harnett County on September 15, 1862, for the war. Deserted the same day.

BIRD, BRIGHT D., Private
Resided in Harnett County where he enlisted at age 32, October 30, 1861. Captured at Roanoke Island on February 8, 1862. Paroled on an unspecified date. "Mustered" at Richmond, Virginia, August 15, 1862. No further records.

BISHOP, NATHAN M., Private
Born in Harnett County* where he resided as a farmer prior to enlisting in Harnett County at age 20, October 30, 1861. "Escaped" from Roanoke Island when the island was captured on February 8, 1862. Enlisted in Company H, 50th Regiment N.C. Troops, March 24, 1862.

BRADLEY, ALEXANDER D., Corporal
Resided in Harnett County where he enlisted at age 21, October 30, 1861. Mustered in as Private. Captured at Roanoke Island on February 8, 1862. Paroled on an unspecified date. Returned to duty on or about September 15, 1862. Promoted to Corporal in May, 1863-April, 1864. Present or accounted for through December, 1864.

BRADLEY, ANDERSON, Private
Resided in Harnett County where he enlisted at age 19, October 30, 1861. Captured at Roanoke Island on February 8, 1862. Paroled on an unspecified date. Returned to duty on or about September 15, 1862. Deserted at Petersburg, Virginia, August 5, 1864.

BRADLEY, STEPHEN, Private
Resided in Harnett County where he enlisted at age 18, September 15, 1862, for the war. Hospitalized at Williamsburg[?], Virginia, May 20, 1864, with a gunshot wound. Place and date wounded not reported. Furloughed on June 6, 1864. Reported absent without leave in November-December, 1864.

BULLARD, JOHN A., Private
Resided in Harnett County where he enlisted at age 23, September 15, 1862, for the war. Deserted on December 9, 1863. Returned to duty prior to June 1, 1864, when he was wounded in the left hand at Cold Harbor, Virginia. Reported absent without leave on November 10, 1864. Returned to duty subsequent to December 31, 1864. Captured near Goldsboro on or about March 15, 1865. Confined at Point Lookout, Maryland, April 3, 1865. Released on June 23, 1865, after taking the Oath of Allegiance. [North Carolina pension records indicate he was wounded at Fort Harrison, Virginia, September 1, 1864.]

BURNS, ALLEN, Private
Resided in Harnett or Chatham County and enlisted in Harnett County at age 22, October 30, 1861. Present or accounted for until captured at Roanoke Island on February 8, 1862. Paroled at Elizabeth City on February 21, 1862. Transferred to Company E, 8th Regiment N.C. State Troops, October 31, 1862.

BUTTS, GEORGE D., Private
Resided in Harnett County where he enlisted at age 18, October 30, 1861. Present or accounted for until captured at Roanoke Island on February 8, 1862. Died at Roanoke Island on February 11-15, 1862, of disease.

BUTTS, SAMUEL A., Private
Resided in Harnett County where he enlisted at age 16, October 30, 1861. Captured at Roanoke Island on February 8, 1862. Paroled on an unspecified date. Returned to duty on or about September 15, 1862. Present or accounted for through December, 1864.

BYRD, RICHARD, ———
North Carolina pension records indicate that he served

in this company.

CAMPBELL, WILLIAM, Private

Enlisted in Wake County. Enlistment date reported as July, 1861; however, he was not listed in the records of this company until March-April, 1864. Reported present for duty in March-April and November-December, 1864. No further records. [May have served previously in Company E, 10th Regiment N.C. State Troops (1st Regiment N.C. Artillery).]

CANADY, THOMAS W., Private

Resided in Harnett County where he enlisted at age 29, October 30, 1861. Present or accounted for until captured at Roanoke Island on February 8, 1862. Paroled at Elizabeth City on February 21, 1862. Discharged on September 20, 1862, by reason of disability.

CARTER, NATHAN, Private

Resided in Harnett County where he enlisted at age 29, October 30, 1861. Present or accounted for until captured at Roanoke Island on February 8, 1862. Paroled at Elizabeth City on February 21, 1862. Discharged on January 20-21, 1863, by reason of disability.

CARTER, NOAH, ———

North Carolina pension records indicate that he served in this company.

CASTLEBURY, BRITTON, Private

Resided in Harnett County where he enlisted at age 47, October 30, 1861. Captured at Roanoke Island on February 8, 1862. Paroled on an unspecified date. Discharged on October 4, 1862, under the provisions of the Conscription Act.

CHRISTIAN, GEORGE W., Private

Born in Cumberland County and resided in Harnett County where he was by occupation a "soldier" prior to enlisting in Harnett County at age 19, October 30, 1861. "Escaped" from Roanoke Island during the Federal attack of February 8, 1862. Enlisted in Company F, 50th Regiment N.C. Troops, March 21, 1862.

CUTTS, JOHN ALLEN, Private

Resided in Harnett County where he enlisted at age 34, October 30, 1861. Captured at Roanoke Island on February 8, 1862. Paroled at Elizabeth City on February 21, 1862. Returned to duty on or about September 15, 1862. Reported absent without leave in March-April, 1864. Returned to duty on an unspecified date. Mortally wounded at or near Fort Harrison, Virginia, on or about September 29, 1864.

DEAN, BURWELL, Private

Resided in Harnett County where he enlisted at age 18, October 30, 1861. Captured at Roanoke Island on February 8, 1862. Paroled at Elizabeth City on February 21, 1862. Returned to duty on or about September 15, 1862. Present or accounted for through December, 1864.

DEAN, JAMES G., ———

North Carolina pension records indicate that he served in this company.

DEAN, JOSEPH, Private

Resided in Harnett County where he enlisted at age 28, October 30, 1861. Captured at Roanoke Island on February 8, 1862. Paroled on an unspecified date. Discharged on October 4 or November 20, 1862. Reason discharged not reported.

DENNIS, HENRY, Private

Resided in Harnett County where he enlisted at age 18, October 30, 1861. Captured at Roanoke Island on February 8, 1862. Paroled at Elizabeth City on February 21, 1862. Returned to duty on or about September 15, 1862. Deserted at Greensboro on December 21, 1864.

DENNIS, JOSEPH, Private

Resided in Harnett County and enlisted at James Island, Charleston, South Carolina, at age 36, March 25, 1863, for the war. Deserted at Raleigh on December 27, 1864.

DEWAR, JOHN P., Sergeant

Resided in Harnett County and was by occupation a farmer prior to enlisting in Harnett County at age 17, October 30, 1861. Mustered in as Corporal. Captured at Roanoke Island on February 8, 1862. Exchanged on an unspecified date. Returned to duty on or about September 15, 1862. Promoted to Sergeant on February 11, 1863. Hospitalized at Danville, Virginia, on or about June 4, 1864, with a gunshot wound of the left arm. Place and date wounded not reported. Returned to duty on June 10, 1864. No further records.

DRAKE, GEORGE FRANCIS, Private

Resided in Chatham County and enlisted in Harnett County at age 21, September 15, 1862, for the war. Captured near Drewry's Bluff, Virginia, on or about May 16, 1864. Confined at Point Lookout, Maryland, May 19, 1864. Released on May 13, 1865, after taking the Oath of Allegiance.

FAISON, JOHN P., Private

Resided in Harnett County where he enlisted at age 25, October 30, 1861. Captured at Roanoke Island on February 8, 1862. Paroled on an unspecified date. "Mustered" at Richmond, Virginia, August 15, 1862, but was "left at home without leave." No further records.

FAUCETT, WILLIAM H., Private

Resided in Harnett County where he enlisted at age 28, September 15, 1862, for the war. Present or accounted for through April, 1864. No further records.

GASKINS, AMETACUS, Private

Resided in Harnett County and enlisted at Sullivan's Island, Charleston, South Carolina, at age 17, September 21, 1863, for the war. Died at or near Richmond, Virginia, on or about July 29, 1864. Cause of death not reported.

GASKINS, CORNELIUS H., Private

Resided in Harnett County where he enlisted at age 17, October 30, 1861. Captured at Roanoke Island on February 8, 1862. Paroled at Elizabeth City on February 21, 1862. Returned to duty on or about September 15, 1862. Killed at Fort Wagner, Charleston, South Carolina, July 17, 1863.

GILBERT, JOHN QUINCEY, Private

Resided in Harnett or Wake County and enlisted in Harnett County at age 18, October 30, 1861. Captured at Roanoke Island on February 8, 1862. Paroled on an unspecified date. Transferred to Company F, 15th Regiment N.C. Troops (5th Regiment N.C. Volunteers), on or about March 20, 1863.

GREGORY, ALFRED BUCK, Private
Resided in Harnett County where he enlisted at age 33, October 30, 1861. Present or accounted for until captured at Roanoke Island on February 8, 1862. Paroled at Elizabeth City on February 21, 1862. Returned to duty on or about September 15, 1862. Hospitalized at Richmond, Virginia, May 17, 1864, with a gunshot wound of the left hip. Place and date wounded not reported. Died in hospital at Richmond on May 18, 1864, of wounds.

GREGORY, JOHN N., Corporal
Resided in Harnett County where he enlisted at age 27, October 30, 1861. Mustered in as Private. Captured at Roanoke Island on February 8, 1862. Paroled at Elizabeth City on February 21, 1862. Returned to duty on an unspecified date. Promoted to Corporal on February 11, 1863. Promoted to Sergeant on June 10, 1863. Wounded at Fort Wagner, Charleston, South Carolina, on or about July 18, 1863. Returned to duty and was reduced to the rank of Corporal prior to May 1, 1864. Company records indicate he was captured by the enemy on or about June 1, 1864; however, records of the Federal Provost Marshal do not substantiate that report. No further records.

GRIFFIN, JOHN W., Private
Resided in Harnett County where he enlisted at age 25, October 30, 1861. Captured at Roanoke Island on February 8, 1862. Paroled at Elizabeth City on February 21, 1862. Returned to duty on or about September 15, 1862. Deserted on December 27, 1864. Captured by the enemy in Chatham County on an unspecified date. Paroled on April 29, 1865.

GRIFFIN, WILLIAM J., Private
Resided in Harnett County where he enlisted at age 31, October 30, 1861. Captured at Roanoke Island on February 8, 1862. Paroled at Elizabeth City on February 21, 1862. Returned to duty on or about September 15, 1862. Reported absent without leave in November-December, 1864.

HAIGWOOD, JOHN C., Private
Resided in Harnett County where he enlisted at age 35, October 30, 1861. Captured at Roanoke Island on February 8, 1862. Paroled at Elizabeth City on February 21, 1862. Returned to duty on or about September 15, 1862. Died in hospital at Petersburg, Virginia, April 25-26, 1864, of ''gastritis.''

HORN, PLEASANT, ———
North Carolina pension records indicate that he served in this company.

HOWINGTON, JOHN H., Private
Resided in Harnett County where he enlisted at age 22, October 30, 1861. Captured at Roanoke Island on February 8, 1862. Paroled at Elizabeth City on February 21, 1862. Returned to duty on or about September 15, 1862. Died at Summerville, South Carolina, September 15, 1863, of disease.

HOWINGTON, JOHN R. J., Private
Previously served in Company E, 8th Regiment N.C.

State Troops. Transferred to this company in November-December, 1862. Hospitalized at Raleigh on June 20, 1864, with a gunshot wound. Place and date wounded not reported. Deserted on September 1, 1864.

HOWINGTON, WILLIAM, Private
Resided in Harnett County where he enlisted at age 24, October 30, 1861. Present or accounted for until captured at Roanoke Island on February 8, 1862. Paroled at Elizabeth City on February 21, 1862. Returned to duty on or about September 15, 1862. Present or accounted for through December, 1864.

JEFFERSON, SIDNEY, ———
Enlisted in Harnett County. Date of enlistment not reported. Reported present in company records dated November-December, 1861. Was apparently dropped from the rolls of the company prior to January 1, 1862. No further records.

JOHNSON, D. W., Private
Resided in Harnett County and enlisted in Moore County at age 18, April 16, 1863, for the war as a substitute for Private A. M. McKay. Deserted on July 11-12, 1863.

JOHNSON, DAVID W., Private
Resided in Harnett County where he enlisted at age 18, October 30, 1861. Present or accounted for until captured at Roanoke Island on February 8, 1862. Exchanged on an unspecified date. Died at Wilmington on January 18 or January 27, 1863, of disease.

JOHNSON, GREEN W., Private
Resided in Harnett County where he enlisted at age 20, October 30, 1861. Present or accounted for until captured at Roanoke Island on February 8, 1862. Paroled at Elizabeth City on February 21, 1862. Returned to duty on or about September 15, 1862. Deserted on September 24, 1863.

JOHNSON, JOHN A., Private
Resided in Harnett County and was by occupation a farmer prior to enlisting in Harnett County at age 20, October 30, 1861. Present or accounted for until captured at Roanoke Island on February 8, 1862. Paroled at Elizabeth City on February 21, 1862. Returned to duty on or about September 15, 1862. Hospitalized at Danville, Virginia, on or about June 4, 1864, with a gunshot wound of the left side. Place and date wounded not reported. Returned to duty on September 26, 1864. Present or accounted for through December, 1864.

JOHNSON, NORMAN T., Private
Resided in Harnett County where he enlisted at age 18, October 30, 1861. Present or accounted for until captured at Roanoke Island on February 8, 1862. Paroled at Elizabeth City on February 21, 1862. Returned to duty on or about September 15, 1862. Present or accounted for through February 28, 1865. [North Carolina pension records indicate he was wounded at Fort Harrison, Virginia, September 30, 1864.]

JONES, SIDNEY J., Private
Resided in Wake County and enlisted in Harnett County at age 19, October 30, 1861. Present or

accounted for until captured at Roanoke Island on February 8, 1862. Paroled at Elizabeth City on February 21, 1862. Died ''at home'' on March 20, 1862. Cause of death not reported.

JONES, WILLIAM, Private
Resided in Harnett County where he enlisted at age 33, October 30, 1861. Present or accounted for until captured at Roanoke Island on February 8, 1862. Paroled at Elizabeth City on February 21, 1862. Hospitalized at Goldsboro on or about December 6, 1862. Returned to duty prior to May 1, 1863. Present or accounted for through December, 1864.

LANIER, BIAS D., 1st Sergeant
Resided in Harnett County where he enlisted at age 21, October 30, 1861. Mustered in as Sergeant. Promoted to 1st Sergeant on February 11, 1863. Captured at Fort Harrison, Virginia, September 30, 1864. Confined at Point Lookout, Maryland, October 5, 1864. Died at Point Lookout on or about December 16, 1864, of ''chronic dysentery.''

LANIER, JAMES H., Private
Previously served in Company F, 15th Regiment N.C. Troops (5th Regiment N.C. Volunteers). Transferred to this company on March 20, 1863. Present or accounted for through December, 1864.

LANIER, JOHN G., Private
Resided in Harnett County where he enlisted at age 18, October 30, 1861. Present or accounted for until captured at Roanoke Island on February 8, 1862. Paroled at Elizabeth City on February 21, 1862. Returned to duty on or about September 15, 1862. Died in hospital at Richmond, Virginia, June 25, 1864, of a gunshot wound of the right foot. Place and date wounded not reported.

LANIER, W. B., Private
Enlisted in Ivor Station, Virginia, February 15, 1864, for the war. Present or accounted for through December, 1864. [North Carolina pension records indicate he was wounded at ''Bentonville in April, 1865.'']

LEE, LEMON P., Private
Enlisted in Harnett County on September 15, 1862, for the war. Reported absent without leave during January-April, 1863.

McALISTER, JOSEPH H., Sergeant
Resided in Harnett County where he enlisted at age 17, October 30, 1861. Mustered in as Private. Present or accounted for until captured at Roanoke Island on February 8, 1862. Paroled at Elizabeth City on February 21, 1862. Returned to duty on or about September 15, 1862. Promoted to Corporal on February 11, 1863. Promoted to Sergeant in May, 1863-April, 1864. Wounded at Fort Wagner, Charleston, South Carolina, July 18, 1863. Returned to duty prior to May 1, 1864. Present or accounted for through December, 1864.

McDONALD, NORMAN, Private
Resided in Harnett County where he enlisted at age 47, October 30, 1861. Present or accounted for until captured at Roanoke Island on February 8, 1862. Paroled at Elizabeth City on February 21, 1862. Discharged on October 4, 1862, under the provisions of the Conscription Act.

McKAY, A. M., Private
Enlisted in Harnett County on September 15, 1862, for the war. Discharged on April 16, 1863, after providing Private D. W. Johnson as a substitute.

McLEAN, ALEXANDER, Private
Resided in Harnett County where he enlisted at age 28, September 15, 1862, for the war. Wounded at White Hall on December 16, 1862. Returned to duty prior to March 1, 1863. Present or accounted for through December, 1864.

McLEAN, DANIEL C., 1st Sergeant
Resided in Harnett County where he enlisted at age 38, October 30, 1861. Mustered in as 1st Sergeant. Present or accounted for until captured at Roanoke Island on February 8, 1862. Paroled at Elizabeth City on February 21, 1862. Discharged on October 4, 1862, under the provisions of the Conscription Act.

McLEAN, HECTOR, Private
Resided in Harnett County and enlisted at age 24, October 30, 1861. Present or accounted for until captured at Roanoke Island on February 8, 1862. Paroled at Elizabeth City on February 21, 1862. Returned to duty on or about September 15, 1862. Present or accounted for through December, 1864. [North Carolina pension records indicate he was wounded at Cold Harbor, Virginia, May 31, 1864.]

McLEAN, MALCOLM, Private
Resided in Harnett County where he enlisted at age 21, October 30, 1861. Present or accounted for until captured at Roanoke Island on February 8, 1862. Paroled at Elizabeth City on February 21, 1862. Returned to duty on or about September 15, 1862. Deserted on August 10, 1864.

McLEOD, DANIEL, Private
Born in Harnett County* where he resided as a farmer prior to enlisting in Harnett County at age 25, September 15, 1862, for the war. Present or accounted for through December, 1864.

MARTIN, JOHN A., Private
Resided in Harnett County where he enlisted at age 40, October 30, 1861. Present or accounted for until captured at Roanoke Island on February 8, 1862. Paroled on an unspecified date. Reported absent in Harnett County in January-February, 1863. Listed as a deserter in March-April, 1863.

MATHEWS, JOHN W., Corporal
Resided in Harnett County where he enlisted at age 26, October 30, 1861. Mustered in as Corporal. Present or accounted for until captured at Roanoke Island on February 8, 1862. Exchanged on an unspecified date. Discharged on September 20, 1862, by reason of disability. Paroled at Avin's Ferry on April 26, 1865.

MATTHEWS, JOSEPH, Private
Resided in Harnett County where he enlisted at age 17, October 30, 1861. Present or accounted for through March 26, 1865.

MELVIN, ISAAC, Private
Enlisted at Camp Whiting on February 13, 1863, for the war. Wounded at Fort Wagner, Charleston, South

Carolina, July 18, 1863. Hospitalized at Charleston where he died of wounds. Date of death not reported.

MESSER, JOHN, Private
Born in Wake County and resided in Harnett County where he was by occupation a farmer prior to enlisting at James Island, Charleston, South Carolina, at age 46, March 24, 1863, for the war. Hospitalized at Raleigh on January 18, 1865, with a gunshot wound of the right leg. Place and date wounded not reported. Returned to duty on January 24, 1865. Retired to the Invalid Corps on February 20, 1865.

MESSER, WILLIAM T., Private
Resided in Harnett County where he enlisted at age 25, September 15, 1862, for the war. Wounded at or near Fort Wagner, Charleston, South Carolina, on or about July 16, 1863. Returned to duty prior to May 1, 1864. Deserted on August 10, 1864.

MILLER, GEORGE W., Private
Resided in Alabama and was by occupation a "moulder" prior to enlisting at Camp Martin at age 46, October 30, 1862, for the war as a substitute. Present or accounted for through December, 1864.

MORRISON, DANIEL, Private
Resided in Harnett County where he enlisted at age 23, October 30, 1861. Present or accounted for until captured at Roanoke Island on February 8, 1862. Paroled at Elizabeth City on February 21, 1862. Returned to duty on or about September 15, 1862. Reported absent without leave on October 1, 1864. [North Carolina pension records indicate he was wounded in the hip at Drewry's Bluff, Virginia, July 1, 1864.]

MORRISON, MARTIN, Private
Resided in Harnett County where he enlisted at age 20, October 30, 1861. Present or accounted for until captured at Roanoke Island on February 8, 1862. Paroled at Elizabeth City on February 21, 1862. Returned to duty on or about September 15, 1862. Present or accounted for through December, 1864. [North Carolina pension records indicate he was wounded in the right hip at Cold Harbor, Virginia, in 1863, and was wounded in the back at Fort Harrison, Virginia, in September, 1863.]

NORDEN, ALEXANDER, Private
Resided in Harnett County where he enlisted at age 33, October 30, 1861. Present or accounted for until captured at Roanoke Island on February 8, 1862. Paroled at Elizabeth City on February 21, 1862. Returned to duty on an unspecified date. Reported absent sick in January-April, 1863. Reported present for duty in March-April, 1864. Deserted on August 10, 1864. [North Carolina pension records indicate he was wounded in the arm and left thigh at Chaffin's Farm, Virginia, April 1, 1863.]

NORDEN, JOHN N., Private
Resided in Harnett County where he enlisted at age 25, October 30, 1861. Present or accounted for until captured at Roanoke Island on February 8, 1862. Paroled at Elizabeth City on February 21, 1862. Returned to duty prior to May 1, 1863. Present or accounted for through December, 1864.

PARKER, WILLIAM A., Sergeant
Resided in Harnett County where he enlisted at age 20, October 30, 1861. Mustered in as Private. Present or accounted for until captured at Roanoke Island on February 8, 1862. Paroled at Elizabeth City on February 21, 1862. Returned to duty on or about September 15, 1862. Promoted to Corporal on February 11, 1863. Promoted to Sergeant in May, 1863-April, 1864. Present or accounted for through December, 1864.

PARTIN, GEORGE P., Private
Resided in Harnett County and enlisted in Wake County at age 23, September 15, 1862, for the war. Deserted on December 9, 1863. Returned to duty subsequent to April 30, 1864. Captured at Globe Tavern, Virginia, August 19, 1864. Confined at Point Lookout, Maryland, August 22, 1864. Paroled at Point Lookout on or about March 14, 1865, and transferred to Boulware's Wharf, James River, Virginia, where he was received on March 16, 1865, for exchange.

PRINCE, MALCOLM M., ———
Negro. "Helped in building the breastworks, and forts at Wilmington, North Carolina, and Fort Hill." No further records.

RAY, NIVEN, Corporal
Resided in Harnett County where he enlisted at age 38, October 30, 1861. Mustered in as Corporal. Present or accounted for until captured at Roanoke Island on February 8, 1862. Paroled at Elizabeth City on February 21, 1862. Discharged on October 4, 1862, under the provisions of the Conscription Act.

RISING, GEORGE W., Private
Resided in Harnett County where he enlisted at age 47, October 30, 1861. Present or accounted for until captured at Roanoke Island on February 8, 1862. Paroled at Elizabeth City on February 21, 1862. Discharged on October 4, 1862, under the provisions of the Conscription Act.

SANDERFORD, JAMES, Private
Resided in Harnett County where he enlisted at age 28, October 30, 1861. Present or accounted for until captured at Roanoke Island on February 8, 1862. Exchanged on an unspecified date. Returned to duty on or about September 15, 1862. Deserted on December 13, 1863. Paroled at Greensboro on or about April 28, 1865.

SAPPS, A., Private
Place and date of enlistment not reported. Captured by the enemy on an unspecified date. Reported in a Federal hospital at Farmville, Virginia, from April 7 through June 15, 1865.

SENTER, CHARLES H., Private
Resided in Harnett County where he enlisted at age 42, October 30, 1861. Present or accounted for until captured at Roanoke Island on February 8, 1862. Paroled at Elizabeth City on February 21, 1862. Discharged on October 4, 1862, under the provisions of the Conscription Act.

SENTER, MALCOM J., Private
Resided in Harnett County where he enlisted at age 19, September 15, 1862, for the war. Present or accounted for through December, 1864.

SHIPP, NATHANIEL M., Private

Previously served in Company G, 7th Regiment N.C. State Troops. Enlisted in this company in Harnett County on September 15, 1862, for the war as a substitute. Transferred to Company G of this regiment on February 12, 1864.

SMITH, DANIEL, Private

Resided in Harnett County where he enlisted at age 22, September 15, 1862, for the war. Deserted on December 29, 1864.

SMITH, HUGH, Private

Resided in Harnett County where he enlisted at age 22, October 30, 1861. Present or accounted for until captured at Roanoke Island on February 8, 1862. Paroled at Elizabeth City on February 21, 1862. Returned to duty on or about September 15, 1862. Hospitalized at Richmond, Virginia, May 17, 1864, with a gunshot wound. Place and date wounded not reported. Died at Richmond on May 18, 1864, of wounds.

SMITH, HUGH H., Private

Resided in Harnett County and enlisted at age 18, October 30, 1861. No further records.

SMITH, JAMES H., Private

Resided in Harnett County and enlisted in New Hanover County at age 18, April 17, 1863, for the war. Captured at Fort Harrison, Virginia, September 30, 1864. Confined at Point Lookout, Maryland, October 5, 1864. Paroled at Point Lookout on or about March 17, 1865, and transferred to Boulware's Wharf, James River, Virginia, where he was received on March 19, 1865, for exchange.

SMITH, JOHN H., Private

Enlisted in Harnett County on October 30, 1861. Present or accounted for until captured at Roanoke Island on February 8, 1862. Paroled at Elizabeth City on February 21, 1862. Returned to duty prior to May 1, 1863. Hospitalized at Richmond, Virginia, May 14, 1864, with a gunshot wound of the head. Place and date wounded not reported. Died prior to December 18, 1864. Place and cause of death not reported.

SMITH, MELTON J., Private

Resided in Harnett County where he enlisted at age 20, October 30, 1861. Present or accounted for until captured at Roanoke Island on February 8, 1862. Paroled at Elizabeth City on February 21, 1862. Returned to duty on or about September 15, 1862. Present or accounted for through December, 1864.

SMITH, WILLIAM, ———

North Carolina pension records indicate that he served in this company.

SPENCE, GEORGE D., Private

Resided in Harnett County where he enlisted at age 35, September 15, 1862, for the war. Present or accounted for through December, 1864.

SPENCE, NEELL A., Private

Enlisted in Harnett County on September 15, 1862, for the war. Deserted on November 27, 1862.

SPENCE, WILLIAM, Private

Resided in Harnett County where he enlisted at age 33,

October 30, 1861. Present or accounted for until captured at Roanoke Island on February 8, 1862. Paroled at Elizabeth City on February 21, 1862. Returned to duty on or about September 15, 1862. Deserted on December 13, 1863. Returned to duty prior to May 1, 1864. Captured near Petersburg, Virginia, June 16, 1864. Confined at Point Lookout, Maryland, June 24, 1864. Transferred to Elmira, New York, on or about July 27, 1864. Released at Elmira on July 3, 1865, after taking the Oath of Allegiance. [North Carolina pension records indicate he was wounded at White Hall in December, 1862.]

STEPHENSON, S. D., ———

North Carolina pension records indicate that he served in this company.

STEWART, ALEXANDER, Private

Resided in Harnett County where he enlisted at age 53, October 30, 1861. Present or accounted for until captured at Roanoke Island on February 8, 1862. Paroled at Elizabeth City on February 21, 1862. Discharged on October 4, 1862, under the provisions of the Conscription Act.

STEWART, ALFRED W., Private

Resided in Harnett County where he enlisted at age 33, October 30, 1861. Mustered in as Private. Promoted to Musician prior to January 1, 1862. Present or accounted for until captured at Roanoke Island on February 8, 1862. Paroled at Elizabeth City on February 21, 1862. Returned to duty on or about September 15, 1862. Reduced to ranks in May, 1863-April, 1864. Captured at Wise's Fork on March 10, 1865. Confined at Point Lookout, Maryland, March 30, 1865. Released on June 20, 1865, after taking the Oath of Allegiance. [North Carolina pension records indicate he was wounded in the right leg at Fort Fisher on January 1, 1865.]

STEWART, JOSEPH A., Sergeant

Resided in Harnett County where he enlisted at age 23, December 31, 1862, for the war. Mustered in as Private. Promoted to Corporal on February 11, 1863. Promoted to Sergeant in May, 1863-April, 1864. Wounded at or near Fort Wagner, Charleston, South Carolina, July 16, 1863. Returned to duty prior to May 1, 1864. Present or accounted for through April, 1865.

STEWART, WILLIAM J., Private

Resided in Harnett County where he enlisted at age 18, October 30, 1861. Present or accounted for until captured at Roanoke Island on February 8, 1862. Paroled at Elizabeth City on February 21, 1862. Returned to duty prior to May 1, 1863. Present or accounted for through December, 1864. [North Carolina pension records indicate he was wounded in the left hand at Cold Harbor, Virginia, October 1, 1863.]

STINSON, H. M., Private

Place and date of enlistment not reported. Captured by the enemy on an unspecified date. Confined at Elmira, New York, where he died on May 17, 1865. Cause of death not reported.

STRICKLAND, JOHN, Private

Resided in Harnett County where he enlisted at age 29, October 30, 1861. Present or accounted for until captured at Roanoke Island on February 8, 1862.

Paroled at Elizabeth City on February 21, 1862. Returned to duty on or about September 15, 1862. Present or accounted for through December, 1864.

STRICKLAND, WILLIAM S., Private
Resided in Harnett County where he enlisted at age 25, October 30, 1861. Present or accounted for until captured at Roanoke Island on February 8, 1862. Paroled at Elizabeth City on February 21, 1862. Returned to duty prior to May 1, 1863. Deserted on December 9, 1863. Returned to duty on an unspecified date. Hospitalized at Richmond, Virginia, May 16, 1864, with a gunshot wound of the left hand. Place and date wounded not reported. Returned to duty on or about June 2, 1864. Wounded in the head at Cold Harbor, Virginia, on or about June 3, 1864. Hospitalized at Richmond where he died on June 20, 1864, of a ''fracture[d] skull.''

SWINSON, JOSEPH, Private
Resided in Harnett County where he enlisted at age 33, September 15, 1862, for the war. Mustered in as Private. Promoted to Musician prior to March 1, 1863. Reduced to ranks in May, 1863-April, 1864. Deserted on December 2, 1863. Returned to duty prior to May 1, 1864. Present or accounted for through December, 1864. [Served also in Company G, 2nd Regiment Confederate Engineering Troops.]

THOMAS, J. D., Private
Enlisted in Harnett County on September 15, 1862, for the war. Discharged on January 28, 1863, by reason of disability.

THOMAS, JOSEPH MARTIN, Private
Resided in Harnett County where he enlisted at age 22, September 15, 1862, for the war. Present or accounted for through December, 1864.

THOMAS, THOMAS H., Corporal
Resided in Harnett County where he enlisted at age 22, September 15, 1862, for the war. Mustered in as Private. Promoted to Corporal in May, 1863-April, 1864. Captured at Cold Harbor, Virginia, June 1, 1864. Confined at Point Lookout, Maryland, June 11, 1864. Transferred to Elmira, New York, July 12, 1864. Paroled at Elmira on March 2, 1865, and transferred for exchange. Furloughed for thirty days on March 9, 1865.

THOMASON, LOUIS, Private
Resided in Wake County and enlisted in Harnett County at age 52, September 15, 1862, for the war as a substitute. Present or accounted for through January 1, 1865.

THRAILKILL, NEILL A., Private
Resided in Harnett County where he enlisted at age 31, September 15, 1862, for the war. Company records indicate he was captured by the enemy on September 30, 1864; however, records of the Federal Provost Marshal do not substantiate that report. No further records.

TRUELOVE, A. R., Private
Resided in Harnett County and enlisted at Sullivan's Island, Charleston, South Carolina, at age 19, October 30, 1863, for the war. Wounded in the head at Drewry's Bluff, Virginia, May 16, 1864. Reported absent without leave on August 11, 1864. [North Carolina pension records indicate that he survived the war.]

TRUELOVE, J. A., ———
North Carolina pension records indicate that he served in this company.

TRULOVE, JOHN, ———
North Carolina pension records indicate that he served in this company.

TRULOVE, THOMAS D., Private
Resided in Harnett County where he enlisted at age 34, September 15, 1862, for the war. Reported absent without leave on June 25, 1863.

TUTOR, J. H., Private
Enlisted at Petersburg, Virginia, July 27, 1864, for the war. Deserted from hospital at Raleigh on March 7, 1865.

TUTOR, JAMES A., Private
Resided in Harnett County where he enlisted at age 19, September 15, 1862, for the war. Present or accounted for through December, 1864. Captured at or near Raleigh on or about April 15. 1865.

TUTOR, JOE A., ———
North Carolina pension records indicate that he served in this company.

TUTOR, OWEN, Private
Resided in Harnett County where he enlisted at age 52, September 15, 1862, for the war as a substitute. Present or accounted for through April, 1864. No further records.

TUTOR, REUBEN S., Private
Resided in Harnett County and enlisted at James Island, Charleston, South Carolina, at age 18, August 31, 1863, for the war. Present or accounted for through December, 1864.

WEATHERS, JAMES H., Private
Enlisted in Harnett County on September 15, 1862, for the war. Deserted on December 25, 1862.

WEATHERS, JESSE D., Corporal
Resided in Harnett County where he enlisted at age 21, October 30, 1861. Mustered in as Private. Present or accounted for until captured at Roanoke Island on February 8, 1862. Paroled at Elizabeth City on February 21, 1862. Returned to duty on or about September 15, 1862. Promoted to Corporal in May, 1863-April, 1864. Captured at Drewry's Bluff, Virginia, May 16, 1864. Confined at Point Lookout, Maryland, May 24, 1864. Paroled at Point Lookout on or about March 15, 1865, and transferred to Boulware's Wharf, James River, Virginia, where he was received on March 18, 1865, for exchange. Furloughed for thirty days on March 23, 1865.

WEATHERS, RICHARD, Private
Enlisted in Harnett County on September 15, 1862, for the war. Present or accounted for until he was sent home on sick furlough on December 25, 1862. Listed as a deserter in March-April, 1863.

WEST, ALEXANDER, Private
Resided in Harnett County where he enlisted at age 34, September 15, 1862, for the war. Present or accounted for through December, 1864.

WEST, DANIEL R., Private
Resided in Harnett County where he enlisted at age 29,

September 15, 1862, for the war. Killed at Cold Harbor, Virginia, on or about June 1, 1864.

WEST, JACOB, Private
Place and date of enlistment not reported. Reported present for duty in November-December, 1864. No further records.

WEST, LEVI, Private
Enlisted at Petersburg, Virginia, April 15, 1864, for the war. Present or accounted for through December, 1864.

WESTER, JOHN H., Private
Resided in Harnett County where he enlisted on October 30, 1861. Present or accounted for until captured at Roanoke Island on February 8, 1862. Paroled at Elizabeth City on February 21, 1862. Returned to duty on or about September 15, 1862. Wounded at White Hall on December 16, 1862. Reported absent sick during January-April, 1863. Returned to duty prior to May 1, 1864. Deserted on December 27. 1864.

WETHERS, STEPHEN, Private
Resided in Harnett County where he enlisted at age 18, October 30, 1861. Died at Roanoke Island on December 20, 1861, or January 15, 1862, of disease.

WILSON, MONROE, Private
Resided in Harnett County where he enlisted at age 17, October 30, 1861. Reported absent without leave in November-December, 1861. Returned to duty prior to February 8, 1862, when he was captured at Roanoke Island. Exchanged on an unspecified date. "Mustered" at or near Richmond, Virginia, on or about August 15, 1862. No further records.

YARBROUGH, JOHN W., Private
Resided in Harnett County where he enlisted at age 25, October 30, 1861. Present or accounted for until captured at Roanoke Island on February 8, 1862. Paroled at Elizabeth City on February 21, 1862. Returned to duty prior to May 1, 1863. Deserted on or about December 5, 1863.

COMPANY K

This company was raised in Craven County and enlisted at New Bern on November 21, 1861. It was then assigned to the 31st Regiment N.C. Troops and designated Company K. After joining the regiment the company functioned as a part of the regiment, and its history for the war period is reported as a part of the regimental history.

The information contained in the following roster of the company was compiled principally from company muster rolls for January-April, 1863; March-April, 1864; and November-December, 1864. No company muster rolls were found for November 21, 1861-December 31, 1862; May, 1863-February, 1864; May-October, 1864; or for the period after December, 1864. Valuable information was obtained from primary records such as the Roll of Honor, discharge certificates, medical records, prisoner of war records, and pension applications. Secondary sources such as postwar rosters and histories, cemetery records, and records of the United Daughters of the Confederacy also provided useful information.

OFFICERS

CAPTAIN

WHITTY, JOSEPH
Resided in Craven County and enlisted at age 31. Appointed Captain on November 21, 1861. Captured at Roanoke Island on February 8, 1862. Paroled at Elizabeth City on February 21, 1862. Returned to duty on or about September 15, 1862. Present or accounted for through January 1, 1865.

LIEUTENANTS

BALLENGER, JOSEPH D., 2nd Lieutenant
Resided in Craven County and enlisted at age 18, November 21, 1861. Mustered in as Sergeant. Captured at Roanoke Island on February 8, 1862. Paroled at Elizabeth City on February 21, 1862. Appointed 2nd Lieutenant on or about September 17, 1862. Resigned on April 15, 1864. Reason he resigned not reported. Resignation accepted on April 23, 1864. Paroled at Goldsboro on May 15, 1865. "Came in for parole." [North Carolina pension records indicate he was wounded in the thigh at Malvern Hill, Virginia, and was wounded in the head at Cold Harbor, Virginia.]

BERRY, JOHN H., 2nd Lieutenant
Served as 2nd Lieutenant in Company E of this regiment. Reported in command of this company in November-December, 1864.

BOWEN, EDWARD J., 1st Lieutenant
Resided in Craven County and enlisted at age 27. Appointed 1st Lieutenant on November 21, 1861. Defeated for reelection when the regiment was reorganized on or about September 17, 1862. Reappointed 1st Lieutenant of this company on October 21, 1863. Reported absent without leave on October 16, 1864.

DARDEN, GEORGE F., 2nd Lieutenant
Resided in Craven County and enlisted in Wake County at age 29, September 15, 1862, for the war. Mustered in as Private. Promoted to 1st Sergeant the same date. Appointed 2nd Lieutenant on June 22, 1863. Wounded in the mouth at Cold Harbor, Virginia, on or about June 1, 1864. Returned to duty prior to September 30, 1864, when he was captured at Fort Harrison, Virginia. Confined at Old Capitol Prison, Washington, D.C., October 6, 1864. Transferred to Fort Delaware, Delaware, October 21, 1864. Released at Fort Delaware on June 17, 1865, after taking the Oath of Allegiance.

GARDNER, WILLIAM N., 3rd Lieutenant
Resided in Craven County and enlisted at age 18, November 21, 1861. Mustered in as Private. Appointed 3rd Lieutenant on or about September 17, 1862. Reported present but under arrest in March-April, 1863. "Cashiered" in April, 1863.

GASKINS, THOMAS H., 1st Lieutenant
Resided in Craven County and enlisted at age 25. Appointed 2nd Lieutenant on November 21, 1861. Captured at Roanoke Island on February 8, 1862. Paroled at Elizabeth City on February 21, 1862. Promoted to 1st Lieutenant on or about September 17, 1862. Resigned on September 20, 1862, in order to enlist in another unit. Later served as 1st Lieutenant of Company B, 1st Battalion N.C. Local Defense Troops.

NONCOMMISSIONED OFFICERS AND PRIVATES

ANDERSON, ELI, Private
Resided in Craven County where he enlisted at age 29, November 21, 1861. Captured at Roanoke Island on February 8, 1862. Paroled at Elizabeth City on February 21, 1862. Returned to duty on or about September 15, 1862. Hospitalized at Danville, Virginia, on or about June 4, 1864, with a gunshot wound. Place and date wounded not reported. Returned to duty on June 26, 1864. Captured near Fort Harrison, Virginia, September 30, 1864. Confined at Point Lookout, Maryland, October 5, 1864. Released on June 22, 1865, after taking the Oath of Allegiance.

ANDERSON, JOHN W., Corporal
Resided in Craven County and enlisted at age 27, November 21, 1861. Mustered in as Corporal. Captured at Roanoke Island on February 8, 1862. Paroled at Elizabeth City on February 21, 1862. Died in Craven County on March 24, 1862. Cause of death not reported.

ANDERSON, JOSHUA, Private
Resided in Craven County where he enlisted at age 21, November 21, 1861. Captured at Roanoke Island on February 8, 1862. Paroled at Elizabeth City on February 21, 1862. Returned to duty on or about September 15, 1862. Deserted in December, 1862. Returned to duty prior to May 1, 1863. Reported absent sick from June 15, 1864, through December, 1864. No further records.

AVIRETT, STEPHEN, Private
Resided in Craven County where he enlisted at age 37, November 21, 1861. Captured at Roanoke Island on February 8, 1862. Paroled at Elizabeth City on February 21, 1862. Returned to duty on or about September 15, 1862. Reported ''absent, sick at home'' prior to March 1, 1863. ''Confined at home by paralysis.'' Dropped from the rolls of the company prior to May 1, 1863.

BANKS, E. J., Corporal
Enlisted in Wake County on September 15, 1862, for the war. Mustered in as Corporal. Died in hospital at Columbia, South Carolina, March 25, 1863. Cause of death not reported.

BANKS, OLIVER P., Private
Resided in Craven County and enlisted at age 40, November 21, 1861. Discharged on November 21, 1862, under the provisions of the Conscription Act.

BARHAM, T. J., Private
Previously served in Company H of this regiment. Transferred to this company on June 13, 1863. Captured at Fort Harrison, Virginia, September 30, 1864. Confined at Point Lookout, Maryland, October 5, 1864. Paroled at Point Lookout on or about February 13, 1865, and transferred to Cox's Wharf, James River, Virginia, where he was received on February 14-15, 1865, for exchange.

BARRINGTON, JESSE S., Corporal
Resided in Craven County where he enlisted at age 28, November 21, 1861. Mustered in as Private. Captured at Roanoke Island on February 8, 1862. Paroled at Elizabeth City on February 21, 1862. Returned to duty on or about September 15, 1862. Promoted to Corporal in May-August, 1864. Present or accounted for until September, 1864, when he was reported absent without leave.

BENNETT, JOSIAH, Corporal
Resided in Craven County and enlisted in Wake County at age 31, September 15, 1862, for the war. Mustered in as Private. Present or accounted for until hospitalized at Richmond, Virginia, May 14, 1864, with a gunshot wound of the hand. Place and date wounded not reported. Promoted to Corporal in May-August, 1864. Reported absent without leave in September, 1864.

BENNETT, WILLIAM E., Sergeant
Resided in Craven County where he enlisted at age 28, November 21, 1861. Mustered in as Corporal. Captured at Roanoke Island on February 8, 1862. Paroled at Elizabeth City on February 21, 1862. Returned to duty on or about September 15, 1862. Promoted to Sergeant on October 8, 1863. Company records indicate he was captured at or near Fort Harrison, Virginia, September 30, 1864; however, records of the Federal Provost Marshal do not substantiate that report. No further records.

BIRD, BENJAMIN A., Private
Previously served in Company C, 1st Battalion N.C. Junior Reserves. Transferred to this company on January 12, 1865. Paroled subsequent to April 26, 1865.

BRADLEY, GEORGE W., Private
Previously served in Company C, 1st Battalion N.C. Junior Reserves. Transferred to this company on January 12, 1865. No further records.

BRINSON, HENRY B., Private
Resided in Craven County and enlisted at age 43, November 21, 1861. Captured at Roanoke Island on February 8, 1862. Paroled at Elizabeth City on February 21, 1862. Discharged on November 21, 1862, under the provisions of the Conscription Act.

BRINSON, JEROME B., Private
Resided in Craven County and enlisted at age 28, November 21, 1861. Captured at Roanoke Island on February 8, 1862. Paroled at Elizabeth City on February 21, 1862. Failed to return to duty when the regiment was reorganized on or about September 17, 1862. Company records dated January-February, 1863, indicate that he was absent without leave and ''says [he] won't come.'' Dropped from the rolls of the company prior to May 1, 1863, by reason of ''being in the Yankee lines or in such other place as that he can not be got at.''

BRINSON, JOHN C., Private
Resided in Craven County where he enlisted at age 20, November 21, 1861. Mustered in as Corporal. Captured at Roanoke Island on February 8, 1862. Paroled at Elizabeth City on February 21, 1862. Returned to duty on or about September 15, 1862. Reduced to ranks prior to January 1, 1863. Captured at Globe Tavern, Virginia, August 19, 1864. Confined at Point Lookout, Maryland, August 22, 1864. Exchanged on March 15, 1865.

CARRIKER, M. W., Private
Resided in Cabarrus County and enlisted at age 39, May 26, 1863, for the war. Wounded at Fort Wagner, Charleston, South Carolina, July 18, 1863. Died at or near Charleston on July 26, 1863, of wounds. ''A brave

man and good soldier."

CIVILS, WILLIAM T., Private

Resided in Craven County and enlisted in Wake County at age 21, November 21, 1861. Captured at Roanoke Island on February 8, 1862. Paroled at Elizabeth City on February 21, 1862. Failed to return to duty when the regiment was reorganized on or about September 17, 1862. Dropped from the rolls of the company in March-April, 1863, by reason of "being in the Yankee lines or in such other place as that he can not be got at."

CLAYTON, D. M., Private

Previously served in Company C, 1st Battalion N.C. Junior Reserves. Transferred to this company on January 12, 1865. No further records.

CLAYTON, G. P., Private

Previously served in Company C, 1st Battalion N.C. Junior Reserves. Transferred to this company on January 12, 1865. No further records.

COPPLE, JACOB, Private

Resided in Randolph County and enlisted at Camp Holmes at age 36, May 20, 1863, for the war. Wounded in the right thigh at or near Fort Harrison, Virginia, September 30, 1864. Reported absent wounded through December, 1864.

CROSS, J. R., Private

Resided in Davidson County and enlisted at Camp Holmes at age 18, May 28, 1863, for the war. Wounded in the left thigh at or near Fort Harrison, Virginia, September 30, 1864. Reported absent wounded through December, 1864. Paroled at Greensboro on May 9, 1865.

CUMBO, CALVIN, Private

Resided in Craven County and enlisted at age 22, November 21, 1861. Captured at Roanoke Island on February 8, 1862. Paroled at Elizabeth City on February 21, 1862. Died in Craven County on March 6, 1862. Cause of death not reported.

CURTIS, SAMUEL C., Private

Resided in Craven County and enlisted at age 18, November 21, 1861. Captured at Roanoke Island on February 8, 1862. Paroled at Elizabeth City on February 21, 1862. Discharged on November 21, 1862. Reason discharged not reported.

DEAL, STEPHEN S., Sergeant

Resided in Craven County where he enlisted at age 20, November 21, 1861. Mustered in as Private. Captured at Roanoke Island on February 8, 1862. Paroled at Elizabeth City on February 21, 1862. Returned to duty on or about September 15, 1862. Promoted to Corporal the same date. Promoted to Sergeant in May-December, 1864. Wounded in the arm at Cold Harbor, Virginia, May 31, 1864. Furloughed on June 7, 1864. Returned to duty on an unspecified date. Reported present for duty in November-December, 1864.

DIXON, CALEB, Sergeant

Resided in Chowan County where he enlisted at age 18, November 21, 1861. Mustered in as Private. Promoted to Sergeant prior to March 1, 1863. Present or accounted for through April, 1864. No further records.

DIXON, ROWLAND, Private

Resided in Craven County and enlisted at age 24, November 21, 1861. Failed to report for duty. No further records.

DOUGLASS, D. H., Private

Resided in Orange County where he enlisted at age 21, May 18, 1863, for the war. Reported absent without leave on December 27, 1864. Paroled at Greensboro on or about May 17, 1865.

DOUGLASS, JAMES F., Private

Resided in Orange County where he enlisted at age 26, May 18, 1863, for the war. Hospitalized at Richmond, Virginia, May 16, 1864, with a gunshot wound of the right forearm. Place and date wounded not reported. Furloughed for sixty days on June 3, 1864. Reported absent without leave on December 27, 1864. Paroled at Greensboro on May 15, 1865.

EDNEY, DECATER, Private

Previously served in Company C, 1st Battalion N.C. Junior Reserves. Transferred to this company on January 12, 1865. No further records.

EUBANKS, EZEKIEL, Private

Resided in Craven County and enlisted at age 22, November 21, 1861. Captured at Roanoke Island on February 8, 1862. Paroled at Elizabeth City on February 21, 1862. Declined to reenlist when the regiment was reorganized on or about September 17, 1862.

EUBANKS, LOTT, Private

Resided in Craven County and enlisted at age 24, November 21, 1861. Declined to reenlist when the regiment was reorganized on or about September 17, 1862. Dropped from the rolls of the company in March-April, 1863, by reason of being within the enemy lines "or in such other place as that he can not be got at."

EUBANKS, THOMAS, Private

Resided in Craven County and enlisted at age 27, November 21, 1861. Declined to reenlist when the regiment was reorganized on or about September 17, 1862. Dropped from the rolls of the company in March-April, 1863, by reason of being within the enemy lines.

FAULK, JOHN L., Private

Resided in Columbus County where he enlisted at age 39, May 20, 1863, for the war. Reported absent without leave on March 1, 1864. Returned to duty subsequent to April 30, 1864. Reported absent without leave on November 15, 1864.

FILINGHAM, WILLIAM H., Private

Resided in Craven County and enlisted at age 22, November 21, 1861. Captured at Roanoke Island on February 8, 1862. Paroled at Elizabeth City on February 21, 1862. Enlisted in the Union Army at Washington, North Carolina, prior to March 1, 1863.

FORNES, LACY A., Private

Born in Craven County where he resided as a farmer prior to enlisting in Craven County on November 21, 1861. Captured at Roanoke Island on February 8, 1862. Paroled at Elizabeth City on February 21, 1862. Discharged on November 21, 1862, under the provisions of the Conscription Act. Discharge certificate gives his age as 16.

FOY, ALEXANDER, Private
Resided in Craven County and enlisted in Wake County at age 18, September 15, 1862, for the war. Captured at Fort Harrison, Virginia, September 30, 1864. Confined at Point Lookout, Maryland, October 5, 1864. Paroled at Point Lookout on March 17, 1865, and transferred to Boulware's Wharf, James River, Virginia, where he was received on March 19, 1865, for exchange.

FRY, FRANKLIN, Private
Resided in Davidson County and enlisted at Camp Holmes at age 23, May 20, 1863, for the war. Present or accounted for through December, 1864. Paroled at Greensboro on or about May 5, 1865.

GARTON, JAMES P., Private
Previously served in Company C, 1st Battalion N.C. Junior Reserves. Transferred to this company on January 12, 1865. No further records.

GATTEN, JAMES W., Private
Resided in Craven County where he enlisted at age 21, November 21, 1861. Captured at Roanoke Island on February 8, 1862. Paroled at Elizabeth City on February 21, 1862. Reported absent sick during January-April, 1863. Reported absent without leave from July 4, 1863, until February 4, 1864, when he returned to duty. Captured at Fort Harrison, Virginia, September 30, 1864. Confined at Point Lookout, Maryland, October 5, 1864. Paroled at Point Lookout on January 17, 1865, and transferred to Boulware's Wharf, James River, Virginia, where he was received on January 21, 1865, for exchange.

GREEN, JESSE, Private
Resided in Nash County and enlisted at Camp Holmes at age 29, May 29, 1863, for the war. Wounded in the left lung at or near Fort Harrison, Virginia, September 30, 1864. Hospitalized at Richmond, Virginia, where he died on October 24, 1864, of wounds.

GWALTNEY, EVERETT, Private
Resided in Craven County where he enlisted at age 42, November 21, 1861. Captured at Roanoke Island on February 8, 1862. Paroled at Elizabeth City on February 21, 1862. Returned to duty on or about September 15, 1862. Deserted in December, 1862. Returned to duty prior to May 1, 1864. Died in hospital at Richmond, Virginia, December 6, 1864, of "diarrhoea ch[ronic]."

HAM, D. S., Private
Resided in Forsyth County and enlisted at Camp Holmes at age 29, May 20, 1863, for the war. Reported absent without leave from January 1, 1864, until April 14, 1864, when he returned to duty. Wounded at or near Cold Harbor, Virginia, May 31, 1864. Reported absent without leave in November-December, 1864. Paroled at Greensboro on May 19, 1865.

HAMMOND, EDWARD, Private
Resided in Jones County and enlisted at age 45, November 21, 1861. Captured at Roanoke Island on February 8, 1862. Paroled at Elizabeth City on February 21, 1862. Discharged on November 21, 1862, under the provisions of the Conscription Act. [May have served later in Company G, 2nd Regiment N.C. State Troops.]

HARDISON, LEVIN, Private
Resided in Craven County and enlisted at age 47,

November 21, 1861. Discharged in December, 1861, by reason of disability.

HARDISON, ROBERT B., Private
Resided in Craven County and enlisted at age 28, November 21, 1861. "Never reported by reason of confirmed rheumatism."

HARDISON, WILLIAM P., Corporal
Resided in Craven County where he enlisted at age 19, November 21, 1861. Mustered in as Private. Captured at Roanoke Island on February 8, 1862. Paroled at Elizabeth City on February 21, 1862. Returned to duty on or about September 15, 1862. Wounded in the shoulder at White Hall on December 16, 1862. Returned to duty prior to March 1, 1863. Promoted to Corporal on September 4, 1863. Wounded in the elbow at or near Drewry's Bluff, Virginia, May 16, 1864. Died in hospital at Richmond, Virginia, June 7, 1864.

HARTNETT, THOMAS, Private
Previously served in 2nd Company H, 40th Regiment N.C. Troops (3rd Regiment N.C. Artillery). Transferred to this company in July, 1863. Present or accounted for through December, 1864. [May have served also in the 2nd Regiment Confederate Engineers.]

HEATH, LEWIS S., Corporal
Resided in Craven County where he enlisted at age 41, November 21, 1861. Mustered in as Private. Captured at Roanoke Island on February 8, 1862. Paroled at Elizabeth City on February 21, 1862. Returned to duty prior to May 1, 1863. Promoted to Corporal in May, 1863-April, 1864. Wounded in the left foot and captured at Fort Harrison, Virginia, September 30, 1864. Hospitalized at Fort Monroe, Virginia. Confined at Point Lookout, Maryland, January 14, 1865. Paroled at Point Lookout on or about March 17, 1865, and transferred to Boulware's Wharf, James River, Virginia, where he was received on March 19, 1865, for exchange.

HERRITAGE, JAMES S., Private
Resided in Jones County where he enlisted at age 39, April 4, 1863, for the war. Captured at Fort Harrison, Virginia, September 30, 1864. Confined at Point Lookout, Maryland, October 5, 1864. Paroled at Point Lookout on or about March 17, 1865, and transferred to Boulware's Wharf, James River, Virginia, where he was received on March 19, 1865, for exchange.

HODGES, H. B., Private
Resided in Johnston County and enlisted at Camp Holmes at age 34, May 25, 1863, for the war. Received a "harvest furlough" of ten days on June 25, 1863, and failed to return. Reported absent without leave through December, 1864.

HULL, C. H., Private
Resided in Lincoln County and enlisted at Camp Holmes at age 28, May 20, 1863, for the war. Present or accounted for until December 18, 1864, when he was reported absent without leave.

IPOCK, BRYCE, Private
Resided in Craven County and enlisted at age 24, November 21, 1861. Failed to report for duty. Dropped from the rolls of the company in March-April, 1863, by

reason of being "in the Yankee lines."

JACKSON, JOHN W., Private
Resided in Craven County and enlisted at age 30, November 21, 1861. Failed to report for duty with this company, apparently by reason of having "joined the navy."

JOLLY, JOHN H., Private
Previously served in Company B, 40th Regiment N.C. Troops (3rd Regiment N.C. Artillery). Transferred to this company on November 21, 1861. Captured at Roanoke Island on February 8, 1862. Paroled at Elizabeth City on February 21, 1862. Declined to reenlist in the company when the regiment was reorganized on or about September 17, 1862.

JOYNER, BENJAMIN F., Private
Resided in Craven County and enlisted at age 32, November 21, 1861. Discharged on December 31, 1861, by reason of "hernia."

KNIGHT, J. H., Private
Enlisted at Camp Holmes. Date of enlistment not reported. First listed in the records of this company in November-December, 1864. No further records.

LANGLEY, ENOS, Private
Resided in Craven County where he enlisted at age 24, November 21, 1861. Captured at Roanoke Island on February 8, 1862. Paroled at Elizabeth City on February 21, 1862. Returned to duty on or about September 15, 1862. Reported absent without leave on January 1, 1864.

LANGLY, DAVID, Private
Resided in Craven County where he enlisted at age 35, November 21, 1861. Captured at Roanoke Island on February 8, 1862. Paroled at Elizabeth City on February 21, 1862. Returned to duty prior to May 1, 1863. Died in Craven County on July 26, 1863, of "smallpox."

LEE, ABRAM, Private
Resided in Craven County and enlisted at age 18, November 21, 1861. Present or accounted for through December, 1861. No further records. [May have served later in Company K, 2nd Regiment N.C. State Troops.]

LEE, ELIAS, Private
Resided in Craven County and enlisted at age 35, November 21, 1861. Captured at Roanoke Island on February 8, 1862. Paroled at Elizabeth City on February 21, 1862. Returned to duty on or about September 15, 1862. Furloughed home in November, 1862, and later "sent aff[i]davit of age" to his company commander. Never returned to duty. Dropped from the rolls of the company in March-April, 1863, by reason of "being in the Yankee lines."

LONG, DANIEL, Private
Resided in Columbus County where he enlisted at age 35, April 20, 1863, for the war. Wounded in the face and blinded at Drewry's Bluff, Virginia, May 16, 1864. Furloughed for sixty days on July 26, 1864.

McKENZIE, J. M., Private
Resided in Mecklenburg County where he enlisted at age 26, April 15, 1863, for the war. Present or accounted for through April 12, 1864. No further records.

McLAUGHLIN, W. H., Private
Resided in Rowan County and enlisted at Camp Holmes at age 36, May 27, 1863, for the war. Died in hospital at Petersburg, Virginia, April 28, 1864, of "pneumonia."

McMILLEN, N., Private
Resided in Cumberland County and enlisted at age 18, May 27, 1863, for the war. Deserted on June 18, 1863.

MARTIN, VAN B., Private
Resided in Craven County and enlisted at age 22, November 21, 1861. Captured at Roanoke Island on February 8, 1862. Paroled at Elizabeth City on February 21, 1862. Died in Craven County on March 17, 1862. Cause of death not reported.

MASON, BENJAMIN F., Sergeant
Resided in Craven County where he enlisted at age 26, November 21, 1861. Mustered in as Sergeant. Captured at Roanoke Island on February 8, 1862. Paroled at Elizabeth City on February 21, 1862. Returned to duty on or about September 15, 1862. Reported absent without leave from January 15, 1864, through April, 1864. Returned to duty on an unspecified date. Reported present for duty in November-December, 1864.

MEADOWS, EDWARD HUGHES, Sergeant
Born in Craven County where he resided prior to enlisting in Wake County at age 19, October 20, 1862, for the war. Mustered in as Private. Promoted to Sergeant prior to March 1, 1863. Wounded in the right hand and wrist at Cold Harbor, Virginia, on or about June 1, 1864. Retired to the Invalid Corps on October 27, 1864.

MILLER, CONSTANTINE, Private
Resided in Craven County and enlisted in Wake County at age 30, September 15, 1862, for the war. Mustered in as Private. Promoted to Corporal prior to March 1, 1863. Reduced to ranks prior to May 1, 1863. Deserted to the enemy on or about March 27, 1864. Took the Oath of Allegiance on May 10, 1864.

MITCHELL, E., Private
Resided in Lenoir County and enlisted in Wake County at age 52, October 20, 1862, for the war as a substitute. Reported absent without leave on January 1, 1864.

MITCHELL, HARVEY, Private
Resided in Craven County where he enlisted at age 21, November 21, 1861. Captured at Roanoke Island on February 8, 1862. Paroled at Elizabeth City on February 21, 1862. Returned to duty on or about September 15, 1862. Wounded at Fort Wagner, Charleston, South Carolina, July 18, 1863. Reported absent wounded through April, 1864. Reported absent sick in November-December, 1864.

MITCHELL, JAMES, Private
Resided in Craven County where he enlisted at age 18, November 21, 1861. Captured at Roanoke Island on February 8, 1862. Paroled at Elizabeth City on February 21, 1862. Reported absent sick in January-February, 1863. Dropped from the rolls of the company in March-April, 1863, by reason of being "in the Yankee lines." Returned to duty prior to May 1, 1864. Present or accounted for through December, 1864.

MORGAN, MARL, Cook

Negro. Joined the company on October 15, 1862, as a cook. Present or accounted for through December, 1864.

MORRIS, JOSEPH, Private

Resided in Craven County and enlisted at age 45, November 21, 1861. Captured at Roanoke Island on February 8, 1862. Paroled at Elizabeth City on February 21, 1862. Discharged on November 21, 1862, under the provisions of the Conscription Act.

MORRIS, LEVI M., Private

Resided in Orange County and enlisted at age 38, November 21, 1861. Captured at Roanoke Island on February 8, 1862. Paroled at Elizabeth City on February 21, 1862. Reenlisted in the company on November 21, 1862, but "never returned." Listed as a deserter and dropped from the rolls of the company in March-April, 1863. Roll of Honor indicates that he "went to the enemy at Washington, North Carolina."

MYERS, A. L., Private

Resided in Davidson County and enlisted at Camp Holmes at age 20, May 23, 1863, for the war. Present or accounted for through December, 1864.

MYERS, WILLIAM AMBROSE, Private

Resided in Davidson County and enlisted at Camp Holmes at age 18, May 27, 1863, for the war. Captured at Fort Harrison, Virginia, September 30, 1864. Confined at Point Lookout, Maryland, October 5, 1864. Released on June 12, 1865, after taking the Oath of Allegiance.

NELSON, JOSEPH, ———

North Carolina pension records indicate that he served in this company.

NOBLES, WILLIAM M., Private

Resided in Craven County and was by occupation a farmer prior to enlisting in Craven County at age 33, November 21, 1861. Captured at Roanoke Island on February 8, 1862. Paroled at Elizabeth City on February 21, 1862. Returned to duty on or about September 15, 1862. Wounded in the right arm at or near Cold Harbor, Virginia, May 31, 1864. Reported absent wounded through April 26, 1865.

NORRIS, PATRICK, Private

Resided in Craven County and enlisted at age 23, November 21, 1861. Captured at Roanoke Island on February 8, 1862. Paroled at Elizabeth City on February 21, 1862. Returned to duty on or about September 15, 1862. Deserted to the enemy on or about November 6, 1862.

PARISH, DANIEL S., Private

Resided in Craven County and enlisted at Petersburg, Virginia, April 1, 1864, for the war. Captured at Bentonville on March 22, 1865. Confined at Hart's Island, New York Harbor, April 10, 1865. Released on or about June 17, 1865, after taking the Oath of Allegiance.

PEARCE, JAMES R., Private

Resided in Craven County and enlisted at age 37, November 21, 1861. Mustered in as 1st Sergeant. Captured at Roanoke Island on February 8, 1862.

Paroled at Elizabeth City on February 21, 1862. Reduced to ranks subsequent to February 21, 1862. Died in hospital at Goldsboro on December 27, 1862, of "pneumonia."

PERRY, JAMES, Private

Resided in Chatham County and enlisted at Camp Holmes at age 32, May 28, 1863, for the war. Hospitalized at Richmond, Virginia, June 14, 1864, with a gunshot wound. Furloughed for thirty days on July 30, 1864. Reported absent without leave in October, 1864.

PERVIS, JAMES M., Private

Resided in Craven County where he enlisted at age 18, November 21, 1861. Captured at Roanoke Island on February 8, 1862. Paroled at Elizabeth City on February 21, 1862. Returned to duty on or about September 15, 1862. Captured at Fort Harrison, Virginia, September 30, 1864. Confined at Point Lookout, Maryland, October 5, 1864. Paroled at Point Lookout on January 17, 1865, and transferred to Boulware's Wharf, James River, Virginia, where he was received on January 21, 1865, for exchange.

PIPKIN, ISAAC, Private

Resided in Craven County where he enlisted at age 18, November 21, 1861. Captured at Roanoke Island on February 8, 1862. Paroled at Elizabeth City on February 21, 1862. Returned to duty on or about September 15, 1862. Hospitalized at Richmond, Virginia, May 17, 1864, with a gunshot fracture of the left arm. Place and date wounded not reported. Deserted on or about August 15, 1864.

PITTMAN, RICHARD H., Private

Resided in Craven County where he enlisted at age 19, November 21, 1861. Captured at Roanoke Island on February 8, 1862. Paroled at Elizabeth City on February 21, 1862. Returned to duty on an unspecified date. Reported absent in hospital in January-February, 1863. Reported absent sick at home in May, 1863. Deserted on or about June 15, 1863.

PITTMAN, SPENCER C., Private

Resided in Craven County where he enlisted at age 18, November 21, 1861. Captured at Roanoke Island on February 8, 1862. Paroled at Elizabeth City on February 21, 1862. Returned to duty on or about September 15, 1862. Wounded at White Hall on December 16, 1862. Returned to duty prior to March 1, 1863. Present or accounted for through December, 1864.

POWELL, WILLIAM H., ———

Negro. Joined the company at Camp Mangum on October 15, 1862. Served as a cook. Present or accounted for through December, 1864.

POWERS, BENJAMIN, Private

Resided in Craven County where he enlisted at age 28, November 21, 1861. Company records dated January-February, 1863, state that he was absent and "won't join the co[mpany]." Company records dated March-April, 1863, indicate he was dropped from the rolls by reason of being "in the Yankee lines." Reported present for duty in March-April, 1864. Discharged on November 1, 1864, by reason of being overage and because he had "served three years." No further records.

RADCLIFFE, THOMAS, Private
Resided in Robeson County and enlisted at age 34, May 13, 1863, for the war. Reported absent without leave in November, 1863. Listed as a deserter on or about February 24, 1864.

RAWLS, JOSHUA M., Private
Resided in Craven County and enlisted at age 18, November 21, 1861. Died at Washington, North Carolina, in December, 1861. Cause of death not reported.

RAY, A. C., Private
Resided in Robeson County where he enlisted at age 38, May 13, 1863, for the war. Present or accounted for through January 21, 1865.

RHODES, JAMES H., 1st Sergeant
Born in Onslow County where he resided as a farmer prior to enlisting in Craven County at age 28, November 21, 1861. Mustered in as Sergeant. Captured at Roanoke Island on February 8, 1862. Paroled at Elizabeth City on February 21, 1862. Returned to duty on or about September 15, 1862. Wounded at White Hall on December 16, 1862. Rejoined the company prior to May 1, 1863. Promoted to 1st Sergeant on October 8, 1863. Wounded in the right thigh at Drewry's Bluff, Virginia, May 14, 1864. Reported absent wounded until February 16, 1865, when he was retired to the Invalid Corps by reason of disability from wounds.

RICH, JOHN F., Private
Resided in Craven County and enlisted at age 18, November 21, 1861. Discharged on November 21, 1862, under the provisions of the Conscription Act.

ROGERS, JOSEPH, Private
Previously served in Company K, 51st Regiment N.C. Troops. Enlisted in this company at Camp Holmes on May 5, 1863, for the war. Present or accounted for through December, 1864; however, he was reported absent sick during much of that period.

ROWE, BARNEY H., Private
Resided in Craven County where he enlisted at age 21, November 21, 1861. Captured at Roanoke Island on February 8, 1862. Paroled at Elizabeth City on February 21, 1862. Declined to reenlist when the regiment was reorganized on September 17, 1862. Dropped from the rolls of the company in March-April, 1863, by reason of being "in the Yankee lines."

SIMPKINS, EPHRAIM, Private
Resided in Craven County and enlisted at age 24, November 21, 1861. Discharged on July 16, 1862, by reason of disability.

SIMPSON, JAMES D., Private
Born in Carteret County and resided in Craven County where he was by occupation a farmer prior to enlisting in Craven County at age 44, November 21, 1861. Captured at Roanoke Island on February 8, 1862. Paroled at Elizabeth City on February 21, 1862. Discharged on November 21, 1862, by reason of the expiration of his term of service.

SMITH, CHARLES, Private
Resided in Craven County and enlisted at age 20, November 21, 1861. Died at Washington, North Carolina, in December, 1861.

SMITH, ZIMMERIA, Private
Resided in Forsyth County and enlisted at age 29, May 27, 1863, for the war. Killed at Fort Wagner, Charleston, South Carolina, July 18, 1863. He was "a brave and good soldier."

SNELL, SHADE A., Private
Resided in Beaufort County and enlisted at Camp Whiting at age 16, February 1, 1863, for the war. Present or accounted for through December, 1864.

SPEAR, N. HARRELL, Private
Resided in Craven County where he enlisted at age 25, November 21, 1861. Captured at Roanoke Island on February 8, 1862. Paroled at Elizabeth City on February 21, 1862. Deserted at or near Washington, North Carolina, in November-December, 1862.

STEWART, J. R., Private
Place and date of enlistment not reported. Company records dated March-April, 1863, indicate he was dropped from the rolls of the company by reason of being "in the Yankee lines."

STEWART, WILLIAM R., Private
Resided in Craven County where he enlisted at age 21, November 21, 1861. Company records dated January-February, 1863, indicate he was absent within the enemy lines near New Bern. No further records.

STILLY, W. J., Private
Born in Beaufort County and resided in Craven County where he was by occupation a farmer prior to enlisting in Craven County at age 52, November 21, 1861. Captured at Roanoke Island on February 8, 1862. Paroled at Elizabeth City on February 21, 1862. Discharged on November 21, 1862, by reason of the expiration of his term of service.

SUTTON, ALFRED, Private
Resided in Craven County where he enlisted at age 46, November 21, 1861. Captured at Roanoke Island on February 8, 1862. Paroled at Elizabeth City on February 21, 1862. Declined to reenlist when the regiment was reorganized on September 17, 1862.

SUTTON, CHARLES, Private
Resided in Craven County where he enlisted at age 22, November 21, 1861. Captured at Roanoke Island on February 8, 1862. Paroled at Elizabeth City on February 21, 1862. Deserted in December, 1862. Dropped from the rolls of the company in March-April, 1863, by reason of being "in the Yankee lines." Roll of Honor indicates that he deserted twice and later enlisted in the Union Army.

SUTTON, SAMUEL, Private
Enlisted in Wake County on September 15, 1862, for the war. Transferred to an unspecified unit on August 3, 1864. No further records.

SUTTON, STEPHEN, Private
Resided in Craven County where he enlisted at age 19, November 21, 1861. "Never reported after enlisting." Dropped from the rolls of the company in March-April, 1863, by reason of being "in the Yankee lines."

SWAIM, ANDREW, Private

Resided in Forsyth County and enlisted at Camp Holmes at age 28, May 27, 1863, for the war. Reported absent without leave on January 1, 1864. Returned to duty on or about April 18, 1864. Reported absent without leave on December 25, 1864.

SWAIM, C., Private

Resided in Forsyth County and enlisted at Camp Holmes at age 23, May 27, 1863, for the war. Reported absent without leave on January 1, 1864.

SWAIM, GEORGE, Private

Resided in Forsyth County and enlisted at Camp Holmes at age 36, May 27, 1863, for the war. Reported absent without leave on December 25, 1864.

TAYLOR, GEORGE, Private

Resided in Craven County where he enlisted at age 19, November 21, 1861. Captured at Roanoke Island on February 8, 1862. Paroled at Elizabeth City on February 21, 1862. Dropped from the rolls of the company in March-April, 1863, by reason of being within the enemy lines. [North Carolina pension records indicate he was wounded in the head and leg at Cold Harbor, Virginia, June 1, 1864.]

TAYLOR, ISAAC, Private

Resided in Craven County and enlisted at age 25, November 21, 1861. Died at Roanoke Island on December 20, 1861. Cause of death not reported.

THOMPSON, H. P., Private

Resided in Robeson County where he enlisted at age 22, May 13, 1863, for the war. Captured at Fort Harrison, Virginia, September 30, 1864. Confined at Point Lookout, Maryland, October 5, 1864. Paroled at Point Lookout on or about March 17, 1865, and transferred to Boulware's Wharf, James River, Virginia, where he was received on March 19, 1865, for exchange.

THOMPSON, JOHN, Private

Resided in Ireland and enlisted at age 31. Enlistment date erroneously reported as March 21, 1861. Deserted in November, 1861.

TINGLE, RICHARD H., Sergeant

Resided in Craven County where he enlisted at age 30, November 21, 1861. Mustered in as Corporal. Captured at Roanoke Island on February 8, 1862. Paroled at Elizabeth City on February 21, 1862. Promoted to Sergeant on an unspecified date. Deserted to the enemy in October, 1862.

TRUETT, JOSEPH, Private

Resided in Craven County and enlisted at age 18, November 21, 1861. Captured at Roanoke Island on February 8, 1862. Paroled at Elizabeth City on February 21, 1862. Declined to reenlist when the regiment was reorganized on September 17, 1862, and was reported to be "with the enemy."

WARREN, A. O., Private

Resided in Beaufort County and enlisted at Camp Holmes at age 31, May 28, 1863, for the war. Reported absent without leave on January 1, 1864.

WHITFORD, STEPHEN, Private

Resided in Craven County and enlisted at age 18, November 21, 1861. Failed to report for duty. Dropped from the rolls of the company in March-April, 1863, by reason of being "in the Yankee lines."

WIGGINS, ALEXANDER, Private

Resided in Craven County where he enlisted at age 20, November 21, 1861. Captured at Roanoke Island on February 8, 1862. Paroled at Elizabeth City on February 21, 1862. Returned to duty on or about September 15, 1862. Reported absent without leave on November 16, 1862. Returned to duty on or about March 5, 1863. Wounded in the neck and shoulder at Fort Wagner, Charleston, South Carolina, July 18, 1863. Retired to the Invalid Corps on October 25, 1864, by reason of disability.

WIGGINS, FREDERICK, Private

Resided in Craven County and enlisted at age 19, November 21, 1861. Captured at Roanoke Island on February 8, 1862. Paroled at Elizabeth City on February 21, 1862. Died in Craven County on March 6, 1862. Cause of death not reported.

WIGGINS, MAJOR, Corporal

Resided in Craven County where he enlisted at age 22, November 21, 1861. Mustered in as Private. Captured at Roanoke Island on February 8, 1862. Paroled at Elizabeth City on February 21, 1862. Promoted to Corporal in June, 1862. Returned to duty on or about September 15, 1862. Present or accounted for through April, 1864. No further records.

WILCOX, ALEXANDER, Private

Resided in Craven County and enlisted in Wake County at age 30, September 15, 1862, for the war. Present or accounted for through December, 1864.

WILLIAMS, EDWARD N., Private

Resided in Beaufort County and enlisted at age 47, November 21, 1861. Captured at Roanoke Island on February 8, 1862. Paroled at Elizabeth City on February 21, 1862. No further records.

WILLIS, ALEXANDER, Private

Resided in Craven County where he enlisted at age 18, November 21, 1861. Captured at Roanoke Island on February 8, 1862. Paroled at Elizabeth City on February 21, 1862. Returned to duty on or about September 15, 1862. Present or accounted for through April, 1864. No further records.

WILLIS, FREEMAN, Private

Resided in Cleveland County and enlisted at Camp Holmes at age 38, May 26, 1863, for the war. Wounded in the thigh at or near Fort Wagner, Charleston, South Carolina, July 16, 1863. Died at Charleston on October 27, 1863. Cause of death not reported.

YORK, J. R., Private

Resided in Randolph County and enlisted at Camp Holmes at age 28, May 26, 1863, for the war. Captured at Fort Harrison, Virginia, September 30, 1864. Confined at Point Lookout, Maryland, October 5, 1864. Paroled at Point Lookout on or about November 1, 1864, and transferred to Venus Point, Savannah River, Georgia, where he was received on November 15, 1864, for exchange. Paroled at Greensboro on May 14, 1865.

MISCELLANEOUS

Civil War records indicate that the following soldiers served in the 31st Regiment N.C. Troops; however, the companies in which these soldiers served are not reported.

CLEMER, ANDREW, Private

Place and date of enlistment not reported. Deserted to the enemy on an unspecified date. Took the Oath of Allegiance on or about October 11, 1864.

CLEMER, L. J., Private

Place and date of enlistment not reported. Deserted to the enemy on an unspecified date. Took the Oath of Allegiance on or about October 11, 1864.

GALTNEY, A. D., ———

Place and date of enlistment not reported. Died at or near Richmond, Virginia, on or about December 6, 1864.

HOWELL, A., ———

Place and date of enlistment not reported. Listed as a deserter on February 24, 1864.

McCARTY, JAMES, Private

Place and date of enlistment not reported. Deserted to the enemy on an unspecified date. Took the Oath of Allegiance on or about April 14, 1865.

MORROW, JAMES, Private

Resided in New Hanover County. Place and date of enlistment not reported. Deserted to the enemy on an unspecified date. Took the Oath of Allegiance at Fort Monroe, Virginia, March 20, 1864.

PEGRAM, HENRY J., ———

North Carolina pension records indicate that he served in this regiment.

TURRENTINE, M. H., 2nd Lieutenant

North Carolina pension records indicate that he served in this regiment.

VAUGHN, C. P., Private

Place and date of enlistment not reported. Captured at or near Raleigh on or about April 16, 1865. No further records.

WEST, ISAAC A., ———

North Carolina pension records indicate that he served in this regiment.

WEST, JOSEPH T., ———

North Carolina pension records indicate that he served in this regiment.

WHITTEN, J. P., ———

Place and date of enlistment not reported. Died at or near Richmond, Virginia, on or about October 19, 1864. Cause of death not reported.

This index contains citations for soldiers listed in the foregoing rosters and for a variety of entries, including all persons, place and regiments, that appear in the unit histories. Alternate spellings of some surnames are cross-referenced. Because this index composed primarily of personal names, a modified form of the letter-by-letter mode of alphabetizing has been employed whereb each entry is alphabetized by letter *only* to the point where the first comma appears; secondary alphabetization is utilized for a words following the first comma. This method permits the placement of entries such as ''Stanly Guards'' at the end, rather tha awkwardly in the middle, of the Stanly surname section. Depending on the information available concerning their given name soldiers with the same surname are divided into two individually alphabetized groups (for each letter of the alphabet) compose of (1) soldiers for whom initials only or an initial plus a given name (*e.g.*, C. Melvin Rogers) are available, and (2) soldiers f whom a given name plus an initial (*e.g.*, Charles M. Rogers) or several given names are available. Place names are placed *afte* identical surnames; for example, the entry for Jackson, Mississippi, appears after the entry for Jackson, Thomas J.

Normell, L., 16
Norris. *See also* Morris
Norris, C. F., 451
Norris, James, 368
Norris, John, 51
Norris, Joseph, 368
Norris, Patrick, 510
Norris, Reuben, 368
Norris, Timothy, 368
Norriss, William W., 368
North, Joshua, 339
North Anna River, Virginia, 6, 108, 320
North Carolina Guards, 31
North Carolina Units
  1st Regt. N.C. State Troops, 319
  2nd Regt. N.C. State Troops, 314, 316-320
  3rd Regt. N.C. Artillery.
    See 40th Regt. N.C. Troops
  3rd Regt. N.C. State Troops, 319
  4th Regt. N.C. State Troops, 314, 316-318
  4th Regt. N.C. Volunteers.
    See 14th Regt. N.C. Troops
  5th Regt. N.C. Volunteers.
    See 15th Regt. N.C. Troops
  7th Regt. N.C. State Troops, 1, 99-106
  8th Regt. N.C. State Troops, 425
  8th Regt. N.C. Volunteers.
    See 18th Regt. N.C. Troops
  9th Regt. N.C. Volunteers, 1
  10th Regt. N.C. Volunteers.
    See 20th Regt. N.C. Troops
  11th Regt. N.C. Troops, 426
  12th Regt. N.C. Troops, 318
  13th Regt. N.C. Troops, 7
  14th Regt. N.C. Troops, 314, 316-318
  15th Regt. N.C. Troops, 4-5
  18th Regt. N.C. Troops, 99, 101-107, 109, 314
  20th Regt. N.C. Troops, 323
  22nd Regt. N.C. Troops, 7
  25th Regt. N.C. Troops, 2, 99
  26th Regt. N.C. Troops, 1-2
  27th Regt. N.C. Troops, 1-7
  28th Regt. N.C. Troops, 99-110
  29th Regt. N.C. Troops, 232-235
  30th Regt. N.C. Troops, 314-321
  31st Regt. N.C. Troops, 424-429
  33rd Regt. N.C. Troops, 99, 101-107, 109
  35th Regt. N.C. Troops, 2
  37th Regt. N.C. Troops, 99, 101-107, 109
  39th Regt. N.C. Troops, 233, 235
  40th Regt. N.C. Troops, 438
  44th Regt. N.C. Troops, 5
  46th Regt. N.C. Troops, 2-5
  48th Regt. N.C. Troops, 2-5
  49th Regt. N.C. Troops, 7, 316
  51st Regt. N.C. Troops, 425-427

56th Regt. N.C. Troops, 4
61st Regt. N.C. Troops, 425
Northcut, James D., 486
Northeast Cape Fear River, North Carolina, 428
Norton. *See also* Newton, Norden
Norton, Balis, 252, 309
Norton, James S., 121
Norville. *See also* Nevill
Norville, James, 378
Norwood, Alvis, 69
Norwood, David, 389
Norwood, Francis M., 389
Norwood, R. W., 329
Nowell. *See also* Normell
Nowell, A. J., 493
Nowell, J. J., 493
Nowell, J. R., 488
Nowell, James Alvin, 459
Nowell, Jonathan, 486
Nowell, W. H., 493
Nowles, William R., 329
Nunn, Benjamin F., 39
Nunn, Henry S., 43
Nunn, Jesse I., 43
Nunn, William H., 69

O

Oakley, David, 348
Oakley, J. W., 358
Oakley, William Lewis, 389
Oar. *See also* Orr
Oar, James D., 244
Oates, David W., 104
Oberman. *See also* Overman
Oberman, Isaiah, 58
Oberry. *See also* Berry
Oberry, H., 486
O'Brian, Alexander P., 389
O'Briant, William G., 389
O'Brien, Alfred D., 389
O'Connell. *See* Connell
Odham. *See also* Oldham
Odham, R., 88
Odom. *See also* Odum
Odom, David M., 408
Odom, Jacob E., 408
O'Donnell. *See also* Donnell
O'Donnell, John, 468
Odum. *See also* Odom
Odum, Elisha, 88
Odum, James P., 88
Ogburn, Joseph P., 451
Ogburn, N. S., 329
Ogle, Lucius H., 252
O'Hagan, Charles James, 74
Oldham. *See also* Odham
Oldham, William P., 185
Old Topsail Sound, North Carolina, 426
Olive, L. T., 451
Oliver, Abram R., 88
Oliver, Allison W., 269

Oliver, Jabez B., 269
Oliver, Joseph M., 269
Oliver, William B., 451
Oliver, William H., 16
O'Neal. *See also* Neal
O'Neal, Daniel, 398
O'Neal, E. A., 316, 318
O'Neal, Hardy, 358
O'Neal, J. B., 16
O'Neal, John, 378
O'Neal, Loftin M., 358
Orange & Alexandria Railroad, Virginia, 102
Orange Court House, Virginia, 2, 5, 108, 315, 319
Orange Guards, 61
Orange Plank Road, Virginia, 5, 105-106, 108, 316-317
Orange Turnpike, Virginia, 5, 105, 10[
Ormand, Robert Dixon, 126
Orr. *See also* Oar
Orr, Nathan D., 413
Orr, Thomas J., 419
Orrell, Adolphus Lafayette, Sr., 27
Orrell, James A., 27
Ottaway, John, 389
Outen. *See also* Outtan
Outen, W. R., 422
Outlaw, James B., 35
Outlaw, William, 43
Outlaw, William R., 486
Outtan. *See also* Outen
Outtan, W. K., 486
Overman. *See also* Angerman, Oberm[
Overman, Benjamin F., 486
Overman, Ezekiel, 16
Overman, John, 16
Overman, Thomas C., 16
Overton, W. R., 79
Owen. *See also* Owens
Owen, Elias P., 205
Owen, Wilbur F., 27
Owens. *See also* Owen
Owens, D., 88
Owens, Edward M., 88
Owens, H. J., 88
Owens, James, 378
Owens, Robert, 378
Ownby, Oliver Deaton, 297
Ownley, William F., 59
Oxford, North Carolina, 381
Ox Hill, Virginia, 103
Oxley, Elbert H., 79
Oxley, Wilkes, 79

P

Pace, W. W., 493
Pack. *See also* Pike
Pack, Reason A., 181
Pack, Thomas, 244
Packard. *See* Pickard
Packer. *See also* Parker
Packer, Stephen, 309

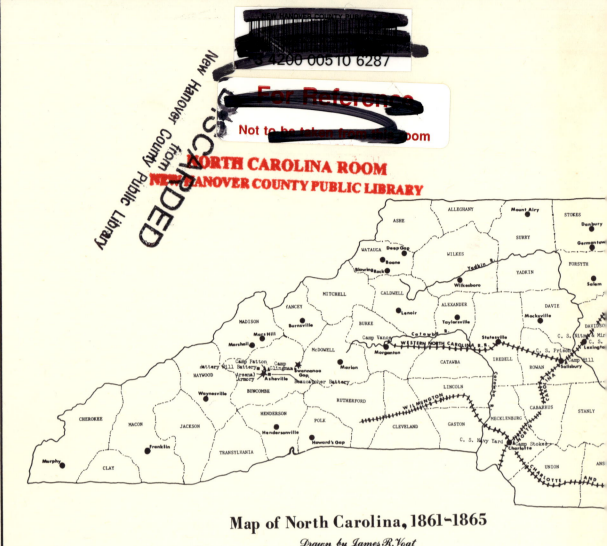

Map of North Carolina, 1861–1865

Drawn by James R. Vogt

This map locates the principal camps, forts,
towns, railroads, and engagements fought in
the State during the Civil War.

LEGEND

● – Towns
■ – Forts and batteries
▲ – Camps of instruction
★ – Engagements
╫ – Railroads

NCR